Tahiti

& French Polynesia Guide

Open Road *is* Travel!

–OPEN ROAD TRAVEL GUIDES–

Whether you're going abroad or planning a trip in the United States, take Open Road along on your journey. Our books have been praised by **Travel & Leisure**, **The Los Angeles Times**, **Newsday**, **Booklist**, **US News & World Report**, **Endless Vacation**, **American Bookseller**, **Coast to Coast**, and many other magazines and newspapers!

Don't just see the world – experience it with Open Road!

About the Author

Jan Prince has lived in Tahiti and Moorea since 1971. She is a travel writer and journalist, and has also written about Tahiti for Fodor's travel guides, *The Los Angeles Times*, *Time Magazine*, *Tahiti Magazine*, *Pacific Islands Monthly*, and many other publications. She is currently a writer for the *Tahiti Beach Press*, the islands' only English-language publication.

You may e-mail her at janprincemoorea@mail.pf only for questions and comments relating to this book—not to assist in travel or other arrangements. Please understand that she cannot help you with real estate, employment or immigration inquiries.

Open Road *is* Travel!

Open Road Publishing has guide books to exciting, fun destinations on four continents. As veteran travelers, our goal is to bring you the best travel guides available anywhere!

No small task, but here's what we offer:

• All Open Road travel guides are written by authors with a distinct, opinionated point of view – not some sterile committee or team of writers. Our authors are experts in the areas covered and are polished writers.

• Our guides are geared to people who want to make their own travel choices. We'll show you how to discover the real destination – not just see some place from a tour bus window.

• We're strong on the basics, but we also provide terrific choices for those looking to get off the beaten path and experience the country or city – not just see it or pass through it.

• We give you the best, but we also tell you about the worst and what to avoid. Nobody should waste their time and money on their hard-earned vacation because of bad or inadequate travel advice.

• Our guides assume nothing. We tell you everything you need to know to have the trip of a lifetime – presented in a fun, literate, no-nonsense style.

• And, above all, we welcome your input, ideas, and suggestions to help us put out the best travel guides possible.

૨૭

Tahiti

& French Polynesia Guide

Open Road *is* Travel!

Jan Prince

Open Road Publishing

4th Edition

Contents

~

Sidebars

Maps

Sidebars

Tahiti & French Polynesia Guide
᭒

1. INTRODUCTION

Unlike many armchair travelers and other romantics I harbored no childhood dreams to escape to Tahiti—the Isle of Illusion and Love under the swaying palms. Surely I had heard the magical name "Tahiti" when I saw the old movies about the South Seas, but they made no lasting impression on me.

But when I saw a picture of Bora Bora in a *Sports Illustrated* magazine in January 1968, I was swept away by the beauty of the island. For the next six months I read every book on Tahiti and the South Pacific that I could find in the Public Library in Houston, where I was living at the time.

When I arrived in Tahiti later that year I was prepared to accept Tahiti as she is, not as a starry-eyed tourist. I could even appreciate the wonder and beauty of a volcanic black sand beach. I knew that I would like the smell of a coconut fire and the musty odor of copra. I longed to hear the rumble of the surf crashing on the coral reef and the squawking cries of the sea birds as they fished in the lagoon. I also knew that I would enjoy the fun loving Tahitian people, their dignity, humor and sensuous dances. I understood that it was more important to absorb the colorful sights, sounds and fragrant smells of the people and scenery around me than to see Tahiti through the lens of a camera.

My husband and I spent three weeks on Tahiti, Moorea and Bora Bora, and returned again in 1970 to do it all again. When we moved to Tahiti in 1971, I chose to discover my own Tahiti. That's what I've been doing ever since. I've experienced Tahiti as an American tourist and as an expatriate full-time resident, as a journalist, travel writer and tour guide. I've explored most of the inhabited islands in five archipelagoes, traveling by airplanes, luxury liners, inter-island cargo ships, small fishing boats and by private sail boats. I've stayed in all the best hotels, at several of the pensions and hostels, and I've lived for weeks at a time with Polynesian families in the outer islands. I learned to speak French with an American accent and enough of the Tahitian language to be understood. However, you can get by with English, gestures and smiles almost everywhere you go in these islands.

French Polynesia is not just another destination for vacations. It is a completely different world; a different lifestyle made up of the special light in the sky, the special color of the water, the special smile of the people.

Along with the travel information you'll find in this book are tidbits of my own experiences in Tahiti and Her Islands, which are officially known as French Polynesia. I'm confident that the travel advice in this book will help you discover your own Tahiti!

Chapter 2

OVERVIEW

Visitors to **Tahiti** often ask me which is my favorite island in French Polynesia, which island I think is the prettiest and which island I think they would most enjoy visiting.

Although I do have my favorites, each island has its own beauty, charm and specific personality. Almost everywhere you go in French Polynesia you will meet hospitable, friendly people, which helps to give meaning to the natural assets of the island. The latter question is dependent on the amount of time and interest you have to explore the islands, the people and the culture.

From the first moment I laid eyes on the lagoon of **Bora Bora** I was entranced. Each time I have returned to Bora Bora over the years I still gasp in awe at the beautiful colors of the lagoon. I find myself gazing at Otemanu and Pahia mountains from all angles around the island, and especially when I'm taking a boat trip around the lagoon.

The mountains and bays of **Moorea** are simply breathtaking, and this is the cleanest island of the Society group, with neatly trimmed lawns and flower gardens. Here you will find the flavor of the islands by sitting beside the lagoon at sunset time and listening to Tahitian musicians playing their guitars and ukuleles and singing their favorite Polynesian songs.

Tetiaroa is a sanctuary for thousands of sea birds that lay their eggs on the white powdery sands of the beaches. Here you can easily observe crested terns, brown noddy birds, red- and blue-footed booby birds, white-bellied gannets, petrels, the beautiful white fairy terns with black eyes, and the occasional red-breasted frigate birds, whose fledglings of fluffy white feathers are larger than their mothers are. The Hotel Tetiaroa Village and the airstrip are now closed and the future of this atoll remains unknown since the death of owner Marlon Brando on July 1, 2004. However, you can still visit one part of this lovely atoll by boat from Tahiti. At 42 kilometers (26 miles) from Tahiti, it is just the right distance for a day-tour that will take you over in the morning and bring you back at night. You can walk to Bird Island, have a picnic on the beach and swim in the enclosed lagoon.

The island of **Huahine** is very special to me because of the Polynesian people who live in the quiet little villages, fishing and planting vegetables and fruit in their little *fa'apu* farms in the valley. As you drive around the island you can still feel the history of Huahine when you visit the stone *marae* temples in Maeva Village.

Raiatea and **Tahaa** are ideal for sailboat chartering, and there are five yacht charter companies based in Raiatea. There are numerous *motu* islets inside the protected lagoon where you can drop anchor, watch a magnificent sunset behind Bora Bora, and listen to the roar of the surf on the reef as you fire up the barbecue on the stern of the boat, while a huge tropical moon rises above the sea.

Tahiti is still the land of double rainbows for me, the regal Queen of the Pacific, and the Diadème Mountain, which can best be viewed from the Fautaua bridge east of Papeete, is even shaped like a crown. A drive around the island of Tahiti will reveal seascapes that are reminiscent of all the island groups of Polynesia. Tahiti is an island that's alive with color, from the flamboyant flowers to the bright *pareo* clothing to the pink, yellow, orange, blue and green houses you'll see beside the circle island road. There are numerous waterfalls in the verdant valleys and you'll find challenging hikes in the mountains if you want to get off-track.

Tahiti is perhaps the most magical and beautiful island of all, but she will not reveal her treasures to you as readily as the smaller islands do. You have to get away from the mainstream of hotels and Papeete to feel the essence of this seductive island, which remains constant amidst the apparent changes of modern life. If you can appreciate the special beauty of a black sand beach of volcanic sand, or a quiet stroll through a forest of *mape* (Tahitian chestnut) trees, then you'll feel some of the spirit of old Tahiti.

Many of us who live on Polynesia's high islands dream of escaping to the **Tuamotu atolls**, where we can get lost between the immensity of sea and sky. Rangiroa, Manihi, Fakarava and Tikehau are the islands that may beckon to you, like a siren call. Here you can live on fish and lobster and coconuts, and scuba dive among an abundance of wild life in the wonderfully clear lagoons that attract professional underwater photographers from the world's top magazines.

The mysterious **Marquesas Islands** hold a fascination for an increasing number of voyagers, who seek the authenticity of lifestyle that is still lived in the isolated valleys of these distant islands of brooding beauty. The wood carvers on each island create magnificent sculptures for their churches, and to sell in the artisan centers. The young people dance the traditional *haka* and

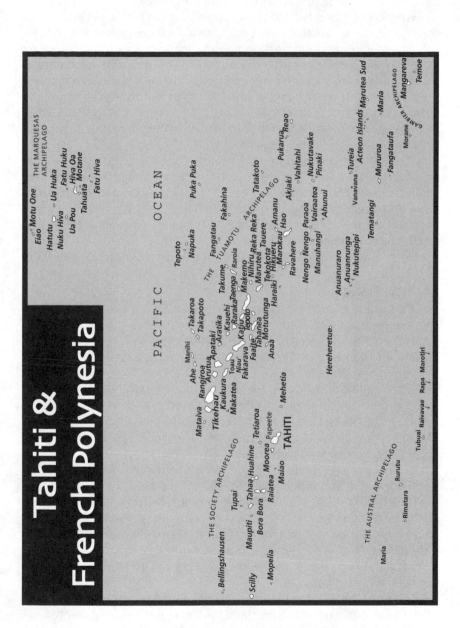

bird dance, and the wild horses, goats and cattle watch the scenery from their pastures on the precipitous cliffs overlooking the bays.

Whenever I hear a *himene* group singing the old Polynesian hymns and chants, I am carried away in spirit to the **Austral Islands**, where the villagers gather in their Protestant meeting houses almost nightly to practice their songs for the Sunday church services. I can almost smell the *couronnes sauvages*, the necklaces of flowers and herbs that are placed around your shoulders when you arrive on the joyful island of Rurutu. And I can see the handsome, muscled young men who spend their days in the taro fields, while the women sit on *peue* mats on their terraces or in their living rooms, weaving hats, bags and mats from pandanus fronds.

The **Gambier Islands** represent another page from Polynesia's colorful and often tragic past. Under the severe staff of Father Honoré Laval, the docile, gentle people of Mangareva were converted to Catholicism and lost their lives under the forced labor of building churches. A neo-gothic city of 116 buildings of coral and stone and a cathedral for 2,000 people is a reminder of the priest who had a driving need to build.

Here's a quick preview of what Tahiti and French Polynesia can offer you:

Society Islands

The **Society Islands** are the main tourist destinations in French Polynesia. They are the islands the furthest west in French Polynesia, and the home of more than three-quarters of the population. They are divided into the **Windward Islands** or *Iles du Vent* and the **Leeward Islands** or *Iles sous le Vent*, so named because of their position in relation to the prevailing wind.

The Windward Islands include the high islands of **Tahiti** and **Moorea**, and the uninhabited volcanic crater of **Mehetia**; plus the coral atoll of **Tetiaroa**, the late Marlon Brando's former retreat. The mostly flat island of **Maiao** still has its doors closed to the outside world, and visitors are not encouraged to spend the night ashore.

In the Leeward Islands the high islands of **Huahine, Raiatea, Tahaa, Bora Bora** and **Maupiti** lie 180 to 260 kilometers (112 to 161 miles) northwest of Tahiti. The atolls of **Tupai, Mopelia, Scilly** and **Bellinghausen** are the westernmost islands of the Society group. These four atolls are either uninhabited or have no tourist facilities, but you can visit by sailboat from Bora Bora. Richard Postma's *Taravana*, which operates out of the Hotel Bora Bora, is frequently chartered by movie stars and other adventurous couples to explore this hidden paradise.

The high islands of the Leeward and Windward Society group are some of the most beautiful islands in the world, offering countless photogenic scenes of saw-tooth mountain ranges, deep blue bays, green valleys and sparkling turquoise lagoons inside the fringing or barrier reefs. These are the names you've heard so much about: Tahiti, Moorea, Huahine, Raiatea, Tahaa, Bora Bora and Maupiti. On most of these islands you can explore the valleys, waterfalls and *marae* stone temples on a safari tour, or while hiking with a guide or on your own. In the opalescent lagoons you can swim, snorkel, scuba dive, water-ski, jet-ski, surf, kitesurf and windsurf, paddle an outrigger canoe, feed the sharks and rays, go sailing and picnic on the *motu*. And you can photograph the island, lagoon and reef while parasailing or taking a flight-seeing helicopter tour. The airport and hotel on **Tetiaroa** were both closed in early 2004, but you can still explore this privately owned atoll during a day's sailing excursion from Tahiti.

Tuamotu Islands

The **Tuamotu Archipelago** consists of two parallel island chains of 77 coral atolls and one upraised island, located between the Society and Marquesas Islands. These specks of land form one of the world's largest collections of atolls in the vastness of the blue Pacific. They are strewn across ten latitudes and stretch more than 1,500 kilometers (930 miles) from northwest to southeast and more than 500 kilometers (310 miles) from east to west. Forming the shapes of a doughnut, a bean or cigar, an egg or a slice of pie, several of these half-drowned atolls enclose lagoons that are inhabited by the black-lip *Pinctada Margaritifera* oyster, which produces the world's finest quality black pearls.

One of these atolls is **Rangiroa**, which is the second-largest atoll in the world, with a lagoon that is so large it could accommodate the entire island of Tahiti within its perimeter. You'll find international class accommodations on Rangiroa, **Manihi**, **Tikehau** and **Fakarava**, as well as thatched roof bungalows or rooms in pensions. There are also guest facilities with families on the atolls of **Ahe**, **Anaa**, **Apataki**, **Hao**, **Kaukura**, **Mataiva**, **Takapoto** and **Takaroa**. Several of the Tuamotu atolls are uninhabited due to a lack of water.

Lagoon excursions on Rangiroa include snorkeling through the pass, along with hundreds of fish and sharks. You can watch the dolphins, look at the fish through a glass bottom boat, visit the *motu* islets around the vast lagoon, picnic on a *motu,* fish inside the lagoon or open ocean, and parasail above the immense watery playground. Scuba diving in the Tuamotus is rated world class by the experts, especially in Rangiroa, Manihi, Fakarava, Tikehau and Mataiva. Manihi's lovely lagoon is a haven for the black lipped oyster, and you can visit a pearl farm, picnic on a *motu*, snorkel, go line or drag fishing, join a sunset cruise and learn to scuba dive. Tikehau has an unspoiled lagoon with pink sand beaches just waiting for a footprint, and Fakarava is becoming so popular with scuba divers that a hotel and several pensions have been built, with more projects planned for the near future. Wherever you go in the

Tuamotus you will find a warm reception, laughter, music, lots of fresh air and sunshine, and an abundance of fresh fish.

Marquesas Islands

The **Marquesas Islands** lie northwest by southeast along a 360-kilometer (223-mile) submarine chain seven to ten degrees south of the Equator. Two geographical groups are separated by 96 kilometers (60 miles) of open ocean, with a combined land area of 1,279 square kilometers (492 square miles). The southern group consists of the four high islands of **Fatu Hiva**, **Tahuata** and **Hiva Oa**, which are inhabited, plus **Mohotani** and the small uninhabited islet of **Fatu Huku**.

The northern group comprises the three high islands of **Ua Pou**, **Nuku Hiva** and **Ua Huka**, all inhabited, plus the small islets of **Motu Iti**, **Eiao** and **Hatutu**, which are uninhabited. The most important island, Nuku Hiva, is about 1,500 kilometers (932 miles) northeast of Tahiti, and Hiva Oa, in the southern group, lies 1,400 kilometers (868 miles) northeast of Tahiti. The Marquesas Islands are younger than the Society Islands and do not have protective coral reefs. The wild ocean beats endlessly against the craggy, sculpted coasts, unbroken by any barriers for almost 6,400 kilometers (4,000 miles).

Accommodations are available on all the inhabited islands, either in small hotels or in family pensions. Most of the rooms and meals are reasonably priced in the Marquesas, but the cost of land and sea transport is very expensive. Read the information on the *Aranui* in the chapters on *Planning Your Trip* and *Eco-Tourism and Travel Alternatives*. This is the best way to visit the Marquesas Islands, unless you want to stay a few days on one or more of the islands. You can also take an Air Tahiti flight to the Marquesas and board the *Aranui* there and fly back to Tahiti if you prefer.

In the Marquesas you can visit restored archaeological sites with giant stone tikis, hike to waterfalls and high plateaus and ride horses to remote villages. You can scuba dive among a wealth of wild sealife, charter a sailboat for a dive and sail outing through the islands, go deep sea fishing, and watch the wood carvers at work.

Austral Islands

The **Austral Islands** are the southernmost island chain in French Polynesia, lying on both sides of the Tropic of Capricorn and extending in a northwest-southeasterly direction across 1,280 kilometers (794 miles) of ocean. They are part of a vast mountain range, an extension of the same submerged chain that comprises the Cook Islands.

The Austral Islands include the high islands of **Rurutu**, **Tubuai**, **Rimatara**, **Raivavae** and **Rapa**, plus the low, uninhabited islands of **Maria** (or Hull) and the **Marotiri** (or Bass) **Rocks**. These islands lie between 538 and 1,280 kilometers (334 to 794 miles) south of Tahiti, and are separated from one another by a great distance of open ocean. These are French Polynesia's more temperate islands, where taro and potatoes, cabbages and carrots are grown for the market in Papeete.

You can fly to Rurutu, Raivavae and Tubuai, and you'll need a boat to get to the other islands. An airport is now being built on the island of Rimatara, while the people of Rapa have voted against this intrusion on their solitude. Raivavae is the most beautiful of the Austral Islands and Rurutu is second in natural beauty but the most lively of all the group. You'll enjoy the communal spirit that exists here, in the taro fields, the artisan shops and in the churches of Rurutu. The people are enthusiastic in both work and play, and they keep their culture alive with annual tours to visit the religious and historic sites of the island.

You can visit the island by horseback or four wheel-drive vehicle, picnic on a white sand beach and hike to waterfalls and limestone grottoes with stalactites and stalagmites. Tubuai is noted for its sandy beaches of various shades, its *motu* islets and fish-filled lagoon. Raivavae has the most beautiful *motu* I have ever seen, where you can still collect *pahua* (tridacna clams) in shallow water, but certain parts of the lagoon is known to be contaminated with *ciguatera*, which prohibits the consumption of fish.

Gambier Islands

At the southern end of the Tuamotu Archipelago are the **Gambier Islands**, a cluster of 10 rocky islands surrounded on three sides by a barrier reef. The largest and most northerly of this group is **Mangareva**, a high island located 1,650 kilometers (1,023 miles) southeast of Tahiti. Other high islands

Tahiti, Where Love Lives

"Tahiti, where love lives" is one of the most popular slogans adopted by the Tahiti Tourist office to promote Tahiti and Her Islands to the American market. This campaign is aimed at busy executives from homes where both husband and wife work and have very little time to spend together.

When you choose the Islands of Tahiti for your vacation, you will find a complete change of scenery and a rhythm of life that is slow and relaxed, very conducive to romance. Tahiti is still the Island of Love. Here we take the time to enjoy one another. Time to simply be. One of Tahiti's favorite expressions is Haere Maru, which means "take it easy." That's what you'll learn to do when you get here.

&

sharing the lagoon are **Aukena**, **Akamaru** and **Taravai**, with several *motu* islets lying inside the barrier reef. The airport of **Totegegie** is built on one of the flat islets across the lagoon from Rikitea, the principal village of Mangareva. Productive black pearl farms in Mangareva provide employment and the exquisite pearls grown here are sold in Papeete and throughout the world.

You will find clean and comfortable accommodations on the island of Mangareva. In addition to visiting the churches of Father Laval, you can take boat trips to the other islands and *motu* islets that share the lagoon, visit pearl farms and enjoy a cool, pleasant climate.

Chapter 3

SUGGESTED ITINERARIES

Choosing Your Dream Islands

The wholesale tour operators who specialize in package programs to Tahiti and Her Islands offer vacation choices ranging from three to 15 days, which will allow you to visit from one to five islands. Some of these programs will schedule you to fly direct from the airport in Tahiti to one of the outer islands, and they sometimes include an overnight stay in Tahiti on the way back home. If you add Moorea to your itinerary, then I suggest that you fly direct from Tahiti to Moorea, providing you don't have to wait too long at the airport in Tahiti. Better yet, schedule an international flight that will allow you to connect from Tahiti to Moorea immediately after arrival at the Tahiti-Faa'a International Airport. The first Air Moorea flight from Tahiti to Moorea begins at 6am. If your overseas flight arrives in Tahiti in the middle of the night, as some of them do, you may want to pre-register in a hotel in Tahiti and continue your trip the next day.

The most important idea is for you to get settled into your hotel as quickly as possible, take a refreshing shower and nap, and go swimming in the lagoon when you awaken. As soon as you get out of your traveling clothes and into your swimsuit, shorts or *pareo*, you'll feel yourself starting to relax.

If you are staying on the island of Tahiti you owe it to yourself to visit Moorea at least for a day. You can hop aboard an inter-island fast catamaran for a 30-minute trip or you can take a 10-minute air shuttle flight to get to Moorea. And if you are staying on Moorea and want to go shopping and sightseeing in Tahiti, you can commute to Tahiti in the morning and return in the afternoon, the same as I do. Details for this inter-island connection are given in the *Moorea* chapter.

One of the statements I hear the most often from visitors when they arrive in Moorea is: "Oh, how I wish I had come here first." I assume this means that they wouldn't have continued their trip to other islands had they known how much they would like Moorea. You will too.

The suggested itineraries in this chapter were taken from the 2004 brochures and from the Internet specials offered by the tour operators. Some of the summer special program rates are applicable only during the low seasons of November, December and January, excluding the Christmas and New Year's holidays. In July 2005 Air Tahiti Nui will begin a direct flight service three times a week from New York to Tahiti and on to Sydney, which will generate new programs and more choices. I suggest that you check out the promotions advertised by the various hotels on their websites, as well as the bargains offered by the tour operators on the Air Tahiti Nui website and on their own individual websites. These addresses are listed in the chapters on *Planning Your Trip, Ecotourism*, or in each island destination chapter.

One Island, One Hotel

If your ideal vacation is to fly to one island, check into a hotel, unpack and settle in, then I suggest that you choose a hotel on Tahiti, Moorea or Bora Bora. Whether your vacation lasts for two days or two weeks, you'll find enough activity to keep you busy on land and in the lagoon. You'll be delighted with the choices of restaurants available and you'll enjoy the entertainment provided by the various hotels and restaurants. You'll have time to get to know a few of the locals and learn something about the culture of the Polynesians, if you so desire, and you can set your own pace for meals, activities and leisure time.

Pleasant Holidays can book you at the Club Bali Hai on Moorea for 6 nights for $955 per person, which includes 1 free night. Swain Tahiti can put you in the Hotel Tiare Tahiti in downtown Papeete for 7 days/6 nights, starting at $1,259 per person, or you can pay a little more and choose another hotel in Tahiti for your one island stay. Tahiti Legends advertises 6 days at the Sofitel Ia Ora Moorea from $1,479 per person, which includes free breakfasts for two. If you don't mind spending one night in Tahiti before heading out-island, there are several options for your one island, one hotel vacation. Brendan Tours has a 6-day/5-night "Tahiti On Sale" special from $1,269. You'll spend 1 night at the InterContinental Resort Tahiti and 4 nights at the InterContinental Resort Moorea, where you will be served free American breakfasts each morning. Tahiti Legends suggests a 7-day/6-night "Stay Put" program that includes 1 night at the InterContinental Resort Tahiti and 5 nights at the Bora Bora Lagoon Resort, yet you'll only pay for 3 nights. The starting cost of $1,879 per person also includes a 3-course dinner for two on Bora Bora. Tahiti Legends also has a "Stay Put" program that allows you to stay at the Hotel Kia Ora in

Rangiroa for 6 nights and pay for 3 nights, then 1 night at the InterContinental Resort Tahiti, starting at $1,569 per person.

The Main Tourist Islands

If you only want to stay on **Moorea** and **Tahiti**, I suggest you spend the first few nights on Moorea and the final part of your visit in Tahiti. All the tour operators have several options to consider. Almost everyone yearns to see **Bora Bora**, yet there are some visitors who deny themselves this privilege, claiming that it is too expensive or that they don't have time. If you think you'll never pass this way again, then I urge you to indulge yourself and just go ahead and do it. I do not recommend a day tour to Bora Bora, because so much of your time is spent at airports and just getting there and back to Tahiti in one day. Do spend at least one or two nights, and be sure to take an outrigger tour to discover the incredibly beautiful lagoon and motu islets. If your budget will stretch that far, then book yourself and your significant other into an overwater bungalow for the complete Bora Bora experience.

Huahine and **Taha'a** are now counted among the main tourist islands, especially since the opening of luxurious international hotels. The package programs offered by tour operators can also include the island or **Raiatea**, which still retains its flavor of old Polynesia, and has accommodations in several guest houses called pensions, as well as a 3-star international class hotel.

Islands & Atolls

There are several packages that combine Society Island stays with a chance to visit one or more atolls in the **Tuamotu** Archipelago. Tahiti Legends advertises an 8-day special package starting at $2,249 that will take you to the Pearl Resorts on Moorea and **Tikehau**, with one night in Tahiti. They also have an 8-day package from $2,439 that includes three nights at the Bora Bora Pearl Beach Resort, with 3 breakfasts, 3 nights at the **Manihi** Pearl Beach Resort with 3 breakfasts and dinners, and 1 night at the InterContinental Resort Tahiti. Tahiti Travel Planners has a 15 day/14-night package that includes Moorea, Bora Bora, Taha'a and Tikehau, starting at $3,849 per person during the high season of June 1-October 31.

Swain Tahiti sells a 10-day/9-night "Secrets of French Polynesia" program that includes 4 nights at Le Taha'a Private Island & Spa, 4 nights at the Manihi Pearl Beach Resort and 1 night in Papeete. They also have a 14-day/13-night "Indulgent Retreats" package that starts at $4,855 per person. This includes 1 night in Papeete, 4 nights at the Bora Bora Pearl Beach Resort, 4 nights at Le Taha'a Private Island & Spa, and 4 nights at the Tikehau Pearl Beach Resort. You can also upgrade to overwater bungalows.

Off the Beaten Track

Air Tahiti offers an interesting choice of "air passes" that will allow you to island hop among the Societies, the Tuamotu, the **Marquesas** and the **Austral Islands**. Air Tahiti also specializes in vacations off the beaten tourist track. Their "Island Adventures" program includes an 18-day/17-night package with lodgings in Maupiti, Raiatea, Huahine, Bora Bora, Rangiroa, and Tikehau, as well as other programs that combine islands and atolls. Details are given in Chapter 6, *Planning Your Trip*.

Tahiti Legends has a 9-day "Marquesas Discovery" package from $3,855 per person that will take you way off track to Nuku Hiva and Hiva Oa, where you will spend 3 nights on each island in a Pearl Resort hotel. You'll also have 3 nights at the InterContinental Resort Tahiti. The program includes 6 breakfasts, 1 lunch, 6 dinners, 4x4 expeditions, archaeological tours, helicopter transfers and lots of other benefits.

Honeymoons

Tahiti and Her Islands provide the ideal setting for a romantic honeymoon, and the deluxe hotels with overwater bungalows are a favorite destination for newlyweds and other lovers. All the tour operators have honeymoon programs, or they can create a personalized package according to your wishes. I suggest that you also contact the hotels of your choice for information on their honeymoon programs.

Tahiti Legends has a Honeymoon Brochure that features "Moorea Romance", an 8-day honeymoon from $6,500 per couple; "Bora Bora Fantasy", 8 days from $8,000 per couple, the "Ultimate Honeymoon", which takes you to Moorea, Bora Bora and Taha'a for 13 days, starting at $12,600, and even a "Honeymoon Cruise" aboard Bora Bora Cruises' world-class luxury cruise yacht, plus pre- and post-cruise stays. This 11-day package starts at $11,300.

Islands in the Sun advertises a 6-day Honeymoon package at the Sheraton resorts, starting at $2,100 per person. This includes round-trip airfare on Air Tahiti Nui, inter-island airfare, a garden bungalow for 3 nights at the Sheraton Moorea Lagoon Resort & Spa, a lagoon view bungalow at the Bora Bora Nui Resort & Spa for 2 nights and a dayroom at the InterContinental Resort Tahiti. This price also includes 5 American breakfasts, a Honeymoon cake, a half-bottle of French champagne, a gift of Tahitian vanilla in Tahiti and a mother-of-pearl gift in Bora Bora. Upgrades to overwater bungalows are available. E-Tahiti Travel recommends a VIP Honeymoon for 11 days/11 nights, starting at $5,884, excluding international airfare. This package gives you one night in a panoramic view room at the InterContinental Resort Tahiti, 3 nights in an overwater bungalow at the InterContinental Resort Moorea, 3 nights in an overwater bungalow at the Bora Bora Nui & Resort, 2 nights at the Hotel Kia

Ora Rangiroa, and 2 nights at the Kia Ora Sauvage on Rangiroa. The package includes MAP (half-board meals) in Tahiti, a private lagoon tour in Bora Bora, and AP (full board) meals at the Kia Ora Sauvage.

Stepping down into the lagoon from the steps of your overwater bungalow is an unforgettable sensual delight, and there are many other pleasures to be enjoyed in these units. Unfortunately, privacy is not one of them. Most of the overwater bungalows are built too close together to provide total discretion. Why not stay at a luxurious villa on a private island, where there are no neighbors to share your passion, albeit unwittingly. Read the information on Private Island and Mai Moana Island in the *Bora Bora* chapter.

Family Vacations

Jean-Louis Delezenne of Fly Tahiti Vacations specializes in family vacations on the island of Moorea, where he has a house beside the ocean at Temae near the airport. He believes, and I agree, that some of the best bargains, as well as the best times, can be had by staying in a family pension or guest house, and some of them even come equipped with a kitchen. Linareva and Fare Arana on Moorea are two of his favorite choices, and mine as well. Or you could rent Fare Hamara, a private house located in the heights of Opunohu Bay on Moorea. See details in the *Moorea* chapter.

However, if you want to get out of the kitchen during your vacation, then Jean-Louis can put together a package for you with accommodations at a family pension that serves meals. Or he can book you in a moderately priced hotel on the island(s) of your choice, where you can feed your family at reasonable costs in nearby restaurants and snacks, which are small restaurants serving local style food as well as French or Chinese cuisine. Good family type hotels include the Royal Tahitien and Ia Orana Villa on Tahiti, Moorea Village, Hotel Hibiscus and Les Tipaniers on Moorea, Bora Bora Beach Lodge and Matira Beach on Bora Bora and the Relais Mahana on Huahine. Or why not charter a sailing catamaran in Raiatea and take your family on a different kind of visit to the Leeward Society Islands of Huahine, Taha'a and Bora Bora. Other suggestions for family travel may be found in the chapter on *Taking the Kids*.

Spa Experience

Another category of theme vacations has been added to the tour operators' brochures with the opening of elegant spas in several of the deluxe hotels in Tahiti, Moorea, Taha'a and Bora Bora. Honeymooners and Hedonists are now enhancing their vacations with fruit, flower or coconut scented body scrubs, body wraps and masks, cleansing, hydrating or exfoliating treatments, rain showers, aromatherapy, acupressure, lomi-lomi, reflexology, or relaxing massages for two under the light of the silvery moon. These spas are described in each of the island destination chapters. Or you can get a copy of Tahiti Legends' Vacations & Honeymoons brochure for details on their programs that will take you to the Spas of Tahiti for your own rejuvenating escape. "Polynesian Caress" is a 7-day vacation at the Sheraton Resorts in Tahiti and Moorea, starting from $3,195 per person.

This includes international and inter-island airfare, all transfers and baggage handling, welcome flower lei, traditional farewell shell lei, 1 night in Tahiti, 6 nights in Moorea, room tax and VAT, 7 Continental breakfasts, a Mandara Experience spa package, Tiki Village dinner show on Moorea, rental car on Moorea (8 hours), and a full-day outrigger canoe excursion with motu picnic on Moorea. An 8-day "Tahitian Inspirations" package starts at $4,645 and takes you to the InterContinental Resorts on Moorea and Bora Bora, complete with a Mahana Spa Experience on Moorea, plus a lot of other extras. "Island Indulgence" is an 8-day package for the Sheraton Moorea Lagoon Resort & Spa and the Bora Bora Nui Resort & Spa, starting at $4,625. You also get the Mandara Spa Experience and the "Bora Bora Sampler" Spa Experience.

Sailing & Cruising Vacations

Should you prefer a sailing vacation, "shared yacht cruising" or "sail and dive" program, this information is given in the chapter on *Planning Your Trip* and in the individual destination chapters of *Moorea*, *Raiatea*, *Tuamotu* and *Marquesas Islands*. Most tour operators include some interesting sailing cruise packages in their brochures.

Sunspots International has combined a 7 day/6 night cruise aboard Bora Bora Cruises' luxury yacht *Tu Moana*, with a pre-cruise room for one night and a post-cruise stay for 2 nights at Le Meridien Tahiti, which sells for $3,982 per person double occupancy. Islands in the Sun has an 11-day package from $4,819, which includes 6 nights on board *Tu Moana*, 1 night at the InterContinental Resort Tahiti, 3 free nights at the InterContinental Resort Moorea, a free breakfast in Tahiti and free breakfast and dinner in Moorea, plus a circle island tour in Moorea.

If you have already visited the Society Islands or just want to get off the track to discover another facet of Polynesia, the *Aranui* cargo/passenger ship offers 16-day round-trip voyages from Tahiti to the Marquesas Islands. This is my favorite cruise. The details are given in the chapters on *Planning Your Trip* and *Ecotourism*. Pleasant Holidays sells a package that includes the *Aranui* cruise plus one night at the Radisson Plaza Resort in Tahiti, starting at $4,785 per person in double occupancy.

Dive Vacations

There are scuba diving clubs on 13 of the islands and atolls that are included in this guide, and on at least three more Tuamotu atolls that are not covered here, due to lack of space. Therefore, you can combine diving with any type of holiday you choose. Some of the larger dive clubs have facilities on two or more islands and they provide packages that allow you to dive on the islands of your choice. See each island destination chapter for more information. See information on *Aqua Tiki* and *Tahiti Aggressor* in the *Planning Your Trip* chapter to learn how you can cruise and dive in the Tuamotu atolls.

World of Diving & Adventure Vacations is a tour operator specializing in Multi-Island Dive packages. Their Value Dive-Pak Moorea starts at $1,490 per person and includes 4 nights at the Moorea Village and 6 single tank dives with Bathy's Club. Their add-on packages include inter-island airfare, 3 nights in a hotel, 2 days of 2-tank boat dives, plus transfers and taxes. The add-ons are priced from $590 to $990 and include diving in Tahiti, Bora Bora, Manihi or Rangiroa.

Surfing Vacations

You can create your own surfing holiday by reading the destination chapters in this guide and choosing the hotels or pensions on each island that will put you closest to the surfing spots. Pension Bonjouir on Tahiti Iti is a favorite lodging for surfers who compete in the Billabong Pro Tahiti surf competitions that are held every year during the month of May. There are also several other pensions in this area where surfers are welcome all year long. Moorea and Huahine also have special lodging for surfers that include kayaks or speedboats to take you to the surfing passes.

An 11-day "Surf Voyager" package in the Tuamotu atolls is promoted by Wavehunters, based on 10 surfers aboard the *Cascade*, starting at $3,550 per surfer, depending on the season. Details are outlined in the chapter on *Planning Your Trip.*

Kayak Holidays

Almost all the international class hotels, as well as most of the family pensions located beside the lagoon, provide kayaks for their guests, or you can rent a kayak to discover the lagoon. Wilderness Travel organizes sea kayaking adventures in the Tuamotu atolls. The land costs for their 2004 programs began at $4,795 per person for 7-8 members. By publication time no announcement had been made for 2005. Tahiti Outfitters is owned by Moorea resident Frank Murphy, who leads kayak expeditions in the Tuamotu and Austral Islands, which can also include bone fishing, salt-water fishing and fly-fishing. See information in chapter on *Ecotourism.*

&

Fishing & Sport Charter Vacations

Deep-sea fishing charters are available on almost all the islands listed in this guide. See details in each destination chapter and in the chapter on *Planning Your Trip*.

Chapter 4

LAND & PEOPLE

Land

Tahiti and Her Islands, officially known as **French Polynesia**, are sprinkled over 5,030 million square kilometers (almost two million square miles) of ocean in the eastern South Pacific, between the longitudes of 134º28' and 154º40 west and the latitudes of 7º50' and 27º36' south. Papeete, the capital of French Polynesia, is located on Tahiti, the largest island, and lies at 17º32' latitude south and 149º34' longitude west.

French Polynesia is east of the International Date Line. Tahiti is 6,200 kilometers (3,844 miles) from Los Angeles, 3,900 kilometers (2,418 miles) from Auckland, New Zealand, 4,700 kilometers (2,914 miles) from Noumea, New Caledonia, 5,700 kilometers (3,534 miles) from Sydney, 8,800 kilometers (5,456 miles) from Tokyo, 7,500 kilometers (4,650 miles) from Santiago, Chile, and 17,100 kilometers (10,602 miles) from Paris. The most northerly island in the Marquesas archipelago, Eiao, also known as Hatutu, is more than 2,000 kilometers (1,240 miles) from the Austral Island of Rapa, the most southerly island.

The word Polynesia means "many islands." The total land area of these 118 Polynesian islands and atolls adds up to only 3,500 square kilometers (1,365 square miles). The territory is geographically and politically divided into five archipelagoes: the Society Islands, Austral Islands, Marquesas Islands, Tuamotu Islands and the Gambier Islands. These island groups differ in terrain, climate and, to a lesser degree, the people. Most of the land in the archipelagoes is in the form of high islands, which are the eroded mountaintops of ancient volcanoes.

The High Volcanic Islands
All the Polynesian islands are basically of volcanic origin. They were formed millions of years ago when volcanoes erupted from a rising column of magma in the asthenosphere called a "hot spot." The earth's crust, or lithosphere, is divided into approximately a dozen plates resting on a flexible magma known as the asthenosphere. Magma escapes from accretion zones along dorsals formed on these plates and disappears within subduction zone troughs back into the magma. The hot spots remain stationary even though the Pacific lithospheric plate moves 7 to 10 centimeters a year in a westward direction, and periodic reactivation of these hot spots over millions of years has resulted in a linear distribution of the Polynesian islands in a southeast-northwest direction.

Five strips of islands correspond to a succession of hot spots along the Pacific seabed. The MacDonald hot spot, southeast of Rapa, is believed to have come to life 15 or 20 millions of years ago, and is still intermittently active. Tahiti is estimated at 2.6 million years in age, whereas Bora Bora seems to have come into existence between three and four million years ago.

The volcano becomes extinct when the magma is no longer expelled through the vent. The lava on top collapses, forming a huge caldera basin, which eventually erodes and forms valleys. As the island sinks slowly into the ocean, coral begins to grow on the underwater sides of the island. These corals are millions of microscopic polyps that attach themselves to a permanent base and produce a hard outer skeleton. Generations of these rocklike formations build upon one another, creating barriers hundreds of feet deep that surround the island shores, forming a fringing reef connected to the island.

When the island disintegrates, the coral remains at the surface of the water, reaching for the light it needs to survive. A circular crust is eventually formed above the volcano, which is called a barrier reef. A channel of varying width fills with water to form a lagoon between the fringing reef and the barrier reef.

This process may take millions of years. The Society archipelago illustrates the different stages of this evolution. The island of Mehetia, which is near a hot spot, is a young island with no coral reef; Moorea is a high island with a coral reef; Bora Bora is nearly an atoll with a barrier reef; and Scilly is an atoll.

The Low Coral Atolls
During **Charles Darwin's** visit to Tahiti in 1842 he climbed a mountain and discovered that the flat coral atoll is actually a high island that has sunk deeper into the ocean when the original volcano disappeared completely under the water. The old volcanic core still remains underneath the atoll, but all you see is the coral ring, which encircles the lagoon. The coral rim of the atoll indicates how big the island once was. A series of small coral islets, strung together by often-submerged coral reefs, are seldom more than a quarter of

a mile wide and only a few feet above the sea. Inside this narrow strip of coral the lagoon can be the size of a salt-water pond or as big as an inland sea.

White beaches of coarse and fine coral sand create a border between the sea and the green oasis of coconut forests, flowering trees and scented bushes. The live coral gardens of the reefs and inner lagoons are filled with a fantastic variety of tropical fish, sharks, rays, turtles, crustaceans, and other marine fauna.

Flora

From the moment you step off your plane in Tahiti you become aware that you are surrounded by flowers. The first scent is the sweet perfume of the beautiful white **Tiare Tahiti** (*Gardenia taitensis*), that a smiling *vahine* offers to welcome you to this luxuriant land of flowers.

This traditional custom of the islands existed long before there were passenger ships and airplanes. Until recently, when the Tahitians were traveling between the islands, they were adorned with crowns and leis of flowers. This sign of the traveler is still a custom in some of the remote islands, but the health department now prohibits transporting food and plants from Tahiti to the outer islands because of the fruit fly and other destructive insects.

"Say it with flowers" is a way of life in Tahiti. Walk through the public market in the heart of downtown Papeete and just watch for a few minutes as the vendors sell their brilliantly colored anthuriums, birds of paradise, asters, carnations, red and pink ginger flowers, delicate orchids, vivid roses, and myriads of varied bouquets. You won't be complaining about the prices here.

Or stroll around to the side of the market late in the afternoon and see the Tahitian grandmothers and little girls creating the decorative flower crowns and leis for the evening's merrymakers. Anyone who is going out to dinner and who wants to feel festive has only to walk by the flower stands and suddenly there are flower covered arms thrust from all directions, filling your nostrils and senses with a captivating aroma.

A drive around the island will give you an opportunity to see the many varieties of flowers flourishing in the rich soil of Tahiti. Especially in the spring and summer months (October-March) you will find a wonderful display of flowering trees and vines. The most readily identified belong to the *cassia* family: the *cassia grandis*, coral shower tree; *cassia fistula*, golden shower tree; *cassia javanica*, pink and white shower tree; and the lovely peach and cream colored *cassia hybrida*, the rainbow shower tree. One of the most exotic stars in this springtime show is the jade vine, *Strongylodon macrobotrys,* from the forests of the Philippines, whose cascading green flowers resemble sharks' teeth.

The pink and purple flowers you see bordering many of the streets in the urban areas of Tahiti are cousins to the crepe myrtle you know back home.

Named *lagerstroemia speciosa*, this tree is a native of India and is also called crepe myrtle in Tahiti. The *koelreuteria* or goldenrain tree, the jacaranda, with its lovely blue-violet bell-shaped flowers, the *tabebuia pentaphylla* or Tecoma tree, with its masses of lavender-pink, trumpet-shaped flowers, and the *bauhinia varigate*, known as the orchid tree, are some of the delightful sights that Tahiti's springtime brings. The Royal Poinciana, also called flamboyant or flame tree, *delonis regia*, grows to a height of 40 feet, and this most regal of all of Tahiti's springtime exhibits is in full bloom each Christmas, providing a huge canopy of red, scarlet and yellow blossoms. With their shiny green fern-like foliage, these showy trees make a brilliant contribution to the holiday season.

Take a tour to the Botanical Gardens in Papeari, where you can walk through 340 acres of exotic plants, shrubs, fruits and flowers that were brought from all the tropical countries by **Harrison Willard Smith**. He left his job as physics professor at the Massachusetts Institute of Technology to settle in Tahiti in 1919. Smith spent the rest of his life importing plants for his gardens.

How to Wear Your Flowers

"They are very fond of flowers," wrote Captain Cook, when he first visited Tahiti in 1769. "Especially of the Cape Jasmine (Gardenia taitensis, known as the Tiare Tahiti), of which they have great plenty planted near their houses; these they stick into the holes of their ears and into their hair..."

Many of the visitors to Tahiti have noticed that there is a custom of conversing through the wearing of flowers, and this language of the flowers still exists. Learn to read what they are saying when you see a big, husky man digging a ditch and wearing his Tiare Tahiti bud behind his ear; or when you see a young lady with her long hair coifed so nicely for that special evening and laced with orchids; when you see the proud Tahitian grandmothers with their woven hats and a hibiscus behind an ear.

When you wear your flower behind your right ear—it means you are single, available and looking. When you wear your flower behind your left ear—it means you are married, engaged or otherwise taken. When you wear flowers behind both ears—it means you are married but are still available. When you wear your flower backward behind your ear—it means "follow me and you'll find out how available I am." When you wear a flower backward behind both ears—it means anything goes. And when you see the young vahine with flowers in her hair—it means she's desperate, you'd better hurry up!

☙

Here you will discover a forest of Tahitian *mape* chestnut trees *(Inocarpus fagifer)*, plus gardens of indigenous and imported trees and plants. These include the perfumed pua *(Fabrea berteriana)*, ylang-ylang *(Cananga odorata)*, pitate jasmine *(Jasminum rex)*, queen of the night *(Epiphyllum oxypetalum)*, ixora or jungle flame *(Ixora macrothyrsa)*, lipstick plant *(Bixa orellana)*, Indian lotus *(Nelumbium Nelumbo nucifera)*, Mickey Mouse plant *(Ochna kirkii)*, pagoda flower *(Clerodendron speciossisimum)*, dwarf poinciana *(Poinciana pulcherrima)*, shrimp plant *(Beloperone guttata)*, white bleeding heart *(Clerodendron thomsonae)*, chenille plant *(Acalpha hispida)* candle bush *(Cassia alata)* elephant ear *(Alocasia macrorrhiza)* and many more.

Called the "Grandfather of Trees" by the Tahitians, Smith distributed his seeds and cuttings to his neighbors in Papeari, encouraging them to beautify their surroundings. He even held a contest each year to see who had the prettiest garden, and Papeari was long considered to be the "flower district" of Tahiti. Thanks to the Tahitians' natural love of flowers, the entire island is a botanical garden today.

Here in the Polynesian islands, we incorporate flowers into our daily lives. Both men and women can be seen wearing a fragrant blossom behind their ears, even while performing the most humdrum tasks. Often you can hear them softly singing to themselves. Wearing flowers does make you want to sing.

Traditional Tahitian Food Plants

Plants have always served as an essential part in the daily social and economic life of the Polynesians. Their ancestors, who were sailors and fishermen, had a plant-based culture. Plants provided the islanders with food, utensils, ornaments, drugs and material of all kinds, On all the islands and atolls of French Polynesia you will find the graceful coconut palm, the "tree of life" to the Polynesians, which can be used in dozens of ways. Other trees and plants that provide traditional Tahitian foods are breadfruit, bananas, *fei* plantains, taro, tarua, manioc, arrowroot, sweet potato and yams. Complimentary food plants include: sugarcane, pandanus, *mape* (Tahitian chestnut), ti or *auti (cordyline fruticosa)*, *vi* Tahiti or Tahitian apple *(Spondias dulcis)*, kava *(Pometia pinnata Forster)*, *nono (Morinda citrifolia)*, small ginger roots called *rea*, bamboo, the candlenut tree *(Aleurites molucanna)*, the wild hibiscus called *purau (Hibiscus tiliaceus)*, the *hotu* fruit of the *Barringtonia asiatica*, and varieties of purslane and cress, as well as several types of ferns.

Imported Food Plants

The European explorers, botanists, sailors, missionaries, traders and civil servants brought many species of economic flora to Tahiti, which flourish on most of the islands today. Among these food plants you will find varieties of: avocado, bay rum tree, Brazilian plum, cantaloupe, cashew nut, cayenne pepper, citron, coffee, custard apple, grapefruit, guava, gooseberry tree, jackfruit, Java almond, lime, lychee, mamee apple, mandarin, mango, orange, pakai, Panama cherry, papaya, passion fruit, pineapple, pistachio, pomegranate, quenette, rambutan, sea grape, soursop, Spanish plum, Surinam cherry, star apple, sugar apple, tamarind, vanilla and watermelon.

Chinese Gardens
Chinese immigrants brought their garden vegetables with them, which they plant in the high valleys of Tahiti. These colorful vegetables can best be seen at the Papeete market, where you will recognize varieties of bok choy, cabbages, carrots, cilantro, cucumbers, eggplant, ginger root, green peppers, jicama, lettuce, long beans and snap beans, parsley, pumpkins, soy bean sprouts, spinach, squashes, tomatoes, watercress, white radishes and zucchini.

Sacred Trees of Old Polynesia
The sacred trees of old Polynesia were chosen for their medicinal value, and the quality of their wood, bark, leaves or roots. Some of these trees are still used for carving into furniture, *umete* bowls, platters, small canoes, tikis and ceremonial clubs. These precious trees are the *tamanu* or *ati* (*Calophyllum*

The Mystical-Magical Intoxicating Ti Plant
The ancient Tahitians had 13 varieties of the **ti plant** (Cordyline terminalis or fructicosa) that they called **auti**. The most sacred of all ti plants in old Tahiti was the Ti-'uti, which was a fine variety planted chiefly in the marae enclosures for the gods and religious uses. Beautiful varieties of ti have been introduced in recent years, but it is still the glossy green leaves that were worn by orators, warriors and enchanters that are worn today by dancers, high priests and firewalkers.

This small tree of the Liliaceae family is believed to possess mystical-magical qualities that will protect the house from fire, and hedges of auti surround many of the homes in the islands. The broad leaves are used as food wrappers and to line the pits where breadfruit is preserved by fermentation. The ti is also used in traditional healing for diarrhea, vomiting, abscesses or ear infections. The root can be cooked in the underground stone oven to replace the breadfruit and the taro, and the large fibrous tuber was formerly made into candy. This root is very rich in sugar, and during the reign of King Pomare II, natives from the Sandwich Islands (now Hawaii) taught the Tahitians how to build a still and produce a potent liqueur from the auti root.

҈

inophyllum), the *tou* (*Cordia subcordata*), rosewood or *miro* (*Thespesia populnea*), banyan or *ora* (*Ficus prolixa*), *aito* or ironwood (*Casuarina equisetifolia*), *reva* or *hotureva* (*Cerbera odollam*) and the *pua* (*Fagraea berteriana*).

Land-Based Fauna

There are no snakes in Tahiti and Her Islands and there are no poisonous spiders or fearsome land animals, except for the centipede (*Scolopendra subspinipes*), which lives in dark, humid areas, under rocks and in palm frond structures. Its bite is venomous and very painful to humans. It is nocturnal by nature and its diet is made up exclusively of cockroaches, while the centipede itself is a delicacy for chickens. So don't strangle the roosters that crow outside your hotel window all night long!

Almost every home in the Polynesian islands has a few house pets in the form of the *mo'o*, a yellow lizard that lives on the ceilings, where they feed on mosquitoes and other flying insects and bananas if they're available. Sometimes these critters find their way into hotel rooms, which has been known to disrupt the tranquility of the human occupants. These geckos are harmless, but they do seem to occasionally take delight in dropping "whitewash" on inappropriate places, such as your bed or head. The reptile population includes four gecko species and three lizard species, none of which are to be feared.

Here you will find the yellowish-red Tahitian dog, some of whom are descendants of the barkless vegetarian dogs who crossed the ocean aboard the double-hulled voyaging canoes of the pioneer Polynesians. They eat meat these days and sometimes they bark all night, in tandem with the cocks.

Along with the dog, the pig was the only domestic animal known to the Polynesian before the arrival of the Europeans. Both animals were raised for food. The pig is still baked in the underground ovens for special feasts, and dogs are still served in a "special Chinese sauce" during big celebrations. Some of the pigs have taken to the bush and men on the high islands organize wild boar hunts.

Captain Wallis gave a cat to the high chiefess Purea in 1767, and it found a mate somewhere, because today cats abound in all the inhabited islands and atolls.

The little Polynesian rat and its cousins, who arrived aboard ships and boats, are threats to coconut trees without the metal bands. The *Rattus norvegicus*, a large brown rat, carries Tahitian meningitis and other contagious diseases. They also steal birds' eggs and fruit, and love to make their nests in thatched roofs.

In the Marquesas Islands you will see wild goats, sheep and cattle grazing on the precipitous cliffs overlooking the sea. Wild and tamed horses roam the plains of Ua Huka. The ancestors of these small horses were brought from Chile by Dupetit-Thouars in 1842.

A land crab called *tupa* lives in holes in the ground close to the lagoon and as far as a mile inland. When I first visited Bora Bora as a tourist I expended a lot of effort in trying to annihilate the tupas. When you cover up one of the holes they just disappear into their extensive underground network and surface from another hole. Now I know better and I feed the tupas who live beside my house. They're also edible if you pen them up and feed them coconut for ten days. Mine are getting pretty big now, but I'll just keep on feeding them.

Some would-be entrepreneur got the idea to import the African snail (*Achatina fulica*) in 1967, because he knew the French like their *escargots*. His snails were not a culinary success and what's more, they gobbled up plants in most of the gardens. Another carnivorous species, *Euglandina rosea*, was brought in to combat this greedy snail, but instead of attacking the *Achatina*, it almost wiped out the *Partula*, the tiny local snails whose shells are used by the Polynesians for making necklaces.

The mosquito and *nono* (sandfly) are two obnoxious pests that can truly ruin your vacation if you don't protect yourself from their stings. They particularly favor visitors, so be sure to bring a good insect repellent with you. I've listed a few suggestions under the Health category in the *Basic Information* chapter.

The insect population in this part of Polynesia includes the beautiful butterfly, *Danaida plexippus*, which you'll see in the daytime. The *Rhyncogonus* beetle that lives in the Marquesas Islands is found nowhere else in the world. There are about forty nocturnal species of moths, including the *Lepidopter sphingidae*, which feeds on leaves and vegetable stalks at night, and the Queensland fruit fly (*Dacus tryoni*). Pesticides are used in massive quantities, especially on the island of Tahiti, which is a concern for the public because of the risks of pollution and toxic effects in rivers and lagoons. Fresh water shrimps and eels live in the rivers and streams.

Birds
The early Polynesians and European explorers brought birds (manu) into these islands, and during the past two centuries other species have been introduced from Asia, Africa, Australasia and the Americas. Habitat changes and introduced species of birds are believed to be accountable for the extinction of certain species that formerly inhabited the Windward Society Islands. There are presently 104 known species of birds found in Tahiti and Her Islands.

Of the 27 species of sea birds nesting here, only nine reproduce in the Pacific, and Murphy's petrel (*Pterodroma ultima*) is the only species that lives in Polynesia all the time. The birds you may see include terns, boobies, noddies, frigatebirds, petrels and the graceful white tropicbirds (phaetons), identified by two long white plumes that form the tip of the tail as they soar high over the valleys from the rocky cavities where they nest. Twenty-one species of migratory sea birds have been observed as they fly from the North to the South Pacific. The white sand beaches and the bushes on the *motus* inside the reef on Tetiaroa atoll are nesting grounds for several species of sea birds, and the Tuamotu atolls have numerous bird islands. Almost a million sooty terns (*kaveka*) live on a small island offshore Ua Huka in the Marquesas Islands.

Thirteen species of land-birds coming from North America and Siberia reach these islands on a regular basis. They include two ducks and a cuckoo from New Zealand. Among the 30 species of nesting birds, almost half can be found only in French Polynesia. They include two herons, two salanganes, two warblers, one swallow, one duck, one rail, one of the limicoles, three parakeets, four wood kingfishers, four flycatchers and nine pigeons. Thirteen introduced species include the harrier, which lives in the Society Islands, and the eagle owl in the Marquesas.

The main land bird you will see is the Indian Mynah (*Acridotheres Tristis*), which was imported to Tahiti around 1903 to eradicate a beetle that was destroying the young coconuts. The cheeky Mynah also wiped out several species of birds by robbing their nests. The turtledove (*geopelia striata)* was introduced in 1950, and the red-tailed bulbul (*Pyconotus cafer*), a native of Asia, was introduced more recently, brought in from Rarotonga in the Cook Islands. The Tahitians gave the name *vini* to several small finch-like birds, which include the chestnut-breasted mannikin (*Lonchura Castaneothorax*), common waxbill (*Estrilda Astrild*), red-browed waxbill (Estrilda Temporalis), crimson-backed tanager (*Ramphocelus dimidiatus*) and the gray-backed white-eye (*Zosterops Lateralis*).

The Tahiti Lorikeet (*Vini peruviana*) disappeared from Tahiti around the end of the last century, when the Swamp Harrier was introduced. This pretty little blue and white bird, also known as *lori-nonette*, is still found on some of the Tuamotu atolls, but is on the endangered species list, along with the *pihiti (Vini ultramarine-Kuhl)* of the Marquesas Islands and all the other lorikeets.

The *mo'a oviri* or wild cock is a Jungle fowl of the *Gallus Gallus* family, which was introduced by the early Polynesians. The roosters are brightly colored with red, green and black feathers, and the hens are beige, brown or black. These birds can fly for several yards and they live in a free state, not really belonging to any family, but roost in trees and bushes close to a good source of food, such as my house. The roosters crow at all hours of the night, especially during the full moon, and of course, when you're trying to take a nap in the afternoon. I buy rice and bread for them and imported frozen chickens for myself. Their biggest enemies, apart from the Swamp Harrier, are little Tahitian boys, who catch the roosters and use them as fighting cocks.

Ocean, Reef & Lagoon Fauna

In a 1985 census, the world's greatest scientists specializing in coral reefs met in Polynesia and inventoried 800 species of shore fishes, with 633 species reported in the Society Islands. During a 2002 expedition 49 new fish species were discovered in the Marquesas Islands, bringing the total inventoried to 415 species. A 1990 study of fish in Rapa counted 268 species, and 10 more species were added during a 2002 study in Rapa. During the past five years several black and white killer whales (*Orcinus Orca*) have been sighted numerous times in the Marquesas Islands, especially around Nuku Hiva, where there is a scuba diving center. The remains of a giant calamary were found floating on the ocean's surface outside the reef of Moorea in 2002. It was estimated to be 5 meters (16.4 feet) long.

The oceanic slope is the richest part of a coral reef, and this is where you will have a better chance of finding crayfish or rock lobsters (*Panulirus penicillatus* called *oura miti*) and slipper lobsters (*Parribacus antarticus* called *tianee* in Tahitian). The near surface zones of the reef abound with surgeonfish, parrotfish, wrasses and red mullets. The external reef is also inhabited by various species of triggerfish, soldier-fish, squirrelfish, bass, perch, rock cod, angelfish, demoiselle-fish, mullet, and gray sharks and moray eels. You may also come across a green turtle (*Chelonia mydas*) or see a rare jellyfish or an occasional sea snake in this underwater zone.

Most of the mollusks and crustacea are found on the reef flats, which are also favored by pencil sea urchins and holothurians (sea cucumbers, called *rori* in Tahitian). The trigger-fish, puffer-fish, rock cods, box-fish, rascass and butterfly cod make their permanent homes here, and parrot-fish, surgeon-fish, angel-fish and small sharks, usually the harmless black-tipped and white-tipped variety, will visit the reef flats at high tide. Submerged coral plateaus act as passages between the oceanic slopes and the lagoons, and are the homes for echinoderms, particularly sea urchins, clam shells, octopus, small sponges and anemones, annelid worms and a variety of crabs. Lizardfish, puffer-fish and trumpet-fish are also common in this area. At high tide small schools of red mullet, jacks and parrotfish cross the zone on their way from the ocean to the lagoons.

On the lagoon slopes, as well as in the passes and the cracks in the reef (*hoa*), which have a sandy bottom sloping gradually to the center of the lagoon, is the favorite area of sponges, sand crabs, seashells (littorinids, nerites, ceriths), oysters, pearl oysters, cowries, strombs, spider shells, cones, all types of holothuria, *Ophiuridae*, starfish, *taramea*, some species of sea urchins (*vana*), soles, sand goby (*avaava*), leopard rays and some red mullets.

The coral outcrops and pinnacles are habitats of bivalve mollusks, including the colorful velvet-mantled reef clam (*Tridacna maxima*), called *pahua* locally. Numerous small species of fishes also gather here: surgeonfish, angelfish, butterfly fish, soldier-fish, harp-fish, butterfly cod, trumpet-fish, box-fish, porcupine-fish and trigger-fish.

There is almost no living coral or algae on the bottom of the lagoons, which are colonized by clamshells, pearl oysters, stony oysters and ark shells.

Spider shells, a rare helmet shell or conch shell live on the softer sand bottom, but the majority of shells, including the pencil shells, miters, harp shells, olives, ceriths and several cones, remain hidden in the sand during the daytime.

The open lagoon waters are the habitat of roving fishes, including unicorn-fish (*ume*), *rotea*, *kukina*, coral trout (*tonu*), chameleon sea bass (*hoa*), lagoon sharks and stingrays. The (*lutjanus*) snappers, sweetlip, flying fish, garfish, great barracuda (*ono*), sea-pike barracuda (*tiatio*), jacks and mullets come and go between the lagoon and the ocean, and the silver scad (*ature*) also visit the lagoon for brief periods during certain seasons.

The flora of the fringing reefs is rich, and trochus are abundant in many parts of the fringing reef, but the fishes found here are usually in the juvenile stage. These may include moray eels, rock eels, rascasse, surgeonfish, wrasses, gobies, blennies and angelfish.

Three types of rays are found in Polynesian waters, and they are not aggressive unless threatened. The biggest danger is when a bather treads on a ray that is buried in the sand in shallow water. The most spectacular and famous member of the family is the giant manta ray (*Manta alfredi (Macleay), fafa piti)*, that has a wingspan up to 25 feet across and may weigh almost two tons. The spotted eagle ray (*Aetobatis nari nari Euphrasen*) is the "bird ray" (*fai manu*) to the Tahitians because of its protruding head and narrow snout. They feed on mollusks and are one of the most important predators of the valuable pearl oysters in the lagoons of the Tuamotu and Gambier Islands. Several species of rays equipped with venomous spines on their tails are found in Polynesia. The stingray (*Himantura sp., fai iu)* live near coral reefs or in the brackish water of some large bays around the high islands. The pectoral fins or wings of these species, as well as those of most other rays, are tasty and considered a delicacy, sometimes appearing on the menu in seafood restaurants in Tahiti and Moorea.

Sea turtles (*honu*) were once reserved for the high chiefs and priests of Tahiti, as this marine reptile was held *tapu* (sacred and forbidden). The three species living in Polynesian waters are the leathery turtle, the green turtle and the hawksbill turtle, which are on the list of endangered species and, therefore, *tapu*. However, these turtles are still massacred for their flesh and carapaces.

The most important commercial fishes found in the ocean depths surrounding French Polynesia include several species of the tuna family, principally, the yellow fin tuna (*Neothunnus albacora macropterus, aahi)*, which are fished year round. Along with the tuna, the mahi mahi dolphinfish (*Coryphaena hippurus*) is the favorite fish served in restaurants. The great barracuda (*Sphyraena barracuda, ono*), the wahoo (*Acanthocybium solandri, paere*), the deep-water swordfish (*Xyphias gladius, haura or meka*), and the salmon of the gods (*Lampris Luna)*, are also served in seafood restaurants. The bonito (*Katsuwonus pelamis, auhopu)* is the most commonly caught fish, and is preferred by most Tahitians to any other fish, but the taste is a bit too "fishy" for most visitors. Many other species of edible fish abound in this oceanic wonderland, which are taken home by the local fishermen for their own dinner.

Roughly one-third, or 25 species, of the species of dolphins and whales in the world are found in the waters of Tahiti and Her Islands. The spinner dolphins (*Stenella longirostris*) are the easiest to find around Tahiti and Moorea because they live the closest to shore. The humpback whales (*Megaptera novaeangliae*) can be seen and heard offshore Moorea between July and October, when they come up from Antarctica to mate and give birth. They also escape the austral winters by visiting the Australs, Gambier and Tuamotu Islands, as well as the Leeward Society group and the Marquesas Islands.

According to Richard H. Johnson, an American marine biologist and local shark specialist living in Tahiti, there are an estimated 35 species of sharks in French Polynesian waters. These include: (*Alopias Vulpinus*) common thresher shark (*mao aero*), (*Carcharhinus Albimarginatus*) silvertip shark (*tapete*); (*Carcharhinus Amblyrhynchos*) gray reef shark (*raira*); (*Carcharhinus Falciformis*) silky shark (*tautukau*); (*Carcharhinus Galapagensis*) Galapagos shark; (*Carcharhinus Leucas*) bull shark; (*Carcharhinus Limbatus*) blacktip shark (*oihe*); (*Carcharhinus Longimanus*) oceanic whitetip shark (*mao parata*); (*Carcharhinus Melanopterus*) blackfin reef shark (*mauri*); (*Galeocerdo Cuvier*) tiger shark (*mao tore tore*); (*Negaprion Acutidens*) South Pacific lemon shark (*arava*); (*Triaenodon Obesus*) reef whitetip shark (*mamaru*); (*Isurus Oxyrinchus*) mako or short-finned mako shark (*mao aahi*); (*Nebrius Concolor*) Indo-Pacific nurse shark (*mao rohoi);* (*Rhincodon Typus*) whale shark; (*Sphyrna Lewini*) scalloped hammerhead shark (*mao tuamata*); (*Sphyrna Mokarran*) great hammerhead shark (*tamataroa*);and (*Sphyrna Sp.*) squarehead hammerhead shark (*mao afata*).

Natural Dangers
The ocean, coral reef, lagoons and coral gardens do have a few inhabitants that are not man's best friend. Sea snakes are rare in Polynesia and only one species (*Pelamis platurus*) is occasionally seen and caught along the coasts of some of the islands. This bi-colored snake has a brownish back and yellow belly and its venom is dangerous to humans. The theory is that these serpents hitchhiked on the bottoms of ships arriving in Tahiti from islands to our west, where the snakes are prevalent.

The natural dangers you want to avoid in the lagoon are: the "crown of thorns" starfish, called *taramea* in Tahitian; the sting of the jellyfish; burns from the Holuthurian or sea cucumber, also called sea leech, *rori* in Tahitian, and its cousin with spaghetti-like sticky tubules; burns from the sea anemone; the sting of the stone fish, called *nohu* in Tahitian; the sting of the scorpion fish and fire coral; the sting of sea urchin spines, called *vana* in Tahitian; and the highly poisonous varieties of cone shells, members of the *Conidae* family. There are 60 species of cones in Polynesia, but the most dangerous are the geographic, textile, marbled, aulicus and tulip cones. The best way to protect yourself from any of these unpleasant encounters is to wear plastic reef sandals or other appropriate shoes when walking in the lagoon or on the reef, and to watch where you put your hands and body when snorkeling or scuba diving.

The moray eel rarely attacks humans, but it will bite when it is provoked and feels threatened. Keep your hands safely out of the crevices or cavities in the coral, where the moray eel may be lurking.

Shark attacks occur most frequently in the atolls, along the exterior of the barrier reefs and in the shallow fissures between the exterior reef and the interior lagoons. Some of these attacks happen when a spear fisherman is trailing a string of fish behind him. Several scuba diving and snorkeling excursions include feeding the sharks and moray eels, who have been "tamed" by repetitious feedings.

You can avoid any potential problems by remembering to swim only in the areas where you see the locals swimming; do not swim in the ocean at night; leave your bright jewelry at your hotel when you go swimming, snorkeling or scuba diving, as it can reflect the sun and refracted light in the water, and attract the attention of moray eels and sharks; and wear protective footwear when you're swimming in the lagoons and walking on the reef.

People

The census of November 2002 counted 245,516 residents of French Polynesia, an increase of 11.8 percent since the last census of 1996, for an average annual growth rate of 1.8 percent. The demographic distribution during the 2002 census included 75 percent of the population living in the Windward Society Islands, 12.3 percent in the Leeward Society Islands, 3.6 percent in the Marquesas Islands, 2.6 percent in the Austral Islands and 6.5 percent in the Tuamotu and Gambier Islands.

The highest growth rate was in the Windward Islands of Tahiti, Moorea and Maiao, which recorded 21,538 more inhabitants since 1996 for an increase of 13.2 percent. The commune of Moorea-Maiao had the biggest population explosion of all the 48 communes, with an increase of 21.6 percent. Moorea now has 14,226 inhabitants, while its sister island of Maiao has only 324 people.

Of the 30,221 people living in the Leeward Islands, Bora Bora has the largest population, with 7,295 inhabitants. There was a migratory deficit of 173 inhabitants as well as a natural growth of 821 people for the Marquesas Islands, where the total population of the six islands numbers only 8,712. In six years, since the last census, the growth rate is 8 percent. The Austral Islands had a loss of population of 2.7 percent, because the people go to Tahiti to work. When they have earned enough money to build a house they often return to their island. In the Tuamotu-Gambier Islands, which had a total of 15,973 people, the 2002 census showed a strong migratory deficit of 1,149 people, which was compensated by a natural growth of 1,641 people. Some of the communes in this archipelago, such as Hao and Tureia, were directly affected by the loss of military personnel with the pullout of the CEP (Centre d'expérimentations du Pacifique) following the end of the French nuclear tests in the Tuamotu archipelago. Some atolls, such as Makemo, attract large families who work in the pearl farming business, while Napuka lost 20 percent of its population compared with 1996, because its lagoon does not provide many natural resources.

No census results have yet been published (July 2004) to let us know the percentage of males and females or their age segments. The 1996 census reported 52 percent males and 48 percent females, and 42.6 percent were in the 0 to 19-year-old group. The birth rate on January 1, 2002 was 19.6 percent, down from 20.2 percent at the same time in 2001. Women are having their children later than in years past, or they are having fewer children because contraceptive means are better known and used or because they are prolonging their studies.

The 1996 census counted 49,574 residences in French Polynesia, with an average of 4.3 people per habitation. When the 2002 census was taken this figure had increased by 22.6 percent for a total of 60,755 residences, while the population growth was only 12.6 percent during that same period. Due to more plentiful housing the number of people occupying each household has diminished from 5.24 percent in 1977 to 3.99 percent in 2002. Now it's more the nuclear family (mother, father, children) rather than having various generations under one roof, as it used to be. This can signify better living conditions, but it also means that more old people are living alone.

The death rate in January 2002 was 4.5 percent, compared to 4.9 percent a year earlier. Life expectancy remains 68 years for men and 72 years for women. This shorter life span in the tropics can be attributed to bad health habits: too much alcohol and tobacco and the consumption of too many sweet and fatty foods.

Road accidents also take their toll, especially on the group under the age of 30. In 2003 there were 439 injuries and 38 deaths due to traffic accidents, compared to 52 deaths in 2002. A new record of 8,175 4-wheel vehicles registered was set in 2001, which was 60% more than in 1997, and in 2002 there were 7,242 new 4-wheel vehicles registered. Another record was set in 2003 with a total of 11,508 vehicles (4-wheels and 2-wheels) added to the already crowded roads. The 2002 census revealed that 72 percent of the homes in French Polynesia owned at least one car, compared to 68 percent in 1996.

The census no longer includes a breakdown by ethnic groups, which were formerly classified as Polynesians, those of Polynesian-European or Polynesian-Chinese mixed race, Europeans and Chinese, or French citizens of Chinese origin. The 1988 census reported that Polynesians and assimilated races accounted for 83 percent of the population, Europeans represented 12 percent, and the Asians comprised 5 percent. The Polynesians and the Chinese born in French Polynesia are French citizens.

As of May 1, 2004, the minimum wage in French Polynesia was set at 650,88 CFP per hour or 110.000 CFP per month, for a 39-hour workweek or 169 working hours per month. Employees are covered by a French government insurance program (CPS) that includes health, workman's compensation and retirement benefits. The employer pays the majority of the premiums, as well as five weeks' vacation pay for each employee per year. There were 60,300 salaried employees in 2003, with an unemployment rate of 12 percent.

The Polynesians

The majority of the people who live in the five island groups of French Polynesia are the **Maohi** people or Eastern Polynesians. Whether they live in the Society Islands, the Marquesas, Tuamotu-Gambier or Austral Islands, they are commonly referred to as **Tahitians**. The Polynesians refer to one another according to their island or archipelago, such as a Marquesan, a Paumotu (native of the Tuamotu Islands), a Rurutu or Rapa Iti, Mangarevan, and so forth.

Two distinct racial types settled the Marquesas Islands and some of the Marquesans have longer, narrow heads. The Marquesan women have the reputation of being the prettiest of all Polynesian women. There are striking differences in the Paumotu physical types, as well as their language and culture. Some of the men on the Tuamotu atolls are big strapping fellows, with wide flat noses, while others are more squat, with big heads, small button noses and dark brown skin. Still others have thin lips, aquiline features, slim bodies and light tan skin. The Austral Islanders resemble their neighbors in the Cook Islands, with almost blue-black hair, Spanish eyes and heavy beards. In Mangareva and the other Gambier Islands the earliest settlers appear to have been castaways from the Tuamotu archipelago, the Marquesas and Rarotonga.

Although their ancestors' idea of beauty included shutting the chiefly children inside special "fattening" houses, where they became enormous while their skin was lightened from lack of sunlight, many of today's Tahitians have adopted the western world's concept of beauty. Therefore, they are even prouder of themselves when they've bronzed their bodies for hours on the beaches, even though their skin is naturally of an amber or golden brown color.

Their hair is usually thick, black and shiny and can be curly, wavy or straight, depending on how much Chinese or Spanish blood is mingled with the Polynesian traits. They anoint their hair and soft, smooth, velvety skin with *monoi*, a wonderful emollient made from coconut oil and different flowers and herbs, which makes them smell divine and practically glow under the rays of the sun.

The Polynesians are among the tallest people in the world, broad and muscular in structure. Most of them have short, broad, well-shaped heads with high cheekbones and strong jaw lines. The average Polynesian nose is long, broad and high, with a straight profile and a depression at the root. The lips are full but not Negroid, and their teeth are perfectly shaped and very white, although today's sugary diet leaves some of them snaggle-toothed. Their long and wide almond shaped eyes reveal an ancestry that began centuries ago in Southeast Asia or Malaysia, and they are a liquid brown or hazel color. The eyes of both the men and women are very expressive, sometimes sparkling with fire, and sometimes melting with softness. Their eyes are deep-set with heavy lids and their long, thick, black eyelashes are definitely enviable.

The Tahitian male has very little body hair, although several of them wear mustaches and little goatee beards. His shoulders are often very wide and strong, and his chest is well developed and tapers down to a nice, slim waist and flat stomach. His long, well-shaped legs with the prominent thigh muscles also have nicely developed calf muscles from years of playing soccer on the beach or sports field. His big feet, which are normally flat with the toes wide apart, are good for climbing coconut trees, and he has the dexterity of an amphibious animal in the water. A Tahitian man's sports usually come before everything else. If the Saturday afternoon soccer game is canceled because the playing field is three feet under water, he quickly becomes *fiu* (bored, fed up, non-talkative, non-responsive) and nothing can appease him. Fidelity to his wife or mistress is not in his vocabulary, and several of the handsomest youths are not averse to more or less discreet bisexual relationships.

The young *vahine* usually has an erect carriage, graceful walk and perfectly proportioned body. She looks fabulous in a string bikini, *pareo,* or a Parisian gown. Some of these modern ladies are well educated, intelligent, sophisticated and liberated. They're at home in the islands and the big cities of the world, at ease among different kinds of people and circumstances.

Although some of the Polynesians remain wiry and slim all their lives, the majority has a tendency toward corpulence in their adult years. The men convey an impression of giant strength, reserve power, and unconscious poise. Some of the women are tall and majestic, with broad shoulders and other masculine features. Their movements are slow, dignified and full of pride, with an undulating movement of their bodies and long pliant fingers.

The first European visitors to Tahiti were impressed by the personal cleanliness of the people. They may take three or four cold water showers a day, and both sexes use a lime as their natural deodorant, or they will sometimes rub the sweet smelling kernel of the pandanus fruit under their armpits. A group of dancers or workers or spectators on a hot day smell only of soap, *monoi* or flowers. Being dirty or wearing dirty clothes was traditionally a matter of shame. There are, of course, exceptions to this custom.

The Polynesians resemble or even exceed the Greeks in their intense worship of beauty, and there are many legends of bold sea rovers who made long and perilous voyages to distant lands to win a famous beauty, whose bodily charms are described in a most detailed and realistic manner. The beautiful languorous people of Tahiti are devoted to pleasure and the joy of the moment.

Polynesian Aristocracy

The first Europeans to discover Tahiti found a highly evolved aristocratic society that was divided into three distinct groups. The first was the Arii or princely caste, whose king or Arii Rahi, was considered a sacred being. The Raatira were minor chiefs and landowners, and the Manahune were the common people. The Arioi were a kind of sect or religious fraternity that originated in Bora Bora. Their rank in the society was identified by their tattoos. They excelled in dancing and good manners and lived totally promiscuous lives, killing their children at birth. They traveled like troubadours from island to island, performing erotic ballets and political skits.

The Manahune or *kaina* of today's Tahiti still forms the majority of the population. These Polynesians are the blue-collar workers, at the bottom end of the economic structure, with the least political power in French Polynesia.

The Chinese

Soon after the American Civil War began on April 12, 1861, the Southern states could no longer supply cotton to the textile mills in England. To fill this shortage, gentleman adventurers were sent to various parts of the world to establish cotton plantations. To Tahiti came William Stewart, a 37-year old Scotsman, who acquired 17,000 acres of fertile plains and rugged hills in Tahiti's south coast districts of Papara and Mataiea, in an area known as Atimaono. When the Tahiti Cotton and Coffee Plantation Company was formed, Stewart received permission from the Governor to import **Chinese laborers** to work in the cotton fields at Atimaono, because the Tahitians refused to become field hands.

The first contingent of 329 Chinese laborers arrived in Tahiti from Hong Kong on February 28, 1865. These workers were from a district around

Canton and the Kwangtung Province, who spoke the Hakka dialect. Eleven months later Atimaono had a total of 1,010 Chinese workers, who lived in five villages separated according to ethnic groups. In addition to the Chinese coolies, Stewart had also recruited Cook Islanders, Gilbertese, Easter Islanders and even some Tahitians to plant cotton, coconut trees, coffee, sugar cane, fruit trees and vegetable gardens.

Rumors of Stewart's tyrannical manner of running the Atimaono plantation included tales of workers being deprived of their food, fined, beaten, imprisoned in solitary confinement and even incarcerated in fetters. In 1867 a Chinese worker named Chim Soo was reportedly executed by guillotine.

Stewart was cleared of this murder and a number of other charges against him, but his fortunes began to fail when the American Civil War was over and the Southern states were once again producing cotton. Stewart's career as cotton king was ended in 1873 and he was bankrupt when he died at the age of 53.

There was no money to send the Chinese home, so most of them took jobs to earn their return fare. About a hundred of these Chinese workers remained in Tahiti and began growing vegetables on rented land, opening small stores in Tahiti and several of the outer islands. Gradually they acquired wealth and today they are integrated in all the professions, but are primarily the merchants of French Polynesia.

Many of the Chinese intermarried with the Tahitians and were eventually allowed to become French citizens, when several families changed their names to sound more "Frenchified." Today Mr. Wong has Chinese cousins who use the name of Vongue, but most of them honor the traditions of their Chinese ancestors, including the commemoration of the death of Chim Soo, the martyred Chinese coolie of Atimaono.

The French

French people from all walks of life began arriving in Tahiti as early as 1843, when the Protectorate was created in Tahiti, with Papeete as the government capital. French civil servants, lawyers, *notaires*, small businessmen, schoolteachers, medical professionals, missionaries and military men settled here, often intermarrying with the most important families of Tahiti.

Most of the French live on the island of Tahiti and her sister island of Moorea. There are small settlements of French *fonctionnaires* or retired civil servants living on Raiatea, Tahaa and Bora Bora, and in the Marquesas Islands of Hiva Oa and Nuku Hiva, with just a scattering of French on the more isolated islands.

The Expatriates

When the census was taken in 1996 there were 1,017 **expatriates** living in French Polynesia. The majority of that number consisted of the wives and concubines of the French military personnel stationed in Tahiti. Most of them have since returned to France. The number of expatriates was not reported for the 2002 census. There are some 300 Americans living in French Polynesia, primarily in the Society Islands, where they are employed in tourism and the black pearl industry, or they have retired from business.

Even though the French and other Europeans have never settled in large numbers in French Polynesia, there has been a recent influx of French moving to the Territory, and the open door policy France has granted to the citizens of the European Union is causing great concern in Tahiti. Although the local government has been assured by France that this does not mean that a Belgian or Dutchman will take the jobs that would normally be filled by Polynesians, there is still a feeling of skepticism and doubt among the local population.

The Demi

A *demi* is a Polynesian with mixed blood. The first half-caste or *demi* was born about nine months after the Spanish caravel *San Lesmes* was wrecked on the reef of Amaru in the Tuamotu atolls in 1526. After that came more Spaniards, followed by the Dutch and then the British sailors, who arrived in Tahiti in 1767. The French followed and then Tahiti became a favored destination for sea rovers, merchants, lotus-eaters, writers, painters and wastrels.

Throughout the years the pure Polynesian stock has been diminished by contact with the French, English, Americans, Germans, Russian, Swedish, Norwegians, Spanish, South Americans, Japanese, Africans—you name it. The *demi* is often very attractive and reasonably intelligent, and usually has a pretty good education, and a good job with the local government, quite frequently obtained through family connections. The *demi* can also be one of the most confused people you'll ever meet, because they live between two cultures.

On one hand they want to be sophisticated and snobbish French, and on the other hand, they are happiest when they're slurping up the *ma'a* Tahiti with their fingers and singing *kaina* songs in Tahitian during a boozy *brinque*. Some of them are adept at combining the two contrasting cultures. There's a saying in Tahiti that describes the dilemma of the average Tahitian-European person: "When he wakes up the morning, the *demi* doesn't know which side of the bed to get out of."

The Very Friendly People of Tahiti

During a 1981 interview on the *East-West Connection* television program in Los Angeles, the hostess asked Tahiti's Minister of Tourism: "What is the racial breakdown of the majority of the people?" He replied: "We used to say in Tahiti that the whole world slept with Tahiti."

☙

Chapter 5

A SHORT HISTORY

General History of French Polynesia
The Polynesian Migrations

Archaeologists, ethnologists, anthropologists, linguists and other scholars have long debated the questions of when, why, and how the pioneer Polynesians crossed thousands of miles of open ocean to settle on these islands in the Eastern Pacific that are now called **French Polynesia**.

New archaeological evidence and improved techniques of radiocarbon dating may refine the theories, but at present most of the experts who study this subject agree that the Australoid ancestors of the Melanesian, Micronesian and Polynesian people came from Southeast Asia. They walked across the land mass that existed in the final Ice Age to reach what are now the Indonesian islands of Sumatra, Java and Borneo, and on to Australia and New Guinea, which were then joined, settling in the Southwest Pacific around 30,000 BC. A group of dark-skinned people called the Papuans also came from Southeast Asia, arriving in the southwestern Pacific area between 7,000 and 3,500 BC. Several thousands of years later, between 3,000 and 1,000 BC, a group of lighter-skinned Austronesians from Asia forced the Papuans to moved further inland in what is now Irian Jaya and Papua New Guinea.

Some of these wanderers then set out to explore the more eastern South Pacific islands, eventually settling on every speck of land that could support life. They sailed eastward in their huge double ocean going canoes, using the sun, stars, wind, ocean currents, and the flight patterns of birds as their guides, referring to their crude stick charts to navigate to new islands. Carrying 100-500 people on board these canoes made of lashed planks with sails of pandanus matting, they brought with them their women and children, pigs and dogs, coconuts and taro, breadfruit tree seedlings and roots, shrubs and trees, as well as flowering plants, which were to be used for food, clothing, medicines, and other household needs. Historians believe this eastward progress occurred over 5,000 years, and departures from a settled island were necessitated due to overpopulation, food and water shortage or because of internal fighting.

The Polynesian culture is believed to have evolved in the central Pacific, in Tonga or Samoa, which they called Havaiki, their ancestral religious center. After a pause of 1,000 years, a migratory wave from this "cradle" of Polynesia brought the new explorers even farther eastward, and some archaeologists believe that as far back as 500 BC the first of these double-hulled canoes reached the Marquesas Islands. A tall and stately race of proud and cultured people settled on some of the 20 islands, which they called *Te Fenua Te Enata*, or *Te Henua Te Enana*, "The Land of the Men."

During this time Mangaia in the Cook Islands was also settled, and due to its close proximity to the Society Islands, the speculation is that Tahiti and the Leeward Society Islands were also occupied by the Polynesians much earlier than radio-carbon dating has indicated.

In 1972 **Dr. Yosihiko H. Sinoto**, the senior anthropologist from the Bernice Pauahi Bishop Museum in Honolulu, began excavation of two archaeological sites on Huahine, and unearthed a village community that existed between 850 and 1200 AD, which had been destroyed by tidal waves. This "Polynesian Pompeii" included remnants of a wooden voyaging canoe that had been preserved by the mud for 1,000 years.

During the next migratory movement of the Polynesians, some 500 years after arriving in the Marquesas, the voyaging canoes sailed south and west to the Tuamotu Archipelago and Mangareva, north to the Hawaiian Islands, and even farther eastward to discover and populate Easter Island, all around 850 AD. The great Polynesian migrations then proceeded southwest, with canoes departing from the new religious and cultural center of Havaiki, Raiatea in the Leeward Society Islands, around 1,000 AD. These voyagers settled in Rarotonga in the Cook Islands and in New Zealand, completing a triangle of Polynesian colonization. The Polynesian people of French Polynesia, the Cook Islanders, Easter Islanders, native Hawaiians and the Maoris of New Zealand all speak variations of the Maohi language, the native tongue of their Marquesan ancestors.

In 1947 **Thor Heyerdahl**, a Norwegian ethnologist, and his crew of five Viking scientists, sailed the *Kon Tiki* balsa raft a distance of almost 5,000 miles (8,000 kilometers) from the shores of Peru to French Polynesia. They crashed onto the coral reef of Raroia in the Tuamotus 101 days later. Heyerdahl wanted to prove that the South American Indians were capable of reaching the Polynesian shores in their primitive rafts, and could have been the ancestors of the Polynesian race.

Although Heyerdahl's theory was dismissed by all the experts who study the South Pacific languages and culture, more than fifty years after the *Kon Tiki* drifted across the Pacific, he was still unrepentant in his theories about Pacific settlement. Spanish adventurer **Kitin Muñoz**, one of Heyerdahl's disciples, launched a similar project in May 1997. Muñoz built a 70-ton reed raft in Easter Island, which he named *Mata Rangi*. He wanted to prove that the Polynesians were able to explore the ocean in all directions aboard rafts made from the *totara* reeds, which grow in Peru's Lake Titicaca, in the crater lakes of Easter Island, in Rapa and in Mangareva in French Polynesia, and in many other parts of the world. The *Mata Rangi* sank after only 18 days at sea, but Kitin Muñoz then built the 3-masted *Mata Rangi II* totara reed raft in the Atacama desert in Chile. The 70-ton boat was 29 meters (96 feet) long when Kitin and his crew of nine brave men left Chile, and by the time they arrived in Taiohae Bay in the Marquesas Islands 88 days later, they had less than half the raft left intact. The cords that held the bundles of totara reeds in place had been eaten away by a multitude of teredo worms, the mollusks that are known as the «termites of the sea», which live in tropical waters.

Once they were safely ashore in Taiohae Bay the remains of Kitin's amputated boat were carried away by the tide, but his enthusiasm and determination remained strong, as well as his intent to build yet another reed raft to sail all the way to Japan. Although that hasn't happened there is yet another *KonTiki* type adventure being planned by six Scandinavian men, including Olav Heyerdahl, the son of Thor, who died in 2001 at the age of 87. Olav will be the carpenter aboard the balsa raft, which will be called *Tangaroa*, named for the Polynesian god of the sea. These Norwegian and Swedish adventurers plan to leave Peru on April 28, 2005, following the exact same route as the one taken by Heyerdahl from Peru to French Polynesia. They will employ satellite communication links to minimize the inherent risks of such a crossing and their focus will be on nature and the environment.

Yet another adventurer will be retracing the route of the *Kon Tiki* starting in January 2005, when Maud Fontenoy of France will leave Peru to row across the Pacific in a specially designed boat that is 7 meters (23 feet) long and 1.60 meters (5.2 feet) wide. This 26-year old woman has already succeeded in rowing across the Atlantic and she expects to cover the 8,000 kilometer (4,960 miles) distance in less than five months, arriving in Tahiti at the end of May or early June 2005.

European Exploration

In 1513 the Spanish explorer **Vasco Nuñez de Balboa** crossed the Isthmus of Panama and sighted the mighty Pacific Ocean. Seven years later, in 1520, **Ferdinand Magellan**, a Portuguese in the service of the Spanish, sailed to the Philippines, but the only island he sighted in Polynesia was the atoll of Puka Puka in the northeastern Tuamotu archipelago. The Spanish caravel

San Lesmes was wrecked on the reef in Amaru in the Tuamotus around 1526 and the shipwrecked sailors supposedly married Polynesian women. In 1595 **Alvaro de Mendaña de Neira** was searching for the Solomon Islands, which he had discovered in 1567, and during this second voyage into the South Seas he discovered the southern group of the Marquesas Islands. In 1606, 80 years after the disappearance of the *San Lesmes*, **Pedro Fernández de Quiros**, who had been Mendaña's chief pilot, discovered a number of the Tuamotu Islands before continuing on to other island groups further west. This was the last of the Spanish explorations in the Pacific during that era.

In 1615-16 the Dutch explorers **Le Maire** and **Schouten** discovered several atolls in the Tuamotus, and in 1722 **Jacob Roggeveen**, another Dutch captain, sailed through the Tuamotus and passed the island of Makatea on his way to the Society Islands, where he sighted Maupiti in the Leeward Society Islands. But he failed to see Bora Bora, Raiatea or Tahaa, all high islands that are visible from Maupiti.

The Dutch were then followed by the British, with **Commodore John Byron**, grandfather of the famous poet, discovering more of the Tuamotu atolls aboard the *H.M.S. Dolphin* in 1765. If any of the European explorers found Tahiti, they left no record of their discovery.

The *Dolphin* returned to the South Seas in 1767 under the command of **Captain Samuel Wallis**, who discovered the island of Tahiti, and anchored in Matavai Bay on June 23, 1767. He was followed just 10 months later by French **Admiral Louis Antoine de Bougainville**, who also discovered Tahiti, and claimed the island for France during his visit in April 1768. In April 1769, Lieutenant **James Cook**, aboard the *H.M.S. Endeavour*, made his first trip to Tahiti. He returned again as Captain James Cook in 1773, 1774 and 1777. Cook visited Moorea and discovered the Leeward Islands of Raiatea, Tahaa, Huahine, Bora Bora, Tupai and Maupiti, which he named the Society Islands as they lay contiguous to each other.

In 1772 Spanish captain **Don Domingo de Boenechea** anchored his ship, the *Aguilla*, in the lagoon of Tautira on the Tahiti Iti peninsula. After claiming the island for his country and king, Boenechea sailed for Peru, but returned in 1774 to establish the first long-term European settlement on the island, with two missionaries and two military men. The Spanish rule ended in Tahiti following the death of Boenechea, when the missionaries returned to Peru.

The story of **Captain William Bligh** and the mutinous crew aboard the *H.M.S. Bounty* provided a colorful chapter in Tahiti's history, following their arrival at Point Venus in 1788.

The English Protestant missionaries from the London Missionary Society (LMS) arrived aboard the *Duff* and landed at Point Venus on March 5, 1797, to convert the Tahitians to the Gospel. **George Pritchard** of the LMS gained the confidence of **Queen Pomare IV** and convinced her that Tahiti should be under the protection of England. Although **Queen Victoria** was unwilling to declare Tahiti a protectorate of England, a power struggle between the English Protestants and the French Catholic missionaries in Tahiti almost brought England and France to the brink of war. The end result was that Queen Pomare IV and the LMS missionaries lost their battle with the French, under the guns of *La Reine Blanche*, a French warship commanded by **Admiral Dupetit-Thouars**. Tahiti became a French protectorate in 1842 and guerrilla rebellions on Tahiti and some of the other islands resisted the French invasion until 1846, when France gained control over Tahiti and Moorea.

French Colonialism
Tahiti and her dependencies became a full-fledged French colony on December 29, 1880, when the century-old reign of the Pomare family formally came to an end and French nationality and rights were bestowed on all Tahitians.

The Pomare's dominions included Tahiti, Moorea, Maiao, Mehetia, the Tuamotu islands and Tubuai and Raivavae in the Austral Islands. The French had already annexed the Marquesas Islands in 1842. The island of Rapa became a French protectorate in 1867 and was annexed in 1881. The Gambier Islands were annexed in 1882; Raiatea and Tahaa were annexed in 1887, although the warriors in Raiatea resisted French control until the end of the century. The other Leeward Society Islands were annexed in 1888, Rurutu was annexed in 1900, and Rimatara was annexed in 1901.

In 1903 the *Etablissements Français de l'Océanie* (EFO), or French Territories of Oceania, were established, incorporating all of the French holdings in the Eastern Pacific into one colony. Copra, cotton, mother-of-pearl shell, phosphate, vanilla and fruits were exported in exchange for manufactured goods. By 1911 there were about 3,500 colonists, mostly French, living in Polynesia, plus the Chinese immigrants who had been brought to Tahiti in the 1860s to work in the cotton fields of Atimaono.

Although Tahiti was geographically far from the main theaters of the two world wars, the colony was politically involved because of its French connection. During World War I almost 1,000 Tahitian soldiers fought against the Germans in Europe, and the town of Papeete was bombarded by two German cruisers on September 22, 1914, when they sank a French navy ship in the harbor.

During World War II young men from Tahiti joined the Pacific Battalion, were shipped to Europe, and fought side by side with the forces of the Free French. Bora Bora was used as a military supply base for the American forces, with 5,000 soldiers, sailors and Seabees arriving on the small island in 1942. Besides a few cannon in the hills and some old Quonset huts, the only reminders of the American presence in Bora Bora today are some blue-eyed Tahitians with light hair and skin.

French Polynesia

A 1957 statute changed the *Etablissements Français de l'Océanie* colony into a French Overseas Territory, with the official name of French Polynesia. In the early 1960s a large harbor was built in Papeete, an international airport was opened in Faaa, the French established the *Centre d'expérimentations du Pacifique* (CEP), the Pacific Experimentation Center in Tahiti, and MGM brought a big film crew to make another movie of *Mutiny on the Bounty*. All of these rapid changes brought French Polynesia into the modern age, accompanied by problems of inflation, unemployment, housing problems, pollution, emotional instability, juvenile delinquency and political discontent among an increasing number of the population.

French Nuclear Testing

French Polynesia entered the nuclear age in 1963 when the French chose the Tuamotu atolls of Moruroa, 1,200 kilometers (720 miles) southeast of Tahiti, and Fangataufa, 40 kilometers (24 miles) south of Moruroa, as sites for the *Centre d'expérimentations du Pacifique* (CEP), Pacific Experimentation Center. Although the local political parties protested the invasion, President Charles de Gaulle responded by outlawing political parties.

On September 11, 1966, De Gaulle watched from an offshore French warship as the first nuclear test was carried out, exploding in the atmosphere almost 600 meters (2,000 feet) above the turquoise lagoon of Moruroa. Between 1966-1974, the French made 41 atmospheric tests in Moruroa and Fangataufa, and between 1975-1991, some 134 underground tests were completed, by drilling a shaft deep into the coral foundation under the lagoons. President François Mitterand suspended the nuclear testing in April 1992 and most of the 7,750 employees of the CEP returned to France or to their islands in French Polynesia. In June 1995, France's newly elected president, Jacques Chirac, announced a new series of eight nuclear tests, to be completed by the end of May 1996.

The shock of this announcement reverberated around the world, and on September 5, 1995, when a 20-kiloton explosion was carried out in Moruroa, the result was disastrous for France, and especially for French Polynesia's tourism and economy. Severe rioting broke out in Papeete, with several buildings burned, the Tahiti-Faaa International Airport terminal was partially burned, and the vehicles in the parking lot were damaged and burned. On January 27, 1996, France made its sixth and final nuclear test at Fangataufa, and two days later President Chirac announced that the tests were finished forever.

Some of the 1,500 workers, technicians and scientists, brought from France and Tahiti for these tests, finished their work and studies and went home, while the French Army and Legionnaires dismantled the two nuclear bases.

Internal Autonomy Government

In 1977 a statute passed by the French parliament in Paris granted administrative autonomy to French Polynesia, and domestic or internal autonomy was given in 1984, consolidated in 1990 and extended in 1996. On February 12, 2004, the French government gave French Polynesia the status of a French Overseas Country, rather than a Territory, which means that the Assembly of French Polynesia can adopt "laws" in the most important areas, and not just "resolutions", or acts of an administrative nature. This revision of the Constitution also enlarges the field of responsibilities of French Polynesia, which can negotiate international agreements with foreign states, in matters relevant to its responsibility. It also may become a member of international organizations and have representation in foreign states.

The French Polynesian Government consists of a president, who is elected for a five-year term by the Assembly and Council of Ministers whom he appoints before submitting the list to the Assembly's vote. The Assembly consists of 57 members, who are elected every five years by votes and who represent the five archipelagoes. The French Polynesian Government is represented in the French Parliament by two deputies and one senator, plus an advisor in the French Social and Economic Council.

A French High Commissioner represents the State in French Polynesia, and the Republic of France controls defense, law and order, justice, worldwide international responsibility and the currency. The French *gendarmes* have brigades on all the larger islands and each *commune* has one or more Tahitian *mutoi* policemen, whose duties may include directing school traffic and tracking down scooters or cars that were "borrowed" on a Saturday night. His job also includes keeping peace in his own neighborhood. There are also other branches of law enforcement in Tahiti, including the secret service police and the municipal police who patrol the "hot spots" of downtown Papeete on weekends, searching for drinking minors, drugs, fights and vehicles with boom boxes blaring at top volume, which are all illegal.

Today the Tahitian flag, white with red borders at top and bottom, with an emblem representing a double outrigger sailing canoe, flies side by side with the tri-color of the French flag. The archipelagoes also have their own emblems. The Territorial anthem "Ia Ora 'O Tahiti Nui" is sung or played wherever French Polynesia participates in international meetings or sports events throughout the Pacific. You can listen to this anthem and learn all about the French Polynesian Government at *www.presidence.pf.*

Post-Nuclear Progress Pact for Self-Sufficiency

A **Progress Pact** between the French Polynesia and the French State was signed in January 1993, to compensate for the loss of financial resources due to the ending of the CEP French nuclear tests in the Tuamotu Islands. A 10-year adjustment law and development contracts for five-year periods were adopted in 1994, with the State providing assistance in the fields of education, training, research, health and transport infrastructures, agriculture, tourism and housing.

When French President Jacques Chirac decided in 1996 to halt all nuclear testing, France committed itself to maintaining the same amount of spending in CFP in French Polynesia. The spending level agreed to was 18 billion French Pacific francs (about US $1.8 million dollars) per year for 10 years, which was made possible by a reconversion fund. This agreement for strengthening the economic autonomy was signed between the French State and French Polynesia on July 26, 1996, and was valid until 2005. President Chirac has now removed all boundaries on the reconversion fund payments so that French Polynesia is supposed to receive 18 billion CFP per year forever and ever.

Tax incentive measures for investments include the "Flosse Law", which complements a national measure known as the "Pons Law," and the French Polynesia Investment Code.

On January 1, 1998, a Value Added Tax (VAT, TVA in French) went into effect. The VAT for the year 2004 includes 6 percent tax for room rates, prepaid meal plans and transfers between the airport or boat dock and your hotel or pension. All other food and beverages consumed in hotels, restaurants and snack bars have a VAT of 10 percent. Transfers provided other than by the hotels and pensions, as well as all tours, excursions and activities you choose at your hotel or from a private company, also carry a 10 percent VAT. There is a VAT of 10 to 16 percent applicable to anything purchased in a shop, store or boutique.

The government's original objective was to increase the VAT to an average of 15 percent over the first five years, and to eliminate a 10 percent tax on all imported goods during the first two years, and all local customs duties during the next three years, at a rate of one-third less per year. The customs taxes since 2002 are 15 percent, compared to more than 30 percent in 1997. However, new taxes were added in 2002 on soft drinks, alcoholic beverages, cigarettes and automobiles.

French Polynesia's main economic resources are tourism and pearl farming. In recent years, deep-sea commercial fishing has also experienced a promising development, particularly with an increase in exports. Agricultural products, such as fruit, flowers and nono or noni (*Morinda citrifolia*), have also had export successes.

Histories of the Bigger Islands: Tahiti, Moorea, & Bora Bora
TAHITI
Wallis Discovers King George III Island
Captain Samuel Wallis of the British Royal Navy, and his crew of 150 men, who were sailing the *H.M.S. Dolphin* during its discovery voyage, sighted the tall mountains of Tahiti Iti and Tahiti Nui five days before anchoring in

Matavai Bay on June 23, 1767. The exhausted and scurvy-ridden men aboard the 32-gun frigate had left England eight months before in search of *terra Australis Incognita*, the great land mass that King George III and his geographers were convinced lay somewhere between Cape Horn and New Zealand, in balance with the northern hemisphere.

While searching for a safe anchorage the *Dolphin* was surrounded by canoes bearing more than 800 men. When the British sailors invited the natives aboard the ship, one of them climbed the mizzen chains and stood on the awning above the deck while the white men showed him trinkets. A friend soon joined him, and as the two men stood on the ship's deck, a billy goat butted the first fellow from behind. In terror they jumped overboard and swam ashore. They soon returned to the ship with other natives, who carried banana shoots. These curious natives inspected the goats and sheep, hogs and fowl, and then began to take everything they could lay their hands on.

Wallis' men began to trade trinkets, axes and other items in exchange for food and water. Although there were skirmishes, with some of the natives throwing stones and the white men discharging their guns, friendly relations and traffic were soon restored, although the foreigners soon learned that the natives were great pilferers.

Upon entering the beautiful harbor of Matavai Bay on June 23, the *Dolphin* struck a deep-sea rock the Tahitians called Hiro's Rock, after one of their demigods. This rock is now called Dolphin Rock on the maps.

As Wallis was too weak from scurvy to claim the new land in the name of the British King, the second lieutenant, **Tobias Furneaux**, hoisted a pennant on a long pole and went ashore on June 26, and took possession of the land Wallis called "King George's Island." The bay was named Port Royal.

Following a consultation by the Tahitian chiefs and counselors, the people formed a large torchlight procession with drums and conch trumpets to bear away the flag on its staff. The natives understood the significance of the white men planting their flag on Tahitian soil, and they sought the aid of their gods to drive the strangers away.

Imagine the surprise and joy of the men aboard the *Dolphin* the next morning when they found their ship surrounded by some five hundred canoes containing four thousand athletic paddlers and loaded with fruit, coconuts, fowl and young pigs. But the most astonishing sight to their sea-weary eyes was that of the fair young girls, standing in the middle of each canoe, nude to the waist, "who played a great many droll, wanton tricks." While the hungry sailors were enjoying the free strip tease, the Tahitian men began to hurl fist-sized stones at the men on board the *Dolphin*. The sailors retaliated by firing the ship's cannons at the canoes, killing forty or fifty of the Tahitians and sinking a great number of the canoes. After a second attack that the men of the ship easily won, the Tahitians decided to be friendly and peaceful.

The men of the *Dolphin* spent the next five weeks trading earrings, nails and beads for foodstuffs. Then they began to engage in a "new sort of trade...it might properly be called the old trade," according to **George Robertson**, master, whose journal is the best account given. When the men had emptied their sea chests to exchange their possessions for the ladies' favors, they began to remove the iron nails and cleats from the ship. This carnal exchange began with a 20- or 30-penny nail. As demand outgrew the supply, the size of the nails increased to a 40-penny and some of the *vahines* demanded as much as a seven- or nine-inch spike. Two-thirds of the men even pulled out the nails on which they had hung their hammocks.

The high **Chief Amo** of the powerful Teva clan of Papara was also in charge of Ha'apape (now called Mahina), the district where the *Dolphin* was anchored. Amo's wife **Purea** was chiefess of Ha'apape, and when Amo returned to Papara, Purea hospitably received Captain Wallis and his people. She personally carried Wallis ashore and had the sick men taken to a guesthouse, where they were massaged with coconut oil and healed with traditional Tahitian medicines until they recovered their health. In exchange for her kindness, Captain Wallis presented Purea with a looking glass, some turkeys, a gander, a goose and a cat.

On July 27 the *Dolphin* left Tahiti, and on passing Moorea, Wallis named the island York, after the Duke of York. Wallis sailed back to England without looking further for the southern continent.

Bougainville's New Cytherea-Island of Love

Just nine months after Wallis had departed, the French explorer **Louis Antoine de Bougainville** was the second visitor from Europe to claim Tahiti for his country. Bougainville led an expedition of two ships, the *Boudeuse* and the *Etoile*, and he was also searching for the mythical *terra Australis Incognita*. In passing through the coral atolls of the Tuamotu Islands, Bougainville named them the Dangerous Archipelago, because the outlines of the low islands were indistinct and dangerous to pass.

Bougainville's visit to Tahiti lasted from April 6-14, 1768, but he did not visit Matavai Bay, remaining instead on the eastern coast of Hitia'a, where he was anchored too close to the reef. During his visit Bougainville lost six anchors in eight days. He was kindly received by **Chief 'Ereti** of Hitia'a, who allowed the Frenchmen to stay in sheds on the bank of a stream while they collected water for the ships. But the chief made it clear that the visit was to be strictly limited.

One unusual incident marked this landing, when the Tahitians spotted a woman among the 314 officers and men of the two ships. Although she had sailed from France disguised as a man, the Tahitians knew immediately that she was a woman. Her secret was revealed to her shipmates when one big Tahitian man grabbed her up to run off to the hills to give her a personal welcome. Her name was **Jeanne Baret** and she had sailed as the valet of Bougainville's naturalist, **Dr. Philibert de Commerçon**. Jeanne Baret became the first white woman to visit Tahiti and to circumnavigate the world.

Bougainville, not knowing that his new island had already been "discovered" by Wallis and claimed for England, proclaimed French sovereignty over the island he called New Cytherea or the New Island of Love. He found the Tahitian love rites similar to the ancient worship of Aphrodite-Venus, whose birthplace was the Greek island of Cythera or Cytherea. Bougainville was an enlightened spirit, a mathematician, diplomat, and a sophisticated *bon vivant*. Inspired by **Jean-Jacques Rousseau's** philosophy that Europeans were overly civilized and should get back to a more natural state, Bougainville coined the phrase 'noble savage'. When he sailed away from Tahiti, Bougainville took with him a young man from Hitia'a named **Ahutoru**, a living noble savage who became the first Tahitian to discover Europe.

Cook at Point Venus

Lieutenant James Cook, who later came to be known as Captain Cook, England's most famous explorer, was the third European discoverer to visit Tahiti. Cook's ship, the *H.M.S. Endeavour*, anchored in Matavai Bay on April 13, 1769.

Cook's expedition was to take an astronomer either to the Marquesas Islands or to New Zealand for the purpose of observing the transit of the planet Venus across the sun. This event was to take place on June 3, 1769, and there would be no further opportunity to witness such a phenomenon again until 1874. Astronomers were eager to take advantage of this rare occurrence, as it would enable them to ascertain the distance of the earth from the sun, the fundamental base line in all astronomical measurements. The Royal Society had sent expeditions to various parts of the world, but Cook's ship was the only one to visit the Southern Hemisphere.

Two months before Cook left for the South Seas, Wallis returned to England with the disappointing news that he had not found the great southern continent. When he learned of the imminent voyage Cook was to command, Wallis suggested King George III's island as the ideal spot to establish an observatory. Wallis told Cook that he and his men would find hospitable natives and an abundance of food and water on this island he discovered during his world circumnavigation just two years before.

Cook's expedition consisted of eighty-four officers and seamen and eight civilians. The civilians included **Joseph Banks**, a young botanist who later became president of the Royal Society; **Dr. Daniel Solander**, an eminent Swedish botanist and zoologist who had studied with the great Linnaeus; and astronomer **Charles Green**, who, in addition to supervising the observation of Venus, provided Cook with precise estimates of longitude, which was indispensable on such a discovery voyage.

When Cook anchored in Matavai Bay, seven weeks before the transit of Venus was expected, the *Endeavour* was given an enthusiastic welcome by the Tahitians. Crowds of natives greeted the ship with the now customary friendliness, and immediately recognized four of the officers who had visited the island with Wallis.

The high chiefess Purea did not greet Cook as the sovereign of Ha'apape, as she had received Wallis, because the Teva clan had been conquered by other chiefs, whose leader was Vairaatoa, or Tu, who later became known as **King Pomare I**.

The first thing Cook did upon arrival in what was then known to the English as King George III's Island was to build a fort to protect the astronomer and his instruments. He chose the same site that Wallis had selected, the strip of land between the beach and the river. In less than three weeks' time the fort was finished, which was 150 feet long and 80 feet wide, with five-foot high walls and two four-pounder cannons.

These precautions proved superfluous, however, for the Tahitians, especially the women, were so friendly and hospitable that the British sailors forgot their duties. Taking a lesson learned from Wallis about the nail-removing fiasco, Cook posted regulations concerning trade with the natives. He ordered that no iron be exchanged except for provisions. He also asked his men to treat the natives with "all imaginable humanity" and to use every fair means of cultivating their friendship. The natives appreciated this treatment and came to know the Englishmen affectionately by their "Tahitianized" surnames—*Tute* (Cook), *Opane* (Banks) and *Tolano* (Solander).

The major problem Cook encountered was constant pilfering. From time to time he was obliged to take one or more of the chiefs hostage against the return of missing objects. The most important item taken was the quadrant, an essential instrument for astronomical observation. Although the instrument was eventually returned, the culprit had removed it from its box and taken it apart to see what was inside, and consequently, the quadrant was useless.

On the day of the observation, there was not a cloud in the sky and the scientists were able to witness every phase of the transit from the fort at Point Venus, named in honor of the occasion. A small party took measurements from a *motu* islet inside the reef of Moorea. However, it was subsequently found that the readings were of little value because of unforeseen optical distortion caused by the irradiation of the sun.

Cook's expedition stayed in Tahiti for three months, during which time he learned much about the Tahitian way of life. He observed the native customs, manners, religion and law. He described the people's appearance (explaining their tattoos), cooking methods, foodstuffs and apparent social and political order. He also made a trip around the island in a longboat and drew a complete and accurate map of the whole coastal region of Tahiti.

By this time Cook had learned what the natives called their island and began using the name he understood it to be—Otaheite. When he asked them the name, they replied, "This is Tahiti," and in their language it sounded like Otaheite.

Several of the things Cook learned about the Tahitian way of life shocked the 41-year old seaman. "It is this," he wrote in his Journal, "that more than half of the better sort...have enter'd into a resolution of injoying free liberty in Love, without being Troubled...by its consequences. These mix and Cohabit together with the utmost freedom, and the Children who are so unfortunate as to be thus begot are smothered at the Moment of their Birth." He noted that couples lived together for years, destroying all children. His reference was to the Areoi Society that was in existence at that time, and their meetings during which "the Women in dancing...give full Liberty to their desires." He was also aghast that "both sexes express the most indecent ideas in conversation without the least emotion" and that "chastity...is but little valued. The Men will very readily offer the Young Women to Strangers, even their own daughters, and think it very strange if you refuse them; but this is merely done for the sake of gain."

However, the Tahitian people were suffering consequences of having enjoyed free liberty in love. Cook found, to his distress, that many of them, as well as his own men, were suffering from venereal disease. How they caught it is a toss-up between the men on Cook's ships or the former discoverers. The English blame the French and vice-versa.

In years to come, the ravages of venereal disease, as well as other illnesses the Europeans introduced to the islands, such as tuberculosis, small pox, measles and alcoholism, as well as the guns they brought to the natives, helped to reduce the population at an alarming rate. Cook gave the estimate of the population at over 200,000. Just 36 years later it was determined to be 8,000.

Cook and his men sailed away from Tahiti on July 13, 1769. Heading westward, he anchored in Moorea's Opunohu Bay, and took a longboat to explore Pao Pao, which he named Cook's Bay. Cook also discovered the Leeward Islands of Huahine, Raiatea, Tahaa, Bora Bora, Maupiti and Tupai, located about 100 miles northwest of Tahiti. He named these six islands the Society Islands "as they lie contiguous to each other." (During the second half of the 19th century the Society Islands name was extended to comprise Tahiti and Moorea). Cook also discovered two islands in the Austral group and several of the Tuamotu atolls, before sailing on to claim New Zealand, Australia, and several other islands for his country. He returned to Matavai Bay again, as Captain Cook, on three separate occasions in 1773, 1774 and 1777, during his second and third voyages of exploration. Today there is a monument to this great discoverer at Point Venus.

"Breadfruit Bligh" & The Bounty

In the following years many ships called at Tahiti, some anchoring in Matavai Bay and others stopping at Tahiti Iti, "little Tahiti" on the Taiarapu peninsula. One of the most famous ships to drop anchor in Tahitian waters was the *H.M.S. Bounty*, commanded by Lieutenant William Bligh. The *Mutiny on the Bounty* saga is well known, as it was imaginatively told by co-authors **James Norman Hall** and **Charles Nordhoff**, two Americans who moved to Tahiti after fighting in World War I. Erroll Flynn starred in the first *Bounty* movie, which was filmed in Australia. Clark Gable and Charles Laughton played the major roles in a black and white *Mutiny on the Bounty* in 1935, which was mostly filmed in Santa Catalina, off the California coast. In 1962 MGM released another *Mutiny on the Bounty* film, starring Marlon Brando, Trevor Howard, and the Tahitian beauty, Tarita, which was filmed at Point Venus and in Bora Bora. A slightly different version entitled *The Bounty*, starring Mel Gibson and Anthony Hopkins, was filmed on Moorea in 1984. Without the bountiful *Artocarpus altilis* or breadfruit tree, one of history's greatest sea dramas might never have occurred.

Bligh first visited Tahiti with Captain Cook aboard the *Resolution*, and had taken note of the breadfruit that was the staple diet of the Tahitians. When he returned to England, Bligh contacted his wife's uncle, who had several large plantations in Jamaica, as well as a number of ships. The English merchants in the West Indies then made a petition to King George III, requesting permission to bring small breadfruit trees from Tahiti to plant in their islands, which they intended to use as a cheap and nourishing means of feeding their slaves. Cook and others had spoken highly of this substitute for bread, which the strong and healthy Tahitians ate daily. The King agreed to their request and Bligh was appointed Captain of the voyage. He had no problem finding a crew willing to sail to Tahiti, as word had spread around Europe about the friendly and welcoming Tahitian *vahines*.

Captain Bligh began having problems with his *Bounty* crew even before the ship arrived in Tahiti's Matavai Bay on October 26, 1788. And once ashore, they had to wait five months in Tahiti before the breadfruit would be at the right stage for transplanting. The sailors happily accepted this respite from Bligh's tight discipline, and willingly adapted to the Tahitian *aita pea pea* (no problem) philosophy of life, complete with all the pleasures any sailor could ever imagine.

Bligh moved his ship from Matavai Bay to Papeete, where he had better protection from the wind. Thereafter, all the visiting ships followed suit and Papeete became the center of activity on the island of Tahiti.

While the breadfruit trees were being gathered and loaded onto the ship, Bligh became excessively severe with his men as the time drew nearer for their departure. When the *Bounty* weighed anchor on April 4, 1789, and headed toward the Leeward Islands of the Society group, Bligh was faced with a moody, belligerent crew.

The punishments Bligh meted out for his men, and his insults to his officers were too harsh to endure after the idyllic life the men had enjoyed in Tahiti. Acting Lieutenant Fletcher Christian was especially disturbed, and his fury finally exploded into a dramatic mutiny, which is remembered as the most famous mutiny in history.

Bligh was hauled out of bed early on the morning of April 28, tied up and dragged on deck. He and 18 of his officers and men were put into an open launch, and the only supplies they received were a 28-gallon cask of water, 150 pounds of bread, some wine and rum, a compass, a quadrant, some canvas, and lines and sails. Then the boat was set adrift in the open ocean, a few miles from Tofua in the Tongan Islands, whose inhabitants were extremely un-friendly in those days.

Bligh's success in sailing the small open boat across 5,800 kilometers (3,600 miles) of ocean to Timor and Batavia in the Dutch Indies, is one of the most remarkable voyages in history. Only one man died during this crossing, and six others died after reaching shore.

The twenty-five men who remained aboard the *Bounty* consisted of Fletcher Christian's followers, as well as the sailors who had nothing to do with the mutiny. Christian sailed the *Bounty* to Tubuai, 568 kilometers (355 miles) due south of Tahiti in the Austral Islands, but they were unable to stay there because the natives were so hostile. The *Bounty* then returned to Tahiti and on June 6 anchored in Matavai Bay. For the next ten days the men loaded pigs, goats, a cow and a bull, cats and fowl, plus nine Tahitian men, eight women and nine children, and set sail once again for Tubuai.

Although Fletcher Christian tried to settle his group in Tubuai, they were forced to give up the idea, after a hundred natives were killed in skirmishes. They retreated to Tahiti for supplies, and when the *Bounty* left Matavai Bay for the last time, some of the British sailors remained ashore at Point Venus. Aboard the ship with Christian were eight of his fellow mutineers, six Tahitian men, twelve Tahitian women and one little girl. This small group reached the uninhabited island of Pitcairn, where they burned the *Bounty* and began a new life ashore. There was no news of Christian and his party for 18 years.

The 16 men who chose to remain in Tahiti settled down with their wives and families. Two of them had died by the time the H.M.S. *Pandora* anchored in Matavai Bay in 1791, but **Captain Edward Edwards**, who had been sent from England in search of the mutineers, arrested the remaining 14 men. The *Pandora* was shipwrecked and four of the men were drowned before they could reach England for their trial. During a court martial inquiry in England, three of the men were condemned to death and hanged, and the remaining seven were set free. **Peter Heywood** wrote the first Tahitian dictionary in prison while awaiting his trial.

Captain Bligh had also undergone a trial by the English court, which cleared his name for any guilt in the *Bounty* mutiny, and he sailed back to Tahiti, arriving in Matavai Bay on April 10, 1792, as commander of the *H.M.S. Providence* and her armed tender, the *Assistance*.

A native war was in progress when he arrived in Tahiti, but he eventually went ashore to supervise the building of storage sheds for the young breadfruit trees he had come to collect. In his journal Bligh recorded his disappointment in seeing the degeneration of the Tahitian people due to the influence of deserters from the various ships that visited Tahiti. "...little of the ancient customs of the Otaheitans remains...It is difficult to get them to speak their own language without mixing a jargon of English with it, and they are so altered that I believe in future no Europeans will ever know what their ancient customs of receiving strangers were," he wrote. He also noted that they were "...no longer clean Otaheitans, but in appearance a set of ragamuffins with whom it is necessary to observe great caution."

Bligh remained in Tahiti for three months, collecting 2,126 breadfruit trees and 500 other plants to take back to the West Indies. The breadfruit seedlings were planted in St. Vincent and in Port Royal, Jamaica. When the trees grew and began to bear fruit, the Negro slaves refused to eat the starchy breadfruit because they didn't like the taste of the stuff.

The Arrival of the Gospel — A Different Kind of Conqueror

On March 3, 1797, the people of Tahiti felt several earthquake shocks, which were accompanied by a high sea and a terrible storm. This was the first time they had ever experienced an earthquake, and they were completely terrorized by these strange happenings. The first shock took place early in the morning, which drove the people out of their houses in confusion. At noon another shock occurred and the frightened people threw themselves prostrate upon the ground and cried out to their gods for mercy. At sunset a third shock caused many to hold night vigils, fearful that some awful calamity was at hand. On the following day, March 4th, the amazed people sighted the London missionary ship *Duff* offshore the peninsula of Tahiti Iti. They understand that this foreign ship was the cause of the commotion, and in consequence, named it *te-rapu* (The Stirrer), a name they have always retained.

By the time the *Duff* anchored in Matavai Bay on March 5, a Sunday morning, more than a hundred natives were dancing and capering on the decks of the ship, eager to make friends with the missionaries. Although the Tahitians were unarmed, Captain Wilson ordered the great guns to be hoisted out of the hold to keep the natives in awe. Instead of being intimidated by the guns, the Tahitians helped to place them into their carriages.

Aboard the ship were 18 missionaries destined for Tahiti, who settled into their new quarters on Point Venus in the former house of Captain Bligh. Most of these men were in their early 20s and only five of them were married and had their families with them. The London Missionary Society (LMS), which was composed of Episcopalians, Methodists, Presbyterians and Independents, had chosen Tahiti as their first foreign country because they felt they would not have so many difficulties in Christianizing the heathen natives. The Reverend **Doctor Thomas Haweis**, the founder of the LMS, had read the accounts of Samuel Wallis, James Cook and William Bligh, who had written of their voyages to Tahiti. The shocking lack of puritanical behavior of the fun-loving Tahitians presented a certain challenge to the LMS leader. He decided that a South Seas island would be a suitable place for their mission, as the climate was good, food plentiful, there were no religious prejudices, and the government seemed monarchical, but of the mildest nature.

One of the first problems the Englishmen encountered was how to deal with the beautiful and seductive Tahitian *vahines*. Several of the young missionaries were sent home soon after arriving in Tahiti because they succumbed to the alluring charms of the idolatrous women, which was an unforgivable sin according to their vows.

Among the missionaries were carpenters, bricklayers, shoemakers, tailors, weavers and a harness maker. There were only four ordained ministers in the group, who soon learned that there was more to apprehend from being caressed and exalted by the natives, than from being insulted and oppressed.

The missionaries had difficulty learning to speak the language well enough to preach the gospel in Tahitian, and the natives would scoff and ridicule them and laugh when the missionaries said that Jehovah was the only true God and their pagan rites and human sacrifices should be abolished.

Some of the Tahitians felt that the missionaries should pay them to attend the mission school, and among the students was the oldest son of **Pomare II**, the powerful chief whom the missionaries thought of as king of Tahiti. His father, Tu, who had been designated as King Pomare I by the Europeans, died in 1803.

It was not until May 18, 1819, that the missionaries baptized their first convert on the island of Tahiti, who was King Pomare II. It had taken 22 long years of hard work, persistence and tremendous faith to achieve this goal. Although they suspected that Pomare wanted to be baptized for his own personal and political gain, they had to accept him in order to get the rest of the people into the church. Following his conversion, the heathen idols and temples were destroyed in favor of the Christian religion.

Although the Tahitians seemed to accept the outward forms of Christianity, many of them still retained their old ways. The missionaries made every effort to enforce their puritan standards on the islanders, who had to cover their bodies with hot clothing. They were forbidden to sing any songs but hymns, nor were they allowed to dance, wear flowers, tattoo their bodies, or sleep together in the big houses, where they formerly enjoyed indiscriminate sex. However, the women were still as free and easy in sex matters with foreign seamen who arrived in increasing numbers aboard the whaling ships. And drunkenness among the men became common, with King Pomare II one of the worst offenders. His behavior continued to shock the puritanical missionaries, as he continued his sexual relations with both sexes. He died in 1821 at the age of 47, from a combination of alcoholism, elephantiasis and dropsy. His young son, **Pomare III**, who was being educated by the missionary **Henry Nott**, died at the age of six.

The Reign of Queen Pomare IV

Pomare II's 14-year old illegitimate daughter, Aimata, was then crowned **Queen Pomare IV**, but her accession to the crown was without pomp or ceremony. The young queen had been married at the age of ten to a chief from Tahaa named Tapoa, but she later divorced him and took a new consort named **Arifaaite**. Although her wild behavior shocked the missionaries, Queen Pomare IV eventually grew into her majestic role and she ruled Tahiti, Moorea and part of the Austral and Tuamotu groups for 50 years.

In 1827 the Protestants built their first church, made of coral stones, which was erected on the site of Marae Taputapuatea at Papetoai in Moorea, which had been a royal stone temple.

The Protestant missionaries were the only soul-savers in Tahiti for almost forty years before any competitive religions arrived on the island. In 1835 a group of Catholic missionaries landed on the island of Mangareva, 900 miles southeast of Tahiti. They eventually made their way to Tahiti, and the Protestants used all their influence to prevent the Catholics from opening a new mission.

When two Catholic priests refused to leave Tahiti, even upon written orders issued by Queen Pomare IV, **Father Honoré Laval** and **Father François Caret** were forcibly removed from the island.

The French Protectorate

When the French government learned how their Catholic priests had been treated by the Queen of Tahiti, they retaliated by sending the frigate V*enus*, under the command of **Captain Abel Du Petit-Thouars**, who arrived in 1836 to punish the Tahitian sovereign for the insult done to France in the person of the priests. The full reparation demanded that Queen Pomare write a letter of apology to the King of France, pay an indemnity of 2,000 Spanish dollars for losses suffered by the two priests, and to honor the French flag with a twenty-one gun salute. **George Pritchard**, the most prominent missionary, and two other English residents provided the money, and the French commander provided the flag and the gunpowder for the salute. Queen Pomare wrote the required letter of apology.

Du Petit-Thouars also proposed a treaty of perpetual peace be drawn up between Tahiti and France, specifying that Frenchmen would be allowed to come and go and to trade in all the islands of the government of Tahiti, where they should be received and protected as the most favored foreigners.

As soon as he left the island, Queen Pomare and four of her principal chiefs wrote a letter to **Queen Victoria**, asking for British protection. At the persuasion of George Pritchard, the Queen of Tahiti had appealed to the Queen of England on previous occasions, asking to be made a protectorate of the British crown. Queen Victoria, who was having her own problems with France, expressed her concern for Tahiti's difficulties, but replied that it would be impossible to fulfill any defensive obligations towards the government and inhabitants of Tahiti.

Soon after receiving the letter from Queen Victoria, Queen Pomare was away from Tahiti, visiting the island of Raiatea, while George Pritchard—who had left the London Missionary Society to become the British Consul of Tahiti—was away in England. During their absence the newly appointed French consul, **Jacques Antoine Moerenhout**, a Belgian Catholic who had served for a time as the American consul in Tahiti, took advantage of this time to persuade four of Tahiti's chiefs into signing a document he had prepared, stating that Tahiti wished to be made a French protectorate.

When this petition was received by the French government, in 1842 they once again sent Du Petit-Thouars, who had been promoted to Rear Admiral, back to Tahiti aboard the flagship *La Reine Blanche*. The French had been looking for a base in the Pacific for their warships, whalers and merchant vessels, and since they had already decided to take over the Marquesas Islands, they found it convenient to establish the French protectorate in Tahiti as well.

The Tahitian chiefs admitted that they had not understood the document they had signed, but in spite of Queen Pomare's protests, the French began to take hold in Tahiti. Du Petit-Thouars used his threats and troops to force the Queen to sign a letter accepting the proposal to place the government of Queen Pomare under the protection of France's **King Louis Philippe**. Du Petit-Thouars then appointed a provisional government that included a Royal Commissioner, a military governor and a captain of the port of Papeete.

Six months later, when news of the French protectorate reached England, the Parliament accepted the French action, stipulating that the work of the Protestant missionaries should continue. Soon it came to the attention of the English that France had actually taken full possession of Tahiti in 1843, when the Tahitian flag had been replaced by the French flag, after 500 French troops had surrounded Queen Pomare's palace in Papeete, forcing the dispossessed queen to take refuge aboard an English ship in the Papeete harbor. Then George Pritchard arrived in England on July 26, 1844, aboard the H.M.S. *Vindictive* with the news that he had been arrested by the French and deported from Tahiti.

Both the French and the English governments felt humiliated by the affairs that had transpired in Tahiti, and tempers rose on both sides of the channel between the two countries. In hopes of maintaining an *entente cordiale* with Great Britain, King Louis Philippe offered to pay Pritchard 25,000 francs from his own funds. Although this offer was rejected, an accord was reached between the two governments when France apologized to England for the treatment Pritchard had suffered, and he was paid an equitable indemnity for his losses.

For three more years this affair was heatedly discussed in all circles and kept alive in the French parliament. Although France and England carefully avoided war during this time, the Tahiti problems eventually contributed to the overthrow of the government and monarchy in France in 1848, and the indemnity was never paid.

Back in Tahiti, meanwhile, the natives resisted the French presence for three years with a series of skirmishes with the military troops that had been sent over to secure the French protectorate. Queen Pomare once again sought refuge in Raiatea, where she wrote another pleading letter to Queen Victoria, beseeching her help. Queen Victoria never answered the letters, yet the Tahitian people did not want to believe that England had deserted them.

After France and England had come to terms over the George Pritchard affair, and Queen Pomare's sovereignty was restored in early 1845, she refused to return to Tahiti under French rule. She stayed in exile for two more years, and was then persuaded by a Tahitian chiefess to give up the useless struggle. After agreeing to accept the French protectorate in 1847, Queen Pomare returned to Tahiti, and remained a figurehead until she died on September 17, 1877. The Paris Evangelical Missionary Society took over from the English Protestant missionaries in 1863.

King Pomare V, the son of the queen, ruled for three years, but he lacked his mother's pride in the Tahitian heritage, preferring drinking and gambling on the visiting ships, rather than assuming any duties of his kingship. On June 29, 1880, he gave France right of sovereignty of his dependencies in exchange for an annual pension and money for his wife and two brothers. Pomare V, the last King of Tahiti, drank himself to death in 1891. The Pomare descendants are now trying to reclaim the lands they lost during the French takeover.

MOOREA

Archaeologists have found evidence of settlements on Moorea as early as 900 AD. Stone *marae* temples, somberly hidden in a grove of *mape* Tahitian chestnut trees in the Opunohu valley, are mute remains of a once powerful religion.

The first European who reported sighting this island was **Captain Samuel Wallis**, who sailed past in 1767 and named it **York Island**, after the Duke of York. When **Captain James Cook** came to Tahiti to record the transit of the planet Venus across the sun in 1769, he sent a party of scientists from Matavai Bay over to York Island, where they camped out on a small sand bank called

Irioa, and set up their telescopes for the June 3rd transit. Cook's ship anchored in Opunohu Bay in 1777, during his third voyage to Tahiti, yet Pao Pao Bay became known as Cook's Bay.

Pomare I of Tahiti conquered the Marama chiefs of Moorea in 1790, and following his death in 1803, **King Pomare II** retreated to Moorea whenever necessary to avoid his warring enemies in Tahiti. Following his defeat in 1808 the king withdrew to Moorea and befriended the remaining missionaries in Papetoai village, who had also fled Tahiti when their mission station was burned at Point Venus. Pomare II helped **Henry Nott**, a missionary bricklayer, translate the Bible into Tahitian. A second mission station was opened in Afareaitu village, where **Reverend William Ellis** installed the first printing press in the South Seas. King Pomare II printed the first page in 1817, and the Gospel of Saint Luke, written in the Tahitian language, was published the following year.

In 1813 the missionaries erected a place for public worship in Papetoai village, and they made their first Christian convert in 1815 when the **High Chief Patti** denounced his idolatrous gods. He later became the first Tahitian deacon, preaching in the church the missionaries built in 1827 on the site of the royal Marae Taputapuatea in Papetoai village. The octagonal shaped Ebenezer church you see there today was rebuilt in 1889 and has since been restored. A spring in the churchyard is said to produce healing water, and a 2-meter- (6.5 foot-) high basaltic stone stands in the church courtyard. This kneeling stone was brought to Moorea from the big Marae Taputapuatea in Raiatea, the sacred island. The first Christian marriage was performed in the missionaries' original church, and the South Seas Academy, the first school, was opened in Afareaitu in 1821. Moorea also had the first plantations of sugar cane, cotton, coffee and rice.

King Pomare II regained his power in Tahiti in 1815 and when he returned to rule in Tahiti, he took his Christian teachings with him. In May 1819 he became the first Christian convert on the island of Tahiti, where he was baptized at Papaoa in Arue.

Queen Pomare IV also used Moorea as a place of refuge when the French raised their flag on Tahiti. When the French protectorate was established in Tahiti in 1843, Moorea also came under French rule. Today Moorea is one of the Windward Islands of the Society Archipelago, along with Tahiti, Tetiaroa and the little island of Maiao.

BORA BORA

Historians believe that the first Maohi or Polynesian settlers on Vavau sailed their double-hulled voyaging canoes into the island's beautiful lagoon sometime during the ninth century. The name of the island was changed to Porapora in the early 1700s, during the reign of **Chief Puni**, "The Terror" of all the nearby islands. This land of brave warriors distinguished their island by conquering their neighbors on Tahaa, Raiatea, Maupiti and Tupai, and they muffled their paddles to silently approach an island at night, thus surprising their sleeping enemy. Because of these warfare tactics the island of Vavau became known by the poetic name of *Porapora i te hoe manu* (first born of the silent paddle).

In 1769 **Captain James Cook** sailed past Porapora in the *Endeavour* and claimed all the Leeward Islands for his Britannic Majesty. During his third voyage in 1777, in command of the *Resolution* and *Discovery*, Cook landed on Porapora in a ship's boat, instead of sailing the ships through the narrow passage. He recorded the event in his ship's log, writing the island's name as BolaBola. At the time of Cook's arrival Chief Puni was a half-blind old man whose forces had conquered all the islands except Huahine. Puni died around 1786.

Porapora's warriors were sent to Tahiti in 1815 to help fight the traditionalists who still practiced the cult of Oro, which involved human sacrifices. At the invitation of the islanders the first Protestant missionaries landed on Porapora in 1820 and built a church in Vaitape in 1822. The first husband of **Queen Pomare IV**, **King Tapoa II**, was from Porapora, and when France claimed a protectorate over Tahiti and its dependencies, he maintained peace on Porapora until his death in 1860. The Pomare rule ended when the Leeward Islands became a French possession in 1888.

The American Armed Forces who were stationed on Porapora in World War II called the island Bora Bora. Although there is no "B" in the Polynesian language, common usage prevails.

In February 1942 the 1,500 Polynesians who lived on Bora Bora awoke to find five gray transport ships and several escorting warships of "Operation Bobcat" lying out in the lagoon. This joint U.S. Navy-Army task force had been sent to construct a military base for supplying fuel to Allied shipping during their long journeys across the South Pacific. The military installations on Bora Bora's main island included a small seaplane base, a submarine base, port facilities, an adequate water system, a good road and bridges around the island, Quonset huts, cannons and bunkers for the anti-aircraft guns. A beer garden for weekend relaxation was built on the white sand beach of Matira Point, and a sports facility there included a baseball diamond.

By 1943 the Seabees had constructed an airstrip on Motu Mute on the northern side of the lagoon. Almost 5,000 troops were involved in the "friendly invasion" of Bora Bora, until June 1946, when the base was decommissioned and turned over to the French. When they departed the Americans left behind some 175 light-skinned, blue-eyed babies. Many of these children died due to lack of proper nutrition following the decampment of "Operation Bobcat."

Several of the men who were stationed on Bora Bora during World War II returned after the war, some to visit their *vahines* and children, and others to rekindle fond memories. The landing strip they built on Motu Mute was used for international air traffic until the Tahiti-Faaa International Airport was opened in 1961, and continued to be used for inter-island flights for many years after. The old airstrip can still be seen when you arrive by plane at the newer runway on Motu Mute.

Chapter 6

PLANNING YOUR TRIP

When to Go

"When is the best time to go to Tahiti?" is a question I'll answer by asking you: "What do you want to do once you get here?"

If you want to scuba dive, you'll have the best underwater visibility during the dry season. If you want to snorkel and swim in the limpid lagoons, then come between October and June, when the water temperature is at least 80º Fahrenheit. If your goal is to photograph the most marvelous sunsets, complete with a "green flash", then come in July or August, when the evening skies are more likely to be free of clouds. If you want to see Tahiti dressed in her most beautiful finery of flowering trees and ripening fruits, then come in the "springtime" months of October through December. If you want to surf the huge rollers, make your reservations for January through March.

If you intend to catch a record-setting marlin, then your guess is as good as the experts, who tell me they're now reeling in the big ones all year long, rather than just during the summer months. If you want to see the humpback whales, they come up from Antarctica between mid-July and early October, and play around just offshore, in the passes and sometimes in the bays of the Society Islands. They also visit the Austral Islands, and you can join a whale-watching expedition organized by a scuba diving company on the island of Rurutu. If you want to charter a yacht and sail from island to island, the balmy trade winds blow most of the year, and are most pleasant from May to September. If your interest is outrigger canoe racing, the biggest competitions are in July, September and October. And if you want to party with the Polynesians during the biggest celebration of the year, then reserve now for a room during the Heiva Festivals that begin in late June, reach a peak in July and continue throughout most of August.

You may want to consult the *Calendar of Events* chapter before making your decision, as well as checking out the legal holidays in French Polynesia, which are listed in Chapter 7, *Basic Information*.

Another thing to keep in mind may be the school holidays, which can influence the availability of international and domestic flights, as well as accommodations in the small hotels and family operated hostels or pensions. The students in the Society Islands have a two-week vacation in mid-October, a month's holiday from mid-December to mid-January, another two weeks the first half of March, a week at the beginning of May, and a seven-week rest from early July until the last week in August. Schools in the Marquesas, Australs and Tuamotu/Gambier Islands keep the same basic holiday schedule, except for October, when they have only a three-day break during the third week in March, when they get the entire month off, and their May break is taken during the third week of the month. If you have any questions about the exact dates, the Tahiti Tourist office can answer them.

This means that from Christmas to the beginning of January, the end of February or beginning of March, the Easter period, the beginning of May, the longer northern-summer holiday in July-August and the beginning of October are likely to be busier.

Climate & Weather

The climate of these islands is usually benign, sunny and pleasant, and the cool, gentle breezes of the South Pacific Ocean and the northeasterly trade winds provide a natural air-conditioning system. Meteorologists consider the months of November through March as the "rainy" season, when the climate is warmer and more humid, and April through October as the "dry" season, with a cooler, drier climate.

November through May is definitely warmer than the rest of the year. Most of the rain falls during the warmer season, but there are also many days of sunshine during these months, with refreshing trade winds.

The central and northern Tuamotus have warmer temperatures and less rainfall than in the Society Islands. There are no mountains to create cooling night breezes, as the elevation of these atolls ranges from six to 20 feet above sea level. They can experience desert-like hot periods between November and April, with devastating storms and cyclones.

The Marquesas Islands are closer to the equator, and temperatures and humidity tend to be slightly higher than in Tahiti, with more rainfall in verdant Fatu Hiva and more arid conditions in Ua Huka. The Marquesas archipelago lies in the midst of a trade wind belt from the northern latitudes, bringing northeasterly winds most of the year, with seasons that are reversed to those in the Society Islands. Although there is no real rainy season, trekking through the steep valleys to visit tikis and archaeological sites in the Marquesas can be a very steamy and often muddy hike at any time of the year.

The climate in the Australs is more temperate and less rainy than in Tahiti, and the seasons are more clearly defined. These islands lie at the southern boundary of the southeast trade winds, which blow from November to March. In the cold season, from May to September, the winds are more variable and generally westerly, with temperatures of 50 to 70 degrees Fahrenheit.

French Polynesia is on the far eastern edge of the South Pacific cyclone (hurricane) belt, and has suffered serious damage from the destructive El Niño effect. The Leeward Society Island of Maupiti was 95 percent destroyed by Cyclone Osea in November 1997. Bora Bora suffered extensive damage caused by Cyclones Martin and Osea in November 1997, and the Tuamotu atoll of Mataiva suffered major destruction caused by tropical depression Veli that hit the atoll in January 1998. All the islands have recovered from these upheavals and with the exception of a rare tropical depression there have been no significant weather problems since then, apart from too much rain or not enough rain.

Dry Season

In July, August and September the *mara'amu* trade winds can bring blustery, howling weather and rain from the south. But the rains don't always accompany these chilling winds. I lost the roof of my house one year in July during the *mara'amu* and I looked up to see a beautiful, bright sky filled with a moon and stars.

The dry seasons are sometimes too dry in many of the islands, when we suffer droughts and water rationing. This is especially true during July, August, and September, when the fire trucks have to replenish water tanks in some of the hotels on Moorea. We have also had a shortage of water in January, but our visitors enjoyed the bright, sunny days when they could work on their tans in the midst of Tahiti's so-called rainy season.

Winter storms in the southern latitudes, down around the "Roaring 40s" south of the Austral Islands, can stir up some powerful waves, with 16-foot swells damaging homes and hotels throughout the Society Islands.

These inclement weather conditions should not affect your vacation plans, as the months of July through September are especially beautiful in the islands, with day after day of glorious sunshine, and cool nights good for snuggling and gazing at the Southern Cross and other tropical stars. If your hotel is located on the southern coast of any of the Society Islands, just bring along a windbreaker or sweater, and throw an extra blanket on the bed.

Wet Season

"Is it going to rain during my vacation/honeymoon?" I get several e-mail inquiries on that subject every year. The answer is "it's highly possible". But don't let it stop you from coming. A guest activities manager in one of the resort hotels answers questions about the rainy season by stating that in these islands we have a short season of the long rains and a long season of the short rains. If I had to guess which is when, I would say that November through March would be the short season of the long rains, and the rest of the year is the long season of the short rains. During the height of the rainy season, it can rain very heavily for days and days. During this time the trade winds stop and the temperature and humidity levels rise. When this happens the mugginess may make you feel hot, sticky and irritable if you stay indoors. The best thing to do is to take a walk in the refreshing rain or swim in the lagoon to cool off.

It's true that you cannot work on your tan during this weather, but you can tour around the island and watch the double rainbows over the emerald green valley when the sun breaks through the clouds for a few minutes. This is also a great time to go shopping for your own special black pearl!

Rainfall & Sunny Days

The yearly average for **rainfall** recorded at the Tahiti-Faa'a airport in 2001 was 1,679 millimeters (67.16 inches) and in 2002 it was 1,061 millimeters (42.44 inches). The meteorologists counted 2,633 hours of **sunshine** for 2001 and 2,896 hours for 2002. The 2003 statistics have not yet been published, and 2004 is much drier than in previous years.

Temperatures

The weather bureau in Tahiti keeps a record of the temperatures in all the island groups of French Polynesia. The yearly average temperature at the Tahiti-Faa'a International Airport for 2001 was a balmy 79.7 degrees Fahrenheit or 26.5 degrees Celsius. The average for 2002 was 80.6 degrees Fahrenheit or 27.0 degrees Celsius. The hottest months are January through April, with an average high of 87 degrees Fahrenheit for this period. The coolest months of the year are July and August, with an average low of 68 degrees Fahrenheit, compared to 74 degrees Fahrenheit during the nights in January, February and March. It's during these "winter" months that I can exchange my habitual *pareos* for "real" clothes such as tee-shirts, pants and long dresses, which are too hot to wear most of the year. Some people laugh when I tell them that I sometimes sleep under three blankets in July and August, when the temperature drops to the mid-60s. Then they experience a couple of rainy days or the chilling *mara'amu* winds from the south, and they're looking for a warm cover themselves.

In the Austral Islands, especially in Rapa, the southernmost island, which is below the tropical zone, the temperature sometimes drops to 41 degrees Fahrenheit in July and August. Good snuggling weather! You can get a 10-day weather report for Tahiti on the Internet at *www.weather.com*, and at *www.tahitiplanet.com/webcam.htm* you can get the weather plus the sunrise, sunset, moon and star movements. Another site is *www.weatherunderground.com*.

What to Pack

Casual and cool are the keywords to packing for this tropical climate. Light, loose, wash and wear garments of cotton and other natural fabrics are best. Unless you are taking a cruise ship to Tahiti you can leave your formal dining clothes and coats and ties at home. Women should pack a few pairs of shorts and slacks, along with a couple of skirts and tops or comfortable dresses, plus one or two swimsuits. Men will be properly dressed in shorts and tee shirts almost everywhere, except for dinner in a few hotels, fancy restaurants and nightclubs, where you'll have to put on long pants, an open-neck shirt and shoes. You can both buy some colorful *pareos* once you are here to complement your wardrobes. Yes, men wear them too! But only around the hotel grounds or on the beach. Most Polynesians do not wear their *pareos* to town.

Both men and women will be in style in sandals or flip-flop rubber thongs, and be sure to include aqua socks or protective footgear, such as old tennis shoes, for walking on the coral reef and in the lagoons. Plastic sandals can be purchased in the islands for about $15, which can be worn in the lagoon and while walking in the valleys.

A lightweight sweater or windbreaker will feel good on cool evenings, especially during the months of July-September, and anytime you are on the sea at night. Along with a hat or visor, don't forget to pack a good pair of sunglasses along with your sun block or screen. A folding umbrella or a lightweight plastic rain coat or poncho that fits into a pocket or purse may also come in handy during tropical rain showers, which are refreshing rather than cold.

Some of the budget hotels and hostels or pensions do not supply face cloths, and in some of the backpacker's lodgings you will have to bring your own soap and towel. A universal sink plug is handy for most lavabos and bathtubs. Other useful items include an alarm clock, portable clothes line and pegs, small bags of soap powder, clothes hangers, beach towel, pocket flashlight, corkscrew, tin opener or Swiss Army knife, plastic fork and spoon, folding plastic insulated cup and zip-lock plastic bags to contain anything spillable. Bring a small first-aid kit containing your personal medicines, aspirin, indigestion tablets, vitamins, insect repellent, antiseptic cream, aloe gel, Band-Aids or other sticking plasters. Pack your toiletries and just a few cosmetics, and you may want to bring along your binoculars. Remember to put your sharp items in your luggage to be checked, rather than in your carry-on bag. On two occasions I've had nail scissors taken away by the security people at the domestic airport in Tahiti because I left them in my purse or carry-on luggage.

Don't forget to bring your camera, and make sure you know how to operate it before you get here, to prevent losing that perfect shot. Be sure to include lots of film and a waterproof bag to protect your camera from salt and spray during boat excursions. Also pack a small travel bag in which to carry your things when you're on tours and excursions.

Hair-dryers are provided in the luxury hotels, and if you bring a hair-dryer, make sure it can convert to 220 voltage, or bring a small adapter (trans-former). Always ask at your hotel reception before plugging in your electrical appliances. You may want to bring your own supply of reading material. You can exchange books at most hotels. Some folks bring their own booze, which is expensive here. Last but not least—bring your passport, airline tickets, driver's license, traveler's checks, cash and all your international credit cards.

Entrance Requirements
Passports/Visas

All U.S. citizens and nationals can apply for a passport by completing the application form DSP-11, which is available in U.S. post offices. You can also obtain this form from the **U.S. Passport Agency** (*Tel. 202/647-0518*), which has offices in Boston, Chicago, Honolulu, Houston, Los Angeles, Miami, New Orleans, New York, Philadelphia, San Francisco, Stamford, Connecticut, and Washington, D.C. You can also download a form from the website of the U.S. State Department at *www.travel.state.gov*. Complete the form and return it to the Passport Agency or to your nearest post office or federal courthouse.

All non-French citizens must have a valid passport to enter French Polynesia, as well as an airline ticket back to their resident country or to at least two more continuing destinations. Your passport or travel document must be valid for at least three months following the last day of your stay in French Polynesia.

Citizens of Argentina, Bolivia, Brunei, Chile, Costa Rica, Croatia, Czech Republic, Ecuador, Estonia, Guatemala, Honduras, Hungary, Japan, Latvia, Lithuania, Malaysia, Mexico, New Zealand, Nicaragua, Panama, Paraguay Poland, Salvador, Singapore, Slovakia, Slovenia, South Korea, the USA and Uruguay do not require a visa for stays of less than 30 days in French Polynesia. If you think you will want to extend your stay in French Polynesia beyond the one-month visa exemption, you should apply for a three-month visa at a French Consulate office prior to coming to Tahiti.

Citizens of the European Union, Andorra, Australia, Bulgaria, Cyprus, Iceland, Liechtenstein, Malta, Monaco, Norway, St. Martin, Switzerland and the Vatican may visit without a visa for up to three months. Nationals from all other countries require visas which may be obtained from the French Embassy or French Consulate in the country of residence. The visa must be endorsed "valid for French Polynesia", which applies also to aliens holding temporary visitor's permits (one year in metropolitan France).

A foreigner with a residence card for the US is not exempt from having a visa for visiting French Polynesia. This visa exemption is subject to change at short notice. It is advisable to contact the nearest French Consulate or an airline serving Tahiti for specific information.

If there is some unforeseen reason why you will need to extend your visa once you are here, you can ask for another month or two at the Immigration office at the Tahiti-Faa'a airport, *Tel. 80.06.01*. This must be done at least one week before the exemption expires. The Police Air Frontière (PAF) who control this office have sometimes refused requests for visa extensions because they want you to get the visa before you arrive in Tahiti. All visitors must have a sufficient amount of resources to cover their planned stay in French Polynesia. Temporary residency visas for up to one year are more difficult to obtain, and have to be applied for at a French Consulate or Embassy before you arrive in French Polynesia.

French nationals require only a National Identity Card to stay in French Polynesia. However, the Delphine passport is necessary when transiting via the US.

In the US
• **Embassy of France**: 4101 Reservoir Rd., NW, Washington, DC 20007-2185, *Tel. 202/944-6200, Fax 202/944-6166; www.info-france-usa.org.*
• **French Consulates**: New York: 10 E. 74th St., New York, NY 10021, *Tel. 212/606-3644/606-3688; Fax 212/606-3670; E-mail: visa@consulfrance-newyork.org.* San Francisco: 540 Bush St., San Francisco, CA 94108, *Tel. 415/397-4330, Fax 415/397-7843; E-mail: visa@consulfrance-sanfrancisco.org.* Los Angeles: 10990 Wilshire Blvd., Suite 300, Los Angeles, CA 90024; *Fax 310/479-4813; E-mail: visa@consulfrance-losangeles.org.*

Other French consulate offices are in Atlanta, Boston, Chicago, Houston, Los Angeles, Miami, New Orleans and Washington, DC. Residents of those cities are required to apply there. If there is no French consulate in your town, please contact the French Embassy in Washington, DC, listed above.

U.S. Consulate in Tahiti

A Consular Agency of the United States opened in Tahiti in 2004, after an absence of 38 years. This office is located in Punaauia on the upper level of the Tamanu Iti Center. Christopher Kozely, the vice consul, cannot issue or renew passports, but his services include helping Americans who have problems due to sickness or death or who have lost their passports. You can contact this office at B.P. 10765, Paea, Tahiti 98711, French Polynesia; *Tel. 689/42.65.35; Fax 689/50.80.96; E-mail: usconsul@mail.pf; or ckozely@mail.pf.* In US *917/464-7457.*

∂

In Canada
- **Embassy of France:** 42 Sussex Drive, Ottawa, Ontario, KIM 2C9, *Tel. 613/789-1795, Fax 613/562-3735: www.ambafrance-ca.org.*
- **French Consulate**: Toronto: 130 Bloor St. West, Suite 400, Toronto, Ontario M5S 1N5, *Tel. 416/925-8041, Fax 416/925-3076.* Vancouver: 1100-1130 West Pender St., Vancouver, BC V6E 4A4; *Tel. 604/681.4345; Fax 604/681-4287.*

Making Reservations

It is so much simpler to talk with your favorite travel agent to take care of all the reservations and details in planning your trip to Tahiti and Her Islands. Or you can arrange your entire trip by yourself, by contacting the airlines and hotels directly or going through one of the travel agencies in Tahiti. The airlines have special fares and passes, which will cost you less if you reserve two weeks to a month in advance. The airfares also vary according to whether you go in the high or peak season, the shoulder season or the basic season. Check with the airline companies to learn which season will be in effect when you want to fly. If you are traveling on a tight budget, ask for their lowest fares, and be sure to learn what restrictions apply.

Some of the "discounter" travel agents buy airline seats and hotel rooms at wholesale prices. You may want to get a list of discounter travel agents, as well as worldwide discount air fares, from the Web site *www.etn.nl/discount.htm#disco.* Also check Internet specials at *www.Discountairfares.com* and the Internet Travel Network at *www.itn.*

Some consolidators or "bucket shops" who buy and resell seats on the major international airlines include: **Air Brokers International**, *Tel. 800/883-3273*; *E-mail: sales@airbrokers.com; www.airbrokers.com;* **Concorde International Travel**, *Tel. 800/207-7300; www.concordetravel.com;* **Council Travel**, *Tel. 800/226-8624; www.counciltravel.com;* **STA Travel**, *Tel. 800/781-4040; www.sta.travel.com;* **Travel Bargains**, *Tel. 800/AIR-FARE; www.1800airfareflycheap.com;* and the **Smart Traveller**, *Tel. 800/448-3338 or 305/448-3338* in the U.S.

The Internet websites offer some of the best deals you'll find on airfare, as well as hotels and car rentals. Two of the most popular travel sites are **Microsoft Expedia**, *www.expedia.com*, and **Travelocity**, *www.travelocity.com*. Before you shop for flights online, be sure to call the airlines or a travel agent to find out the lowest fare published.

Using Travel Specialists/Agents

Contact the Tahiti Tourist Board for brochures, schedules and information.
- **Tahiti Tourism North America**, 300 Continental Boulevard, Suite 160, El Segundo, CA 90245; *Tel 310/414-8484; Fax 310/414-8490; E-mail: tahitilax@earthlink.net; www.GoToTahiti.com.*

The following list includes only the wholesale travel companies, tour operators and travel agencies that have been approved by the Tahiti Tourist office in Los Angeles. Should your local travel agency need additional brochures and information, they can contact one of these companies, who are financially sound and have a well trained staff with a good knowledge of Tahiti and Her Islands. Some of the wholesalers also work directly with the public.

U.S.

- **Brendan Worldwide Vacations**, *Tel. 800/421-8446 or 818/428-6000; Fax 818/722-6492; E-mail: info@brendantours.com; www.brendantours.com.* This family owned business has been in operation for 36 years and offers some interesting packages to Tahiti and French Polynesia.
- **Fly Tahiti Vacations**, 5910 Edinger Ave, Huntington Beach, CA 92649; *Tel. 866/9Tahiti or 714/274-0379; E-mail: flytahiti@yahoo.com; www.flytahiti.com.* Owner Jean-Louis Delezenne is a Frenchman living in Southern California who also has a home in Moorea. He worked as a French chef, then for AOM, before forming his own travel agency in 2001. He works with travel agents and the public, specializing in family vacations in the smaller hotel structures and pensions around Moorea, as well as in luxury tailor-made packages at 4- and 5-star hotels in Tahiti and Her Islands. He has a staff of 8 people in French Polynesia and I recommend him personally, as I know that he is a real go-getter who stays on top of the latest information about special airline fares, hotel promotions, package deals and anything else concerning tourism and life in French Polynesia. He truly knows the meaning of personalized service, which he happily offers to each and every customer.
- **Happy Vacations**, *Tel. 800/877-3853; Fax 831/461-0150; E-mail: sales@happytours.com; www.happytours.com.* This package wholesaler has been in business since 1969 and specializes in the Caribbean, Hawaii, Tahiti, Fiji, Cook Islands, Cancun and the Maya Riviera. They do not sell to the public directly.
- **Islands in the Sun**, 2381 Rosecrans Ave., Suite 325, El Segundo, CA 90245, *Tel. 800/828-6877, 310/536-0051, Fax 310/536-6266; E-mail: info@islandsinthesun.com; www.islandsinthesun.com.* The late Ted Cook founded this company in 1965 and since then thousands of travelers have booked their South Pacific vacations through this well informed and very helpful team.
- **Maeva Tours**, 7084 Miramar Road, Suite 203, San Diego, CA 92121; *Tel. 800/799-6991 or 714/999-0050; E-mail: info@maevatours.com; www.maevatours.com.* Maeva Tarahu-McNicol is a very busy young Tahitian woman who has lived in the States for 20 years. Her Tahiti and Beyond programs offer "a la carte service with a touch of innovation" and a complete package of services especially tailored to the needs of each

individual client or group. Among her 10 employees are 4 Polynesians who act as guides for visiting Tahitians who book through her inbound agency.
- **Manuia Tours and Travel**, 59 New Montgomery Street, San Francisco, CA 94105; *Tel. 415/495-4500; Fax 415/495-2000; E-mail: manuiatravel@yahoo.com*. Owner Pascale Siu asked me to include her small agency as she is from a big Chinese family in Tahiti and is the only French-Tahitian owned travel agency in San Francisco. They specialize in individual and personalized services, including Honeymoon packages and stays in Family Pensions.
- **Newmans South Pacific Vacations**, *Tel. 800/421-3326 or 310/348-8282; Fax 310/215-9705; E-mail: newmans@newmansvacations.com; www.newmans.com*.
- **Pacific Destination Center**, 18685 Main Street, #622, Huntington Beach, CA 92648; *Tel. 800/227-5317 or 714/960-4011; Fax 714/960-4678; E-mail: sales@pacific-destinations.com; www.pacific-destinations.com*. Owner Jeanette Ryan has arranged vacations for her satisfied clients for more than 20 years.
- **Pleasant Tahitian Holidays**, *Tel. 800/448-3333 or 800/742-9244; Fax 805/379-4573; www.pleasanttahiti.com or www.2tahiti.com*. This is a big wholesale company that also sells packages to Hawaii and several other destinations.
- **Qantas Vacations**, 300 Continental Blvd., Suite 350, El Segundo, CA 90245; *Tel. 800/641-8772; Fax 310/535-1057; E-mail: booknow@qantasvacations.com; www.qantasvacations.com*.
- **Sunspots International**, 1918 N.E. 181st Street, Portland, OR 97230; *Tel. 800/334-5623 or 503/674-4325; Fax 503/661/7771; E-mail: info@sunspotsintl.com; www.sunspotsintl.com*.
- **Swain Tahiti Tour**s, 6 W. Lancaster Ave., Ardmore, PA 19003; *Tel. 800/227-9246; Tel. 610/896-9595; Fax 610/896-9592; E-mail: Info@swaintours.com; www.swaintahiti.com*. This is the Pacific Division of Far & Wide, headed by Swain Australia's founder and president, Ian Swain. Their brochure includes cruise options, wedding packages, custom tours to the Austral and Gambier Islands, independent travel and escorted tours.
- **Tahiti Legends**, 19891 Beach Blvd., Suite 107, Huntington Beach, CA 92648; *Tel. 800/200-1213, 714/374-5656; Fax 714/374-7262; E-mail:info@tahitilegends.com; www.legendsluxurytravel.com*. Their 72-page brochure simply makes you dream of your own trip to the islands, and their well-trained staff are not only very familiar with Tahiti and Her Islands, but are truly in love with the islands, the people and the hotels, cruise ships and tourist activities. They also publish a 12-page Tahiti Honeymoons brochure.

• **Tahiti Travel Planners**, (New Millennium Travel LLC), 461 Durand NE, Suite #100, Atlanta, GA 30307; *Tel. 800/772-9231 or 404/378-4983; Fax 404/ 378-8430; E-mail: info@gotahiti.com; www.gotahiti.com.* This is the only travel agency in the Southeastern States that specializes solely in vacations to Tahiti and French Polynesia. Among their numerous recognitions by travel magazines, all their agents have received the Tiare Award distributed by the Tahiti Tourist office for outstanding knowledge about these islands. Once a package is booked and confirmed, the client's price is locked in and guaranteed not to increase. Their *www.gotahiti.com* website includes the largest collection of hotel photographs of any Tahiti focused website, plus more than 300 package options for travel packages. Their *www.tahitimoons.com* website includes a Honeymoon Registry program.

• **Tahiti Vacations**, *Tel. 800/553-3477; Fax 818/773-8282; E-mail: reservations@tahitivacations.net; www.tahitivacation.com.* This is the wholesale tour operator for Air Tahiti, the domestic airline of French Polynesia. They offer some interesting packages to Tahiti and Moorea, as well as choices for all the other islands served by Air Tahiti.

Canada
• **Island Escapes by Goway**, *Tel. 800/387-8850 or 604/264-8088; Fax 604/ 267-2111; E-mail: Info@goway.com; www.goway.com.*
• **Fun Sun Vacations,** *Tel. 800/938-6786 or 780/421-1272; Fax 780/420-0589; E-mail: T.Brown@FunSunVacations.com; www.funsunvacations.com.* This 48-year old Canadian owned family business is one of Canada's top 3 tour wholesalers and sells through retail travel agencies.

Diving
• **PADI Travel Network**, 30151 Tomas Street, Rancho Santa Margarita, CA 92688-2125; *Tel. 800/729-7234 or 949/858-7234, ext. 2; E-mail: ptn1@padi.com; www.padi.com.* They have packages for scuba divers.
• **World of Diving & Adventure Vacations**, 301 Main Street, El Segundo, CA 90245; *Tel. 800/Go-Diving or 800/900-7657 or 310/322-8100; Fax 310/ 322-5111; E-mail: mail@worldofdiving.com; www.worldofdiving.com.*

Travel agencies in Tahiti are mentioned in various parts of this book. Here is the list of Destination Management Companies recommended by Tahiti Tourisme. You may want to contact one or more of these inbound agents when planning your trip, as they can give you detailed information about every aspect of traveling in French Polynesia. You should know in advance that a handling fee may be charged if they make reservations for you to stay in the family pensions or bed & breakfast type guesthouses.

- **Dream Travel Tahiti**, B.P. 6014, Faa'a, Tahiti 98702. *Tel./Fax 689/53.34.74; E-mail: info@dreamtraveltahiti.com; www.dreamtraveltahiti.com.* This travel agency is headed by Didier Alpini, who also manages Aquatica, a 5-star PADI Dive Center based at the InterContinental Tahiti Resort. This travel agency specializes in "green" tourism, with hiking, trekking, 4WD safaris, golf, participation in local sports such as marathons, as well as cruising and diving holidays. They also handle reservations for the outer islands of French Polynesia.
- **E-Tahiti Travel**, B.P. 42692, Fare Tony, Papeete, Tahiti 98713, *Tel./Fax 689/ 83.51.60; E-mail: sales@etahititravel.com; www.etahititravel.com.* This is a new agency that is located on the 4th floor of the Vaima Center, Suite 124, in downtown Papeete. The French and Tahitian staff live year-round in Tahiti and have put together packages for all budgets.
- **Marama Tours**, B.P. 6266, Faa'a, Tahiti, 98702. *Tel. 689/50.74.74; Fax 689/82.16.75; E-mail: maramatours@mail.pf; www.maramatours.com.* This company was founded in 1973 by Mata and Emile Cowan, a Polynesian family whose children also grew up in the tourist business and now take active roles in managing this popular agency.
- **Paradise Tours**, B.P. 2430-98713, Papeete, Tahiti, *Tel. 689/42.49.36; Fax 689/42.48.62; E-mail: paradise@mail.pf.* This is one of the oldest agencies in Tahiti handling inbound tours.
- **South Pacific Tours**, B.P. 1588, Papeete, Tahiti 98713. *Tel. 689/80.35.00; Fax 689/80.35.12; E-mail: in-bound@spt-tahiti.pf. www.south-pacific-tours.com.* In addition to being the biggest inbound agency in Tahiti for the Japanese market, they also handle clients from the U.S.A. and Europe.
- **Tahiti Nui Travel**, B.P. 718, Papeete, Tahiti 98713. *Tel. 689/54.02.00; Fax 689/42.74.35 / 41.39.23; E-mail: sales@tahitinuitravel.pf; www.tahitinuitravel.com.* This is Tahiti's largest travel agency, and handles inbound tours for individuals and groups from all countries. They have a well-earned reputation for their professionalism.
- **Tahiti Tours**, B.P. 627, Papeete, Tahiti 98713. *Tel. 689/54.02.50; Fax 689/ 42.50.50; E-mail: sales@tahititours.pf; www.tahiti-tours.com.* This agency has been in business for more than 45 years and is owned by Tahiti Nui Travel. They handle a lot of inbound tours and local excursions and day tours and they are the American Express representatives in Tahiti.
- **Tekura Tahiti Travel**, B.P. 2971, Papeete, Tahiti 98713. *Tel. 689/43.12.00; Fax 689/42.84.60, E-mail: go@tahiti-tekuratravel.com; www.tahiti-tekuratravel.com.* The knowledgeable English-speaking staff can book your hotel rooms, guest houses, villas, transfers, excursions, diving, cruises, yacht charters, sailboats, domestic flights, boat transportation to outer islands and car rentals.
- **Haere Mai Association**, B.P. 4517, Papeete, Tahiti 98713. *Tel. 689/ 50.14.05; Fax 689/50.14.06; E-mail: haere-mai@mail.pf; www.haere-*

mai.pf; www.haere-mai.com. This association was created in 1997 and represents 184 of the 256 family pensions and guesthouses in all the archipelagoes of French Polynesia. Their office is located in Fare Manihini, adjacent to the Tahiti Manava Visitors Bureau, on the Papeete waterfront. Contact them for online booking and information.

Website Forums and **Bulletin Boards** are also a good source of information on deciding which islands to visit and where to stay. Not only do they have trip reports and photos of various hotels, pensions, activities and tourist sites in French Polynesia, but also you have access to an endless number of opinions on each subject. The most popular ones with a Tahiti Forum in English are: *www.tahiti-explorer.com; www.polynesianislands.com/fp*; and *www.tahititalk.com.* If you're planning to visit the islands by cruise ship, then tune into the Cruise Critic forum, *www.cruisecritic.com*, and find out what former passengers have to say about the ship and shore excursions you'll be taking.

Getting to French Polynesia
Baggage Allowances and Storage
Airline regulations for international flights entitle each first-class or business-class passenger to a baggage limit of 30 kilograms (66 pounds). Economy-class passengers are allowed 20 kilograms (44 pounds). All passengers are allowed a carry-on bag that will fit under your seat, which means that it cannot exceed total measurements of 115 centimeters (45 inches). Only first-class or business-class passengers are allowed a second carry-on bag. All passengers may carry a small handbag on board, and most airlines will also allow you to board with one other accessory, such as a portable computer or camera bag, providing it does not weigh more than 7 kilograms (15 pounds).

Air Tahiti, the domestic inter-island company in Tahiti, has a baggage limit of 10 kilograms (22 pounds for each passenger). If you have a ticket connecting with an international flight within seven days, the baggage limit is 20 kilograms (44 pounds).

A baggage storage room at the Tahiti-Faa'a airport terminal, *Tel. 86.60.61*, is open daily from 5am to 12:30am, except for Monday night, when they close at 7pm because there are no flights. On Sunday they close for lunch between 12-1:30pm. Their rates for 24-hour storage are 395 CFP for a small bag, 640 CFP for a medium bag and 755 CFP for a large bag. The hotels offer free baggage storage for their guests.

Dangerous Goods
The following items are prohibited in both hold and carry-on baggage: compressed gas or other explosives, inflammable liquids, corrosives, poisons, irritants, and substances or materials that are oxidizing, toxic, radioactive or

magnetized. Safety regulations prohibit certain articles from being carried into the aircraft cabins. These include firearms, munitions, knives, scissors and other sharp or pointed instruments.

Some articles containing dangerous goods are permitted as carry on or checked baggage, such as toilet articles, perfumes and a thermometer for medical use. Matches and lighters are to be carried on your person only. Contact your airline representative for a complete list.

By Air From North America

All international flights arrive at the **Tahiti-Faa'a International Airport** on the island of Tahiti. The airline companies serving Tahiti from North America usually depart from the Los Angeles International Airport, for a 7 1/2-hour direct flight to Tahiti. If you are flying to Los Angeles from another city or state, be sure to allow sufficient time between flights to make the connection. When your flight lands in Los Angeles it takes a while to transfer your bags from a domestic airline terminal to the international terminal. Due to increased safety measures, airport check-in time is now three hours before each international flight departure.

The following airline companies have one or more flights weekly between Los Angeles and Tahiti. Extra flights are added during the high seasons, which vary. The busiest seasons are generally the months of July and August and the Christmas-New Year's season. Once you arrive in Tahiti and want to check on arriving or departing flights you can contact the Tahiti-Faa'a International Airport at *Tel. 86.60.61.*

Airlines Serving Tahiti from Los Angeles

AIR FRANCE, *in US Tel. 800/321-4538 / 800/237-2747; in Canada 800/ 667-2747; in Tahiti Tel. 689/47.47.47; Fax 689/47.47.90. www.airfrance.com.* France's international carrier has three Paris-Los Angeles-Papeete flights a week, code-sharing with Air Tahiti Nui. The Air France Tahiti office is on rue LaGarde in downtown Papeete.

AIR NEW ZEALAND, *in US Tel. 800/262-1234 / 310/615-1111, Fax 648-7017; in Canada Tel. 800/799-5494 (English) or 800/663-5494 (French); Fax 604/606-0155; in Tahiti Tel. 689/54.07.47, Fax 689/42.45.44; www.airnewzealand.com or www.airnz.co.nz.* Air New Zealand has four flights a week from Los Angeles to Tahiti, code-sharing with United Airlines. The Tahiti office is on the ground floor of the Vaima Center, on the corner of rue Jeanne d'Arc and rue du General du Gaulle.

AIR TAHITI NUI, *in Los Angeles, Tel. 877/824-4846 or 866/835-9286 (U-FLY-ATN); Fax 818/670-0549; E-mail: res@airtahitinui-usa.com; in Tahiti Tel. 689/45.55.55; Fax 689/46.02.20; info@airtahitinui.pf; www.airtahitinui.com or www.flyatn.com.* This is Tahiti's international airline company, and shouldn't be confused with Air Tahiti, which is the national carrier. Air Tahiti Nui has seven flights a week from Los Angeles to Papeete, code-sharing with Qantas, and six flights a week from Paris to LAX and Papeete, code-sharing with Air France. They currently have four Airbus 340-300 airplanes with 6 first class, 24 business class and 264 economy class seats. A fifth Airbus A340-300 will be added to the fleet in July 2005, when Air Tahiti Nui begins operating 12.5 hour non-stop flights from New York to Papeete every Monday, Thursday and Saturday, covering a distance of 6,289 statute miles. In 2003 Air Tahiti Nui was named "Best Pacific Airline" by Skytrax, and a six-month poll of 4.4 million passengers on 140 airline companies voted Air Tahiti Nui and its cabin staff fourth best airline in the world for welcome, service and comfort on board. Passengers are welcomed in traditional Tahitian style by smiling Polynesian hostesses who offer them a Tiare Tahiti flower when they board Air Tahiti Nui in Los Angeles and Paris. The airplanes provide individual movie screens in front of the seats, with a choice of six films, as well as telephones and music. The Air Tahiti Nui office in Papeete is located on rue Paul Gauguin at the Pont de l'Est.

QANTAS AIRWAYS, *Tel. 800/227-4500; Tel. 689/50.70.64; Fax 689/ 43.10.52; E-mail: qantas@southpacificrepresentation.pf; www.qantas.com* no longer flies to Tahiti, but maintains a code share agreement with Air Tahiti Nui for the Los Angeles to Tahiti service. The Tahiti office is located upstairs at the Vaima Center in Papeete.

By Other Air Routes

AIR CALEDONIE INTERNATIONAL, in US *Tel. 310/670-7302*; in Noumea *Tel. 687/26.4400*; in Tahiti *Tel. 689/85.09.04; Fax 689/85.09.05; E-mail: acippt@mail.pf; www.aircalin.nc*. Aircalin has a direct flight from Noumea, New Caledonia, to Tahiti each Saturday, with an Airbus A320 airplane. The Tahiti office is on the first floor upstairs at the Tahiti-Faa'a International Airport.

AIR NEW ZEALAND, *in US Tel. 800/262-1234 or 310/615-1111; in Tahiti Tel. 689/54.07.47; Fax 689/42.45.44; www.airnewzealand.com* has three direct flights a week from Auckland and two weekly flights from Auckland and Rarotonga, with a third flight added in July-August that also stops in Rarotonga. The Tahiti office is on the ground floor of the Vaima Center, on the corner of rue Jeanne d'Arc and rue du General du Gaulle.

AIR TAHITI NUI, *Tel. 689/45.55.55 in Tahiti; www.airtahitinui.co.jp or www.airtahitinui.com* has two direct flights from Tokyo to Papeete each week and one flight from Tokyo and Osaka to Papeete under a code-share agreement with Japan Airlines. You can also fly from Auckland to Papeete three times a week. Air Tahiti Nui and Qantas have a code share program that provides connections from Australia to New Zealand and on to Tahiti and Los Angeles. In July 2005, when Air Tahiti Nui receives its fifth Airbus 340-300, it will begin direct service from Sydney to Tahiti every Saturday and Monday.

HAWAIIAN AIRLINES, *in the continental US, Alaska and Canada Tel. 800/367-5320; in Honolulu 808/838-1555; in Tahiti Tel. 689/42.15.00; Fax 689/45.14.51; E-mail: ppt.admin@hawaiianair.pf; www.hawaiianair.com.* There is only one regular flight a week between Honolulu and Tahiti, departing Honolulu each Saturday. The Tahiti office is located upstairs at the Vaima Center in Papeete.

LAN AIRLINES, *in US Tel. 800/735-5526; in Tahiti Tel. 689/42.64.55; www.lanchile.com.* LAN (formerly LAN Chile) has two flights per week from Santiago, Chile and Easter Island. The Tahiti office is located upstairs at the Vaima Center in Papeete.

QANTAS AIRWAYS, in US *Tel. 800/227-4500;* in Tahiti *Tel. 689/50.70.64; Fax 689/43.10.52; E-mail: qantas@southpacificrepresentation.pf; www.qantas.com.* Qantas code shares with Air Tahiti Nui for a flight from Auckland to Papeete each Thursday, and with Air Tahiti Nui and Polynesian Airlines for a flight from Sydney and Auckland to Tahiti each Tuesday and Saturday. The Tahiti office is located upstairs at the Vaima Center in Papeete.

By Passenger Ship

Tahiti's brief cruise ship season usually begins in November and ends in April, with most of the passenger liners calling during the months of January through March. The average number of cruise ships that call in Tahiti and Her Islands is only a dozen for the entire season.

These include Russian flag-carriers such as the *Bremen, Delphin, Columbus and Maxim Gorky*, whose passengers are primarily from Eastern Europe. The *Deutschland, Albatros, Astor, Saga Rose* and the *Europa* (now the *Superstar Aries)*, are some of the ships that call in Tahiti and Her Islands. Their passengers are mostly Germans and other Europeans, who are visiting 40 countries in 101-129 days during their round-the-world cruise. The *Clipper Odyssey, Seven Seas Mariner, Crystal Harmony, Star Princess, Topaz, Olympia Voyager, Prinsendam* (former *Seabourn Sun*), the *Crown Princess* and the former *Crown Odyssey* (now the *Norwegian Crown*) have also visited Tahiti and several of the outer islands, including Raivavae, Rapa, Mangareva and Raroia. The *Queen Elizabeth 2* visits Tahiti and Moorea during her world cruises and will return in January 2005. Other ships cruising around the world in 2005 will be the *Seven Seas Voyager* and *Crystal Serenity*. Ship day in Tahiti usually is limited to an early morning arrival in the harbor and a late afternoon departure, allowing enough time to make a tour of the island, perhaps to explore the coral gardens or tropical valleys and shop for post cards and souvenirs.

South Pacific cruises also include Tahiti, Moorea, Raiatea and Bora Bora in their itineraries, and some of the ships are now calling at the Marquesas Islands, as well as Rangiroa and Fakarava in the Tuamotu Archipelago, in their shore programs. The passengers enjoy these remote islands for their unexploited natural beauty. The 2005 and 2006 schedules for the 688-passenger *Tahitian Princess* include 10-day cruises to French Polynesia and the Cook Islands, and 10-day round-trips from Papeete to the Marquesas Islands, Rangiroa, Raiatea, Bora Bora and Papeete. In April 2005 the *Pacific Princess* will make a 15-day cruise from Sydney to Bora Bora, Raiatea, Moorea and Papeete, and in April 2006, the new *Diamond Princess* will have a 29-day cruise from Hawaii to Tahiti and the South Pacific and end in San Francisco.

By Private Boat

The best way to visit Tahiti and Her Islands is, of course, the leisurely way. Hundreds of cruising yachts from all over the world pass through the islands each year, with some boats stopping only long enough to get provisions for the next leg of the journey, while others linger until the authorities ask them to move on.

Their contact with the villagers in remote islands is often rewarding for all concerned, with the "yachties" often getting involved in the daily lives of the friendly Polynesians. Outgoing visitors are frequently invited to join in volleyball and soccer games and fishing expeditions. The young people will take you to hunt for tiny shells that are strung into pretty necklaces, and the women will teach you how to weave hats, mats, and baskets from palm fronds. You can also eat delicious seafood direct from the shell while standing on a Technicolor reef. In the evenings, you can sit on the pier under a starlit sky and watch the Southern Cross as you listen to the young men from the village playing melodic island tunes on their guitars and ukuleles.

There's a sailing adage that goes: "A month at sea can cure all the ills of the land." However, a month at sea with an incompatible crew can make you ill or want to kill. Sailing to Tahiti sounds so very romantic, and many people do realize their life-long dreams of anchoring inside an opalescent lagoon and tying a line around a coconut tree. It takes a month and sometimes much longer to sail from the US West Coast or Panama to the Marquesas Islands, the first landfall in French Polynesia. This long crossing is also disastrous for many relationships, so it is very important to know the dispositions of the other people on the yacht, and to be as easy-going and tolerant as you can be.

Valid passports and tourist visas are required for the captain and each crewmember. The Immigration Service in French Polynesia can issue a three-month visa that is good for all of French Polynesia. In addition to the required visa, each crew member must also deposit money into a special account at a local bank or at the Trésorerie Générale that is equal to the airfare from Tahiti back to their country of origin. Crew changes can only be made in harbors where there is a *gendarmerie*, and the Chief of Immigration must be advised of any crew changes.

Customs Allowances

Entering French Polynesia

In addition to your personal effects, when you come to French Polynesia you may legally bring in duty free: 200 cigarettes or 100 cigarillos or 50 cigars or 250 grams of smoking tobacco, 50 grams of perfume, .25 liter of *eau de toilette*, 500 grams of coffee, 100 grams of tea and two liters of spirits. Visitors under 17 years of age are not allowed to import tobacco or spirits. Each traveler over the age of 15 years can bring in 30.000 CFP and under 15 years the limit is 15.000 CFP.

Before importing any telephone or telecommunications items, please contact the office of the French High Commissioner for French Polynesia, Postal and Telecommunications Division, *Tel. 689/53.22.44; Fax 689/53.28.01*. Prohibited items include narcotics, copyright infringements (pirated video and audiotapes), guns and weapons of all kinds, ammunition, dangerous drugs, counterfeit items or imitation brand names. Cultured pearls of non-French Polynesian origin are prohibited.

No domestic pets can be imported without authorization from the Food and Veterinary Department, *Tel. 689/42.81.47, Fax 689/42.08.31*. The importation of live animals, animal products and products of animal origin is subject to prior authorization. Plants and plant products are subject to phytosanitary control. For further information you can contact the Department of Agriculture, B.P. 100, Papeete, Tahiti, or at Tahiti-Faa'a Airport, *Tel. 689/82.49.99*, or at the Port of Papeete, *Tel. 689/54.45.85*. The Department of Customs and Indirect Duties also publishes information on the web site of the Ministry of Economics, Finance and Industry at: *www.finances.gouv.fr/douanes*.

Returning Home

US customs allows an exemption of $800 in goods for each US resident, including one liter of liquor, 200 cigarettes and 100 cigars. A Know Before You Go brochure is published by US customs, which you can read at *www.usacustoms.com*.

US law allows the importation, duty-free, of original works of art. Because of concessions made to developing countries, jewelry made in Tahiti may qualify as original art, and thus be duty-free. The US customs has waived the import duty on Tahitian black pearls or black pearl jewelry made in French Polynesia, so you will not be charged duty by the customs for these purchases. California residents will be charged a State tax on black pearls if you declare them. If you purchase black pearls or jewelry, make sure to get a certificate from the place of purchase stating that the jewelry was made in the islands. See information on VAT Tax Refunds in *Basic Information* chapter.

Canadian residents have a personal exemption of Can$750 if they are absent from Canada for at least 7 days. You can learn all about their regulations at *www.canadaonline.com*.

Traveling On Your Own

Having the time to be flexible in your travels and being open to adventure and new experiences can bring you infinite rewards in discovering wonderful places and people. If you like to travel "by the seat of your pants" you can come to Tahiti without a hotel reservation and let serendipity be your guide.

You can usually get a hotel room or a bed in a hostel or family pension on the most popular tourist islands without any advance notice if you are willing to settle for whatever accommodation is available. I have found spur-of-the-moment lodgings for friends who wanted to spend a couple of days in Bora Bora during the July Festival, which is normally overbooked at that time of year. Although Polynesians are now more discerning about inviting strangers into their homes, there are still numerous visitors who get "adopted" by a local Tahitian, French or Chinese family. One woman I know went to Huahine where she intended camping out, but she was invited to stay in the home of a Tahitian woman she met, who has a *roulotte* on the boat dock in Fare. The *Tahiti Beach Press* receives several letter each year, written by tourists who want to nominate a local resident for the "Mauruuru Award" because that local has been exceptionally kind to them. The hospitality extended to our visitors includes everything from giving a free ride and a tour around the island to inviting the tourist to their homes for a shower, a meal and quite often, free room and board for several days.

Tourism is very far from reaching the level of saturation in these islands, and the only long lines you'll find are at the buffet tables in the hotels during a special event. You can usually get a last-minute seat on an airplane, a cabin on an inter-island ship, a berth on a sailboat, or a place on any of the tours and excursions that are available on each island. However, it is certainly recommended to reserve in advance if you want to avoid delays, especially for airline flights.

Getting Around Tahiti & Her Islands
BY AIR

AIR MOOREA, Tahiti-Faa'a International Airport, B.P. 6019, Papeete, Tahiti; (Papeete) *Tel. 689/86.41.41; Fax 689/86.42.99*; (Moorea) *Tel. 689/55.06.01; 55.06.09; E-mail: reservation@airmoorea.pf; www.airmoorea.com.* The Air Moorea Terminal is in a separate building to the left of the main terminal as you exit Immigration and Customs in Tahiti. Just follow the arrows on the marked walkway.

Air Moorea operates an air-shuttle service between Tahiti and Moorea, with a fleet of Britten Norman and Twin-Otter aircraft, plus Dornier 228 planes in pool with Air Tahiti. Most of the flights leave Tahiti every hour on the hour and depart from Moorea at 15 minutes past the hour, but there are exceptions during the busy period of the day when extra flights are added. There are up to 40 scheduled round-trips daily between Tahiti and Moorea, with the first Tahiti-Moorea flight at 6am. On Monday, Tuesday and Wednesday the last flight to Moorea leaves Tahiti at 6pm. Air Moorea also operates night flights to connect with the arrival of Air Tahiti Nui service from Los Angeles, with flights scheduled at 7:30 and 8pm on Friday and Sunday, and at 7:30, 8:00, 10:30 and 11pm on Thursday and Saturday. The first Moorea-Tahiti flight is at 6:15am and the last flight is at 6:15pm on Monday-Wednesday. The night flights from Moorea to Tahiti leave Moorea at 7:45 and 8:15pm on Friday and Sunday, and on Thursday and Saturday the Moorea-Tahiti night flights are at 7:45, 8:15, 10:45 and 11:15pm. Reservations are recommended for the 10-minute hop between the two airports. For the daytime service the one-way fare is 3.100 CFP and starting at 7:30pm the one-way fare is 4.700 CFP for residents or non-residents. At publication time the Air Moorea website listed a one-way fare of 8.000 CFP for the night flights, but they confirmed by telephone that the one-way fare is actually 4.700 CFP.

AIR TAHITI, Tahiti-Faa'a International Airport, B.P. 314, Papeete, Tahiti; reservations *Tel. 689/86.42.42/86.40.00; information on flight arrivals 689/86.41.83; Fax 689/86.40.99; E-mail: reservation@airtahiti.pf; www.airtahiti.aero.* The main ticket office, *Tel. 47.44.00,* is located on the corner of rue du Genéral de Gaulle and rue Edouard Ahnne, across the street from Fare Loto in downtown Papeete. Office hours are Monday to Friday 7am to 5pm and on Saturday from 8 to 11am. The airport office, *Tel. 86.41.84 / 86.41.95,* is open daily from 5:30am to 5pm, and the Moana Holidays office *Tel. 50.26.26,* at the Moana Nui Shopping Center in Punaauia, is open all day Monday to Friday 8am to 6pm and on Saturday mornings from 8am to 12pm..

Tahiti Vacations is the Air Tahiti subsidiary in the US. You or your travel agent can contact them at *Tel. 800/553-3477* or *Tel. 310/337-1040; Fax 818/773-8282; E-mail: reservations@tahitivacations.net.*

Air Tahiti Network

Air Tahiti operates domestic scheduled flights between the islands of French Polynesia, with a network of more than 40 islands, covering all five archipelagoes. A modern fleet of twin-turboprop aircraft comprises four ATR 42-500 planes with 48 seats, five ATR 72-500 planes with 66 seats, two Dornier 228 planes with 19 seats, and a Twin-Otter plane with 19 seats that is based in the Marquesas Islands. All the aircraft have high wings, offering you great views of the beautiful islands if you are seated by the window. Your travel agent can arrange an air pass for you to visit several islands, which is the most popular and least expensive means of island hopping.

Air Passes

Air Tahiti offers five different **air passes** with two extension possibilities, which all begin in Papeete. There are also two **Blue Passes** that cannot be

An Air Tahiti Adventure

One of the most exhilarating feelings in the world for adventurers is to step off a plane onto new territory, a place you've never explored. This excitement is intensified when you land on a tropical island that you have longed to visit since you were a child. Some of us believe that the further you have to go to get there, the more rewarding your experience will be once you arrive. Remember the old song that goes: "Far away places with strange sounding names, far away over the sea, those far away places with the strange sounding names are calling, calling me." **Air Tahiti** can take you to 40 far-away places with such beautiful names as Arutua, Huahine, Bora Bora, Tikehau, Fakarava, Kaukura, Manihi, Takapoto, Pukarua, Mangareva, Ua Huka, Nuku Hiva, Raivavae and Rurutu. Just pronouncing these mellifluous names can give you wanderlust.

Getting there truly is half the fun when you fly Air Tahiti. Imagine sitting in a comfortable seat inside a quiet modern aircraft and looking out the window at the incredibly blue Pacific Ocean and the magnificent islands below. Air Tahiti flies low enough so that you can see the fern-covered crenellated mountain ranges of the high islands and the sapphire and emerald lagoons inside the coral atolls. They all seem to be a mirage, a dream or a movie setting for a South Pacific film. Adding to the exotic feeling is the intoxicating perfume wafting from the flowers worn by the islanders when they travel.

It is a Polynesian custom to welcome people with floral leis when they arrive and to send them off on their journeys wearing leis and crowns of flowers, sweet smelling herbs, ferns and colored leaves. On the smaller islands almost everyone in the village goes to the airport to meet the incoming flights, and most of them bring several leis to place around the necks of their family and friends who are arriving or departing. The Rurutu airport turns into a veritable flower garden before the arrival of each Air Tahiti flight, when the flower vendors set up shop in the waiting area. The fragrance of the sauvage (wild) leis fills the air, a sweet and pungent combination of ylang ylang, sweet basil, Tiare Tahiti, avaro, and dried pineapple, threaded together with red twirls of the porohiti fruit. You'll smell the same wonderful melange of perfumes at airports in the Marquesas Islands, with the addition of sandalwood, pandanus fruit, spearmint, gingerroot and other mysterious herbs. In the Tuamotu Islands you'll smell the Tiare Tahiti gardenias that adorn the floral crowns of the islanders, who may also be wearing multiple strings of brightly colored shells.

In addition to providing a means of reliable, quick and comfortable transportation, Air Tahiti is also a source of education into the Polynesian culture, which can be very entertaining.

combined with extensions. All the air passes are subject to special conditions. Rates quoted are for adults, but children's fares are also available. Contact the carrier for more information or go to: *www.airtahiti.pf.*

Air Passes to the Society Islands

Pass MD230 is called the **Discovery Pass**, which will take you from Tahiti to Moorea and on to Huahine and Raiatea, and the 2004 fare is 23.000 CFP. Pass MD 215 is called the **Bora Bora Pass**, which lets you visit all six of the major islands in the Society group: Tahiti, Moorea, Huahine, Raiatea, Bora Bora and Maupiti. You are not allowed to transit in Papeete within the pass nor to fly back to Papeete before the end of the pass, which is sold for 32.500 CFP.

Air Passes to the Society Islands & Tuamotu Archipelago

Pass MD220 is the **Lagoon Pass**, which costs 37.000 CFP and combines a visit to Moorea with Rangiroa, Tikehau, Manihi and Fakarava. One transit is allowed through Papeete between Moorea and the Tuamotu Archipelago. Pass MD213 (**Bora Bora-Tuamotu Pass**) is one of the most popular choices, especially for honeymooners and scuba divers. This pass costs 47.500 CFP and takes you from Tahiti to Moorea, Huahine, Raiatea, Bora Bora and Maupiti in the Society group, and on to Rangiroa, Tikehau, Manihi and Fakarava in the Tuamotu atolls.

A **Blue Pass** (Code BD216) takes you to Huahine, Raiatea, Bora Bora and Moorea, and is sold for 22.000 CFP. It is subject to specific conditions and cannot be combined with the Austral or Marquesas Islands extensions. A **Discovery Blue Pass** (Code BD236) for 16.000 CFP is good for Huahine, Raiatea and Moorea.

Air Pass to the Marquesas Islands

You can also visit the islands of Nuku Hiva, Hiva Oa, Ua Pou and Ua Huka with an Air Tahiti **Marquesas Pass**, which is priced at 60.000 CFP from January 1 to March 31 and from November 1 to December 31. From April 1 to October 31 this same pass is 65.000 CFP.

Air Pass Extensions

Should you wish to discover some of the more remote archipelagoes you can take advantage of two Air Pass Extensions, which must be purchased with one of the four basic Air Passes available. The extensions to the Marquesas or Austral Islands can be used either before or after the pass, and you can buy both extensions if you so choose. A stopover in Tahiti is permitted before or after the extensions.

Code A is the **Austral Islands Extension,** which includes the islands of Rurutu and Tubuai, for an additional 20.000 CFP. Code M is a **Marquesas**

Extension that will take you to the islands of Nuku Hiva and Hiva Oa for an additional 45.000 CFP.

Air Tahiti Day Tours

Air Tahiti offers day tours to Huahine, Raiatea, Bora Bora and Tahaa, which can only be booked locally less than seven days prior to departure. They include the round-trip airfare from Tahiti, picnic or lunch, and excursions, and rates are subject to change without notice. Whether you travel by yourself, with a partner or a group, you may be able to join others who have booked for the same tour. If you cancel your day tour a cancellation fee will apply, and the amount charged will depend on the tour. To arrange a day tour you can contact Air Tahiti in Papeete, *Tel. 689/86.43.43; Fax 689/86.40.99*, or call your local travel agent. See more information under *Excursions & Day Trips* in **Tahiti** chapter.

Island Stays

Air Tahiti's **Island Adventures** specializes in off the beaten track stays in all five island groups, with ready made packages at preferential prices that include round-trip air fares between Tahiti and the outer island chosen, plus accommodations in a hotel, hostel or family pension, meeting and greeting with flower leis and travel documents, ground transfers and most of the government taxes. Depending on your package, you may also have one, two or three daily meals included, and an excursion thrown in.

Here is a sampling of packages proposed by Island Adventures: the Manava package for 11 nights and 12 days starts at 92.250 CFP per person with accommodations in Moorea, Huahine and Bora Bora; the Orama package for 17 nights and 18 days, from 164.900 CFP per person, includes lodgings in Maupiti, Raiatea, Huahine, Bora Bora, Rangiroa, and Tikehau; the Apatea Nui package for 17 nights and 18 days begins at 167.650 CFP per person and takes you from Papeete to Moorea, Huahine, Bora Bora, Rangiroa, Tikehau and back to Papeete; and the 4-night Austral Islands package takes you to Rurutu and Tubuai for 65.700 CFP per person. All the packages are detailed on *www.islandsadventures.com*, which is also in English, or you can fax them at *689/86.42.67*.

Baggage

The normal baggage allowance of 10 kilograms (22 pounds) is raised to 20 kilograms (44 pounds) on most destinations if you have arrived in Tahiti less than 7 days before the first Air Tahiti flight. If you purchase your domestic flights locally then your limit is 10 kilograms. Excess baggage fares vary according to destination. Rather than having to pay for excess baggage at each inter-island flight, you may choose the special round-trip rate available upon check-in at the Tahiti or Moorea airports.

Reconfirmations
You are not required to reconfirm your reservations with Air Tahiti, except in the following conditions. If Air Tahiti has no contact number for you then you should reconfirm a day before your scheduled flight. If you take a flight for which you have no reservation or if you should choose to travel by other means, then you should reconfirm any subsequent reservations you've already made with Air Tahiti. If you are flying on board a 19-seat Dornier 228 aircraft to the Eastern Tuamotu, the Gambier Islands or to Marquesas Islands you should reconfirm a week in advance. Air Tahiti advises that you verify the departure time of your flight in the event of a delay or flight cancellation, at *Tel. 86.42.42.*

Other Information
Check-in time for Air Tahiti flights is one hour in advance of your flight. If you haven't checked in by 20 minutes before flight departure your reservation will be canceled. All Air Tahiti flights are non-smoking. Air Tahiti issues two new timetables every six months, one for local distribution and the other for overseas markets.

Charter Flights
AIR TAHITI, Tahiti-Faa'a Airport, B.P. 314, Papeete, Tahiti 98713. *Tel. 689/86.40.12/86.42.42; Fax 689/86.40.69; E-mail: reservation@airtahiti.pf; www.airtahiti.aero*. Aircraft available for charter within French Polynesia includes four ATR 42-500 planes with 48 seats, five ATR 72-500 planes with 66 seats, two Dornier 228 planes with 19 seats.

AIR MOOREA, Tahiti-Faa'a Airport, B.P. 6019, Faa'a, Tahiti 98702. *Tel. 689/86.41.41 (Papeete), Tel. 689/86.42.42 (reservations); Tel. 689/55.06.01 (Moorea); Fax 689/86.42.99; E-mail: reservation@airmoorea.pf; www.airmoorea.com*. Air Moorea has 30-minute flight-seeing tours over Moorea, and other charter flights can be arranged.

AIR ARCHIPELS, Tahiti-Faa'a Airport, B.P. 6019, Faa'a, Tahiti 98702. *Tel. 689/81.30.30; Fax 689/86.42.69; E-mail: reservation@airarchipels.pf; www.airarchipels.com*. This small airline is used for charters and emergency flight service. The fleet includes two Beechcraft Super King B200 aircraft, each with seven VIP passenger seats or nine high density seats.

WAN AIR, Tahiti-Faa'a Airport, B.P. 6806, Faa'a, Tahiti 98702. *Tel. 689/ 50.44.11 /cell 77.03.79; Fax 689/86.61.72; E-mail: lliparo@wanair.pf*. This company is owned by Robert Wan, who also owns several black pearl farms in the Tuamotu and Gambier Islands. He is the world's largest exporter of black pearls and uses his aircraft to visit his pearl farms. His fleet includes an 18-passenger Beechcraft 1900-D and a 32-place Dornier 328-300 jet, which can be chartered on request to visit all five archipelagoes of French Polynesia and some of the neighboring island groups. In 2005 he will add a Falcon 50 Jet to his fleet for VIP charters.

BY HELICOPTER

POLYNESIA HÉLICOPTÈRES, B.P. 424, Papeete, Tahiti 98713. *Tel. 689/ 86.60.29; Fax 689/86.61.29; cell 78.65.05; E-mail: helico-tahiti@mail.pf; www.polynesia-helicopteres.com.* This company is also known as Heli Inter Polynesie. One AS 350 BA Ecureuil (Squirrel) 5-seat helicopter is based in Tahiti, providing sightseeing flights and charters on request to visit Tahiti and Moorea. There is also an AS 350 BA Ecureuil 5-passenger helicopter based in Bora Bora, and one 5-passenger Ecureuil based permanently in the Marquesas Islands, where they provide transfers from the Nuku Hiva airport to Taiohae village and other nearby islands, as well as photographic flights. A private charter is 168.000 CFP per hour.

See further information in the destination chapters on Tahiti, Moorea, Bora Bora and Nuku Hiva in the Marquesas.

BY INTER-ISLAND PASSENGER BOATS & FREIGHTERS
Windward Society Islands

Tahiti and Moorea are connected by two fast catamarans that provide 30-minute crossings several times daily between Papeete and the Vaiare ferry dock in Moorea. **Aremiti V**, *Tel. 689/50.57.57* in Tahiti and *Tel. 689/56.43.24* in Moorea, *Fax 689/50.57.56,* transports 700 passengers, 30 lightweight cars and 2-wheel vehicles. At publication time there was a question of whether this new catamaran would continue to be used for the Moorea line because of its large size, which protesters claim is unfair to the 306-passenger **Moorea Express**. If the court decides in favor of the **Moorea Express**, then the 495-passenger **Aremiti IV** catamaran, which also carries cars and 2-wheel vehicles, will be put back on the Tahiti-Moorea run and the **Aremiti V** will either be assigned to the Leeward Islands route or sold. The **Moorea Express**, *Tel. 689/ 82.47.47* in Tahiti and *Tel. 689/56.43.43* in Moorea; *Fax 689/42.10.49,* has between 5-7 departures daily from Tahiti to Moorea or from Moorea to Tahiti, carrying passengers and 2-wheel vehicles.

Passengers, cars and larger vehicles are transported on this route by the **Aremiti Ferry,** *Tel. 689/50.57.57/56.43.24,* and the **Moorea Ferry,** *Tel. 689/ 82.47.47/56.34.34,* for the 50-minute trip across the Sea of Moons, as the channel is called. For rates and schedules see *Arriving by Boat* and *Departing by Boat* in the **Moorea** chapter.

Leeward Society Islands

HAWAIKI NUI, B.P. 635, Papeete, Tahiti, *Tel. 689/45.23.24, Fax 689/ 45.24.44; E-mail: sarlstim@mail.pf.*

The Hawaiki Nui leaves the Motu Uta dock in Papeete each Tuesday at

4pm and arrives in Huahine on Wednesday at 2am, in Raiatea at 4:30am and in Bora Bora at 8am. The ship leaves Bora Bora on Wednesday at 10:30am, arrives in Tahaa at 3pm, then departs Tahaa at 3:30pm for Raiatea, arriving at 6pm. It leaves Raiatea at 6:30pm and heads straight back to Papeete, arriving on Thursday at 7am.

The Thursday trip leaves Papeete at 4pm, and the ship arrives in Raiatea at 2:30am on Friday, departs at 3:30am for Bora Bora, arriving at 5:30am. It leaves Bora Bora on Friday at 7:30am for Tahaa, arriving at 11:30am, then departing at 12pm for Raiatea, arriving in Uturoa at 1pm. Departure time from Raiatea is at 1:30pm on Friday, arriving in Huahine at 3:30pm, then departing for Tahiti at 4:30pm, arriving in Papeete at 5am on Saturday. The cost of sleeping on deck is 1.750 CFP per person for each adult and 900 CFP for a child under 12 years. The one-way cost of a berth in a 2-berth cabin with shared toilet is 4.950 CFP from Papeete to all the Leeward Islands. Meals are available on board the ship. Note: All passengers must sleep in a cabin during the Thursday trip from Tahiti to the Leeward Islands because the ship is carrying fuel during that voyage.

VAEANU, operated by Société Coopérative Ouvrière de Production Ihitai Nui. B.P. 9062, Motu Uta, Tahiti, *Tel. 689/41.25.35; Fax 41.24.34.*

This freighter is 79 meters (264 feet) long and 12 meters (39 feet) wide, with a draft of 6 meters (19 feet). In 1981 this ship began its career in Polynesian waters as the *Aranui*, cruising to the Marquesas and Tuamotu Islands. It was sold and renamed in the early 1990s and now serves the Leeward Society Islands with three round-trips each week from Papeete. There are accommodations for 32 passengers in 2 triple cabins, 12 double cabins and one individual cabin, with deck space for 58 passengers. There is also a dining room on board.

This passenger/cargo ship departs from the Motu Uta quay in Papeete at 4pm on Monday, Wednesday and Friday, arriving in Huahine the following morning at 12:30am, in Raiatea at 3:30am and reaches Tahaa at 6am and Bora Bora at 10am. The return trip leaves Bora Bora each Tuesday and Thursday at 11:30am, arriving in Raiatea at 2:30pm, in Huahine at 5pm, and in Papeete at 2am the following morning. The *Vaeanu* leaves Papeete each Friday at 4pm, arriving in Huahine on Saturday at 12:30am, Raiatea at 3:30am, Tahaa at 6am and Bora Bora at 10am. The ship spends each Saturday night in Bora Bora, departing at 8:30am on Sunday for Tahaa, arriving at 11am, and departing at 12pm for Raiatea, arriving in Uturoa at 1pm, then leaves at 2pm for Huahine, arriving at 4pm, leaving again at 4:30pm and arriving in Papeete at 1am Monday.

The one-way fare between Papeete and all the Leeward Society Islands for deck passengers is 2.120 CFP per person. A berth in a 3-person cabin costs 4.400 CFP with shared bath facilities; 4.929 CFP in a 2-berth cabin with a wash basin; and 5.989 CFP in a 2-berth cabin with a private bathroom.

Inter-island deck fares are 1.060 CFP between Huahine and Raiatea, 1.400 CFP between Huahine and Tahaa, 1.690 CFP between Huahine and Bora Bora, 800 CFP between Raiatea and Tahaa, 1.400 CFP between Raiatea and Bora Bora or between Tahaa and Bora Bora. Reservations for cabin space must be paid in full before 9am on the fixed date of departure from Papeete, and all passengers are boarded at 4pm. No alcohol or drugs are allowed on board.

TAPORO VII, *Tel. 42.63.93*, makes three weekly voyages between Tahiti and the Leeward Islands, carrying freight but no passengers.

MAUPITI EXPRESS II, B.P. 612, Bora Bora 98730. *Tel/Fax 689/67.66.69 (Bora Bora; Tel./Fax 689/66.37.81 (Raiatea); cell phone 78.27.22*. This new 140-passenger launch was constructed in Raiatea and began service at the end of September 2004, transporting passengers between Raiatea, Tahaa, Bora Bora and Maupiti. Owner-Captain Gérald Sachet operated the *Keke II* and *Keke III* service between Tahiti and Moorea during the 1970s and 1980s, with his father Pierre Sachet. Gérald also worked aboard the *Aranui* before starting his career with the first *Maupiti Express*.

Each Monday, Wednesday and Friday the *Maupiti Express II* leaves Vaitape quay in Bora Bora at 7am. The boat stops in Tahaa then continues to Uturoa, arriving at 8:45am, docking at the Uturoa quay where all the Tahaa boats tie up. The boat leaves Raiatea at 4pm on Monday and Wednesday, and arrives in Bora Bora at 5:45pm. On Friday it leaves Raiatea at 2pm, arrives in Bora Bora at 3:45pm, then departs again at 4pm, arriving in Raiatea at 5:45pm, and leaves Uturoa at 6pm for Bora Bora, arriving at 7:45pm. On Sunday the *Maupiti Express II* leaves Bora Bora at 4pm, arrives in Raiatea at 5:45pm, then departs at 6pm and arrives in Bora Bora at 7:45pm. The one-way fare between Bora Bora, Tahaa and Raiatea is 2.500 CFP, and 3.500 CFP for a round-trip ticket. The captain is not allowed to transport passengers from Raiatea to Tahaa only, but the boat does make a brief stop in Tahaa.

The *Maupiti Express II* departs from the Vaitape quay in Bora Bora each Tuesday, Thursday and Saturday at 8:30am for Maupiti, an open ocean trip that takes 1 hour and 45 minutes, arriving in Maupiti at 10:15am. It leaves Maupiti the same afternoon at 4pm, returning to Bora Bora. The one-way fare between Raiatea and Maupiti is 3.500 CFP and round-trip costs 5.500 CFP. Passengers under 12 years pay half-fare. If you want to take a day-trip from Bora Bora to Maupiti, you should contact Gérald Sachet at the above cell phone number. He also has a small boat in Maupiti that is used for lagoon tours and his wife runs the Pension . See information on Maupiti Poe Iti Tours under *Lagoon Tours* in this chapter.

Marquesas Islands

ARANUI 3, *operated by Compagnie Polynésienne de Transport Maritime, 2028 El Camino Real South, Suite B, San Mateo, California 94403; in US*

Tel. 800/872-7268 or 650/574-2575; Fax 650/574-6881; www.aranui.com. The Tahiti office is located at Motu Uta, across the harbor and bridge from Papeete, Tel. 689/42.62.40/43.76.60; Fax 689/43.48.89; E-mail: aranui@mail.pf. See more information in Chapter 11.

In my opinion the *Aranui* is the best way to visit French Polynesia if you have the time and interest to enjoy an authentic experience of ship-day in a small secluded valley in the Marquesas Islands. The *Aranui 3* was custom-built in Rumania and began service in March 2003, replacing the *Aranui 2*, offering the same friendly atmosphere that has made the world-wide reputation of the Aranui ships and Polynesian crew. The *Aranui 3* is a working cargo/copra ship—not a cruise ship in the usual sense, where you put on your best finery to dine at the captain's table. You'll be more practically dressed in a cool shirt or blouse and shorts or pants that you don't mind getting wet and dirty when you get into the whaleboat for shore excursions. And don't forget your plastic sandals, protective hat, sunglasses, sunscreen and a good repellent against mosquitoes and *nonos* (sand fleas). The 200-passenger *Aranui 3* was specially designed with added space and the passengers' comfort in mind. The air-conditioned ship is 117.65 meters (386 feet) long, 17.68 meters (58 feet) wide and cruises at a speed of 15 knots. There are accommodations for 208 passengers in 63 standard "A" cabins, 12 deluxe cabins, 10 suites with a balcony, and a dormitory with 30 bunk style beds. All the cabins and suites have a telephone and personal safe.

The 10 spacious suites all have picture windows and some suites even have a balcony. In addition to a queen-size bed with reading lights, there is a desk, chest of drawers, hanging closet, comfortable chairs and coffee table in the sitting space, a refrigerator, television with video channel, private bathroom with bathtub/shower, and a selection of amenities. A suite costs $4,950 per person.

The 12 deluxe cabins are large outside cabins with picture windows, a queen-size bed or two twin beds, refrigerator and private facilities with bathtub/shower, for $4,200 per person. The 63 standard "A" class cabins, are all outside, with two lower berths and private facilities with showers, for $3,500 per person. The class "C" dormitory style accommodations for 30 passengers are located on the restaurant deck. They are air-conditioned but have no private facilities. These upper and lower berths are $1,980 per person.

The public facilities of the *Aranui 3* include an air-conditioned reception, colorful dining room with your choice of seating, a non-smoking lounge-library, boutique, video room, meeting rooms, elevator, gym, and infirmary with a doctor. There are two bars and lounges, a sun deck and salt-water swimming pool. Special marine facilities make it easy for you to fish, swim, snorkel and go scuba diving. There is daily maid service, twice-weekly laundry service and trained hostess and guides. Organized shore excursions include picnics, Marquesan feasts, guided hikes to waterfalls, stone tikis and archaeological sites, visits to wood carvers and artisan workshops, plus inland and upland tours by 4-wheel drive vehicle.

The *Aranui 3* leaves Tahiti 16 times a year for 16-day round-trip voyages to the Marquesas Islands, with a stop at the Tuamotu atoll of Takapoto on the outbound trip, and in Fakarava atoll on the return voyage. The *Aranui* means "The Great Highway" in the Tahitian language and it serves as a lifeline to the Marquesas Islanders, as the ship calls at each principal village and several remote valleys, for a total of at least 15 stops on all six inhabited islands. The big cargo holds contain food, fuel, cement and other building materials, trucks, fishing boats, beer, bedding and other necessities to offload in the distant Marquesas Islands. Copra, citrus fruit, fish and barrels of *noni* (*Morinda citrifolia*) are embarked to take back to Papeete.

Watching the *Aranui*'s muscular crew perform their tasks is part of the attraction and charm of this voyage. Even if hydraulics are not your favorite thing, you'll enjoy watching a pickup truck being loaded from the ship's hold onto a barge or double platform balanced on top of two whale boats lashed together. What's even more interesting is to see how the crew gets the truck safely ashore while the waves are bouncing the whaleboats up and down.

On-board guest lecturers are experts in their fields of Marquesan art, archaeology, history or customs, and they accompany the passengers ashore to enrich their visit by explaining the meaning of the designs in wood carvings, the stone tikis, the *paepae* platforms and *tohua* meeting grounds in the valleys. While you're watching the young people dance for you in the villages, tasting special Marquesan food and visiting the archaeological sites, the Marquesan men and boys are helping the *Aranui* crew to load burlap bags of copra in the whaleboats to be shipped to the copra processing plant in Papeete. A trip aboard the *Aranui* will give you many opportunities to meet the friendly and natural Polynesians, far removed from the normal tourist scene.

The 2005 rates quoted here are based on per person double occupancy and include three meals a day with wine at lunch and dinner, plus picnics and programmed meals on shore, as well as guided excursions. Activities such as horseback riding, scuba diving and helicopter tours are optional. Add 50 percent for single occupancy. Children 3 to 15 years sharing a cabin with adults are charged $860 per person. Adults sharing a cabin with three Pullman beds will have a 25 percent reduction from the full fare for the third person. The estimated Port tax for all passengers is $75 per person. In addition to the rates quoted here, you will pay a Cruise tax of $105 plus a Tourism tax of $105 per person.

The *Aranui* itinerary given here may vary with each voyage, depending on departure date and the freight to be delivered, but the ship will call at most of these villages during each trip.

Day 1 – Departure from dock in Papeete, Tahiti, at 7pm

Day 2 – Takapoto, Tuamotu Islands
Day 3 – At Sea
Day 4 – Ua Pou (Hakahau-Hakahetau), Marquesas Islands
Day 5 – Nuku Hiva (Taiohae)
Day 6 – Nuku Hiva (Taiohae-Taipivai)
Day 7 – Hiva Oa (Atuona)
Day 8 – Fatu Hiva (Omoa-Hanavave)
Day 9 – Hiva Oa (Puamau-Hanaiapa)
Day 10 – Ua Huka (Haavei)
Day 11 – Ua Huka (Hane-Vaipaee-Hokatu)
Day 12 – Nuku Hiva (Hatiheu-Anaho-Aakapa)
Day 13 – Nuku Hiva (Taiohae) Ua Pou (Hakahau)
Day 14 – At Sea
Day 15 – Fakarava, Tuamotu Islands
Day 16 – Arrival back in Papeete at 9am

TAPORO VI, operated by Compagnie Française Maritime de Tahiti, B.P. 368, Papeete, Tahiti, *Tel. 689/42.63.93/43.89.66; Fax 689/42.06.17; E-mail: taporo@mail.pf.* It is based at the Motu Uta quay.

This freighter can transport 12 passengers, either on deck or in two air-conditioned cabins, each containing four berths. Departures from Papeete are made every 15 days, with visits to Takapoto, Tahuata, Fatu Hiva, Hiva Oa, Tahuata, Nuku Hiva, Hiva Oa, Ua Pou and Ua Huka, returning to Papeete on the 10th day. Three meals daily are served on board but there are no arranged activities for passengers. The full cruise fare to the Marquesas in a cabin, with meals, is 64.000 CFP per person, and the full cruise with meals, sleeping on deck, is 44.000 CFP. One-way fares are half the full cost.

Tuamotu Islands

Before planning a trip to the Tuamotu and Gambier Islands aboard any of the ships listed below, you should verify if the vessel is still in service. The treacherous reefs of the atolls are a graveyard for ships that have been wrecked on these coral shores. These distant atolls were named the Dangerous Archipelago for a good reason. During the past few years some of the older ships were destroyed by fire and/or sank at sea. Because these freighters are allowed to carry only 12 passengers, the owners have asked me not to list their ships anymore because they cannot even meet the needs of the inhabitants of the atolls. The offices of these *goëlettes* (tramp boats) are located in the port area of Motu Uta, reached by bridge across the Papeete harbor.

ST. XAVIER MARIS STELLA III, operated by Société Navigation Tuamotu, B.P. 14160, Arue, Tahiti 98701; *Tel. 689/42.23.58; Fax 689/43.03.73; cell 77.22.88; E-mail: maris-stella@mail.pf.* The office is in a warehouse on the inter-island goëlette pier at Motu Uta.

This 207-foot long red-hulled steel ship began its service to the Tuamotu atolls in June 2001. Only 12 passengers are allowed on board and meals are served. In April 2004 the office told me that the passenger berths need to be repaired and the passengers now sleep on the deck, so bring a sleeping bag or a *peue* woven mat. The ship reaches Rangiroa after 20 hours at sea, then continues on to all the western Tuamotu atolls: Ahe, Manihi, Takaroa, Takapoto, Arutua, Apataki, Kaukura, Toau, Fakarava, Kauehi, Raraka, Niau and Papeete. Only one day is spent in each port and the itinerary changes according to the freight on board. The ship leaves Papeete every 15 days and it takes 10 days to make the round-trip circuit. The one-way deck fares, with 3 meals per day included, are 7.710 CFP for Rangiroa and Tikehau, 8.484 CFP for Manihi and 11.830 CFP for Fakarava.

MAREVA NUI, operated by Siméon Richmond, B.P. 1816, Papeete, Tahiti 98713. *Tel. 689/42.25.53, Fax 689/42.25.57.* The office is at the Motu Uta inter-island cargo ship pier.

This is a 181-foot steel ship that transports passengers and cargo between Tahiti and the western Tuamotu atolls, with departures from Papeete every 15 days for the 8-day round trip voyage. There are 12 passenger berths and no cabins. The ship calls at Makatea, Mataiva, Tikehau, Rangiroa, Ahe, Manihi, Takaroa, Takapoto, Raraka, Kauehi, Apataki, Arutua, Kaukura, Niau, Fakarava, and then returns to Papeete. The one-way fares start at 3.800 CFP for deck passage to Makatea, Mataiva or Tikehau, and the most expensive fare is 8.200 CFP for a berth to the last stop on the itinerary, which may be Fakarava, Manihi or Takapoto. Three meals a day cost 2.200 CFP per person per day.

VAI AITO, B.P. 9777, Motu Uta, Tahiti 98715. *Tel. 689/43.99.96/ 50.96.09; Fax 689/43.53.04; E-mail: snathp@mail.pf.* The office is at the Motu Uta inter-island cargo ship pier.

This is a 150-foot long steel hull ship that makes two to three voyages to the Tuamotus a month, with Tikehau the first port-of-call, followed by Rangiroa, Manihi, Ahe, Aratika, Kauehi and Fakarava, before returning to Papeete seven or eight days later. There are no cabins on board and the costs of 12 passengers sleeping on the deck are: 5.353 CFP for Papeete to Tikehau or Rangiroa, 10.706 CFP to Manihi, and escalate up to 18.735 CFP to go to Fakarava. Rates include three meals a day. The round-trip voyage is 27.560 CFP.

NUKU HAU, managed by Roland Paquier of S.T.I.M., B.P. 635, Papeete, Tahiti 98713, *Tel. 689/54.99.54/45.24.44,* is based at the Motu Uta quay.

This is a 210-foot cargo ship that can take 12 passengers from Tahiti to the eastern Tuamotu and Gambier Islands during the 20-day round-trip voyages it makes once every 25 days. There is no cabin space but you will be served three meals a day on board. The itinerary includes Hao, Nego Nego, Tureia, Vanavana, Marutea Sud, Rikitea, Tematangi, Anuanuraro, Nukutepipi and Hereheretue, before returning to Papeete. The one-way fare is 7.950 CFP for deck space, plus 1.950 CFP per day for the meals.

TAPORO VIII, owned by Morton Garbutt, B.P. 368, Papeete, Tahiti 98713. *Tel. 689/42.63.93; Fax 689/42.06.17*. It is based at the Motu Uta quay.

This 213-foot steel ship carries freight and passengers to the eastern atolls of the Tuamotu Archipelago and to Rikitea village on the island of Mangareva. The itinerary changes according to freight to be delivered, but usually includes Anaa, Hikueru, Marokau, Hao, Amanu, Nego Nego, Tematangi, Moruroa, Rikitea (Gambier), Marutea Sud, Tureia, Reao, Tatakoto, Vahitahi, Nukutavake, Pinake, Vairaatea, Hao, Hereheretue and back to Papeete. The ship leaves Tahiti about once a month for the 23-day round trip voyage, and can carry 12 passengers on deck. There are no cabins. The fares start at 7.851 CFP for transportation to Anaa and increase up to 43.590 CFP if your destination is Hereheretue. The one-way fare to Rikitea in the Gambier Islands is 33.534 CFP. All rates include meals.

Other ships serving the Tuamotus are **Cobia III**, *Tel./Fax 43.36.43*, **Dory III**, *Tel./Fax 42.30.55*; **Hotu Maru**, *Tel. 41.07.11, Fax 42.77.67*; and **Kura Ora III**, *Tel. 45.60.00; Fax 45.55.44.*

Austral Islands

TUHAA PAE II, operated by Société Anonyme d'Economie Mixte de Navigation des Australes, B.P. 1890, Papeete, Tahiti, *Tel. 689/50.96.09; Fax 689/42.06.09; E-mail: snathp@mail.pf.*

This is a steel hull ship, 59 meters (196 feet) long, that carries passengers and supplies to the Austral Islands. It makes three voyages a month from Tahiti to the Austral Islands, calling at Tubuai, Rimatara, Raivavae and Rurutu, then returning to Papeete. The itinerary may vary. The ship visits Rapa once every two months. The cabins are very basic, usually with four bunk beds, no portholes and no air. The showers and toilets are on a separate level from the cabins. The local passengers sleep in berths in a big open room up top, which is cooler but not private. Bring your own toilet paper, booze, towels, soap and electric fans (220 volts). The dining room serves simple but good food. There are no shore activities programmed. You can hitch a ride with some of the islanders who come to the ship to collect their merchandise from Tahiti or to load their taro and other vegetables that are being shipped to Papeete.

The one-way fares from Tahiti to Rurutu, Rimatara and Tubuai are 4.046 CFP on the deck, 5.664 CFP in a berth on deck, and 7.789 CFP for a berth in a cabin. The one-way fares to Raivavae are 5.832 CFP on the deck, 8.164 CFP in a berth on deck, and 11.226 CFP for a berth in a cabin. Meals are 3.080 CFP per day in the cafeteria and 5.060 CFP per day in the officers' dining room. The one-way fare from Tahiti to Rapa starts at 7.974 CFP on the deck, and escalates up to 15.330 CFP for a berth in a cabin. A round-trip voyage from Tahiti to Rapa and return is 23.361 CFP for one person, plus meals.

BY CRUISE SHIPS BASED IN TAHITI

M/S PAUL GAUGUIN is operated by Radisson Seven Seas Cruises (RSSC), which is based in Fort Lauderdale, Florida, *Tel. 877/505-5370* (RSSC Expert), *Tel. 866/213-1272* (Travel Agent near you); *Tel. 954/776-6123, ext. 456* (Charters & Incentives); *www.rssc.com.*

The *Paul Gauguin* is 156 meters (512 feet) long, 20.80 meters (68 feet wide), with a draft of 5.10 meters (17 feet), and it weighs 1,230 tons. The 160 outside cabins can accommodate 318 passengers, who pay from $2,210 to $8,740 for a standard 8-day/7-night cruise, depending on stateroom and season. The cost of a 10-day Christmas cruise is $4,835-$16,495, and the 11-day New Year's sailing is $5,325-$18,145. Single supplements and port taxes are added to all cruises. RSSC operates a charter flight service for the *Paul Gauguin* clients with round-trip add-on fares from several gateway cities in the USA. Free economy air specials and special cruise discounts are offered at various times of the year. Pre- and post-cruise packages are also available for those who wish to spend more time on their favorite islands.

The *Paul Gauguin* was named the "World's Best Cruise Ship" in a survey of more than 32,000 people for the *Conde Nast Traveler's* 16th annual "Best in the World" Readers' Choice Awards. The results were published in the February 2004 edition of the magazine, rating the *Paul Gauguin* with an overall 97.7 (out of 100), in a rating of 75 ships. It also received awards for the "Best Overall Cruises", "Best Food at Sea", and "Cruise Critic Editor's Pick" in 2003.

The 320-passenger *Paul Gauguin* was built in France to be based year-round in Tahiti, and in January 1998 it began regular 8 day/7 night cruises in the Society Islands. All of the 160 staterooms and suites have sweeping ocean and lagoon views and half of the staterooms have private balconies or verandas. The Owner's Suite has 457 square feet of living space plus a veranda. The three largest of the Grand Suites each has 529 square feet, including a private balcony and veranda. There are deluxe suites with verandas, veranda suites, junior suites with balconies, and exterior cabins with windows or portholes in categories D, E and F. The smallest cabin is 205 square feet.

The air-conditioned staterooms and suites have individual temperature control and are decorated in a contemporary motif, with exotic woods and warm colors. They each contain a queen-size bed or twin beds, white marble appointed bathroom with a real bathtub and shower, hair dryer and terry cloth robes, closed circuit television and video player, direct dial telephone, safe, numerous shelves and spacious closets. There is also a refrigerator stocked with soft drinks and mineral waters, with a complimentary bar set-up on your embarkation. A staff of more than 250 employees includes a sufficient number of cabin stewards to provide individual service round-the-clock.

The 9-deck ship has two elegant restaurants, an outdoor grill, plus a 24-hour room service menu. Passengers can choose single, open seating dining at their leisure to enjoy gastronomic meals featuring Mediterranean cuisine, as well as Polynesian specialties and a barbecue evening. Menu selections are inspired by **Jean-Pierre Vigato**, a two-star Michelin chef at the Parisian restaurant Apicius. Fare Tahiti is an on-board museum, gallery and special information center with books, videos and other materials on the ethnic art, history, geography and culture of Tahiti and Her Islands. In addition to two bars and lounges, there is a duty free boutique and black pearl shop, a panoramic nightclub and piano bar, a disco, casino, hospital and beauty salon. A full spa and fitness center is operated by **Carita of Paris**, and includes a steam room, as well as aromatherapy, thalassotherapy, massage, facials and full beauty services. The fully equipped Fitness Center features Lifecycles, Liferower, Treadmill, Stairmasters and weight machines. In addition to the swimming pool, there is a nautical sports center with a retractable water sports platform. Water-skiing, windsurfing, sailing, kayaking and snorkeling are offered, as well as a full scuba dive program for novices and experts. Nightly entertainment is presented in the main lounge. The "Gauguines" or "Gauguin's Girls" are 12 pretty Tahitian *vahines* who sing and dance and act as gracious hostesses aboard the ship.

Rates include all meals, preselected wines with meals, non-alcoholic beverages and mineral waters, Captain's Welcome Cocktail, all nautical sports from the Marina nautical sports center except scuba diving, tips, welcome at the Tahiti-Faa'a International airport and transfer to a first-class hotel, use of hotel rooms for the morning on departure day, brunch at the hotel, transfers from the hotel to the *Paul Gauguin* in the afternoon, and transfers from the ship to the airport at the end of the cruise for international departure.

During the standard 8-day/7-night cruise the passengers board the *Paul Gauguin* each Saturday afternoon, with departure time at 10pm. The ship reaches Raiatea on Sunday morning, departing on Monday for Tahaa, where the passengers have use of a private islet between the barrier reef and the main island. The *Paul Gauguin* arrives in Bora Bora each Tuesday morning and remains inside the world-famous lagoon until Wednesday at 6pm, then it cruises to the island of Moorea, where it anchors in Cook's Bay, allowing the passengers two days and a night to explore Moorea. On Friday evening at 6pm the ship leaves Moorea to return to Papeete for the final night, and the passengers disembark on Saturday morning.

In its program for 2005 the *Paul Gauguin* has included a 14-night Solar Eclipse Cruise from April 2-16 that will take passengers from Papeete to the Tuamotu atolls, Pitcairn Island, Hiva Oa and Nuku Hiva in the Marquesas Islands, back to Fakarava in the Tuamotus and then to Moorea and Papeete. The total/hybrid eclipse will take place on April 8. This voyage is priced from $5,970 to $20,559 per person, in double occupancy, plus port charges of $290 per person.

TAHITIAN PRINCESS, 24305 Town Center Dr., Santa Clarita, CA 91355, *Tel. 800/PRINCESS or 661/753.0000; Fax 661/753.0136; www.princess.com.* The 684-passenger ship *Tahitian Princess* was formerly operated as the *R-4* for Renaissance Cruises before joining the Princess Cruises fleet. Since December 2002 the 594-foot long *Tahitian Princess* has offered year-round cruises in Tahiti and the South Pacific. The old world decor features elegant cherry-colored wood finishes, lush window treatments, and cozy upholstered furnishings in a design scheme that evokes a British country house hotel feeling. The 342 cabins give you a choice of eight accommodation categories, with the most elaborate being the 10 owners' suites with 786 to 982 square feet of living space. 73 percent of the staterooms feature balconies (that are not very private), and the size of the accommodations varies from the spacious owners' suites to the "G" class cabin, with 146 square feet. All the cabins have twin or queen-sized beds, a touch-tone telephone, remote controlled television with CNN, the Discovery Channel, sports and movies, including some that are not yet out on video. There are individual temperature controls, ample closet and drawer space, a personal safe, vanity with mirror, hair dryer (reportedly terrible), full-length mirror and a spacious bathroom with French-milled soaps, shampoos and body lotions. There is also 24-hour room service and a crew of 386 to take care of the passengers.

The Club dining room has open seating for breakfast and lunch, and passengers are assigned tables and tablemates for the two dinner seatings. The Sterling Steakhouse Grill features carved-at-the-table prime rib and several choices of steaks. Sabatini's features a multi-course Italian-style feast, and The Panorama serves a breakfast buffet each morning and is transformed into a pizzeria in the evenings. Meals are available 24 hours a day, with hot dinners served in the Bistro from 11 pm to 4am, and a continental breakfast available at 4am in The Panorama Buffet. Other public areas include the purser's lounge area on deck four, where there is a winding staircase that looks just like the one in the movie *Titanic*. In addition to the Cabaret Lounge and Club Bar, there are two very small gift shops, an Internet room with six terminals, a laundromat, nice card room and a gorgeous library with unlocked bookshelves. The highlight of the ship's entertainment is provided by a dance and musical performance presented by Polynesians of all ages who come on board in Raiatea. A Polynesian buffet is served that evening.

The smallish swimming pool is flanked by two whirlpools and the pool deck has a small walking-running promenade deck and a well-used ping-pong table. The spa offers Steiner services, with four treatment rooms, a steam room, thalassotherapy pool and sundeck, and a beauty salon. There is a small but adequate fitness facility and numerous classes such as aerobics, Pilates and yoga. As this is not really a cruise for young kids, there are no dedicated children's facilities. If the ship does have more than 20 kids registered to sail, then Princess assigns a dedicated children's counselor. There are two formal nights per 10-day cruise, when the passengers dress in "resort casual formal" clothes. The rest of the time the cruise is resort casual.

For 2005 the *Tahitian Princess* offers 26 voyages from Papeete to Huahine, Rarotonga (Cook Islands), Raiatea, Bora Bora, Moorea and back to Papeete to complete the 10-day cruise. Prices for this voyage start at $1,395 per person in double occupancy. At publication time there were nine cruises listed for 2006, but this number may increase in the coming months. There are also eight 10-day cruises programmed for 2005 and two for 2006 that will take you from Papeete to Moorea, through the Tuamotu atolls to Nuku Hiva and Hiva Oa in the Marquesas Islands, back to Rangiroa, Raiatea, Bora Bora and Papeete.

On April 12, 2005, the *Tahitian Princess* will operate a 12-day cruise from Papeete to Honolulu, and on May 3, 2005, the ship will leave Honolulu for Papeete on a cruise of 11 days. Both cruises include stops in Moorea, Bora Bora, Christmas Island, Hilo, Maui and Kauai.

The **Pacific Princess**, formerly the R-3 for Renaissance Cruises, is an identical sister-ship to the *Tahitian Princess*. It is no longer based year-round in Tahiti, but does visit on occasion. On April 23, 2005 the Pacific Princess will make a 15-day cruise from Sydney to Auckland, Suva, Pago Pago, Bora Bora, Raiatea, Moorea and Papeete. Then on May 7, 2005, the *Pacific Princess* will begin a 12-day cruise from Papeete to Moorea, Bora Bora, Christmas Island, Hilo, Maui, Kauai and Honolulu, following in the wake of the *Tahitian Princess*, which leaves for Hawaii on May 3.

TU MOANA and **TI'A MOANA** are sister ships owned by Bora Bora Cruises, P.O. Box 40186, Fare Tony, Papeete, Tahiti 98713; *Tel. 689/54.45.05; Fax 689/ 45.10.65; E-mail: resa@boraboracruises.com; www.boraboracruises.com.* You can also book through Orient Express Hotels, Trains & Cruises. USA/Canada *Tel. 800/223-6800.*

These two sister ships were built in Australia to the specifications of Bora Bora Cruises (BBC) and the interior design is Swedish. Since their delivery in 2003 the ships are based year-round in the Leeward Society Islands. If you are looking for a quiet, intimate, low-key cruise, their programs offer a nice escape from all the stress and craziness that we can experience in our daily lives. Former passengers have described their cruise on board the *Tu Moana* "like being a guest on a billionaire's mega yacht." The *Ti'a Moana* will be put into service on demand.

Each of the ships is 69.1 meters (226.7 feet) long, with a beam of 13.8 meters (45.3 feet) and a draft of 2.3 meters (7.5 feet). There are 30 ocean view cabins for 60 guests on three of the five decks, with a choice of queen size, double or twin beds. The bedding is quality European linen with Bora Bora Cruises exclusive Kenzo bed-throw. Each guestroom has large windows, individually controlled air-conditioning, a writing desk with stationery, flat screen LCD television, individual DVD/CD player, telephone, mini-bar refrigerator, personal combination lock safe, under-bed baggage storage area, bathroom with adjustable shower-head with temperature control, Philippe Starck designer basin, fitted hairdryer, cotton bathrobes, Bora Bora Cruises exclusive hypo-allergenic bathroom amenities, plus a hand-blown glass fruit bowl containing fruit.

The public facilities in the fully air-conditioned ships include a panoramic restaurant, 2 bars, a reading room and Internet area, library of books, DVD movies and CD music, a gallery showcasing local artists, a boutique, spa and fitness center, 2 outdoor Jacuzzis, shaded outdoor lounges and sundecks, observation lounge, reception and concierge, excursion office, aft "yacht beach" deck and watersports platform for tenders, kayaks, swimming and fishing. An open seating dining room serves gourmet meals with special diet and kosher meals available on request. The ship's personnel are recruited by a specialized agency in Monaco and the waiters are trained to give the best dining experience possible.

The 7-day/6-night Lagoon Yacht Cruise itinerary begins each Monday in Bora Bora, with a visit to Tahaa on Tuesday, followed by a late night lagoon cruise to Faaroa Bay in Raiatea. The ship spends Wednesday in Raiatea and cruises to Huahine on Thursday, then back to Raiatea on Friday and on to Bora Bora early Saturday morning. You will disembark the ship in Bora Bora after lunch on Sunday. During this memorable week, in addition to having the pleasure of cruising among the beautiful Leeward Islands in a unique, exclusive and exotic manner, you will also be treated to some innovative experiences. These include: a champagne breakfast served in the lagoon; munching popcorn while watching the movie "Tabu", which is screened under the stars on a *motu* islet; feasting on traditional Tahitian foods cooked in an underground *ahima'a* oven and served on a *motu*; a beach barbecue in what could be a movie setting; cruising around the island of Tahaa at sunset time with a glass of bubbling champagne to toast the occasion; paddling up the Faaroa River by kayak or joining a motorized outrigger canoe tour; visiting a black pearl farm to learn all about how these magical gems are produced; and photographing the children of Raiatea as they dance for you on board the ship. Optional activities and excursions include daily massages on board the ship or on the *motu*, horseback riding on the beach, chasing mahi mahi with a local fisherman, trekking a verdant valley to a waterfall, feeding the rays and sharks, taking a 4x4 safari tour, visiting the lagoon aquarium, taking a tour by outrigger speed canoe, Waverunner or Quad bike, helicopter flights, deep-sea fishing and scuba diving.

The rates from January 3, 2005 to January 1, 2006 for a Lagoon Yacht Cruise aboard the *Tu Moana* or *Ti'a Moana* are 459.427 CFP per person, based on double occupancy. The charge for single occupancy guests is 826.969 CFP per person. The cost of two adults and one child 2-12 years old in one cabin is 459.427 CFP per person. Extra or older children are required to reserve an extra guestroom to ensure that BBC safety and comfort standards are met. Children younger than 2 years are not accepted on board. Reduced rates are given for advance purchase. A Romantic Honeymoon supplement is an additional 35.800 CFP per person, which is designed for those guests celebrating marriage, re-marriage, vow renewal or a special anniversary. This cruise enhancement includes a chilled bottle of Roederer Cristal vintage champagne, ceremonial Polynesian high priest's blessing and exclusive Bora Bora Cruises gifts. A Festive Season supplementary charge of 35.800 CFP per passenger will be added to the New Year's voyage of December 26, 2005 to January 1, 2006.

All Bora Bora Cruises include gourmet cuisine throughout (from breakfast Monday to lunch on Sunday), a number of unique events and activities, transfers to/from Bora Bora Airport, mineral waters, tea/coffee/espresso, and all local taxes. Port charges of 14.320 CFP per adult passenger are compulsory.

WINDJAMMER BAREBOAT CRUISES, *Tel. 800/327-2601; www.windjammer.com*, was testing Polynesian waters at publication time with a series of six 10-day cruises aboard the **M/V Amazing Grace**, a 257-foot long ship that carries 94 passengers as well as cargo to replenish the fleet of Windjammer's sailing vessels in the Caribbean. Taking time off from her usual duties, the *Amazing Grace*'s six cruises started on September 26 and the final cruise was scheduled for November 15, 2004. She left Papeete on Sunday, called at Huahine on Monday, at Bora Bora on Tuesday, then spent Wednesday at sea, arriving on Thursday in Rangiroa in the Tuamotu Islands. On Friday the next port-of-call was Aitutakii in the Cook Islands, then the ship sailed back to the Leeward Society Islands to call at Tahaa on Sunday and at Moorea on Monday, arriving back in Papeete on Tuesday. The costs of these 10-day voyages were priced from US $1,975 to $2,075 according to the cabin chosen.

If this trial period proves positive, Windjammer Bareboat Cruises will base the **S/V Polynesia** in Tahiti in 2005. This graceful old 4-masted sailing schooner is 248-feet long and was built in 1938 as one of the last of the great Portuguese Banks fleet. It was acquired by Windjammer in 1975 and has 112 passenger berths and a crew of 45. If all goes as planned, the *Polynesia* will replace the 4-masted sailing ship, **Wind Star**, which was scheduled to leave Tahiti at the end of 2004.

BY CHARTER BOAT

If your romantic spirit is stirred at the sight of a white-sailed ship beating out to the wide sea, you can put yourself aboard your dream by chartering a sailboat in Tahiti. Comfortable modern yachts of every description are available for chartering by the day or week, with bases in Tahiti, Moorea, Raiatea, Tahaa, Bora Bora, Rangiroa and Fakarava. Please check each island section for details on chartering a sailboat.

Billowing sails, white against the horizon, beckon you to "come aboard" one of the sleek yachts you see gliding gracefully across the lagoon, within the protective embrace of the barrier reef that encloses Raiatea and Tahaa. Sailing conditions are ideal in the Leeward Islands and a large variety of yachts can be chartered in Raiatea for bare-boating, day-sailing or for longer excursions with skipper and crew.

ARCHIPELS, B.P. 1160, Papetoai, Moorea 98729. *Tel. 689/56.36.39, Fax 689/56.35.87; E-mail: archimoo@mail.pf; www.archipels.com.*

Archipels Croisières is based in Opunohu Bay on the island of Moorea. Five deep-sea Fontaine Pajot 57 sailing catamarans can be chartered to cruise the Leeward Society Islands, the Marquesas Islands or the Tuamotu atolls. Individuals can choose a "by the cabin" shared-boat cruise, paying 213.500 CFP per person during the low season and 234.000 CFP in the high season for a 7 day/6 night Leeward Islands cruise. An 8 day/7 night Marquesas Islands cruise from Nuku to Ua Huka, Hiva Oa, Fatu Hiva, Tahuata and back to Nuku Hiva, is 256.500 CFP per person all year round. A 7 day/6 night Tuamotu cruise from Fakarava to Toau and Rangiroa is 220.500 CFP year round, and it costs 124.000 to 133.500 CFP per person for a 4 day/3 night Tuamotu cruise inside the atoll of Rangiroa, or 93.000 to 102.000 CFP per person for a 3 day/2 night cruise inside the immense lagoon of Rangiroa. The rates include meals, hotel services aboard in double occupancy cabins, and organized shore activities such as 4x4 excursions. You can also charter the entire yacht for 238.000 to 287.500 CFP per day, depending on the season, with a skipper and hostess/cook included.

Three yachts are kept in Raiatea for sailing the Leeward Islands and another yacht is based year-round in Rangiroa for cruising the Tuamotu Islands. Please see information in the *Moorea, Raiatea* and *Rangiroa* chapters.

THE MOORINGS, B.P. 165, Uturoa, Raiatea 98735. *Tel. 689/66.35.93; cell 78.35.93; Fax 689/66.20.94. E-mail: moorings@mail.pf; www.moorings.com.* North American reservations: *Tel. 800/669-6529,* outside US and Canada *Tel. 727/535-1446.* The nautical base is located at Apooiti Marina in Raiatea and has an average fleet of 25 yachts. Please see further information in *Raiatea* chapter.

STAR VOYAGE PACIFIQUE, Contact Jérôme Touzé at The Moorings, *B.P. 165, Uturoa, Raiatea 98735. Tel. 689/66.35.93, cell 78.35.93; Fax 689/66.20.94; E-mail: moorings@mail.pf.* This French-owned company has turned their 4 yachts over to Bruno Cadoret of The Moorings to charter. Please see further information in *Raiatea* chapter.

SUNSAIL, B.P. 331, Uturoa, Raiatea 98735. *Tel. 689/60.04.85; Fax 689/66.23.19; E-mail: stardustyc@mail.pf; www.sunsail.com.* This nautical base is located at PK 12.5 in Faaroa Bay, 8 miles from Uturoa, with a fleet of 20 sailing yachts. Please see further information in *Raiatea* chapter.

TAHITI YACHT CHARTER, Tahiti office: Monette Aline, B.P. 608, Papeete, Tahiti 98713; *Tel. 689/45.04.00; Fax 689/42.76.00; E-mail: tyc@mail.pf; www.tahitiyachtcharter.com.* North America reservations: Mark Wakeman, *Tel. 800/404-1010; E-mail: marimktg@ix.netcom.com.* Raiatea base: *Tel. 689/66.28.86; Fax 689/66.28.85.*

The office is located in Papeete and the yacht base is at the Apooiti Marina in Raiatea. You can charter a monohull or catamaran bareboat or with provisions and captain and crew. Charter rates start at 289.379 CFP for an 8-day/7 night cruise aboard a Tobago 35 catamaran with 3 cabins during the low seasons (January 10-March 27 and August 28-January 1). A crewed monohull Prototype Australe OFD 54 with 3 cabins can accommodate six passengers for a week's cruise, starting at 1.026.252 CFP for the boat, crew and all meals. Please see more information in *Tahiti* and *Raiatea* chapters.

Other Charter Yachts described in the Island chapters include: **ATARA ROYAL**, based in Raiatea; **CATAMARAN TANE**, based in Raiatea; **BISOU FUTÉ**, and **FAI MANU**, based in Tahaa; **EDEN MARTIN**, based in Huahine; and **O'HANA**, based in Bora Bora.

BY SURF/FISHING BOAT AND SPORT CHARTERS
CASCADE, *Tel./Fax 689/43.70.70; cell 689/73.78.10; 881631468727 sat/phone on boat; E-mail: chris@tahitianbluewaterdream.com; www.tahitianbluewaterdream.com / www.wavehunters.com/tuamotus.*

Cascade is a 64-foot steel motor vessel with 4-star live-aboard accommodations for 10 surfers or fishermen in 6 cabins. There are 3 heads, 3 showers and an outdoor deck shower. The large saloon is furnished with plush couches, color TV, DVD, CD stereo and a full selection of the latest surf magazines and surf videos. A French chef prepares fine cuisine in the stainless steel kitchen that is equipped with microwave, gas oven hot plates, water maker, ice maker and a big freezer. Meals include just-caught fish, as well as fresh seafood, meats, poultry, pastas, vegetables and fruits. A barbecue is on the outside deck and dining is both inside and outdoors. Full category 1 safety equipment includes life rafts, life jackets and flares. *Cascade* has two powerful engines (V8 550 Turbo GM Detroit Diesels), as well as a 14-foot Dory with a 25hp engine. There is a Jet Ski on board, along with a kite surfer (Robbie Nash model), 2 kayaks, snorkel and spearfishing gear, and state-of-the-art fishing equipment. For an optional charge passengers also have use of *Cascade*'s unprecedented Surfboard Quiver of over 60 surfboards shaped by top international shapers for Tahitian style waves. This saves you from the hassle and expense and risk of loss in checked airline baggage when you bring your surf boards with you. There is no scuba gear on board, but divers can link up with licensed scuba dive operators in the Tuamotu atolls.

Owner Chris O'Callaghan is an Australian who grew up on Sydney's southern beaches, making his reputation early on as one of the most talented surfers in Australia. As he matured he sought ways to combine his passion for water sports with his desire for traveling and making friends. Chris is now based in Tahiti as the contest director for Billabong, who sponsors the World Cup Tournament (WCT) Pro Surfing Championships in Teahupoo on Tahiti Iti every year during the month of May. Chris has joined forces with Moana David, a Tahitian-French fellow who is an experienced seaman, surfer and fisherman. Moana operated the land-based camp, Moana Surf Tours, for 10 years before taking to the sea aboard the *Cascade*. They have hosted most of the world's top surfers, taking them to remote atolls in the Tuamotus where they can catch the wave of their choice without fear of colliding with other surfers. Chris and Moana said that there are two surf seasons in these islands. From November through March, the summer season, the swells are from the North and can reach up to 8 feet. From April through October, which are considered the winter or cooler months in the Southern Hemisphere, there are big southerly storms from Antarctica and New Zealand that can bring good surfing waves. The water temperature from November to February is 27º C (80.6º F), and in July and August it is 24-25º C (75º-77º F).

Surfers are charged about US $250 each per day, based on the full load of 10 people for a 10-day trip. There is a 4-day minimum for these charters and singles can also book. This cost covers accommodation and food on board, the use of snorkeling and spearfishing equipment, drop off to the waves and pick-up, plus use of the washing machine. It does not cover any airfare or surfboard rental. Tall-boy Hinano beer is sold for $2 per bottle on board the boat. Wine is also available for purchase.

Live aboard charters for surfing or deep-sea fishing begin in Rangiroa during the months of November through April and end in Fakarava. The rest of the year the charter begins in Fakarava and ends in Rangiroa. Surfing stops depend on where the best waves are that day. Chris and Moana keep a close wave watch by Sat-Nav. Specialized trips can be made to suit charterers who wish to book out the whole boat, and the *Cascade* is available for all kinds of tours—surfing, diving, adventure and fishing excursions.

Wavehunters advertises a 2005 Tuamotu 11-day "Surf Voyager" package, based on 10 surfers aboard the *Cascade*, for $3,550 per surfer during the South Season and $3,850 per surfer during the North Season, including all flights. The 11-night "Surf Voyager" Full Boat cost without flights or surf board rental is $22,000 during the South Season and $25,000 during the North season, with a maximum of 10 surfers.

A 2005 Tuamotus 7-day "Surgical Strike" package, including all air flights, 7 days/nights on board Cascade with board rental is $3,225 per person for individuals and $2,850 per person for groups, based on 10 passengers. The "Surgical Strike" Full Boat cost without flights or board rental is $15,000. **Warning**: These trips fill up very quickly, so early reservations are definitely advised.

TARAVANA ISLAND SPORT CHARTERS BORA BORA, B.P. 186, Bora Bora. *Tel. 67.77.79 (evening) or cell 689/72.30.99 (day); Fax 689/60.59.31; E-mail: taravana@mail.pf; www.taravana.com.* Based at the Hotel Bora Bora.

Captain Richard Postma is an American who has 25 years of sailing experience in French Polynesia and for most of that time he has lived in Bora Bora. *Taravana*, his 50-foot state-of-the-art custom Lock Crowther-design ocean cruising catamaran, is equipped for comfort, stability and sportfishing. *Taravana* is the first sailboat in the world designed to be competitive in international big game tournaments. Each of her spacious double cabins offers queen-size bunks and semi-private facilities and the boat is well designed for both day, overnight and extended charters. On a day cruise you can explore Bora Bora's beautiful protected lagoon or ocean sail and sportfish near the atoll of Tupai, the island closest to Bora Bora. It takes 1 1/2 hours to cross the 10-mile channel and you can sportfish on the way to the reef, enjoy superb snorkeling and have lunch on the calm side of the lagoon.

Half-day charter cruises cost 90.000 CFP for the boat and 120.000 CFP for full-day cruises. Famous Hollywood stars who want to get away from it all find the privacy and tranquility they seek when they charter the *Taravana* for an overnight sail. Some movie stars have even gotten married aboard Richard's famous catamaran. The cost of this romantic cruise is 220.000 CFP for two people or 260.000 CFP for four passengers. These rates do not include tax. Quotes for six passengers are given on request. The overnight charter rates include 3 meals a day plus wine with lunch and dinner, served by a staff of two professionals. A 2-day cruise can easily include visits to the nearby islands of Tahaa and Raiatea.

By Live-Aboard Dive Boats

AQUA TIKI, contact Patrice Poiry at Aqua Polynésie, *Tel. 689/73.47.31; Sat/phone on boat 06 60525060; E-mail: aquapol@club-internet.fr; www.aquatiki.com.*

Aqua Tiki is a 46-foot Bahia deep-sea catamaran that provides Dive Cruises in the Tuamotu atolls. On the 8-day/7-night cruise you embark in Fakarava and visit the north and south ends of the atoll, then sail to Kauehi and Toau and back to Fakarava, where you disembark. Six passengers/divers can sleep in the 3 double guest cabins, each with its own bathroom. There is a television and VCR player on board, as well as full scuba diving equipment. There are also 10-day/9-night cruises and 15-day/14-night cruises in the Tuamotus, as well as 8-day/7-night cruises in the Leeward Islands. Please see information under Fakarava in *Tuamotu* chapter. From mid-February to mid-April 2005 the *Aqua Tiki* will be in the Marquesas Islands, operating dive cruise charters out of Taiohae Bay in Nuku Hiva.

TAHITI AGGRESSOR, *Aggressor Fleet, Limited, P.O. Box 1470, Morgan City, LA 70381-1470; Tel. 800/348-2628 or 985/385-2628; Fax 985/384-*

0817; E-mail: tahiti@aggressor.com; www.aggressor.com. Tahiti contact: Gérard Seidl, Tel. 77.15.06; Fax 689/42.79.91.

The *Tahiti Aggressor* is a 106-foot, 18 passenger, handicapped-diver accessible, catamaran that is based year-round in Rangiroa, offering a live-aboard dive program that takes guests to explore the passes and channel entrances of the Tuamotu Atolls, which usually include Rangiroa, Apataki, Toau and Fakarava. The boat offers nine double cabins, each with a private bathroom. There is also a salon with entertainment center, wet bar, hot tub and partially covered sun deck. The air-conditioned yacht has 110-volt power on board. The *Tahiti Aggressor* is one of 12 worldwide franchises and the boat was built to U.S. Coast Guard standards with a full complement of safety equipment.

Diving is available from the mother ship; however, most dives are made from the high- speed 18-passenger dive skiff, which is lifted to the main level for easy boarding. Nitrox rental and certification is available and scuba gear can also be rented with advance reservations. A full line of underwater cameras can also be rented for the charter. The Tuamotu itinerary is recommended for advanced divers only, and they must all complete a pass flying course before plunging into the swift currents, which can sometimes exceed five knots. 7-day dive cruise rates for January 1, 2005 to January 7, 2006, are $2,895 per person in deluxe accommodation and $2,695 per person in double accommodation. From January 7, 2006 to January 6, 2007, the rates will be $100 more per category. These prices include local airport transfers on the day of departure and return, around-the-clock service from a professional crew, on-board accommodations, delicious meals, between-dive snacks, soft drinks, local beer and wine. Special dietary requests may be made in advance. Airfare, local taxes and fees, hotel stays, day rooms, insurance, nitrox, crew gratuity and dinner Friday on evening are not included in the charter rates. There is also a Cruising/ Tourism tax of $120 per person to be paid on board.

The *Tahiti Aggressor* offers two itineraries: charterers board in Rangiroa and disembark in Fakarava one week, then the next charter will board in Fakarava and disembark in Rangiroa. The standard scuba itinerary is Saturday-to-Saturday with 5.5 days to Eat, Sleep and Dive. An overnight stay is required in Papeete to accommodate the flights to the Tuamotus. Guests may board Saturday afternoon. Diving begins Sunday morning and ends Friday at noon. The *Tahiti Aggressor* returns to port on Friday afternoon. Guests may spend the afternoon shopping or sightseeing until the evening cocktail party hosted by the crew. After the party, everyone will dine at a local restaurant. This is the only meal not included in the charter. Check-out is Saturday morning.

Scuba Diving Conditions & Requirements

The clear, tropical waters of Tahiti and Her Islands are ideal for year-round diving, providing a diversity of magnificent dive sites in the lagoons, passes and outer coral reefs. Because French Polynesia covers such a vast area, with varying degrees of latitude and longitude, the underwater scenery is different from archipelago to archipelago, from island to island. The average water temperature is 29 º Celsius / 85º Fahrenheit during the summer months of November to March, and 25º Celsius / 79º Fahrenheit during the Austral winter months of April to October. Underwater visibility is normally good up to distances of 30 meters (100 feet).

All non-certified scuba divers must have a certificate from a doctor indicating that you are in good health. A medical exam can be taken in Tahiti for the necessary papers, and examinations are available to obtain diving diplomas.

Around the island of Tahiti you will find some of the best scuba diving conditions for the beginner or the veteran diver who needs a reorientation. Due to the location of dive centers on the west coast of the island, in the lee of the prevailing easterly winds, you will find minimal currents and calm surface conditions. There is good visibility, with colorful small reef fish, friendly moray eels, eagle rays, small white-tip sharks and nurse sharks. Dive attractions also include a sunken inter-island schooner and a seaplane, and a vertical cliff on the outer reef that descends to infinity from a plateau 4.5 meters (15 feet) deep.

Moorea's special diving features are the feeding of moray eels, barracuda and large lemon sharks, plus a friendly encounter with leopard rays and large Napoleon fish. A sunken ship is clearly seen in the translucent waters of Papetoai.

Bora Bora is famous for its multihued lagoon, but also for the abundance of large-species marine life that inhabit this environment, especially the graceful manta rays that are sometimes found in groups of 10 or more, swimming inside the lagoon and in the pass.

In the lagoon surrounding Huahine Nui and Huahine Iti you can feed sharks and see large schools of barracudas, big red snappers, tuna, turtles, rays and Napoleons.

The lagoon that is shared by Raiatea and Tahaa attracts large schools of pelagic fish, leopard rays and a few manta rays. Divers can watch or join in the feeding of the large blue-green Napoleon fish, pet moray eels, and observe white-tip, black-tip and gray sharks.

In the Tuamotu atolls you will find world-class diving in luminescent waters with very good visibility inside the lagoons and passes. Rangiroa is one of the top diving destinations in the world. This is the largest atoll in the Southern Hemisphere and the second largest in the world, after Kwajalein in the Marshall Islands. Rangiroa's two most famous diving spots are the Avatoru and Tiputa passes through the coral reef. Schools of sharks, squadrons of eagle rays, jacks, tuna, barracuda, manta rays, turtles and dolphins swim

Scuba Diving Terms

For the uninitiated in the vernacular of scuba diving, **PADI** is the **Professional Association of Diving Instructors**. An OWDI is an overwater diving instructor. The PADI system of training divers is used in North America. The techniques differ from those of the French system of **CMAS** (**Conféderation Mondiale des Activités Subaquatiques**), which is the World Underwater Federation. Most of the diving monitors and instructors in Tahiti and Her Islands are qualified to teach both PADI and CMAS.

The **FFESSM** is the **Fèderation Française des Activités Subaquatiques**, or French Underwater Federation. A level of B.E. training in the FFESSM equals a CMAS one star rating; the first echelon or level equals a two-star rating in CMAS; and autonomous diver equals a three-star rating in CMAS. In France a monitor (moniteur) is more qualified than an instructor. A moniteur d'Etat is the equivalent of a State instructor, with levels of BEES 1, 2 or 3. BEES 3 is the highest level you can reach, except for a moniteur federal, who is not supposed to accept money for giving lessons. All the instructors and monitors in Tahiti are paid for their services.

through these passes when the very strong currents from the ocean flow into the lagoon or rush back out to sea.

Manihi is famous for the black pearl farms inside its crystal clear lagoon. Excellent diving conditions are favorable for beginners and experienced divers. The sites include a beautiful variety of coral gardens, big Napoleon fish, black-tip reef sharks, gray sharks, eagle and manta rays, schools of snappers and big tuna fish. One favorite site is a breathtaking wall that drops 3 to 1,350 meters (10 to 4,500 feet). When the famous French diver Jacques Cousteau explored the lagoon in Tikehau he said that it contained more fish than any of the other lagoons in this part of the Pacific. The inhabitants ship parrotfish and other lagoon fish from the Tikehau lagoon to Tahiti by airplane and fishing ships. Fakarava is the second largest atoll in the Tuamotu archipelago, where scuba diving is the most spectacular in the Garuae Pass, which is one kilometer (.62 miles) wide and 16 meters (52 feet) deep.

Experienced divers will be treated to a panorama of underwater life that includes manta rays, dolphins, barracudas, tiger sharks, hammerhead sharks and whale sharks. A dive center is now open on the atoll of Makemo, where a virtually unexplored scuba diver's paradise awaits discovery. Some of the dive boats include Toau, Kauehi, Tahanea and Aratika on their itinerary.

The northern group of the Marquesas Islands offers underwater caves with large fauna, recommended for adventurous, experienced divers only. Some of the world's most famous underwater photographers come here to dive and photograph the dozens of manta rays, leopard rays, stingrays, friendly hammerhead sharks and pigmy killer whales that inhabit the open waters surrounding the islands.

In the southern latitudes of the Austral Islands the humpback whales are a big attraction for scuba divers just offshore the island of Rurutu. These mammals, which are 14 to 18 meters (46 to 59 feet) in length, are seen during the months of July through October, when they come up from Antarctica to mate and give birth, while escaping the austral winters. Several humpbacks also visit Moorea, Tahiti and the Tuamotu atolls.

There are more than 30 scuba diving clubs in French Polynesia, located on the islands of Tahiti, Moorea, Huahine, Raiatea, Tahaa and Bora Bora in the Society Islands, the atolls of Rangiroa, Tikehau, Manihi, Fakarava, Makemo and Hao in the Tuamotu archipelago, on Nuku Hiva in the Marquesas Islands, and on Rurutu and Tubuai in the Austral Islands. Please check each destination chapter for information on the most popular diving clubs used by tourists.

BY CAR

In the Society Islands most of the roads that circle the islands are paved. There are a few places in Raiatea and Tahaa where the road is not sealed but they are pretty well graded. Following heavy rains there are frequently holes in the road that can be very dangerous, especially if you are driving a scooter or bicycle. In most of the Marquesas Islands the 4-wheel drive vehicles (called 4x4, pronounced "cat-cat") are usually rented with driver, because the roads are abominable. You can rent a self-drive 4WD in Atuona on the island of Hiva Oa. Rangiroa has a paved road between the two passes and there's nowhere else to go by car. The Austral Islands have mostly unpaved roads, which you can drive in a normal car, except for some places in Rurutu, where a 4WD is required.

You will drive on the right side of the road in French Polynesia, just as you do in North America and continental Europe. A valid diver's license from your State or home country will be honored here. Should you buy an international driver's license, which is not at all necessary, you will still need to show your normal driver's license in order to rent a car or scooter. The minimum age is 21 years to rent a 4WD vehicle and to rent two wheel vehicles the driver must be 18 or 19 years old, depending on the island.

Speed limits are 40 kilometers per hour (24 miles per hour) in the towns and villages, 60 kilometers (37 miles per hour) on the winding roads of most of the islands and 80 to 110 kilometers (50 to 68 miles per hour) on a short stretch of freeway leading from Tahiti's west coast to downtown Papeete. Seat belts are mandatory for the driver and passenger in the front seats of vehicles on all islands, and helmets are required for anyone riding a motorcycle or scooter.

Anyone driving a two-wheel vehicle should remember to go single file. There are no bicycle paths in these islands and some of the local drivers are in a mighty big hurry to get somewhere, even with nowhere to go. After all, they take their driver's lessons from the French!

You should also be alert for drunk drivers, especially late at night, and young boys doing "wheelies" on bicycles or scooters, often with no lights at night. You also have to look out for children and dogs when you pass through the villages around the island.

Liability Insurance

Vehicle insurance includes third party liability insurance. It is possible, depending on the conditions of the driving license and age, to take a comprehensive insurance that covers collision, damage and waiver.

Automobile Rental

Europcar and **Avis-Pacificar** are the biggest names for rental cars in French Polynesia, although **Hertz** also has offices in the more popular tourist islands. There are also a few individuals who rent cars, scooters and bicycles. See information for each island in the *Getting Around Town* section.

BY PACKAGE TOURS

The travel agencies listed in this chapter can suggest package tours that include international air travel to French Polynesia, accommodations, some meals, ground transfers, inter-island travel by airplane or boat, and some tours and excursions. Should you decide on a tour package, be sure to read the fine print so that you will understand what you are paying for. You don't want to limit yourself to eating all your meals in the same hotel when there are enticing restaurants to explore on the island.

Accommodations

According to figures released by Tahiti's Tourism Service, at April 30, 2004, there were 48 international class hotels on 11 islands in French Polynesia. When the Radisson Plaza Resort opened in Tahiti in August 2004, the 165-room hotel brought the number of classified hotel rooms to a total of 3,336. Although there were several more hotels waiting for government approval to begin construction, the only projects that were actually underway at publication time were on the island of Bora Bora. The Ritz Carlton is building 80 bungalows on Motu Ome, scheduled to open at the beginning of 2006, and the Hotel InterContinental Bora Bora will open 112 bungalows on Motu Piti Aau in March 2006. The Four Seasons project has received authorization and will begin construction of 110 bungalows in January 2005 on Bora Bora's Motu Tofari.

The April 2004 figures also included 256 non-classified small hotels, guesthouses, bed and breakfast lodgings, hostels and homestays, locally referred to as *family pensions*. These establishments offer a total of 1,273 rooms, with accommodations for 3,472 people. In addition to the pensions officially recognized by the tourism officials, there are several other non-registered lodgings available for guests.

The up-market hotel accommodations include air-conditioned deluxe rooms with direct dial international telephones, modem hookups, individual safes, satellite television and room service, similar to American hotel or motel rooms, usually in concrete buildings of two or more levels. Most of the newer hotels also offer these conveniences in their deluxe Polynesian style bungalows.

Mid-range rooms are available in small hotels, which may be an air-conditioned room in downtown Papeete, a self-contained, totally equipped house on Moorea or Huahine, or an attractive bungalow on a motu in Bora Bora, with a ceiling fan, cooking facilities and television.

The typical Polynesian style bungalows can be very elegant, especially when they are built overwater, with a glass panel or table in the floor, allowing you to have a peek at what the fish are doing in the coral gardens below. These bungalows often have thatched roofs of woven pandanus leaves and woven bamboo walls. The interior walls are sometimes covered with pandanus matting from Indonesia, and a chic Polynesian decor incorporates all the flamboyant colors you'll find in the tropical gardens, or it reflects the softer colors of the lagoon. The most deluxe hotels have replaced the Polynesian furnishings with a neutral decor of off-white, cream and beige, adding accent colors with cushions. Most of the newer bungalows have air-conditioning, large bathrooms with a bathtub/shower, bathtub and separate shower, or Jacuzzi and separate shower. They also have lighted dressing tables and living areas, plus a terrace or veranda, and the overwater bungalows have steps leading into the lagoon, with a shower on the landing. To answer the demands of their American guests, the hotel rooms most frequently chosen by honeymooners are also equipped with a CD player and television and machine for DVD films. Some of these hotels have also added a spa whose services include a relaxing massage for two, often at the edge of the lagoon at sunset time or under the starry sky.

The small *fare* (FAH-rey) often has a thatched roof, overhead fan and colorful linens and curtains. Some are screened, and most have a porch or terrace. In the family-operated guesthouses and *pensions* you usually have a private room or bungalow. In some *pensions* you have cooking facilities and in others you eat what your hosts prepare. You may have a bathroom to yourself with a hot water shower, or share the outdoor facilities which may have a cold water shower. On some of the more arid islands your water supply may be limited; you may have to dip half a coconut shell into a barrel of water to take your bath. Backpackers' lodgings and campgrounds are available on several islands. Check the accommodation information for the individual islands.

International Hotel Chains

The 54-unit Hotel Bora Bora is operated by the exclusive **Amanresorts**. North America Reservations: *Tel. 800/421-1490*, Los Angeles *Tel. 818/587-9650; Fax 818/710-0050; E-mail: hotelborabora@aol.com; www.amanresorts.com;* Central Reservations Office: *Tel. 689/60.44.11; Fax 689/60.44.22; E-mail: reservations@hotelborabora.pf.*

Orient Express Hotels operates the 80-bungalow Bora Bora Lagoon Resort. US Reservations: Orient Express *Tel. 800/860-4095 / 843/965-8600 (direct line); E-mail: sales@bblr.net; bblr@mail.pf; www.boraboralagoonresort.orient-express.com.*

The Beachcomber hotels in Tahiti (263 units), Moorea (143 units) and Bora Bora (64 units) became members of the **Inter-Continental Resort** chain in June 2001, and are now part of the **Bass Hotels & Resorts** empire. In addition to managing the hotels, InterContinental now owns 16% of Tahiti Beachcomber Sociètè Anonyme (TBSA), the Tahiti-based company that is headed by American Dick Bailey. The Beachcomber name will be dropped at the end of 2004, and the hotels will then be called InterContinental Resort Tahiti, InterContinental Resort Moorea, InterContinental Moana Beach Bora Bora, and a new 112-unit hotel will open in May 2006 in Bora Bora that will be called InterContinental Resort and Spa Bora Bora. North America Reservations: *Tel. 800/327-0200; E-mail: tahiti@interconti.com; www.interconti.com.*

Starwood Hotels & Resorts manage the 200-unit Sheraton Hotel Tahiti Resort & Spa, the 106-unit Sheraton Moorea Lagoon Resort & Spa and the Bora Bora Nui Resort & Spa, with 120 premium units, which is a member of the Luxury Collection. North America reservations: *Tel. 800/782-9488; E-mail: reservations.tahiti@sheraton.pf; www.sheratonsintahiti.com.* These three hotels are owned by Tahiti resident Louis Wane, who is also building the 80-bungalow Ritz Carlton in Bora Bora. He is the brother of Robert Wan, who owns black pearl farms and Tahiti Pearls boutiques. They spell their family name differently.

Club Mediterranee, US reservations, *Tel. 800/528-3100; www.clubmed.com* has 150 units at the Club Med Bora Bora. The Club Med Moorea closed its 350-bed village in November 2001 and no announcement has been made of re-opening. **Le Méridien Hotels**, North America reservations, *Tel. 800/543-4300, E-mail: sales@lemeridien-tahiti.com; www.lemeridien-tahiti.com*, operate the 150-unit Le Méridien Tahiti and the 100-unit Le Méridien Bora Bora.

The French company **Sofitel Coralia**, US reservations *Tel. 800/763-4835, E-mail: reservation_tahiti@accor-hotels.com; www.sofitel.com*, has the 224-

room Maeva Beach in Tahiti, the 110-unit Sofitel Ia Ora Moorea, the 61-unit Sofitel Heiva Huahine, the 64-unit Sofitel Marara Bora Bora and the 30-bungalow Sofitel Coralia Motu. In August 2004 Sofitel took over management of the new 80-room 3-star Bora Bora Beach Resort and the new 38-unit Rangiroa Beach Resort, which now operate under the **Novotel** branch of the **Accor Group**. These two hotels were built on the sites formerly occupied by Tahiti Resort Hotels, a chain of five hotels that was taken oven by **Nouvelles Frontières** of France in 1999. Nouvelles Frontières no longer has a hotel property in French Polynesia. Sofitel also handles the promotion for the 63-unit Hotel Kia Ora Rangiroa and the 5- bungalow Kia Ora Sauvage in Rangiroa.

In July 2004 **Outrigger Hotels & Resorts** took over management of the 41-unit Te Tiare Beach Resort, a 4-star American-owned hotel in Huahine. US reservations can be made at *www.outrigger.com* or by contacting the hotel directly at *Tel. 689/60.60.50; Fax 689/60.60.51; E-mail: welcome@tetiarebeachresort.pf; www.tetiarebeachresort.com.*

Locally-owned Hotel Chains

Financière Hôtelière Polynésienne (FHP) is a Tahiti company comprised primarily of Air Tahiti and Banque Socredo, along with private investors. They own the 5-star Le Taha'a Private Island & Spa, with 60 deluxe suites, which is a member of the prestigious **Le Relais et Chateaux** association. Another 5-star holding of FHP is the 80-unit Bora Bora Pearl Beach Resort. Their 4-star hotels are the 41-unit Manihi Pearl Beach Resort, the 38-unit Tikehau Pearl Beach Resort, the 95-unit Moorea Pearl Resort, the 20-unit Nuku Hiva Keikahanui Pearl Lodge and the 20-unit Hiva Oa Hanakee Pearl Lodge. All the properties marketed as **Pearl Hotels** are managed by **South Pacific Management** (SPM). US contact: Kahi Arnaud, *Tel. 310/649-2528; Fax 310/649-2520; E-mail: kahi.arnaud@spmhotels.pf; www.pearlresorts.com.*

Hotel Management & Services (HMS) is owned by Dick Bailey, an American resident of Tahiti, who also heads the company that owns the InterContinental hotels in French Polynesia. HMS manages the Hotel Le Maitai Polynesia in Bora Bora, with 74 units, and the Hotel Maitai Dream Fakarava, with 30 units. Reservations: *Tel. 689/86.51.46/86.51.08; Fax 689/86.51.90; E-mail: booking@maitaipolynesia.pf; hms@mail.pf; www.hotelmaitai.com.*

Chapter 7

BASIC INFORMATION

Listed here, in alphabetical order by topic, are practical information and recommendations for your trip to Tahiti and Her Islands.

Business Hours

Several of the small restaurant/snacks and the Papeete Municipal Market, **le Marché**, open around 5am, and between 7:30-8am the post office, government offices, banks, airline offices, travel agencies and boutiques open. Many of the shops and offices still close for lunch between 12pm and 1:30 or 2pm, while others are now remaining open through the lunch period. Except for the restaurants and sidewalk cafés and bars, most of Papeete is closed down by 6pm.

The suburban shopping centers remain open until 7 or 8pm. Most businesses close at noon on Saturdays and all day Sunday and holidays. The food stores are open on Saturday afternoon and usually open on Sundays and holidays from 6 to 8am, with a few *magasins* remaining open until noon and then reopening between 5 and 7pm.

Cost of Living & Travel

French Polynesia can be very expensive and it can also be affordable, depending on how you choose to go. I've been living in Tahiti and Moorea since 1971 and I have never ceased to be amazed at the costs. We pay the same prices as you will when we go to the restaurants and grocery stores, take a taxi or buy gas for our automobiles. Only recently have the residents begun to benefit from reductions on inter-island airfares, hotel rates and some of the excursions. Even the French visitors are surprised at the cost of living in Tahiti and Her Islands. The Japanese don't find it too expensive, but many Americans spend their entire vacation complaining about the cost of Coca-Cola, beer, water and food. Some of these tourists are so concerned with how much money they're spending that they cannot even enjoy their vacations.

Even though some of the prices here are still astronomical compared to what you'll pay in the United States, Canada or wherever you are, they are actually lower for many items than we paid a few years ago. I remember when a package of celery, or a head of cauliflower or broccoli cost 1.300 CFP! Today, in Moorea I pay 795 CFP a kilo for broccoli imported from Australia, and it is only 245 CFP a kilo at a big super market in Tahiti. I pay 285 CFP per kilo for cauliflower imported from the USA, while it is only 180 CFP a head in Tahiti. Imported celery is 380 CFP for 16 ounces. Locally grown frisée lettuce is 550 CFP a kilo, green peppers are 760 CFP per kilo, cucumbers are 370 CFP a kilo and locally grown tomatoes are 570 CFP a kilo. The Papeete Public Marché sells watermelons from Maupiti or Huahine for 180 CFP a kilogram and cantaloupe from those islands are 200 to 290 CFP per kilogram, depending on the type of melon. The same fruit would cost double the price in Moorea. A bottle of Chateau Toutigeac Bordeaux wine is 995 CFP in Tahiti, 1.490 CFP in Moorea and 2.600 CFP in Raivavae.

With the opening of the "mega" markets (Carrefour, Hyper-U Tropic Import, Cash and Carry, Price Club, Hyper Champion and Casino) in Tahiti, competition brought the prices down a little. Larger supermarkets have also opened in the outer islands, providing a wider choice of goodies at slightly lower prices. But then, the value added tax brings them up again.

Hotel Rates

You won't find many real bargains for a hotel room in Tahiti and Her Islands, unless you get way off the tourist track or stay at a hotel with a construction project underway. Have a look at the prices listed in the *Where to Stay* sections of each island chapter and you will see that the cost of a standard room in a deluxe hotel in Tahiti is 30.000 to 35.000 CFP double, with the exception of the Sofitel Maeva Beach, where the rack rates for the low seasons in 2005 start at 18.400 CFP. The Sofitel la Ora in Moorea will charge 19.800 CFP for a garden bungalow and 45.400 CFP for an overwater bungalow during the low season, because they are planning a big construction project. The Sofitel Marara in Bora Bora has also dropped its rates due to a planned addition and big changes on that property.

Overwater bungalows are the most popular accommodations with honeymooners, and are priced from 62.000 to 80.100 CFP during the low season on Moorea, at 46.000 CFP on Raiatea, 65.000 CFP on Rangiroa, 70.000 CFP on Huahine, 60.000 CFP on Manihi, 70.000 CFP on Tikehau, and up to 115.000 CFP on Taha'a. Bora Bora's 10 hotels with overwater bungalows start at 39.000 CFP at TOPdive and escalate up to 136.000 CFP per night during the high season at the Bora Bora Nui Resort & Spa.

The rates for a standard double room in a medium-priced classified hotel start at 8.500 CFP in Tahiti, 10.000 CFP in Moorea, 22.000 CFP in Huahine, 18.500 CFP in Raiatea, 21.000 CFP in Bora Bora, 23.000 CFP in Rangiroa, and 18.000 CFP in Nuku Hiva.

You will find some of the least expensive accommodations in the pensions, bed and breakfast guesthouses, backpacker's lodgings and family homes. Some of their rates, however, are higher than you would pay in a moderate priced hotel. The economy lodgings on Tahiti are usually priced between 5.000 CFP and 14.000 CFP for a room for two with no meals. On Moorea you can get a room or bungalow with no meals for 4.300 to 16.900 CFP double; or a small backpacker's cabin for 2.500 CFP a day. Rooms in Raiatea start at 4.700 CFP double, sharing bath and kitchen facilities, and on Huahine you can find a room for two from 4.350 to 15.000 CFP. Bora Bora's pensions charge 6.000 to 20.000 CFP per couple for a room or garden bungalow, and on Maupiti you will have breakfast and dinner included with the cost of your bungalow, from 10.000 to 22.800 CFP double. In Rangiroa the room or bungalow with a modified American plan (MAP), called *demi-pension*, ranges from 10.000 to 28.000 CFP double, and many of these pensions will serve you lunch on request. In the more remote Tuamotu atolls you are usually served three meals a day (*pension complete*), but you can also rent a bungalow or room with no meals or just breakfast and dinner.

The cost of a room or bungalow in Tikehau with full-board or American Plan (AP) meals is 14.000 to 21.000 CFP double, and in Fakarava you will pay 14.000 to 35.000 CFP per night with accommodations and all meals. Some of these facilities require a two or three night minimum stay. A bed in a dormitory costs 2.300 to 2.500 CFP per person on Tahiti, 1.600 to 2.600 CFP per person on Moorea, 1.650 to 2.000 CFP on Huahine, and 2.500 to 3.250 CFP on Bora Bora. If you bring your tent you can rent camping space for 1.200 CFP per person per day on Tahiti, 1.100 to 1.800 CFP a day on Moorea, 1.250 CFP a day on Huahine, 1.000 to 2.000 CFP a day on Raiatea, 1.000 to 2.000 CFP a day on Maupiti, 1.800 to 2.300 CFP on Bora Bora, and 800 to 3.000 CFP a day on Tikehau.

Transportation Costs

Tahiti's public transport system is in the process of being modernized, with new buses replacing the traditional *le truck*, which has a brightly painted wooden cabin mounted on the rear of a flatbed truck. A four-year renewal program began in 2002, and eventually the only *le truck* you will be able to see in Tahiti will be those used to transport groups of tourists on a folkloric tour of the island. See information under Le Truck in *Tahiti* chapter. Transportation is provided during the daylight hours, with night service provided from downtown Papeete to the airport and hotels on the west coast, as far as Sofitel Maeva Beach. The last run depends on what is happening in Papeete. Each *le truck* or bus has a specific route, with the destination shown on top of the cab. The minimum fare is 120 CFP, which will get you from your hotel to downtown, and you'll have to pay 200 CFP at night. The Tahiti Manava Visitors Bureau can give you specific details on where to catch *le truck* or the bus to your destination.

Taxi fares will be one of your biggest shocks when you arrive in Tahiti, but the rates have not increased in a few years. Some of them have even been lowered. The legal taxi rates are supposed to be visibly displayed inside the cab and posted at the taxi stands. The flag-fall or minimum rate between 6am and 8pm is 1.000 CFP, which is increased by 120 CFP for every kilometer after the first one. The minimum rate between 8pm and 6am is 1.500 CFP and 240 CFP per kilometer. Between the airport and the hotels in Papeete the fare should be 1.500 CFP during the day, and 2.500 CFP at night. The daytime rate from the west coast hotels to the airport is 1.000 CFP and 1.500 CFP at night, except for the Hotel Le Méridien, which costs 2.000 CFP during the day and 3.500 CFP at night.

A trip to the Gauguin Museum on Tahiti's south coast will cost 10.000 CFP round-trip, and a trip around the island of Tahiti is officially 21.000 CFP, but the driver will usually charge between 15.000-20.000 CFP. The cost for renting a taxi is 4.000 CFP per hour. Taxi drivers tell me that they have taximeters but they don't use them because the customer has to pay more with the meter running than when paying a set fee.

You will also be charged 100 CFP extra for each large bag of luggage transported and 50 CFP for the smaller bags. Extra heavy bags cost more.

Rental cars are available on most of the islands listed in this guide. You'll find the lowest fares on Tahiti, where you can rent a car starting at 1.900 CFP a day, plus a minimum of 42 CFP per kilometer. A Europcar package rate with car rental, unlimited mileage and insurance starts at 8.350 CFP a day on Tahiti and Moorea, 8.400 CFP on Huahine, 8.300 CFP on Taha'a, 9.000 CFP on Raiatea, 8.850 CFP on Bora Bora and 8.400 CFP for an 8-hour rental on Rangiroa.

Gasoline is sold by the liter (4 liters = 1.06 gallons), and in Moorea you'll pay 128 CFP per liter for unleaded gas, or 512 CFP per gallon, which is used by most of the rental cars. Diesel fuel is 99 CFP a liter or 396 CFP per gallon. These rates are down from the 2002 edition of this guide. Costs are a little higher on the outer islands. Most service stations sell Total and Mobil products, and Shell has a few stations on the island of Tahiti and Moorea.

Electricity

The current is 220 volts, 50 cycles in most hotels and family homes. Some of the newer upscale hotels have outlets for both 220 and 110 volts. Most hotels provide 110-volt outlets for shavers, and hair dryers are usually provided. It's best to ask the management before you plug in hair dryers, battery chargers and computers. Adapters are usually necessary for American appliances, as the French plugs have two round prongs. You can bring your adapters with you or buy them at a general store in Tahiti. The hotels sometimes, but not always, have a transformer or converter for your electrical appliance.

Festivals & Holidays

All the islands in French Polynesia celebrate New Year's Day, Missionaries Day (March 5), Good Friday, Easter, Easter Monday, May Day (May 1, which is Labor Day), May 8, which was also Victory Day 1945, Pentecost (seventh Sunday after Easter), Pentecost Monday, Ascension Day (June 1), Internal Autonomy Day (June 29), Bastille Day (July 14), Assumption (August 15), All Saints Day (November 1), Armistice Day 1918 (November 11) and Christmas Day.

All government offices, banks, airline offices, travel agencies and most private offices are closed on these days. If the holiday falls on a Thursday or Tuesday, quite often the businesses will make a bridge, giving their employees an extra day off to enjoy a long weekend.

See Chapter 8, *Calendar of Events*.

Getting Married

Tahiti, the Island of Love, has long been a favorite honeymoon destination for lovers of all ages. Getting married in Paradise has also become a popular activity for some of our visitors. In Tahiti, Moorea, Huahine, Taha'a and Bora Bora couples from around the world are now saying "Oui" at the Mairie (Town Hall), "Hai" in the wedding chapels at the hotels, and "Eh" while standing in front of a Tahitian high priest.

Young Japanese couples choose to get married in French Polynesia to avoid the exorbitant costs of a wedding "correctly" done in Japan, which averages around $50,000 for some 80 guests. Travel agencies and hotels in Tahiti take care of all the details, and the prospective newlyweds are already legally married according to Japanese law before they leave home. Along with their rented wedding clothes and rings, they bring a certificate of marriage, which has been completed and officially stamped at their own town hall. This paper must be translated and stamped at the French Embassy in Japan before a wedding can be performed in Tahiti.

Tying the knot in French Polynesia requires several steps and official stamps. For non-French applicants each person needs to furnish a birth certificate, must be of legal age, and must present a certificate of celibacy to prove that they have never been married. If they are divorced or widowed they must have the legal papers to prove that too. Birth certificates are required for any children of either party, and all these papers must be translated into French by a legal translator who has been granted an official stamp. All birth certificates must have been issued or translated in French within three months prior to application.

In addition, each spouse has to provide a pre-marriage medical certificate issued within the last two months. In order to verify if the projected marriage is not contrary to public order, the municipal authority has the right to demand a customary certificate from the foreign authorities, which can be either the ministry or consulate of your country. A certificate of residency is necessary to prove that one or both of the future spouses has an address or has established residency in one of the communes of French Polynesia for a minimum of one month's continued residency prior to the marriage date. The wedding will be performed at the Mairie in that commune.

The marriage bans will be posted for 10 days in the commune where the wedding will take place and in the last place of residence of the future spouse not residing in French Polynesia. If one of the applicants has neither address nor residence in French Polynesia, the wedding bans must be published in his/her place of residence and must be verified by a certificate of publication.

Tiki Village in Moorea specializes in creating authentic Polynesian weddings. Most lovers, however, get married back home and splurge for a fun-filled colorful wedding ceremony in the authentic tradition of old Polynesia. And it's not just newlyweds who are getting married in the Tahitian style, but also loving couples who are celebrating their anniversaries, who wish to renew their vows to one another. Non-binding Polynesian weddings are also being performed at some of the international class hotels in Tahiti, Moorea, Huahine and Bora Bora.

Honeymoon Hotels

Most of the hotels with overwater bungalows have special honeymoon packages. Some of these hotels will upgrade honeymooners to overwater bungalows if there is a vacancy. Check the *Where to Stay* section of each island and contact the hotels directly for special programs for honeymooners. The sailboat charter companies also have cruising honeymoon programs.

Health Concerns

On the island of Tahiti you will have access to a large government hospital, two private clinics and numerous specialists who provide good medical and dental services. In addition to the allopathic doctors, you have alternative health care in the form of homeopathic medicine, acupuncturists, Chinese herbalists, traditional Tahitian healers, massage therapy, magnetizers and thalassotherapy. Many of these specialists speak English. Moorea, Raiatea, Nuku Hiva and Tubuai have small hospitals, and all the other islands have medical centers, infirmaries or dispensaries. The more populous islands also have pharmacies and dentists. In Tahiti and Moorea there are optical services, where you can have minor repairs made to your eyeglasses or new glasses made, and should you need emergency attention for your hearing aid, that is also available in Papeete.

All the islands maintain hygienic controls to combat potential epidemics of tropical diseases, such as the dengue fever, which is also known as "breakbone" fever, because of the intense pain in the head and muscles. This viral disease is carried by the *Aëdes aegypti* mosquito, which also lives indoors and bites during the daytime. In addition to a high fever, excruciating headache, pain in the joints and small of the back, and general feeling of weakness, the victims also develop an itchy body rash. Unfortunately, there is no vaccine, and you cannot take aspirin for the pains, as it may cause the stomach to bleed. The doctors can treat this disease with a *dengue cocktail*, which is an injection of Vitamin C and other vitamins, but the symptoms can last from a week to 10 days. There are several forms of *dengue*, and the most severe type can cause death in children, although this is very rare in French Polynesia.

Leptospirosis or Weil's disease has some of the same symptoms as the dengue: high fever, severe headaches, chills, muscle aches, vomiting, jaundice, red eyes, abdominal pain, diarrhea or a rash. This is caused by bacteria of the genus *Leptospira* and affects humans and animals. Most of the cases reported in French Polynesia are caused by dried rat urine that is mixed with the food, water or soil. You can also get this disease from swimming downriver from pigpens. In addition to causing kidney damage, meningitis, liver failure and respiratory distress, the disease is usually fatal. Be sure to wipe off the tops of all bottles and cans before drinking, because rats live in all the storerooms in the tropics. Better yet, drink from a clean glass.

Malaria is not present in the islands of French Polynesia, and the inhabitants generally have a high standard of health. There is an occasional outbreak of conjunctivitis, and some of the long time residents have suffered from filariasis or elephantiasis, an insect-borne disease that attacks the lymphatic system. Preventive medicine is distributed free every six months in all the islands, which keeps this disease well under control, and it is not a threat to the short-term visitor.

Pests & Pets

Mosquitoes are tropical pests, and in addition to the high cost of living and the noise of the roosters, the biggest complaints in French Polynesia are about the hungry mosquitoes that just love fresh blood from our visitors. There's not much you can do about the inflated prices and the crowing rooster you'd love to throttle at 2-3-4-5am, but you can avoid being bitten. In the high-end hotels, you will find an electric diffuser or mosquito destroyer that uses a bottle of liquid or blue pastilles, treated with Allethrin, to ward off mosquitoes. Other lodgings usually provide mosquito coils that you can burn, or you can buy them at any food store.

Bring a good mosquito repellent with you or go to the pharmacy once you're here and buy your defense products. I have found Dolmix Pic cream to be effective, which is sold in pharmacies. Aerogard spray or lotion is a good Australian product and can be purchased in the supermarkets. Tourists have also reported satisfactory results with *monoi* oil mixed with citronella, and this is available in most supermarkets, small *magasins* and hotel gift shops. My favorite anti-mosquito cream is Rid, which is made in Australia, but it is not sold in Tahiti. It is available in other Pacific Island groups, however. Be aware that mosquitoes will bite you day and night, and are most active when the weather is hot and sticky, which means during our rainy seasons. You have to remember to reapply your mosquito protection throughout the day or evening, especially if you are perspiring or swimming, as the water and sweat wash the product away.

On some of the islands, especially in the Marquesas, you may encounter the *nono*, which is a minuscule "no-see-um" sand fly with a nasty sting. They are most prevalent at daybreak and late in the afternoon, when they come to chew on your ankles. You might not even know you've been bitten until hours later, when the itching starts. Do not scratch it, however, as that will only aggravate the pain and cause an infected sore. Slathering yourself in oil is the best way to keep these little buggers at bay, as they just slide off your skin. Any kind of oil will do, although Avon's Skin So Soft from the States, or *monoi* oil, which is sold all over French Polynesia, will certainly smell better than cooking oil. Daily doses of 500 milligrams of vitamin B1 will help to ward off the pesky nonos.

If you do get stung by a mosquito, nono, wasp or bee, or cut yourself on coral, a good first aid treatment is to squeeze fresh lime juice on the wound to avoid infection. Cuts and scratches infect easily and take a long time to heal, so it is important to prevent any problems. Creams are also sold to take away pain from stings. Just remember to include an antibacterial cream in your traveling first aid kit, which you should definitely pack for your trip. The ingredients of such a kit will vary according to your own needs. The most important items to include would be any prescription drugs you take. Bring an extra pair of eyeglasses if you use them.

Ciguatera

More than 400 species of lagoon and reef fish are potential carriers of **ciguatera**, a poisoning from eating infected fish. This phenomenon existed in some of the coral islands before the arrival of the first Europeans, and is caused by a microscopic marine organism that lives on or near the coral reef, especially reefs that have been disturbed by shipwrecks, port construction and other developments.

The larger carnivorous fish, such as the parrot fish, surgeon fish, coral bass, sea perch, snappers and jack fish are all potential carriers of ciguatera, as well as the big barracuda, as they tend to store the toxins found in the smaller coral fish on which they feed. The open ocean fish, such as mahi mahi, tuna, swordfish, salmon of the gods and marlin and other pelagics do not carry the ciguatera toxin.

If you catch your own fish, it is best to get the advice of the local people before you cook it. They know which spots are more likely to be affected by ciguatera. The seafood served in the restaurants of French Polynesia is as safe as you'll find anywhere. Just avoid eating the head, gonads, liver and viscera of the fish.

Drinking Water

The Department of Health in French Polynesia reports that the tap water in Papeete has been treated with chlorine and is potable, and the water on the island of Bora Bora and Tahaa is drinkable. For the rest of the island of Tahiti and on all the other islands, it is advisable to drink bottled water. Eau Royale and Vaimato are two companies in Tahiti that sell bottled water, and the lab tests have given a higher rating to Vaimato for purity and cleanliness. There are also several brands of bottled water imported from France. Some of the hotels have water filter systems.

Sunshine

More vacations have been ruined from an overdose of sun than from any other factor. So many of the elderly tourists, who come ashore from their air-conditioned cruise ships, walk along the road in the heat and humidity of the noonday sun. Back home they drive round and round the parking lot, hoping to find a parking place close to the entrance to the shopping center or super market. When they come here they decide to walk the equivalent of several blocks or even kilometers, with the sun blazing on their heads.

I have escorted groups of American doctors to Marlon Brando's atoll of Tetiaroa for a day tour. No matter how much they were warned about the dangers of the sun, when it was time to fly back to Tahiti in the afternoon, every doctor in the group, including the dermatologists, was red as a boiled lobster. The Tahitian name for white people is *popa'a*, which is derived from the Tahitian word for "red lobster."

Fair-skinned people have to be especially careful in the tropics. Do your jogging, take your walk and work on your tan at the beginning of the morning or in the late afternoon, when distant clouds low on the horizon filter the ultra violet rays. During your picnic on the *motu* or while riding in any open boat, make sure you apply a sufficiently strong sunscreen or sunblock (containing 25 to 50 sunburn protection factor) on all the exposed parts of your body. Wrap up like a mummy if there is no sun protector on the boat. Don't forget to rub the lotion on your feet and reapply the sunblock throughout the day, as you sweat and swim. Always wear a hat when exposed to the sun, and protect your nose and lips with zinc or a similar barrier cream.

Should you forget this advice and get yourself "cooked" while vacationing in Tahiti and Her Islands, there are several remedies to ease the pain and help the healing process. These include applying tomato juice or vinegar to the sunburned parts, as well as Calamine lotion, aloe vera gel, tamanu oil, and a range of other products, which are available at the pharmacies in your country and in Tahiti.

Diarrhea

The abundance of tropical fruits you'll find so tempting in Tahiti are also very good for you if you exercise moderation. If you go overboard on the mangoes, papayas, *pamplemousse* (sweet grapefruit), bananas, pineapple, passion fruit, custard apples, rambutan, carambola (Chinese star apples), watermelon and other delicious fruits, you may regret it. Your system is not accustomed to so much Vitamin C, which can have a cataclysmic effect on your bowels.

The change of water, food and climate are the primary reasons for an upset digestive system. Drink bottled mineral water, eat in balanced proportions and get plenty of rest, and you will most likely avoid any disruptive problems. When you're packing for your trip to Tahiti be sure to include a remedy for treating diarrhea. There are many products on the market from which to choose, such as Imodium and Lomotil.

Should symptoms of diarrhea manifest, it would be best to avoid the consumption of raw vegetables and chilled beverages. Eat steamed white rice and boiled eggs and yogurt, and drink lots of bottled water to restore body fluids lost through dehydration. My French doctor in Moorea (a general practitioner) said that the best cure for diarrhea is a hearty shot of *pastis*, the licorice-flavored milky liquor that Mediterranean Frenchmen love to drink while smoking their *gitanes* cigarettes and sitting at a table with friends in a sidewalk café. You mix it with water and it actually tastes like medicine.

Sex in the South Seas

Exercise the same precautions you would apply back home. Since the arrival of the first European ships in 1767, Tahiti has earned a worldwide reputation as a sexually permissive port-of-call. Even with the strong influence of all the missionaries and church groups that have worked for over 200 years to change the sexual mores of the Polynesians, the promiscuous practices have not been completely eliminated.

Papeete is a hot spot of very young female prostitutes and *mahu* (male transvestites), who frequent the nightclubs and bars and hang out on the corner of Boulevard Pomare and Avenue Prince Hinoi, looking for a pick-up.

Safe sex in Tahiti often means that when boy meets girl for a clandestine rendezvous, they are both reasonably sure that his wives and girlfriends and her husband and/or boyfriends are not going to catch them in the act—this time. Even though there is an on-going educational program on the dangers of unprotected sexual encounters, there is still a reticence to put the knowledge into action. Thankfully, French Polynesia today has one of the lowest rates of the Acquired Immune Deficiency Syndrome (AIDS) virus, known as SIDA in French, with 0.06% of the population testing HIV positive. This terrible disease has already claimed several lives in Tahiti, however, and all the other sexually transmitted diseases are prevalent here as well.

Vaccinations

No immunizations are required for entry into French Polynesia unless you are arriving from an infected area. The U.S. State Department has a 24-hour **Travel Advisory**, *Tel. 202/647-5225; www.travel.state.gov/travel/ warnings.html* for up-to-date overseas health information, as well as crime and politics in foreign countries. The US Center for Disease Control in Atlanta, Georgia, gives travel advisories on an **International Traveler's Hotline**, Tel. 404/332-4559, Fax 404/332-4565; www.cdc.gov/travel/blusheet.htm.

Maps

Free maps of each island are available at **Tahiti Manava Visitors Bureau**, including a good map of downtown Papeete. The *Tahiti Beach Press* includes maps of Papeete and the islands of Tahiti, Moorea and Bora Bora. You'll also find maps in the bookstores and newsstands. Pacific Promotion's *39 Tourist Maps of Tahiti and Her Islands* sells for about 1.500 CFP and includes the locations of all hotels and pensions. Librairie Klima, *Tel. 42.00.63*, at Place Notre Dame in Papeete, sells oceanographic charts of the islands. Nauti-Sport, *Tel. 50.59.59*, in Fare Ute, also sells French nautical charts of Polynesia, and Marine Corail, *Tel. 42.82.22*, has charts. The Topographie Section of the Service de l'Urbanisme, *Tel. 46.82.18*, is located on the 4th floor of the Administrative Building at 11 Rue du Commandant Destremeau, where you can find topographical maps of the islands.

Money & Banking

The **French Pacific franc**, written as **CFP,** or **XPF** in banking circles, is the official currency of French Polynesia. One of the banks in Tahiti told me that CFP stands for *cour de franc Pacifique*, and in the currency exchanges on the Internet CFP means *comptoirs français du Pacifique franc*. The colorful CFP notes, which may look like play money to you, are issued in denominations of 500, 1.000, 5.000 and 10.000 francs (CFP); and coins are 1, 2, 5, 10, 20, 50 and 100 francs (CFP).

The CFP franc has been anchored to the euro since January 1, 1999, on a fixed parity basis. With 1.000 CFP you have 8,38 Euros **(1 euro = 119,33 CFP)**. Even though the French franc was replaced by the Euro starting January 1, 2002, the French Pacific franc (CFP) will continue, for the time being, to exist as a separate monetary entity. This currency is valid only in the French Overseas Countries and Territories of the Pacific: French Polynesia, New Caledonia and Wallis and Fetuna.

Euro bank notes and coins began circulating in French Polynesia on January 1, 2002, and the French franc was withdrawn from the market in June 2002. The 7 Euro bills are in denominations of 500, 200, 100, 50, 20, 10 and 5. The 8 coins are the 2 Euro coin, the 1 Euro coin, and cents—50, 20, 10, 5, 2 and 1 Euro cents. The local banks will accept Euro bills, just as they accept American dollars, but they will not accept Euro coins or American coins. The stores, shops, boutiques and other small vendors will not accept even the Euro bills. Most shops will accept American dollars, but you probably won't get good exchange rates in the process.

The exchange rate for the US dollar fluctuates daily in the banks and by the second on the Internet. The US dollar's highest daily level to date in 2004 (as of October 17, 2004) was 98.267 CFP, which occurred on May 13. The daily dollar exchange rate has been below 100 CFP since November 7, 2003. To determine the approximate amount of CFP you will get for one US dollar, check in your local newspaper for the number of Euros per dollar, and multiply that amount by 119,33. (Example: Today's exchange rate for the dollar is 0.802 Euros. Therefore, $1 = 0.802 Euros x 119,33 = 95,7 CFP or XPF, as it is also written).

If you have access to the Internet you can get currency conversions on *www.xe.com/ucc/full.shtml.*

Quick Currency Conversion Trick

A quick way to get an approximate dollar equivalent to the **CFP** is to drop the last two zeros of the price tag in Tahiti, then add or subtract the percentage difference between the actual rate and 100 CFP. For example, the cost of a pareo may be 1.000 CFP, which is easy to think of as $10 + 5% ($0.50) = $10.50; and a black pearl for 150.000 CFP is $1,500 + 5% ($75) = $1,575.

To be more exact than the conversion shown above, you should divide the cost of the item by the current exchange rate to determine the US dollar equivalent. At this writing, the exchange rate is **95.7 CFP per US dollar**, which means that you would actually pay $10.45 for your *pareo* and $1,567.40 for that beautiful black pearl. When you want to find the CFP rate in comparison to the US dollar, you multiply the amount of dollars you have to spend by the exchange rate.

Bargaining or price haggling is not a custom in French Polynesia, but it is widely practiced in the black pearl industry. So, don't hesitate to ask for a discount when you're negotiating the purchase of a black pearl. This same technique should not be used when you're buying the $10 *pareo* or a $30 woven bag.

Ready Cash

Banque de Polynésie and Socredo Banque have offices at the International Airport of Tahiti Faa'a, where you can buy French Pacific francs as soon as you arrive in Tahiti, and exchange your leftover francs for US dollars just before you leave.

Banque de Polynésie, Banque de Tahiti and Banque Socredo have offices on most of the main islands. Banking hours are generally from 8am to 3:30pm, Monday through Friday, with branch offices closing two hours for lunch and remaining open until 5pm and on Saturday morning. All the banks accept and issue travelers checks and have a currency exchange counter. Be prepared to pay the bank charge of 500-600 CFP per transaction.

The automatic teller machine (**ATM**) is called a *distributeur*. All the banks listed above are now equipped with this handy service, even in most of the outer islands. Socredo and Banque de Polynésie also have ATM windows at the Tahiti Faa'a Airport. Most, but not all, of these machines will accept your Visa and Mastercard transactions, as well as Eurocard, but they do not accept American Express or Diner's. Although you may see the Cirrus logo on the ATM, these machines will process only Cirrus from France.

You can get cash advances with your Visa and Mastercard inside the banks, which are limited according to the type of credit card you have. American Express cash advances can be transacted at Tahiti Tours in Papeete and some of the banks are now able to handle American Express transactions as well.

Currency Exchanges

Banque de Polynésie has a currency exchange booth *in the baggage area* that is open for international flight arrivals, as well as a bank *in the main terminal* that is open for international arrivals and departures. It would be advisable to exchange some dollars for CFP (francs) before leaving the airport.

All the main banks have a currency exchange window and most of the branch offices will also exchange currency. You can also exchange your dollars for CFP at your hotel, which is sometimes necessary, but you will not receive as good a rate as you'll get at the banks.

A Currency Exchange office is located in the Fare Manihini building, adjacent to Tahiti Manava Visitors Bureau on the Papeete waterfront, beside the passenger ship dock, *Tel. 43.22.77*. They are open on Monday, and Wednesday through Friday, from 8:30am to 12pm and from 1 to 4pm. On Saturday they are open from 8:30am to 3:30pm, and they are closed all day Sunday and Tuesday. They will supposedly give you the legal exchange rate for your dollars and other foreign currencies.

A mobile Currency Exchange van sets up shop in the parking lot beside the boat dock in Moorea for the arrival of each passenger ship.

Credit Cards & Personal Checks

Visa is the most widely accepted credit card in the tourist islands of French Polynesia. The international class hotels and some of the black pearl shops will accept all major credit cards, and some restaurants and shops accept Mastercard. Most restaurants, boutiques and shops will not accept American Express or Diner's Club cards, but American Express has taken a few steps forward recently and convinced more shop and restaurant owners to use their services.

All the banks in Tahiti can help you with any questions regarding Visa and Mastercard. **Tahiti Tours**, *Tel. 54.02.55*, is the local representative for American Express services; **Socredo Bank**, *Tel. 41.51.23*, handles JCB; and **Banque de Polynésie**, *Tel. 46.66.66*, is the representative for Diner's Club. Some of the small hostels and pensions do not accept credit cards.

To secure a reservation in a hotel or hostel, you may send a personal check for the required deposit, but once you arrive, most businesses will not accept personal checks unless they are written on a local bank account. Some of the owners of art galleries and black pearl shops will occasionally accept a personal account on a foreign bank if you are making a big purchase.

To get the best exchange rate for your dollar I recommend charging your hotel bill, restaurants, activities, black pearls, gifts and all other purchases on your credit cards. You will need some local cash in your pocket for incidentals, and if you have CFP left over at the end of your stay, then apply it to your hotel bill.

Movies & Videos

The impact of movies showing the South Sea Islands has been so motivating that several people moved down here to live forever after seeing films such as *Tabu, Sadie Thompson* (also known as *Rain*), *Return to Paradise*, one or more versions of *Mutiny on the Bounty*, and the 1958 release of *South Pacific*, starring Mitzi Gaynor, John Kerr and Rosanno Brazzi.

I was once the tour guide for a group of Japanese tourists, who sang "Bali Hai," "Bloody Mary," "Happy Talk" and other songs from *South Pacific* all day, as we drove around the island of Tahiti. This movie was not made in Tahiti, nor did the book or film ever indicate that Tahiti, Moorea or Bora Bora was the setting, yet many people still assume otherwise. The former Bali Hai hotels on Moorea, Huahine and Raiatea, as well as the Club Bali Hai on Moorea, were named for the movie, not the other way round. The "Bali Hai" mountain on Moorea (Mou'a Roa or 'long mountain' in Tahitian) does not even resemble the "Bali-ha'i" of the original movie. Still, escapist dreams are very good for tourism and for the well being of the dreamer.

ABC Productions made a remake of *South Pacific* in 2000, which was shown on American television and is now available in VHS and DVD. Actress Glenn Close played the role of a much older Nurse Nellie Forbush, and Harry Connick, Jr. is an aging First Lieutenant Joseph Cabel. The role of the sexy French planter who wants to marry Nellie Forbush was played by Rade Sherbegia (*Mission Impossible 2*). Although most of the movie was filmed at Port Douglas in Queensland, Australia, ABC Productions chose Opunohu Bay in Moorea for the scenes that include the spectacular beauty of the island of Bali-ha'i and the Mou'a Roa mountain. Thus, the legend became reality and the mountain named Bali Hai by the Hotel Bali Hai "boys" is now immortalized on film as the famous Bali-ha'i peak that beckons to the sailors across the sea.

Movies to Set the Mood

Here is a list of movies that were either filmed in Tahiti, or supposedly used stories or settings from Tahiti. Perhaps you can locate a few of these in your local video rental stores. And you, too, can dream of Tahiti and Her Islands.

White Shadows in the South Seas (1927) was the first movie filmed in French Polynesia, which was shot in the Marquesas, and based on the book by Frederick O'Brien. The lovely "Polynesian" in the movie was Mexican actress Raquel Torres. *The Pagan* (1928) starred Ramon Navarro and Dorothy Janis. *Tabu* (1931) was filmed in Bora Bora, a Murnau-Flaherty production, starring Anna Chevalier as Reri. *Never the Twain Shall Meet* (1931) was a story about Tahiti, with Conchita Montenegro, that was filmed in Hawaii.

Bird of Paradise (1932), with Dolores Del Rio and Joel McCrea, was also made in Hawaii. *Mutiny on the Bounty* (1935), based on Charles Nordhoff and James Norman Hall's *Bounty Trilogy*, starred Charles Laughton as Captain Bligh, Clark Gable as Fletcher Christian and Mamo Clark as Maimiti. Most of this movie was filmed on Santa Catalina, off the California coast. This was the second *Bounty* movie; the first was an Australian production, starring Erroll Flynn. *Hurricane* (1937), John Ford's production based on Nordhoff and Hall's book of the same name, was the first of the "South Seas" films starring Dorothy Lamour and Jon Hall. *Aloma of the South Seas* (1941) was a story about Tahiti that was filmed in Puerto Rico, starring Dorothy Lamour and Jon Hall.

Son of Fury (1942), with Tyrone Power and Gene Tierny, was a Tahiti setting filmed at 20th Century Fox in Hollywood. *The Moon and Sixpence* (1941), Somerset Maugham's book about Paul Gauguin, starred George

Sanders and Elena Verdugo (an Hispanic) who played the role of a Tahitian *vahine*. *South of Tahiti* (1941) starred Mexican actress Maria Montez as a Tahitian. The *Tuttles of Tahiti* (1942) was an amusing film based on *No More Gas*, a book by Nordhoff and Hall, starring Charles Laughton and Jon Hall. *Bird of Paradise* (1951) was a remake of the film of 1932, with Debra Paget and Louis Jourdan, a story about Raiatea that was filmed in Hawaii. *Drums of Tahiti* (1953) was a made-in-Hollywood film with Dennis O'Keefe and Patricia Medina. *Cinerama South Sea Adventure* (1958) was filmed in Bora Bora, with Tahitian actress Ramine Allen-Buchin.

Enchanted *Island* (1958) was based on Herman Melville's book *Typee* about the Marquesas Islands. It was filmed in Mexico, with Dana Andrews and blue-eyed Jane Powell, who played a Polynesian. *Mutiny on the Bounty* (1962), MGM's successful film, was filmed in Tahiti and Bora Bora. Trevor Howard played the role of Captain Bligh and Marlon Brando was cast as the mutinous Fletcher Christian. Tarita Teriipaia, from Bora Bora, was Brando's Tahitian lady in the movie, and thus began a real-life relationship. *Tiko and the Shark* (1963) was also filmed in Bora Bora by MGM, with Hawaiian actors. *Donavan's Reef* (1963) was supposed to be Tahiti after World War II, but it was filmed on Kauai in Hawaii, with John Wayne, Lee Marvin and Dorothy Lamour.

Hurricane (1978) was the Dino de Laurentiis version of the Nordhoff and Hall book, which was also filmed on Bora Bora. Mia Farrow and Hawaiian Dayton Ka'ne played the lead roles. James Norman Hall's daughter, Nancy Hall, and her husband Nick Rutgers, were also in the film. *Beyond the Reef*, also known as *The Boy and The Shark*, was filmed on Bora Bora by de Laurentiis, immediately following the *Hurricane*, using some of the same decor. Dayton Ka'ne and Tahitian Keahi Farden were the stars. *The Bounty* (1984) was another movie version of the famous mutiny, which was filmed in Moorea with Mel Gibson as Fletcher Christian and Anthony Hopkins as a more sympathetic Captain Bligh. The *vahines* were all Tahitian. *A Love Affair* (1994) was a Warner Brothers movie filmed in Moorea, starring Warren Beatty and Annette Bening.

Tahiti has several private companies that produce video films on all the islands, from the land, sea and sky. The quality of the color is excellent and most, but not all, of these films are compatible with the American video systems. The Tahiti Tourisme office has a selection of promotional films for sale. Tahiti Music, in front of the Notre Dame Cathedral in Papeete, a large choice of commercial films, as well as Odyssey, a big new bookstore-music shop behind the Cathedrale.

Post Office & Courier Services

You can leave your American stamps at home because they won't be acceptable for mailing your postcards overseas from any of the islands in French Polynesia. I say this because I've met several Americans who do bring their stamps to Tahiti, thinking they'll be saving money on postage. Each country has its own postal system, and in Tahiti this is an important source of revenue for the country.

When we go on vacation most of us wait until the last few days before we mail our "Wish you were here" postcards home. As the airmail service from Tahiti to most overseas destinations takes anywhere from six to ten days to arrive, chances are the card will not get there before you do. If you post your mail from the international airport it will probably get processed faster and be put on the next departing flight.

The cost of mailing letters weighing less than 20 grams is 130 CFP to all international destinations except France and French Overseas Departments and Territories. Stamps can be purchased from all post office counters and from the hotel boutiques. A few of the newsstands and tourist shops also sell stamps, but you will have to go to the post office and stand in line if you want to make sure you've added enough postage to the envelope. The post offices have begun installing stamp machines as well as a postage scale for do it yourself weighing and stamping.

Addressing a Letter to French Polynesia

When addressing a letter or package to anyone living in French Polynesia, it is necessary to include the name of the person, hotel or business, the B.P. (boite postale) number, the town or village where the post office is located, the island, the zip code if known, and the country. Example: **Jan Prince, B.P. 298, Maharepa, Moorea, 98728 French Polynesia**. On some of the islands the PK number is used instead of a B.P., which should always be followed by the name of the village and any other specifics you may have, then the name of the island and country. Example: **Jan Prince, Chez Wilder, PK 12.5, côté montagne, Pihaena, Moorea, French Polynesia**.

Zip codes are a relatively recent addition to our postal services and many people still don't know what their zip code is. I haven't included the name of the country in the addresses given in this book, but each address should always include the name of the island, followed by French Polynesia.

☙

The main post office is on Boulevard Pomare in downtown Papeete. Services include stamps for letters and parcels, express delivery service, international telephone calls, telegrams, telex, fax, phone cards and a philatelic center. This post office is open Monday to Friday 7am to 6pm, and on Saturday from 8 to 11 am for postal services, and until 6pm for telephone and fax service. The post office inside the international terminal at the airport is open Monday to Friday 6-10:30am and from 12-2pm, and on Saturday 6 to 9:30am. Closed Sunday. You can also make international phone calls from this small office. There are post offices on all the inhabited islands of French Polynesia, which are open Monday through Thursday 7am to 3pm, and on Friday 7am to 2pm.

General Delivery mail service is available at all the post offices. On the envelope you should write the person's name, c/o Poste Restante, and the name of the island, and make sure that this is followed by French Polynesia.

B.P. = *bôite postale* or post office box

You will note that most of the addresses listed in this book show the initials B.P., which stand for *bôite postale*, the equivalent of post office box in the US. You can write P.O. Box or B.P. and your letter to French Polynesia will be processed with no problem.

PK = *poste kilometre*, the number of kilometers from the *mairie* or post office

Should you be given an address with a PK number instead of B.P., on the island of Tahiti, this indicates how many kilometers that person lives from the *mairie* (town hall) in Papeete. On other islands, such as Moorea, the 0-kilometer can be at the post office. PK stands for *poste kilometre*, and when you're driving around Tahiti, Moorea, Huahine, Raiatea, Tahaa and Bora, you will see the kilometer markers on the mountainside of the road. Look for the red-capped white painted stone or concrete markers with the kilometer number painted in black on two sides.

For Stamp Collectors

The Philatelic Center of the Offices Des Postes et Télécommunications in Tahiti is located in the main post office, where you can buy sets of collector stamps, along with a stamped "first day" envelope. The themes for these beautiful stamps include the fruits, flowers, fishes and fauna of Polynesia, along with pictures of pretty *vahines*, fancy hats, outrigger sailing canoes, old *goelette* schooners and lovely seascapes. All the major post offices in the islands also carry selections of these collectors' items. You can also order stamps from home: Centre Philatélique de Polynésie Française, Office des Postes et Télécommunications, 98709-Mahina, Tahiti, French Polynesia, *Tel. 689/41.43.35; Fax 689/45.25.86;* or through the Internet, *E-mail: phila@mail.opt.pf, www.tahiti-postoffice.com.*

⊱

Courier Services

DHL Worldwide Express, *Tel. 83.73.73, Fax 83.73.74,* is located in the Immeuble Te Motu Tahiri Faa'a building on the right at the exit of the Tahiti-Faa'a International Airport, B.P. 6480, Tahiti. Open Monday through Thursday 7:30am to 4pm and on Friday until 3pm, and do not close at lunch. They provide 4-day delivery service from Tahiti to the USA. They charge 4.600 CFP to ship 500 grams to the United States.

Federal Express (Fedex), *Tel. 45.36.45,* has an office in the Immeuble Polyfix building in Faaa. Open Monday through Friday from 7:30am to 12pm and 1:30 to 5pm. They charge 4.960 CFP to ship 500 grams to the United States.

Publications about Tahiti
Newspapers & Magazines

Tahiti Beach Press is an 18-page English language magazine that is published monthly and distributed weekly for visitors. You will find it in hotels in Tahiti, Moorea, Huahine, Raiatea, Bora Bora and Rangiroa. You can also pick up a copy at Tahiti Manava Visitors Bureau, the airports, ferry docks, car-rental agencies, and in the restaurants and businesses that advertise in the *Tahiti Beach Press*. A one-year subscription to this publication is $37 for airmail postage to the U.S. Address your subscription request to *Tahiti Beach Press,* B.P. 887, Papeete, Tahiti 98713, French Polynesia. *Tel. 689/42.68.50; E-mail: tahitibeachpres@mail.pf.*

La Dépêche de Tahiti and *Les Nouvelles* are Tahiti's two daily French-language newspapers. The *International Herald Tribune, USA Today, Time* and *Newsweek* are sold at Le Kiosk in front of the Vaima Center on Boulevard Pomare and at La Maison de la Presse on Boulevard Pomare in Papeete. The copies you can find in Tahiti will not be the most current editions. You can also find newspapers and magazines on Moorea at Kina Booksellers, adjacent to the post office in Maharepa, at Supersonics in Le Petit Village, and in the boutiques of the larger hotels. La Maison de la Presse in Bora Bora also carries magazines and newspapers. *Tahiti Pacifique Magazine* is a popular monthly publication in French, with a long list of subscribers. *Air Tahiti Magazine* is published in French and English, a quarterly on-board magazine that is also available for subscription.

Books

In 1968, when I knew that I would be coming to Tahiti, Moorea and Bora for a three-week vacation, I visited the Public Library in Houston, Texas, each week for six months prior to getting on the airplane. During that period I checked out each available book on Tahiti and the South Pacific, and thoroughly did my homework before making my first visit. During my 34-year residence in Tahiti and Moorea, I have had access to the best private libraries in Tahiti, and have made my own collection of reference books and armchair favorites of old tales of the romantic South Seas. Yet, I have not even touched the tip of the iceberg in discovering the wealth of published material on Tahiti and Her Islands.

Due to the limits of space available for the subject, I will give you an abbreviated list of recommended reading and reference material, which you may still find in the public libraries, specialized book stores and secondhand shops. Free catalogs of publications may be requested from: **Bishop Museum Press**, P.O. Box 19000-A, Honolulu, HI 96817-0916, *Tel. 808/848-4135;* **University of Hawaii Press**, 2840 Kolowalu Street, Honolulu, HI 96822; **The Book Bin**, 351 NW Jackson Street, Corvallis, OR 97330; **Mutual Publishing**, 2055 N. King Street, Suite 201, Honolulu, HI 96819; **Colin Hinchcliffe**, 12 Queens Staith Mews, York, Y01 1HH, England; and **Société des Océanistes Catalogue**, Musée de l'Homme, 75116, Paris, France. You can also buy books about Tahiti and Her Islands, including this travel guide, online at *www.amazon.com* and *www.bn.com.*

Reference Books
Ancient Tahiti (Bulletin 48 Bernice P. Bishop Museum, Honolulu) by Teuira Henry, is based on material recorded by her grandfather, the Reverend J. M. Orsmond, who came to Moorea as a Protestant missionary in 1817. This is my primary reference book for the plants, flowers, trees, religion, culture and legends of the Society Islands.

Ancient Tahitian Society (The University Press of Hawaii, Honolulu, 1974) is a three-dome collection by Douglas L. Oliver. These scholarly studies are an excellent reference for the history and culture of the Tahitians.

Bengt Danielsson, a Swedish anthropologist and historian, who crossed the Pacific from Peru to the Tuamotus with Thor Heyerdahl aboard the *Kon-Tiki* raft in 1947, settled in Tahiti until his death in 1997, and published a wide variety of books. They include: *The Happy Island* (London, 1952), *Work and Life on Raroia* (Stockholm, 1955), *From Raft to Raft* (London, 1960), *Forgotten Islands of the South Seas, Love in the South Seas* (Mutual, 1986), *Tahiti-Circle Island Tour Guide* (Les Editions du Pacifique, 1976), and *Moruroa Mon Amour—the French Nuclear Tests in the Pacific* (1977), by Bengt & Marie-Thérèse Danielsson.

Fatu-Hiva—Back to Nature (Penguin Books, 1976) is Thor Heyerdahl's account of the sojourn he and his wife undertook for more than a year on this lonely island in the Marquesas Archipelago, just before the outbreak of World War II.

History and Culture in the Society Islands (Honolulu, 1930), *Marquesan Legends* (Honolulu, 1930), *Polynesian Religion* (Honolulu, 1927), and *The Native Culture in the Marquesas*, Honolulu, 1923), all by Craighill Handy. *Landfalls of Paradise: The Guide to Pacific Islands* (Western Marine Enterprises, Inc., Marina del Ray, California, 1986), by Earl Hinz, who sailed the South Pacific aboard his yacht *Horizon,* along with his wife Betty. They dropped anchor in Honolulu for several years, where Earl wrote his books and magazine articles. Finally, they gave up the sea and now live in the desert near Las Vegas.

Pacific Islands Yearbook (Fiji Times), editors Norman and Ngaire Douglas, is a good reference book on all the islands, which is updated on a regular basis.

Polynesian Researches (1829) by William Ellis, is a two-volume work by a missionary who spent nearly six years in the South Sea Islands. *Polynesia's Sacred Isle* (Dodd, Mead & Company, New York, 1976), by Edward Dodd, is part of a three-volume *Ring of Fire* set about the island of Raiatea.

Ra'ivavae—An expedition to the most fascinating and mysterious island in Polynesia (Doubleday & Company, Inc., New York, 1961). Author-anthropologist Donald Marshall describes life on Ra'ivavae, one of the Austral islands south of Tahiti.

Return to the Sea (John deGraff, Inc., New York, 1972), by William Albert Robinson, is the story of Robinson's 70-foot brigantine *Varua,* in which he sailed to Tahiti in 1945, to settle in Paea, where his house still stands. Robinson used *Varua* as a floating laboratory to travel throughout the Pacific Islands, helping to eradicate the filariasis parasite transmitted by mosquitoes that causes elephantiasis.

Robert Suggs, an American archaeologist who did seminal work for the American Museum of Natural History of New York in the Marquesas Islands during the 1950s and 1960s, has written *The Island Civilizations of Polynesia* (New American Library, Mentor Books, New York, 1960), *Hidden Worlds of Polynesia* (Harcourt, Brace and World, New York, 1963) and *Marquesan Sexual Behavior* (Harcourt, Brace and World, New York, 1966), which are interesting reading and good reference books for anyone interested in the Marquesas Islands. His latest book is *Manuiota'a, Journal of a Voyage to the Marquesas Islands,* which was written with Burgl Lichtenstein and published by Pa'eke Press in 2001.

Many archaeologists and historians who specialize in the South Seas consider Patrick V. Kirch the expert authority on Polynesian pre-history. His works include *On the Road of the Winds: An Archaeological History of the Pacific Islands Before European Contact,* (University of California Press, May 2000), *The Lapita Peoples: Ancestors of the Oceanic World (The Peoples of South-East Asia and the Pacific),* (Blackwell Publishers, December 1996), *The Evolution of the Polynesian Chiefdoms* (Cambridge University Press, reprint edition August 1989), and *Historical Ecology in the Pacific Islands: Prehistoric Environment and Landscape Change* (co-authored with Terry L Hunt, Yale University Press, March 1997).

Tahiti, Island of Love by Robert Langdon, is a popular account of Tahiti's history, and it's easy reading. *Tahitian Journal* (University of Minnesota Press,

1968) is a diary written by George Biddle between 1917 and 1922, along with paintings and drawings by the author. The setting is Tautira on the Tahiti-Iti peninsula, where Biddle lived among the Tahitians. *Tahitians—Mind & Experience in the Society Islands* (University of Chicago Press, 1973) by Robert I. Levy is an anthropologist's reference book for anthropologists, containing a wealth of cultural information. *The Journals of Captain James Cook* (Cambridge University, 1955, 1961, 1967), edited by J. C. Beaglehole, were published in three volumes.

Novels, Island Tales & Modern Accounts

Come Unto These Yellow Sands (Bobbs-Merrill Company, 1940) by author, artist and anthropologist Earl Schenck, combines fact with fiction in a captivating tale that takes us to various islands of the South Pacific, including Tahiti, Bora Bora and to the distant atolls of Hikueru and Vahitahi in the Tuamotus, the Dangerous Archipelago.

Manga Reva—the Forgotten Islands (Mutual Publishing Paperback Series, Tales of the Pacific, Honolulu, 1931) by Robert Lee Eskridge, tells the story of an American artist who arrived in Tahiti in 1927 aboard the SS *Makura*, became friends with Queen Marau, and set off for the remote Gambier Islands to discover the "Forgotten Islands." His book tells about Father Laval, the "mad builder priest" who ruled the Gambier Islands with a Jesuit rod early in the nineteenth century, and killed thousands of Polynesians who built his great Cathedral of the Jungles in Manga Reva.

Mystic Isles of the South Seas (Garden City Publishing Company, Inc., New York, 1921) by Frederick O'Brien, is based on his visit to Tahiti during one of three journeys he made to the South Seas. His story of Lovina Gooding, the colorful character who owned the Tiare Hotel in Papeete, is classic. O'Brien's *White Shadows in the South Seas* are about the Marquesas Islands, and *Atolls of the Sun* feature the Tuamotu Archipelago.

Numerous Treasure (Jacobsen Publishing Company, Inc., New York, 1930) is a Romantic Novel by Robert Keable, whose former home still stands on a bluff in Papeari, overlooking Port Phaeton and the Tahiti-Iti peninsula.

Planter's Punch (Appleton-Century-Crofts, Inc., New York, 1962) by Margaret Curtis, is an autobiographical account of an English opera singer who met and married wealthy American Carl Curtis in 1932 while sailing to the South Seas aboard the *Stella Polaris*. Curtis took his new bride home to Tahiti to live in his big white rambling house on a coconut plantation in Mahina. This house is still standing and has been known throughout the years as the Brander House, the Curtis Mansion, Martin Mansion and the White House.

Point Venus (Little, Brown and Company, 1951) by Susanne McConnaughey, is a fictional account of the English Protestant missionaries in Tahiti during the era of Queen Pomare and the French takeover.

Rainbow in Tahiti (Hammond, Hammond & Co., Ltd., London, 1951) is Caroline Guild's story of a charmed, easy life in Tahiti in the 1920s and 1930s, where she and her husband, Eastham, had an estate in Paea, near the fern grottos of Mara'a. Due to the influence of Zane Grey, who also lived in Tahiti at that time, the Guilds took up sports fishing. Carolyn landed an 823-pound black marlin in New Zealand to set a world's record.

South Sea Idylls (James R. Osgood & Co., Boston – 1873), was written by Charles Warren Stoddard, about life in the Marquesas Islands during his visit in the 1800s. This is one you'll have to search for in specialized shops.

Tahiti (Grant Richards Ltd., London) by Tihoti, the Tahitianized name of George Calderon, who visited Tahiti in 1906. He was killed in the war in Gallipoli in 1915, and the book was completed from his notes. This is truly a collector's item and is illustrated with Calderon's drawings of the people he met while wandering around the island of Tahiti.

Tales of the South Pacific (1947) and *Return to Paradise* by James A. Michener, are all-time classics by a very descriptive writer.

The Blue of Capricorn (1977) by Eugene Burdick, takes you from Polynesia, to Melanesia and Micronesia.

The Bounty Trilogy (1932) by Charles Nordhoff and James Norman Hall, comprises the three volumes of *Mutiny on the Bounty, Men Against the Sea* and *Pitcairn's Island.*

The Dark River (1946) by Charles Nordhoff and James Norman Hall, is set in the wild and natural *fenua 'aihere*—the Land of Forests—of the Taiarapu peninsula on Tahiti-Iti. The descriptions of this savage beauty transport us right onto the scene of this lonely land.

The Hurricane (1935) by Charles Nordhoff and James Norman Hall, is an exciting story set in the Dangerous Archipelago of the Tuamotus.

The Lure of Tahiti—An Armchair Companion (Edited by A. Grove Day and published by Mutual Publishing Company, Tales of the Pacific, Honolulu, 1986). An entertaining selection of stories by 17 authors, including Rupert Brooke, Paul Gauguin, Jack London, Pierre Loti, Charles Darwin, William S. Stone, James Norman Hall, James A. Michener and some of the early explorers.

The Moon and Sixpence (Penguin Books, 1945-1977), first published in 1919, is W. Somerset Maugham's story of Charles Strickland, a London stockbroker, who abandons family and career to become a painter in Tahiti, suggested by the life of Paul Gauguin.

To Live in Paradise (*Armand Denis,* 801 W. Covina Blvd., San Dinas, CA 91773, *Tel. 626/909-8931*). Published in 1996, this book by Renée Roosevelt Denis, a long-time resident of Tahiti and Moorea, is an autobiography that takes us from Bali to Haiti to Tahiti. Renée's book is filled with tales of adventure with her grandfather, André Roosevelt, her famous parents, her Tahitian husband and children, her years with Club Med in Moorea and her meetings with Marlon Brando on his private atoll in Tetiaroa. This book is currently available in all the bookstores in Tahiti and Moorea and in the hotel gift shops on all the major tourist islands.

Two-Thirds of a Coconut Tree (Little, Brown and Company, 1963) is the most hilarious book I've ever read about Tahiti. Author H. Allen Smith and his wife, Nelle, spent six months in Tahiti just after the international airport opened in the early 1960s. Although local residents recall Smith as being drunk the whole time he was here, his written humor was always intact. He calls names and says what he feels about everyone.

Typee: a Real Romance of the South Seas; Omoo; a Narrative of Adventures in the South Seas, a Sequel to Typee and Marquesas Islands by Herman Melville are all based on Melville's experiences in the islands.

Together Alone is a 2004 publication written by my Scottish neighbor in Moorea, Ron Falconer that tells the true story of his experiences sailing around the world and settling on Caroline Island, an uninhabited atoll in Kiribati, now known as Millennium Island. Ron spent almost four years on this desert island, along with his French wife and their two children who were under the age of five years. In this book you will meet some of the characters that still live on Moorea, Tahiti and Ahe, in the Tuamotu Islands. Published by Random House, Australia-Bantam Books and priced at $22.95 Australian. You can order it from: *Special Orders Dept., Dymocks Sydney, 424-428 George Street, Sydney, NSW 2000; Tel. (02) 9235 0155; Fax (02) 9233 7009; E-mail: specialorders@dymocks.com.au-; www.dymocks.com.au.* Reader's Digest has bought the condensed rights to this book, to be published in January 2005.

Books Available in English in Tahiti

I am including this list so that you will know what to look for when you come here. Some of the books are available in the States. You might also contact the following bookstores in Tahiti that carry the best selection of books in English, as well as the individual publishers.

Galerie "Point Art" is the Polynesian section of the **Librarie du Vaima**, B.P. 2399, Centre Vaima, Papeete, Tahiti, *Tel. 689/45.57.44/45.57.57, Fax 689/45.53.45;* **Odyssey**, *Tel. 54.25.25*, is behind the Cathedral, adjacent to the Aorai building; **Archipels**, B.P. 20676, 68, rue des Remparts, Papeete, Tahiti, *Tel. 689/42.47.30, Fax 689/45.10.27.* For books on art and Paul Gauguin, as well as the pamphlets listed below, contact the **Paul Gauguin Museum** at B.P. 7029, Taravao, Tahiti, *Tel. 689/57.10.58, Fax 689/57.42.10.* For the brochures published by **Pacific Promotion**, contact Teva Sylvain at B.P. 625, Papeete, Tahiti 98713, *Tel. 689/42.43.11, Fax 689/42.25.98.* **Erwin Christian** books can be purchased from Kea Editions, B.P. 5, Bora Bora, French Polynesia, *Fax 689/67.75.49, www.tahitibooks.com.*

A Tahitian and English Dictionary (Haere Po No Tahiti, 1985) with introductory remarks on the Polynesian language and a short grammar of the

Tahitian dialect. This was first printed in 1851 at the London Missionary Society's Press. *Fa'atoro Parau* is a 684-page illustrated Tahitian/English-English/Tahitian dictionary written by Sven Wahlroos, Ph.D., also known as Taote Tivini, that can be ordered from the **Academie Tahitienne** (Fare Vana'a), *Tel. 689/50.15.50*. Their mailing address is BP 2609, Papeete, Tahiti, French Polynesia. You can also order it directly from the **University of Hawaii bookstore** for US $70, at *2840 Kolowalu St., Honolulu, HI 96822-18883; E-mail: uhpbooks@hawaii.edu.*

Atoll (Scoop - Tahiti, 1992) is an illustrated 44-page pamphlet by Jean-Louis Saquet, that illustrates the geology of the atolls, the surrounding lagoon, coral reefs and ocean shelf, and the flora and fauna that inhabit these "desert isles" of dreams.

Birds of Tahiti (Les Editions du Pacifique, 1975) with text by Jean-Claude Thibault and photographs by Claude Rives, features the land and sea birds of the Society Islands.

Black Pearls of Tahiti (Tahiti, 1987) by Jean Paul Lintilhac, is an informative, authoritative and factual book, with good photographs, providing all you want to know about the black pearls.

Bora Bora (Les Editions du Pacifique, 1974, 1980), with text by Erwin Christian and Raymond Bagnis, features the wonderful photography of Bora Bora resident, Erwin Christian.

Bora Bora, Impressions of an Island (Kea Editions, 1996), contains 95 photos by Erwin Christian.

Diving in Tahiti—a Diver's Guide to French Polynesia (Les Editions du Pacifique, 1991) by Thierry Zysman has an introduction to diving in French Polynesia, plus detailed descriptions and photographs of specific dive sites in Tahiti, Moorea, Huahine, Raiatea, Tahaa, Bora Bora, Rangiroa and Manihi.

Fishes of Polynesia (Les Editions du Pacifique, 1972, 1987), by residents Raymond Bagnis, Philippe Mazellier, Jack Bennett and Erwin Christian, is a coffee-table book with photos and descriptions of the lagoon, reef and ocean fish, and their scientific, Tahitian and English names.

Guide to Navigation and Tourism in French Polynesia (Editions A. Barthélemy & Editions Le Motu, 2001), by Patrick Bonnette and Emmanuel Deschamps; *www.editions-barthelemy.com*. This is a handy guide for cruising yachts or yacht charterers who want to know about the approaches, passes, navigational signals, anchorages, port facilities and land services in all five archipelagoes of French Polynesia. Translated from French to English by Jan Prince.

Hiva Oa, Glimpses of an Oceanic Memory (Departement Archeologie, 1991) by Pierre Ottino and Marie-Noële de Bergh-Ottino, reports on their archaeological work on Hiva Oa, and their scholarly 50-page booklet is filled with historical information and maps on the Marquesas Islands.

Islands of Tahiti (Kea Editions, 1991) by Raymond Bagnis, with photos by Bora Bora resident, Erwin Christian, is a coffee-table book on all the island groups of French Polynesia.

Moorea (Millwood Press, Wellington, New Zealand, 1974) is a photographic book by James Siers.

Noa Noa by Paul Gauguin is an autobiographical account of his life in Tahiti.

Plants and Flowers of Tahiti (Les Editions du Pacifique, 1974) with text by Jean-Claude Celhay and photography by Bernard Hermann, is a colorful 143-page reference book that is very helpful for amateur botanists.

Sharks of Polynesia (Les Editions du Pacifique, 1978), with text and photography by Richard H. Johnson, an American marine biologist and shark expert, who operated a nautical activities center in Tahiti for 20 years before he retired.

Tahiti Blue and Other Modern Tales of the South Pacific (Les Editions de Tahiti, Tahiti, 1990) by Alex du Prel. He is also editor of *Tahiti Pacifique Magazine*, which he publishes monthly in French from his home on Moorea.

Tahiti from the Air (Les Editions du Pacifique, 1985) by Erwin Christian and Emmanuel Vigneron, has aerial photos of French Polynesia as it was in the mid-1980s.

Tahiti, the Magic of the Black Pearl (Tahiti, 1986) by Paule Solomon is poetic, ethereal and has beautiful photographs.

Tahiti—The Other Side (Institute of Pacific Studies of the University of the South Pacific, in association with Editions Haere Po No Tahiti, 1983) is a social study made by Marc Cizeron, Marianne Hienly and several others, to reveal the people who live on the mountainside of Tahiti, far from the postcard scenery and glamour of a Polynesian Paradise.

Tahitian Glimpses (Kea Editions, 2002) by Erwin Christian, is a collection of black and white photos taken by Christian between 1962-2002 to celebrate his 40 years of residence in French Polynesia.

Tahitian Island Cooking (Arapoanui Edition, 1988), with text by Jean Galopin and photography by Jean-Claude Bosmel, is a beautifully presented coffee-table book that will have your mouth watering when you read Galopin's recipes, which he prepares and serves in his Auberge du Pacifique Restaurant in Punaauia, on Tahiti's southwest coast.

Tatau—Maohi Tattoo (Tupuna Productions, 1993) by Dominique Morvan, photographs by Claude Corault and Marie-Hélène Villierme, traces the resurgence of traditional tattooing in French Polynesia. Black-and-white photos of the geometrical Polynesian tattoos.

The Dance of Tahiti (Les Editions du Pacifique, 1979), by Jane Freeman Moulin, presents the traditional dances of Tahiti from A to Z, along with photos and illustrations of the movements.

The Marquesas (Les Editions du Pacifique, 1982), with text by Greg Dening and photography by Erwin Christian, presents Te Henua Te Enata, the Land of Men.

The Tahiti Handbook (Editions Avant et Après, 1993) by Jean-Louis Saquet covers French Polynesia's geography, history, and natural history with general information on marine life, plant life, canoe design and arts and crafts.

Tuamotu (Les Editions du Pacifique, 1986), with text by Dominique Charnay and photographs by Erwin Christian, covers the history, geography, flora and fauna, and daily life in the remote atolls of the Tuamotu archipelago.

Underwater Guide to Tahiti (Les Editions du Pacifique, 1977, 1980), with text by Raymond Bagnis and photography by Erwin Christian, presents the reefs and lagoons, the living environment, distribution of living organisms and the species of inhabitants in this threatened submarine world.

Paperback editions of books by James Norman Hall, such as *My Island Home*, *The Far Lands*, *Dark River*, and other favorites, can be purchased at the James Norman Hall House and Library on the mountainside at PK 5.5 in Arue, *Tel. 50.01.61/50.01.60; E-mail: jamesnormanhall@mail.pf; www.jamesnormanhallhome.pf.*

Pamphlets/Booklets Sold in Tahiti

Pacific Promotion Tahiti has published a number of pamphlets on Tahiti and Her Islands, which are filled with the colorful photographs of owner Teva Sylvain, who also issues calendars and post cards. These publications include: *Circle Island Tour Guide to Tahiti, Souvenir Guide to Bora Bora, 39 Tourist Maps of Tahiti and Her Islands, Tupai Island, Flowers of Tahiti, Orchids of Tahiti, The Fishes of Tahiti, Natural Dangers in Tahiti, Bora Bora-History and Gls in Paradise* (text by Thomas J. Larson & Alex W. du Prel), *Gauguin and the Tahitian* (text by Loana Sanford) and others.

The Société des Océanistes and Les Nouvelles Editions Latines in Paris have issued several informative pamphlets that are sold in the bookstores in Tahiti and the hotel boutiques in the islands. These include booklets on *Ancient Tahiti, Ancient Tahitian Canoes, Bora Bora, Botanical Garden of Papeari, Bougainville in Tahiti, Cartographic Handbook of French Polynesia, Childhood in Tahiti, Dancing in Tahiti, Gauguin in Tahiti, Huahine, Moorea, Painters in Tahiti, Pomare—Queen of Tahiti, Protestant Church at Tahiti, Sacred Stones & Rites of Tahiti, Short Flora of Tahiti, Stamps and Postal History of Tahiti, Tahiti From Word to Paper, Tahitian Catholic Church, Tahitians of the Past, The Fairyland of Useful Shells, Traditional Art of Tahiti, Useful Plants of Tahiti, Whaling Off Tahiti,* and others.

Radio

Radio Television Française d'Outre-Mer (RFO), also known as Radio Tahiti or Radio Polynésie, (FM 89), is the official station, which operates with

French and Tahitian broadcasts on several AM and FM frequencies. Some of the mayors in Tahiti have their own FM radio stations, where political messages in French and Tahitian are interspersed with a musical mélange of rap, rock, reggae, religion and Tahitian favorites, as well as death announcements and other local news. The most popular of these are Radio Tefana (92.8, 97.4), Radio Maohi (88.2-94.8), Radio 1 (98.7, 90.9), Star FM (96.4, 97.8, 105.9), Tiare FM (89.9 Papeete, 98.3 Moorea) and Radio Bleue.

Should you bring your Walkman or other transistor radio with you, then you can just turn the dial from 88.6 to 106, until you find music to your liking. French Polynesia has 19 radio stations with only temporary authorization, including 4 religious stations and several political stations. Some of these stations, such as Radio Rurutu, Radio Marquises and Radio Bora Bora, can only be heard in the immediate transmission zone. There are 14 new radio stations that will share 60 new frequencies that have been made available. Don't rely on your radio for soft music for dreaming while you contemplate the clouds or classical music for a superb sunset. You'll have a hard time finding it. More than half the population here is under 20 years old, and the music is played primarily for that audience.

Retiring in Tahiti, Buying Land or Houses in French Polynesia

If you have a dream of living in Tahiti and Her Islands, then I suggest that you come here on a visit first and get a feel of the place before you take the next step. Spending a relaxing vacation on a small island in the middle of the South Pacific is quite different from living so far removed from the choices and conveniences of life in a big modern country. The complexities are even more magnified if you do not speak or read and write French, which is the official language of French Polynesia.

In the past it was possible, although not easy, for foreigners to buy land or houses here, and some American couples have retired quite happily in these islands. Others divide their time between their homes in the States and their "fares" on Tahiti, Moorea, Huahine or wherever in the islands. They can have the best of both worlds. During the past few years, however, it has become increasingly difficult for non-Polynesians to buy property here. The government's approvals or denials are made on an individual basis.

Another option to actually buying the land is to take a long-term rental or a lease for 30 years or more. There are about 30 real estate agencies in Tahiti that can answer your questions regarding the purchase of land, houses, villas, condos and apartments. Tahiti Sun Travel's network can answer some of your questions on this subject: *www.papeete.com/business/realestate*. Philippe Giraud, who operates Bora Bora Parasailing, also owns *www.dream-islands.com,* and he can answer your questions about real estate matters. Realtor Jeanine Sylvain and her daughter Maima speak English and the agency has a good reputation in the business. You can contact them at *Tel. (689)*

43.98.31, cell 689/77.01.15; Fax 689/41.05.44; E-mail: jsylvain@mail.pf; www.jeanine-sylvain.com. Other realtors are listed under *www.tahiti-realestate.com;* or go to *www.tahitiweb.com,* then click on *annuairedessites.pf.* Please do not contact me with questions about real estate. I have no experience with realtors and cannot tell you the correct price of land or houses.

Shopping

All the main tourist islands have souvenir shops and arts and crafts centers, where you can find hand-painted *pareos*, locally made T-shirts, carved Marquesan bowls, ceremonial spears, drums, ukuleles, tables and tikis, plus tapa bark paintings, Tahitian dancing costumes, basketry and woven hats, shell jewelry, mother-of-pearl creations, *tifaifai* bed covers, vanilla beans, Tahitian music and video films, *monoi* oil, soaps and perfumes, and beautiful black pearls. See information in each Island chapter.

Tahitian Black Pearls

The emerald and turquoise lagoons of the Tuamotu and Gambier Islands of French Polynesia are a natural haven for the black-lipped oyster, the *Pinctada Margaritifera* (*Cumingi variety*), which produces the world's finest black pearls. At the beginning of the 19th century the lagoons of Polynesia were filled with pearl oysters, also called *nacres*. From 1802-1940 the smoky gray mother-of-pearl shell was sought after as material for buttons. With the introduction of watertight diving glasses the divers could go deeper and deeper to find oysters of an acceptable size, as they exhausted the ready supply. With the advent of synthetic buttons and the depletion of accessible oysters in the lagoons, the adventurous days of the famous South Seas pearl divers ended after World War II, with controlled diving seasons continuing into the 1960s.

During the highlight of the pearl diving days there was an average of one black pearl found among 15,000 oysters killed. The *Pinctada margaritifera* came very close to extinction, until researchers experimented with techniques to harvest the spawn of the *nacre* to collect the baby spats that would grow into oysters.

The first trials were made at culturing black pearls in the lagoon of Hikueru in 1962 and in Bora Bora in 1964, using the grafting technique that was invented in Japan in 1893, and refined by Mikimoto in the early 1900s. The first undersea pearl farm was established in the lagoon of Manihi in the 1970s, and the culturing of black pearls has slowly grown from an isolated experiment into an industry. In 1976 the Gemological Institute of America (G.I.A.) gave formal recognition to the authentic character of the cultured pearls of Tahiti, and in 1989 the official designation of this gem became "Perle de Culture de Tahiti," the label decided upon by the *Confederation Internationale de la Bijouterie Joaillerie et Orféverie* (CINJO). Today there are about 900 more or less functioning pearl farms, essentially in the Tuamotu and Gambier atolls, with a few small pearl farms in the Society Islands of Huahine, Tahaa, Raiatea and Maupiti.

The Tahitian black pearl is French Polynesia's biggest export item and the most sought after souvenir purchase made by visitors to Tahiti and Her Islands. Just a few years ago the black pearl was virtually unknown in the United States, and today you can buy black pearl jewelry through the Home Shopper's Channel on television, as well as on E-bay and several other websites on the Internet. Some of the black pearl merchants in French Polynesia also have their own shopping websites.

When you shop for your black pearls you can make a better choice if you know what to look for in choosing a quality pearl. The main criteria are size, shape, surface quality, luster and color.

Size: Although you can find a few black pearls with a diameter of 7 or 7.5 millimeters, they usually start at 8 millimeters. The average size is 9.5-11.5 millimeters, and anything over 16.5 millimeters is very rare and often valuable. The bigger the pearl, the more it costs. The largest round Tahiti pearl on record is the Robert Wan, which measures 20.92 millimeters (over 13/16 of an inch) and weighs 12.5 grams. This beauty is on display at Tahiti Pearl Museum in Papeete.

Shape: The shape or form of the pearl is judged by roundness and symmetry. They are graded as round, semi-round, semi-baroque, baroque and circle. The round pearls are rare, therefore more expensive, but a drop or pear-shaped pearl that is perfectly symmetrical can be as expensive as a round pearl.

Surface quality: In 2001 the French Polynesia Assembly adopted measures that revised the classification of Tahiti's cultured pearls. The pearls are graded Gem, A, B, C, and D quality according to the number of flaws, pits, scratches and rays that blemish the surface.

A "Gem" quality pearl is extremely rare, as it is perfect, with no blemishes. "A" category pearls have no more than one imperfection or a group of localized imperfections concentrated over less than 10% of a pearl's surface. These pearls also have a very beautiful luster. "B" category pearls are defined as those with some imperfections "concentrated" over less than a third of their surface and with a beautiful or average luster. Instead of just having imperfections over less than a third of their surface, the imperfections must now be concentrated. The majority of pearls are "C" quality, those with "light concentrations" of imperfections over less than two-thirds of their surface and an average luster. Before the new ruling in 2001, the imperfections did not have to be lightly concentrated over less than two-thirds of a pearl's surface. "D" category pearls are pearls with "light" imperfections over more than two-thirds of their surface and "no deep imperfections;" or "D Category" pearls are those with deep concentrations "over less than half of their surface" and with "a soft luster." When I sold pearls I used to tell people that a "D" quality pearl looks like your dog has been chewing on it, leaving lots of tooth marks. Some pearl shops have recently started grading their pearls as AAA, AA, B+, B-, C+, C-, and so on.

Luster or orient: The most important criteria in judging the quality of a black pearl are its luster or orient. Luster is the reflective quality or mirror-like shine on the pearl's surface. Orient is the iridescence or radiance from the inner-layer quality of the pearl. The thicker the mother-of-pearl (nacre) covering the nucleus inside the pearl, the more light it reflects. From the grafting to the harvesting of a black pearl, a period of 18 to 24 months is necessary to achieve the desirable thickness that produces a fine quality pearl with a good luster and orient. The minimum nacre thickness required was formerly set at 0.6 millimeters, but the Tahitian government increased the minimum thickness to 0.8 millimeters, effective July 1, 2002. Reputable pearl dealers sell only those pearls with a nacre thickness of 1.5 to 2 millimeters, which can be determined by knowing the size of the nucleus that was grafted into the oyster and measuring the diameter of the finished pearl. No x-rays are needed for this information, but some of the more aggressive pearl dealers use gimmick advertising, claiming that you will receive an x-ray of the pearl you buy.

Color: The color of a black pearl may range from white to lunar gray, with gradations of cream, peacock green, rainbow tints, aubergine (eggplant), blue, pink and golden. Robert Wan of Tahiti Pearls introduced a new and very rare cherry colored pearl to the market in May 2002, and since then has added one or two other color categories of pearls with just a nuance of varied color. Black pearls are rarely black, which may come as a surprise to you, but they are called black pearls because they come from the black-lipped oyster.

The color of the pearl depends on the color of the mantle or lip of the donor oyster used to graft into the producing oysters during the cultivating process. The grafter trims the outer mantle, the epithelium, of a donor oyster and cuts it into about 50 small pieces. Then he takes one tiny sliver of this living cell and transplants it into the gonad gland of a three-year old oyster, along with a nucleus, a small white round ball that is made from the shell of the Mississippi River mussel. The grafted oysters are then placed in wire nets and suspended from platforms under the lagoon, where they live for 18 to 24 months while the oyster is covering the nucleus with up to 16,000 micron-thin layers of mother-of-pearl, which is comprised of aragonite. The pearls that are produced from the slivers of mantle from one oyster will all be different, as there are no two pearls exactly alike.

Color is also affected by the mineral salts present in the water, the degree of salinity, the plankton that the oysters feed on, and the water temperature. Although some pearl sales people will tell you that the nuances of color do not affect the price of a pearl, they actually do. Pearls with a prevalence of white or gray are priced lower and black pearls with rare hues, such as rainbow, aubergine, fly-wing green and shiny black, are more expensive.

Where to Buy Your Pearls

There are numerous pearl shops in Tahiti, and if you have the stamina and the perseverance, you can check out all the most obvious boutiques and sales rooms in downtown Papeete and at the hotels. Tahiti Pearls is the biggest supplier of fine quality black pearls in the world, and they have an exquisite collection of pearls and jewelry made with pearls. At Tahiti Pearl Museum in the Vaima Center on rue Jeanne d'Arc in Papeete, you can watch a video film and see a replica of a pearl farm, which will give you a basic education on pearls. You'll also enjoy looking at their beautiful but very pricey black pearl jewelry.

In addition to the pearl shops in the Vaima Center and on the waterfront street, be sure to walk through the Quartier du Commerce behind Tahiti Sports, where you also have several choices of black pearl shops. And just a little further down Boulevard Pomare toward the Moorea Ferry dock is My Pearls, on the corner of Avenue Prince Hinoi. This is one of my favorite shops and I am attracted to their window displays every time I walk by. I personally like the settings and quality of pearls, and I like the sales lady, Mai, who is also the manager. She speaks good English and is very friendly and knowledgeable about pearls.

My recommendation for choosing your pearl is to find a sales person you like and a pearl that "winks" at you. I sold pearls on a part-time basis in Moorea for five years, and I learned that certain pearls naturally attract the attention of the person who should be wearing them. They have their own magic, you know. In the outer islands, such as Moorea and Bora Bora, some of the pearl shops are owned by people who have their own pearl farms and jewelers, or they own the shop, so there's no middle man to pay. Therefore, they can sell the pearls at a lower price than in Papeete. Plus you have the advantage of being able to walk outside the boutique and look at the pearls in the natural light, which truly brings out the beauty of this living jewel, especially in the early morning, at sunset time and on cloudy days. The same tactic won't work on a bright sunny day at noon.

People often ask if a pearl costs less when you buy it from a pearl farm, such as on Manihi, Rangiroa and Fakarava. The answer is yes, but the best pearls are usually shipped to Tahiti to be set into jewelry, or sold at auction to the big name buyers from overseas. Most of the smaller pearl farms belong to a co-operative that sells their pearls at an international auction held twice a year. Although these producers are not legally allowed to advertise their pearls, they are not opposed to selling a few pearls if you happen to be staying in their pension (guesthouse) and ask where you can buy pearls. In Tahiti and Moorea you will find black pearl pendants mounted in 18-carat gold starting around $100.

Get a receipt and a certificate of origin and authenticity for each pearl you buy. You can claim a tax refund (Value added Tax or VAT) for black pearl jewelry you purchase in French Polynesia, but this exemption does not cover unset pearls or precious stones. See information under *Taxes* in this chapter. Keep in mind there is no import duty on black pearls when you pass through US Customs on your way home.

You will probably be warned against buying black pearls from street vendors. This notice is to protect you against the possibility of receiving stolen goods and buying inferior merchandise. Customs officials at the international airport in Tahiti now have three powerful x-ray machines that can see everything in your suitcases, carry-on bags and containers. Some people have been caught trying to leave Tahiti with quantities of inferior quality black pearls that haven't been claimed as export items. Normally, these reject pearls (also called caca pearls) are dumped into the ocean under controlled conditions.

Smuggling Tahiti cultured pearls out of the country will get you into a lot of expensive trouble. An American tourist heading for Honolulu was caught by the x-ray machine with 220 reject pearls. Another person with a ticket to Easter Island had a cooler filled with pork ribs and two raw ducks. The x-ray machine revealed two sacks of mediocre quality pearls stuffed inside the ducks. If you buy pearls in quantity you will have to present your pearls to the Service de la Perliculture to receive an export certificate, once they have determined the quality of the pearls you have purchased.

The following websites will help you in learning more about Tahiti's black pearls: **GIE Perles de Tahiti**, *www.perlesdetahiti.com,* is the Tahiti-located official promotional organization for Tahiti black pearls. They have an on-line newsletter that includes the latest regulations concerning the black pearl industry in French Polynesia. They will also tell you how to take care of your black pearls. **Tahiti Pearls**, *www.tahitiperles.com,* is the website of Robert Wan, Tahiti's "pearl baron," who owns the Pearl Museum in Papeete. He also publishes a quarterly newsletter online. The **Black Pearl Gem Company** in Moorea is one of my favorite black pearl shops. Owner Marc Collins has set up a beautiful website, *www.blackpearlgemco.com,* that lets you select and purchase your pearls on-line. **Pacific Pearl Colors** has set up a website, *www.pacificpearlcolors.pf,* which may answer your questions concerning the colors of Tahiti's pearls.

Staying Out of Trouble

When you're packing your bags for a trip to Tahiti please do not include any drugs that are illegal in your country. They are also illegal here and the French Immigration and Customs authorities do not consider the importation of any stupifiants as a light matter. "Dope dogs" are trained to sniff out anything suspicious in your luggage when it's unloaded from the plane, and new x-ray machines now make it possible for the officials to see everything inside your suitcases. Heavy fines and jail sentences are a sure way to ruin a good vacation. Should you decide to risk it anyway, then please use discretion and do not give or sell any illegal drugs to a local person. This is a very small place and news travels amazingly fast via the "Coconut Radio."

When I first came from Houston, Texas, to Tahiti as a tourist in 1968 I remember that I was so afraid of theft that I took my handbag with me when I took a ride across the beautiful Bora Bora lagoon aboard an outrigger sailing canoe. Inside the bag were my passport, return plane tickets, traveler's checks, money, driver's license and other important papers. After I moved to Tahiti I learned to relax more and to leave the watch and handbag in my hotel room when I went out in a boat. Many times there were no doors to lock and no windows to close.

Due to the increasing hotel room thefts, most of the rooms are now more protected. Experience has taught me to lock the valuable papers inside the safe provided in some of the hotels, or at least to lock the door to the hotel room or bungalow, and to close the windows.

For police, dial 17.

The shops, boutiques and especially the *roulottes* (mobile diners) in Papeete have their share of thefts, and you should watch out for purse-snatchers in the city, which also includes pre-teenage girls. The delinquency problems are not so pronounced that you have to be afraid to take your eyes off your suitcase at the airport. Please don't let fear ruin your vacation, when you should be relaxed and carefree, but just be cautious and use the same common sense that you would use when traveling anywhere.

If you want to discover Papeete-by-night, stay in the main stream of lighted streets, sidewalk cafés and bars, where lots of people are on the streets. Avoid drunk Tahitians and you'll enjoy yourself more. A municipal police station is close to Papeete's municipal market, adjacent to the Loto (lottery) building on rue Edouard Ahnne. You can also dial 17 at any telephone booth without having to deposit coins and you will be connected to the *gendarmerie*, the French national police station.

Women Traveling Alone

If you're a woman traveling alone or with a girlfriend, then you should be aware that the crime rate in Tahiti is very low compared to most cities anywhere in the world, but you should still use caution. Back in the 1970s and 1980s, in my pub-crawling days, I used to feel totally at ease running around in Papeete at any time of the night, popping into a nightclub here and there to see what was going on and to dance the night away. Experience has since taught me to heed my own advice and avoid drunk men and dark streets.

Another word to the wise for women alone: do not sunbathe in the nude or even topless on secluded beaches. Some of the Tahitian males see this as an open invitation, and they will pursue you, even if it takes all day. This warning needs to be heeded in the remote islands as well as in the more popular tourist islands.

A form of rape called *mafera* existed in these islands long before the Europeans arrived, not to be confused with *motoro*, the traditional courtship practice of a fellow slipping into his girlfriend's bed or onto her *peue* mat for consensual sex. The difference between the two customs depends on whether or not the girl agrees. If she does, then they are simply making love. If she objects and he does it anyway, then it is *mafera* or rape. Older Tahitian men on various islands claim that neither custom is practiced on their island today because the young people are better educated now. Others say that the *tane haere po* (guy who creeps around in the dark) is more interested in smoking his *pakalolo* (marijuana) than peeking or crawling through windows. Whatever the reasons may be, there are fewer cases of rape reported today than in past years.

Tahitian men can be very charming and are always ready for sexual encounters. Many of them have told me that they do not notice whether a woman is young or old, fat or skinny, pretty or not. What they see is a woman. One of their favorite expressions is: "Age makes no difference. It's love that counts." What woman would want to argue with that philosophy? Should you succumb to the erotic mist that covers these tropical isles, then be sure that you provide your own protection against sexually transmitted diseases, which exist in Tahiti and Her Islands just as they do back home. Do not rely on your partner for anything except a brief moment of pleasure, which is not even guaranteed.

A woman visiting the islands by herself is often open to all kinds of experiences, which may include being invited to stay in the home of a Tahitian family. Should this happen to you, then chances are you'll create a lifelong friendship and wonderful memories. Just use your female intuition in making your decision.

Taxes
Value Added Tax (VAT)

A 5 percent government tax is added to the cost of a room in the classified hotels and cabins of cruise ships based in French Polynesia. The pensions and guesthouses are not subject to this tax.

A Value Added Tax (VAT), (TVA in French) was added in 1998 on all goods and services, and was aimed at gradually replacing the customs duties, which were to be regularly reduced. A VAT tax has been in effect since 2002 that adds 6 percent to all rented accommodations, including hotel rooms, pensions and family stays, as well as "room and meal" packages, and it covers transfers that the hotel provides between the airport or boat dock and the hotel or pension. If transfers are made by a taxi or transfer service, VAT is 10 percent. A 10 percent VAT also applies to all restaurants and snacks, as well as all activity and excursion services.

A 6 percent VAT applies to all inter-island transportation by air and boat, including charter flights and chartered boat trips. The 6 percent VAT applies to non-alcoholic beverages, medicines, books, newspapers and magazines. Alcoholic beverages are taxed 16 percent.

Most of the rates quoted in this guide do not include the VAT. I have indicated the addition of VAT wherever I was sure, and I believe that some of the restaurant prices given also include the VAT, although it was not always specified by the managers. The cost of local transportation, activities and excursions may increase without notice to compensate for the VAT; therefore, the rates quoted in this book are subject to change at any time.

Visitors Tax or Municipal Tax

All visitors staying in a classified hotel, guest house, family pension or campground on the island of Tahiti must pay a visitor's tax or municipal tax, regardless of what type of accommodation they buy. This ruling also applies to visitors staying on the islands of Moorea, Bora Bora, Huahine, Tahaa, Raiatea, Bora Bora, Rangiroa, Tikehau and Fakarava. The tax amounts to 150 CFP per person, per day, for anyone staying in a classified hotel. Guests staying in pensions, hostels or campgrounds pay a visitors tax of 50 CFP per day, Passengers on board the cruise ships pay a tax of 500 CFP per day.

All children ages 2-12 accompanied by a parent are exempt from this tax. Each municipal government that imposes the visitors tax is supposedly using this money to safeguard the environment, create public toilets, maintain public sites, seashores and valleys, improve garbage collection, support major tourist events such as the Hawaiki Nui outrigger canoe races, the Marathon, Heiva, Festival of Arts, and New Year's programs, help to pay for the installation of potable water, the creation of strategic sites such as green tourism, panoramic lookouts and maintaining the marae stone temples, and creating access to the beaches and archaeological sites.

VAT Tax Refunds

If you are visiting French Polynesia for less than six months you can claim a tax refund (Value Added Tax or VAT) for eligible goods you take home. The value of purchases from any single store, tax included, must total at least 5.000 CFP. All the goods must be taken back with you, in your carry-on or checked luggage, when you leave French Polynesia. All tax refunds must be claimed within six months of purchasing the goods. Not all stores are participating in the tax-free program; therefore, prior to your purchase, verify this with the store concerned. If they do participate, you will have to prove that you are not a resident of French Polynesia and that you are 15 years old or over.

At the Tahiti-Faa'a International Airport you should present the three copies of the Retail Export Form, as well as the goods purchased under the tax-free program. Customs will retain the pink copy #3 and will stamp the other two copies. You need to return the stamped pink copy #2 to the store for your refund. The green copy #4 is for your records.

Do not forget to keep the goods with you at all times when you apply for Customs endorsement of the Retail Export Form at Tahiti-Faa'a International Airport. Customs officers may want to check them. Within a reasonable period of time, once you are back home, you should receive the amount of refunded tax from the store, credited directly to you credit card.

Once you are back home, you may still claim the tax refund if the Retail Export Form has not been endorsed by Customs upon leaving French Polynesia. However, the process is time consuming and may be more expensive than the amount of tax refund that you are claiming.

There is no refund for tax you pay on food products and beverages, tobacco products, medicine, firearms, unset precious stones and pearls, cultural property, automobiles, motorcycles, boats, planes, as well as their parts and accessories. Nor is there a refund on taxes for purchases of a commercial nature (in such quantities that it is reasonable to believe they are not intended for your personal use).

Telephones & Telecommunications

Dial 19 to reach a long-distance operator in Tahiti from any of the islands of French Polynesia. They all speak good English and are very efficient and courteous. Dial 3612 for information on telephone numbers within French Polynesia, and 3600 for international information. The telephone numbers for government offices, hotels and other private businesses, as well as all home phone numbers, contain only six digits.

Public pay phones are easily identifiable booths of metal and glass, with black letters on a yellow background. There are several phone booths in the most populous islands, and you will probably even find a public phone in the most remote village of the Marquesas Islands, the Gambier, or Rapa in the Austral Islands.

There are a few pay phones that still take coins, but most of them require a *télécarte*, a phone card that you can buy at any post office and in many shops and newsstands. These plastic cards are often decorated with some of the same scenes as the postage stamps, and are collectors' items as well. A 40-unit card costs 1.550 CFP, and a digital readout on the phone states how many units remain on your card as you talk with your party.

Calling Tahiti

When dialing direct to Tahiti and Her Islands, dial the proper International Access Code + 689 (Country Code) + the local number. The International Access Code if calling from the US is 011. Therefore, if you were calling me at the *Tahiti Beach Press*, you would dial 011+689+42.68.50.

The same codes apply when sending faxes. When transmitting telex messages from the US, the code 702 or 711 + FP must precede the telex number. You can look up telephone or fax numbers in French Polynesia online at *www.annuaire.pf.*

Calling Home from Tahiti

To call overseas from anywhere in Tahiti and Her Islands, dial 00, then the country code (1 for the US and Canada), followed by the area code and phone number. You can dial direct from your hotel room or by going to the nearest post office or phone booth. In the post offices you give the postal clerk the number you are calling and she will direct you to one of the booths when your call is placed.

Automatic direct dial calls to Hawaii, the US mainland or Canada from Tahiti at any time during the day or night, Sundays and holidays included, cost 103 CFP per minute. This rate also applies to metropolitan France, New Zealand, New Caledonia, Australia, Japan and the Cook Islands. The cost of calling most European countries is 171 CFP per minute from 6am to 12am and 103 CFP per minute from 12am to 6am. To call Mexico, South America, Asia or Eastern Europe, you will pay 205 CFP per minute day or night.

At the post office you can pay directly for the call, place a collect call or charge the call to your AT&T, MCI or similar long-distance calling card if you live in the US or Canada. If you live in Hawaii and have a Hawaiian Telephone Company GTE card, that is also acceptable. Canadians with a Teleglobe Canada card can also use it in Tahiti.

You can now dial 1-800 numbers direct from French Polynesia, but these calls are billed at the normal rate of 103 CFP per minute.

Calling Within Tahiti and Her Islands

When calling from a fixed phone to a fixed phone, intra-island calls (on the same island) cost 34 CFP for every 4 minutes. Inter-island calls (such as from Tahiti to Huahine or Rangiroa to Nuku Hiva) cost 34 CFP for every 2 minutes and 30 seconds minute between 6am and 10pm, and 34 CFP for 5 minutes between 10pm and 6am. Just dial the six-digit telephone number, as there are no area codes within the territory.

Many individuals and businesses now carry their cell phones wherever they go. These numbers have a prefix of 7 or 2. If you are calling from a fixed telephone to a mobile vini (cell) phone, the local cost is 60 CFP per minute from 6am to 6pm during the week, from Monday to Friday. The price is reduced to 34 CFP per minute between 6pm and 6am Monday through Friday, and the 34 CFP per minute rate applies day and night on weekends and holidays. These rates include taxes.

Calling from Hotels

Whether you dial direct from your hotel room or go through the hotel switchboard, the surcharge can often double the cost of your international call.

Cellular or Mobile Phones

If you want to bring your own cell phone with you when you visit French Polynesia, make sure that it is an unblocked phone that can operate on a 900-megahertz system. If you have a Global System for Mobiles (GSM) phone you can buy a prepaid SIM card for French Polynesia at Cellular Abroad in Santa Monica, CA., *Tel. 800/287-3020; www.cellularabroad.com.* Or you can wait until you get to Tahiti and have a new Vini chip inserted in your cell phone at a post office or wherever Vini phones or recharge cards are sold. (Vini is the name of a small finch that lives in these islands and it is also the name used by the Tikiphone department of the telephone company). Save your original chip to put back in once you are on your way home. The cost of this prepaid Vini chip/phone card is 5.500 CFP, which gives you a calling credit of 30 minutes of local calls or 13 minutes of international calls.

You will also be given a local phone number. This number can be reached from overseas by dialing 011+689+your six-digit mobile phone number. This phone number is valid for 180 days unless you replace it with your original chip. If you want to continue the service, make sure you buy a replacement card before the credit is used up. The recharge cards cost 4.400 CFP for 44 minutes, 1.650 CFP for 16 minutes and 550 CFP for 5 minutes.

You will also have voice mail service when you buy the Vini card. Be sure you specify that you want an English-speaking version; so that you will understand when she tells you how much credit you have left. Because your credit can be used up very quickly, it's best if you buy a phone card (*télécarte*) for long conversations. If you're on a yacht or somewhere else where a phone isn't available, then quickly call your family and friends on your cell phone and ask them to call you back.

The Tikiphone GSM 900 MHz network in French Polynesia covers 97 percent of the most populated areas and major islands of French Polynesia. There are blackout zones, however, where you won't be able to communicate in this manner. For further information, contact Tikiphone Customer Service in Papeete in the OPT (*Office Postes Télécommunications*) building at the Pont de l'Est, *Tel. 689/48.13.13; Fax 689/48.72.48; www.vini.pf.*

Other options are to rent a cell phone in the US from InTouch USA, *Tel. 800/872-7626; www.intouch-global.com,* or from RoadPost, *Tel. 888-290-1606 or 905/272-5665; www.roadpost.com.* In Tahiti you can buy a cell phone for 9.900 CFP or you can pay up to 70.000 CFP for a more deluxe model. You can also rent a Vini phone in Papeete from **Telephone+**, *Tel. 83.13.14; Fax 83.13.00; E-mail: telephone.plus@mail.pf.* The cost is 700 CFP for 24 hours, 3.500 CFP per week and 10.000 CFP per month. Prices include the cell phone and charges, but do not include the SIM cards and phone calls. A deposit of 20.000 CFP is required. Credit cards accepted. Delivery service is available to hotels in Papeete and Faa'a, or you can go to the Téléphone+ Faaa office, which is located in the Air Tahiti building at the entrance to the airport, next to La Cafetes restaurant.

Television

Télé Polynésie and Tempo are two free channels televised by Radio Television Française d'Outre-Mer, RFO Tahiti, the French government-owned station. Télé Polynésie reaches most of the remote island groups of French Polynesia, with direct broadcasts replacing the recorded programs that used to arrive in the outer islands a week or two after the event. Tahiti Nui Satellite (TNS) provides 22 channels of cable service, including CNN and TCM in English, Tahiti Nui Television (TNTV), with local news and other programs in French and Tahitian, and Canal+, another cable service. Most hotels in the Society Islands have access to the TNS programs, especially CNN, which is the version made for the Asia-Pacific region rather than the United States programs you are used to seeing.

Has television changed the lives of the Polynesians? My answer is an unqualified yes! The old adage that "ignorance is bliss" was still in effect when I first came here, and I have seen the changes as the people have evolved or degenerated with their newly acquired knowledge, which is due in a very large part to the television programs they've absorbed, like a dry sponge sucks in water. Several people have no television in their homes, nor do they want one. But they are usually expatriate Americans, French or European residents who came here to get away from too much exposure to the news and other forms of distraction.

Time

The island of Tahiti, as well as all the rest of the Society Islands, the Tuamotu Archipelago and the Austral Islands, is 10 hours behind Greenwich Mean Time. These islands are in the same time zone as Hawaii, and are two hours behind US Pacific Standard Time and five hours behind US Eastern Standard Time. You'll add one-hour difference in time between Tahiti and the US when daylight saving time is in effect in the US. This means that between the first Sunday in April and the last Sunday in October, when it is noon in Tahiti, it is 6pm in New York and 3pm in Los Angeles; and between the last Sunday in October and the first Sunday in April, when it is noon in Tahiti, it is 5pm in New York and 2pm in Los Angeles.

The Gambier Islands, which form the most eastern archipelago in the territory, are an hour ahead of the rest of French Polynesia, and a half-hour ahead of the Marquesas Islands, which are a half-hour ahead of the Tuamotus, Societies and Australs. Therefore, when it is noon in Tahiti, it is 12:30pm in the Marquesas and 1pm in the Gambier Islands.

French Polynesia is east of the International Date Line, with the same date as the US. These islands are one day behind Tonga, Fiji, New Zealand and Australia. Tahiti is 20 hours behind Australian Eastern Standard Time.

Tipping

The brochures published by the Tahiti Tourist office state that tipping is not expected in Tahiti and Her Islands. In tour guides and brochures you will read that tipping is considered contrary to the Polynesian custom of hospitality, or that a Tahitian will be offended if you try to tip them.

It is still true that tipping is not the custom here, nor will you be expected to tip, even if someone does render a service beyond the call of duty. No one here has a hand out in anticipation of a tip, although I run across a European or half-European eager beaver occasionally, who makes it more than obvious that he expects a tip. However, if you do want to tip someone, you will make them happy and you'll feel good about it yourself, because you are probably accustomed to tipping back home. Just keep in mind that it is not required. Some American visitors have started bringing gifts of candy to distribute to people instead of giving them tips.

The *Tahiti Beach Press* prints a notice in each weekly publication, encouraging tourists to write a letter of thanks (*mauruuru* means "thank you" in Tahitian) to the magazine if someone has been especially nice or has gone out of their way to help the visitor. This letter nominates that helpful person for the Mauruuru Award, which is presented once a year during a special luncheon held at a restaurant in Tahiti. The winners can be people who work in the tourist industry, as well as any other resident, and they are awarded a round-trip airline ticket on Air Tahiti Nui to California, New Zealand or France.

Tipping at Hotels & Restaurants

In the US and other countries when you are presented the bill in restaurants and bars there is a printed form that includes a place to add tips. I never saw this type of bill in Tahiti and Her Islands until 2004, when I stayed at the Bora Bora Nui and ate in the restaurants there. It took a long time getting here.

At the bottom of the menu in some restaurants you'll occasionally see a notice that tips are appreciated. There may also be a "Tips Accepted" sign posted in some obvious place inside the restaurant. At the Linareva floating restaurant in Moorea a huge bottle containing dollars and francs sits on a table near the entrance to the converted ferryboat. I asked one of the waitresses what happens to the money when the jug is full, and she said that all the employees get to spend a weekend on another island, or they divvy up the tips among all the staff. Other restaurants use the tips for their Christmas party. Some of the restaurants on Moorea and Bora Bora offer free pick-up service, but the driver displays a sign (in English only) inside the van stating that tips are not included. One driver in Moorea even comes right out and says that tips are expected. One of the managers at a popular restaurant on Bora Bora pointed out that when you tip someone, that money goes right back into the local economy and keeps the flow going, because the employee may use the tip to buy a beer after work—maybe at his bar.

The bellmen or *bagagistes* in the hotels also appreciate the tips they receive, even though the hotel management discourages this practice. I've asked many of these young men how they feel about receiving tips, and some of them said that they just indicate to the hotel guest to put the money in their shirt pockets, and that way they can truthfully say they didn't have their hand out.

Tipping Guides

I worked as a free-lance tour guide in Tahiti for 17 years, in addition to my newspaper job, and I can assure you that all of the tour guides and drivers happily welcome tips. Some of the European guides have also told me that they make it clear to the tourists that they want tips. This is exactly the attitude that the Tahiti Tourist office is trying to prevent, and Tahitian guides and drivers do not use this aggressive approach.

Tipping Taxi Drivers

Chances are you won't feel much inclined to tip taxi drivers when you discover how expensive the fares are. But it's still up to your discretion whether to tip. The president of the taxi drivers' union in Tahiti said that only one percent of people tip them, and these tippers are Americans.

Weights & Measures

French Polynesia is on the metric system, but for your convenience, I have converted kilometers to miles, meters to feet, kilos to pounds, liters to gallons, and Celsius to Fahrenheit, where appropriate. To facilitate your own conversions, here are the equations:

1 meter = 3.28 feet	1 foot = 0.30 meters
1 meter = 1.09 yards	1 yard = 0.91 meters
1 square meter = 10.7639 square feet	1 square foot = 0.09 square meter
1 square meter = 1,1960 square yards	1 square yard = .08 square meter
1 hectare = 2.4710 acres	1 acre = .04 hectares
1 kilometer = .62 miles	1 mile = 1.61 kilometers
1 liter = 1.06 quarts	1 quart = 0.95 liters

4 liters = 1.06 gallons	1 gallon = 3.79 liters
1 kilogram = 2.20 pounds	1 pound = 0.45 kilograms

Temperature Guide

0º Celsius = 32º Fahrenheit	=	Freezing point of water
10º Celsius = 50º Fahrenheit	=	Winter in the Austral Islands
20º Celsius = 68º Fahrenheit	=	Comfortable for you, chilly for some of Tahiti's residents
30º Celsius = 86º Fahrenheit	=	Quite warm-almost hot
37º Celsius = 98.6 Fahrenheit	=	Normal body temperature
40º Celsius = 104º Fahrenheit	=	Heat wave conditions
100º Celsius = 212º Fahrenheit	=	Boiling point of water

Where to Find More Information

• **Tahiti Tourisme**, B.P. 65, Papeete, Tahiti 98713, French Polynesia. *Tel. 689/ 50.57.00; Fax 689/43.66.19; E-mail address: tahiti-tourisme@mail.pf; www.tahiti-tourisme.pf.* This is the main office for overseas promotion, across the street from the Cultural Center on Boulevard Pomare in the Paofai section of Papeete, just before the entrance to the RDO freeway. A tour guide to the small hotels and pensions, plus video films, posters, T-shirts, caps and sun visors can be purchased in the promotional materials department.

• **Tahiti Tourisme Overseas Representatives**

• **North America,** 300 Continental Boulevard, Suite 160, El Segundo, CA 90245; *Tel 310/414-8484; Fax 310/414-8490; E-mail address: info@tahiti-tourisme.com; www.tahiti-tourisme.com.*

• **Europe** (France, Belgium, Switzerland, Luxembourg, The Netherlands, Eastern and Central Europe), Tahiti Tourisme Paris, 28, Boulevard Saint-Germain, 75005 Paris; *Tel. (33) 01 55 42 64 34; Fax (33) 01 55 42 61 20; E-mail: tahititourisme@tahiti-tourisme.fr; www.tahiti-tourisme.fr; Website in German language: www.tahititourisme.de*

• **Italy**, Aigo, Plazza Caiazzo, 3, 20124 Milano; *Tel. (39) 02 66 980 317; Fax (39) 02 66 92 648; E-mail: Tahiti@tahiti-tourisme.it; www.tahiti-tourisme.it*

• **Spain/Portugal**, Orense, 85, Edificio Lexington, 28020 Madrid, Spain; *Tel. (34) 915 678 415; Fax (34) 915 714 244; E-mail: info@tahitiysusislas.com; www.tahitiysusislas.com*

• **United Kingdom**, BGB & Associates, 7 Westminster Palace Gardens, Artillery Row, London SW 1P 1RL; *Tel. 44 (0) 20 7233 2300; Fax 44 (0) 20 7233 2301; E-mail: virginia@bgb.co.uk. Also info@tahiti-tourisme.co.uk; www.tahiti-tourisme.co.uk*

• **Northern Europe**, Tahiti Tourisme, 3, Larsbjørnsstraede, DK-1454 Copenhagen K, Denmark; *Tel. (45) 33 37 71 12; Fax (45) 33 32 43 70; E-mail: info@tahiti-tourisme.dk; www.tahiti-tourisme.dk*

· **South America, Oficina de turismo de Tahiti y sus islas, Av.** 11 de Septiembre 2214, Of.116, Casilla 16057 – Santiago 9, Chile; *Tel. (562) 251 2826; Fax (562) 233 1787; E-mail: Tahiti@cmet.net; www.entahiti.cl*

· **Australia**, 12 Ann Street, Surry Hills NSW 2010, Sydney; *Tel. (61) 2 9281 6020; Fax (61) 2 9211 6589; E-mail: info@tahiti-tourisme.com.au; www.tahiti-tourisme.com.au*

· **New Zealand**, 200 Victoria West Street, Suite 2A, P.O. Box 106192, Auckland, NZ; *Tel. (64) 9 368 5262; Fax (64) 9 368 5263; E-mail: info@tahiti-tourisme.co.na; www.tahiti-tourisme.co.nz*

· **Japan**, Tahiti Tourist Promotion Board, TCAT 42-1 Nihonbashi Hakozakicho, Chuou-ku, Tokyo 103-0015 Japan; *Tel. (81) 3 3639 0468; Free number (81) 0120 635 326; Fax (81) 3 3665 0581; E-mail: info@tahiti-tourisme.jp; www.tahiti-tourisme.jp*

· **Asia Regional Office** (Singapore, Taiwan, Thailand, Hong Kong and China), Tahiti Tourist Office c/o Pacific Leisure Group, 8/F Maneeya Center Building, Lumpini, Patumwan 518/5 Ploenchit Road, Bangkok 10330 Thailand; *Tel. (66) 2 652 05 07; Fax (66) 2 652 05 09; E-mail: eckard@plgroup.com*

· **Tahiti Manava Visitors Bureau**, B.P. 1710, Papeete, Tahiti 98713, French Polynesia. *Tel. 689/50.57.12; Fax 689/50.55.47; E-mail: infos@tahiti-manava.pf.* This office is on the harbor side of the Papeete waterfront in Fare Manihini. Here you will find brochures and informational sheets on lodgings, activities, tours and excursions, ferries, boats and air services to the outer islands, maps and anything else related to tourism. English-speaking Tahitian personnel are on duty from 8am through 5pm Monday through Friday, and from 8am until noon on Saturday.

· **Service of Tourism**, B.P. 4527, Papeete, Tahiti 98713, French Polynesia. *Tel. 689/47.62.00; Fax 689/47.62.02; E-mail: sto@tourisme-gov.pf; www.service-du-tourisme.pf.* This office is in charge of regulations concerning tourist activities, cruises and charter boats, tourist transportation, travel agencies and tourist accommodations.

· **Ministry of Tourism,** French Polynesia Government, The Presidency, B.P. 2551, Papeete, Tahiti 98713. *Tel. 689/47.24.40; Fax 689/42.61.36; E-mail: tourisme@tourisme.gov.pf; www.tourisme.gov.pf.*

· **Chamber of Commerce**, **Industry and Trade**, B.P. 118, Papeete, Tahiti 98713. *Tel. 689/47.27.00; Fax 689/54.07.01; E-mail: cci.tahiti@mail.pf; www.ccism.pf.* Use this contact for questions regarding any business or trade in Tahiti.

· **Diving in Tahiti and Her Islands**, B.P. 6014, Papeete, Tahiti 98702. *Tel. 689/53.34.96; Fax 689/53.34.74; E-mail: gieplongee@mail.pf; www.diving-tahiti.com.* This is the representative office for all scuba diving centers in French Polynesia.

• **Haere Mai Federation**, B.P. 4517, Papeete, Tahiti 98713. Tel./Fax *689/ 42.16.17; E-mail: haere-mai@mail.pf; www.haere-mai.pf; www.haere-mai.com.* This association was created in 1997 and represents most of the family pensions and guesthouses in all the archipelagoes of French Polynesia. Contact this office for online booking and information.
• **Te Fare Tauhiti Nui Cultural Center** (**House of Culture**), B.P. 1709, Papeete, Tahiti 98713, French Polynesia. *Tel. 689/54.45.44, Fax 689/ 42.85.69; E-mail: Tauhiti@mail.pf; www.maisondelaculture.pf.* The House of Culture is in charge of selected cultural events throughout the year. There is a library on the premises.
• **Société des Etudes Océaniennes**, c/o Territorial Records, Tipaerui, B.P. 110, Papeete, Tahiti 98713, French Polynesia. *Tel./Fax 689/41.96.03; E-mail: d.r.koenig@mail.pf.* Researchers may obtain permission to use the library and archives of the Oceanian Studies Society.
• **Friends of Tahiti**, P.O. Box 2224, Newport Beach, CA 92659; *E-mail: friendsoftahiti@welcome.to; www.welcome.to/friendsoftahiti.* Te Mau Hoa No Tahiti is the Tahitian name for this cultural and charitable association, whose objectives include promoting friendship and cultural understanding between the people of French Polynesia and the United States through education, cultural arts exposure and travel. If you live in Southern California perhaps you can join them for their Tahitian galas and fundraiser programs, which include traditional Tahitian buffets and dance shows.

Useful Websites
TahitiWeb is the Internet guide to Tahiti's Websites: *www.tahitiweb.com*; **Tahiti Tourisme in France,** *www.voyagetahiti.com*; **Tahiti Live** for information on small hotels and guesthouses, *www.tahitilive.pf*; **Tahiti Guide**, *www.tahitiguide.com*, also has tourist information. Have a look at *www.tahitirealestate.com* if you want to rent or buy a house, bungalow or apartment in Tahiti and Her Islands. For information on the specific islands, most of them have their own website, which you can reach by typing the name of the island, preceded by *www. (moorea.com, raiatea.com, borabora.com, rangiroa.com, marquises.com, tahiti.com and papeete.com*), or you can type the name of the island plus the word «island» and you'll get another site, such as mooreaisland.com, huahineisland.com and so on. Some of these sites are owned by the Tahiti Travel Net and others belong to other travel agencies, who can help you plan your trip. If you want to find information about the **French Polynesia Government**, go to *www.presidence.pf.*
Websites for online news from Tahiti also offer English translations. To keep up with what's happening in French Polynesia, go to *www.tahitipresse.pf; www.tahiti1.com*, or *www.tahitiplanet.com*, which also has a webcam.

Chapter 8

CALENDAR OF EVENTS

You can contact **Tahiti Manava Visitors Bureau**, *Tel. 689/50.57.12; Fax 689/50.55.47; E-mail: infos@tahiti-manava.pf; www.tahiti-manava.pf* for further information and specific dates of programmed events in this chapter. The Tahiti Tourist Office is Los Angeles should also have this information, *Tel. 310/414-8484.*

January

Kaina Island Tour. The Tahiti Manava Visitors Bureau organizes a circle island tour called the Kaina Island Tour, which takes place every other year on the first Sunday of the New Year. The next event will be in January 2006. Following a tradition in Tahiti you will ride in a flower decorated *le truck*, complete with a band of musicians playing the guitar, ukulele and "gut-bucket" bass, and singing "kaina" style Tahitian songs, while you rattle two spoons in a beer bottle and sing along until you're hoarse.

There are normally about 10 *le trucks* and 300 people on this tour and you stop at several of the most beautiful natural sites to visit waterfalls, public gardens, parks and beaches, with a traditional Tahitian breakfast and lunch served beside a beach, followed by a dance show. This 12-hour tour ends on the beach at Point Venus, with the election of a King and Queen and a fire dance is performed against the golden rays of the setting sun.

February

Chinese New Year. Tahiti's Chinese community will welcome in the Year of the Rooster on February 9, 2005, and the Year of the Dog will make its appearance on January 29, 2006. Celebrations include parades, the Dance of the Lion and Dragon, and open house at the Chinese temple in the Mamao suburb of Papeete, with traditional dances, martial arts demonstrations, food tasting, calligraphy, paintings and fortune telling. This colorful event ends two weeks later with a Parade of Lanterns and a fireworks show over Papeete harbor.

Tahiti Nui Sunrise Marathon. A 42,195-kilometer scenic marathon is held each year on the island of Moorea on the second Saturday of February. This is an increasingly popular event that attracts competitors from all over the world. A 21-kilometer Mini-Marathon and a 6-kilometer Fun Run are also held in conjunction with the international event. The next marathon is set for February 12, 2005. You can get more information from Way Beyond, *www.wayb.com or www.moorea-events.org.*

World Cup Jet Sport Competitions. The top Jet Ski champions from the USA, Brazil, France, Portugal and other countries will compete for the world title in Tahiti from February 14-27. Contact André Trimaille, vice-president of the Tahiti Jet Club, at *Tel. 689/48.37.96.*

Tahiti Nui Triathlon. The first edition of this event will take place on February 19, 2005, on the island of Moorea, when contestants will swim 2 kilometers, bike for 99 kilometers and run for 21 kilometers. Contact *www.moorea-events.org.*

Heritage Days is a three-day event that is held at the Museum of Tahiti and Her Islands at the end of February. Some aspect of the Polynesian culture is featured, such as dancing, music, the cultural center or the museums.

March

Missionaries Day. March 5 is a public holiday each year to commemorate the arrival of the first English Protestant Missionaries on March 5, 1797. Reenactment ceremonies are held in the Evangelical churches and at some of the stadiums in the Society Islands and special celebrations are sometimes held in the Austral Islands.

National Women's Day. The women's associations from throughout French Polynesia meet in Papeete on March 8 to discuss the Women's Condition. Songs, dances and skits punctuate these well-attended colorful meetings.

Tahiti International Billfish Tournament (T.I.B.T.) or the **Raiatea International Billfish Tournament (RIBT)** is held every year at one of these two islands during the month of March. Blue marlins weighing more than 500 kilos (1,010 pounds) have been caught by Polynesian fishermen ever since Zane Grey discovered the Tahitian waters in the 1930s. The best-recorded catch so far was the 707 kilo (1,560-pound) blue marlin caught by the Bonnet/Tavanae team in 1986. Contact *www.worldbillfishseries.com.*

May

Billabong Tahiti Pro. Each year during the month of May the top 44 professional surfers in the world face the impressive rollers offshore Teahupoo on Tahiti-Iti. This event is part of the World Cup Tournament (WCT) of international surfing. Surfers and spectators enjoy the friendliness, warmth and local color provided by the residents of Teahupoo, the little village at the end of the road on the Tahiti-Iti peninsula, closest to the surfing action. Contact *www.billabong.com* for dates of surfing competitions.

Traditional Maohi Sports Festival in Tahiti. This demonstration of traditional Polynesian sports includes fruit-carriers' races, javelin throwing, coconut tree climbing, husking coconuts, stone lifting competitions and lots of *maa Tahiti*, food cooked in an underground oven.

"Me" is celebrated during the month of May in each Evangelical parish throughout the islands. This religious festival is also a fundraising event and the money collected not only finances the churches' projects but is also given as aid to the underprivileged. At the end of the ceremony a huge feast is prepared by the church members to thank everyone for their generosity.

Miss Dragon is elected in Tahiti each year in May or June. The winner then represents Tahiti's Chinese community in the Miss Asia Pacific beauty pageant.

Raid Moorea. The second edition of this event will be divided into Fun and Aito categories. The Fun race will be held on May 14, 2005, with individuals and teams competing in a 15-kilometer mountain bike trial, an 8-kilometer foot race in the mountains and a 3-kilometer kayak race in the lagoon of Moorea. On May 28, 2005 the Aito adventure race on Moorea will include a 25-kilometer mountain bike trial, a 12-kilometer foot race in the mountains and a 5-kilometer kayak race. Contact A.S. Te Moorea Club, *Tel./Fax 689/56.34.56; E-mail: Moorea@sjs.pf; www.moorea-events.org*.

Commemoration of the Arrival of the *Bounty*. This re-enactment ceremony takes places every two years on the island of Tubuai, where Fletcher Christian and the *Bounty* mutineers tried to settle in 1789. The next event will be in May 2006.

June

World Environment Day. This event on or near to June 5th includes a special environmental awareness program throughout French Polynesia, involving school children, youth and church groups and visitors. Guided tours are organized to visit the beautiful valleys, such as Fautaua, Papenoo and Lake Vaihiria, and a trek to the top of Aorai, 2,066 meters (6,776 feet) altitude, Tahiti's second highest mountain.

Annual Tahiti International Pro/Am Golf Open. This popular event is sponsored by the Australasia Pro Golf Association Tour (PGAT) and it attracts golfers from many parts of the world, who compete for the cash prizes at the

Olivier Breaud International Golf Course in Atimaono, on Tahiti's south coast of Papara. Contact *www.pgatour.com/au*.

Tahiti Nui Cup. The Leeward Islands Regatta attracts yachting enthusiasts from various countries who sail from Raiatea to Huahine, Tahaa and Bora Bora. This event also includes Polynesian dancing, culture, parties and lots of fun.

Miss Tahiti Contest. Lovely and talented young *vahines* compete for the coveted title of Miss Tahiti during the first part of the month. The winner then goes to Paris to vie for the title of Miss France.

Heiva Upa Rau. These are the Polynesian music awards, which are held annually, when the best singers and musicians receive prizes from Tahiti's Cultural Center and the local recording studios.

July

Heiva Nui. The Heiva Cultural Festival is the biggest event of the year. It begins in late June or early July and continues for almost a month. There are daily activities, but the main events are scheduled for Thursday-Sunday each week. In addition to traditional Polynesian sports such as stone lifting, fruit carrier races, copra preparation and javelin throwing, Tahiti's competitions also include outrigger sailing canoe races, bicycle races and a beer race of restaurant and bar waiters. Outrigger paddle canoe races are held inside the lagoon and in the open ocean. The program includes a fire walking ceremony, song and dance competitions and all-night balls. Carnival type rides and fairground booths called *baraques* are set up in two locations, where the kids of all ages can munch popcorn and cotton candy and jump on the Ferris wheel, merry-go-round and other thrilling rides.

Heiva Rima'i Crafts Festival. This is a star attraction during the Heiva activities in Tahiti, with dozens of exhibits of handcrafts from all the island groups. Live concerts, song and dance competitions, Polynesian meals and various games accompany daily demonstrations of traditional arts and crafts. The Crafts Festival is a 3-week event held at the Aorai Tini Hau hall in Pirae. The program for 2005 will be held June 23 through July 17, and will include 150 arts and crafts stands.

Heiva Festivals on all the Islands. The schedules vary, but these festivals usually begin during the month of July. Each island has traditional sports competitions, including fruit carriers' races, javelin throwing, copra chopping contests and outrigger canoe races, arts and crafts stands and games for children. The singing and dancing contests are the highlight of each festival, which usually lasts from four to six weeks. The most popular outer island festivals take place on Bora Bora, Raiatea, Tahaa and Huahine.

Anniversary of Internal Autonomy Day with a Hiva Vaevae Parade in Papeete. Each year on June 29 the biggest folkloric parade of the year is held along Boulevard Pomare in downtown Papeete. This celebration is to commemorate the anniversary of a French parliamentary statue that was adopted in 1984, giving French Polynesia increased self-governing powers. In Tahiti you will see all the dance groups, youth groups, church groups, sports groups and special interest groups parading on foot, roller blades, bicycles, motorcycles, horses, in pirogues, cars and trucks and aboard decorated floats. **French Bastille Day Holiday Parade**. France's National Holiday of July 14th is celebrated throughout French Polynesia with parades, parties and all night balls. Large hotels also organize special evenings for this event. A military parade is staged on Boulevard Pomare along the Papeete waterfront, followed by a champagne party at the residence of the French High Commissioner. Horse races and bicycle races are usually scheduled for that afternoon.

Tahiti World Kneeboard Horue Surfing Championships. The 2004 edition of this annual surfing competition was held July 10-25, 2004 at Popoti Bay in Papara, on Tahiti's southwest coast. First prize was US$5,000. This annual event is organized by the Popoti Surf Club, *Tel. 689/57.4818; E-mail: qch.Tahiti@netcourrier.com / mainasage@mail.gov.pf; www.horue.pf.*

Annual Te Aito Individual Marathon Outrigger Canoe Race. Almost 300 individual outrigger canoe racers compete in this 20-kilometer course in Tahiti's Matavai Bay, which is held at the end of July. The Aito (Polynesian warrior) winners of this race qualify to compete in the Super Aito competitions.

August

Mini Heiva Festivals. The InterContinental Resort Tahiti invites the winners of the Tahiti Festival song and dance competitions to perform during a Mini Heiva Festival that is held over a period of three or more evenings. Gastronomic feasts are served on the hotel's *motu*, followed by first class entertainment. Some of the other hotels also host special Mini Heiva dinners and shows.

Super Aito Individual Outrigger Canoe Channel Race. Along with the local paddlers who qualify for this most important individual va'a competition, foreign paddlers are invited to join the 4-leg race that is held over a 4-day period in mid-August or early September. The first three legs take place in Tahiti and the fourth leg is a distance of 21.5 kilometers (13.3 miles) starting at Moorea's Temae Beach and ending at Place To'ata in Tahiti. Women's competitions are also held. The winners receive cash prizes.

Tahiti Agricultural & Floral Fair. Farmers from all five archipelagoes of the territory gather in Tahiti for this big event, which is held in late August or early September. Along with stands of fruits, vegetables and flowers, there are displays of arts and crafts, black pearls and other local products, as well as *ahima'a* (earth ovens) with Polynesian food to go.

September

World Tourism Week. Tahiti, Moorea, Huahine, Raiatea, Tahaa and Bora Bora all participate in this annual celebration in honor of our visitors. World Tourism Day is September 27, and that entire week is filled with traditional singing and dancing shows, arts and crafts exhibits, and Polynesian bands playing music in the streets while hostesses distribute flowers to tourists. The airports, hotels, tourist offices, *les trucks*, banks and other offices are decorated with flowers for the occasion.

Annual Tahiti Flower Show. Floralies is the biggest floral exhibit of the year, organized by the Harrison Smith Association at Place Tarahoi in Papeete. This festival of tropical colors and scents, which usually coincides with World Tourism Day, is dedicated to Tahiti's "Grandfather of the Trees," Harrison W. Smith, who created the Botanical Gardens in Papeari on Tahiti's south coast.

Raid Painapo. This annual event is held on the island of Moorea, with teams of 3 making a trail run of 25 kilometers across the Opunohu Valley, where pineapple (painapo) plantations slope down the mountainside. The third edition was held on September 25, 2004.

October

Tahiti Aito Man Triathlon is an international 1/2 Ironman Triathlon that is usually held in late October. This annual competition features 3.8 kilometers of swimming, 180 kilometers of bicycling, and 42.195 kilometers of running. The 2004 edition was held on the island of Raiatea. Contact Way Beyond at *www.wayb.com/triathlon.*

Hawaiki Nui Outrigger Canoe Race. This is a four-day marathon race between the Leeward Islands of Huahine, Raiatea, Tahaa and Bora Bora, with more than 100 canoes and hundreds of paddlers. This is the ultimate va'a competition, which is held each year in October.

November

All Saints Day. The graves in the cemeteries and in the yards of private homes are weeded and cleaned in preparation for this annual event. Flower stands are set up all around the island of Tahiti on this public holiday, which takes place on November 1, when families decorate the graves with dozens of fresh and plastic flowers. That night the cemeteries are lighted with candles as the families sing hymns and recite prayers for their departed loved ones.

Tahiti Nui Roller Marathon. The 6th edition of the Tahiti Nui Roller marathon, the Tahiti Black Pearl Inline Marathon, was scheduled to be held in Moorea on November 7, 2004. The 2003 event took place on Tahiti Iti, and the venue and date for the 2005 competition had not been announced at publication time. This great show combines sports, beautiful scenery and a lot of local color, plus hundreds of in-line skaters from various countries. Contact

Way Beyond Running, *Tel. 877/230-2495; E-mail: tahitiroller@wayb.com; www.wayb.com.*

Moorea Triathlon. This competition is held in late November on the island of Moorea, when athletes can swim for 500 meters, bike for 15 kilometers and run for 5 kilometers in the Sprint category, or swim for 1,000 meters, bike for 40 kilometers and run for 10 kilometers in the Short Olympic category. Contact *www.moorea-events.org.*

December

Tiare Tahiti Days. Tahiti's national flower, the fragrant white Tiare Tahiti (*gardenia taitensis*), is honored during this three-day annual event. On the major tourist islands of Tahiti, Moorea and Bora Bora, the airports, hotels, some restaurants, tourist offices, post offices and banks are decorated with garlands of Tiare Tahiti blossoms, and Tiare Tahiti flowers are presented to tourists on the streets.

Christmas in Tahiti. Santa Claus or "Papa Noel" arrives in Tahiti by outrigger canoe, jet ski, helicopter or horse, accompanied by Polynesian musicians as he distributes candies to the children in Papeete. The major hotels in the tourist islands and several restaurants offer special menus and entertainment on Christmas Eve and Christmas Day, which also include roast turkey with chestnut dressing. And the perfect French wine to accompany the meal, of course!

Chapter 9

TAKING THE KIDS

Tahiti and Her Islands are a haven for the young! So bring your kids and let them enjoy the attention they'll receive from the friendly Polynesians, who adore babies and little children. If they're still young enough to be picked up easily, that will be even more fun for the child and the Tahitians, who love to kiss and hug little people, little puppies and anything that is still a baby. When they get older and bigger, that's another story for the animals and local kids, but the Tahitians will still treat visiting children with genuine warmth and patience.

International airline companies and Air Tahiti give preferential seating to families traveling with children. Kids generally pay only half the adult fare on international airline routings. Air Tahiti gives at least a 50 percent discount to children between two and eleven years and the fare for babies less than two years is 10 percent of the adult fare. Most of the hotels, hostels, guest houses and pensions will let the kids stay for free if sharing a room with their parents, or they only charge for an extra bed.

Your travel agent can make all the reservations for you, securing spacious bulkhead seats on airlines and determining which flights are least crowded. They can also seek out the best deals on lodging and meals.

When traveling with children of any age, make sure their vaccinations are up to date and bring their health records and any special medications they made need. In the event of an emergency, there are medical facilities on all the islands. Mamao hospital in Tahiti has a modern pediatric department. Make sure that your repatriation insurance also covers your child.

Rascals in Paradise, One Daniel Burnham Court, Suite 105-C, San Francisco, CA 94109, Tel. 415/921-7000; Fax 415/775-0900; E-mail:

trips@rascalsinparadise.com; www.rascalsinparadise.com. They organize South Pacific tours for families with kids, including visits with local families.

Traveling with Babies

Hopefully, you'll be at least two people to bring a baby on a long airplane flight to Tahiti. Bring a suitcase filled with baby supplies, including a sufficient supply of disposable diapers, food, light clothes that cover the whole body, a sun hat, favorite toys, Q-Tips, baby wipes, a first aid kit with sun block, mosquito repellent, baby aspirin, thermometer and a treatment for diarrhea. The supermarkets and small *magasin* stores carry fresh or powdered whole milk, bottled mineral water, dry cereals that must be cooked, canned fruits and jars of baby food, but you'll pay much more for these items in Tahiti than you will back home.

Bring a stroller with sunshade or cloth carrier for your baby, or a car seat-sleeper combination. Only a few of the hotels can provide cribs and high chairs for babies.

Toddlers & Little Tikes

Along with the shorts, T-shirts, sweater, waterproof shoes and sun hat you pack for your small children, you should also include some of their favorite snacks, books and toys. If they're big enough to snorkel, pack their own snorkel gear, plus a bucket and shovel and inflatable beach ball. In their first-aid kit be sure to include some preventive drops for swimmer's ear. Cleanse and treat any minor cuts or abrasions immediately to prevent staph infection. Make sure they're protected from the hot tropical sun and mosquitoes and that they drink a sufficient amount of water throughout the day.

Juniors & Adolescents

The warm climate, natural setting, aquatic games and lack of poisonous creatures make Tahiti and Her Islands a paradise for children of all ages. Many of the hotels have swimming pools and beach activities, such as outrigger paddle canoes, pedal boats and windsurf boards. Swimming or playing in the reef-protected lagoon waters is also relatively safe, as long as you keep an eye on the little ones, because there are no lifeguards. Children enjoy lagoon excursions, picnics on the *motu*, feeding the fish, rays and sharks, sailing and other water activities. Some of the scuba diving centers will accept divers as young as four years. Some of the hotels and guesthouses provide bicycles for their guests, or you can rent them on most of the islands.

McDonald's is located in downtown Papeete and there is another outlet next to the Marina Taina in Punaauia, which has a pool and playground equipment for children. On several of the islands you'll find hamburgers, sandwiches, pizzas, tacos, pancakes and crêpes. All the food stores carry some

American snacks and good ice cream. Most of the hotels have children's menus and give special discount rates for buffets and Tahitian feasts for children under 12 years of age. The more luxurious hotels have room service, which can be convenient for families, and several of the moderate range hotels and family pensions provide kitchen facilities.

Babysitters

Hotels that welcome children generally have no problem arranging babysitters. If you're staying in a pension or guesthouse, ask your hostess to find a babysitter for you.

Special Activities at Hotels

The **InterContinental Resort Moorea** has a Kids Only Club for their guests who are from 4 to 10 years old. The activities desk opens at 8:30am and the program is from 9am to 4:30pm on Monday through Friday. The children get lunch and an afternoon snack, in addition to the organized activities, for a cost of 6.000 CFP. The children will be supervised while learning to swim in a reserved part of the swimming pool or in the lagoon, playing Olympiad games on the beach, visiting the hotel's botanical gardens and sampling tropical fruit. They will learn how to wear a *pareo* and dance the *tamure*, how to make floral crowns or paint a *pareo*, or play croquet and *petanque*, a game of French bowls. Rainy day activities include drawing, singing, arts and crafts and watching movies.

Also at the InterContinental Resort Moorea, the kids who are a minimum of 4 years old can learn to scuba dive with the instructors from Bathy's Club, which is on the hotel premises. This optional activity is 3.500 CFP per child. Another option is to have an interactive session with the dolphins in the shallow water at the Dolphin Center on the hotel grounds. See further information in the *Moorea* chapter.

Chapter 10

ECOTOURISM

Ecotourism, as defined by the Ecotourism Society, is "responsible travel that conserves environments and improves the welfare of the local people." This definition applies not only to developing countries where the land and culture is being exploited by external forces but to all destinations. Ecotourism aims to keep the money generated by tourism in the local economy in order to preserve the area's landscape, culture and economy.

The Ecotourism Society of America defines an ecotour as: "Purposeful travel to natural areas to understand the culture and natural history of the environment, taking care not to alter the integrity of the ecosystem, while producing economic opportunities that make conservation of the natural resources beneficial to local people."

Ecotours can vary from bird watching safaris to botanical investigations to tours that focus on local dance styles, or language, or archaeological interests. What they have in common is that they use local guides, seek to educate the client about the natural and cultural world and the environmental issues surrounding it, and actively promote the conservation of each tour site.

The development of ecotourism is a direct response to public interest in the environment, which has risen dramatically in the last three decades. The market for ecotourism has taken a well known fact—that beautiful pristine environments and unspoiled cultures are good for tourism—and turned it into a defining edict: that ecotourists want to learn about these places and cultures, and that they want to have something to do with conserving them.

French Polynesia is an ideal region for ecotourism as it offers many unspoiled areas of terrestrial and marine flora and fauna to explore, and the Maohi culture is still largely intact. Even though there are environmental problems (some directly related to high-end tourism), even on the more populated islands of Tahiti and Moorea there are still places where an interested person or group can spend a quiet day in a natural setting. There are other islands, such as Huahine, Raiatea and Tahaa, which are better preserved, and many islands in the Tuamotu, Marquesas and Austral archipelagoes are still relatively wild. Almost all of the islands are accessible by air.

Tahiti's Tourism Ministry designated 20 tourist sites for upgrading in 2004 to create "green promenading", the new term (replacing "green tourism") to designate places set aside for ecology-minded visitors. All 20 sites are located on the island of Tahiti. The upgrading involves improved signs to indicate access to the sites and more cultural information about the site.

The Tourism Minister has compiled a list of 190 sites of interest to tourists on Tahiti, which include the *marae* and sanctuaries that have been found in the high valley of Papenoo. The Haururu Association of Papenoo was created in 1994 to protect and develop this valley, where it is believed that between 6,000 and 10,000 people lived at one time. The first signs of human settlement date from 1500 to 1650 AD, and the Papenoo Valley was occupied at various times until it was finally deserted around 1850. The Haururu Association has built 15 *fare* shelters at Fare Hape for groups or families who wish to discover the Papenoo Valley and its restored *marae*, petroglyphs, walking trails and waterfalls. There are also 5 camping sites, a sheltered area with picnic tables and benches, a meeting area for seminars, and a kitchen with hot and cold water, stove, refrigerator, freezer, pots, pans and cooking gas. People staying in the *small fare* shelters, as well as campers, should bring their own sheets, blankets, pillows and towels, as well as their dishes and food and they must take their own garbage with them when they leave. There are separate toilet and shower facilities for men and women. The Haururu Association does not provide transportation for people to get to the Fare Hape site, but they will transport your bags and equipment from the first bridge, called Mamao, for a round-trip fee of 10.000 CFP per vehicle. Then you can hike into the valley.

For more information see **Fare Hape** under *Where to Stay* in the *Tahiti* chapter. You might also want to have a look under **Relais de la Maroto** in the *Tahiti* chapter, which is a mountain inn above Fare Hape, where your entertainment is provided by walking through the natural beauty of the Papenoo Valley.

Listed below are some of the most popular eco-activities and adventures in French Polynesia, as well as companies that support sustainable tourism and operate eco-tours to Tahiti and Her Islands.

Dr. Michael Poole, CRIOBE, B.P. 1013, Papetoai, Moorea; *Tel./Fax 689/ 56.14.70; E-mail criobe@mail.pf; www.drmichaelpoole.com* is an American marine biologist who has lived in Moorea for more than 17 years, studying the 24 local occurring species of dolphins and whales, some of whom live year-round in the waters surrounding Moorea and Tahiti. For his Ph.D. in marine biology, Michael studied at the University of California at Santa Cruz, with

Doctor Kenneth Norris, the world's foremost authority on dolphins and whales. Michael chose to come to Moorea for his research work, where the University of California at Berkeley has a biological research station, the Gump Center, located beside Cook's Bay.

He is currently the Director of the Marine Mammal Research Program at the Centre de Recherches Insulaires et Observatoire de l'Environnement (CRIOBE), a French biological research station of the University of Perpignan, in Opunohu Bay on Moorea. Michael is also a Research Associate with the National Oceanic Society in Southern California. To carry out his research projects, which take him to several other islands in French Polynesia, he depends on grants from foundations, businesses, philanthropists and individuals. He also offers internship programs to interested individuals who wish to participate in the research as "hands-on" field assistants.

Michael has identified over 200 spinner dolphins (*Stenella longirostris*), of which 120 presently live around Moorea, and over 300 humpback whales (*Megaptera novaeangliae*).

It was Michael's research that demonstrated that these whales come up from Antarctica to mate and give birth between July and October. These giant mammals can be seen off Moorea, and Michael has a whale sighting and stranding network set up throughout the islands of French Polynesia. Michael's proposal to create a whale and dolphin sanctuary within French Polynesia's exclusive economic zone (half the size of the continental US), and his draft legislation to completely protect these animals, was passed by French Polynesia's territorial government on 13 May 2002.

In addition to his internship programs, Michael and his staff lead 3-4 hour eco-tours, Dolphin & Whale Watching Expeditions, twice a week, to give visitors an opportunity to observe and learn about the dolphins and whales in their natural environment. The enthusiasm he and his staff feel for the mammals they study is very contagious. Michael is a man who truly loves his work, a teacher who enjoys sharing his knowledge with people.

Aranui 3, Compagnie Polynésienne de Transport Maritime, 2028 El Camino Real South, Suite B, San Mateo, California 94403; *in US Tel. 800/972-7268 or 650/574-2575; Fax 650/574-6881; E-mail: aranui@mail.pf; www.aranui.com.*

The 208-passenger ship *Aranui 3* offers 16-day round-trip voyages from Papeete to the Marquesas Islands. The ship stops in Takapoto in the Tuamotu archipelago on its way to the Marquesas and in Fakarava on the return trip, and it visits several valleys on all six of the inhabited Marquesas Islands.

If you want to get off the beaten path of tourism and discover the authentic lifestyles of the Polynesian people, the *Aranui* offers the best opportunity for this experience. The passengers who choose the *Aranui* are normally well-educated, travel-wise people who have an idea of where they're going, and usually they have already done some background reading on the

Marquesas before boarding the ship. An onboard library and video films will help to further your knowledge during the trip. Multi-lingual guest speakers lecture on Marquesan history, culture, archaeology, art, flora and fauna.

Shore excursions to Marquesan archaeological sites include *me'ae* stone temples, *tohua* assembly places, *paepae* house platforms, stone tikis and petroglyphs. Your guides will take you to the Catholic churches to see the magnificent wooden sculptures carved by Marquesan artisans, and to the handcrafts centers to purchase *umete* bowls, platters, tikis, war clubs, saddles and ukuleles carved from beautiful local woods. You will also find tapa bark cloth, made and painted entirely by hand, carved stones and coconut shells, fragrant *monoi* oils, sandalwood leis and smoky-flavored dried bananas.

Guided trips take you to visit small museums, a botanical garden, vanilla and coconut plantations and noted gravesites, including those of the French painter Paul Gauguin and Belgian singer Jacques Brel in Hiva Oa. You can hike through a tropical rain forest in Fatu Hiva, ride a horse across the island of Ua Huka, picnic on a mountain in Nuku Hiva, see the flower stones (*phonolitis*) in Ua Pou, and enjoy traditional Marquesan *kai kai* feasts that include fresh lobster and curried goat cooked in coconut milk. Optional activities include scuba diving with the orcas, manta rays and sharks offshore Nuku Hiva and you can also scuba dive and snorkel in the magnificent lagoon of Fakarava on the voyage back to Tahiti.

Rates for the 16-day voyage, including accommodations, all meals, wine and guided excursions, range between $1,980 and $4,950 per person. See detailed information in the *Planning Your Trip* chapter.

M/S Paul Gauguin is operated by Radisson Seven Seas Cruises (RSSC), which is based in Fort Lauderdale, Florida, *Tel. 877/505-5370* (RSSC Expert), *Tel. 866/213-1272* (Travel Agent near you); *Tel. 954/776-6123, ext. 456* (Charters & Incentives); *www.rssc.com.*

During the summer season of 2004 the 318-passenger cruise ship *Paul Gauguin* offered an environmental program for its passengers, and especially the children on board during the weekly cruises from Tahiti through the Society Islands. A Jean-Michel Cousteau team of experts from Ocean Future Society helped the participants to become familiar with the flora and fauna of French Polynesia, as well as its legends, coral reef and the human impact on this environment. Jean-Michel Cousteau has also collaborated with Radisson Seven Seas Cruises on conferences held aboard the *Paul Gauguin* during its special 14-day cruises to the Marquesas Islands.

In its program for 2005 the *Paul Gauguin* has included a 14-night Solar Eclipse Cruise from April 2-16 that will take passengers from Papeete to the Tuamotu atolls, Pitcairn Island, Hiva Oa and Nuku Hiva in the Marquesas Islands, back to Fakarava in the Tuamotus and then to Moorea and Papeete. The total/hybrid eclipse will take place on April 8. This voyage is priced from $5,970 to $20,559 per person, in double occupancy, plus port charges of $290 per person. See detailed information on the *Paul Gauguin's* regular cruises in the *Planning Your Trip* chapter.

Cox & Kings, *Tel. 800/999-1758; E-mail: tours@coxandkingsusa.com; www.coxandkingsusa.com.* Tahiti: Islands in Time is the name of a 15-day eco-adventure tour to Tahiti, Moorea, Bora Bora and Rangiroa. You will camp on a private island, climb a volcano, spend a day with a reef ecologist, snorkel in pristine lagoons and share a Tahitian feast in a private home. The cost is $5,235 per person in double occupancy, plus round-trip airfare between Los Angeles and Papeete. They also offer Hidden Polynesia mini-tours, with a choice of camping on a private island in Rangiroa for $775; a Natural History & Culture of Moorea experience, for $1,325; Gauguin's Island, The Culture and Natural History of Tahiti, for $585; and Climb Tahiti's Mt. Aorai for $585. Private yacht charters can also be arranged. Original signature events that can be added to the grand tour Islands in Time or combined with your own one-of-a-kind journey, include Ancient Polynesian Beliefs for $175, Tahitian Culinary Adventure for $350, Whale Watching Expedition for $395, Coral Reef and Island Exploration for $485, and a Helicopter Adventure for $975. All rates are per person.

Explorers' Corner, LLC, 1201 Monterey Avenue, Berkeley, CA 94707; *Tel. 510/559-8099; Fax 650/966-8060; www.explorerscorner.com.* A rugged kayaking trip in the remote atolls of French Polynesia and day hiking in the lush mountains of Tahiti are features of a "Rangiroa Expedition" that sells for $3,790 per person for land costs. You will spend 5 nights in hotels, 7 nights in tented camps and 2 days getting to and from your home. From Tahiti you will fly to Rangiroa for a kayaking trip inside the lagoon of the world's second largest atoll. In Tahiti you will hike and camp on Aorai Mountain, and you will also cross the "Sea of Moons" to visit the island of Moorea. A 12-day Exploratory Trip to Raivavae in the Austral Islands was added to the kayaking excursions offered in late 2004. This eco-adventure includes 5 nights in hotels and 4 nights in tented camps and is sold at $4,090 for land costs. Check their website for upcoming expeditions.

Wilderness Travel, *1102 Ninth Street, Berkeley, CA 94710; Tel. 800/368-2794 or 510/558-2488; Fax 510-558-2489; E-mail: info@wildernesstravel.com; www.wildernesstravel.com.* This company organizes extraordinary cultural, wildlife and hiking adventures. Their 2005 itinerary also includes a once-in-a-lifetime "Solar Eclipse in the South Pacific" cruise aboard the *Orion*, a 106-guest ship that will follow in the "Wake of the Bounty" from Tahiti to Bora Bora, to the coral atolls of the Tuamotus, onward to the legendary Marquesas Islands, down to the Gambier Islands, over to Pitcairn and then continuing to Easter Island and Chile. In addition to the ship's naturalists and cultural historians, an expert astronomer will lecture on eclipses and other astronomical subjects. The voyage begins in Papeete on February 19, 2005 and ends in Chile on March 16, and starts at $13,695 per person, depending on the cabin type chosen.

They also organize sailing and sea kayaking adventures in Tuamotu atolls, paddling the inner lagoons to learn about reef ecology, stargaze at night and listen to legends and tales of the islands. The land costs for their 2004 programs began at $4,795 per person for 7-8 members. No announcement had been made for 2005 at publication time.

Expert Guides & Lecturers for Groups or Individuals

Tahiti Outfitters, *Tel. 689/56.31.74, E-mail: ecotours@mail.pf; www.tahitioutfitters.com (note: this website was not yet operational in September 2004).* Frank Murphy is a geographer and biologist who spent four years as resident director of the University of California Berkeley Biological Research Field Station in Moorea, and still works with them for special projects, living year-round on Moorea. He has extensive experience organizing and conducting natural history tours and university field courses in California, Mexico and French Polynesia. He is a former vice-president of Iaora Tahiti Ecotours, and he is now an outfitter for adventure travel groups from all over the world, such as Explorers' Corner, Cox & Kings and Wilderness Travel. Frank will take you on kayak expeditions in the Tuamotu and Austral Islands, bone fishing, salt-water fishing and fly-fishing. He will do customized tours on request.

Mark Eddowes, *Tel. 689/79.88.00; E-mail: eddowestane@hotmail.com.* Mark, who is British, is a professional archaeologist who has worked for the archaeology department of the Museum of Tahiti and Her Islands for several years. He was also vice-president of Iaora Tahiti Ecotours, which no longer exists. Mark has conducted research and led numerous archaeological and historical tours in all of the island groups of French Polynesia. He has worked with special interest groups from the Smithsonian Institute, Harvard and other universities. He specializes in cultural tourism and speaks English, French and Tahitian. He lives in Huahine and lectures aboard the *Paul Gauguin* passenger ship, guiding tourists on archaeological and historic tours in Bora Bora and Moorea.

Heidy Baumgartner-Lesage, *Tel. 689/50.44.50; E-mail: heidy@mail.pf.* Heidy is German-Swiss and speaks English and French as well as her native language. She is a professional archaeologist who has lived in Tahiti for several years, and for about 10 years she was a hostess-guide aboard the *Aranui*, leading passengers to visit the archaeological sites in the Marquesas Islands. Heidy now works as escort-guide for the Elder Hostel groups who visit French Polynesia and other South Pacific Islands. She will work with other special interest groups on request.

Dr. Robert C. Suggs, *365 E. Fairbrook Drive, Boise, ID 83706; Tel. 208/429-1619; Fax 208/429-1825; E-mail: mongonui@msn.com; www.marquesasnow.com.* Doctor Suggs is the leading authority on the Marquesas Islands and a major contributor to Marquesan and Polynesian archaeology. He was a

Research Assistant at the American Museum of Natural History for four years and conducted the first stratigraphic excavations in the Marquesas in 1956-8 for the American Museum. He provided the archaeological world with its first solid evidence of the Melanesian/Western Polynesian origins of the Marquesan culture. He received his Ph.D in Anthropology from Columbia University in 1959, and is the author of eight books on the Marquesas and Polynesia, as well as numerous articles.

His first book, *The Island Civilizations of Polynesia*, was published in 1960 and translated into eight languages. *The Archaeology of Nuku Hiva, Marquesas Islands, French Polynesia*, was a monograph for the American Museum of Natural History, Volume 49. *Modern Discoveries in Archaeology* and *Lords of the Blue Pacific*, a book for juveniles, were both published in 1962. *Hidden Worlds of Polynesia*, published in 1963, was a chronicle of a year that Doctor Suggs and his wife Rachel spent in Nuku Hiva in 1957 and 1958. He also authored *Marquesan Sexual Behavior*, and *Human Sexual Behavior: Variations in the Ethnographic Spectrum*. His latest book, published in 2001, is *Manuiota'a, Journal of a Voyage to the Marquesas Islands*, which he co-authored with Burgl Lichtenstein.

Since 1956 he has made more than 18 additional trips to the Marquesas for further research, and he is an experienced guide, multilingual interpreter, lecturer and tour group leader in the Marquesas and throughout the Pacific. He is fluent in English, French, German, Italian, Indonesian and Marquesan, and reads Russian, Portuguese and Spanish. In addition to lecturing aboard the *Aranui*, Doctor Suggs has also cruised as guest speaker aboard the *World Discoverer* and the *Royal Viking Sun*, on behalf of the Smithsonian Institute. He lectures on Geology of Polynesia, The Marquesas Today, Polynesian Settlement, Marquesan Prehistory, Tiki and Tapu, Temples, House Platforms and Tribal Plazas, and Marquesan Tattooing, as well as Famous European Visitors to the Marquesas.

Dominique Leoture, *Tel. 77.57.61; E-mail: leodom@mail.pf; www.magicmoorea.com*; Internet-based US voicemail and fax *718/247-3220*.

Dominique is an exclusive registered tourist agent and guide living on Moorea, who speaks English, French, Spanish and Portuguese. He is very active in environmental programs on Moorea and also leads trail hikes into Opunohu Valley. He is available to take you on a leisurely, never hurried island tour of Moorea or to other islands in French Polynesia, walking in the forests, to waterfalls and beaches, adapting his services according to your wishes. Dominique grew up in Brazil and he is a multi-talented artist and artisan who designs and makes black pearl jewelry and flutes. He also designs websites.

Chapter 11

FOOD & DRINK

I've listened to big beefy American men comparing prices while standing in a hotel swimming pool beside Moorea's Cook's Bay, totally ignoring the incredible beauty of the mountains and lagoon, as they talked about how they managed to cut costs on their trip to Moorea. One of them bragged that he had collected free packages of coffee, tea, sugar, cream, mustard, ketchup, mayonnaise, crackers and other condiments from the fast food outlets in his town, and had brought them along.

Others described all the snacks, soft drinks and alcohol they had packed into a cooler for the trip. These people were not eating in the hotel or nearby restaurants. They spent their week surviving on processed snack foods they brought with them, plus the crusty French *baguette* bread, luncheon meats, cheese and crackers bought at the nearest food store. Although the hotel had (it is now closed) a no-food-in-the-room policy, it was usually ignored, and some of the guests were unwilling to spend 200 CFP for a cup of coffee in the hotel restaurant.

If you decide to travel on a very tight budget, try not to let the high prices occupy so much of your attention that you cannot even enjoy these magnificent islands. You may want to have a look in the larger supermarkets in Tahiti, where there are deli counters with a varied selection of prepared foods. The smaller *magasins* in Tahiti and the outer islands sell tasty take-away meals of rice with chicken, meat or fish, and containers of *poisson cru* for about 700-800 CFP. The mobile diners, *les roulottes*, are found in all the Society Islands, where you can have a good meal for about 1.200 CFP. There are also small, inexpensive restaurant/snacks, which are listed under *Where to Eat* for each island.

You can buy a soft drink for 135 CFP in the supermarket and you'll pay around 150-180 CFP at a few of the *roulottes* and snack bars, but this same canned drink will cost you up to 450 CFP in a hotel bar. Tahiti's favorite locally brewed beer is Hinano, which sells for about 185 CFP for a small bottle and 190 CFP for a can in grocery stores, and from 350-600 CFP in restaurants and bars. Most restaurants serve *vin ordinaire* (table wine) by the carafe, and an acceptable quality of Bordeaux can be purchased at the grocery stores for around 1.200-1.500 CFP.

For most of us, one of the greatest pleasures of traveling to a foreign country is to sample the local cuisine. If your budget allows a few meals in a restaurant while you're visiting Tahiti, Moorea, Bora Bora or any of the other islands in French Polynesia, then chances are you will have a superb meal.

Helpful hints in ordering from a French menu should include a translation of how you want your steak cooked. Bleu = rare; Saignant = medium-rare; à Point = medium; and Bien Cuit = well done. If you have the audacity to order a steak bien cuit, however, most French chefs will send it out to you when it is about half cooked.

La Nouvelle Cuisine Tahitienne

The hotels and restaurants in Tahiti have earned a reputation among gourmet visitors for serving choice cuisine. The chefs have united the flavors of Europe and the Orient, spiked with a fresh tropical island accent. Whether he came from France, Switzerland, Italy, South America or Asia, each newcomer brought his little sprig of thyme, his chili pepper, soybean or ginger, perhaps to ward off the effects of home sickness in a foreign land.

Culinary choices feature French *haute cuisine*, seven-course Imperial dinners from the provinces of China, Vietnamese *nems*, Italian pasta, Algerian *couscous*, Spanish *paella*, spicy West Indian specialties and Alsatian *choucroute*. These imaginative and creative chefs have also introduced a *nouvelle cuisine Tahitienne* that is a combination of the traditional recipes of their own home countries and the fresh bounty of the Polynesian waters and fruit orchards. Dishes may include fresh local snapper infused with vanilla sauce, a lagoon *bouillabaisse*, reef clams in garlic butter, sautéed crab with ginger, *varo* with champagne and cream, roast duck with papaya or chicken drumsticks with *fafa* and taro.

To accompany these memorable meals are fine French wines and champagnes, locally brewed beer, or a selection of imported beers and wines. Most of the bars bill themselves as a "Bar Americaine" and serve mixed cocktails. Freshly squeezed orange, grapefruit or pineapple juices are some times available, or you will be served fruit juices from the cartons of the Moorea Fruit Juice Factory and Distillery. Perrier and a wide variety of carbonated waters are stocked, as well as the most popular soda pops, sometimes including carbonated diet drinks. Bottled waters from Tahiti and

France are also served, and can cost as much as 850 CFP for a bottle of sparkling water such as San Benedetto, while in the supermarkets it is only 155 CFP.

Snack Bars, Fast Food, Salons de Thè & Patisseries

You'll find an abundance of small restaurants in Tahiti and Her Islands that are advertised as Snacks or Restaurant/Snacks. Most of these places are clean and serve daily specials of local style home cooking. The food is usually delicious and inexpensive. The choices often include *poisson cru* with coconut milk, beef or lamb stew, an assortment of curry dishes, fresh lagoon fish, chicken and vegetables, prawns in garlic sauce, pork and taro, chow mein, or *maa tinito haricots rouge*, which is a Chinese dish of red beans, macaroni, pork or chicken, Chinese vermicelli noodles and a few more good things.

Fast foods have definitely arrived on the scene in Tahiti, with international and local style hamburger stands popping up all over the island. McDonald's has a prime site in downtown Papeete. There is also a McDonald's adjacent to Marina Taina in Punaauia on Tahiti's west coast, which replaced a Kentucky Fried Chicken site that closed soon after opening. The McDonald's counter at the Tahiti-Faa'a Airport sells only muffins, soft drinks and ice cream. These days you hardly have to pause at all in your shopping to have a bite to eat. You can walk up to a sidewalk food stand and order a *casse-croûte*, a ham and cheese *croissant*, a small pizza or a *panini* sandwich. Or you can beat the heat of the Papeete streets while enjoying some of the world's best ice cream.

Salons de thè serve a variety of teas and *infusions*, as well as *espressos* and vanilla flavored coffee from Pacific plantations. *Patisseries* provide people watching in air-conditioned comfort while nibbling on your choice of flaky pastries.

Les Roulottes

Les roulottes (not roulettes) are mobile diners (roach coaches) that set up shop each evening near the cruise ship dock at Place Vaiete on the Papeete waterfront. They serve hot meals until the wee hours of the morning. These colorful food vans provide good, fast food at reasonable prices, as well as a barstool or a table with chairs, where you can sit and watch the waterfront scene of Papeete-by-night.

You can order barbecue steaks, chicken and *brochettes* (shish kabob), served with French fries, *poisson cru*, or *salade russe*, which is potato salad with beets. Specialty diners serve pizza cooked in a wood-burning stove, *couscous*, grilled fish and chips, Tahitian food, barbecue veal and freshly wokked hot delicacies from the provinces of China. Your dinner can be a veritable moveable feast, with a tempting choice of *crêpes* for dessert. No alcohol is served here, but the bars and nightclubs are just across the street.

Place Vaiete has been modernized and is now an attractive, well-lit and popular gathering place at night because of the 30 roulottes that rent space here and also because of the free music concerts frequently presented in the music gazebo. In addition to public restrooms there is also a special place where the *roulotte* owners can wash dishes and pots and pans. These facilities and all of Place Vaiete are kept clean at all times by a special group of women called the "Gippettes," who are government employees. Their male counterparts, the "GIP" (*groupements d'intervention polynésiens*), provide security around Papeete's public properties.

Drinking Laws

Beer, wine and all other alcoholic beverages are sold in the larger supermarkets and magasins in Tahiti and most of the outer islands. However, laws have been imposed restricting the sale of alcoholic beverages in some areas after 5pm Monday through Saturday and all day on Sundays and holidays. You can buy beer and booze on Sunday mornings before 10am in some of the shops and in others not at all. This law is still in effect in Tahiti's commune of Faa'a, where the Sheraton Hotel Tahiti and InterContinental Resort Tahiti are located. In the commune of Mahina, on Tahiti's northeast coast, the stores cannot sell cold beer at all, but you can buy beer to take home and chill. If you are staying in an area where the restrictions still apply, then be sure to do your shopping before 5pm and before Sunday. If you forget, you can still drink at your hotel bar or in restaurants, of course. The legal age for buying alcohol is 18 years.

&

Tahitian Feasts

Several hotels and individually owned restaurants in Tahiti and the other tourist islands feature regular Tahitian feasts. The *tamaara'a* (tah-mah-AH-rah-ah) is Tahiti's equivalent to the luau served in Hawaii, only much more authentic. This feast features *maa Tahiti* (MAH-ah), foods that are cooked for several hours in an underground *ahima'a* (ah-HEE-mah-ah) oven. These usually include roast pig, *taro* root, *tarua* root, breadfruit, yams, bananas, *fei* (fey-ee) plantains, *fafa* (taro leaves cooked with chicken and coconut milk that tastes like spinach), and accompanied by coconut sauces. Dessert is a gooey pudding called *po'e*, (PO-eh), which is made with bananas, papaya, pumpkin or other fruits and flavored with coconut milk.

The national dish of Tahiti is *ei'a ota* (ee-ah OH-ta), which the French call *poisson cru*. It's made with small cubes of fresh tuna or bonito fish that have been marinated in lime juice and mixed with chopped tomatoes, grated carrots, thinly sliced onions and cucumbers and coconut milk. It's delicious and even better with a French *baguette*. If you have an adventurous palate then you'll want to try *fafaru*, slices of fish marinated in a stinky sauce that most Tahitians just adore. The traditional manner of eating *maa Tahiti* is with your fingers, although forks are normally supplied. Most hotel restaurants also serve a buffet of Continental foods along with the Tahitian dishes. In hotels the *tamaara'a* is normally accompanied by Tahitian music and an hour-long folkloric dance show. The colorfully costumed entertainers perform the traditional dances of Tahiti and the musicians play exciting music on their drums, guitars and ukuleles. The dancers may even invite you to dance the *tamure*.

Meals for the Health-Conscious, Vegetarians, & Vegans

Tahiti is not a paradise for dieters or vegetarians, and even less so for vegans. Most of the restaurants serve rich dishes made with real butter, knowing that few people go out to diet. It is difficult to get a piece of grilled fish or steak without having a generous serving of parsley butter on the top. French chefs are also very partial to crême fraiche, a thickened fresh cream that is served on most meals you order in a French restaurant. Vegetarians probably won't mind this unless they are pure vegans. Lagoon fish and prawns are sometimes served with the heads intact, so if you're squeamish about having your dinner looking at you, order a fish filet or something else. Vegetarians usually have a choice of rice, potatoes, carrots, green beans and salads, plus fresh fruits, French cheeses and tempting desserts. A few restaurants do have vegetarian plates and sandwiches. These are indicated in the *Where to Eat* section of each island.

Health conscious visitors will find whole grains, breads, cereals, crackers, dried legumes, nuts and fruits at La Vie Pacifique, a health food store located on rue Jean Gilbert in the Quartier du Commerce in downtown Papeete. They also carry vitamins, soya milk and vegetable juices. Another source for these items is at La Vie et Sante, *Tel. 50.82.56*, a health food shop operated by the Seventh Day Adventist Church, located on Cours de l'Union Sacrée in Fautaua. Take Avenue Prince Hinoi from downtown Papeete towards Pirae and turn right at the Seventh Day Adventist Church. Most of their products come from France and New Zealand. The large supermarkets in Tahiti, such as Carrefour in Punaauia and Arue, Champion in Papeete and Hyper U in Pirae, carry a line of health food products, including soya milk and tofu. You can buy fresh tofu, as well as fresh fruits, vegetables and herbs, at Le Marché, the public market in the center of Papeete.

On Moorea you can usually find soya milk and tofu at Champion Fare Toa in Afareaitu and at Supermarché Are in Pao Pao. Champion Fare Toa has a special organic (bio) section that contains a small selection of Swedish (Björg) products of whole grain pastas, breads, cereals, galettes, lentils, soup, bouillon, herbal salt and a few bottled or packaged sauces with low sodium and sugar. I even found polenta there, but never have I found corn meal in these islands, except at Supermarché Cecile (years ago) and at the Adventist store. Most of the supermarkets on Moorea carry fresh and dried fruits and nuts, fresh vegetables and supplies for spring rolls. I also checked the supermarkets in Bora Bora and Raiatea and found that they had long life soya milk and tofu on the shelves. Most of the supermarkets have yogurt, including the low sugar and added bifidus Nature yogurt by Yoplait.

If you have lodgings with access to a kitchen, you should have no problems finding enough nutritious food to eat while visiting Tahiti and Her Islands. Otherwise, you'll have to pick and choose carefully from the hotel menu, or have a heart to heart talk with the chef de cuisine.

Chapter 12

BEST PLACES TO STAY

Hotel Bora Bora

Point Raititi in Bora Bora. Tel. (689) 60.44.60, Fax (689) 60.44.66; Reservations Tel. (689) 60.44.11, Fax (689) 60.44.22, US & Canada Bookings toll free at (800) 421-1490, E-mail: reservations@hotelborabora.pf; www.hotelborabora@aol.com. Year round (EP) Rack Rates between $700 and $1.000 per double bungalow per night (EP). Special Honeymoon Packages Available.

You will be greeted with a glass of champagne as soon as you arrive at the Hotel Bora Bora boat dock on board their private launch, and you will be treated as a very special guest throughout your stay. The management and staff know the meaning of personalized service and this is what you will receive.

The Hotel Bora Bora is my favorite hotel anywhere in the world. This establishment is to the hotel industry what the QE 2 is to the cruise ship business: it has stately, royal class and the comfort of a privileged country club. The Hotel Bora Bora is as solid to me as the Otemanu Mountain that rises from the heart of the island behind the hotel.

Since it's opening in June 1961, the Hotel Bora Bora has frequently been rated in guidebooks as one of the world's top resort hotels and has been a member of the prestigious Amanresorts since 1988. This luxurious resort has attracted some of the world's most discriminating travelers and it is a favored destination for stars of the cinema, television and stage, plus several leaders in politics and business. Many of these personalities return again and again, where they can still find the magical charm that entranced them during their first visit. Often these repeat visitors celebrate their special wedding anniversaries in the same bungalow where they spent their first honeymoon. Some of them have given the name of the bungalow to their babies, who were conceived while the parents were spending their honeymoon at the Hotel Bora Bora. And several of these children come to this hotel years later for their own honeymoons.

Seventeen acres of luxuriant tropical flowers and exotic foliage border three lovely beaches of fine white sand. Sea birds nest in the fronds of the towering coconut palms and the surf tenderly laps the shore. The vast sparkling lagoon of Bora Bora is a tableau of at least seven shades of blue and green. The coral gardens are one of the hotel's best attributes. The hotel management encourages the guests to feed the fish in the lagoon, and there are hundreds of tropical fish of every hue, including the graceful manta rays, who perform their ballet nightly next to the boat dock and below the steps of the overwater bungalows.

Amidst this exclusive setting on the peninsula of Point Raititi, the Hotel Bora Bora offers 50 individual guest bungalows. Eighteen superior bungalows are located on the palm-studded beachfront, offering a spacious bedroom, bathroom and sitting area leading to a small patio facing the sea. Each bungalow has a hammock nearby, where you can enjoy the beach and sea breeze. Fifteen overwater bungalows are situated on the fringing reef section of the lagoon surrounded by a wealth of marine life. Each of the luxurious units features a spacious bedroom with a king-size four-poster bed, a bathroom with a venetian blind indoor panel and a sundeck terrace with a pandanus shade that overhangs the top level and a shower at the water level next to the steps set into the lagoon.

A newer category of accommodation at the Hotel Bora Bora offers *fares* or villas, a Tahitian term for home. All *fares* are 1,200 square feet (117m) with a living room, bedroom with a king-size four-poster bed, en suite sitting room, bathroom and large sundeck. Five premium *fares* (numbers 3, 6, 21, 27 and 29) are situated in prime beach locations on the Matira - South side of the resort. Twelve pool *fares* are surrounded by a rock garden wall for added privacy, enclosing a small plunge pool and outdoor sun pavilion.

All the spacious bungalows are built in the Polynesian style with hand-tied thatched pandanus roofs, ceiling fans and natural woods. The decor is neutral with plenty of natural light, drawing the vivid colors of the lagoon and gardens into every room. All accommodations have freestanding bathtubs and separate showers, hair-dryers, private bars, coffee and tea facilities, telephones, radio/cassette players, personal safes and dual 110/220 voltages. The king size mattresses make you feel like you are indeed floating on air and are the most comfortable of any hotel bed in Bora Bora. Well, perhaps the beds at the Bora Bora Nui could tie for that credit. But the Hotel Bora Bora definitely has my vote for their bathroom amenities. Instead of placing plastic bottles of shampoo, conditioner, lotion, and etcetera in your bathroom, they present their specially selected products in attractive glass flacons. They have even added a light monoi oil, which is difficult to find.

The main building of the Hotel Bora Bora is located on a bluff overlooking Point Raititi. From the Matira Terrace Restaurant you can watch the hotel's outrigger sailing canoe skimming across the lagoon while you enjoy a bountiful breakfast buffet. The French *chef de cuisine* ensures that the menu upholds the reputation of the hotel, and each dinner is a gourmet's treat. The Pofai Beach Bar is ideal for light lunches while you're relaxing on the beach.

High-tide Tea is served on the beach late in the afternoon, flavored with fresh vanilla beans from the island of Tahaa, and accompanied by banana or coconut cookies. My favorite place to watch the sunset behind the island of Maupiti is from the Matira Terrace Bar, where colorful cocktails are accompanied by Polynesian musicians playing some of the romantic songs of the island.

The reception area, guest relations and activities desks, and the Puiaia boutique are located in the main building. Sibani Perles presents the Nilo collection of fine jewelry in a separate bungalow on the hotel's premises, and another bungalow is used for massages, body and beauty treatments. The hotel's two complimentary tennis courts, basketball court and volleyball court are located across the road.

Fare Raititi game room is set up for billiards and you'll also find a paperback book exchange, video and television with international broadcasts. Other free of charge activities include snorkeling, outrigger paddle and sailing canoes and a twice-daily shuttle bus service to Vaitape village.

Paid activities include circle island tours, horseback riding, jeep safaris, parasailing, helicopter excursions, and a full range of nautical activities. See details under *Where to Stay* and the *Activities* sections in chapter on *Bora Bora*.

Honeymooners are welcomed at the Hotel Bora Bora as very special guests. A 3-night *Honeymoon Escape* includes a room and a variety of inclusive offerings and activities. Should you desire to exchange or reaffirm vows the hotel will arrange a *Polynesian Ceremony* on the beach at sunset. A *Marriage of Hearts Ceremony* includes a private two-hour sunset sail aboard a catamaran, a non-binding sentimental ceremony performed during the cruise in Tahitian and English by the captain, fragrant flower leis, and champagne and canapés. Contact the hotel directly for details on these programs. When you return to the Hotel Bora Bora with your children, be assured that baby-sitting service is available.

Kia Ora Sauvage Rangiroa

Motu Avea Rahi is a private islet 25 miles or one hour by boat from Hotel Kia Ora in Rangiroa, Tel. (689) 93.11.17, Fax (689) 96.02.20; E-mail: resa@hotelkiaora.pf; www.hotelkiaora.com. Year round (EP) Rack Rates 40.000 CFP per double beach bungalow per night, Meal Plan with Breakfast,

Lunch & Dinner (AP) is 7.600 CFP per person, Round-trip Boat Transfers between Hotel Kia Ora and Motu Avea Rahi 10.000 CFP per person.

Do you harbor secret dreams of escaping to a desert isle, far, far away, and living the simple life—a modern version of Robinson Crusoe's experience? Are you looking for a little haven of peace, where you can fish for your dinner, breathe pure sweet air, sunbathe *au naturel*, listen to the thunder of the surf on the reef, and gaze at the Southern Cross or an enormous full moon?

Kia Ora Sauvage (KOS) is lost from the big world and all its problems. You have to go a little further these days to find a paradise of peace and tranquility. First you have to fly to Tahiti, then to Rangiroa, and then take an hour's boat ride across the lagoon to get there. But it's definitely worth the trip.

Five little thatched roof bungalows are located on the white sand beach of a 4-hectare (9.88-acre) islet named Motu Avae Rahi, which means "isle of the big moon." I've stayed here four times during the full moon, and during my second trip, in April 1997, all the guests stood on the beach under the enormous bowl of the sky and gazed at the huge full moon, the Hale-Bopp comet, the Southern Cross and the other wonders of the celestial universe, while the manager gave us a lesson in astronomy.

Michel Chevalier has been one of the managers at Kia Ora Sauvage every other month since it opened. He is assisted by Tetuanui and Meme Potini, who cook fabulous meals, and by Moise and Kiri, who keep the grounds clean, catch fish and perform numerous other tasks. They are replaced by Bernard and Mahine and their team on a month-on, month-off basis. They all do a super job of taking care of their visitors in this miniature version of paradise, and the guest book sings their praises on every page.

Each of the five attractive and comfortable bungalows accommodates two or three people. The bedspreads on the king-size bed and single bed are made of fabric in a tapa cloth design. There is a writing desk with stool, bedside tables, mosquito nets over the bed and mosquito coils. A step-down bathroom has a coral floor, a tiled shower, now with hot water, and a huge clamshell lavabo. You can sit on your covered terrace and read or watch the small lagoon sharks swimming close to the white sand beach as they arrive for their twice-daily feeding when your hosts clean the fish for lunch and dinner.

In keeping with the *sauvage* or wild, natural theme, the hotel has no electricity. Two lighted petrol lamps are placed on your steps each evening, and you should also bring a small flashlight.

The manager makes twice-daily radio contact with the Hotel Kia Ora, to learn of new arrivals and to order food supplies and more ice for the rum punches and other drinks he'll prepare for you at the bar. He blows a *pu* (triton) shell to summons you to meals, which are served family style inside the restaurant or under the shade of Tiare Kahaia trees on the beach. Fresh lagoon fish and shellfish from the coral reef are daily fare, which are supplemented by creative salads, chicken and meat dishes.

You can work off the calories by paddling an outrigger canoe to a nearby *motu*. You can also go spear fishing with your host or accompany him to the fringing reef to collect *maoa* sea snails and *pahua* clams for dinner. You'll walk through incredible walls of crystallized coral that rise six feet above the sea. These miniature cathedrals are called *feo*, which are fossils that are said to be more than four million years old. Your host will also invite you to come along to explore *motu* islets that are even wilder than Kia Ora Sauvage. You are free to do whatever you want, or nothing at all. That's the whole idea of playing "cast-away."

Most visitors are already looking forward to coming back just as soon as they arrive at Kia Ora Sauvage. Some of them extend their stay because they have found the Robinson Crusoe deserted island of their childhood fantasies. One visitor wrote in the guest book: "KOS teaches us that electricity, wake-up calls, phones, television, etc., are not what's important. KOS is the family, the company, the food. It's reading a book in a hammock. It's the feeling that the most important thing you have to do is not getting to work on time, but catching the sunset."

Manihi Pearl Beach Resort

On Manihi atoll in the Tuamotu Archipelago, just an hour and 15 minutes by direct flight from Tahiti. Tel. (689) 96.42.73, Fax (689) 96.42.72, Fax 607/273-5302, E-mail: sales@spmhotels.pf; www.pearlresorts.com. Year round (EP) Rack Rates from 28.000 CFP per double beach bungalow per night and 60.000 CFP for a premium overwater bungalow. Honeymoon Packages are available. Meal Plan with Breakfast & Dinner (MAP) is 7.500 CFP per person, Meal Plan with Breakfast, Lunch and Dinner (AP) is 10.000 CFP per person.

Manihi is a world removed from time and care, a tiny green oasis floating in the desert of the sea, with a name as exotic as the trade winds and coconut trees, and a lagoon as pretty as a mother-of-pearl shell. Manihi Pearl Beach Resort is the only hotel on the atoll and it is one of the most beautiful and pleasant resort hotels you'll find anywhere.

Manihi Pearl Beach Resort was the first of a chain of eight deluxe Pearl Hotels to be built in French Polynesia. The 5 standard beach bungalows, 17 superior beach bungalows, 14 deluxe overwater bungalows and 5 premium overwater bungalows are located on the site of the former Kaina Village, a small hotel that opened in 1977 and was operated until the end of 1995 by Mareva and Guy Coquille, who still live on the same *motu* as the hotel.

I think that the overwater bungalows in this hotel are some of the most attractive of all the deluxe accommodations in French Polynesia. The roof is thatched pandanus fronds and the wooden walls are covered with matting of pandanus fibers. The soft blonde-beige hard wood furniture matches the golden tones of the split bamboo trim, and geometric Polynesian tattoo designs are carved into the wood between the wall and ceiling, around the full-length mirror and around the exterior base of the bungalow. The king size bed or two twin beds and day bed have neutral beige covers with accent cushions the color of the turquoise and emerald lagoon, which is visible from almost every angle of the bungalow.

The glass top coffee table that allows you to view the fish below your bungalow has become almost *de rigeur* in overwater bungalows, but the Manihi Pearl Beach Resort gives you additional fish watching possibilities with windows on two sides of a writing desk, where you'll also find a telephone and small lamp. Glass panels in the bathroom keep you in touch with what's happening in the lagoon at all times. A light can be turned on at night to attract the fish and you can even watch a family of blue, green, turquoise and red parrotfish nibbling their dinner while you're brushing your teeth after your own meal! A fish identification card is placed in the desk drawer of the overwater bungalows to help you recognize the various species of fish you're seeing.

The lagoon is always in view if you choose to open the shutters between the bathroom and bedroom. A triple sliding glass door leads to the terrace, with heavy blackout curtains for privacy and light beige sheers for diffused lighting. The railing of the terrace is made of decorative *miki miki* branches, fragrant bushes that grow on the coral shores of the atolls. Two *chaises longues* welcome sunbathers and lagoon gazers, and a curved stairway leads you down into the warm waters of liquid crystal.

There are two entrances to the 17 superior beach bungalows, which also have an indoor garden with a coral floor. You can spend hours lying in a hammock along the white sand beach. You can also walk across a shallow part of the lagoon to a small islet, where you can relax in a lounge chair and read your favorite beach book.

In addition to the fabulous bungalows at Manihi Pearl Beach Resort, I also like the big fresh water swimming pool between the white sand beach and the lagoon. The restaurant serves very good French cuisine and some local dishes. Activities are centered around the lagoon, with emphasis on scuba diving. The Manihi Blue Nui dive center is on the premises, offering exciting dives inside the lagoon, the pass and in the open ocean.

Because the Manihi Pearl Beach Resort is a small hotel, it is easy to get to know the employees and other guests. The feeling here is that of a small village, yet you still have all the privacy you desire.

InterContinental Resort Tahiti

Beside the lagoon at Point Tata'a on the border of Faaa and Punaauia, facing the island of Moorea. Tel. (689) 86.51.10, Fax (689) 86.51.30, E-mail: reservationspf@interconti.com; www.tahiti-interconti.com. Low Season (EP) Rack Rates from 31.370 CFP per double room per night and from 46.540 CFP per double bungalow per night, Meal Plan with Breakfast & Dinner (MAP) is

8.065 CFP per person, Meal Plan with Breakfast, Lunch & Dinner (AP) is 11.570 CFP per person. Special Honeymoon Packages Available.

This is Tahiti's "can-do" hotel, whose motto is "We know what it takes." The professional staff is very efficient and the management makes sure that your stay will be more than satisfactory. This is a favorite hotel for honeymooners, business people, incentive groups and individual travelers.

This hotel opened as a Travelodge in June 1974 and the name was changed to Beachcomber in 1979, when it became a member of the Southern Pacific Hotel Corporation (SPHC). The Parkroyal title was later added and the 5-star Beachcomber Parkroyal rose to an international dimension. In 2000 SPHC was taken over by Bass Hotels & Resorts, whose holdings of more than 3,200 hotels in 100 countries include the Inter-Continental hotels. In June 2001, all three of the Beachcomber Hotels (Tahiti, Moorea and Bora Bora) dropped the Parkroyal title when they became members of the prestigious Inter-Continental Resort chain. At the beginning of 2005 they will all drop the Beachcomber title and this hotel then be known as InterContinental Resort Tahiti.

The InterContinental Resort Tahiti has 170 recently renovated rooms in the original three-story buildings. These units overlook the gardens or lagoon, and offer a choice of king-size or twin beds, plus a sitting area and a private balcony or terrace. An extension of two more 3-story buildings added another 60 and a presidential suite in 1999, offering five-star spacious accommodations, with a panoramic view of the hotel grounds, the Lotus swimming pool, the lagoon and the island of Moorea across the Sea of Moons. The decor is tropical colonial, with bamboo, wood and wicker furniture, wooden floors, and a canopy and padded headboard for the bed. A shuttered window between the bedroom and bathroom can be opened if you want to gaze at the lagoon while soaking in the big oval bathtub. There is also a separate shower with two adjustable showerheads, and there are two lavabos of black marble.

All rooms and bungalows have adjustable air-conditioning, separate bathrooms with bathtubs and courtesy soaps, *monoi*, bath gel, shampoo, conditioner, body lotion, shaving set, toothbrush and lots of other amenities. Each room has blackout curtains, a stocked mini-bar, coffee and tea making facilities, personal safe, hair-dryer, make-up mirror, color television with cable, direct dial telephone, data line, twice-a-day maid service, and same-day laundry and dry-cleaning service. Three free laundromats are provided for your convenience. Room service is available round-the-clock.

The overwater bungalows are built in the Polynesian style, with thatched roofs and natural woods. In addition to the air-conditioning they also have a ceiling fan, screened windows and sliding glass doors, as well as private balconies and sun decks with steps leading into the lagoon. There are 17 deluxe overwater bungalows grouped around a private island, reached by a bridge from the main property. These are usually chosen by guests who enjoy swimming off their balcony. Fifteen beautifully appointed junior suites are built over the lagoon at the legendary Point Tata'a, which you can reach by the Beachcomber's *le truck* or electric cart or a leisurely stroll through the hotel gardens. The water is deeper here and the current is sometimes too choppy for good swimming. But these units provide the most intimacy. Imagine yourself reclining on a deck chair at night, drinking fine French champagne and gazing at the Southern stars from the privacy of your overwater balcony. On request, guests staying in the overwater bungalows can be served breakfast by outrigger canoe, for 5.940 CFP per person.

The latest addition to the hotel accommodations is the Bora Bora Villa, which is also built on the private motu. This prestige unit is a model of the 80 overwater villas that are being built for the InterContinental Resort & Spa Bora Bora, programmed to open in May 2006. There is a flat screen television with cable and DVD player in the living room and the separate bedroom, as well as a desk facing the lagoon in each room. The headboard of the king-size bed is wood with inlaid mother-of-pearl and all the modern style wooden furniture has the simple lines of Japanese or Indonesian decor. Satin sheets and pillows adorn the bed. An espresso coffee machine is provided in the living room, along with a selection of 9 coffees from Les Grands Crus de Nespresso. The large bathroom is equipped with a bathtub and separate shower stall with a rain shower nozzle overhead, and there are two separate his and hers lavabos, as well as an adjustable lighted makeup mirror. The spacious terrace is half covered and half solarium, complete with a table for romantic dinners for two or breakfast delivered by outrigger canoe. You can step down into the lagoon for a swim and have a shower on the way back up to the terrace, and there is also a fish-watching glass table in the living room that gives you a window into the lagoon.

In the reception area of the main building is a lobby with comfortable sofas and easy chairs. There are desks for guest activities, rental cars, excursions, and day trips to outer islands. Also on this level you'll find a duty free gift shop and newsstand, a Tahiti Pearls boutique, and function rooms that are used for conferences, seminars and art shows. One of the hotel's three bars is in the corner of the lobby, and is open from 11pm to 3am, serving drinks and snacks for late arrivals. You can take the elevators or the stairways to the ground level, where you will find the spacious Tiki Bar and open-air Tiare Restaurant, which has all-day dining. The air-conditioned Hibiscus Restaurant is on the second floor and is used for special occasions. Le Lotus Restaurant is built over the lagoon and offers the most romantic setting of any restaurant on the island, with a lovely view of Moorea.

The 30 acres of landscaped tropical gardens surrounding the hotel include a 1-mile jogging track and exercise area. Also provided free for guests are the use of snorkel gear, kayaks, volleyball, and petanque (French bowls), as well as tennis balls and rackets to play on two floodlit courts. Guests have free access to two large fresh water swimming pools, an outdoor Jacuzzi and two white sand beaches. At the Aquatica Nautical Pavilion on the hotel premises you join a free excursion to feed the Moray eels, or get a free boat transfer to sunbathe on the hotel's private pontoon within the reef-protected lagoon. You can also book a Dolphin cruise or a sunset cruise aboard the *Enjoy* sailing catamaran. Water sports include snorkeling safaris, jet-skiing, water-skiing and scuba diving.

Cultural activities may include a folkloric marketplace, demonstrations of Tahitian cuisine, tifaifai quilt making, pareo dyeing, basket weaving, and how to make leis from flowers and shells. Happy Hour is held in the Tiki Bar from 4:30-5:30pm every afternoon, and Thursday nights are especially lively, when Happy Hour is extended from 4:30-6:30pm and a very popular local musician entertains the crowds who come to meet their friends and enjoy the ambience. A Rotisserie Dinner with a Tahitian dance show is held in the Tiare Restaurant each Wednesday night. A *Soirée Merveilleuse* Seafood Buffet Extravaganza is held each Friday night, with a team of dancers and musicians performing a torch-lit show beside the pool. A Saturday night Bounty Dinner also includes a "Bounty" show presented by Les Grands Ballet de Tahiti, the island's best dance group.

Upcoming projects planned for InterContinental Resort Tahiti include building a marina, a spa, a museum and enlarging the parking lot.

This hotel receives my highest recommendation for your place to stay on the island of Tahiti. See more information under *Where to Stay, Where to Eat* and *Nautical Centers & Clubs* in the *Tahiti* chapter.

Sheraton Moorea Lagoon Resort & Spa

Beside the lagoon at PK 14 between Cook's Bay and Opunohu Bay on the island of Moorea. Tel. (689) 55.11.11; Fax (689) 55.11.55; US and Canada Bookings toll free at (800) 782-9488, E-mail: tahiti@sheraton.pf; www.sheratonsintahiti.com, www.sheraton.com. Low Season (High Season) EP Rack Rates between 32.400 CFP (36.000 CFP) and 80.100 CFP (89.000 CFP) single/double per night. Meal Plan with Breakfast & Dinner (MAP) is 7.217 CFP per person, Meal Plan with Breakfast, Lunch & Dinner (AP) is 10.189 CFP per person. Special Honeymoon Packages Available.

In the second edition of this book I wrote that I had watched this hotel going up, as it is close to the house where I live year-round on Moorea. I also wrote that guests staying here would have one of the most romantic views of the setting sun and rising full moon of any hotel site in Tahiti and Her Islands. I mentioned that I had taken an outrigger canoe ride beside the overwater units on the evening of the Harvest Moon in September and had watched the huge gold orange globe rise majestically from the sea, a scene that was absolutely spellbinding. That's a good enough reason for choosing to stay here, but there's a lot more to learn about this hotel, which is owned by a Chinese man from Tahiti. The general manager and his staff are French, and the rest of the employees are all Polynesian. Although the Sheraton is managed by an American company, there are no Americans working here on a full-time basis. Three or four students from Hawaii were sent to Moorea by Sheraton Hotels & Resorts in 2004 as part of their hotel training program, but their assignment lasted only three months. During that period the hotel guests were happy to have the help of English-speaking people at the guest relations desk.

The Sheraton Moorea Lagoon Resort & Spa opened in September 2000 on the site that was formerly occupied by the Moorea Lagoon, a hotel that closed in 1998. Soon after the opening of the new hotel I went to have a look at the finished product and to toast this accomplishment with a champagne cocktail at the main bar. Ever since that first sunset visit I have been back time and again (it's only two minutes away) to enjoy the magical sunsets from the end of one of the arms or piers that houses some of the overwater units. There are benches placed here for gazing at the sea and sky, and honeymooners meet other couples here with their champagne and cameras. They compare the positive and negative aspects of their bungalows and the hotel's amenities and services.

In January 2002 I stayed in one of the overwater bungalows for three nights during the full moon. I obviously have lots to say about the hotel, but the most significant comment is that I would like to move into bungalow 109 and stay there forever! It's a horizon overwater unit facing the sunset and the bungalow closest to the end of the pier. I was eating my room-service breakfast one morning in my air-conditioned room and listening to the American news on CNN when I looked out toward the overwater terrace and saw a vivid double rainbow arching over the lagoon, with one end touching the red roof of the Protestant Church in Papetoai village and the other end dipping into the blue Pacific ocean. That incredible sight instantly brought me back to the present, with a lovely reminder of why I live in Polynesia and why you will want to stay in this hotel. That night I watched the sunset and the moonrise in this romantic setting.

Most guests love the thatched roof Polynesian style hotel, which is located in 12 acres of very colorful tropical gardens, coconut palms and gnarled old tamanu trees, along a white sand beach. The 106 air-conditioned units consist of 52 garden and beach bungalows and 54 bungalows over the water. There are double bungalows for families, smoking and non-smoking rooms and units for handicapped guests in wheelchairs.

Upon arrival at the Sheraton Moorea Lagoon you will be greeted with a flower lei, a cold face cloth and a glass of fruit punch. After completing your registration one of the friendly Tahitian valets will drive you and your luggage to your room in an electric golf cart. If you have booked an overwater bungalow be prepared for a wonderful surprise when he opens the door of your room. The golden-orange walls provide a warm setting for the rich-grained wood furniture in this spacious bungalow. Your eyes are immediately drawn to the picture postcard scenery of the shimmering turquoise lagoon and velvet green mountains beyond your terrace. You have a feeling of being suspended in space above the water, which indeed you are. It's simply stunning!

All the bungalows are air-conditioned and also have a ceiling fan. The rooms contain a king-size bed or two double beds and there is a sofa bed and writing table. The furniture is made of local semi-precious woods, and includes tables and padded lounge chairs on the partially shaded terraces. The overwater bungalows have steps that let you shimmy down into the warm lagoon, which is about 4 feet deep, and there is an outdoor shower on a landing above the water. The overwater units also have a long glass floor and a glass table for fish watching, and you are guaranteed an interesting performance of jewel-colored fish in these coral-rich waters. Thousands of new fish and more coral were added to this area in 2004 and you'll find some of the best snorkeling on Moorea in the vicinity of the overwater bungalows.

The rooms also have electronic door locks, smoke detector, fire sprinkler system, blackout draperies, alarm clock/radio, 110/220 volt electrical outlets, computer data port, personal safe, mini bar, coffee/tea making facilities, remote control color television with CNN and other programs by satellite, CD players, international direct-dial telephone with a set in the bedroom and another beside the toilet. The hotel provides electric mosquito machines, which are certainly not needed in the overwater units. Guests staying in the overwater bungalows also have use of two sets of snorkeling gear and two robes, and an iron & board are in the closet. Twice daily maid service is provided and room service is available 24 hours a day. Next day laundry service is also available. A pillow menu in each room offers you a choice of wide, neck, heart, bongon, round, sleep body, TV pillow, diabolo, or goose down.

All the bathrooms have a claw-footed tub and a separate shower with degree controlled faucets, and a private toilet. There are also bidets in the overwater bathrooms. All units have an extendible lighted makeup mirror and full-length mirror and hair dryer. A nice selection of Sheraton soaps, shampoos, bath gel and other toiletries is replenished daily.

The resort's public buildings carry out the theme of Polynesian architecture with enormous thatched roofs, local woods, and shell lamps hanging from the ceiling. The gardens are carefully landscaped with basaltic boulders and huge hibiscus flowers of every hue. Walkways take you from the spacious reception area and activities desk past gardens of white ginger, ixora and other lush tropical plants. Waterfalls cascade into fern-rimmed pools where golden carp frolic and swim. Tahiti Perles jewelry shop displays chokers and earrings of high quality black pearls. Kaimana Boutique is a shopper's dream of tropical clothing, *tifaifai* wall hangings and unusual gift items.

At the end of this walk is a terrace overlooking the white sand beach and turquoise lagoon of diamonds dancing in the sun. You can sit here and sip a colorful cocktail ordered from a special drink menu from the Eimeo Bar. Marianne is the name of the pretty bartender, and she knows how to make a really good frozen Margarita, which is most unusual in these islands where a Maitai is the most popular cocktail. You can get two drinks for the price of one during the daily Happy Hour, which is held at sunset, between 6 and 7pm, while you listen to a Tahitian trio playing island favorites. Entertainment is also provided once a week by a French couple or other resident musicians. Most of the hotel guests watch the sunset from the terraces of their bungalows or from the end of the pier, or they are still snorkeling among the purple coral gardens and brightly painted fishes during this magical moment. Several diners eventually wander into the Arii Vahine restaurant across from the main bar. The musicians also change rooms and continue to sing their haunting songs from the Tuamotu Islands while the customers dine on French cuisine, which is surprisingly ample compared to the attractively presented but skimpy portions of *la nouvelle cuisine* that most upscale restaurants serve. A theme buffet is held on Tuesday night and a Seafood Buffet is featured each Saturday evening, and each of these special events is accompanied by a Polynesian dance show.

On the beach level is the Rotui Grill and Arearea Bar, between the beach and the infinity swimming pool. From 11:30am to 5pm you can order sandwiches, light meals and refreshing beverages. There is also a beach *fare* beside the pool, where you can get towels. You can even get the kinks of a long plane flight massaged out of your neck, shoulders and back while relaxing beside the pool. Mandara Spa has a special chair for this purpose and a staff of well-trained massage therapists who will work wonders on your aches and pains. Be sure to visit this haven of tranquility for an unforgettable indulgence in your own comfort. They're also on the beach level and are open daily from 8am to 8pm. You and your partner can even have a double massage performed under the light of the Polynesian moon.

Behind Mandara Spa is a business center, where you can log onto the Internet and check your E-mail. Bring along any books you've finished reading and make an exchange in the small library. Next door to Mandara Spa is a meeting/function room for conferences and banquets up to 100 people. Then you'll come to the Nautical Activities Center, where you can check out a kayak, outrigger paddle canoe or a pedal boat at no charge. Or you can sign up for boat excursions, picnics on the motu, a Dolphin Watch, shark and ray feeding and many more activities. Should you prefer, you can rent a boat you pilot yourself and order a picnic from the restaurant to take to the motu for a day's outing. Across the road from the hotel is a Fitness Center with Technogym equipment, two changing rooms, lockers and showers. There are also two lighted tennis courts that are open from 7:30am to 9pm and free to in-house guests.

Other services provided include short-term baggage storage, wrapping parcels, baby accessories, such as bottle warmers, high chair, crib and toiletries, as well as baby-sitting. You may also want to rent a video player recorder from the hotel's Guest Services to watch the tape filmed during your Tahitian wedding ceremony, a non-binding exchange of vows that can be performed at Moorea's Tiki Village. Should you prefer a legal wedding in Moorea, you will have to reside a minimum of four weeks in French Polynesia before the ceremony can be performed at City Hall. And if you decide on this course of events, then perhaps you'll be living in bungalow 109 instead of me!

An expansion project has been announced to add 22 suites over the lagoon, which the hotel owner and management hope to begin in November 2004 and complete in 2005. This extension is supposed to start from the overwater pier just beyond bungalow 109, where the honeymooners and other romantics like me go to sit and watch the sunset. When these new units are built I will no longer be able to see the sunset at all from the pier in front of my house, except by looking through the pilings of the bungalows built over the lagoon on stilts. Yet, when I go to the Sheraton to enjoy Marianne's two-for-one Margaritas and the sunset, the security guard at the gate asks me my name and the nature of my business, which he writes down in his report. The Sheraton Moorea Lagoon is the only hotel in French Polynesia where local residents are questioned before being allowed to enter the public property.

Chapter 13

TAHITI

Queen of the Pacific

Polynesian mythology tells of a lovely *vahine* named Terehe, who defied the gods of great Havai'i on the island of Raiatea by swimming in the river during a period of sacred restriction. The angry gods caused the young maiden to be overcome by a feeling of numbness and she sank to the bottom of the river and was swallowed by a giant eel. Terehe's spirit then possessed the eel, who thrashed about, tearing away the earth between Raiatea and Tahaa. The eel's body was magically transformed into a fish, which swam away from Havai'i toward the East. Tu-rahu-nui, artisan of Ta'aroa, the supreme god, guided the fish in its course, and the warrior Tafai used a powerful ax to cut the sinews of the fish, to stabilize the new land. Thus were formed lofty mountain ranges, winding gulfs, an isthmus, bluffs and caves. The insouciant soul of Terehe lives today in this transplanted land called **Tahiti**.

Tahiti Nui Mare'are'a, Great Tahiti of the Golden Haze, the Polynesians sang. This is Tahiti of many shaded waters; various are the songs of the birds. Great Tahiti, the mounting place of the sun. The Tahitian people of old had to boast, because the people of Raiatea, the sacred island of Havai'i, regarded Tahiti as a plebeian island with no gods.

When the Europeans discovered Tahiti, beginning with the arrival of English Captain Samuel Wallis in 1767, followed by Frenchman de Bougainville, Captain James Cook, Captain Bligh and the famous *Bounty* crew, they too shouted the praises of this seductive island, where dreams are lived. Explorers, artists, writers and poets, sea-weary sailors and beachcombers of all makes spread the word. The myth of Tahiti as an earthly paradise was born.

Throughout the years Tahiti has become known as the Land of the Double Rainbows, the Romantic Isle, Beloved Island, Isle of Illusion, Island of Love, the

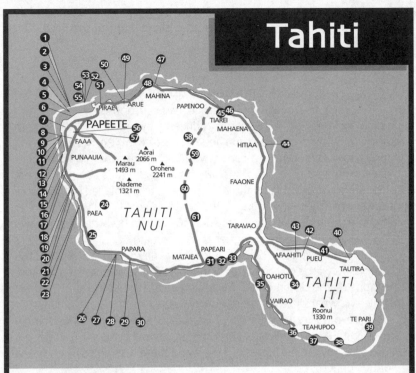

Tahiti

1. Public Market
2. Vaima Center
3. Tahiti Pearl Museum
4. Mahina Tea
5. Chez Myrna
6. Sheraton Hotel Tahiti
7. Tahiti-Faa'a International Airport
8. Chez Lola
9. Pension Damyr
10. Tahiti Airport Lodge
11. InterContinental Resort Tahiti
12. Hotel Sofitel Maeva Beach
13. Ia Orana Villa
14. Lagoonarium
15. Museum of Tahiti
16. Le Meridien
17. Pension de la Plage
18. Chez Armelle
19. Pension Otaha
20. Taaroa Lodge
21. Relais Fenua
22. Pension Te Miti
23. Marae Arahurahu
24. Maraa Grottos
25. Hiti Moana Villa
26. Papara Village
27. Fare Ratere
28. Papara Surfing Beach
29. Atimaono Golf Course
30. Matoa Gardens
31. Vaipahi Gardens & Waterfall
32. Gauguin Museum
33. Botanical Gardens
34. Taravao Plateau
35. Pension Chayan
36. Tauhanihani Village
37. Teahupoo Surfing Site
38. Te Pari Village
39. Pension Bonjour
40. Captain Cook's Anchorage
41. Pueu Village
42. Punatea Village
43. Fare Maithe
44. Bougainville's Anchorage
45. Fa'arumai Waterfalls
46. Blowhole
47. Point Venus
48. Tahara'a Lookout
49. Radisson Plaza Resort
50. James Norman Hall House & Library
51. Hotel Royal Tahitien
52. Mamao Hospital
53. Pension Puea
54. Hotel Royal Papeete
55. Hotel Prince Hinoi
56. Hotel Le Mandarin
57. Hotel Tiare Tahiti
58. Papenoo Valley
59. Fare Hape site
60. Relais de la Maroto
61. Lake Vaihiria

Amorous Isle and the World's Most Glamorous Tropic Isle. Tahiti, the living Spirit of Terehe, is hailed as the most famous island in the South Seas—Queen of the Pacific.

A Tahitian Prophecy

The ancient Tahitian seer named Pau'e prophesied: "There are coming children of the glorious princess, by a canoe without an outrigger, who are covered from head to foot." **King Pomare I**, hearing him say so, inquired how a canoe without an outrigger could hold its balance and not upset; so to illustrate his subject, Pau'e took an 'umete (wooden trough) and set it afloat with a few stones placed in it in a pool of water close by; then turning to the King he said: "What will upset that 'umete without an outrigger. It is balanced by its breadth, and so also is the canoe without an outrigger that is coming."

Pau'e also said: "There will come a new king to whom this government will be given, and new manners will be adopted in this land; the tapa and the cloth-beating mallet will go out of use in Tahiti, and the people will wear different, foreign clothes."

Three days afterwards Pau'e died, and a little later the Dolphin arrived with Captain Wallis, when the people exclaimed: "There is the canoe without the outrigger of Pau'e, and there are the children of the glorious princess!"

When the Dolphin coasted the Taiarapu peninsula of Tahiti Iti, the natives approached the ship, headed by a man who held up a banana shoot, which to them was an effigy of their own persons, and after a welcome speech, he dropped it into the sea, signifying that their intentions were friendly and that the sea was sacred to all, for the Tahitians regarded it as a great moving marae or temple.

— Extract from *Ancient Tahiti* by Teuira Henry

Arrivals & Departures
Arriving By Air

If you are flying from a cold country to Tahiti, then make sure you can take off heavy garments once you arrive here, especially if you are continuing on to Moorea, Bora Bora or any of the other outer islands. You'll probably arrive in the cooler hours of the dawn, but once the sun rises you'll be sweltering in sweaters, woolens and polyesters. So layer your traveling clothes.

If you are on a package tour you will be met inside the baggage room or immediately outside the Customs area of the **International Airport of Tahiti-Faaa**. The tour operators hold signs listing the names of their arriving guests.

Banque de Polynésie has a currency exchange booth in the baggage area, and another branch with an ATM machine in the main terminal, and Banque Socredo has an ATM and currency exchange machine in the terminal. If you need to make a phone call, book a room or continuing flight, rent a car, pick up a map, post a letter, go to the restroom, eat or drink, shop for a gift or check your E-mail, you can do it all inside the modern airport terminal.

The airport is located at PK 5.5 (3.4 miles), west of downtown Papeete. A taxi ride between 8pm and 6am will cost you 2.500 CFP to go downtown, and 1.500 CFP to go to the InterContinental Resort Tahiti, Sofitel Maeva Beach and any hostels and guest houses that are on the west coast in the vicinity of the airport, except for Le Méridien, which is 3.500 CFP at night. The taxi driver will also charge you 100 CFP for each large bag, 50 CFP for small bags and more for extra heavy bags. If you arrive in the daytime and want to save money, you can walk out to the main road and catch *le truck*. When you leave the airport you'll turn right on the main road (Route 1) to go to the west coast hotels and turn left to go downtown and to the east coast. You have a choice of the old coastal route or the freeway, (Route 5), which is called the RDO. You'll see the freeway entry almost in front of the airport.

If you are flying to Moorea you can push your baggage cart to the Moorea terminal, which is to the left of the main terminal. Just follow the signs. The first flight to Moorea is at 6am. If you are flying to any of the other outer islands the Air Tahiti counter is at the extreme right of the main terminal when you come out of the Customs area. A baggage storage room next to the flower/shell stands is open daily from 5am to 12:30am, except for Monday night, when they close at 7pm because there are no flights that evening. On Sunday they close between 12-1:30pm for lunch. Storage rates are 395 CFP for each small bag, 640 CFP for medium bags and 755 CFP for big bags, for a maximum of 24 hours. The hotels have a baggage storage room, which is free for their guests.

Arriving By Boat

If you arrive in Tahiti on board a passenger cruise ship you will disembark at the **Quai d'Honneur**, the visitor's dock in downtown Papeete. A currency exchange office is located in the building adjacent to the Tahiti Manava Visitors Bureau at the quay. Tour buses, taxis, guides and tourism representatives meet each ship's arrival, and a Tahitian dance show is often performed for the visitors. A covered reception area with public restrooms and telephones has been built adjacent to the Visitors Bureau for the convenience of ship passengers.

Before arriving in the port of Papeete by yacht you must notify the port authorities via channel 12 of HF 26 or 38 Khz of your arrival. You can anchor at the quay or beside the beach close to the Protestant church, and you are supposed to check in with Immigration as soon as possible. If you arrive on a

Friday afternoon then you'll have to wait until Monday morning before checking in, as offices for Immigration, Customs and the Harbormaster are all closed on weekends and holidays. Their offices are all in the same building beside the Quai d'Honneur, to the far right of Tahiti Manava Visitor's Bureau when approaching from the harbor side.

The Harbormaster's office, *Tel. 50.54.51*, is open Monday to Thursday from 7 to 11:30am and from 12:30 to 4pm, and on Friday to 3pm. The office hours for Immigration, *Tel. 43.94.90*, are Monday to Friday from 7:30am to 12am and from 2 to 5pm. The Customs office, *Tel. 42.01.22*, is open Monday to Thursday from 7am to 2:45pm, and on Friday from 7am to 1:30pm.

You will have to complete a Port Documentation form at the Port Captain's office, *Tel. 50.54.62*. This paper contains information for boats that are entering, moving or leaving the port. It also includes port fees if you want to tie up at the yacht quay along the waterfront. These charges are 288 CFP per day for electricity, 100 CFP per day or 2.000 CFP per month for water, a one-time fee of 1.000 CFP for garbage pick-up and 120 CFP francs a day per meter length of your boat for wharfage fees. Boats are no longer allowed to anchor in Papeete Harbor.

Anchorages are available at the Yacht Club in Arue, at the Marina Taina in Punaauia, and at the Tahiti Nautic Center at Port Phaeton in Taravao. Yachts are no longer allowed to anchor at Maeva Beach. This practice is tolerated by the harbormaster only during a four-month period each May through August, in the height of the cruising season. Each crewmember is required to have a return air ticket or pay a repatriation bond to your home country. See more information in Chapter 6, *Planning Your Trip*.

Departing By Air

You should reconfirm your international flight no later than 72 hours before your departure date. Check-in time for departing international flights is 3 hours prior to departure. You can exchange your francs for dollars at the Banque Socredo or Banque de Polynésie offices inside the terminal. Once you pass Immigration and go into the international departure lounge, you will find a few duty free shops that sell cigarettes, liquors, French perfumes, Tahitian music, black pearls and various gift items.

Departing By Boat

The cruise ship company or travel agency that arranges your cruise will give you details of what you will do when you arrive in Tahiti to board a passenger ship. Groups are met at the airport and transferred to a hotel until time to board the ship, when they will be transferred by boat to the Quai d'Honneur in Papeete, where the ship is moored.

If you are departing by private yacht you must advise the Immigration office in Papeete of your final departure, and the Police Air Frontière (PAF) who run this office will issue a release from the bond that you were required to post upon arrival. This document must be presented to the *gendarmes* on the last island you visit before leaving French Polynesia, and your bond will be refunded.

Orientation

Tahiti is located in the Windward Islands of the Society archipelago of French Polynesia. This is the largest of the 118 islands and atolls, with a population of around 170,000 people living in 12 *communes* on Tahiti Nui (big Tahiti) and Tahiti Iti (little Tahiti), also known as the Taiarapu peninsula.

Tahiti Nui and **Tahiti Iti** are shaped as a turtle, a lady's hand mirror or a reclining figure 8. Geologists say that these two majestic green islands emerged from the sea in separate volcanic births millions of years apart. Comprising a total of 1,042 square km. (402 square miles) of land, Tahiti Nui and Tahiti Iti are joined by the narrow isthmus of **Taravao**, 60 kilometers (37 miles) from the noise of **Papeete** by the south coast and 54 kilometers (34 miles) by the north coast.

The circle island tour around the coastal road of Tahiti Nui is 114 kilometers (71 miles). Away from the metropolitan area close to Papeete the paved roads are two lanes, with very few straight stretches, and there are usually no streetlights and very few guardrails at the edge of the seaside cliffs. The east coast is less developed, with numerous waterfalls and deep verdant valleys, modest homes and beautiful flower gardens beside the road. Here you will find the golden-brown sands of the volcanic beaches and cool streams ferrying tiny boats of flower blossoms to the sea. A fringing reef borders the shoreline in a few places, but most of the coast is battered by the waves of the frequently turbulent open ocean.

The west coast is much more congested, with houses and traffic, and high fences around the luxurious homes that often conceal ocean views to the motorists. A few white sand beaches border the shoreline and the shimmering turquoise lagoon is protected by a coral reef. Beyond the reef, across the Sea of Moons, is the island of Moorea.

Tahiti Iti has 18 kilometers (11 miles) of paved road on the eastern and western coasts and a 7-kilometer (4 mile) interior road that leads past dairy farms and citrus groves to a panoramic view of the Plateau of Taravao. Beyond the road's end of the peninsula's southern tip lies the *fenua 'aihere*, the magnificent bush land, and the steep sea cliffs known as Te Pari. You can explore this coast by boat or hike across the rivers and volcanic bluffs.

PAPEETE

The busy, bustling town of **Papeete**, on Tahiti's north coast, is the capital of French Polynesia. This is the administrative center for the 245,516 people (census of November 2002) who live in the five archipelagoes that comprise this French Overseas Country.

Papeete (Pah-pay-eh-tay) is a Tahitian word meaning «a basket of water». The town is spread along the waterfront on Tahiti's north coast, 5 kilometers (3 miles) east of the airport, facing the island of Moorea across the Sea of Moons. Papeete harbor is an international port, as well as home base for the *Paul Gauguin* cruise ship, the *Aranui 3* and other inter-island ships, copra freighters, fishing boats, ferries and a small fleet of French naval ships.

Among the winding streets of Papeete and its environs you will find the government operated medical center and hospital, two private clinics, pharmacies, French and Tahitian government offices, tribunal courts, *gendarmerie*, municipal police, port authorities and post office with international communications. Services also include the tourist bureau, banks, airline offices, shipping and travel agencies, television and radio stations, newspapers in French, English and Tahitian, hotel and technical schools, lycée and university, cathedrals and temples, sports centers and stadiums, health clubs and gyms, a cultural center, museums, art galleries, movie theaters, shopping centers, boutiques, crafts centers and a public market.

Tahiti's former government, who lost their majority during the 2004 elections, then won it back four months later, has taken some definitive steps in improving the public facilities in the capital of Papeete, with changes being made at an incredible pace for life in the tropics. Starting in 1999 a third traffic lane was added to ease the flow of cars, le trucks and other heavy-duty diesel-engine vehicles, along with the numbers of scooters and motorcycles that are constantly darting in and out among the cars. Roundabout traffic circles were created to eliminate the traffic lights, thereby helping to reduce the bottleneck backups. Pedestrian crossings were added, but you still have to be very careful when crossing the street in front of oncoming cars and scooters, as some drivers never heard of right-of-way.

The yacht quay along the waterfront street of Boulevard Pomare was rebuilt and now has an attractive boardwalk. Planters of colorful bougainvillea, benches, street lamps and discreetly hidden garbage cans are welcome changes for the international yachts that tie up to the wharf. The sidewalk around Temarii a Teai Square, adjacent to the Tahiti Manava Visitors Bureau in Fare Manihini, was also paved in the same Bomanite design as the yacht quay. This is a popular meeting place for strollers who want to sit in the sun or shade, smell the briny air and feel the breezes as they watch the activity along the waterfront from a quieter distance. You may also see a few street people hanging out here, lounging on the benches and drying their laundry on nearby bushes. Bougainville Park, beside the main post office, was also redone, providing a very pleasant place for adolescents to meet for after-school munching, giggling, smoking and smooching in the park. This is the only green space open to the public besides the gardens of the Papeete town hall.

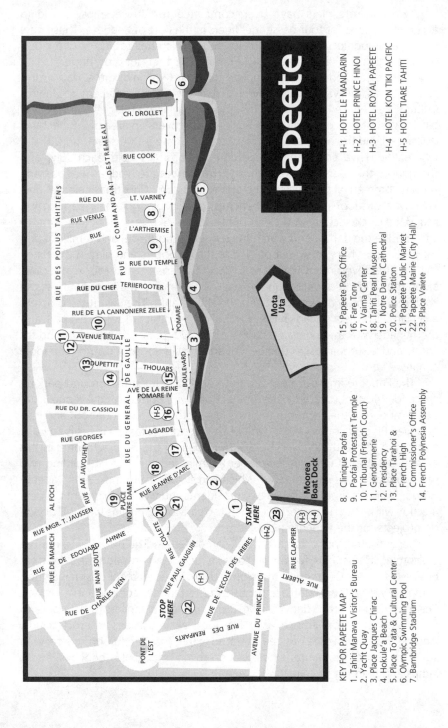

Papeete

Mota Uta

Moorea Boat Dock

CH. DROLLET

RUE COOK

LT. VARNEY

L'ARTHEMISE

RUE DU TEMPLE

TERIIEROOTER

RUE DE LA CANNONIERE ZELEE

RUE DU CHEF

RUE DU COMMANDANT DESTREMEAU

RUE DES POILUS TAHITIENS

RUE DU

RUE VENUS

RUE

AVENUE BRUAT

DUPETTIT

THOUARS

DE GAULLE

AVE DE LA REINE POMARE IV

POMARE

BOULEVARD

RUE DU DR. CASSIOU

LAGARDE

RUE GEORGES

RUE DU GENERAL

RUE AM JAVOUHEY

AL FOCH

RUE MGR. T. JAUSSEN

RUE DE EDOUARD AHNNE

RUE DE MARECH

RUE NAN SOUTPD

RUE VIEN

RUE DE CHARLES

RUE JEANNE D'ARC

PLACE NOTRE DAME

RUE COLLETTE

RUE PAUL GAUGUIN

RUE DE L'ECOLE DES FRERES

RUE DES REMPARTS

AVENUE DU PRINCE HINOI

RUE CLAPPIER

RUE ALBERT

PONT DE L'EST

START HERE

STOP HERE

KEY FOR PAPEETE MAP

1. Tahiti Manava Visitor's Bureau
2. Yacht Quay
3. Place Jacques Chirac
4. Hokule'a Beach
5. Place To'ata & Cultural Center
6. Olympic Swimming Pool
7. Bambridge Stadium

8. Clinique Paofai
9. Paofai Protestant Temple
10. Tribunal (French Court)
11. Gendarmerie
12. Presidency
13. Place Tarahoi & French High Commissioner's Office
14. French Polynesia Assembly

15. Papeete Post Office
16. Fare Tony
17. Vaima Center
18. Tahiti Pearl Museum
19. Notre Dame Cathedral
20. Police Station
21. Papeete Public Market
22. Papeete Mairie (City Hall)
23. Place Vaiete

H-1 HOTEL LE MANDARIN
H-2 HOTEL PRINCE HINOI
H-3 HOTEL ROYAL PAPEETE
H-4 HOTEL KON TIKI PACIFIC
H-5 HOTEL TIARE TAHITI

Two concrete piers have been completed for cruise ships, providing accommodations for four passenger liners in the Port of Papeete. These new piers are in addition to the Quai d'Honneur, which has room for two cruise ships or one luxury liner that is 240 meters (787 feet) long or longer.

Work is still underway to complete the boardwalk along the waterfront, extending all the way to the Olympic swimming pool adjacent to Tahiti's Cultural Center (Te Fare Tauhiti Nui) and Tahua To'ata (Place To'ata), a few blocks west of the center of town. Place To'ata covers an area of 2.5 hectares (6.2 acres) and the amphitheater can accommodate 3,000 spectators. This is where the Heiva song and dance competitions are held each July, and throughout the year song and dance performances are held, as well as trade shows, commercial fairs, arts and crafts exhibits and Christmas celebrations. There are outdoor restaurants, benches, public telephones, a parking lot, round-the-clock security and clean public toilets. Sweethearts come here to stroll beside the harbor and watch the sunset or moonrise, and families bring their little ones here to skate board, ride their scooters and play in the tangy salt air. The government has plans to build two snacks and four restaurants along the renovated waterfront, as well as continuing the boardwalk all the way from the ferry dock to the Sheraton Hotel Tahiti. They want to complete a big landfill project on which they can build a 5-hectare (12.3 acres) park and promenade with three green sections, plant 500 trees, add a playground for sports and leisure, a suspended beach, and installations for outrigger paddle canoes.

The Papeete improvement program also includes underground parking space for 240 cars, located in the area of Boulevard Pomare and Avenue Bruat at the far end of the yacht quay. This is just in front of a roundabout and is to be called Place Jacques Chirac. One of the President Flosse's ideas is to build a museum above the ground here. After opening the Bounty Tunnel in this area in October 2002, the government eliminated the idea of building two more tunnels in the Papeete area, which had included a tunnel under Papeete Harbor. At press time, Tahiti has two presidents and two governments. A new election will be held in early 2005, so it is too early to determine who will decide on projects for the Papeete waterfront.

Several other projects have been completed and help to create a more welcoming atmosphere for visitors to Papeete. A few years ago the side street beside the Vaima Center was transformed into an open-air pedestrian center, complete with sidewalk cafés and musical entertainment on special occasions. This may include samba dancers from Brazil, flamenco dancers from Spain and can-can dancers from France, as well as local jazz musicians and rock bands. Another pedestrian area has been created in the Quartier du Commerce, with street paving of Bomanite concrete resembling bricks, plus benches, street lamps and planters of colorful flowers.

Place Vaiete (Tahua Vaiete, adjacent to the passenger ship dock), has been transformed into an attractive modern square, with benches, a waterfall, public toilets that are kept open and very clean 24 hours a day and round-the-clock security guards. About sunset time every day a maximum of 30 *roulottes* arrive to set up their tables and chairs or high stools for the evening. Some of these mobile dining vans are still cooking steak-frites, grilled fish and bro-chettes of lamb hearts when the nightclubs and bars close at 2-3am. Free concerts draw the crowds to the bandstand in Vaiete Square on weekends and holidays. This is a pleasant, clean and safe place to bring the family and spend the evening.

The sidewalks along Boulevard Pomare, which were formerly broken and even dangerous, have been redone. On the waterfront side they are generally safer, although there is still a hole here and there that you must watch out for so that you don't sprain an ankle. On the town side of Boulevard Pomare trash pick-up still needs improvement, and people still litter the streets and sidewalks while they're walking around near the market or waiting for *le truck* or *le bus* just across the street from the Tahiti Manava Visitors Bureau.

The crime rate for purse snatching and other petty thefts has been reduced due to the presence of more security personnel patrolling the streets. A municipal police station is now located near the public *marché*, which is the center of town. You will see the occasional street person sitting on the sidewalk near the entrance to a shop, but it is rare in Tahiti for anyone to ask passersby for money. Juvenile delinquency, on the other hand, remains a problem, but the statistics have been lower in 2003-2004 than the two previous years.

Prostitutes of all sexes (including Polynesia's third sex, the *mahu*) are rampant. You'll find them in the bars, sidewalk cafés and nightclubs on Rue des Ecoles and near Avenue Prince Hinoi, and some of them are glamorously attired in satins, sequins, feathers, makeup and wigs when they patrol the streets at night. The street surveillance teams also keep an eye on their behavior. A new anti-noise law was passed in 2004 to eliminate the loud music booming from cars and 4WD vehicles in downtown Papeete or anywhere on the island.

Getting Around Town
Car Rentals
Note: The minimum age for renting a 4-wheel vehicle is 21 years and for 2-wheel vehicles it is 18 or 19 years, depending on the island. The driver must have a valid driver's license of one-year minimum from his country of residence or an international driver's license corresponding to the class of vehicle rented. You will have to pay a guarantee deposit when renting cars, scooters and bicycles. When you rent a car, do not leave anything at all inside the car when you're not in it. All major credit cards are accepted.

• **Avis**, *in US Tel. 800/230-4898; in Tahiti, Tel. 689/54.10.10/ Fax 689/ 42.19.11; E-mail: avis.tahiti@mail.pf; www.avis-tahiti.com.* The main office for **Avis-Pacificar** is at 56 Rue des Remparts at the Pont de l'Est in Papeete, and there are also sales offices at the Tahiti-Faaa International Airport, *Tel. 85.02.84* and in Taravao, *Tel. 85.02.84.* A 3-door Twingo rents for a forfeit price of 9.609 CFP per day, with unlimited mileage and insurance. A 3-door air-conditioned Peugeot 106, Ford Ka or Twingo costs 11.495 CFP per day, and a 4-door Mercedes with air-conditioning and automatic drive is 26.675 CFP per day. A Suzuki Samurai 4WD vehicle costs 12.797 CFP per day. Rentals are available for several days and by the week or month.

• **Europcar**, *in US Tel. 800/227-7368; in Tahiti, Tel. 689/45.24.24; Fax 689/ 41.93.41; www.eurocar.com.* The main sales office is on Avenue Prince Hinoi in Papeete, and there are branch offices at the Tahiti-Faaa International Airport, *Tel. 86.61.96;* at all the major hotels and in Taravao. A 3-door Fiat Panda rents for 1.900 CFP per day and 42 CFP per minute or a forfeit price of 8.350 CFP with unlimited mileage and insurance. You can also rent an automatic drive air-conditioned Mazda 6 Sedan for 19.500 CFP per day, and Europcar offers a variety of other choices, including an air-conditioned Kia mini-bus for 22.000 CFP per day.

• **Hertz**, *in US Tel. 800/654.3001; in Tahiti, Tel. 689/42.04.71 (Office), Tel 689/82.55.86 (Airport); Fax 689/43.49.03; E-mail: hertz@mail.pf.* They have a sales counter at the Tahiti-Faaa International Airport and sales desks at the major hotels. A 3-door Peugeot 106 or 4-place Opel Corsa costs 2.240 CFP per day, 44 CFP per kilometer and 1.500 CFP for insurance, or a package price of 9.520 CFP per day. An air-conditioned Opel Corsa, Peugeot 206 or Toyota Yaris rents for 12.520 CFP per day, and a 5-place air-conditioned Peugeot 307 with automatic transmission rents for 17.780 CFP per day.

• **Tahiti Rent A Car**, *Tel. 689/81.94.00,* has an office at the airport. Forfeit rates start at 5.320 CFP for a one-day package of 50 kilometers for a 3-door Hyundai, paying 872 CFP for each additional hour, or 8.454 CFP per day for unlimited mileage. An air-conditioned Renault Twingo or Peugeot 106 costs 10.701 CFP per day for the package price.

• **Daniel Rent-A-Car**, *Tel. 689/81.96.32/ 82.30.04; Fax 689/85.62.64; E-mail: daniel.location@mail.pf.* They have a sales counter at the airport. A 4-seat Peugeot 106 rents for 8.019 CFP per day with unlimited mileage and a 5-place Peugeot 206 with air-conditioning is 10.794 CFP per day. Other choices are available.

Taxi & Limousine Service

A taxi stand is located at the Tahiti-Faaa International Airport, *Tel. 86.60.66,* at the Vaima Center, *Tel. 42.60.77,* at the Papeete Market, *Tel.*

43.19.62, and at Mana Rock Cafe, *Tel. 42.35.98*. Your hotel reception can also call a taxi for you. A taxi ride between the airport and downtown Papeete is 1.500 CFP during the day and 2.500 CFP between 8pm and 6am. The taxi fare between the airport and the west coast hotels, as far as Sofitel Maeva Beach, is 1.000 CFP during the day and 1.500 CFP at night. The daytime fare from the airport to Le Méridien is 2.000 CFP and 3.500 CFP at night. Between the InterContinental Resort Tahiti and downtown Papeete you will pay 1.800 CFP in the daytime and 3.000 CFP at night, and from Le Méridien Tahiti to Papeete the fare is 2.500 CFP during the day and 4.500 CFP at night. From the airport to the Royal Tahitien the taxi fare is 2.000 CFP during the day and 3.500 CFP at night, and to the new Radisson Plaza Resort the daytime fare is 2.500 CFP and 4.500 CFP at night. The official cost of a circle island tour by taxi is 21.000 CFP, but you usually can make an agreement with the taxi chauffeur and pay between 15.000-20.000 CFP. The hourly rate for a taxi is 4.000 CFP. Drivers charge 100 CFP for each big bag transported. See hotel rate structures in the *Basic Information* chapter.

Carl's Taxi, *Tel. 77.13.69/82.22.72*, is operated by Carl Emery, who has been a tour guide in Tahiti for 20 years. He grew up in Australia and speaks excellent 'Aussie' English. He has a 7-passenger air-conditioned mini-van that he uses for private taxi service and tours, and he charges 15.000 CFP for a half-day circle island tour and 25.000 CFP for a full-day tour, which can be divided among seven people.

Mami Elisa Taxi, *Tel. 72.46.31*, is available 24-hours a day to drive you wherever you want to go. I have used her on several occasions and she is very reliable as well as friendly.

Robert Gavin Taruia, *Tel. 74.92.72; Fax 83.77.89*, provides private limousine service with two air-conditioned Peugeot 607 cars. He charges 4.500 CFP for 2 passengers for private transfers from the International Airport of Tahiti-Faa'a to any hotel on the island. His hourly rate is also 4.500 CFP for private tours or sightseeing. He was originally from Hawaii and has lived in Tahiti for 22 years.

Te Reva Nei, *Tel. 56.20.01/71.81.24; E-mail palomat2002@yahoo.fr*. This small company will transport you to the Tahiti Iti peninsula, provide personalized Night-Out tours to visit unique restaurants and popular night entertainment spots, drive you on a shopping tour or city tour. A private all day tour is 60.000 CFP for a minimum of 6 passengers and a private half-day tour is 45.000 CFP.

Tour & Transport Companies

When you book your visit to Tahiti through a travel agent, your ground transportation is normally part of the package. If you are traveling on your own, you can save money by contacting one of the following tour and transport companies to drive you between your hotel and the airport or ferry dock. Be sure to reserve at least one day in advance. See more contact details in Chapter 6, *Planning Your Trip.*

- **Marama Tours Tahiti**, *Tel. 50.74.74; Fax 82.16.75; E-mail: maramatours@mail.pf*
- **Paradise Tours**, *Tel. 42.48.33/42.49.36; Fax 42.48.62; E-mail: paradise@mail.pf*
- **Tahiti Nui Travel**, *Tel. 54.06.71; Fax 42.76.80; E-mail: sales@tahitinuitravel.pf*
- **Tahiti Tours**, *Tel. 54.02.50; Fax 42.50.50; E-mail: sales@tahititours.pf*
- **Tekura Tahiti Travel**, *Tel. 43.12.00; Fax 42.84.60; E-mail: go@tahiti-tekuratravel.pf*

Le Truck & "Busscar" Transportation System

Tahiti's public transport system has traditionally been provided by *le truck*, which is a brightly painted wooden cabin mounted on the rear of a flatbed truck. Wooden benches along each side of the cabin are sometimes supplemented by a long wooden bench in the middle of the aisle, especially for the most distant destinations on Tahiti Iti or Taravao on the isthmus between Tahiti Nui and Tahiti Iti. These colorful vehicles operate during the daylight hours, with night transportation provided from downtown Papeete to the airport and hotels on the west coast, as far as Sofitel Maeva Beach. The last run depends on what is happening in Papeete. Each *le truck* has a specific route, with the destination usually painted on the top or sides of the vehicle.

Tahiti's famous *le truck* is now being phased out as they are replaced with modern buses, which are locally called "**Busscar**." When this new system becomes fully operational there will be 26 lines in service and the 250 buses will be painted according to the zone they serve. The red buses are for the urban zone from Pirae to Punaauia; orange is for the West coast, from Punaauia to Taravao and Teahupoo, and green is for the East coast, between Tautira and Papeete. New lines will be created, such as a service between Tautira and Teahupoo on the Tahiti Iti peninsula, and an "express" bus between the University and the sports stadium in Arue. Line Nº 20 will be an "omnibus" that operates between Outumaoro and Arue. The name and number of the zone served is also shown on the front of the bus, just like buses in the United States.

The authorized bus stops, which are presently indicated by a blue sign with a drawing of *le truck*, will also be changed eventually. The minister of transportation promises that the drivers of the busscars will respect their schedules and that the bus fares will remain the same as those charged *by le truck*, but passengers already have to wait up to half an hour for their bus. The minimum fare is 120 CFP, which will get you from your hotel to downtown, and you'll have to pay 200 CFP at night. The one-way fare to the end of the road in Teahupoo or Tautira on the Tahiti Iti peninsula is 300 CFP. The Tahiti

Manava Visitors Bureau can give you specific details on where to catch the bus to your destination.

So, with all this modernization program, what will happen to the beloved *le truck*? Some of them will be kept in Tahiti to transport groups of tourists who arrive aboard the passenger liners or for "Kaina Island" tours around Tahiti. Other *le trucks* will be shipped to the outer islands, such as *le truck* that recently began a twice-daily service on the atoll of Rangiroa.

Where to Stay
DOWNTOWN PAPEETE
Moderate

HOTEL LE MANDARIN, *B.P. 302, Papeete, Tahiti 98713. Tel. 689/ 50.33.50; Fax 689/42.16.32; E-mail: chris.beaumont@mail.pf; www.hotelmandarin.com. EP Rates: standard room 13.000 CFP single, 15.000 CFP double; mini-suite 15.000 CFP single, 17.000 CFP double; third person 2.000 CFP. Continental breakfast 950 CFP; American breakfast 1.650 CFP; meal plan with breakfast and dinner 3.950 CFP per person; meal plan with breakfast, lunch and dinner 5.900 CFP per person. No charge for children under 12 years old sharing room with parents. Add 5% hotel tax to room rates and 6% value added tax to room rates and prepaid meal plans. A 10% value added tax is applicable to all other services and a 150 CFP municipal tax is charged per person per day. All major credit cards.*

On Rue Colette in downtown Papeete, two blocks inland from the waterfront and across the street from the Mairie of Papeete (City Hall). 38 air-conditioned rooms on five floors, with elevator. Each room has a queen size bed or twin beds, private bathroom with shower, refrigerator or mini-bar, tea and coffee facilities, television and international direct dial telephone. Restaurant Le Plaza, in the same building, and Restaurant Le Mandarin, around the corner, are two first-rate air-conditioned Chinese restaurants and bars, and there is also a coffee shop in the hotel. The rooms were renovated in 2000 with new furniture, carpets and television sets. This Chinese-owned hotel offers a convenient location for downtown activities, and rates second for quality of the accommodations. Rental cars and island tours and excursions can be reserved at the reception desk.

HOTEL TIARE TAHITI, *B.P. 2359, Papeete, Tahiti 98713. Tel. 689/ 50.01.00/50.84.62; Fax 689/43.68.47/42.99.14. No E-mail. Blvd. Pomare, on waterfront adjacent to Papeete Post Office. EP Rates: Standard room 15.295 CFP single/double; harbor view room 16.950 CFP single/double; panoramic view 18.615 CFP single/double; panoramic suite #502 is 20.280 CFP. Third person 2.925 CFP. Continental breakfast 1.100 CFP per person. Rates include all taxes. All major credit cards.*

This hotel opened in 1997, adjacent to the Papeete Post Office on the waterfront of Boulevard Pomare. It is the best choice for the downtown area and reservations have to be made well in advance. The 38 deluxe rooms are located in a five-story building with an elevator. 13 of the 18 rooms facing the post office have a balcony and terrace; the 16 seafront rooms overlooking the yacht quay, harbor and Moorea also have balconies and terraces, as well as the 3 panoramic rooms and the panoramic suite, #502. Each room has air-conditioning, telephone, cable television and a hair dryer on request. Breakfast is served in the cafeteria above the reception. Several restaurants, bars and boutiques are less than a block away.

HOTEL PRINCE HINOI, *B.P. 4545, Papeete, Tahiti 98713. Tel. 689/42.32.77; Fax 689/42.33.66; E-mail: hotelprincehinoi@mail.pf; www.hotel-princehinoi.com. EP Rates: 12.800 CFP single; 13.600 CFP double; 14.500 CFP triple. Continental breakfast 1.250 CFP, American breakfast 1.500 CFP. Add 5% hotel tax to room rates and 6% value added tax to room rates, plus 150 CFP municipal tax per person per day. A 10% value added tax is applicable to all other services. All major credit cards.*

A six-story concrete building on the corner of Boulevard Pomare and Avenue Prince Hinoi in the heart of Papeete's "hot" district, where you'll find the nightclubs, bars and discos. There are also lots of restaurants in this vicinity. The 72 air-conditioned rooms are very basic, but clean, with telephone and television, and a private bathroom with shower or bathtub/shower. There is an elevator and you can order breakfast in the street level dining room. Weekend nights are usually noisy in this area, but the location is convenient to getting around.

HOTEL KON TIKI PACIFIC, *B.P. 111, Papeete, Tahiti 98713. Tel. 689/54.16.16; cell 78.45.69; Fax 689/42.11.66; E-mail: kontiki@mail.pf. EP Rates: single 11.250 CFP; double 14.730 CFP; twin bed room 15.840 CFP. Continental breakfast 850 CFP per person. Add 5% hotel tax to room rates and 6% value added tax to room rates, plus 150 CFP municipal tax per person per day. A 10% value added tax is applicable to all other services. All major credit cards.*

This 7-story hotel is popular with the French military men, as it is located at the lower end of Boulevard Pomare, opposite a naval base in the Papeete harbor. It is only two or three blocks from the downtown center. 20 of the 36 air-conditioned rooms have deep balconies facing the waterfront, where you can watch the Moorea ferries coming and going. You may hear some noise coming from the nearby discos on the street level when they are in full swing on weekends, but the air-conditioners in the rooms drown out a lot of exterior sounds. The rooms on the back facing the mountains are quieter. The television sets are more or less functional. Each room is equipped with a telephone and small refrigerator, and there is a bathtub/shower in the tiled bathroom. There is no restaurant, but breakfast will be brought to your room if you order it from reception in advance.

Economy
   MAHINA TEA, *B.P. 17, Papeete, Tahiti 98713. Tel. 689/42.00.97. A 10-minute walk from downtown area, in Sainte-Amélie valley behind the gendarmerie on Avenue Bruat. EP Rates room single/double: downstairs room 5.000 CFP; upstairs front or back room 6.000 CFP; room with 2 single beds 7.000 CFP. Monthly and yearly rates available on request. Add 6% value added tax to room rates and 50 CFP per person per day for municipal tax. No credit cards.*

   This family-operated hotel is still a bargain for budget travelers who want to be within walking distance of downtown Papeete. There are 16 rooms with private bathrooms and hot water, 14 rooms with a double bed and 2 rooms with a single bed. The 15 studios with kitchen and private bathroom are usually rented by the month. The rooms are basic but clean, linens are provided, and some of the rooms have balconies. The reception area on the ground level also doubles as a communal television room. A few of the clients have lived here for years and others are students from the outer islands. Manager Rose Ceran-Jerusalemy can help you organize your excursions. There is a small grocery store next door.

   CHEZ MYRNA, *B.P. 790, Faaa, Tahiti 98702. Tel./Fax 689/42.64.11; E-mail: dammeyer.family@mail.pf. In Tipaerui valley, a five minute walk inland from Rue du Commandant Destremeau. EP Rates: room 4.240 CFP single, 5.830 CFP double; extra person 1.590 CFP. Transfers 1.060 CFP 6am-6pm, 1.590 CFP 6pm-6am. Rates include all taxes. No credit cards.*

   Myrna and her husband Walter Dahmmeyer have a clean concrete two-bedroom house with a double bed in each room. There's hot water in the shared bathroom and house linens are furnished. Guests also share the living room with television. Myrna is a good cook and she'll serve your meals on the terrace. You can also walk to nearby restaurants, snack bars and magasins.

NORTHEAST COAST: ARUE – PIRAE
Deluxe
   RADISSON PLAZA RESORT TAHITI, *B.P. 14170, Arue, Tahiti 98701. Tel. 689/48.88.88; Fax 689/48.88.89. Reservations: Tel. 689/48.88.00; Fax 689/48.88.89; E-mail: sales-tahiti@radisson.com; www.radisson.com. On Lafayette Beach in Arue Commune, 7 kilometers (4.3 miles) northeast of Papeete. EP Rates single/double: Ocean View room 32.000 CFP; Ocean View room with Jacuzzi and kitchenette 38.000 CFP; Ocean View suite 42.500 CFP; Ocean View duplex suite 45.000 CFP; extra person 7.000 CFP. Children 3-12 years of age are complimentary if sharing with their parents and using existing bedding. Complimentary cots for infants 0-3 years. Transfer charge from airport is about 2.500 CFP. Add 5% hotel tax to room rates and 6% value added tax to room rates. A 10% value added tax is applicable to all other services and a municipal tax of 150 CFP is charged per person per day. All major credit cards.*

The Radisson Plaza Resort was originally planned as a residence hotel with kitchens and large balconies overlooking 2,600 feet (792 meters) of black sand beside the lagoon at Lafayette Beach on Tahiti's northern coast of Arue. The seven concrete buildings that are spread out around an 8,611 square foot (800 square meter) swimming pool were already under construction when the owner decided to upgrade his project to that of a 5-star hotel.

This luxury resort, which is an affiliate of Carlson Hotels, held its official opening in August 2004 with only 50 rooms available to the public, and all 165 rooms were opened a month later. All the guest rooms and suites are located on 4 levels and there are elevators and underground parking for 50 cars. There are no garden or mountain rooms. Each unit overlooks the ocean and they all have the same size balcony or lanai, which is 140 square feet (13 square meters), thus creating an external living room. Louvered shutters assure privacy at one end of the lanai. There are 50 standard rooms, 32 rooms with a double Jacuzzi on the covered balcony, 4 rooms with a kitchenette on the covered balcony, 52 suites and 27 duplex suites. There are 12 inter-connecting suites and rooms with a balcony in addition to the lanai.

All the suites are furnished with a king size bed or two double beds and a sofa bed and can accommodate four people and a baby bed. Each of the rooms has a king size bed or two twin beds, individually controlled air-conditioning, work desk, color television with satellite, local and IDD telephones with two lines, voice mail and modem connection, bathroom with shower and bathtub or shower and Jacuzzi, bathrobes, bathroom scale, broadband Internet access, voltage of 220/60 hz, personal safe, minibar, coffee and tea making facilities, hair dryer and daily housekeeping service. The suites also have an iron and ironing board, and guests staying in the rooms also have access to iron and board on request. There are no CD or DVD players. Room service is available.

The guest rooms and suites, as well as the restaurant, bar, lounge, reception and all other public areas are decorated in a mixture of trendy modern and exotic Polynesian, with furnishings from all over the world. Hiti Mahana, the resort's signature restaurant, overlooks Lafayette Beach and historic Matavai Bay, with a seating capacity of 152, including 52 seats in an air-conditioned area. Under the direction of Executive Chef Christian Pageot, the menu offers a mix of local Tahitian, South East Asian dishes and international Mediterranean cuisine. A local Tahitian buffet is served on Friday nights, complete with a Polynesian dance show. Saturday nights feature a Mediterranean buffet. See further information under *Where to Eat* in this chapter.

The resort's Lafayette Bar is named for the (in-)famous Lafayette after hours nightclub that was located here from the 1940s through the early 1970s. This new upmarket bar has quickly become the gathering place for Tahiti's young international set of beautiful people who come to listen to the music played by Patrick Roche and his Radisson Band. The special cocktail of the house is the pisco sour, which is a drink from Peru and Chile and has nothing at all to do with Tahiti, but it's still good. The James Norman Hall Lounge is the perfect place to relax with a cup of coffee or tea while waiting to meet a friend or business associate. Located to the right of the reception area, guests checking into the hotel in the morning will be invited to sit, relax and enjoy a complimentary beverage of juice or coffee. In the afternoon they will be able to order from the beverage list and enjoy the picturesque view of Matavai Bay. They can also walk across the road (watch out for traffic) to visit the James Norman Hall Home and Library.

Le Spa is a full-service spa on the resort's third floor and is reached by elevator. A trained staff welcomes hotel and non-hotel guests for treatments on appointment. Hotel guests can use their room key for access to the air-conditioned Fitness Center, which is adjacent to Le Spa. In addition to the Star Trac Pro equipment, there are locker rooms, two showers, a sauna and a steam room. In addition to the extensive cardio fitness and free-weight equipment, there are professional yoga and aquagym classes available. See more information under *Massages and Spas* in this chapter. At the entrance to the Radisson you will find a Frederic Missir Black Pearl Boutique, a Prokop Boutique featuring local pottery and jewelry, and an interesting arts and crafts shop with colorful displays of *tifaifai* quilts, pareos, woven hats and bags, mother-of-pearl jewelry and drums.

The hotel bills itself as offering "the most comprehensive meeting facilities on the island with the largest, non-obstructed ballroom in all of French Polynesia, offering more than 2,500 square feet (232 square meters) of space." These meeting rooms and events spaces are named after some of the famous European explorers and ships that visited Tahiti and especially Matavai Bay in the latter half of the 1700s. These include the Endeavour Room, Captain Samuel Wallis Room, Captain James Cook Room, Captain Louis A. Bougainville Room, the Dolphin Meeting Room, the Restaurant Hiti Mahana, the Lafayette Bar, the Endeavour patio and Endeavour garden. The Commune of Arue is also rich in Tahitian history, and several members of the royal Pomare family are buried near the new hotel.

The resort's large fresh water swimming pool overlooks the beach and features a Jacuzzi and full service pool bar and a menu of light snacks. The Radisson Plaza Resort Tahiti Watersports Fare is a comprehensive sports center; open daily from 8:30am to 4:45pm. Snorkeling equipment and kayaks are complimentary for guests. A floating pontoon will be built for easy pick-up by excursion boats. The Tahara'a Diving Center at the Beach House is located adjacent to the Radisson at the foot of Tahara'a Hill. They provide guided snorkeling tours for 4.900 CFP per person, and water-skiing for 2.750 CFP for 10 minutes or a 20-minute lesson for beginners at 3.850 CFP. A Dolphin Visit also includes a guided snorkeling tour, an historical overview of Matavai

Bay and a coconut demonstration for 4.900 CFP. Scuba diving starts at 6.500 CFP for an introductory dive or a Fun dive for certified divers, and a private half-day diving excursion is 78.000 CFP. You can rent a Jet-Ski for 8.250 CFP for 30 minutes or 12.950 CFP for one hour; rent a surfboard or bodyboard for 1.500 CFP for one hour and 3.000 CFP for a half-day and take a surf or body board lesson starting at 4.800 CFP, with equipment, transfers and insurance included. A 2-day program will introduce you to Fly Surfing and costs 19.000 CFP for beginners and 11.000 CFP for advanced fly-surfers. You can also rent a speedboat with driver for 16.700 CFP per hour for a maximum of 4 passengers, or go deep-sea fishing for the morning or afternoon for 16.500 CFP per person. An athletic half-day deep-sea fishing adventure is 66.000 CFP for 4-6 people.

At the excursion desk in the hotel lobby you can rent a car or Quad, sign up for a 4-wheel drive mountain safari, a circle island tour, Papeete discovery tour, Bounty Tour and other specialized tours. Guided nature walks and hiking excursions into the valleys can also be arranged, or you can go flightseeing by helicopter for a 20-minute flight over Tahiti or a 35-minute flight over Moorea. For details on land excursions, hiking and helicopter tours, look under appropriate headings in this chapter.

Like all the favorite Honeymoon Hotels in Polynesia, Radisson Plaza Resort Tahiti also has special packages for newlywed guests and other loving couples. A "Sizzling Romance" romantic dinner in the restaurant is 29.950 CFP for two, a Starlight Dinner is 30.430 CFP, and a "Delicious Sunset" private lanai dinner is 36.590 CFP. A bed of flowers is 12.000 CFP, a bottle of Louis Roederer champagne with 8 canapés is 10.000 CFP, and a music trio will play for a half-hour for 25.000 CFP. A Polynesian Wedding Ceremony is 66.500 CFP and a Royal Polynesian Wedding is 174.500 CFP. Please contact the hotel directly for all details.

Moderate
   HOTEL ROYAL TAHITIEN, *B.P. 5001, Pirae, Tahiti 98716. Tel. 689/ 50.40.40; Fax 689/50.40.41; Reservations Tel. 689/50.40.45; E-mail: royalres@mail.pf; www.hotelroyaltahitien.com. On the beach in Pirae, on Tahiti's north shore, 4 kilometers (2.5 miles) east of Papeete. EP Rates: Standard room 17.000 CFP single/double; 20.000 CFP triple. Add 5% hotel tax to room rates and 6% value added tax to room rates. A 10% value added tax is applicable to other services. All major credit cards.*

Although this is an old hotel that was built in the 1960s, it is still very popular with travelers who want to be close to Papeete but away from the noise and dirt of the city. They also appreciate the moderate rates and beautiful grounds. About 60 percent of the guests are from France and Europe and 20 percent are American. The 40 air-conditioned rooms are located in two-story motel-type structures beside a spacious garden with flowering trees and a small river meandering toward the sea. The carpeted rooms have a telephone, refrigerator and tea/coffee facilities, bathtub/shower and a private balcony or terrace overlooking the tropical gardens. Tahiti's royal family once owned this land. You can swim in the lagoon beside a black sand beach, relax in a Jacuzzi spa and sunbathe on the adjacent wooden deck, or you can cool off under the waterfall in the tropical swimming pool in the garden. Meals are served in the thatched roof Tahitian style dining room or under the shade of huge almond trees on the terrace. There is also a snack *fare* adjacent to the swimming pool. This is a favorite destination for local diners and the Happy Hour crowd who come to the spacious bar on Friday evenings to dance to tunes played by Tahiti's favorite musicians. For more information see *Where to Eat* in this chapter.

AIRPORT AREA: FAAA-PUNAAUIA
Deluxe
   SHERATON HOTEL TAHITI, *B.P. 416, Papeete, Tahiti 98713. Tel. 689/ 86.48.48; Fax 689/86.48.40; Reservations Tel. 689/86.48.49, Fax 689/ 86.48.40; E-mail: reservations.tahiti@sheraton.pf; www.sheratonsintahiti.com. 190 guest rooms and 10 suites beside the lagoon in Auae, 1.6 kilometers (1 mile) from downtown and 3.5 kilometers (2.2 miles) from the airport. Year-Round EP Rates single or double: lagoon view room 30.000 CFP; superior lagoon view room 32.000 CFP; deluxe lagoon view room 37.000 CFP; one-bedroom suite 55.000 CFP; two-bedroom suite 85.000 CFP; additional bed 7.000 CFP. Add 5% hotel tax to room rates and 6% value added tax to room rates and prepaid meal plans. A 10% value added tax is applicable to all other services and a 150 CFP municipal tax is charged per person per day. All major credit cards.*

   This deluxe hotel opened in July 1999 on the site that was occupied by the famous Hotel Tahiti from the early 1960s until March 1997, when it was closed to make way for the new 200-unit structure. The site was enlarged by landfill, providing 6.2 acres (2.5 hectares) of lagoon front property that can be reached from a mountainside parking lot by way of an overhead passage across the busy road. A stone fence separates the hotel grounds from the circle island road.

   The soundproof rooms and suites are located in five concrete buildings with low-rise four and five story wings. The upstairs rooms are reached by three elevators and long winding passageways that are decorated with paintings by local artists and an enviable collection of *tifaifai* (Tahitian patchwork quilts). The rooms are categorized according to their view, and they all have private balconies that overlook the lagoon.

   Each unit has central air-conditioning, either two double beds or a king size bed, sheer and blackout draperies, computer data ports, phone with voicemail, cable color television with remote control, iron and board, alarm clock radio, electronic door locks, in-room safe, refrigerator with mini-bar service, coffee & tea makers, full tub with shower, makeup mirror and hairdryer. There are cribs and connecting rooms available, as well as five rooms equipped for the disabled, and there are also non-smoking floors. Some of the higher-priced rooms have an extra terrace, a larger bathroom with a bidet, and a solarium.

The rooms and suites are all attractively decorated in pleasant, homey colors of apple green and sunshine yellow or gold, with quilted bedspreads in a traditional Hawaiian patchwork design. The polished wood floors and the Polynesian artwork add cheery warmth to the décor. The one-bedroom junior suites have a 180-degree view from the two balconies overlooking Papeete harbor and the island of Moorea, and there are two lavabos in the bathrooms. All rooms have daily maid service and next day laundry and dry cleaning service on request. Room service is available from 6:30am to 10pm.

The public areas of the Sheraton Hotel Tahiti include a reception area with 24-hour front desk service, valet service, a currency exchange, multilingual concierge service, a Kaimana Boutique, Tahiti Perles shop, Europcar rental agency, travel desks and a beauty salon. A business center adjacent to reception includes a computer with Internet connections. A fitness center contains Star Trac exercise equipment, and even includes a special spring floor for aerobics. The Mandara Spa, next to the fitness center, is part of a chain of some 60 spas located throughout the world. Qualified technicians offer a range of services, such as facials, manicures, pedicures, floral Jacuzzi baths, body wraps, a choice of relaxing massages, body scrubs, essential oil treatments and other pampering touches. This spa is open daily from 8am to 8pm and also has a sauna and steam room, which guests may use free of charge.

The Restaurant Moevai is built over the water, where breakfast, lunch and dinner are served. The Terrasse He'epu'enui («to set in a cloudless sky») is open daily from 11am to 9pm, serving light meals. Poolside beverage service is also available. Drinks are served in Quinn's Bar from 10am to midnight. Meeting and banquet facilities can accommodate up to 500 people. For further information see *Where to Eat* in this chapter.

An infinity swimming pool with a five-foot deep grotto and waterfalls faces the lagoon and the spacious green lawns of the Sheraton Hotel Tahiti. You can climb the steps above the pool to the 16-person whirlpool spa, and relax your body while gazing at the sunset and the island of Moorea. There is no beach here, but you can dive from the pier built over the lagoon. Snorkeling equipment, outrigger canoes, pedal boats and kayaks are free for in-house guests. A new nautical center was added to the hotel's facilities in 2002, and it is managed by Bernard Begliomini, who also heads the TOPdive Tahiti scuba dive center on the premises. During the Tahitian arts and crafts demonstrations that are held at the Sheraton Hotel Tahiti several times a week, you can learn how to make floral garlands, weave coconut leaf plates, baskets and seasonal ornaments. You can participate in any number of daily activities, which are listed with the Guest Services Desk in the lobby, and you can arrange for your tours and excursions at the travel desks.

The hotel also has a list of suggested "Romantic Touches" for lovers, which includes a massage in the Mandara Spa, a black pearl, a flower covered bed and romantic dinners with champagne. You can even order a traditional Tahitian Wedding Ceremony to be performed in the hotel gardens. This non-binding wedding includes the blessing by a Polynesian high priest, a band of local musicians and villagers, beautiful leis and crowns of flowers for the couple, a bridal bouquet, a Tahitian wedding certificate made of *tapa* cloth, a pathway of petals, a traditional drink served in a coconut, and *pareu* cloth costumes for both bride and groom to wear during the ceremony. You can have a professional photographer take pictures of this big momentous event. Contact the hotel directly for details.

INTERCONTINENTAL RESORT TAHITI *(formerly **Tahiti Beachcomber Inter-Continental**), B.P. 6014, Faaa, Tahiti. 98702. Tel. 689/86.51.10; Fax 689/86.51.30; E-mail: reservationspf@interconti.com; www.tahiti.interconti.com. Beside the lagoon at the border of Faaa and Punaauia, 7 kilometers (4.3 miles) west of Papeete and 2 kilometers (1.2 miles west) of the airport. EP Rates single/double, low season-high season: garden view room 31.370-34.610 CFP; ocean view room 35.020-38.680 CFP; panoramic room 41.160-45.430 CFP; overwater bungalow on the motu 46.540-51.350 CFP; overwater bungalow on the lagoon 60.750-67.060 CFP; panoramic suite 68.620-75.710 CFP; third person 15 years and older add 6.000 CFP. Child under 15 years of age free of charge when sharing parent's room. MAP half-board meal plan with breakfast and dinner is 8.065 CFP per person; AP full-board meal plan with breakfast, lunch and dinner is 11.570 CFP per person. Add 5% hotel tax and 6% value added tax to room rates, plus 150 CFP municipal tax per person per day. A 10% value added tax is applicable to other services. All major credit cards.*

The Hotel Tahiti Beachcomber Inter-Continental celebrated its 30-year anniversary in September 2004 and still remains the premier international hotel of Tahiti. Although the management has announced that the Beach-comber name will be dropped at the beginning of 2005, local residents as well as many tour operators and tourists will certainly continue to call it the Tahiti Beachcomber. It is located in 12 hectares (30 acres) of lush tropical gardens on the western shore of Tahiti, facing the island of Moorea, built among palm trees and grassy lawns, and has its own white sand beaches and lagoon. The 263-accommodation units include 170 fully renovated garden and lagoon view rooms, each with 307 square feet (28.5 square meters) of floor space plus a balcony. An extension of 60 panoramic view rooms is located in two additional three-story buildings. These units were completed in 1999, and offer 414 square feet (38.5 square meters) of living space, plus a wide terrace overlooking the sandy bottom swimming pool adjacent to the Lotus Restaurant and the island of Moorea. The panoramic suite is also in this section. There are 15 junior suites over deep water at the Restaurant Lotus end of the property, which have 38.5 square meters (414 square feet), excluding the terrace and deck. On a private motu across a bridge from the main hotel property are 17 overwater bungalows with 30.5 square meters (328 square feet) of living space. All rooms and bungalows have air-conditioning, direct dial telephone, data line, cable television and private terrace or private balcony, and are equipped with 110 volt and 220 volt outlets, hairdryers, private safes, mini bar, refrigerator, tea and coffee making facilities. Each bathroom is also garnished with special soaps, bath gels, shampoos and other toiletries.

The hotel's public areas and guest services include two restaurants and three bars, 24-hour reception, concierge, public relations, tour and travel desks, car rental desks, duty free boutique, Tahiti Pearls black pearl shop, 24-hour room service, guest laundry rooms in each section, meeting rooms and private function facilities, nautical activities center, tennis courts, two swimming pools, a jogging track, volley ball court, French bowls, sunbathing reef pontoon, and a helipad.

After transforming the original swimming pool beside the Tiare Restaurant into a much larger pool, with a waterfall and Jacuzzi, the InterContinental's private lagoon was made into an enclosed lagoonarium, where guests can swim among the colorful tropical fish without any danger. The Fare I'a Reserve project has now been completed, providing a constant flow of seawater for the fish, corals and seashells that were added. Guests now gather each day at 9am and 3pm to help the attendant feed the fish. The Tiki Bar has been enlarged, offering more covered and open air seating on the terrace. Diners can easily watch the Polynesian dance shows while seated at their tables on the 3-level terraces of the Tiare restaurant, when these extravaganzas are performed on the deck beside the pool each Wednesday, Friday and Saturday night. A daily program of cultural activities takes place at the Tiare swimming pool or Tiki Bar, which includes an arts and crafts exhibit, pareu dying and tying demonstrations, dance lessons, and lessons on how to create floral crowns, tifaifai patchwork bed covers, or how to make the famous Tahitian fish salad called *poisson cru*.

On making a reservation at the InterContinental Resort Tahiti for honeymooners, and when you mention "Honeymoon" on the reservation document as well as on the voucher, guests receive special gifts and treats on their arrival at the hotel. A catalog of 'Romantic Ideas' has been prepared for honeymooners and other lovers, which tells you all about the Romantic Touches that can be added. These include flowers, champagne and canapés served in the room, a Tahitian musical trio, a private mini dance show and various gifts you can buy. A one-hour Traditional Tahitian Wedding Ceremony can be staged for 180.250 CFP, or you can have a 45-minute Traditional Tahitian Ceremony for 117.400 CFP. Photographs and video films are extra. A Romantic Gourmet

Dinner for Two will cost you 24.200 CFP per couple when it is served in the Lotus Restaurant. Should you opt for a Degustation Dinner at the Lotus Restaurant, be prepared to pay 29.350 CFP per couple, and if you want the Degustation Dinner served on the terrace of your overwater bungalow, it will cost you 32.450 CFP per couple. All the Romantic Dinners include a half-bottle of champagne. *The low season is from January 1 to May 31 and November 1 to December 31. High season is June 1 to October 31.

See more information under *Where to Eat* and *Nautical Centers & Clubs* in this chapter and in the *Best Places to Stay* chapter.

HOTEL LE MERIDIEN TAHITI, *B.P. 380595, Tamanu, Punaauia, Tahiti 98718. Tel. 689/47.07.07; Fax 689/47.07.08; Reservations Tel. 689/47.07.26, Fax 689/47.07.28; in North America 800/543-4300; E-mail: sales@lemeridien-tahiti.com; www.lemeridien-tahiti.com. Beside the lagoon in Punaauia, 15 kilometers (9.3 miles) from downtown Papeete and 9 kilometers (6 miles) west of the international airport. 150 units.EP Rates: single/double: lagoon view room 35.000 CFP; junior suite 50.000 CFP; overwater bungalow 50.000 CFP; senior suite 70.000 CFP; presidential suite 85.000 CFP. No charge for child under 12 years sharing room with parent. American Buffet Breakfast 2.925 CFP, Lunch 4.160 CFP, Dinner 4.160 CFP, MAP half-board meal plan with breakfast and dinner 7.791, AP full-board meal plan with breakfast, lunch and dinner 11.655 CFP. Lunch or dinner at Le Carré is 8.019 CFP. Add 5% hotel tax to room rates and 6% value added tax to room rates, plus 150 CFP municipal tax per person per day. A 10% value added tax is applicable to other services. All major credit cards.*

Le Méridien Tahiti opened in June 1998, on 4.5 hectares (11.12 acres) of land close to the Museum of Tahiti and Her Islands and just 20 minutes from the Atimaono International Golf Course. Facilities include 12 air-conditioned overwater bungalows with thatched roofs, and 130 air-conditioned guestrooms and 8 suites in four-story concrete buildings. The overwater bungalows are 60 square meters (646 square feet) in size and feature a spacious living area opening onto an outdoor deck providing direct access to the lagoon. The suites include 5 junior suites, 2 deluxe suites and one presidential suite. From each room you can see the lagoon and the island of Moorea across the Sea of Moons. All the rooms and bungalows are decorated in a brightly colored tropical French contemporary motif, with tiled floors. Amenities include international direct dial telephones, cable televisions, mini-bars, personal safes, coffee and tea facilities, hair dryers, a range of Le Méridien toiletries, separate bathtubs and showers and handy makeup mirrors. Room service is available from 6:30am to 11pm and laundry service and ironing are also available.

In addition to a business center, Made in Paradise boutique, Sibani Perles, travel agency and car rental desk in the main building, there are five conference and banquet rooms accommodating from 20 to 500 people. La

Plantation is the main restaurant, which offers a very large variety of specialties combining the subtleties of French cuisine and the original, exotic savors of Polynesian cuisine. Le Carré is an elegant beachside restaurant serving gastronomic cuisine for lunch and dinner and it is best to reserve. The main bar, L'Astrolabe, serves exotic cocktails while you listen to the rhythms of piano jazz. You can get panini sandwiches and burgers at the Pool Bar during the day. A Polynesian Night is presented in La Plantation restaurant each Friday evening, with a Polynesian buffet for 7.100 CFP, and the Toa Reva dancers perform an extravaganza show and fire dance around the pool. A cold buffet is served at noon each Saturday and Sunday. Please see further information under *Where to Eat* in this chapter.

The 2,500 square meter (26,910 square feet) sand bottom swimming pool, prolonged by a stream, is claimed as the largest in the world. This vast watery playground is located in the hotel gardens, close to the beach, and is a gathering place for hotel guests. Free activities also include snorkeling equipment, kayaks, aquagym classes, ping-pong, badminton, bacci ball, and tennis on the hotel's court. You can scuba dive with Eleuthera Plongée, join a snorkeling safari, sailing cruise, or a dolphin/whale watch expedition, go deep sea fishing, charter a private boat for a half-day's outing, play golf or discover Tahiti's charms on a circle island tour. You can also opt for a relaxing massage in your room. The travel desk in the lobby can book your tours and excursions or rent you a car for your own personal explorations. Le Méridien operates a shuttle bus service twice a day aboard a «le truck' that will take you to Papeete and back for 1.000 CFP per person. Or you can walk out to the circle island road and catch a local bus and pay the one-way fare of 130 CFP.

Le Méridien also has a program for Honeymooners, including a non-binding Polynesian wedding ceremony and honeymoon dinner. Contact the hotel directly for details.

Superior

HOTEL SOFITEL MAEVA BEACH, *B.P. 60008, Faaa, Tahiti 98702. Tel. 689/86.66.00; Fax 689/43.84.70; Reservations 689/86.66.66; Fax 689/ 41.05.05; E-mail: reservation_tahiti@accor-hotels.com; www.sofitel.com. Beside the lagoon in Punaauia, 7.5 kilometers (4.6 miles) west of Papeete and 2.5 kilometers (1.5 miles) west of the airport. Low season-High season EP Rates single/double: garden view room 18.400-20.600 CFP; lagoon view room 22.350-24.700 CFP; panoramic room 24.150-26.650 CFP; suite 36.550-40.900 CFP; third person add 5.000 CFP. Note: The high season rates are in effect between July 1 and October 31. During the low season you can get some really good room rates, such as the 9.800 CFP room for 1-3 people they were advertising in January 2004. No charge for child under 12 sharing parent's room. American breakfast 2.400 CFP, set lunch menu 2.950 CFP, set dinner menu 5.050 CFP. Half price for child under 12 years old. Add 5% hotel* *tax to room rates and 6% value added tax to room rates, plus 150 CFP municipal tax per person per day. A 10% value added tax is applicable to other services. All major credit cards.*

The Maeva Beach is operated by the Sofitel Coralia French hotel chain, which also has hotels in Moorea, Huahine and Bora Bora. This hotel opened in 1969, offering a fabulous view of the island of Moorea across the Sea of Moons. Accommodations include 218 air-conditioned rooms in a 7-story pyramid shaped building. These consist of 202 standard rooms, 14 rooms with a scenic view and two suites. Each room is tiled and has a terrace or balcony, bathtub/shower, separate toilet, direct-dial phone, cable television, personal safe, mini refrigerator, tea and coffee facilities, hair-dryers and makeup mirrors. Room service is available from 6:30am to 10pm. In the lobby are desks for car rentals, tours and activities, plus a gift and sundries shop. Seminars and banquets can be held in the Paevai Room, which seats 250 people theater style; in the 70-seat Gauguin Room; and in the Diadème Room, which has 15 seats.

In addition to a big swimming pool, there are two lighted tennis courts and a golf driving range. Each day's activities are printed on individual sheets in French and English and displayed in the lobby. You can join an Aquagym class or take swimming lessons for adults in the pool, sunbathe on the hotel's private pontoon, learn to play golf or tennis, take a guided city tour, circle island tour or safari tour in the mountains, visit Tahiti's museums, go on a snorkeling and fish-feeding safari, go scuba diving, and sign up for a sunset cruise, deep sea fishing or water-skiing.

The Sakura is a Japanese teppanyaki restaurant adjacent to the hotel lobby and the Bougainville, on the ground level, is an open-air restaurant for 200 people. Breakfast, lunch and dinner are served in this open-air restaurant, which overlooks the lagoon. Polynesian dance shows are presented in the Bougainville restaurant at 8pm each Friday during a Barbecue Buffet for 4.800 CFP, and each Sunday another dance show is performed during the Tahitian *tamaara'a* luncheon feast, which has become a popular tradition at the Maeva Beach and costs 5.800 CFP. From 11:30am to 5pm you can get sandwiches, hamburgers and salads at the Moorea Bar beside the swimming pool, and from 9:30am to 10:30pm you can enjoy your favorite cocktails at this outdoor bar. Happy Hour is held here daily from 5 to 6pm and from 9 to 10pm, when drinks are half-price. A musical group plays rock, country and blues at the Moorea Bar each Friday and Saturday from 4 to 6pm and a Polynesian trio then plays island tunes from 6 to 7pm and there is also musical entertainment from 9 to 11pm at the Moorea Bar. A Polynesian trio entertains at the adjacent Bougainville restaurant each Sunday from 7 to 9pm. See information under *Where to Eat* in this chapter.

Honeymooners have the option of adding a romantic touch to their stay at the Maeva Beach, with a special VIP welcome, a honeymoon gourmet dinner for two and other special treats. Contact the hotel directly for their programs.

Moderate
  IAORANA VILLA, *B.P. 380853, Tamanu, Punaauia, Tahiti 98718. Tel. 689/54.49.11; Fax 689/54.49.14; E-mail: iaoranavilla@mail.pf. On the lagoon and mountainside at PK 10.8 in Punaauia, between the airport and Le Méridien. EP Rates single/double: standard room on seaside or mountainside 8.500 CFP; deluxe air-conditioned room on mountainside 9.990 CFP; air-conditioned junior suite with kitchenette on mountainside 12.210 CFP; air-conditioned bungalow with kitchenette on seaside 13.320 CFP. Weekly and monthly rates available. Add 150 CFP municipal tax per person per day. All other taxes included. All major credit cards.*

  This hotel was built in the late 1960s, after the French nuclear tests began in the Tuamotu atolls of Moruroa and Fangataufa. For more than 30 years it operated as a rest and recreation center for French military personnel who worked for the *Centre d'expérimentations du Pacifique* (CEP) The military closed this R&R camp in March 2001, and it reopened a few months later as a public hotel under local management. Although the clientele still includes some military families, the ambience is definitely Polynesian, especially on weekends, when the bar does an active business to the dance tunes played by a Tahitian band.

  The location is good if you are looking for a moderate priced hotel on Tahiti's west coast. The thatched roof reception area, small boutique, restaurant, bar, dance floor and outdoor terrace all face the lagoon, offering a lovely view of Moorea. There's a small swimming pool near the narrow manmade white sand beach. A few lounge chairs, picnic tables and palapa-type shelters are scattered along the beach and on the gravel-covered ground beneath the Australian pine trees that border a small peninsula. Low and high dive boards are a natural attraction for Tahitian kids who spend the weekend days somersaulting from the boards into the lagoon. This noise doesn't seem to bother the family of noddy birds that nest in the top branches of the shade trees; all is quiet again on Monday morning once the children have returned to school. A marina here has two dozen slips for small boats, and you can see the big luxury yachts that are moored at Marina Taina, just a short distance up the coast.

  Only 63 bungalows and rooms of the original 81 have been renovated. These include the 26 bungalows in the gardens on the lagoon side of the road that are rented for 13.320 CFP a night. None of the hotel's accommodations actually faces the lagoon. The bungalows are typical of the Tahitian hotels built in the 1960s. The walls are yellow bamboo and the roofs are thatch pandanus fronds. Each bungalow is square in back and round in front, with concrete steps only—no terrace or balcony. There is an air-conditioned bedroom with a squeaky double bed and two bunk beds in the living room, which is cooled by a ceiling fan. The living room also contains a mini-refrigerator, microwave oven, electric plate, telephone, television, a 2-place rattan sofa, two chairs and a writing desk. Mosquitoes ate me up when I stayed in one of these bungalows, even though I burned a mosquito coil that was provided. As long as you stay in the air-conditioned bedroom you're all right. The junior suites on the mountainside across the circle island road also have air-conditioners in the bedrooms, as well as beds for two adults and two children, equipped kitchens and television. The deluxe rooms on that side of the road are also air-conditioned and have a refrigerator and television, and the standard rooms on the lagoon side have fans and refrigerators.

There is a restaurant here but no breakfast is provided. An à la carte lunch is served, with a daily special that is advertised on a chalkboard beside the road. Dinner is available only on Friday and Saturday evenings, and the young Polynesian management team plans to organize a Tahitian feast every other Sunday at noon. See *Where to Eat* in this chapter. A Tahitian band plays music at the Tiki Bar during lunch on Thursday through Saturday, and there is live *kaina* music each Sunday from 12-11pm. If you're in the mood to dance local style (Tahitian waltz, fox trot and *tamure*), this is definitely the place to be on Sundays.

Economy

CHEZ LOLA, *B.P. 6102, Faaa, Tahiti 98702. Tel./Fax 689/81.91.75; cell phone 78.08.52. PK 4.5 mountainside in the Sainte-Hilaire neighborhood in Faaa Commune, one kilometer inland from airport. Free round-trip transfers in the daytime and 800 CFP per car at night. EP Rates: room and breakfast 5.000 CFP single, 7.000 CFP double/triple. Reduced rates starting on third night. Dinner on request. All taxes included. No credit cards.*

Lola rents out two bedrooms in her family home, which is a modern concrete house above the airport. Each room has a double bed and a fan. There's hot water in the bathroom, which you'll share with the other guests. House linens are provided. You'll also have use of the living room, dining room, television and terrace. Not only does Lola meet you at the airport upon arrival, but she will also drive you to the main road to catch *le truck* to Papeete, and come to fetch you at the airport after you've finished your sightseeing and shopping. You'll enjoy her generous meals.

PENSION DAMYR, *B.P. 6492, Faa'a, Tahiti 98702. Tel./Fax 689/83.69.13; cell 70.81.31. On the mountainside at PK 5 in the Aubry quartier of Faa'a, overlooking the airport and the island of Moorea. Free round-trip transfers provided. EP Rates: room with communal bathroom 5.500 CFP single; 6.500 CFP double, breakfast included. 1.500 CFP for third person. Studio with private bathroom 8.000 CFP single/double, 9.500 CFP triple, 10.500 CFP for 4 people. Breakfast included first day. Seventh night free. Add 6% value* *added tax to room rates and 50 CFP per person per day for municipal tax. No credit cards.*

Daniel and Myrtille Duquenne have a large property with 2 rooms for guests in the house, who share a bathroom with hot water, as well as the dining room and terrace. Each room has a double bed, large closet and electric fan. There is also a completely equipped studio with a private bathroom and hot water, kitchen, dining room and terrace, plus cable television, a ceiling fan in the bedroom and an electric fan in the living room. A *magasin* store is about 650 feet away. This pension was recommended to me by an American man who owns a house in Moorea and flies in and out of Tahiti several times a year, always using these facilities when he is arriving or departing in the middle of the night. I have also booked American and Australian friends here and they were all very impressed with the cleanliness of the house, as well as the friendliness and efficiency of the hosts.

TAHITI AIRPORT LODGE, *B.P. 2580, Papeete, Tahiti 8713. Tel. 689/ 82.23.68/79.30.84; Fax 689/82.25.00. PK 5.5 Cité de l'Air in Faaa, overlooking airport. Round-trip transfers between airport and pension 1.500 CFP per person. EP Rates: room with one twin bed, sharing bathroom 5.000 CFP; room with two twin beds, sharing bathroom 6.000 CFP double; room with a double bed and private bathroom 8.000 CFP single/double. Extra bed 2.000 CFP. Breakfast 500 CFP. All taxes included. No credit cards.*

This two-story colonial style house, with a panoramic view of the lagoon and the island of Moorea, is just a three-minute ride from the airport and five minutes from downtown. It has six attractively decorated bedrooms on two levels with single or double beds, and both communal and private bath facilities with hot water. Owners Charles and Marguerite Topa-Bredin will take you around the island, to visit the archaeological sites, to the beach, or on a picnic. Backpackers consider this dorm the nicest accommodation in the airport area and the Tahiti Manava Visitor's Bureau and Haere Mai Association have received good reports from travelers who have stayed here. It is run by an elderly couple who lock the gate at night, but will wait up for all the guests to arrive safely back at the pension before going to bed. Marguerite will drive you to one of the nearby restaurants or snack bars for your dinner.

Economy to Moderate
SOUTHWEST COAST: PUNAAUIA TO MATAIEA
PENSION DE LA PLAGE, *B. P. 381593, Tamanu, Punaauia, Tahiti 98718. Tel. 689/45.56.12; Fax 689/82.85.48; E-mail: laplage@mail.pf; www.pensiondelaplage.com. PK 15.4 on mountainside in Punaauia Commune, 9.5 miles from downtown. Look for the sign beside the road. EP Rates: room without kitchen 7.500 CFP single, 8.500 CFP double; extra bed 2.000 CFP. Room with kitchen 8.900 CFP single, 9.900 CFP double; extra bed 2.000. Breakfast 900 CFP; basket meal 1.500 CFP; dinner 2.500 CFP per person. Add*

6% value added tax to room rates and 50 CFP per person per day for municipal tax. Mastercard, Visa.

This pension opened in 2001 and is close to the Tamanu shopping center, the Museum of Tahiti and Her Islands and several restaurants, including those at Le Meridien hotel. Even though the name indicates that it is a guesthouse on the beach, it is actually on the mountainside, with access to the beach, which is only 100 meters away. You can take Le Truck from Papeete or in front of the airport to get here.

There are 12 rooms located in two one-story concrete buildings, each with a double bed or single beds, and private bathroom with hot water. The bright, cheerful rooms have bamboo furniture, a refrigerator, ceiling fan and television, and they open onto a terrace facing the swimming pool and flower gardens. Some of the units have a kitchenette. You can also have Corinne Magri-Tetard, the owner, cook your meals for you.

CHEZ ARMELLE, *B.P. 380640, Tamanu, Tahiti 98718. Tel. 689/58.42.43/ 77.79.99; Fax 689/58.42.81; E-mail: armelle@mail.pf; www.pension-armelle.com. PK 15.5 on seaside in Punaauia Commune, 9.6 miles from downtown. Look for the Chez Armelle sign on the road shortly after the Mobil Station and Plage de Toaroto sign. Take the small access road to the right past the first home and head toward the beach. Round-trip transfers 2.500 CFP per person at night. EP Rates: room 5.880 CFP single; 7.520 CFP double. Additional bed 1.000 CFP. Bungalow 8.630 CFP single/double. Add 2.000 CFP per day for air-conditioning. Breakfast included. Meals on request. Special long-term rates. All taxes are included. Mastercard, Visa.*

This pension/snack is located beside the coral sand beach, close to the Museum of Tahiti and Her Islands and to Taapuna, one of Tahiti's most popular surfing spots. Each of the eight rooms in the house has a double bed, ceiling fan and a private bathroom with hot water. There is also a bungalow for 3 people, with a double bed and a single bed, fan, and private bathroom with hot water. House linens are furnished. Air-conditioning is available on request. You'll share the living room and shaded beachside patio with the other guests. Bicycles, snorkeling equipment, kayaks and outrigger paddle canoes are provided for guest use. Armelle opened this pension in 1993 and turned it over to her three sons in 1998. One of them, Raimana Riviere, is now in charge and he will arrange island tours and excursions for you. The snack is open daily, serving dinner specials for 1.500 CFP, and Armelle will prepare a special dish or dessert on request.

PENSION OTAHA, *B.P. 380231, Tamanu, Punaauia, Tahiti 98718. Tel. 689/58.24.52; Fax 689/58.22.65; cell 71.55.54; E-mail: paemiti@hotmail.com; www.pensionotaha.com. PK 17.3 on seaside in Punaauia Commune, 17.3 kilometers (10.7 miles) from downtown and 12 kilometers (7.4 miles) from the airport. EP Rates: 2-bedroom house in garden, with kitchen 7.500 CFP per room single/double; garden room with outside kitchen 10.500 CFP single/*

double plus a child; beach bungalow with local style kitchenette 11.000 CFP single/double plus a child; room with kitchen and sitting room 10.500 CFP single/double plus a child; studio with private bathroom and terrace with kitchen 9.000 CFP single/double plus a child; bed in garden dormitory 2.800 CFP; bed in beach dormitory 3.500 CFP. Add 6% value added tax to room rates and 50 CFP per person per day for municipal tax. No credit cards. Two-night minimum stay required.

Titaua Schenck runs this increasingly popular pension beside the white sand beach in Punaauia, and she speaks English. There's a big sign beside the road and you get off Le Truck right at the driveway to the pension. All guests have access to a washing machine, kayaks and snorkeling gear. There are restaurants, snack bars and roulottes, as well as various Chinese *magasin* stores selling food in this area.

TAAROA LODGE, *B.P. 498, Papeete, Tahiti 98713. Tel/Fax 689/58.39.21; Cell 689/78.84.26; E-mail: taaroalodge@mail.pf; www.taaroalodge.com. PK 18.2, beside the beach in Punaauia behind Snack PK 18. Round-trip transfers 1.500 CFP per person. EP rates: room 5.000 CFP per person; dormitory 2.300 CFP per person per day; bungalow for 1-3 people 10.000 CFP per day; bungalow for 4-8 people 16.000 CFP per day. Add 6% value added tax to room rates and 50 CFP per person per day for municipal tax. Mastercard, Visa.*

Ralph Sanford, who is an avid surfer, opened his guesthouse in 1998 and welcomes surfers, backpackers and anyone else who wants to stay beside one of Tahiti's nicest beaches. He has a large chalet style wooden bungalow from New Zealand, with a bedroom and double bed on the ground floor, complete with a private bathroom and hot water. On the mezzanine is a 7-mattress dormitory, whose occupants share a bathroom with hot water. All guests have use of the kitchen, dining room and big terrace. Two new bungalows overlooking the lagoon are wooden kit houses from New Zealand, which have a double bed and a single bed in each, as well as a refrigerator, microwave oven and facilities for coffee and tea. They also have a small covered terrace, where you can sit and watch Moorea and the sunset. No meals are served, but the Sanfords will bring you fresh bread and fruit in the mornings, and there is a restaurant/snack in front of the house. Mahana Park is less than 500 feet down the road, where you'll find a restaurant and a snack bar. You can catch *le truck* to the airport or town in front of the house.

RELAIS FENUA, *B.P. 381585, Tamanu, Punaauia, Tahiti 98718. Tel. 689/ 45.01.98/77.25.45; Fax 689/45.30.03; E-mail: relais.fenua@mail.pf; www.relais-fenua.pf. PK 18.25 on mountainside in Punaauia, right across the road from Taaroa Lodge and 150 meters from the public beach of Mahana Park. Round-trip transfers 2.000 CFP per person. EP Rates: Room 7.900 CFP single, 8.500 CFP double, 8.900 CFP triple; air-conditioned family room 9.900 CFP 1-4 people. Reduced rates after 14 days. Breakfast 900 CFP per person; take-away dinner 900 CFP per person. All taxes are included. Mastercard, Visa.*

This six-room concrete house was built in 2001 and contains colonial style rooms for singles, doubles and families. The rooms have either 2 single beds or a king size bed and 2 single beds, and one room can accommodate handicapped guests. There are air-conditioners in the family rooms and ceiling fans in the other rooms, and each room has a mini-bar, hair dryer and television, plus a private bathroom with hot water. Public rooms include a living room and library/office, which is furnished with a bar, television set, stereo, DVD player, telephone, fax, computer with Internet connections, safety box, ironing board and iron. Local style meals can be ordered to eat in the communal dining area. There is a boutique of local arts and crafts on the premises, and a small swimming pool and whirlpool are located in the tropical garden. Public transportation is provided by Le Truck, which passes along the coastal road just 100 meters in front of the property. This guesthouse is convenient to scuba diving centers, marinas, the Museum of Tahiti and Her Islands, the Lagoonarium and the big hotels on Tahiti's west coast.

TE MITI, *B.P. 130088, Moana Nui, Punaauia, Tahiti 98717. Tel./Fax 689/ 58.48.61; Cell 689/78.60.80; E-mail: pensiontemiti@mail.pf; www.pensiontemiti.com. PK 18.6, mountainside, 11.5 miles from Papeete in Lotissement Papehue, in Paea Commune, 100 meters (328 feet) after the Paea sign, across road from Mahana Park public beach. Round-trip transfers 1.000 CFP per person in daytime and 2.500 CFP at night. EP Rates: (Breakfast included) small room single/double 6.000 CFP; medium size room 6.500 CFP; large room 7.000 CFP; dormitory 2.500 CFP per person. Rates are reduced by 500 CFP for 7 nights and more. All taxes included. Mastercard, Visa.*

A "Bed and Breakfast" sign on the mountainside of the circle island road points the way to this hostel, which is located on a quarter-acre of land with lots of fruit trees. This pension is a good choice for surfers and sunbathers, as it is just 200 meters (218 yards) from Tahiti's prettiest white sand beach at Mahana Park. Three clean, modern houses provide five bedrooms, with ceiling fans and plenty of storage space, mosquito nets and house linens. There are also two dormitories with 4 beds each. Guests share two kitchens, three bathrooms with hot water, a television corner and several spacious patios. A refrigerator is provided for guests but there are no cooking facilities. There are restaurants, snacks and *magasin* food stores nearby. Snorkeling gear is available for guest use. This is a highly rated hostel according to the tourist feedback at the Tahiti Manava Visitor's Bureau. Frédéric and his wife are a young, dynamic couple who treat their guests very well.

HITI MOANA LODGE, *B.P. 10865, Paea, Tahiti 98711. Tel. 689/ 57.93.93; Fax 57.94.44; cell 74.16.67; E-mail: hitimoanavilla@mail.pf; www.papeete.com/moanavilla. At PK 32, 19.8 miles from Papeete beside the lagoon in Papara Commune, 10 minutes from golf course and surfing beach. One-way transfers from airport 1.500 CFP per person. EP Rates: garden view bungalow without kitchen 8.500 CFP single/double; lagoon view bungalow* *without kitchen, 9.000 CFP single/double CFP; lagoon view bungalow with kitchen 11.500 CFP for 1-4 people; Mara bungalow beside pool with lagoon view and kitchen 13.000 CFP for 1-4 people. Extra bed 1.000 CFP. Breakfast 900 CFP per person. All taxes are included. Mastercard, Visa.*

This is a very clean and modern pension built in a lovely flower garden between the road and the lagoon in Papara, just 10 minutes by car from the international golf course and the international surfing beach of Taharuu. There are four concrete studios with tiled floors, each with a double bed in the separate bedroom and two single beds in the living room, plus a private kitchen, private bathroom with hot water, television, ceiling fans and a covered narrow terrace facing the lagoon. Paved walkways also lead to the four new bungalows that are built in the local government approved FEI style with wood shake roofs, a double bed in the sleeping/living room, a private bathroom with hot water, ceiling fan, television and a terrace overlooking the flower garden and lagoon.

All the rooms are very attractively decorated in bright Polynesian motifs. In addition to a swimming pool, you'll also have the advantage of a private pontoon. Paddle canoes, kayaks, and an aluminum boat with motor are available for additional fees, and you can also rent a car at reduced rates. Steve Brotherson, the owner, has a mini-bus that he uses for circle island tours for 4-7 passengers for 5.000 CFP each. He was the 2001 president of the Haere Mai Association of Family Pensions, and is very knowledgeable about Tahiti's history and current events, plus he speaks good English. The Restaurant Nuutere is across the street and supermarkets and snack bars are close by. A washing machine is available for guest use for 1.000 CFP, and there is a public telephone booth beside the road in front of the pension. I've had some good feed back from people who stayed here and were very happy with this nice pension.

RELAIS DE LA MAROTO, *B.P. 20687, Papeete, Tahiti 98713. Tel. 689/ 57.90.29/72.98.21; Fax 689/57.90.30; E-mail: maroto@mail.pf. Turn left at the sign at PK 46.5 in Mataiea Commune, 28.8 miles from Papeete. Transfers from bottom of valley 3.500 CFP for adult and 2.500 CFP for child under 12 years. Drive up the winding, unpaved mountain road, past Lake Vaihiria 473 meters (1,551 feet) and keep climbing. EP Rates: standard room 3.500 CFP single, 7.000 CFP double; bungalow 15.000 CFP single/double; suite 25.000 CFP single/double; extra bed 3.000 CFP per adult, 1.000 CFP per child. Continental breakfast 1.200 CFP; American breakfast 1.700 CFP. Lunch and dinner à la carte. MAP package from Saturday afternoon to Sunday morning with room, dinner and breakfast 10.500 CFP. Other packages available. All taxes are included. American Express, Mastercard, Visa.*

If your preferences include quiet mountain retreats in a cool, peaceful setting of tree ferns, waterfalls, archaeological sites and wild beauty in every imaginable shade of green, then you'll be happy at Maroto. This is Tahiti's only mountain lodging, located in the center of the island in the historic Papenoo Valley, at the convergence of Vaituoru and Vainavenave rivers. In pre-Christian days this valley was formerly inhabited by thousands of Maohi people. Several of the basaltic house platforms, petroglyphs, meeting sites and *marae* temples of stone have been restored, and you can hike from the hotel to explore the interior of the island, where you'll find tunnels, grottos, caves and lava tubes.

The hotel buildings were originally used to house construction crews who built several hydroelectric dams in the Papenoo Valley. The interior part of these buildings was completely renovated in 2001 and again in 2003 and there are now 26 standard rooms for guests, as well as 3 newly built bungalows and 2 suites. All the units contain a queen size bed and there are also single beds in the bungalows and suites. Each accommodation has a private bathroom with hot water and a terrace overlooking the mountain peaks and lush valley. Another large building houses the reception area, living room, convention room, dining room, bar, kitchen and game room The restaurant serves French cuisine and Te Ana, their wine cellar, is supposed to be the most prestigious in all of the South Pacific, with wines priced from 2.500 to 140.000 CFP a bottle, including Napa Valley's best labels.

You can get to La Maroto by 4-wheel drive vehicle from Mataiea or through the Papenoo Valley. If you decide to drive up this tortuous mountain road make sure you have a strong 4x4, and be especially careful during the frequent rains, as the roads can be very slippery. You can also drive to the bottom of Papenoo Valley and the Relais de la Maroto will send someone to transfer you to their small family hotel. Note the cost of transfers above. You can also go by helicopter. Or you can join a full-day Across the Island Tour with Tahiti Safari Expedition (See information under *Mountain & Waterfall Tours*), which stops at the restaurant here for lunch. You can walk from the hotel to the restored *marae* in the Papenoo Valley.

TAHITI ITI PENINSULA (Little Tahiti)

Transfer service by mini-bus is available from Papeete or the airport to Tahiti Iti. *Tel. 54.81.81 or 78.76.85, or Tel. 56.20.01/71.81.24.* The one-way fare is 5.500 CFP for one or two passengers and 3.000 CFP per person for more than two passengers. You can also take Le Bus or Le Truck public transportation for 300 CFP and if you want to return to Papeete the same day, be sure to check with the driver before boarding the vehicle.

Economy to Moderate

PENSION CHAYAN, *B.P. 8836, Taravao, Tahiti 98719. Tel./Fax 689/57.46.00; cell 72.28.40; E-mail: pensionchayan@mail.pf; www.pensionchayantahiti.pf. On mountainside at PK 14 in Vairao, on west coast of Tahiti Iti. EP Rates: bungalow 14.150 CFP single/double; extra bed 3.000 CFP; no charge for child under 4 years; 1.500 CFP for child 4-12 years. Breakfast 500 CFP, lunch or dinner 2.000 CFP per* *person per day. Add 6% value added tax to room rates and 50 CFP per person per day for municipal tax. Mastercard, Visa.*

Chayan is a contraction of Chantal and Yannick Salmon, the young owners of this 4-bungalow pension they opened in December 2002, between the mountain and the lagoon of Vairao. Although they are on the mountain side of the road, their guests have access to a small beach and a pier built over the lagoon. Their own verdant property has a waterfall and basin in the back yard, and in the middle flows a stream where fresh water eels swim and feed. The four concrete bungalows are far enough apart to insure privacy. Each unit has two rooms with two double beds and a bathroom and porch. In a big central *fare* there is a large kitchen and a big terrace for eating family style. Rental kayaks are available for 500 CFP a half-day, and boat excursions will take you to the Vaipoiri River in Tahiti Iti for 3.500 CFP per person, or to visit the petroglyphs for 6.000 CFP. A shuttle boat will transport surfers to the passes for 1.500 CFP per person, and you can also go scuba diving with a qualified instructor from a nearby dive club.

TAUHANIHANI VILLAGE LODGE (La Vague Bleue), *B.P. 66, Taravao, Tahiti 98719. Tel./Fax 689/57.23.23; cell 74.81.82; E-mail: kotyvaguebleue@mail.pf; www.waybe.com/tauhanihanilodge_tahiti//htm. Beside the lagoon at PK 16 in Teahupoo village, 76 kilometers (47 miles) from the airport. Round-trip transfers 4.000 CFP per person. EP Rates: garden bungalow 12.000 CFP single/double; beach bungalow 14.000 CFP single/ double; extra bed 2.000 CFP for adults and 1.000 CFP for child 5-12 years. Continental breakfast 1.000 CFP, (complete) American breakfast 1.500 CFP, lunch or dinner 2.500 CFP. Special package for 3-4 surfers in room, plus breakfast and dinner for 6.500 CFP per person. Rates include all taxes. American Express, Mastercard, Visa.*

Koty and Réné Manuireva have 5 new local style FEI (government approved and subsidized) bungalows on their property at the edge of the lagoon in the middle of Teahupoo village, yet they are 200 meters (656 feet) from the road, facing the famous Hava'e Pass that even international surfing champions find awesome and challenging. They have two sons who surf and take care of the family pension and everyone here speaks English. Each bungalow has a king size bed and two single beds, a ceiling fan or electric fan, color television, a private bathroom with hot water shower, and a covered terrace. There is a small beach here and kayaks for the guests, who are of all ages and from many countries. They also have a big outrigger canoe and a boat they use for excursions to explore the wild coast of Te Pari at the south end of Tahiti Iti, for picnics on the motu, visits to Vaipoiri grotto and to shuttle the surfers out to the big waves. Le Perroquet Bleu (The Blue Parrotfish) is the name of the on-site restaurant, where Koty serves family style meals. This may be shrimp from the river or the shrimp farm in Vairao, or fish from Rangiroa (she doesn't want to take the fish from the lagoon in Teahupoo because she wants to leave them for guests to admire), plus filling meals for hungry surfers. Tauhanihani is a flirtatious Tahitian expression that translates to, as the old song goes, "put your arms around me honey, hold me tight..." and La Vague Bleue is the Blue Wave.

TE PARI VILLAGE, *B.P. 697, Papeete, Tahiti 98713. Tel. 689/42.59.12/ 42.01.49; cell 689/78.91.12; Fax 689/42.59.12; E-mail: teparivillage@yahoo.fr. 2 kilometers (1.2 miles) beyond the end of the road in the Fenua Aihere (wild land), a 30-minute walk or a 10-minute boat ride from the Teahupoo dock on the south coast of Tahiti Iti. One-way mini-bus transfer from airport to boat dock in Teahupoo 2.700 CFP. Free round-trip boat transfers between boat dock and pension. AP Rates: bungalow with all meals and excursion 10.450 CFP per person; half-price for child 3 to 12 years old; day tour excursion 5.500 CFP per person with lunch included. Add 6% value added tax to room rates and 50 CFP per person per day for municipal tax. No credit cards. Minimum stay of 2 nights during week and 1 night on weekends.*

Vanina Teamotuaitau and Désirée Liant have built four attractive bungalows in a big grassy area beside the lagoon in a tropical paradise. There are 5-hectares (12.4 acres) of coconut groves, fruit trees, coffee and vanilla plantations and flowers everywhere. Three of the four units contain a double bed, terrace and private bathroom with hot water, and there is one bungalow with two double beds. The bungalows are spacious, clean and attractively decorated with Tahitian fabrics and a mosquito net. All guests share the living room and dining area. A five-minute boat ride takes you to the most fabulous surfing spot in Polynesia and you can hike to the waterfalls and tropical jungle of Te Pari cliffs. Canoes and kayaks are provided for guests and you can swim, dive and visit the grotto of Vaipoiri. This is a good pension for guests who prefer a quiet, peaceful environment. Most of the clientele are French people who live in Tahiti and want to get away for the weekend or a few days. Although this pension does not attract surfers, it is a good place for lovers who enjoy gazing at the stars hand in hand or romantics who thrill at the sight of the full moon rising right out of the ocean in front of their eyes.

LE BONJOUIR, *B.P. 8255, Taravao, Tahiti 98719. Tel. 689/77.89.69/ 73.42.69; E-mail: bonjouir@mail.pf; www.bonjouir.com. Beside the lagoon on the south coast of Tahiti Iti in an area called Te Pari, a 12-minute boat ride beyond the end of the road and the Teahupoo boat dock. A one-way mini-bus transfer between airport and Teahupoo boat dock 3.000 CFP per person. Round-trip boat transfers between Teahupoo dock and pension 1.600 CFP per person. Private parking 500 CFP per day. EP Rates: bungalow and private bathroom for 2-6 people 9.500-15.000 CFP; studio for 2-6 people 5.000-7.000 CFP; ocean view room with communal bathroom for 2-3 people 7.000-8.000; bed in dormitory for groups 2.500 CFP; camping 1.200 CFP per person per day. Meal plan with breakfast and dinner 4.000 CFP. Surfer packages* *available. Add 6% value added tax to room rates and 50 CFP per person per day for municipal tax. No credit cards.*

Bonjouir is a French word to describe the BEST feeling you EVER had! World-class surfing champions have discovered the exciting waves in the Teahupoo pass, which has created a need for accommodations in this remote area. Many of the top surfing champions stay at Pension Bonjour for two weeks every May during the Billabong Pro Tahiti surf competition. Owner Annick Paofai speaks good English and is very outgoing. She also calls her pension the 'Eden of Tahiti'. Here you will find 3 bungalows, 3 *fares*, 5 studios, 2 rooms, a big dormitory for large groups, and a campground on a lush green property that is located between the mountains and the lagoon on the peninsula of Tahiti Iti. Some of these units face the jungle and mountains and others have a view of the ocean and jungle. A river flows through the property and access to the pension can be made only by boat from Teahupoo on the west coast or Tautira on the east coast of Tahiti Iti.

This untamed bush land provides a tranquil refuge for individuals or groups who want to get off the beaten track. The bungalows have double and single beds for 2-3 people in two units and up to 6 people in the big bungalow, and private bathrooms with hot water. Most of the bungalows are equipped with private kitchens and they all have patios. The beds are covered by mosquito nets, and the sheets, towels, pillows and blankets are provided. One of the studios has a private bathroom and you can share the kitchen with the people who sleep in the rooms and dormitories. The campers also share the communal bathrooms and cooking facilities, and they can take a 4-kilometer (2.5-mile) hike along the seashore to buy food at the *magasin* store in Teahupoo. The pension also operates a shuttle boat service twice a day that will take you to Teahupoo and back for 1.600 CFP per person.

Six-course meals prepared in the pension's main restaurant feature international cooking with a Tahitian flair, according to Annick Paofai, who describes the ingredients as "fresh local products caught out front or raised out back and picked just hours ago," adding that you just have to try her famous papaya goulash or coconut jam. Breakfast costs 1.000 CFP and dinner is 3.000 CFP. Beer, wine and cocktails are also available.

Kayaks and outrigger canoes are free for guest use, but you should bring your own snorkeling gear. Video, music and television are available in the restaurant/bar area, and there are facilities for soccer, volleyball and bacci ball. You can also swim, hike, go fishing in the river or lagoon or chill out in a hammock under the big Fare Pote'e gazebo. A shuttle boat is available to transfer surfers to the famous spots of Hava'e, Te Ava Iti and to the Vairao pass, for 1.000-1.500 CFP, depending on which pass you choose. Activities also include hiking into the interior of Te Pari and exploring the lagoon and nearby *motu* islet. The mornings here are especially magnificent, as you can see the sun rising from behind the horizon of the sea. A special sunset cruise or moon cruise can be arranged, as well as picnics on the motu. **Moana Paofai's Eden Day Adventure Boat Trip** to explore the Fenua Aihere and Te Pari costs guests of the pension 3.500 CFP per person, including lunch, and if you are not staying at Le Bonjouir the cost is 7.000 CFP per person. This is an outrigger excursion for six or more passengers that takes you to visit the southern coast of Tahiti Iti, exploring a hidden tributary, hiking through a rain forest to enter a cave and swim in the refreshing clear waters of the underground grotto of Vaipoiri. If you come for an Eden Day Tour Moana will meet you at the Eden boat beside the lagoon just before the end of the road in Teahupoo. If you rent a car to get here then you can leave it in his private parking area. You can also get a round-trip mini-bus transfer.

   PUNATEA VILLAGE, *B.P. 20756, Punaauia, Tahiti 98713. Tel./Fax. 689/ 57.71.00; cell 689/77.20.31/72.17.01; E-mail: punatea-village@mail.pf; www.punatea.com. On seaside at PK 4.7 in Afaahiti on the east coast of the Tahiti Iti peninsula, 64.7 kilometers (40 miles) from Papeete. EP Rates: bungalow 9.000 CFP single/double; room 5.500 CFP single/double; extra bed 2.000 CFP for adult and 1.000 CFP for child 3-12 years. Breakfast 500 CFP; lunch 1.500 CFP; dinner 2.000 CFP. Add 6% value added tax to room rates and 50 CFP per person per day for municipal tax. Mastercard, Visa.*

   This pension opened in February 2001 and is built on 18.5 acres of land beside the lagoon in Afaahiti, between Taravao and Pueu. There are four separate bungalows and a building containing five rooms, all built of wood and cedar shake roofs in the FEI style that has become the "norm" for pensions that receive special financial support from the local government. Each of the bungalows contains a double bed and a convertible sofa, a private bathroom with hot water, plus a kitchen and covered porch. There are ceiling fans and electric mosquito repellants. People staying in the rooms share the bath facilities. Owner/manager Titaua Bordes speaks English and is very helpful with her guests.

   Meals are served family style in two dining *fares* by the sea. Tapas made of various Tahitian foods are available to nibble on each Sunday afternoon while dancing to the music played by a Tahitian band. Tahitian feasts are organized on occasion, as well as wedding receptions and other parties. Free activities for guests include a fresh water swimming pool, swings for kids and volleyball net. Paid activities include horseback riding, trips to visit a private waterfall, picnics on Motu Nono and boat excursions to Te Pari on the end of the peninsula. In addition to the health benefits of breathing the fresh salty air and hiking in the tropical jungle of Tahiti Iti, Punatea Village has also added a massage chair and Japanese sauna, an infrared machine to help eliminate poisons from the system, so that you will return home feeling like a new person.

   FARE MAITHE, *B.P. 7141, Taravao, Tahiti 98719. Tel./Fax. 689/57.18.24; E-mail: rmo@tahitinui.net; www.chez-maithe.com. Beside the sea at PK 4.5* *in Afaahiti, on the east coast of the Tahiti Iti peninsula, 64.5 kilometers (40 miles) from Papeete. No transfers provided. EP Rates: room 7.000 CFP single/ double; air-conditioned room 8.000 CFP single/double; add 2.000 CFP per day for extra bed. All taxes included. No credit cards.*

This small guesthouse is located 20 meters from the sea, overlooking Motu Nono. There are two attractively decorated rooms with a double bed and a private bathroom with hot water. One of the rooms is air-conditioned and both rooms have a ceiling fan, and sheets and towels are furnished. Guests share the fully equipped kitchen, dining room, living room with television, and a terrace. Snorkeling equipment, bicycles, books and games are available. Maithé can arrange lagoon excursions, trips to the waterfalls and Te Pari cliffs, as well as a picnic outing to Motu Nono.

EAST COAST – PAPENOO VALLEY
Economy

FARE HAPE, *Hauururu Association, B.P. 110382, Mahina, Tahiti. Tel. 689/ 78.89.13/78.89.73; Fax 689/48.00.95. In Papenoo Valley, about 18 kilometers (11.2 miles) from the circle island road and Papenoo Village. EP Rates: small fare 3.000 CFP per day for 1-5 people; camping 1.500 CFP per person per day. No credit cards.*

The Hauururu Association of Papenoo was created in 1994 to protect and develop the Papenoo Valley, where it is believed that between 6,000 and 10,000 people lived at one time. Some archaeologists have estimated that up to 20,000 people inhabited this valley. Dr. Kenneth P. Emory of the Bernice P. Bishop Museum in Honolulu first excavated this site in 1926. Some 190 *marae* and sanctuaries have been found in the high valley, especially since the road was built to construct hydroelectric dams.

The first signs of human settlement date from 1500 to 1650 AD, and remains show that the inhabitants worked with tools of stone. Between 1650 and 1815 AD they created a series of terraces on which they built their *marae* temples and house sites. The *fare hau pape* was the home of the high chief of this area, and it appears that all activity ceased around 1815. Between 1825 and 1840 the *fare haupape* was once again occupied, with the addition of a kitchen on the front veranda. The Papenoo Valley was finally deserted around 1850.

The Fare Hape site is located in a lovely setting just below the Relais de la Maroto (Maroto Inn). There is even a sparkling waterfall that cascades into a refreshing pool, a favored destination for swimmers who stop for a picnic while visiting the interior valley by 4WD vehicle, usually during a Safari tour. The Hauururu Association has built 15 *fare* shelters that will sleep 5-6 people in each. Bring your own sheets, pillows, blankets and towels. There are also 5 camping sites, but you must bring your own tent. A sheltered area has picnic tables and benches, a meeting area for seminars, and a kitchen with hot and cold water, stove, refrigerator, freezer, pots, pans and cooking gas. People staying in the *small fare* shelters, as well as campers, should bring their individual dishes and food and take their own garbage with them when they leave. There are separate toilet and shower facilities for men and women.

Several of the *marae* in the Fare Hape site have been restored and there are also archery platforms, house foundations and a huge boulder carved with petroglyphs. If you come here without a guide, you can hire a local guide for 4.000 CFP per hour. On request, he will take you to visit the nearby site of Anapua, where a *marae* resembling an airstrip was built on top of a grotto. Some Tahitians say that this is where the souls of the ancient Maohi people took off after they left their bodies. Other walks will take you to the Tahinu site of 19 restored *marae* and to visit the Maroto waterfalls. The Haururu Association does not provide transportation for people to get to the Fare Hape site, but they will transport your bags and equipment from the first bridge, called Mamao, for a round-trip fee of 10.000 CFP per vehicle. Then you can hike into the valley.

Other Family Pensions, Guest Houses, Surf Lodges, Dormitories & Camp Sites

Motel Pension Puea, *Tel. 85.43.43; E-mail: pension.puea@mail.pf*, at 87 Rue Octave Moreau in Farepitii, has 8 rooms from 6.500 CFP single/double.

Heitiare Inn, *Tel. 83.33.52*, PK 5, Faa'a, near airport, has 13 rooms from 7.500 CFP single/double.

Le Bellevue, *Tel. 58.47.04; E-mail: jacques.richard@freebel.net*, on the mountainside at PK 16.5 in Punaauia, has a studio for 25.000 CFP single/ double. Weekly and monthly rentals available.

Papara Village, *Tel. 57.11.11; E-mail: paparavillage@mail.pf*, at PK 38 on the mountainside in Papara, with 3 bungalows and swimming pool from 12.000 CFP single/double.

Fare Ratere, *Tel. 57.48.19; E-mail: yannfareratere@mail.pf*, at PK 39.2 on the seaside in Papara, has 2 beach bungalows from 12.000 CFP single/ double and 3 duplex garden studios from 9.500 CFP single.

Chez Jeannine, *Tel./Fax 57.07.49/77.27.37*, PK 4, Taravao Plateau on Tahiti Iti, has 5 rooms for 5.000 CFP single/double and 4 bungalows for 7.900 CFP single/double.

Meherio Iti, *Tel. 78.83.74/72.45.50*, on the seaside at PK 11.9 in Vairao, has 3 bungalows for 8.000 CFP single and 10.000 CFP double.

Pension Vaiani, *Tel./Fax 57.96.16*, on the seaside at PK 16.9 in Teahupoo, has 3 rooms with 10 dormitory beds and communal bathroom, for 6.500 CFP per person MAP. This no frills lodging is designed for surfers.

Pueu Village, *Tel./Fax 57.57.87*, on the seaside at PK 9.8 in Pueu on the east coast of the Tahiti Iti peninsula, has 4 new bungalows for 9.000 CFP single/double. Owner Victor Van Cam is also building 6 rooms in a concrete building. Swimming pool on premises, which used to be the Hotel Te Anuanua.

Where to Eat
HOTEL RESTAURANTS
INTERCONTINENTAL RESORT TAHITI, *Tel. 86.51.10. PK 7, Faaa. Open daily for breakfast, lunch and dinner. All credit cards. Add 10% tax.*

Tiare Restaurant is the main restaurant, offering all day dining. An Express breakfast is served from 5:30-10:30am for 1.130 CFP, a Continental breakfast is a cold buffet between 5:30-10:30am for 2.225 CFP, and a full American breakfast buffet for 2.710 CFP is served from 7-10:30am. This buffet also includes Japanese breakfast foods such as miso soup, rice and pickled vegetables. Light meals and a *table d'hôte* menu are served between 11am and 3:30pm. Sandwiches are 1.175-1.735 CFP, pizzas are 1.650-1.855 CFP, paninis are 1.900 CFP and pasta is 1.900-2.060 CFP. Between 11:30am and 2:30pm you can also choose your own combinations to be wokked for 2.215 CFP. The *table d'hôte* luncheon menu of the day is 4.020 CFP for a 3-course meal. Dinner is served from 6:30 to 10pm, featuring local specialties and international cuisine. Hot or cold appetizers are 1.130-2.400 CFP, and Tahitian specialties are 2.575-3.810 CFP, which include pan-fried veal medallion and shrimp, served with a shellfish sauce, vegetables and exotic rice, deep fried salmon with basilic sauce, and Moorea shrimp, pineapple and Tahitian rum flambé. Other specialties are marinated duck filet for 3.400 CFP and roast lamb for 2.730 CFP. Desserts are 880-1.130 CFP. The set dinner menu is 5.995 CFP.

A Rotisserie Barbecue Dinner is featured on Wednesday night, followed by a Tahitian dance show, for 6.225 CFP per person. The most popular event of the week is the *Soiree Merveilleuse*, the Marvelous Evening, for 7.680 CFP, which is held on Friday night. Following a seafood buffet that includes oysters on the half shell and rock lobster tails, entertainment is provided by one of the best professional dance groups of Tahiti. This show often includes fire dancing under the stars on the white sand beach. A Bounty Dinner and Show is held on Saturday nights, with a special buffet of imaginative dishes prepared with local products and a musical re-enactment of the "Mutiny on the Bounty" story of Captain Bligh and Fletcher Christian performed by Les Grands Ballet de Tahiti, the premier dance group of Tahiti. This costs 7.120 CFP per person. A Tahitian brunch for 3.500 CFP is served in the Tiare restaurant every Sunday morning, which gives you the opportunity of tasting some very unusual treats such as *taioro*, *firi firi* and vanilla coffee laced with coconut milk.

Following Tahiti's Heiva Festival held each July, the InterContinental Resort Tahiti presents the Mini-Heiva, a program of several sumptuous buffets and performances by the winning song and dance groups. And throughout the year, in addition to the special evenings each week, the hotel organizes other festive events. If you happen to be in Tahiti then, you don't want to miss it. The prices quoted above include taxes.

Le Lotus is an overwater restaurant adjacent to a sandy bottom swimming pool with an outdoor Jacuzzi and swim-up bar. From 10am to 6pm you can sip a tropical cocktail from your underwater barstool as you gaze at the beautiful island of Moorea across the Sea of Moons, and watch the outrigger canoe paddlers glide past in the opalescent lagoon. This is one of Tahiti's most beautiful and romantic restaurants and you'll think you're in a movie setting of the South Seas.

The hotel management signed a partnership agreement in 2001 with Paul Haeberlin of Alsace and his restaurant, l'Auberge de l'Ill, one of the grand names of French gastronomy, who received a three-star rating by Michelin in 1965 and still hold this rating. A Haeberlin chef now collaborates with the Lotus' own Chef Franck David to combine Tahiti's fresh products with the recipes from l'Auberge de l'Ill.

Le Lotus is open daily 12-2:30pm and 6:30-9:30pm. You should reserve. Lunch can be a two-course Fine Bouche meal for 4.200 CFP or a 3-course Gourmet meal for 4.900 CFP, or you can order à la carte. Small salads are 2.100 to 3.000 CFP and large salads are 2.900 to 4.400 CFP. The main course choices include rack of lamb for 3.600 CFP, beef tenderloin with green pepper sauce for 3.800 CFP and grilled veal tenderloin saltimboca for 4.200 CFP. Desserts are 1.300 to 1.500 CFP.

The à la carte dinner menu proposes cold appetizers for 2.950 to 3.400 CFP, which include fresh and smoked salmon tartare or goose liver and fig skewer on a pastry. Hot appetizers are priced from 2.950 to 3.800 CFP and include Thai fried shrimp served in a fresh apple or a pastilla of duck confit. Your main course may be lamb filet with a Haeberlin purée for 4.400 CFP, boned pigeon with foie gras in a pastry crust with pork and truffle sauce for 4.900 CFP, or veal filet with asparagus and fresh mushrooms in flaky pastry for 5.600 CFP. The 2-course Fine Bouche menu is 6.900 CFP, the 3-course Gourmet menu is 8.200 CFP and the 4-course Degustation menu is 9.600 CFP. A platter of French cheeses is 1.300 CFP and desserts are 1.300 to 1.500 CFP. The menu changes frequently. You can choose your wines and champagnes from an extensive menu, and toast one another to the musical accompaniment of your old favorites that are played softly on the piano as you dine.

LE MERIDIEN, *Tel. 47.07.07. PK 15, Punaauia. Open daily for breakfast, lunch and dinner. All credit cards.*

La Plantation is the hotel's main restaurant, where you can order a Continental breakfast from 5:30-6:30am for 1.900 CFP. An American buffet breakfast is 3.100 CFP and the brunch served on Sundays and holidays is 3.900 CFP. You can also order à la carte, which includes coffee, tea or hot chocolate with milk for 400 CFP, French toast (2) or pancakes (2) for 550 CFP each, and a ham or cheese omelet for 900 CFP. The luncheon menu includes appetizers for 1.300-1.990 CFP, seafood pasta for 2.100 CFP, grilled fish for 2.700-2.900 CFP and meats for 2.500-3.100 CFP. A 3-course set menu is 4.160 CFP, or you can order from the snack menu, which offers a Croque Monsieur (ham and cheese sandwich) for 1.300 CFP, a Club sandwich for 1.500 CFP, burgers for 1.650-1.800 CFP, lasagna for 1.650 CFP, and desserts for 1.300 CFP. A cold buffet is served from 12-3pm on Saturday and Sunday for 2.600 CFP.

A Polynesian Night is presented each Friday evening with a seafood buffet for 7.100 CFP, and the Toa Reva dancers perform an extravaganza show around the pool, which includes a spectacular fire dance. **L'Astrolabe**, the main bar, serves exotic cocktails. The **Pool Bar** serves light snacks such as panini sandwiches and burgers.

Le Carré is a gastronomic restaurant beside the beach, where you can sit on the sundeck under a big umbrella at lunchtime or under the stars at night while dining by candlelight. Inside the square restaurant are square tables and chairs, square place settings, napkins and dishes, all designed to carry out the theme of Le Carré—the square. Formula dining is possible by choosing Le Carré Salé for 6.700 CFP, giving you a hot or cold starter and main course of your choice, or Le Carré Sucré for 5.400 CFP, which is the main course and dessert. Le Grand Carré for 8.500 CFP includes the starter, main course and dessert.

The menu of gourmet cuisine suggests cold appetizers such as a mosaic of mahi mahi and salmon with seaweed, tomato and green lemon emulsion for 2.800 CFP, a trilogy of poisson cru for 2.900 CFP, a corolla of scallops with poached egg, home smoked salmon and soy vinegar for 3.400 CFP, roasted goat cheese with tapenade, olive oil and balsamic vinegar for 3.500 CFP, or duck foie gras, preserve, stew of pig's trotter with thyme for 3.500 CFP. Hot starter courses are 2.800 to 3.600 CFP, the chef's suggestions are 3.200 CFP, and the fish and seafood choices are priced from 3.400 to 3.900 CFP. These include roasted shrimp with vanilla, a duet of risotto brouilly and saffron flavor, or roasted John Dory, infusion of beetroot with coriander, a fan of zucchini flower and duet of glazed vegetables. The meat and poultry dishes are 3.600 to 3.900 CFP. Two of the suggestions are filet of beef and foie gras with truffle sauce, served with duchesse of potatoes, or surprise of lamb filet with potatoes and tapenade. You can also select cheeses from the trolley for 1.800 CFP a serving. All desserts are 1.800 CFP and the list includes papaya tarte tatin; hazelnut soufflé and sweet icing; and savarin cake with rum and fine fruit mousse. Gourmet vegetarian dishes are also listed on the menu for 2.800 to 3.300 CFP. Pan sautéed tofu and vegetarian pasta is one suggestion, and mixed salad leaves with a tart of sautéed vegetables is another.

The wine cabinet is filled with select choices of wine from Spain, Chile, Argentina, Australia and California, priced from 3.135 to 10.460 CFP. Red Bordeaux wines are 2.670 to 78.320 CFP, and champagnes are 7.820 to 25.230 CFP. Dessert wines include Château d'Yquem 1989 Sauternes for 58.810 CFP. Exotic coffees are 350 to 1.200 CFP, and after dinner *digestifs* are

450 to 1.700 CFP per glass. There are even cigars from Cuba for 1.600 to 3.000 CFP, or from the Dominican Republic for 1.260 to 2.110 CFP.

RADISSON PLAZA RESORT TAHITI, *Tel. 48.88.88. Open daily for breakfast from 6:30-11am, lunch from 12-3pm, and dinner from 6:30-10pm. All credit cards.*

Restaurant Hiti Mahana is the resort's signature restaurant, overlooking Lafayette Beach and Matavai Bay, and it is the only restaurant in Tahiti that offers both indoor, air-conditioned seating, as well as alfresco dining. The breezes are sometimes a little too windy, as I experienced a few days after the hotel opened in August 2004. We had to move to keep from having our table settings blown away. The seating capacity is 152, including 52 places in the glassed-in area with air conditioning. The menu offers a mix of local Tahitian, South East Asian dishes and international Mediterranean cuisine. Friday and Saturday nights feature special themed buffets, with a local Tahitian and seafood buffet on Friday nights, complete with Tahitian dance shows. This Matavai Feast costs 6.360 CFP. The Saturday night Mediterranean buffet is inspired by the cuisine of Italy, South of France, Spain and Northern Africa, and costs 6.180 CFP. A Sunday brunch buffet is 3.900 CFP.

A Continental buffet breakfast is 2.000 CFP and a full American buffet breakfast is 2.640 CFP. A set luncheon menu with appetizer, main course and dessert is 3.640 CFP, and a 3-course set dinner menu is 5.000 CFP. The à la carte menu for lunch and dinner lists starter courses from 850 CFP, for a bowl of pineapple and carrot soup with fresh chives, to 1.950 CFP for a Thai beef filet salad on a bed of glass noodles. The grill and main course choices are priced from 1.950-3.100 CFP, and include king prawns in a *ragout* of tomato and basil on white rice and sautéed eggplants; grilled honey lamb filet, served with soya flavored vegetables and sweet potatoes; and tournedos of beef and polenta, sautéed with balsamic vinegar accompanied with sun dried tomato and wild thyme. The "sweet ending" desserts are 900-1.350 CFP, featuring the Croquant Radisson, which is a dark chocolate mousse, puff pastry with hazelnut cream and biscuits. White wines are priced from 2.500-8.250 CFP, red wines are 2.410-13.170 CFP, and the *grand cru* vintage Bordeaux wines are 14.190-23.760 CFP.

Lafayette Bar is on the hotel's upper level and is open from 4pm until late at night. The resort's signature drink is the Pisco Sour, and an extensive variety of cocktails, beers, spirits, wines and champagnes can be served on request.

SHERATON HOTEL TAHITI, *Tel. 86.48.48. Open daily for breakfast, lunch and dinner. All credit cards.*

Restaurant Moevai is built over the water, serving breakfast from 6-10:30am, lunch from 12-2pm, and dinner from 6:30-10pm. The menu lists appetizers from 1.500-2.500 CFP, fish and seafood from 2.350-3.000 CFP and chef's classics for 2.100-3.350 CFP. Desserts are 1.000-1.200 CFP and may be kiwi pie with corossol sorbet, coconut soufflé with Grande Marnier or baked papaya crumble. A business lunch is 4.650 CFP, which includes an appetizer, main course, dessert and a glass of house wine.

Terrasse He'epu'enui («to set in a cloudless sky») is open daily from 11am to 9pm, serving light meals. Poolside beverage service is also available. Drinks are served in **Quinn's Bar** from 10am to midnight. There was a lot of activity around the restaurant and bar areas when this hotel opened in July 1999, with local clientele attending the Polynesian buffet that was served at noon on Friday, followed by an afternoon of drinking and dancing to live Tahitian music. There were also seafood buffets with a dance show, Tahitian breakfasts on Sunday morning and other lively activities. The service was very slow and even non-existent at times, which must have eventually taken a heavy toll, because all the special breakfasts, brunches, buffets and dance shows had been eliminated when I checked in August 2004. The only entertainment was a Tahitian singer performing in the bar on weekends. Meeting and banquet facilities can accommodate up to 500 people.

SOFITEL MAEVA BEACH, *Tel. 86.66.00. PK 7.5 Punaauia. Open daily for breakfast, lunch and dinner. All credit cards.*

Restaurant Bougainville, on the ground level, is an open-air restaurant for 200 people. A breakfast buffet is served from 5:45-10am and costs 1.950 CFP for a Continental breakfast and 2.400 CFP for a hot American breakfast. The lunch/dinner menu lists salads and appetizers from 800 to 1.800 CFP, including poisson cru for 1.100 CFP. The self-serve salad bar is 2.050 CFP. Grilled fish and meats range from 1.750 CFP for roast pork to 2.550 CFP for beef tenderloin. Desserts are 600-1.150 CFP. If you prefer a quick and light meal, you can order an omelet for 1.150 CFP, spaghetti for 1.250 CFP, burgers for 1.350 CFP or a Club sandwich for 1.450 CFP. Polynesian dance shows are presented in the Bougainville restaurant at 8pm each Friday during a Barbecue Buffet for 4.800 CFP, and each Sunday another dance show is performed during the Tahitian *tamaara'a* luncheon feast, which has become a popular tradition at the Maeva Beach. This buffet and show costs 5.800 CFP per adult and includes a welcome punch, wine, draft beer or soft drink, and the price is 2.900 CFP for a child 6-11 years old.

Some of the Polynesian employees who work in the Bougainville restaurant have been here for many years. They are very friendly and seem to truly enjoy their work, whether it's cooking omelets for breakfast or bringing you the bill for your meal. From 11:30am to 5pm you can get sandwiches, hamburgers and salads at the Moorea Bar beside the swimming pool, and from 9:30am to 10:30pm you can enjoy your favorite cocktails at this outdoor bar. Happy Hour is held here daily from 5 to 6pm and from 9 to 10pm, when drinks are half-price. Musical entertainment adds to the ambience on weekends.

Sakura is a Japanese restaurant located adjacent to the main lobby of the Sofitel Maeva Beach. Open daily 6:30pm to 9:30pm. Teppanyaki cooking is the main attraction, with choices of chicken breast, sirloin steak, tenderloin, shrimp, salmon or lobster. Special combinations include steak and salmon for 2.950 CFP, chicken and shrimp for 4.300 CFP, and filet mignon and lobster for 6.500 CFP. You can also order a combo of sashimi and sushi for 1.300 CFP, and tempura is priced from 1.100 to 2.100 CFP. A honeymoon menu is 16.000 CFP. The accompanying vegetables are different from those you are normally served in this type of restaurant, which usually include mushrooms and bean sprouts, but these are missing from the Sakura's table. Nonetheless, all the chefs (no Japanese) are kept busy and reservations are a must.

ROYAL TAHITIEN, *Tel. 50.40.40. On waterfront in Pirae at the Hotel Royal Tahitien. All credit cards. Open daily for breakfast from 6:30 to 11am, for lunch from 11:30am to 2pm, and for dinner from 7-9:30pm (until 10pm on Friday nights).*

You can dine on an open deck overlooking the black sand beach and lagoon, or inside the Polynesian style restaurant, which has an intricately woven pandanus ceiling that is reminiscent of Tahiti of yesteryear, "la belle epoch". You can choose a French style breakfast for 930 CFP, a Continental breakfast for 1.450 CFP, an American breakfast for 1.730 CFP, or a Tahitian breakfast for 1.900 CFP. You can also order à la carte eggs with bacon, ham or sausages for 730 CFP, poisson cru for 1.550 CFP or grilled horse steak for 1.800 CFP. A cup of Tahitian coffee with vanilla and coconut cream is 370 CFP.

The lunch or dinner menu suggests poisson cru for 1.750 CFP, nems and sashimi for 1.800 CFP or shrimp cocktail for 2.050 CFP. Salads are 1.550-1.680 CFP and soups include gaspacho for 850 CFP, or onion soup for 1.050 CFP. Some of the house specialties are tartare of tuna or steak for 1.900 CFP, tuna sashimi for 1.900 CFP and shrimp curry for 2.780 CFP. Special Island dishes include chicken and fafa (taro leaves) for 1.980 CFP and breaded mahi mahi in coconut milk for 2.050 CFP. A vegetarian dish of Chinese style sautéed vegetables is 1.200 CFP, fish and seafood choices are 1.980-3.040 CFP, grilled lobster is 3.240 CFP and meats are 1.500-2.880 CFP. These include veal kidneys in Porto wine for 1.980 CFP, breaded veal cutlet Cordon Bleu for 2.180 CFP, and a T-bone steak for 2.880 CFP. A *plat du jour* is served at lunch for 1.950-2.250 CFP. A 3-course tourist menu is 3.400 CFP. If you prefer a lighter meal, you can order a hamburger, cheeseburger or mahi mahi burger for 1.280 CFP, all served with fries. A Club sandwich with fries is 1.350 CFP. Desserts are priced from 680-900 CFP and include bananas flambé, coconut pie or a banana split. You can order house wine by the carafe for 1.500 CFP a liter, or choose a bottle of wine from 1.500-8.580 CFP.

Each Friday evening is a big occasion at the Royal Tahitien, when local residents gather around the bar and terrace to celebrate the end of the work week. A live orchestra plays music for dancing until midnight, and a special barbecue dinner of roast veal on a spit is 3.700 CFP per person.

IAORANA VILLA, *Tel. 54.49.11. On the lagoon and mountainside at PK 10.8 in Punaauia, between the airport and Le Méridien. All credit cards. Open daily for lunch and on Friday and Saturday night for dinner. No breakfast is served.*

A chalkboard beside the old circle island road along the coast lists the *plat du jour*, which may be blanquette de veau, mahi mahi, meka, espadon (swordfish), or curry, priced at 1.500 CFP. This is a pleasant place to eat while gazing at the lagoon and listening to the live band that plays music every day during lunch. You might also want to order a drink from the Tiki Bar, an authentic Polynesian watering hole that attracts local customers. A live band plays local tunes during lunch on Thursday, Friday and Saturday, and from noon to 11pm on Sundays. In August 2004 the manager said that they will start serving Tahitian food every other Sunday for 3.500 CFP.

RESTAURANTS IN DOWNTOWN PAPEETE
Deluxe

CORBEILLE D'EAU, *Tel. 43.77.14. Blvd. Pomare, Paofai. American Express, Mastercard and Visa. Open for lunch and dinner, except for Saturday noon and all day Sunday and holidays. Reserve.*

You won't find the daily luncheon specials listed on a sidewalk chalkboard at this small, elegant restaurant. The name is the French version of Papeete, which means "water basket" and it's located in the block just west of the Protestant Temple across from the waterfront. If you're walking from downtown it is worth the few extra steps to experience the gastronomic French cuisine that is served in a very intimate air-conditioned setting. The menu changes very frequently, with appetizers ranging from 1.700-3.300 CFP, and the main courses including four to six choices each of meat and fish, which are priced from 2.900 to 4.300 CFP per dish.

You may decide on the *carpaccio de foie gras de canard aux asperges* or *crevettes fraîches sautées á la crème de saumon fumé*. If you're in the mood for meat, the *filet de boeuf rôti á la créme aux morilles* is an excellent choice. You may choose from the *chariot de desserts* for 1.800 CFP. You may not understand what you're reading on the menu, but the *maître d'hotel* will graciously explain it all to you, as well as suggesting the appropriate wines for your meal. Some Americans find this place too "precious", too snobbishly French with a cold atmosphere and nothing interesting to eat.

Superior

L'O A LA BOUCHE, *Tel. 45.29.76. Passage Cardella. American Express, Mastercard and Visa. Open for lunch and dinner. Closed Saturday noon and all day Sunday. Reserve.*

Bruno and Jean-Charles have one of the best-rated restaurants in Tahiti, right in the heart of Papeete. The name indicates that you'll be salivating when you order their original specialties of *la nouvelle cuisine Française*. You may want to start with the cold Vichyssoise soup for 1.400 CFP, the parrotfish terrine with a lime cream dressing for 1.750 CFP, an endive and Bayonne salad with Roquefort cheese for 1.750 CFP, or snails with butter and garlic in flaky pastry for 1.750 CFP. A vegetarian platter is 1.660 CFP, and you can order a small or large portion of tuna carpaccio or tuna/beef tartare for 1.100 or 1.750 CFP. The fish and seafood main courses range from 2.800 to 3.000 CFP and the meat and poultry dishes are 2.650 to 3.400 CFP. Perhaps your taste buds will tempt you to try the *choucroute de perroquet à la moutarde ancienne* for 2.800 CFP, or you may prefer the *magret de canard caramélisé aux epices et au miel*, for 2.950 CFP. The Coquille St. Jacques with shrimp is another good choice for 2.950 CFP. This air-conditioned restaurant has a very bright modern French décor and a faithful clientele.

LE RUBIS, *Tel. 43.25.55. 16 rue Jeanne d'Arc, on the street level of the Vaima Center, between the waterfront and the Catholic church in the center of Papeete. All major credit cards. Open Monday through Saturday for lunch and Tuesday through Sunday for dinner. Closed Sunday noon and Monday night. Reserve.*

Acajou, one of Tahiti's top chefs, who was the manager and chef of this 100-seat gourmet restaurant, has now retired, and left his well-trained assistant in charge of the kitchen.

The menu still includes Acajou's famous French onion soup for 890 CFP, his crispy fried shrimp with cocktail sauce for 2.895 CFP, his shrimp curry with coconut milk for 2.995 CFP, and his fisherman's cassolette for 2.995 CFP. Starter courses are 890-3.975 CFP, salads are 1.875-2.995 CFP, poisson cru is 1.795 CFP, tartares or carpaccios are 1.895 to 2.595 CFP, fish and seafood is 1.895 to 2.995 CFP, meats and poultry is 1.895 to 3.500 CFP, and a Chateaubriand Henry IV for two is 6.850 CFP. Daily specials are around 1.900 CFP and may be a tuna tartare, veal and white sauce, or curried pork and wild rice. The menu at Le Rubis contains an extensive selection of tempting dishes, such as stewed rabbit cooked in St. Emilion wine sauce, baby lamb with Provence herbs and flaky puff pastry with salmon, dill and basil, cooked in a Riesling wine sauce. The menu also suggests a wine to accompany each dish. Le Rubis is a wine bar and will serve you a glass of fine wine for 700 to 1.150 CFP, or you can choose a bottle from 130 different labels in the wine cellar.

ROYAL KIKIRIRI, *Tel. 43.58.64. Rue Colette, between Rue Paul Gauguin and Rue des Ecoles. Mastercard, Visa. Open Monday through Saturday 11:30am-2pm, and Wednesday-Saturday 7-9:30pm. Closed all day Sunday and at night on Monday and Tuesday.*

This is an undiscovered gem of a restaurant for people who enjoy French or Chinese cuisine and Tahitian specialties. The small, simply decorated restaurant is air-conditioned and is located above the Kikiriri nightclub. What I really like is the selection of fish, which can be mahi mahi, moon fish, grouper, parrot fish, red snapper or various lagoon fish, steamed whole with ginger and green onions, salted lemon or black beans. Cold appetizers are priced between 800 and 1.850 CFP, New Zealand oysters are 2.350 CFP, hot appetizers are 1.500-2.250 CFP, fish dishes are 1.950-3.100 CFP, seafood is 1.700-2.680 CFP, a seafood platter is 4.650 CFP, shrimp and lobster tails are 5.950 CFP, and meats and poultry are 1.750-4.950 CFP, including veal scallop Milanese style for 1.950 CFP. Chinese dishes start with appetizers for 980 CFP, chow mein special for 1.450 CFP, and main courses for 1.300-2.800 CFP include a spicy tofu dish with minced pork and chicken for 1.450 CFP. Desserts, from 650 to 1.350 CFP, include fresh local fruits such as papaya baked with citron.

They offer a tourist menu every Tuesday, which is *ma'a tinito haricots rouge* (Chinese food with red beans) for 1.600 CFP, and each Friday they alternate between prime rib for 4.000 CFP and *ma'a Tahiti* (Tahitian food), also for 4.000 CFP. A big buffet for gourmands is presented on the last Saturday night of each month, and the price of 5.000 CFP includes a Tahitian dance show. Afterwards, you can go downstairs and dance in the air-conditioned Kikiriri nightclub, one of the most popular discos in Papeete.

Moderate to Superior
   LA ROMANA, *Tel. 41.33.64/45.25.50/72.67.32. 3 Rue du Commandant Destremeau. American Express, Mastercard and Visa. Open for lunch Monday-Friday from 11am to 2pm and for dinner Monday-Sunday from 6-10pm. Closed for lunch on Saturday and Sunday and open for dinner. Free pick-up service.*

This is a very active lunchtime restaurant near the complex of government offices, and the dinner business is very slow. Starr and Mehiti Teriitahi bought the restaurant in 2001 and have added a free pick-up service for tourists who want to get out of their hotels for dinner. The décor of this large restaurant is reminiscent of Tuscany, with a restful, old world decor, and soft lighting. The menu suggests starter courses for 1.450-2.500 CFP, including a Javanese tuna for 1.800 CFP, carpaccio of mahi mahi with pesto sauce for 1.800 CFP and raw shrimp for 2.200 CFP. Fish and seafood are priced from 2.350-2.900 CFP, meats are 2.300-3.600 CFP, and chef's specialties are 1.950-2.950 CFP. These include breaded veal scallop Milan style, grilled lamb, grilled T-bone steak, osso bucco, and tournedos Rossini. A child's menu is 1.250 CFP with 2 choices. Entertainment is provided on the last weekend of each month, featuring, among others, the local "King" (Elvis impersonator), Rocky Gobrait.

   LA SAIGONNAISE, *Tel. 42.05.35. Ave. Prince Hinoi. Visa. Open for lunch and dinner. Closed Sunday.*

To reach this Vietnamese restaurant if you're walking from downtown Papeete, follow Avenue Prince Hinoi from the waterfront to the first traffic light, and continue straight ahead, walking on the left side of the street until you see the restaurant in the next block. You can relax in the small, air-conditioned dining room while choosing your meal from a varied menu. In addition to the soups and salads, which are light and pleasing to the palate, you'll want to try some of Jeannot's house specialties, such as the *nems*, a Vietnamese omelet or the very light and tender fried balls of pork, which are priced from about 1.200 to 4.500 CFP.

LE CAFE DES NEGOCIANTS, *Tel. 48.08.48; www.lecafédesnégociants.pf. 10 Rue Jean-Gilbert, Quartier du Commerce. Mastercard, Visa. Meals served from 8am to 1am Monday-Friday and Saturday night. Closed Saturday noon and all day Sunday.*

You will find this small air-conditioned French bistrot from the waterfront street of Boulevard Pomare by following the side street behind *La Maison de la Presse*. There are also tables outside, beside the pedestrian street. Some of the regular clients are black pearl dealers, who have their jewelry shops and offices on this street. Musical concerts are shown on a big screen starting at 4:30pm and Happy Hour is from 5 to 6pm, with reduced prices on beer and cocktails. Live musical groups perform on occasion, usually on weekends. The menu includes a creative selection of salads for 1.600 to 2.250 CFP. Baguette sandwiches are 850 to 1.100 CFP, a cheeseburger is 1.650 CFP, and a vegetarian plate is 1.400 CFP. A variety of carpaccios, poisson cru and tartares are 1.450 to 2.250 CFP, grilled mahi mahi is 1.850 CFP, meats are 1.900 to 3.200 CFP and desserts are 1.050 to 1.300 CFP. They carry an extensive menu of fine French wines from 2.300 to 12.200 CFP. Breakfast can be ordered à la carte or formula. A Continental breakfast is 900 CFP, an American breakfast is 1.000 CFP and a Maohi breakfast is 1.500 CFP. Tapas are available at night only, for 350 to 980 CFP, and include crostinis of tomatoes, mozzarella and salsa verde, samoussas, chorizo tortilla, and shish kabobs of chicken, tuna or shrimp.

LE GALLEINI, *Tel. 42.01.29. Hotel Royal Papeete, Blvd. Pomare. All major credit cards. Open for lunch daily except Sunday and for dinner nightly except Tuesday and Sunday.*

This air-conditioned restaurant may be a bit run down at the heels but it is one of Papeete's hidden culinary treasures, and you will be happily surprised with the food, service and prices. The menu offers several mouth-watering selections of French and local style cuisine. Cold appetizers are priced at 1.230 to 2.520 CFP and hot starter courses are 880 to 2.800 CFP. Salads are 950 to 1.510 CFP, fish and seafood dishes range from 1.700 to 2.350 CFP, poultry is 2.100 to 2.570 CFP and meat choices are 1.650 to 2.560 CFP. The specialty of the house each Thursday, Friday and Saturday for both lunch and dinner is the tender California style prime rib *au jus*, served with baked potatoes and horseradish sauce, for 2.160, 2.770 or 3.880 CFP for a small, medium or large portion, respectively. My favorite dish here is the *poisson cru* with coconut milk, which is a meal in itself for 1.500 CFP. You'll like the dessert trolley also, with its tempting selection of cakes, puddings and pies for 800 CFP per serving.

LE MANDARIN, *Tel. 50.33.50. 26, Rue des Ecoles. All major credit cards. Open daily from 11am to 1:30pm and 6 to 9:30pm except Saturday and Sunday noon.*

If you're in downtown Papeete and are in the mood for good Chinese food, this air-conditioned restaurant just around the corner from the Hotel Mandarin is one of the better restaurants. The upstairs dining room is decorated in an elaborate Chinese Mandarin motif and serves authentic Cantonese specialties, using local seafood and fresh produce. The menu changes weekly, featuring unusual dishes such as soup made from chicken and *bêche de mer* (sea cucumber), *cigale de mer* (slipper lobster) and steamed *limande* (flounder). Soups are priced from 700-1.200 CFP, appetizers are 750-2.500 CFP, fish dishes are 990-1.700 CFP, seafood is 1.200-3.200 CFP, poultry dishes are 1.600-2.400 CFP, meats are 1.600-2.000 CFP, specialty items are 1.200-3.700 CFP and noodles are 950-1.950 CFP. A tourist menu for two people is 2.300 CFP per person and includes three dishes. The talented chef will also prepare you an unforgettable dinner of Peking duck or *ta pen lou* (Chinese seafood fondue) if you give him a day's advance notice. The wine cellar contains a varied selection of the best of Bordeaux. Live music is also performed during lunch on Friday and in the evenings on weekends.

LE MARAICAIBO, *Tel. 85.31.11. In Aorai building just behind the Cathedral in downtown Papeete. Open Monday-Saturday at 9am for coffee. Lunch is served from 11:30am-2:30pm and dinner is served from 6:30-9pm. The bar stays open all day. Closed Monday night and all day Sunday. American Express, Mastercard, Visa.*

Look for the Pirate statue on Rue Edouard Ahnne, or if you are visiting the Odyssey book and music store, you can also enter the building from the Cathedral side. The menu offers a selection of salads for 750-2.400 CFP, cold plates for 1.550-2.150 CFP, hot starter courses for 1.650-2.550 CFP, fish dishes for 1.700-3.400 CFP and meats for 1.800-2.950 CFP. Specialties include gambas with a spicy or rum sauce for 2.500 CFP, frog legs for 2.550 CFP, seafood gratin for 2.350 CFP and filet of beef Rossini for 2.950 CFP. A tourist menu is 2.900 CFP for 3 courses. Desserts are 850-1.150 CFP. The Route du Rhum bar has stools that are usually occupied by a few customers who linger for a *digestif* or *pression* after a long lunch. The air-conditioning system isn't efficient enough to offset the cigarette smoke, which adds to the atmosphere of a pirate's hangout.

MOANA ITI, *Tel. 42.65.24. Blvd. Pomare. American Express, Mastercard and Visa. Open for lunch and dinner. Closed Sunday.*

Since 1973 Jean-Jacques has been serving fine French cuisine in his air-conditioned restaurant across from the waterfront, in the block just west of Avenue Bruat. His specialties include rabbit simmered in white wine, for 2.050 CFP, and *tournedos* (tenderloin of beef) with *cèpes*, for 2.650 CFP. Chateaubriand for two is 4.300 CFP. The fresh seafood dishes, according to season, may be raw oysters, marinated mussels or grilled salmon, imported from France. He also carries a good selection of moderate priced wines. The restaurant and the stale air could use a freshening up and the reception you get here is not the friendliest in town, but the food is still good.

MORRISON'S CAFE, *Tel. 42.78.61. On fourth level of the Vaima Center. Mastercard, Visa. Open for lunch and dinner. Closed Saturday noon and Sunday.*

Take the private outside elevator between L'Oasis and Air New Zealand to reach this rooftop restaurant with air-conditioned dining or a table on the garden terrace. Workers from the travel agencies and airline offices in Papeete meet here for lunch to gossip while feasting on the *plat du jour*, low calorie salads or specialties from the garden menu. There are several salad choices for 1.450 to 1.800 CFP. Fish dishes are 1.650 to 1.950 CFP, meats are 1.750 to 2.950 CFP, a mixed grill is 2.150 CFP, roast duck leg is 1.950 CFP and filet mignon with green pepper sauce is 2.650 CFP. A wine cellar now fills the space that was formerly occupied by a swimming pool, and carries a large selection of wines from the vineyards of France. As a very young man, owner "Pasha" Allouch used to wash dishes in a restaurant in Houston, Texas, where Jim Morrison and The Doors rock band were playing. He became such a Jim Morrison fan that he named his restaurant after the famous singer, and during special weekends this is a gathering place where you may hear rock or jazz music performed by visiting American groups or local musicians.

RESTAURANT JIMMY, *Tel. 43.63.32. 31, Rue des Ecoles (behind the Papeete Mairie). Mastercard, Visa. Open Monday-Saturday from 11am to 2pm; Monday-Thursday from 6 to 9:30pm; and Friday and Saturday night from 6 to 10pm. Open holidays from 6 to 9pm. Closed Sunday. Reserve.*

This is absolutely a "must try" recommendation if you like Thai, Vietnamese or Chinese food. President Jacques Chirac ate here when he visited Tahiti in 2003 and he reportedly enjoyed his dinner just as much as I do when I have the occasion to eat some of the excellent food here. Teresa and Feye Sisengehanh bought this restaurant in January 2001 and have turned it into an ideal place to meet for lunch or dinner. The air-conditioned restaurant has seating for 100 people on two levels and there is a very pretty aquarium on the ground floor. Teresa, who is from Vancouver, takes care of the front part, and the waitresses are well trained, friendly and very efficient. Feye, who is originally from Laos, performs magic in the kitchen, preparing each wonderful dish on order. They receive the necessary spices from family and friends in Thailand and France and they grow their own cilantro and other herbs or know where to find them year-round in Tahiti.

The Thai section of the menu lists starter courses for 900-1.600 CFP, which include fish beignets with lemon grass, and shrimp salad with lemon grass. The potages are 1.450-1.980 CFP, sautéed noodles with chicken, peanuts, eggs and bean sprouts is 1.100 CFP, curry dishes from Thailand are 1.450-1.650 CFP and Thai "sticky" rice is 650 CFP a serving. The delicious beef filet mignon with Thai curry is listed on the daily specials sheet and costs 2.500 CFP. There are also a lot of other tempting choices on this list.

Vietnamese dishes start with soup from 1.100-1.200 CFP, shrimp spring rolls for 950 CFP, nems for 1.050 CFP, rice and noodle dishes from 950-1.100 CFP and chicken with caramel for 1.400 CFP is another choice in this category. One dish you really have to try is the steamed Vietnamese raviolis, listed as Banh Cuôn for 1.100 CFP. Feye makes these by hand and they are flavored with cilantro and other marvelous and mysterious flavors. Order them as one of your starter courses. I always want more because they are so good.

Chinese specialties are 900-2.200 CFP, and include all my favorites, such as lemon chicken, for 1.000 CFP, Chinese poisson cru for 1.200 CFP (the best I ever ate), aubergine (eggplant) satay for 1.700 CFP, pork with oyster sauce for 1.900 CFP, and Cantonese rice for 1.000 CFP. They also have vegetarian dishes from 900-1.400 CFP, including tofu with spicy sauce or cooked with black mushrooms, sautéed vegetables and eggplant sautéed with garlic. Beef dishes are 1.450-1.800 CFP, and a selection of 8 shrimp dishes costs 1.980-2.200 CFP. Beignets of bananas, pineapple, taro or apples are served for dessert, priced from 450 to 600 CFP. Wine is sold by the half bottle for 1.600-2.800 CFP and a full bottle is 3.800-14.000 CFP.

Moderate

DRAGON D'OR, *Tel. 42.96.12. Rue Colette. All major credit cards. Open for lunch and dinner. Reserve. Closed Monday.*

This is the tried and true Chinese restaurant of Tahiti, and it is still consistently the very best Chinese restaurant on the island or anywhere in French Polynesia and probably in the South Seas. It is located in the heart of Papeete across the street from the Papeete Mairie (Town Hall). Robert Wong, who also owns the Hotel Royal Papeete, opened this restaurant in 1964, and his family still serves mouthwatering specialties from Canton.

This was the first Chinese restaurant I visited when I moved to Tahiti in 1971, and I'll never forget my lesson on how to eat *nems*, the Vietnamese egg rolls that are so popular in Tahiti. You wrap your *nem* in a leaf of lettuce, add fresh mint leaves and dip it into a special Chinese sauce. Then enjoy a taste treat that will have you asking for more. They are priced at 980 CFP. I later added *chop soy special* for 1.400 CFP to my repertoire of culinary favorites when I'm lunching alone here. On top of the crispy noodles the chef piles a sumptuous concoction of meat, chicken, shrimp, broccoli, snow peas, celery, mushrooms and other Chinese vegetables. More recently, I have discovered the dish that Ricky, the English-speaking manager (grandson of Robert Wong) called "Chinese tacos." This is ground beef mixed with some crunchy water chestnuts and "mille delices" (a thousand delights) spices. You wrap it in a lettuce leaf the same as you would fold up a taco. It's absolutely yummy! It is priced at 1.780 CFP. They also have a seafood or vegetarian filling for this dish.

Most people eat family style when two or more dine in Chinese restaurants. This way you'll have a larger variety of foods, which should definitely include the Chinese style *poisson cru* that is a specialty of the "Golden Dragon" and is priced at 1.300 CFP. The decor in this comfortable, air-conditioned restaurant never changes. The walls are decorated with murals of China, complete with twinkling lights. You can sit at the bar while waiting for your table if you forget to reserve.

JACK'S, *Tel. 42.50.58. Vaima Center, Lower Plaza. All credit cards. Open daily for lunch and dinner except Sunday noon. Open Sunday night. Best to reserve.*

If you're feeling a little homesick or you are not too adventurous in your eating preferences, then you'll feel better once you walk into this restaurant, which is decorated in the old country style of America, complete with checkered tablecloths. This was formerly called Jack Lobster but the new owner shortened the name. The menu choices will have your mouth watering even before you taste the Texas burger or fish and shrimp burger for 1.675 CFP, the chicken, shrimp or beef fajitas for 1.850 to 2.450 CFP, the rice Jambalaya for 1.975 CFP, or the chimichangas for 2.100 to 2.150 CFP. If you're really hungry you may want to order the 700-gram (28 oz.) T-bone steak for 2.775 CFP or the special ranchero platter of baby spare ribs, chili, grilled chicken and baked potato, served with a Corona beer and a shot of tequila, for 3.850 CFP. Use the stairway behind the Kiosque newspaper stand on the Boulevard Pomare side of the Vaima Center. Be sure to get there before the lunch crowd arrives, because the place fills up quickly. There is a Blues Night on the first Friday of each month.

LA BRASSERIE DES REMPARTS, *Tel. 42.80.00. Rue des Remparts at the Pont de l'Est in Papeete. Mastercard, Visa. Open Monday to Friday from 6:30 am to 10pm and on Saturday from 10am to 3pm. Closed all day Sunday.*

Although this restaurant is easy to get to in downtown Papeete, it is not a place where you'll find tourists. However, the savvy travelers who use this guide will probably be pleased to discover this French style brasserie, where you can get great food for a good price. Owner Bernard Procureur is from Belgium and formerly owned Le Pêcheur and l'Aventure restaurants on Moorea. His house specialty is mussels (in season) and french fries, and you may want one of the 15 Belgian beers he sells to drink with your meal.

You can order breakfast until 10am, and the choices include *poisson cru* or a portion of thick "rostis" potatoes, as well as omelets and eggs and bacon. Between 11am and 3pm there is non-stop service, with daily bistro type specials that include homemade cassoulet, sausage, sweet breads, tripe, ray wings with caper sauce, magret of duck with apples, lamb chops and filet of pork cooked in beer, which is very tasty. Between 6-10pm his homemade *choucroute* (sauerkraut), served with pork, sausages and potatoes, is a favorite for 2.100 CFP. Bernard also serves light snacks and *casse-croûte* sandwiches all day, as well as pie, *crêpes* and waffles to accompany a cup of hot tea.

The wood and copper bar is a favorite meeting place for young Frenchmen, who sit on the high stools, sipping a beer of *espresso café* and smoking cigarettes. They listen to the recorded jazz music playing softly in the background, as they eye the pretty girls who pass by or walk in. Just like in the brasseries in France.

L'APIZZERIA, *Tel. 42.98.30. Blvd. Pomare. Mastercard, Visa. Open from 11:30am to 10pm with nonstop service. Closed Sunday.*

Here is a garden restaurant serving Italian specialties and French food on the waterfront since 1968. Located 228 yards west of the Papeete Post Office, this is a very popular restaurant with the luncheon crowd. In addition to a choice of 16 succulent pizzas (960 to 1.580 CFP or mini pizzas for 420 to 820 CFP) cooked in a wood-burning oven, you may also want to try the lasagna for 1.600 CFP or a pasta dish from 850 to 1.750 CFP. Choices of 12 salads are well prepared and priced from 1.080 to 2.280 CFP, and the *poisson cru* for 1.480 CFP is freshly prepared on order. Mahi mahi dishes are 2.380 to 2.480 CFP, shrimp is 2.580 CFP, veal sautéed in Marsala wine is 2.290 CFP, and a barbecued steak is 1.680 CFP. The only drawback here is the roar of the traffic, which passes just beside the shaded terrace. Desserts are 580-890 CFP and the wine list includes Italian vinos for 1.620 to 4.970 CFP, as well as French wines for 1.840 to 8.210 CFP. If you want to talk and be heard, then take a table inside. Parking is available on the mountain side of the restaurant.

LA TERRASSE API, *Tel. 43.01.98. Rue du General de Gaulle. Mastercard, Visa. Open 6am to 7pm. Closed Sunday.*

This indoor-outdoor restaurant was formerly called Big Burger and is located on the corner of Fare Tony, across the street from the Vaima Center. This was perhaps the first of the "fast-food" restaurants, but the tendency here is to linger over a meal or a beer *pression* rather than eating on the run. Therefore, they added covered terraces and changed the name, and the customers do enjoy a leisurely lunch and time for people watching. The menu still includes a choice of burgers from 650 to 900 CFP and a hotdog costs 600 CFP, but there's a lot more besides. You can order an American breakfast for 800 CFP, which includes bacon and eggs, juice, toast, and coffee, tea or chocolate. Omelets are 500-1.200 CFP. They have a very good selection of fresh salads for 1.200 CFP, including their *salade Niçoise* (Mediterranean salad), which is consistently the best and most generous in town. Add a few slices of crusty French bread and a glass of red wine for 600 CFP and you've got a very satisfying meal. Their daily luncheon specials are plentiful and cost 1.350 to 2.150 CFP. These may be filet of mahi mahi, veal, chicken, duck or beef dishes. You can also order a slice of raspberry pie, fresh pastry or tiramisu for 650 CFP each.

LE JANOKO, *Tel. 45.30.13. Fare Tony. Mastercard, Visa. Open Monday to Friday from 6am to 5pm, and on Saturday from 6am to 3pm. Closed Sunday.*

With a few tables inside the restaurant and several more placed in the passageway leading from Tahiti Art on Boulevard Pomare into the Fare Tony building, this is a good meeting place for shoppers, working folks who want a reasonably priced lunch and for those who like to get away from the street noises while eating breakfast in the morning or drinking a cup of coffee or cocktail during the afternoon. Daily luncheon specials include dishes such as quiche, mussels and fries, turkey scallop, mahi mahi with green pepper sauce, calamaries with Armoricaine sauce, and seafood pasta, priced between 1.400-2.200 CFP.

LE MANAVA, *Tel. 42.02.91. Corner of Ave. Bruat and Ave. Commandant Destremeau. American Express, Mastercard and Visa. Restaurant is open Monday through Friday for lunch only. Closed Saturday and Sunday.*

Specialties from the Pèrigord region of France are featured in this air-conditioned restaurant, which is located near the government buildings downtown. The luncheon crowd includes politicians, judges and business people, who may order the *plat du jour,* which can be *blanquette de veau* for 1.500 CFP, with a *salade de choux* for 800 CFP, or an onion tarte for 800 CFP. Appetizers are 600 to 2.000 CFP, salads run about 500 to 1.850 CFP, the fish main courses range from 1.950 to 2.350 CFP, and the meats cost 1.850 to 2.850 CFP. This is the restaurant where you may find liver and onions on the menu, and you might want to try the *rognon de veau à l'ancienne,* for 2.250 CFP, or the *confit de lapin à la crème de pruneaux et à l'armagnac,* for 2.500 CFP. You can also stop for a cup of coffee or glass of wine and sit at the bar inside or in the gazebo restaurant outside. The bar stays open at night even though the restaurant is closed.

LES TROIS BRASSEURS, *Tel. 50.60.25. Blvd. Pomare, across street from Moorea ferryboats. E-mail: les3brasseurs@mail.pf; www.3brasseurs-tahiti.com. Mastercard, Visa. Open daily 7am to 1am with continuous food service.*

This sidewalk restaurant and microbrewery continues to be one of the most frequented spots in Tahiti, attracting a varied clientele of business people, white collar and blue collar workers, the crews and passengers from cruise ships, tourists from hotels, bed and breakfast pensions and yachts, and people like me, who come over by boat from Moorea for the day and stop by for a glass of delicious beer before taking the fast catamaran back home. The name means the three brewers, and it is Tahiti's first and only boutique brewery, serving four qualities of beer, which are not pasteurized, but are taken fresh from the copper holding tank into your glass. These choices include blond, amber, white and brown beer, which you can order by the glass, mug or pitcher.

They also offer all the services of a classic restaurant and bar. A snack menu lists a Club sandwich and fries for 900 CFP and a cheeseburger or chicken burger and fries for 1.100 CFP. In addition to daily luncheon specials for 1.350 CFP you can choose from a variety of appetizers and salads from 850 to 1.500 CFP, fish for 1.250 to 1.950 CFP, and grilled meats from 1.700 to 1.950 CFP. Their brasserie plates offer horse steak for 1.500 CFP, grilled pork and lentils for 2.100 CFP, or *choucroute* (sauerkraut, heaping portions of pork, and boiled potatoes) for 2.100 or 2.600 CFP. Another specialty is their homemade 'Flammekeuches', or flambé tarts, made with cheese, onions, mushrooms, bacon, white cheese, fresh cream and other ingredients, which you slice like a quiche and eat with your fingers to accompany your brew. They are priced from 950 to 1.500 CFP. Desserts are 700 to 900 CFP.

LOU PESCADOU, *Tel. 43.74.26. Rue Anne-Marie Javouhey. Mastercard, Visa. Open 11am to 2:30pm and from 6:30 to 11pm. Closed all day Sunday.*

This open air, very lively Italian restaurant is the kind of place where you can whoop and shout. This is Tahiti's most popular pizza parlor, and you can also order Italian or French Provençal specialties. Mario, the owner-chef, sets the ambiance with good cheer, good smells and good food. Even the decor is boisterous and happy, with murals of waterfront scenes from the Mediterranean coast, Chianti wine bottles tied to the support posts, with checkered tablecloths and bottles of spicy olive oil on the tables. There is a well-stocked bar, where you can order *kir* or *pastis* or your favorite cocktail. The waitresses are mostly big Tahitian "mamas" who have been with Mario for many years, and they all wear ample sized tee-shirts sporting Mario's face with a grizzled beard. These friendly and hard-working girls have been known to dance on the tabletops with Julio Iglesias and other visiting celebrities. You'll find Mario's place behind the Cathedral of Notre Dame, on the same street as the Clinique Cardella. He closes every year between December 15 and January 15, and May 1-10.

SUSHI BAR, *Tel. 45.35.25. On second level of Vaima Center. All major credit cards. Open Monday through Saturday 11:15am to 2pm and for dinner on Thursday, Friday and Saturday, from 6:15 to 10pm. Closed Sunday.*

A tempting selection of sushi sells for 80 to 400 CFP a piece, or you can order 10 regular pieces for 1.000 CFP, 12 deluxe pieces for 1.500 CFP, and on up to 60 pieces for 8.800 CFP. *Poisson cru* made from fresh yellowfin tuna is 1.100 CFP, tuna sashimi, tartare or carpaccio is 1.400 CFP, and salmon sashimi is 2.000 CFP. You can eat in the small restaurant or order in advance for take away sushi.

Economy to Moderate

LE MARCHE, *(Papeete Public Market), Tel. 42.25.37. Rue Edouard Ahnne, one block inland from Blvd. Pomare. Visa. Open 5am-4pm. Closed Sunday.*

On the ground floor of the public market are take-out counters where you can get a selection of very good Chinese pastry, sandwiches, *casse-croûtes* and fries. Coffee and soft drinks are also available here, but you have to eat and drink standing up.

Go up the escalator to the second floor of the public market and you will find a cafeteria-style restaurant where you can eat breakfast, lunch or a snack, and you can order a freshly squeezed pineapple juice or orange juice. *Couscous* is served each Thursday for 1.400 CFP and Friday is *maa Tahiti* day, for 2.000 CFP. A live Tahitian band keeps you entertained while you eat, playing music from 11am-1:30pm. (You are not allowed to take food from the first floor to eat upstairs).

LE RETRO, *Tel. 42.86.83. Street level of Vaima Center, Blvd. Pomare. All major credit cards. Open daily with non-stop service until 11pm.*
This is an all-purpose restaurant for breakfast, lunch and dinner, a snack, *salon de thé* and bar. The service isn't the world's fastest, however, and you'll have a good chance to practice your discipline of patience while waiting for someone to take your order if you're sitting at one of the sidewalk tables. But if you're not in a hurry, this is a great place to people watch, as it is on the waterfront street across from the boat docks. The menu changes daily, and includes salads for 380 to 1.400 CFP, *poisson cru* for 1.350 CFP, burgers for 610 to 770 CFP, paninis for 440 to 580 CFP, pizza for 800 to 1.900 CFP, pasta for 800-1.550 CFP, fish and shellfish for 1.850 to 2.250 CFP, and meats for 1.650 to 2.250 CFP. Daily specials are 1.600 CFP and with dessert are priced around 1.900 CFP.

MARKET COFFEE, *Tel. 45.60.70. 4 Rue Edouard Ahnne. Open Monday-Saturday from 5:30am to 2:30pm, Friday and Saturday nights from 5:30 to 10:30pm, and on Sunday from 7-11am. Mastercard, Visa.*
If you feel in the mood for a breakfast of poisson cru along with your bacon and eggs, then this is the place to go. For 1.000 CFP you have a choice of: a fresh fruit plate, croissant or pain au chocolat; grilled local fish; pua roti (roast pork); poisson cru and omelets; poisson cru and bacon and eggs; poisson cru and marinated chicken legs; poisson cru and fried chicken; or sautéed beef with vegetables. Each item is served with coffee, tea, chocolate, bread, butter and jam. You can also order breakfast à la carte for 500-1.950 CFP. The Sunday brunch is 1.500 CFP. Lunch and dinner choices include salads for 900-1.400 CFP, appetizers for 1.300-2.000 CFP, lagoon or deep ocean fish and seafood for 1.400-2.150 CFP, and meats for 1.550-2.000 CFP. Desserts are 600 CFP. You can also order beer for 460-650 CFP, cocktails for 900-1.000 CFP or bottled wines. Seafood is the Friday night special, with frequent entertainment by a local band, and Saturday is karaoke night, which can also be a lot of fun.

PATACHOUX, *Tel. 83.72.82, cell 78.95.90. In Fare Tony Center between Snack Hollywood and La Terrasse Api on Rue LaGarde. No credit cards.*
This is a very popular pastry and chocolate shop, as well as a bakery, take-away service and snack restaurant with tables on a covered terrace beside a

pedestrian street in the heart of Papeete. You can order ham croissants for 300 CFP, a slice of pizza for 450 CFP, a Croque Monsieur with ham and blue cheese for 620 CFP, sandwiches with smoked turkey, roast chicken, smoked pork, roast veal, lamb or steak from 580 to 950 CFP, or fish sandwiches from 735 to 1.100 CFP. Salads are priced from 980 to 1.450 CFP, poisson cru or sashimi is 1.250 CFP, and luncheon daily specials of fresh fish and vegetables are 1.450 CFP.

This is definitely the place to satisfy a sweet tooth, and you can also get chocolates, pastries, cakes and breads to take with you. If you have a car you may want to stop at their **Pastryland** shop *on the seaside at PK 12.5 in Punaauia, Tel. 45.03.33.*

Economy

LA MARQUISIENNE, *Tel. 42.83.52. Rue Colette. No credit cards. Open Tuesday-Friday 5am-5pm, on Saturday 5am until 2pm and on Sunday until 8:30am. Closed Monday.*

The smell of the coffee will lure you into this air-conditioned pastry shop, but you won't regret following your nose, because you'll discover a wonderful selection of French pastries, cakes, pies, quiches, slices of pizza and sandwiches that will make you glad you came. And the coffee is as good as it smells. You might even find me in here, enjoying a *café au lait* and a big, crispy *croissant.*

LE FESTIVAL DES GLACES *is a fast food counter in front of Le Retro on the corner of Blvd. Pomare and Rue LaGarde. No credit cards.*

You can choose one of the 13 *casse-croûte* sandwiches listed for 300 to 500 CFP, a hot dog for 250 CFP, a cheeseburger for 500 CFP, or order a hot Italian panini sandwich for 300 to 450 CFP. They also have pizzas. American friends living in Moorea claim they get the best ice cream in the world here, with a choice of 38 flavors, including apricot, kiwi, cantaloupe, peach, pear, mango, passion fruit, or something more familiar, such as chocolate praline. They've even added sugarless ice cream, which they advertise is a good choice for diabetics and people on diets.

LE MOTU, *street level of Vaima Center, on the corner of Rue General de Gaulle and rue Georges LaGarde. No credit cards.*

This kiosk *on the back side of the Vaima block* serves a good selection of takeout sandwiches, cheese *croissants* and crusty *casse-croûtes*, as well as soft drinks and ice cream. A Tahitian hotdog is 360 CFP and a Parisian hotdog with cheese is 460 CFP.

L'OASIS DU VAIMA, *Tel. 45.45.01. Street level of Vaima Center, on corner of rue Jeanne d'Arc and Ave. General de Gaulle. No credit cards. Open 6am-6pm. Closed Sunday.*

You can buy a sandwich or *casse-croûte* from the kiosk counter and eat as you go, or you can sit on the covered dining terrace and watch the daily drama of people passing, while sipping a cold *pression*. You can serve yourself from the salad bar and dine on the daily specials of French food in the air-conditioned restaurant a few steps up.

McDONALD'S TAHITI, *Tel. 53.37.37. Rue General de Gaulle. No credit cards. Open daily 6am-10:30 or 11pm.*

McDonald's has been firmly established in Tahiti since 1996 and this was the first location to open. School kids, government officials and visiting South Pacific dignitaries all stand in line to order their Big Macs, fries and soft drink. You won't find the bargains here that you are used to back home - a double cheeseburger meal is 690 CFP. But that doesn't keep the people of Tahiti from flocking here on a regular basis. There is also a big McDonald's in Punaauia and a small kiosk at the Tahiti-Faa'a airport that doesn't sell burgers.

SNACK GABY, *Rue Edouard Ahnne, across from Papeete Public Market. No credit cards. Open for lunch only. Closed Sunday.*

This is where I go when I want to eat well, but quickly and inexpensively. Gaby, who is Chinese, lived in California and speaks very good English. His restaurant is very clean and you can choose the daily specials, mostly Chinese dishes such as chicken and lemon sauce, chow mein, beef and vegetables or *maa tinito haricots rouges*, from a cafeteria style display of prepared foods. It will cost you about 1.000 CFP for full portions and you can also order small portions. His clients are mostly Tahitians, who eat an early lunch. The food is sold out by 1pm.

SNACK ROGER, *Tel. 42.80.38. Place Notre Dame. No credit cards. Closed Sunday.*

This is a quiet restaurant at mid-morning, where you can linger over a coffee or tea for 250 CFP, or order an omelet for 600 CFP. But watch out for the hungry herd that arrives at lunchtime, to devour Roger's daily specials. A chef's salad is 850 CFP, Salade Niçoise is 900 CFP, Chinese poisson cru is 1.150 CFP, duck with olives is 1.100 CFP and roast pig with frites is 1.100 CFP.

TIKI SOFT C@FE, *Tel. 88.93.98; E-mail: tikisoft@mail.pf; www.tikisoft.pf; www.tikisoftcafe.com. Rue des Remparts at the Pont de l'Est. No credit cards. Open Monday through Friday 8am to 10:30pm, on Saturday from 8am to 3pm, closed Sunday.*

This was Tahiti's first cyber bar. You can order a coffee and *croissant* breakfast, and for lunch you have a small selection of sandwiches and salads. This is a busy place throughout the day as people wait their turn to get on-line at one of the three computers, which cost 250 CFP for 15 minutes. Clients who eat here at noon get 10 minutes' free access. Happy Hour is held each Friday between 6-7:30pm. Buy two beers and get the third beer free.

RESTAURANTS EAST OF PAPEETE TO MAHINA
Deluxe
LE BELVEDERE, *Tel. 42.73.44. Fare Rau Ape Valley, Pirae. American Express, Mastercard, Visa. Open daily for lunch and dinner.*

You will feel on top of the world in this rustic and cheerful setting, 600 meters (1,800 feet) above the sea, overlooking Point Venus and Moorea. Tetiaroa atoll is visible some 42 kilometers (26 miles) to the north. The mountains of Huahine, an island 150 kilometers (93.2 miles) from Tahiti, can be seen on a clear evening at sunset, with the help of a telescope on the terrace.

Le Belvedere's bright yellow *le truck* provides unforgettable transportation from your hotel, and you will feel and smell the change of air as *le truck* winds up the one lane road with some 70 hairpin curves, climbing through the Fare Rau Ape Valley. Wild mountain ferns mingle their fragrance with the scent of the tall eucalyptus trees that grow in a wild profusion of verdure, along with giant mangoes, cashew trees, *casaurina* pines, acacias and wild hibiscus *purau* trees. By the time you get to the restaurant you will probably have begun to make friends among the other passengers, who are also laughing a little nervously while eyeing the precipitous drop-off on one or both sides of the road.

You can come for lunch and a swim in the pool. You can take the first dinner service that gets you to the restaurant in time to photograph a panoramic sunset. Or you can come later for a romantic dinner under the stars. Whatever the time of day, you will be rewarded with breathtaking seascapes. You can also get to Le Belvedere by helicopter, enjoying a bird's eye view of the scenery *en route*.

The restaurant is a combination of a wooden Swiss chalet and Polynesian decor. There are four dining areas, but you will probably want to sit on the terrace for the best view, if the air isn't too chilly. That expression is not normally used to describe any other place in these tropical islands. During the "winter" months of June, July and August, the manager sometimes has to close the windows of the restaurant and light a fire in the fireplace, just like in a real Swiss chalet!

The *fondue bourguignonne* (beef fondue) is a specialty, with tender slices of New Zealand beef that you cook to your own taste. This is accompanied by a salad bar, hot French fries, tasty sauces and carafes of white or red wine, with ice cream and coffee served afterward. The cheese fondue and seafood fondue are also great favorites for couples or large groups, who have a great time trying to recapture a piece of meat or shrimp that fell into the cooking pot. Other favorite selections include French onion soup, mahi-mahi, *couscous* and pepper steak. The ride back down the mountain is always a happy one, and you'll probably join the rest of the revelers in singing, if the group is convivial.

The tourist menu, which includes transportation, a choice of beef or cheese fondue, fish or steak, is 5.200 CFP per person. The seafood fondue is 4.250 CFP. Reserve for your transportation. Pick-up at the hotels on the west coast begin at 11:30am for lunch, 4:30pm for sunset and dinner, and 7pm for the last service. If you have a plane to catch during the night and are looking for a place to spend your last evening in Tahiti, why not take advantage of the Belvedere's free *le truck*, who will pick you up somewhere near the airport, ferry dock, tourist office or hotel, and drop you off at the airport after a long, leisurely dinner. You can either store your luggage at the airport or you can arrange to bring them along with you to the restaurant.

Superior
LE LION D'OR, *Tel. 42.66.50. Rue Afareii, Pirae. All major credit cards. Open for lunch and dinner. Reserve. Closed Saturday noon and all day Sunday.*

This is an excellent seafood restaurant just five minutes from Papeete via Avenue Prince Hinoi to Pirae, on the right side of the road adjacent to the Banque de Tahiti and a pharmacy. The air-conditioned restaurant is upstairs, with a lovely decor of pink and white linens and fresh flowers on the tables. Seafood choices include grilled lobster, mahi-mahi stuffed with shrimp, escargots and their special seafood platter. Perhaps you will prefer frog legs, tournedos Rossini, Roquefort steak or *steak tartare au cognac*, followed by a selection of salads and something sinfully delicious from the dessert menu.

Moderate to Superior
BEACH HOUSE TAHARA'A, *Tel. 85.22.42. PK 7, on the beach of Tahara'a Hill in Arue. Mastercard, Visa. Open daily 10am to 1am except on Sunday night, when they are closed.*

This gastronomic restaurant, bar and nautical center is at the foot of the old Hotel Tahara'a (now closed), and is reached by a private road that winds down the hill from the Tahara'a lookout point. There are parking places down below for 40 cars, and because this popular place fills up quickly on weekends, a shuttle service from the lookout point to the restaurant is provided from Friday night through Sunday afternoon. French and Tahitian specialties are served in the restaurant overlooking the black sand beach and the open waters of Matavai Bay. Poisson cru is 1.600 CFP, escargots are 1.800 CFP, carpaccio of red tuna is 2.000 CFP, mahi mahi is 2.600 CFP, shrimp curry is 2.800 CFP, magret of duck is 3.000 CFP and beef filet with morilles is 3.200 CFP. A 3-course tourist menu is 3.500 CFP. Happy Hour is held every Thursday from 6-7:30pm with two drinks for the price of one, with live Brazilian music that attracts a good audience of local residents. Owner Guillaume Louis said that he will start a free pick-up service for tourists in 2005, which will be sure to increase his business. He also operates a nautical activities center on the premises, including the Tahara'a Diving Center. In addition to renting small motorboats and kayaks, you can join a 3-hour Dolphin and Whale Watch excursion for 7.000 CFP per person. See more information under *Nautical Centers & Clubs* and *Scuba Diving* in this chapter.

DAHLIA, *Tel. 42.59.87. PK 4.2, Arue. All major credit cards. Open 10:45am to 1:15pm and 6:30 to 9pm. Closed Sunday.*

This air-conditioned restaurant is located on the seaside, across the road from the French military base in Arue. It has a very good reputation for the quality of its food, but my most recent experience was not positive. Maybe the cook was off that day. You can choose shrimp for 1.760-2.950 CFP, poultry for 1.370-2.000 CFP, and meats for 1.590-2.020 CFP. A *teou fou* (tofu) cassolette with 8 delices is 1.960 CFP and other specialties are 1.090-2.870 CFP. The sizzling platters are very popular and cost 1.640-2.950 CFP. Seasonal additions are algae, crab, lobster, cuttlefish and river shrimp for 1.600-3.980 CFP. You can even order a whole turbot for 12.500 CFP and abalones with oyster sauce for 8.600 CFP.

FARA'E, *Tel. 42.70.50. PK 3.6, Arue, on the mountainside near the round point at Camp Arue military base. Mastercard, Visa. Open for lunch and dinner. Closed Sunday.*

You can eat on the terrace or in the air-conditioned dining room, which smells of cigarette smoke when the place gets filled up at noon. The menu is quite extensive and includes seven kinds of Chinese soup for 980 to 1.500 CFP, crab rolls (6) for 1.400 CFP, lemon chicken for 1.300 CFP, 11 shrimp dishes for 1.980 to 2.650 CFP, braised pork for 1.980 CFP, lobster and ginger for 3.850 CFP and stuffed deboned Peking duck for 3.600 CFP. You can order *ta pen lou* for two every night without advance notice, which is most unusual. This is also called Chinese fondue, and consists of shrimp and other seafood, chicken and beef, which you cook in a pot of hot broth at your table. The cost is 3.950 CFP per person for the two of you, and if there is a third diner, the cost remains the same as for two people.

LE CHEVAL D'OR, *Tel. 42.98.89. Farepitii, Taunoa. Visa. Open Monday through Saturday for lunch and dinner. Closed Sunday.*

Whenever I eat here I always order the *riz Cantonnais Cheval D'or*, which is fried rice with bits of shrimp and fish, the house specialty of the "Golden Horse" for 1.200 CFP. Some of my other choices are the eggplant stuffed with fish paste, and shrimp cooked in a spicy sauce and served on a sizzling platter. The prices are 1.200-2.000 CFP per dish and the roast suckling pig in coconut sauce, which is served only on weekends, is 2.400 CFP. This air-conditioned restaurant is almost always packed with Chinese, French, Tahitian and American residents, which gives me the impression that it's a popular restaurant with everyone who knows how to find it. You'll need transportation and a map to get here from downtown. The simplest way is to turn right from Boulevard Pomare at the first street past the Hotel Royal Papeete, and follow Avenue du Chef Vairaatoa about 12 blocks until you come to Cours de l'Union Sacrée. Turn left and head toward the sea, where you'll find the restaurant in front of you where the inland road ends.

RESTAURANTS WEST OF PAPEETE TO PAEA
Deluxe

COCO'S, *Tel. 58.21.08. PK 13.5, (seaside) Punaauia. American Express, Mastercard and Visa. Open daily for lunch and dinner. Reserve.*

This is where you definitely want to go to celebrate romance, that special occasion or simply because you're in the mood for divine French food. You will be enchanted from the moment you walk through the entrance and feel, as well as see, the magnificent tropical setting of casual elegance, with orchids and ferns, a gentle surf kissing the shore and romance in the air. This is old Tahiti at its best—a thatched roof and woven bamboo covering the walls, the soft glow of gas lamps, colorful paintings by resident artists, pink tablecloths and gentle music wafting through the air. You begin your evening with a glass of champagne on the lawn beside the lagoon, watching the last rays of the sunset fade into mauve and purple behind the peaks of Moorea. Your dining table may be inside the open dining room or in the gardens. Owner Hervé Gérard has a frequently changing menu of *la nouvelle cuisine Française*, which is attractively presented, gracefully served and very pleasing to the palate. An American style bar is separate from the dining room and serves all your favorite beverages.

This is one of the few restaurants in Tahiti that presents a silent menu without prices to a woman if she is with a man, and it is his decision whether to remain silent and discreet or convince her to pay half of the meal (or pick up the whole check)

The menu is changed every six months. Sumptuous specialties in May 2004 included appetizers of pure French duck liver for 3.650 CFP, freshwater shrimp ravioli flavored with crayfish bisque served with light *vana* (sea urchin) mousse, for 2.850 CFP, and savory lobster tail for 3.600 CFP. The seafood choices for 2.750 to 2.950 CFP included tropical bass, filet of sole au gratin and freshwater shrimp fricassee with curry and mango chutney. The main dishes offered roasted rack of lamb, thick duck breast, simmered veal rib, roasted French pigeon, and filet mignon of beef with a red wine sauce, priced from 2.800 to 3.350 CFP. Set menus are suggested for 5.300-12.100 CFP to allow you to sample up to five courses. The regular wines are priced from 2.600 to 25.400 CFP and there are 14 different champagnes on the impressive wine menu. Wine connoisseurs will appreciate the prestige wines and there is also a selection of prestige liqueurs, as well as cigars and coffees.

AUBERGE DU PACIFIQUE, *Tel. 43.98.30. PK 11.2, (seaside) Punaauia. American Express, Mastercard and Visa. Open for lunch and dinner Monday-Saturday. Closed Sunday.*

Owner Jean Galopin was a cook at Maxim's and Tour d'Argent in Paris, and he has been setting new taste trends in Tahiti since 1968, harmoniously blending the abundance of nature and the eternal traditions of *haute cuisine*. He was named a Maître Cuisinier of France in 1987 and a Master Chef of America in 1982. He has published two beautifully illustrated books, entitled *Tahitian Island Cooking* and *Cocktails of Tahiti and Her Islands*, which you can buy in the book shops in Tahiti or order through the Internet.

Auberge du Pacifique is located beside the lagoon and you can dine in an air-conditioned salon or on a covered terrace overlooking the island of Moorea. The frequently changing menu always offers exotic choices, which may include wild game of rabbit, venison or pheasant during the months of October through December, and other specialties from the various regions of France throughout the year.

Pressed duck is the *pièce de resistance*, which you should order in advance, or you can order on the spot from the extensive menu. Try the grilled shrimp salad with a slightly sweet dressing for 2.580 CFP, which is truly excellent. Other starter courses include escargots for 2.190 CFP or a lobster salad with brandy and artichoke hearts for 2.990 CFP. The fish dishes are 2.450 to 3.250 CFP, slipper lobster is 3.990 CFP and rock lobster is 3.950 CFP. The meat choices range from 2.580 to 4.200 CFP. Among them you will find tenderloin of beef, veal filet with mushrooms or a grilled New York steak. A duck steak with mushrooms is 3.480 CFP, veal sweetbreads and cream sauce is priced at 2.990 CFP and deer cooked in a wine sauce is 2.990 CFP. The homemade sorbets are made of lime, mango, pineapple and soursop, for 890 CFP each, or you can choose your sweets from the trolley of homemade desserts for 1.250 CFP. Crêpes Suzettes are 1.150 CFP or you can share a Baked Alaska for two for 2.240 CFP. You can opt for the 3-course tourist menu for 4.990 CFP, or you may want to sample the seven courses on the tasting menu for 9.500 CFP. Be sure to visit the air-conditioned wine cellar, which is stocked with an excellent selection of the best *crus* of France, with some very special bottles priced up to 225.000 CFP.

Superior
CAPTAIN BLIGH, *Tel. 43.62.90. PK 11.4 (seaside), Punaauia. American Express, Mastercard and Visa. Open for lunch and dinner. Closed Sunday night and Monday.*

Just seven miles from Papeete, on Tahiti's "Gold Coast" overlooking Moorea, this may be the largest overwater restaurant in the South Seas, with seating for more than 300 diners. A deluxe seafood buffet is served each Friday and Saturday night for 4.990 CFP, which includes a dance performance by Marguerite Lai and her award winning "O Tahiti E" group. Live music is played each Sunday during the noon buffet of *ma'a Tahiti* (a Tahitian feast) for 3.750 CFP. On the à la carte menu you will find salads for 600 to 900 CFP, *poisson cru* for 1.350 CFP, shrimp cocktail for 1.600 CFP, a seafood plate for 1.800 CFP, filet mignon for 2.500 CFP and steak and lobster for 3.800 CFP. A pier beside the restaurant leads to the Lagoonarium, where you can play peek-a-boo with the fish, turtles and sharks you see through the windows of underwater tanks. When you dine in the restaurant you get free admission to the Lagoonarium.

CASABLANCA, *Tel. 43.91.35. Marina Taina, PK 9 (seaside), Punaauia. Mastercard, Visa. Open daily for lunch and dinner.*

This is a popular restaurant with French residents of Tahiti who like a nautical scene while dining, and this is also the place usually recommended to visitors by people working at the travel desks in the hotels on Tahiti's west coast. If you enjoy traditional French cuisine, you'll be sure to like the food and the view of Moorea just beyond the boats, lagoon and reef. I found the open-air décor attractive, the service excellent and the food highly commendable. You will appreciate the light lunch selections, such as tuna tartare with potatoes or other vegetables, and *Couscous Royale* is served every Wednesday at lunch and dinner, for 2.600 CFP. The starter courses are priced from 1.300 to 2.200 CFP; the fish dishes are 2.450 to 2.800 CFP, a lobster tail is 3.500 CFP, and the meat choices range from 2.450 to 3.400 CFP. A delightful taste treat is the *foie gras* served with artichoke hearts. A 3-course Discovery menu is 4.600 CFP, and there is also a children's menu. Desserts are 800-1.200 CFP and coffees are 300-1.200 CFP. The wine menu includes some of the *grands crus* for 68.000 a bottle, or you can pay 600-700 CFP for a glass of good wine. A musical discovery evening takes place each Friday and Saturday night.

LA ROSE DES VENTS, *Tel. 86.60.61, ext. 3320. Second floor of Tahiti-Faaa airport, PK 5,5, Faaa. All major credit cards. Open Monday through Friday 12-2pm. Closed nights and weekends.*

This small, intimate air-conditioned restaurant can be reached by taking the elevator adjacent to the Manureva Bar and Snack shop on the ground level of the airport. It's a convenient place to dine if you are waiting for a flight or happen to be in the vicinity of the airport and are looking for a good restaurant. There are mirrored walls, nice table linen and fresh flowers on the tables, and the food is excellent. *Poisson cru* with coconut milk is 1.500 CFP, tuna tartare or sashimi are priced at 1.600 CFP, a rapid lunch is 2.900 CFP, and a three-course meal is 3.500 CFP. The *plat du jour* is priced around 2.300 CFP and may be a filet of parrotfish, steak tartare with frits, a big slice of beef with a wine sauce, or some other French delicacy. The only negative point here is that you can smell the cigarette smoke from other tables.

Moderate to Superior

LE CIGALON, *Tel. 42.40.84. PK 15, Tamanu, (seaside) Punaauia between Tamanu Center and Hotel Le Méridien. Mastercard, Visa. Open Tuesday-Sunday 12-3pm and 7-9pm. Closed Monday.*

This air-conditioned restaurant has a menu of cold appetizers for 1.480-

2.350, hot appetizers for 1.750-2.850 CFP, fish and seafood dishes from 2.350 to 2.750 CFP, chicken and meat choices for 2.080-2.720 CFP, pasta for 1.120-1.950 CFP and pizzas from 970-1.500 CFP. French specialties include a dozen escargots for 1.850 CFP, sea urchins for 1.880 CFP and tournedos Rossini for 3.850 CFP. Desserts are 580-950 CFP.

WESTERN GRILL, *Tel. 41.30.56. On seaside at PK 12.6 in Punaauia, near school 2+2=4. Visa. Open Monday-Friday 11:45am-2:30pm and 7-9:30pm. Closed Saturday noon and open Saturday night 7-9:30pm. Closed all day Sunday. Reservations are a must, and it's best to reserve two days in advance for weekends.*

If the name doesn't prepare you for this experience, then you'll certainly get the idea when you walk through the swinging saloon doors into this frontier scene right out of the old Wild West. Cowhide rugs, longhorn chairs, wagon wheels, gunny sacks, horseshoes, guitars, serapes, sombreros, leather saddles, Native American pictures, dream catchers and woven art, gold mining pans, lassos, miniature covered wagons, and a ceiling covered with old flags all provide the rustic décor for this most unusual restaurant. Of course there's a long wooden bar and country music, and it's only natural that the waiters are dressed in western gear, complete with big cowboy hats.

The paper place mat menus list a mouth-watering choice of good grub, starting with an El Paso plate, Grand Canyon plate, Beans and Duck Surprise and Pioneer's Onion Rings, priced from 890 to 1.990 CFP. Then there's the Country salad, Wyoming salad, Montana salad, and Commanchero salad, from 990 to 1.790 CFP. Fish of the Day is listed, along with Shrimp Tequila, Maine sole and poisson cru, from 1.490 to 1.890 CFP. Grilled meats, from 1.590 to 2.790 CFP, include Western Wings, Dalton Brochettes, Geronimo lamb ribs, Cheyenne pork sausages, a Texas platter, Dakota steak, Nebraska filet and Magnum beef ribs. Then come the specialties, featuring barbecue ribs and baked potatoes, Rio Grande chicken, Cowboy steak burgers, Cajun alligator, Buffalow stew, Beef or Chicken Fajitas and Rio Bravo Rabbit, from 1.490 to 2.890 CFP. A Western Menu for 1.490 CFP includes 3-courses, and the Little Red Skin's Menu for kids under 10 is 990 CFP and includes free cotton candy. Desserts are 450 to 890 CFP, with such treats as Calamity Jane pie, Desperado Dish, Rodeo Dessert, Louisiana Bread Pudding and homemade brownies. Saloon Desserts with a kick include Colonel Custer, Blizzard, Cactus, Nevada, Kansas and Mississippi, each priced at 890 CFP. They've thought of everything but corn on the cob. A Hinano pression (draft beer) is 450 CFP, cocktails are 790 to 990 CFP, and the wines are priced from 1.790 to 11.450 CFP. So you can wet your whistle while you gnaw away on your smoked ribs, which are served with an authentic tasting BBQ sauce.

Gérald Mingo, one of the waiters, is also a comedian, singer, dancer, choreographer and drag queen artist. He has created a Western show that combines all his talents mentioned above, which is performed every Thursday,

Friday and Saturday night. Getting into the Western Grill any night of the week is difficult, but you really must reserve well in advance if you want to see this show. There are two meal services during the weekend.

Moderate

CÔTÉ JARDIN, *Tel. 43.26.19, Moana Nui Shopping Center, PK 8.3, Punaauia. Mastercard, Visa. Open daily 7am to 8pm.*

This is a handy place to rest and people watch while you're shopping at Carrefour or waiting for someone who is browsing around the mall. You can sit at a table on the mall level or go upstairs to the air-conditioned dining room, where you can order from an interesting menu that includes 12 kinds of pizza from 1.150 to 1.450 CFP, salads for 695 to 1.695 CFP, pasta dishes from 1.295 to 1.595 CFP, *poisson cru* for 1.295 CFP, Japanese sashimi for 1.795 CFP, fish dishes for 1.595 to 2.350 CFP, or grilled meats for 1.395 to 1.995 CFP. Daily specials are priced around 1.695 CFP, and you can order wine by the glass, carafe or bottle. Fresh fruit juices are 495-795 CFP, a Hinano pression is 420 CFP and they also have a list of Belgian beers. Most of the prices have increased by 200-300 CFP within the past two years, but you can still order pancakes for breakfast for 300 CFP or an omelet for 795 CFP.

SNACK CARO, *Tel. 43.87.43. PK 10.2 (mountainside), Punaauia. No credit cards. Open for lunch and dinner. Closed Sunday.*

Nothing fancy about this place, where you can eat on a shaded terrace or in the dining room. The attraction at Caro's is the high quality of the mouth-watering Chinese food, which is served cafeteria style. You will be happily pleased with the food and prices, which include lemon chicken for 950 CFP and poisson cru for 1.150 CFP. No alcoholic beverages served.

Economy

CHOCOLATINE, *Tel. 43.26.31. Moana Nui Shopping Center, PK 8.3, Punaauia. No credit cards. Open daily 7am to 7pm.*

This busy snack stand is located at the exit doors of Carrefour super market. They sell casse-croûtes for 230-320 CFP, panini sandwiches for 350 CFP, hamburgers for 500 CFP, salads for 550 to 900 CFP, sashimi for 950 CFP, and a daily lunch special for 1.300 CFP. Service is cafeteria style. Italian ice cream is 260 CFP and there is a good selection of soft drinks and fresh juices.

MACDONALD'S TAHITI, *Tel. 48.07.07. Taina Beach, PK 9, Punaauia. No credit cards. Open daily 9:30am-10pm.*

This is the second MacDonald's outlet in Tahiti, which opened in December 1999 on the site that was occupied for a brief time by one of the two Kentucky Fried Chicken outlets that are now both gone. You'll find all the familiar burgers and fries and fast service here and there is also a drive-through window and games for the kids in the parking lot. There is a white sand beach behind the restaurant with an entry into the lagoon.

PACIFIC BURGER / LE CIGALON SNACK, *Tel. 42.40.84. PK 15, Tamanu (seaside), Punaauia. Mastercard, Visa. Open Tuesday-Friday 10:30am-3pm, Saturday-Sunday 10:30am-9:30pm.*

This snack bar/pizzeria is in between the Tamanu Center and Hotel Le Meridien. Look for the sign Le Cigalon from the road, which is the adjacent restaurant under the same ownership. Pacific Burger is a very popular spot for families because of the small swimming pool and playground in front, and also because the food is very good and not expensive. You can munch on 13 choices of burgers and hot dogs, priced from 420 to 850 CFP, or 28 types of pizza, from 990 to 1.680 CFP. There are also salads, *poisson cru* and lots of other goodies to eat and drink. A Hinano draft beer (*pression*) is 390 CFP and a milk shake is 580 CFP. Be sure to specify if you want your meat well done as they have a tendency to undercook their hamburgers. The pizza oven opens at noon and in the evening from 6-9pm.

ROULOTTE SABOR LATINO, on the mountainside at PK 18.7 in Punaauia, is open from 11am to 11pm during the week and a little later on weekends if business is good. This is the only roulotte in Tahiti that specializes in Chilean and Mexican food. Andrea, her husband Pedro and her brother Diego have set up their roulotte not far from several family pensions as well as the Manu Ura beach. They claim they make their empanadas, tacos, fajitas lomito, churrasco and pollo dishes with love. Prices are very reasonable, from 300-800 CFP.

ROULOTTE PAEA PIZZA, *Tel. 77.26.12*, on the mountainside at PK 19 in Paea, has a wood burning pizza oven in their mobile diner. Owners Daniel and Isabelle Zeichen from France offer a choice of 20 pizzas from 1.000 to 1.300 CFP.

RESTAURANTS AROUND THE ISLAND
Superior

NUUTERE, *Tel. 57.41.15, cell 79.41.55. PK 32.5, Papara (mountainside). American Express, Mastercard, Visa. Open for lunch and dinner. Closed Tuesday.*

For many years this restaurant was noted for its gastronomic French cuisine served in a pleasant Tahitian setting of thatched roof, tropical gardens, wicker furniture, white tablecloths and freshly cut flowers on the table. Unfortunately, the restaurant and garden now have a shabby, neglected appearance, with dead leaves on the interior and exterior plants, broken shell lamps and a crying need for paint on the outside walls. The menu is just as big and impressive as ever, and the quality of the food depends on what you order. Chef's specialties include duck with passion fruit for 1.900 CFP, rabbit stewed in red wine for 2.100 CFP, filet of veal with mango for 2.800 CFP and filet of paru fish with ginger butter for 3.100. You can also order a horse steak for 2.800 CFP, filet of kangaroo for 3.100 CFP or wild pig (*pua oviri*) for 2.800 CFP. Cold starter choices include *maoa farcis* (stuffed sea snail) for 1.600 CFP, stuffed crab for 1.900 CFP, and a dozen fresh oysters from New Zealand, for 2.400 CFP. A selection of salads is available for 1.600 to 1.800 CFP, fish dishes are priced from 1.800 CFP to 2.900 CFP, and meats are 1.800 to 3.600 CFP. Lobster is 3.500-5.200 CFP. A 3-course tourist menu is 2.800 CFP, and a Discovery menu is 4.300 CFP. Desserts are 800-1.100 CFP. The wines are from the best vineyards in France and include some of the *grands crus* from Bordeaux, for 40.000 to 137.000 CFP a bottle. They also carry a selection of beers from Belgium and France.

Moderate to Superior
   AUBERGE DU PARI, *Tel. 57.13.44. PK 17.8, Teahupoo, Tahiti-Iti. Mastercard, Visa. Open Tuesday, Wednesday, Thursday, Saturday and Sunday for lunch and dinner. Closed Monday and Friday. Reserve for dinner on weekends.*

   This simple open-air restaurant is located beside the lagoon in Teahupoo village, almost at the end of the road on the west coast of the Tahiti-Iti peninsula, with a good view of the famous international surfer's spot of Hava'e Pass. Although it is no longer a gourmet restaurant, the food is good and it is still a nice place to linger over a long lunch of shrimp, crab, or lobster while sharing a bottle of wine and gazing at one another and the distant white line of the coral reef across the blue lagoon. Choices include poisson cru for 1.600 CFP, a dozen snails for 1.700 CFP, stuffed mussels for 1.850 CFP, spicy prawns for 2.600 CFP, raw shrimp for 2.600 CFP, crab with vinaigrette for 3.200 CFP, stuffed hot crab for 3.300 CFP and a seafood platter for two for 8.800 CFP. Wines are 3.200-4.500 CFP a bottle.

   CHEZ LOULA ET REMY, *Tel. 57.74.99. Turn off from circle island road onto Tautira road and drive to Taravao center. Take first road to right after post office. All major credit cards. Open Tuesday through Sunday for lunch and Tuesday through Saturday for dinner. Closed Sunday night and all day Monday.*

   It is worth a drive from Papeete to Taravao just to eat at this restaurant. Remy used to own the restaurant Chez Remy in the Tamanu Center in Punaauia. Now he and his family are attracting a happy clientele in Taravao, and it's his two half-Tahitian daughters who are turning out such fabulous meals in the kitchen. Remy, a rotund Frenchman, wears a baseball cap as he circulates among the various sections of his restaurant, which include an air-conditioned room for 15 people, and he creates a noisy, lively atmosphere with his *joie de vivre*. This is not a fancy place, but the customers don't seem to mind the plastic flowers on their tables, if there are any at all. They come here again and again for the superb quality of the food. Don't expect the young surfer waiter to pour your wine or to give great service. Be patient and tolerant and you will be rewarded by an excellent meal.

I highly recommend the shrimp and ginger for 2.450 CFP. It's heavenly—what more need I say? The mahi mahi with basil is served with pasta and a pesto sauce for 1.950 CFP, and it is also very good. The salad choices are priced from 900 to 2.500 CFP. The tuna tartare is served with fries and a green salad for 1.850 CFP. Poisson cru is 1.300 CFP and a dozen escargots cost 1.760 CFP. A Neptune plate for 2.600 CFP consists of sashimi, carpaccio, tuna tartare and seaweed, and a Reef plate for 4.150 CFP contains shrimp, *cigales* (slipper lobster) and rock lobster, all flambéed with Armagnac. Dishes including locally grown shrimp cost 2.450 to 2.580 CFP, and fresh river shrimp is 2.350-2.480 CFP. Grilled lobster Maori, flambéed with Armagnac, is 3.800 CFP, and grilled meats run between 1.750 and 2.990 CFP. Desserts include apple pie for 790 CFP, profiteroles for 850 CFP, floating island for 750 CFP and sorbets, up to 990 CFP. A 3-course tourist menu is 2.950 CFP. Wines are priced from 1.500-9.990 CFP.

GAUGUIN MUSEUM RESTAURANT, *Tel. 57.13.80. PK 50.5, Papeari. American Express, Mastercard, Visa. Open daily for lunch only.*

You'll enjoy this luncheon stop whether you are touring the island by rental car, by taxi or in a 50-passenger bus with guide. This popular restaurant is built over the lagoon in Papeari, 50.5 kilometers (31 miles) west of Papeete and just 364 meters (400 yards) west of the Paul Gauguin Museum and Harrison Smith Botanical gardens. Chances are you'll be able to admire a double rainbow over Tahiti-Iti while dining on stuffed crab, grilled mahi mahi, shrimp dishes and Continental cuisine, complete with yummy homemade coconut, papaya or lime pie. Appetizers are 1.600-2.000 CFP, salads are 1.000-1.650 CFP, poultry dishes are 1.950-2.400 CFP, grilled meats are 2.000-2.400 CFP, seafood is 1.950-2.500 CFP, Juliette's famous shrimp curry is 2.400 CFP, grilled lobster is 3.600 CFP in season, and desserts are 600 CFP. Or you may prefer the buffet of salads and Tahitian food, with fresh fruits and coconut for dessert, for 2.550 CFP. A special buffet is presented each Sunday and on holidays for 3.400 CFP. You can also order a sandwich for 700 CFP or an omelet for 1.300 CFP. The maitai rum drinks are a house specialty, and after a few of these, you'll be happier if you're not driving. Englishman Roger Gowan and his Chinese wife, Juliette, opened the restaurant in 1968, and are still on the job, greeting guests and running back and forth between the kitchen or bar and the dining rooms, making sure that the service is smooth and efficient. The staff includes people from the neighborhood in Papeari, some of whom have worked in the kitchen right from the beginning. Be sure to look at the fish and sharks in the enclosures beside the restaurant.

L'OISEAU ROUGE, *Tel. 48.19.99. PK 18.2 on seaside at Manu Ura beach in Mahana Park, Punaauia. Visa. Open 9am to 10pm Thursday through Sunday, serving lunch and dinner. Closed Monday-Wednesday.*

The open-air restaurant overlooks Manu Ura (Red Bird) beach and the gardens of Mahana Park. The restaurant manager will rent you a lounge chair with bright yellow padded cushions and an umbrella for 1.000 CFP a day and you can recline on the wooden deck and work on your tan.

When I was there in August 2004 the menu included poisson cru for 1.600 CFP, tuna sashimi for 1.800 CFP, a trilogy of tuna sashimi, poison cru and grilled tuna for 2.200 CFP, fish dishes for 1.800-2.400 CFP and meats for 1.800-2.500 CFP. A child's menu was 1.400 CFP. You could order wines by the glass for 500 CFP or 2.200-12.000 CFP per bottle. When I called the manager less than a week later, he said that he was changing the menu, the days open and closed and the entertainment and special events, so it's best to check when you arrive.

Between 4:30-6:30pm each Sunday there is a Happy Hour with music for dancing at sunset and the cocktails are half-price. Although this restaurant is closed three days a week, you can get something to eat and drink at the Red Bird Café, just a few steps away, beside the road at Mahana Park.

Moderate

CLUB HOUSE, *Tel. 57.40.32. PK 40,2 in Papara, at the Atimaono Golf Course. American Express, Mastercard, Visa. Open daily 11:30am-3pm and on weekends until 4pm.*

This is the Golf Course restaurant and is open to the public. It is managed by Skip Anderson, an American ex-pat who also owns the Beach Burger and knows his food as well as plays a mean game of golf. Salads are priced from 450-1.350 CFP; cold appetizers include poisson cru with coconut milk for 1.300 CFP, and other raw tuna dishes for 1.350-1.450 CFP; hot appetizers are 1.450-1.550 CFP; fish and shellfish are 1.850-2.350 CFP, including pan fried mahi mahi with tartar sauce, a rare find in these islands. You can also order jumbo shrimp in herb, tomato and wine sauce, or shrimp curry in coconut cream sauce. Veal and Poultry selections are priced from 1.350-2.150 CFP and include pan fried veal Italian style with pasta (Veau à la Milanese). Charbroiled steaks and other meats are priced from 1.750 to 2.700 CFP, with a choice of grilled lamb chops, grilled duck breast, a 12-ounce rib eye steak with grilled onions or Montreal black pepper sauce, and a 15-ounce portion of rib eye steak. Maybe you'd better finish playing your 18 holes before diving into the generous portions of food served here. Or at least take a siesta in the shade before continuing your circle island tour.

RESTAURANT SNACK MOTU OVINI, *Tel. 57.17.59. PK 51.5, Papeari. Mastercard, Visa. Open daily 9:30am to 5:30pm.*

After you've visited the Paul Gauguin Museum and strolled through the Harrison Smith Botanical gardens, you'll be able to quench your thirst or enjoy a full meal in the restaurant beside the parking lot. You can sit beside the lagoon or dine in the open sided building, which is fancy, but there's usually a good breeze. Choices include salads for 700-800 CFP, poisson cru for 1.200 CFP, cheeseburgers with fries for 1.200 CFP, daily specials of fish for 1.700-

2.300 CFP, shrimp cocktail for 1.950 CFP, shrimp curry for 2.100 CFP, fricassee of lobster for 3.300 CFP, meats for 1.750-1.950 CFP, and desserts for 600-750 CFP. Fresh juice is 500 CFP and Hinano beer is 400-550 CFP. Ma'a Tahiti (Tahitian food) is served each Sunday for 2.600 CFP.

RESTAURANT L'EURASIENNE, *Tel. 57.07.49, cell 77.27.37. PK 4, Taravao Plateau. Mastercard, Visa. Open daily for lunch and dinner.*

Jeannine serves Vietnamese and French specialties to guests staying in her family pension (Chez Jeannine) or to anyone else who drops in for a bite while driving around on the Taravao Plateau. Her Nems (spring rolls) made with shrimp or crab are 800 CFP, crispy ravioli is 1.000 CFP and shrimp fritters are 1.000 CFP. A choice of Vietnamese soup costs 900-1.100 CFP, chow mein is 1.400-1.800 CFP, chicken wings are 1.500 CFP, Vietnamese crêpes are 1.600 CFP, fish with ginger sauce is 1.800 CFP and other choices of chicken, duck, fish, beef and seafood dishes range from 1.500-2.500 CFP. French cuisine is priced from 1.500-2.400 CFP. Hinano beer is 350-400 CFP and there is also a wine list.

Economy to Moderate
BEACH BURGER, *Tel. 57.41.03. PK 39, Papara. Mastercard, Visa. Open daily 9:30am to 8pm.*

This very popular restaurant-snack is located near the surfing beach in Papara and is a convenient roadside stop when you're driving around the island. American owner, Skip Anderson, also runs the pro-shop at the nearby golf course.

Hot dogs are 270 CFP, hamburgers are 430 CFP, a bacon cheeseburger is 500 CFP, and french fries are 350 CFP. You can also get a combo of hamburger, fries and coke for 760 CFP, and other combos are available for less than 850 CFP. Salads start at 400 CFP, *poisson cru* is 1.200 CFP, steaks are 1.220 to 1.350 CFP and a dozen fried shrimp costs 1.950 CFP. You can order a milk shake or a chocolate sundae for 490 CFP, a Hinano beer for 400 CFP and a half-carafe of house wine for 540 CFP. There are also daily specials and it is all good eating.

CHEZ MYRIAM, *Tel. 57.71.01. PK 60, Taravao. Mastercard, Visa. Open Monday-Saturday 7am-11pm and on Sunday from 9am to 3pm.*

This friendly restaurant and open terrace snack bar is on the mountainside at the crossroads of Tahiti-Nui and Tahiti-Iti. Myriam is a Chinese-Tahitian lady who speaks English and likes to meet people, and she serves traditional French cuisine and quality Chinese food. You can order a *poisson cru* with coconut milk for 1.200 CFP or shrimp curry with coconut milk for 1.900 CFP. On the last Saturday of each month she serves *ma'a Tahiti* (Tahitian food), for 2.500 CFP a plate, which is complete with all the traditional foods, including roast pig. You can also get a simple casse-croûte sandwich on French baguette bread for 200-500 CFP.

MÉMÉ CHOU, *Tel. 52.12.13. PK 40, Hitia'a. No credit cards. Open 11:30am-2pm Tuesday through Sunday and on Friday and Saturday nights to 8-9pm. Closed Monday.*

You'll be pleasantly surprised when you stop at this east coast restaurant-snack on the mountainside, because it is noted for the great food Mémé Chou serves. You can order *poisson cru* with coconut milk for 1.000 CFP, or chow mein at the same price. She serves *ma'a tinito* (a Chinese dish of pork and red beans and macaroni) for 1.000 CFP, and has a *plat du jour* for 1.400-1.500 CFP, which may be steak and fries, fresh lagoon fish or shrimp and rice. Her Friday special is *couscous* for 1.400 CFP, and for Sunday lunch you can sample her *ma'a Tahiti* (Tahitian food) for 1.800 CFP. She doesn't make *casse-croûte* sandwiches, but serves real homemade style meals. Tour buses sometimes stop here to look at the blue-eyed fresh water eels that live in the river beside her restaurant.

Seeing the Sights
Papeete Highlights

The best way to visit Papeete is to take a walking tour, which you can do on your own or with a guide. You'll enjoy the walk more if you do it in the cool of the morning. Everyone gets going early around here, so you won't have any problems with closed shops if you begin your stroll around 7:30am.

Your first stop should be at the **Tahiti Manava Visitor's Bureau** on the waterfront side of Boulevard Pomare, at the corner of Rue Paul Gauguin. This building is also called Fare Manihini, which is the Tahitian word for "Visitor's House." The helpful hosts and hostesses speak good English and will give you a map of the city and answer any questions you may have. You can also follow the map shown here, taken from the *Tahiti Beach Press*.

Just outside the Visitor's Bureau on the right is the **Captain Tamarii a Teai Square**, named in honor of a former Tahitian merchant marine officer. This is an attractive place with benches and shade trees, where you can relax and enjoy watching the sailboats and bonito boats after your stroll. Some of the phone numbers on the informational panels may be out of date, but they also show maps, and give information on the birds and fish that are found around Tahiti.

All set to go? Walk along the renovated **yacht quay** and check out the sailboats from many countries around the world whose owners are living their dreams of cruising the South Pacific. You'll also see the catamarans and dive boats that are loading passengers for a day sail to Moorea or Tetiaroa. Across the Papeete harbor you'll see container ships and inter-island cargo vessels docked at **Motu Uta**, and chances are you'll also see one of the fast catamarans and ferries that connects Papeete with Moorea. This is one of the busiest French-owned harbors in the world, due to the passenger traffic between Tahiti and Moorea.

Walking along the quay past the **Bounty Tunnel** you'll come to a traffic roundabout where **Avenue Bruat** joins **Boulevard Pomare**. There's major construction going on here and all along this end of the waterfront. Walking will be a lot easier once the boardwalk is finished, but in the meantime, just watch your step and don't get run over. In the area called **Hokule'a Beach** you'll see several outrigger canoes on supports. You may even be able to watch some of Tahiti's canoe teams practicing for the next big race, which is a national passion. The Hokule'a stele has been temporarily removed until the construction work is completed. This is a monument in the form of twin canoe hulls imbedded in stone, which was erected in honor of the Hokule'a, a replica of an ancient Polynesian voyaging canoe that was built in Hawaii. It is sponsored by the Hawaiian Voyaging Society to retrace the sailing routes of the Polynesian pioneers who settled the tiny specks of land that make up the Polynesian triangle. The *Hokule'a* made its first voyage to Tahiti in 1976, navigating by the winds, stars and sea currents, and arrived in Tahiti to an overwhelming welcome by thousands of Tahitians. The beach here is polluted and swimming is not allowed.

Your destination on this side of the street is **Place To'ata**, also called **Tahua To'ata**, which opened in time for the **Heiva Festival** activities in June 2000. This is an immense outdoor theater and meeting place, complete with restaurants, public restrooms and showers and exhibit space. It's a great place to sit on a bench among the flower gardens and watch the activity in the harbor, as well as the families who bring their children to skate or ride their scooters in the fresh air. There are restaurants and very clean restrooms here, complete with toilet paper, which is not the case in all public restrooms in Tahiti.

The **Maison de la Culture** at Fare Tauhiti Nui, adjacent to Place To'ata, is Tahiti's cultural center, library and theater/concert hall. Here you'll find a snack bar and public toilets, but those at Place To'ata are better. The **Olympic swimming pool** is just beyond the cultural center, and beyond that is the **Artisan Center**, where you can buy arts and crafts made in Tahiti and Her Islands.

When you get ready to head back toward the center of town, perhaps you will prefer to walk past the swimming pool and go up the stairs to the crossover to get to the other side of the road. Or you can use the designated crossing in front of Place To'ata. Trying to get across the five lanes of traffic can be quite tricky and even dangerous in Papeete, even though there are pedestrian zones and a few traffic lights. Once you've negotiated getting across Boulevard Pomare, you'll soon come to the **Clinique Paofai**, then the **Protestant Temple**, which used to be part of the Evangelical Society of French Polynesia. In mid-2004 all the former Evangelical churches changed their name to Maohi Protestant Church. The missionaries from the London Missionary Society brought the Gospel to Tahiti in 1797 and the Protestant religion was predominant in the Windward Society Islands until the year 2000, when a poll revealed that 45 percent of the population is Catholic and 34 percent is Protestant.

Continue on down Boulevard Pomare to Avenue Bruat and turn right. Walk a block and cross the street on Rue du Commandant Destremeau, which changes to Rue du General de Gaulle at this corner. Walk a block or two up Avenue Bruat and see the government buildings.

Here you'll find the French court or tribunal, the Police station, the *gendarmerie*, and the **Presidential Palace**, the impressive building that houses the offices of the President of French Polynesia. When Oscar Temaru, leader of the independence party, replaced autonomist Gaston Flosse as President in June 2004, he opened the building and grounds to the public rather than limiting it to the privileged elite. At publication time, Temaru's party continued to occupy the presidency even though Flosse had regained his power, and both men claimed to be president. More than 500 employees work in this showcase. Across the street is the **Ministry of Culture**. Go back to Rue du General de Gaulle and continue back toward the center of town, passing more government buildings.

On your right is **Place Tarahoi**, where Queen Pomare IV lived in an elaborate mansion before the French took control in 1842, and used Tarahoi as their headquarters. The offices and home of the **French High Commissioner** are located in the building on the right. Against the fence in the parking lot is the **Pacific Battalion Monument**, a tribute to the French Polynesians who fought with General Charles de Gaulle's Free French forces during World War II. This monument was moved from the waterfront during the construction of the traffic roundabout and boardwalk in front of Avenue Bruat. If Gaston Flosse is still president when it is inaugurated, he will name this site **Place Jacques Chirac**.

To the left of the French High Commissioner's office is the French Polynesia **Assembly** building, where the local politicians have a good go at one another during their hot debates. In front of the building is a monument to **Pouvanaa a Oopa** (1895-1977), a man from the island of Huahine who was a decorated hero fighting for France during World War I. He became an even bigger hero to the Tahitian people when he was sentenced to prison in France while seeking independence for his own country. After spending 15 years behind bars during the 1960s and 1970s Pouvanaa returned to Tahiti, but was sent back to France again, this time as Tahiti's representative in the French Senate.

Cross Rue du General de Gaulle again in the crosswalk between Place Tarahoi and the rear of the **Papeete Post Office**. Double back toward the West for a few yards until you see the green oasis of **Bougainville Park** on your right, adjacent to the post office. A gurgling stream meanders through the tree-shaded gardens. This was Queen Pomare's favorite bathing pool when she lived at Place Tarahoi, and it was from this little river that Papeete received its name: *Pape* (pah-pey) means water in the Tahitian language; and *ete* (eh-tey) means basket; therefore, Papeete means water basket. Before the houses were equipped with water pipes, the people used to come to this spring with their gourds wrapped in woven leaves and take the *pape* home in their *ete*.

Although this park was named for the French explorer, Louis Antoine de Bougainville, he never laid eyes on this site, because he spent his entire brief visit to Tahiti on the east coast of Hitiaa. However, he was the first French discoverer, and his statue stands between the **two cannons** that are adjacent to the sidewalk on the Boulevard Pomare side of the park.

The cannon nearest the post office was taken from the *Seeadler*, a World War I German raider that belonged to the luckless Count Felix von Luckner. His ship ran aground on Mopelia atoll, in the Leeward Society Islands in 1917, after having captured 14 British, French and American ships in the South Pacific. The other gun comes from the *Zélée*, a small French navy vessel that was sunk in Papeete harbor in 1914 when the German raiders *Scharnhorst* and *Gneisenau* bombarded Papeete.

After you've walked around the cannons, continue on toward the center of Papeete on Boulevard Pomare. Turn right on Rue Jeanne d'Arc beside the **Vaima Center** and you'll see the **Cathédrale de l'Immaculée Conception**, which is usually called the **Cathedral of Notre Dame**. This cathedral was built in 1875 and has been restored a few times. If the door is unlocked go inside, where it is quiet and cool, and look at the paintings of the Crucifixion.

Cross over to the left side of the street at the Pharmacie de la Cathédrale, which is on the corner opposite Place Notre Dame. Walk past Tahiti Voyages travel agency and Tahiti Music and turn left at the end of the block. The sidewalk here is usually quite crowded with Tahitians who are shopping or hanging out, talking with friends. Walk past the police station and you'll see the public market, the **Marché Municipale**, which is the heart and breadbasket of Papeete. The Tahitian "mamas" and even young men sell orchids, anthuriums, ginger flowers, roses, and other flowers of every imaginable hue.

Past the flower vendors inside *le Marché* you'll see traditional Tahitian fruits and tubers on the left of the aisle and vegetables sold by the Chinese are on the right. The fish and meat markets are off to the right and upstairs you'll find all kinds of locally made products, including some nice *tifaifai* bed covers or wall hangings and lots of seashells. Outside *le Marché* are hundreds of colorful *pareos*. The cotton ones were made in Tahiti and the uni-colored ones with fringe are imported.

When you leave *le Marché*, go out the door closest to the counters selling woven hats, bags and grass skirts. Walk straight ahead on Rue Colette for one block until you come to Rue Paul Gauguin. Turn right at the corner and you'll see the **Mairie of Papeete** on the left. This impressive building is the town hall, called *Hôtel de Ville* in French and *Fare Oire* in Tahitian. This building is a replica of Queen Pomare's royal palace that once stood at Place Tarahoi. The elaborate building, with crystal chandeliers and pink marble imported from Italy, was inaugurated in 1990. Former French President **François Mitterand** was the guest of honor for the dedication ceremonies. Walk up the steps into the building and take the elevator to the third floor. There are frequent art exhibits on display in the room to the left as you get off the elevator. Don't hesitate to walk around the building and admire the decor, and be sure to see the stone carvings in the gardens all around the outside of the building. They were made by sculptors living in Tahiti, the Marquesas and Easter Island.

Following your tour of the town hall, walk back toward the waterfront and the Tahiti Manava Visitors Bureau. Cross Boulevard Pomare to the harbor side, and as you approach Fare Manihini, take a little detour to the right to have a look at the modern **Place Vaiete**, also called **Tahua Vaiete**, which has an all-new look since February 2001. This square was the site of the first territorial parliament in 1945. It was also the place where the 4th Festival of Pacific Arts was held in 1985. For many years the traditional song and dance competitions took place here during the July celebrations, and the carnival type stalls, carousel, Ferris wheel and *papio* rides for children were built next to the amphitheater.

Today this square has been enlarged to a tiled area of 1,200 square meters (129,167 square feet). A low stone wall encloses Place Vaiete and there are benches and a waterfall, toilets that are open and kept clean 24 hours a day, and round-the-clock security guards. The roulottes (mobile diners) still set up shop here in the evenings, but they are now limited to 30, and there is even a washroom where they can clean their dishes and pots and pans. Many of the roulottes bring their own linoleum to spread under their vans to protect the tile from grease spots, and some of them place tables and chairs beside the roulotte for more comfortable dining. Local musicians give free concerts in the bandstand and the audience sits on the low wall, the benches and the tiled floor of the square.

If this two-hour walk is too long for you, it can be shortened by crossing Boulevard Pomare at Avenue Bruat, after you have visited the waterfront and had a look at the yachts. You can head inland on Avenue Bruat to see the government buildings and continue the above itinerary from there. You will eliminate the extra walk to the Cultural Center and Protestant Temple.

You can also take an organized **Papeete Discovery Tour** for 3.000 CFP, plus a 600 CFP entry fee to the Musée de la Perle (Black Pearl Museum) at Tahiti Pearls. This tour can be booked through your hotel activities desk or with any of the local travel agencies in downtown Papeete, and is normally available only in the afternoons.

Around the Island

Most tour drivers follow the northeast coast through Papeete's neighboring *communes* of Pirae, Arue and Mahina. Ask your driver to stop at the **James Norman Hall House and Library**, at PK 5.5 in Arue. It is well worth a visit. See information under *Museums & Special Sightseeing Stops* in this chapter. From the **Tahara'a Lookout Point** at PK (poste kilometre) 8.1 in Arue you can see historic Matavai Bay. When **Captain James Cook** sailed the *Endeavour* into this bay in 1769, he sighted a single tree (*Erythrina indica*) with bright red-orange flowers growing on the promontory above the bay. He used the tree as a navigational landmark and named this reference point "One Tree Hill." Although the gnarled old tree has disappeared, this lookout provides a spectacular panoramic view of the island of Moorea, the Sea of Moons, the coral reef and lagoon, and Tahiti's majestic fern-softened mountains.

The next stop will be at **Point Venus** *at PK 10 in Mahina*. This historic site beside Matavai Bay is where English **Captain Samuel Wallis** of the *H.M.S. Dolphin* came ashore in 1767, to become the first European to discover Tahiti. When Captain Cook led an expedition of scientists to Tahiti to observe the transit of the planet Venus across the sun on June 3, 1769, he named the site Point Venus. **Captain William Bligh** and the *Bounty* crew came here in 1788 to collect breadfruit plants, and representatives of the **London Missionary Society** waded ashore in 1797, in search of souls to save.

In addition to the monuments in honor of Captain Cook and the missionaries, you'll see a lighthouse, snack bar, arts and crafts stands, toilet facilities, tropical gardens and a black sand beach, usually decorated with topless sunbathers, mostly French women. Raise your gaze from the bare twin peaks on the beach and look up at the double summit of Tahiti's highest mountain, Mt. Orohena, reaching 2,241 meters (7,353 feet) high into a crown of clouds. Point Venus is a lovely spot to photograph the bathing beauties as well as the tropical sunset, with a magnificent view of the nearby island of Moorea.

Continuing along the east coast you'll see the surfers riding the waves offshore Papenoo, before coming to the **Blow Hole of Arahoho** and the **Three Cascades of Fa'arumai** in Tiarei at PK 22. The Vaimahuta waterfall is easily reached in five minutes by walking across the bridge over the Vaipuu river and following a well defined path under a cool canopy of wild chestnut (*mape*) trees and *Barringtonia asiatica* (*hutu*) trees. Countless waterfalls cascade in misty plumes and broken curtains down the mountainside to tumble into a crisp, refreshing pool. This is a good swimming hole, but don't forget your mosquito repellent.

Back on the circle island road you will pass country villages, modern concrete homes and modest little *fare* huts brightly painted in yellow, pink and blue. Flowers and hedges of every shape and hue border the road and breadfruit, mangoes, papaya and banana trees fill the luxuriant gardens.

Birdhouse-shaped boxes stand by the road in front of each home, ready to receive the daily delivery of fresh French *baguettes* that are baked by the Chinese and eaten by the Tahitians as their staple food.

At PK 37.6 in Hitiaa your guide may point out a plaque beside the bridge. The French explorer, **Louis Antoine de Bougainville**, made a deed of annexation in April 1768, when his ships *Boudeuse* and *Etoile* dropped anchor just inside two islets offshore the village. Bougainville proclaimed French sovereignty over the island, which he named New Cytherea. He placed the deed in a bottle and buried it in the ground between the river and the beach. Bougainville's ships lost six anchors during his 10-day visit.

At PK 60 you'll be in the village of Taravao, the isthmus that connects Tahiti Nui with Tahiti Iti, the Taiarapu peninsula. If you're saving your discovery of Tahiti Iti for another delightful day, then continue on to **Papeari**, where you'll find the **Paul Gauguin Museum** and the **Harrison Smith Botanical Gardens** (see information under *Museums* and also under *Gardens* in this chapter.

Most tour buses stop for lunch in the vicinity of Taravao or Papeari, where you have a good selection of restaurants and snack bars. The most popular luncheon choice is the **Gauguin Museum Restaurant**, *Tel. 57.13.80*, at PK 50.5 in Papeari. This very spacious restaurant and bar is built over the lagoon, just 400 yards west of the Paul Gauguin Museum and Harrison Smith Botanical gardens. (See description in the *Where to Eat* section).

Land of the Double Rainbow

When you stop at the Vaipahi Gardens and Cascade in Mataiea, look out over the lagoon and perhaps you'll catch sight of a double rainbow arching over the peninsula of Tahiti Iti. This is where I fell in love with Tahiti during my first visit to the island in 1968. There's magic in the air here, a haunting beauty that touches the soul.

The latter half of your tour will take you to the **Vaipahi Gardens and Cascade**, at PK 49 in Mataiea. If you are making the island tour on your own, then stop at the **Vaima River**, PK 48.5 in Mataiea, very close to the public gardens. This is one of Tahiti's favorite watering holes, complete with underground springs that bubble up like a cold Jacuzzi. Leave your car in the parking lot and wade waist-deep through the clear, refreshing river. Wild hibiscus *(purau)* trees lend their shade and purple water hyacinths add their color to the scene. This is a welcome treat on a hot sunny day.

On the southwest coast you'll pass the **Atimaono Golf Course**, *Tel. 57.40.32*, at PK 40.2, where international championship tournaments are played each July. A little further on you'll see the black sand beach of **Papara**, where world-class surfers compete. Several of the tour guides will stop at the **Ava Tea Distillery and Tasting Room,** *Tel. 53.32.43,* on the mountainside at PK 26.2 in Paea. They moved into a new building in February 2002. You can learn how the liqueurs and *eau de vie* are made from coconuts, gingerroot, *pamplemousse* grapefruit, mangoes and other tropical fruits. You are welcome to taste all the flavors, and if you imbibe too much and drowse on the bus, then you can take the **West Coast Tour** another day to see what you missed. If you are touring on your own, keep in mind that they close at 5:30pm and are not open at all on Sundays.

The side road leading into the valley to the **Marae of Arahurahu** is at PK 22.5 in Paea. Follow the road to the parking area and walk a few steps to the two restored open-air stone temples, which were used in pre-Christian days for religious ceremonies, meetings, cultural rites, sacrifices and burials. There is no entry fee to visit the *marae* except during special performances that take place during the **Heiva I Tahiti Festival** in July and August. These colorful reenactment ceremonies choose various themes, such as the crowning of a king and royal weddings, with a cast of dozens of beautifully costumed Tahitian dancers, musicians, warriors and *tahua* priests. No performances have been held here during the past 2-3 years, however.

The **Grottos of Mara'a** at PK 28.5 in Paea, are joined by a flower-bordered walkway. The **Paroa cave** is the largest of three natural grottos, where overhead springs drip through wild ferns and moss, forming a pool where children play. **Queen Pomare** used to bathe here and **Paul Gauguin** wrote of swimming inside this cave. Drops of water from the overhead ferns reflect rainbow hues in the rays of the afternoon sun. No entry fee.

On the west coast of the island you'll see a sign on the seaside at PK 15.7 in Punaauia, directing you to the **Museum of Tahiti and Her Islands (Musée des Iles)**. Some of the tour guides stop here. See information under *Museums.*

In the communes of Paea and Punaauia, you will catch only glimpses of Tahiti's lovely beachfront properties behind the walls and thick hedge fences that protect them from the road. You may even see some old Polynesian style homes that are built of pandanus and woven bamboo. The millionaires' modern villas are up in the mountains, overlooking the island of Moorea. Here suburbia Tahiti blends the past with today. The thatched roof *fare*, colonial mansions and concrete homes are neighbors with schools, shopping malls, used car lots and video shops. Supermarkets sell foods for all tastes and boutiques sell surfboards and beachwear from California and Hawaii.

From 1897 to 1901, the artist **Paul Gauguin** lived in a comfortable villa at PK 12.6 in Punaauia, before he left for the Marquesas Islands in search of a wild and savage beauty. Your guide may point out the **2+2=4 school** that was built adjacent to Gauguin's former property.

Museums & Special Sightseeing Stops

Le Musée de la Perle is also called **The Robert Wan Pearl Museum**, *Tel. 45.21.22; Fax 45.48.92; E-mail: museeperle@tahitiperles.pf; www.tahitiperles.com.* Located on the street level of the Vaima Center on Rue Jeanne d'Arc in Papeete. Open Monday-Saturday from 8am to 7pm and on Sunday from 9am to 7pm. Entry is 600 CFP. The museum has seven promenades and themes that teach you many lessons about the history and culture of the black pearl, a gem that has been regarded as a wonder and a mystery to man and woman since time immemorial.

James Norman Hall House and Library, *Tel. 50.01.61/50.01.60; E-mail: jamesnormanhall@mail.pf; www.jamesnormanhallhome.pf.* On mountainside at PK 5.5 in Arue. Open daily except Sunday and Monday from 9am to 4pm. Entry is 600 CFP for adults, 500 CFP per person for groups, and free for school students. This colonial style green house is a replica of the famous author's original home, and his library of more than 3,000 books is displayed in numerous bookshelves. James Norman Hall and Charles Nordhoff, both American heroes of World War I, moved to Tahiti in 1920. Hall wrote 17 books by himself and co-authored 12 books with Nordhoff. Their most famous works included *Mutiny on the Bounty*, *Men Against the Sea*, *Pitcairn's Island*, *The Hurricane,* and *The High Barbaree.*

Hall's office library contains his original writing desk and typewriter and is arranged exactly as it was on the day he died in 1951. The house is filled with antique wooden furniture, family pictures, Hall's poems written to his family, his favorite paintings, gramophone and other personal effects. One of the three Oscars awarded to his son, the late Conrad L. Hall, for his achievements as a cinematographer in Hollywood films, is also on display. Be sure to visit Mama Lala's Tea Room, named in memory of Hall's wife, Sarah Winchester Hall.

Paul Gauguin Museum, *Tel. 57.10.58.* Beside the lagoon at PK 51.2 in Papeari, adjacent to the Harrison Smith Botanical Gardens. Open daily 9am to 5pm. Entry is 600 CFP for adults and 300 CFP for people 12-18 years old. This is a memorial to the late French artist, with only a few original carvings and wood blocks located in the Salle Henri Bing. Reproductions of Gauguin's paintings and carvings are exhibited in three buildings beside the sea. In the second building you can see where the originals of Gauguin's works of art are located today. Three ancient stone *tiki* from Raivavae in the Austral Islands stand in the gardens surrounding the museum, and now the people of Raivavae want them returned to their original sites.

Museum of Tahiti and Her Islands (Musée des Iles or Te Fare Iamanaha), *Tel. 54.84.35,* on the sea side at PK 15.7 in Punaauia, at Fisherman's Point (Pointe des Pêcheurs). Open from 9:30am to 5:30pm. Closed Mondays. Entry is 600 CFP for adults, free for students. This modern museum presents the natural environment, Polynesian migrations, history, culture and ethnology in four exhibit halls. On display are stone and wooden tiki, hand-hewn canoes, intricate sculptures, tapa bark, seashells and other traditional Polynesian objects and tools. The museum has a collection of old books about Tahiti's colorful past, as well as more recent publications. When I was here in August 2004 all the books and posters were locked away in drawers and it took about 45 minutes to buy a book. Walk out to the beach and watch the surfers before you continue your tour. Breathe deeply and smell the fresh salty air.

If you plan to visit the museum by public transportation, you should know that the last bus for Papeete passes in front of the Tamanu shopping center at 4pm, except during the Heiva Festival, when they run a little later.

Lagoonarium, *Tel. 43.62.90,* at PK 11.4 in Punaauia at the Captain Bligh Restaurant. Open daily 9am to 5:30pm. Entry is 500 CFP for adults and 300 CFP for children 3 to 12 years old. No entry charge if you eat in the restaurant. Four big fish parks are built into the lagoon, filled with thousands of fish, sharks and moray eels. The walls of the Lagoonarium are covered in coral, shells and sea urchin spines, and glass cases contain collections of seashells, mother-of-pearl shells, black pearls and other treasures from the sea. If you arrive at noon you can watch the daily shark feeding show.

Parks & Gardens

Mahana Park, *Tel. 48.19.99,* is beside the lagoon at PK 18.2 in Paea. Open daily. No entry fee. This public park covers a one-acre grassy lawn and parking area and borders a white sand beach facing the island of Moorea. The tranquil lagoon is good for swimming. There are public toilets and showers and you can rent a lounge chair and beach umbrella for 1.000 CFP at the restaurant L'Oiseau Rouge (red bird in French). You can picnic at one of the tables under the trees or dine in the restaurant. The Manu Ura (red bird in Tahitian) Café is a small snack beside the road that is open all day except Monday and Tuesday.

Le Jardin de Mataoa, *Tel. 57.37.24,* on the seaside at PK 34.500 in Papara. Open Monday to Friday from 10am to 4pm, and on weekends and holidays from 1 to 4pm. Entry is 720 CFP for adults and half price for children 6 to 12 years. This is a privately owned flower garden. Their greenhouse contains a magnificent collection of birds of paradise, anthuriums, heliconias, ginger flowers, orchids and vanilla, as well as a small pineapple plantation. In addition to tasting fresh tropical fruits, you will learn how to make floral arrangements and garlands, as well as watching a demonstration of how to marry or cross pollinate the vanilla orchid during its blooming season. You can also order flowers to be delivered at the airport to take home with you. See information on Tahiti Fleurs under Shopping in *Tahiti* chapter.

Harrison W. Smith Botanical Gardens, *Tel. 57.11.07,* at PK 51.2 in Papeari, adjacent to the Paul Gauguin Museum. Open daily 9am to 5pm. Entry is 500 CFP for adults and half price for children under 12 years. Protect yourself from mosquitoes and stroll through the 137 hectares (340 acres) of tropical gardens, streams and water lily ponds. You will see hundreds of trees, shrubs, plants and flowers gathered from tropical regions throughout the world by Smith, who was an American physics teacher who escaped to the South Seas in 1919 and created his own Garden of Eden in Tahiti.

The most impressive part of this park is a natural forest of Tahitian *mape* trees, with their convoluted roots above the ground. This grove provides a cool and pleasant walk, with a small stream meandering through the shaded garden. Main attractions in the gardens are two huge land turtles, which were brought to Tahiti in the 1930's from the Galapagos Islands. These pets placidly pose for photographs and will stop eating to raise their long wrinkled necks and stare at the cameras.

Motu Ovini is on the point of land adjacent to the parking lot for the Gauguin Museum, Harrison W. Smith Botanical Gardens and the Restaurant Snack Motu Ovini. Harrison Smith lived here until his death in 1948, and his house stood here for several decades afterward. Walk to the end of the denuded terrain adjacent to a big gazebo (Fare Pote'e) structure built over the water, and here you will find excellent swimming, with underground springs blending with the salt water of the lagoon, providing buoyancy that will keep you floating for hours. You'll find fresh water showers, toilets and changing rooms on the premises. This used to be an outstanding natural setting, with wonderful shade trees and flowers, but Tahiti's former government had all the trees and plants cleared away in preparation for a big event that was supposed to have taken place here when French President Jacques Chirac came to Tahiti in late July 2003. A house was even built for Chirac on the premises, but it is no longer there. A big space was also cleared in the Botanical Gardens to make way for a helipad for Chirac's arrival, but the gathering and entertainment never took place. A GIP (local government guard) lives on the premises and he said that people can come here and swim and even picnic, but no alcohol is allowed and the Fare Pote'e is off limits to the public. There is no entry fee.

Vaipahi Gardens and Cascade, on the mountainside at PK 49 in Mataiea. Open daily. Free entry. Take a pleasant stroll through these public gardens and discover a sparkling waterfall at the end of a short path. Huge tree ferns and giant leaves of elephant ear plants provide a natural setting for the cascade, which is a popular photographic choice for travel brochures on Tahiti. The gardens are filled with luxuriant vegetation, including *rambutan* fruit, fragrant *pua* flowers, ground orchids and the exotic jade vine. Crotons and hibiscus add to the flamboyance in these gardens of dancing color. You can enjoy a picnic at a table on the seaside if you are touring the island by private car.

Guided Island Tours of Tahiti Nui (Big Tahiti)
You can book your sightseeing tours through the travel desk at your hotel in Tahiti and see the island with a knowledgeable guide aboard an air-conditioned bus, mini-van or Mercedes luxury car.

A **Half Day Circle Island Tour** starts at 3.700 CFP plus entrance fees to the museums and gardens visited, or 4.950 CFP-5.500 CFP including entrance fees. These tours operate daily between 8:30am and 12:30pm, or between 1:30 and 5:30pm. A **Full Day Circle Island Tour** starts at 4.400 CFP with a pickup at your hotel at 9:30am, returning around 3:30 to 4pm. The full day tour with two entries and lunch is 8.150 CFP. The **Bounty Tour**, which takes you to visit the James Norman Hall Home & Library, Tahara'a View Point, Point Venus, the Tomb of King Pomare V, Pirae City Hall, Chinese Temple and Papeete City Hall, is a four-hour excursion in the morning or afternoon, and sells for 3.600 CFP.

A knowledgeable guide who speaks good English is essential for your introduction to the sights and stories of Tahiti. For 17 years I worked as a tour guide in Tahiti, in addition to my journalistic endeavors, and I will recommend the best guides so that you'll be able to make an agreeable choice when you book a tour.

Bernie's Circle Island Tour, sold by Paradise Tours, *Tel. 42.49.36*, will surely please even the most reticent of visitors. Bernie Kamalamalama, who is part Hawaiian, advertises that his tour is worth his weight in pleasant memories for you, and that's really saying a lot. Bernie would make his Polynesian ancestors very proud, as they believed that bigger is better. In addition to being one of the sweetest and most helpful people you'll meet anywhere, Bernie is also a very good guide.

Marama Tours Tahiti, *Tel. 50.74.74*, has a number of guides who do a good job of telling Tahiti's tales. Teva Cowan was taught by his dad Emile, who taught me to be a guide way back when. Emile and his wife Mata, both Polynesians, are owners of the company.

Adventure Eagle Tours, *Tel. 77.20.03*. William Leeteg is the son of Edgar Leeteg, the famous black velvet painter who lived in Moorea until he died in a motorcycle accident in 1953. William has a great sense of humor and will maybe even sing for you as he drives you in his air-conditioned 9-seat mini-bus to visit the island. He has a half-day West Coast Tour, and Grand Circle Island Tour of Tahiti, with morning or afternoon departures. William also arranges private tours on request.

Guided Island Tours of Tahiti Iti (Little Tahiti)
Te Reva Nei, *Tel/Fax 56.20.01; cell 71.81.24; E-mail: palomat2002@yahoo.fr* is owned by a young Polynesian couple who use their 8-passenger mini-bus for tours of Tahiti Iti. The 5-hour excursion takes you along the West Coast of Tahiti Nui to Taravao, up to the **Plateau of Taravao**,

then down the West Coast of Tahiti Iti to Teahupoo and the famous Surf Spot. This tour costs 7.000 CFP per person. The 8-hour excursion for 8.500 CFP combines sightseeing on Tahiti Iti and Tahiti Nui. They offer private tours for 45.000 CFP per half day and 60.000 CFP for an all-day outing. This company also provides transfers from Papeete or the airport to any pension or the Teahupoo boat dock on Tahiti Iti.

You can also buy a copy of Bengt Danielsson's *Circle Island Tour Guide* and rent a car for a do-it-yourself excursion. If you have the time and the inclination, I suggest that you take a guided tour around Tahiti Nui (big Tahiti) and on another day rent a car and drive around the island, stopping where you choose and exploring both coasts of Tahiti Iti (little Tahiti), as well as driving up the Plateau of Taravao, where you will see horses and cattle grazing in rolling green pastures bordered by eucalyptus trees and orange groves.

Mountain & Waterfall Tours

Excursions by four-wheel drive vehicle (4x4) are designed for you to get off the beaten track and up into the mountains and valleys of Tahiti. The "Queen of the Pacific" will disclose a few of her mysteries and magic as you are driven in air-conditioned or open-air Land Rovers or other 4WDs through the tropical forests of giant ferns, centuries old Tahitian *mape* chestnut trees, wild mango and guava trees, and more waterfalls than you can count.

A **Half-Day Mountain Tour** can be made in the morning or afternoon. This excursion takes you to a height of 4,500 feet up **Mount Marau** via the **Tamanu Canyon**. Or you can choose a **Half Day East Coast Tour**, which also takes you to Mount Marau and the Tamanu Canyon, plus you will see the **Blowhole of Arahoho** and the **Fa'arumai Cascades of Tiarei**. This tour is noted for the numerous waterfalls you will see.

A **Full Day Across the Island Tour** takes you from **Mataiea** in the south to the **Papenoo Valley** in the north, crossing the main crater of Tahiti. You leave the circle island road at PK 47.5 in Mataiea and follow the winding track that leads 11.2 kilometers (7.4 miles) up to **Lake Vaihiria**. At an altitude of 465 meters (1,550 feet) above the sea, this is Tahiti's only fresh water lake. The scenery along the way seems almost vertical, with a saw-tooth mountain range, deep ravines and tumbling cascades above and below you. As you snake to dizzying heights around the curves you will pass small catchment lakes, dams and hydroelectric substations.

After you traverse the **Urufau Tunnel**, which is 110 meters (361 feet) long, your guide will probably stop to let you look out over the Papenoo Valley. It is believed that from 10,000 to 20,000 Maohi people once inhabited this area, and the valley was totally deserted by 1850. At this height of (780 meters) 2,558 feet you will have an impressive view of Tahiti Nui's great extinct volcano. A junction in the road near the tunnel leads to the **Relais de la Maroto** (Maroto Inn), where some tours stop to have lunch. If you have brought your own lunch, then your driver will usually continue on to a site in the Papenoo Valley that is known as **Fare Hape**. This is an area rich in archaeological sites, and some 190 *marae* and sanctuaries have been found in the high valley since the road was built. After a refreshing swim under a sparkling waterfall and a satisfying picnic lunch eaten at a table under a big covered shelter, you can walk with your guide to visit the Fare Hape site. Several of the *marae* temples have been restored and there are archery sites, house foundations and a huge boulder carved with petroglyphs.

Tahiti Safari Expedition, *Tel. 42.14.15; E-mail: tahiti.safari@mail.pf; www.tahiti-safari.com.* Patrice Bordes is the go-getter owner who has five Land Rovers and he advertises that all his guides speak English. He offers a choice of two half-day treks or a full-day excursion, all starting from the Papenoo side of the island. He charges 5.500 CFP for a half-day mountain tour of Papenoo Valley and 9.800 CFP for a full-day tour across the island from Papenoo to Mataiea, with a picnic lunch included. You also have the option of stopping for lunch at Le Relais de la Maroto, a hotel and restaurant located in the mountains of the Papenoo Valley. These tours were recommended by *Géo Magazine* for their efficiency and expertise. Patrice was the pioneer of the inner island tours in 1990, and he's still the leader. These excursions are not for pregnant women or anyone who is frail, as the unpaved roads can be quite bumpy, and most uncomfortable if you are sitting on the bench in the back. These lush green valleys get a lot of rain and you will also get wet unless the side flaps are closed, creating a hothouse effect for the passengers, who can no longer see the misty beauty of the rainforest. Patrice advises his passengers not to wear the color blue as it attracts mosquitoes.

Patrick Adventure, *Tel. 83.29.29, Cell 79.08.09; E-mail: patrickaventure@mail.pf; www.papeete.com.* Patrick Cordier has a 9-passenger Mazda 4WD and he is a very knowledgeable guide who covers the entire range of subjects concerning Tahiti: the history, culture, legends, geology, archaeology, agriculture, botany, religion, foods, modern life and everything else any visitor would want to know about an island and its people. His full day tour is 6.500 CFP and also takes you around the island of Tahiti Nui. Bring your own lunch to eat at a picnic table in the covered shelter at **Fare Hape**, and then swim in the pool under the waterfall just behind the picnic area. Patrick takes you to visit the restored *marae* temples on the premises. He also has a half-day mountain tour to visit Tahiti's east coast for 4.500 CFP. Children pay half-price on all his tours.

Natura Excursions, *Tel. 43.03.83; Cell 79.31.21; E-mail: natura.explo@mail.pf; www.natura-exploration.com.* Owner Arnaud Luccioni advertises half-day Landrover tours to Mount Marau or to the Papenoo Valley for 5.000 CFP and 3.000 CFP for children 4-12 years old. His full-day exploration to follow the tracks of the Bounty mutineers who hid out in Papenoo Valley is 7.500 CFP, including a picnic lunch, and children pay 4.500 CFP. Kids under 4 years old are free.

Marama Tours Tahiti, *Tel. 50.74.74 or Cell 78.40.11; E-mail: philippe@mail.pf.* Teva Cowan heads a team of guides who will take you on a half-day morning or afternoon tour to visit Mount Marau, for 5.500 CFP. The full-day cross-island Maroto trek by 4WD with a picnic is 9.800 CFP.

Helicopter Tours
A helicopter tour offers the best of Tahiti's scenic sights, giving you a close-up look at the tallest mountains, dipping into the lush green valleys to hover like a hummingbird in front of a sparkling waterfall, and soaring over the lagoon, reef and sea. Go early in the morning before the clouds veil the view.
Polynesia Hélicoptères, *Tel. 689/86.60.29; cell 78.65.05; Fax 689/ 81.61.29; E-mail: helico-tahiti@mail.pf; www.polynesia-helicopter.com.* A 5-seat "Squirrel" AS 350 BA helicopter is based at the Tahiti-Faa'a airport and is available for tourist flights around Tahiti, transfers to Moorea and specific charters on request. A 20-minute flightseeing tour of Tahiti is 15.700 CFP and a 35-minute "Moorea Discovery" tour for a minimum of four passengers costs 25.500 CFP per person with a departure from the Faa'a Airport in Tahiti. Private transfers from a hotel in Tahiti to a hotel in Moorea are 52.000 CFP, and a private charter is 168.000 CFP per hour.

Nightlife & Entertainment
Reputed as the South Seas heart of hedonism, Papeete by night is prowl-about time. The shops are closed and nightclubs swing. Sounds of techno, disco, zouk, beguine, reggae, calypso, rock, rap, waltz and jazz compete with the pulsating rhythm of the *tamure*, Tahiti's tantalizing national dance.

Some of Tahiti's larger hotels feature folkloric dance shows and Tahitian orchestras for dancing, and there are frequent all-night balls presented by the various sports clubs and friendship organizations on the island. These events always include live music and entertainment and the Tahitians never tire of seeing their professional or amateur dance groups performing the *ori Tahiti*. After the show the beautifully dressed Tahitians, Chinese and French diners fill the dance floor, where they glide so gracefully to the upbeat tunes of the fox trot and Tahitian waltz. When the tempo suddenly erupts into the sensual *toere* drumbeat of the hip-swiveling, rubber-legging *tamure*, the floor is suddenly packed with Tahitians, who involve their whole being—body, mind and soul—into vigorously performing their favorite dance.

Most of the bars, nightclubs and casinos are located in the heart of Papeete, along the waterfront street of Boulevard Pomare and rarely no more than one block inland. The nightclubs and casinos require proper attire. This means that the women cannot wear shorts and the men should wear a shirt, rather than a tank top, plus shoes, rather than rubber thongs or going barefoot. The nightclubs usually charge an entry fee for men, which includes one drink, and unescorted ladies get in free most of the time, sometimes with the bonus of a complimentary first drink. Some of these nightclubs change ownership and names frequently, so don't be surprised if you don't find the place you're looking for. Just ask a few people at your hotel to give you the new name, and you'll probably get mixed answers.

Local Style

LE ROYAL KIKIRIRI, *Tel. 43.58.64, on Rue Colette between Avenue Prince Hinoi and the Mairie of Papeete (town hall).*

This place started out as a true Tahitian bar, where the musicians tuned up for an evening of *kaina* music, playing the songs of the islands on their guitars and ukuleles, strumming the chords of a gut bucket bass or rattling two spoons together in a beer bottle. The revelers enthusiastically sang and danced as they got happy on Hinano beer or Johnny Walker whisky, and the chairs had a hard time staying upright in the general melee. This bar has now been transformed into a chic air-conditioned nightclub that attracts a completely different type of clientele. For several years it has been one of the choice nightspots in Papeete, where good-looking, well-dressed young people gather to dance to live and recorded Tahitian and disco type music. Open Wednesday through Saturday from 10pm to 3-4am. Happy Hour is held each Friday from 6 to 9pm. Closed Sunday.

LE ROYAL TAHITIEN, *Tel. 50.40.40*, in Pirae, is the Happy Hour gathering place for many of Tahiti's office workers each Friday afternoon, when local residents come to dance at the bar and on the terrace to the tunes of Polynesian music played by a live band. A special barbecue dinner is also served for those who feel like diluting their booze with some veal cooked on a spit. The security is good here and no fights take place, according to manager Lionel Kennedy, an expatriate Aussie, who is also a musician.

Discos & Jazz

LE PIANO BAR, *Tel. 42.88.24*, on Rue des Ecoles, the street behind Mana Rock Café. They have enlarged their dancing space by taking over the shop next door. If you want to see a female impersonator strip show Tahitian style, this is the place to go. I used to enjoy going here back in my "heyday" when I lived on the island, and my young female friends who are in the know about Papeete after dark still prefer the Piano Bar to any other nightclub. The transvestite *mahu* dancers, Polynesia's "third sex," are friendly and may even ask you to dance in front of the mirrors with them, regardless of your sex. If you can stand the smoke, this can be a fun place, and is quite harmless, unless you try to make out with someone else's boyfriend.

LE PARADISE, *Tel. 42.73.05*, on Boulevard Pomare, across from the French naval station. Le Paradise normally has a European ambiance, but it can also resonate to an Afro-Caribbean rhythm. This is a complex of Le Night restaurant, Le Paradise nightclub and Le Chaplin's brasserie, cocktail and video lounge. Open daily from 10am to 3am, except for Monday night, when the nightclub is closed. The restaurant is closed Friday and Saturday nights. You can sing *Karaoke* at Le Chaplin's from Wednesday through Saturday. Men pay an entrance fee of 1.500 CFP to get into Le Paradise, which includes a drink. This is the second choice of "best" nightclubs chosen by my swinging friends in Tahiti.

MANA ROCK CAFÉ, *Tel. 50.02.40, on the corner of Boulevard Pomare and Rue des Ecoles.*

The bar is open daily from 8am to 3am and to 4am on weekends. The decor of wood, ironworks and mosaics extends from the sidewalk café to the air-conditioned salon upstairs, which overlooks the Port of Papeete. A brasserie-snack menu includes grilled meats and salads, and the bar serves beer on tap as well as mixed drinks. Live and recorded music is played for disco dancing, and you can check your E-mail messages at the cybercafé upstairs.

Let the Music Play

The Tahitian custom of inviting someone to dance is rather subtle. You are sitting at the bar or a table, alone or with friends. A young man begins to stare at you, trying to get your attention, or perhaps returning your own flirtatious glance. When he catches your eye, he just lifts his eyebrows and nods his head toward the dance floor. You can ignore him, shake your head negatively, or raise your own eyebrows in a positive reply and meet him on the dance floor. Tahitian men assume that if a woman isn't dancing with anyone, she is available to dance with him, even if she is sitting with a man.

Dancing with a Tahitian **tane** involves little or no conversation. Normally there is no desire for introductions before or during the first few dances. People are there to dance, and grab a feel, perhaps, but not to talk. Each trip to the floor lasts for the duration of two songs, played to similar tempos. This gives you a good opportunity to get to know one another, with little or no conversation transpiring between you. But there is definitely a communication going on.

If you continue to dance with the same man, for the first hour or so of the evening he is very polite and dances beautifully, as he holds you at a respectful distance. He smells divine, wearing the best perfume of his sister, wife or live-in vahine, the mother of some of his children. After he has drunk a few bottles of Hinano beer he becomes more relaxed and informal. Also much more intimate. He squeezes you close and his hands become freer in their wanderings around your body. He might ask you to leave with him after the dance, as he nuzzles your neck and presses his body close to yours. The next hour after that is when you have to start holding him up, if you are still on the scene by that time.

☙

The Rue des Ecoles has been transformed into a pedestrian street and this is one of the most popular meeting places in Papeete. It's a good place to sit at a table on the sidewalk and people watch as you sip your suds or blow in your bubbles. You'll see most of Papeete's *demi-monde* swish by if you stay long enough.

MORRISON'S CAFÉ, *Tel. 42.78.61*, in the Vaima Center, with a private elevator located on Rue General de Gaulle, adjacent to the Air New Zealand office.

This is an indoor/outdoor restaurant and café, where the sounds of sweet jazz sing out over the rooftops of Papeete, played by American or French musicians who are frequently imported to liven up the scene. This café is named after Jim Morrison (of The Doors), and the musical ambiance is a combination of American rock music, jazz and modern Tahitian rock bands.

CLUB 106, *Tel. 42.72.92*, on Boulevard Pomare adjacent to the Moana Iti restaurant.

This is one of the oldest private dance clubs in Papeete. There's no entry charge, but you must take care of your "look" to be permitted. Simply ring the bell at the front door downstairs and then join Papeete's "in crowd" and dance to taped music for all tastes. Open nightly.

Here are some of the other night spots: **Ba-Zik** (ex-Glamour, ex-Krypton and a few other names) is an "in" disco for the young and chic crowd, located above Le Newport Restaurant on the corner of Boulevard Pomare and Avenue Bruat. If you like techno sounds, this is the place to go. **Le Saxophone**, next to the Piano Bar, is new and hot. **Le Manhattan**, next to the Hotel Kon Tiki on Boulevard Pomare, features "toere rock" by local musicians, but is not currently one of the preferred night spots. **Shark** (ex-Zizou), across from the ferry dock on Boulevard Pomare, combines a local ambience with recorded disco tunes. **Café des Négociants**, *Tel. 48.08.48*, in the Quartier du Commerce, frequently has live rock bands, and **Market Coffee**, *Tel. 45.60.70*, on Rue Edouard Ahnne, has live local music on Friday night and a karaoke show on Saturday night. **Place Vaiete** on the waterfront near the ferry dock, has free concerts and dance performances on some weekends.

Outside of town on the West Coast the **Western Grill**, *Tel. 41.30.56*, at PK 12.6 in Punaauia presents a Western Show and Drag Show during two dinner services every Thursday, Friday and Saturday night, featuring the talented Gerald Mingo, who is also a cowboy waiter. Reservations are required. Way on down the road, **Le Safran**, *Tel. 57.96.96*, is a restaurant at the Tahiti Nautique Marina in Taravao, that has live entertainment on Saturday night, often presenting American expatraite, Bubba Shaky Bill Sawyer, and the Moorea Blues Explosion.

On the Northeast Coast of Tahiti, the **Beach House Tahara'a**, *Tel. 85.22.42*, is a gourmet French restaurant and bar that attracts a local partying crowd, especially on Thursday evenings, when Happy Hour is held between 6-7:30pm, with two drinks for the price of one. A live Brazilian band adds a lot to the laid back ambience.

Friendly Bars

My favorite hangout is **Les Trois Brasseurs (3B)**, on Boulevard Pomare, a sidewalk cafe, restaurant and full service bar across the street from the boat dock for the Moorea ferryboats, very close to the Royal Papeete. This is Tahiti's only microbrewery, and they serve four different beers straight from the vats to your glass or pitcher. Whenever I go into Papeete for business, I always try to save enough time for at least one glass of lager beer before I board the *Aremiti* catamaran for my return trip to Moorea in the late afternoon. And I usually find a few other Moorea residents here, also enjoying a cold brew. You can order food from the menu all day long. This place is usually packed in the evenings and live music is played on special occasions.

Bar Taina is in the same block as Les Trois Brasseurs, and is a bar preferred by Tahitians and French military men. Couples or women without escorts may find the atmosphere a little too rough, but men in search of meeting a friendly Tahitian *vahine* or *mahu* may find it to their liking. Hervé, the French manager, speaks English. You can drink on the covered terrace outside and dance to recorded music inside the bar. There's a live Tahitian band every Friday night.

Jacky's Bar inside the **Hotel Royal Papeete** is a friendly and comfortable meeting place for American expatriates, residents of the outer islands and older locals. Jacky, the bartender, has been serving drinks here for 35 years. The bar is air-conditioned and has a few stools and tables.

Even if you don't find a place particularly friendly, such as the sidewalk café **Le Retro** in the Vaima Center, you can still enjoy people watching while having a drink, a cup of coffee or a meal. Down at the other end of Boulevard Pomare, on or near Rue des Ecoles and Avenue Prince Hinoi, are a variety of bars, where you will see a continuous parade of young prostitutes, both male and female, as they make their nightly rounds looking for business. You'll also see French soldiers from the military bases and young French sailors off the ships, who are looking for some action.

Ia Orana Villa in Punaauia claims to have the only Tiki Bar in Tahiti. This is another popular watering hole for Tahitians and French military personnel, and the handsome young hotel manager, Jean-Pierre Viatje, who is half Tahitian, claims that it is a very friendly place indeed. You can sit on a barstool and talk with the fellow next to you or take a table overlooking the swimming pool and lagoon. There's usually Tahitian music in the air, either canned or live.

Sports & Recreation
Quad Excursions
D-Tour Tahiti, *Tel. 70.99.53*, is based at the InterContinental Resort

Tahiti, offering you another way to discover the island. You will have an unforgettable experience when you join a guided ATV outing into the Papenoo Valley, up to the heights of Mount Marau or the Belvedere in the Fare Rau Ape Valley. Protective goggles and head gear provided and closed shoes are obligatory. The hotel travel desks sell this tour for 12.000 CFP for a 2-hour excursion to Belvedere, 14.000 CFP for a 2-hour sunset excursion at the Belvedere, 17.000 CFP for a half-day trip to Mount Marau, and 20.000 CFP for a full-day trip to the Papenoo Valley. Rates are cheaper if you go direct to D-Tour Tahiti.

Golf
If golf is your game you can tee off at the **Olivier Breaud International Golf Course of Atimaono,** at PK 40.2 in Papara, *Tel. 57.43.41; Fax 57.49.68; E-mail: skiptahiti@yahoo.com.* Located between the mountains and the sea 25 miles from Papeete on Tahiti's southwest coast, you'll find an 18-hole course 6,900 yards long, par 72, mostly flat, and well known for some of the world's toughest par 3's. The greens are planted with hybrid Bermuda grass from Hawaii. Two artificial lakes and wide, hilly fairways surrounded by fruit trees add to the beauty and pleasure of this course, which attracts professional and amateur golfers from overseas, who compete in the annual Tahiti International Pro/Am Open, held each July or August. This event is now part of the Australian PGA circuit.

A modern Club House has locker rooms and showers for men and women, a full bar and a restaurant serving French and local foods with service to 4pm. There is a swimming pool, spa pool and a driving range, plus a pro shop and boutique for sales and rentals. The course is open daily from 8am to 4pm and the Club House stays open to 6pm. The green fees are 5.500 CFP for 18 holes and 3.300 CFP for 9 holes, which include all taxes. You can rent a sack of clubs for 2.500 CFP, a pull cart for 650 CFP, and an electric car is 4.600 CFP for 18 holes and 2.900 CFP for 9 holes.

Hui Popo Golf Tours, *Tel. 57.40.32; Fax 57.49.68; E-mail: skiptahiti@yahoo.com,* is managed by Skip Anderson, who is also in charge of the Club House. He provides round-trip transfers by air-conditioned mini-bus from the Port of Papeete or any hotel to the golf course and back, for 4.250 CFP per person, with a minimum of two passengers. Skip offers 7 golf packages from 20.500 CFP per person to 34.900 CFP for two people. The deluxe 18-hole package #1 includes: a set of clubs, golf car, golfer's lunch, green fee, round trip transfers, free practice balls and a souvenir & play package, for 23.900 CFP for one golfer and 34.900 CFP for two people. A Golfer's Lunch Menu consists of a salad and main course, plus a glass of wine, soft drink or a Hinano beer, and costs 1.850 CFP per person.

Tahiti Nui Travel, **Tekura Tahiti Travel and Marama Tours** travel desks located in some of the hotel lobbies also sell a golf package for 23.500

CFP per person and 34.500 CFP per couple, which includes round-trip transportation between your hotel or ship and the golf course, the green fee, a set of clubs, practice balls, a golf car, golfer's lunch and the souvenir and play package.

Hiking

Feel like taking a hike? Tahiti's mountains and valleys and rugged Te Pari coast offer an interesting choice of treks. Even though you may be tempted to set out on your own to discover the lava tubes, burial caves and hidden grottos, my advice is to go with a guide and the proper equipment. The weather can be variable in the heights, and sudden downpours can suddenly swell the rivers, making them impassable for several days.

Polynesian Adventure, *Tel./Fax 43.25.95, cell 77.24.37; E-mail: polynesianadv@mail.pf; http://www.polynesianadv.fr.st.* Vincent Dubousquet is a professional guide who specializes in 30 different hikes on Tahiti and Moorea, including exploring the lava tubes. Following are some of his most popular hikes.

The **Fautaua Valley** is one of the easiest walks, which most people accomplish in four to seven hours. The waterfall here was the romantic setting described in *The Marriage of Loti*, a novel written by a French sailor named Louis Marie Julien Viaud, who came to Tahiti in the 1880s. A minimum of two people is required for this half-day outing, or to visit other valleys on Tahiti's east coast, including **Le Belvedere**, **Tuauru** or **Faananu**. The cost for a half-day hike is 5.100 CFP per person, plus there is an access fee of 600 CFP per person to visit the Fautaua Valley and another 600 CFP to get to the Diademe Pass.

Half-day hikes to the west coast valleys of **Vaipohe** or **Mateoro** are rated easy to sportive and also cost 5.100 CFP per person for a minimum of two people.

All-day easy to medium level hikes can be made to the **Fautaua Valley**, the **Hamuta** Pass 900 meters (2,952 feet) high on the **Aorai** trail, to the basaltic organs of **Tuauru Valley** in Mahina, to **Te Faaiti Valley** in Papenoo, which is a park with natural Jacuzzis, or to **Faananu Valley** in Tiare, all on the east coast. The west coast hikes can take you to the canyon of **Vaipohe Valley** in Paea, or to **Mateoro Valley** in Papara, where there is a small canyon and lots of flowers. All these hikes require a minimum of two people and cost 6.700 CFP per person, plus an access fee of 600 CFP per person to enter the Fautaua Valley.

You should be in good physical condition and not subject to vertigo to climb to **Fare Ata**, the second refuge, at a height of 1,810 meters (5,937 feet) on **Mount Aorai**, which at 2,066 meters (6,776 feet), is the second highest peak on Tahiti. Vincent includes this one-day hike in his "sportive" level, which requires a minimum of two people. Other rugged hikes are to the **Teovere**

Pass in Papeete, which gives you a good view of the Fautaua Valley and **Le Diadème**, the crown mountain; to the high waterfalls of **Te Faaiti Valley** in Papenoo; and to **Vaihi Valley** in Hitia'a with lovely waterfalls and a view of the east coast. You'll need at least four hikers to go to the **Lava Tubes**, river and tunnels in Hitia'a; up to the refuge of Faaroa and the rugged cliffs of **Te Pari** in Teahupoo; or to **Vaipoiri Grotto** on Tahiti Iti. Each of these tougher treks costs 8.800 CFP per person and you will have to pay an access fee of 600 CFP to get to Teovere Pass.

Two or three hikers can divide the total cost and still make the treks that normally require a minimum of four. All material is provided for the hikes in Tahiti Iti and Hitiaa, including shorty wetsuits, headlamps and gloves. Boat transfers are also provided on the Tahiti Iti treks. Ground transfers are free up to 35 kilometers from pick-up point to the trail entrance. Cold meals and a drink are furnished for 1.000 CFP per person. Minimum age for these hikes is 12 years.

Polynesian Adventure also has two-day camping hikes into the valleys of Tahiti Nui and Tahiti Iti, for 16.900 CFP a person, including meals. Vincent Dubousquet also leads all-day treks in Moorea.

Le Circuit Vert, *Tel. 57.22.67; Fax 57.21.67*. Zena Angelin has specialized in trekking the Te Pari coast since 1986. He takes you beyond the road's end on the peninsula of Tahiti Iti to the **fenua 'aihere**, the magnificent bush land and the formidable sea cliffs known as **Te Pari**. Only the most physically fit bodies and adventurous souls attempt this challenging trek around the untamed coast. The monumental Te Pari cliffs, with their ravines strung in plumes of falling water, descend straight into the ocean. Slippery barriers of basaltic rock guard this isolated coast, and fuming rollers splash with unrestrained force against the solid wall.

During the day you will visit old *marae* temples, burial caves, grottos and rocks carved with petroglyphs. In the evening you can fish, catch lobsters on the reef and search for fresh shrimp in the rivers. The hikes can start from the village of Teahupoo on the west coast or from Tautira on the east coast. Zena charges 15.000 CFP per person for a 2-day camping expedition and 17.000 CFP per person for a 3-day excursion. Rates include, taxes, road and boat transfers, equipment and meals.

Presqu'ile Loisirs, *Tel. 57.00.57*. Mataa'e Rangimakea can guide you on the easiest or the most difficult one- or two-day hikes on the Tahiti Iti peninsula, including Te Pari. He leads 3-day/2 night treks with bivouac for 4-6 people.

Tahiti Evasion, *Tel. 74.67.13/56.48.77; E-mail: tahitievasion@mail.pf; www.tahitievasion.com*. Eric LeNoble leads day hikes into Fautaua Valley and Orofero Valley, which are rated as family outings without difficulty. For confirmed hikers, he will take you up to a height of 1,400 meters (4,522 feet) on Mount Aorai. He charges 8.900 CFP per person if there are two hikers, 6.900 CFP per person for three hikers and 5.200 CFP each for four hikers. He also leads 3-day hikes to the Pari and Fenua Aihere wild lands of Tahiti Iti, including a 2-night bivouac on the beach. You need to be in good physical condition and able to walk on varied terrain for this trek, which costs 23.500 CFP per person for a minimum of two people.

Tiare Mato Excursions, *Tel. 43.92.76, cell 77.48.11; E-mail: tiaremat@mail.pf; http://www.tiaremato.free.fr.* Guillaume Dor specializes in canyoning, hiking and 4WD excursions. One-day canyoning trips take you to the lava tubes of Hitia'a, to the heights of Orofero or to Maroto in the Papenoo Valley. He also leads hikes and all level trekking for one or two days, ranging from the first category for easy walks to the fifth category for confirmed mountain climbers, using ropes and rappel techniques. He furnishes all equipment except your shoes, personal clothing and sandwich.

Tahiti Manava Visitors Bureau on the Papeete waterfront has a list of the qualified tour guides on all the islands. Other well-known guides include: Hervé Maraetaata of **Mato-Nui Excursions**, *Tel. 78.95.47*; Serge Pihatarioe of **Puarai Excursions**, *Tel. 42.41.65*; Noella Tutavae of **Hina Trekking**, *Tel. 78.36.31*; and Fabien Tetaz of **Tahiti Rando-Trek**, *Tel. 73.04.69*.

Horseback Riding

Most of the horses in Tahiti are from the Marquesas Islands, descendants of Chilean stock. The equestrian clubs now have thoroughbreds from New Zealand as well. You can ride by the sea or in the mountains with a guide, who will take along a picnic lunch upon request. The **Club Equestre de Tahiti**, at the Pirae Hippodrome race track, *Tel. 42.70.41*, and **L'Eperon de Pirae**, *Tel. 42.79.87*, in a nearby stable, have both races of steeds for your riding pleasure.

Ranch Rauvau, *Tel 20.20.68*, is located at PK 2.5 on the Taravao Plateau of Tahiti Iti. You'll need to reserve in advance if you wish to explore "little Tahiti" by horseback, but the magnificent views are worth the effort. There are 16 horses available for riding for 2.000 CFP per hour, 6.000 CFP for a half-day outing with picnic, and 8.000 CFP for an all-day ride with picnic. The basic tourist ride costs 3.000 CFP for 1 1/2 hours in the saddle. This ranch is also called L'Amour de la Nature A Cheval (Love of Nature by Horseback).

Tennis

Tahiti's climate is ideal for playing tennis year-round, by scheduling a match in the early morning or at sunset time, to avoid the hottest hours of a tropical day. Tennis courts are located at the following hotels: **Le Méridien**, **InterContinental Resort Tahiti** and **Sofitel Maeva Beach**.

Sports clubs and private tennis clubs also have their own courts, where you can play for a nominal fee and meet some of the local resident players. These include the **Tennis Club of Fautaua**, just to the west of downtown Papeete, *Tel. 42.00.59*; **Fei Pi Tennis Club** at PK 3.2 in Arue, *Tel. 42.53.87*; and the **Excelsior Tennis Club** in the Mission Quarter of Papeete, *Tel. 43.91.46*.

Deep Sea Fishing
Zane Grey put Tahiti on the world map of outstanding deep-sea fishing spots in the 1930s, when the American novelist had his own fishing camp in Vairao on the Tahiti Iti peninsula. Game fishing has become a year-round sport in Tahiti, and your chances are very good of reeling in a big blue marlin, sailfish, swordfish, yellow fin tuna, mahi mahi, wahoo, ocean bonito or tiger shark. You may also catch jack crevally, blue crevally, rainbow runner, dogtooth tuna and barracuda just outside the reef.

You have a choice of several professional fishing boats throughout the islands, whose crews compete in local tournaments in preparation for the **Tahiti International Billfish Tournament**, which is held every two years, usually in Raiatea and the Leeward Islands. Alban Ellacott is the president of this association, *Tel. 54.41.54; Fax 43.28.45.*

Haura Club of Tahiti, *Tel. 42.37.14/77.09.29*, presided by Georges Poroi, is based at Marina Taina in Punaauia. This is the game fishing club or marlin club of Tahiti.

Tahiti Sporting & Adventure, *Tel. 689/41.02.25/41.02.27; Fax 689/ 45.27.58; E-mail: marina@mail.pf*, is a government operated nonprofit company located at the Marina Taina in Punaauia. They will book fishing boats that are represented by the organization.

Chrisnat, *Tel./Fax 689/41.96.63; cell phone 78.97.53.* Jean-Louis Casabianca owns this 36-foot cabin cruiser, which is based *at the Marina Taina*. It has a flying bridge and a 510 horsepower turbo diesel engine, and can be chartered for half- or full-day trips to Moorea or for billfishing.

Napuka, *Tel. 42.18.34/41.02.25*, is a deluxe air-conditioned 61-foot Davis sport fishing boat that accommodates up to 10 passengers, charging 140.000 CFP for half-day fishing excursions and 200.000 CFP for full-day outings.

Tohitika, *Tel. 77.82.25; E-mail: tohitika@mail.pf*, is a 58-foot Ocean Alexander trawler operated by Pacific Pearl Charter.It can accommodate up to 10 passengers in 3 air-conditioned cabins. An all-day cruise or fishing expedition is 100.000 CFP.

Heremana (ex-Horea Royal II), *Tel. 50.48.00/41.02.25; E-mail: emalmezac@satnui.pf*, is a custom 47 Davis Sports Fisherman with twin diesel engines for 30-knot speed, full electronics, tuna tower, fish finder, Rupp riggers, Murray Brothers chair, Penn International reels (130, 80 and 50 pounds), and light tackle (30 and 20 pounds). The luxurious salon, galley and two staterooms are fully air-conditioned. A half-day outing is 110.000 CFP and a full-day charter is 150.000 CFP.

Traditional Fishing, Lagoon Tours, and Dolphin & Whale Watching
Ruahiti Tour, *Tel. 42.99.88, cell 72.20.46*, is a *poti marara* open fishing boat that is used by Polynesian fisherman in search of mahi mahi and flying

fish (marara). Half- and full-day excursions in the open sea for a maximum of 4 people will introduce you to traditional fishing techniques. The half-day outing is 30.000 CFP and the all-day trip with a picnic is 50.000 CFP. You can book this at your hotel travel desk or call directly. Ruahiti Tour also provides sunset charters to fish for the marara flying fish. You can also join a snorkeling and fish feeding excursion that will show you the lagoon, take you to look for dolphins and even do some whale watching during the season from July through October.

Jet-Ski Excursions
   D-Tour Tahiti, *Tel. 70.99.53; www.tahiti-dtour.com* is based at the InterContinental Resort Tahiti Nautical Center. Guided jet-ski excursions will take you to the Tahara'a cliff on Tahiti's northeast shore, with a stop for swimming and exploring a white sandbank. Rates start at 12.000 CFP for one hour.

Massages & Spas
   Mandara Spa, *Tel. 86.48.48*, is located at the Sheraton Hotel Tahiti. Treat yourself to a relaxing footbath, an aromatic floral Jacuzzi bath, Mandara body scrub, exotic facial, aromatic hair bath, aromatherapy massage, sports massage, stone massage, reflexology massage, manicure, pedicure, steam bath, sauna, Vichy shower, or a combination of indulgences.
   Le Spa, *Tel. 48.88.88*, is on the upper level of the Radisson Plaza Resort in Arue, where it is billed as the first full-service spa on the island of Tahiti. They even carry their own clothing line and products created exclusively for Le Spa. There are two single and two double treatment rooms with jet baths, saunas, steam rooms, a rainfall shower and a full-service salon for facial care, makeup, manicure and pedicure. Signature treatments feature black sand and volcanic stones as well as indigenous fruits such as mango, guava, papaya, coconut and vanilla. Massages are priced from 9.000 CFP for 50 minutes to 16.000 CFP for 80 minutes, and there are also duo massages. A selection of baths followed by a 50-minute massage starts at 15.000 CFP for 80 minutes, and body scrubs and body masks are 8.000 to 17.000 CFP. An 80-minute papaya mask facial is 16.000 CFP. Body care packages include treatments from 3 1/2 to 5 hours, priced from 26.000 to 41.000 CFP. A 24-hour fitness center with cardio and strength training equipment as well as a yoga center is located next to Le Spa.
   Rikardo "The Relaxer," *Tel. 73.18.18*, is a one-man massage service operated by Richard Hammill, an American expatriate resident of Tahiti. He is located in the Tiniouru Medical Building, behind the Cathedral, across the road from Odyssey bookstore. He's on the first level, which Americans know as the second floor.
   Philippe Girodeau, *Tel./Fax 689/56.40.42, cell phone 77.54.79*, will bring his massage table to your room and make you feel like a new person after

he works on your body, mind and soul. He opens your chakra energy centers and heals your aches and pains with magnetism and a pair of very strong hands. He charges 8.000 CFP, but the massage usually lasts more than an hour. He lives in Moorea and goes to Papeete a couple of times a week on request.

Frederic Precloux, *Tel. 42.23.30*, is a chiropractor who studied at the Los Angeles College of Chiropractic. He speaks very good English and his office is located behind the Cathedral in Papeete, in the Tiniouru Medical Building, facing the Odyssey bookstore. He's on the second floor, just above the street level.

Nautical Centers & Clubs

Aquatica Dive Center and Nautical Activities, *Tel. 53.34.96; cell 77.60.61; E-mail: resa@aquatica-dive.com; www.aquatica-dive.com*, is located at the **InterContinental Resort Tahiti** and is open daily from 8am to 1pm and 2 to 5pm. Guests of the hotel can use the snorkeling equipment free for one hour. Otherwise, the cost is 1.000 CFP for the mask & snorkel and 1.000 CFP for fins, with a 5.000 CFP deposit. The same rules apply for tennis rackets and balls and use of tennis courts. You can rent a kayak or pedal boat for 1.800 CFP for one hour (the first hour is free and a 10.000 CFP deposit is required). You can sunbathe and swim from a floating pontoon in the lagoon for 1.000 CFP, with free boat transfers included. A non-guided snorkel trip is 3.500 CFP and a guided Snorkeling Safari is 6.000 CFP per person. You can join a Dolphin Cruise for 9.000 CFP, take a 10-minute water-ski lesson for 4.500 CFP, or sign up for a Sunset Sailing Cruise aboard the *Enjoy* for 5.000 CFP, rent the boat with skipper for an hour for 20.000 CFP, or for the day for 100.000 CFP. You can hire a Jet-Ski for 12.000 CFP an hour, or an ATV Quad for a 4-hour guided excursion, for 15.000 CFP. A half-day deep-sea fishing charter is 40.000 CFP and 60.000 CFP for the whole day. Aquatica Dive Center charges 6.000 CFP for an exploration dive, 6.500 CFP for a beginner's dive, 7.000 CFP for night diving, and 11.000 CFP for a two-tank dive. Even if you are not staying at the hotel, you can take part in the activities by making reservations. See more information under *Scuba Diving* in this chapter.

Le Méridien Tahiti Watersports Activities Center, *Tel. 47.07.07*, is open daily from 8am to 6pm. Snorkeling equipment and kayaks are free for Le Méridien hotel guests, as well as the Aquagym classes that are held in the sandy bottom swimming pool. Snorkeling excursions cost 5.900 CFP, the Dolphin Watch is 7.000 CFP, a 3-hour Whale Watch (July-October) is 11.000 CFP, and a 4-hour excursion by private boat is 60.000 CFP for a maximum of 4 passengers. You can rent an Aquatic camera at the swimming pool activities counter for 2.300 CFP. The Eleuthera scuba dive center is based here, offering all levels of diving and lessons. They charge 6.500 CFP for the first dive or fun dive, and 12.200 CFP per person for a two-tank dive.

Water-Skiing Club of Tahiti, (Ski Nautique Club de Tahiti), *Tel. 45.39.36; cell 77.22.62; Fax 41.26.09; E-mail: pluviaud@mail.pf; www.papeeteonline.com/ sites/tahiti-waterski.* This club is located beside the lagoon between the InterContinental Resort Tahiti and Sofitel Maeva Beach. Patrick Pluviaud, the fully qualified monitor will help you perfect your water-skiing techniques on the wakeboard, ski-tubes, by mono-ski or barefoot. A floating pontoon in the lagoon is available for sunbathing and swimming.

Tahara'a Nautical Center, *Tel. 85.22.42*, is located beside the Beach House Tahara'a Restaurant and Bar at the foot of the lookout point on Tahara'a Hill. You can rent a kayak for 600 CFP single and 800 CFP double; a small boat with a 6 h.p. engine is 4.500 CFP per hour, 16.000 CFP for a half-day and 27.000 CFP for the whole day, and you don't need a pilot's license to drive it. A Dolphin and Whale Watch costs 7.000 CFP per person for a 3-hour excursion. You can also scuba dive with a qualified instructor for 5.900 CFP per dive. The Tahara'a Diving Center provides all levels of dives and lessons, charging 6.500 CFP for a Fun dive or introductory dive, and 12.200 CFP for a 2-tank dive.

Marinas

Marina Taina, *B.P. 13003-98717, Punaauia, Tahiti; Tel. 689/41.02.25; Fax 689/45.27.58; cell 78.92.46/71.21.67; E-mail: marina@mail.pf*. This modern marina is located at PK 9 in Punaauia, on Tahiti's west coast, facing the island of Moorea. Whether you want information on chartering a sports fishing boat, a luxury motor yacht or a safe mooring for your own sailboat, you can contact manager Philippe Ollitet and his efficient staff. There are berths and moorings for about 700 boats. The dock can handle up to six units at a time (stern to). The fees are 100 CFP per foot per day to accommodate yachts less than 82 feet in length, and 150 CFP per foot per day for yachts 83 feet and longer. A 10% value added tax is also applicable. These rates will be raised in 2005 following completion of a work project that will add about 50 more places for small boats. Their services include electricity, fuel, fresh water, mail handling, office communication, on-board telephones, cable television, car rental, laundry service and much more. The Eleuthera Dive Center, Haura Fishing Club and the Casablanca restaurant are all on the premises, as well as a shipchandler, repair shop and a marine gas station.

Tahiti Nautic Center Marina, *B.P. 7305-98719, Taravao, Tahiti; Tel. 689/ 54.76.16; Fax 689/57.05.07; E-mail: tnc@mail.pf; www.tahitinauticcenter.pf*. Located at PK 56 in Taravao, beside Phaeton Bay, with berths for 40 boats up to 50 feet long catamarans and a maximum draft of 2 meters. On the premises are a restaurant, clubhouse, laundry service, naval shipyard, superstructure store and mechanical workshop.

For information on anchoring in the **Port of Papeete** see information in this chapter under *Arrivals & Departures, By Boat*.

Sailing Charters
Tahiti Yacht Charter, *Tahiti office: Monette Aline, B.P. 608, Papeete, Tahiti 98713; Tel. 689/45.04.00; Fax 689/42.76.00; E-mail: tyc@mail.pf; www.tahitiyachtcharter.com. North America reservations: Mark Wakeman, Tel. 800/404-1010; E-mail: marimktg@ix.netcom.com. Raiatea base: Tel. 689/66.28.86; Fax 689/66.28.85.*

Tahiti Yacht Charter is now a 100% locally owned company since it was bought back from VPM in October 2002. They have been established in French Polynesia for 15 years, chartering bareboats or crewed boats. They have a fleet of 14 boats, mainly catamarans, including 3 new boats from April 2004, all based at the Apooiti Marina in Raiatea, with Papeete as a possible departure point. Rates and details are listed under *Sailing Charter Yachts* in the *Raiatea* chapter.

Day Sailing & Boat Excursions
You'll find day sailing and other boat excursions easy to arrange once you're here, simply by booking with your hotel activities desk or walking along the quay at the Papeete waterfront, across from the post office, and talking with the captain of the boat you choose to fulfill your dream.

Enjoy, *Tel. 86.51.10/77.80.04*, is a 12-meter (40-foot) Fontaine Pajot sailing catamaran based at the InterContinental Resort Tahiti. This yacht with skipper can be chartered for 20.000 CFP per hour or 100.000 CFP per day for private day-sailing excursions for a maximum of 10 passengers. A sunset cruise, including a drink, costs 5.000 CFP, and a Dolphin Cruise is 8.000 CFP per person.

Jet France, *Tel. 56.15.62/45.04.00*, is a 22.5-meter (75 foot) maxi sailing catamaran owned by Jean-Jacques Besson that is based at the yacht quay in Papeete. Day cruise charters to Tetiaroa leave Papeete each Wednesday, Saturday and Sunday at 7am and return at 6-7pm. You will have about five hours ashore at Tetiaroa, and they will guide you to visit Bird Island. Bring your own lunch and drinks. The captain takes a minimum of 10 and a maximum of 24 passengers and per person fare is 11.000 CFP. A dive-cruise is 14.000 CFP.

Biotherm II, *Tel. 24.12.19/41.04.09; E-mail: biotherm2@mail.pf.* This is a 60-foot racing trimaran formerly owned by Florence Arthaud, who sailed her boat in some of the world's most famous races, such as the Route du Rhum, La Baule/Dakar, Ostar and the San Francisco Trophy. A maximum of 10 passengers now have the pleasure of sailing across the Sea of Moons from Tahiti to Moorea or to the atoll of Tetiaroa during a day cruise. Sunset cruises, diving cruises for the day and private charters are also available. Contact Pierre-Philippe Tricottet for details and rates.

L'Escapade, *Tel. 72.85.31, Satellite Tel. 00.872.76.25.24.382; E-mail: escapade@mail.pf; www.escapade-voile.pf.* This 46-foot aluminum Sea Breeze sailboat is owned by Anne-Marie and Paul Gasparini, who have 20 years' experience in sailing, spent cruising around the world with their family, and chartering in the Caribbean. You can join them for a relaxing day in Tetiaroa, with departures from the Papeete waterfront quay at 6am on request. You will arrive in Tetiaroa at 10:15am and visit the motu islets, the seabird sanctuary and swim in the clear warm lagoon. Lunch is served on board and the boat leaves Tetiaroa at 3:15pm, arriving in Tahiti at 7:30pm. Departures are made from Moorea each Tuesday and Thursday, with breakfast, lunch and drinks included for the price of 11.000 CFP per person.

Tahiti Cruise/Margouillat, *Tel. 72.23.45; E-mail: mahi@mail.pf; www.tahiticruise.pf.* Margouillat is a 43-foot catamaran based at Marina Taina in Punaauia that can accommodate eight passengers in 4 double cabins for a long cruise and 13 people for a day sail. Daily cruises with or without meals will take you around Tahiti, Moorea or Tetiaroa, on outings to discover the dolphins and whales, or for sunset cruises for groups. A weekend in Moorea cruise of two days and one night departs from Papeete on Saturday morning and returns on Sunday evening, or you can arrange cruises of 3 days to 3 weeks or more. A skipper and hostess will accompany you. Contact Jean-Marie Libeau.

Scuba Diving

The protected lagoons, passes and outer coral reefs offer ideal conditions for scuba diving year-round and you'll discover an abundance of dive clubs on the island of Tahiti. The diving instructors are highly qualified and speak English to varying degrees. Safe, dependable boats are used to take you to discover several beautiful locations, which may include "**The Aquarium**," a calm, clear, fish feeding site; "**The Wrecks**," a ship and aircraft on the same dive; and "**The Tahiti Wall & Shark Cave**," an outer reef drop-off with canyons, crevices and shark cave. The small reef sharks and moray eels are fed by hand.

Aquatica Dive Center *Tel. 689/53.34.96/77.60.01; Fax 689/53.34.74; E-mail: resa@aquatica-dive.com; www.aquatica-dive.com.* This is a 5-star PADI Center "Gold Palm IDC" #6313, Scubapro SEA center and NITROX scuba diving center based at the Nautical Activities Center at InterContinental Resort Tahiti. Manager Didier Alpini is a CMAS** certified monitor and a PADI master instructor. He and his qualified instructors will take you to explore a stunning underwater world, promising the best dives in Tahiti. The 2004 rates are 6.000 CFP for an exploration dive, 6.500 CFP for a beginner's lesson, 7.000 CFP for night diving, and 11.000 CFP for a two-tank dive. A 3-day Open Water course is 60.000 CFP and 4 Open Water dives are 32.000 CFP. A Diving Day in Moorea can be organized for a minimum of 6 divers for 19.500 CFP per person. Didier Alpini also heads Dream Travel Tahiti; selling adventure sports and diving packages. Free pick-up service is provided for divers on reservation.

Eleuthera, *Tel. 689/42.49.29; Fax 689/43.66.22; E-mail: eleut@tahiti-dive.pf; www.tahiti-dive.pf.* This is a 5-star PADI center located at Marina

Taina in Punaauia. The managers are Nicolas Castel and Joshua Rouger, who are International CMAS ** and *** instructors, BEES 1 federal instructors, Sea-Guides and PADI, OWSI and ANMP certified instructors. They will provide a total of four outings per day, including ocean dives at 9am and 2pm. They offer programs from beginners to certified divers, specifically adapted to each level. They can also organize your own excursion to dive Moorea or Tetiaroa.

Fluid, *Tel. 689/70.83.75; Fax 689/85.45.45; E-mail: fluid@mail.pf*. Yannis Saint-Pè is a scuba dive instructor who provides personalized service aboard his boat **Fluid** for up to six divers or snorkelers. He can take up to six divers or snorkelers and he also provides all the material and gear necessary for diving. He will take you from Paea on Tahiti's west coast to Motu Martin on the north coast of Mahina, around the island of Tahiti, or to visit the sister island of Moorea. He also works with the catamaran *Biotherm* to visit Tetiaroa during a day tour, where you can dive inside the protected lagoon or on the outer reef. His rates are 30 to 40 percent higher than those charged at dive clubs, but Yannis offers personal service like you would get on a luxurious yacht.

Scuba Tek Tahiti, *Tel./Fax 689/42.23.55; E-mail: plc.scubatek@mail.pf; www.chez.com/scubatek*. This center is located at PK 4, at the Yacht Club of Arue, and is managed by Pascal Lecointre, an international monitor CMAS ***, FFESSM national instructor and PADI OWSI monitor. He is also a sea guide and has a diving school for young people. This is a NITROX dive center.

Tahara'a Diving Center, *Tel. 85.22.42*, is located beside the Beach House Tahara'a Restaurant and Bar at the foot of the lookout point on Tahara'a Hill. Guillaume Louis, who owns the Beach House Restaurant and Bar, is also a qualified diving instructor. He charges 5.900 CFP per person for a Fun dive. He also works with the new Radisson Plaza Resort, which is adjacent to the dive center. They charge 6.500 CFP for a Fun dive or introductory dive, 12.200 CFP for a 2-tank dive or night dive, 28.500 CFP for 5 fun dives, 56.000 CFP for 10 Fun dives, 78.000 CFP for a half-day of private dives, 65.200 CFP for an Open Water course, 39.600 CFP for an advanced Open Water course, 18.300 CFP for a 3-dive package on the East Coast, and 22.800 CFP for a Best of Tahiti 4-dive package.

Tahiti Plongée, *Tel. 689/41.00.62/43.62.51; cell 77.16.49; Fax 689/42.26.06; E-mail: plongée.tahiti@mail.pf; www.tahitiplongee.pf*. This dive center is based on the grounds of the ex-Hotel Bel Air between the InterContinental Resort Tahiti and Sofitel Maeva Beach. Henri Pouliquen has been teaching children and first time divers the necessary basics of scuba diving since 1979 and has a very good reputation in Tahiti for his success and his gentle personality. He holds a CMAS *** international rating and can deliver all levels of CMAS certification.

TOPdive Tahiti, *Tel. 86.49.06; cell 70.55.55/77.13.07; Fax 83.51.26; E-mail: topdivetahiti@mail.pf; www.topdive.com*. Bernard Begliomini heads this dive center based at the Sheraton Hotel Tahiti, a PADI center and a Scubapro S.E.A. Center with personal dive trainers. Bernard swam the channel between Tahiti and Moorea in 4 hours, 2 minutes and 57 seconds on April 3, 2002. He and his team provide snorkeling tours, scuba diving, open water training, wall dives, wreck dives and night dives. Public rates for scuba diving start at 6.500 CFP for an introductory dive, fun dive or night dive; a CMAS* (one star) course is 49.900 CFP; and a package of 10 dives is charged at the rate of nine dives, which comes to 58.500 CFP. The diving rates include taxes and all equipment. This package can be used at TOPdive centers in Bora Bora, Moorea, Rangiroa, Fakarava and Tahiti. Nitrox scuba diving is also available and costs 7.800 CFP for an exploratory dive, 15.500 CFP for 2 tank dives, 29.000 CFP for Nitrox certification and 71.100 CFP for a Nitrox Inter-island 10-dive package.

Iti Diving International, *Tel./Fax 689/57.77.93; cell phone 78.77.93; E-mail: itidiving@mail.pf; www.itidiving.pf.* This center is based at the Riri Point in Vairao, on the west coast of Tahiti Iti, approximately 60 kilometers (37 miles) from Papeete. Gilles Jugel is an international CMAS** monitor, a 1st degree French federal instructor, BEES 1 and PADI OWSI instructor. He has a very good reputation as a dive master and teacher, and can give exams in all categories for FFESSM, CMAS and PADI certification. He speaks good English and Italian as well as his native French.

Although this center is not close to any of Tahiti's big hotels, it would definitely be worth your time to rent a car and drive down to the Tahiti Iti peninsula for a very different experience, far removed from the metropolitan area of Tahiti. The exploratory dives go out at 10am, 2pm, and 4pm. You can drive to the center from your hotel in about an hour, or you can stay in a family owned pension on the Tahiti Iti peninsula.

Most of the dozen or so proposed dives are made in the lagoon or oceanside, and the peninsula is the only place in French Polynesia where you can dive along sheer underwater walls rich with gorgoneas even at shallow depths, and thus accessible to all levels of certified divers. Depending on your dive site you may see white-tip sharks, black-tip sharks, giant wrasse, jack fish, moray eels, angel fish, parrot fish, surgeon fish, butterfly fish, emperor fish, clown fish in their anemones, schools of porcupine fish, schools of tropical Dorado and all kinds of trigger fish.

One of the sites is described as a hole in the lagoon, where divers have seen eagle rays, sting rays, small dog-tooth tuna, groupers, batfish, porcupine fish, toad fish, all kinds of gobies, stone fish, scorpion fish, lion fish and nudibranches. If you look carefully, you may also see sailfin leaf fish and anglerfish, as well as seven finger shells and cones. Gilles will also take you to the Tetopa Grotto, which is the only one in French Polynesia, besides in the Marquesas Islands, which can be explored. It is an easy dive for all levels of certified divers and a lamp is necessary. I have a letter from a man who dove for two days with Gilles and he said that he saw six big napoleon wrasse together at one dive site, and some black coral and a few soft corals, which are very rare for this part of the Pacific. But his biggest thrill was to snorkel with some humpback whales and about 60 dolphins. The whales come up to these tropical waters from the Antarctic during the months of June or July through October.

Gilles charges 5.800 CFP for a first dive or fun dive, and 7.200 CFP for a night dive, a PADI certification dive or a first dive with special diving logbook from Tahiti. A four-dive individual package is 22.000 CFP, and a 10-dive individual package is 52.000 CFP. The dive center is open seven days a week and the first dive or lesson takes place at 8am.

Surfing/Flysurfing

The Tahitians claim that their Maohi ancestors invented surfing, and the chiefs of Tahiti used to compete with one another on long wooden boards. Surfers come to Tahiti from all around the world to surf the edges of the passes, and international surfing champions have found challenging waves offshore Teahupoo at the end of the Tahiti Iti peninsula. Between October and March strong swells from the north bring sizable waves, and from April to September the Antarctic winds from the south produce powerful waves that are great for riding the tube.

Prime surf spots include the break at the mouth of the **Papenoo River** at PK 17 on Tahiti's northeast coast. Southwest of Papeete the **Taapuna pass** at PK 15, close to Fisherman's Point in Punaauia, is a favorite reef break spot for local surfers. Further along the coast you'll find the **Taharuu black sand beach** at PK 36 in Papara, where the waves are good enough for the popular **Horue open**, an international competition held each July. The **Billabong Pro Tahiti** is part of the World Championship Tour (W.C.T.). This competition takes place in May, and is reserved exclusively for the 44 best surfers in the world. Accompanying the big name surfers are the international press and crowds of spectators who flock to the beautiful untamed coastline of **Te Pari**, at the southern tip of Tahiti Iti. The passes of **Hava'e**, **Te Ava Ino** and **Tapueraha** are good for riding the waves to the left, and **Te Ava Piti** pass sends you to the right.

Tura'i Mata'are Surf School, *Tel. 77.27.69; E-mail: surfschool@mail.pf*, is operated by Olivier Napias (contact him through the Kelly Surf Shop in the Fare Tony Center in Papeete). Morning and afternoon classes in surfing or bodyboarding are given by a certified surf instructors, and all material, transportation and insurance is included. Surfboard rentals cost 1.500 CFP per hour, 3.000 CFP for a half-day and 4.000 CFP for a full-day.

Moanareva, *Tel./Fax 42.45.28, cell 72.07.75; E-mail: courrier@moanareva.com/moanareva@mail.pf; www.moanareva.com*. Bruno Sutter and Gerald Fournier operate this surf school at Point Venus in Mahina, with introductory classes in surfing or body-boarding. Boards, transfers and insurance included. Board rentals on request.

Spectator Sports

Soccer is Tahiti's favorite sport, and during the *futbol* season enthusiastic crowds gather at the **Fautaua Stadium** near Papeete on weeknights and during weekends to cheer their team to victory.

Outrigger canoe racing is the top traditional sport. At almost any time of the year you will see the muscled young men practicing for the next big *pirogue* race. The racing season begins around May, and the best teams of male and female paddlers compete in the Heiva Festival races in July, which are held inside the lagoon and in the open ocean. More races are held in August and September to select the teams who will compete in the **Hawaiki Nui Pirogue Race** that is held each November. During this three-day event, the paddlers race from Huahine to Raiatea, then to Tahaa and on to Bora Bora.

Tahitian-style **horse racing** is held on special occasions at the **Pirae Hippodrome**, where jockeys used to ride bareback, wearing only a brightly colored *pareo* and a crown of flowers. Safety regulations now require saddles and helmets. You can place your bets, but the payoffs are very small.

Cockfighting is another Sunday afternoon event. Although it is officially illegal, everyone seems to know where the fights will take place on a certain day. Ask at your hotel for specific details.

Almost every weekend in Tahiti or Moorea you will find a marathon or triathlon or bicycle-racing event going on. Other competitions are held for Hobie Cats, wind surfers and jet-skiers, as well as tennis, golf, *petanque* or bacci-ball, volleyball, basketball, boxing, archery, rugby and track.

Shopping

Tahiti is not a shopper's paradise, but some of the merchandise is different from what you're used to seeing back home. Made-in-Tahiti items can be good souvenir purchases, but be aware that some of the wooden masks, clothing and pearly shells that are sold in boutiques and curio shops were imported from Indonesia or the Philippines. The *pareu* or *pareo*, which is called a sarong or lava lava in other countries, is Tahiti's national garment. It is made from a piece of cotton fabric approximately two yards long and one yard wide and tie-dyed, airbrushed or hand painted. You will find these in shops along the Papeete waterfront, at sidewalk stands, in arts and crafts centers all around the island, in hotel boutiques, and displayed at the colorful kiosks set up permanently outside and upstairs at **le Marché**, the municipal market in the heart of Papeete.

One of the nicest selections of hand painted pareos, shirts, caftans (boubou) and beach cover-ups is at **Le Tiare de Tahiti** boutique on the second level of the Vaima Center. Fabrics to make your own *pareos* or brightly patterned shirts and dresses are sold by the meter at **Tahiti Art**, **Tahiti Beach**, the **Venus** fabric stores and other Chinese-owned shops in the vicinity of the public market.

Polynesian style bikinis, beachwear and ball gowns are fabricated by local factories and couturiers in attractive hand-blocked materials. You'll find the choicest selections in the hotel boutiques, and in dozens of shops in Papeete, including **Tahiti Art**, **Marie Ah You**, **Celina** and **Tiare Shop** on Boulevard Pomare, **Anémone** on Rue Marechal Foch, **Shop Gauguin Curios** on Rue Gauguin, **Tamara Curios** in Fare Tony Center, **Vaima Shirts**, **Bikini Boutique** and several other shops in the Vaima Center. **Tahiti Shirts**, on Boulevard Pomare, carries several lines of quality shirts that are designed by young artists in Tahiti. **Tahiti Art** also sells wall hangings, tapestries, lampshades, candles, jewelry boxes, paintings and engravings, all with Polynesian designs.

Sports and Surf clothes are sold all over town, as well as in the Moana Nui (Carrefour) center in Punaauia, where you will find **Kelly Surf**, **Tahiti Sport** and **Graffity**.

Hinano Boutique, beside the Cathedral, sells tee-shirts, dresses, swim-suits, caps, cups, glasses, ashtrays and all sorts of gift items bearing the famous Hinano beer label.

The three curio shops I knew that sold local arts and crafts have all closed, but you should look upstairs at **le Marché** for carved Marquesan bowls, ceremonial spears, drums, ukuleles, tables and tikis, plus many other gift items. You can also shop upstairs and downstairs here for Tahitian dancing costumes, basketry and woven hats, plus shell jewelry, mother-of-pearl creations, *tifaifai* bed covers or wall hangings, embroidered cushion covers and wood carvings. The **Artisan Village** adjacent to Tahiti's Maison de la Culture (cultural center) on the Papeete waterfront in Tipaerui should have some interesting carvings. Handcrafts stands or artisan centers are located in almost every village around the island, and the major hotels have arts and crafts demonstrations several times a week. You can buy very pleasing souvenir gifts directly from the person who created them.

Monoi oil is an especially nice and inexpensive purchase, and is made from coconut oil and the essence of flowers. The most popular fragrance is that of the Tiare Tahiti, the white gardenia. Other floral choices of *monoi* are made with Pitate, Ylang Ylang, Tipanie (Frangipani or Plumeria), and you can also buy vanilla, coconut and sandalwood scented *monoi* products. *Monoi* oil can be used as a moisturizing lotion, a perfume, suntan lotion, mosquito repellent, hairdressing and a massage lotion. This can be purchased, along with *monoi* soaps, shampoos, bath gels and balms, in pharmacies, super markets, hotel boutiques and in many shops in Papeete and all around the island. Tamanu oil and creams are also popular, as well as beauty and health products made from the Tahitian noni fruit.

Tahitian vanilla beans make an unusual souvenir item, and are found in **le Marché** and in souvenir shops and grocery stores. Candies, cookies, *confitures* and coconut toddy, all Tahiti products, are good for gifts. And don't forget the Tahitian musical choices, in cassettes, compact disks and on video and DVD films of the islands.

French perfumes are sold at prices lower than in Paris or New York, plus there are French fashions, crystal ware and French *patés* and cheeses. Duty Free Shops are found in Papeete and at the International Airport of Tahiti-Faaa. Very French-y style lingerie is on display in several of the shop windows. **Vahine's Secret**, beside the Cathedral, carries name brands of lace bras and thongs or strings, such as Calvin Klein, Aubade, Morgan, Simone Pérèle, Diesel and the Rien Collection.

Gastronomic gift items can be found at **Boutique Comtess du Barry** on Rue Edouard Ahnne in Papeete. In addition to a large selection of French wines, champagnes, apéritifs and digestifs, you'll find bamboo platters and wicker baskets filled with fois gras, confit de canard, jars of baba au rhum, fruit confitures, gourmet nuts and French chocolates. If you are looking for a good Cuban cigar, then go to **Les Alizés** on the street level of the Vaima Center, which is between Air New Zealand and the movie theater. They import about 60 different brands of Cuban and Davidoff cigars into French Polynesia and sell them to several hotels and restaurants in Tahiti, Moorea, Bora Bora and Rangiroa. Due to 100 percent import duty the Cuban and Davidoff cigars are very pricey. Enjoy them here, but remember that it is illegal to take these cigars into the United States.

However, you can take some of Tahiti's exotic flowers home with you by contacting one of the **Tahiti Fleurs** representatives in Tahiti, Moorea or Bora Bora and placing your order in advance, *Tel. 57.37.24* – ask them which outlet is nearest to your hotel. You will pick up your bouquet of anthuriums, birds of paradise, heliconias or orchids at the Tahiti-Faaa airport just before passing through Immigration. You can add a package of 60 Tiare Tahiti buds or take home a fragrant lei of 80 Tiare Tahiti flowers. You can also order some delicious pineapples to take home for yourself or as a special gift for friends and family. Reserve your pineapples at all **Tahiti Nui Travel** desks in the hotels in Tahiti, as well as in several hotels on Tahiti, Moorea and Bora Bora, *Tel. 57.37.24*. Call to find out your nearest contact.

Gift packages wrapped in red and white pareo cloth can be ordered to take home by calling *Tel. 48.33.11 or 78.12.10*. These packages contain pareos, greeting cards made of tapa bark cloth, vanilla from Tahaa, Marquesan carvings, Tahitian music, *monoi* soap, Tahitian colognes and other surprises.

Ariki Boutique is on the mountainside in the Punaruu Industrial Zone in Punaauia, *Tel. 58.48.42, E-mail: jones@mail.pf; www.vanillaproducts.com*. Open Monday-Saturday 9am to 6pm. Free factory tours will take you on a guided visit through a brewery, rum distillery and chocolate factory. In the boutique you can taste liqueurs and shop for your gifts and souvenirs among more than 102 items produced in the factory. These include Noa Noa vanilla flavored coffee, Noa Noa noni juice, South Pacific chocolate covered macadamia nuts, Oa Oa coconut soap, Ariki beer, Empire Whisky, Tahiti Nui white or brown rum, Somov Vodka, and Tahitian Tiki Coffee Liqueur.

The highlight of this visit is a cheeseburger that American Marc Jones, owner of Ariki Boutique, advertises as "The Best on the Islands." The smell of it cooking will draw you over to the wood fire on the terrace, where you can order a delicious cheeseburger and a soft drink. A special each Friday is the barbecued veal that is roasted over a spit. Italian sausages are also available on Fridays, when Ariki Boutique stays open until 7pm. If you're staying at Le Méridien, it's just a 5-minute walk from the hotel.

Art Galleries

Galerie Winkler, *Tel. 42.81.77*, is located on Rue Jeanne d'Arc in Papeete, where you will find a variety of paintings, pottery, sculptures and other art works. **Galerie Les Tropiques**, *Tel. 41.05.00*, is on the corner of Boulevard Pomare and Rue Cook, a few blocks west of the Vaima Center. Frequent exhibits feature the works of resident artists.

Galerie Olivier Creations, *Tel. 48.29.36*. Rue Paul Gauguin, facing Air Tahiti Nui office, between the Papeete Mairie and the Pont de l'Est. The paintings of Joannis and Thierry Fiérin are among the exhibits of paintings by contemporary resident artists you'll find in this interesting gallery.

Faaturuma Galerie, *Tel. 43.21.54*, is on the second floor of the Vaiete building on Boulevard Pomare. Among the exhibits are some lithographs by the late Bobby Holcomb, a half-Hawaiian artist and singer who lived on the island of Huahine. **Au Chevalet**, *Tel. 42.12.55*, is at 158 Boulevard Pomare in Fariipiti. **Ganesha**, *Tel. 43.04.18*, is on the second level of the Vaima Center, with paintings, tapa bark cloth, wood and stone carvings, traditional culture and contemporary art.

Astronomy Club

The **Astronomers Club of Tahiti** (SAT) invites the public to an open house every 15 days at their observatory in the Cité de l'Air overlooking the International Airport of Tahiti-Faa'a. You can come alone or with a group to gaze at the celestial lights above the island through their powerful telescopes. To find out exact date of observation, call *82.17.83* or *77.99.57;* E-mail: *astronomie.tahiti@inorbit.com; www.astrosurf.com/ sat.* Check out their web links, which include *www.southernstars-observatory.org*, the English language website of Roland Santallo, who has a privately owned observatory in Faa'a.

࿓

Galerie Paul Gauguin, Tel. 43.44.34, is on Rue des Remparts at the Pont de l'Est, facing the OPT building. Their limited collection includes an original Ravello painting, works by Rosine Masson, Daniel Duprat, wood sculptures, albums of vintage Tahitian music, and exquisite original nacre and pearl jewelry by Li Léon. **Matete Art**, Tel. 82.92.88, at 54 Rue Paul Gauguin above Restaurant Koke, has reproductions of Paul Gauguin paintings and Polynesian landscapes.

Where to Buy Black Pearls

Tahiti's biggest export item is the black pearl, which is also the most sought-after souvenir item. Exquisite jewelry, fashioned of black pearls, 18-karat gold and diamonds, can be purchased in Tahiti, as well as pearls set in crystallized Pyrex and pure crystal, or braided coconut fibers, plus unset pearls of all sizes, shapes, quality and prices. Shops selling these jewels of the sea are found on practically every block in downtown Papeete, in addition to all the hotel boutiques.

I like the creative settings and quality of pearls at **My Pearls**, Tel. 43.24.69, on the corner of Avenue Prince Hinoi and Boulevard Pomare, as well as the friendliness and knowledge of Mai, the lady who manages the shop. She's a real professional, but not pushy, and she speaks very good English, as well as several other languages. Alain, Mai's partner in My Pearls, has registered 250 of his jewelry designs since 1986. **Vaima Perles**, Tel. 42.55.57, upstairs in the Vaima Center, is another good shop for creative designs, and **Dany's Black Pearl**, Tel. 54.58.89, on Boulevard Pomare, has nice selections of pearl jewelry. **Tahiti Pearl Market**, Tel. 54.30.60, at 25 Rue Colette, between the Papeete Marché and Mairie, has 150,000 pearls direct from the producer's pearl farm, from which you can make your selections. They will even help you to drill your pearls and create you own jewelry.

Tua at **Ariihau Nui Pearls & Handicrafts**, Tel. 42.66.12, is my contact for good yet inexpensive pearls. Her shop is upstairs at Le Marché (the Papeete Market). Take the escalator and walk through the restaurant and you will find Tua at the 4th or 5th shop on the left. You'll see the pearls in a showcase, as well as jillions of tie-dyed pareos, mother-of-pearl jewelry, carved artifacts and many more items. Tua and her children keep busy making all these items, which they also sell to boutiques and shops throughout the islands. She takes credit cards, including American Express. The photographs on the wall are of her great-great-grandmother, Teha'apapa, known as the warrior queen, who was the last queen of Huahine. The biggest names in the pearl business here are **Tahiti Perles** and **Sibani**, who have some exquisite showpieces and shocking prices to match. See more information on black pearls under Shopping section of Basic Information chapter.

Tattoos

Aroma Tattoo Art, *Tel. 78.06.73; E-mail: demonaroma@yahoo.com.* Aroma Salmon is located upstairs at the Papeete public market, along with his brother, Manu Salmon of **Manu Tattoo Art.** They are both professional tattoo artists. Their parents, Manihi and Tila Salmon, own Pension Motu Aito Paradise in Fakarava. Both brothers speak English. You'll also find some good tattoo artists from the Marquesas Islands on this level of the Papeete market.

Excursions & Day Trips

These are the main travel agencies that can arrange your day tours to suit your requests. See more information on Air Tahiti in *Planning Your Trip* chapter.

Air Tahiti, *Tel. 689/86.43.43; Fax 86.40.99; www.sejoursdanslesiles.pf.* They have offices at the Tahiti-Faa'a Airport and in downtown Papeete.

Marama Tours Tahiti, *Tel. 689/50.74.74; Fax 689/82.16.75; E-mail: maramatours@mail.pf; www.maramatours.com.* They have a travel desk at Sofitel Maeva Beach and Sheraton Hotel Tahiti.

Tahiti Nui Travel, *Tel. 689/54.02.00; Fax 689/42.74.35; E-mail: sales@tahitinuitravel.pf; www.tahiti-nui.com.* This is the largest travel agency, with travel desks in most of the hotels. You can also visit their main office in the Vaima Center in Papeete.

Tahiti Tours, *Tel. 689/54.02.50; Fax 689/42.50.50; E-mail: sales@tahititours.com; www.tahiti-tours.com.* This agency is an affiliate of Tahiti Nui Travel, with an office on Rue Jeanne d'Arc in Papeete, the street between Boulevard Pomare and the Notre Dame Cathedral in the center of town. They can arrange day tours and island excursions.

Tekura Tahiti Travel, *Tel. 689/43.12.00, Fax 689/42.84.60; E-mail: go@tahiti-tekuratravel.pf; www.tahiti-tekuratravel.com.* Tekura has an office on the third level of the Vaima Center in Papeete, and she is also represented at hotel travel desks. She can organize interesting programs for individual travelers and specializes in incentive groups.

Day Tour to Moorea

Moorea is only 17 kilometers (11 miles) across the channel from Tahiti, and the rugged profile of her mountains beckon you to cross the **Sea of Moons**, so named by the ancient Polynesians, and come on over to have some fun. This is where the residents of Tahiti go when they need to "escape" for a day or weekend. If your plans don't include a stay on Moorea, then a day tour is certainly on the "must do" list.

You can book your excursion with any of the travel agencies listed above, who will make all the arrangements so that you can be totally carefree. Following are some of the standard tours:

A **Moorea Island Tour** with lunch at the InterContinental Resort Moorea includes all transfers in Tahiti and Moorea, the round-trip by fast catamaran, a full circle island tour of Moorea, plus a drive up the mountain to the **Belvedere** lookout point and a stop at the *marae* stone temples in Opunohu Valley. This excursion leaves your hotel in Tahiti at 8:30am and you'll return at 5:30pm. The hotel travel desks sell the Moorea Day Tour by boat for 10.250 CFP, plus 3.450 CFP for a 2-course light lunch at the hotel. Should you wish to go by boat and return to Tahiti by plane, the cost is 13.900 CFP, and if you prefer to fly both ways you will pay 14.100 CFP.

A **Dolphin Encounter** can be combined with a **Moorea Day Tour** at the InterContinental Resort Moorea. The cost of going by boat and returning by air, plus a Dolphin Encounter at Dolphin Center is 29.900 CFP. Lunch at the hotel is optional and costs 3.450 CFP for a 2-course meal. If you want the above plus a Circle Island Tour it costs 33.900 CFP. Should you prefer the Dolphin Encounter plus a 4-wheel drive Safari Adventure instead of the normal circle island tour, the day tour will cost 35.700 CFP, but you will see more of the natural beauty of the mountains and valleys. You can also choose a Snorkeling and Ray Feeding lagoon excursion instead of a land tour for 35.600 CFP.

The **Moorea Day Tour at Tiki Village**, from Tuesday to Sunday, which sells for 13.950 CFP, going and returning by boat, also leaves your hotel at 8:30am, returning at 5:30pm. The cost includes all transfers, the fast catamaran, lunch and a bus tour from the boat dock in Moorea through **Cook's Bay** to the **Moorea Distillery and Fruit Juice Factory** and the **Belvedere** lookout point, and on around the island. The beach at Tiki Village is not as pretty as some others on the island, and the lagoon is very shallow and warm close to the shore. But you will certainly find all the entertainment you want. Here in this typical **Polynesian village**, you'll see Tahitians weaving palm fronds, dying *pareos*, making floral crowns, sculpting wood or stone, tattooing and creating jewelry from black pearls. You can paddle a canoe and go snorkeling in the coral gardens. You can eat lunch in the **Papayer Restaurant** and watch a mini-show of **Polynesian dances** performed in the white sand. Should you choose to go to Moorea by boat and return to Tahiti by air, your cost will be 16.450 CFP, and air/air will cost 16.695 CFP.

You can also visit Moorea quite easily on your own. The least expensive way will cost you a minimum of 2.640 CFP for land and sea transportation. You can catch le *truck* from your hotel to downtown Papeete for 120 CFP, get off on Boulevard Pomare by the Banque de Polynésie, cross the street to Fare Manihini, the Tahiti Manava Visitors Bureau, and walk along the wharf a couple of blocks until you come to the dock for the Moorea ferries. You'll see the ticket office for *Aremiti* catamaran *(Tel. 50.57.57)* inside the building on the waterfront that sells ferryboat tickets to Moorea. A one-way fare is 900 CFP for adults. The *Aremiti* is air-conditioned and comfortable. The service from Papeete to Moorea starts at 7:30am Monday through Friday, and at 7am and 7:30am on Saturday and Sunday, respectively. Visitors usually like to take the boat that leaves Papeete at 9am daily. You will arrive in Moorea just 30 minutes later, which gives you time for a full day of discovering this lovely island.

You can reserve a guided tour of Moorea through your travel desk in Tahiti, or you can rent a car or a scooter in the main terminal at the **Vaiare** boat dock in Moorea. Both **Avis** and **Europcar** have sales counters here.

Should you decide on the least expensive way, just walk to the parking lot in front of the terminal, where you will see several buses, and at least two of them will be loading passengers. The first bus in line usually serves the **North Coast** of Moorea, passing by the hotels Sofitel Ia Ora Moorea, Moorea Pearl Resort, Le Kaveka, Club Bali Hai, Sheraton Moorea Lagoon, InterContinental Resort Moorea, Les Tipaniers, Club Med (closed), Hibiscus, Vaimoana and Moorea Village. The second bus goes around the **South Coast** of Moorea, passing by Hotel Linareva, the Tiki Village, Moorea Village, Hotel Hibiscus and Vaimoana, stopping at Le Petit Village, which is within easy walking distance of the hotels in that vicinity. Be sure to ask the bus driver which direction he's headed, and you pay him 300 CFP before boarding the bus. There's just one standard fare.

The **best beach** on the island is adjacent to the **Sofitel Ia Ora**, which is the nearest hotel to the ferry dock. If your desire is to swim in crystal clear water and just hang out around the beach and swimming pool, then this is your answer. Talk with the people in charge of activities and decide how you can best spend your day. You can paddle an outrigger canoe, kayak or pedal boat, take a ride on a glass bottom boat or a boat trip to the *motu*. You can also join a tour bus to explore the highlights of Moorea.

If you want to see the coastal sights of Moorea, then take one of the buses to **Haapiti**, and get off at the end of the line, which is at the **Moorea Visitors Center** in Le Petit Village. From there you can walk across the street to the island's **second best white sand beach**. You can also choose one of the hotels in the vicinity as your home for the day. They all have public showers and toilets and you'll find several restaurants, snack bars, boutiques and **black pearl shops** within easy walking distance of Le Petit Village.

If you visit Moorea on a Sunday, you may want to go to the **Hotel Moorea Village**, where a traditional Tahitian feast is prepared in the underground oven. Be sure to take pictures when the oven is opened at 12:30pm. A buffet of Tahitian food and international dishes includes wine. If you get here early enough you can join a morning tour. There is a white sand beach and you can swim in the lagoon or in the hotel's fresh water swimming pool. You can also spend your day at **Painapo Beach**, where you can swim, snorkel, rent a kayak and have lunch at **The Other Place**, which includes a snack bar and restaurant beside the lagoon. They are open only on weekends. A Tahitian feast on

Sundays is accompanied by live music and costs 3.500 CFP for all you want to eat. To get here you should take the South Coast bus from the ferry dock.

The buses depart from **Le Petit Village** one hour before each arrival and departure of the ferries. Therefore, if you are taking the last *Aremiti* from Moorea to Tahiti, which leaves at 4:45pm Monday through Friday, at 4:20pm on Saturday and at 5pm or 7pm on Sunday, just stand beside the road an hour before departure time and wave for the driver to stop.

When you get back to Papeete you'll have to walk back to the stop for *le truck*, where you'll find a *le truck* that will take you to the hotels on the west coast, but there will be fewer of them running on weekends.

Day Tour to Bora Bora

Booking your Day Tour to Bora Bora with the travel agent at your hotel tour desk is the easiest way to have all the details taken care of for you. Your departure time depends on the day you want to go, as the **Air Tahiti** flight schedule varies. You will be picked up at your hotel around 6am, approximately one hour before your scheduled flight. The flight time to Bora Bora is 50 minutes in a very comfortable ATR 72 aircraft. The airport is located on **Motu Mute**, an islet that lies within the barrier reef, separated from the main island by the multihued lagoon. The Bora Bora shuttle boat to **Vaitape village** leaves the airport 20 minutes after your arrival, and you can admire the changing blues and greens of the lagoon during the 25-minute crossing. Transfers from the boat dock in Vaitape to the hotels are made by mini-van or *le truck*.

Should you choose to spend a day on a *motu*, the **Bora Bora Lagoonarium** will send a boat to the airport dock to pick up a minimum of 4 passengers. When you choose this excursion you will tour the island by outrigger speed canoe, watch the shark feeding, snorkel inside the natural aquarium and eat a picnic lunch on the *motu*. You will not see Bora Bora by land. This tour is sold for 49.100 CFP, including round-trip airfare from Tahiti, transfers and lunch. It is available every day except Saturday.

A day tour at the **Sofitel Marara Bora Bora** is sold in Tahiti for 51.900 CFP, which includes the round-trip transfers between your hotel and the airport in Tahiti, the round-trip airfare to Bora Bora, the round-trip transfer by *le truck* between the boat dock in Vaitape village and the hotel, and a nice lunch. This price also includes the use of snorkeling equipment and beach towels, plus a circle island tour by outrigger speed canoe with shark feeding. A day tour that takes you to the **InterContinental Moana Beach Resort** requires a minimum of 12 people and is sold for 62.900 CFP per person, including airfare, transfers, lunch and excursion. You will be met at the Vaitape boat dock and transferred to the hotel, where you will be welcomed with a tropical fruit punch. Then you will be shown to a Day Hospitality Bungalow to put on your swimsuit and around 9am you will board a motorized outrigger canoe for a lagoon tour around the island. Stops will be made for you to dip into the water to watch a thrilling shark feeding show, swim with the stingrays, and to wade ashore on a palm-shaded *motu* to taste a coconut and fresh fruit. Around 12:45pm the boat will bring you back to the hotel, where you can shower and change before having lunch in the Noa Noa Restaurant or Terrace beside the beach. A tourist menu includes a starter course, main course and dessert. Drinks are not included. You will have ample time to swim and snorkel in the blue-silk lagoon. In mid-afternoon, depending on your return flight, you will be transferred back to the airport on Motu Mute, 1 hour and 45 minutes before your flight departure.

Air Tahiti has a package price of 30.100 CFP per person for a Bora Bora Day Tour. This includes round-trip airfare from Tahiti, the Air Tahiti shuttle boat transfer from the airport to Vaitape Village, a mini-bus transfer to Chez Nono at Matira beach, where you will join an outrigger canoe excursion around the island, stopping to feed the sharks and sting rays and snorkeling in the coral gardens, a barbecue picnic on a *motu* islet and transfers back to the airport. You must book this tour seven days prior to departure and a minimum of two people is required.

You can create your own Day Tour to Bora Bora, but you will need to get a current copy of the Air Tahiti schedules. The **Tahiti Tourist** office in Los Angeles can mail this to you on request. The normal round-trip airfare from Tahiti to Bora Bora was 25.500 CFP through October 31, 2004. Some of the travel agencies in Tahiti do not recommend a Bora Bora Day Tour because of the travel time and cost involved. They will try to sell you an overnight trip instead, which I also recommend, simply because it takes a lot out of your day just to get to where you're going and then get back to Tahiti that evening.

Day Trip to Huahine
Air Tahiti has a Huahine Day Tour for 23.600 CFP per person that includes round-trip airfare from Tahiti, meeting and greeting at the airport, land transfers in Huahine, a lagoon excursion by outrigger canoe, a 4x4 Safari Tour and a local style meal served on a motu islet. You must book this tour seven days prior to departure.

Day Tour to Raiatea
Air Tahiti sells a day tour to Raiatea for 26.800 CFP, including round-trip airfare from Tahiti, land transfers in Raiatea and lunch. You begin your adventure with a guided excursion to visit a black pearl farm and botanical garden, then a boat trip to visit the Faaroa River, explore the sacred Taputapuatea Marae, followed by a picnic barbecue and Tahitian food served on a white sand motu islet. In the afternoon you have time for sunbathing, swimming and snorkeling. You must book this tour seven days prior to departure.

Day Tour to Tahaa
Air Tahiti offers day trips to Tahaa, which begin with a 40-minute flight from Tahiti to Raiatea, arriving at the Uturoa airport before 8 or 9am. You will then board an outrigger speed canoe for Tahaa, where you will visit a black pearl farm, a vanilla plantation and the lagoonarium to see rays, turtles, sharks and lots of fish. Lunch will be served under a traditional *fare* shelter on a white sand motu and then you can snorkel in the coral gardens. You can watch for dolphins on the boat trip back to the airport. The cost is 26.000 CFP per person and includes the round-trip airfare, meet and greet at the airport, excursion and lunch. This tour must be booked seven days prior to departure.

Practical Information
Books, Newspapers and Magazines
La Maison de la Presse, *Tel. 50.93.93*, is on Blvd. Pomare across the street from Place Vaiete. **Librairie du Vaima**, *Tel. 45.57.57*, is on the top level of the Vaima Center in Papeete. **Librairie Archipels**, *Tel. 42.47.30*, is on Rue des Remparts, across from the Mairie of Papeete (town hall). **Odyssey**, *Tel. 54.25.25*, is behind the Cathedral, adjacent to the Aorai building. They have books, CD's, DVD's and office supplies.

Cell Telephone Rental
Telephone +, *Tel. 83.13.14; Fax 83.13.00; E-mail: telephone.plus@mail.pf.* You can rent a mobile Vini phone for 700 CFP for 24 hours, 3.500 CFP per week and 10.000 CFP per month. Prices include the cell phone and charges, but do not include the SIM cards and phone calls. A deposit of 20.000 CFP is required. Credit cards accepted. Delivery service is available to hotels in Papeete and Faa'a, or you can go to the Téléphone + Faaa office, which is located in the Air Tahiti building at the entrance to the airport, next to La Cafetes restaurant.

Churches & Religious Services
Many religions and denominations are represented in French Polynesia. The Protestants formerly held the membership majority of practicing Christians in Tahiti, with 60 percent in 1962 and 47 percent in the 1990s. A study in 2001 revealed that the Catholics now predominate with 45 percent, while the Protestants have dropped to 34 percent of the population in Tahiti. The Mormons make up 7 percent, the Seventh Day Adventists comprise 6 percent, the Sanito church has 3 percent, the Jehovah's Witnesses number 2 percent, and the other 3 percent is comprised of Buddhists, Jewish, Bahai, Assembly of God, and other religions. Only 28 percent of the population attends church on a regular basis.

Following are the main numbers for the religious offices on the island of Tahiti:
• **Protestant Evangelical Church, (Maohi Protestant Church)** *Tel. 46.06.00*

- **Catholic Church**, *Tel. 50.30.00* (Cathedrale parish), *Tel. 50.23.51* (Archdiocese)
- **Mormon Church**, *Tel. 50.55.05*
- **Seventh Day Adventists**, *Tel. 50/82.50/50.55.05* (regional office)
- **Sanito**, *Tel. 54.55.30*
- **Jehovah's Witnesses**, *Tel. 54.70.00*
- **Assembly of God Pentecostal Church**, *Tel. 45.36.61*
- **Christian Center of the Good News Church**, *Tel. 82.05.72*
- **Church of the New Testament**, *Tel. 43.84.71*
- **Alleluia Church**, *Tel. 42.95.88*
- **Neo-Apostolic**, *Tel. 57.93.02*
- **Israelite Synagogue**, *Tel. 41.03.92, cell 72.66.17*
- **Naropa Buddhist Cente**r, *Tel. 57.64.91, 74.71.88*
- **Tibetan Gelugpa Buddhism**, *Tel. 57.49.32*

Church services on Sunday morning will offer you an insight into the Tahitian culture away from the hotel scene. You'll enjoy the singing, which is best in the Protestant churches or temples, formerly called **Eglise Evangelique**. This name was changed in 2004 to **Eglise Maohi Protestant**. The missionaries taught the Tahitians to sing the old time hymns in the early 1800s, and over the years the people have transformed the old religious songs into their own versions called himene. The singing is a capella, with the men sitting behind the women and the kids running around everywhere. Hats are worn to church but not flowers. Be prepared to sit on the side up front, where you can look at the parishioners and they can smile back at you. They are used to visitors and will warmly welcome you.

Clubs & Associations
- **Alcoholics Anonymous**, *Tel. 43.21.63*
- **Chamber of Commerce, Industry and Trade in French Polynesia**, *Tel. 47.27.00*
- **Department of Culture and Patrimony**, *Tel. 54.17.17*
- **Kiwanis Club of Papeete**, *Tel.42.04.10*
- **Kiwanis Vahine Club of Papeete**, *Tel. 42.16.79*
- **Lion's Club**, *Tel. 42.44.44*
- **Polynesian Cultural Center (Te Fare Tauhiti Nui)**, *Tel. 54.45.44*
- **Red Cross**, *Tel. 42.02.76*
- **Rotary Club**, *Tel. 50.52.23; www.rotary-tahiti.org/*
- **Société des Etudes Oceaniennes**, *Tel. 41.96.03*
- **Soroptimist**, *Tel. 83.61.60*
- **Tahitian Academy (Fare Vana'a)**, *Tel. 42.61.47*
- **Women's Council of French Polynesia,** *Tel. 57.11.94*

Consulates
Consular Agency of the United States, *B.P. 10765, Paea, Tahiti 98711, Tamanu Iti Center, (1st floor), Punaauia. Tel. 689/42.65.35, Fax 689/50.80.96, E-mail: usconsul@mail.pf / ckozely@mail.pf. Fax in USA 917/464-7457.* Consular sessions are held each Tuesday between 10am-12pm. You can contact Christopher Kozely 24 hours a day for emergencies only at *cell 21.93.19.*

Other Consular Agents: Australia and Canada, Marc Siu, *Tel. 689/ 46.88.06; Fax 689/43.39.26.* **Austria, Switzerland and Leichtenstein**, Paul Maetz, *Tel. 689/ 43.21.22; Fax 689/43.91.14.* **Belgium**, Pierre Raynal, *Tel. 689/42.94.89; Fax 689/43.90.05.* **Chile**, Daniela Pasqualetto, *Tel. 689/ 43.89.19; Fax 689/43.61.62.* **Denmark**, Claude Girard, *Tel. 689/54.04.54; Fax 689/54.04.55;* **Finland**, Jean-Pierre Fourcade, *Tel. 689/43.60.67.* **Germany**, Claude Eliane Weinmann, *Tel. 689/42.99.94.* **Great Britain**, Marc Allain, *Tel. 689/41.98.41, cell 70.63.82.* **Israel**, Serge Cohen-Solal, *Tel./Fax 689/42.41.00; cell 77.39.99.* **Italy**, Lucia Grolli, Tel. *689/43.45.01; Fax 689/ 43.45.07.* **Japan**, Narii Faugerat, *Tel. 689/45.45.45; Fax 689/43.12.60.* **Korea**, Bernard Baudry, *Tel. 689/43.64.75; Fax 689/45.45.74.* **Norway**, Morton Garbutt, *Tel. 689/43.79.72; Fax 689/42.06.17.* **New Zealand**, Ron de Groot, *Tel. 689/54.07.40; Fax 689/42.45.44.* **The Netherlands**, Albert Engelbertus Den Breejen, *Tel. 689/42.49.37; Fax 689/43.56.92.* **Sweden**, Jacques Solari, *Tel. 689/42.73.93.*

Currency Exchange
Banque de Polynésie, Boulevard Pomare, *Tel. 46.66.66*, open Monday to Thursday 7:45am to 3:30pm, Friday 7:45am to 4pm, Saturday 8am to 12pm; **Banque de Tahiti**, Rue Cardella, *Tel. 41.70.00*, open Monday to Friday 7:45am to 3:30pm; **Banque Socredo**, Rue Dumont d'Urville, *Tel. 41.51.23*, open Monday to Thursday 7:15am to 3:30pm, Friday 7:15am to 2:30pm. There are several branch offices of these banks in downtown Papeete and around the island of Tahiti, with various business hours, and all the major locations have an ATM. See sections on *Ready Cash and Currency Exchanges* in Chapter 7.

Hospitals & Doctors
You can find English-speaking doctors, dentists, nurses and other medical personnel in Tahiti, but they are not common. The Mamao Hospital and the two private clinics are open 24 hours. There is also a hospital in Taravao. See Health Concerns in *Basic Information* chapter for further details.

Mamao Hospital, *Tel. 46.62.62* (switchboard), *Tel. 42.01.01* or *15* (emergency), is the government operated medical center on Avenue Georges Clemenceau in Mamao, a suburb just east of Papeete. Taravao Hospital, *Tel. 54.77.77* (switchboard), *Tel. 57.76.76* (emergency). **Clinique Cardella**, *Tel. 46.04.00* (switchboard), *Tel. 46.04.25* (emergency), and **Clinique Paofai**, *Tel. 46.18.18* (switchboard), *Tel. 46.18.90* (emergency), are two privately owned clinics in Papeete. **S.O.S. Medecins**, *Tel. 42.34.56*, is an emergency unit of doctors and other medical personnel, who will come to the hotel to attend to your needs.

Optique Vaima is now called **Krys Vaima** in the Vaima Center, Tel. *42.77.54*, and **Pacific Optic**, Rue Yves Martin in the Quartier du Commerce, one block inland from Boulevard Pomare, *Tel. 42.70.78*, will repair your glasses while you wait.

Surdité de Polynésie, *Tel. 43.33.04*, in the Quartier du Commerce close to the Tracqui store will solve your hearing aid problems while you're in Tahiti.

Internet Service – Cyber Cafés

Cybernesia, *Tel. 85.43.67; E-mail: cybernesia@mail.pf; www.cybernesia.pf.* This cyber café is on the third level of the Vaima Center above the Concorde Cinema. There are 8 last generation Pentium IV Integra computers with Internet access. Other services include color printing, copies and CD engraving. Open Monday-Friday 9am to 6pm and on Saturday 10am-3pm.

Dpi @ Business Center, *Tel. 50.84.95; E-mail: digital@mail.pf; www.dpi.pf.* This business center and cyber café is located at the Tahiti-Faa'a Airport at the entrance to the domestic terminal. Services include Internet access, E-mail, color copying, scanning, documents copied to digital files, digital photo cards transferred and CD-Rom engraving.

La Maison de la Presse, *Tel. 50.93.93*, is on Blvd. Pomare facing Place Vaiete. There are 9 computers upstairs, all with flat monitors. The rates are 250 CFP for 15 minutes, 500 CFP for 30 minutes and 1.000 CFP per hour. Open Monday and Tuesday from 7am to 7pm and on Wednesday through Saturday until 10pm.

Mana Rock Café, *Tel. 50.02.40*, is on the corner of Blvd. Pomare and Rue des Ecoles. There are two computers, with the Internet rates starting at 250 CFP for 15 minutes. Access to this service is available daily from 11am to 10pm.

Tiki Soft C@fe, *Tel. 88.93.98; E-mail: tikisoft@mail.pf; www.tikisoft.pf; www.tikisoftcafe.com.* Rue des Remparts at the Pont de l'Est. No credit cards. Open Monday through Friday 8am to 10:30pm, on Saturday from 8am to 3pm, closed Sunday. This was Tahiti's first cyber bar and is a busy place throughout the day as people wait their turn to get on-line at one of the three computers, which cost 250 CFP for 15 minutes. Clients who eat in the small restaurant at noon get 10 minutes' free Internet access. Happy Hour is held each Friday between 6-7:30pm.

Laundry Service

All the larger hotels provide laundry service, and can arrange to have your dry cleaning done. **Lavex Sa M'Plaix**, *Tel. 41.26.65*, is the name of an automatic laundry on Boulevard Pomare in downtown Papeete, close to

Broadway Tobacco shop between Avenue Prince Hinoi and Rue Clappier. They're open Monday to Friday 6am to 5pm, and Saturday on request. Closed Sunday. They will wash, dry and fold up to 4 kilograms (8.8 pounds) of laundry for 1.000 CFP, and you can pick it up at the Broadway. They charge 4.000 CFP to iron a basket of clothes. There is also a self-service laundromat called **Laverie**, *Tel. 43.71.59*, which is located at 64 Rue Gauguin, facing the Papeete Mairie (town hall) near the Pont de l'Est. They charge 750 CFP to wash 8 kilos of clothes and 750 CFP for the dryer, plus 100 CFP for the soap powder. Ironing is also available.

Pharmacies / Drugstores

There are half a dozen pharmacies in the Papeete area, and several around the island. One of the easiest to find in Papeete is the **Pharmacie du Vaima**, *Tel. 42.97.73*, on Rue de Général de Gaulle at Rue Georges La Garde, behind the Vaima Center close to MacDonald's Hamburgers. The pharmacist is Nguyen Ngoc-Tran, who speaks English.

Pharmacie Moana Nui, *Tel. 43.16.98*, is in the Carrefour shopping mall in Punaauia, convenient to the InterContinental Resort Tahiti and Sofitel Maeva Beach. **Pharmacie Tamanu**, *Tel. 58.20.34*, is located in the Tamanu shopping center in Punaauia, next door to Le Méridien. The pharmacies rotate night and weekend/holiday duty, so it is best to check with your hotel to find out which one is available should you need medical supplies after hours. The medicines sold in French Polynesia are French brands.

Police

The main headquarters of the French gendarmerie, *Tel. 46.73.67*, is located on Avenue Bruat in Papeete. There are also brigades in Faaa, Punaauia, Paea, Papara, Taravao, Tiarei and Arue.

Restrooms

There are public toilets on the Papeete waterfront at the passenger ship dock, just outside the **Tahiti Manava Visitor's Bureau.** The public facilities at **Tahua Vaiete** (Place Vaiete) and **Tahua To'ata** (Place To'ata), on opposite ends of the waterfront, are kept clean 24-hours a day by a team of Tahitian government employees. You'll also find public toilets in the building that houses the **Moorea Ferry** freight bureau, at the ferry dock on the Papeete waterfront. Bring your own paper just in case, and do not be surprised if some of the public facilities are not clean. You can also use the restrooms in the restaurants downtown.

Around the island, you'll find public restrooms at the main tourist stops, such as Point Venus, the Blowhole of Arahoho and the Three Cascades of Tiarei, the Paul Gauguin Museum, the Vaipahi Gardens and Waterfall, and at the Grottoes of Mara'a.

Chapter 14

MOOREA

Scientists say that **Moorea** (Mo-oh-RAY-ah) is shaped like an isosceles triangle, and romantics believe the island is in the form of a heart. I think it looks like a swimming turtle. Geologists say that Moorea is twice as old as Tahiti and once contained a volcano that reached 3,300 meters (11,000 feet) into the sky. Polynesian legend tells us that Moorea was created when a magical fish swam from the lagoon of Raiatea and Tahaa to become the island of Tahiti; and the second dorsal fin of this enormous fish grew into land that was called "Aimeo i te rara varu" for the eight mountain ridges that separate the island. The traditional shortened name of this island was Aimeho, Aimeo or Eimeo. Following a vision by one of the Polynesian high priests, the name was later changed to Moorea, which means, "yellow lizard."

Moorea offers you the tropical South Seas island that you expect to find when you fly to Tahiti, just 17 kilometers (11 miles) across the Sea of Moons. Some people say it's worth the airfare to Tahiti just to see Moorea. Others say that Moorea was created so that people on Tahiti would have something to stare at across the sea.

Moorea's magnificent beauty covers an area of 136 square kilometers (53 square miles), which is the south rim of a crater that was formed following cataclysmic explosions eons ago. The lofty cathedral-shaped peaks and jade velvet spires that you will see reflected in the lapis lazuli waters of **Cook's Bay** and **Opunohu** (belly-of-the-stone-fish) **Bay** are the basaltic remains of the crater's interior wall.

The volcanic peaks of the mountain range resemble a fairy castle or a serrated shark's jaw, dominated by **Tohive'a** (hot spade) at 1,207 meters (3,983 feet), **Mou'a Roa** (long mountain), with an altitude of 880 meters (2,904 feet), resembles a shark's tooth. This is the most photographed of the

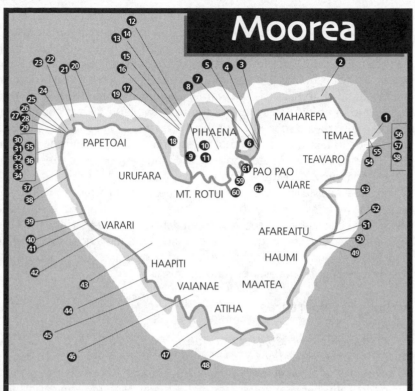

Moorea

1. Temae Airport
2. Moorea Pearl Resort
3. Hotel Kaveka
4. Club Bali Hai
5. Motel Albert
6. Cook's Bay
7. Village Temanoha
8. Fruit Juice Factory
9. Fare Oa Oa B&B
10. Pension Aito
11. Pension Motu Iti
12. Sheraton Moorea Lagoon Resort & Spa
13. Fare Nani
14. Village Faimano
15. Chez Francine
16. Fare Vaihere
17. Fare Hamara
18. Opunohu Bay
19. Les Tipaniers Iti
20. Papetoai Temple
21. Pension Marie-Lou
22. InterContinental Resort Moorea
23. Dolphin Center
24. Les Tipaniers
25. Pension Anahoa
26. Club Med (closed)
27. Dream Island
28. Villa Fare Coralina
29. Le Petit Village
30. Hotel Hibiscus
31. Fare Vaimoana
32. Camping Nelson
33. Pension Teataura
34. Moorea Camping
35. Fare Auti Ura
36. Moorea Village
37. Fare Matotea
38. Fare Manuia
39. Tiki Village
40. Fare Chez Edith
41. Painapo Beach
42. Residence Linareva
43. Haapiti Camping
44. Haapiti Surf Lodge
45. Tarariki Village
46. Nature House of Mou'a Roa
47. Fare Arana
48. Fare Auti
49. Waterfalls
50. Chez Pauline
51. Pension Te Ora Hau
52. Motu Ahe Lagoonarium
53. Vaiare Ferry Dock
54. Sofitel Ia Ora
55. Temae Public Beach
56. La Baie de Nuarei
57. Fare Maeva
58. Motu Temae B&B
59. Marae Titiroa
60. Le Belvedere Lookout
61. Opunohu Valley Ranch
62. Pineapple Fields

spectacular wonders, and it is often pointed out to visitors as "Bali Ha'i." **Mou'a Puta** (split rock), the 830 meter- (2,739 foot-) high mountain with a hole in its top, is a tempting challenge for hikers. The hole is said to have been made by the spear of Pai, a favorite son of the gods of old Polynesia, who was warned that Hiro, god of thieves, wanted to steal the sacred **Rotui** Mountain and take it home to Raiatea. The warrior Pai threw a spear from Tahiti that pierced the top of Mou'a Puta and the noise woke up all the roosters on Moorea, who crowed so loudly that the thieves were forced to flee. But Hiro did manage to take a piece of Rotui's crest and this stolen land can be seen on top of a mountain in Raiatea, covered with the *toa* (ironwood) trees similar to those that grow on **Mou'a Rotui**.

Moorea's crystalline lagoons, filled with gardens of fanciful coral and exotic sea creatures, are said to have been a gift from Ruahatu, king of the ocean. This benevolent god specially created the azure waters of the fjord-like bays. Tane, the Polynesian god of beauty, bordered the lagoons with white sand beaches and planted an abundance of fragrant white Tiare Tahiti blossoms among the majestic coconut palms.

Arrivals & Departures
Arriving By Air
Air Moorea, *Tel. 86.41.41 in Tahiti; Tel. 55.06.01 in Moorea; Fax 86.42.99; E-mail: reservation@airmoorea.pf; www.airmoorea.com.* 10-minute air taxi service is provided daily between Tahiti and Moorea with up to 40 round-trip flights between the sister islands. The Air Moorea terminal in Tahiti is located 300 meters (984 feet) from the **International Airport of Tahiti-Faaa** and the domestic terminal. You have to pay 100 CFP to use the luggage carts and you can retrieve your money when you attach it to the luggage rack, just like in other airport terminals. You can push the carts from one terminal to another, following a sidewalk painted red that also has arrows. There are restrooms, a public telephone, a snack and bar counter in the small Air Moorea terminal in Tahiti.

The 19-passenger Twin Otter DHC6/300 planes depart from the Faaa airport in Tahiti every hour on the hour from 6am to 6pm. Additional flights are added on the half-hour during peak times before 10am and after 3pm. There is no 4pm departure except on Friday and Sunday, but there is a 4:30pm flight daily. Reservations are required if you want to specify a certain flight time. The one-way fare is 3.100 CFP. Air Moorea also provides night service from Tahiti to Moorea on Thursday, Friday, Saturday and Sunday, corresponding with the arrival of Air Tahiti Nui international flights from Los Angeles. This service makes it possible for you to go directly to Moorea without having to book an overnight room in Tahiti. On Thursday and Saturday the flights leave Tahiti at 7:30pm, 8pm, 10:30pm and 11pm. On Friday and Sunday the flights leave Tahiti at 7:30pm and 8pm. The one-way cost for these connections is

4.700 CFP for the night flights for residents or non-residents. You must reserve in advance and check-in closes 15 minutes before each departure.

Air Tahiti, *Tel. 86.42.42*. Some of the Air Tahiti ATR flights from Papeete to the Leeward Islands of Huahine, Raiatea and Bora Bora stop in Moorea, but passengers do not leave the aircraft in Moorea.

You can also charter an airplane to Moorea with **Air Moorea**, *Tel. 86.41.41* or **Air Tahiti**, *Tel. 86.42.42*, **Air Archipels**, *Tel. 81.30.30*, and **Wan Air**, *Tel. 50.44.17, cell 77.03.79*. Helicopter flights can be organized with **Polynesia Hélicoptères**, *Tel. 86.60.29*.

The modern **Temae Airport** terminal in Moorea has restrooms, a restaurant-bar, car rental agencies, and information counters for tour and excursion companies. Taxi service is usually available for all arriving flights, and there is a taxi phone at the main entrance. There is no bus or *le truck* service provided directly to the airport. If you are not carrying heavy bags and wish to walk about four blocks to the main road to catch *le truck*, you want to be sure that you schedule your arrival with that of the ferries from Tahiti, when the public transportation service will be operating. You can stand beside the Total Station and wave down the first bus that passes, which will be going toward Cook's Bay. **Torea Nui Transport** provides land transfer service for 500 CFP per person during the day and 1.000 CFP at night. See details under *Tour & Transport Companies* in this chapter.

Arriving By Boat

The **Moorea Boat Dock (Gallieni Wharf)** in Papeete, a couple of blocks east of the Tahiti Manava Visitors Bureau on the waterfront, is where you will find the two fast catamarans and two ferries that transport passengers between Tahiti and Moorea. You can buy tickets in the building adjacent to **Snack Moana Café** adjacent to the ferry dock. Be sure to verify the schedules before or when you get to the ticket window, because they are subject to change at any time without much advance notice.

Aremiti V, *Tel.50.57.57* in Tahiti and *Tel. 56.43.24* in Moorea. This big new aluminum fast catamaran was built in Australia and was originally supposed to provide service to the Leeward Society Islands. But when the **Aremiti IV** developed engine problems and went into dry-dock in mid-2004, the new government gave permission for the *Aremiti V* to take over the fast catamaran service between Tahiti and Moorea. The air-conditioned *Aremiti V* is 56 meters (184 feet) long and 14.4 meters (47 feet) wide, with 2 bridges and 3 passenger salons, a snack bar with tables in the rear, clean toilets, lots of television screens, comfortable seating for 700 passengers, including 70 places on the upper sundeck, and space for 30 passenger cars and scooters. The crossings from quay to quay take 30 minutes. Promotional fares at press time included a one-way adult fare for 900 CFP, 742 CFP for people over 60 years and 450 CFP anyone between 4-23 years.

The *Aremiti V* leaves Papeete each Monday through Thursday at 6:10am, 7:30am and 9am, 12pm, 4:05pm and 5:30pm, with the exception of Wednesday, when the 12pm departure actually leaves at 12:20pm. The same schedule applies for Friday with the addition of an extra crossing, leaving Papeete at 2:40pm. The Saturday departures from Papeete to Moorea are at 7am and 9am, 12:15pm, 2:40pm and 4:05pm. On Sundays the boat leaves Papeete at 7:30am and 9am, and at 3:30pm, 4:50pm and 6:20pm. See further information on the **Aremiti** boats under *Inter-Island Cruise Ships, Passenger Boats & Freighters* in the chapter on *Planning Your Trip*.

Aremiti Ferry, *Tel. 50.57.57* in Tahiti and *Tel. 56.43.24* in Moorea. This is a 272-foot long steel hull catamaran that transports cars, big trucks and construction equipment, and up to 500 passengers between the two islands. A one-way crossing takes 50 minutes. There are toilets, an air-conditioned lounge and a snack bar on board. This boat is not recommended for people who have difficulty climbing steep stairs. The *Aremiti Ferry* leaves Papeete for Moorea on Monday through Friday at 6am, 9am and 11:45am. On Monday through Thursday afternoons the ship leaves Tahiti at 3:10pm, and on Friday the ship leaves Tahiti at 2:30pm and 5pm. On Saturdays the *Aremiti Ferry* leaves Papeete at 7am and 9:30am, and at 12pm. The hours on Sunday are 7:45am, 3:30pm and 6pm. The one-way passenger fares are 900 CFP per adult, 742 CFP for people over 60 years and 450 CFP anyone between 4-23 years. Occupants of vehicles being transported round-trip on board the *Aremiti Ferry* benefit from reduced rates: the round-trip fare for adults is 1.484 CFP and 848 CFP for people between 4-23 years of age. The round-trip cost to transport a passenger car starts at 4.505 CFP.

Moorea Express, *Tel. 82.47.47* in Tahiti, *Tel. 56.43.43* in Moorea. This fast catamaran is owned by the same company as the Moorea Ferry, who bought the aluminum boat in France, where it had served a long career. The air-conditioned catamaran is 41.60 meters (136 feet) long and can transport 306 passengers, as well as scooters and bicycles, from dock to dock in 30 minutes. There is a snack bar on board but no meals are served. One-way fares are 900 CFP per adult, 450 CFP for a student and 716 CFP for a senior of 60 years or more. The one-way fare for a bicycle is 212 CFP and 742 CFP for scooters, vespas and motorcycles. On Monday through Thursday Moorea Express leaves Tahiti for Moorea at 6:10am, 7:25am, 9:05am, 12:05pm*, 4:05pm and 5:20pm. *The Wednesday departure is at 12:20pm. Each Friday the Moorea Express leaves Papeete at 6:10am, 7:25am, 9:05am, 12:05pm, 2:40pm, 4:05pm and 5:20pm. The Saturday departures from Papeete are at 7:05am, 9:05am, 12:05pm, 1:45pm, 3:45pm and 5:30pm, and the Sunday schedule is 7:20am, 9:05am, 3:30pm, 4:50pm and 6:20pm.

Moorea Ferry, *Tel. 82.47.47* in Tahiti and *Tel. 56.34.34* in Moorea. This is a 190-foot long steel hull ship that can transport 300 passengers, cars, heavy trucks and freight during the one-hour crossings between Tahiti and Moorea.

On board are an air-conditioned lounge, a snack bar and toilets. The one-way adult fare is 848 CFP and half-price for children 4 to 12 years and for seniors over 60 years. Lightweight cars are 2.650 CFP one-way, 4WD vehicles are 3.180 CFP and bicycles are 212 CFP. The Papeete-Moorea schedule for Monday through Friday has departures at 6:15am and 10am, 2pm and 4:45pm. The *Moorea Ferry* leaves Papeete each Saturday at 6:30am and 9:30am and at 12pm and 5:15pm. On Sundays it leaves Papeete at 7:30am, 4:15pm and 6:45pm.

You will find public telephones, car rental agencies, taxi service, toilets, fruit stands and snack bars at the two terminal buildings on the **Vaiare Ferry dock or quay**.

Public ground transportation in Moorea is provided by buses or *le truck*, with vehicles waiting in front of the new terminal upon the arrival of the catamarans and ferries from Tahiti. Give the driver the name of your destination and verify that you're getting onto the right bus, as one goes on the north coast to **Cook's Bay** and onward to the **Club Med** area, and the other bus heads in the opposite direction, towards **Afareaitu** and on to **Haapiti** and the **Club Med** area, by way of the south coast. You pay the driver 300 CFP before boarding, and pull the cord, ring the bell or holler "stop" when you want to get off.

Departing By Air

Air Moorea, *Tel. 55.06.01*. The first flight from Moorea to Tahiti is at 6:15am daily, and the last flight is at 6:15pm Monday through Wednesday, at 11:15pm on Thursday and Saturday and at 8:15pm on Friday and Sunday. The hourly flights leave Moorea at a quarter past the hour (7:15am, 8:15am, 9:15am, etc.) and extra flights are added at a quarter to the hour (6:45am, 7:45am, 8:45am, 9:45am, 4:45pm, 5:45pm) during the peak times before 10:15am and after 4:15pm during the week. An exception to the hourly rule is that there are flights daily at 4:45pm and no 4:15pm flights except on Friday and Sunday. It is best to pick up an Air Moorea schedule when you arrive or check out their flights by Internet, as they are subject to change without notice. Reservations are imperative for the early morning and late afternoon flights and are strongly advised for all flights. Check-in no later than 15 minutes before the flight.

The regular fare from Moorea to Tahiti is 3.100 CFP and the night fare is 4.700 CFP. This latter rate applies to the Air Moorea flights that connect with Air Tahiti Nui's international departures. The scheduled night flights from Moorea are at 7:45pm, 8:15pm, 10:45pm and 11:15pm on Thursday and Sunday, and at 7:45pm and 8:15pm on Friday and Sunday. This service can be used to catch your Hawaiian Airlines flight to Honolulu, or any other flights leaving Tahiti during the middle of the night or early morning hours. This Air

Moorea flight from Moorea to Tahiti is also subject to an earlier departure; therefore, be sure to check in at the airport one hour in advance.

Air Tahiti, *Tel. 86.42.42/86.41.84* on weekends in Tahiti or *Tel. 55.06.00* in Moorea, provides ATR service from Moorea to the Leeward Islands. You can fly direct from Moorea to Huahine once a day. There are three flights a day between Moorea and Bora Bora, including direct service or with a stop in Huahine or Raiatea. There are direct flights from Moorea to Raiatea on Monday, Tuesday, Wednesday and Sunday, and the Friday flight stops first in Bora Bora. One-way fares to Huahine or Raiatea are 12.500 CFP and 17.900 CFP to Bora Bora.

Departing By Boat
The **Aremiti V Catamaran**, *Tel. 56.43.24*, leaves Moorea for Papeete Monday through Friday at 5:30, 6:50, and 8:10am. A 10:50am departure is made on Monday, Tuesday Thursday, and Friday, and on Wednesday at 11:30am, to coincide with the school program. The afternoon boats leave Moorea at 3pm and 4:45pm Monday through Thursday, and at 1:50pm, 3:20pm and 4:45pm on Friday. On Saturday the boat leaves Moorea at 6am, 7:45am and 10:50am, and at 1:50pm, 3:20pm, and 4:45pm. The Sunday schedule is at 8:10am, 2:50pm, 4:10pm and 5:40pm. Ticket counters for the *Aremiti* catamaran and ferry are located at the new terminal of the Vaiare Ferry dock in Moorea. One-way fare is 900 CFP for adults, 742 CFP for seniors over 60 years and 450 CFP for anyone between 4-23 years old.

The **Aremiti Ferry**, *Tel. 56.43.24*, leaves Moorea for Papeete Monday through Thursday at 7:30am and 10:30am, at 1:15pm and 4:20pm Monday through Thursday, and on Friday at 7:30am, 10:30am, 1pm, 3:45pm and 6pm. The Saturday departures from Vaiare are at 8:15am and 10:30am and at 4:20pm. The Sunday ferry leaves Vaiare at 2:30, 5pm and 7pm. One-way fare is 900 CFP for adults, 742 CFP for seniors over 60 years and 450 CFP for anyone between 4-23 years old.

Moorea Express, *Tel. 56.43.43*, provides fast catamaran service from Moorea to Tahiti with departures each Monday through Thursday at 5:30am, 6:50am, 8:10am, 10:50am, 2:50pm and 4:40pm. *The Wednesday departure is at 11:30am instead of 10:50am. Each Friday the *Moorea Express* leaves Vaiare dock at 5:30am, 6:50am, 8:10am, 10:50am, 1:50pm, 3:20pm and 4:40pm. On Saturday the departures are at 6am, 7:45am, 11am, 12:45pm, 2:50pm and 4:50pm. The Sunday departures are at 6:30am, 8am, 2:50pm, 4:10pm and 5:40pm. One-way fares are 900 CFP per adult, 450 CFP for a student and 716 CFP for a senior of 60 years or more. The one-way fare for a bicycle is 212 CFP and 742 CFP for scooters, vespas and motorcycles.

Moorea Ferry, *Tel. 56.34.34*, provides passenger and car service between Moorea and Papeete on Monday through Friday at 5am and 8:15am. Afternoon service is at 12:30pm and 3:30pm on Monday, Tuesday, Wednesday and Thursday, and at 12:30pm and 3:15pm on Friday. The Saturday departures from Moorea are at 5am, 8am, 10:45am, and at 4pm. The *Moorea Ferry* leaves Vaiare on Sunday at 6am, 3pm and 5:30pm. The ticket window is in the old terminal and the one-way fare is 848 CFP per adult, 424 for children 4-12 years and for seniors 60 years old. One-way fares to transport cars starts at 2.650 CFP, a bicycle is 212 CFP and other 2-wheel vehicles are 424 CFP.

Orientation

A paved road hugs the coast for 60 kilometers (37 miles) around Moorea, where you'll see thatched roof *fares* with bamboo walls, little shacks with tin roofs and lovely villas with stone walls. The census of November 2002 counted 14,226 inhabitants and most of them live on the mountainside of the road, with a sprinkling of homes along the white sand beaches. Gardens of fruit and flowers border the road and during the summer months (November-March) you will see the flamboyant red or yellow Royal Poinciana trees in bloom.

You can happily take pictures on this beautiful island without having electric lines mar the photograph. All the cables are underground. However, you now have to shoot the scenery while trying to avoid the streetlights that have been placed beside the road in the touristic sections of the island. The 591 lampposts were in place a year or so before the lights were turned on during the Christmas season of 2003. Although there has been a lot of grumbling about these lights, they are helpful for tourists who wish to walk beside the road at night when searching for a place to eat, and they also help drivers to better negotiate the twists and curves along the coastal road at night, while trying to avoid the kids on bikes, people walking in the road and dogs lying or just standing on the pavement.

Moorea doesn't have a town and until recently there was no central shopping area on the island. The administrative center is in the village of **Afareaitu**, which most visitors never see except from a tour bus. Located on the eastern coast facing Tahiti, this sleepy little settlement contains the principal *mairie* (town hall), local government offices and hospital. Most of the churches, schools, supermarkets, small *magasin* stores, banks, boutiques and restaurants are located in the villages of **Maharepa, Pao Pao, Papetoai** and **Haapiti**. Most of the hotels, hostels, family pensions and campgrounds are found beside **Cook's Bay** or beside a white sand beach in **Haapiti**, although you can now find accommodations all around the island. The **Raihau Center** in Maharepa is adjacent to the **Socredo Center** that includes a bank, post office, newsstand, snack stand and a few other shops. The **Centre Noha** is across the road. This area is slowly building up with new boutiques and pearl shops opening here and there. At PK 2.7 in Tiaia, **Centre Tumai** is a new shopping area located on both sides of the road between Maharepa and the airport in Temae. You will find interesting clothing and souvenir shops here, as well as a snack shop and a computer store with Internet service.

Aroa Beach is a 65-unit 5-star hotel project on the Northeast point of Temae, which is awaiting government approval of the building contract. Investors from New Caledonia want to build 6 beach villas, 17 garden bungalows, 24 connecting rooms and 18 bungalows over the water. In September 2004 plans were announced for a 4-star **Legend's Resort** hotel project to be built on the hillside across the road from the InterContinental Resort Moorea. If this project survives the impact study and gets the go-ahead on a building contract, then work will proceed to build 50 autonomous villas of one to three bedrooms on a property of 71,800 square meters (772,849 square feet) overlooking the lagoon. There will be 15 large villas, each with three bedrooms, entrance, living room, kitchenette, large bathroom, and a deck with a Jacuzzi, for a total surface area of 153 square meters (1,646 square feet). The 35 small villas will each contain one bedroom, but will feature the same commodities as the larger units, for a surface total of 100 square meters (1,076 square feet). Each villa will be built of tropical wood with roofs of pandanus, situated in a grove of coconut palms. There will also be a restaurant-bar, prepared foods to eat in the privacy of the villa, a tennis court, swimming pool and gated parking lot.

The **Pacific Golf and Resort Development Company** announced plans a few years ago to build an international class 18-hole golf course near the Temae airport, as well as a 5-star hotel with 150 rooms. Although the work was supposed to have begun in April 2002, the designated swamp and land remain the same as before. Another hush-hush deal is now in the works that includes a 5-star hotel in a choice spot as well as an 18-hole golf course to be built in Opunohu Valley.

Although you will still have to wait until these projects become a reality before you can tee off in Moorea, there are many enjoyable ways to spend your vacation on this special island. The beautiful clear lagoon invites you to come on in for a swim, or you can snorkel, scuba dive, water-ski and jet-ski. You can view the fish and coral through a glass bottom boat or Aquascope, wear a Jules Verne type helmet to walk on the sandy bottom of the lagoon gardens with Aqua Blue, or grab onto a motorized Sea Trailer and snorkel to the reef. You can zoom across the lagoon in a motorboat, kayak, pirogue or lagoon jet, and you can let the tradewinds propel you on a flysurf or windsurf board. There are sailing excursions, beach barbecues, shelling expeditions and fishing trips. You can take a Dolphin & Whale Watching Expedition, sunset cruise or moonlight cruise. Professional lessons are available for all water sports, as well as for tennis at various hotel courts, and for horseback riding in Opunohu Valley. You can take your aerial photos during a helicopter ride or airplane tour of Moorea, and you can soar above the lagoon on a parasail.

You can also discover the island by rental car, scooter, bicycle or on foot. Guided tours will show you Moorea's most breathtaking scenery, around the coastal road, in the interior valleys, up the mountains and to the Atiraa waterfalls of Afareaitu. You can visit a fruit juice factory and distillery, and sample a tall cool drink at a lively Happy Hour. At the hotels and at Tiki Theatre Village you can photograph traditional dance shows, learn to tie a *pareo*, grate a coconut and dance Tahitian style. You can even "get married" in a traditional non-binding Polynesian ceremony.

Moorea's excellent restaurants and snack bars have menu selections for all tastes and prices for all budgets. The highlight of your culinary explorations in Moorea should include a *tamaara'a*, an authentic Tahitian feast.

Getting Around Moorea
Car, Scooter & Bicycle Rentals
• **Albert Rent-a-Car**, facing Club Bali Hai, *Tel. 56.19.28*, Moorea Pearl Resort, *Tel. 56.30.58*, InterContinental Resort Moorea and Club Med, *Tel. 56.33.75*. You can rent a 3-door Fiat Dixie or Citroen Saxo for 5.500 CFP for 4 hours, 7.000 CFP for 8 hours, 8.000 CFP for 24 hours and 14.500 CFP for 2 days. A Peugeot 106 or Hyundai Atos 5-door car with radio is 6.000 CFP for 4 hours up to 17.000 CFP for 2 days. Longer rentals available. C 50cc scooters rent for 4.000 CFP for 4 hours, 4.500 CFP for 8 hours, 5.000 CFP for 24 hours and 9.000 CFP for 2 days. Insurance and free mileage are included in all rentals.
• **Avis-Pacificar** has a sales office at the Moorea Airport, *Tel. 56.32.61*, and the Vaiare Ferry Dock, *Tel. 56.32.68*, at Club St. Jacques facing Club Med, *Tel. 56.50.07*, and at Club Bali Hai, *Tel. 56.52.04*. A 3-door Ford Ka, Peugeot 106 or Renault Twingo rents for 5.500 CFP for 4 hours, 6.500 CFP for 8 hours and 8.000 CFP for 24 hours. A 5-door air-conditioned Ford Fiesta rents for 6.000 CFP for 4 hours, 8.000 CFP for 8 hours and 9.000 CFP for 24 hours. An automatic drive 5-door Peugeot 206 with air-conditioning and radio starts at 8.900 CFP for 4 hours. You can also rent a 2-seat Suzuki Samurai 4WD vehicle or pick-up truck for 7.000 CFP for 4 hours, 9.000 CFP for 8 hours or 10.500 CFP for 24 hours. Rates include taxes, unlimited mileage and insurance, or you can rent a car without mileage and insurance included. Rentals are available for several days and by the week or month. Beach bikes can be rented for 1.110 CFP per day and 6.600 CFP per week, including taxes.
• **Europcar** has a main office facing Club Med in Haapiti, *Tel. 56.34.00*; sales offices at the Moorea Airport, *Tel. 56.41.08*; Vaiare Ferry Dock, *Tel. 56.28.64*; InterContinental Resort Moorea, *Tel. 56.16.16*; and Sofitel Ia Ora, *Tel. 56.12.90*. A 3-door Fiat Panda or Seicento rents for 6.000 CFP for 4 hours, 7.000 CFP for 8 hours and 8.350 CFP for 24 hours. You can also rent an air-conditioned 5-door Daewoo N Sedan with automatic drive for 11.500 CFP for 4 hours, 14.500 CFP for 8 hours, and 18.000 CFP for 24 hours. There are several other choices and all cars can be rented by the month. Scooter rates start at 4.500 CFP for 4 hours, a Quad is also 4.500

CFP for 4 hours and a special 2-person Quad is 7.200 CFP for 4 hours. Europcar also has a special overnight rate of 4.000 CFP if you rent a car at 5pm and return it the next morning by 8am. These rates include taxes, unlimited mileage and insurance. Fuel and flat tires are not included.

- **Tehotu Location Scooter**, *Tel. 56.52.96/56.37.24*, has an office at the Vaiare ferry dock, where you can rent a scooter for 4.500 CFP for 4 hours, 5.000 CFP for 8 hours, 5.500 CFP for 24 hours. The scooter is insured and you will be required to wear a helmet, which is included.
- **Rent A Bike**, *Tel. 71.11.09*, is beside the road adjacent to Le Petit Village in Haapiti. Free pick-up service is available. They rent bicycles for 1.000 CFP for 4 hours, 1.500 CFP for 8 hours and 1.900 CFP for 24 hours.

Some of the hotels and pensions rent bicycles to their guests. Check with your hotel activities desk for details.

Taxis

You'll find a taxi stand at the airport, *Tel. 56.10.18*, from 6am to 6:30pm. They are all equipped with taxi meters, and the following rates are just to give you just an idea of how much you will be paying. The actual fare may be a little more or a little less than listed here. The fare between the airport and ferry dock is 1.500 CFP for a distance of 2.4 miles (3.9 kilometers). It will cost you about 1.000 CFP from the airport to the Hotel Sofitel Ia Ora, 1.500 CFP from the airport to the Moorea Pearl Resort, 1.800 CFP to the Hotel Kaveka in Cook's Bay, 2.000 CFP to the Club Bali Hai in Pao Pao, 2.500 CFP to the Sheraton, 3.800 CFP to the InterContinental Resort, 4.000 CFP to Club Med area and 4.300 CFP to the Moorea Village.

Tour & Transport Companies

Some of the Tour and Transport Companies handle round-trip transfers between the airport or ferry dock and your hotel. They will also provide taxi service if you want to dine out in the evening or arrange a special shopping tour. The best deal you can get is with Loulou and Mate at Torea Nui Transport, *Tel. 56.12.48/77.01.52*. They have an office at the Moorea Airport and they provide a transfer service from the airport to any hotel on the island for 500 CFP. When you buy your Tahiti-Moorea airline ticket at the Air Moorea counter in Tahiti, ask for a land transfer, which is only 500 CFP. Once you arrive at the airport in Moorea, go to the Torea Nui Transport counter and show them your transfer ticket and they will drive you to your destination on Moorea.

While you are on Moorea you can also use their transfer services in the day time hours to get from one hotel to another, to one side of the island to the other, to go shopping, or whatever, as long as it is on the main road, for just 500 CFP one way. You have to reserve in advance. Their last transfer is at 5:15pm except on Thursday, Friday, Saturday and Sunday nights, when Air

Moorea has flights that coordinate with the arrival of Air Tahiti Nui international flight service from Los Angeles. On these nights Torea Nui will pick you up at the Moorea airport when the plane arrives at 7:30pm and 8pm and drive you to your hotel or pension. On Thursday and Saturday they will also pick you up at 10:30pm and 11pm when the Air Moorea flights arrive from Tahiti.

Buses & Le Truck

Public transportation is provided by eight companies who rotate the service, using various kinds of buses and a couple of the traditional wooden bodied *les trucks*. Some of these vehicles are hand-me-downs from the big transport companies in Tahiti. The Bluebird buses and yellow school buses were brought in from California, and are in pretty good shape, but the advertising space inside the bus is void of the publicity you will find anywhere in the States. All these vehicles operate schedules that coincide with the arrivals and departures of the fast catamarans and ferries from Tahiti, and with the school programs.

The **bus terminals** are located beside the Moorea Visitors Bureau at Le Petit Village opposite Club Med in Haapiti, and at the Vaiare Ferry dock. The buses leave Le Petit Village Monday through Saturday at 4:45am, 5:45am, 6:45am, 9:45am, 1:45pm, 2:45pm and 3:45pm. The Sunday schedule is 6:45am, 1:45pm, 2:45pm and 4:45pm. It is best to be at the Moorea Visitors Bureau 15 minutes in advance of departure time. From Le Petit Village terminal the buses and *le truck* head in both directions around the island to get to the Vaiare Ferry dock. You just stand beside the road and wave to the driver to stop, and you pay 300 CFP when you get off.

You can use this service for other purposes in addition to your arrival and departure transfers, and you can even go around the island for 600 CFP, as long as you coordinate your plans with the bus schedules, which the drivers normally adhere to. There have been some problems with the 2:30pm buses not showing up, but they are usually dependable.

Where to Stay
AIRPORT & MOTU TEMAE
Deluxe

HOTEL SOFITEL IA ORA MOOREA, *B.P. 28, Maharepa, Moorea, 98728. Tel. 689/55.03.55, Fax 689/56.49.52; E-mail: HO566-gm@accor-hotels.com; Reservations 689/86.66.66, Fax 689/41.05.05. In US Tel. 800/SOFITEL (763-4835); E-mail: reservation_tahiti@accor-hotels.com; www.sofitel.com. Beside the lagoon at PK 2 in Temae, on northeast coast facing Tahiti, 2 kilometers (1.2 miles) from the airport and 2 kilometers from the ferry dock. 110 bungalows. 2005 Low Season (High Season) EP Rates single/double: garden bungalow 19.800 CFP (22.700 CFP); beach bungalow 26.300 CFP (29.900 CFP) CFP; deluxe beach bungalow 36.400 CFP (41.500 CFP); overwater* *bungalow 45.400 CFP (52.200 CFP). Note: Low Season is January 1-June 30, 2005 and November 1-December 31, 2005. High Season is July 1-October 31. 2005. Third person 5.000 CFP. American breakfast 2.400 CFP; set luncheon menu 2.950 CFP; set dinner menu 5.050 CFP per person. Add 5% hotel tax to room rates and 6% value added tax to room rates and meal plans, plus 150 CFP municipal tax per person per day. A 10% value added tax is applicable to other services. All major credit cards.*

The 110 Polynesian style bungalows are spread over the lagoon and throughout 35 acres of gardens. Your accommodation choice includes 47 garden bungalows, 33 beach bungalows, 10 deluxe beach bungalows and 20 overwater bungalows. All rooms have a bathroom with shower, a mini-refrigerator, individual safe and direct dial phone. The garden and beach bungalows have ceiling fans and the 10 deluxe beach bungalows and 20 overwater bungalows each have air-conditioning, ceiling fan, hair dryer, color television and tea and coffee facilities. The overwater bungalows have a window floor for fish watching and snorkeling gear is provided. There is also a covered terrace and a solarium, plus steps leading into the lagoon and a shower to rinse off when you come out of the water. All the bungalows have thatched roofs and woven bamboo walls and they are decorated in a tasteful Tahitian style, using bamboo, woven pandanus mats and *tifaifai* appliqué bed covers. The windows and doors are screened and there is an electric mosquito repellent in the rooms. Each of the land bungalows has a terrace overlooking Moorea's best white sand beach and clearest lagoon, where swimming and snorkeling offer year-round pleasures.

La Perouse is a Tahitian-style open-air restaurant, where dinners are served, featuring Tahitian and international cuisine. The Molokai restaurant is on the beach, adjacent to a spacious bar, where you can enjoy breakfast and lunch in an informal indoor-outdoor setting, while gazing at the lagoon and the island of Tahiti across the Sea of Moons. You'll find a conference and banqueting room, black pearl shop and a gift shop on the property. An activities desk and car rental desk are also located in the lobby. Baby sitting services are available on request.

Among the spacious grounds are a nautical activities center, two tennis courts, a volleyball court and an infinity swimming pool beside the white sandy beach. Complimentary sports and leisure activities include Polynesian outrigger paddle canoes, snorkeling equipment, aqua gym in the swimming pool, parlor games, *petanque* (French lawn bowls), volleyball, a coconut show, slide show and *pareo* show. Rental bicycles start at 500 CFP for one hour. A wide range of optional lagoon activities can be organized, such as a half-day circle island tour by bus, for 3.300 CFP, a half-day Safari Tour by 4WD vehicle, for 4.500 CFP, or a visit to the Tiki Village Cultural Center for a Polynesian feast and dance show, which costs 8.850 CFP per person, including round-trip transportation. You can also enjoy a professional massage for 10.000 CFP for one hour or get a tribal style tattoo. See further information under *Nautical Activities Centers* in this chapter. The tour and activities desk in the reception area can also help you book horseback riding and helicopter flights.

Four theme buffets per week are held at La Perouse Restaurant (see information under *Where to Eat* in this chapter). A mini dance show is presented at the Bar Molokai on Friday afternoon at 6:30pm and a Polynesian dance show with fire dancing takes place at La Perouse restaurant on Saturday at 8pm.

The Ia Ora also has its own wedding chapel, which is very popular with Japanese couples and other newlyweds who get married officially back home and then add the romantic touch with a wedding ceremony performed in the chapel beside the white sand beach. Wedding and Honeymoon Celebration packages can be requested direct from the hotel.

The French Accor Group that owns the Sofitel Ia Ora has announced plans to add 19 new bungalows over the water and 11 new bungalows in the garden, rebuild 49 of the existing bungalows as slightly larger accommodations, and renovate most of the remaining bungalows. They intend to tear down the existing La Pérouse Restaurant, which will be replaced by six or ten new garden bungalows and a multi-purpose hall for conferences, seminars and marriages. A small Italian theme restaurant for 30 or 40 people will be built near the existing Molokai Restaurant, which will involve building a new kitchen. The Molokai will be enlarged to a capacity of 240 diners. The objective is to provide a restaurant area close to the lagoon and around an open-air dance area. A spa and massage facility will be built and the swimming pool will be enlarged and a children's pool will be added. Every time anything is published about this project, the numbers are different, but the latest figure indicated that the hotel will end up with a total of 137 bungalows. These changes have been put on hold several times, and the work was postponed once again until October 2004. This project supposedly will be completed in two stages of eight months each, so that the hotel will not have to be completely closed.

Superior

LA BAIE DE NUAREI, *B.P. 605, Maharepa, Moorea 98728. Tel. 689/ 56.15.63 / 56.55.09; Fax 689/56.41.81; E-mail: labaiedenuarei@mail.pf; www.labaiedenuarei.com. Adjacent to the public beach on Motu Temae, 5 minutes from the airport and 10 minutes from the ferry dock. EP Rates: Bungalow Sakura 17.600 CFP single/double, 19.800 CFP triple and 22.000 CFP for four people; Bungalows Vaiki and Vahia 15.400 CFP single/double, 17.600 CFP triple. Breakfast and all taxes included. No credit cards.*

There are three bungalows behind the fence in this exclusive compound owned by Tamara Kindynis-Tamagna, who also operates a Thalassotherapy-Balneotherapy spa and beauty institute on the premises. See section on

Massages and Spas in this chapter. The Sakura bungalow-studio sleeps 2-4 people and is equipped with an American type kitchen, a spacious bathroom and a ceiling fan. The Vaiki and Vahia bungalows will accommodate 2-3 people and each has a kitchen, dining room and a bathroom paved with stones from Moorea. Each unit is different and very tastefully decorated, as you can see on her website. House linens are furnished and guests have free use of bicycles, snorkeling equipment and a small boat with paddles. A nice white sand beach and lagoon are just outside the pension.

Moderate

FARE MAEVA, *B.P. 3170 Temae, Moorea 98728. Tel./Fax 689/56.18.10; cell 74.10.14; E-mail: faremaevamoorea@mail.pf. On the ocean side on Motu Temae, 4.5 kilometers (2.8 miles) from the ferry dock and 2 kilometers (1.2 miles) from the airport. One-way transfers from ferry dock 1.500 CFP for 2 people and 1.000 CFP from airport. EP Rates: bungalow 8.500 CFP single/ double. Mattress on floor 1.000 CFP. Continental breakfast on request 995 CFP per person. Add 6% value added tax to room rates and 50 CFP per person per day for visitor's tax. A 10% value added tax is applicable to other services. No credit cards.*

This modern and clean family pension is located just after Kerebel Jeweler on Temae motu, which is really a peninsula connected to the main island. Follow the dusty road beside the airport landing strip and look for the sign. There are three garden bungalows, each with a double bed, well-equipped kitchen and private bathroom with hot water. The sheets and towels are changed every three days. There is also a small terrace plus a *fare pote'e* for each unit, complete with a table and chairs. The trees and plants here are similar to those found on an atoll and the beachy scene is accented by a yard filled with white sand. You also have access to a nice white sand beach, but there is no lagoon here, just the reef and open ocean. The public beach, which does have a nice lagoon, is very close by and one of Moorea's most popular surfing spots is also in this vicinity. Your hostess, Maeva Jacquemin, is a young Polynesian-French woman who specializes in arts and crafts. She teaches her guests how to make *poisson cru*, dye and tie a *pareo*, and how to open and grate a coconut. There are two bikes available for guests to use.

COOK'S BAY AREA: MAHAREPA TO PAO PAO
Deluxe

MOOREA PEARL RESORT & SPA, *B.P. 3410, Temae, Moorea 98728. Tel. 689/55.17.50; Fax 689/55.17.51; www.pearlresorts.com. Reservations: Tel. 689/50.84.52; Fax 689/43.17.86; E-mail: sales@spmhotels.pf. Beside lagoon at PK 5, between Moorea airport and Cook's Bay, 5 kilometers (3 miles) from the airport and 9 kilometers (5.5 miles) from the Vaiare ferry dock. 95 units. 2005 Low Season (High Season) EP Rates single/double: garden* *room 27.000 CFP; family room 30.000 CFP; garden bungalow 34.000 CFP; garden pool bungalow 39.000 CFP; beach bungalow 39.000 CFP; premium beach bungalow 49.000 CFP (52.000 CFP); overwater bungalow 51.000 CFP (54.000 CFP); premium overwater bungalow 62.000 CFP (65.000 CFP); third person 5.000 CFP. Note: Low Season is from January 1-May 31, 2005 and from November 1-December 31, 2005. High Season is from June 1-October 31, 2005. Meal plan with breakfast and dinner 7.900 CFP per person; meal plan with breakfast, lunch and dinner 11.100 CFP. Full American breakfast 2.500 CFP; Continental breakfast 2.000 CFP. One or two children between 3 and 12 years old sharing parent's room are free of charge on accommodation basis and have 50% discount on meals (excluding beverages). Babies and children under 3 years old are free of charge on accommodation and meals. Add 5% hotel tax to room rates and 6% value added tax to room rates and prepaid meal plans, plus 150 CFP municipal tax per person per day. A 10% value added tax is applicable to other services. All major credit cards.*

This 4-star hotel opened in June 2002 on the site of the former Hotel Bali Hai, which closed in January 2001. The Moorea Pearl Resort is situated on 8 acres of land just two miles from Cook's Bay. This traditional Polynesian style hotel offers 28 overwater bungalows, 9 beach bungalows, 28 garden bungalows (18 with private pool) and 30 garden and family rooms. All units are air-conditioned and the bungalows also have a ceiling fan. The garden rooms and family rooms with mezzanine have one king size bed or two twin beds plus a sofa, and all the other units have a king-size bed and sofa.

All units feature a sundeck, coffee/tea making facilities, mini bar, hair dryer, safety box, satellite television with in-house video, IDD telephone and an Internet outlet/fax line. In addition, the overwater bungalows have bathtubs and separate showers, glass tables to view the aquatic life of the lagoon, a large sundeck and sitting area with direct access by steps to the water. The beach bungalows and overwater bungalows also have a CD player. Two garden bungalows are specially equipped for guests in wheelchairs, and public areas and the pool are easily accessible. There are wide cement paths, ramps and an elevator.

The hotel has two restaurants, a bar, boutique/black pearl shop, and an activities desk where you can rent a car or bicycle or book an excursion. A 108-person conference room opened in 2004, which can be used as three separate rooms, complete with all the audio-visual equipment for meetings. The Manea Spa, which also opened in 2004, offers a complete range of relaxing and esthetic treatments. Room service, laundry service, secretarial services, currency exchange, public Internet service, babysitting on request and a daily newsletter are all available.

There is a 7,500 square foot infinity edge swimming pool, which you can see by Webcam on the hotel's website. There is also a Nautical Activities Center and the Moorea Blue Diving scuba center. Guests have free use of snorkeling gear, outrigger paddle canoes and kayaks, and they can also play beach volleyball, badminton, ping-pong and petanque (French bowls).

The Autera'a Bar and Terrace is a popular place for local residents as well as visitors, and you can actually get a good frozen Margarita here, as well as a good choice of other exotic cocktails at prices lower than at most other hotels on Moorea. This becomes a lively place around sunset, when there is often a trio of Tahitian musicians playing island songs and guests gather to learn how to make their own crown of flowers. A Barbecue buffet and dance show takes place each Wednesday night at the Mahanai Restaurant, and a Seafood buffet and dance show is held on Saturday nights. See more information under *Where to Eat* in this chapter.

Honeymooners and all other lovers have a choice of Romantic Rendez-vous programs. These include Romantic Welcomes, Romantic Interludes, Romantic Escapades, and Polynesian Wedding Ceremonies, complete with champagne and photos. Contact the hotel directly for details.

Moderate

KAVEKA, *B.P. 373, Maharepa, Moorea 98728. Tel. 689/56.50.50; Fax 689/56.52.63; E-mail: kaveka@mail.pf; www.hotelkaveka.com. Beside lagoon at PK 7 on east side of Cook's Bay, 7 kilometers (4.3 miles) from the airport and 11 kilometers (7 miles) from the ferry dock. EP Rates single/double: lanai bungalow 11.500 CFP; garden bungalow 13.500 CFP; lagoon side bungalow 15.500 CFP; lanai bungalow with air conditioning 17.500 CFP; garden bungalow with air-conditioning 18.500 CFP; beach bungalow 19.500 CFP, beach bungalow with air-conditioning 23.500 CFP. Add 3.000 CFP for third person. No charge for child under 12 sharing room with parents. Add 4.200 CFP for MAP breakfast and dinner. Room rates include all taxes. A 10% value added tax is applicable to other services. Deposit required. American Express, Mastercard, Visa.*

There are 28 wooden bungalows in the gardens, at the edge of the lagoon and beside a small white sand beach that slopes into the warm water of Cook's Bay. This 2-star hotel offers a multi-millionaire's view of the postcard scenery of mountains, coral reef, sea and sky. Four new bungalows were added in April 2004, which are duplex garden units that provide larger accommodations than the original bungalows. These new bungalows are all air-conditioned and have a ceiling fan, television, refrigerator, a double bed and two single beds, a bathroom with a hot water shower, a tiled floor and a large covered terrace with two lounge chairs. All the waterfront units have refrigerators. Most of the 23 original units have already been renovated, providing 3 single beds (2 pushed together to form a double bed), a small table and ceiling fan, plus a small private bathroom with a hot water shower. Two units in each category are air-conditioned and all bungalows have a terrace except the lanai rooms, which are sold as a bare bones, no frills package deal. Although some of the bungalows are quite spartan, you can rent refrigerators, televisions and cell phones on request. There are no coffee/tea makers in any of the bungalows, but they all have a private safe in the closet and they are also furnished with blackout curtains. Greg Hardie, the owner, has changed all the bed and bath linen and now provides face cloths for his guests. The linens are changed daily. A high rock wall around two sides of the property helps to eliminate noises from the road while giving the hotel more privacy as well as a new updated look. A new beach has been created in front of the lagoon side bungalows, and plans include adding a pontoon and entry into the water through the basaltic rocks that protect the waterfront.

This hotel is adjacent to the dock where the ships' tenders land their passengers, and some of these visitors wander over to the Kaveka to spend a little time ashore, soaking up the sun, looking at the view and swimming in the lagoon. There's good snorkeling close to the hotel pier, but the pier itself is not open to the general public. There are kayaks, bicycles, snorkeling gear, sun umbrellas and beach chairs for rent. Signs are posted at the reception desk and in the garden, stating prices for the use of the hotel's facilities, including the telephone and Internet services. You can also use your own laptop to log onto the Internet for 700 CFP for 20 minutes. You can watch CNN and other channels on the television in the reception/lounge area, where you will also find shelves of exchange books in various languages. Restaurant Kaveka is built overwater, providing indoor or outdoor dining and a truly breathtaking view of Cook's Bay. Please see more information under *Where to Eat* in this chapter.

CLUB BALI HAI, *B.P. 8, Maharepa, Moorea 98728. Tel. 689/56.13.68, Fax 689/56.13.27, E-mail: reservations@clubbalihai.pf; www.clubbalihai.com. Beside the lagoon at PK 8 in Cook's Bay, near Pao Pao village, 8 kilometers (5 miles) from the airport and 12 kilometers (7.5 miles) from the ferry dock. 44 air-conditioned rooms and bungalows. EP Rates single/double: garden room with kitchen and mountain view 10.000 CFP; bayview room 12.000 CFP; beach bungalow with kitchen 17.000 CFP; overwater bungalow with kitchen 21.000 CFP. Third adult 3.500 CFP. Add 5% hotel tax to room rates and 6% value added tax to room rates, plus 150 CFP municipal tax per person per day. A 10% value added tax is applicable to other services. All major credit cards.*

Club Bali Hai overlooks the panoramic beauty of Cook's Bay and the surrounding mountains of cathedral peaks and spires. The 44 air-conditioned units include 13 overwater bungalows, 6 beachfront bungalows, 5 garden rooms with no kitchen, and 20 rooms in a two-story colonial style building. Most of the rooms in the 2-story building have kitchenettes and they all have coffee machines. A bayview room will be quieter as the road traffic can be quite noisy, but the advantage of the mountain view rooms is the lower price plus a kitchenette. The overwater and beach bungalows are Polynesian in decor, with a bedroom, separate kitchen/dining area and terrace facing the spectacular scenery. The floors and bathrooms are tiled and there are plenty of mirrors in the bedroom and bathroom. These units are furnished with a ceiling fan, a queen size bed in the bedroom and a twin bed in the living room, with a door in between for a little privacy, although the wall does not extend all the way to the ceiling. The kitchen contains a stove and oven, as well as a microwave and coffee/tea making facilities. The windows are screened, but not the sliding door leading to the sundeck. All the bathrooms have hot water showers. Club Bali Hai is a hotel with a Vacation Time-Share program, which is affiliated with Resort & Condominium International (RCI).

The Blue Pineapple (l'Ananas Bleu) is an excellent snack bar located on the hotel premises beside the bay. Matahi Hunter and his wife Virginia and their crew serve breakfast and lunch daily from 7am to 3pm, which you can enjoy while gazing at the magnificent view of the mountains overlooking Cook's Bay. They also serve wine and beer, but there are no other alcoholic beverages available, unless you bring your own booze to the poolside in the afternoon and listen to Muk McCallum, one of the three "Bali Hai Boys", talk story about the old days at Hotel Bali Hai. Muk is there every day at 5:30pm except on Wednesdays and he brings the ice and the entertaining answers to your questions. The other two founders of a chain of Bali Hai Hotels were Hugh Kelley, who died a few years, and Jay Carlisle, whom you will probably meet around the snack bar.

The hotel staff, headed by Rose Tetuamahuta, the pretty and efficient manager, are all Tahitians who have worked for the Hotel Bali Hai and/or Club Bali Hai for years. Rose always takes time to give personal attention to her guests, answering individual questions in her calm, caring manner. Club Bali Hai has a big boutique at the hotel entrance next to the reception area and you can watch CNN on a television in the lounge beside the reception desk. There is also a good selection of books to swap. A public phone is on the wall near the reception and you can buy a phone card from Rosalie in the boutique. Internet service is just 1/2 a mile from the hotel. There are also several very good restaurants near the hotel and most restaurants in the Cook's Bay area provide free transportation for dinner.

Club Bali Hai offers their guests a free tennis court, a fresh water swimming pool with a waterfall and a white sand beach with good swimming in Cook's Bay. Work was completed in September 2004 to enlarge the beach area and to put new tile all around the swimming pool. Free activities also include *tupa* crab races on Monday evening, a *pareo*-tying demonstration on Tuesday evening and a Tahitian dance show on Wednesday evening. Hiro Kelley of **Hiro's Tours/What to Do on Moorea Tours** has an activities desk at the hotel and he also has rental kayaks for 1.000 CFP per hour. Avis has a desk in the lobby and other rental cars, scooters and bikes can be rented across the street. For more information on optional activities, see *Lagoon Excursions, Snorkeling & Picnics on the Motu* in this chapter.

Check the Internet on the Club Bali Hai website, as they often have specials that can mean big savings for your next vacation on Moorea.

VILLAGE TEMANOHA, *B.P. 94, Maharepa, Moorea 98728. Tel./Fax 689/ 55.25.00, cell 77.17.00; Fax 689/55.25.01; E-mail: villagetemanoha@mail.pf; www.temanoha.com. In Pao Pao Valley behind school, 10 kilometers (6 miles) from the airport and 14 kilometers (9 miles) from the ferry dock. One-way transfer 1.000 CFP per person. EP rates: Fare Tiare bungalows 10.000 CFP single/double; 12.000 CFP triple; Fare Rotui bungalows 11.000 CFP single/ double; 13.000 CFP triple. No charge for child under 5 years. Continental breakfast 1.000 CFP. Add 6% value added tax to room rates and 50 CFP per person per day for visitor's tax. A 10% value added tax is applicable to other services. No credit cards.*

There are 6 high quality wooden bungalows with 40 or 50 square meters (431 or 538 square feet) of living space built around a swimming pool in a tropical garden of 5,000 square meters (53,820 square feet) at the foot of Mount Rotui and Mount Mouaputa. You'll have cooler temperatures and a wonderful view of the cathedral shaped mountains from this elevation, and the quiet setting is ideal for those who enjoy meditating, taking long walks, lying beside the pool with a book and simply being. Each bungalow contains a double bed and a single bed with mosquito nets, a small living room, equipped kitchen, mini bar, private bathroom of bamboo, wood and river stone paving and a hot water shower, plus a covered terrace. There is a ceiling fan in the living room, split bamboo wall coverings, natural tapa on the doors, teak furniture and a television and electric mosquito repellent in each bungalow. Housekeeping service is provided and breakfast is served on request. Bicycles are available for 1.000 CFP per day. The rocky road from Pao Pao to the pension is recommended for 4WD vehicles only, but once you arrive you will want to stay. Hosts Christa and Mathieu Castellani will help you arrange your island tours. Some of the drivers provide free pick-up service, including Alfredo's restaurant.

Economy

MOTEL ALBERT, *B.P. 27, Pao Pao, Moorea 98728. Tel. 689/56.12.76; Fax 689/56.58.58; E-mail: motel.albert@laposte.net; http://motelalbert.free.fr. Mountainside at PK 8 in Pao Pao, across from Club Bali Hai, 8 kilometers (5 miles) from the airport and 12 kilometers (8 miles) from the ferry dock. EP Rates: room 5.000 CFP single/double; bungalow 8.500 CFP for 4 people; additional person 1.000 CFP per day. Minimum 2 nights or add 1.000 CFP to rates. Add 6% value added tax to room rates and 50 CFP per person per day for visitor's tax. A 10% value added tax is applicable to other services. No credit cards.*

This is a good choice if you are traveling on a tight budget and want to be in the Cook's Bay area, where you can see the famous mountains surrounding the bay. You'll also be within easy walking distance of supermarkets, restaurants and snacks. There are 16 units on a hillside slope and flat ground decorated with fruit trees and pretty flower gardens, and 9 are units available for rent by the night, week, month or year. These include 5-person wooden bungalows on stilts, each with two bedrooms, living room, a spacious kitchen with regular stove and big refrigerator, large screened in terrace, screened windows and sliding glass doors, and private bathroom with hot water shower. The decor is old Polynesia with pareo cloth bedspreads and curtains. There are also 7 rooms with one or two double beds, a kitchen and private bathroom with hot water shower. The Polynesian owners have plans to renovate these rooms, but they are still in great demand and in constant use. You can rent a bicycle for 1.000 CFP a day at the reception or reserve a car with Albert Rent A Car next door.

OPUNOHU-PAPETOAI AREA
Deluxe
   SHERATON MOOREA LAGOON RESORT & SPA, *B.P. 1005, Papetoai, Moorea 98729. Tel. 689/55.11.11; Fax 689/55.11.55; E-mail: reservations.tahiti@sheraton.pf; www.sheratonsintahiti.com, www.sheraton.com. Beside the lagoon at PK 14 between Cook's Bay and Opunohu Bay, 14 kilometers (8.7 miles) from the airport and 18 kilometers (11 miles) from the ferry dock. 106 bungalows. 2005 Low Season (High Season) EP Rates single/double: Garden bungalow 32.400 CFP (36.000 CFP); Superior Garden bungalow 37.800 CFP (42.000 CFP); Beach bungalow 51.300 CFP (57.000 CFP); Overwater bungalow 71.100 CFP (79.000 CFP); Horizon Overwater bungalow 76.500 CFP (85.000 CFP); Premium Horizon Overwater bungalow 80.100 CFP (89.000 CFP); Premium Horizon Overwater Suite bungalow (opening mid-2005) 99.000 CFP (110.000 CFP). Note: Low Season is January 1-March 31, 2005 and November 1-December 22, 2005. High Season is April 1-October 31, 2005 and December 23, 2005-January 1, 2006. Extra bed 10.000 CFP. MAP breakfast and dinner 7.217 CFP per person; AP breakfast, lunch and dinner 10.189 CFP per person. American breakfast buffet 2.548 CFP. Add 5% hotel tax to room rates and 6% value added tax to room rates and prepaid meal plans, plus 150 CFP municipal tax per person per day. A 10% value added tax is applicable to other services. All major credit cards.*

This hotel opened in September 2000 with 106 bungalows facing the lagoon and the entrance to Moorea's beautiful Opunohu Bay. An expansion plan was announced in September 2004 that will add 22 Horizon Overwater Suite bungalows, scheduled to be finished in mid-2005. You will then have a choice of garden, beach or overwater bungalows, plus the new overwater suites.

All the bungalows are equipped with individually controlled air conditioning, ceiling fan, smoke detector system, black-out drapes, private terrace with outside shower, direct-dial phone, color television with cable, Internet access, alarm clock/radio, CD player, individual safe, mini-bar, coffee/tea making facilities, and ironing-board with an iron. The bathroom features a bathtub and a separate shower, a hairdryer, telephone and a make-up mirror. A pillow menu offers you a choice of various sizes and shapes of head rests, from feather soft to firm.

In addition to a restaurant, beach grill and three bars, the hotel services include room service from 6am to 10:15pm, 24-hour front desk service, 24-hour security, laundry and dry cleaning service, valet service, guest ice machines, multilingual concierge service, pre-registration service, currency exchange, banquet and meeting facilities, daily newsletters and a business center with Internet connections.

There is a boutique and black pearl shop, and in the lobby you will find a guest relations desk and excursions and activities desk and car rental agency. A nautical activities center is next to the beach, where you can book all water sports including scuba diving. Mandara Spa, also on the beach level, has a sauna and steam room, which hotel guests can use at no extra charge. There is also a Jacuzzi and Vichy shower, and the trained massage therapists provide an interesting choice of relaxation treatments. There is a fantasy swimming pool and a Jacuzzi in the gardens beside the main buildings, and across the road is a fitness center and two lighted tennis courts.

See more information under *Where to Eat*, *Nautical Activities Centers*, *Scuba Diving*, and *Massages & Spas* in this chapter and in the chapter on *Best Places to Stay*.

Moderate
PENSION MOTU ITI, *B.P. 189, Paopao, Moorea 98728. Tel. 689/ 55.05.20; Cell 74.43.38; Fax 689/55.05.21; E-mail: pensionmotuiti@mail.pf; www.pensionmotuiti.com. Beside lagoon at PK 13.2 between Cook's Bay and Opunohu Bay, 13 kilometers (8 miles) from the airport and 17 kilometers (11 miles) from the Vaiare ferry dock. EP Rates single/double: garden bungalow 10.500 CFP; beach bungalow 12.000 CFP; extra bed 1.650 CFP; dormitory 1.650 CFP per person. Rates include all taxes. American Express, Mastercard, Visa. Reserve.*

Auguste Ienfa and his wife Dora opened this small hotel and restaurant in mid-2002 and have enjoyed an 80 percent occupancy year-round ever since. They have not raised their rates and will keep the same prices for 2005. Their five modern Polynesian style bungalows are built beside the lagoon in Pihaena between Cook's Bay and Opunohu Bay, within easy view of the Sheraton Moorea Lagoon Resort & Spa.

Pension Motu Iti offers the same spectacular sunsets and full moon risings as the big hotel does, but at more affordable prices, and with very personable and attentive service. Three of the bungalows are beside the water, with the two garden bungalows just behind. Each unit has a wood shingle roof and the interior walls are covered with *pueu* matting. They are furnished with big bamboo furniture, including a king-size bed with a bright bedspread that is pretty and in good taste with the rest of the décor. There is a writing desk, a closet with shelves and hanging space, a ceiling fan, television, bathroom with tiled shower and an ample supply of clean hot water. The windows and sliding glass door are unscreened, but each room is equipped with an electric machine for mosquito repellent. There are chairs on the terrace and a faucet is placed beside the steps at the front entrance to rinse off sandy feet. You can have room service on your terrace for breakfast, lunch or your favorite drinks.

Upstairs over the reception area is a dormitory for 15 cots, which is also cooled by a large opening on the lagoon side, as well as a series of fans. There are two clean bathrooms provided downstairs for people sleeping in the dorm.

There is a parking lot for guests, with a high stone wall to help keep road noises to a minimum. Paved walkways connect the reception, restaurant and bungalows, and Dora's attractively landscaped flower gardens add a lively touch to the clean and pleasant scene. An overwater *fare* provides shelter as well as a sundeck for guests who want to spend a few quiet hours reading, napping in a lounge chair or gazing at the sea and sky. This is an ideal place to be at sunset, feeling the gentle breeze of the tradewinds as you sip your favorite cool beverage and watch Nature's spectacular show. Kayaks are provided free of charge and Auguste will drive you to the Sheraton to join a tour or excursion.

The Motu Iti restaurant is open to the public and the dining room is on a covered terrace facing the lagoon. The ceiling is trimmed with woven bamboo and the tables and chairs are teak. Breakfast, lunch and dinner are served daily, and the prices are right. See more information under *Where to Eat* in this chapter.

Auguste also operates an Internet service, with two computers and all his wealth of knowledge in his former career as a banker to assist you with any computer questions you need answered. He charges 250 CFP for 15 minutes on-line. A small boutique is the next addition on the agenda. You can visit Pension Motu Iti on their website.

FARE NANI, *B.P. 61572, Faaa, Tahiti 98702. Tel./Fax 689/56.19.99; Cell 79.89.73. Beside the lagoon in Pihaena at PK 14.1, between the Sheraton Moorea Lagoon Resort and Village Faimano, 14 kilometers (8.7 miles) from the airport and 18 kilometers (11 miles) from the ferry dock. EP Rates: fare 10.000 CFP for two adults and two children under 12 years. Third person 1.000 CFP; child 12 years and older 500 CFP. All taxes are included. No credit cards.*

Maeva Bougues, one of Tahiti's best songwriters, operates this little pension. She speaks good English and Spanish in addition to French and Tahitian, her native language. Each of the three little thatched roof *fares* has a double bed with mosquito net and small electric fan, a lounge with sofa and mattresses, a kitchen and outside bathroom with cold water. Paddle canoes are available for exploring the lagoon and there is a small white sand beach, with shade provided by gnarled old wild hibiscus (*purau*) trees. You have to walk under them to see the lagoon and sunset, but they add to a feeling of privacy. Maeva also has houses for rent on a short-term basis, including a 2-bedroom house next door to her pension, which has a nice white sand beach and wonderful view of the lagoon and sunset.

VILLAGE FAIMANO, *B.P. 588, Maharepa, Moorea 98728. Tel. 689/ 56.10.20, Fax 689/56.36.47; E-mail: faimanodenis@mail.pf; www.faimanovillage.com. Beside the lagoon at PK 14.1 in Pihaena, close to the Sheraton Moorea Lagoon Resort, 14 kilometers (8.7 miles) from the airport and 18 kilometers (11 miles) from the ferry dock. EP Rates: garden bungalow 8.500 CFP 1-3 people; beach bungalow 9.500 CFP single/double; 10.500 CFP triple; family bungalow 12.500 CFP 4-6 people per day. Add 6% value added tax to room rates and 50 CFP per person per day for visitor's tax. A 10% value added tax is applicable to other services. Mastercard, Visa.*

This is my favorite seaside pension and offers good value for money. The location is very pretty, with a white sand beach and clear lagoon for easy swimming. This is a very popular weekend destination for Tahiti residents, and the ambiance is often local, which means Tahitian music and songs. Your choice of 7 Polynesian style bungalows includes two family size *fares*, each with two rooms with a double bed, one or two single beds in the living room, plus a kitchen and private bathroom with solar hot water. Or you can rent one of the five smaller *fares*, each with a bedroom and double bed, single beds in the living room, kitchen and private bathroom with solar hot water. Each bungalow has a barbecue grill and television. Bikes, outrigger paddle canoes and kayaks are free of charge for guest use and you can sunbathe on a floating dock within a few laps from the shore. The reception is also a communal room with books and games. Faimano, who is Tahitian, and her French husband, Denis Feildel, who own the pension, have now retired to Tahaa, and Faimano's niece Valerie takes care of the guests. She speaks a little English.

FARE HAMARA, *Tel. 689/56.25.65. On mountainside at PK 16.4 in Papetoai, overlooking Opunohu Bay and Pass. Reservations: Bob Hammar, 3324 Soundview Drive, University Place, WA 98466; Tel. 253/564-0180; E-mail: hamara@harbornet.com; www.farehamara.com. EP Rates: 2-bedroom house $1,400 per week.*

Bob Hammar is a part-time resident of Moorea. Fare Hamara is a Lindal cedar home pre-cut from a kit, with a 25-foot ceiling, 2 bedrooms, a living-dining room, a well-equipped kitchen with a tiled counter and all American appliances, a big bathroom with a double shower, and a wrap-around terrace. This well-planned octagon-shaped house can sleep 8 people cozily. There is a personal safe in the walk-in closet, ceiling fan, washing machine and clothes dryer, a gas stove and 110 and 220-volt electrical outlets. The windows and sliding glass doors are screened and there is a barbecue grill on the terrace. From this height you can see humpback whales in Opunohu Bay during the months of July through October.

FARE VAIHERE, *B.P. 1806, Papetoai, Moorea 98729. Tel./Fax 689/56.19.19; cell 74.07.57; E-mail: farevaihere@ifrance.com; www.farevaihere.com. Beside the lagoon at PK 15.5 in Opunohu Bay, 15.5 kilometers (9.6 miles) from the airport and 19.5 kilometers (12 miles) from the ferry dock. EP Rates: small bungalow plus breakfast 15.000 CFP single/double; family bungalow 25.000 CFP 1-6 people; add 1.000 CFP per day for extra bed. All taxes included. Mastercard, Visa.*

This new family pension offers a taste of old Moorea, with local style architecture and woven bamboo walls, on the verdant east coast of Opunohu Bay. Look for a sign with the design of a breadfruit leaf at the entrance, and then turn into the driveway for protected parking beside the property. There are 4 bungalows for a maximum of 3 people and a family *fare* that can accommodate 8 people. Each of the smaller units has a double bed and a single bed and a large bathroom with hot water shower. They are furnished with a desk, refrigerator/bar, a kettle with supplies of coffee, tea and capuccino, a ceiling fan, mosquito net and a teak terrace. These three bungalows are rented as a bed and breakfast with a continental breakfast include in the price. The big family *fare* has all the comforts of a small villa, including 3 bedrooms, 2 bathrooms with hot water, a kitchen, dining room, living room, television and terrace. There is also a communal *fare pote'e* that serves as a kitchen and dining room for clients. On the mezzanine is a television and DVD player and library.

The French family who own Fare Vaihere are Curil and Florence Morize and their three children, aged 14, 11 and 5 at publication time. This is a good choice for vacationing families, as there are bicycles, kayaks and snorkeling gear provided, and you can swim and fish off the end of the long pier. Smaller kids can play in the shallow water beside a narrow beach. The owners also have a 24-foot motorboat that can be used for à la carte nautical excursions and they will help you organize any of the other excursions available on Moorea.

WEST COAST: PAPETOAI TO HAAPITI
Deluxe

INTERCONTINENTAL RESORT MOOREA, *B.P. 1019, Tiahura, Moorea 98729. Tel. 689/55.19.19, Fax 689/55.19.55, E-mail: reservationspf@interconti.com; www.moorea.interconti.com. Beside the lagoon at PK 24 between Papetoai and Haapiti, 24 kilometers (14.8 miles) from the airport and 28 kilometers (17.3 miles) from the ferry dock. 143 rooms and bungalows. 2005 Low Season (High Season) EP Rates single/double: lanai room 32.550 CFP (36.470 CFP); garden suite bungalow 37.550 CFP (42.030*

CFP); beach suite bungalow 46.050 CFP (51.520 CFP) CFP; overwater suite bungalow 64.640 CFP (72.350 CFP); Teremoana lanai suite 64.640 CFP (72.350 CFP). Note: Low Season is January 1-May 31, 2005 and December 1-31, 2005. High Season is June 1-November 30, 2005. Third person 15 years or over 6.000 CFP. Continental breakfast 2.225 CFP; American breakfast 2.710 CFP; MAP with breakfast and dinner 8.065 CFP; AP with breakfast, lunch and dinner 11.570 CFP. Add 5% hotel tax to room rates and 6% value added tax to room rates and prepaid meal plans, plus 150 CFP municipal tax per person per day. A 10% value added tax is applicable to other services. All major credit cards.

In June 2001, all three of the Beachcomber Hotels (Tahiti, Moorea and Bora Bora) dropped the Parkroyal title, when they became members of the prestigious Inter-Continental Resort chain. By the end of 2004 they will drop the Beachcomber name and the Moorea hotel will become InterContinental Resort Moorea. This property covers 17 acres of land on a mini-peninsula on the northwestern side of Moorea, between Opunohu Bay and the tourist hotels and shops in the Club Med area of Haapiti.

The 17-year old hotel has 48 air-conditioned Lanai rooms, including 2 handicapped rooms, and 1 suite located in colonial style two-story concrete buildings, each with a king-size bed or two twin beds and a balcony or lanai overlooking the lagoon. The 16 garden suite bungalows, 28 beach suite bungalows and 50 overwater suite bungalows are all built in the traditional Polynesian design with thatched roofs. These units have a separate sitting area with a writing desk, a king-size bed and a sofa bed. All the bungalows are air-conditioned and also have ceiling fans in the living room and bedroom, and in the bathrooms there are separate bathtubs and showers and a private toilet section. Standard amenities in all rooms and bungalows include international direct dial telephones with 2 sets, color television with local channels, CNN, ESPN, Canal +, in-house video movies, radio and music. There is a fully stocked self-service mini-bar/refrigerator in each room and bungalow, as well as complimentary tea and coffee making facilities, a personal electronic safety box, a hair dryer, 240/110-volt electrical outlets and complimentary grooming items. All the bungalows have a private balcony with table and two armchairs and 2 snorkeling masks. The overwater bungalows are just at the edge of the lagoon and have steps leading into the water and mats for sunbathing. A romantic breakfast will be delivered by a floral decorated canoe to your overwater bungalow on request.

An enormous thatched roof building houses the reception, Fare Nui restaurant for 250 diners, Fare Hana poolside restaurant for 80 people, Motu Iti bar with seating for 70 people, a conference room for 80-100 diners or 150 theater-style seats, a concierge service and public relations activities desk, taxi, car and bike rental desk, gift shop and black pearl shop. Guest services include twice a day maid service, next day laundry and dry cleaning service (Monday to Friday), iron and ironing board on request, currency exchange, and mail and postal service. In-room dining is available 24 hours a day and a special romantic touch for guests staying in the most of the overwater bungalows is to order breakfast served to your balcony by flower decorated outrigger canoe.

Guests have free use of the hotel's fresh water swimming pool, two tennis courts and white sand beaches, and snorkeling equipment and outrigger paddle canoes are also provided. Paid activities at the nautical sports center include kayaks, glass-bottom boat, speedboats, Aquascope underwater boat, Aquablue excursions, catamaran excursions, water-skiing, jet-skiing, boat transfers to a nearby motu, snorkeling excursions and picnics on the motu, ray and fish feeding tours, deep sea fishing, parasailing and sunset cruises. Bathy's Club has a scuba dive center here and also offers shark-feeding excursions. See more information under *Nautical Activities Center*.

The Moorea Dolphin Center (ex-Dolphin Quest) is a big attraction for people who want to play with the dolphins in an enclosed environment, or you can take a Dolphin Watch excursion with Dr. Michael Poole and see the wild spinner dolphins that live year-round in the natural environment of the open ocean surrounding Moorea. Helicopter rides are available with a landing pad on the hotel grounds. In addition to a daily program of activities presented at the hotel, you will also have an interesting choice of excursions to discover the romantic beauty of Moorea's seashore and interior valleys. Should you feel in the mood to just relax and be pampered, you can treat yourself to a fresh floral bath and massage at Héléne'Spa, located on the hotel grounds.

A musical duo plays songs from the islands around the bar at sunset, and various activities are organized in the lobby or at the Motu Iti bar. These include *pareo*-tying demonstrations, *tamure* lessons, learning how to prepare Tahitian marinated fish and watching video films on the black pearl. The weekly entertainment program begins on Monday evening with Polynesian Night, when a buffet of Tahitian and seafood specialties is served and the Mamas of Moorea dance for you in the Fare Nui restaurant at 8:15pm. The dinner and show costs 6.402 CFP. Barbecue Night is held each Wednesday beside the swimming pool, accompanied by a Polynesian show, and it is also 6.402 CFP.

The *Soirée Merveilleuse* held each Saturday evening is a gastronomic buffet featuring a variety of fresh seafood, usually served on the beach under the stars and tropical moon. A Tahitian dance group performs on a stage set between two graceful coconut trees. This costs 7.810 CFP. A Sunday Buffet lunch is served in the Fare Hana beside the pool, to the tune of a musical trio.

A Kids Only Club has a program of the day Monday through Friday for children 4 to 10 years old. Activities include supervised swimming in the pool or lagoon, beach Olympics, tropical fruit tasting, a discovery tour of the botanical garden, arts and crafts, weaving floral crowns and stringing shell leis, dying *pareos* and other creative games. A full day's activities cost 6.000 CFP per child.

The InterContinental Resort Moorea has a catalog of "Romantic Ideas," "Celebrations of Romance" and "Romantic Touches" for honeymooners and other lovers. You can also exchange vows in a non-binding wedding ceremony for 168.000 CFP. A Polynesian mini-wedding ceremony is 119.000 CFP.

DREAM ISLAND, *B. P. 1175, Papetoai, Moorea 98729. Tel. 689/ 77.84.70; Fax 689/56.38.81; E-mail: darmin@mail.pf; www.dream-island.com. 3 deluxe houses on a private motu facing Club Med in Haapiti. All taxes included. No credit cards.*

If you are looking for a dream house to rent on a private motu islet, Kolka Muller and his wife Josy have just the answer for you. Three deluxe houses are surrounded by unspoiled beauty on a white sand beach just a five minute boat ride from the main island. Fare Polynésie is a 3 bedroom, 2 bath house with a private apartment, large lounge, kitchen, dining room and two terraces, for US$500 a night, $2,950 a week or $9,500 a month. Fare Pacifique has 2 bedrooms, 2 bathrooms, a lounge, kitchen and 2 terraces and rents for US$450 a night, $2,550 a week or $8,500 a month. Fare Gauguin has 2 bedrooms, a master bathroom and one other bathroom, a lounge, kitchen and dining room, for $350 a night, $1,050 a week or $6,900 a month. These rates are for four people maximum per house. Each additional person will be charged $340 extra per week. Each house is equipped with a television, telephone, lovely furnishings and homey touches. Check out the photos on their website.

VILLA CORALLINA, *B.P. 19, Maharepa, Moorea 98728. Tel. 689/ 77.05.90 or 76.11.11; Fax 689/56.36.65; E-mail: info@villacorallina.com; corallina@mail.pf; www.villacorallina.com. 2-bedroom villa on the west side of Motu Fareone, across the channel from Club Med in Haapiti, 27 kilometers (16.7 miles) from the airport and 5 minutes by boat from main island. EP Rates: 48.000 CFP single/double; 72.600 CFP triple. Add 6% value added tax to room rates and 50 CFP per person per day for visitor's tax. No credit cards. Minimum stay 3 nights.*

Marco Ciucci's Villa Corallina offers 2 double rooms, 2 bathrooms, a living room, dining room, breakfast area, fully equipped kitchen, beach terrace with barbecue, a private white sand beach with lounge chairs and 6,000 square meters (64,583 square feet) of private grounds on a quiet motu islet, providing panoramic views of the lagoon, coral reef, deep ocean and open skies. Using only hardwoods and quality materials, the interior walls are lined with woven bamboo mats. Tiki sculptures, tapa paintings and mother of pearl and coral ornaments are all inspired by the theme of the ocean. Amenities include ceiling fans, two television sets, a video player and VCR library, a CD player in the rooms and in the living room, cellular phone, fax, books, refrigerator, freezer and house linens. Guests have free use of snorkeling equipment, two kayaks and outrigger paddle canoe. The housekeeping and beach maintenance are assured daily by the staff. A courtesy shuttle will transfer you to the main island or to the Fare Vai Moana restaurant. No children under 12 years allowed.

FENUA MATA'I'OA, *B. P. 1192, Papetoai, Moorea, 98729. Tel. 689/55/ 00.25; Fax 689/55.00.26; E-mail: eileenb@mail.pf; www.fenua-mataioa.com. Beside the lagoon in Tiahura Village, between the InterContinental Resort Moorea and Hotel Les Tipaniers. EP Rates: Room for two people 30.000 CFP; Princesse Maimiti Royal Suite 50.000 CFP; additional person is 5.000 CFP per day, including taxes. Mastercard, Visa.*

Do not confuse this unique lodging with a family pension, as it is an exclusive, elegant *residence* located in a gated community. Eileen Bossuot, the hostess, is a former designer for the Relais et Chateaux properties in France, and she and her husband Serge have filled their lagoon-side home with all the treasures of their many voyages throughout the world, including Eileen's collection of 2,500 owls. The décor is a blend of Tahitian, French Provincial, European and Asian, and each item has its own story. Along with the mirrors, lamps, sconces, and objets d'art, there are many colorful tableaux that were painted by Moorea's resident artists. Fenua Mata'i'oa offers a choice of six rooms for two or three guests or a 2-level duplex suite with beds for four guests. All the rooms are air-conditioned and furnished with a king-size bed, large sleeping sofa, color satellite television, music system, DDD telephone with modem data port, mini-bar and large terrace, all lovingly decorated. Each of the rooms also has a private bathroom with a large shower, two lavabos, toilet, hair-dryer and tasteful décor. In the suite the upstairs bedroom has a private safety box, and the bathroom contains a Jacuzzi bathtub and shower.

Guests can enjoy their meals in the privacy of their rooms, on the pier or in the small interior or exterior dining rooms that are so invitingly decorated. Continental or American breakfasts are served, salads and light lunches are available, and dinner consists of refined cuisine, with special theme evenings presented. Drinks are served throughout the day and late into the evening at the Honomai Bar. There is no beach here, but lounge chairs and palapa type thatched roof umbrellas line the wooden deck beside the lagoon and there is a nice Jacuzzi pool in the garden. Snorkeling equipment is provided at no extra charge, as well as kayaks, bicycles and electric scooters. Optional land and lagoon excursions can be arranged including ray feeding, trips to the motu and sunset cruises.

Moderate

HOTEL LES TIPANIERS, *B.P. 1002, Papetoai, Moorea 98729. Tel. 689/ 56.12.67, Fax 689/56.29.25; E-mail: tipaniersresa@mail.pf; www.lestipaniers.com. Beside the lagoon at PK 25 in Haapiti, 25 kilometers (15.5 miles) from the airport and 29 kilometers (18 miles) from the ferry dock. 22 bungalows. EP Rates: standard superior bungalow near beach with fridge and no kitchen 13.850 CFP single/double, 15.100 CFP triple, 16.500 CFP* *quadruple; local style thatched roof bungalow in garden with kitchen 13.850 CFP single/double, 15.900 CFP 3-4 people; local style thatched roof bungalow on beach with kitchen 15.750 CFP single/double, 16.600 CFP 3-4 people; vanilla style bungalow in garden with kitchen 14.900 CFP 1-3 people, 16.800 CFP 4-6 people. Garden room 6.800 CFP single/double. Add 4.600 CFP per person for breakfast and dinner. Continental breakfast 1.250 CFP, American breakfast 1.700 CFP, Dinner 3.350 CFP. Children under 10 years old free in parents' bungalow, meals à la carte. Add 5% hotel tax to room rates and 6% value added tax to room rates and prepaid meal plans, plus 150 CFP municipal tax per person per day. A 10% value added tax is applicable to other services. All major credit cards.*

"Les Tipaniers" means frangipani or plumeria, the trees of white, pink, orange and yellow flowers you will see and smell throughout the gardens of this very Polynesian style hotel. The 22 thatched roof bungalows are rather close together and the best choice is one of the beach bungalows, where you can sit on your terrace and admire the white sandy beach and aquamarine lagoon. Across this watery playground are three *motu* islets, which you can reach by outrigger paddle canoe, kayak or small motorboat. All the bungalows have a porch or terrace, as well as screens on the windows but not on the sliding glass doors. The thatched roof bungalows are built in the local Polynesian style, offering a choice of superior standard bungalows with refrigerator and no kitchen or 13 bungalows with fully equipped kitchens. The vanilla style bungalows, with a different type roof and gingerbread trim, are built in the French colonial style and will accommodate up to six people. All the bungalows were renovated in 2003 and this hotel enjoys 80 percent occupancy year-round.

The beachside restaurant-bar is open for breakfast, lunch and sunset cocktails, and the main restaurant is open for dinner. See information under *Where to Eat* in this chapter. Free activities include outrigger paddle canoes, volleyball, ping-pong, pétanque (French bowls) and bicycles. Paid activities include mountain bike rentals, sailing, boat shuttle to the motu, deep sea fishing, glass bottom boat, horseback riding, island tours, rental cars, scuba diving and hiking. Tip'Nautic activities center is on the premises and will arrange your outings on the lagoon. See more information under *Nautical Activities* in this chapter. Scubapiti is a dive center based at the hotel, with a qualified instructor. See more information under *Scuba Diving* in this chapter. The hotel management also promotes hiking in Moorea and Tahiti with Tahiti Evasion. See more information under *Hiking* in this chapter. You can easily walk to several restaurants, shops, boutiques and black pearl shops from this hotel, and some of the restaurants on Moorea provide free transportation from the hotels.

LES TIPANIERS ITI, *an annex to the main hotel, is located beside the lagoon at PK 20 in Papetoai, 4 kilometers (2.5 miles) from Hotel Les Tipaniers,*

20 kilometers (12.4 miles) from the airport and 24 kilometers (14.8 miles) from the ferry dock. 5 local style bungalows with kitchens can accommodate up to four people. EP Rates: 7.950 CFP for 1-3 people per night and 8.500 CFP for 4-5 people per night. Special rates are given for long stays. Add 4.600 CFP per person for breakfast and dinner at the main hotel. Add 5% hotel tax to room rates and 6% value added tax to room rates and prepaid meal plans, plus 150 CFP municipal tax per person per day. A 10% value added tax is applicable to other services. All major credit cards.

"Little Tipaniers" has five thatched-roof bungalows with kitchenettes and beds for 3 or 5 people. A sun deck type wharf overlooks the entrance to magnificent Opunohu Bay. You have access to all the activities available at Les Tipaniers. A complimentary shuttle van will transfer you to the main hotel for dinner on request.

CLUB MEDITERRANEE MOOREA, *B.P. 575, Papeete, Tahiti 98713. Tel. 689/42.96.99, Fax 689/42.16.83; www.clubmed.com. Beside the lagoon at PK 26 in Haapiti on northwest coast, 26 kilometers (16 miles) from the airport and 30 kilometers (18.6 miles) from the ferry dock.*

This 350-room club closed November 30, 2001. No press release or official notice has been issued to announce a reopening.

HOTEL HIBISCUS, *B.P. 1009, Papetoai, Moorea 98729. Tel. 689/ 56.12.20, Fax 689/56.20.69, E-mail: hibiscus@mail.pf; www.hotel-hibiscus.pf. Beside the lagoon at PK 27 in Haapiti, next door to Club Med, 27 kilometers (16.7 miles) from the airport and 31 kilometers (19.2 miles) from the ferry dock. 29 bungalows and 12 air-conditioned rooms. EP Rates: garden bungalow with fan 13.200 CFP single, double or triple; beach bungalow with fan 15.400 CFP single, double or triple. Add 1.650 CFP for additional bed. Air-conditioned room 15.000 CFP double; air-conditioned studio 25.000 CFP 4-5 people. Continental breakfast 1.060 CFP, American breakfast 1.750 CFP, add 5.250 CFP per person for breakfast and dinner (half-board); add 8.250 CFP for all meals (full board). Add 5% hotel tax to room rates and 6% value added tax to room rates and prepaid meal plans, plus 150 CFP municipal tax per person per day. A 10% value added tax is applicable to other services. All major credit cards.*

The 29 thatched roof bungalows are compact but comfortable, and with the aid of brightly colored tie-dyed sheets and curtains the decor is quite cheery. Each bungalow contains a double bed and a single bed, with space to add another single bed. They have tiled bathrooms with hot water showers, a separate toilet compartment, double sinks, a kitchen corner with a mini-refrigerator and three-burner hot plate, plus cooking and eating utensils, wardrobe closet, ceiling fan, and a covered terrace with table and chairs, where you can enjoy your meals in privacy. There are also 10 air-conditioned rooms and 2 air-conditioned studios in a new 2-story building that opened in 2003 beside the swimming pool. Each room has a bathtub/shower, a double bed and a single bed, a kitchenette and a balcony or private garden. The 2 studios can accommodate four people. Should you feel like eating out, you can try the French, Italian and Tahitian home-style food at Le Sunset Restaurant, built over the white sand beach in front of Hotel Hibiscus.

In addition to a fresh water swimming pool in the spacious gardens, and a white sand beach, you also have an interesting selection of ways to explore the lagoon. You can paddle an outrigger canoe to the three *motu* islets across the lagoon, or pay 7.000 CFP for a two-hour rental of a 4-passenger motorboat that doesn't require a permit. Cata-Jet offers guided excursions aboard a 2-place boat that is a combination of a catamaran and a jet-ski, and they also have kayaks to rent. You can rent a bicycle at the hotel reception desk, sign up for island tours or check your e-mail with the Internet service provided, which costs 375 CFP for 15 minutes and 1.500 CFP per hour.

This hotel attracts a mid-range clientele and is favored by Europeans, as well as New Zealanders. Owners Sylvette and Jean-Claude Perelli, who bought Hotel Hibiscus in 1993, are very helpful and friendly, and will make sure that your visit is a happy event. In 2003 the French government's secretary of tourism awarded them a bronze medal for service rendered to the tourism industry.

FARE VAI MOANA, *B.P. 1181, Papetoai, Moorea 98729. Tel. 689/ 56.17.14; Fax 689/56.28.78; E-mail: farevaimoana@mail.pf. Beside the lagoon at PK 27 in Haapiti, west of Club Med, 27 kilometers (16.7 miles) from the airport and 31 kilometers (19.2 miles) from the ferry dock. 14 bungalows. EP Rates are for 1-4 people and include 2 Continental breakfasts per day: garden bungalow 13.000 CFP, ocean view bungalow 15.000 CFP, beach bungalow 17.300 CFP. Add 2.700 CFP for 5th person. Continental breakfast 1.200 CFP; American breakfast 1.650 CFP; add 4.800 CFP per person for Continental breakfast and set dinner menu. Add 5% hotel tax to room rates and 6% value added tax to room rates and prepaid meal plans, plus 150 CFP municipal tax per person per day. A 10% value added tax is applicable to other services. All major credit cards.*

This small hotel is built along a white sand beach, close to other hotels, restaurants, boutiques and black pearl shops. The white concrete bungalows are topped with pandanus roofs, attractively decorated with bamboo furniture and precious woods and seashells. Each bungalow has a mezzanine and can sleep up to five people. They are equipped with a ceiling fan, refrigerator, safety box, private bathroom with hot water shower, and a small terrace facing the lagoon. The windows are not screened.

The thatched roof restaurant is open to the sea, with a Polynesian flavor that includes posts carved as Marquesan tikis. You can play games in the salon or watch the sunset from the central patio. You can also rent a bike at reception. In October 1999, the hotel was taken over by the same company that owns Les Tipaniers and Tipaniers Iti, but the management is independent from the other two hotels. The restaurant benefits from the cuisine of a French chef from Agen, near Bordeaux. See more information under *Where to Eat* in this chapter.

HOTEL MOOREA VILLAGE, *B.P. 1008, Papetoai, Moorea 98729. Tel. 689/56.10.02, Fax 689/56.22.11; Reservations: Tel. 689/56.30.95; E-mail: mooreavillage@mail.pf. Beside the lagoon at PK 27 in Haapiti, west of Club Med, 27 kilometers (16.7 miles)) from the airport and 31 kilometers (19.2 miles) from the ferry dock by the north coast. 80 bungalows. EP Rates: garden bungalow without kitchen 9.500 CFP single, 10.500 CFP double; beach bungalow without kitchen 12.000 CFP single, 13.000 CFP double; garden bungalow with kitchen (3rd & 4th row) 18.000 CFP 1-4 people; garden bungalow with kitchen (2nd row) 20.000 CFP 1-4 people; garden bungalow with kitchen (1st row) 22.000 CFP 1-4 people; beachfront bungalow with kitchen, 27.000 CFP for 1-4 people. Extra mattress 1.000 CFP. No charge for child under 12 years sharing bungalow with parents. Add 4.600 CFP per person for breakfast and dinner, and 5.800 CFP per person for 3 meals daily. Continental breakfast is 950 CFP and American breakfast is 1.500 CFP. Add 5% hotel tax to room rates and 6% value added tax to room rates and prepaid meal plans, plus 150 CFP municipal tax per person per day. A 10% value added tax is applicable to other services. All major credit cards.*

Tekeani Gendron is a lovely young Polynesian lady and former Miss Moorea beauty queen who has taken over management of her family's hotel. She has already started a big renovation program to give the bungalows and all public areas of Moorea Village a new look. This includes painting, replacing broken tiles in the restaurant and bar, redoing the pool area and tennis court and changing the curtains, bedspreads and other furnishings in the bungalows.

Australians and New Zealanders especially appreciate the value for money aspect this hotel offers, as well as the location, service and wide range of activities available. The 80 Polynesian style bungalows, all with verandas, are located in the garden or along a white sand beach. Some of the bungalows have thatched pandanus roofs and others have redwood roofs. They all have woven bamboo walls, screened windows and sliding glass doors with screens, plus a spacious private veranda. Each bungalow has a double bed in the bedroom and two beds in the living room. There is an overhead fan, hanging closet and a full-length mirror in the bedroom, and a television in the living/dining area. The bathroom has a shower with hot water. The newer bungalows have American style plugs, but don't forget that the electricity is 220 volts. Kitchens are included in 14 bungalows, providing all the necessary equipment and supplies you'll need to prepare meals: a refrigerator, 4-burner stove, sink, toaster, coffee maker, dishes, pots and pans.

The restaurant and bar overlook the beach and lagoon, with a long dining terrace on stilts in the sand. Between the reception and activities area and the boutique is a good size swimming pool, also facing the sea. A tennis court is across the street and a volleyball net is on the beach.

You'll never have to complain about having nothing to do at the Moorea Village, because something's almost always going on. Free activities include snorkeling equipment, tennis rackets and outrigger paddle canoes. A free boat trip to the *motu* in front of Club Med leaves the hotel daily at 9:30am and returns at 2:30pm, which gives you a lot of time to swim and snorkel.

The hotel organizes a barbecue picnic on their private motu on Thursdays, for 2.800 CFP per person. Each Saturday evening the pace steps up for the hotel's barbecue buffet, with a *pareo* show and fire dance around the pool for 3.600 CFP per person. Sunday is Tahitian *tamaara'a* day, when the *ahima'a* underground oven is opened to reveal the roast suckling pig, breadfruit, taro and other Tahitian foods. The bowls of food are served family style and you eat with your fingers in true island fashion. The price of 3.900 CFP also includes wine and coffee and a Tahitian dance show.

You can rent a bicycle at the reception desk for 600 CFP for 2 hours, 1.000 CFP for 4 hours, 1.200 CFP for 8 hours and 1.500 CFP for 24 hours.

The activities desk in the reception area, *Tel. 56.57.11*, has a complete list of exciting and unusual tours and excursions. Be sure to meet Tepua, the Tahitian name for an outgoing Canadian woman who sailed to Tahiti with her French husband and decided to stay. Now she has a nice Tahitian *tane* named Tautu who will create an original tattoo for you. See information under *Tattoos* in this chapter. Tepua is very well organized and can book the best excursions for you. Contact her at Tel. 689/27.73.91 or E-mail: tapuavahine@hotmail.com.

RESIDENCE LINAREVA, *B.P. 1 H, Haapiti, Moorea 98729. Tel. 689/ 55.05.65 (Bungalows); Tel. 689/55.05.66 (Restaurant); Fax 689/55.05.67; E-mail: linareva@mail.pf; www.linareva.com. Beside the lagoon at PK 34 in Haapiti, 21 kilometers (13 miles) from the ferry dock and 25 kilometers (15.5 miles) from the airport around the south coast. EP Rates for 2005: air-conditioned garden studio with kitchenette 11.500 CFP single, 13.500 CFP double; air-conditioned garden bungalow with kitchenette 10.500 CFP single, 12.500 CFP double; beachfront studio with kitchenette 12.500 CFP single, 14.500 CFP double; 15.500 CFP triple; beach bungalow with kitchenette 14.500 CFP single, 16.500 CFP double; 17.500 CFP triple; beachfront suite with kitchenette 19.500 CFP up to 4 people; air-conditioned beach bungalow with kitchen 19.500 CFP double, 23.500 triple, 24.500 CFP for 4 people and up to 26.500 CFP for 6 people; lagoon view villa with kitchen 24.500 CFP up to 4 people, up to 27.500 CFP for 7 people. Extra bed 1.300 CFP. No charge for children under 2 years. Rates include all taxes except a visitor's tax, which is 50 CFP per person a day for anyone 12 years and older. Minimum of 2 days' stay required. American Express, Mastercard, Visa.*

Eric Lussiez and Florian Pilloud, who own the very popular floating restaurant Linareva-Le Bateau, also have eight units in the gardens overlooking a beach and Moorea's sunset sea. This small family hotel has a 3-tiare rating from the Tahiti Tourist office and each unit is lovingly and tastefully decorated with a Polynesian touch. You have a choice of an air-conditioned garden studio, air-conditioned garden bungalow, beach studio, beach bungalow, beach suite, air-conditioned beach bungalow and lagoon view villa. There are king size, double and single beds, according to the unit chosen. All the kitchens are well equipped with stove and refrigerator, toaster and coffee maker, and cleaning products are provided daily. They also have a ceiling fan, television, safety box, library of books, private tiled bathroom with hot water shower, and a covered terrace. Daily maid service is provided, and you can even have breakfast delivered to your room. Bicycles, snorkeling gear, outrigger canoes, kayaks and barbecue grills are free for guest use, and there's a sunbathing deck beside the restaurant and bar. There is a public phone in the garden and an Internet service in the reception/boutique area, which you can pay for with a local phone card. If you have access to the Internet you can also take a virtual tour through the bungalows and studios. Eric and Florian are also building a family pension on a private motu in Fakarava. Read about it in the *Tuamotu* chapter.

FARE MATOTEA, *B.P. 111, Haapiti, Moorea* **98729**. *Tel. 689/56.14.36; Fax 689/56.32.54; E-mail: mtt@mail.pf; www.farematotea.com. Beside the lagoon at PK 28.7 in Haapiti, 25 kilometers (15.5 miles) from the ferry dock and 29 kilometers (18 miles) from the airport, by way of the south coast. EP Rates: 9.010 CFP bungalow for 1-4 people per day; 10.600 CFP for 5-6 people per day. Deposit required. Minimum stay 2 nights, discount for longer stays. Add 6% value added tax to room rates and 50 CFP per person per day for visitor's tax. A 10% value added tax is applicable to other services. American Express, Mastercard, Visa.*

Nine houses are placed rather far apart on a very spacious grassy property by the sea. Five of the *fares* contain one room with a double bed and two sofa beds, and the other four units each have two rooms with a double bed in each room. There is also a private kitchen. All units have private bathrooms with hot water. Linens are furnished. You'll need a car or scooter to get around. Outrigger paddle canoes are provided. The owners don't speak much English but they are nice and laid back in the South Seas style.

HAAPITI SURF LODGE, *Haapiti, Moorea 98729. Tel./Fax 689/56.40.36; cell 72.64.84; E-mail: haapitisurf@mail.pf. Located on the mountainside at PK 22.5 in Haapiti. Round-trip transfers included. EP Rates: 8.500 CFP single/ double for first night, with digressive rates for longer stays. Extra bed 1.500 CFP per day. No charge for child under 12 years. Add 6% value added tax to room rates and 50 CFP per person per day for visitor's tax. A 10% value added tax is applicable to other services. No credit cards.*

There are 4 modern white concrete bungalows on the mountainside overlooking the surfing pass of Haapiti, where the spinner dolphins play inside the lagoon year round and the humpback whales swim just beyond the reef between July and early November. Petero Tehuritaua, the young Tahitian owner, built his surfing lodge in 2001 and has everything well organized for his guests. Each clean and attractively furnished bungalow has a double bed, television, ceiling fan, equipped kitchen and a bathroom with hot water and a bathtub/shower, as well as a terrace with a dining table and individual barbecue grills. One of the units is a Honeymoon bungalow, built a little higher than the other three, offering a better view of the lagoon, the pass and the romantic tropical sunsets. Guests with children can put up a tent in the yard beside their bungalow. There is also an outdoor shower.

Petero provides his guests with kayaks and bicycles at no charge, and he will also take you on a tour of the island in his 4WD. There is a long pier on the beach side of his property, where you can fish and swim. You can buy fish from vendors on the road or bike to the nearest magasin store for food supplies, which is only a kilometer away. Meals can be provided on request for charter groups of 8-10 people. They will even provide laundry service for long-stay guests.

Economy
CAMPING NELSON, *B.P.1309, Papetoai, Moorea 98729. Tel./Fax 689/ 56.15.18; E-mail: campingnelson@mail.pf; www.camping-nelson.pf. Beside the lagoon at PK 27.1 in Haapiti, 27.1 kilometers (17 miles) from the airport and 31.1 kilometers (19.5 miles) from the ferry dock. EP Rates: Maire room 4.300 CFP single/double; Fare 4.500-4.700 CFP single/double; Aito room 5.800 CFP single/double; dormitory 1.600 CFP per person; camping 1.100 CFP per person per day. Discounts starting second night. Rates include all taxes. Mastercard, Visa.*

In addition to a spacious campground by the sea, this clean and well maintained backpacker's hostel offers 3 *fares* with a double bed and small terrace, 1 Fare Hoe with a double bed and terrace facing the lagoon, 1 Aito room with a double bed and small refrigerator, plus a terrace facing the lagoon, 15 Maire rooms with a double bed or two single beds, and 10 dormitory rooms with two single beds per room. Everyone shares the 7 toilets, 7 showers with cold water and the lavabos and there is also a toilet and shower for handicapped guests. The communal kitchen and dining room are adjacent to the reception area. This is a popular campground and backpacker's hangout, and the office has all the information on activities available on land or sea. Miranda and Delia Flohr, the two daughters of the owners, take care of the reception and helping guests. You can also rent a bicycle and kayak from them. A small beachfront snack on the premises opens at night and there are several restaurants, snacks, magasin stores and souvenir shops in the imme-diate neighborhood.

MOOREA CAMPING, *Haapiti, Moorea 98729. Tel. 689/56.14.47; Fax 689/56.30.22; E-mail: einui@hotmail.com. Beside lagoon at PK 27.5 in Haapiti, 500 meters from Club Med, 27.5 kilometers (16.7 miles) from the airport and 31.5 kilometers (19.2 miles) from the ferry dock. EP Rates: room 2.500-3.800 CFP single/double; bungalow 4.800–5.800 CFP single/double, 6.000-7.000 CFP triple, 6.500-7.500 CFP 4 people; bed in dormitory 1.200-1.800 CFP per day, camping 1.100-1.500 CFP person per day. Rates include all taxes. No credit cards.*

This is a gathering place for backpackers and campers and adventurers from all parts of the globe. There is a pretty white sand beach here and some organized activities are available at reduced rates. The simple accommodations are in need of updating, but that project remains on standby until the owners complete the land division of the property. There are four bungalows for two people, one bungalow for 3 people, and one bungalow for four people. Nine rooms have double or single beds, and there 4 berths in each of the seven dormitory rooms. A communal kitchen and dining room is built beside the beach, and the communal bathrooms have cold water. House linens are furnished but you bring your own soap and towel. You can camp in the gardens, under the trees or beside the beach. Bikes and kayaks can be rented at reception. Check-in is at 11am and checkout is at 9am.

HAAPITI CAMPING, *B.P. 41, Maharepa, Moorea 98728. Tel./Fax 689/ 56.43.02; cell 78.93.65; E-mail: tablesaw@mail.pf; www.haapiti.com. On mountainside at PK 23.5 in Haapiti, in front of the surfing pass. One-way transfer from ferry dock or airport 500 CFP per person. EP Rates: Camping 1.500 CFP per person for one night and 1.000 CFP starting 2nd night. Bungalow with 4 single beds 2.000 CFP per person for one night; bungalow/ dormitory for 10 people 2.500 CFP per person for one night or 5.000 CFP if there are only two people; bungalow for 4 people 6.000 CFP double for one night; bungalow for 3 people 9.000 CFP double for one night. All rates are reduced starting second night. Breakfast on request. Add 6% value added tax to room rates and 50 CFP per person per day for visitor's tax. A 10% value added tax is applicable to other services. No credit cards.*

Look for the Haapiti Camping sign beside the circle island road just past the Eglise de la Sainte Famille, the Catholic Church with twin towers. Forming a backdrop is the back side of the incredible shark's tooth peak of Mou'a Roa and the crenellated mountain range that resembles a fairy castle. Follow the dirt road into the valley until you see the campground and bungalow complex on the right. Mark Walker, an American expatriate who has lived in French Polynesia for many years, is a builder and wood worker who has bought 5,000 square meters (53,820 square feet) of grassy land in this valley. After building toilets and showers, Mark opened up his hidden paradise to campers in search of a quiet place to set up their tents. Then he began a building project that is still on going, and by the end of 2004 he plans to have 8 bungalows completed for guests. Each unit will be different and will include a Japanese style bungalow with bamboo and shoji screens. Other bungalows will be built around rocks and an *aito* tree (Australian pine) that Mark planted soon after he bought the property. Accommodations range from a bed in a dormitory to a studio for two or bungalows for four, six and even ten people.

The bungalows are very well thought out and creatively constructed. Among the units already completed when I visited in mid-2004 was a 10-person bungalow with screened windows, a kitchen with stove and refrigerator, private sleeping spaces, reading lights and two firemen-type poles that can be used by people sleeping in the loft beds. This building contains bathrooms with kohu wood and red cedar, plus bamboo towel racks. The facilities consist of 4 sinks, 4 showers and 4 toilets, half of them inside for the people in the big bungalow and the other half outside for the use of campers. Bring your own towels and soap. A big communal kitchen with a gravel floor can also serve as a sleeping area for four people. Mark has built beds with mosquito nets for this area. There are also beds in the communal lounge area and another studio with bathroom is located behind Mark's workshop. He rents tents for 1.500 CFP each, kayaks for 1.000 CFP, bicycles for 1.000 CFP and charges 1.000 CFP for a load of washing. There is a public phone on the premises, as well as a small sitting pool, a swing, volleyball and badminton nets and an area for playing petanque (French bowls). In addition to surfing the pass in Haapiti, Mark's guests enjoy hiking over the mountains and participating in the other activities that are available on Moorea.

NATURE HOUSE OF MOU'A ROA (La Maison de la Nature du Mou'a Roa), *B.P. 2018, Papetoai, Moorea 98729. Tel. 689/56.58.62; cell 72.62.58; Fax 689/56.40.47; E-mail: mouaroa@mail.pf. On mountainside at PK 21 in Vaianae Valley between Haapiti and Atiha. EP Rates: room 2.700 CFP. Room with breakfast and dinner 5.000 CFP; room with breakfast, lunch and dinner 6.500 CFP. Add 50 CFP per person per day for visitor's tax. A 10% value added tax is applicable to other services. No credit cards.*

Whether you spend a day, a weekend or a week at this agricultural farm hidden in the valley of Vaianae at the foot of Mou'a Roa Mountain, you will have various choices of how to experience a «green» vacation. You will sleep in a big colonial style house that contains 9 bedrooms with 3 or 6 beds in each room, plus a living room, dining room, library and video room, an activities room, kitchen and four bathrooms. Electricity is generated by renewable energy including solar panels, and all the fruits and vegetables grown on the farm are biologic. All meals feature Polynesian food made from fresh local products, including shrimp from the nearby river.

This lodging is owned by Maite Buisson and Bernard Genton, who enjoy a back-to-nature lifestyle that they willingly share with the children and adults who visit. A half-day of activities, sports and nature includes an introduction to archery, trekking and swimming, river canyoning and practice in climbing on an artificial wall. Maite takes care of the food preparation and Bernard will guide you on hiking and camping excursions. Special programs are also available for children during their school vacations.

Superior
FARE ARANA, *B.P. 3351, Temae, Moorea 98729. Tel./Fax 689/56.44.03; E-mail: patcoucuret@mail.pf. On mountainside at PK 19.5 in Atiha, 15 minutes from the ferry dock and 20 minutes from the airport. EP Rates: bungalow 16.900 CFP single/double; add 2.000 CFP for third adult and 1.000 CFP if third party is a child. Reduced rates for long stays. Breakfast on request 1.500 CFP per person. Rates include taxes. No credit cards.*

A pack of friendly dogs welcomes you to the "beach in the sky" and if you don't see hosts Patrice and Nathalie Coucuret right away, then you can ring the bell at their outdoor flower decorated reception area at the bottom of the spacious walkway covered with soft white sand. This happy French couple will make you feel at home before you even have a chance to visit their fabulous place. Fare Arana is built high on a hillside overlooking Avarapa Bay, offering panoramic views of the ever-changing colors of the lagoon and ocean. This is truly a place to relax in an elegant hammock under the shade of a *fare potée* or sunbathe on a *chaise longue* beside the swimming pool. The verdant gardens are filled with fruit trees and flowers, providing the perfect setting for three thatched roof bungalows of high quality and craftsmanship. Each two-level concrete bungalow is air-conditioned and has 70 square meters (753 square feet) of living space. There are two double beds or one or two single beds with mosquito nets, plus a private bathroom with hot water shower, a living room with television, ceiling fan, bamboo and teak furniture, and screened windows and doors. There is a dining table with chairs in the living/dining room, or you can eat at the table on the terrace, adjacent to the well-equipped kitchen. An open sundeck is furnished with comfortable lounge chairs and steps lead down to the gardens and pool area.

Unless you want to just stay put in one place, it would be best to rent a car, as this pension is off the beaten track. I met some people there who own a restaurant in New Zealand and they hadn't gone anywhere since they arrived four days earlier. They were perfectly content to lie around the pool and read while their son played in the pool with a couple of Tahitian boys. Two kayaks are provided free for guests who want to explore the lagoon.

AFAREAITU TO VAIARE
Moderate
TE ORA HAU, *B.P. 4005, Maharepa, Moorea 98728. Tel./Fax 689/ 56.35.35; cell 77.48.22; E-mail: pensionteorahau@mail.pf; www.teorahau.com. Beside lagoon at PK 8.2 in Afareaitu, facing Motu Ahi, 4.2 kilometers (2.6 miles) from the Vaiare ferry dock and 8.2 kilometers (5 miles) from the airport.*

EP Rates: Fare Ata 10.000 CFP single/double, and 12.500 CFP for 4 people; Fare Hina and Fare Manu 20.000 CFP for 4 people. Add 6% value added tax to room rates and 50 CFP per person per day for visitor's tax. No credit cards.

You'll sleep to the sounds of the ocean in this environment that resembles that of the Tuamotu Islands, complete with a white sand beach, sea breezes blowing through the pandanus trees, and a motu islet right in front of you. In the distance, however, you can clearly see the island of Tahiti with its mountains and houses. Your Polynesian hostess, Heipua Bordes, has three large wooden bungalows or *fares* that are completely equipped with a kitchen, washing machine and bathroom with hot water shower. Fare Ata is suitable for two adults and two children. Fare Hina is a one-story bungalow and Fare Manu has two levels, and both units can accommodate up to six people. All three bungalows are clean, modern and very tastefully decorated and the bed linens are changed every three days. Barbecue grills and kayaks are provided free of charge for guests. Heipua is well versed in the culture and legends of Polynesia and she has taught her cleaning staff to speak a little English. No meals are provided, but you can shop for groceries at Champion Fare Toa, which is 1.7 miles from the pension. Cars, scooters and bicycles can be rented at the nearby ferry dock in Vaiare.

Other Family Pensions, Guest Houses, Surf Lodges, Dormitories & Camp Sites

Motu Temae Bed and Breakfast Fare KiRiHai, *Tel. 689/56.13.41*. 1 bungalow with breakfast for 10.000 CFP single/double beside beach on Temae Motu near airport. Reduced rates after one night. Dinner on request. "Cool" setting in artists' home and English is spoken.

Fare Piti Vacation Home, *689/Tel.56.46.77; E-mail: k.wong@mail.pf*. On mountainside at PK 8.7 in Pao Pao Valley, up road at the Garage Renault sign, between Station Mobil and Restaurant Alfredo's. When the Hotel Bali Hai closed in 2001 Luc and Kristin Wong bought one of the hotel's bungalows plus the roof from the pool bar, and now have two Polynesian style bungalows joined by an open-air kitchen and dining area. There are 3 bedrooms including an air-conditioned room with a private balcony, with sleeping accommodations for 6 people on 2 queen size beds and a double bed. There is a full kitchen with all the equipment and table settings, a dining area, full bathroom, washer-dryer and wrap-around lanai with views of Cook's Bay. The cost of $1,100 per week includes all taxes and transfers from airport or ferryboat dock.

Aito Pension, *Tel./Fax 689/56.45.52, cell 20.82.84*. 4 rooms with or without kitchenette beside lagoon in Pihaena, from 5.500 CFP to 12.500 CFP single/double. English spoken. **Fare Oa Oa Bed & Breakfast**, *Tel./Fax 689/ 56.25.17; E-mail: fareoaoa@magicmoorea.com; www.fareoaoa.com*. 4 rooms and dormitory with shared bathroom and kitchen on mountainside in Pihaena, from 2.500 CFP to 4.500 CFP. English spoken. **Chez Francine**, *Tel. 689/56.13.24*. 1 room with or without kitchenette in Opunohu Bay, from 6.500 CFP to 12.500 CFP single/double. English spoken.

Pension Marie-Lou, *Tel. 689/72.93.15; Fax 689/56.27.11; E-mail: bgml@mail.pf.* 1 self-sufficient guesthouse with 2 bedrooms in Papetoai village, 12.000 CFP single/double. Meals and laundry on request. She speaks good English. **Pension Anahoa**, *Tel. 56.35.32; www.pension-anahoa.com.* 2 upscale wooden bungalows on beach at PK 25 in Tiahura Village before Club Med area, for 26.500 CFP per day, including breakfast. Restaurant on premises serves snacks for lunch and set dinner menu.

Moorea Fare Auti Ura, *Tel. 689/56.14.47.* 6 bungalows with kitchens on mountainside at PK 27, across road from Moorea Camping, for 7.000 CFP. Mastercard, Visa. **Pension Teataura**, *Tel. 689/56.22.01.* 5 simply furnished studios with kitchenettes behind Chez Capo Restaurant in Haapiti, for 9.000 CFP single/double 1st night and 7.000 CFP 2nd night. Monthly rental 70.000 CFP.

Fare Manuia, *Tel. 689/56.26.17.* 6 fares in garden and on beach at PK 30 in Haapiti, from 10.200-16.000 CFP for 4-6 people per day. English spoken. **Fare Chez Edith**, *Tel. 689/56.35.34.* 2 garden bungalows and 2 beach bungalows beside lagoon at PK 32.5 in Varari, starting at 13.000 CFP double. **Tarariki Village**, *Tel. 689/55.21.05; E-mail: pensiontarariki@mail.pf.* 6 rustic bungalows, tree houses and 2 dormitories beside beach in Vaianae, near surfing pass. Dorm 1.700-2.600 CFP, room 2.300-3.200 CFP, bungalow 5.500-7.500 CFP single/double. **Fare Aute**, *Tel. 689/56.45.19/78.23.34.* 2 well-equipped bungalows for 4 or 6 people include kitchens, TV and washing machine, on the white sand beach at PK 16.2 in Atiha, for 10.700 CFP single/double. No English. **Chez Pauline**, *Tel. 689/56.11.26.* 5 rooms in an old colonial style wooden house at PK 9.8 in Afareaitu village, 4.000 CFP single/5.500 CFP double.

For a complete list of lodgings, contact **Tahiti Tourisme** at *Tel. 689/50.57.00, Fax 689/43.66.19, E-mail: tahiti-tourisme@mail.pf; www.tahiti-tourisme.pf.* You can also check out the website for **Moorea Visitors Bureau**: *www.gomoorea.com.* I will be the Forum Moderator and supply the site with information.

Where to Eat
AIRPORT & MOTU TEMAE
Deluxe

SOFITEL IA ORA MOOREA, *Tel. 55.03.55. La Perouse Restaurant is open daily for breakfast and dinner and Le Molokai Restaurant and Bar on the beach is open daily for lunch. All credit cards.*

The Continental breakfast at **La Perouse Restaurant** is 1.900 CFP and an American breakfast is 2.400 CFP. The dinner menu includes starter courses for

1.600 CFP, the main course for 2.500 CFP and desserts for 1.100 CFP. A 3-course dinner menu du jour is 5.050 CFP and a child's 3-course meal is 1.300 CFP. Theme nights include an Italian buffet on Monday for 5.000 CFP, a Round the World buffet on Tuesday for 5.000 CFP, a Seafood buffet on Thursday for 6.430 CFP and a Polynesian buffet on Saturday for 5.380 CFP. The Saturday night buffet is accompanied by a Polynesian dance show.

Lunch at **Le Molokai Restaurant** is served daily between 12-3pm. The starter course includes *poisson cru*, carpaccio of tuna or Molokai salad for 1.450 CFP each. Burgers and fries are 1.580 CFP, grilled fish and meats are 1.990 CFP, a salad bar and grillade is 2.990 CFP, and specials such as fish and chips are served each day for about 2.300 CFP. Desserts are 880-990 CFP and wines are priced from 1.570 to 7.140 CFP. A buffet lunch is served each Sunday noon for 3.650 CFP.

COOK'S BAY AREA: MAHAREPA TO PAOPAO
Deluxe
MOOREA PEARL RESORT & SPA, *Tel. 55.17.50. Mahanai Restaurant is open daily for breakfast, lunch and dinner. Matiehani Restaurant is open for dinner. Autera'a Bar & Terrasse serves lunch and cocktails. All credit cards.*

The **Mahanai Restaurant** opens onto the view of the swimming pool, lagoon and overwater bungalows. A Continental breakfast is 2.000 CFP and a full American breakfast is 2.500 CFP. A set luncheon menu is 3.200 CFP and the set dinner menu is 5.400 CFP. A Barbecue buffet is held each Wednesday night for 5.900 CFP, followed by a Polynesian dance show, and a Seafood buffet and dance show takes place each Saturday night, for 7.100 CFP per person.

You can also eat your lunch while sitting at the spacious **Autera'a Bar & Terrasse** facing the pool. A choice of menus allows you to eat between 12 and 2pm or between 12 and 4:30pm. Interesting selections include a panini or crostini for 950 CFP, a pita sandwich or Caesar salad with grilled chicken for 1.450 CFP, a club sandwich for 1.600 CFP, a Moorea salad with shrimp and pineapple for 1.650 CFP, burgers and fries for 1.550 CFP up, and a Polynesian plate for 2.100 CFP, which includes sashimi, tuna tartare, poisson cru and Nems (spring rolls).

Matiehani is the name of the air-conditioned restaurant that opened in September 2004. This gourmet restaurant serves dinner only and seats just a dozen people.

HONU ITI, *Tel. 56.19.84, PK 8, beside Cook's Bay, Pao Pao. Mastercard, Visa. Open daily 11:30am-2pm and 6-9:30pm. Courtesy shuttle.*

In 1974 Roger Igual won France's most prestigious diploma for chefs—the Concours National de la Poêle d'Or. That same year he brought his cooking skills to Tahiti, and since 1991 Roger has been serving his gourmet specialties to Moorea diners. The overwater terrace of his Honu Iti restaurant provides a privileged setting, where you can gaze at the romantic scenery of Cook's Bay, bordered by pineapple fields and fairy castle mountains, while enjoying some of the island's finest French cuisine. In the evening you can feed the rays and fish that swim close to the terrace, hoping for handouts.

A starter course that is guaranteed to please is the snails in puff pastry, for 1.800 CFP. If you're having a main course then perhaps you'd like to share this first course with your dining partner. The sauce for this dish is the best on the island. The French onion soup is also good and costs 1.400 CFP, and an appetizer of warm goat cheese on toast is 1.600 CFP. Fish and seafood specialties are priced from 2.600-3.200 CFP, and include a mixed seafood casserole for 2.900 CFP and scallops served with leeks for 3.200 CFP. Roger's famous Tournedos Rossini (3.400 CFP) are the very best, which is beef tenderloin with goose liver in Madeira sauce. His meat and poultry dishes are priced from 2.600 to 3.500 CFP, and include *magret de canard* and *foie gras* for 3.500 CFP. Desserts are 1.200 to 1.400 CFP and include the chef's special apple pie with ice cream, as well as homemade sorbets and Roger's famous profiteroles.

The red wines are priced from 3.200 to 7.300 CFP, the white wines are 3.400 to 4.900 CFP, and the rosé wines are 1.800 to 3.500 CFP. The *grands crus* wines are 5.700 to 47.000 CFP. Free transportation is provided from Sheraton Moorea Lagoon, Moorea Pearl Resort, Hotel Kaveka and Club Bali Hai.

Superior
LE MAHOGANY, *Tel. 56.39.73, PK 5, mountainside, Maharepa. Mastercard, Visa. Open 11am-2:30pm and 6-9:30pm. Closed Wednesday. Pick-up service available.*

This indoor-outdoor restaurant is located beside the Moorea gym, Moorea's only health club, and when coming from the ferry dock or airport this will be the first restaurant you'll see. A street-side chalkboard lists the daily specials, which may be fresh sautéed duck foie gras with apples for 2.750 CFP, couscous royal for 1.950 CFP, or grilled lobster for 3.950 CFP. In addition to a varied menu of French cuisine, they also serve a few Chinese dishes, including good chow mein for 1.250 CFP or chow mein special with shrimp for 1.850 CFP. Their sashimi (1.550 CFP) is made with fresh red tuna and presented over a bed of chopped cabbage, served with an excellent sauce. The shrimp curry with coconut sauce (2.250 CFP) is highly recommended. The soups and salads are priced from 950 to 2.150 CFP; seafood dishes are 1.750 to 2.450 CFP and meat dishes cost between 1.950 and 2.850 CFP. Burgers and fries for 950 CFP are served at lunchtime, along with a selection of salads from 600 to 1.100 CFP, and grilled rib eye steak for 1.650 CFP.

The ambience in this popular restaurant is laid back and friendly and you should reserve for dinner. They provide free transportation from the hotels, but don't be in a hurry when you come here, because the service is rather slow, with only two waitresses taking care of a large group of diners.

LE COCOTIER, *Tel. 56.12.10, PK 4.7, mountainside, Maharepa. Diners, Visa. Open daily 11:30am-2pm and 6:30-9pm. Free pick-up service provided between Sofitel Ia Ora and Sheraton.*

Pascal Mathieu, the manager and chef, has turned this small restaurant into one of the best dining spots on the island, with a varied menu of well prepared dishes that are guaranteed to please even the most discerning guest. Pascal's partner, François, will seat you according to your request, in the open-air restaurant, on the terrace, where there is a barbecue grill, or inside the air-conditioned dining room with 35 seats.

The menu lists the classic French dishes, with starter courses from 750 to 2.100 CFP, fish choices from 2.150 to 2.350 CFP, meats from 2.050 to 2.950 CFP, and desserts from 850 to 1.450 CFP. A chalkboard on the wall lists the chef's suggestions of the day, which may be a Polynesian plate for 1.850 CFP, papio fish (pompano) with dill sauce for 2.350 CFP, filet of hoki fish from New Zealand for 2.350 CFP, *calamars armoricaine* for 2.950 CFP, or *St. Jacques au calvados* for 2.950 CFP. The choices of wines range from 1.760 CFP to 19.100 CFP and include a few of the *grands crus* from the best vineyards of France. Some of Pascal's regular clientele are French doctors and schoolteachers living on Moorea, who meet here frequently to savor his cuisine. He reveals some of his recipes in his book on *La Cuisine Tahitienne*, published in French and English. A musical duo performs each Wednesday night and a theme night is presented once a month, with a special menu and entertainment.

LES NOUVEAUX MONDES, *Tel. 56.44.24, lesnouveauxmondesmoorea@yahoo.fr. PK 7.4, mountainside in Cook's Bay. Mastercard, Visa. Open daily 11am-2pm and 6-10pm. Free pick-up service available.*

This was formerly Caprice des Iles and had been closed for a couple of years when Jean Santa Maria, a Spanish man, bought it and opened the New Worlds for the pleasure of Moorea's gourmet diners. This includes not only a restaurant, but also a boutique shop with a selection of curios, food items, vintage wines, liqueurs, champagnes, gifts, souvenir items, pareos and pearls.

The menu features French and Tahitian cuisine, with specials such as candied leg of lamb in garlic and herbs, kidney and calf sweetbreads in Madera sauce, frog legs in Provençal sauce, scallop and shrimp kebab, coq au vin, mussels and fries, and bouillabaisse with seafood and shellfish. Appetizers are priced from 1.650 to 1.800 CFP, seafood is 2.100 to 2.800 CFP, flamed lobster with cognac is 3.900 CFP, meat choices range from 1.900 to 3.400 CFP and an extra charge is made for your choice of sauce, which may be blue cheese, red wine, Hollandaise, buttery garlic cream, or ginger sauce. Desserts are 800 to 1.450 CFP, a selection of cheese is 1.850 CFP and French wines are priced between 1.850 and 8.650 CFP per bottle. Wine by the glass is also available.

A new snack section beside the road has a grill where you can order a hamburger or a Japanese yakitori brochette.

ALFREDO'S, *Tel. 56.17.71, VHF Channel 69; E-mail: chrismar@mail.pf; www.alfredosofmoorea.com. PK 8.5, mountainside, Cook's Bay, Pao Pao Mastercard, Visa. Open daily 11am-2:30pm and 5:30-9:30pm. Pick-up service available.*

This indoor-outdoor restaurant can seat 100 and on Thursday and Sunday evenings it is often filled with American tourists and other lively people who come for "party night". This is when my Scottish neighbor, Ron Falconer, plays his body harp and harmonica and sings songs from the 1960s and 1970s, plus a few Scottish ballads. As the evening progresses the show really gets "Rollin' on the River" and you can also get up and sing with Ron if you feel in the mood. Or you can dance the jitterbug or rock 'n roll. Some people enjoy themselves so much that they come back for dinner almost every night during their week's stay.

I go here occasionally for the fun, ambiance and music and to have a good giggle with owner Christian Boucheron, a Frenchman who lived in the States for 21 years. Christian and his guests enjoy joking together and his dedicated team offers friendly service. Some people love the food and others find it only so-so, but they enjoy the music and atmosphere. The menu gives you a choice of Italian or French cuisine. For 500 CFP you can order garlic bread to nibble on while you sip your cocktail, beer or glass of wine. Appetizers start at 1.050 CFP and a fresh spinach salad with warm bacon dressing costs 1.650 CFP. The pasta dishes are priced from 1.650 CFP to 2.150 CFP and there is a choice of 5 pizzas for 1.550 to 1.650 CFP. Seafood is 2.100 to 2.650 CFP and meats are 2.150 to 2.950 CFP, including my favorite, escalope de veau Milanaise for 2.750 CFP. This is a breaded veal scallop with a tomato-garlic sauce and is served with spaghetti, green beans and carrots, as are most of the dishes. There is also osso bucco for 2.950 CFP. The special dishes include fettuccine Alfredo's for 3.250 CFP and grilled beef tenderloin for 3.850 CFP. A 3-course tourist menu is 4.900 CFP. The wine list includes half-bottles of Bordeaux.

Be sure to reserve for Thursday and Sunday evenings. Transportation is provided from the hotels, all the way from the Sofitel Ia Ora to the Moorea Village. A sign in the van states in English that the transfer is free but tips are expected.

Moderate to Superior

LE SUD, *Tel. 56.42.95/71.17.49; E-mail: lesud.moorea@mail.pf. PK 5.5, seaside on Cook's Bay, Maharepa. Mastercard, Visa. Open for lunch 11:30am-2pm and for dinner 6:30-9pm. Closed Sunday night and all day Monday.*

This restaurant is catty-corner across the road from the shopping center where the Banque Socredo and the post office are located. Françoise and Dominique Bandol feature cuisine from the South of France, with such specialties as *Aïoli Provençal, Bourride Sètoise, Confit d'Agneau* and *Jarret de Porc Braisé*, priced from 1.700 to 2.850 CFP. You can add homemade olive oils that contain garlic and spices or hot peppers. The salads are 1.450 to 2.250 CFP and starter courses are 1.350 to 2.250 CFP. The mahi mahi with leek sauce is 2.300 CFP, shrimp à la Provençale is 2.350 CFP, a small bouillabaisse is 2.500 CFP and seafood paella for two people is 5.900 CFP. Desserts are priced from 550 to 1.050 CFP and Bordeaux wines are 2.450 to 5.000 CFP. Pickup service is available to Moorea Pearl Resort and they will split the cost of a taxi for transfers from other hotels.

Moderate
    MARIA TAPAS, *Tel. 55.01.70; E-mail: mariatapas@mail.pf, is a "cyberbodega" in the Kikipa Center at PK 6 in Maharepa. Mastercard, Visa. Open Monday through Wednesday from 8:30am to 11pm, and Thursday through Friday from 8:30am to 1am. Closed Saturday noon and all day Sunday. Open Saturday night until 1am. Meals served until 9:30pm during week and until 11pm on Thursday, Friday and Saturday. Free transportation provided for lunch or dinner.*

    This combination restaurant, snack, bar and cybercafé serves salads from 400 to 1.500 CFP and burgers from 1.100 to 1.400 CFP. Tex-Mex specialties include chicken, fish or beef tacos for 1.000 CFP, enchiladas for 1.200 CFP, chicken wings for 1.200 CFP, and Mexican chicken nuggets for 1.400 CFP, accompanied by guacamole, crème fraiche and green salad. You can order barbecue from the grill for 1.600-1.900 CFP, or cook your own meat with Fondue Bourguignonne for 2.000 CFP, or Fondue Bressane chicken for 2.000 CFP. The beer menu includes 30 choices from all over the world. There is live musical entertainment on Thursday nights and half-price beer is served during Happy Hour between 6-7pm each Thursday and Friday. A special theme evening is held on the second Saturday of each month when Herenui, the new owner of Maria Tapas, performs his spectacular fire dancing. Herenui was Tahiti's first Carnival King and a former Tiki Theatre Village dancer. There are three computers in the cybercafé, including one Macintosh, plus a scanner and printing facilities. Internet charges are 250 CFP for 15 minutes.
    HOTEL KAVEKA RESTAURANT, *Tel. 56.50.50, PK 7, Maharepa. All credit cards. Open daily for breakfast, lunch and dinner.*
    This spacious overwater restaurant has a fantastic view of Cook's Bay and the peaked mountains that fringe the mirror-like waters of the bay and lagoon. This is an especially agreeable place to cool off during the hot tropical summers, while enjoying a glass of cold beer or a good meal prepared by one or more of the three chefs in the kitchen.
    An American breakfast buffet is 1.500 CFP and with a hot plate the cost is 2.000 CFP. A Continental breakfast of coffee, tea or chocolate, plus bread, butter and jam, is 750 CFP. The luncheon and dinner menu includes an

appealing list of appetizers, priced from 500 to 1.000 CFP, and salad plates for 1.800 CFP. Beef, bacon, chicken or Mahi Mahi burgers and fries are 1.200 CFP and sandwiches on baguette bread are 750 CFP, with choices including tuna, chicken, ham, beef, egg, and BLT (bacon, lettuce and tomato). An order of nachos is 800 CFP. You can order shrimp cocktail for 950 CFP, onion soup for 950 CFP, fish soup for 1.050 CFP, and a choice of 15 pizzas from 1.150 to 1.500 CFP. The fish and seafood dishes are 1.100 to 2.400 CFP, the poultry choices are 1.800 to 2.200 CFP, the beef dishes are 2.000 to 2.300 CFP, and pasta is 1.600 CFP. A new addition to the menu is Chinese food, priced from 1.200 to 1.800 CFP per dish. Desserts include a cheese plate for 900 CFP, a banana split for 900 CFP, and chocolate mousse for 1.000 CFP. Carlo Rossi white wine is 350 CFP for a glass or 1.300 CFP for a carafe, and bottled red wine is 1.300 to 6.000 CFP. A child's menu with dessert is 1.300 CFP.

ALLO-PIZZA, *Tel. 56.18.22, is on the mountainside at PK 7.8 in Pao Pao, across the road from the French gendarmerie. Open Tuesday through Saturday from 11am to 2pm and from 5 to 9pm. Closed all day Sunday and Monday.*

You have a choice of 40 thin crust pizzas cooked in a wood burning pizza oven, priced from 900 to 1.900 CFP. These include Regina, Chorizo, Vegetarian, Hawaiian, Moorea, Primavera, Armenian and much more. Each pizza offers 8 delicious slices. Be sure to try the homemade chocolate mousse and freshly baked bread. You can eat at one of the few tables provided on a small terrace or take it to your room. They will also deliver to your hotel.

BLUE PINEAPPLE (l'ananas bleu), *Tel. 56.12.06. Club Bali Hai Bar, Pao Pao. Mastercard, Visa. Open daily 7am-3pm.*

Be sure to treat yourself to breakfast, lunch or a snack at this friendly waterside restaurant and enjoy the pleasure of the incomparable view of Cook's Bay, yachts in the harbor and pineapple fields on jagged mountain slopes across the bay. I recommend the hamburgers with fries for 800 CFP, cheeseburger with fries for 900 CFP, fishburger and fries for 1.350 CFP, and the *poisson cru* for 1.250 CFP. For lunch Matahi serves grilled fish or beef curry for 1.700 CFP or shrimp curry for 1.980 CFP. You can order soft drinks, juice, a milkshake and even a banana split. Beer is 450-460 CFP and a glass of red wine is 550 CFP.

I also like to eat here on Sunday mornings or holidays, when owner Matahai Hunter prepares a typical Tahitian breakfast of marinated fish with coconut milk, grilled fish, *taioro* (sour coconut sauce with onions), *firi firi* (a figure 8 donut), and coffee flavored with vanilla and sweetened with coconut milk and sugar. If that sounds too heavy for your appetite, perhaps you'll prefer a glass of fresh pineapple juice for 500 CFP. You can also order pancakes for 650 CFP, eggs with ham or bacon or a Spanish omelets for 850 CFP, or steak and eggs for 1.400 CFP.

CHEZ JEAN-PIERRE, *Tel. 56.18.51, PK 9, beside the quay in Cook's Bay, Pao Pao. Mastercard, Visa. Open 11am-2:30pm and 6-9:30pm. Closed Monday night, all day Wednesday and Sunday noon.*

The specialty here is Chinese food, quickly prepared and served in their two dining rooms adjacent to the fishing boat dock at Cook's Bay. Most of the dishes are priced around 1.350-1.550 CFP, and the shrimp specialties are 1.950 CFP. Each Saturday night Jean-Pierre Tetuanui, who is Tahitian with a Chinese wife, Micheline, serves succulent suckling pig roasted to a crisp, accompanied by a bowl of coconut milk. This is good and very popular with local residents, so it is best to get there early.

Economy to Moderate
CARAMÉLINE, *Tel. 56.15.88, PK 5, Maharepa, in shopping center on mountain side, along with Socredo Banque and the post office. Mastercard, Visa. Open daily 7am-5pm.*

Here is the ideal place to sit and write your post cards while enjoying something good to eat and drink. You can exchange your dollars at the bank, buy post cards at Kina newsstand, write them at Caraméline and mail them at the post office, all in the same small center.

Breakfast is available all day at this popular snack and pastry shop. A Continental breakfast is 990 CFP, an American breakfast is 1.550 CFP, and a Tahitian breakfast that includes fish and coconut milk is 1.780 CFP. In addition to a tempting selection of ham and cheese croissants, quiches and pizzas, you may want to try a *pain bagnat* filled with chicken, tuna or ham for 650 CFP. A hot dog is 330 CFP, a cheeseburger is 520 CFP, crêpes are priced from 320 to 1.300 CFP, salads are 450 to 830 CFP, and *poisson cru* with coconut milk is 950 CFP. After 11am they serve a daily special for 1.300 to 1.600 CFP, which may be steak and fries, garlic shrimp or mahi mahi with rice or fries. Along with fresh fruit juices, fresh limeade and Hinano beer, you will also have a good choice of ice creams, 25 flavors of milkshakes for 480 CFP, and a banana split or pineapple split for 720 CFP. Don't forget to check out the pastry counter inside.

Economy
JULES ET CLAUDINE, *PK 9, beside the quay and fish market in Cook's Bay, Pao Pao. No credit cards. Closed Sunday.*

This is a stationary *roulotte* where you can order your *casse-croûte*, *poisson cru, steak-frites*, chow mein or other quickly prepared foods, and sit at the tables in the courtyard of Te Fare Hotu Rau, the Fish Cooperative. Or you can take it with you. The servings are generous and you can eat for 1.200-1.500 CFP. The quality of the food varies, but is usually good.

SNACK ROTUI, *Tel. 56.18.16, PK 9.5, beside Cook's Bay, just after Are's Supermarket in Pao Pao. No credit cards. Closed Monday.*

You can sit on a stool at the sheltered counter, eat at one of the tables in back or pick up a sandwich and soft drink, a *poisson cru*, chow mein, or other prepared Chinese dishes served with rice for 700 CFP. Don't resist having a piece of yummy chocolate cake at this popular fast food snack. The tuna *casse-croûtes* for 180 CFP and the big nems or spring rolls for 150 CFP are also good here, and you'll have a good view of the sailboats anchored in Cook's Bay.

PAOPAO TO HAAPITI
Deluxe
SHERATON MOOREA LAGOON RESORT & SPA, *Tel. 55.11.11. Arii Vahine Restaurant serves breakfast and dinner daily and lunch is served at Rotui Pool Bar & Grill. Snacks and cocktails are available in the Eimeo Lounge Bar. All major credit cards.*

In the **Arii Vahine Restaurant** an American breakfast buffet is 2.548 CFP. The dinner menu includes French onion soup for 1.000 CFP, starter courses from 1.500-1.800 CFP, fresh homemade pasta and risotto from 1.900-2.100 CFP, fish dishes from 2.300-2.950 CFP and meats from 2.400-3.400 CFP. These may include pan seared veal with white wine sauce for 2.400 CFP, roast duck breast with lemon and honey sauce for 2.900 CFP, pan-fried shrimp with white butter served in a pineapple for 2.950 CFP or roasted rack of lamb with a garlic cream sauce for 2.900 CFP. A vegetarian dish is also available. A Mediterranean buffet is presented each Tuesday evening for 6.000 CFP, which includes a Polynesian dance show. A special Seafood Buffet on Saturday night is 7.000 CFP per person, and also includes a traditional dance show. A musical trio plays around the **Eimeo Bar** at sunset (6-7pm) and in the restaurant every night except Tuesday and Saturday. Happy Hour also takes place at sunset, with two drinks for the price of one.

Rotui Pool Bar & Grill serves lunch daily from 11:30am to 3pm, and you dine under a beach umbrella to shade you from the tropical sun. The choices include salads, burgers, poisson cru, sashimi and grilled steaks. Between 3-5pm you can order snacks at the Rotui Bar, along with a frosty pression of Hinano beer, milkshakes and other drinks and cocktails. This same snack menu is available upstairs at the Eimeo Lounge Bar between 5-9pm. It includes assorted vegetables with a dip for 750 CFP, guacamole for 750 CFP, quiche for 950 CFP, an Asian platter of spring rolls, samoussas and pork dumplings for 1.000 CFP, hamburger with fries for 1.350 CFP, pizzas for 1.300-1.500 CFP, and a Caesar salad with grilled chicken breast for 1.500 CFP.

INTERCONTINENTAL RESORT MOOREA, *Tel. 55.19.19. Fare Hana Restaurant is open daily for breakfast and lunch and Fare Nui Restaurant is open daily for dinner. All credit cards.*

An Express breakfast for 1.130 CFP is served for early risers and departures in the **Fare Hana Restaurant** beside the swimming pool. A Continental breakfast from the cold buffet is 2.225 CFP and the full buffet or American breakfast is 2.710 CFP. Breakfast delivered by outrigger canoe to guests in overwater bungalows is 5.560 CFP per person. Luncheon choices include small or large portions of Caesar salad with a choice of grilled chicken, shrimp or tuna, from 1.415-1.870 CFP. Poisson cru or sashimi costs 1.750 CFP, sushi and medium cooked tuna is 1.800-3.500 CFP, a shrimp and pineapple salad is 2.050 CFP, parrot fish filet is 2.320 CFP, sautéed Moorea shrimp is 2.650 CFP, and a grilled steak is 2.650 CFP. Quiche is served for 1.340 CFP a slice, pizzas are 1.430-1.650 CFP, a steak sandwich is 1.175 CFP and a hamburger with fries is 1.175 CFP. The set 3-course luncheon menu is 4.020 CFP. A Sunday Buffet lunch is served in the Fare Hana to the tune of a musical trio.

Fare Nui Restaurant features gourmet à la carte dining, as well as a fixed 3-course dinner menu, which is priced at 5.995 CFP. Each Monday a buffet of Tahitian and seafood specialties is served and the Mamas of Moorea dance. The Polynesian Night dinner and show costs 6.225 CFP. Barbecue Night is held each Wednesday beside the swimming pool, accompanied by a Tahitian dance show, and it is also 6.225 CFP. The *Soirée Merveilleuse* on Saturday evening is a gastronomic buffet featuring a variety of fresh seafood, usually served on the beach under the stars and tropical moon. A Tahitian dance group performs on a stage set between two graceful coconut trees. This costs 7.680 CFP.

Moderate to Superior
   AITO RESTAURANT, *Tel. 56.45.52, cell 20.82.84. Beside lagoon at PK 13.1 between Cook's Bay and Opunohu Bay. Lunch and dinner served daily. Mastercard, Visa.*

   In the third edition of this book I wrote that every island needs a funky beach-shack restaurant where you can eat deliciously prepared fish served by a "boozy" Corsican, and that Jean-Baptiste Cipriani and his Aito Restaurant play this role in Moorea. Since then the restaurant has been cleaned up and improved, with a new entrance that is now visible from the small parking area. Now you don't have to walk through the beauty parlor to get to the restaurant, as the beauty parlor no longer exists. Jean-Baptiste still drinks his 10 glasses of scotch and Coke every day, and Vanina, his lovely lady, still makes the best carpaccio of tuna on the island. This restaurant has become my favorite hangout, as well as a "must" place to visit again and again for other residents and visitors, many of whom have read about the "funky" restaurant on the Internet Tahiti forums or in the *Tahiti Beach Press*. Everyone I have ever taken here just loved the setting, the food and Jean-Baptiste, who is a real character.

   Aito Restaurant is a thatch-covered terrace at the edge of the lagoon. Tall Australian pines (*aito* in Tahitian) shade the small beach and you may even see a wire basket of *pahua* (reef clams) or rock lobsters sitting in the shallow edge of the lagoon. A couple of big *aito* trees grow right through the floor and sagging palm-frond ceiling of the restaurant, and a series of Plexiglas windows can be propped open with a stick so you can enjoy the fresh ocean breezes.

This is a most delightful place to be on a hot summer's day, when you can feel the tradewinds blowing, gaze across the sparkling lagoon to the white line of spume on the reef and watch the gray herons and white fairy terns as they fish nearby.

Whenever he has the time, Jean Baptiste also fishes for some of the food he serves. But most of it is supplied by the local fishermen, from the fish market or during his trips around the island very early each Sunday morning. That's when he returns with an excellent choice of fresh lagoon fish. A sign beside the road advertises the catch of the day. Ask Jean-Baptiste which fish is the freshest and order accordingly.

The menu lists stuffed mussels for 1.600 CFP, poisson cru with coconut milk for 1.650 CFP, tuna carpaccio with basil for 1.800 CFP, grilled ume or other lagoon fish for 1.850 CFP, grilled Mahi Mahi with macadamia nuts for 1.950 CFP, shrimp in a fine champagne sauce for 1.980 CFP or fried filet of parrotfish breaded in grated coconut and served with coconut milk, for 1.950 CFP, which is an Aito special. Another house specialty is the bouillabaisse for 3.800 CFP, or the bouillabaisse royale for 5.200 CFP, which includes the soup, a bowl of squid, mussels, scallops and other seafood to dump into the liquid, and a plate of steamed lagoon fish. It's delicious and plentiful. Vana (sea urchins), varo (sea centipede), fresh pahua (reef clams) and lobster are seasonal and are listed on the board beside the road when Jean-Baptiste has received a fresh supply. The chef's specials are also listed on a chalkboard inside the restaurant. These usually include shark with a choice of sauces, octopus curry, homemade terrines, as well as some Corsican dishes, such as Tagliatelle à la Cargesienne for 1.650 CFP, Chicken Sartenaise for 1.850 CFP, Red tuna à la Bonifacienne for 2.600 CFP, or Corsican style steak for 2.400 CFP. An entrecôte (rib eye steak) can be prepared with a variety of sauces for 1.950 CFP.

Jean-Baptiste puts small bowls of pepper sauce on the table, which he describes as hot, hotter and hottest. He grows them himself and they go well with the food he serves, accompanied by crunchy baguette bread and butter and washed down with yet another drink or bottle of wine. Desserts are priced from 750 to 1.100 CFP and may include coconut or banana pie, tarte tatin or a pineapple surprise.

You will never be hurried here. Several times I have arrived at 1pm with friends and we left hours later, sometimes at 7pm, feeling quite "boozy" ourselves. We had Bloody Mary's with hot pepper sauce, several bottles of wine with our meal, liqueur in our desserts and in our coffee, plus an after-dinner drink offered by Jean-Baptiste, who used to own a bar in Papeete. He carries a good selection of after-dinner drinks, as well as some really cold Hinano beer. Thank goodness I live very close to Aito Restaurant and can just stumble home to bed!

Very conveniently, Jean-Baptiste also operates **Aito Pension**, which is on the same premises. He has 4 rooms with private bathrooms to rent, and three rooms also have their own kitchen. They are priced from 5.500 CFP to 12.500 CFP, with special discounts after the third night. He serves breakfast, lunch and dinner to his pension guests, provides them with free snorkeling gear and even has rental bikes.

Jean-Baptiste provides free round-trip transfers for lunch or dinner guests staying at the Sheraton Moorea Lagoon and Club Bali Hai or in family pensions in those areas. He said that he would come to get you at the InterContinental Resort Moorea if he feels in the right mood.

Moderate
MOTU ITI, *Tel. 55.05.20. Beside lagoon at PK 13.2 between Cook's Bay and Opunohu Bay. Breakfast, lunch and dinner served daily. Mastercard, Visa.*

This small restaurant is located on a covered terrace beside the lagoon at Pension Motu Iti. A Continental breakfast of coffee, juice, fresh fruit, bread, butter and jam is 800 CFP, and you can order eggs or fish if you want a more substantial meal in the mornings. For lunch or dinner you have 7 choices of salads from 850 to 1.100 CFP, burgers from 900 to 1.150 CFP, with a plate of fries for 400 CFP, thin crust pizzas from 1.050 to 1.300 CFP, fish dishes from 1.000 CFP to 2.150 CFP, and poultry and meats prepared in traditional French style from 1.700 to 1.950 CFP. You can also order Chinese specialties, such as lemon chicken for 950 CFP, tamarind duck for 1.100 CFP, and Mahi Mahi Cantonese for 1.800 CFP. Desserts include coconut pie, tarte tatin (apple pie) and profiteroles, each for 950 CFP. A tourist menu is 1.450 CFP. Cocktails, wine and beer are also served. Tahitian food can be prepared for groups.

WEST COAST: HAAPITI
Deluxe
LINAREVA-LE BATEAU, *Tel. 55.05.65, PK 34, Haapiti. All credit cards. Open daily 11am-3pm and 5-10pm. All major credit cards.*

When the *Tamarii Moorea* finished its long career ferrying passengers and freight between Tahiti and Moorea, it metamorphosed as a floating restaurant, safely anchored in the lagoon in front of Hotel Linareva. Eric Lussiez and Florian Pilloud lovingly restored the old boat, outfitting the dining room and bar with large windows, polished wood, shining brass and nautical antiques. They run a good ship-restaurant and their Tahitian waitresses, who have been with them for many years, are very friendly and efficient.

Whether you are touring Moorea with a guided tour or rental vehicle, you'll want to stop here for lunch and return again for dinner. This is not only Moorea's most unusual restaurant, with a panoramic view of the reef and mountains, but the cuisine is also highly praised by Moorea's most discerning gourmets. It is one of the best restaurants on the island because of the varied selection of appetizers and fish dishes offered. The menus are printed in French and English on two chalkboards, with appetizers on one board and the main courses on the other.

The first course choices cost from 890 to 2.550 CFP and include chilled cucumber soup, Greek salad with feta cheese, fried calamaries, crab gratin, endive salad with Roquefort cheese, salmon sashimi and fresh New Zealand oysters. The main course fish dishes are priced from 2.150 to 3.850 CFP, offering mahi mahi in ginger sauce, parrot fish in vanilla sauce, barracuda in a pink pepper sauce, jackfish in a tarragon sauce, salmon of the gods, lagoon fish and shrimp curry with coconut sauce. Reef lobster is seasonal and prices vary according to weight. There are meat dishes that range from 2.450 to 3.850 CFP. The dessert menu may tempt some of you, but I like to order the Colonel, which is lime sorbet with vodka, for 1.350 CFP. Light and heady! A 3-course tourist menu is 3.350 CFP. The bar serves a wide range of exotic cocktails and the wines are 1.910 to 24.400 CFP per bottle. Coffees are 290 to 1.150 CFP.

An unexpected treat in this small restaurant is a Tahitian dance show performed by the waitresses. Sometimes the Tahitian cook comes out of the kitchen and dances, and I have even seen Eric and Florian performing the Tahitian *otea* for their guests. Free round-trip transportation is provided from hotels and pensions within the limits of the InterContinental Resort Moorea and Pension Terariki. Reserve before 6pm for this service.

Superior
LA PLANTATION, *Tel. 56.45.10, PK 26, on mountain side just past Le Petit Village in Haapiti. American Express, Mastercard, Visa. Open 11am to 2pm for lunch and 6 to 10pm for dinner, closed all day Wednesday. Free pick-up service.*

This large open-air restaurant has seating for 60 inside and almost as many on the partially shaded terrace by the street. French cuisine, fish and crustaceans are featured, as well as pizzas and traditional foods from the lagoons of Polynesia. Luncheon specials are printed on the sidewalk chalk-board and may feature slipper lobster (cigales de mer) or fresh crab. Appetizers are priced from 1.400 to 2.500 CFP, seafood is 2.200 to 3.700 CFP, shellfish is 2.100 to 2.950 CFP and meats are 1.850 to 3.400 CFP. A 3-course tourist menu is 2.950 CFP. Wines from Bordeaux and Bourgogne are featured.

Moderate to Superior
LE MAYFLOWER, *Tel. 56.53.59, PK 27, Haapiti, seaside. Open Tuesday through Sunday 11:30am-2:30pm and 6:30-10:30pm. Closed all day Monday. American Express, Mastercard and Visa.*

This restaurant is beside the road next door to Hotel Hibiscus. It was called l'Aventure until Laurence and Bertrand Papin took it over in 2004. They named it Le Mayflower because Americans identify with that name and also because of the nautical decor, which includes an old oak barrel, photos of ships, wooden ceiling, walls and floor, brass lights, oil lamps and thick cords of rope. An intimate ambience is added by soft lighting and soft music, live plants, pink tablecloths and fresh flowers on the table.

Bertrand is a young chef from the Loire region of France, whose impressive *haute-cuisine française* has pleased Moorea diners for years, first at Le Cocotier, then at Le Pitcairn restaurant, just down the road from the Mayflower. Appetizers are priced from 950 to 2.300 CFP, fish and seafood dishes are 1.700 to 2.550 CFP, and meat and poultry choices are 1.900 to 2.850 CFP. His specialties change nightly, of course, and may include *terrine maison* for 1.300 CFP, meka (swordfish) with garlic cream sauce for 1.950 CFP, calamaries with amoricaine sauce for 2.050 CFP and fricassée of duck with *trompettes de la mort* mushrooms for 2.100 CFP. A child's menu of chicken nuggets and ice cream is 1.200 CFP, and a 3-course tourist menu is 3.800 CFP. Desserts sometimes include apple pie for 900 CFP, *crème brûlée* for 900 CFP, lemon sherbet with vodka for 1.150 CFP and Moorea profiteroles, with banana, and pineapple ice cream with black and white chocolate sauce and whipped cream, all for 950 CFP. Wines are priced from 2.250 to 9.300 CFP and should be detaxed, therefore less expensive by the time you come here. This is definitely a restaurant worth trying and returning to again and again.

LE PITCAIRN, *Tel. 56.55.46, PK 27.5 in Haapiti. Open for lunch and dinner daily except Thursday noon. Mastercard, Visa.*

I cannot recommend this restaurant since it changed hands in early 2004. Please do not confuse it with Laurence and Bertrand Papin, the excellent couple who used to run this place but now own Le Mayflower. Maryse may be considered a good cook by some people, but I got sick eating a small portion of poisson cru, sashimi and tuna carpaccio for 1.800 CFP. And her French husband, who acts as waiter, could do with a little underarm deodorant as well as a few manners in how to serve the clients. Take your business to Le Mayflower and you won't regret it.

FARE VAIMOANA, *Tel. 56.17.14, PK 27, Haapiti, seaside. Open daily for breakfast, lunch and dinner. All major credit cards.*

This hotel restaurant is not visible from the road, but it is well worth a little detour toward the lagoon at the same lane that leads to Camping Nelson. You can watch the action on the beach and lagoon while eating in the attractive little restaurant. A Continental breakfast is 1.200 CFP, and an American breakfast is 1.650 CFP. A big Tahitian breakfast is served each Sunday for 2.200 CFP. A luncheon menu suggests burgers from 950 to 1.250 CFP, a plat du jour for 1.200 CFP or a seafood plate for 2.150 CFP. Their seafood platters are very popular and are priced from 4.250 to 4.650 CFP. A child's menu is 900 CFP. The à la carte menu lists starter courses from 1.550 to 2.100 CFP, fish and seafood for 1.900 to 2.900 CFP, and meats from 1.900 to 2.400 CFP. Desserts are 700 to 950 CFP. The chef de cuisine is from Agen, France, near the Bordeaux region, and his specialties are very well prepared.

PAINAPO BEACH / THE OTHER PLACE, *Tel. 55.07.90, E-mail: painapo@mail.pf; is on the seaside at Painapo Beach, PK 33 in Haapiti. Open for lunch Saturday and Sunday only. Mastercard, Visa.*

The Other Place (TOP) is the name of the restaurant at Painapo Beach Village, but it is better known as Painapo Beach. At publication time it was open only on weekends, when lunch is served non-stop from 10am to 5pm. Tables and chairs are placed under the shade of almond trees overlooking the lagoon, or you can eat inside the big thatched roof dining room with a white sand floor. A platter of *poisson cru*, red tuna sashimi, carpaccio of tuna and tuna tartare makes a nice lunch for two and costs about 3.950 CFP. This is served with taro and breadfruit chips and rice. Add a few slices of fresh French baguette and a nice bottle of wine, and you might not even have room for dessert. Other specials include a selection of cooked fish, shrimp, fresh *pahua* (tridacna clams) from the reef or crab with garlic or ginger sauce. Maa Tahiti (Tahitian food) is served each Sunday noon, accompanied by a live band, for 3.500 CFP. You can order sandwiches, salads and other light meals, as well as drinks, at the thatched roof snack bar beside the road. See more information under *Tahitian Feasts* in this chapter.

Moderate

LES TIPANIERS, *Tel. 56.12.67, PK 25, seaside, Haapiti. All credit cards. Beach Bar Restaurant open daily 7-9:30am and 12-2 p.m. Main restaurant open daily for dinner 7-9pm. Best to reserve. Free pick-up service for dinner from InterContinental Moorea Resort & Spa to Moorea Village.*

This is one of the most delightful places to spend the day, swimming in the lagoon, participating in a variety of water sports, or reading in the shade beside a white sand beach. Breakfast and lunch are served in the beachside restaurant. You can order burgers and sandwiches for 950 to 1.350 CFP, salads from 520 to 1.350 CFP, and pasta for 980 to 1.500 CFP, mahi mahi, meka or salmon of the gods for 1.700 CFP or grilled meats for 1.700 CFP, with a choice of sauces. Take-away sandwiches are less than 500 CFP. Tahitian singer Nile plays music at the beach bar each Thursday from 5:45-6:45pm.

Pizzas and fine Italian cuisine are served for dinner in the main restaurant in the gardens, featuring pasta, spaghetti, lasagna and fettuccine, from 980 to 1.550 CFP. French dishes include fish soup for 1.050 CFP, mahi mahi with vanilla sauce for 1.800 CFP, and lamb sirloin with goat cheese for 1.950 CFP. My Scottish neighbor Ron Falconer plays the body harp and harmonica and sings folk songs, blues and old favorites from the 1970s every other Saturday night, starting at 7pm in the main restaurant.

RESTAURANT IRENE, *Tel. 56.15.93, PK 25.5 on mountainside, between Le Tipaniers and Le Petit Village in Haapiti. Open for breakfast Sunday only* from 7:30 to 10:30am. Open for lunch and dinner Tuesday through Sunday noon. Closed Sunday night and all day Monday. Mastercard, Visa.

This is a very popular and friendly local style restaurant featuring seafood and Polynesian cooking. Meals are served on the open-air terrace and inside the restaurant. Starter courses are 500 to 1.200 CFP, chicken is 1.200 to 1.500 CFP, meats are 1.500 to 1.700 CFP and shrimp dishes are 1.800 CFP. Specialties include poisson cru for 900 CFP, tuna curry with coconut milk for 1.200 CFP, raw shrimp with coconut milk for 1.500 CFP, tuna with passion fruit sauce and salad for 1.500 CFP, and poulpe a l'ail (octopus and garlic) for 1.980 CFP. Desserts are 400 to 700 CFP, with such delights as fried bananas and ice cream or baked papaya with ice cream.

IGUANE ROCK CAFÉ, Tel. 56.17.16, PK 26 in Le Petit Village in Haapiti. Open daily with non-stop service from 7am to midnight. Mastercard, Visa.

This is an ice cream parlor, bar, snack, pizza parlor and a full service restaurant, with a menu offering French, Tahitian and Chinese foods. The dining rooms can seat 150 people and a special area is provided for children, where they play in security while the parents dine in tranquility. Burgers are 1.200 to 1.500 CFP, pizzas are 1.300 to 1.500 CFP, and salads range from 1.000 to 1.600 CFP. Pasta is 1.500 to 1.600 CFP, poisson cru, sashimi or tuna carpaccio are 1.600 CFP, and meats are 1.600 to 1.800 CFP. A choice of grilled meats includes buffalo steak for 2.600 CFP. Desserts are 700 to 800 CFP. There is a cybercafé here in the back, with Internet connections.

LE SUNSET, Tel. 56.26.00, PK 27, on the beach at Hotel Hibiscus, Haapiti. Mastercard, Visa. Open daily for meals from 12 to 2:30pm and from 5:45 to 9:30pm.

Here you can eat pizzas, grilled meats and homemade pastas or sip a cold beer while sitting at a picnic table on the open deck overlooking the white sand beach, the lagoon and the motu islets in front of Club Med. Or you can sit inside the restaurant and look at the enormous rubber trees that grow at the edge of the hotel's spacious lawn. Sandwiches are 600 CFP, burgers with fries are 1.200 CFP, salads are 1.200-1.300 CFP, sashimi or poisson cru are 1.400 CFP, a choice of 11 thin crust pizzas are 1.200 CFP, fish dishes are 1.600-1.900 CFP, steaks are 1.900-2.900 CFP, the plat du jour is 1.800 CFP, a 3-course tourist menu is 2.800 CFP and the kids' menu offers several choices for 1.300 CFP. Desserts are 600-1.100 CFP and wines are 2.025-2.985 CFP per bottle. Draft beer is 350 and 600 CFP.

CHEZ CAPO, Tel. 56.54.89; cell 77.56.56, on seaside at PK 27.3 in Haapiti. Open for lunch and dinner Sunday through Thursday. Closed Friday and Saturday noon and open for dinner both nights. Mastercard, Visa. Reserve.

This is one of the best restaurants on the island for local style food, but you can also get such familiar items as hamburgers and fries for 800 CFP. Starter courses are 900-1.300 CFP and hot dishes are 1.200-1.500 CFP.

Specialties include excellent poisson cru, grilled fish, shrimp dishes, lemon pork, pahua (clam) curry, goat curry or goat with five spices, all accompanied by either breadfruit, taro, manioc, tarua, banana, or fei (Tahitian plantain). A Saturday night Polynesian buffet with veal on a spit is 3.500 CFP and a Tahitian band plays music. Ma'a Tahiti is served each Sunday at noon for 3.000 CFP, presenting all the traditional Tahitian foods that are cooked in the *ahima'a* underground oven, as well as the accompanying dishes. Live music adds to the festive occasion. Capo has a plant and flower nursery and his restaurant is always decorated with brightly colored flowers and hanging baskets of ferns and other greenery.

LE PAPAYER, *Tel. 55.02.50, PK 30, at Tiki Village in Haapiti. American Express, Mastercard, Visa. Open Tuesday-Saturday 12-3pm and 6-10pm. Closed Sunday and Monday.*

This is a good luncheon choice while you are visiting the traditional Tahitian style Tiki Village. The thatched roof open-air restaurant overlooks the lagoon and coral reef, providing a beautiful view as well as good food. Starter courses are 650 to 1.250 CFP, fish dishes are 1.500 to 2.000 CFP, meat and poultry choices are 1.400 to 1.700 CFP and desserts are 400 to 800 CFP. A 3-course tourist menu is 2.700 CFP. A mini-show is provided at 1pm by the young dancers and musicians from the Tiki Theatre Village. If you feel like becoming a Tahitian Chief and wining and dining your Princess in tropical splendor, then reserve the Royal Floating Fare, a private houseboat, where your lunch will be served by canoe and set upon a glass bottom table on the terrace. You can enjoy your meal and admire the beautiful multicolored fish while taking in the spectacular surroundings.

A big buffet of Tahitian food and international dishes is served in Le Papayer restaurant each Tuesday, Wednesday, Friday and Saturday evening, when the Tiki Theatre Village dancers and musicians present a spectacular Polynesian show. Please see further information in the *Nightlife & Entertainment* section of this chapter.

Economy to Moderate

LE MOTU, *Tel. 56.16.70, PK 26, Haapiti, in St. Jacques Center, right across street from Club Med. Mastercard, Visa. Open non-stop 9:30am-8pm. Closed Sunday night and Monday night.*

This is a good choice for salads from 600 to 1.400 CFP, crêpes for 800 to 1.000 CFP, 15 choices of pizzas from 1.050 to 1.300 CFP. Sashimi, carpaccio of tuna and poisson cru are 1.300 CFP. You can choose from 13 kinds of burgers for 470 to 800 CFP and a plate of fries is 450 CFP. Steaks are 1.500 to 1.800 CFP and daily specials are 1.400 to 1.600 CFP. They have an unusual selection of sandwiches that are served on half a loaf of the crusty French *baguette*. My favorite is the ground beef sandwich, which is grilled hamburger meat, with lettuce, tomatoes, onions and mayonnaise spread on a *baguette*.

It is much bigger and better than the hamburgers on buns and costs 450 CFP. It's not on the menu they give you at the tables because most people get it to go. The bar is well stocked and there are several imported beers and soft drinks in the cooler. They also have Internet service in an air-conditioned room.

SNACK COCO D'ISLE, *Tel. 56.59.07. Next to road on lagoon side at PK 27.5, Haapiti. Mastercard, Visa. Open 11:30am-3pm and 6:30-9:30pm. Closed Sunday.*

This unpretentious snack with a thatched roof and gravel floor is conveniently located near the campgrounds on Moorea's sunset coast. Prices are geared toward people on a low to medium budget and special rates are given for take-away meals. The menu lists several choices of sandwich baguettes for 600 to 800 CFP, burgers and fries are 900 CFP, a double cheeseburger with fries is 1.300 CFP, salads are 1.200 CFP or less and *poisson cru* is 1.400 CFP. Special full meals for a Backpacker, Globetrotter or Adventurer are 1.500 to 1.700 CFP and consist of cooked tuna, salmon of the gods, chicken or ground beef. These same dishes are 1.300 to 1.500 CFP for take-away service.

The portions are plentiful and good and the fries are thickly sliced from fresh potatoes. You can also order pizzas for 1.000 to 1.500 CFP. Desserts start at 200 CFP for a scoop of ice cream and go up to 700 CFP for a banana split or profiteroles. A glass of juice is 250 CFP, soft drinks are 320 CFP, a big bottle of Hinano beer is 550 CFP, a glass of wine is 280 CFP and a carafe of wine is 1.100 CFP. A child's menu with ice cream is 1.000 CFP. Owners Jean-Pierre and Norma are both very friendly folks.

Economy

A L'HEURE DU SUD ROULOTTE, *PK 26, on mountainside between Le Petit Village and La Plantation restaurant. No credit cards.*

Look for a vertical sign advertising Sandwiches just past the Rent-A-Bike shack. This stationary roulotte has a good reputation for its casse-croute sandwiches on French baguettes, priced from 400 to 470 CFP. You can also get a hamburger and fries for 750 CFP or a cheeseburger for 50 CFP more. A chef's salad is 900 CFP and they also serve pain bagnat sandwiches to go.

ROYAL CHICKEN, *Tel. 78.53.53. Beside road on lagoon side next to Magasin Aimeo at PK 27 in Haapiti. Open Tuesday through Sunday 11am-1:30pm and 6-7:30pm. Closed Monday except on holidays. No credit cards.*

This is the domain of the famous Chicken Man, a personable Frenchman named Alain who lived in the USA for two years and speaks English. You can read about him in the Tahiti Forums on the Internet. He is conveniently located close to the campgrounds and backpacker lodgings, as well as the hotels on Moorea's sunset coast. Alain specializes in Provençale style rotisserie chicken and rosemary herbed potatoes to go, preferably with advance reservations.

You can order a chicken sandwich for 360 CFP, a quarter portion of chicken for 350 CFP, half a chicken for 650 CFP or a whole chicken for 1.200 CFP.

DANIEL'S PIZZA, *Tel. 56.39.95. PK 34.1 seaside, close to Linareva in Haapiti. No credit cards. Open 11am-9pm. Closed Thursday.*

This is where you'll find the best pizza on the island. Daniel has built a wood-fired pizza oven in his garage and you can sit on a stool and eat at the wooden counter or take it with you. He offers 13 choices of pizza priced from 1.200 to 1.400 CFP. No alcohol is served. Look for his sign beside the road on the seaside just before you get to Hotel Linareva.

MAATEA-TEMAE
Moderate

CHEZ TEINA SNACK RESTAURANT, *Tel. 56.29.29 / 78.42.55, PK 13,200 on seaside in Maatea. Open Tuesday through Thursday and on Sunday 11am-1:30pm and 6-10:30pm; on Friday and Saturday 11am-1:30pm and 6-9pm. Closed Monday. No credit cards.*

Open since June 2004 this small and clean air-conditioned restaurant serves the best Chinese food on the island. Prices range from 180 CFP for a taro beignet to 1.500 CFP for shrimp crystal, except for the specialties, which are available only on Saturday night. This is when you can have Peking duck for 1.600 CFP per serving or roast suckling pig with coconut milk for 2.200 CFP per serving. Their lemon chicken for 950 CFP is excellent, as well as their *poisson cru* with coconut milk for 1.050 CFP. They also do a good take-away business.

PAULINE RESTAURANT, *Tel. 56.11.26, PK 9, on mountainside in center of Afareaitu village. Open daily for lunch and dinner. No credit cards.*

This old restaurant is now under the management of a Frenchman whose menu includes a hamburger and fries for 1.000 CFP, Chinese dishes for 950 to 1.200 CFP, salads for 700 to 1.200 CFP, fish and seafood for 1.300 to 1.800 CFP and meat dishes for 1.300 to 3.900 CFP. You can order poisson cru, carpaccio of beef or tuna, raw shrimp, tuna sashimi, and tuna or beef tartare for 1.200 to 1.300 CFP. Duck with guava and pineapple is 1.500 CFP and a seafood platter for two is 14.000 CFP, which includes lobster, crab, shrimp, reef clams, slipper lobster and sea urchin. There are also daily specials, such as mussels and french fries. Desserts are 400 to 650 CFP. You can order wine, beer and other drinks and you can eat inside or outdoors, where clean white sand is spread under the tables.

Pauline Teariki was a pioneer of tourism in Moorea, and operated her pension and adjacent restaurant until she died in October 1996, when she was 83 years old. There is no charge to visit Pauline's small museum collection of wood and stone *tiki*s, which she found in the mountains and valleys of Moorea.

Tahitian Feasts
CHEZ CAPO RESTAURANT, *Tel. 56.54.89, cell 77.56.56; PK 27.3, Haapiti on lagoon side of road. Mastercard, Visa.*
Sunday noon is ma'a Tahiti day in most Tahitian homes, and Chez Capo offers a truly Polynesian experience that will make you feel you are visiting a Tahitian family. Capo and his friendly staff all dress in pareo fabrics and wear leis and crowns of fragrant flowers. The open-sided restaurant is decorated with brightly hued hibiscus, ginger flowers, bird of paradise and hanging baskets of ferns and other greenery. You'll eat your fafa poulet, roast pig, breadfruit, taro, bananas, po'e and other traditional foods to the tune of live music. The cost is 3.000 CFP per person.
   HOTEL MOOREA VILLAGE, *Tel. 56.10.02, PK 27, Haapiti, American Express, Mastercard, Visa.*
   Sunday is Tahitian *tamaara'a* day, when the *ahima'a* underground oven is opened at 12:45pm to reveal the roast suckling pig, breadfruit, taro and other Tahitian foods. This is the most authentic Tahitian feast you'll find in a hotel on Moorea, and it also includes a Tahitian dance show. The servings of roast suckling pig, *poisson cru* and Tahitian vegetables are very generous. You can even have *fafaru* if you feel adventurous. You eat with your fingers and you'll still be licking them when the Tahitian dance show begins after lunch. The cost of 3.900 CFP per person includes wine and coffee.
   HOTEL SOFITEL IA ORA MOOREA, *Tel. 55.03.55, PK 2, Temae. All major credit cards.*
   The Tahitian underground oven is opened at 6:30pm each Saturday evening and a *tamaara'a* buffet of Tahitian food is served in La Perouse Restaurant, followed by a Polynesian dance show at 8pm, which may also include fire dancing. The cost of 5.380 CFP per person is for the food and show only. Drinks and wine are extra.
   PAINAPO BEACH / THE OTHER PLACE, *Tel. 55.07.90, on the seaside at Painapo Beach Village, PK 33 in Haapiti. Mastercard, Visa.*
   A genuine and delicious Tahitian feast is served buffet style each Sunday at noon. This food tastes like it was cooked in a Tahitian underground *ahima'a* (which it was), and not in the oven of a gas-burning stove, like some of the hotels cook their *maa* Tahiti. All the traditional favorites are included: *poisson cru* with coconut milk, *pua'a chou* (a pork stew with cabbage and carrots), *poulet fafa* (chicken and taro leaves with coconut milk), roast breadfruit, *fei*, (mountain plantains), cooked bananas, sweet potatoes, taro and tarua, (root vegetables) baked fish, roast pig, three kinds of *po'e* desserts with coconut milk (pumpkin, banana and papaya), and both fresh and fermented coconut milk sauces to dip your food into. *Fafaru* (a stinky but good tasting fish once you've acquired the taste for it) is also on the buffet table, covered with a plate to hold the smell inside. This excellent food costs 3.500 CFP per person, and you may even get to listen to Ronald Sage, the owner, singing with the Tahitian

band that plays music for dancing. There is usually a fire dance performed as part of the entertainment. You can eat outdoors under the shade of almond trees or inside the thatched roof dining area with a sand floor.

TIKI THEATRE VILLAGE, *Tel. 55.02.50, PK 30, Haapiti, American Express, Mastercard, Visa.*

A big buffet of Tahitian food, as well as grilled meats and fish, is served in Le Papayer Restaurant each Tuesday, Wednesday, Friday and Saturday evening, when the Tiki Theatre Village dancers and musicians present a spectacular Polynesian show, complete with fire dancing. The *ahima'a* underground oven is opened as part of the cultural visit through the village. Even if you don't like the looks or tastes of Tahitian food, there are other, more familiar choices of foods served. The total price for unlimited welcome punch, the dinner buffet with all the house wine you want, a guided visit through the Tiki Village and a dance show with 60 performers is 7.700 CFP. Round trip bus transfers from the airport, the boat dock or any hotel on the island is 1.150 CFP. The cost of dinner and the transfers also entitles you to come back to visit Tiki Village during the daytime without paying an entry fee. Please see further information in *Nightlife & Entertainment* section of this chapter.

Seeing the Sights

Look for the **PK** (*poste kilometre*) markers on the mountainside of the road, which are placed one kilometer (.62 miles) apart. The signs are in concrete in the shape of Moorea, which resembles a heart. PK 0 is located at the old post office in **Temae**, close to the airport road. If you're coming from the airport and turn right onto the circle island road, you'll soon see the PK 1 marker opposite Lake Temae, which is actually a swamp.

The distance markers continue on around the northwest coast to the village of **Haapiti** to PK 35, and then there's a gap in the numbering system. Here you'll want to photograph the **Mou'a Roa** and **Tohivea mountains** that rise in the distance behind the soccer field. On the seaside is a Protestant Church. The next marker you'll see will be PK 24, where another lovely landscape of the mountains is visible from the courtyard of the Catholic Church, **Eglise de la Saint Famille**. The PK numbers then descend from PK 24 to PK 4, where you'll find the Ferry dock at **Vaiare Bay**, and then on down to PK 0, where you'll see the old Temae post office again. The new post office is in the commercial center of **Maharepa** at PK 5.

At the end of Opunohu Bay at PK 18 you can leave the circle island road and turn left onto a partially paved inland road that passes through the **Opunohu Valley**. Here you will see horses, cows, sheep and goats grazing in verdant green pastures under the shadow of Moorea's sacred **Rotui Mountain**. There is an agricultural school in this valley and the students look after the livestock. Beside this road, in a forest of *mape* Tahitian chestnut trees, are restored *marae* temples of stone and ancient archery platforms, where the

Maohi chiefs and priests used to worship and play. **Le Belvedere** is a popular destination at the top of a steep and winding road, and from the **Lookout Point**, at the end of a torturous road, you have the visual pleasure of **Cook's Bay** and **Opunohu Bay** far below, which are separated by Mt. Rotui. You continue on along the *route des ananas* (the pineapple road), where you'll see the mountain slopes of Pao Pao valley covered with pineapple plantations. Forests of mahogany, teak, acacia and mangoes border the rutted red dirt road, which leads you back to the circle island road at PK 9 in the village of **Pao Pao**.

Land Tours
The **Circle Island Tour** takes you by minivan or large bus on a 3 1/2 to 4-hour voyage along the coastal road, winding around Cook's Bay and Opunohu Bay and inland to the Opunohu Valley, with stops at *marae* of Titiroa and the other Polynesian stone temples and archery platforms in this area, the Belvedere Lookout, pineapple fields, vanilla plantation, and to the Moorea Fruit Juice Factory & Distillery, where you can taste different liqueurs made with the fruits of Moorea. This tour sells for 3.000 CFP up.

The **Mountain Safari Tours** and **Photo Safari Excursions** are also usually half-day tours, varying according to the guides, which sell for 4.000 to 4.950 CFP. In addition to the sights and sites mentioned above, these 4WD excursions also take you off the main road to discover groves of oranges and pamplemousse (grapefruit), gardens of lush tropical fruits, medicinal plants, rosewood, tamanu, coffee plantations, soft green meadows and a jungle undergrowth of ferns and bamboo. The highlight of this excursion is a visit to the waterfalls of Afareaitu, which includes a 15-minute hike uphill and a refreshing splash under the cascade of water. You will discover Moorea from the mountain to the sea and learn all about the history, culture and daily lives of the people of Moorea.

Here are some of the companies and guides who will be happy to show you Moorea:

Aimeo Safari Tours, *Tel. 56.14.11 or 78.85.29.* Heitapu Hunter has received rave reviews from many people who have taken his half-day tours, which take you off-track to visit his private family domain in the Pao Pao valley.

Albert Transport & Activities, *Tel. 55.21.10 / 55.21.11; Fax 56.40.58; E-mail: alberttransport@mail.pf.* Rico Haring manages this family business, providing a combined circle island tour and interior island tour by air-conditioned bus with shopping at Moorea Black Pearls and Heivai Black Pearls, their two family-owned boutiques. They also offer a **Photo Safari Excursion** by 4WD. Albert's guides are usually his sons, who grew up in the tour business. They don't let the facts stand in the way of a good story and they may even entertain you with tales of their many wives and girlfriends, following in the footsteps of their dear old dad. Private tours are also available by air-conditioned car and taxi service is also available.

Hiro's Tours / What To Do On Moorea, *Tel. 78.70.10 / 70.51.08*. Hiro Kelley has an activity desk in the reception area of Club Bali. His 4WD Safari Tour operates daily except Sunday, departing at 8:15am and returning at 12:30pm, for 3.500 CFP per person. Hiro's guides speak English and know the history and legends of Moorea.

Inner Island Safari Tours, *Tel. 56.20.09; Fax 56.34.43; E-mail: inner-saf@mail.pf.* Alex and Ghislaine Mahotu operate half-day inner island photo tours in air-conditioned and open jeeps. They also take you to "Magic Mountain," where you will climb the side of a crater for a 360-degree view. Be sure to bring your camera. These are very well informed guides, who speak good English.

Julienne's Safari Tour, *Tel. 56.48.87/78.65.40; E-mail: vdirosa@mail.pf; www.tahiti1.com/safari/index.htm.* Julienne's half-day 4WD tours take you to some extra places you'd not normally visit on a tour. In addition to all the other stops mentioned in this section, she also takes you to see the dolphins at the InterContinental Moorea, to Le Petit Village, to see the fresh water eels in Papetoai, to the public beach of Toatea, to the ferry boat dock to see the fruit vendors, to the Agricultural School snack bar, and even to the pharmacy. Tourists are happy with her tour.

Moorea Explorer, *Tel. 56.12.86; E-mail: mooreaexplorer@mail.pf; www.moorea-explorer.com.* This company has a big fleet of yellow buses, vans and 4WD vehicles, all decorated with fish. You'll see them everywhere on the island. They'll take you on a half-day full Circle Island Tour (Belvedere) by air-conditioned bus, or you can sign up for the Aito Safari Off-Road Moorea, a half-day tour by 4WD. They also offer a Private Safari and a Private Sunset Safari, as well as a Local Art and Handicraft Private Discovery that will take you to meet the famous local artists, sculptors, carvers, and tattoo masters in their homes.

Salvatore Mura, *Tel. 56.18.92*, has a 14-passenger Mercedes van that he uses for private tours around the island. A 4-hour tour is 15.000 CFP for the bus. He speaks English, French and Italian.

Torea Nui Transport & Safari, *Tel. 56.12.48/77.01.52, E-mail: enttoreanui@mail.pf.* They offer a half-day Safari Tour by 4WD and they also operate a transfer service for only 500 CFP per person, providing transportation from the airport or ferry dock to your hotel, or from your hotel to other locations on the island. You must reserve in advance. See additional information under *Tour & Transport Companies* in this chapter.

Special Activities & Sightseeing Stops Around the Island

Agricultural Lycée of Opunohu has a **Fare Boutique**, *Tel. 56.11.34*, on the right as you drive up the mountain to visit Le Belvedere. In addition to tasting the delicious fresh fruit juices, you can buy their vanilla and coffee beans, dried bananas, crystallized fruits, homemade jams and hand-painted *pareos.* You can also visit the high school farm and see the vanilla plantations, greenhouse, tropical orchards and vegetable gardens. The Fare Boutique has maps of three discovery walkways that will take you along marked paths for hikes of one or two hours for each choice. Open Monday to Thursday from 8am to 4:30pm, on Friday from 8am to 3pm, and on Saturday from 8am to 12pm. If you want to hike a trail be sure to arrive at least two hours before closing time.

Fare Vanille, *Tel. 56.37.22, cell 77.63.71; E-mail: sachamartin@mail.pf* on the mountainside at PK 6.7 in Afareaitu. Sacha Martin is a young man from Tahiti whose company, Pacific Natural Products, produces and sells vanilla beans, vanilla powder, sugar, perfume and other by-products. Learn how the vanilla vine is planted, how the orchids are "married" by hand and how the bean pods are dried to produce fragrant vanilla. Free admission.

Moorea Fruit Juice Factory and Distillery, *Tel. 55.20.00*, on the mountainside at PK 12 in Cook's Bay. Boutique open Monday-Saturday 9am-4pm. Visit distillery Monday-Thursday. You can taste the various liqueurs, including the prize-winning ginger brandy, and you can take home Rotui fruit juices, Paina Colada (*paina* means «drunk» in Tahitian), Ava Tahiti chocolate and coconut liqueur, Tahiti Drink rum punch, bottles of Tahitian rum and a whole range of Tahiti-Manutea confections and candies made with local fruits. You can also order fresh pineapple to be delivered to the Tahiti-Faa'a International Airport in time for your flight home.

Nature House of Mou'a Roa, *Tel. 56.58.62, cell 72.62.58,* is located in the Vaianae Valley between Haapiti and Atiha. You turn off the circle island road at PK 21 (there is a sign) and walk up the valley until you come to the big colonial house that was built in 1900. It is surrounded by lush green foliage and tropical flowers and twin rivers flow through the property. Be sure to sample the farm's homemade organic jams, honey and dried fruit. Phone ahead if you want to stay for lunch. You may even want to participate in one of the sports activities organized by Bernard Genton. These include archery, rope rappelling down to the river, mountain skating, riding mountain bikes and hiking. See more information under *Where to Stay* in this chapter.

Painapo Beach, *Tel. 55.07.90*, is on the seaside at PK 33 in Haapiti. Just look for the giant sized tattooed warrior beside the road. It is open every weekend and you can spend the day in this welcoming place. Bring your swimsuits, towels, protective shoes and snorkeling equipment, and rent a kayak to explore the lagoon or just take it easy on the beach, playing in the lagoon and sipping a cold beer under the shade of big almond trees on the big grassy lawn overlooking the beach and lagoon. There is no admission charge and there are toilets and showers. You can also order sandwiches, salads and other light meals, as well as drinks, at the thatched roof snack bar, or you can enjoy a fresh fish platter at a table under the shady trees. See more information under *Where to Eat* and *Tahitian Feasts* in this chapter.

Motu Moea, *Tel. 56.55.37, cell 74.96.96*, also known as Motu Tiahura, is across the channel from Les Tipaniers and the Club Med beach. You can spend a few hours snorkeling in the coral gardens, enjoying the private white sand beach or lounging in a hammock under the shady trees in this privileged setting. **Restaurant La Plage** serves lunch, specializing in French and Tahitian cuisines. Boat transfers are provided at 10am and 12pm, returning at 2pm and 4pm. From the InterContinental Resort Moorea the round-trip boat costs 980 CFP; from Hotel Hibiscus the cost is 750 CFP; and from Les Tipaniers it costs 700 CFP.

Maiau Beach, *Tel. 70.78.58*, is on Motu Moea (Motu Tiahura). A private section of the white sand beach has been transformed into a protected environment where organized groups, clubs or associations can spend the day on the beach, take a private snorkeling tour, sunset cruise or enjoy a feast of *ma'a Tahiti* cooked in an underground *ahima'a* oven. See *Tuatini Activities Moorea* under *Nautical Activities Centers* for information.

Temae Beach is where the locals go to swim, play games on the beach and in the water and have picnics on the white sand. A good surfing spot is also located nearby. This is also the starting or ending point for outrigger canoe races, international marathons and other big events. There are public toilets and showers, as well as trashcans, but unfortunately, the whole area gets littered during busy holidays or long weekends. Turn off the circle island road across from the old post office at PK 0, and follow the dirt road for about one kilometer, bearing left where you see a fork, and you can park in the shade across from the public park. You can also walk down the beach from the Sofitel la Ora to get here.

Nightlife & Entertainment

Several of the hotels have barbecues, special theme evenings, and especially Tahitian feasts, followed by Tahitian dance shows. The regular events are listed for each hotel in the *Where to Stay* section of this chapter. More entertainment is added during the high seasons of July-August and for the Christmas-New Year holidays. The *Tahiti Beach Press*, an English-language publication that is distributed free to all the hotels each week, has a Special Events page that will inform you where the action is on any night of the week.

Tiki Theatre Village, *Tel. 55.02.50*, at PK 30 in Haapiti, is a cultural and folkloric center that you can visit by day or four evenings a week. Multilingual guides lead you through the village of thatched roof fares where you will see demonstrations of how to carve tikis from stone, how to sculpt wooden bowls, weave a hat, make a floral crown and tie-dye a pareo. You can get a traditional Tahitian or Marquesan tattoo and learn how the ancient Tahitians built their homes and meetinghouses. You can swim in the lagoon, paddle an outrigger canoe, visit their black pearl farm in the lagoon or sunbathe on the beach. You can also browse around in the Tiki Village boutique, black pearl shop and the Maison du Jouir art gallery, where Paul Gauguin prints are priced from 10.000 CFP to 45.000 CFP. You can enjoy lunch in Le Papayer restaurant and watch a mini-dance show at 1pm. Tiki Village is open Tuesday-Saturday from 11am to 3pm. They are closed on Sunday and Monday. The entrance fee to the village during the daytime is 2.200 CFP and transportation from the hotels, airport or boat docks is 1.150 CFP per person. If you rent a car from Avis or Europcar there is no entrance charge during the day.

Each Tuesday, Wednesday, Friday and Saturday evening the 60 dancers and musicians at the Tiki Theatre Village present a Polynesian extravaganza. The program begins at 6pm with a welcome fruit drink or rum punch. You will be immersed in the culture and tradition of Polynesia, with demonstrations of arts and crafts and dancing techniques. After the opening of the *ahima'a* underground oven a bountiful buffet is set out, featuring Tahitian specialties, Continental cuisine, barbecued fish, chicken and meats, along with a salad bar and dessert table.

While you are enjoying your meal you'll be treated to a very lively demonstration of how to wear the *pareo*. After dinner the big show gets underway at 8:45pm in the open-air theater with a white sand floor. This spectacular dance show includes several fire dancers, all muscular men with beautiful tattoos. Everyone here works very hard and puts all their energy and enthusiasm into entertaining you. I highly recommend this **Great Polynesian Revue**. The cost of the buffet dinner, all the punch you want, as much wine as you wish to drink during dinner, plus the extravaganza show, is 9.050 CFP, including transportation. The cost of dinner and the show also entitles you to visit the Tiki Village during the daytime without paying an additional entry fee. The cost of seeing the show without dinner is 3.500 CFP, plus 1.150 CFP if you want a round-trip transfer. Reserve at your hotel or *Tel. 55.02.50.*

Ron plays the auto harp and harmonica and sings songs from the 1960s and 1970s, plus a little country and Celtic folk songs. You can catch his act at **Alfredo's** every Thursday and Sunday evening and at **Les Tipaniers** every other Saturday night.

Special all-night balls are held at the sports stadiums (Salles Omnisports) on occasion, usually on a Saturday night. These *bals* are usually sponsored by soccer teams, outrigger canoe teams and other sports groups, and provide the perfect occasion to meet some of the local young people and to learn how to dance Tahitian style.

Sports & Recreation
All Terrain Vehicle/Quad
   ATV Moorea Tour, *Tel. 56.16.60/cell 70.73.45; E-mail: jqmoorea@hotmail.com*. Located at PK 24.6 in Tiahura, across road from

InterContinental Resort Moorea. Free pick-up. A 2-person ATV 4WD can be rented with a guide for 2 hours for 13.000 CFP or 4 hours for 18.000 CFP.

Hiking

Opunohu Agricultural College has opened three circular trails that you can walk alone or with a guide, where you can see the work of the school students and explore one section of the Opunohu domain. A small brochure with the detailed notes on the plant life on the trails is available in four languages (French, English, German and Spanish). Ask for information on guided tours at the Fare Boutique on the right side of the road leading to Le Belvedere lookout.

Moorea Hiking, *Tel. 79.41.54; E-mail: hiro@magicmoorea.com.* Hiro Damide and Dominique Leoture operate 3-hour hikes in Opunohu Valley for families and older people. They start at the Marae Titiroa and hike up a trail to the Belvedere lookout and return to the *marae*, explaining the geology, plants, birds, and Polynesian culture along the way. The hikers are served fresh pineapple, *pamplemousse* (grapefruit) and other fruits and the cost is 4.000 CFP per person. A 5-hour hike into the Opunohu Valley is 6.000 CFP. Hiro will be your qualified guide when you hike across the island from Vaiare to Haapiti. This is a full day trek for 6 people and costs 10.000 CFP per person. Hiro also leads mountain climbing expeditions up Rotui Mountain and Moua Puta, the mountain with the hole in the top. Each of these all-day hikes is 10.000 CFP

Polynesian Adventure, *Tel./Fax 43.25.95, cell phone 77.24.37; E-mail: polynesianadv@mail.pf.* Vincent Dubousquet is a specialized professional guide who will accompany you on a day's hike to walk across the mountains of Moorea from Vaiare to Pao Pao or to visit the Three Coconut Trees pass. These are easy to medium level walks for a minimum of four people and each hike costs 6.700 CFP per person. He will take you for a day's hike to Mou'a Puta or Rotui Mountain, or to cross Moorea from Haapiti to Vaiare, walking over two passes. You should be in good physical condition and fit for these hikes, which also require a minimum of four people. Each hike costs 8.800 CFP per person. The above rates do not include taxes, food and drinks and boat transfers from Tahiti. Bring a casse-croûte sandwich and water.

Randonnées Pacifique / Tahiti Evasion, *Tel./Fax 689/56.48.77, cell phone 21.46.25; E-mail: tahitievasion@mail.pf; www.tahitievasion.com.* Michel Veuillet is the guide who will take you into the green sanctuary of Moorea's valleys and mountains for half- or full-day treks. He will introduce you to the archaeological sites in the Opunohu Valley during a hike through the forest of Tahitian chestnut trees (*mape*). This is an easy 3-hour walk that starts at 8am and costs 3.500 CFP per person. Another relatively easy hike takes you to the *marae* temples in Opunohu Valley and then to the Three Coconut Trees pass. This 4-hour trek starts at 8am and costs 4.000 CFP per person. You can also climb up to the Three Coconut Trees pass and explore Opunohu Valley for a marvelous view of Cook's Bay and Opunohu Bay during a half-day hike that starts at 7:30am and costs 4.000 CFP per person. A minimum of two people is required and transfers are included.

An all-day hike takes you to the waterfalls in Afareaitu and on to Mou'a Puta, the mountain with a hole in the top. From this height you will have a magnificent 360-degree view of the island of Moorea and you can also see Tahiti from here. You must be in good physical condition and not subject to vertigo to attempt this climb. A minimum of two people is required and transfers and a picnic are included for the cost of 6.000 CFP per person.

Horseback Riding

Opunohu Valley Ranch, *Tel. 56.28.55, cell 78.42.47*, is located on the *route des ananas* (pineapple road) in Opunohu Valley, on the right side of the road past the turn-off for Le Belvedere, 2 kilometers (1.2 miles) from the circle island road at Opunohu Bay. Terai Maihi, who formerly operated the Tiahura Ranch, has horses for 6 riders. He leads 2-hour guided excursions through mountain trails and into the valley, passing the river, forests of Tahitian chestnut trees (*mape*) and pineapple plantations. The morning ride is from 8:30 to 10:30am and the afternoon ride is from 3:15 to 5:15pm. He is closed on Sunday afternoon and all day Monday. Each 2-hour ride is 5.500 CFP per person.

Helicopter Tours

Polynesia Hélicoptères, *Tel. 689/86.60.29; cell 78.65.05; Fax 689/81.61.29; E-mail: helico-tahiti@mail.pf; www.polynesia-helicopter.com*. A 5-seat "Squirrel" AS 350 BA helicopter is based at the Tahiti-Faa'a airport and is available for tourist flights, transfers to Moorea and specific charters on request. A 35-minute "Moorea Discovery" flight-seeing tour for a minimum of four passengers costs 25.500 CFP per person with a departure from the Faaa Airport in Tahiti. A 15-minute flight over Moorea costs 15.700 CFP per person (minimum of four passengers) when it leaves from the Temae Airport in Moorea. Private transfers from a hotel in Tahiti to a hotel in Moorea are 52.000 CFP, and a private charter is 168.000 CFP per hour.

Boat Rentals, Kayaks, Cata-Jet, Jet-Ski and Wave Runners

Cata-Jet is located on the beach at Hotel Hibiscus, *Tel. 56.43.37 or 77.88.49*. They rent catajets with an awning and 6 HP or 25 HP engines that you can drive yourself without a license if you are at least 16 years old. The 6 HP catajet costs 6.000 CFP for one hour and a two-hour guided excursion on the 25 HP catajet is 13.000 CFP for two people. You can also rent a catajet at all the big hotels.

Moorea Locaboat, *Tel. 78.13.39*, is located on the beach at Hotel Hibiscus and on the beach beside Fare Condominium. Sylvie and Francis have small boats with a 6 horsepower engine that you can rent without a license. The rates are 7.000 CFP for 2 hours, 9.000 CFP for 4 hours, and 11.000 CFP for 8 hours, gas included. They also provide transfer service from anywhere on the island.

Moorea Mahana Tours, *Tel. 56.20.44 / 55.19.38 / 55.10.19/ 55.10.27.* This company is operated by Moise and Félicie Ruta, who are based at the InterContinental Resort Moorea and at the Sheraton Moorea Lagoon. They provide boat transfers to the motu. They charge 16.700 CFP for one hour to rent a 5-passenger Spyder boat with captain. An Aquavision boat with a 4 horsepower engine is 6.500 CFP for 2 hours, 8.500 CFP for 4 hours and 10.500 CFP for 8 hours. You can rent a jet-ski or wave-runner with a guide daily from 8:30am to 4pm, for 8.250 CFP for a half-hour or 12.950 CFP for an hour. They also have boat tours around the island, picnics on the motu, water-skiing and parasailing. See information under each heading in this chapter.

Moorea Pearl Resort Activities, *Tel. 55.17.50*, rents jet skis for 9.500 CFP for 30 minutes and 14.000 CFP for one hour. Their small motorboats are 8.000 CFP for 2 hours and 10.000 CFP for 4 hours.

Nati Miti, *Tel. 56.57.47 or 74.16.25*, rents 16-foot Hobie Cats for one or two people for 5.000 CFP per hour with a skipper. Call for details.

Sofitel Ia Ora Activities, *Tel. 55.03.55*, rents kayaks for 500 CFP for 30 minutes and 800 CFP for one hour, pedal boats for 1.000 CFP for 30 minutes and 1.500 CFP per hour, and a round hydra-jet boat with a joystick is called a Coco-Jet, which rents for 3.000 CFP for 30 minutes and 4.500 CFP for one hour.

Deep Sea Fishing

Tea Nui Services, *Tel./Fax 56.35.95; E-mail: teanuiservices@mail.pf.* Captain Chris Lilley has a 31-foot Bertram Flybridge Sportfisher named *Tea Nui* that is professionally equipped with Penn International reels and all that you need to realize your dream of catching marlin, tuna, wahoo or mahi mahi offshore Moorea. Chris, who is an American resident of Moorea, has more than 20 years' experience in local waters. The *Tea Nui* is based at InterContinental Resort and they charge 61.600 CFP for a half-day private charter or 15.400 CFP per person for a minimum of 4 and a maximum of 6 people for a half-day fishing excursion. These rates include 10% value added tax. The Sheraton charges 16.500 CFP per person for 4-6 people and 66.000 CFP for a private half-day charter on board the *Tea Nui*, including taxes.

Moorea Fishing Charters, *Tel. 77.02.19; E-mail: halfon@mail.pf*, is operated by Jean Pierre Halfon. His 29-foot Riviera fishing boat has a flybridge, 200 HP diesel Volvo engine and luxury accommodations for six guests. There are two game fishing chairs, two outriggers and all the fishing equipment is provided. This boat is available for fishing or cruising, looking for dolphins and whales (in season). The charter rates start at 15.000 CFP for a minimum of 3 people for 4 hours of fishing, and go up to 95.000 CFP for 8 hours for a maximum of 5 people on a private charter. A Taxi Boat service is also provided for a maximum of 8 passengers, for 15.000 CFP per hour during the day and a 30 percent supplement at night.

Dolphin & Whale Watching Eco-Tours

Dolphin and Lagoonarium Tour, *Tel. 78.42.42,* is operated by Paul Courset and Harold Wright, who worked with Club Med on Moorea until it closed in 2001. Their fully covered catamaran *Rava IV* makes daily trips around the island to look for the spinner dolphins and they also sight humpback whales between July and late October. Another highlight of this excursion is an hour's visit to Motu Ahi, where the tourists can snorkel among the fish, sharks, rays and turtles in the enclosed lagoonarium. Then they are served rum punch, juice, water, coconut and pineapple under the shade on the beach. A cameraman is on board to record this memorable occasion and you can buy a video or DVD film that may even show you caressing a nurse shark. This tour lasts for 4-5 hours and costs 7.000 CFP per person. Pick-ups from Les Tipaniers, Hotel Hibiscus, Vaimoana and Moorea Village start at 8am and the boat leaves the last dock at 8:30am.

Dolphin & Whale Watching Expeditions is owned by Doctor Michael Poole, *Tel/Fax 56.23.22; cell 77.50.07; www.drmichaelpoole.com,* whose fiberglass boat will seat up to 40 people. On Sunday and Thursday mornings a 3-4 hour Dolphin & Whale Watching Expedition (see sidebar) is guided by Doctor Michael Poole or his staff, which takes you through the lagoon and outside the reef to search for, observe and learn about the dolphins and whales that inhabit local waters. Free fruit and juice are provided, and time permitting, a snorkeling stop is offered inside the lagoon. This tour costs 6.700 CFP for adults, half price for children 3-12, and free for children under 3. Supplementary excursions are sometimes made on Tuesdays, and special group charters can be arranged.

Manu Eco Tours Catamaran, *Tel./Fax 56.28.04; cell 72.62.22 / 79.03.28. Manu* is a 10.8 meter (36-foot) motorized catamaran owned by Bernard Calvet, which operates out of the Nautical Center at the InterContinental Resort Moorea. A 4-hour eco-tour around the island takes you to look for dolphins and whales (between July and late October), and also includes snorkeling with the rays and fish, for a minimum of 4 passengers and a cost of 8.200 CFP per person. A 3-hour snorkeling and ray-feeding cruise for a minimum of four people costs 6.800 CFP each, departing daily at 9:30am and 1:30pm. and also includes a visit to Cook's Bay and Opunohu Bay. A half-day private charter for 6 passengers is 45.000 CFP. You can also join a sunset cruise on board. See information under *Sunset Cruises* in this chapter.

Moorea Boat Tours, *Tel/Fax 56.28.44; cell 78.68.86; E-mail: mooreaboattours@mail.pf.* Heifara Dutertre has a 32-foot boat *Naia,* which can seat 30 people, and *Tohara*, a 28-foot boat for a maximum of 12 people. A half-day tour will take you into the open ocean to look for dolphins and whales (in season), for 6.700 CFP. If you find the dolphins early in the day he will make one or two snorkeling stops, let kids water-ski behind the boat or the passengers can take turns fishing. Captain Dutertre also rents his boat with skipper for private tours for 60.000 CFP. These charters start at 8:30am and end around 3:30pm, during which time the passengers can swim with the stingrays, snorkel and go ashore for lunch at one of the restaurants, which is optional.

Dolphin & Whale Watching Expeditions

Dr. Michael Poole, *Tel/Fax 56.23.22; cell 77.50.07; www.drmichaelpoole.com,* is an American marine biologist who lives in Moorea and has devoted his life's work to the study of dolphins and whales. He is a very good teacher who loves sharing his knowledge with other people. The enthusiasm he feels for the mammals he studies in their natural environment is very contagious. Michael and his staff lead 3-4 hour **Dolphin & Whale Watching Expeditions** on Thursday and Sunday mornings. A maximum of 40 passengers are picked up at their respective hotel docks between 8 and 9am, and Michael or one of his staff boards the boat at the Moorea Pearl Resort pier. The search begins, as you head through the lagoon or through a pass into the open ocean. The wild spinner dolphins (Stenella longirostris) are the easiest to find and the most fun to watch because of their acrobatic aerial leaps. Michael and his staff will tell you that 120 of these mammals live around Moorea all the time.

When the sea is calm and the mammals seem approachable, you can sometimes swim with the rough-toothed dolphins, pilot whales and humpback whales. The giant humpback whales can be seen and heard singing off Moorea between July and October, when they come up from Antarctica to mate and give birth. These are the most exciting mammals to watch as they frolic close to the shore and splash in the vicinity of the surprised surfers, who ride the waves beside the passes.

Lagoon Excursions, Snorkeling, Shark & Ray Feeding, & Picnics on the Motu

"A Coconut Cookout with Maco", *Tel. 56.36.05*. Maco is a very lively Tahitian fellow who operates Manahau Tours that is based at the Sofitel Ia Ora. Each Tuesday, Friday and Sunday, between 9am and 3:30pm, Maco offers a unique picnic and snorkeling adventure. He will take you by boat to visit Cook's Bay and Opunohu Bay, and if you wish, you can get into the water and watch him feed the reef sharks and stingrays. Maco will then take you to a private motu islet, where you will have plenty of time to relax on the white sand beach or swim and snorkel in the coral gardens, while he prepares your lunch of chicken and fish grilled on a barbecue. Salads, fresh tropical fruits, beer, wine and juice, soda, water and dessert are included in the price of 7.500 CFP. Maco will even show you how to open your own coconut and how to wear the *pareo*. You'll enjoy his humor. Bring your snorkel gear, towel, sunscreen, camera and protective shoes. Free pick-up at your hotel or pension. Manahau Tours also performs Polynesian wedding ceremonies on Maco's special little motu.

Moorea Mahana Tours, *Tel. 56.20.44*. They have excursions from the InterContinental Resort Moorea and Sheraton Moorea Lagoon that will take you in a covered outrigger speed canoe to visit the two bays, snorkel and feed the stingrays, from 3.900 to 4.290 CFP, or 5.500 to 7.360 CFP, including a picnic on the motu. A full-day Dolphin Watch boat tour around the island with a picnic on the *motu* is 9.100 CFP per person.

Moana Lagoon Excursions, *Tel. 55.21.10 / 55.21.11; Fax 56.40.58; E-mail: alberttransport@mail.pf*. This excursion is operated by Albert Transport and Activities and has earned a good reputation for their barbecue picnic on the *motu*, which takes place every Tuesday, Wednesday, Friday and Sunday. You'll stop to feed the sharks and stingrays and go snorkeling and shelling, in addition to viewing Cook's Bay and Opunohu Bay from the water. The hotel pick-ups start at 8:45am and the all-inclusive cost is 6.000 CFP.

Moorea Camping, *Tel. 56.14.47*, has a 3-hour shark and ray feeding tour at 10am and 2pm for a minimum of 8 passengers, which includes a fruit-tasting stop on the motu. The regular price is 2.000 CFP and for Moorea Camping guests it costs 1.500 CFP.

Te Aho Nui Activities, *Tel. 56.10.02/56.31.42 or 79.09.58*. Patrice Pater is known as "the man who dances with sharks." His 30-foot motorized outrigger canoe departs daily at 9:30am from the beach at Moorea Village. Escorted by the sea birds across the sparkling lagoon of turquoise and blue, his first stop is to feed the rays in their abode of clear, shallow water. You'll never forget the second stop, when Patrice calls to his friends the reef sharks. You will be amazed at the rapport and inter-action between Patrice and these wild creatures when you see how carefully he handles a shark he picks up in his hands to bring to the boat to show his passengers. You can get into the water if you want to, but you can see the main events of this incredible show and still keep dry inside the canoe if you prefer. Other lagoon inhabitants who come to feed from Patrice's loving hands may be a moray eel or even a barracuda he has tamed. You will certainly agree that it's true romance between man and moray when Patrice performs a mouth-to-mouth feeding. Then he will take you to Opunohu Bay to a site called "Le Tiki", where you can snorkel among several huge stone tiki statues that were carved by Tihoti, a multi-talented resident artist of Moorea. Patrice also picks up passengers at the Hotel Hibiscus, and the tour ends between 12:15 and 12:30pm. The cost is 3.500 CFP per person.

Hiro's Tours / What To Do On Moorea, *Tel. 78.70.10 / 70.51.08*. Hiro Kelley's **Motu Picnic Tour** is very popular with tourists and features photo stops, a visit to Cook's Bay and Opunohu Bay, an exciting Shark Show and Ray Feeding, plus a sumptuous barbecue picnic on a motu islet, with punch, wine, beer and soft drinks included. This 5 1/2 hour tour is 6.000 CFP and includes free pick-up service from your hotel or pension. A 2-hour **Sunset Cruise** of Cook's Bay is 4.000-5.000 CFP. See information under *Sunset Cruises* in this chapter. Hiro's team of friendly Tahitian guides will also take you on a 1 1/2 hour **Snorkeling Excursion** for 1.000 CFP a person, departing Club Bali Hai at 1:30pm each Monday, Wednesday and Saturday. Hiro Kelley is the son of the late Hugh Kelley, one of the famous "Bali Hai Boys", and his activity desk at Club Bali Hai can also book other island excursions.

Massages & Spas

Hélène'Spa, *Tel. 689/55.19.70; Fax 689/55.19.80; E-mail: helenespa@mail.pf; www.spa-tahiti.com* is located at the InterContinental Resort Moorea. Hélène Sillinger is a qualified professional, certified in naturopathy. Services include natural and tropical massages, hand and foot reflexology, body scrubs, body wraps in fresh banana leaves, a bath with fresh flowers, a rain shower, a traditional river bath at sunset and masks with fresh fruit and plants. She also provides manicures, pedicures, makeup, waxing, body scrubs, face care, hair care, Bach Flowers remedies, bionutrition advice and natural aesthetic care. You can even get a Polynesian tattoo on request. She charges 15.100 CFP for a 55-minute natural massage, 10.900 CFP for a 25-minute wrap with tamanu oil, fresh papaya or pineapple; 8.400-14.200 CFP for facials, and 8.000 CFP for a full leg waxing.

La Baie de Nuarei, *Tel. 689/56.55.09; Fax 689/56.41.81; E-mail: labaiedenuarei@mail.pf' www.labaiedenuarei.com*. Adjacent to the public beach on Motu Temae, 5 minutes from the airport and 10 minutes from the ferry dock. Tamara Kindynis-Tamagna operates this spa, beauty institute and thalassotherapy-balneotherapy center. You can have a Swedish, Californian, shiatsu, relaxing or energetic massage, a bath with seawater and algae, a jet shower with seawater or spring water to drain lymph nodes, or a multi-jet treatment with essential oils. You can also have a facial, a treatment for heavy legs, waxing, plucking and several other beauty treatments.

Mandara Spa, *Tel. 689/55.10.40; Fax 689/55.11.55; E-mail: tahiti@mandaraspa.com; www.mandaraspa.com*. is located at the Sheraton Moorea Lagoon Resort & Spa. You'll love this place from the moment you walk in the door. Mandara Spa originated in Bali and the unique spa treatments you'll receive here reflect the beauty, spirit and tradition of Asia. The staff of technicians includes massage therapists who are available to pamper you, and a menu of indulgences will tempt all your hedonistic tastes. You may choose a relaxing footbath, an aromatic floral Jacuzzi bath, a Mandara body scrub, exotic facials, an aromatic hair bath, an aromatherapy massage, sports massage, hot stone massage, reflexology massage, a manicure, pedicure, steam bath, sauna, Vichy shower, or a combination of indulgences.

An Exotic Island Facial cleanses, exfoliates and rehydrates your skin and costs 12.500 CFP. A 50-minute Heaven and Earth reflexology massage focuses on your head and feat, and costs 12.500 CFP. A Sunset or Moonlight Massage lasts for 50 minutes and costs 13.500 CFP. Couples enjoy being massaged at the same time in their private bungalow or on the ocean terrace deck, as the sky colors itself beautiful. This double pleasure costs 25.000 CFP. A Mandara Experience begins with a body scrub of your choice and is followed with a full session massage or facial for 80 minutes and costs 17.000 CFP. The Polynesian Indulgence is the ultimate pampering package that lasts for 3 hours and costs 27.000 CFP. A basic manicure with polish is 5.500 CFP and an aromatic pedicure with polish is 6.000 CFP. There's lots, lots more.

Manea Spa, *Tel. 55.17.97*, is a new spa at the Moorea Pearl Resort and Spa that opened in 2004. Isabelle, the manager, is noted for her knowledge and experience in various massage techniques, including reflexology for head, hands and feet. She uses only 100 percent natural products for her treatments, which range from a 30-minute massage for 6.500 CFP to a 3 hour and 20 minute Manea Manea combination for 30.000 CFP. The spa facilities include a Hammam, Jacuzzi and Vichy shower.

Harmony-Beauté, *Tel. 56.55.54*, is located at PK 12.800 on the mountainside in Pihaena, between Cook's Bay and Opunohu Bay, close to the Sheraton. Chantal and Hélène are two French women with magical fingers, who can give you a facial, drain the lymphatic glands, pluck your eyebrows, wax your face, legs and body, apply permanent makeup for your eyes and lips, give you a manicure and pedicure and massage your body. A one-hour facial is 5.500 CFP, manicures are 3.800-5.000 CFP, full leg waxing is 4.600 CFP, and a 45-minute relaxing massage is 6.000 CFP.

Philippe Girodeau, *Tel./Fax 689/56.40.42, cell 77.54.79*, is my preferred massage therapist. He will bring his massage table to your room and make you feel like a new person after he works on your body, mind and soul. He opens your chakra energy centers and heals your aches and pains with magnetism and a pair of very strong hands. He charges 8.000 CFP, but the massage usually lasts more than an hour.

Nautical Activities Centers
InterContinental Resort Moorea Nautical Activities Center, *Tel. 55.19.19*. You'll find a variety of interesting activities here, which are available to hotel guests and anyone else who wants to explore the lagoon. In addition

to snorkeling, windsurfing, scuba diving, day sailing, parasailing, fishing, lagoon tours, and pedal boat rentals, you can also get a round-trip boat transfer to a *motu* for 980 CFP, water-ski for 2.500 CFP for a 10-minute tour, join a snorkeling and ray-feeding expedition in the lagoon for 6.800 CFP, take a sunset cruise for 3.500 CFP, view the coral gardens through the windows of the *Aquascope* half submarine for 3.500 CFP, or through an Aquablue diving helmet as you Aqua-Walk on the bottom of the lagoon for 6.500 CFP.

Moorea Pearl Resort & Spa Activities Center, *Tel. 55.17.50*. Hotel guests can use the snorkeling equipment, kayaks and outrigger canoes free of charge. A glass bottom boat ride is 3.500 CFP, a sunset cruise is 7.500 CFP, a Jet Ski is 9.500 CFP for a half hour or 14.000 CFP for an hour, and a Cata-Jet is 7.000 CFP for 2 hours. You can go snuba diving for 6.000 CFP or scuba diving with Moorea Blue diving for 6.850 CFP. You can also go deep-sea fishing, dolphin and whale watching, water skiing, parasailing, or join a Motu Picnic excursion, complete with ray feeding, a visit to the two bays and snorkeling for 6.000 CFP.

Sheraton Moorea Lagoon Resort & Spa Nautical Activities Center, *Tel. 55.11.11*. Guests staying in the hotel have free use of the kayaks, outrigger paddle canoes and pedal boats that you see lined up on the white sand beach. Most of all the other nautical activities are handled by Moorea-Mahana Tours, except for scuba diving, which is managed by TOPdive-M.U.S.T., who charges 6.500 CFP for all dives, and the *Tea Nui* fishing boat.

Snorkeling equipment is free and 45-minute snorkeling lessons are given every day at 2:30pm for 2.900 CFP. A Jet Ski with guide is 8.250 CFP for 30 minutes or 12.950 CFP for one hour. A speedboat with pilot is 16.700 CFP per hour, a boat tour with ray feeding is 4.290 CFP, a circle island tour with a picnic on the motu is 9.100 CFP, or you can go directly to the motu at 10pm for the picnic and return to the hotel at 2:30pm for 7.360 CFP. A half-day deep-sea fishing charter for 1-5 people is 16.500 CFP each, and a private fishing charter is 66.000 CFP for a half-day outing. This is just a sample of the activities available.

Sofitel Ia Ora Moorea Nautical Activities Center, *Tel.55.03.55*. You can rent a pedal boat for 1.000 CFP per half-hour or 1.500 CFP per hour, a kayak for 500/800 CFP, a motorized sea trailer for 1.500/2.500 CFP, a coco jet for 3.000/4.500 CFP, a wakeboard for 3.000 CFP or take a ride on the Aquascope Yellow Submarine for 5.000/8.000 CFP for two people. You can join a snorkeling excursion daily except Sunday for 2.500 CFP, go fishing in the lagoon for 7.500 CFP, walk underwater with Aquablue for 6.000 CFP, or visit the Lagoonarium for 5.000 CFP. A Dolphin & Whale Watch with Dr. Michael Poole is available on Thursday and Sunday, for 6.700 CFP, and each Tuesday, Friday and Sunday you can take a boat tour to a motu for a picnic, snorkeling and swimming, stopping to feed the sharks and stingrays on the way. This tour costs 7.500 CFP per person. Deep-sea fishing costs 15.000 CFP per person for a half-day outing, and scuba diving is 5.800 CFP per dive, available daily at 8am, 10am and for beginners at 2pm, who must pay 6.300 CFP.

Tip'Nautic, *Tel. 56.12.67, cell 78.76.73*, is a nautical base located at Hotel Les Tipaniers, open daily from 9am to 6pm. You can rent snorkeling gear for 500 CFP, a kayak for 500 CFP for 1 hour, take a guided tour by kayak for 2.500 CFP for 2 hours, or you can catch a boat to the motu for 700 CFP a person, water-ski for 15 minutes for 2.500 CFP. You can join a **Shark and Ray Discovery** excursion for 3.000 CFP, or combine the shark and ray feeding with a 3-hour boat tour around the island for 5.800 CFP per person. Manager Jean-Marcel Grosrenaud has an 8-passenger motorboat for these excursions and he is a qualified sports teacher. He will even give you a 30-minute swimming lesson for 1.600 CFP.

Tuatini Activities Moorea, *Tel./Fax 56.17.85, cell 74.32.50; E-mail: glassbottomboatmoorea@hotmail.com*. Their headquarters are located behind the bicycle rental *fare* adjacent to Le Petit Village. In addition to 2-hour glass bottom boat excursions for 3.500 CFP, they will transfer you to the motu for 700 CFP per person or take you on a sunset cruise with maitai punch for 5.500 CFP. A new activity is a Maiau Beach picnic on the motu for a feast of ma'a Tahiti, which will be cooked in an underground *ahima'a* earth oven on the beach. They will also teach you how to make *poisson cru* and tie a *pareo*. This all day outing is 15.000 CFP per adult and 10.000 CFP for a child under 10 years. Private tours include snorkeling beside the coral reef and at the entrance to Opunohu Bay to see the underwater tikis, plus ray and shark feeding and a picnic. The rates for 2-12 people are 60.000 CFP for a half-day and 100.000 CFP for a full day excursion.

Sailing – Charter Yachts

Archipels, B.P. 1160, Papetoai, Moorea, 98729. *Tel. 689/56.36.39, Fax 689/56.35.87; E-mail: archimoo@mail.pf; www.archipels.com*. The main office for Archipels Croisières Polynésienne is on the mountainside at PK 17 in Opunohu Bay.

François Profit, the general manager, will help you plan your own sailing holiday aboard one of the five Archipels 57 sailing catamarans, whether you want to visit the Leeward Society Islands or the Tuamotu atolls. Each catamaran has a Fiberglass hull, is 17.5 meters (57 feet) long and 8.20 meters (28 feet) wide, with a draft of 1.20 meters (4 feet) and 160 square meters (190 square yards) of sail area. The 4 air-conditioned guest cabins, each with its own private bathroom, can sleep a total of 8 passengers. There's a spacious living area, galley, 2-crew cabin and large cockpit protected by a permanent sunroof. Technical equipment includes 2 engines, a generator, fresh water maker, large refrigeration space, icemaker, dishwasher and washing machine. An inflatable dinghy with a motor, snorkeling and fishing equipment, two ocean kayaks, cassette deck and compact disk player, television and video are some of the leisure equipment available, and each yacht has radio transceivers, navigational equipment, automatic pilot and radar.

Archipels Croisières charters primarily to individuals or "by the cabin" in a shared-boat cruise, or you can charter the entire yacht by the day. This rate includes fuel for the boat and dinghy, all meals and hotel services aboard, organized shore activities and airport/yacht transfers. The per-passenger rates also include meals and hotel services aboard, double occupancy cabins, airport/yacht transfers and all the excursions and events specified in the program you choose.

The 2004 low season in the Society Islands and the Tuamotu atolls is from January 3 to April 30 and from October 23 to December 17. The high season is May 1 to October 22 and from December 18 to January 2, 2005. This may change by a few days in 2005. A 7-day/6-night Leeward Islands cruise in low season is 213.500 CFP per person and 234.000 CFP in high season. A Marquesas Islands cruise of 8 days/7 nights is 256.500 CFP year round, and a 7 day/6 night Tuamotu cruise from Fakarava to Toau to Rangiroa is 220.500 CFP in all seasons. A 4 day/3 night Tuamotu cruise inside the atoll of Rangiroa is 124.000 to 133.500 CFP per person, or 93.000 to 102.000 CFP per person for a 3 day/2 night cruise inside the Rangiroa lagoon. You can also charter the entire yacht by the day for 238.000 to 287.500 CFP with a skipper and hostess/cook included.

Scuba Diving

A qualified English-speaking instructor heads each dive center in Moorea. All diving equipment is available, and dive packages with special lodging can be arranged. If you are not a certified diver bring a health certificate from your doctor with you. The protected lagoons, passes and outer coral reefs offer ideal conditions for scuba diving year-round in water temperatures that range from 77º to 86º F. There are more than a dozen dive sites no deeper than 75-90 feet that you can discover with the following diving professionals.

Bathy's Club, *B.P. 1247, Papetoai, Moorea, 98729. Tel. 689/56.31.44 / 55.19.39; cell 78.15.38; Fax 689/56.38.10, E-mail: bathys@mail.pf; www.baths.net; www.dive-moorea.com.* This is one of the two PADI five-star centers in French Polynesia, and it is located at the InterContinental Resort Moorea. Four PADI instructors, headed by Juan-Pedro and Corinne Duran-Lopez, speak English, French and Spanish, and are very experienced in underwater guided tours inside the lagoon, on the coral shelf and in the open ocean around Moorea. The dive gear is new, safe and comfortable, and includes 30 top of the line Scubapro jackets, 25 Scubapro regulators and 40 wet suits in 14 different sizes. A maximum of 25 divers can be divided between two fast and safe aluminum boats that were specially built for diving. Full service features air fill, professional video service, dive shop, certification, and lessons for beginners or certified divers. A specialty of Bathy's Club is feeding

Moorea's Best Dive Sites

Moorea's dive sites offer special treats of feeding the large lemon sharks and a rendezvous with the friendly giant-sized Napoleon fish. Divers also see black and white-tip sharks, gray sharks and moray eels. The water is clear with insignificant currents, assuring easy dives that attract scuba divers from all over the world. One of the most popular sites is "Le Tiki", where you'll be able to see wild sharks, including lemon sharks more than 2.4 meters (8 feet) long. The Toatai Pass through the barrier reef offers drift diving among nurse sharks, leopard rays and schools of jackfish. A site known as "Napoleon Plateau" offers Napoleon fish that weigh up to 80 pounds, as well as sharks. Inside the lagoon is a site called "The Wreck", which is an artificial haven for fish, with the ship's hull spread over 82 feet, complete with anchors, chains and a gangway. Other sites include the "Ray Corridor," "The Canyon," "The Blue Island," the "Shark Dining Room," the "Bali Hai Wall," "Temae," "Atiha," the "Avamotu Pass" and the "Taotaha Pass," all offering a concentration of eels, barracudas, coral fish, rays or sharks. The depths for these dives is usually 60 to 70 feet, with an average visibility of 150 feet and sometimes more than 250 feet. Many of the dive spots are less than 10 minutes by boat from the shore.

the sharks and meeting stingrays that live inside the lagoon. Open daily from 8am to 6pm, with four dives per day. A Fun Dive last 40/45 minutes and costs 6.900 CFP and an Initial Dive of 25/30 minutes is 7.800 CFP, with all equipment included for any dive. Shark feeding costs 2.000 CFP extra.

Ia Ora Diving, *Tel. 689/55.03.55, ext. 4982; Fax 689/56.49.52; E-mail: iaoradiving@mail.pf; www.iaoradiving.pf.* This PADI dive center is located on the beach at the Sofitel Ia Ora and is open daily from 8am to 5pm. Two qualified English-speaking instructors are available to take you to the most interesting sites in their fast 28-foot dive boat that can accommodate 12 divers. All equipment is provided, including shorty wetsuits. Certified divers leave the hotel beach at 8am and 10am and pay 5.800 CFP per exploratory dive. Beginners can have an introductory dive at 2pm, which costs 6.300 CFP.

Moorea Blue Diving Center, *Tel. 689/55.17.50; E-mail: mooreabluediving@mail.pf; www.mooreabluediving.com.* This small dive center is based at the Moorea Pearl Resort & Spa. Raphael, the diving instructor and owner/manager, has had several years' experience diving in Moorea, formerly with M.U.S.T. and then with Club Med. An initiation dive is 7.500 CFP, an exploration dive is 6.850 CFP, and a night dive is 8.500 CFP. A package of 5 Fun dives is 32.500 CFP and 10 Fun dives costs 59.500 CFP. The rates include all the equipment, which is new.

Moorea Fun Dive, *B.P. 737, Maharepa, Moorea 98728. Tel./Fax 689/ 56.40.38; E-mail: fundive@mail.pf; www.fundive.pf; www.divemoorea.com.* This dive shop is adjacent to Moorea Camping at P.K. 27 in Haapiti, and is operated by Roland and Edmee Imfeld. Edmee is a PADI master scuba diver trainer, a Nitrox instructor and a CMAS** international instructor. Roland is a PADI master instructor, Nitrox instructor and CMAS** international, and Remy is a CMAS** international instructor, BEES1 and underwater photographer, with 15 years' experience diving in French Polynesia. Their equipment includes a 24-foot aluminum boat for 14 passengers, but they limit the diving to 10 people with one dive guide for a maximum of 5 divers. All the necessary equipment is provided and they also make pick-ups from hotels and pensions within a 5-minute drive from the dive center. They charge 5.500 CFP for an exploration dive, 10.000 CFP for two dives and 27.300 CFP for a 6-dive package.

Scubapiti Moorea, *B.P. 563, Maharepa, Moorea, 98728. Tel. 689/ 56.20.38; Fax 689/56.47.79; E-mail: scubapitidaniel@mail.pf; www.scubapiti.com. Hotel Les Tipaniers Tel. 689/56.12.67.* Daniel Cailleux runs this popular dive center, which is located on the property of Les Tipaniers in Haapiti. He is a French State supervisor BEES 1, 1st degree French federal monitor, CMAS instructor, and monitor for PADI and ANMP (Association National des Moniteurs de Plongée). Daniel and his highly qualified instructors are available to take you for an exploration or first dive for 5.500 CFP. A 5-dive package is 26.000 CFP and a 10-dive package is 48.000 CFP. These rates include all the equipment, and lower rates are available if you bring your own diving gear. They will also give you lessons that will enable you to obtain a level one ANMP certification in just a few days, which is recognized by PADI. The boat transport for a maximum of 10 kilometers (6.2 miles) is included in the prices. While you are exploring the underwater world of clown fish, groupers and sharks, one or two camera men will follow you to video tape your dive, which you can then see on an instant replay system. This tape is available for purchase as a souvenir of your vacation memories. The center is open daily.

TOPdive - M.U.S.T. (Moorea Underwater Scuba Diving Tahiti), *B.P. 336, Maharepa, Moorea, 98728. Tel. 689/56.17.32 Fax 689/56.15.83; E-mail: info@topdive.com; www.topdive.com.* The main office of this PADI dive center is located beside the pier at the Cook's Bay Resort (the hotel is now closed), and they also have a branch at the Hotel Sheraton. Manager and dive master Nicolas Buray is assisted by four qualified instructors, offering beginner, certified and night dives, each for 6.500 CFP. The 8am exploration dive includes shark feeding and 2-tank dives are also available each morning. A Fun dive can be made at 2pm and Introductory dives and lessons are given by appointment only. All the equipment used is Scubapro, and they dive with 12-liter steel tanks (15 liter tanks are available on request). A package of 10 dives is charged at the rate of nine dives, which comes to 58.500 CFP. The diving rates include taxes and all equipment. This package can also be used at TOPdive centers in Bora Bora, Rangiroa, Fakarava and Tahiti. At publication time it was announced that TOPdive Moorea will also offer Nitrox scuba diving in the near future.

Sunset Cruises

Hiro's Tours/What to Do on Moorea, *Tel. 78.70.10/70.51.08.* A Cook's Bay Sunset Cruise departs from the Club Bali Hai dock at 4pm each Monday, Wednesday and Saturday, for a 2-hour sunset celebration on board Hiro Kelley's modern version of the famous Bali Hai Liki Tiki ("Leaky Tiki") catamaran. A Tahitian band plays Polynesian songs, and there is even a pareo demonstration show. Rum punch, beer, wine and soft drinks are included for the price of 5.000 CFP, with a discount of 1.000 CFP if you combine it with Hiro's other tours.

Manu Catamaran, *Tel./Fax 56.28.04; cell 72.62.22 / 79.03.28. Manu* is a 10.8 meter (36-foot) motorized catamaran that operates out of the Nautical Center at the InterContinental Resort Moorea. The sunset cruise leaves the dock every afternoon at 5pm and returns at 6:30pm, for a minimum of four and a maximum of 12 passengers. Drinks are included in the price of 3.500 CFP.

Tuatini Activities Moorea, *Tel./Fax 56.17.85; cell 74.32.50; E-mail: glassbottomboatmoorea@hotmail.com.* A 2-hour sunset cruise aboard a glass bottom boat on the lagoon in Haapiti includes maitai punch and costs 5.500 CFP per person.

Water-Skiing

Moorea Mahana Tours, *Tel. 56.20.44,* charges 3.800 CFP for beginners at the InterContinental Resort for five tries in 20 minutes. Certified water-skiers pay 2.500 CFP for a 10-minute round. Beginners at the Sheraton Moorea Lagoon pay 3.850 CFP for 20 minutes and certified skiers pay 2.750 CFP for 10 minutes.

More Water Fun

Aqua Blue, *Tel. 56.53.53, E-mail: aquablue_pf@hotmail.com* is a novel way to say hello to the fish in the lagoon in Moorea. This activity is based at the InterContinental Resort Moorea. You do not have to be a certified diver nor even a swimmer to discover this new sensation, and you can wear a simple swimsuit for the experience. A certified diving instructor will accompany you and help you to put on a funny looking yellow diving helmet that looks like those used in Jules Verne's movie, *20,000 Leagues Under the Sea.* The helmet weighs 40 kilograms (88 pounds), but you don't feel the weight when you are under the water, and you can actually walk around on the bottom of the lagoon just as you would walk on any land. An air hose connected to a compressor on board the boat allows you to descend to a depth of 3 to 5 meters (10 to 16 feet). Your Aqua-Walk lasts 35 minutes and costs 6.500 CFP.

You can also recreate the pioneer diving techniques of the 1930s when you are outfitted in an authentic hard helmet, canvas diving suit and heavy boots, and your air is supplied by an authentic René Piel pump from that era. All the equipment conforms to security norms and you will have a qualified and enthusiastic team of PADI and BEES1 diving instructors to accompany you. An optional photo/video service is available to record your unforgettable dive to a depth of six meters (20 feet), which lasts for 35 minutes.

Aquascope, *Tel. 55.19.19.* You'll find this excursion at the InterContinental Resort Moorea. Aquascope is a half submarine that puts you under the surface of the water, where you can view the coral gardens and colorful fish without getting wet. The cost is 3.500 CFP and you can take a ride every day, every hour between 9am and 12pm.

Moorea Dolphin Center (ex-Dolphin Quest), *Tel. 55.19.48; Fax 56.16.67; E-mail: dqmoorea@dolphinquest.org; www.dolphinquest.org.* This organization is based at the InterContinental Resort Moorea. You can participate in encounter programs with trained dolphins that live inside a lagoon park. A one-hour Dolphin Experience is available at 9am and 3pm for anyone over 12 years old, and costs 11.500 CFP. This encounter combines elements of hands-on contact, education, fun and adventure. A one-hour Honeymoon Package costs 28.000 CFP and includes sharing a special romantic encounter with your partner, complete with a photo. An Ocean Adventure lasts for two hours and takes you underwater with a mask where you will experience stingrays, fish and other colorful ocean animals. Then you will meet the dolphin family for games, feeding, training signals and learning about their unique personalities. This program is open for anyone 16 years and older and costs 24.000 CFP. Kid's Ocean Adventure is a one-hour adventure for the 5- to 11-year olds and costs 7.000 CFP per kid. They will play ocean games, say hello to the playful stingrays and then slip into the shallow water to meet the dolphin. They will also receive a Dolphin diploma to proudly display to friends at home.

Lagoonarium of Moorea, *Tel. 78.31.15; Fax 43.89.30; E-mail: lagoonarium@mail.pf,* is operated by Teiki Pambrun on Motu Ahi, at PK 8 in Afareaitu. Look for the Lagoonarium's creative wooden sign beside the road and stop here for a shuttle boat service to the motu. The fee is 2.300 CFP for each adult and 1.500 CFP per child, which allows you to spend the day on the motu, snorkeling in a lagoonarium filled with tropical fish of all colors. You'll see parrotfish, butterflyfish, surgeonfish, red snapper, small tunafish, loach, jackfish, picassofish and wrasses, as well as moray eels, stingrays small blacktip reef sharks and a turtle. There are even two friendly nurse sharks you can pet. Face masks and snorkels are provided and kayaks and diving equipment can be rented and diving is available with advance reservations. You may want to bring a sandwich and drink, or you can buy your lunch and water, soft drinks or beer from a little snack stand on the motu. Teiki's family also carries a supply of steaks, chicken legs, merguez sausages and chips that you can buy and cook yourself on the barbecue grills provided. Some of the organized lagoon excursions come here for their barbecue picnic on the motu. There is a Tahitian style outhouse and a few simple A-frame shelters for those who want to spend the night in this *sauvage* environment. Just remember that it is not a hotel or pension, but an opportunity to sleep on a motu and commune with Nature. This is a popular destination for groups of school children, who enjoy the hands-on education Teiki treats them to when he leads them into the water. If you are coming from Tahiti you can telephone in advance and they will pick you up at the Vaiare boat dock and take you back for your return boat, charging 600 CFP per person for the round-trip transfers.

Lakana Fly Kite Surfing, *Tel. 27.31.76; E-mail: bdflyfr@yahoo.fr.* David is a young Frenchman who gives lessons in kite surfing and he speaks good English. He is based next door to Les Tipaniers on the site of the former Moorea Beach Club. His rates are 12.000 CFP for 2 hours, 20.000 CFP for 4 hours and 40.000 CFP for 12 hours of lessons, which are spread out over several days.

Polynesian Parasailing, *Tel. 56.20.44*, is a way to let you float over Moorea's lagoon without getting your feet wet. You have a 10-12 minute ride aloft, up to 180 meters (600 feet) above the lagoon, where all you can hear is the wind. This activity is available at the InterContinental Resort Moorea for 6.650 CFP per person or 9.900 CFP tandem for one adult and one child; the Sheraton Moorea Lagoon charges 6.710 per person for a minimum of 2 people; and the Moorea Pearl Resort & Spa charges 7.700 CFP per person and 10.400 CFP for one adult and one child.

Shopping

When you take a guided circle island tour of Moorea the bus or 4-wheel drive vehicle will most likely stop at a boutique and a black pearl shop, which are probably owned by the guide's family or friends. If you rent a car or scooter or bike around the island you'll have a better chance of finding out which shops you prefer.

My favorites are the shops that sell locally made products, rather than clothes, pareos and souvenir items imported from Bali. **Boutique Polynesia**, *Tel. 56.19.27*, is in the Centre Tumai on the mountainside at PK 2.7 in Tiaia, between the airport and Maharepa. Jean-Luc, the talented owner, creates his own jewelry from black pearls, nacre, bone, tou, tutu, purau and other local wood. He also sells Marquesan wood sculptures, pareo outfits, shirts and lamps made by Tahiti Art, and he carries Te Mana shirts from Tahiti for men and women. His wife has **Boutique Océane** across the road, where half the merchandise is locally made and half is imported. **Green Lagoon Gallery**, *Tel. 56.18.30*, on the mountainside around PK 3.8 in Tiaia, presents oil canvases by Nataly Jolibois and sculptures of driftwood, wood and metal and wood and stone by Hans Jörg Stübler.

There are a few curio shops and boutiques in and close to the Maharepa Center, where you'll also find the post office and banks. **Michou Creations** is a well-known dressmaker whose shop is next to Le Pêcheur Restaurant at PK 6 in Maharepa. **Club Bali Hai** has increased the size of their boutique and placed it at the entrance to the hotel next to the road. You might find the perfect souvenir item or *pareo* in there. **Honu Iti Boutique**, PK 8.5 in Cook's Bay, has Tahitian clothing and souvenirs, as well as pareos and trinkets imported from Indonesia. They also have some black pearl jewelry. **Kaimana Boutique** at the Sheraton Moorea Lagoon Resort & Spa is well-stocked with gift items, silk painted pareos, tropical clothing, men's shirts and T-shirts, and some pretty wall hangings or bed covers called *tifaifai* in Tahitian.

L'Atelier du Chat, *Tel. 56.47.86*, is on the mountainside close to the InterContinental Resort Moorea. Bruno and Nathalie sell Oceanian Art and sculptures. Down the road on the lagoon side, **Outre-Mers** is a nice boutique at PK 25 in Tiahura. They have some really pretty *pareos* and unusual souvenir items.

In the Club Med area of Haapiti you'll find a number of boutiques that carry *pareos*, T-shirts, swimsuits and gift items. **Little Blue Boutique**, in the Saint Jacques Center, has locally made clothes and gift items. **Le Petit Village** is a small shopping center with an ABC store, three black pearl shops, plus boutiques and a magazine stand. **Paki Paki** is a clothing shop at PK 27 on the mountainside in Haapiti, between Hotel Hibiscus and Moorea Village. The Tahitian style dresses and gowns are made by seamstresses in Moorea and are quite expensive but original. **Linareva Boutique**, *Tel. 55.05.65*, at PK 34.5 in Haapiti, sells original necklaces made by Mama Fauura, a noted artisan who lives in Tahiti. **Marie Couture**, *Tel. 70.49.26*, on the lagoon side of the road at PK 6.3 in Afareaitu, makes Tahitian style clothes to order.

You should also visit the **bazaars** at the boat docks in Cook's Bay and Papetoai village when the *Paul Gauguin*, the *Tahitian Princess* or visiting passenger liners are in port. Local artisans set up display stands under awnings to sell their *pareos*, tee-shirts, dresses and beachwear, costume jewelry made of shells and mother-of-pearl, woven hats and bags and numerous other souvenirs that are made in Moorea.

Shopping for Black Pearls

Black Pearl Gem Company (BPGC), *Tel. 56.36.68*, is open daily from 9am to 6pm. Look for the sail-like canopies on the attractive building across the road from Club Med.

Marc Collins, who is half-American and half-Chinese from Tahiti, grew up in Mexico City. He heads this family owned and operated business that produces, wholesales and retails black pearls. They specialize in premium quality and stunning top-of-the line colors, including blue, green, purple and the rare peacock. The BPGC collection of jewelry designs features the work of award-winning goldsmiths and designers from around the world, and their in-store designer can work with you in creating one-of-a-kind jewelry for you. They also offer an extensive range of pearls for all budgets.

The sales consultants at BPGC are trained by the Gemological Institute of America, and the service is friendly and helpful, never pushy. Everyone here speaks very good English, in addition to a few other languages. The air-conditioned showroom is designed to make shopping for your pearls an enjoyable and memorable experience. You are welcome to help yourself to a beer, soda or bottle of water kept on ice at the back of the shop. Informative brochures answer your questions about black pearls, and transportation by courtesy shuttle is provided on request.

Marc will organize private pearl parties for groups. He prints the invitations you can distribute to all the people in your group, and he provides buses and mini-vans for the round-trip transfers from your hotel. The group arrives at Black Pearl Gem Company after the shop has closed for its normal business day, and you are greeted with flower leis, a Tahitian musical trio, glasses of very good French champagne and Marc's entire sales staff. This is a delightful way to shop, as they keep on pouring the champagne. Even then, there is no pressure to buy. You will be given a certificate of authenticity and origin for each pearl you buy, which is also backed by an unconditional 30-day money-back guarantee. BPGC also provides global shipping and you can browse their online catalogue at *www.blackpearlgemco.com*.

EVA PERLES, *Tel. 56.10.10*, is next to the Banque de Tahiti in Maharepa. Eva and Thierry Frachon are the very amiable hosts in this pleasant shop, and their selection of fine black pearl jewelry will be sure to please you. Eva was trained as an art metalist in Wisconsin during her college years, and now uses this knowledge to design and fabricate a lot of the jewelry she sells. She has also completed the pearl course given at the Gemological Institute of America, as well as the Accredited Jewelry Professional training. Her first goal is to educate people so that they will be free to choose the best for themselves, no matter where they buy their pearls. She never pushes for a sale, choosing instead to share her passion with the visitor, opening them up to the uniqueness of this magical gem, to recognize the true beauty of each pearl, even though that beauty may not be perfect. Eva also displays some of her paintings in the gallery, as well as works by other resident artists.

Golden Nugget Perles, *Tel. 56.13.05*, is on Motu Temae close to the public beach and the Sofitel Ia Ora. You take the coral sand road opposite the post office at PK 0 in Temae and follow the signs pointing to Kerebel Jeweller. Kerebel is a goldsmith who creates most unusual jewelry, which often reflects his interest in the American Southwest. Some of his masculine rings are a golden or silver eagle set with a big black pearl.

Heivai Black Pearls, *Tel. 55.00.80,* is across the road from Club Bali Hai in Pao Pao, and **Moorea Black Pearls**, *Tel. 55.01.40,* is across the road from InterContinental Resort Moorea. Anyone who takes a circle island tour or 4WD Safari with Albert Transports and Activities will certainly stop at one or both of these pearl shops, as they are owned by Albert's son, William Haring, and his wife Tania. She creates the jewelry designs and has won a gold trophy in an international jewelry competition. Like all the Haring family, William is a hard worker and dedicated salesman.

Island Fashion Black Pearls, *Tel. 56.11.06,* at PK 6.9 in Pao Pao, is open Monday through Saturday from 9am to 6pm. Owner Ron Hall is an American from California, who sailed to Tahiti with Peter Fonda aboard the yacht *Tatoosh* in the mid-1970s. Ron met a wonderful Tahitian lady named Josée, who was also a professional dancer, and very wisely chose to marry her and remain in "Paradise." Ron managed hotel bars, taught snorkeling and shelling and then opened his Island Fashion Boutique, selling Hawaiian style shirts, bikinis, beach wear and *pareos*.

He then added showcases of black pearl jewelry set in 18-carat gold, and became one of the first successful black pearl salesmen on the island. Some of his customers return time and again to add to their collection from Ron's impressive selection of quality black pearls and black pearl jewelry. Ask him to give you a "pearl school" lesson in how black pearls are produced. You may even be lucky enough to meet Josée, Ron's most precious gem, who is the mother of his two children. Their son, Heimata, has now joined the family business, which is expanding to include a new shopping center on the mountainside right across from the boat dock where cruise ship passengers come ashore in Cook's Bay. Transportation from your hotel is provided on request.

Van der Heyde Art Gallery, *Tel. 56.14.22,* next door to Island Fashion, is owned by Aad van der Heyde, a Dutch artist whose oil paintings are displayed all around his enclosed garden, as well as a few works by other resident artists. Inside his shop you'll find authentic primitive art from throughout the South Pacific, more of Aad's paintings, coral and wood sculptures from the French Polynesian Islands, and displays of black pearl jewelry. Aad said that he was the first person in Moorea to sell black pearls. In addition to his collection of cultured pearls, he also sells unset *keshis*.

Woody Art Gallery, *Tel. 56.17.73 or 56.37.00.* is beside the lagoon at PK 23.9 in Papetoai. Woody Howard is an American resident of Moorea who creates exquisite sculptures from the roots of trees and local wood. He has now added a black pearl showroom to his gallery.

Tattoos

Masters of the art can design tattoos for those of you who wish to wear a permanent souvenir of your trip to Moorea. The cost of a Maohi tattoo depends on the design, and you'll pay around 10.000 CFP for a simple drawing.

Chimé Tattoo, *Tel. 689/56.24.16; E-mail: tahiti-tatau@netcourrier.com*, is located beside the lagoon at PK 10.8 in Haumi, between the villages of Afareaitu and Maatea. This is a combination boutique, tattoo shop and mini-museum of traditional tattooing instruments from different countries. You have a choice of techniques for your tattoo, which are all performed hygienically. Chimé has won several international tribal tattoo competitions in Europe and has lived in various countries with his wife, Barbara, who is Dutch. They both speak English. Their boutique carries a small production of tattoo-influenced designs in tee shirts and fisherman/aikido type pants, as well as tattoo paintings and shell jewelry.

Gilles, *Tel. 689/77.58.23*, is a Frenchman whose tattoo *fare* is located on the white sand beach at Sofitel Ia Ora. He has several books of designs to choose from and he does a good business with tourists.

Purotu Tattoos, *Tel./Fax 56.22.92, cell 77.57.59*, is located on the mountainside at PK 5.5 in Maharepa. Purotu is noted for his original designs and he is also a talented artist and sculptor.

Roonui Tattoo, *Tel. 689/56.37.53; E-mail: tatauroonuilynda@yahoo.fr*. Roonui Anania has won several international tattoo competitions for Tribal Tattoos. He has moved his shop and is now located on the mountainside at PK 24 in Tiahura, across the road from the InterContinental Resort Moorea.

Tautu Tattoo, *Tel. 689/56.57.11 / 27.73.91; E-mail: taututattoo@hotmail.com*. The Tatau by Tautu shop is next door to Magasin René Junior in the hotel area of Haapiti. His exclusive Polynesian designs are applied in good hygienic conditions, he speaks English, and he also plays guitar and sings. Tautu's ladylove, Tepua, is a Canadian woman who organizes activities and excursions at the Moorea Village. She will happily answer any questions you may have about getting a tattoo.

You can also get tattooed at **Tiki Village**.

Practical Information
Banks
All the banks are closed on weekends and holidays. They charge a commission for each transaction, which varies from bank to bank.

Socredo Banque is in the same shopping center as the Maharepa Post Office, *Tel. 55.07.00*, and you'll find an ATM ready cash window here. Open Monday through Friday 8am-12pm and 1:30-4:30pm.

Across the road in the Centre Noha is the **Banque de Polynesie**, *Tel. 55.05.80*. Open Monday through Friday 7:45am-12pm and 1:15-3:45pm. They have an ATM window. There is also a branch with an ATM window located in Le Petit Village in the Club Med area of Haapiti, *Tel. 55.04.30*. Open 8am-12pm and 1:30-4:30pm.

Banque de Tahiti is on the lagoon side near the Maharepa Post Office, *Tel. 55.00.55.* They have an ATM window and are open 8am-12pm and 1:30-4:30pm.

Books, Newspapers & Magazines
• **Kina Maharepa** is in the same commercial center as the Post Office and Socredo Banque, *Tel. 56.22.44.*
• **Supersonics** is in Le Petit Village in the Club Med area of Haapiti, *Tel. 55.05.30.*

Churches
If your hotel is in the Cook's Bay area, the Protestant church at PK 5 in Maharepa is a good choice. The Protestant church Ebenezer at PK 22 in Papetoai Village is octagonal and was built on the site that was once the royal Marae Taputapuatea, where heathen gods were worshipped. The first church in the South Seas was built here in 1827 and rebuilt in 1889. It has since been restored a few times. Another Protestant church is located at PK 35 in Haapiti, and the beautiful Catholic Church, Eglise de la Saint Famille Haapiti, is at PK 24 on the mountain side.

Saint Joseph's Chapel at PK 10 beside Cook's Bay contains a large mural depicting a Polynesian Nativity scene, painted in 1946 by Swedish artist Peter Heyman. The members of this little church wrote a letter to the Pope, asking permission to have a religious painting made, with Mary, Joseph and the Christ child portrayed as Polynesians. The Pope agreed to their proposal, stipulating that the painting should be a mural so that it would always remain in the church and not be transported elsewhere. When the building began to deteriorate, a new church was built next door, where services are still held. A wealthy Moorea resident had the chapel restored in 1999, and it is now used for weddings, baptisms and other special occasions.

Dentist
Dr. Fréderic Avet has an office in the Centre Noha, opposite the post office in Maharepa, *Tel. 56.32.44.* He has modern equipment and good dental knowledge and techniques. Most of the expatriate Americans living in Moorea go to him.

Doctor
Dr. Christian Jonville, who speaks good English, has an office in the Centre Noha, opposite the post office in Maharepa, *Tel. 56.32.32.* The office hours are 7am to 12pm and 2 to 6pm Monday through Friday, 7am to 12pm on Saturday, and 8 to 10am on Sunday. Dr. Pierre Champion, *Tel. 56.44.63,* is my favorite all-purpose doctor and his office is located above the pharmacy in Maharepa. He has the same hours as Dr. Jonville. Dr. Hervé Paulus has an office

in Le Petit Village, opposite Club Med, *Tel. 56.10.09*. He specializes in sports injuries. He is closed Thursday afternoons.

Drugstores
Pharmacie Tran is at PK 6.5 in Maharepa, *Tel. 55.20.75*. The hours are 7:30am to 12pm and 2 to 6pm Monday through Friday, 8am to 12pm on Saturday and 8 to 11am on Sundays and holidays. Dr. Tran is Vietnamese and speaks good English. In case of emergency, knock on the door. The **Pharmacie of Haapiti** is located on the mountainside at PK 30.5, *Tel. 56.38.37/56.41.16*.

Hospital
The 20-bed government **Hospital of Afareaitu** is at PK 9 in Afareaitu Village, *Tel. 56.24.24/56.23.23*. Seriously ill or injured patients are evacuated by helicopter or airplane to Mamao Hospital in Tahiti.

Internet Service
Iguane Rock Café, *Tel. 56.17.16*, is in Le Petit Village in Haapiti. Open daily 9am to 7pm. Mastercard, Visa. There are four computers and the charge of an Internet connection is 20 CFP per minute.

Cyberc@fé, *Tel. 56.16.70* is at Le Motu Pizzeria, PK 26, Haapiti, in St. Jacques Center, across street from Club Med. Open Tuesday through Saturday 9:30am-8pm and Sunday morning. Closed Sunday night and Monday night. They have an air-conditioned room with computers, 17-inch flat faced screens, Azerty and Swerty keyboards, a printer and Internet connections for 20 CFP per minute.

Maria Tapas, *Tel. 55.01.70; E-mail: mariatapas@mail.pf,* is a "cyberbodega" in the Kikipa Center at PK 6 in Maharepa. Mastercard, Visa. Open Monday through Wednesday from 8:30am to 11pm, and Thursday through Friday from 8:30am to 1am. Closed Saturday noon, but they are open Saturday night until 1am. Closed all day Sunday. There are three computers, including one Macintosh, plus a scanner and printing facilities. Internet charges are 250 CFP for 15 minutes.

Moorea Vision, *Tel. 55.01.75, E-mail: mooreavision@netcourrier.com,* This Internet connection is at PK 9 in Pao Pao village, located across the road from the Ecole Maternelle de Pao Pao in Cook's Bay. You can get on-line Monday through Friday from 7am to 5pm, and on Saturday from 8 to 11am. Closed Saturday afternoon and all day Sunday. During school holidays (July/ August), they open at 8am Monday through Friday. They have three computers in back of the store. The cost is 250 CFP for 15 minutes and 1.000 CFP per hour. Printing is 100 CFP per page.

System Tek, *Tel. 55.20.70*, has Internet connections on the mountainside in the Centre Tumai at PK 2.7 in Tiaia, between the airport and Maharepa.

Tiki@Net, *Tel. 56.39.42, E-mail: tikinet@mail.pf*, is located in the back room of Arts Polynésiens boutique in Le Petit Village. They are open Monday-Saturday 8:30am to 6:30pm and on Sunday from 8am-12pm. They charge 20 CFP per minute for Internet connections.

Internet service is also available at the InterContinental Resort Moorea, Sheraton Moorea Lagoon Resort & Spa, Moorea Pearl Resort, Sofitel la Ora, Hotel Hibiscus, Residence Linareva and Pension Motu Iti.

Laundry

La Laverie Beatrice, *Tel. 56.17.19 / 70.64.65*, operates a pick up and delivery laundry service Monday-Saturday. They charge 750 CFP to wash 5 kilos of clothes and 750 CFP to spin dry 5 kilos. Ironing is also available for 200 CFP per piece.

Marina

The **Marina of Vaiare**, *Tel./Fax 689/56.26.97*, has a welcome pier with a pontoon for yachts and deep-sea fishing boats up to 60 feet long.

Police

The French *gendarmerie* is at PK 7 in Maharepa, *Tel. 56.13.44*. Open daily 7am to 12pm and 2 to 6pm.

Post Office & Telecommunications Office

The **Maharepa Post Office**, *Tel. 56.10.12*, is located in the shopping center at PK 5.5. Hours are 7:30am-12pm and 1:30-4pm Monday through Thursday, and on Fridays it closes at 3pm. It's also open on Saturdays 7:30-9:30am. All telecommunications and postal services are available here. **Papetoai Post Office**, *Tel. 56.13.15*, is on the lagoon side in the center of Papetoai village. Open Monday through Thursday from 8am to 12pm, and from 1:30 to 4pm and until 3pm on Fridays. Open on Saturday from 8 to 10am. Most hotel boutiques also carry a few postage stamps.

Tourist Information

Moorea Visitors Bureau, *Tel. 56.29.09*, www.gomoorea.com, has an office at Le Petit Village shopping center opposite Club Med. The English-speaking hostess is on duty Monday to Thursday from 8am to 12pm and 1 to 5pm and on Fridays from 8am to 12pm and 1 to 4pm. Closed weekends and holidays.

Wedding Ceremonies

Tahitian Weddings are performed at the **Tiki Theatre Village** for lovers who get married back home and want to splurge for a fun-filled colorful wedding ceremony in the authentic tradition of old Polynesia. It's not just newlyweds who are getting married in the Tahitian style, but also loving couples who are celebrating their anniversaries or who want to renew their vows. The ceremony takes place on a marae stone altar with a Tahitian priest officiating. **Olivier Briac** and his Tiki Village artisans will transform you into a Tahitian prince and princess for your wedding ceremony for a marriage made in Paradise. Costs vary from 75.000 CFP for a Motu Wedding, 110.000 CFP for a Princely Wedding, 135.000 CFP for a Royal Wedding and 195.000 CFP for a Deluxe Wedding. Contact Olivier Briac at B.P. 1016, Haapiti, Moorea, *Tel. 55.02.50, Fax 56.10.86, E-mail: tikivillage@mail.pf; www.tikivillage.pf.*

Sofitel Ia Ora Moorea, *Tel. 55.03.55,* has a wedding chapel, which is popular with Japanese couples, and **Moorea Beachcomber Inter-Continental Resort**, *Tel. 55.19.19*, also performs Polynesian non-binding weddings and renewal of vows.

Chapter 15

HUAHINE

Huahine (WHO-ah-HEE-nay) is a magical island. I discovered the special qualities of Huahine in 1977, when I was shipwrecked on the reef in Parea, on the south end of Huahine Iti, during a dark and stormy night, while sailing with American friends aboard their luxury yacht. The story has a happy ending, because the yacht was saved and we were adopted into a Tahitian family in Parea. I stayed there for six weeks just because the people were so nice.

On that first morning in Parea, from the cockpit of the yacht that was embedded on the coral reef, I watched the early dawn turning the whole world pink from the mountains to the village to the sea. There is a certain light and color of the air on this island that I haven't found anywhere else. The senses are heightened so that the colors of nature seem more vivid, the air more calm, yet at the same time charged with a feeling of anticipation. I realized that I was listening more intently for—perhaps the primeval call of the jungle.

I still have the same feeling for Huahine. The people are happy and relaxed and they have maintained their traditional lifestyle of fishing and farming. Family and friends are more important than television and Internet. The mountains of Huahine form the shape of a beautiful Tahitian woman when seen from the sea in the moonlight. And there's a definite aura of sexual energy in the air.

Huahine is 175 kilometers (110 miles) northwest of Tahiti, the nearest of the Leeward Society Islands to the capital of Papeete. The two islands that comprise **Huahine-Nui** and **Huahine-Iti** (big and little Huahine) are connected by a bridge and have a combined surface area of 73 square kilometers (28 square miles). Legend claims that the two islands were once united and the isthmus was formed when Hiro, a great warrior and god of thieves in

Huahine

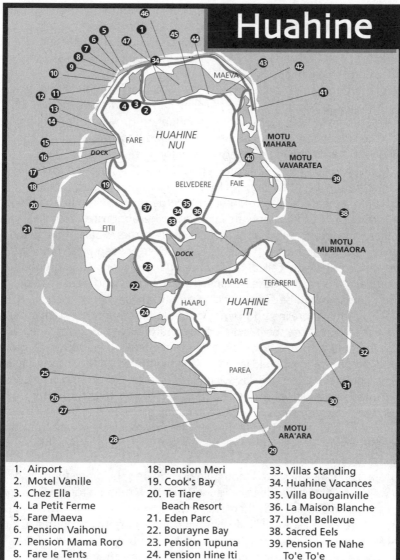

1. Airport	18. Pension Meri	33. Villas Standing
2. Motel Vanille	19. Cook's Bay	34. Huahine Vacances
3. Chez Ella	20. Te Tiare	35. Villa Bougainville
4. La Petit Ferme	Beach Resort	36. La Maison Blanche
5. Fare Maeva	21. Eden Parc	37. Hotel Bellevue
6. Pension Vaihonu	22. Bourayne Bay	38. Sacred Eels
7. Pension Mama Roro	23. Pension Tupuna	39. Pension Te Nahe
8. Fare Ie Tents	24. Pension Hine Iti	To'e To'e
9. Chez Lovina	25. Pension Mauarii	40. Huahine Pearl Farm
10. Fare Tehani	26. Relais Mahana	41. Hotel Sofitel Heiva
11. Rande's Shack	27. Avea Bay	42. Camping Vanaa
12. Pension Ariitere	28. Pension Te Nahe	43. Stone Fish Traps
13. Chez Enite	Parea	44. Archaeological Sites
14. Chez Guynette	29. Marae Anini	45. Fare Potee Museum
15. Fare Center	30. Ariiura Camping	46. Pension Fetia
16. Chez Henriette	31. Panorama	47. Lake Fauna Nui
17. Pension Poetaina	32. Maroe Bay	

Polynesian mythology, sliced his canoe through the island, dividing it and producing two beautiful bays on each side of the isthmus. Folklore tells us that Hiro used the Leeward Islands as his favorite hangout, and on Huahine you can see Hiro's paddle and parts of his anatomy in the stone formations of the cliffs overlooking the channel.

A common barrier reef surrounds the two islands, with several passes providing openings from the sea to the deep harbors. Offshore *motu* lie inside the reef, where watermelons and cantaloupe are grown in the white coral sand. These islets are surrounded by white sand beaches, ideal for a picnic outing with snorkeling in the living coral gardens.

A paved road winds 32 kilometers (20 miles) around the two islands, passing through the little villages of Fare, Maeva, Faie and Fitii on Huahine Nui, and Haapu, Parea, Mahuti, Tefarerii and Maroe on Huahine Iti. The modest homes of the 5,750 inhabitants are built beside the lagoon in the small villages. Another paved road, called *la route transversale*, crosses part of the island of Huahine Nui, and is best explored by Land Rover or Jeep or any four-wheel drive vehicle, which are called 4x4 (*quatre-quatre* in French and pronounced like cat-cat). This road is close-hemmed by giant ferns and vines that look as though Tarzan might be seen swinging around these parts.

Skirting the shoreline and climbing a little higher into the fern-covered mountains, you will see spectacular views of natural bays and seascapes, with the white foam of the indigo ocean leaping into spray on the coral reef, giving birth to sapphire and emerald lagoons. One multihued bay near the village of Haapu is pointed out on tours as "Gauguin's palette." All around both islands are plantations of vanilla, coffee and taro, and groves of breadfruit, mango, banana and papaya. Trees of *purau* and kapok grow among tangled masses of untamed wilderness. Swiftly flowing streams make their way from their mountain origins, winding through the *mape* forests to form delightful pools for fresh water shrimp.

Mou'a Tapu is the sacred mountain overlooking the prehistoric village of Maeva, which is built beside Lake Fauna Nui. The mountain forms a pyramid, and the people of Maeva say there is a power spot on its summit, which is 429 meters (1,407 feet) high. A tiki of white coral and a Tiare Taina (gardenia) bush are found here. You can reach this spot by going up the road where the television antenna is located on the southern side of the mountain.

According to ethnohistory, Maeva was the ancient capital of Huahine, and all its ruling families lived there and worshipped in their individual *marae* temples of stone. The great Marae Manunu on the coral islet on the opposite side of Maeva Village was the community temple for Huahine Nui, and Marae Anini at Point Tiva in Parea was the community *marae* for Huahine Iti.

Huahine's Archaeological Sites

The royal village of **Maeva** was the traditional headquarters of Huahine, the capital of a complex and highly centralized system of government. This was the only place in the entire Polynesian triangle where the royal families lived side by side. The people of Maeva say that the sacred mountain of Mou'a Tapu protected them. Each of the eight district chiefs of Huahine held court at Maeva and ruled in his province through envoys. Each royal household had a marae stone temple in Maeva as well as in his provincial seat. When the children of each household approached maturity, they, too, each had a temple erected. Consequently, there are some 200 marae in Maeva.

Doctor Yosihiko H. Sinoto, Senior Anthropologist of the Bernice P. Bishop Museum in Honolulu, restored several of the marae temples in Maeva Village and on nearby Matairea Hill in 1967 and 1968. He also restored the stone fish weirs in Lake Fauna Nui, which were used by the ancient fishermen of Maeva.

In 1972 Doctor Sinoto began excavation of two archaeological sites on the grounds of the former Hotel Bali Hai in Huahine. Over a period of years he and his assistants unearthed a village community that existed between 850 and 1200 AD, which had been destroyed by tidal waves.

Doctor Sinoto has restored some 200 sites, including 35 marae temples, plus council platforms and housing sites on Matairea Hill in Maeva Village. Inside the Fare Pote'e, an oval-shaped traditional meeting house that is built over Lake Fauna Nui, is a museum where you can pick up a map of Matairea Hill. Follow the cultural and scenic hiking trail to visit the restored sites and learn the story of the royal village.

European Discovery

Lieutenant James Cook (who was later promoted to Captain) was the first European to discover Huahine, when he anchored the *Endeavour* in the harbor of Farenui-Atea on July 15, 1769. You can see the islands of Raiatea, Tahaa and Bora Bora from Huahine, which Cook named a Society of Islands, 'because they lay contiguous to one another'.

Cook returned to Huahine in 1773 aboard the *Resolution*, along with the *Adventure*, under the command of Captain Tobias Furneaux. When the two ships set sail, a young man from Raiatea who lived in Huahine went with them. His name was Mai but the Englishmen call him Omai. He became the first Tahitian to discover England, where he was presented to King George III on July 17, 1774. Cook brought Omai back to Huahine in 1777 during his third and final voyage to the South Seas.

After Cook's departure there were few Europeans who visited Huahine, until 1808-09, when a party of Protestant missionaries from the London Missionary Society made it their headquarters for nearly a year. When Christianity was adopted in Tahiti in 1818 the missionaries returned to Huahine and opened a station. The Reverend William Ellis in *Polynesian Researches* tells a first-hand account of this story.

Huahine's warrior-queen Teha'apapa defended her island against the aggressions made by the men of Bora Bora, and she won a great naval battle against the forces of Tahiti's Queen Pomare, who tried to gain control of Huahine. In 1846 Teha'apapa won a land battle against French troops at Maeva, and 24 Frenchmen are buried in Maeva Village, surrounded by seven broken cannon. Huahine defended its independence until 1888, when the regent Marama accepted the French protectorate. In 1898 Huahine became a French colony, but it was not until 1946 that the people of Huahine became French citizens, 58 years after the residents of Tahiti.

Arrivals & Departures
Arriving By Air
Air Tahiti has three to six flights daily between Tahiti and Huahine. The 35-minute non-stop flight is 10.000 CFP one-way for adults, and 18.300 CFP round-trip, tax included. There is also a daily direct flight from Moorea, which costs 12.500 CFP one-way. You can fly from Raiatea to Huahine every day except Sunday for 5.200 CFP, and with one to three daily flights from Bora Bora, for 7.500 CFP. **Air Tahiti reservations**: Tahiti, *Tel. 86.42.42/86.41.84;* Moorea, *Tel. 55.06.00;* Huahine, *Tel. 68.77.02/60.62.60.*

If you have hotel reservations then you will be met at the airport and driven to your hotel. There are also taxis at the airport, as well as **Avis** and **Europcar** counters. There are public phones. Brochures of hotels, pensions and activities are available in a wall rack close to the arrival gate. A couple of boutiques and Dorothy Levy's **Vakalele** snack bar are located in the airport terminal.

You can also get to Huahine by chartering an airplane in Tahiti from **Wan Air**, *Tel. 50.44.17, cell 77.03.79;* **Air Archipels**, *Tel. 81.30.30;* or **Air Tahiti**, *Tel. 86.42.42.*

Arriving By Boat
All the inter-island transport boats dock at the quay in Fare village, the main town of Huahine, and it would be advisable to arrange with your hotel or pension to have someone meet you when you arrive in the middle of the night. The car rental agencies will also meet you at the Fare quay. A travel agency and visitors information center is across the street from the quay.

Hawaiki Nui, *Tel. 45.23.24/Fax 45.24.44, E-mail: sarlstim@mail.pf.* This 12-passenger ship leaves the Motu Uta dock in Papeete each Tuesday at 4pm and arrives at Fare quay in Huahine on Wednesday at 2am. The Thursday trip leaves Papeete at 4pm, and arrives in Huahine on Friday at 3:30pm, after visiting Raiatea, Bora Bora, Tahaa and Raiatea again. The cost of sleeping on deck is 1.750 CFP per person and a berth in one of the 4 double cabins costs 4.950 CFP from Papeete to all the Leeward Islands. Passengers must sleep in cabins on the Thursday voyage as the ship also transports fuel. Meals are available on board.

Vaeanu, *Tel. 41.25.35; Fax 41.24.34, E-mail: torehiatetu@mail.pf*. This ship can transport a total of 90 passengers, with 32 berths in cabins and 58 places on the deck. It departs from the Fare-Ute quay in Papeete at 4pm on Monday, Wednesday and Friday, arriving in Huahine at 12:30am the following morning. The ship continues on to Raiatea, Tahaa, Bora Bora and Raiatea again, then stops in Huahine on its way back to Tahiti each Tuesday and Thursday at 5pm and each Sunday at 4pm. One-way fares for deck passengers are: 2.120 CFP from Tahiti to Huahine; 1.690 from Bora Bora; 1.400 CFP from Tahaa and 1.060 CFP from Raiatea. A berth in a cabin costs 4.400 to 5.989 CFP per person depending on accommodations chosen, and the entire cabin can be rented for 9.858 to 13.197 CFP. Meals are served on board. Reservations for cabin space must be paid in full before 9am on the fixed date of departure from Papeete.

Departing By Air

You can fly from Huahine to Raiatea or Bora Bora or return to Moorea or Tahiti by **Air Tahiti**, *Tel. 68.77.02 or 60.62.60* in Huahine. Tickets can be purchased at the airport. If you already have reservations and a ticket and need to reconfirm your flight, most hotels will take care of this for you or you can do it yourself one day in advance. Check-in time at the airport is one hour before scheduled departure.

Departing By Boat

You can continue on to Raiatea, Tahaa and Bora Bora by boat from Huahine, or you can return to Papeete.

Hawaiki Nui, *Tel. 68.78.03* (Huahine); *Tel. 54.99.54* (Tahiti), leaves Huahine for Raiatea, Bora Bora, Tahaa and back to Raiatea each Wednesday at 2:30am. On Fridays it leaves Huahine for Tahiti at 4:30pm, arriving in Papeete on Saturday at 5am.

Vaeanu, *Tel. 68.73.73* (Huahine); *Tel. 41.25.35* (Tahiti), leaves Huahine at 1:30am each Tuesday, Thursday and Saturday for Raiatea, Tahaa and Bora Bora and back to Raiatea and Huahine (also stopping again in Tahaa on the Sunday voyage). The return trips from Huahine to Papeete leave Fare each Tuesday and Thursday at 5:30pm, arriving in Papeete at 2am the following day. On Sundays the ship leaves Huahine at 4:30pm for Papeete, arriving each Monday at 1am.

Orientation

To get from the airport in Huahine to the hotels you will turn right to reach the road that circles the island of Huahine-Nui. When you come to this road you will turn right to go to the main village of **Fare** (pronounced Fah-rey) and the land base for Te Tiare Beach Resort. Turn left if you want to go to **Maeva Village**. You can drive in either direction to reach Huahine-Iti, where Hotel Relais Mahana and a few pensions are located. If you arrive by boat you will disembark on the dock at Fare, right in the center of Huahine's "downtown" area. Fare looks like a sleepy little village, shaded by acacia and South Seas almond trees, but it certainly wakes up on boat days when the passenger or supply ships arrive. Then you have traffic jams in the center of the village.

On the waterfront street opposite the quay are the Banque de Tahiti, a couple of snack bars and small restaurants, two pensions, car, scooter and bicycle rentals, service station, scuba diving center, a supermarket, general merchandise and clothing stores, boutiques, a photo shop and jewelry shop. The post office, *gendarmerie*, private doctors, pharmacy and a 15-bed dispensary are within easy walking distance. **Note**: The hotel on the end of Motu Maeva, which operated as the **Sofitel Heiva** since the opening in 1989, ceased to be part of the Sofitel chain as of October 1, 2004. The hotel has been sold and will no longer be used for public lodging. The Huahine Country Club and Spa Resort is a project to build 2 deluxe hotels of 100 and 150 rooms, an 18-hole golf course, a marina, 2 condominium projects, 331 villas and a large shopping center in Tefarerii on Huahine Iti. This should begin in 2005 and be completed in 2007.

Getting Around Huahine
Car, Scooter & Bicycle Rentals

Avis Fare Nui, *Tel. 68.73.34; E-mail: avis.tahiti@mail.pf*. They have a sales counter at the airport and at the Mobil service station behind the Super Farenui store in Fare village. A 3-door Peugeot 106 rents for 6.050 CFP for 4 hours, 7.150 CFP for 8 hours and 8.250 CFP for 24 hours. A 5-door Saxo with air-conditioning costs 8.250 CFP for four hours, 9.350 CFP for 8 hours and 10.450 CFP for 24 hours. These rates include taxes, unlimited mileage and insurance. Gas is extra.

Europcar has a sales office facing the post office in Fare, *Tel. 68.82.59*; at the Port of Fare, *Tel. 68.88.03*; and a sales desk at the Relais Mahana, *Tel. 68.71.62*. A 3-door Twingo rents for 6.200 CFP for 4 hours, 7.200 CFP for 8 hours, 8.400 CFP for 24 hours and 15.100 CFP for 48 hours. A 5-door air-conditioned Peugeot 206 rents for 8.900 CFP for four hours, 9.900 CFP for 8 hours, 11.600 CFP for 24 hours and 21.000 CFP for 48 hours. Scooter rates are 4.900 CFP for 4 hours, 5.500 CFP for 8 hours and 5.900 CFP for 24 hours. These rates include unlimited mileage and third party insurance. Gas is extra.

Hertz/Huahine Location, *Tel. 68.76.85; E-mail: huahinelocation@mail.pf; www.huahinelocation.com.* Their sales office is located on the waterfront in Fare village and they have a counter at the airport. A 3-door Twingo is 5.500 CFP for 24 hours, and an air-conditioned 5-door Clio or Peugeot 106 rents for 6.600 CFP for 24 hours. Scooters rent for 4.000 CFP for 24 hours. Rentals are also possible for two or three days for cars and scooters. These rates include unlimited mileage and insurance. Gas is extra.

Bicycles/Boats/Kayaks

Europcar, *Tel. 68.82.59,* rents bikes for 1.200 CFP for 4 hours and 1.600 CFP for 8 hours. Longer rentals possible.

Huahine Lagoon, *Tel. 68.70.00,* on the quay of Fare adjacent to Pension Chez Guynette. You can rent a beach bike for 1.000 CFP for 4 hours and 1.500 CFP for 8-24 hours. They also have kayaks for 500 CFP per hour or 1.500 CFP for 4 hours. A 6 HP boat costs 8.000 CFP for 8 hours and a 15 h.p. boat for 2 passengers is 10.000 CFP for 8 hours.

Taxis

Taxi service is provided by **Enite Excursions,** *Tel. 68.82.37, cell 73.05.07,* and a couple of other taxis that wait at the airport and boat dock.

Le Truck

The local transportation service, *le truck,* operates between the boat dock in Fare and the outlying villages around Huahine Nui and Huahine Iti, coordinating their runs with the arrivals and departures of the inter-island ferries and school hours. The name of the destination is painted on the wooden sides of each *le truck.* Although the fares are affordable for all budgets, hopping aboard a *le truck* is not recommended if you don't know your way around Huahine, and especially if you don't speak any French or Tahitian. But if you are adventurous, this is a fun way to discover the island and its inhabitants.

Where to Stay
HUAHINE NUI
Deluxe

TE TIARE BEACH – AN OUTRIGGER RESORT, *B.P. 36, Fare, Huahine 98731. Tel. 689/60.60.50; Fax 689/60.60.51; E-mail: welcome@tetiarebeachresort.pf; www.tetiarebeachresort.com. Reservations in US and Canada: Tel. 800-OUTRIGGER (688-7444); E-mail: reservations@outrigger.com; www.outrigger.com. Located on the coast of Fitii, 20 minutes by boat from the main village of Fare. 41 bungalows. 2005 EP Rates single/double: garden bungalow 32.000 CFP; premium garden bungalow 38.000 CFP; beach bungalow 52.000 CFP; overwater bungalow 56.000 CFP; deep overwater bungalow 70.000 CFP; third adult 5.000 CFP. MAP meal plan* for breakfast and dinner 7.600 CFP; AP meal plan for breakfast, lunch and dinner 10.800 CFP per person; Continental breakfast 1.800 CFP; full American breakfast 2.400 CFP; Outrigger Canoe Breakfast 3.750 CFP; Honeymoon breakfast 4.750 CFP; Honeymoon dinner in the restaurant 11.000 CFP; Dinner under the Stars 12.600 CFP; one-way boat transfer 2.500 CFP; private boat transfer with champagne 10.000 CFP. One or two children between 3 and 12 years-old sharing parents' room are free of charge on accommodation basis and have 50% discount on AP/MAP plans (except beverages), and Airport/Hotel/Airport transfers when provided by the hotel. Babies and children under 3 years are free of charge on accommodations, meal plans and airport/hotel transfers provided by the hotel. Add 5% hotel tax to room rates and 6% value added tax to room rates, prepaid meal plans and transfers. A 10% value added tax is applicable to all other services and a municipal tax of 150 CFP is charged per person per day. All major credit cards.

This 4-star hotel is owned by American businessman Rudy Markmiller, and was managed by Tahiti-based South Pacific Management as a Pearl Resort from its opening in March 1999 until July 2004, when the Honolulu-based Outrigger Hotels & Resorts took over the management contract. An "Escape to Luxury" program is in effect through March 31, 2005, allowing guests the fifth night free if they stay at Te Tiare Beach Resort for four nights at published retail rates. With the "Gourmet Escape" program, guests who stay four nights at published retail rates will receive a complete breakfast and dinner for two each day at no additional cost.

Honeymooners and other lovers especially appreciate this 4-star hotel because it is so private and peaceful, a welcome retreat, a world removed from time and care. It opened in March 1999 with 19 garden bungalows, 6 beach bungalows, 5 lagoon bungalows and 11 deep overwater bungalows, beside and over the lagoon in the district called Fitii. The hotel property can be reached only by boat, about a 12-minute ride from Fare village to the resort. All of the 41 bungalows face west, so guests may enjoy the island's spectacular tropical sunsets as well as admire the nearby islands of Raiatea and Tahaa. Your first impression when you arrive here will be a sense of spaciousness and total tranquility. You will also discover how uniquely different this resort is. The reception, lobby, lounge, main bar, restaurant and boutique have all been built over the lagoon, suspended over the water on sturdy concrete pilings. The motif of this complex is tastefully Polynesian, with a huge thatched roof, ceiling fans, shell chandeliers, rattan tables and chairs, bamboo and woven pandanus decorations, and a Tahitian trio playing island tunes in the evening, while lovely vahines dressed in Polynesian colors and flowers take your order and serve you an excellent meal that combines French and local style cuisine.

On land the hotel site covers 11.40 hectares (28.17 acres) of tropical plants and flowers, including 3.5 hectares (8.65 acres) of flat ground. The deluxe bungalows, which are decorated in a modern Polynesian style, are among the largest rooms you will find in Tahiti and Her Islands. You may not even want to leave your room because they are so comfortable. You don't even have to go out to eat if you want to order from room service, which is available from 7am to 9:30pm.

Each bungalow features a king-size bed and a living room with sofa, chairs and tables, air-conditioning and ceiling fan, a wet bar, refrigerator, coffee and tea facilities, television with cable channels in French and video channels in French and English, international direct dial telephones and a separate dressing room in which you will find a personal safe. The overwater bungalows have a large Jacuzzi bathtub and a separate shower with powerful water pressure. (The water at Te Tiare Resort comes from a fresh underground spring, which is filtered, offering you a very high quality of drinking water.) All the bathrooms have separate toilets and hair dryers. There is twice-daily maid service to bring you more towels, bath gels and lotions. All the doors and windows are screened and you even have blackout curtains for more privacy. The terraces for these units are L-shaped and partially covered, with deck chairs for sunbathing or reading and snoozing in the shade. A ladder leads down a few steps into the shallow lagoon, which shades from silk green to aquamarine and turquoise blue.

Next to the lagoon are a free form swimming pool and beach bar, as well as the water sports facilities. Complimentary activities include scheduled boat transfers to and from the main town of Fare, snorkeling equipment, outrigger paddle canoes, kayaks, beach volleyball, ping-pong, French bowls and board games. Optional activities include land tours by 4WD, horseback riding, sunset catamaran cruises, deep sea fishing, shark feeding, island tour by outrigger speed canoe, picnic on a motu, jet-skiing, scuba diving and sailboat excursions. Car, scooter and bicycle rentals, as well as Jeep safaris and other land excursions, are operated from the Te Tiare land base in Fare village. Private tours for two people are also available, such as a Jet Ski tour for 35.000 CFP per couple, a shark feeding expedition for two for 30.000 CFP, an outrigger canoe excursion around the island for 50.000 CFP per couple, and an outrigger canoe tour around the island with picnic for 80.000 CFP. You can also enjoy a relaxing massage in the privacy of your bungalow for 10.000 CFP per hour, and you can practice your asanas with a yoga teacher for 6.000 CFP per person.

Special evenings at the Ari'i Restaurant at Te Tiare Resort include a Friday night Exotic Buffet for 6.800 CFP, which is accompanied by a Polynesian dance group. A Prime Rib Dinner Under the Southern Cross is served on Friday nights, also with a dance group, for 6.000 CFP. See more information under *Where to Eat* in this chapter.

Various cultural demonstrations, such as how to make flower leis, pandanus bracelets, coconut palm hats, tie a *pareo* or dance the *tamure*, are given each evening at the Hawaiki Nui Bar at 6pm, while a trio of Tahitian musicians plays romantic island songs to complete your dream come true.

Honeymooners and couples celebrating anniversaries or other special events can contact the hotel directly for a list of the Romantic Rendez-Vous programs that are designed especially for lovers. These even include non-binding Polynesian wedding ceremonies, such as the Matairea for 104.500 CFP and Topa Mahana for 156.200 CFP, including taxes.

Family Pensions, Guest Houses, Bed & Breakfast, Backpackers'
Lodgings, & Campgrounds
Moderate

MOTEL VANILLE, *B.P. 381, Fare, Huahine 98731. Tel./Fax 689/68.71.77; E-mail: yvesmotelvani@hotmail.com; www.motelvanille.com. Located beside the road 1 kilometer (0.62 miles) from the airport, 1 kilometer from the beach, and 1 kilometer from Fare village. Free round-trip transfers. 6 units. EP Rates: «fare» 8.900 CFP single/double, 11.900 CFP triple; extra bed 1.800 CFP. Breakfast and dinner add 2.900 CFP per person. Prices include a 6% value added tax on room rates and meal plans. A 10% value added tax is applicable to all other services and a municipal tax of 50 CFP is charged per person per day. Mastercard, Visa.*

This small family hotel is the first lodging you come to when leaving the airport, as it is built on the corner between the airport road and the circle island road. There are 6 bungalows with a choice of sleeping accommodations for 2, 3 or 4 people. Each bungalow has a private bathroom with hot water, and a terrace. All the Tahitian style *fare* units are built of local woods, bamboo and thatched roofs, and the windows are screened. They are set in a tropical garden around a swimming pool, which is good for people who prefer a pool to the ocean. Unfortunately, there's not even a view of the ocean from here. Bicycles are free for guests if you want to go exploring or to the village. A restaurant-snack is located on the premises. See more information under *Where to Eat* in this chapter.

PENSION POETAINA, *B.P. 522, Fare, Huahine 98731. Tel./Fax 689/ 68.89.49; cell 78.86.39; E-mail: pensionpoetaina@mail.pf; www.poetaina.com. Located on the mountainside of the road in Fare village, 3 kilometers (1.8 miles) from the airport and 1 kilometer (.62 miles) from the ferry dock. Free round-trip transfers. EP Rates: room with fan and shared bathroom 8.480 CFP single/double; air-conditioned room with private bath 11.130 CFP single/ double; 12.930 CFP triple; 18.330 CFP for 6 people; family room with private bathroom, kitchen and electric fan 12.720 CFP single/double; 14.520 CFP triple. Breakfast included for all rooms. Rates include all taxes except a municipal tax of 50 CFP per person per day. Mastercard, Visa.*

Jean-Pierre Amo and his wife Damiana have built a big three-story white concrete house in the South Seas colonial style, with a huge sun deck on the top floor. There are four rooms with a double and single bed, sharing two communal bathrooms and hot water; three air-conditioned family rooms with a double bed, single bed and private bathroom; and one family room with a king size bed, single bed, private bathroom and kitchenette. Downstairs is a living room with television and activity area, a kitchen and dining room, which are all shared, as well as the big terrace and swimming pool. Jean-Pierre has a cute little *le truck* that he uses to transport his guests to and from the airport and village. He also operates Poetaina Cruises, providing a choice of lagoon excursions and picnics on the motu. Bicycles, horseback riding, scuba diving and all other activities can be arranged through the pension. Poetaina Restaurant is located in Fare village facing the fishermen's wharf. Guests staying in Pension Poetaina are driven to the restaurant and back for dinner on request. The half-board meal plan is 2.000 CFP per person, which includes the appetizer, main course and a dessert. Or you can order from the menu and pay a little extra. See *Where to Eat* and *Lagoon Excursions* in this chapter.

LA MAISON BLANCHE, *B.P. 332, Fare, Huahine 98731. Tel. 689/ 60.63.05; Fax 689/60.63.06; E-mail: lamaisonblanche@mail.pf. PK 10, beside Maroe Bay. EP Rates: room with Continental breakfast 8.600 CFP single/ double; dinner on request 2.500 CFP per person. Add 6% value added tax to room rates, meal plan and transfers. A 10% value added tax is applicable to all other services and a municipal tax of 50 CFP is charged per person per day. No credit cards.*

This bed and breakfast pension consists of two bedrooms in a white colonial style house at the end of the road overlooking Maroe Bay. Each room contains a queen size bed covered by a mosquito net and an electric fan. You share the house and facilities with the friendly hosts, Patricia and Michel Mauren, who speak English.

LA PETITE FERME, *B.P. 12, Fare, Huahine 98731. Tel./Fax 689/68.82.98; E-mail: lapetiteferme@mail.pf; www.la-petiteferme.com. Located on the seaside next to the main road at PK 3, between the airport and Fare village and a kilometer (.62 miles) from the beach. EP Rates: bungalow 5.250 CFP single, 7.900 CFP double, 9.450 CFP triple; 13.150 CFP for 5 people. Room with breakfast 3.900 CFP single, 4.400 CFP double; add 500 CFP for one night stay; MAP room with breakfast and dinner 5.700 CFP per person; dormitory with breakfast 1.850 CFP per person; add 500 CFP for one night stay; MAP bed with breakfast and dinner 3.650 CFP per person per day. Rates include 6% value added tax. A 10% value added tax is applicable to all other services and a municipal tax of 50 CFP is charged per person per day. No credit cards.*

The main activity at this equestrian center is naturally riding the horses in the stable of «The Little Farm», but all the other organized land and lagoon activities are also available. The accommodations include a 5-person bungalow with beds, mosquito nets, electric fan, big kitchen, terrace and private bathroom with hot water. There is also a room with a double bed, and a 6-bed dormitory, all sharing a communal bathroom. House linens are furnished.

Transfers are free during the daytime and cost 1.000 CFP at night. See more information under *Horseback Riding* in this chapter.

HOTEL BELLEVUE, *B.P. 21, Fare, Huahine 98731. Tel. 689/68.82.76; Fax 689/68.85.35. Located on the mountainside overlooking Maroe Bay, 6 kilometers (4 miles) from the airport and 5 kilometers (3 miles) from the ferry dock in Fare village. Round-trip transfers 1.600 CFP per person. 10 garden bungalows. EP Rates: bungalow without kitchen 6.000 CFP single, 7.000 CFP double, 8.000 CFP triple; bungalow with kitchen 7.000 CFP single, 8.000 CFP double, 9.000 CFP triple. Add 6% value added tax to room rates. A 10% value added tax is applicable to all other services and a municipal tax of 50 CFP is charged per person per day. Mastercard, Visa.*

Most visitors to Huahine see the Hotel Bellevue when they are riding around the island in a tour bus. It is perched on the top of a knoll overlooking the panoramic scenery of Maroe Bay and the hills beyond. This is one of those places that is discovered by travelers who have the time to get to know an island, its people and its delightful secrets.

Each of the 10 colonial style bungalows contains a double bed with mosquito net, a private bathroom with hot water provided by solar heating, and individual terraces overlooking the fresh water swimming pool and the view of Maroe Bay. Four of these units are now equipped with their own kitchen, and guests staying in the other six bungalows without kitchens share the communal kitchen.

This small hotel is owned by Eliane and François Lefoc, a Chinese couple from Huahine who were once noted for the delicious seafood they served in their restaurant, before they turned the kitchen over to their guests. The Lefocs do not speak much English, but they say a lot with their eyes and gestures. Eliane will drive you to Fare village for supplies or you can also walk down to the road and catch *le truck*.

PENSION VAIHONU, *B.P. 302, Fare, Huahine 98731. Tel. 689/68.87.33; Fax 689/68.77.57; cell 73.70.97/71.96.03; E-mail: vaihonu@mail.pf; www.iaorana-huahine.com/fr/vaihonu.html. Located beside the sea at PK 1 in Fare, between the airport and the village. Free round-trip transfers. EP Rates: duplex cottage 7.200 CFP single/double, extra bed 1.650 CFP; beach cabin 3.020 CFP single, 4.350 CFP double; dormitory 1.650 CFP per person; camping 1.200 CFP per person. Minimum stay is 2 nights at rates quoted. Add 500-1.000 CFP per person for one-night stays. MAP half-board meals (break-fast and dinner) 2.600 CFP per person; MAP full-board meals (breakfast, lunch and dinner) 4.200 CFP per person. Rates include 6% value added tax on room rates. A 10% value added tax is applicable to all other services and a municipal tax of 50 CFP is charged per person per day. Mastercard, Visa.*

This is the lodging I recommend if you want to be near the ocean, the airport and close to Fare village. Etienne Faaeva, the owner and manager, is a Huahine resident who has worked in tourism in Tahiti and Huahine for several years, and his English is excellent. His facilities are clean and attractive and the atmosphere is laid back and fun. If you are coming from Fare village look for the dirt road just past La Petite Ferme; turn left there and head toward the sea; turn left again at the last road before you get to the end at Fare Maeva; continue a short distance until you see the Vaihonu sign.

Available for guests are three small beach huts facing the sea, two twin or duplex cottages, a six-bed dormitory and a campground for a dozen tents. The concrete duplex cottages are equipped with two double beds upstairs, and a bright, cheerful kitchen and dining area, plus a bathroom and terrace on the ground level. The windows are screened and the floors are tiled. The three beach huts, built of wood and a sheet metal roof, contain one double or two twin-size beds. The six-bed dormitory has mosquito nets over each bed, plus a big ceiling fan. It is adjacent to the communal kitchen and outdoor dining terrace, which both have floors of white coral. The communal bathroom has cold-water showers. Sheets are furnished to all guests except the campers, but you must bring your own towels.

If you don't want to cook your own meals, you can order from Etienne's menu, which features Chinese and local style dishes. Etienne also owns Huahine Explorer and can organize your safari excursions and other activities. This is a family of excellent musicians, and chances are you will be in residence during one of Etienne's frequent barbecue parties, when you can listen to the beautiful island songs they sing while playing the guitar and ukulele.

FARE MAEVA, *B.P. 675, Fare, Huahine 98731. Tel. 689/68.75.53; cell 72.89.60; Fax 689/68.70.68; E-mail: faremaeva@mail.pf; www.fare-maeva.com. Located beside the sea on the outskirts of Fare, 3 kilometers (1.8 miles) from the ferry dock and 1 kilometer (.62 miles) from the airport. Free round-trip transfers. EP Rates: room with breakfast 6.360 CFP single/double; bungalow and breakfast 9.640 CFP single/double; additional adult 1.590 CFP; child under 12 years 1.060 CFP per day. Restaurant on premises. Rates include 6% VAT. A 10% value added tax is applicable to all other services and a municipal tax of 50 CFP is charged per person per day. Mastercard, Visa.*

Ten yellow concrete bungalows with sheet metal roofs are built in a garden setting 20 meters (66 feet) from the sea. Each small unit is furnished with cheerful colors and contains a double bed or two single beds, a lounge and dining area with a portable fan, plus a completely equipped kitchen, private bathroom with cold water, and a terrace. Two bungalows have easy access for handicapped guests. There are also 10 rooms with a double bed and a private bathroom with hot water. The Restaurant Tehina is part of the pension, where you can eat all your meals if you don't want to cook. Their specialty is barbecue. The dining tables are placed on a covered terrace beside the small swimming pool, overlooking the ocean. There is a *fare potée* (gazebo shelter) where groups can eat. You can also rent bicycles here and the reception people will help you organize your tours and excursions.

Economy

CHEZ GUYNETTE CLUB-BED, *B. P. 87, Fare, Huahine 98731. Tel./Fax 689/68.83.75; E-mail: chezguynette@mail.pf. In the center of Fare village, opposite the ferry dock and 3 kilometers (1.9 miles) from the airport. 7 rooms and an 8-berth dormitory. EP Rates: room 4.400 CFP single, 5.400 CFP double, 6.400 CFP triple; for one night only add 300 CFP per person; bed in dormitory 1.750 CFP; for a one-night stay the dormitory bed is 2.000 CFP per person. Rates include all taxes. All major credit cards except American Express.*

This is my favorite place to stay in Huahine when I want to meet all kinds of interesting people while sitting on the terrace facing the road and beach in the middle of Fare village. If you arrive in Huahine by inter-island ferryboat you can walk across the road from the boat dock and you'll be at Chez Guynette, which is operated by my friend Marty Temahahe, an American expatriate who bought the pension in April 1998. The hostel has 7 large rooms, each with a double bed and one or two bunk beds, and a private bathroom with hot water. There is also an 8-bed dormitory, sharing a communal bathroom with hot water, and a big, clean and homey kitchen where you can cook your own food. The windows are all screened and each room has an electric fan. Linens are furnished. Marty and her Tahitian husband, Moe, gave Chez Guynette a thorough face-lift in 2004. The beds all have new mattresses and there are new bed linens and bright curtains in all the rooms. All the floors have new tiles and they have even added an Internet room with three Cyberpoint computers. In the reception area Marty has all the information posted on the activities available on Huahine. You'll enjoy eating the breakfasts and snacks prepared in the local style even if you're not sleeping in the pension. See information under *Where to Eat* in this chapter.

You'll be right in the center of village life on a small tropical island here, with the benefit of walking across the road to a white sand beach for a wonderful swim in the warm lagoon, or watching the inter-island freighters and luxury passenger ships coming and going.

PENSION ENITE, *B.P. 37, Fare, Huahine 98731. Tel./Fax 689/68.82.37. Located at the end of the waterfront street in Fare. Round-trip airport transfers 1.200 CFP per person. MAP Rates: room with breakfast and dinner 8.000 CFP single; 6.500 CFP per person if there are two or more people; child 2-12 years 4.500 CFP. Room with one double bed 5.000 CFP per person per day; room with a double bed and single bed 6.000 CFP per person per day; room with two double beds 7.000 CFP per person per day. Add 6% value added tax to room rates, meal plan and transfers. A 10% value added tax is applicable to all other services and a municipal tax of 50 CFP is charged per person per day. No credit cards.*

This is one of the oldest pensions on the island, with eight rooms located next to the lagoon, providing single or double beds. Guests share a living room and a bathroom with hot water. Owner Enite Temaiana has earned a worthy reputation for the cuisine she serves her guests in the open-air restaurant. She also operates a taxi service and will take you on excursions around the island.

CHEZ LOVINA, *B.P. 173, Fare, Huahine 98731. Tel. 689/68.88.06/ 68.88.06; cell 72.51.12; Fax 689/68.88.06. Located between the circle island road and the sea 1 kilometer (.62 miles) north of the ferry dock in Fare and 2 kilometers (1.2 miles) from the airport. Round-trip transfers 1.200 CFP to airport, 600 CFP to the quay. EP Rates: fare 4.500 CFP single, 6.500 CFP double; additional person 1.500 CFP per day; family fare 6.550 – 20.700 CFP per day; bed in dormitory 1.800 CFP per person per day; camping 1.250 CFP per camper per day; for breakfast and dinner add 3.700 CFP per person per day, for breakfast, lunch and dinner add 6.000 CFP per person per day. Discount for longer stay. Add 6% value added tax to room rates, meal plan and transfers. A 10% value added tax is applicable to all other services and a municipal tax of 50 CFP is charged per person per day. Mastercard, Visa.*

Backpackers and campers discovered Lovina's place many years ago and it became very popular in this circuit. Her business has slowed down during the past few years, however, and some say that Lovina is *fiu* (fed up or tired of it all), but she keeps hanging in there anyway. Centuries old sacred tamanu trees and stately fruit trees shade the thatched roof bungalows and campground. The five *fare* type accommodations have a double and single bed and share a communal bathroom with cold water. There are also three family bungalows with two double beds and four single beds, a kitchen and private bathroom with cold water. Guests staying in the 15-bed dormitory share a kitchen, dining room and bathroom with cold water. There is a restaurant-snackbar on the property, and Lovina also operates a taxi service and will pick you up at the airport or ferry dock if you have reserved. If your boat arrives in the middle of the night, you can also find your way to the pension and sleep on one of the sofas in the reception area, and check in the next morning. Special rates sometimes drop the cost of the camping site and a camping hut. Lovina speaks good English and knows all about the history and legends of the island.

PENSION FETIA, *B.P. 73, Fare, Huahine 98731. Tel. 689/72.09.50; Fax 689/68.83.71; E-mail: pension-fetia@caramail.com; www.ifrance.com/ polynesie-pension-fetia. On the beach at Motu Maeva, 2.5 kilometers from the airport and 5 kilometers from boat dock in Fare village. Free round-trip transfers. EP Rates: house for one couple 7.000 CFP; house for 5 people 10.000; house for 5-10 people 15.000 CFP. Breakfast 500 CFP, dinner 2.500 CFP per person. Add 6% value added tax to room rates, meal plan and transfers. A 10% value added tax is applicable to all other services and a municipal tax of 50 CFP is charged per person per day. No credit cards.*

Réjane and Pierre Ah-Min are a Polynesian couple who welcome you to their family pension in a coconut grove beside the ocean shore on Motu Maeva. Pierre took great care in building the five guest bungalows, which are essentially made of natural materials such as wood, bamboo and stone. There are two bungalows for a couple, two bungalows with a bedroom and a mezzanine that can sleep up to five people, and one big bungalow for up to 10 guests. Each bungalow, *fare* or house has mosquito nets over the beds, a private bathroom and a kitchen. Réjane is noted for her food, which may be grilled fish with a coconut milk sauce, rice or pasta and a pie or fruit salad. She will prepare *ma'a Tahiti* or grilled lobster on request. Meals are served family style in the big open sided dining area, which has a coral floor and a lovely view of the sea. You can sometimes see humpback whales swimming close to the beach during the months of July through October.

RANDE'S SHACK, *B.P. 112, Fare, Huahine 98731. Tel./Fax 689/68.86.27; E-mail: randesshack@mail.pf. On the beach between the airport and boat dock, a short walk from Fare village. EP rates: one-bedroom house for 3 people, $60 per night; two-bedroom house for 4-5 people, $100 night. Minimum of 3 nights required. Add 6% value added tax to room rates. A 10% value added tax is applicable to all other services and a municipal tax of 50 CFP is charged per person per day. No credit cards.*

American expatriate Rande Vetterli and his Moorean wife Emere have two fully equipped houses that are set in a garden full of fruit trees. The houses are very clean and completely screened, with full kitchens, private bathrooms, hot water, linens, washing machines and bicycles. You will need to provide your own toiletries and car transportation and there is no maid service available. A 5-minute walk or less along the white sand beach or on the road will bring you to Fare village, where you can find restaurants and supermarkets. You can also spend hours snorkeling in the marvelous lagoon in front of your bungalow or walk down the beach to the site where the Hotel Bali Hai used to stand, and swim in this lost paradise. Rande's Shack is highly recommended by discerning Canadian friends who visit Huahine frequently.

HUAHINE ITI
Moderate

RELAIS MAHANA, *B.P. 30, Fare, Huahine 98731. Tel. 689/60.60.40; Fax 689/68.85.08; E-mail: relaismahana@mail.pf; www.relaismahana.pf. Located at Avea Bay on Huahine's best white sand beach, (25 kilometers) 15.5 miles from the airport, on the southwest side of Huahine Iti, just outside Parea Village. 22 garden and beach bungalows. EP Rates: garden bungalow 22.095 CFP single/double, 25.943 CFP 3-4 people; beach bungalow 24.685 CFP single/double, 28.463 CFP 3-4 people. One child under 12 years can have a bed free of charge in the double bungalow of parents; child 12 years or older is charged 1.509 CFP when sharing room with parents. One-way transfers from airport 1.336 CFP per adult and 1.002 CFP for children under 12 years. Rates include hotel taxes and VAT on hotel rooms. A 10% value added tax is applicable to all other services and a municipal tax of 150 CFP is charged per person per day. All major credit cards.*

This small hotel was built in 1985 and has been remodeled two or three times. The grounds and the 22 shingle-roofed bungalows are kept clean and well maintained. The hotel was sold in March 2001 to private investors whose staff and personnel know how to welcome guests in the traditional friendly style that has made Polynesia so famous.

There are 12 bungalows for one or two people, including 7 beach and 5 garden units, and 10 bungalows will sleep three or four people in 4 beach and 6 garden units. One of the beach bungalows is equipped to receive disabled guests with a wheelchair. The bungalows for one or two people are equipped with a large double bed, and a single bed, and there are two double beds in the rooms for four people. All the bungalows have a ceiling fan in the bedroom, a mini-bar, desk, a bathroom with hot water showers and a terrace with a plastic table and chairs.

There is a restaurant and bar in the main building, where breakfast and dinner are served. Lunch is normally served on the terrace, where there is a barbecue grill. See more information under *Where to Eat* in this chapter. Also in the main building you'll find a reception desk and interesting boutique, plus an Internet Point computer. Free activities include pedal boats, bicycles, canoes, kayaks, snorkeling equipment, ping-pong, books, tennis and swimming pool. The paid activities include water-skiing, snorkeling excursion, jet-ski excursions, lagoon excursions, Land Rover safari tours, horse riding and shark feeding. Mahana Dive is an on-site scuba dive center with a qualified dive instructor, and a Europcar representative is on duty in the reception area every morning between 8am and 12pm, providing rental cars and scooters.

The hotel grounds along the white sand beach are partially shaded by enormous trees. These include tamanu, almond, miro (rosewood), tahinu, tiare kahaia and purau (wild hibiscus) trees. A bench has been built into the convoluted root system of an ancient almond tree that has grown together with a tamanu tree, a coconut palm and some bushes. This is a wonderful place to relax and watch the sunset. I sat here while it rained one afternoon and never even got wet because the overhead branches are so thick.

The white sand beach curves along the aqua and deep turquoise waters of Avea Bay, which offers some of the island's best coral gardens for snorkeling. This bay is also a haven for cruising yachts. One day while I was staying in one of the beach bungalows on the tree-shaded side of the hotel property, I watched some Tahitian people casting their nets at the water's edge for *ouma* (baitfish). Then they fished for larger catch from the end of the hotel's long pier. On the beach four small children made sand castles while their parents tried to communicate in French and English. The American family was staying at the hotel for a month and the French family, who also had a tiny baby, was staying in the hotel's duplex family units next to them. In the bungalow next to me was a 70-year old Swiss woman, a former high-fashion model who wanted privacy. She was also staying at the hotel for a month. The

Relais Mahana has accommodations and facilities to meet most requirements, as long as you keep in mind that this is a 2-star hotel in the intermediary category. This hotel will close for the month of February 2005 to give all the employees a vacation.

PENSION MAUARII, *B.P. 17, Parea, Huahine 98731. Tel. 689/68.86.49; Fax 689/60.60.96; cell 73.90.26; E-mail: vetea@mail.pf; www.mauarii.com. Beside a white sand beach in Parea, 17 kilometers (10.6 miles) from the ferry dock and 19 kilometers (11.8 miles) from the airport. 4 bungalows, 4 rooms and a mezzanine. EP Rates: room in big house 7.500 CFP double; mezzanine 9.000 CFP double; room on beach 9.000 CFP double; garden bungalow 10.000 CFP double; garden bungalow with refrigerator 13.000 CFP double, 15.500 CFP triple, 18.000 CFP quadruple; beach bungalow 15.000 CFP double; 17.500 CFP triple. MAP half-board plan with breakfast and dinner 4.000 CFP per adult and 2.500 CFP per child per day; AP full-board plan with breakfast, lunch and dinner 6.500 CFP per adult and 4.000 CFP per child per day. Transfers from airport 3.000 CFP. Add 6% value added tax to room rates, meal plan and transfers. A 10% value added tax is applicable to all other services and a municipal tax of 50 CFP is charged per person per day. American Express, Mastercard, Visa.*

This pension is located on Huahine Iti beside a beautiful white sand beach just outside Parea village. The main building is a deluxe Polynesian style *fare pote'e* or traditional meeting house, with a dining terrace over the edge of the lagoon. The two big bedrooms each contain a king-size bed and mosquito net, and guests share the bathroom with hot water shower, as well as the kitchen and large living room. The mezzanine has 2 mattresses on the floor and guests use the communal bathroom downstairs. The four bungalows are beside the lagoon or with a garden view, offering a variety of accommodations for four to six people, with a private bathroom and hot water shower. Two new beach rooms with a hammock on the deck were added in 2001, and they have a private bathroom outside. All the bungalows have ceiling fans and mosquito nets over the beds and they are all clean and attractively decorated. There are also communal bath facilities. The restaurant has a very good reputation for its food, and the menu includes fish and seafood specialties, as well as tasty Chinese dishes. See more information under *Where to Eat* in this chapter.

Marcelle Flohr owns the pension and restaurant and her energetic young son, Vetea Breysse, has taken over the management. They are both fluent in English. This is the pension I would choose if I wanted to be beside a white sand beach and close to Parea village. Vetea has added Internet facilities and now calls his place a "Cyber Pension." He charges 500 CFP for 15 minutes to connect to the Internet. There is also a pay phone on the premises. You can rent a car, scooter or bicycle at the Europcar desk, or sign up for an island tour by 4WD vehicle or boat. You can also paddle one of the kayaks that are free for guests and discover the lagoon on your own. Maraamu Sailing is based at

Pension Mauarii, and you can join Captain Pierre Altier for a day sail aboard a catamaran or Hobie Cat. You can also learn to kite surf at this active pension.

Economy

ARIIURA CAMPING, *B.P. 145, Fare, Huahine 98731. Tel./Fax 689/ 68.85.20. Located on a white sand beach in Parea village, 18 kilometers (11.2 miles) from the ferry dock and 20 kilometers (12.4 miles) from the airport. EP Rates: Cabin with two single beds 5.000 CFP double; Garden cabin 4.500 CFP single/double; Beach cabin 4.900 CFP single/double; Cabin on seaside 3.800 CFP per person; Polynesian tent or camping 1.250 CFP per camper per day. Add 6% value added tax to room rates and transfers. A 10% value added tax is applicable to all other services and a municipal tax of 50 CFP is charged per person per day. No credit cards.*

I have received several good reports about this campground, as well as letters sent to the *Tahiti Beach Press* recommending the Tahitian owner, Hubert Bremond, for the Mauruuru Award because of his friendly, helpful manner. There are 8 simple cabins on the white sand beach of Parea, with a double bed and mosquito net in each unit. Household linens are supplied. The communal kitchen, dining room and bathroom with cold water are shared with the campers. There is also a snack bar on the premises. Mr. Bremond's sons will guide you on a hiking tour, teach you all about the medicinal plants still used by the Polynesians, or take you by boat to visit the lagoon and *motu* islets.

Other Family Pensions, Guest Houses, Bed & Breakfast, Villas Backpackers' Lodgings and Campgrounds on Huahine Nui and Huahine Iti

Chez Ella, *Tel. 689/68.73.07*, has 2 houses and a cottage, all with kitchens, next door to Motel Vanille near the airport. Pension Mama Roro, *Tel./Fax 689/68.84.82*, has two bungalows with kitchens close to the sea and airport, across the road from Pension Vaihonu. Pension Ariitere, *Tel. 689/ 74.40.30; Fax 689/68.82.26; E-mail: pensionariitere@mail.pf*. There are 4 bungalows, a pool, free bikes and kayaks, with meals on request in this pension in Fare, 10 minutes from the village and 3 minutes from the beach. Pension Meri, *Tel. 689/68.82.44, cell 79.56.11; E-mail: mataireameri@yahoo.fr*, has 5 fares with kitchens on the mountainside in Fare village.

Fare Tahitini, *Tel. 68.89.42*, is upstairs above the store next to the gendarmerie just before you reach the Te Tiare base in Fare village. Chez Henriette, *Tel. 689/ 68.83.71*, has 6 bungalows with kitchenettes in Haamene Bay; Pension Hine Iti, *Tel./Fax 689/68.74.58*, has a 3-story house for six people in Haapu. Pension Tupuna, *Tel./Fax 689/68.70.36; cell 79.07.94; E-mail: lorettafranck@yahoo.fr*, is in a coconut plantation near Bourayne Bay, with 3 very small local style bungalows.

In the Maroe Bay area there are houses and villas to rent. A car and boat are included with some rentals: **Residence Loisirs Maroe**, *Tel. 689/42.96.09/ 68.88.64*, with a 4-bedroom villa; **Villas Standing**, *Tel. 689/82.49.65; Fax 689/85.47.69*, with 4 houses; **Villa Bougainville**, *Tel./Fax 689/68.81.59*, with 3 villas; and **Huahine Vacances**, *Tel./Fax 689/68.73.63*, with 3 villas.

Pension Bourgeoise or **Te Nahe Toetoe**, *Tel./Fax 689/68.71.43 or 78.13.53*, is in Faie and has simple rooms as well as a dormitory, plus meals, free bicycles and pirogues. They also own **Pension Te Nahe** in Parea on Huahine Iti. Backpackers and campers will find inexpensive accommodations at **Vanaa Camping and Snack**, *Tel. 689/68.89.51*, on Motu Maeva, which has 13 small *fares* and a campground.

Where to Eat

If you want to see what's happening in Fare village or elsewhere around the island, the following restaurants and snack bars serve good food for reasonable prices. You'll also find a few *roulottes* (mobile diners) and small snack bars on the quay of Fare, which are open when the inter-island boats arrive from Papeete or Bora Bora during the wee hours of the morning.

Deluxe

TE TIARE BEACH RESORT, *Tel. 60.60.50. Open daily for breakfast, lunch and dinner. All major credit cards.*

The Arii Restaurant and Hawaiki Nui Bar are built over the water and the Beach Bar serves snacks and drinks beside the swimming pool and white sand beach. Breakfast, lunch and dinner are served in the Arii Restaurant, which is open to the sea breezes. Nonetheless, this is the only restaurant in all of French Polynesia where I have been given a choice of seating in the "Smoking" or "Non-Smoking" sections. A breakfast buffet starts the day off right with a varied choice of fresh fruits, cereals, breads and pastries, yogurts, breakfast meats, and cheeses, as well as eggs, bacon, sausages, potatoes and Japanese soups, salted plums and radish. The Continental breakfast is 1.800 CFP and the full American breakfast is 2.400 CFP.

Lunch choices include salads, soups, burgers and grilled fish or meats. The Caesar salad with parmesan is 1.200 CFP and a mahi mahi burger with fries is 1.450 CFP. Pasta is 1.250-1.600 CFP and shrimp tempura with tartar sauce is 2.000 CFP. A set lunch menu is 3.200 CFP and a set dinner menu is 5.200 CFP. The *à la carte* dinner menu offers starter courses for 1.200-1.950 CFP, such as pumpkin cream soup for 1.200 CFP, flaky pastry with goat cheese and apple sprinkled with honey and served with a green salad for 1.450 CFP, and roasted tuna with cajuan served with pineapple chutney for 1.500 CFP. The fish dishes are priced from 1.850 to 2.500 CFP and a Pacific "bouillabaisse" for two costs 7.800 CFP and should be ordered the day before. Meat and poultry dishes are 1.850-2.800 CFP, and include lemon chicken, grilled prime rib of beef, breast of duck and grilled New York steak served with green pepper sauce. A Surf and Turf combination of beef filet and reef lobster is 3.200 CFP. A special vegetarian menu is also available. The pastry chef does a good job of tempting you to try his rich desserts, such as warm creamy chocolate cake served with vanilla ice cream, for 1.200 CFP, a crystallized lemon parfait, caramelized apple with vanilla, for 1.200 CFP, or a crème brûlée with coconut for 1.100 CFP.

Special evenings at the Ari'i Restaurant include a Friday night Exotic Buffet for 6.800 CFP, which is accompanied by a Polynesian dance group. A Prime Rib Dinner Under the Southern Cross is served on Friday nights, also with a dance group, for 6.000 CFP.

Moderate

RELAIS MAHANA, *Tel. 60.60.40. Te Nahe Restaurant is open daily for breakfast, lunch and dinner. All major credit cards.*

Breakfast and dinner are served in the two dining rooms and you eat lunch outside on the terrace. Some of the tables are partially covered by the roof of the restaurant, while others are open to the elements, or covered by a big umbrella. Containers of carnelian and purple bougainvillea border the dining terrace. A Va'a (Polynesian canoe) breakfast buffet is 1.696 CFP. If you like your bacon crispy you'll have to ask them to cook it some more, as you'll have to do in most restaurants in French Polynesia. Lunch choices include *poisson cru* for 1.200 CFP, burgers and fries for 1.450 CFP, mahi mahi for 1.750 CFP, or grilled steak for 1.800 CFP. Wine is sold by the carafe or bottle, and you can also order a cold pression of Hinano beer. Hiro Itchner, the bartender, was named best barman in Polynesia in 2000. Try one of his rum drinks served with lychees, vanilla, pineapple and honey. His Bloody Marys are also good.

Chef Michel Prat is of Basque origin and has lived in French Polynesia more than 20 years. He specializes in combining local products with typical European recipes. You'll enjoy his terrine de foie gras with papaya, the fish and shrimp salad with almonds, sesame seeds, tomato petals and olive oil, the oven baked lamb with a taro crust, chicken leg stuffed with fafa (taro leaves), and crisp lobster raviolis, Julienne papaya and grenadine onions. Desserts include ice cream home made with local fruits, and the caramelized banana tarte tatin is just yummy. The à la carte dinner costs 1.400 to 3.500 CFP and the 3-course daily tourist menu is 3.453. Vegetarian meals are prepared on request. A Polynesian buffet with a Tahitian dance show is organized on Saturday nights during the high tourist seasons.

CHEZ MAUARII, *Tel. 68.86.49, beside lagoon at PK 17 in Parea. Open daily 7:30am to 8:30pm with non-stop service. American Express, Mastercard, Visa.*

This beachside restaurant is noted for its fresh seafood specials and local dishes. The menu changes frequently, and the choices may include yellow fin tuna, moonfish, wahoo, mahi mahi, swordfish, shark or lagoon fish, with a variety of sauces, from 1.600 to 3.200 CFP. Poultry dishes are 1.900 to 2.350 CFP and meats are 1.800 to 2.350 CFP. Shellfish choices are priced from 2.300-4.300 CFP and include crab and lobster in season, and *varo*, a sea centipede that is a rare and tasty delicacy from the lagoon. Desserts are 500-700 CFP. You can buy wine by the glass, carafe or bottle, from 300 to 3.500 CFP. For breakfast you can order eggs, bacon or pancakes for 1.500 CFP. A snack menu is served from 12-5pm, offering casse-croûte sandwiches for 600-1.000 CFP, poisson cru for 1.600 CFP, sashimi for 1.900 CFP and tuna tartare for 2.000 CFP. Tahitian food is available any day of the week, including the staple diet of the Polynesians—*punu puatoro* (canned corned beef) and *mitihue* (fermented coconut milk), for 1.500 CFP, or a Polynesian plate for 2.650 CFP, which contains *poisson cru* with coconut milk, chicken and spinach with coconut milk, and pork braised with cabbage, radish and carrots.

LES DAUPHINS, *Tel. 68.78.54, cell 74.56.69, is on the mountainside of the circle island road, adjacent to the post office, a five-minute walk from Fare village. Open daily except Wednesday, from 11:30am-2pm and 5-9pm. Visa.*

Titiane, the Tahitian owner, is noted for her great food, especially the fresh seafood selections from Lake Maeva and the coral reefs, such as lobster for 3.500 CFP, or crab with ginger, also for 3.500 CFP. You can order a steak and fries for 1.300 CFP, or poisson cru for 1.400 CFP, plus a variety of other mouth-watering dishes.

RESTAURANT MATAPIRI, *Tel. 73.76.16, beside the lagoon in Fare, on the road to Fitii, just past the Gendarmerie and the Hotel Te Tiare land base. Open for lunch Wednesday through Sunday from 11am-2pm and for dinner Tuesday through Sunday from 6-9pm. Closed all day Monday and at noon on Tuesday. Mastercard, Visa.*

Pierre and Dominique Seybald formerly managed Restaurant Le Cocotier in Moorea, the Rangiroa Beach Club and their own restaurant Le Kai Kai, also in Rangiroa. Then they asked themselves, "How about Huahine?" and consequently, they opened Restaurant Matapiri in March 2004. Matapiri is the name of the land at this site. The non-smoking section of this steak house restaurant is air-conditioned and smokers sit in the open section. Pierre is a French chef de cuisine and his dishes include veal escalope with cream sauce, mussels and fries, and beef filet with Roquefort sauce, as well as the local favorites of grilled mahi mahi, shrimp curry or shrimp with ginger sauce.

RESTAURANT BAR TE MARARA, *Tel. 68.81.70, is at the edge of the lagoon at the beginning of Fare Village when you come from the airport. Open daily, from 10am to 10pm Sunday-Thursday, and from 10am to midnight on Friday and Saturday. Mastercard, Visa.*

Marc Garnier has taken over this popular restaurant and at press time he was in the process of buying it from Edna and Guy Flohr, who opened Te Marara in the early 1970s. Marc also owns Huahine Nautique. He has added a Happy Hour with half-price drinks between 5:30-6:30pm on Sunday through Thursday, a local band on Wednesday nights and live music for dancing on Friday and Saturday nights. The menu features fresh fish such as mahi mahi and tuna for 1.600 CFP, poisson cru for 1.200 CFP, a dozen fresh New Zealand oysters for 1.600 CFP, plus flounder and salmon for 1.800 CFP, which are also flown in weekly from New Zealand. You can also get a filet mignon steak for 1.800 CFP.

RESTAURANT VANILLE, *Tel. 68.71.77, is located at Motel Vanille close to the airport. Open Tuesday through Sunday for lunch and dinner. Closed Monday. Mastercard, Visa.*

The dining room faces the gardens and swimming pool and you are served by Ronan and Nathalie, who take care of the pension. She prepares the meals, which let you begin with a plate of raw vegetables, *poisson cru*, sashimi or tuna tartare. The main courses may be fish steak with lemon sauce, mahi mahi or wahoo with Roquefort, curry, black butter or green pepper sauce, shrimp dishes, chicken with cashew nuts and honey, or rib-eye steak and vegetables. The wine list is good and reasonably priced. The MAP half-board rate for guests staying in the pension is 2.900 CFP per person for breakfast and dinner.

RESTAURANT POETAINA, *Tel. 68.80.50/68.89.49; cell 78.86.39, is on the Fare waterfront facing the fishing dock. Open Tuesday through Sunday for lunch and dinner. Closed Monday. Mastercard, Visa. Free transfers provided for lunch or dinner.*

Poerava Amo, whose parents own Pension Poetaina, manages this small restaurant that specializes in seafood and Chinese dishes prepared by a chef imported from China. Local bands entertain on special occasions. This restaurant is popular with local residents as well as tourists.

EDEN PARC, *Tel. 68.86.58; Fax 68.84.04; E-mail: info@edenparc.org; www.edenparc.org. Located in Vaiorea Bay at Port Bourayne, close to Fitii Village. Open Monday through Saturday from 9am to 4pm. Closed Sunday. Closed annually from mid-December to mid-January. No credit cards.*

Biologically grown fruits and vegetables and fresh seafood are served in this lush tropical setting. You can order a 2-course exotic lunch for 1.000 CFP, a 3-course ocean lunch for 2.200 CFP, or a tropical 3-course lunch for 2.500 CFP. The dishes may consist of heart of palm salad and terrine of avocado with seafood, or other healthy choices, and coffee or juice is included. They also sell produce from the park, such as sun dried bananas, jams, exotic pickles and spices and Huahine vanilla. You can also buy *monoi* oil mosquito repellant here, which you will probably need to use immediately, as this place is notorious for mosquitoes. Some tourists also object to the uncomfortable chairs made of coral rock.

Economy

CHEZ GUYNETTE, *Tel. 68.83.75, facing the waterfront of Fare village. Open daily from 7am to 7pm. Mastercard, Visa.*

This is a great place to eat breakfast or just to stop in for a coffee or beer and meet people while you watch what's happening on the waterfront. My very close friend, Marty Temahahe, and her Tahitian husband, Moe, own the pension and snack bar. Marty is an American who has lived for more than 30 years in the islands. A continental breakfast costs 800 CFP, and if you want eggs you'll pay a little more. You can get a smoothie for 500 CFP, a cup of coffee for 200 CFP, a draft beer for 300 to 400 CFP, a glass of wine for 300 CFP and even a cold drinking coconut for 300 CFP. A coconut costs up to 1.200 CFP in Bora Bora! A cheeseburger with fries is 900 CFP, a Chef's salad or Greek salad is 1.000 CFP and a steak and salad is 1.300 CFP. Aside from their normal luncheon menu, they offer a daily special for 1.000 CFP, which may be sashimi or poisson cru, fish burritos with guacamole and salsa, lasagna, tamale pie, spare ribs or tagliatelle carbonara with salad and garlic bread. The special changes daily. The snack is busy most of the day, and especially in the mornings and late afternoon. Local residents and some of the visitors to Huahine are usually having so much fun that they don't want to go home when it's closing time.

RESTAURANT TEHINA, *Tel. 68.75.53, cell 72.89.60, beside the sea at the Fare Maeva pension at PK 3, near Huahine airport. Open daily for breakfast, lunch and dinner except Sunday noon. Mastercard, Visa.*

This small restaurant specializes in barbecue and fresh local fish dishes. Salads are 600 CFP and starter courses of tuna sashimi, poisson cru, tuna tartare or carpaccio of tuna are each 1.320 CFP. The main courses are also 1.320 CFP each and may be tuna with mustard sauce, shrimp curry or steak with pepper sauce. Grilled lobster (in season and ordered in the morning) is 2.600 CFP. Desserts of fresh fruit, baked papaya, fresh fruit salad or banana split are priced from 250 to 600 CFP.

RESTAURANT VAIHONU, *Tel. 68.87.33, is beside the sea, between the airport and Fare village. Open daily for breakfast, lunch and dinner. Mastercard and Visa accepted.*

Even if you are not staying at Pension Vaihonu, you are welcome to join Etienne Faaeva and his group for a good meal in a relaxed setting beside the sea. He has a tempting menu of Chinese dishes and there is a house specialty every Wednesday and Friday.

HAAMENE PIZZA, *Tel. 68.71.70, is on the mountainside of the road in Fare village on the way to Fitii, between the French gendarmerie and Pension Poetaina. Open Tuesday-Saturday from 12-2pm and every night from 6:30-9pm. Closed Sunday noon and Monday noon. No credit cards.*

American residents of Huahine, as well as visitors, say that the pizzas made by this Polynesian family are the best they have tasted in Tahiti and Her

Islands. You can order from a menu of 14 pizzas that are priced 900-1.500 CFP for a medium pizza for two, and 1.200-1.800 CFP for a large pizza that is plenty for 3-4 people.

VAKALELE, *at the Huahine Airport.*

Dorothy Levy's snackbar is open for all Air Tahiti arrivals and departures. Meeting Dorothy is worth the trip to Huahine. Take the time to order one of Dorothy's special fruit smoothies or a drink and sandwich, and when she's not too busy, she will tell you about the history and culture of the island.

Seeing the Sights

Ariiura Paradise, *Tel. 68.85.20*, is a back-to-Eden garden of revival and conservation of Polynesian herbal medicine. Cecile Tehihira and Hubert Bremond have planted more than 200 varieties of herbs, flowers, ferns, fruits and trees in their hillside garden beside Maroe Bay. Over 150 of these plants are used by the islanders for *raa'u Tahiti*, traditional medicine. Native healers visit the gardens twice a month to collect medicinal plants and to treat people who have health problems. Some of the organized tours stop here. There is no entrance fee but a donation is appreciated.

Eden Parc, *Tel. 68.86.58; Fax 68.84.04; E-mail: info@edenparc.org; www.edenparc.org. The park is open Monday through Saturday, from 7am to 5pm. Restaurant and bar open from 9am to 4pm. No credit cards.*

This tropical garden is located in Vaiorea Bay at Port Bourayne close to Fitii Village. Look for the sign at the junction just past Hotel Bellevue. Gilles Tehau Parzy and his wife Anne have created an ethno-botanical garden of Eden in 3 hectares (7 acres) of fruit trees, flowers and exotic plants. A visit package costs 500 CFP per person and includes three tours. Be sure to protect yourself with mosquito repellent. You can follow the guidebook they give you to visit the **Botanical Orchards**, where you will see exotic vegetables and fruits from many parts of the world. A show on **Eco-Energy Systems** starts at 1pm, and you can also join the **Great Panoramas** tour to admire and photograph the three magnificent bays beyond Eden Parc. You can taste some of the healthy foods grown in the gardens here by ordering an à la carte lunch or a fixed menu. Fresh fruit juices include pineapple, mango, guava, carambola, guanabana, cashew apple, starfruit, papaya, pamplemousse (grapefruit) and banana. In the gift shop you can also purchase vanilla-flavored coffee, tropical herbal teas, sundried bananas, jams, herbs and spices, pickled bilimbi peppers, and monoi insect repellent.

Fare Pote'e is a museum and handcrafts center built over the water at Lake Fauna Nui in Maeva Village. It is a replica of a traditional meeting house of classic Polynesian oval shape, with a high curved roof of pandanus thatch, bamboo walls, and a bamboo covered floor. The exhibits include a variety of useful tools that were used by the Polynesians before the arrival of the Europeans. Kites, canoes, tops and other traditional games are also displayed, as well as musical instruments and a copy of the wooden headrest used by Omai, the first Tahitian to discover England. Arts and crafts made by the residents of Huahine are for sale, and you can get a map of the hiking trails on nearby Matairea Hill, where you can see the restored *marae* temples of stone, the house and council platforms and other work in progress.

Huahine Nui Pearls & Pottery, *Tel. 78.30.20*, owned by Peter and Ghislaine Owen, was for many years Huahine's only black pearl farm. They are open every day and offer a free tour by boat to visit the pearl farm, leaving the Marina of Faie every 15 minutes from 10am to 4pm. Peter, an expatriate American, and his Polynesian wife, Ghislaine, also have some of their creative pottery for sale in the overwater boutique at the pearl farm.

Taravari Pearls Creations, *Tel. 68.83.02/79.88.37*, is a pearl farm and boutique located in Bourayne Bay that you can visit by appointment Monday-Friday from 10am-4pm. Ray Marks, another expatriate American living in Huahine, does the grafting of the oysters, and his Polynesian wife, Arieta, creates the black pearl jewelry. Mastercard and Visa accepted.

Land Tours

Island Eco-Tours, *Tel./Fax 68.79.67; E-mail: pauljatallah@mail.pf; www.www.island-eco-tours.com*. Paul Atallah is an American archaeologist who offers half-day tours by 4WD Ford Ranger that will give you an in-depth briefing on Huahine's unique charm, history, culture and tropical flora as you discover the authentic island, mountains, valleys, rivers, beaches, islets and people. This is also an interesting botanical experience for lovers of nature and green open spaces. But the main advantage that sets Paul's tours apart is his extensive knowledge of the ancient *marae* temples and other archaeological sites. He worked with Professor Yosihiko H. Sinoto to help restore the stone *marae* in Huahine and in other islands and the knowledge he gained through his scientific research helps to make his tours even more interesting. Paul charges 5.000 CFP per person for his tour if you book directly through him.

Huahine Explorer, *Tel. 68.87.33; Fax 68.77.57; E-mail: h-explorer@mail.pf; www.association@iaorana-huahine.com*. Etienne Faaeva has three 8-passenger Land Rovers to take you around Huahine Nui and Huahine Iti to discover the magical wonders of the two islands. Etienne and his brother Daniel are very good tour guides. They speak excellent English and know all about the legends and history of their native island. The Explorer Tour is 4.000 CFP per person and takes you around Huahine Nui and Huahine Iti. You will see the watermelon, cantaloupe and noni plantations, visit the *maraes*, fresh water eels, and enjoy the panoramic views. The 2-hour Cultural Tour is 3.000 CFP and takes you to discover Huahine Nui, to visit the *maraes*, Belvedere lookout, the fresh water eels and the plantations. A Combined Tour is 10.500 CFP, and after you have visited the island by 4x4, you will board a comfortable canoe to visit a black pearl farm, snorkel and swim, and have lunch and a coconut show on a *motu* islet. The tours operate daily and water and fruit juices are served on board during each excursion.

Huahine Land, *Tel. 68.89.21, cell 78.58.31, Fax 68.86.84,* is owned by Joel House, an American who has lived in French Polynesia for more than three decades. He has three 4x4 vehicles and English-speaking guides who lead the half-day excursions. The tour begins at 8am or 1pm and takes you off the track into the hidden valleys and sites of the two islands.

Felix Tours, *Tel. 68.82.26,* offers half-day Circle Island Tours by mini-van with a Polynesian guide. The morning tour starts at 9am and ends at 12:30pm and the afternoon tour is from 1:30 to 5:30pm. You will visit all of the interesting sites on both islands, including some of the most important prehistoric archaeological remains in all of Polynesia. The stops include: Marae Manunu on Motu Maeva, the largest stone temple on Huahine; the ancient stone fish traps in Lake Maeva, which are still in use; the prehistoric archaeological center of Maeva Village; the blue-eyed sacred eels of Faie Village; the Mato Ere Ere panoramic view of Huahine Nui and Huahine Iti at Maroe Bay; a viewpoint of the beautiful Mahuti Bay on Huahine Iti; the picturesque white sand beach at Ave'a Bay on Huahine Iti; and a visit to Fare, the capital and commercial center of Huahine.

Huahine Local Tours, *Tel./Fax 68.89.14.* Pascal Taipuna has air-conditioned buses and he will take you to visit the vanilla plantations, Tahitian chestnut forest of *mape* trees, ancient fish traps and the archaeological sites.

Enite Tours, *Tel. 68.82.37,* has big buses and mini-vans that are used for Circle Island Tours and Archaeological Tours.

Quad Evasion, *Tel. 68.71.38 / 20.33.75, E-mail: oa.oa@mail.pf; www.perso.libertysurf.fr/quad/evasion.html* is owned by Romuald Diez, whose tours will give you a glimpse into the local traditional life around Lake Maeva and its winding beaches between watermelon plantations and coconut groves. There are 2-hour tours and half-day tours, and the rates start at 6.000 CFP per person.

Sports & Recreation
Hiking
Ariiura Camping, at PK 18 in Parea, *Tel. 68.85.20,* leads hiking expeditions into the flatlands, valleys, plateaus and mountains of Huahine. These Camping Ecology outings leave from the Ariiura campground at 9am, and return at 1pm. Your qualified guide is Paul Pureni and his brother, Wilfred Pureni, will teach you all about the traditional medicinal plants that you will see growing along the pathways.

Horseback Riding
La Petite Ferme, *Tel./Fax 68.82.98.* The little farm is located on the ocean side of the road between Fare Village and the airport. Brigitte and Vincent

Pouzet will take you riding on trained Marquesan horses along the beach and on the shores of Lake Maeva for 4.500 CFP for two hours. An all-day trail ride with picnic is 9.800 CFP. Open daily 8am to 6pm. Please reserve at least a day in advance. Boarding house facilities are also available. See *Where to Stay* in this chapter.

Boat Rental

Huahine Lagoon, *Tel. 68.70.00*. Jean-Luc Eychenne rents 13-foot aluminum boats with a 15 HP motor that you need a license to pilot. All safety equipment is included for a maximum of four people. The rates are 5.000 CFP for 2 hours, 7.000 CFP for 4 hours and 10.000 CFP for 8 hours. Masks, fins and snorkel are included, as well as icebox and map of the lagoon. Gas is extra. Rental kayaks and bicycles are also available.

Maraamu Kiteboarding & Sailing School, *Tel./Fax 68.77.10; cell 78.90.69; E-mail: pie@tahitikite.com; www.tahitikite.com*. This nautical activity center is based at Pension Mauarii in Avea Bay on Huahine Iti. Pierre Altier leads private half-day tours aboard Hobie Cat 18 boats for 6.500 CFP per person, or you can rent the boat for 4.000 CFP for one hour and 10.000 CFP for 4 hours. He also gives lessons on board a Hobie Cat 13 and has small boats for children to use with an instructor. You can rent an aluminum boat with a 6 HP motor that you can pilot without a license for 5.000 CFP per hour or 10.000 CFP for 4 hours. A funboard rents for 3.000 CFP for one hour and you can also rent snorkeling gear here. You can learn to fly a kitesurf for 6.000 CFP for one lesson; 4 private lessons cost 20.000 CFP. You can also rent partial or complete kitesurfing equipment.

Deep Sea Fishing

Huahine Sport Fishing, *Tel. 68.84.02; Fax 68.80.30; E-mail: huah.mar.trans@mail.pf*. **Ruau II** is a 36-foot Bertram Hatteras owned by American expatriate, Richard Shamel. He uses tackle approved by the International Game Fishing Association (IGFA) and the tag and release system is used on request. If you contact Rich directly he charges a net price of 60.000 CFP for a half-day fishing excursion and 80.000 CFP for a full day outing. The hotels charge 80.000 CFP for a half-day excursion and 100.000 CFP for a full-day fishing trip. Soft drinks, beer and water are included. Bring your own food.

Lagoon Excursions, Picnics on the Motu, Jet-Ski & Shark Feeding Excursions

Huahine Nautique, *Tel. 689/68.83.15; Fax 689/68.82.15; E-mail: reservation@huahine-nautique.com; www.huahine-nautique.com*. Marc Garnier has a 12-passenger 36-foot long glass bottom boat, 2 speed boats, 4 outrigger speed canoes and 12 Jetskis, as well as an 8-passenger mini-bus that he uses to transfer his clients from their hotel, pension or cruise ship to the marina or boat dock. Marc's tours are highly praised by former customers, and some of the participants on Internet forums say that he offers the best excursions in the Leeward Islands. His tours are well described on his website, and he offers a 10 percent discount on the first activity you book by fax or E-mail one week in advance, and 20 percent off on the second activity.

On the **Island Picnic** tour you will take a boat ride around part of Huahine Nui and all of Huahine Iti by outrigger speed canoe, with stops to visit the stingrays and eagle rays, snorkeling in a big coral garden, and a picnic on a small island called a motu. On the way back to Fare you will stop and watch your guide feeding the black tip lagoon sharks. This full-day excursion is 7.500 CFP per person.

A **Private Picnic** Luxury Lagoon cruise can be made by Jetski or on board Marc's comfortable catamaran, which is complete with a toilet and shower on board, as well as a sunbathing deck and awning for shade. After visiting the black pearl farm in Faie Bay and snorkeling in the coral gardens of Tefarerii, Marc's guide will take you to a motu islet where he will set up a table and chairs in the shallow lagoon and shade them with a gazebo type tent. You will be served a Royal lunch of grilled lobster, marinated fish, baked potatoes, salad, fruit, a coconut tart with vanilla sauce, white and red wine, plus a bottle of champagne. After lunch you continue on around Huahine Iti and return to the dock around 3pm. This unforgettable treat is priced at 80.000 CFP per couple.

Shark Feeding excursions take on another dimension with Huahine Nautique, due to the unique submerged platform that lets you descend from the boat into the lagoon without the risk of getting coral cuts. You can also observe the sharks being fed while standing on the top deck of the glass bottom boat, 4 meters (13 feet) above the water's surface. The morning or afternoon excursion costs 4.200 CFP per passenger.

A 2 1/2 hour **Safari Jet** excursion aboard a 3-seater Bombardier Jetski costs 21.250 CFP per Jetski, and includes a stop on a *motu*, snorkeling in a coral garden, meeting the gray stingrays and spotted eagle rays, and a cocktail in a hotel.

Marc also has special programs for passengers who arrive in Huahine aboard the **Tahitian Princess** cruise. You can join an outrigger excursion for a barbecue picnic on a motu and boat cruise around Huahine Iti, which costs $80 per person, including the excursion, food and drinks. You can also combine the picnic tour with a circle island tour by 4x4 vehicle, which is $100 per person, including the food and drinks.

Poetaina Cruises, *Tel./Fax 68.89.49, cell 78.86.39*, is owned by Jean Pierre Amo, who also operates the Poetaina Pension and Restaurant Poetaina. He has a 43-foot outrigger speed canoe for 6 to 38 passengers and a 43-foot double decker catamaran named *Te Aito* that can accommodate up to 70 passengers. The excursion begins at the Fare quay daily at 9:30am and returns at 4pm, taking you around Huahine Nui and Huahine Iti inside the lagoon, with a stop at Vaiorea motu for snorkeling and a visit to the black pearl farm. Lunch is served in the clear shallow water of the lagoon and you sit with your feet in the water as you dine. This all-day picnic excursion is 7.500 CFP per adult, 4.000 CFP for kids 5-12 years old and is free for those under 5 years. A half-day picnic excursion is 6.000 CFP per adult. You can also join the picnic cruise in the morning and at 1:30pm you will board a 4x4 Land Rover for a Huahine Explorer Safari Tour around the island. The combined tours are 10.450 CFP per adult and 5.225 CFP for children 6-12 years old. Taxes are included in all rates.

Vahine Api Cruises, *Tel. 68.84.02; Fax 68.80.30; E-mail: huah.mar.trans@mail.pf.* Richard Shamel has a 22-foot fiberglass hull boat for 2 to 8 passengers that can be used for personalized or individual transfers on the lagoon. He also has a bodyboard and banana-ski boat. On request he will take you for a sunset cruise.

Vaipua Tour, *Tel./Fax 68.86.42; cell phone 72.10.51; E-mail: here@mail.pf,* is managed by Marie-Colette Teaurai. She has two 30-foot outrigger speed canoes and a 36-foot double catamaran available for half- or full-day cruises for 6 to 60 passengers. You can board the boat at the quay in Fare at 9:30am for an all day excursion inside the lagoon to visit the bays, swim with the rays, snorkel and hunt for shells in the best spots and visit a black pearl farm. Your barbecue lunch of chicken or fresh fish with local vegetables and fruits will be prepared on the white sand beach of Motu Topatii in Tefarerii. Your Polynesian guide will teach you how to weave protective sun hats and other items from the coconut fronds. The tour ends at the Fare boat dock at 4pm. If you are on a cruise ship anchored in Maroe Bay, the catamaran will meet you at the dock there. This tour is 6.000 CFP for adults and half-price for children 5 to 12 years, which they advertise as the "best in the west."

Sailing Yachts

Sailing Huahine Voile, B.P. 661-98731 Fare, Huahine, *Tel./Fax 689/ 68.72.49; E-mail: eden@sailing-huahine.com; www.sailing-huahine.com.* Claude and Martine Bordier have a 50-foot sailboat called the *Eden Martin* that is based in Huahine, offering half- and full-day sailing cruises, sunset cruises and private charters. The half-day cruise departs daily at 9am from the quay in Fare and sails down the lagoon to Motu Vaiorea, where passengers snorkel in the coral garden. Another swimming stop is made at the white sand beach of Hana Iti, then the boat sails back to Fare, arriving at the quay at 1pm. The cost is 6.500 CFP per person. The full-day cruise is 12.500 CFP and lasts from 9am to 5:30pm. The yacht sails down the lagoon to Motu Vaiorea for a snorkel stop in the coral garden, then a swimming stop on the Hana Iti white sand beach. From there it continues sailing down the lagoon to Avea Bay, where lunch is served on board. This consists of carpaccio of tuna or mahi mahi, a chocolate tart, fruit, wine, coffee and mineral water. You can then relax on board or visit the reef by dinghy before sailing back to the quay in Fare.

Snorkeling gear is available on board. A sunset cruise for a minimum of 4 passengers leaves the Fare quay at 4:30pm and returns at dusk. The cost of 5.500 CFP per person includes cocktails, and champagne can be ordered at extra cost.

The *Eden Martin* can also be chartered for 2-5 passengers to cruise the Society Islands or the Tuamotu Archipelago. A 7-day/6-night cruise in the Leeward Islands begins in Huahine, sails to Raiatea, Tahaa and Bora Bora, where the passengers disembark. The cost is 69.000 CFP per day or 483.000 CFP for 7 days, and includes the boat rental, skipper and fuel for the main engine. A 7-day/6-night cruise in the northern Tuamotu Islands begins in Rangiroa and ends in Tikehau. This is a good cruise for scuba divers. The rate of 86.250 CFP per day or 60.370 CFP for the full cruise includes boat rental for 2-5 people, skipper, fuel for the main engine and the boat delivery from Huahine to Rangiroa. A cruise to the central Tuamotu Islands lasts for 12 days/ 11 nights and costs 86.250 CFP or a total of 1,035.000 CFP for 2-5 passengers. You board the boat in Makemo and disembark in Fakarava. You'll sail from Makemo to Tahanea, then to Fakarava.

You can also rent a sailboat from one of the yacht charter companies based in Tahiti, Moorea or Raiatea and sail to Huahine, or you can arrange for a yacht to be delivered to Huahine in time for your arrival. See chapter on *Planning Your Trip*.

Scuba Diving

Mahana Dive, *Tel. 73.07.17; Fax 68.76.63; E-mail: kbi@mail.pf; www.huahine.com/divemahana* is based at Le Relais Mahana in Parea. Annie Brunet is the manager and qualified dive master who will guide you to the underwater wonders of the diving world of Huahine. This center is open to the public, and the cost of an exploratory dive is 5.900 CFP. Baptism dives, daily outings and 4-dive packages are also available.

Pacific Blue Adventure, *Tel. 68.87.21; cell 71.96.55; Fax 68.80.71; E-mail: pba@divehuahine.com; www.divehuahine.com.* This dive shop is located on the quay in the main village of Fare. Theophile Samourcachian is an international PADI and CMAS diving instructor who leads lagoon and ocean dives for beginners and certified divers. He has an outing at 9am and 2pm daily, taking a maximum of 10 divers to the best sites inside the lagoon or in the open ocean, adapting to the diving level of the participants. The cost is 5.800 CFP for one dive, 21.200 CFP for four dives, and night dives are 1.500 CFP more. All equipment is included and transfers are possible. Add 10% VAT to all rates.

Surfing

American surfers discovered the passes of Huahine in the early 1970s, and a couple of them are still here, now sharing their favorite surf spots with their children. The local surfers jealously guard the passes with the best breaks, and a few foreign surfers have been given black eyes when they intrude. The big attraction in Huahine is the consistency and perfect shape of the waves rather than their size. Three of the best breaks are in the Fare area, and another good site is at the Araara pass in Parea on the southern tip of Huahine Iti. Try to find a local surfer to accompany you to the passes, which may eliminate any problems from the other surfers.

Water Skiing
Vahine Api Cruises, *Tel. 68.84.02.* Richard Shamel, at the land base for Hotel Te Tiare, has a banana-ski boat and a kneeboard, plus all the equipment for water-skiing. He charges 10.000 CFP per hour.

Shopping
In addition to the boutiques and black pearl shops in the resort hotels, you can also find original creations and some imported items in the boutiques in Fare and around the island. The **Huahine Lagoon** in Fare is an art gallery and boutique. **Plaisir d'Offrir** on Fare's main street has black pearls and other jewelry and perfumes. **Exotica Boutique** is also located in Fare village.

The **Tima'i Te Nui Taue** has the most original clothing and souvenir items, including pottery made by Peter Owen, an American resident of Huahine, who owns **Huahine Pearl and Pottery** at his black pearl farm in Faie.

Special Services, Massage, Natural Therapy, Relaxation
Patricia Matthews Nanua, *Tel. 68.72.32, cell 77.94.65,* is an Australia expatriate 12-year resident of Huahine who does intuitive healing massages, working with the body's energy. She also gives private yoga lessons. Her base is Te Tiare Resort, and she will also come to your house, room or yacht to work her wonderful magic on your body.

Tattoo Artists
Tihoti (Georges), *Tel./Fax 68.77.27; E-mail: tihotitatau@yahoo.com,* has a very good reputation for his creative Polynesian style tattoos.

Practical Information
Banks
Huahine has two banks, which are located in the main village of Fare. **Banque de Tahiti**, *Tel. 68.82.46,* has an ATM window. Open Monday through Friday 7:45-11:45am and 1:30-4:30pm. **Banque Socredo**, *Tel. 60.63.60,* is located on the mountainside of the circle island road in Fare village and also has an ATM window.

Doctor
There are three private doctors in Fare who speak good English, and the 15-bed government infirmary is on the mountainside in Fare, *Tel. 68.82.48.*

Drugstore
The **Pharmacy of Huahine**, *Tel. 60.62.40,* is on the circle island road of Fare, on the way to the post office, one block inland from the waterfront. Open Monday to Saturday from 7:30 to 11:30am and 2:30 to 5:30pm. The pharmacist speaks English.

Internet
AO API–New World Internet Café is located upstairs above the pharmacy and Huahine Manava Visitors Bureau on the waterfront in Fare Village, *E-mail: aoapi_newworld@hotmail.com.* They also have Xerox facilities and can print out digital photos and color photocopying.
Chez Guynette, *Tel. 68.83.75*, on the waterfront street of Fare, provides Internet services with 3 computers.
Pension Mauarii, *Tel. 68.86.49,* just outside Parea Village on Huahine Iti, is a "Cyber Pension" and they charge 500 CFP for 15 minutes on the Internet.
Te Tiare Beach Resort, *Tel. 60.60.50*, has 3 Cyberpoint computers in their overwater lobby, and you can hook up your laptop to the data port on the telephone in your bungalow.

Police
The French gendarmerie, *Tel. 60.62.05,* is beside the lagoon in Fare.

Post Office and Telecommunications Office
The **Post Office**, *Tel. 68.82.70*, is in Fare on the circle island road. All telecommunications and postal services are available here. Hours are Monday to Thursday from 7am to 3pm, Friday from 7am to 2pm.

Tourist Bureau
Manava Visitors Bureau, *Tel. 68.78.81*, is a tourist information office located on the waterfront street in Fare, Open Monday through Friday from 7:30 to 11:30am. Georgette Itchner is the pretty Tahitian hostess who will give you brochures on all the lodgings and activities and answer your questions with a smile.

Chapter 16

RAIATEA

A panorama of green carpeted mountains, azure shoals and indigo bays greets your eyes as your Air Tahiti flight descends at **Raiatea** (Rye-ah-TEY-ah). The Temehani plateau rises to heights of 792 meters (2,598 feet) in the north, and Mount Tefatoaiati touches the clouds at 1,017 meters (3,336 feet) in the south. Small coral islets seem to float at the edge of the bays, rising from the submarine foundation that surrounds Raiatea and the smaller island of Tahaa. Eight passes provide entry into the vast lagoon.

Raiatea does not have the glamour of its neighboring island of Bora Bora. There are no white sand beaches except around the *motu* islets, and the tourist facilities do not include world-famous luxury resorts. Neither does it have the dramatic skyline of Moorea or the majesty of the mountains of Tahiti. Raiatea's big attractions include the ideal conditions the island and its surrounding lagoon and ocean offer for year-round sailing, scuba diving and fishing. There are five major yacht charter bases on the island, two scuba diving centers and several game-fishing boats.

Raiatea is 220 kilometers (136 miles) to the west-north-west of Tahiti. It is the largest of the Leeward Society Islands, which also include the high islands of Tahaa, Huahine, Bora Bora and Maupiti, plus the coral atolls of Tupai, Mopelia, Scilly and Bellinghausen. It has a surface area of 170 square kilometers (105 square miles) and is shaped rather like a triangle. When I look at a map of Tahaa and Raiatea together and see the barrier reef that protects the two islands, I think that it looks like a *penu*, the phallic-shaped stone pestle used by the Polynesians to prepare their traditional medicines of plants and herbs. Tahaa is the head of the *penu* and Raiatea is the base.

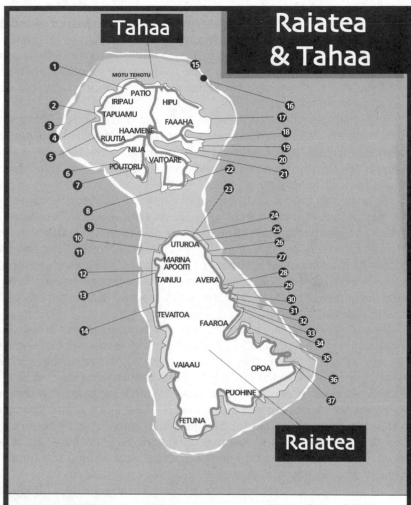

1. Tupenu Village
2. Chez Pascal
3. Le Taha'a Private Island and Spa
4. Au Phil du Temps
5. Chez Louise
6. Pension Vaihi
7. Pension Herenui
8. Hotel Marina Iti
9. Pension Tiare Nui
10. Uturoa Airport
11. Marina Apooiti
12. Sunset Beach Motel
13. Hotel Tenape
14. Marae Tainuu
15. Hotel La Pirogue
16. Hotel Vahine Island
17. Pension Le Passage
18. Chez Patricia & Daniel (Vai Poe)
19. Pension Hibiscus
20. Turtle Foundation
21. Haamene Bay
22. Pension Api
23. B&B Raiatea Bellevue
24. Uturoa Market
25. Hotel Bajoga-Hinano
26. Hotel Hawaiki Nui
27. Pension Tepua
28. Pension Manava
29. Kaoha Nui Ranch
30. Peter's Place
31. Pension Rauvine
32. Pension Yolande
33. Pension Raiatea Village
34. Pension La Croix du Sud
35. Vini Beach Lodge
36. Marae Taputapuatea
37. Hotel Atiapiti

Havai'i, The Sacred Island

Raiatea means "clear sky" and is still referred to as the **Sacred Island of Havai'i**, the ancestral home of the **Maohi** people. The Polynesian Creation Chant tells how Havai'i was created by the god Ta'aroa, as the birthplace of land, the birthplace of gods, the birthplace of kings and the birthplace of man. And it was to Havai'i, deep within the sacred Temehani mountain, that the souls of the dead must return.

According to Polynesian mythology, fragments of the sacred island broke off to create other lands, swimming like a fish to become the Windward Islands of Tahiti, Moorea, Maiao, Mehetia and Tetiaroa. Havai'i was also the cradle of royalty and religion in Eastern Polynesia, as well as the center of the Maohi culture, history and heraldry.

Ta'aroa, the creator god, was considered too aloof for the dynamic religion that soon developed among the ancient Polynesians. He was eventually retired to the background, along with the god **Tane**, while **Oro**, the son of Ta'aroa, came to be revered as the god of war, harvest, music and the founder of the famous Arioi society of troubadours and comedians. Long before Oro was born at Opoa the national *marae* of Havai'i or Havaiki was called Tinirauhinimatatepapa o Feoro, which means "Fruitful myriads who engraved the rocks of Feoro."

When Oro became very powerful and was acknowledged as the supreme every day god of the earth and sky, the name Feoro was changed to Vaiotaha, meaning "Water of the man o' war bird," because this bird was Oro's shadow and the water meant human blood. To his *marae* were taken most of the heads of decapitated warriors, which were cleaned and stacked in shining white rows on the black stones of the temple. The name was later changed to **Taputapuatea**, which means, "Sacrifices from abroad," and it became an international *marae*, where chiefs were brought for investiture. All other *marae* temples were founded by bringing a sacred stone from Taputapuatea or one of its descendant *maraes*.

The sacred pass of **Te Ava Moa** at Opoa in Raiatea offered frequent scenes of grandeur as great double canoes from many islands sailed into the lagoon, streaming long pennants from Hawaii, Tonga and New Zealand. The deep-toned sound of drums and the conch shell trumpets announced the arrival of delegations from island kingdoms throughout the Polynesian triangle, who were members of a friendly alliance.

At Opoa, the **Tamatoa** dynasty was reputed to go back 30 generations to **Hiro**, who was Raiatea's first king. Tradition says that Hiro and his associates built a great canoe and sailed away to Rarotonga and New Zealand, leaving two of his sons behind. One succeeded him as King of Raiatea and the other was the King of Bora Bora. During the meetings of the friendly alliance at Opoa, King Tamatoa was entitled to wear a red feather belt or *maro*, a sign of the highest honor, as he welcomed the visiting delegations. Each group of pilgrims brought human sacrifices to offer to the bloodthirsty Oro, and awesome ceremonies were held in the open-air temple of Marae Taputapuatea for the festivity of the gods, to render respect and sacrifices to Oro on his home soil.

These pagan rites ended with the arrival of the missionaries. Oro and the lesser gods were banished and Marae Taputapuatea is now silent, except for an occasional reenactment ceremony, which does not involve human sacrifices!

European Discovery

Captain James Cook was the first European to discover Raiatea, when he anchored the *Endeavour* in the lagoon at Opoa in July 1769. On board the ship was a man named **Tupia**, a native of Uliatea, as the island was then called. Tupia was the rejected lover of **Queen Purea** in Tahiti, and he and his servant boy Tayeto sailed with Cook when the *Endeavour* left Uliatea 11 days later. Both of the Polynesians died in Batavia in October 1770, of scurvy or malaria or both.

Cook returned to Raiatea in September 1773, and took a young man from Raiatea to England with him. This was a 22-year old fellow named Mai (**Omai**) who was then living in Huahine. Cook brought Omai back to Huahine in 1777 and once again visited Raiatea on a prolonged visit before sailing to Hawaii, where he was killed.

A number of other explorers touched at Raiatea following Cook's visits, but very few of them wrote about their experiences. After them came the traders and whalers, whose primary objective was to recover from scurvy, get provisions and find a woman.

John Williams from the London Missionary Society arrived in Raiatea in 1818, when he was just 21 years old. A few years later he founded the town of Uturoa. The island remained under the influence of the English Protestant missionaries long after Tahiti had come under French control. The people of Raiatea are still predominantly Evangelical. Following a *coup de force* in Tahiti by French **Admiral Du Petit-Thouars** in 1842, there followed a long period of instability. The French did not attempt a real takeover until 1888. In 1897, more than 50 years after the conquest of Tahiti, two war ships filled with French marines mounted a full-scale attack, with massive fire-power, driving the Raiateans back, until the surrogate chief Teraupoo was captured and exiled to New Caledonia. The French flag first flew over Raiatea in 1898.

Raiatea Today

The Raiatea airport is at the northern tip of the island and the town of Uturoa is southeast of the airport. A mostly paved road encircles the island for about 150 kilometers (93 miles), following the contours of the deeply indented coastline, with occasional forays into the exuberant vegetation of the valleys. You can drive for several miles without seeing any houses or people. Raiatea's 11,133 inhabitants live beside the road in Uturoa and in the villages and hamlets of Avera, Faaroa, Opoa, Puohine, Fetuna, Vaiaau, Tevaitoa and Apooiti.

Driving in a southeasterly direction from Uturoa you will see the **Hotel Hawaiki Nui** on your left, and you will pass impressive new homes and lovely flower gardens on both sides of the road. By the time you reach Avera you are in the country. At PK 6 you will see the small family hotel, **Raiatea Village**, just before a curve to the right that takes you down the deeply indented road that winds quietly around the edge of the **Faaroa Bay**. Your senses are heightened as you breathe in the perfumes of fresh mountain ferns, wild mangoes, kava, kapok and ripening breadfruit.

This bay merges with the **Apoomau River**, which is navigable by small ships and boats for a distance of four kilometers (2.5 miles) into the interior. At the mouth of the river is a spring containing effervescent water. A woman from Raiatea told me that people come from Hawaii and New Zealand to drink this water, which is guarded by the spirit of the spring. She said that photos taken here always show an extra person, or part of a face, which is supposedly that of the spirit. But this image fades in time.

A road from Faaroa Bay takes you into the interior of the island for 8 kilometers (5 miles), connecting with Fetuna at the southern tip of the island. Winding through the fertile valleys and wide flatland, you will pass plantations of pineapple, tapioca, papaya and vanilla, and farms with horses, cows, pigs and chickens. Far below the lacy fronds of acacia trees bordering the road you can see the wild, untamed southern coast of Raiatea. If you continue along the coastal route instead of cutting across the valley, you will come to **Marae Taputapuatea** at PK 32, 19.2 miles from Uturoa center, just beyond the village of Opoa. This is Raiatea's most famous landmark. The huge slabs of coral flagstone and basaltic rock slumber under the shade of coconut palms, a shrine to Polynesia's rich and varied Maohi culture.

Between Puohine and Fetuna a new road has been built along an embankment, with small *motu* islets, some with just one coconut tree, within wading distance from the shore. The *motu* beside Nao Nao pass into Faatemu Bay used to be a popular picnic site for cruise ship passengers and local inhabitants, but now that it is being developed with the construction of vacation villas, most of Motu Nao Nao is off limits to the public. The pre-fabricated box-like houses on stilts that you will see are supposedly built to withstand cyclones like those that destroyed the former homes on these sites. The Tahitian government sells these MTR houses to qualified property owners at very low cost.

Along the west coast you will see mountain streams meandering to the sea and gaily-colored cocks following their harem of clucking hens. The fishermen still use stones to enclose their fishponds, instead of wire netting.

You can see them mending their nets on the beach, while their children play in the shallows of the lagoon. There are no stores in these remote settlements, except for the mobile *magasins* operated by the Chinese vendors, who make their daily rounds with fresh *baguettes*, frozen chickens and Piggy Snax.

Tiare Apetahi-Raiatea's Endangered Flower

In the heights of the sacred Temehani Mountain grows the **Tiare Apetahi**, refreshed by the cool, dense clouds and mountain showers. When touched by the first rays of the rising sun, this rare white flower bursts open with a slight exploding sound.

The five-petal Tiare Apetahi is the symbol of Raiatea, and it is believed that this particular variety of the Campanaulacées family grows nowhere else in the world.

Legend says that the delicate petals represent the five fingers of a lovely Tahitian girl who fell in love with the son of a king and died of a broken heart because she could not hope to marry him.

In order to protect the rapidly disappearing Tiare Apetahi, which the flower vendors in Raiatea were selling at the airport, the local government has declared it an endangered species. Offenders may be fined up to one million French Pacific francs if caught. Repeat offenders can be given a maximum fine of six months imprisonment and nine million French Pacific francs.

The lagoon narrows between Vaihuti and Vaiaau Bays, with palm-shaded *motu* islets on the reef edge of the lagoon. Sharp peaks delineate the central mountain chain and in Vaiaau valley are remnants of fortifications that were built by the warriors of Faterehau, the great chiefess of Raiatea, who opposed the takeover by the French in 1897.

Behind Tevaitoa village the magnificent **Temehani Plateau** rises in formidable walls of basalt. The historic peaks shimmer in shades of blue and gray, and countless waterfalls cascade in misty plumes to splash far below into crisp pools fringed with tropical fern trees and shrubbery. **Marae Tainuu** is on the shoreline in the middle of the village. The Protestant church here is the oldest on the island, and partially covers the flagstones of the *marae*. Petroglyphs engraved in the basaltic stones include a Polynesian sundial and 10 turtles, depicting a sort of Polynesian treasure hunt that the Maohi warriors had to perform to achieve valor and esteem.

Copra drying in the sun, pigs grunting in the mud and black pearl farms in the lagoon just beside the road are left behind as you arrive at Apooiti Bay and see the sleek charter yachts moored at **Apooiti Marina**. Soon you round the north end of the island, pass in front of the airport and end your tour back in Uturoa.

Although there is an increase in the flow of traffic in the town center, the lifestyle here is still unhurried and the calm, friendly feeling of a small island lingers still. It is this wonderful magic of Polynesia that tempts you to return again to Raiatea.

Arrivals & Departures
Arriving By Air
Air Tahiti has one to seven direct 40-minute flights daily between Tahiti and Raiatea and one to three daily flights with stops in Huahine, according to the busy or slow seasons. The fare is 11.500 CFP one-way for adults, and 21.000 CFP round-trip, tax included. You can also fly direct to Raiatea from Moorea each Monday, Tuesday, Wednesday and Sunday, with a stop in Huahine on Friday. You can fly direct from Bora Bora to Raiatea daily except Tuesday and Thursday, and there are direct flights from Maupiti to Raiatea each Tuesday, Friday and Sunday. The one-way Moorea-Raiatea fare for adults is 12.500 CFP, between Huahine-Raiatea it is 5.200 CFP, Bora Bora-Raiatea is 5.900 CFP, and from Maupiti to Raiatea the one-way fare is 6.500 CFP. **Air Tahiti reservations**: Tahiti, *Tel. 86.42.42/86.41.84*; Moorea, *Tel. 55.06.00*; Huahine, *Tel. 68.77.02/60.62.60*; Raiatea, *Tel. 60.04.44/60.04.40*; Bora Bora, *Tel. 60.53.53/60.53.00*; Maupiti, *Tel. 60.15.05/67.81.30*.

If you have reservations with a hotel, pension or yacht charter company, then you will be met at the airport and driven to your hotel. Avis and Europcar have sales counters at the airport and there are also taxis that meet the arrival of each flight.

You can also get to Raiatea by chartering an airplane in Tahiti from **Wan Air**, *Tel. 50.44.17, cell 77.03.79*; **Air Archipels**, *Tel. 81.30.30*; or **Air Tahiti**, *Tel. 86.42.42*.

Arriving By Boat
All the inter-island transport boats dock at the quay in Uturoa, the main town of Raiatea, and it would be advisable to arrange with your hotel or pension to have someone meet you when you arrive in the middle of the night. The car rental agencies will also meet you at the Uturoa quay. A Visitors Bureau is adjacent to the quay.

Hawaiki Nui, *Tel. 54.99.54; Fax 45.24.44, E-mail: sarlstim@mail.pf*. This 12-passenger cargo ship has 4 double cabins and deck space. Passengers must sleep in cabins on the Thursday voyage as the ship also transports fuel then. It leaves the Motu Uta dock in Papeete each Tuesday at 4pm and arrives at the Uturoa quay in Raiatea on Wednesday at 4:30am, after stopping in Huahine. The Thursday trip leaves Papeete at 4pm, and arrives in Raiatea on Friday at 2:30am. The ship continues on to Bora Bora and Tahaa and returns to Raiatea on Friday at 1pm on its way back to Huahine and Tahiti. The cost of sleeping on deck is 1.750 CFP per person and a berth in one of the cabins costs 4.950 CFP from Papeete to all the Leeward Islands. Meals are available on board the ship.

Vaeanu, *Tel. 41.25.35; Fax 41.24.34, E-mail: torehiatetu@mail.pf*. This ship can transport a total of 90 passengers, with 32 berths in cabins and 58 places on the deck. It departs from the Fare-Ute quay in Papeete at 4pm on Monday, Wednesday and Friday, stopping in Huahine and arriving in Raiatea the following morning at 3:30am. One-way fare for deck passengers is 2.120 CFP; a berth in a cabin costs 4.400 to 5.989 CFP per person depending on accommodations chosen. Meals are served on board. Reservations for cabin space must be paid in full before 9am on the fixed date of departure from Papeete.

Maupiti Express II, *Tel./Fax 689/66.37.81; Cell 78.27.22*. This new 140-passenger boat began service at the end of September, 2004, replacing the 62-passenger boat that was formerly used to transport passengers between Raiatea and Bora Bora and from Bora Bora to Maupiti. The new boat also docks at the Uturoa quay where all the Tahaa boats tie up. The *Maupiti Express II* arrives in Uturoa direct from Bora Bora and Tahaa at 8:45am each Monday, Wednesday and Friday, and at 5:45pm each Friday and Sunday. The one-way fare from Bora Bora to Raiatea is 2.500 CFP and round-trip is 3.500 CFP. The fares from Maupiti to Raiatea are 3.500 CFP and 5.500 CFP. Passengers under 12 years pay half-fare.

Enota Transport Maritime, *Tel./Fax 65.61.33*. Enota Tetuanui has two 42-foot launches that can transport 57 passengers each between Tahaa and Raiatea. *Te Haere Maru V* leaves from the east coast of Tahaa twice a day, starting from Faaaha, stopping in Haamene (at 6:30am and 12pm) and Vaitoare for the trip to Uturoa. *Te Haere Maru IV* leaves from the west coast of Tahaa twice a day, with stops at Tapuamu (5:30am on Monday and 5:45am Tuesday-Saturday and again at 11:45am), Tiva, Poutoru and Marina Iti, and then makes the 15-minute crossing to Uturoa. One-way fare is 500 CFP.

Tamarii Tahaa, *Tel. 65.65.29* or *20.93.11*, can transport a maximum of 66 passengers in a 46-foot aluminum boat that operates a shuttle service between Tahaa and Raiatea. The boat leaves the Patio boat dock at 5:15am and 11:45am Monday through Friday, and at 5:30am on Saturday. Stops are made at Tapuamu, Tiva, Poutoru and Apu, then continue on to Uturoa, arriving one to one and a half-hours after leaving Patio. The fare is 700 CFP from Patio and the other stops cost 500 CFP per person.

Departing By Air

You can fly from Raiatea to Bora Bora, Maupiti and Huahine, or return to Tahiti by **Air Tahiti**, *Tel. 60.44.44/60.04.40* in Raiatea. There is no direct return flight service between Raiatea and Moorea. Tickets can be purchased at the airport. Check-in time at the airport is one hour before scheduled departure.

Departing By Boat
You can continue on to Tahaa, Bora Bora and Maupiti by boat from Raiatea, or you can return to Papeete with a stop in Huahine.
Hawaiki Nui, *Tel. 54.99.54* (Papeete), *Tel. 66.42.10* (Raiatea); *Fax 45.24.44*, leaves Raiatea for Bora Bora and Tahaa each Wednesday at 5:30am, returning to Raiatea at 6pm and then departs for Tahiti at 6:30pm, arriving in Papeete on Thursday at 7am. It leaves each Friday at 3:30am for Bora Bora and Tahaa and returns to Raiatea at 1pm, and then leaves at 1:30pm on Friday for Huahine and Tahiti, arriving in Papeete at 5am Saturday morning.
Vaeanu, *Tel. 41.25.35* (Papeete), *Tel. 66.22.22* (Raiatea); *Fax 41.24.34*, leaves Raiatea at 5am each Tuesday for Tahaa and Bora Bora, and on its return voyage it leaves Raiatea at 3pm each Tuesday for Huahine and Tahiti, arriving in Papeete at 2am on Wednesday. On Thursday the ship leaves Raiatea at 5am for Tahaa and Bora Bora, then returns to Raiatea at 2:30pm and departs at 3pm for Huahine and Tahiti, arriving in Papeete at 2am Friday. On Saturday the Vaeanu leaves Raiatea at 5am for Tahaa and Bora Bora, and returns to Raiatea at 1pm on Sunday, then departs at 2pm for Huahine and Tahiti, arriving in Papeete each Monday at 1am. The deck fare from Raiatea to Tahaa is 800 CFP, to Bora Bora it's 1.400 CFP, from Raiatea to Huahine is 1.060 CFP and from Raiatea to Tahiti it costs 2.120 CFP. A berth in a cabin is 4.400 to 5.989 CFP.
Maupiti Express II, *Tel./Fax 689/66.37.81; Cell 78.27.22*. The boat departs from the Uturoa quay each Monday and Wednesday at 4pm for Tahaa and Bora Bora, arriving in Vaitape at 5:45pm. On Friday and Sunday it leaves Raiatea at 6pm, arriving in Bora Bora at 7:45pm. During the school period the *Maupiti Express II* leaves Raiatea at 2pm and 5:30pm. The one-way fare is 2.500 CFP. Passengers under 12 years pay half fare. The captain is not allowed to transport passengers from Raiatea to Tahaa only.
Enota Transport Maritime, *Tel./Fax 65.61.33*. Enota Tetuanui has two 42-foot speedboats that can transport 57 passengers each between Raiatea and Tahaa. *Te Haere Maru V* leaves from the boat dock in Uturoa at 10:30am and 4:30pm for the east coast of Tahaa, stopping in Vaitoare, Haamene and Faaaha. *Te Haere Maru IV* leaves from the boat dock in Uturoa at 10:30am and 4:30pm for the west coast of Tahaa, stopping at the Marina Iti, Poutoru, Tiva and Tapuamu. The crossing takes 20 to 45 minutes, depending on your destination. One-way fare is 500 CFP.
Tamarii Tahaa, *Tel. 65.65.29 or 20.93.11*, can transport a maximum of 66 passengers in a 46-foot aluminum boat that operates a shuttle service between Raiatea and Tahaa. The boat leaves the Uturoa boat dock Monday through Friday at 10:30am and 4:30pm and on Saturday at 10:30am only. Stops are made in Apu, Poutoru, Tiva, Tapuamu and Patio. The one-way fare is 500 CFP as far as Tapuamu and 700 CFP to Patio.

Orientation

The town center of **Uturoa** (oo-too-RO-ah), which means, "long jaw," is two kilometers (1.2 miles) south of the airport. This is the second largest town in French Polynesia. Here you will find the administrative seat for the Leeward Islands. Buildings reminiscent of former colonial days stand adjacent to modern government buildings, post office, banks, boutiques, general stores, supermarkets and small restaurants. There is a hospital, *gendarmerie*, courthouse, a Catholic school, a lycée, technical schools and boarding facilities for students from throughout the Leeward Islands. A community nautical center and marina are on the edge of town, and the public market, port facilities and shipping warehouses in the center of Uturoa provide the focal point of a relaxed pace of business life.

Mount Tapioi rises 294 meters (964 feet) behind Uturoa, with a television relay at the summit. You can hike up or drive 3.5 kilometers (2.2 miles) to the top in a 4WD, where you'll enjoy the panoramic view of Tahaa and Huahine, Bora Bora and Maupiti.

Big government projects have modernized Uturoa's public facilities. A new wharf provides 430 meters (1,410 feet) of docking space for the passenger ships that are based in Tahiti or the Leeward Islands year-round, as well as the inter-island cargo/passenger ships from Tahiti. On or adjacent to the quay are a new port captain's office, warehouses, cold storage for fish, public restrooms, arts and crafts center and public gardens. A Gare Maritime shopping mall also embellishes the waterfront, with fancy two-story buildings painted pink. Granite from Portugal was imported to pave rue Tiare Apetahi in front of the mall. In addition to the restaurants, black pearl shops, boutiques, gift shops and florist shop downstairs, the Raiatea Visitors Bureau occupies an enormous space on the ground level, and the post office has a branch upstairs.

Work is still underway to improve Uturoa's downtown area. The public market that was built in 1946 was torn down to build a new modern marché, and a temporary market was erected adjacent to the mairie (town hall). This arrangement doesn't seem to please the habits of the residents, however, as very few sales people or shoppers use the temporary market. The Chinese businessmen in Uturoa are being encouraged to update or rebuild their old wooden stores that added a certain charm to the Uturoa of yesteryear, an image that will soon disappear. A by-pass road is being constructed behind the main street, which will be used for traffic, and the main street will become a pedestrian street.

This modernization program will mean losing the old Fare Vanira, a little wooden shack on the main street to which you are drawn by the enticing aroma of fragrant vanilla wafting on the breeze. This is the oldest building downtown, built in 1938, and it is the domain of "Madame Vanilla," Jeanne

Chane, a lively Chinese woman who sells dried vanilla beans, powdered vanilla and extract. She is the third generation of vanilla experts in her family. If the Magasin Vanira is still standing when you visit Uturoa, be sure to ask Madame Chane to show you her six diplomas and two silver cups she's won as a vanilla professional. Just follow your nose to her store and you'll find her counting her beans— vanilla, that is.

Getting Around Raiatea
Car, Scooter & Bicycle Rentals
Avis (Te Maire) *Tel. 60.00.95; Fax 66.00.96; Cell 71.74.26, E-mail: temaire-raiatea@ifrance.com.* This agency is located next to the Apetahi Mobil station at the airport in Raiatea and is open 7 days a week to rent cars only. A 3-door air-conditioned Twingo is 7.300 CFP for 4 hours and 11.500 CFP for 24 hours. A 5-door air-conditioned Twingo or Clio is 8.300 CFP for 4 hours and 12.530 CFP for 24 hours.

Europcar, *Tel. 66.34.06; Fax 66.16.06; Cell 78.33.53/75.53.74; E-mail: europcar-loc@mail.pf.* Sales offices are located at the airport, at the main office between the airport and Uturoa, and at the Hawaiki Nui Hotel, *Tel. 66.16.06.* A 3-door Saxo or Twingo rents for 5.300 CFP for 2 hours, 6.500 CFP for 4 hours, 7.600 CFP for 8 hours and 9.000 CFP for 24 hours. An air-conditioned 5-door Peugeot 206 costs 8.100 CFP for 2 hours, and escalates up to 12.900 CFP for 24 hours. Scooter rates start at 4.200 CFP for 2 hours. These rates include unlimited mileage and third-party insurance. Gas is extra. Raiatea Location, which represents Europcar, also offers a special Tiare Nui package for 10.930 CFP a day, which includes a Saxo or Twingo and a bungalow, or 17.530 CFP for a Saxo or Twingo, a bungalow for two people and a boat. The simple bungalows are located adjacent to Europcar's main office near the airport. All rates include taxes.

Hertz, *Tel. 66.44.88, Fax 66.44.89*, is located in the office of Raiatea Motors, on the mountainside across the street from the Mairie (town hall) of Uturoa. They also have a counter at the airport, *Tel. 66.44.90.* An air-conditioned 5-door Toyota Maris manual drive car rents for 5.990 CFP for 4 hours, 6.990 CFP for 8 hours, 8.600 CFP for 24 hours and 15.990 CFP for 2 days. A 5-door air-conditioned Toyota Maris with automatic drive rents for 7.330 CFP for 4 hours, 8.450 CFP for 8 hours and up to 20.150 CFP for 2 days. You can also rent a 4x4 Santana pick-up truck for 8.300 CFP for 4 hours up to 19.900 CFP for 2 days. Rates include VAT and unlimited mileage, plus collision insurance.

Bicycles
Europcar, *Tel. 66.34.06*, rents bicycles for 1.500 CFP for 2 hours, 1.800 CFP for 4 hours and 2.400 CFP for 8 hours, tax included. Longer rentals possible. **Vaea Rent A Bike** is on the Uturoa Quay, *Tel. 79.16.61; Fax*

66.27.17. **Odile Locations** is at Sunset Beach Motel in Apooiti, *Tel. 66.33.47.* Other hotels and pensions also rent bikes.

Taxis
Taxis are usually available at the Uturoa airport for each flight arrival, and a taxi stand is located at the boat and ferry dock in the center of Uturoa, *Tel. 66.20.60/66.36.74/72.30.54.* The taxi drivers pride themselves on their good reputation. Taxi fare from the airport to Uturoa center is 1.000 CFP and from the airport to the Hawaiki Nui hotel is 1.500 CFP, plus 100 CFP for baggage. The rate from the port in Uturoa to Hawaiki Nui is 700 CFP. The hourly rate is 4.000 CFP, and 1.800 CFP for waiting time. A circle island tour by private taxi is 20.000 CFP.

Le Truck
A *le truck* service operates between the public market in Uturoa and each village, coordinating their schedules with the arrivals of the ferries and school hours. They charge a minimal fee to transport passengers to their destination in Raiatea.

Taxi Boats
La Compagnie des Taxis-Boat (Corto), *Tel./Fax 65.66.44; cell 79.62.01/ 79.62.02; VHF: 16; E-mail: taxi-boat@mail.pf; www.taxi-boat.com.* William Donzelot and his son Briam have two locally built 23-foot and 28-foot polyester and aluminum boats that will accommodate a minimum of two or a maximum of six passengers. They provide taxi boat service between Raiatea and Tahaa or Tahaa and Raiatea on request, daily from 6am to 6pm. They will pick you up at the airport, the quay in Uturoa or from any boat dock specified. The per person fare from Uturoa to Tahaa starts at 2.000 CFP for Zone 1, the villages closest to Uturoa, and escalates to 4.000 CFP per person for Zone 5, which includes Hipu, Patio and Iripau. Night transfers cost 100 percent more. You can also charter a taxi boat for 12.000 CFP an hour.
Taxi Boat, *Tel. 66.13.33*, also provides taxi boat service.
Tumatahi Taxi Boat, *Tel. 66.25.17 / 79.62.41.* Jean-Luc and Tetuanui operate a taxi service to the *motu* for 3.800 CFP per person.

Where to Stay
Superior
HOTEL HAWAIKI NUI, *B.P. 43, Uturoa, Raiatea 98735. Tel. 689/ 60.05.00; Fax 689/66.20.20; E-mail: maraea.temauri@spmhotels.pf; www.pearlresorts.com. Beside the lagoon, two kilometers (1.2 miles) south of town. Round-trip transfers from the airport or ferry dock: 1.500 CFP per person. EP Rates: garden room 24.000 CFP single/double; garden bungalow 26.000 CFP single/double; lagoon bungalow 34.000 CFP single/double;*

overwater bungalow 38.000-46.000 CFP single/double. Add 5.000 CFP for extra person. Continental breakfast is 1.800 CFP; American breakfast 2.200 CFP; meal plan with breakfast and dinner is 7.600 CFP per person; meal plan with breakfast, lunch and dinner is 10.800 CFP per person. Add 5% hotel tax to room rates and 6% value added tax to room rates, prepaid meal plans and transfers, plus 150 CFP municipal tax per person per day. A 10% value added tax is applicable to other services. All major credit cards.

The 3-star Hawaiki Nui (formerly Raiatea Pearl Resort) is the largest hotel on Raiatea, and it is the only international class resort hotel on the island. It is situated on the fringe of the lagoon in Tepua Bay, with 28 rooms and bungalows built in the Polynesian style with thatched roofs and bamboo furniture. A 100 million franc renovation project began in 2003 and the result is all new interiors, furniture and furnishings. The 8 garden rooms are now air-conditioned; one of the 8 garden bungalows now offers a junior suite, family room or two bedrooms, and the 3 lagoon bungalows and 9 overwater bungalows have new thatch roofs with false ceilings, which will keep the rooms cleaner. The garden bungalows offer a lounge area, and the overwater bungalows have a veranda overlooking the lagoon and steps leading down into the warm blue waters. A glass floor in the overwater bungalows lets you watch the fish at night as they feed in the coral gardens below. All units are screened and equipped with a king-size bed and a single bed, ceiling fan, mini refrigerator, cable television, telephone, coffee and tea making facilities, safety deposit box and hair dryer. An iron and board are available on request.

Pierre Dinard took over as general manager of Hawaiki Nui in 2002 and helped to bring about the renovation project. Pierrot, as he is nicknamed, has managed other hotel properties in French Polynesia and Kiki, his wife, is from Moorea. In addition to the roofs and interior decoration of the bungalows, all the pier walkways to the overwater bungalows and the main pier were redone, the garden was redesigned, the restaurant was enlarged and repainted, an air-conditioned conference room was created that can accommodate 40 people for a seminar, room service was added and all the services were computerized. A cyberpoint was installed in the lobby for guests to connect to the Internet.

The Hawaiki Nui is truly an integral part of the community. The recently formed Rotary Club meets here, as well as the Chess Club. Pierrot began a Happy Hour and resumed the Sunday brunch, which attracts the island's well established residents, including the mayor and his family and older families who arrive on Sunday dressed in Polynesian shirts, lovely *mama ruau* gowns and crowns of flowers. They dance the Tahitian two-step, fox trot and waltz to the tunes of old Polynesia that are played by a 3-piece band.

Adjacent to the Nordby Restaurant is an indoor-outdoor bar and a fresh water swimming pool just outside the restaurant overlooks the lagoon. There is no beach here, but there is a pier for sunbathing. Snorkeling equipment is provided free of charge as well as outrigger canoes and kayaks. Hemisphere Sub Diving Center charges 5.900 CFP to take qualified divers to visit the *Nordby* wreck at the bottom of the giant aquarium close to the hotel pontoon. Pronounced "Nordbou", this 3-masted barque was built of iron in 1873 in Dundee, Scotland, under the name *Glencarn* for a British ship owner. It was sold in 1893 to the Winther Shipbuilders in Denmark. It sank in August 1900 in front of Teavarua pass in 25 meters of water.

Cathy Briy from the hotel's Activities Desk encourages guests to come with her to feed the fish at the end of the pontoon each day at 8:30am. She acts as guide to take you by boat to snorkel in the shallow water beside Motu Ofetaro, opposite the hotel. This excursion leaves the pontoon at 9:30am and costs 2.500 CFP for 1 1/2 hours. For 1.500 CFP per person Cathy will drop you off at Motu Ofetaro and come back later to pick you up, and if you want to picnic on Motu Iriru it will cost 5.500 CFP per person. Cathy can also help you to arrange your tours and excursions by land or sea to discover the mountains, valleys, rivers, *motu* and lagoons of Raiatea and its sister island of Tahaa. A Games Room provides scrabble, checkers and other board games and babysitting is also available at the hotel for 1.000 CFP per hour during the day and 1.500 CFP per hour at night. You can even have a massage therapist come to your room anytime between 8:30am and 8pm.

The Painapo boutique is located beside the hotel entrance, where you can rent a bicycle for 500 CFP for 2 hours, 900 CFP for 4 hours and 1.600 CFP for all day. You can also rent an underwater camera here, as well as leave your film and numeric photos to be developed. Carine, who manages the boutique, is also an underwater photographer who will make a DVD of your dive for 6.500 CFP.

Should you wish to drive yourself around the island, Europcar is represented at the Hawaiki Nui reception desk. See *Where to Eat* in this chapter.

HOTEL TENAPE, *B.P. 1280, Uturoa, Raiatea 98735. Tel. 689/60.01.00; Fax 689/60.01.01; E-mail: hoteltenape@mail.pf; www.raiatea.com/tenape. On the mountainside at PK 9.8 in Tumaraa, 4 kilometers (2.5 miles) from the airport and 7 kilometers (4.3 miles) from the ferry dock. Round-trip transfers 1.500 CFP for maximum 3 passengers. EP rates: room 18.500 CFP single/ double; add 4.000 CFP for additional person; suite 26.500 CFP for maximum 4 people. Continental breakfast 1.400 CFP, American breakfast 1.900 CFP, meal plan with breakfast and dinner 5.300 CFP, meal plan with breakfast, lunch and dinner 8.400 CFP per person. Add 5% hotel tax to room rates and 6% value added tax to room rates, prepaid meal plans and transfers, plus 150 CFP municipal tax per person per day. A 10% value added tax is applicable to other services. Mastercard, Visa.*

This 2-story colonial style hotel opened in 1999, with 15 air-conditioned rooms and a 2-bedroom air-conditioned suite with a living room. The hotel is situated on two hectares (4.9 acres) of land on the northwest coast of Raiatea, with 120 meters (394 feet) of lagoon frontage across the road. Each room contains a king-size bed or twin beds, television, direct dial telephone, individual safe, and a separate bathroom with a hot water shower. The suite has two bedrooms, living room, bathroom and all the other amenities as the rooms. A covered terrace overlooks the lagoon, the islands of Bora Bora and Maupiti, and the spectacular sunsets. This may be a convenient place to stay if you have a car and want to be close to the marina and yacht club.

Public facilities include a restaurant and bar, swimming pool and pool bar, front desk, lounge, activities desk and boutique. There is a helicopter-landing pad on the premises, and you can board an excursion boat from their pier across the road. They work with Europcar, who will come to the hotel to pick you up when you want to rent a car. Other tours and excursions are also available, such as scuba diving, deep-sea fishing, 4WD safari tours, lagoon outings and picnics on the *motu*. The French owners do not speak English, but they said that the French cook speaks English. He has earned a good reputation for the fine cuisine served in the restaurant's lovely and romantic dining room. See *Where to Eat* in this chapter.

A new project to build 10 studios in the garden behind the hotel began in mid-2004, with a plan to construct 2 units at a time. These studios will have kitchens and other facilities for guests who stay for several days or weeks.

Moderate
PENSION TEPUA, *B.P. 1298, Uturoa, Raiatea 98735. Tel. 689/66.33.00; Fax 689/66.32.00: E-mail: pension-tepua@mail.pf; www.raiatea.com/tepua. Beside the lagoon in Tepua Bay, 2.5 kilometers (1.5 miles) south of Uturoa center. Round-trip transfers from Uturoa port or airport 1.000 CFP per adult, 500 CFP for child. EP Rates: studio beside lagoon 13.000 CFP single/double; bungalow beside swimming pool 11.000 CFP; garden studio 9.000 CFP single/double, add 1.000 CFP for extra bed; room with double bed 7.000 CFP single/double; room with single bed 4.500 CFP; dormitory 2.000 CFP per person. Breakfast 1.000 CFP. Meal plan available. Rates include taxes except visitor tax of 50 CFP per person per day. Mastercard, Visa.*

Joe Ungaro-Alves and his wife Guylaine have managed this pension since April 2001. He speaks Portuguese, Spanish, Italian, French and English. Since this couple took over they have renovated, repainted and redecorated whatever needed attention on the premises, hired a new chef and receptionists and other needed personnel. They have also installed a "Cyberpoint" service with Internet connections for guests.

The pension has a seaside bungalow, a bungalow facing the pool, and a garden bungalow; all with a queen size bed and two single beds, ceiling fan, kitchenette and private bathroom. There is a room with a double bed, two rooms with a single bed, and a 12-bunk dormitory. The rooms and dorm have ceiling fans and guests share the bathroom facilities and kitchen. All the

bathrooms have hot water showers. There are refrigerators in all the bungalows and television in the most expensive bungalow.

The restaurant serves breakfast and lunch to the in-house guests and is
open to the public at night, as well as the bar. There is a swimming pool on
the premises and a pier over the lagoon. There's a lot squeezed into one small
space here, and all land and sea activities that are available in Raiatea can be
arranged at the pension.

HOTEL ATIAPITI, *B.P. 884, Uturoa, Raiatea 98735. Tel./Fax 689/
66.16.65; E-mail: atiapiti@mail.pf; www.raiatea.com/atiapiti. Beside the
lagoon at PK 31 in Opoa, near Marae Taputapuatea, 30 kilometers (18.6
miles) from the ferry dock and 32 kilometers (19.8 miles) from the airport.
Round-trip transfers 3.000 CFP per person. EP Rates: beach bungalow 10.600
CFP single/double; garden bungalow-suite 12.500 CFP single/double; third
adult add 1.200 CFP. Breakfast 1.100 CFP. Meal plan with breakfast and
dinner 4.400 CFP, meal plan with breakfast, lunch and dinner 7.000 CFP per
person, half-price meals for children under 12. Rates include taxes except
visitor tax of 50 CFP per person per day. Mastercard, Visa.*

This is the only accommodation available anywhere near the famous
Marae Taputapuatea. Seven modern concrete bungalows with wood shake
roofs are well spaced in a hectare (2.5 acres) of land beside a narrow strip of
white sand beach. The grounds are planted with fruit trees, rainbow shower
trees and lots of flowers—orchids, Tiare Tahiti, gardenias and 45 different
kinds of hibiscus. Each of the 5 beach bungalows has a bedroom with a king-
size bed, living room with tamanu wood furniture, a kitchenette, mini-bar,
bathroom with hot water, and a terrace overlooking the sea and the distant
island of Huahine. The 2 garden bungalow suites contain a lounge with a
double bed and two single beds, a small room with a single bed, a kitchen,
terrace, and a bathroom with hot water. All bungalows have an electric fan
and television and can accommodate up to five people.

Marie-Claude Rajaud, the friendly and energetic French woman who
owns this small family hotel, speaks English and Spanish, and she is a very good
cook. See more information under *Where to Eat* in this chapter.

Free activities include snorkeling from the long pier or pontoon, fishing,
outrigger paddle canoes, feeding the eels, petanque (French bowls), ping-
pong, society games and a lending library. Marie-Claude's young daughter has
a Tahitian dance group who sometimes perform for the guests. Rental bicycles
are available for 1.500 CFP per day, and a single kayak or outrigger paddle
canoe costs 1.000 CFP for a half-day and 1.500 CFP per day for a double canoe
or kayak.

At this pension you will have an interesting choice of optional activities,
including a guided visit to the Marae of Taputapuatea for 1.000 CFP per
person. Guided walking tours take you into the wild southern end of Raiatea,
for a 2-3 hike through Opoa Valley and a swim in the river, for 2.000 CFP per

person. A 2-3 hour hike into the Hotopuu Valley includes a visit to a vanilla plantation and swimming in the basin of a waterfall, for 2.000 CFP per person. If you are interested in history, you will be guided to the Cascade of Faeratai, where there are petroglyphs carved in the boulders beside the river, and you can also bathe in the waterfall. This 3-4 hour hike requires a good physical condition and costs 4.000 CFP per person for 2 to 4 people. Hiking trips to Mount Temehani take about 7 hours and cost 6.000 CFP a person for 2 to 4 people. Boat trips to visit *motu* islets in the vicinity start at 2.000 CFP per person, and a boat trip to Tahaa for the day is 6.000-9.000 CFP, according to the number of passengers and program chosen. Land excursions by 4WD will take you around the island for 6.000 CFP per person or show you the highlights of the southern end for 4.000 CFP for a 2-3 hour tour. You can also horseback riding, scuba diving and deep-sea fishing.

VINI BEACH LODGE, *B.P. 1384, Uturoa, Raiatea 98735. Tel. 689/ 60.22.45/78.48.34; Fax 689/60.22.46; E-mail: vinibeach@mail.pf; www.raiatea.com/vinibeach. On seaside, overlooking Faaroa Bay at PK 12 in Avera, 7.4 miles southeast of Uturoa center. Round-trip airport transfers 800 CFP per person. EP Rates: 10.000 CFP single/double; 1.000 CFP per night for third person and 500 CFP for child 3-12 years old. Rates include taxes except visitor tax of 50 CFP per person per day. No credit cards.*

Five new duplex bungalows opened in 2003 on the hillside in Faaroa, overlooking the Sunsail Yacht base and the Faaroa River. Each bungalow comprises a double bed in the bedroom and twin beds on the mezzanine, with mosquito nets over the beds and a ceiling fan. There is a kitchenette, bathroom with hot water shower and a terrace and balcony.

SUNSET BEACH MOTEL, *B.P. 397, Uturoa, Raiatea 98735. Tel. 689/ 66.33.47; Fax 689/66.33.08; E-mail: sunsetbeach@mail.pf; www.raiatea.com/ sunsetbeach. Beside the lagoon in Apooiti, 5 kilometers (3 miles) from the ferry dock and 2 kilometers (1.2 miles) from the airport. Round-trip transfers are free. EP Rates: bungalow 8.000 CFP single, 9.000 CFP double, 10.000 CFP triple and 11.000 CFP quadruple. Add 1.000 CFP for fifth adult. Camping 1.100 CFP per person per day. Reduced rates for stays exceeding 15 days. No charge for children under 3 years, and 500 CFP for 3-12 year olds. Rates include taxes except visitor tax of 50 CFP per person per day. Mastercard, Visa.*

If you are looking for a quiet, comfortable place to spend several days or weeks, you'll find this small family hotel very suitable for your desires, as it offers one of the best values and most pleasant experiences in the islands. You have to reserve in advance to watch the sunsets here, as this is a very popular lodging for European visitors. The 20 American style wooden cottage type houses or bungalows are placed far apart on a 10-hectare (24.7 acre) property that is still a working coconut plantation. The bungalows are all on the waterfront with a fabulous view of Tahaa and Bora Bora. Each bungalow has screened windows and sliding glass doors, and contains a bedroom with a double bed, a living room with three single beds and television, a picnic table, a fully equipped kitchen, private bathroom with solar hot water, house linens, portable fan, covered terrace and carport. A narrow strip of white sand beach fronts the property, and you can sunbathe on the long private pier or feed the fish at the end of the dock. Snorkeling equipment and outrigger paddle canoes are provided, as well as ping-pong and volleyball. You can rent a bicycle, scooter, car or a motorboat for five people to go to the *motu*. Free car transfers are provided for shopping expeditions in town. An activities book with photos and descriptions of land and lagoon excursions is provided for each bungalow, and if you want to take an excursion they will pick you up at Sunset Beach.

Separated from the bungalows by a large garden is a campground for up to 25 tents, with a large equipped kitchen and big covered dining terrace. Campers share the communal cold-water bath facilities, with access to a pay phone, laundry, luggage room and library on the premises.

Sunset Beach is managed by 33-year-old Moana Boubee, whose grandfather bought this property 48 years ago. After finishing a three-year hotel school course in Tahiti, Moana took over from his mother, Eliane, who is a retired schoolteacher in Raiatea. His enthusiasm and friendliness are welcome assets, and he speaks good English. He has nine employees to help run the estate, which includes plantations of papaya, pineapple, vanilla and copra. There is no restaurant on the premises, but a breakfast including fresh fruit grown on Moana's farm will be delivered to your bungalow on request, for 1.000 CFP. You can also order bread the night before and they will bring it to your bungalow the next morning.

BED & BREAKFAST RAIATEA BELLEVUE, *B.P. 98, Uturoa, Raiatea 98735. Tel./Fax 689/66.15.15; E-mail: raiatea-bellevue@mail.pf. On the mountainside behind the Lycée of Uturoa, two kilometers (1.2 miles) from the airport and two kilometers from the Uturoa ferry dock. Round-trip transfers 1.400 CFP per person. EP Rates including breakfast: 6.995 CFP single, 7.990 double. Rates include taxes except visitor tax of 50 CFP per person per day. No credit cards.*

This Bed and Breakfast guesthouse is located on top of a very steep hill reached by a road north of Uturoa center. Take the first paved road on the left after PK 1 and follow it past the school, upward for 800 meters (2,624 feet). There are 4 very small rooms, each with a double bed, mosquito net, fan, television, and private bathroom with hot water. The rooms are all romantically decorated with Tahitian *tifaifai* bedspreads. Guests share a refrigerator and the terrace. There is a small swimming pool for guests and you'll have a lovely view of the *motu* islets and island of Tahaa from this mountainside location. I received an E-mail from Canadian friends who have traveled extensively throughout the outer islands of French Polynesia, and they reported that the total room size here, including the bathroom, is 9x12 feet. They also complained about the mosquitoes, adding that the fan is too big for the room and there is no air circulation in most of the room. They commended Max Boucher, the owner, for his helpfulness, and said that three restaurants provide pick-up service for dinner.

HOTEL BAJOGA-HINANO, *B.P. 1689, Uturoa, Raiatea 98735. Tel. 689/ 66.13.13; Fax 689/66.14.14; E-mail: bajoga-hinano@mail.pf; www.hotel-hinano-tahiti.com. On the main street in the center of Uturoa, a two-minute walk from the ferry dock. Round-trip transfers from the airport 800 CFP per person. EP Rates: standard room with fan 6.350 CFP single, 7.700 CFP double; standard room with air-conditioning 7.350 CFP single, 8.700 CFP double; extra person 1.350 CFP. Breakfast 600 CFP per person. Rates include taxes except visitor tax of 50 CFP per person per day. Mastercard, Visa.*

This hotel is upstairs in the center of town and is the only lodging in the downtown area of Uturoa. Two French couples bought it in 2002, combined the initials of six children in their families, and came up with Bajoga, then added that to the former Hotel Hinano to make a new identity for the old hotel. The 10 motel-type rooms have been renovated and spruced up and 5 of them have air-conditioning, while the other 5 have ceiling fans. They all have double beds and a single bed, cable television and private bathrooms with hot water shower. Tables and chairs have been added to the interior patio area and breakfast is served here each morning. Although the reception closes at 8:30-9pm, a woman can stay here alone without having to be concerned about someone knocking on her door in the middle of the night, because the door to the street downstairs is locked at night. Chez Michele restaurant is on the ground floor facing the boat dock and several good restaurants and snack bars are just a few steps away.

LA CROIX DU SUD, *B.P. 769, Uturoa, Raiatea 98735. Tel./Fax 689/ 66.27.55; E-mail: tiaregerma@yahoo.fr. On the mountainside at PK 12, overlooking Faaroa Bay. Round-trip transfers 3.000 CFP; free transfers for stays of 3 nights. EP Rates: room and breakfast 7.300 CFP single, 7.700 CFP double; third bed 1.200 CFP; room and MAP plan (demi-pension) 8.900 CFP single, 13.500 CFP double. Rates include taxes except visitor tax of 50 CFP per person per day. No credit cards.*

This pension has a lovely panoramic view from a large covered terrace and is surrounded by a flower garden, with a swimming pool in the front yard. Hostess Annette Germa is Marquesan and worked in the charter boat business for many years with her late husband, Eric Germa. The three bedrooms are clean and attractively furnished, each with a double bed, mosquito net, fan and private bathroom with hot water. House linens are furnished. Activities can be arranged on request.

PENSION TE MAEVA, *B.P. 701, Uturoa, Raiatea 98735. Tel./Fax 689/ 66.37.28; E-mail: temaeva@mail.pf; www.temaeva.com. On the mountainside at PK 23 in Opoa, 25 kilometers (15.5 miles) from the airport and 23 kilometers (14.3 miles) from the boat dock. Free round-trip transfers for 2-*

night stay. EP Rates: bungalow and breakfast 6.800 CFP single, 7.500 CFP double; add 1.000 CFP for 1-night stay. Third person 2.000 CFP per night. Half-pension (breakfast and dinner) 1.800 CFP; complete pension (breakfast, lunch, dinner) 3.200 CFP per person per day. Camping 2.000 CFP single, 2.500 CFP double. Rates include taxes except visitor tax of 50 CFP per person per day. No credit cards.

You'll have a panoramic view of the *motu* islets of Avera from this mountainside retreat, which is 7 kilometers (4.3 miles) north of Marae Taputapuatea. It's far from the sea, far from the main village and tourist attractions, far from noise, far from everything. The two modern style bungalows have a double bed and single bed, fan, refrigerator, terrace and private bathroom with hot water. House linens are supplied and guests can swim in the pool while admiring the view. There is a small fee for using the washing machine and bicycles are provided at no charge. Claudine Leclerc-Hunter, the owner, likes to recount the legends of her island and she enjoys cooking for her guests, serving them *cordon-bleu* cuisine. Campers have a shower and toilet, but no kitchen facilities.

PENSION MANAVA, *B.P. 559, Uturoa, Raiatea 98735. Tel. 689/66.28.26; Fax 689/66.16.66; E-mail: manava@free.fr; www.manavapension.com. On mountainside in Avera, 6 kilometers (3.7 miles) southeast of town. Round-trip transfers are provided. EP Rates: room with shared kitchen and bathroom 4.700 CFP single/double; bungalow with private bathroom and shared kitchen 6.000 CFP per bungalow; bungalow with totally private bathroom and kitchen 7.100 CFP person. Add 1.000 CFP for one night stay only. Add 1.000 CFP for third person. Breakfast on request 600 CFP. Rates include taxes except visitor tax of 50 CFP per person per day. No credit cards.*

Four clean and attractive bungalows and a large house are located in a pretty setting of trees, grass and flowers, across the road from the lagoon. Two bungalows have individual kitchens and toilets with solar hot water. Two bungalows have individual toilets with hot water and share a kitchen. In the large house are two bedrooms with shared kitchen and a communal bathroom with hot water. Each bungalow has screened windows and a covered terrace. Each room has an electric fan and bed linens are furnished. Your very friendly and enterprising hostess, Mrs. Roselyn Brotherson, can serve breakfast on request. If you want to eat dinner in a local restaurant someone from the pension will drive you to the good dining places, and the restaurant will drive you back after dinner or the Brothersons will come get you.

Manava Excursions is across the road, where Andrew Brotherson will take you on an outrigger canoe ride to Tahaa for the day, for 6.000 CFP per adult and half-fare for a child less than 12 years old. Or you can join a half-day boat tour to visit the Faaroa River and Marae Taputapuatea, for 4.000 CFP per adult and half-price for each child. You can be dropped off on a *motu* and picked up later, for 1.500 CFP per person. There are no excursions on Saturday.

PENSION RAUVINE, *B.P. 1175, Uturoa, Raiatea 98735. Tel./Fax. 689/66.25.50; pensionrauvine@mail.pf. Beside the lagoon at PK 8.5 in Avera. Free round-trip transfers. EP Rates: Bungalow 6.500 CFP single/double; add 1.500 CFP for 1-night stay. Add 1.000 CFP per day for extra bed. Rates include taxes except visitor tax of 50 CFP per person per day. No credit cards.*

There are six short-term rental bungalows here, with two beside the lagoon. Each bungalow has a double bed, mosquito net, kitchen with refrigerator and a private bathroom with cold water. House linens are furnished. You can swim or fish from a long pier or watch the sunset from a *fare pote'e*, a little gazebo type shelter beside the pier. Bicycles are free for guests. Rauvine Safari Tours will provide your 4WD excursions to explore Raiatea's inland valleys or you can join a boat tour to visit the lagoon and *motu* islets.

KAOHI NUI RANCH, *B.P. 568, Uturoa, Raiatea 98735. Tel./Fax 689/66.25.46; Cell 689/74.37.13; E-mail: kaoha.nui@mail.pf; www.tahitidecouvrir.com. On mountainside in Avera, 6 kilometers (3.7 miles) southeast of town. Round-trip transfers are free. EP Rates: bungalow 6.500 CFP single/double; add 1.000 CFP for 1-night stays; add 1.000 CFP for third person; room with shared bathroom 3.600 CFP single/double; add 800 CFP for 1-night stays. Breakfast is 800 CFP. Rates include taxes except visitor tax of 50 CFP per person per day. Mastercard, Visa.*

The grounds resemble a Western movie setting, with a corral, bank (reception area) and saloon, which is the mini-bar. Lodging is in two bungalows with a double bed and one or two single beds, a fan, private bathroom with hot water, and a terrace. A four-bedroom house has 2 single beds in each room, with a fan and shared bathroom facilities with hot water. Be aware that the walls do not go all the way up to the ceiling in these rooms. House linens and anti-mosquito products are furnished. Guests have use of the kitchen and share the dining room.

The Kaohi Nui Ranch includes a stable of horses, and 1 1/2-hour ride costs 3.700 CFP, a 2-hour ride is 4.000 CFP, a half-day ride is 5.300 CFP, and an all-day ride is 8.500 CFP. Lessons are also available. You can also rent bicycles, or join an outrigger excursion to visit the Faaroa River, Marae Taputapuatea, coral reef and a motu islet, for 4.500 CFP. A 7 1/2 hour boat excursion to Tahaa is 7.000 CFP, and a boat transfer to a nearby *motu* is 1.500 CFP. A knowledgeable guide leads walks into the valley behind the ranch. A half-day walk is 3.000 CFP and Patrick Marinthe, the owner, also leads hikes to Mt. Temehani, pointing out the local plants along the way and explaining their medicinal properties and uses.

Economy

PETER'S PLACE, *PK 6.2 Avera, Taputapuatea, Raiatea 98735. Tel. 689/66.20.01. On the mountainside in Avera, 3.8 miles southeast of town. Round-*

trip transfers between boat dock and pension 600 CFP. EP Rates: Room 1.200 CFP per person; Camping 1.000 CFP per person per day. Add 6% value added tax to room and camping rates and transfers plus a visitor tax of 50 CFP per person per day. No credit cards.

On the mountainside, 50 meters (164 feet) from the lagoon at Vairahi. This is a popular choice for travelers with limited budgets who don't mind very basic accommodations. There is one large plywood *fare* with eight rooms containing a double or single bed. A rustic bamboo and thatch open-air kitchen and dining room are shared, as well as the bathroom facilities with cold water showers. House linens are available. The campground is large enough for 6 tents and has lots of shade trees. Bring mosquito repellent.

Peter Brotherson, who built and ran this place for years, has now turned the management over to his son-in-law, Pascal Grand. Ask him about activities, which used to include complimentary outrigger paddle canoes and hiking into the valley. Excursions can also be arranged to visit Marae Taputapuatea or explore the lagoon and motu islets.

Other family lodgings include: **PENSION YOLANDE**, *Tel. 689/66.35.28*, has 4 studios with kitchen in a large bungalow beside the lagoon at PK 10 in Avera, starting at 6.000 CFP single. MAP available; **RAIATEA VILLAGE**, *Tel. 689/66.31.62; Fax 689/66.10.65; E-mail: raiatea.village@mail.pf*. 10 bungalows with kitchenettes beside the lagoon at PK 10 in Avera starting at 7.770 CFP single. No restaurant. **PENSION TIARE NUI**, *Tel. 689/66.34.06; Fax 689/ 66.16.06; E-mail: europcar-loc@mail.pf; www.raiatea.com/tiarenui*. Adjacent to Europcar Agency, who has special packages for bungalow and car or bungalow, car and boat rental. EP rates start at 5.300 CFP single for bungalow only.

Where to Eat
Superior
RESTAURANT TENAPE, *Tel. 60.01.00, is located at Hotel Tenape in Tumaraa. Open daily for breakfast, lunch and dinner. Mastercard, Visa.*

This is an attractive open sided restaurant overlooking the hotel's gardens and swimming pool and the lagoon across the road. The dinner atmosphere is romantic, with soft lighting, pink table linen and fresh flowers. The French chef is from the Bordeaux region and he speaks English. He is noted for his delicious cuisine, which includes his specialty of *ris de veau aux morilles*, (veal sweetbread and morilles mushrooms) for 2.900 CFP. Starter courses are priced from 1.200-2.300 CFP and include foie gras; fish and seafood dishes are 2.000-2.800 CFP, and meat dishes are 2.000-2.900 CFP, which include roast duck breast. Desserts average 990 CFP, including the colonel cup, which is lime sherbet with vodka. The wine list suggests good white choices for 1.800 to 4.300 CFP, Bordeaux reds from 2.200 to 10.500 CFP, or Champagne from 6.600 to 11.000 CFP.

HOTEL HAWAIKI NUI NORDBY RESTAURANT, *Tel. 66.20.23. Open daily for breakfast 6:30-10am, lunch 12-2pm, snacks 2-5:30pm, and dinner 7-9:30pm. Sunday brunch 10:30am-2:30pm. All major credit cards.*

A breakfast buffet is served each morning, or you can order à la carte. Continental breakfast is 1.800 CFP and an American breakfast is 2.200 CFP. Lunchtime fare includes a mixed green salad with goat cheese and honeyed apples for 1.450 CFP, two choices of *poisson cru* for 1.220 CFP, and tuna tartare with salsa verde for 1.450 CFP. Burgers, sandwiches and pizza are 1.400 CFP and pasta is 1.250 CFP. The lunch or dinner menu offers a good selection of hot or cold appetizers for 1.000-1.750, fish and shellfish for 1.980-2.600 CFP, roasted lobster for 2.750 CFP, meat and poultry for 1.880-2.650 CFP. The meat dishes include fried spareribs marinated in mango nectar, roasted lamb with pan-fried potatoes, and grilled beef tenderloin, shrimp and mashed sweet potatoes with gravy. The dessert menu lists a dozen choices, including a cheese platter for 850 CFP, banana au gratin on coconut ice cream with vanilla sabayon for 850 CFP, and profiteroles for 990 CFP. The wine list ranges in cost from 1.700 to 13.850 CFP. Special barbecue evenings are also featured, and the bar serves a variety of exotic cocktails.

Moderate
LE QUAI DES PECHEURS (FISHERMAN'S WHARF), *Tel. 66.43.19, is in the Gare Maritime building facing the quay for small boats. Open daily 10am to 10pm. The kitchen is closed from 2 to 7pm, but the pastry shop and bar remain open. Mastercard, Visa.*

This French and seafood restaurant is located in the big, pink Gare Maritime building beside the ship dock. Raiatea residents say that it is one of the best restaurants on the island. You can eat on the terrace overlooking the dock area or inside the restaurant, where the tables are covered with tablecloths. The menu lists starter courses such as *poisson cru* for 950 CFP, shrimp cocktail with fresh coriander for 1.050 CFP, carpaccio for 1.200 CFP, sashimi for 1.300 CFP, and 9 choices of salads priced from 1.200-1.450 CFP. Fish and seafood choices include parrotfish, mahi mahi or tuna for 1.600 CFP, mussels with cream sauce for 1.850 CFP and shrimp curry for 2.200 CFP. Meat and poultry dishes are 1.600-2.500 CFP, including *magret de canard au miel* for 2.400 CFP. Desserts include chocolate mousse or warm coconut pie for 750 CFP and a banana split for 850 CFP. Cocktails are 950 CFP, and wines are 2.300-12.800 CFP.

A lot of the restaurant's business takes place on the covered terrace, where you can watch the action on rue Tiare Apetahi and the port from your table. This is a great place to let yourself be caressed by the sea breezes while you linger over a big mug of *pression* beer or enjoy a cup of coffee and some of the pastries on display in the glass case beside the kitchen. A Tahitian dance show is performed here each Saturday night at 8:30pm. Reserve for this occasion.

RESTAURANT TEPUA, *Tel. 66.33.00, is located at Pension Tepua beside the lagoon in Tepua Bay. Open at night only for public. Breakfast and lunch are served only to in-house guests. Mastercard, Visa.*

This restaurant has a good reputation with residents of Raiatea, who enjoy coming here for dinner. You can order the *menu du jour* or select some specialties from the *à la carte* menu, which features fish, seafood and other fresh local foods, as well as a tropical barbecue. The chef prepares local dishes as well as Asiatic specialties. Plan to spend between 2.400-3.500 CFP per person.

SEA HORSE, *Tel. 66.16.34; E-mail leogite@mail.pf, is in the Gare Maritime building on the quay, next to Le Quai des Pecheurs. Open Monday through Saturday from 10am to 9:30pm. Closed Sunday. American Express, Mastercard, Visa.*

This is a very popular Chinese restaurant. It is open on three sides, giving you a good view of the quay and activities taking place in the harbor. You can buy Chinese food to go, such as chow mein or chop soy, for 1.100 to 1.500 CFP, or you can dine here. A selection of Chinese soups is priced from 800 to 1.700 CFP; spring rolls are served with a sweet and sour sauce for 900 CFP and fried wonton is 900 CFP. Spicy salted shrimp is 1.950 CFP; fish and seafood dishes are 1.350 to 3.800 CFP; beef with satay sauce is 1.500 CFP, lemon chicken is 1.100 CFP, and tofu with eight spices is 1.650 CFP. The list goes on and on, and even includes the Sea Horse Tapenlou for a minimum of two, which is a Chinese seafood fondue for 3.500 CFP per person. On weekends you can order roast suckling pig with coconut milk for 1.800 CFP. Wines are priced from 2.200 to 9.900 CFP a bottle.

JADE GARDEN, *Tel. 66.34.40, is on the mountainside of Uturoa's main street in the downtown shopping area. Open Wednesday through Saturday from 11am to 1pm and 6:30 to 9pm. Closed Sunday, Monday and Tuesday. American Express, Mastercard and Visa.*

I've always enjoyed my meals here, which feature well-prepared Cantonese dishes for 1.500 to 2.300 CFP for the main course. There are 59 choices on the menu, plus the specials, which include stuffed shrimp, seafood cassolette and eggplant with salted fish. The air-conditioned dining room is upstairs and has an elaborate ceiling decorated with gold dragons. The tables are covered with red or pink cloths and a vase of plastic flowers. You pay the owner, Soufa Chung, at the bottom of the stairway when you've finished eating. This building will be torn down eventually, when the street behind the town is finished, and the owner told me that he wouldn't rebuild. If the Jade Garden still exists when you visit Raiatea, be sure to try it out.

MOEMOEA, *Tel. 66.39.84, is between the Uturoa quay and the main street in the center of town. Open Monday through Saturday from 6am to 5pm. Closed Sunday. No credit cards.*

This is my favorite snack-restaurant anywhere in French Polynesia. It's an indoor-outdoor café and very local style, with no pretensions of any sort, and it's usually packed with a noisy, happy crowd. This is where the Tahitian crews from the cruise ships and ferries come to eat, and it's a good place to just hang out, drinking Hinano beer and watching the people who come to town to shop, do their banking and take care of business, but also to visit, gossip and giggle. Many of them end up at the Moemoea, including hotel owners and the mayor of Raiatea. You can watch the boats across the street loading for their trip back to Tahaa.

The reason this place is so popular is not only its location and the friendly waitresses, but the food is just downright delicious! Although it's not the cheapest place to eat in Uturoa, it is still easy on the budget. They serve the very best *poisson cru* you could ever eat and it's a big portion complete with coconut milk. The menu offers five choices of *poisson cru*, from 900 to 1.300 CFP, including the Moemoea special *poisson cru* that you mix yourself. You've gotta love garlic and ginger to order this one. And don't breathe on anyone for the next couple of days! A big cup of plain or vanilla flavored coffee with coconut milk is 300 CFP, eggs and bacon are 700 CFP, fresh fried lagoon fish is also served for breakfast, cooked with onions and soy sauce in the local manner, for 800 CFP. Vana (sea urchin) is 1.500 CFP, when it's in season. Roast pork is 1.200 CFP and a horse steak is 1.000 CFP. Chinese dishes, such as chow mein, chop soy or Kai fan are 1.300 to 1.600 CFP, fried or grilled Mahi Mahi is 1.700 CFP, grilled lobster is 2.850 CFP and burgers are 550 to 600 CFP. Fries are 300 CFP, and ice cream is 300 to 600 CFP. You can also order wine and beer. You also have a selection of fresh juices for 600 CFP, which include pineapple, pamplemousse (grapefruit), lime, orange, papaya, tomato, carrots, corossol, carambola and watermelon, or a mixture of your choices.

RESTAURANT ATIAPITI, *Tel. 66.16.65, is located at Hotel Atiapiti, PK 31, beside the lagoon in Opoa, near Marae Taputapuatea. Open daily for breakfast, lunch and dinner. Guests not staying in their hotel-pension are welcome at lunch only. Mastercard, Visa.*

This is a great place to eat lunch when you are driving around the island, visiting Marae Taputapuatea, or simply looking for some good food. Marie-Claude Rajaud likes to serve fresh fish, crab and lobster from the lagoon, which she says is still not polluted. The river shrimp she prepares can be served with saffron or curry. She also cooks chicken with Coca-Cola, grilled New Zealand beef, and she makes a sumptuous coconut cake. Fresh fruits from the garden are also served. There is a well-stocked bar and a good wine list.

LA VOILE D'OR, *Tel. 66.12.97. This thatched roof open-air restaurant is beside the lagoon at the Apooiti Marina, facing Tahaa and Bora Bora. Open for lunch and dinner Monday night through Sunday noon. Closed Sunday night and Monday at lunch. Mastercard, Visa.*

This was formerly the Tama'a Maitai, and El Carthage restaurants, and became La Voile D'Or (the golden sail) in mid-2001. Poisson cru or sashimi costs 1.300 CFP, a dozen escargots are 1.600 CFP, tuna tartare is 2.200 CFP, lamb curry is 1.850 CFP, filet of beef is 1.950 CFP, and you can choose your sauce, which is extra. A Tahitian buffet is served on the last Saturday night of each month, and the price varies between 2.500-3.500 CFP, which also includes the live music.

BRASSERIE MARAAMU, *Tel. 66.46.64, is in the Gare Maritime building. Open for breakfast, lunch and dinner Monday through Saturday noon. Closed Saturday afternoon and all day Sunday. American Express, Mastercard, Visa.*

This Chinese restaurant is popular with local residents, who sometimes reserve the entire restaurant for private parties. You can have a breakfast of coffee, bread and butter for 300 CFP, *poisson cru* for 650 to 1.000 CFP, eggs or an omelet for 350 to 750 CFP, or fried fish for 800 CFP. The lunch and dinner choices are *ma'a tinito* (Chinese stew with pork, red beans, vegetables and macaroni) for 950 CFP, Chinese dishes of beef, chicken or shrimp for 950 CFP to 1.350 CFP, steak and fries for 1.250 CFP, grilled fish for 1.650 CFP or fried shrimp for 1.750 CFP.

LE NAPOLI, *Tel. 66.10.77, is on the lagoon side of the road between Uturoa village and the airport. Open Tuesday through Friday for lunch and dinner, and on Saturday and Sunday evenings. Closed Saturday noon, Sunday noon and all day Monday. Mastercard, Visa.*

This little restaurant is right beside the road near the airport, with shoji screens and bamboo walls. They serve Italian cuisine and pizzas cooked in a wood oven.

Economy

CHEZ MICHELE, *Tel. 66.14.66, occupies the ground floor of the Hotel Bajoga-Hinano, facing the boat dock. Open for breakfast, lunch and dinner. Closed Saturday night and Sunday. No credit cards.*

You can get Polynesian food at all times in this small in-door, out-door restaurant that has been in business for many years. In addition to *poisson cru*, you will be served *fafa* (Tahitian spinach), *uru* (breadfruit), taro, bananas and other Tahitian specials on request. The quality of the food is usually good, and includes Chinese and European dishes such as steak, chicken and fish, prepared in the local style. There are three choices of daily specials, which cost 1.500 CFP each.

SNACK BAR TEMEHANI, *Tel. 66.14.40, is located at the airport*, and is open according to the Air Tahiti flights, but closed at noon. You can get drinks and ham and cheese sandwiches.

There are small snack stands all around the island where you can buy casse-croute sandwiches on baguette bread, *poisson cru*, *maa tinito* and other local dishes while driving around Raiatea. Look for **Patisserie Arnaud** north of the Raiatea Marina, where you can buy muffins, pies and freshly baked bread. **Restaurant Bellevue** is on the seaside at PK 23 in Vaiaau on the west coast, and **Snack Punaeroa** is at PK 32.5, south of Vaiaau on the southwestern coast. Several rolling food trucks called **Roulottes** park on the Uturoa waterfront at night, serving steak and fries, chicken legs and *salade russe* (red potato salad), *poisson cru*, brochettes of beef hearts, and other grilled fish, along with soft drinks and juices in cartons. The prices are usually about 1.200 CFP per food order. You can also get casse-croûtes and other prepared foods in the well-stocked supermarkets in Uturoa.

Le Club House at the Apooiti Yacht Harbor closed in mid-2004 and the 200-seat restaurant is for sale.

Seeing the Sights

Almost Paradise Tours, *Tel. 66.23.64*, is owned by American Bill Kolans, who will take you in his 8-passenger minibus on a 3-hour tour to visit Marae Taputapuatea and five other *marae* temples. Bill's tours are highly praised by English-speaking visitors, who learn about the migration, anthropology and navigation of the ancient Polynesians. He gives detailed explanations of the rocks, gods, religious ceremonies and human sacrifices performed at this international *marae*. Cost is 4.500 CFP per person.

Hinerani Tours, *Tel. 66.25.75*, is owned by Lysis and Heiariki Terooatea, who have an 8-passenger Land Rover. They will take you into the interior of the island in the Faaroa valley, stopping at a botanical garden, splashing through rivers, and visiting Marae Taputapuatea. This 4-hour tour costs 4.500 CFP for a minimum of 4 people. A new combination excursion takes you by 4WD to visit the botanical garden and the volcanic crater of Faaroa Valley then to Marae Taputapuatea and on to Avera, where you will transfer to a boat and cruise up the Faaroa River, then go to Motu Iriru for a swim and picnic. This all-day excursion is 7.500 CFP for a minimum of 5 passengers and 7.000 CFP per person if there are 8 people.

Jeep Safari Raiatea, *Tel. 66.15.73/78.23.73*, is operated by Mirella and Petero Mou Kam Tse, who have five 4WD vehicles and a motorized outrigger canoe that they use for combined land and lagoon tours. They have daily departures in the morning and afternoon for 4-hour tours through the mountain valleys, with stops at vanilla plantations, Marae Taputapuatea and at a black pearl farm. You will learn about the botanical treasures of the hidden valleys and tropical plantations and all about the cultivation of the black pearl oyster. Boat tours will take you to the *motu* for a picnic.

Raiatea Discovery, *Tel. 66.24.16/78.33.26; E-mail: raidiscovery@mail.pf* is operated daily at 8:30am and 1pm by Maria Cowan and Gérard Duvos. Their 4x4 safari tours by open air Land Rover are 4.400 CFP per person for a minimum of 4 passengers. These cultural and botanical tours take you to Faaroa Bay, to the island crater, Marae Taputapuatea and to visit vanilla plantations.

Raiatea Tourism, *Tel. 66.20.86/78.33.13; E-mail: raiateatourisme@mail.pf; www.raiateatourisme.com*. This company is operated by Christophe Bardou, who can give you an option of guided excursions that last from 1 to 4 hours around the island of Raiatea. A 1-hour tour in an air-conditioned 4WD is 12.000 CFP per vehicle and a 2-hour tour is 16.000 CFP per vehicle, for a maximum of 6 passengers. He also has a 45-place air-conditioned Hyundai bus that can be used to transfer groups between the airport and hotel or pensions downtown or for 3 1/2 hour tours around the island. Catamaran tours are also available.

Special Places to Visit

Marae Taputapuatea, at PK 32 in Opoa, faces Te-Ava-Moa pass on the east coast of the island. This is Raiatea's most famous landmark and the most significant archaeological site in the whole South Pacific area. This international *marae* has been in existence since 1600 AD and was the most important *marae* in eastern Polynesia during the pre-Christian era. Raiatea was then known as Havai'i, the Sacred Island. This marae was not always international and did not always carry the name of Taputapuatea. At a very remote time before the birth of the god Oro it was only the national marae of Havai'i (Raiatea) and its full name was Tini-rau-hui-mata-te-papa-o-Feoro (Fruitful myriads who engraved the rocks of Feoro), and its abbreviated name was Feoro. It contained eight memorial stones representing the eight kings who had reigned over the land. These stones later became eight symbols of the royal insignia of the kings and queens in long succession afterwards. They were named: Te'iva, Feufeu, Nuna'a-e-hau, Te-ata-o-tu, Manava-taia, Paie-o-te-fau-rua and Te-ra'i-pua-tata. On the seashore is **Marae Hauviri** with an investiture stone that served as a royal throne and as a measuring stone for warriors who served as representatives to the outside world. See introduction to *Raiatea chapter* for more information.

Marae Tainuu is located beside the sea at PK 15 in the little fishing village of Tevaitoa on the northwest coast of Raiatea. This marae has one of the most imposing *ahu* altars in the Leeward Islands. Petroglyphs engraved in the basaltic stones include a Polynesian sundial and 10 turtles, depicting a sort of Polynesian treasure hunt that the Maohi warriors had to perform to achieve valor and esteem. The chief's platform, called Taumatini, is at the edge of the road. Upstream from these ruins, on the hill there are several structures. First of all is the Mara'e Tetuira, which belonged to the chief and was considered to be very sacred. Above that a succession of small terraces takes you to the platform of the war chiefs, the *paepae* Taputuari'i.

Chez Lovine Botanical Garden, *Tel. 66.14.45*, is at PK 14,5 in Faaroa Bay. For an admission fee of 200 CFP you can visit a lush garden filled with a wide variety of local plants and flowers, and also learn all about how the vanilla vines are grown.

Mama Kapu's Garden is on the mountainside at PK 31 in Vaihuti in the district of Vaiaau on the west coast of Raiatea. Her garden has 25 species of hibiscus, 18 kinds of bougainvilleas, 17 different *aute* plants, bird of paradise, opuhi ginger flowers, torch ginger and roses in all colors. She also has 30 species of fruit trees, several acres of flowers that she sells to the hotels in Bora Bora, plus a garden of 121 medicinal herbs. A small stream on her property provides irrigation and provides a home for some 40 fresh water eels.

La Vanillère is located at PK 33.5 Opoa in Hotopuu Bay, *Tel. 66.15.61; cell 79.16.56; E-mail: contacts@lavanillere.com or coconut@mail.pf; www. lavanillere.com.* While driving around the island be sure to stop at this vanilla farm with 18,000 vanilla plants and learn how the vanilla orchids are "married" by hand to cross-pollinate the flower that produces the vanilla bean. You can also buy dried vanilla beans, powder, extract and vanilla soap in their farm shop. Guided tour at 2pm Monday-Saturday. Closed Sunday. Admission 300 CFP per person. Hidden in the bushes nearby is a pretty waterfall where you can splash around in the basin, which is called "The Queen's Bathtub."

Magasin Vanira, *Tel. 66.30.06*, on the mountainside in Uturoa center, sells dried vanilla beans, powdered vanilla and vanilla extract. This is the oldest building on the street and may even be destroyed by the time you arrive. If so, ask around to find out where Madame Jeanne Chane has relocated her vanilla business. She is the third generation of the Chane family to buy and sell vanilla, and she has earned two silver cups, six diplomas and other honors for her knowledge. A package of plump, fragrant vanilla beans costs 1.000 CFP.

Black Pearl Farms you can visit include: **Tahi Perles** at PK 4, *Tel/Fax 66.30.97; E-mail: tahiperles@hotmail.com;* and **Vairua Perles** at PK 8,7 in Avera, *Tel. 66.12.12/78.25.62; www.multimania.com/blackpearls.* **Anapa Pearl Farm**, *Tel. 66.34.52, Cell 70.76.07*, who bills themselves as "the best little pearl farm in the South Pacific", is located in Tevaitoa, in front of the Protestant church and Marae Tainuu. They invite the public to call for a free visit. Don't forget your snorkeling gear and they accept all major credit cards. **Rautoanui Perles,** *Tel. 66.29.07*, is also in Tevaitoa.

Nightlife & Entertainment

CLUB ZENITH DISCOTHÈQUE, *Tel. 66.27.49*, is upstairs in the Léogite Building in Uturoa center. The disco opens at 10pm each Friday and Saturday. Entry is free before 11pm and after that the cover charge is 1.500 CFP, including a drink.

LE QUAI DES PECHEURS (Fisherman's Wharf), *Tel. 66.43.19*, in the Gare Maritime building facing the quay for small boats, presents a Tahitian dance show each Saturday night at 8:30pm. Reserve.

Sports & Recreation

Horseback Riding

Kaohi Nui Equestrian Tourism Center is on the mountainside at PK 6 in Avera, *Tel. 66.25.46 / 74.37.13*. Patrick Marinthe leads 1 1/2-hour rides for 3.700 CFP, 2-hour rides for 4.000 CFP, half-day rides for 5.300 CFP, and full-day rides for 8.500 CFP, using saddled Marquesan horses of Chilean stock. A picnic can be arranged for a ride into the valley, stopping to swim at the waterfalls. Lodging is also available.

Hiking

Patrick Marinthe of the Kaohi Nui Equestrian Center, *Tel. 66.25.46 / 74.37.13*, also leads walkers into the valley behind his ranch, explaining the use of the plants and trees that grow in this wild environment. You can stop for a refreshing swim at the waterfalls. A 3-hour hike for a minimum of two people costs 3.000 CFP each, including transfers to the ranch.

Motor Boat Rental

Europcar, *Tel. 66.34.06*, rents boats with a 6-horse power engine that requires no permit or a 15-horse power engine that does require a license. The cost of either boat is 7.000 CFP for 4 hours, 9.300 CFP for 8 hours and 17.400 CFP for 2 days.

Deep Sea Fishing

Game fishing is especially rewarding in the Leeward Society Islands, where prize catches of marlin, yellow fin tuna, mahi mahi and wahoo are frequent events. The Raiatea Haura Club holds local competitions several times a year, and the private charters report good fishing year-round.

Sakario Charter, *Tel. 60.20.15; cell 78.58.18; Fax 66.24.77; E-mail: ariicreation@mail.pf; www.arii-creation.com*. This 28-foot Bertram Flybridge cruiser is owned by Joseph Chaussoy, a multi-talented artist and owner of Arii Creation, which manufactures Polynesian printed fabrics and *pareos* in Raiatea. His fishing boat is available for half-day charters that last for five hours. Full-day charters also include a picnic lunch.

Te Manu Ata Charter, *Tel. 66/21.09/66.32.14; E-mail: temanuatapf@yahoo.fr* is a 28-foot Bertram owned by Jean-Luc Liaut, who also provides half-day fishing expeditions and full-day outings. A 4-hour fishing trip costs 60.000 CFP and an 8-hour outing is 100.000 CFP. Bring your own sandwiches.

Moanavaihi II Charter, *Tel./Fax 66.30.97; cell 72.10.57 / 72.03.38; e-mail: jpconstant@mail.pf*. This fishing boat is owned by Jean Pierre Constant, who is one of the top captains in the Leeward Islands.

Lagoon and Motu Excursions

Faaroa River is a cool, green haven bordered by wild hibiscus *purau* trees and modern homes. One of the most popular excursions is to explore this historic river by outrigger speed canoe. Around the year 1350 hundreds of brave Maohi families left Raiatea from this river, navigating their voyaging sailing canoes by the wind, stars and ocean currents to settle in Hawaii, the Cook Islands, the Samoas and finally in New Zealand. Their Polynesian descendants are called Maori in New Zealand and Tahitians in French Polynesia.

A Day Tour to Tahaa Island takes you on a 30-minute boat ride across the protected lagoon that is shared by Raiatea and Tahaa. On the main island you will visit a picturesque little village and a vanilla farm. Then you will explore the lagoon by boat, visiting a black pearl farm and stopping on a *motu* islet to swim and snorkel in the clear lagoon waters. Most full-day excursions to Tahaa also include a picnic on the *motu*.

Trips to the Motu provide an ideal destination by canoe or speedboat, where you will find white sand beaches, privacy, and time for daydreaming and swimming in the lagoon. Taxi boats are available to drop you off and pick you up later, or you can arrange transfers with your hotel or pension. Should you wish to make a day of it, your hotel will pack a picnic lunch for you or you can buy food already prepared in the supermarkets in Uturoa or order a take-out dish from any of the restaurants and snack stands. Several of the motu islets around Raiatea and Tahaa are off limits to the public, as they are privately owned. Others are partially private while the rest of the motu is open to visitors seeking sun, sand and sea. On these sometimes fiercely protected properties you will see Tabu signs warning you to keep out. Some of the people who operate the boat excursions have access to private motu islets where they take their passengers.

Motu Iriru, located at the entrance to the Iriru pass on the east coast of Raiatea, is open to the public. The government has built a *fare pote'e* shelter here, along with a small changing room, shower, water faucets, toilets with handicap access, picnic tables and barbecue grills. You have to take your garbage away with you. To camp on Motu Iriru you need a permit from the commune of Taputapuatea. There are no mosquitoes, no nonos and no grouchy owners here.

Motu Oatara, on the southeast side of Raiatea in front of Hotel Atiapiti, is also known as Bird Island. There is good snorkeling here.

Motu Nao Nao, on the south end of Raiatea, is still being used by some of the boat service providers who take visitors to enjoy the pretty white sand beach. A 3,000-foot landing strip was built on this 65-acre flat islet by the US Navy Seabees during World War II. This motu is now being developed as a private Tahitian island, where **Vaimahanahana Villas**, *Tel. 60.24.11, Fax 60.24.10*, is building vacation rental houses.

Motu Ceran (Motu Mahaea on a map of Taha'a) has three owners and they have put up fences between their properties. You can visit one part for 300 CFP per day and use the beach. **Motu Atger** (also known as Motu Toahotu) is also privately owned and having conflicts between the owners. Boat excursions take their passengers to visit a lagoonarium or marine park beside this motu and there are toilets on the islet.

Here is just a partial list of the people who provide boat tours in Raiatea and Tahaa. You may also want to look at the lagoon excursions listed in the Taha'a chapter, as many of those excursions begin in Raiatea.

André Topspots, *Tel. 60.05.20, cell 79.22.03; E-mail: andretopspots@mail.pf*. André Huitoofa Taurua offers tours by covered boat for 12 or more people to visit Raiatea and Tahaa. He provides half-day or full-day tours that will take you to the Faaroa river, the Botanical Garden, to Marae Taputapuatea, around the island of Raiatea, to visit a black pearl farm, or to Motu Iriru for a picnic and swim. He also has tours to Tahaa, with or without a picnic on the *motu*. A half-day excursion is 4.000 CFP and a full-day tour is 8.000 CFP for a minimum of 4 people.

Faaroa Tours, *Tel. 66.32.70*, is owned by Noma Wong, who managed the Hotel Bali Hai in Raiatea for several years. (This hotel was also the Raiatea Pearl Resort and is now Hawaiki Nui). Noma has three 36-foot long outrigger speed canoes that are used to take visitors to the Faaroa valley and Apoomau river, with a visit to the Marae Taputapuatea, and a swimming stop on a *motu* islet with a white sand beach. This 4-hour excursion starts at 9am or 12:30pm, costs 4.500 CFP per person, and a picnic can be added on request. She also offers half-day boat tours to Taha'a, or a full-day tour with a barbecue picnic on a *motu*.

Hinerani Tours, *Tel. 66.25.75; E-mail: lysis@mail.pf* has a 27-foot long covered boat for 6 to 12 passengers that leaves from the pier in Uturoa for a full-day excursion of Raiatea. You will visit the Faaroa River, Lovine botanical garden, Marae Taputapuatea and then go to Motu Iriru for a swim and picnic. Changing rooms, restrooms and drinking water are available on the *motu*. This excursion is 6.000 CFP per person. A half-day excursion for 4.500 CFP will take you to the Faaroa River and botanical garden, then direct to the *motu*. Owners Lysis and Heariki Terooatea have 4WD tours.

Jeep Safari Raiatea, *Tel. 66.15.73*, is operated by Mirella and Petero Mou Kam Tse, whose outrigger speed canoe holds 6 to 16 passengers. The boat leaves Raiatea daily at 8am and returns at 5pm, with an excursion inside the lagoon and a picnic on a *motu*.

Manava Excursions, *Tel. 66.28.26, E-mail: manava@free.fr; www.manavapension.com*. This company is owned by Andrew Brotherson of Pension Manava. He provides excursions by a 27-foot longboat with a sun awning, offering half-day trips to the Faaroa Bay, Apoomau river and Marae Taputapuatea for 4.000 CFP. An all-day day trip to Tahaa to visit a black pearl farm, fish park, vanilla plantation and stop for a swim and picnic of grilled fish and fresh fruits at a motu costs 5.500 CFP. He will also take you to a nearby *motu* and return at your convenience, for 1.500 CFP per person. No excursions on Saturdays.

Ofetaro Tours, *Tel. 66.34.46/20.17.73; E-mail: polytrans@mail.pf*. Joseph Sham Koua has two 28-foot boats for 6 to 20 passengers. His tours take you to Motu Ofetaro for a barbecue picnic, where you can paddle a kayak or outrigger canoe, swim and snorkel. The tour also stops at a fish enclosure. Feasts prepared in the Tahitian underground oven can be organized on request, as well as a Tahitian dance show on the *motu*.

Raiatea Discovery, *Tel. 66.24.16/78.33.25; E-mail: raidiscovery@mail.pf* is owned by Maria and Gérard Duvos. They have a 31-foot speedboat for 6 to 12 passengers that is used for tours around the island of Raiatea, a distance of 32 nautical miles. Swimming and snorkeling stops are made on the beach and on a *motu*. This excursion is 6.050 CFP per person, and all-day outings are available on request. They also provide land excursions.

L'Excursion Bleue (formerly Tahaa Pearl Tour), *Tel. 66.10.90/78.33.28; E-mail: tpt@mail.pf; www.tahaa.net*, is owned by Bruno Fabre, who has outrigger speed canoes with awnings that he uses to transport 4 to 12 passengers for half- or full-day excursions. On the all-day tour, from 9am to 5pm, you will visit a vanilla plantation in Faaaha, a pearl farm in Haamene Bay, a Lagoonarium enclosure for sea turtles, sharks and rays on Motu Toahotu, and eat a lunch of fresh foods cooked and served on Motu Mahaea. Then you will have time to swim in the clear water around the motu and again in the coral gardens on Tahaa's west coast. You return to Raiatea on the southwest side of the island, where you may see dolphins playing in the wake of the boat and an incredible sunset off to the west. Bring plastic shoes, a towel and snorkeling gear. This excursion is 11.000 CFP for adults, 5.500 CFP for children under 4-12 years, and 2.000 CFP for 1-3 years. There are hostesses on board as well as an underwater photographer. Bruno works with the *Tahitian Princess* during her visits to Raiatea.

Tumatahi, *Tel. 66.25.17/79.62.41; E-mail: tumatahi@ifrance.com*. Jean-Luc and Tetuanui provide half-day and full-day lagoon excursions that leave at 9am from the Shell station on the quay. On a full-day excursion you will visit a black pearl farm, the Faaroa River, botanical garden, Taputapuatea Marae and swim and picnic on Motu Iriau for 7.000 CFP. A half-day tour is 5.000 CFP per person. You can also join a tour to Tahaa or use Tumatahi's taxi boat service. They will drop you off on a *motu* and come back for you later.

West Coast Charters, *Tel. 66.45.39/79.28.78*. Tony and Marie Tucker are a very friendly couple who speak good English. He's from South Africa and she is French. They offer a program of scenic lagoon excursions around Raiatea and Tahaa aboard their two boats with sun awnings. A full-day circle island tour of Raiatea includes a visit to Marae Taputapuatea and a snorkeling stop at a *motu* for 8.500 CFP. A half-day Raiatea River Tour for 4.000 CFP takes you along Faaroa River and to Motu Iriru for a swim or to snorkel at Motu Oatara. Or you can visit Marae Taputapuatea. A full-day boat trip to Tahaa is 7.500 CFP and takes you to visit a pearl farm and vanilla plantation, to feed the turtles, rays, tropical fish and sharks at a marine park, and snorkeling on a spectacular coral drop and in coral gardens. You'll also visit a private motu.

Sailing Charter Yachts
   Archipels Croisières (Archipels Polynesian Cruises), *Tel. 689/56.36.39; Fax 689/56.35.87; E-mail: archimoo@mail.pf; www.archipels.com.* This yacht charter company has a nautical base at Opunohu Bay in Moorea and three 57-foot sailing catamarans based permanently in Raiatea. Their 7 day/6 night sailing program starts in Bora Bora and calls at Tahaa, Raiatea and Huahine, or they can begin in Huahine and end in Bora Bora, also visiting Raiatea and Tahaa. These cruises are guaranteed to operate with a minimum of two people, and the per passenger cost is 213.500 CFP during the low seasons and 234.000 CFP during high seasons. Please see chapters on Bora Bora and Huahine for sailing schedules and chapter on Moorea for details of company and yachts.

   The Moorings, *B.P. 165, Uturoa, Raiatea 98735. Tel. 689/66.35.93, Cell 78.35.93; Fax 689/66.20.94; E-mail: moorings@mail.pf; www.moorings.com; North American reservations: Tel. 800/669-6529; outside US and Canada 727/535-1446. The nautical base is located at Apooiti Marina, 2 kilometers (1.2 miles) from the Raiatea airport and 4 kilometers (2.5 miles) from the boat dock in Uturoa.*

   The Moorings has been operating in Raiatea since 1985 and has an average fleet of 25 yachts. These consist of monohull sailboats from 36 to 52 feet and catamarans 42 to 47 feet long. You have a choice of 3, 4 or 5 cabins in a frequently renewed fleet. Yachts can be chartered bareboat, ready to sail away or with skipper and hostess/cook. Provisioning is available on request.

   No matter what your level of sailing skill, The Moorings has a yacht and vacation plan that is right for you. If you visit their Website you can select your level of luxury and plan your vacation, then get an estimate of what your cruise will cost. The Moorings is the charter company most frequently chosen by Americans who want a cruising vacation in the Leeward Society Islands.

   Star Voyage Pacifique, *Contact Jérôme Touzé at The Moorings, B.P. 165, Uturoa, Raiatea 98735. Tel. 689/66.35.93, cell 78.35.93; Fax 689/ 66.20.94; E-mail: moorings@mail.pf.*

   This French-owned company has turned their yachts over to The Moorings to charter. The fleet includes two monohulls (36 feet and 42 feet) and two Privilege catamarans (37 feet and 42 feet). The yachts can be chartered with or without crew and you board in Raiatea or Tahaa for a minimum of 3-day cruises in the Leeward Islands.

Sunsail, *B.P. 331 Uturoa, Raiatea, 98735 Tel. 689/60.04.85; Fax 689/66.23.19; E-mail: stardustyc@mail.pf; www.sunsail.com.*

This nautical base was formerly operated by Stardust Yacht Charters and is located at PK 12.5 in Faaroa Bay, 8 miles from Uturoa, with a fleet of 20 sailing yachts. The monohulls include Sun Odyssey 37, 43DS, Oceanis 411, 423 and 473, and Beneteau 50. The catamarans are Athens 38, Belize 43 and Bahia 46. A one-week bareboat charter for a for a Sun Odyssey 37 is 270.286 CFP to 386.634 CFP according to seasons, and for a Bahia 46 catamaran the cost is 572.792 CFP to 818.019 CFP.

The sailing range includes the neighboring Leeward Islands of Raiatea, Tahaa, Bora Bora and Huahine, and with special permission, Maupiti. Two-week charters are also available and one-way cruising is possible. The yachts can be chartered ready to sail away, complete with fuel, water, dinghy and outboard engine, bed linens and towels, barbecue grill and charcoal, snorkeling equipment and with complete provisions on request. Optional services include skippers and hostess-cooks, spinnaker and windsurf boards.

Tahiti Yacht Charter, *Tahiti office: Monette Aline, B.P. 608, Papeete, Tahiti 98713; Tel. 689/45.04.00; Fax 689/42.76.00; E-mail: tyc@mail.pf; www.tahitiyachtcharter.com. North America reservations: Mark Wakeman, Tel. 800/404-1010; E-mail: marimktg@ix.netcom.com. Raiatea base: Tel. 689/66.28.86; Fax 689/66.28.85.*

Tahiti Yacht Charter is now a 100% locally owned company since it was bought back from VPM in October 2002. They have a fleet of 14 boats, mainly catamarans, including 3 new boats from April 2004, all based at the Apooiti Marina in Raiatea, with Papeete as a possible departure point. The monohulls include Feeling 356 DI and 486, Oceanis 411 and 473 and Atoll 43, plus a luxuriously appointed OFD 54. The catamarans are from 35 to 46 feet: Tobago 35, Nautitech 395, Venezia 42, Belize 43 and Bahia 46.

Their sailing range is mainly the Leeward Islands, including Maupiti when weather conditions allow it. You can also sail to the Tuamotu and Marquesas Islands with a Tahiti Yacht Charter skipper on board. Charter rates vary according to seasons; with a Tobago 35 catamaran with 3 cabins starting at 289.379 CFP for an 8-day/7 night cruise during the low seasons (January 10-March 27 and August 28-January 1). This same boat is chartered for 375.894 CFP during the mid-season (March 27-June 26) and for 417.661 CFP during the high season (June 26 to August 28). A new Bahia 46 catamaran with 6 cabins charters for 656.324 CFP, 799.522 CFP or 942.720 CFP, from low to high season. Weekly rates for a Feeling 356 monohull with 3 cabins are 250.596 CFP, 310.262 CFP and 346.062 CFP from low to high seasons, and a new Oceanis 473 with 4 cabins charters for 375.894 CFP, 461.813 CFP and 511.933 CFP according to the time of year. A crewed monohull Prototype Australe OFD 54 with 3 cabins can accommodate six passengers for a week's cruise, starting at 1.026.252 CFP for the boat, crew and all meals.

Atara Royal, *Tel. 66.17.74/78.23.74; Fax 66.17.67; E-mail: myc@mail.pf; www.tahiti-motoryacht.com.* This is a 46-foot Grand Banks Europa motor yacht that can be chartered for short or long cruises in the Leeward Islands or to other archipelagoes of French Polynesia. It was built in 1999 and has two Caterpillar 375 horsepower engines. Accommodations include double cabins plus crew quarters, air-conditioning, water maker, washing machine, micro-wave oven, television, video and DVD players, satellite telephone/fax, two stereos, dinghy with 30 horse-power engine, plus equipment for fishing and water skiing.

A one-week Leeward Island cruise of 7 days/6 nights, including all meals, is 900.000 CFP for 2 passengers and 960.000 CFP for 4 passengers. An "a la carte cruise" through the Leeward Islands is 150.000 CFP per day for 2 passengers and 160.000 CFP per day for 4 passengers, all meals included. A minimum of 2 nights is required. A Honeymoon cruise for 2 passengers is 390.000 CFP for 4 days/3 nights and 780.054 CFP for 7 days/6 nights, all meals included. Days tours are also available.

Catamaran Tane, *Tel./Fax 66.16.87; cell 73.96.90; E-mail: charter.tane@mail.pf; www.raiatea.com/tane.* Martine, Jean-Pierre and Christian are your hosts aboard this 46-foot catamaran that is specially designed for sailing in the tropics. *Tane* has a large, friendly outdoor mess-room that can seat 16 people for meals. Below deck there are two double cabins aft and a double cabin forward, two toilets, 2 showers and lavabos, plus there is an outdoor shower. A Mini Cruise of 5 days/4 nights takes you from Raiatea to Bora Bora (or vice versa), and costs 599.500 CFP for the boat (maximum of 6 passengers) or 275.000 CFP per double cabin. A Discovery Cruise of 7 days/ 6 nights departs from Uturoa and sails to Tahaa and Bora Bora, for a cost of 825.000 CFP for the boat or 395.000 CFP per double cabin. An Open Sea Cruise of 14 days/13 nights will let you discover the islands of Moorea, Huahine, Raiatea, Tahaa, Bora Bora and Tupai. Departure is from Papeete, Tahiti and the cost is 1.500,000 CFP for the boat or 676.500 CFP per double cabin. Rates for these three programs include the crew and food. Private cruises, day cruises and sunset cruises are also available.

Scuba Diving

A short boat ride takes you to the **natural aquarium** at Teavapiti, and 50 different exciting dive spots are found in the four most beautiful passes of the Raiatea-Tahaa lagoon. These include exploring a sunken three-masted yacht, the hull of a Catalina seaplane, feeding gray sharks, barracuda, moray eels and the Napoleon fish that inhabit an underwater wall. The Octopus Grotto is a cave 120 meters (394 feet) long at a depth of 50 meters (55 feet); a dive for experienced divers only. There are rainbow-hued Jack trevally fish, caves of orange corals, black coral forests and dancing coral gardens of blues, violets and yellow.

Hémisphere Sub Plongée, Tel. 66.12.49; cell 79.26.27; Fax 66.28.63; VHF channel 68; E-mail: hemis-subdiving@mail.pf; www.diveraiatea.com is based at the Marina Apooiti. A team of qualified instructors led by dive master Hubert Clot offers French CMAS-certification courses and PADI lessons. Daily diving excursions leave the marina at 8:30am and 4:30pm to discover the lagoon, passes and open ocean depths around Raiatea and Tahaa. Introductory dives are made at 10:30am, and night dives are available on request. A day tour with a picnic lunch on a motu and diving cruises can also be arranged. They also have dive centers at Hawaiki Nui Hotel and Sunset Beach Motel. Rates are 5.900 CFP per dive, 7.000 CFP for a night dive and 50.000 CFP for a 10-dive package.

Te Mara Nui Plongée, Tel./Fax 66.11.88; cell 72.60.19, E-mail: temaranui@mail.pf; www.temaranui.pf. This dive center is located at the Marina in Uturoa and is open daily. Floriane Voisin, the manager, is an international CMAS ** instructor and BEES 1 State instructor. An introductory dive or exploration dive is 5.500 CFP, a night dive is 6.500 CFP and a 10-dive package is 50.000 CFP. Boat transfers to the motu for snorkeling is 1.500 CFP per person round-trip.

Shopping

Coco-Vanille, Tel. 66.17.63, is next to the drugstore on Uturoa's main street. Isabelle is the friendly English-speaking sales person who also makes the darling hand-painted dresses and T-shirts, plus the original patchwork designs of the Tahitian bed covers. They also have quality pearls in pretty colors that come from the Bernard Champon pearl farm in Tahaa, and a selection of paintings by local artists. **La Palme d'Or**, Tel. 66.23.79, on Uturoa's main street, sells black pearl jewelry, and their shop in the Maritime building is **Tehani Jewelers**, Tel. 66.11.11. **Tico Pearls,** Tel. 66.14.00, has an impressive showroom in the Maritime building. They also sell wood and coral sculptures by Mara, Tahiti's most renown coral sculptor. **Rai-Teva,** Tel. 60.04.20, in the Maritime building, is a jewelry shop that carries a good selection of small black pearl earrings. This size black pearl is not easy to find in most shops. They also carry a fashion collection of jeans, tops and other clothes.

Sephora Boutique, Tel. 66.21.21, is in the pink Gare Maritime building on the Uturoa wharf. They carry woven hats, tapa covered photo albums, paintings and other gift items, as well as black pearls. **Te Fare Shop**, Tel. 66.17.17, is behind the Gare Maritime across the street from the Arts and Crafts Village. They offer a colorful selection of Polynesian art deco linens, pottery, basketwork and jewelry. **Arii Boutique**, Tel. 66.35.54, on Uturoa's main street, sells locally made fabrics, pareos and tee shirts, and **Habillez-Moi (Boutique Mariki)**, Tel. 66.44.88, on the mountainside facing the Mairie (town hall), sells clothes for children and women. **Wasa Nui Shop** in downtown Uturoa, Tel. 66.18.00, sells pareos, T-shirts and Indonesian clothes. **My Flowe**r, *Tel. 66.19.19*, is a florist and gift shop in the Maritime building.

Be sure to visit the **Arts and Crafts Village** or **"Fare Mama"** adjacent to the ship dock in Uturoa. There are 10 thatched roof *fares* decorated with *tifaifai* wall hangings, where the artisan mamas display their hand painted dresses and pareos, woven hats and bags, woodcarvings and shell jewelry. You can also find locally made souvenir items The **Hawaiki Nui Association**, *Tel. 66.12.37*, at the airport, sells *pareos* and tee-shirts, wood sculptures, and traditional woven hats and bags, plus seashell jewelry.

Anuanua Art, *Tel. 66.12.66,* is on the mountainside of the main street in Uturoa center. A unique selection of paintings, sculptures, etchings, pottery, tapa, sandalwood and seashell jewelry is on display. Some of the local painters, sculptors and other artists represented are: Erhard Lux, Jean-François Favre, Christian Deloffre, André Marere, Joannis, Martiale, Philippe Dubois, Maryse Noguier, Roland Marti's sculpture and Peter Owen's pottery. Open Monday to Friday 8am to 12pm and 1:30 to 5:30pm, and on Saturday from 8am to 12pm.

Painapo Boutique is located at the Hawaiki Nui Hotel. In addition to T-shirts, pareos and gift items, you can rent a bicycle for 500 CFP for 2 hours or 1.600 CFP for all day, get your film developed, rent an underwater camera or hire Carine, who runs the boutique, to make a video film of your scuba diving adventures. You can contact her at *Tel. 73.03.18; E-mail: carineunderw@hotmail.com*.

Special Services, Massage, Natural Therapy, Relaxation

Institut Vahine Beauté, *Tel. 66.15.16*, is upstairs in a building across the road from the Arts and Crafts Village and the Uturoa wharf. Their services include manicures, pedicures, facial care, waxing, makeup and relaxing massages. **Hau Massages** is operated by Jerome and Jasmine, who will massage you in your room at Hotel Hawaiki Nui. Their rates are 6.000 CFP for a one-hour relaxing massage, 7.500 CFP for a one-hour ayurvedic or shiatsu massage or one-hour foot reflexology. Beauty shops in Uturoa include **Style et Tendance Coiffure**, *Tel. 66.21.77*, and **Tehina Coiffure**, *Tel. 66.10.20*.

Tattoo Artists

Isidore Haiti, *Tel. 66.15.97/72.86.63*, specializes in Marquesan tattoos.

Practical Information
Banks

Raiatea has three banks, which are all located in the center of Uturoa. **Banque de Polynésie**, *Tel.60.04.50*, is open Monday through Friday from 7:45am to 12pm and from 2 to 3:45pm; they also have an ATM window on the port side of the bank. **Banque Socredo**, *Tel. 60.07.00*, is open Monday through Friday from 7:30 to 12pm and from 1:30 to 4pm, and there is also an ATM window outside the bank; **Banque de Tahiti**, *Tel. 60.02.80*, is open Monday through Friday from 7:45 to 11:45am, and from 1:30 to 4:30pm, and they also have an ATM window.

Bookstores
Librarie d'Uturoa is in the center of town, on the mountainside of the main street, *Tel. 66.30.80*. They have calendars and books (in French) about Tahiti and Her Islands.

Drugstore
The **Pharmacie de Raiatea** is on the mountainside of the main street in Uturoa center, across the street from the Catholic Church, *Tel. 66.15.56*, *Tel. 66.35.48* (emergency). It is open Monday through Friday from 7:30am to 12pm and 1:30 to 5:30pm; on Saturday from 7:30am to 12pm and on Sunday and holidays from 9:30 to 10:30am.

Hospital
There is a government hospital close to the boat dock in Uturoa, *Tel. 60.08.00* (all services) and *Tel. 60.08.01* (emergency), which serves all the Leeward Society Islands. Several private doctors and dentists have practices in Raiatea as well as physical therapists (kinésithérapeutes) and there is also an optician, **Te Mata Ora**, *Tel. 66.16.19*.

Internet
Techni-Iles, *Tel./Fax 66.37.81*, is located at the Europcar office and general store, next to the Moemoea restaurant on the waterfront street facing the quay in downtown Uturoa. You can bring your own laptop or use one of the two computers provided in the back room. **ITS** (Informatique Technologie Services) *Tel. 60.25.25,* has moved its Internet services to the Gare Maritime building in the center of Uturoa. They have six computers with flat screens and ergonomically designed keyboards. There are cyber point computers at the Hawaiki Nui hotel and at Pension Tepua that accept phone cards.

Laundry and Dry Cleaning
Bleu des Iles, *Tel. 66.29.64*, is located at the Centre Commercial Tahina and has a free pick-up and delivery service for dry cleaning, pressing and laundry. **Laverie Jacqueline**, *Tel. 66.24.09*, is in Apooiti and will also pick up and delivery your laundry. She's closed Saturday afternoon and all day Sunday.

Police
The French *gendarmerie* is close to the post office in Uturoa center, *Tel. 66.31.07*. The number for the Municipal Police is *Tel. 66.38.97*.

Post Office and Telecommunications Office

The **Post Office** has a branch at the Gare Maritime building on the boat dock in Uturoa, which is open Monday through Friday from 8am to 12pm and 1:30 to 4:30pm, and on Saturday from 8 to 11:30am. The main post office, *Tel. 66.35.50*, is in a modern building north of Uturoa on the main road, facing the hospital. It is open Monday to Thursday 7:30am to 3pm, on Friday from 7:30am to 2pm and on Saturday from 8 to 10am. There is an ATM window here. All telecommunications and postal services can be handled at either office.

Tourist Bureau

The **Raiatea-Tahaa Manava Visitors' Bureau**, *Tel. 60.07.77, Fax 60.07.76, E-mail: raiateainfo@mail.pf.* This information center is located in the Gare Maritime Building on the quay in Uturoa, and is open Monday-Friday from 8am to 12:30pm and from 1pm to 4pm. The hostesses are helpful and speak English.

Yacht Services, Marinas & Nautical Bases

Apooiti Marina is at PK 3 in Apooiti, west of Uturoa center, *Tel. 66.12.20; Fax 66.42.20; VHF 68 or 12; E-mail: noc_fr@yahoo.fr.* This is the home base of The Moorings and Tahiti Yacht Charter. There are 70 berths for boats up to 50 feet with a maximum draft of 8 feet. Free overnight stays for all craft. Contact the marina manager for extended stays. Sailboat rentals, sailing school, sail loft, dive club, 2 restaurants and bars, laundry service.

Uturoa Marina is a public marina in the harbor of Uturoa and is a subdivision of the Equipment Service of Raiatea, *Tel./Fax 66.31.52; Cell 78.36.94 (Port Captain); VHF Channel 16 or 12.* There are 100 berths for boats from 26 feet to 55 feet, and a maximum draft of 3 meters (9.8 feet). Large vessels welcome. Overnight stays for all craft are free. Contact the marina manager for longer stays. A diving club is on the premises and fuel service is available in the Uturoa port complex adjoining the wharf.

Uturaerae Marina is at PK 4.5 in Apooiti. This large marina is on the northwest side of Raiatea and is used by all vessels needing repairs or services, as well as by people on extended stays. It is privately owned by the **Chantier Naval des Iles** (Naval Shipyard of the Islands) and is the base of four companies that service the marine industry, providing construction and repair facilities for 30 vessels from 10 feet to 60 feet, including barges. Maximum draft 2.30 meters (7.5 feet). Dry-docking, ships chandlery, take-away food, point phone. Contact Jacques Freixas or Ariel Badinot on *VHF Channel 72 or Tel. 66.10.10, Fax 66.28.41; E-mail: raiateacarenage@mail.pf; www.raiatea.com/carenage.*

Raiatea Carénage Services, *Tel. 66.26.96, cell 78.22.96; VHF Channel 68 E-mail: raiateacarenage@mail.pf.* This full service boatyard has everything you need to repair your boat and sails and also provides long-term moorage during your absence. It is located at Uturaerae Marina and is managed by Dominique Goché, who speaks English.

Faaroa Nautical Base, *Tel. 60.04.85/66.20.35; Fax 66.23.19; E-mail: stardustyc@mail.pf; www.stardustyc.com/www.sunsail.com.* Moorings available for 25 boats.

Chapter 17

TAHAA

For many years you didn't hear much about the quiet little island of **Tahaa**, which formerly lived in the shadow of its big sister island of Raiatea and within sight of the glamorous island of Bora Bora. Then, without making much hoopla about it, Tahaa began stretching in many directions. Its reputation as Polynesia's vanilla island has now expanded to include three dozen black pearl farms in the clear lagoon waters near the white sand beaches of the *motu* islets, as well as a few family pensions with accommodations for guests.

Word began to spread among cognizant travelers when the 9-unit Vahine Island Private Island Resort was built on a private *motu* a few years ago. In July 2002, the 5-star Taha'a Pearl Beach Resort & Spa opened 60 bungalow suites on Motu Tautau, a lovely little islet just a 5-minute boat ride from the main island of Taha'a. One of its main selling points is a clear view of Bora Bora across the sea. According to the advertising hype, this ultra deluxe hotel was designed to be the most luxurious resort in the entire South Pacific region. The promoters' promises were proven true at the end of 2003 when this hotel was accepted as a member of Relais et Châteaux, which has only 450 members. This chain and The Leading Hotels of the World, Ltd., have created the Luxury Alliance group, representing the most prestigious hotels in the world. Upon acceptance into this elite club, Le Taha'a Private Island & Spa was born, shedding all reference to the Pearl Resorts.

Taha'a now has the attention of hotel developers looking for new properties. Raffles Taimana Resort Taha'a is a project to build a 5-star hotel on three islets (Motu Niuniu, Motu Rohutu and Motu Tauhea), which will be managed by Raffles Hotels & Resorts. Plans are waiting governmental approval for the construction of 65 king, one-bedroom and two-bedroom villas, along with three food and beverage facilities, a meeting room, library,

Raffles Amrita Spa, tennis court and a diving center. More than 80 percent of the resort will be built over the lagoon, providing stunning views of the nearby islands of Raiatea and Bora Bora. China Travel Service is reportedly financing construction of this hotel project. Tahiti's local French newspapers also announced that China Travel Service wants to build a 5-star hotel with 150 rooms on Motu Teotu, the biggest islet offshore the island of Taha'a, but this project is still in the beginning stage. The Taha'a Golf Resort is a project of TB Promotion, who also owns the new Radisson Plaza Resort in Tahiti. La Pirogue is a 3-star hotel that opened 12 units on Taha'a's Motu Porou in June 2004. This small circular island that is known today as Taha'a (or Tahaa) was settled by Maohi pioneers several hundred years ago, estimated between 850 and 1200 AD. They called the island Uporu, a name that is also found in Samoa (Upolu). Polynesian folklore declares that this island was the natal home of Hiro, the famous god of thieves in Polynesian mythology, whose favorite hangout was in the area we now call the Leeward Society Islands. Huge black volcanic boulders on Tahaa's east coast are considered parts of Hiro's body or objects that belonged to him.

During the 17th century the kings of Raiatea and Taha'a fought for possession of Tahaa. Bora Bora's feared warriors were more powerful, and both Taha'a and Raiatea were subjugated to the rule of Bora Bora's King Tapoa, descendant of Puni the Conqueror.

Although the Leeward Islands became a possession of France in 1888, the French flag was raised in Taha'a only in 1897, following years of rebellion.

Several Frenchmen with yachts have chosen the now peaceful island of Taha'a as retirement retreats. There are good marina facilities and all yachts are welcomed.

Taha'a's inhabitants lead quiet, industrious lives, earning their living in agriculture, fishing and breeding livestock. Plantations of sumptuous fruits and vegetables add their lushness to the palette of vibrant colors you'll see all around the island. The produce from Taha'a is sold at the public market in Raiatea and the watermelons are shipped to the market in Papeete.

Taha'a is often called the **Vanilla Island** because of the numerous plantations of this aromatic "black gold" that flourish in the fertile valleys. After the vanilla beans are harvested and laid out to dry, the whole village is filled with the rich perfume of vanilla. You can visit a vanilla plantation and some of the black pearl farms that are built in the warm, clear lagoon near the *motu* islets.

Taha'a has no airport, but there are good port facilities, with service by inter-island ferry and cargo ships several times a week, and water-taxi or shuttle boat service from Uturoa. Taha'a has a *gendarmerie*, infirmary and dispensary, two post offices, a bank and small general stores. Accommodations are available on a small but steadily growing scale, either in traditional Polynesian style hotels, beach and overwater bungalows on a *motu*, a berth aboard a sailboat or a room in a village home. Wherever there is a room there is usually an excellent meal available.

You can paddle a kayak or hire a boat and guide to visit the *motu*, where you can picnic on the white sand beaches. The protected lagoon is also ideal for sailing, windsurfing, snorkeling and fishing. You can hike into the valleys or rent a car or bike to explore the island.

Taha'a still remains virtually undiscovered by the general tourist market, although it is now awakening to the world of tourism. Peace, tranquility and natural beauty combine with the island's friendly, unhurried pace, offering you a relaxed and happy vacation with a taste of Polynesia of yesteryear. Wherever you go on this island you will find that the people smile and wave to you, nod their heads or raise their eyebrows in a traditional Polynesian greeting.

Arrivals & Departures

Arriving By Air

There is no airport on the island of Tahaa. You can fly to Raiatea and take a boat to Tahaa. If you have made reservations at a hotel or pension on Tahaa, your host may send a boat to meet you at the airport. The dock is to the right of the terminal building as you face the street. There is no sign indicating this is where you should wait. You can sit at the snack bar and watch for the arrival of your boat. You can also go to the quay in Uturoa and get a regular shuttle boat to Tahaa or take a private taxi boat.

Arriving By Boat

Vaeanu, *Tel. 41.25.35; Fax 41.24.34, E-mail: torehiatetu@mail.pf*. This ship can transport a total of 90 passengers, with 32 berths in cabins and 58 places on the deck. It departs from the Fare-Ute quay in Papeete at 4pm on Monday, Wednesday and Friday, stopping in Huahine and Raiatea before arriving at Tapuamu quay in Tahaa the following morning at 6am. One-way fare for deck passengers is 2.120 CFP; a berth in a cabin costs 4.400 to 5.989 CFP per person depending on accommodations chosen. Meals are served on board. Reservations for cabin space must be paid in full before 9am on the fixed date of departure from Papeete.

Hawaiki Nui, *Tel. 54.99.54 (Tahiti); Tel. 65.61.59 (Tahaa); Fax 45.24.44, E-mail: sarlstim@mail.pf*. This 12-passenger cargo ship has 4 double cabins and deck space. Passengers must sleep in cabins on the Thursday voyage as the ship also transports fuel then. It leaves the Motu Uta dock in Papeete each Tuesday at 4pm and arrives at the Tapuamu quay in Tahaa on Wednesday at 3pm, after stopping in Huahine, Raiatea and Bora Bora . The Thursday trip leaves Papeete at 4pm, and arrives in Tahaa on Friday at 11:30am after going to Bora Bora and before returning to Raiatea and Huahine on its return trip to Tahiti. The cost of sleeping on deck is 1.750 CFP per person and a berth in one of the cabins costs 4.950 CFP from Papeete to all the Leeward Islands. Meals are available on board the ship.

Maupiti Express II, *Tel./Fax 689/66.37.81; Cell 78.27.22*. The *Maupiti Express II* arrives in Tahaa direct from Bora Bora at 8:20am each Monday, Wednesday and Friday. The one-way fare from Bora Bora to Tahaa is 2.500 CFP and round-trip is 3.500 CFP. The fares from Maupiti to Tahaa are 3.500 CFP and 5.500 CFP. Passengers under 12 years pay half-fare.

Enota Transport Maritime, *Tel./Fax 65.61.33*. Enota Tetuanui has two 42-foot speedboats that can transport 57 passengers each between Raiatea and Tahaa. *Te Haere Maru V* leaves from the boat dock in Uturoa at 10:30am and 4:30pm for the east coast of Tahaa, stopping in Vaitoare, Haamene and Faaaha. *Te Haere Maru IV* leaves from the boat dock in Uturoa at 10:30am and 4:30pm for the west coast of Tahaa, stopping at the Marina Iti, Poutoru, Tiva and Tapuamu. The crossing takes 20 to 45 minutes, depending on your destination. One-way fare is 500 CFP.

Tamarii Tahaa, *Tel. 65.65.29 or 20.93.11*, can transport a maximum of 66 passengers in a 46-foot aluminum boat that operates a shuttle service between Raiatea and Tahaa. The boat leaves the Uturoa boat dock Monday through Friday at 10:30am and 4:30pm and on Saturday at 10:30am only. Stops are made in Apu, Poutoru, Tiva, Tapuamu and Patio. The one-way fare is 500 CFP as far as Tapuamu and 700 CFP to Patio.

Taxi Boats

La Compagnie des Taxis-Boat (Corto), *Tel./Fax 65.66.44, Cell 79.62.01 (William) or 79.62.02 (Briam); VHF: 16; E-mail: taxi-boat@mail.pf; www.taxi-boat.com*. William Donzelot and his son Briam have two locally built 23-foot and 26-foot polyester and aluminum boats that will accommodate a minimum of two or a maximum of six passengers. They provide taxi boat service between Raiatea and Tahaa or Tahaa and Raiatea on request, daily from 6am to 6pm. They will pick you up at the airport, the quay in Uturoa or from any boat dock specified. The per person fare from Uturoa to Tahaa starts at 2.000 CFP for Zone 1, the villages closest to Uturoa, and escalates to 4.000 CFP per person for Zone 5, which includes Hipu, Patio and Iripau. Night transfers cost 100 percent more. You can also charter a taxi boat for 12.000 CFP an hour. They also offer package deals of a taxi-boat plus car rental.

Departing By Air

You can take a boat from Tahaa directly to the airport on Raiatea or go to Uturoa town by taxi boat and take a land taxi to the airport. Air Tahiti's number in Raiatea is *Tel. 60.04.44/60.04.40*.

Departing By Boat

Hawaiki Nui, *Tel. 54.99.54 (Papeete)*, *Tel. 65.61.59 (Tahaa); Fax*

45.24.44, leaves Tahaa each Wednesday at 3:30pm for Raiatea and Tahiti, arriving in Papeete on Thursday at 7am. It leaves Tahaa each Friday at 12pm for Raiatea, Huahine and Tahiti, arriving in Papeete at 5am on Saturday morning. The one-way deck fare is 1.750 CFP and a berth is 4.950 CFP.

Vaeanu, *Tel. 41.25.35* (Papeete); *Fax 41.24.34*, leaves Tahaa at 7am each Tuesday, Thursday and Saturday for Bora Bora, arriving at 10am. Each Tuesday and Thursday the ship skips Tahaa on its voyage back from Bora Bora to Raiatea, Huahine and Tahiti. But on Sunday, after spending the night in Bora Bora, the ship returns to Tahaa, arriving at 11am on Sunday and then continues its voyage back to Raiatea, then to Huahine and Tahiti arriving in Papeete at 1am on Monday. The deck fare from Raiatea to Tahaa is 800 CFP, to Bora Bora it's 1.400 CFP, from Raiatea to Huahine is 1.060 CFP and from Raiatea to Tahiti it costs 2.120 CFP. A berth in a cabin is 4.400 to 5.989 CFP.

Maupiti Express II, *Tel./Fax 689/66.37.81; Cell 78.27.22*. The boat stops in Tahaa each Monday, Wednesday and Friday between Raiatea and Bora Bora. See schedule in the Raiatea chapter.

Enota Transport Maritime, *Tel./Fax 65.61.33*. Enota Tetuanui has two 42-foot launches that can transport 57 passengers each between Raiatea and Tahaa. *Te Haere Maru V* leaves from the east coast of Tahaa twice a day, starting from Faaaha, stopping in Haamene (at 6:30am and 12pm) and Vaitoare for the trip to Uturoa. *Te Haere Maru IV* leaves from the west coast of Tahaa twice a day, with stops at Tapuamu, Tiva, Poutoru and Marina Iti, then makes the 15-minute crossing to Uturoa. The boat begins its journey at 5:30am Monday-Friday during school days, and at 5:45am during vacation time. They also make another trip starting at 11:45am. One-way fare is 500 CFP.

Tamarii Tahaa, *Tel. 65.65.29* or *20.93.11*, can transport a maximum of 66 passengers in a 46-foot aluminum boat that operates a shuttle service between Tahaa and Raiatea. The boat leaves the Patio boat dock at 5:15am and 11:45am Monday through Friday, and at 5:30am on Saturday. Stops are made at Tapuamu, Tiva, Poutoru and Apu, then the boat continues on to Uturoa, arriving one to one and a half-hours after leaving Patio. The fare is 700 CFP from Patio and the other stops cost 500 CFP per person.

Orientation

Tahaa lies three kilometers (2 miles) northwest of Uturoa, sharing the same coral foundation and reef-protected lagoon that surrounds the island of Raiatea. The shape of the island, with its scalloped shoreline, resembles a hibiscus flower. A narrow isthmus separates the deeply indented bays of Apu, Haamene and Hurepiti on the south of the island. Some 60 *motu* islets lie inside the coral reef in the north and this protective barrier is unbroken except by the two navigable passes of Toahotu on the southeast side and Tiamahana on the southwest coast. Yachts and even ships can completely circumnavigate the island inside the lagoon, often accompanied by porpoises.

Tahaa has a land surface of 88 square kilometers (34 square miles), and **Mount Ohiri**, at 598 meters (1,961 feet), is the highest peak of the volcanic mountain range. The mountains are not high enough to attract enough rain to meet the needs of the 4,845 residents, who live in the small villages of Patio, Pahure, Hipu, Faaaha, Haamene, Motutiairi, Vaitoare, Poutoru, Patii, Tiva, Tapuamu and Murifenua. **Tiva** is considered the prettiest village, **Tapuamu** has the main port facilities, **Patio** is the administrative center, and **Haamene Bay** is six kilometers (3.7 miles) long, providing good anchorage and a haven for sailors.

A road winds 67 kilometers (42 miles) through the coastal villages and up mountain roads, where you have panoramic views of the bays, offshore islets and the ever-changing colors of the sea beyond the white foam on the barrier reef.

Getting Around Tahaa
Car & Scooter Rentals
Europcar, *Tel. 65.67.00*. The main sales office is located at the service station on the ferry dock of Tapuamu. A Fiat Panda rents for 5.000 CFP for 2 hours, 6.000 CFP for 4 hours, 7.000 CFP for 8 hours and 8.300 CFP for 24 hours. A 5-door air-conditioned Punto costs 8.100 CFP for 2 hours, 8.600 CFP for 4 hours, and up to 12.900 CFP for 24 hours. These rates include taxes, unlimited mileage and third-party insurance. Gas is extra.

Hibiscus Location, *Tel. 65.61.06, cell 79.28.81*, is located at Hotel Hibiscus in Haamene. The rental rates are the same as those charged by Europcar.

Monique Location, *Tel. 65.62.48*, is located at the ferryboat dock in Haamene. She rents 3-door or 5-door Saxo Citroën cars for 8.990 CFP for 8 hours. Gas is not included.

Bicycles
Vai Poe pension (Chez Patricia and Daniel), *Tel. 65.60.83, cell 78.67.68/79.26.01*, have rental bicycles in Haamene.

Where to Stay
Prestige
LE TAHA'A PRIVATE ISLAND & SPA, *B.P. 67, Patio, Taha'a 98733. Tel. 689/60.84.00; Fax 689/60.84.01; E-mail: welcome@letahaa.com/ letahaa@relaischateaux.com; www.letahaa.com/ www.relaischateaux.com. Reservations: 689/50.84.54; Fax 689/43.17.86; E-mail: info@spmhotels.pf. Located on Motu Tautau, 45 minutes by boat from the airport in Raiatea and 10 minutes by boat from the main island of Tahaa. One-way boat transfer*

from airport in Raiatea 4.000 CFP per person; private boat transfer for two passengers minimum with half a bottle of French champagne, 21.000 CFP per couple; 15-minute helicopter shuttle from the Bora Bora airport 21.000 CFP per person. 60 bungalows. EP rates single/double: Beach villa 90.000 CFP; Tahaa overwater suite 90.000 CFP; Sunset overwater suite 100.000 CFP; Bora Bora overwater suite 115.000 CFP. Continental breakfast 2.400 CFP; American breakfast 2.800 CFP. MAP (half-board) add 9.800 CFP per day; AP (full board) add 13.300 CFP per day. Add 5% hotel tax to room rates and 6% value added tax to room rates and prepaid meal plans. A 6% value added tax is applicable to transfers and a 10% VAT is added to other services. Add 150 CFP municipal tax per person per day. All major credit cards.

Le Taha'a Private Island & Spa is the only hotel in French Polynesia to be accepted as a member of the prestigious Relais et Châteaux association of hotels, and was chosen, along with only 22 other hotels and lodges throughout the world, for the rare privilege of being included in the 2004 promotion of Relais et Châteaux properties.

This 5-star 60-unit resort hotel opened in July 2002 as the Taha'a Pearl Beach Resort & Spa, and the name was changed to Le Taha'a Private Island & Spa when it became associated with Relais et Château at the end of 2003. This traditional Polynesian style hotel is located on Motu Tautau on the coral reef, facing the island of Tahaa on the lagoon side and offering an unsurpassed view of Bora Bora on the ocean side. The hotel grounds cover 16 hectares (40 acres) and encompass a white sand beach that stretches 700 meters (2,296 feet) along the lagoon side of the motu. The 48 overwater suites are 90 square meters (969 square feet) large and are built over the most translucent lagoon imaginable. They are classified according to the views they offer. The 34 Taha'a Overwater Suites face Mount Ohiri on Tahaa's main island; the 6 Sunset Overwater Suites have a view of the lagoon and romantic sunsets; and the 8 Bora Bora Overwater Suites look out over the ocean and the island of Bora Bora. Each overwater unit has a terrace with an open sundeck and a covered sitting area. Steps lead down to another solarium platform and a ladder provides access to the lagoon. At the foot of the majestic bed in the center of the room, there is a see-through "lagoonarium" feature complete with nighttime lighting so that you can watch the tropical fish.

Each of the 12 Beach Villas faces the lagoon. These units are even more spacious, with 180 square meters (1,937 square feet) of living space, including a private enclosed garden and terrace with a small private self-cleaning pool, shaded sitting area and an open sundeck. All the units have air-conditioners and ceiling fans, a full shower and separate bathtub, a king size bed or two twin beds, plus a sofa bed. They all have International Direct Dial phones and Internet access, satellite television with English channels, a hotel movie channel, DVD and CD players, mini-bar, coffee/tea making facilities, individual in-room safe, hair dryer and magnifying mirror. Housekeeping service is provided twice daily and room service is available from 7am to 9:30pm. They will also deliver ice to your room between 4-8pm and the mini-bar is stocked daily. An iron and ironing board can be provided on request and same day laundry service is available with a pick-up before 9am. Fare Mahana consists of 4 transit/day rooms with a sofa bed, shower and closet that is available for guests who arrive before the check-in time of 3pm or check out at 11am and remain on the resort premises until later in the day.

The best local craftsmen have combined their know how and talent to produce a marriage of luxury, elegance and space, using local materials such as bamboo, pandanus and tapa cloth to create an authentic Polynesian style in the suites, villas and public areas, which are built among the trees, providing an excellent view of the lagoon and the island of Tahaa. There are three restaurants, two bars and two boutiques, plus a fresh water infinity swimming pool that is open 24 hours a day. Besides the pool, other free activities include board games, magazines and books at the Tehutu Bar, windsurfing, volley ball, badminton, French bowls, pedal boats, kayaks, outrigger paddle canoes, and a lighted tennis court that is open round-the-clock. You can take a free shuttle boat from Motu Tautau to the main island of Taha'a and go exploring on your own or join an organized tour. At the activities desk in the lobby you can book a circle island tour of Taha'a for 7.500 CFP, rent a jet ski starting at 10.000 CFP for 30 minutes, rent a scooter on the main island for 4.800 CFP for 4 hours, or sign up for a picnic on a motu for 9.900 CFP. Or you can opt for a 15-minute helicopter ride from Bora Bora to the motu helipad adjacent to Le Taha'a Private Island & Spa. A one-way hop is 21.000 CFP per person.

There are also many other ways to spend your day, including snorkeling in the magnificent coral gardens adjacent to the hotel, or lying in a *chaise longue* on Motu Paari, an islet just a few steps from the beach and gazing at the mountains of Bora Bora in the distance. You can also go scuba diving with Blue Nui, which has an on-site dive center. A secretarial service is located in the lobby, as well as computers providing access to the Internet. Manea Spa has a directory of relaxing treatments that include body shaping sessions, treatments using Monoi oils and body and facial care for both men and women. They are located in a bungalow beside a salt lake, which, unfortunately, is a haven for mosquitoes that make their presence known in all the outdoor areas as well as at the reception desk.

If ever a hotel was created with honeymooners in mind, it is here at Le Taha'a Private Island & Spa. One magazine article stated that since the hotel opened in 2002, the management has had to change the mattresses three times in all the bungalows that offer a view of Bora Bora, although the mattresses were guaranteed for five years under normal wear. Apparently, this vision of Paradise acts as an inspiration for lovers. Indeed, when I stayed at the hotel in 2004, the Bora Bora Suites were all being renovated. These are rooms 1-8, with bungalows 2 and 3 providing the best view.

Special Romantic Rendez-Vous services are provided for honeymooners. These include Romantic Welcomes, Romantic Interludes, Romantic Escapades and Polynesian Wedding Ceremonies. All rates are per couple and do not include tax. Guests staying in the overwater suites can order breakfast delivered by outrigger canoe to their terrace for 8.500 CFP. A romantic breakfast on the beach, terrace or at the water's edge is 8.200 CFP. Lunch for two on the little Motu Paari just in front of the hotel property is 18.500 CFP or you can take a boat excursion to visit the lagoon and have a picnic on a private motu for 38.182 CFP. A romantic dinner can be served in the Vanilla restaurant for 22.500, a romantic Milky Way dinner is 31.000 CFP and a private beach dinner is 33.500 CFP. Private excursions are also available for shark and ray feeding, sunset cruises, sunset lagoon tours, private lagoon cruises, private catamaran cruises, and a private champagne cruise on board the Atara Royal yacht. Polynesian wedding ceremonies can be performed on the motu (Te Vaa) for 85.000 CFP, on board a yacht (Te Ruau) for 127.000 CFP, or on a catamaran and motu (Te Arii) for 210.000 CFP. These are non-binding wedding ceremonies and you can contact Le Taha'a Private Island & Spa for a brochure on honeymoon packages. See further information under *Where to Eat, Massages & Spas, Seeing the Sights* and *Scuba Diving* in this chapter.

Deluxe
   HOTEL VAHINE ISLAND, *B.P. 510, Uturoa, Raiatea 98735. Tel. 689/ 65.67.38; Fax 689/65.67.70; VHF radio Channel 68; E-mail: vahine.island@mail.pf; www.vahine-island.com. Located on Motu Tu Vahine (Island of the Woman), a private islet in the Tahaa lagoon, facing Bora Bora, 15 kilometers (9.3 miles) from the Raiatea airport and 12 kilometers (7.4 miles) from the ferry dock in Raiatea. Round-trip boat transfers from Raiatea are 6.000 CFP per person for a minimum of two people. 9 bungalows. EP Rates: beach bungalow 35.000 CFP single/double; overwater bungalow 52.000 CFP single/double. Add 4.000 CFP for child sharing bungalow with parents. Half board meal plan with breakfast and dinner is 7.500 CFP per person; full board meal plan with breakfast, lunch and dinner is 10.500 CFP per person. Breakfast is 2.000 CFP, à la carte lunch is 800-1.600 CFP, and dinner is 5.500 CFP. Note: The hotel offers special rates between October 1 and April 30. For a 4-night stay one night is free and for a 9-night stay three nights are free. Special year-round packages for honeymooners and wedding anniversary celebrants staying 7 nights include a large bottle of champagne, a bouquet of flowers and one free night. Add 5% hotel tax to room rates and 6% value added tax to room rates and prepaid meal plans. A 6% value added tax is applicable to transfers and a 10% VAT is added to other services, and there is also a municipal tax of 150 CFP per person per day. All major credit cards.*
   This private hotel is located on a 10-acre *motu* facing the village of Hipu on Tahaa's northeastern shore. Here you will find white sand beaches,

snorkeling in the coral gardens of the lagoon, a lounge filled with a good selection of books, music and video films, and a calm setting for relaxing. You arrive by a fast covered boat from the airport dock in Raiatea and you will be greeted with floral leis at the hotel pier and escorted to the lounge area, where you will be served a welcome tropical punch. Then you will be taken to your overwater bungalow or to your bungalow on the beach, which is reached by walking through a coconut grove to the ocean side of the *motu*.

The bungalows are built of local wood and bamboo that has been varnished, and there is no plastic used in the construction or decorations. The six beach bungalows are small and are filled with a king-size bed of big bamboo or two twin beds, plus a table and chair and a closet. The beds are covered by a mosquito net. Two sides of the shoji screen walls slide open to give a feeling of more space, and there is a narrow terrace overlooking the lagoon, just big enough for two chairs and a table.

If it is at all possible, stay in one of the three overwater bungalows because they are larger than the beach units. They have a bedroom and sitting area, plus a spacious covered deck with steps leading down into the shallow lagoon. The bamboo furniture and lovely *tifaifai* bed covers, along with the curtains and cushion covers, provide a traditional Polynesian motif. A glass coffee table in the sitting area is a window to the marvelous marine world beneath the bungalow, where you can spy on the comings and goings of the multihued fish. The coral on the white sand bottom attracts a lot of fish both night and day, and you will see some pretty parrotfish, Picasso fish, yellow butterfly fish, electric blue damselfish and many other varieties. All the bungalows have ceiling fans, a mini-bar/refrigerator and private bathrooms with hot water showers. The toilet is in a separate compartment and the shower and lavabo area is closed off by saloon-type swinging doors. Electricity is 220 volts. The water is potable and the telephones have Internet access. Mini bars and hair dryers have been added to the amenities in each bungalow.

The shallow water in the lagoon around Vahine Island is filled with spiny sea urchins and bêche de mer, the elongated black sea cucumber that lives on the white sand bottom. You have to step carefully through these obstacles to get to the deeper water where you can swim and snorkel.

There is no charge for the use of the Polynesian outrigger canoes, the windsurf board and kayaks, and the snorkeling equipment is also provided. There is a volleyball court in the palm shaded grassy garden, and beach games and board games are available. The management can suggest several ways to enjoy the beautiful lagoon between Tahaa and Raiatea and land tours on the main island. Optional activities can be snorkeling trips by boat to another *motu*, visits to a pearl farm, shark feeding excursions, and rental of small motor boats that you pilot yourself to play "castaway" with a picnic on an uninhabited private motu. You can also sign up for scuba diving in Taha'a or Raiatea, jet ski rentals, sport fishing, vanilla tours on Taha'a, a jeep safari in Raiatea, or sailing cruises.

During one of my stays at Vahine Island, the owner's wife (a lovely Tahitian-French woman) and their child were in residence, along with some of their French friends living in London or Paris. One of the interesting activities they organized was to take a helicopter trip from the hotel to Bora Bora and spend the day jet skiing around the lagoon in Bora Bora, then returning to Vahine Island in late afternoon. A helipad on the premises allows you to fly over from Bora Bora or Raiatea and land on Tu Vahine Island. On another day they flew to Tahiti for lunch and shopping and returned to the hotel in time for dinner. This may be a good idea for the guests who are not happy unless they can shop, because there is only a small boutique at the hotel.

The outgoing and very pleasant young manager of Vahine Island is Eric Barbace, originally from Bordeaux. His wife, Nicole, is from Paris and is the hotel's chef de cuisine. The restaurant is renown for its gastronomic meals, and if you are a vegetarian or have other food requests, they will cater to your preferences. The bar serves a variety of exotic cocktails. The restaurant and bar are open to the public, but reservations must be made for meals if you are not staying in the hotel. See more information in *Where to Eat* in this chapter.

Vahine Island was named a member of The Small Hotel Company Collection in 1999, and offers full hotel service, with special care given to honeymooners, who comprise 85 percent of the guests. This charming hotel provides a romantic setting for lovers of all ages who seek a more intimate ambience. See more information under *Where to Eat* in this chapter.

Superior

HOTEL LA PIROGUE, *B.P 668, Uturoa, Raiatea 98735. Tel. 689/60.81.45; Fax 689/60.81.46; E-mail: hotellapirogue@mail.pf; www.hotellapirogue.com. Located on Motu Porou on the northern barrier reef facing Bora Bora, a 30-minute boat ride from the port of Uturoa and 35 minutes by boat from the airport in Raiatea. Boat transfer 6.000 CFP. EP Rates: garden bungalow 22.000-24.000 CFP single/double, 27.000-29.000 CFP triple; beach bungalow 24.000-28.000 CFP single/double; 29.000-33.000 CFP triple, according to seasons. Child 2-12 years 2.000 CFP. Continental breakfast 1.850 CFP; American breakfast 2.250 CFP; MAP half-board with breakfast and dinner add 6.500 CFP per person; AP full board with all three meals add 9.500 CFP per person. Add 6% value added tax to room rates and meal plans and a municipal tax of 50 CFP per person per day. A 10% value added tax is applicable to other services. American Express, Mastercard, Visa.*

This 3-star hotel opened in June 2004 on Motu Porou, a private islet that seems to float on the lagoon inside the coral reef on the northern side of Taha'a, offering a superb view of the lagoon of Taha'a as well as the romantic sunsets over Bora Bora. Giuliano Tognetti and his wife Séverine and their two daughters welcome guests to their cozy little resort, which offers 4 beach bungalows and 4 garden bungalows that are built in the local style of wooden walls and floors and thatched roofs of coconut fronds that were woven by the people of Hipu village. Each bungalow is equipped with a double bed, mosquito net, ceiling fan, television, teak and kohu furniture, DDD telephone and Internet connection for your laptop, a private bathroom with hot water shower, and a small terrace with lounge chairs. Fresh water is piped in from the main island under the lagoon and electricity is provided by solar energy and an electric generator. Household linens are supplied, and there is a restaurant, bar and small boutique on the premises. The restaurant proposes a local menu, with seafood specialties and Polynesian nights organized. Room service is available from 8am to 10pm. Canoes, snorkeling equipment, fishing gear, and bicycles to explore Taha'a Island are all free to in-house guests. They will be picked up at the hotel's private pier for optional boat excursions to visit pearl farms, take a 4WD trip around the island or to join a picnic outing on a motu. A private shuttle boat transfers hotel guests from the port of Uturoa or the airport in Raiatea to La Pirogue on Motu Porou. See more information under *Where to Eat* in this chapter.

Moderate

MARINA ITI, *B.P. 888, Uturoa, Raiatea 98735. Tel. 689/65.61.01; cell 72.30.61; Fax 689/65.63.87; E-mail: marinaiti@mail.pf. Beside the lagoon in Vaitoare, 8 minutes by motor launch from the airport in Raiatea and 10 minutes by shuttle boat from the boat dock in Uturoa. Round-trip boat transfers 3.600 CFP per person. EP Rates: garden bungalow starts at 12.720 CFP single/double; lagoon bungalow starts at 16.240 CFP single/double. Additional bed 2.000 CFP. Meal plan with breakfast and dinner is 5.500 CFP per person; meal plan with breakfast, lunch and dinner is 8.000 CFP per person. Prices quoted include a 6% value added tax to room rates, prepaid meal plans and transfers. A 10% value added tax is applicable to all other services. No credit cards.*

Frenchman Philippe Robin and his wife, Marie Adeline, started the Marina Iti in 1985, providing a comfortable and attractive small hotel where guests felt like they were being welcomed to a private home rather than a tourist lodging. Sixteen years later they tried to retire, but that didn't work out, so they have been back on the job since January 2002, doing the same things they did when they first started out. Marie Adeline does the cooking and Philippe serves the guests, dressed informally in shorts and shirt and bare feet. They both take care of the bungalows and all the other multiple tasks of running a family pension on the island of Taha'a.

There are two double bungalows and a honeymoon bungalow beside the lagoon and one double bungalow in the spacious garden. These units are built of wood, bamboo and shingle roofs, providing 14-18 double or twin beds with mosquito nets. All the bungalows contain a ceiling fan, electric mosquito repellent, private bathroom with hot water shower and a covered terrace.

During my most recent visit in February 2004 I stayed in the bridal suite, which is a round *fare* on the end of the property at the southern-most point on Taha'a. The double foam mattress is placed on a high wooden platform so that you can gaze at the lagoon while reclining in bed, enjoying the caress of the refreshing ocean breezes, along with those of your partner, hopefully. These bungalows may be dated but they offer a glimpse of what accommodations were like during Polynesia's golden era.

The main building of this hotel and nautical base has an open-air lounge, dining room and terrace facing the lagoon and the island of Raiatea. The decor is typical South Seas Island style, with lots of comfortable sofas and chairs of teak and bamboo, shell lamps, ceiling fans, green plants and the golden patina of aged woven bamboo walls. The views of the sunsets here are truly remarkable, looking past the masts of the sailboats that are moored close to the hotel pier. This is a popular gathering place for residents of Raiatea, which is just 10 minutes by boat from the Apooiti Marina. The atmosphere is very European, but some of the hotel's clients are American (the owners speak English). People who live on Tahiti also come over for the weekend and almost anyone with a boat at their disposal heads for the Tahaa Yacht Club, also known as Latitude 16, on weekends and holidays, or else they arrive by shuttle boat from Raiatea. If you plan to do this, you should be aware that there is no return shuttle boat in the afternoon and you will have to order a private taxi boat if you need to get back to Raiatea that evening.

Optional activities available include excursions on board a large double outrigger canoe, outings on motor boats and sailboats, and a variety of choices to discover the islets around Tahaa, with a picnic on an uninhabited *motu*, scuba diving, fishing, visits to pearl farms and fish enclosures, swimming with the rays and looking for dolphins. You can rent a scooter or bicycle at the hotel to explore Tahaa's charms on your own, or you can join a 4WD safari to visit the vanilla plantations, arts and crafts shops and panoramic viewpoints. For more information on the cuisine served see *Where to Eat* in this chapter.

CHEZ PATRICIA & DANIEL (VAI POE), *B.P. 104, Haamene, Tahaa 98734. Tel. 689/65.60.83/78.67.68/79.26.01; Fax 689/65.60.83; E-mail: v.p@mail.pf; www.infotahiti.com. On mountainside in Haamene, 15 minutes by boat from the Apooiti marina in Raiatea and 13 kilometers (8 miles) from the boat dock in Tapuamu. Round-trip taxi-boat transfers from Uturoa to Amaru quay in Haamene 3.600 CFP per person. Round-trip car transfers between Tapuamu and Haamene 1.200 CFP per passenger. 5 bungalows. EP rates: bungalow with breakfast 12.000 CFP single/double. Additional person 1.000 CFP. Half-price for child 3 to 12 years. Meals on request. Add 6% value added tax to room rates and meal plans. A 10% value added tax is applicable to other services. American Express, Mastercard, Visa.*

This small family pension is owned by Patricia and Daniel Amaru, who are some of the most organized people involved in tourism in French Polynesia.

They have built five very clean and attractive thatched roof bungalows situated on a large lot of grassy land facing the lagoon and the family's black pearl farm in Haamene Bay. Two bungalows each have a double bed, a kitchen with a mini-refrigerator stocked with drinks, and a private bathroom with hot water shower. The other three bungalows are family size, with one double bed and two single beds and a small desk or dressing table, all with a Polynesian touch. There is also a kitchen and private tiled bathroom with a hot water shower. The bungalows are all colorfully decorated and have screened windows and television. You can sit on your terrace and admire the flower gardens, filled with bright blossoms of yellow, mauve, champagne or peach colored *monettes*, Tiare Taina (gardenia) bushes, and lots of hybrid hibiscus with huge pink, white, purple, and even green blossoms.

The main family house is used as a gathering place for guests, with a long covered terrace and a big living room and kitchen, where Patricia cooks family style meals on request. She serves only fresh local products, which include fish and seafood, fruits and vegetables. No meat or chicken is served. You can dine in the privacy of your bungalow or on the big terrace. Patricia will also bring breakfast to your room each morning and will even create special cocktails for your Happy Hour enjoyment. On request, she will make you a sandwich for lunch.

A pay phone with a computer connection to Internet is provided for guests on the terrace of the main house. You can make calls with a phone card that is sold at the post office as well as in most of the stores and boutiques. You can also use the laundry facilities for 1.000 CFP per machine load.

Beside the road in front of the pension is the Vai Poe Boutique that sells pearls from their own farm, which is located in the lagoon across the road. A classroom is built over the lagoon where the Amaru daughters or nieces give explanations of black pearl farming in English and French, whenever visitors arrive by cruise ship tender or during guided island tours. Patricia and Daniel have also installed five moorings for boats close to their dock.

Vai Poe Tours is another one of their enterprises. They have 3 very sturdy 4WD vehicles and 4 outrigger speed canoes that are used for land or lagoon excursions. Guests staying in the pension are charged 3.500 CFP for a Safari Tour and 6.500 CFP for an all day excursion with a picnic on a motu. See more information under *Seeing the Sights* and *Sports & Recreation* in this chapter.

PENSION HIBISCUS, *B.P. 184, Haamene, Tahaa 98734. Tel. 689/ 65.61.06/79.28.81; Fax 689/65.65.65; VHF 68; E-mail: hibiscus@tahaa-tahiti.com; www.tahaa-tahiti.com; www.tahiti-tahaa.com. At the end of Haamene Bay, 20 minutes by boat from the Raiatea ferry dock. Round-trip boat transfers between airport and pension 2.000 CFP per person; transfers between Uturoa boat dock and pension 1.700 CFP. EP Rates: bungalow with private bathroom 9.434 CFP single/double, 11.130 CFP triple; plus choices up to 10-person bungalow for 26.500 CFP. Reduced rates for longer stays and* *low seasons. Meal plan with breakfast and dinner add 4.392 CFP per person; meal plan with breakfast, lunch and dinner add 6.629 CFP per person. Meals are half-price for children under 12 years. Rates include taxes. American Express, Mastercard, Visa.*

This is classified as a small family hotel and it is also a nautical base with seven bungalows for rent, including four units that were added in 2003. The smallest bungalow contains two double beds and a single bed, a private bedroom with hot water and a small terrace. The largest bungalow can sleep up to 10 people, with beds downstairs and on the mezzanine, plus a bathroom with hot water. All the bungalows have screened windows and a refrigerator and house linens are provided, and they are built close together in a tight space.

Snorkeling equipment is available and you can swim from the pier, visit the turtle park and go hiking, or you can take a safari tour by 4-wheel drive vehicle, visit a vanilla farm and explore the lagoon by outrigger speed canoe. You can have a picnic on the *motu* or even get married in a traditional Polynesian ceremony. If you want to go scuba diving, the Hemisphere Sud boat will pick you up on the pier across the road from the pension.

The main action is in the lagoon-side restaurant and bar across the road. This 200-seat space opened in 2003 and also serves as a yacht club, decorated with flags and nautical pennants. The ambiance at Leo and Lolita Morou's bar can become quite lively when a group of yachties tie up at the 14 moorings provided at the big pier and adjourn to the "watering hole." If you're looking for a rollicking good time, with lots of sea tales, this is your place. If you seek a tranquil, private environment, maybe the bungalows in back will give you enough distance from the noise to get a good night's sleep. You'll have to go further, however, to escape the sound of the *toere* drums when there is a dance group, so you may as well join them and learn to dance the hip-shaking *tamure*. Be prepared to chip in to pay for the entertainment when Leo passes the hat. He has a reputation for adding a lot of extra charges to the bill. (See more information under *Where to Eat* and *Yacht Services* in this chapter.

LE PASSAGE, *B.P. 150, Haamene, Tahaa 98734. Tel./Fax 689/65.66.75; cell 72.07.71/79.17.17; E-mail: residencelepassage@mail.pf. On the mountainside in Faaaha, a 20-minute boat ride from the airport in Uturoa, Raiatea. Transfers 6.000 CFP per boat. No transfer charge for stays of 3 nights in full-board (AP). Rates: bungalow and breakfast 9.000 CFP per person; bungalow with breakfast and dinner 12.000 CFP per person; bungalow with breakfast, lunch and dinner 15.000 CFP per person. Rates include all taxes except municipal tax of 50 CFP per person per day. No credit cards.*

This small family pension opened in mid-2002 on the side of a hill in Faaaha on the wild east coast of Taha'a, facing the rising sun and overlooking Motu Atara, Vahine Island and Motu Mute, as well as the boat passage near the village of Patio. Bruno and Marie-Thérèse Meunier-Coeroli have created 3 bungalows that are more like a high-class residence than a lodging for tourists. Each of the two smaller bungalows contains a double bed, private bathroom with hot water shower and a covered terrace overlooking the marvelous lagoon. The family unit has a double bed in each of the two rooms, as well as a bathroom with hot water, and their own covered terrace with a panoramic view. The bungalows are painted blue, green or yellow, and each unit is equipped with a mosquito net over the beds, and electric mosquito repellent and an electric floor fan. The furnishings and decorations are all done in good taste.

Kayaks, mountain bikes and ping-pong are available for guests' use, and Bruno also provides them with a 4WD Landrover excursion to see the highlights of the island. His uncovered boat can also be used for transfers between the airport and Le Passage. Just across the road from the pension is Bruno's new wooden pier, where he intends to build a bar and barbecue in 2005. Although there is no beach in this area, he said that snorkeling from the pier is good. Guests can enjoy a day sailing excursion on board the *Shamrock* for 7.500 CFP per person. They can sign up for scuba diving or a lagoon excursion by outrigger canoe that will take them to snorkel in the coral gardens or to feed the rays and sharks. Bruno has also built a *fare potée* shelter in his yard that is used for showings of works by local painters, sculptors and other artists.

The biggest attraction at Le Passage is the gastronomic restaurant, where Marie-Thérèse practices her culinary arts. See more information under *Where to Eat* in this chapter.

PENSION API, *Vaitoare, Tahaa 98734. Tel./Fax 689/65.69.88; E-mail: jjwatlp@mail.pf; www.pensionapi.com. On lagoon-side in Vaitoare, close to Marina Iti. 2 rooms. EP Rates: 8.000 CFP single/double; add 1.000 CFP for extra bed. Breakfast 700 CFP per person; breakfast and dinner 4.000 CFP; breakfast, lunch and dinner 6.000 CFP. Add 6% value added tax to room rates and meals. A 10% value added tax is applicable to other services. No credit cards.*

Constructed of local woods, bamboo and a pandanus roof, this family pension has two rooms for rent in a long rustic building facing the lagoon and the island of Raiatea. Each room has its own bathroom with hot water shower and a communal deck overlooking the landscaped gardens and the lagoon. French owner Jean-Jacques Waterlot and his companion, Laurence, help their guests organize excursions and tours and picnics on the *motu*. Bicycles, kayaks, fishing tackle and snorkeling equipment are provided at no cost. Laurence serves gastronomic meals of French cuisine prepared from local products.

PENSION AU PHIL DU TEMPS, *B.P. 50, Patio, Tahaa 98734. Tel. 689/ 65.64.19/74.71.08; Fax 689/65.64.19; E-mail: moutte.junior@mail.pf; www.pension-auphildu-temps.ifrance.com. On mountainside on Tahaa's* *west coast, near the Tapuamu ferry dock. Boat transfers from the airport in Raiatea to the pension 3.000 CFP per person one way. Free land transfers from Tapuamu dock to pension. 2 bungalows. Rates: bungalow with breakfast 6.000 CFP per person; bungalow with breakfast and dinner 10.000 CFP per person; bungalow with breakfast, lunch and dinner 13.000 CFP per person. Add 6% value added tax to room rates and meal plans. A 10% value added tax is applicable to other services. Visa.*

Two small thatched roof bungalows are built on stilts beside the main house inside a fenced yard across the road from the lagoon and boat dock. Each unit has 2 single beds and a double bed in the mezzanine, a mosquito net, fan, TV, mini-bar and terrace and an exterior private bathroom with hot water. Household linens are provided. Meals are served in the communal dining room. Across the lagoon are Motu Tautau and Le Taha'a Private Island Resort and Spa (Le Relais et Chateaux). This small family pension is owned by Philippe and Babeth Moutte, a French couple who will include all the activities free of charge starting on the third day of your stay, if you choose the complete pension meal plan of three meals a day. Philippe handles all the excursions personally. His 12-passenger boat has a sunroof, and he will take you fishing in the lagoon or outside the reef, for a tour around the island, with stops to see fish parks, the turtle park and for a swim in the coral gardens next to a *motu*. Canoes and tandem bicycles are also available. Land tours by 4WD will take you to visit a vanilla farm, a pearl farm and arts and crafts shops. Babeth is a *cordon bleu* cook, whose specialties include mahi mahi with vanilla sauce, chicken curry and homemade pastries. Philippe also creates original handcrafts.

Economy

CHEZ PASCAL, *PK 1, Tapuamu, Tahaa 98734. Tel./Fax 689/65.60.42. On mountainside in Tapuamu, one kilometer (.62 miles) from the Tahaa ferry dock and 40 minutes by boat from Raiatea airport. Round-trip shuttle boat transfers between Uturoa and Tapuamu 1.000 CFP per person. 4 bungalows and 2 rooms. EP rates: bungalow or room with breakfast 3.000 CFP per person. Bungalow or room with breakfast and dinner 4.500 CFP per person. Bungalow or room with all meals 6.500 CFP. Add 6% value added tax to room rates and meals. A 10% value added tax is applicable to other services. No credit cards.*

If you're looking for total immersion into a Polynesian experience at the lowest rates available, this is the place to stay. There are four large, simply furnished bungalows. Two bungalows have a double bed and a single bed, a terrace and an outside private bathroom with cold water. The other two bungalows have two single beds, all sharing an outside bathroom with cold water. There is also a house with two rooms for guests, each with a double and single bed, sharing the outside bathroom, dining room and kitchen. House linens are furnished and the electricity is solar powered. Meals are served family style, with Pascal and his family joining guests at the table. Pascal can help you rent a car or bicycle, take a 4WD safari tour, hike into the valley, visit a vanilla farm, or explore the lagoon by boat.

Other Family Pensions, Guest Houses, Surf Lodges, Dormitories & Camp Sites

Pension Herenui, *Tel. 689/65.62.60.* 3 bungalows and communal kitchen on mountainside in Poutoru for 8.000 CFP single/double. **Pension Vaihi**, *Tel. 689/65.62.02.* 3 bungalows beside Hurepiti Bay for 8.000 CFP single/double. **Tupenu Village,** *Tel 689/65.62.01.* 5 very basic, musty smelling rooms beside the lagoon in Patio village for 5.000 CFP single/double. **Chez Louise**, *Tel. 65.68.88/72.59.18.* Dormitory for 12, a small room for 2 and a small house for 2 are located across road from Chez Louise restaurant in Tiva village. A bed in the dorm is 2.000 CFP per person.

Where to Eat
Prestige
LE TAHA'A PRIVATE ISLAND & SPA, *Tel. 60.84.00. There are three restaurants and two bars. Add 10% tax to all prices. All major credit cards. Reserve.*

Restaurant Vanille is the main restaurant, situated in the heart of the resort on the upper level among the trees. Breakfast is served from 7 to 10:30am. A Continental breakfast is 2.400 CFP and an American breakfast is 2.800 CFP. Dinner is served from 7 to 9:30pm nightly except Tuesdays. The food is *la nouvelle cuisine Française*, which is very attractively arranged on nice dishes, has a marvelous combination of flavors and leaves you hungry even after you finish your meal. Starter courses are priced from 1.650 to 2.600 CFP, and may include crisp deep-fried shrimp with rosemary on a layer of melted tomato and ginger, and a fresh herb salad for 2.600 CFP. Fish dishes are 2.900-4.500 CFP and lobster gratinée is 6.500 CFP. Pasta is 1.700-2.600 CFP and meat and poultry selections are 2.600-3.750 CFP. Oven braised prime rib for two is 7.800 CFP and a 3-course menu motu is 7.000 CFP. Desserts are 1.300 CFP and include mouth-watering treats such as light lemon mascarpone cream in a caramelized puff pastry with amoretto jelly, or a spicy melting chocolate pyramid with raspberry and bell pepper sherbet. The wine list includes international selections from California, New Zealand and Chile from 3.200-6.650 CFP, French wines priced from 2.750 CFP up to 296.000 CFP for a bottle of Chateau Petrus 1993. Champagnes are 4.800 CFP for a half-bottle of Dela Motte brut to 57.600 CFP for a Salon brut 1995.

The waitresses are Polynesian women from the island of Taha'a who wear white dresses and flowers as they serve the guests. For some of them, this is the first time they have worked outside the home. Patience is needed while waiting for your food and check. On Saturday evenings in the Restaurant

Vanille you can feast on a range of Seafood served buffet style for 8.000 CFP, which includes a dance show.

Restaurant Ohiri is an elegant air-conditioned room with limited seating that is open for dinner only five nights a week (closed on Sunday and Tuesday). It will be necessary to reserve the previous evening if you wish to savor a gourmet *table d'hôte* menu dreamed up by Executive Chef, Véronique Melloul. She prepares theme menus such as Tea & Spice, Cinnamon & Lemon, Crisps & Melts, Honey & Salted Butter and Tomato & Olive, that offer your choice of three dishes for 9.500 CFP or five "degustation" selections for 14.500 CFP. Guests who have had the privilege and pleasure of sampling Véronique's culinary art can only rave about her creative combinations of spiced, sweet and savory tastes. The menu changes every two weeks.

La Plage is the poolside restaurant that gifts you with a magnificent view of the lagoon and Taha'a island while you are enjoying your lunch, served daily from 11:30am to 5:30pm. You can order burgers and light dishes and serve yourself from the salad bar. La Plage is also the setting for Polynesian Evening each Tuesday, when a Polynesian barbecue buffet is served, accompanied by a Polynesian dance group and a fire dance performance. This theme dinner is 6.400 CFP per person.

Tehutu Bar is the hotel's main bar on the upper level, which is open daily except Tuesdays from 3 to 11pm. You can cool off in the swimming pool and swim up for a tropical cocktail at the **Manuia Bar**, which is open daily from 10am to 6pm.

Deluxe

HOTEL VAHINE ISLAND, *Tel. 689/65.67.38. Breakfast, lunch and dinner are served. Breakfast is 2.000 CFP, à la carte lunch is 800-1.600 CFP, and dinner is 5.500 CFP. Add 6% VAT. All major credit cards. Reservations are required for guests not staying in the hotel.*

The complete Continental breakfast is enhanced with local and "house" specialties, such as mango marmalade, vanilla yogurt with locally produced vanilla, fresh tropical salad, toasted French bread, good croissants, coffee and jam. I recall the pleasure of eating my delicious breakfast while looking through the open shoji doors of the dining room and feasting my eyes on the scenery of the white sand beach and turquoise lagoon, as well as the almond and tamanu trees that shaded a sitting area beside the water. Guests have a choice of eating lunch in the dining room or having it served at one of the tables on the beach. A few notable dishes proffered by Chef Nicole for dinner include tuna sashimi with local berries, pickled cabbage and fresh coriander, crispy shrimp with tender baby vegetables in coconut milk, mahi mahi steak flavored with Taha'a vanilla and served with igname (a local root vegetable) chips, salmon of the gods, tagliatelle of vegetables wrapped in a banana leaf, farm raised chicken stuffed with pota (a green leafy vegetable) and creamy curry and coconut sauce, almond tender cake with roasted mangoes and cinnamon honey, chocolate chip pralines in blanc mange coconut, and paper thin pineapple wedges with taro root ice cream.

If you're going to stay at the hotel for a few days, try to persuade Nicole to bake you a coconut cake. The slice I ate was the best I've ever tasted during all the 34-plus years that I've been living under the swaying coconut palms in these islands. Nicole is from Paris and she used to own a gastronomic restaurant in Grasse, France. She picked up a few more culinary ideas when she and her husband, Eric, lived in Kenya and Guadeloupe, and since they have been managing Vahine Island, she has added some local delicacies to her menu.

Superior

CHEZ LOUISE, *Tel. 65.68.88/72.59.18, beside the lagoon in Tiva village. Open daily for lunch and dinner. Add 6% VAT to meals. Mastercard, Visa.*

Louise has earned a good reputation for her crab and lobster and river shrimp specialties and other local style cuisine that is often flavored with vanilla. A marine menu or seafood platter is 4.900 CFP and includes a glass of wine and a surprise for women. A rare treat that you will find on her menu is *cigale de mer*, a very tasty slipper lobster that is priced at 3.350 CFP. Even more delicious and almost impossible to find on anyone's menu is *varo*, which Louise also serves for 5.650 CFP. Special hooks and skills are required to capture these sea centipedes that live in pairs in a hole in the white sand bottom of the lagoon.

Louise is considered "the" specialist in preparing *maa Tahiti* for groups. Prompted by some of the hotels and passenger ships to put the price up so that they can get a commission, she now charges 5.500 CFP per person, which includes a glass of wine. Louise answers the phone with a giggle: "My English no good. My food very good." I'm sure you'll agree. Yachting people can tie their dinghy to the boat dock in front of the restaurant. Louise and her husband Ape also provide simple sleeping accommodations for backpackers on the mountain side of the road.

LA PIROGUE, *Tel. 60.81.45, on Motu Porou. Breakfast, lunch and dinner. Add 6% VAT to meals. American Express, Mastercard, Visa. Reservations are required for guests not staying in the hotel.*

Séverine and Giuliano Tognetti made a good reputation for themselves when they owned a restaurant on Motu Atara, which they laughingly called Yacht Club Atara because so many of their clients arrived on yachts. Now they have opened a 3-star hotel on Motu Porou and they are back in the restaurant business as well, serving fresh fish and seafood, local favorites and international cuisine. A la carte lunch usually consists of poisson cru, sashimi or tuna carpaccio, and a 3-course dinner costs around 5.000 CFP per person.

Moderate
   LE PASSAGE, *Tel. 65.66.75, on mountain side in Faaaha. Breakfast, lunch and dinner. No credit cards. Add 6% VAT to meals. Reservations are required for guests not staying in the pension.*
   The discreetly sophisticated character of the lagoon is the theme chosen by Marie-Thérèse Meunier-Coeroli, who uses local products and organically grown fruits and vegetables from her own garden when preparing her fine cuisine. A menu beside the road announces the specialties of the day, which may be carpaccio of salmon for 1.500 CFP or shrimp curry for 1.800 CFP, with a dessert for 800 CFP. These plats du jour can be served without reservations, and if you call in advance, you can have a delicious 3-course meal for 3.800 CFP.
   MARINA ITI, *Tel. 65.60.87/65.61.01. Breakfast, lunch and dinner. No credit cards. Reservations are required for guests not staying in the pension.*
   The Marina Iti Restaurant is renown for its cuisine, which is made with fresh local products, mainly fish and seafood, but also the fruits and vegetables from an island that is noted for the quality of its vanilla and agricultural produce. Marie Adeline Robin changes the menu daily according to what the fishermen bring her and the tastes of clients staying in the family pension. Although 95% of the dinners contain fish, during my most recent stay I was served a tarte with tomatoes, onions and Roquefort cheese, followed by a pintade with taro patties and slices of fried bananas, with *gateau a l'orange* (orange cake) for dessert. Highly recommended and moderately priced.
   RESTAURANT HIBISCUS, *Tel. 65.61.06. Breakfast, lunch and dinner are served. American Express, Mastercard and Visa. Add 6% VAT to meals. Reservations are required for guests not staying in the hotel.*
   Leo and Lolita Morou have built a new 200-seat restaurant and bar on the dock across the road from their small family hotel. The emphasis is on local specialties and the fish catch of the day and the average meal costs around 4.000 CFP per person. The menu lists old style *poisson cru*, *terrine de fois gras à la papaya*, crab with citron, curried river shrimp, grilled lobster and *varo*, a succulent sea centipede cooked in butter and white wine. The Hibiscus hosts a Tahitian *tamaara'a* feast each Saturday night Guests are expected to chip in to pay the musicians and dancers who entertain.

Economy to Moderate
   RESTAURANT TAHAA MAITAI, *Tel. 65.70.85. On the waterfront in Haamene village. 3 moorings for boats. Open 10am-2:30pm and 6:45-8pm Monday–Friday. Closed Saturday noon and open at night. Open Sunday noon and closed at night. Closed all day Monday. Mastercard, Visa.*
   Frenchman Bruno François serves salads from 600-1.250 CFP, poisson cru for 900 CFP, fish and seafood for 1.300-1.550 CFP, fish catch of the day for 1.250 CFP and meat dishes for 1.250-1.550 CFP. A sandwich is 350 CFP, a

cheeseburger and fries or salad costs 1.150 CFP, 14 choices of ice cream are 150 CFP a scoop, chocolate profiteroles are 450 CFP and home made pastry is 350 CFP. Wine is served by the glass, carafe or bottle. Hinano beer is 400 CFP and 550 CFP, juice is 270 CFP and a 1.5-liter of Coke is 850 CFP. He caters to a local clientele, as well as French residents and visitors from many countries.

SNACK MAC CHINA 99, *Tel. 65.67.81.* In Haamene village across road from post office. Breakfast, pastry shop and Chinese food to go.

Seeing the Sights

Hibiscus Activities, *Tel. 65.61.06,* is located at Pension Hibiscus. Lolita, also known as Tearere Ariitu-Morou, leads excursions by 4WD to discover the summits of Tahaa's lookout points, to visit a vanilla plantation, copra drying platform, a black pearl farm and to explore the fauna and flora of Tahaa, including a stop at the Hibiscus Foundation's turtle reserve. All the boat activities are also available, including snorkeling, tours around the island and picnics on a motu.

Poe-Rani Tours, *Tel. 65.60.25/78.80.25; Fax 65.64.20; VHF 11; E-mail: rani-poe@mail.pf.* Teva and Rooverta Ebb operate Land Rover tours for a minimum of 4 and maximum of 7 passengers. A complete sightseeing tour takes you across the island, to visit a vanilla farm, a cultured pearl farm and a turtle park.

Tahaa Tours Excursion, *Tel./Fax 65.62.18, cell 79.27.56,* is operated by Edwin and Jacqueline Mama. They provide guided tours by two Landrovers that cross the island from Haamene to Patio, stopping to admire the panoramic views from the mountain road. Other stops include a visit to a vanilla farm and a pearl farm.

Vai Poe Excursions, *Tel. 65.60.83/78.67.68 or 79.26.01.* Pension Patricia and Daniel have three 4-wheel drive vehicles that are used for guided circle island tours and 4x4 safaris into Tahaa's mountains and valleys, with stops to visit a vanilla farm and their own pearl farm. A half-day excursion is 4.000 CFP per person. An all day boat and safari excursion from Raiatea includes a picnic on a motu for 7.000 CFP per person.

Vanilla Tours, *Tel. 65.62.46, Fax 65.68.97, VHF 9; E-mail: vanilla.tours@mail.pf.* Alain and Christina Plantier have a 4-hour excursion that takes 4-8 people on a botanical tour and mountain safari by 4-wheel drive vehicle through Tahaa's luxuriant vegetation, across the island, through the mountains and from bay to bay, to view the scenery from these vantage points. You will visit a tropical fruit garden and vanilla plantation, where you will learn about this fragrant "brown gold" and how it is "married" by hand. This tour operates daily except Sunday, departing at 8am from Hurepiti Bay. The cost is 5.000 CFP per adult and 2.750 CFP for children under 12 years. An optional visit to a pearl farm is 500 CFP extra per person. People on yachts can safely bring their boats to Hurepiti Bay, just in front of the pass to/from Bora Bora, and use one of the two moorings provided in front of the Plantier home.

Land tours are also provided by: **Dave's Tour**s, *Tel. 65.62.42*; **Hanalei Tours**, *Tel. 65.67.60;* and **Remuna Tours**, *Tel. 65.63.28/72.93.28;*

Sports & Recreation
Deep Sea Fishing
See the section on Deep Sea Fishing charters in the *Raiatea* chapter.

Lagoon Excursions and Black Pearl Farms
Dave's Tours, *Tel./Fax 65.62.42*, is operated by Dave Atiniu in Haamene. He has a 28-foot locally built Fiberglas boat with a sun awning that he uses for excursions that begin in Uturoa or Taha'a. Full-day excursions include snorkeling in the coral gardens and a picnic on a motu. These tours can also be combined with 4WD land excursions.

Monique Cruise, *Tel./Fax 65.62.48*, is owned by Monique Tuahu *in Haamene*. She has a locally built 27-foot Fiberglas motorboat that is covered for comfortable cruising around the island of Tahaa. Stops are made to visit the fish enclosures, pearl farms and *motu* islets.

Poe-Rani Farm, *Tel. 65.60.25/78.80.25; Fax 65.64.20; VHF 11; E-mail: rani-poe@mail.pf.* is owned by Teva and Rooverta Ebbs *in Haamene Bay*. Guided excursions take you to the pearl farm, where you will learn about how the oysters are grafted and the beautiful black pearls are produced. You can also buy Tahitian products here.

Tahaa Discovery / Motu Pearl Farm, *Tel. 65.66.67; Fax 65.69.18; cell 79.28.92/72.33.01; VHF 08.* Matahiarii Laughlin takes you by 30-passenger motor launch or a 60-passenger covered catamaran on a half-day excursion to visit Motu Pearl Farm, the black pearl farm of the Laughlin family in Faaaha Bay. Demonstrations are available from 9am to 5pm to explain how the pearl is cultivated inside the mother-of-pearl oyster. Their boutique is open from 9am to 10pm and you'll surely want to see their collection of pearls for sale. Optional visits can also be made by 4WD vehicles to visit a vanilla plantation and see the panoramic sights of Tahaa. Tahaa Discovery also specializes in organizing barbecue picnics and Tahitian buffets on the motu for groups up to 200 people. They can provide VIP tours on request.

Tahaa Terapu Tours, *Tel. 65.69.55*, is owned by Reynald Vaiho of Vaitoare. He has a 36-foot locally built wooden motorboat for 6-12 passengers.

Tahaa Tours Excursion, *Tel./Fax 65.62.18, cell 79.27.56.* Edwin and Jacqueline Mama provide lagoon excursions on board their motorized outrigger canoes, which include a visit to a pearl farm and a picnic and swim at a motu. These tours usually originate in Raiatea and can be combined with a 4WD land excursion in Taha'a.

Hibiscus Foundation Saves the Sea Turtles

Leo and Lolita Morou, who own the Hotel-Restaurant Hibiscus in Tahaa, started the **Hibiscus Foundation** in 1992. Their goals are to fight against underwater spearfishing and turtle poachers, and to rescue the turtles that have been injured or accidentally trapped in fish parks inside the lagoon near the passes. When they find these turtles Leo and his volunteer helpers shelter them in a special enclosure for a few days, then tag them for future identification before releasing the turtles into the open ocean. By the end of 2003 the Hibiscus Foundation had saved 1,184 turtles, mostly the Cholera Midas, the green sea turtle, which is the most common and the tastiest. The hawksbill turtle, Eretmochelys imbricata, the large-headed turtle, Caretta caretta gigas, and the lute turtle, Dermochelys coriacea, have also been rescued by Leo and Lolita, and their network of yachting friends.

In the olden days when the arii, the Polynesian chiefs, ruled the people, the honu (turtles) were considered sacred and their meat was reserved only for the kings, priests and keepers of the marae, where the Maohi people worshipped their god Oro. The marae that were dedicated to Oro were distinguished by stones that were shaped in the form of turtle heads, and turtle petroglyphs were carved in the basaltic rocks. The turtles are just as tapu (taboo, sacred or forbidden) today as they were then, because they have been declared an endangered species by the local government.

Vai Poe Farm - **Vai Poe Tours**, *Tel. 65.60.83/78.67.68, cell 79.26.01*. Patricia and Daniel Amaru, who operate a pension in Haamene, also have a black pearl farm and **Vai Poe Boutique** in front of the pension. There is a little classroom where explanations and demonstrations are given in French and English, covering the whole range of black pearl farming, and they even open an oyster to show you the pearl inside. Vai Poe Tours has four boats available for half- or full-day day boat tours that include visits to the Vai Poe pearl farm and boutique, as well as a vanilla plantation and Motu Mahaea, for 4.000 CFP per person. Full-day boat tours also include a visit to a fish park and a picnic on Motu Mahaea, for 6.500 CFP per person.

The Raiatea chapter also lists several tour operators under *Lagoon and Motu Excursions* who provide boat excursions to Taha'a and its motu islets. Some of these guides are: **André TopSpots**, *Tel. 60.05.20*; **l'Excursion Bleue**, *Tel. 66.10.90*; and **West Coast Charters**, *Tel. 66.45.39*.

Charter Yachts
Information on the yacht charter companies is given in *Tahiti, Moorea* and *Raiatea* chapters.

Day Sailing
Bisou Futé Charter, *Tel. 65.64.97/79.11.42; Fax 65.69.08; E-mail: jeanyvon@mail.pf; www.bisoufute.com.* This 51-foot Beneteau monohull is owned by Jean-Yvon Nechachby and is based in Apu Bay, Tahaa. This yacht is available for full-day sailing cruises inside the Raiatea-Tahaa lagoon. Lunch is served on board or on a motu islet. Private cruises can be organized on request to other Society Islands.

Fai Manu Cruises, *Tel. 65.62.52; Fax 65.69.08; E-mail: faimanu@mail.pf; www.faimanu.com.* This 50-foot fast speed catamaran is owned by Louis Corneglio and is based in Apu Bay in Taha'a. A maximum of 16 passengers can sail around the island, with a picnic on request. Weekly cruises are available for 8 passengers.

See information on **Atara Royal** and **Catamaran Tane** under *Charter Yachts* in the Raiatea chapter. They also offer day sailing and sunset cruises.

Massages and Spas
Manea Spa, *Tel. 60.84.00*, is built at the edge of a salt-water lake on Motu Tautau, providing body and facial care for men and women, most of whom are guests at Le Taha'a Private Island & Spa. Body work can be a relaxing massage with monoi oil made from coconut and scented with *tiare Tahiti* flowers or other blossoms and herbs, or you can choose a combination of different techniques, such as petrissage that is used in Swedish massage, or opt for lomi-lomi, acupressure or reflexology. A 30-minute massage starts at 6.500 CFP, a 50-minute massage starts at 11.000 CFP and an 80-minute massage is 15.000 CFP. You can have a 4-hand massage or you and your partner can be massaged in synchronization, leaving you with an unforgettable sensation of harmony. Open air rain showers, exfoliates, body wraps and masks are yours for the asking, and you can even get treated with a Mahana Manea if you stay in the sun too long. Facial care for ladies includes the 50-minute Hohoa Matai treatment for 13.000 CFP and the Hohoa Patitifa, a 50-minute natural treatment using hibiscus, coconut, honey and fruit, for 11.000 CFP. The Hoho'a Tane or Tino Tane for 11.000 CFP are 50-minute hydrating, cleansing and exfoliating treatments for men. The ultimate choice is the Poe Manea (Manea pearl) that is a complete treatment that lasts 3 hours and 20 minutes and costs 30.000 CFP for one person and 53.000 CFP per couple.

Scuba Diving
There are more than 25 recorded dive spots, including 8 passes, around Taha'a and Raiatea, all reachable by boat within 10-25 minutes from Taha'a.

You can see reef sharks and humphead wrasses year-round in water temperatures of 60-80º Fahrenheit. Of special interest to divers are underwater caves and a wrecked ship.

Shark Dive Polynesia, *Tel. 689/65.65.55; Tel./Fax 689/65.65.60; E-mail: shark@dive.pf; www.dive.pf* is based at Universal Scuba Diving Institute (Institut Subaquatique) in Raai Bay at PK 12 near Patio. Bertil Venzo is an International CMAS *** monitor, FFESSM and NAUI dive master. He can give certification in CMAS and FFESSM diving. He specializes in private dives for individuals, couples or groups, and speaks good English, French, Russian, a little Spanish and a little Italian. He works with people staying in hotels, aboard charter yachts or private boats, as well as ship passengers. He charges 36.000 CFP for 1-3 people for a 2-tank dive and for 3-8 people he charges 12.000 CFP per person for the expedition, which is 6.000 CFP for each of the two dives. Night dives are also available. Diving equipment rental is 2.500 CFP per person.

Taha'a Blue Nui Diving Center, *Tel./Fax 689/65.67.78; E-mail: tahaabluenui@mail.pf; www.bluenui.com* is located at Le Taha'a Private Island & Spa on Motu Tautau. Stéphane Hamon is the manager and PADI/CMAS dive instructor who can take certified divers for a Fun dive for 6.700 CFP, a 2-tank Fun dive for 13.000 CFP, an introductory dive or lesson for 7.500 CFP, or a night dive for 8.000 CFP. A package of 5 Fun dives is sold for 31.000 CFP and a 10-dive package is 59.000 CFP, and both packages are available and usable in the four Blue Nui Diving Centers in Taha'a, Bora Bora, Manihi and Tikehau. A CMAS* or PADI Open Water (referral) certification is 8.000 CFP, and after the initiation you must add a minimum of 4 lessons and purchase the diving log book, which costs 2.000 CFP. A private half-day dive is 47.000 CFP. Modern equipment includes a 30-foot aluminum boat with a 140 HP outboard engine and equipment for 15 divers, including shorty wet suits.

Shopping

Motu Pearl Boutique, in Faaaha, *Tel. 65.66.67*, sells black pearls, keishis, mabes and black pearl jewelry. They also sell locally made clothing, *pareos*, curios, and traditional arts and crafts combining mother-of-pearl with local woods and woven coconut fibers. **Poerani Pearls**, *Tel. 65.60.25*, and **Vai Poe Pearls**, *Tel. 65.60.83*, both in Haamene Bay, sell black pearls from their own farms, as well as locally made jewelry and arts and crafts. **Chez Sophie** in Hurepiti Bay, *Tel. 65.62.56*, sells hand painted *pareos*.

Practical Information

Banks

Banque Socredo, *Tel. 65.66.53*, is located in Patio, and **Banque de Tahiti**, *Tel. 65.63.14*, is in the Teva Uri building in Haamene.

Doctors

There is a government operated medical and dental center in Patio, *Tel. 65.63.31*, and a dispensary in Haamene, *Tel. 65.61.03*. Doctor Laurent Jereczek has a private practice in Haamene, *Tel. 65.60.60*, and Doctor Evelyne Kerleau, *Tel. 65.65.67*, has a private practice in Patio.

Drugstore

Pharmacie Tahaa, *Tel. 65.67.69*, is in the Commercial building in Haamene.

Police

A brigade of the French *gendarmerie* is posted in Patio and Haamene, *Tel. 65.64.07*.

Post Office and Telecommunications Office

There is a **Post Office** in Haamene, *Tel. 65.60.11*, and another in Patio, *Tel. 65.64.70*. All telecommunications and postal services are available.

Yacht Services

Hibiscus Yacht Club, *B.P. 184, Haamene, Tahaa 98734; Tel. 689/ 65.61.06/79.28.81; Fax 689/65.65.65; VHF 68-Hibiscus; E-mail: hibiscus@tahaa-tahiti.com; www.tahaa-tahiti.com; www.tahiti-tahaa.com*. The Hotel-Restaurant Hibiscus is at the entrance to Haamene Bay. There are 14 free yacht moorings and services include fresh water, free showers, garbage disposal, message service and, on request, fresh bread can be delivered to your yacht daily except Sunday. You can also catch a ride with the local people to go to church on Sundays.

Tahaa Yacht Club or **Latitude 16 Sud**, *Tel. 689/65.61.01; Fax 689/ 65.63.87; VHF 68; E-mail: marinaiti@mail.pf*. There are moorings for 12 boats near the Marina Iti in Apu Bay. People on yachts have use of the water, showers, laundry facilities, garbage disposal, ice, and Internet services. Be sure to order your bread in advance and make advance reservations for meals in the Marina Iti restaurant.

Chapter 18

BORA BORA

When you tell your friends: "I'm going to **Bora Bora**," you can be sure that this simple phrase will bring envy and longing to their romantic hearts and stir a feeling of wanderlust in their vagabonding souls.

Bora Bora has become the center of tourism in Tahiti and Her Islands. Some of the world's famous stars of stage, cinema and television vacation here, flying directly from the international airport in Tahiti to Bora Bora, without a thought of seeing the other islands of French Polynesia. European royalty, sheiks, maharajas and international jet-setters find the serenity and privacy they seek on this magnificent little island. Cinematographers discover the ideal tropical setting for movies, often starring the islanders themselves.

Bora Bora, perhaps more than any other island in the South Seas, teases the imagination of travel writers, who search for adequate phrases of 'purple prose' to describe the spectacular beauty of its craggy, sculpted mountains, the palm-crowned islets that seem to float just inside the coral reef, surrounded by a confection of white sandy beaches that dip down into a lagoon of opalescent blues and greens.

Bora Bora lies 260 kilometers (161 miles) northwest of Tahiti in the Leeward Society Islands. Your first glimpse of Bora Bora may be from the window of an Air Tahiti plane, at the end of a 50-minute direct flight from Tahiti. Bora Bora from aloft appears as a precious emerald in a setting of turquoise, encircled by a protective necklace of sparkling pearls. You will have a great view of Bora Bora as the ATR-72 banks for landing on Motu Mute. If you are coming directly from Tahiti, the left side of the aircraft usually provides the best scenery. If your flight stops in Raiatea first, then you should sit on the right side for spectacular views of the mountains and lagoon. This all depends on the landing pattern used for that particular flight, of course.

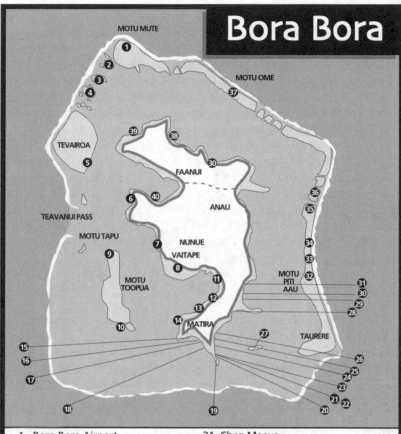

1. Bora Bora Airport
2. Private Island
3. Le Paradis
4. Mai Moana Island
5. Bora Bora Pearl Beach Resort
6. Bora Bora Yacht Club
7. TOPdive Resort
8. Vaitape Boat Dock
9. Bora Bora Lagoon Resort
10. Bora Bora Nui Resort & Spa
11. Moon B&B
12. Chez Rosina
13. Village Pauline
14. Hotel Bora Bora
15. Village Temanuata Lagoon
16. Hotel Matira
17. Matira Beach
18. Chez Nono
19. Chez Robert & Tina
20. InterContinental Moana Beach Resort Bora Bora
21. Chez Maeva
22. Village Temanuata Beach
23. Bora Bora Beach Lodge
24. Le Maitai Polynesia
25. Novotel Bora Bora Beach Resort
26. Sofitel Marara
27. Sofitel Motu
28. Club Mediterranee
29. Chez Teipo
30. Pension Bora Lagoonarium
31. Chez Henriette
32. Hotel InterContinental Bora Bora
33. Relais Matie
34. Eden Beach
35. Le Meridien
36. Lagoonarium
37. Hotel Ritz-Carlton
38. Musée de la Marine
39. Bora Bora Condos
40. Farepiti Wharf

Paul-Emile Victor - The Colors of Bora Bora

Paul-Emile Victor, a French polar explorer, artist and writer, retired to Bora Bora with his wife **Colette**, and lived on Motu Tane in Bora Bora until his death in 1995. His impression of seeing Bora Bora from the cockpit of an airplane in 1958, after a 25-year absence from the island, was published in the 1970s in *Distance*, the in-flight magazine of the former UTA-French airline:

"...Never before had I seen waters the colour of the rainbow or like fireworks, springing right out of some maddened imagination, or from Gauguin's own palette. Waters the colour of bronze, of copper, gold, silver, mother-of-pearl, pearl, jade, emeralds, moonlight or the aurora borealis. The stars themselves seemed to have fallen into the sea, scintillating brilliantly on the lagoon's surface, in bright sunlight...Who could find the words, what poet the images, what painter even the colours, to describe this scene? I give up."

If you arrive in Bora Bora by cruise ship, inter-island ferryboat or by sailboat, you will also be impressed by the kaleidoscope of shimmering iridescence that greets your eye at every turn. Aquamarine. Lapis lazuli. Turquoise. Cobalt. Periwinkle. Sapphire. Emerald. Jade. Ultramarine. Indigo. You'll love counting the shades of color in the sparkling waters of Bora Bora's world-famous lagoon.

Mythology

Polynesian mythology claims that Ofai Honu, a volcanic boulder carved with petroglyphs of turtles, was possessed with godly power and mated with the Pahia Mountain, then called Hohorai. From their union a son was born, whose name was Firiamata O Vavau. This first great chief gave his name to the island and for many years this fabled paradise was known as **Vavau**, which means first-born. Legend says that Vavau was the first island that sprang up after the mythical creation of the sacred island of Havai'i (Raiatea). The beautiful little islet beside the pass of Vavau was named Motu Tapu, the sacred islet.

Geology

Bora Bora was formed by volcanic eruptions some three to four million years ago. It is one of the oldest in the chain of the Leeward Islands. Through eons and centuries it has been eroding and sinking. One to two miles inside the fringing reef rise the sharp cliffs of basaltic rock that form the central mountain chain running through the principal island of Bora Bora. Mount

Otemanu, at 727 meters (2,384 feet), Mount Pahia, at 661 meters (2,168 feet), and Mount Hue at 619 meters (2,030 feet), are the most spectacular chimney peaks of the crater that once spewed molten lava. The center of this sunken volcano lies far beneath the electric blue of Povai Bay, and the smaller islands of Toopua and Toopua-Iti are the opposite walls of the crater, formed when the earth erupted beneath the ocean. The Teavanui Pass is the only navigable break in the coral wall that has formed on top of the caldeira of the sunken volcano.

If you want to see what an atoll is like without heading out to the Tuamotu archipelago, then you should visit a *motu* in Bora Bora. These islets have the same flora and fauna of the atolls, with the advantage of having a high island just a five-minute boat-ride away. Walk along the ocean side of a motu and you will find *miki miki* bushes, sea grape, pandanus, the South Seas rosewood tree called *miro*, the huge *tou* trees with their orange flowers and precious wood so desired by sculptors, *tamanu* trees whose fruit gives us a healing oil for the treatment of deep burns and cuts, the Australian pine, which is called *aito* in these islands, and the *tiare kahaia*, whose decorative branches are used in the construction of the typical Polynesian bungalows built by most hotels.

Legend of Hiro

One of the most famous characters in Polynesian oral history was **Hiro**, god of thieves. Hiro hid out on **Toopua Island**, across Povai Bay from the main island. Using the dragonfly to distract attention, Hiro and his band of thieves robbed their victims at night, between sunset and the first cockcrow. Hiro's constant companion was a white cock, the moa uo. This rooster became excited when Hiro was trying to steal Toopua Island and began to crow, breaking the magic power and so enraging Hiro that he hurled the bird against the face of Pahia mountain, where the imprint still remains. Although Hiro abandoned his plan to steal the island, he detached a large chunk of it that is called Toopua-Iti, the islet that is separated by only a few feet from Toopua.

The view of Bora Bora's famous mountains of **Otemanu** (sea of birds) and the twin peaks of **Pahia** and **Hue** are best photographed through this opening, where just underneath the clear surface of the lagoon lie rocks known as **Hiro's Canoe**. Ashore on Toopua Island are giant stones said to have been left by Hiro and his son Marama, tossed about in a game played by the two giants. Deep inside the coconut forest is a gigantic rock, **Hiro's Bell** that used to reverberate when struck. This basaltic boulder was damaged during the construction of a hotel on Toopua Island, however, and now sits as a silent witness to Polynesia's past.

Go for a walk along the seashore early in the morning and you will see the herons fishing, and during a picnic on the *motu* perhaps you will catch a glimpse of the lovely white fairy tern with its black button eyes.

The Exploitation of Bora Bora

I had not heard of Bora Bora until I read the *Sports Illustrated* magazine mentioned in the sidebar on the next page that showed Erwin Christian water-skiing in front of the Hotel Bora Bora. That was in January 1968. I was so impressed by the beauty of the purple-colored mountains of Bora Bora that I just had to see this scene in person. The article that accompanied the photos stated that the Hotel Bora Bora was the most expensive hotel in the South Pacific, and had the best restaurant. The rates were $35 for a single room and $48 for a double bungalow per day, American plan. The only other hotel on the island was Club Med's Noa Noa, with a few simple bungalows beside the lagoon in Vaitape village.

My husband and I spent two weeks at the Hotel Bora Bora in August 1968, and one of the best memories I have of that visit was the all–day excursion around the island aboard an outrigger sailing canoe. We were the only passengers and we had a helmsman to steer the canoe while another Tahitian fellow stood on the outrigger on either side of the boat, depending on which way the wind was blowing. Sometimes it tipped precariously to the left or right with the gusts of wind. We stopped for a picnic lunch on an uninhabited *motu*, where Hotel Le Méridien is built today. Instead of showing us how to open and use a coconut, tie a *pareo* or cook us a barbecue lunch, our guides took a nap under the palm trees while we ate the lunch that had been prepared in the hotel kitchen. Then we napped too, lying on the palm fronds our guides had gathered for us. In spite of almost constant exposure to the tropical sun, it was an exhilarating trip and one we could never repeat.

When we returned to the Hotel Bora Bora two years later, the circle island tours were done by motor boat. Later the motorized outrigger canoe took the lead and still holds that place of honor today, transporting visitors around the island for a morning or afternoon tour, or an all-day excursion that includes several stops: to feed the sharks, pet the sting rays, admire the manta rays, snorkel in the coral gardens and dine in style on a marvelous *motu* with a white sand beach. There are still several of these uninhabited islets around the island, but some of them are now being developed with 5-star hotels.

Today Bora Bora is an island devoted to tourism, with more luxurious hotels than on any other island of French Polynesia. In addition to the eight major hotels on the main island, at publication time in October 2004, there were six international class hotels in operation on the offshore *motu* islets, with two more 5-star hotels under construction, another getting ready to break ground and two more projects waiting for their building permits.

The **Ritz Carlton**, which may be called the **Royal Bora Bora Resort & Spa**, is scheduled to open at the beginning of 2006 on Motu Ome with 80 bungalows and 5 suites built on stilts over the lagoon, plus 10 beach bungalows, 5 villas and 2 suites with a pool and Jacuzzi. The plans include a panoramic overwater restaurant with a central aquarium in the lagoon, a fresh water swimming pool and spa.

The **Hotel InterContinental Bora Bora** will open in March 2006 with 112 luxury bungalows built on a motu called Tiarepuomu, located on the east side of Bora Bora, 600 meters (1,980 feet) south of Le Meridien hotel. On most maps of Bora Bora this is shown as part of the long Motu Piti Aau islet. There will be 84 overwater bungalows, 16 garden *fares* and 12 day *fares* on the 10 hectare (25-acre) site, which includes 800 meters (2,640 feet) of white sand beach. The hotel will have two restaurants, a bar, a thalassotherapy spa, tennis courts, swimming pool and a full range of nautical activities. There will also be an employee village to provide housing for some of the staff.

The next big hotel project on Bora Bora will be the construction of 110 bungalows and suites over the lagoon and on the 1-kilometer long beach of Motu Tofari, which is also shown as Motu Piti Aau on most maps. Thierry Barbion of TB Promotion in Tahiti, who is building this hotel, also owns the new Radisson Plaza Resort in Tahiti. Work on this new 5-star hotel is supposed to get underway in January 2005 and **Four Seasons Hotels & Resorts** will handle the marketing, management, reservations, restaurants, decoration and spa.

The Société Polynésienne d'Investissement Hôteliers (SPIH), or Polynesian Hotel Investment Company, has applied for a building permit to construct **Hotel Anapa**, a 5-star property on Motu Tevairoa, the same islet where the Bora Bora Pearl Beach is located. Plans call for 30 bungalows to be built over the lagoon and 20 bungalows over an interior lagoon or swampy pond of brackish water. Mosquitoes love swamps as anyone who has ever stayed in the garden pool *fares* at Bora Bora Pearl Beach can testify. In February 2004 **China Travel Service** (CTS) announced plans for a hotel project to be built on Bora Bora, with an opening date for 2007. No further details have been made available since then.

Bora Bora's mayor has agreed that the number of hotel rooms should be limited to 1,500 maximum. At press time there were already 942 international class rooms on the main island and motu islets, and once the Ritz Carlton, InterContinental, Four Seasons and Anapa hotel projects are completed, there will be 1,316 hotel rooms on Bora Bora. If the CTS project does materialize that will mean another 100 or so units, which leaves room for still one more smaller 5-star hotel before the limit is reached.

In addition to the international class hotels, there are also more than a dozen pensions, hostels and lodgings in family homes on the main island and on the *motu* islets. And let's not forget the condos, millionaire's villas and other luxurious accommodations on the main island, as well as on the privately owned motu islets. There's too much traffic on the circle island road and too much traffic in the lagoon, with the cruise ship tenders, hotel shuttle boats, outrigger speed canoes and jet-skis zooming about from the airport to the hotels and village, and back and forth from the main island to the *motu* islets. Bora Bora is not boring at all, contrary to what has been published by jaded travel writers. It truly offers a wonderful experience for anyone who enjoys Nature in a tropical setting. In spite of all the human traffic the lagoon of Bora Bora is still so outstandingly beautiful that I fall in love with it all over again each time I visit the "Pearl of the Pacific."

Erwin Christian

The January 15, 1968 edition of Sports Illustrated magazine included an article on the island of Bora Bora, with a photo of **Erwin Christian** water-skiing in front of the Hotel Bora Bora. The story said that Christian (no relation to **Fletcher Christian**, the Bounty mutineer) had jumped ship in Tahiti in 1963, where he scratched out a living for seven weeks while he explored the mountains and undersea world surrounding the island. His send-off party at the airport was so much fun that Christian changed his mind at the last moment and decided not to board his jet plane.

Instead of going to Bermuda to accept a well-paying and challenging job in the hotel business there, the 27-year old native of Silesia eventually took a job as assistant manager of the Hotel Bora Bora, which at that time was an American-owned hotel with 18 small bungalows that had opened June 1, 1961. Christian soon fell in love with a beautiful and charming local girl named Ate (pronounced Ah-tay), and became a father. He created Moana Adventure Tours and served as director of the vast watery playground that is formed by the world's most beautiful lagoon.

After many years of taking tourists to visit the Bora Bora lagoon aboard his glass bottom boat, to walk on the reef, scuba dive, spearfish, to troll for fish or water-ski behind his runabout, Christian began to concentrate on his photography. He has taken thousands of pictures for post cards, calendars, posters and several coffee table books about Bora Bora and all the other island groups of French Polynesia. The bookstores, newsstands, gift shops and hotel boutiques carry Erwin Christian's photos, and you can see the whole collection when you visit his Moana Arts Boutique, adjacent to the Hotel Bora Bora.

᭪

Arrivals & Departures

Arriving By Air

Air Tahiti has three to seven 50-minute direct flights daily between Tahiti and Bora Bora, as well as flights that stop in Huahine and/or Raiatea. The fare is 13.900 CFP one-way for adults, and 25.500 CFP round-trip, taxes and airport shuttle boat in Bora Bora included. There are three flights daily from Moorea, either direct or stopping in Huahine or Raiatea. The one-way fare from Moorea to Bora Bora is 17.900 CFP, from Huahine to Bora Bora it is 7.500 CFP, and from Raiatea to Bora Bora the fare is 5.900 CFP. You can also fly to Bora Bora from Rangiroa or Tikehau for 23.000 CFP, and from Manihi you'll pay 26.000 CFP. **Air Tahiti reservation**s: Tahiti, *Tel. 86.42.42;* Moorea, *Tel. 55.06.00*; Huahine, *Tel. 68.77.02/60.62.60*; Raiatea *Tel. 60.04.44/60.04.40*; Bora Bora, *Tel. 60.53.53/60.53.00*; Rangiroa, *Tel. 93.11.00*; Tikehau *Tel. 96.22.66*; Manihi, *Tel. 96.43.34/96.42.71.*

The **Bora Bora airport** is located *on Motu Mute*, a 15-minute boat ride to the main village of Vaitape or by 10-15 minutes by luxury launch direct to your deluxe hotel, depending on its distance from the airport.

As soon as you step off the plane you can pick up brochures and get information inside the modern terminal building, which also has a snack bar, boutique and toilets. The boats leave for Vaitape village about 20 minutes after your flight lands in Bora Bora. The voyage across the emerald silk lagoon will help to set the pace for a vacation on a small island, and you can take some fabulous photographs of the island and motu islets during this crossing. If your hotel doesn't have a private launch to the airport, then you will be met at the boat dock in Vaitape village and driven to your hotel. Land transportation from the Vaitape quay to the small hotels, pensions and campgrounds is also provided by *le truck*, mini-vans or taxi. The Air Tahiti office is located on the quay of Vaitape, and there are public phone booths just outside.

You can also get to Bora Bora by chartering an airplane in Tahiti from **Wan Air**, *Tel. 50.44.17, cell 77.03.79*; **Air Archipels**, *Tel. 81.30.30*; or **Air Tahiti**, *Tel. 86.42.42.*

Arriving By Boat

All the inter-island transport boats dock at the Fare Piti quay in Faanui, 3 kilometers (1.9 miles) from Vaitape village. It would be advisable to arrange with your hotel or pension to have someone meet you when you arrive. You can rent a car, scooter or mountain bike across the street. A *le truck* also provides service from the boat dock to the hotels in Matira.

Hawaiki Nui, *Tel. 54.99.54, Fax 45.24.44, E-mail: sarlstim@mail.pf* leaves the Motu Uta dock in Papeete each Tuesday at 4pm and arrives at the Fare Piti quay in Bora Bora on Wednesday at 8am, after stopping in Huahine and Raiatea. The Thursday trip leaves Papeete at 4pm directly to Raiatea and then on to Bora Bora, arriving at the Fare Piti dock on Friday at 5:30am.

Passengers are limited to 12, who sleep on the deck for 1.750 CFP or in one of four cabins containing 2 berths and a toilet. A berth costs 4.950 CFP from Papeete to all the Leeward Islands. Meals are available on board the ship. For the Thursday voyage passengers must have accommodations in a cabin as the ship transports fuel from Tahiti to the Leeward Islands.

Vaeanu, *Tel. 41.25.35, Fax 41.24.34, E-mail: torehiatetu@mail.pf* departs from the Motu Uta dock in Papeete at 5pm on Monday and Thursday, stopping in Huahine, Raiatea, and Tahaa, arriving in Bora Bora Tuesday and Friday at 10am. This cargo ship also carries 90 passengers and has sleeping space for 32 people in cabins with two or three berths, private or shared toilets. The one-way deck fare from Tahiti to Bora Bora is 2.120 CFP, from Huahine to Bora Bora deck fare is 1.690 CFP; and from Raiatea or Tahaa to Bora Bora it costs 1.400 CFP. The one-way fare for a berth ranges from 4.400 CFP to 4.929 CFP and the cabins are 9.858 CFP, 11.978 CFP and 13.197 CFP, depending on the number of berths and toilet facilities. There is a restaurant on board and meals are extra. Reservations for cabin space must be paid in full before 9am on the fixed date of departure from Papeete.

Maupiti Express II, *Tel./Fax 689/66.37.81; Cell 78.27.22*. This new 140-passenger boat began service at the end of September, 2004, replacing the 62-passenger boat that was formerly used to transport passengers from Bora Bora to Maupiti and Raiatea. The *Maupiti Express II* leaves Raiatea at 4pm each Monday and Wednesday and arrives at the Vaitape quay in Bora Bora at 5:45pm. On Friday it leaves Raiatea at 2pm and arrives in Bora Bora at 3:45pm, and on Friday and Sunday it leaves Raiatea at 6pm, arriving in Bora Bora at 7:45pm. On Tuesday, Thursday and Saturday the Maupiti-Bora Bora shuttle leaves Maupiti at 4pm and arrives in Vaitape at 5:45pm. The one-way fare is 2.500 CFP and round-trip is 3.500 CFP. Passengers under 12 years pay half price.

Departing By Air

The main office of **Air Tahiti**, *Tel. 60.53.53/60.53.00*, is at the boat dock in Vaitape village. Most of the hotels take care of reconfirming your departure flight, or you can do it yourself by telephone. The Bora Bora Navette, Air Tahiti's shuttle boat, leaves the Vaitape village dock one hour and 15 minutes before each scheduled departure and check-in time at the Air Tahiti office on Motu Mute is one hour before your flight departs. Air Tahiti flies from Bora Bora to Tahiti five to nine times a day. Most of the flights are direct and the other flights stop in Huahine or Raiatea. There is a daily flight from Bora Bora to Moorea, with a stop in Huahine, daily non-stop flights from Bora Bora to Huahine and direct flights from Bora Bora to Raiatea daily except Tuesday and Thursday. There are no flights between Bora Bora and Maupiti, but you can fly from Bora Bora to Rangiroa daily, to Fakarava each Tuesday and Friday, to Manihi on Monday, Wednesday, Friday and Sunday, and during the high season you can fly to Tikehau daily except Tuesday.

Departing By Boat
   Hawaiki Nui, *Tel. 67.72.39* (Bora Bora), leaves the Fare Piti dock in Bora Bora at 10:30am each Wednesday for Tahaa and Raiatea, then heads directly back to Papeete, arriving at 7am Thursday. On Fridays the ship leaves Bora Bora at 7:30am, stopping in Tahaa, Raiatea and Huahine, and arrives in Papeete at 5am on Saturday.
   Vaeanu, *Tel. 67.68.68* (Bora Bora), leaves Bora Bora at 11:30am each Tuesday and Friday, stops in Raiatea and Huahine, and arrives in Papeete at 2am on Wednesday and Saturday. Buy your ticket at the counter on the dock or on board the ship.
   Maupiti Express II, *Tel. 66.37.81, cell 78.27.22*, leaves Bora Bora for Tahaa and Raiatea at 7am each Monday, Wednesday and Friday, and at 4pm on Friday and Sunday. It leaves for Maupiti at 8:30am each Tuesday, Thursday and Saturday. The trip to Maupiti is 1 hour and 45 minutes and gives you plenty of time to enjoy a day tour on one of the lovely motu islets. See chapter on *Maupiti* for further information. The one-way fare from Bora Bora to Tahaa and Raiatea is 2.500 CFP and round-trip is 3.500 CFP. The same rates apply for the Bora Bora-Maupiti voyage. Passengers under 12 years pay half-fare.

Orientation
   Close to the boat dock in **Vaitape village** you will find the *mairie* (town hall), *gendarmerie*, post office, banks, schools, churches, dispensary, pharmacy, Air Tahiti office, Bora Bora Visitors' Bureau (also called the Tourism Committee), arts and crafts center, food stores, small restaurants and snack stands, shops, boutiques and rental agencies for cars, scooters and bicycles, plus service stations and public telephones. In 2004 the local government announced expansion and face lifting plans for Place Vaitape, the part of Bora Bora's main village where visitors arrive on shuttle boats from the airport. New facilities will include a maritime station, a museum, a large meeting place and a restaurant.
   Bora Bora's main island is only 10 kilometers (5.2 miles) long and 4 kilometers (2.5 miles) wide. A partially paved road circles the coastline, winding 29 kilometers (18 miles) through the colorful villages of Vaitape, Faanui and Anau. You'll see little settlements of modest *fares*, the homes of Bora Bora's 7,295 inhabitants, which are often surrounded by flower gardens.

Getting Around Bora Bora
Car, Scooter & Bicycle Rentals
   Fredo & Fils Rent A Car operates out of the Hotel Bora Bora and from an office in Vaitape, *Tel. 67.70.31; Fax 67.62.07; E-mail: boraboratours@mail.pf*. They rent 3-door Citroën Saxo cars for 4.800 CFP for 2 hours, 6.600 CFP for 4 hours, 7.800 CFP for 8 hours, and 9.240 CFP for 24 hours. These rates include unlimited mileage and insurance. Gas and flat tires are not included. The cars

are insured with a deductible of 100.000 CFP, which the client pays in the event of any accident.

Europcar has its main sales office in Vaitape facing the quay, *Tel. 67.70.15/67.70.03*, with sales desks at all the hotels. A 2-seat Mini Cabriolet rents for 6.750 CFP for 2 hours, 7.050 CFP for 4 hours and 8.750 CFP for 8 hours. A 3-door Fiat Panda or Seicento rents for 5.900 CFP for 2 hours, 6.550 CFP for 4 hours 7.650 CFP for 8 hours and 8.850 CFP for 24 hours. A 5-door air-conditioned Peugeot 206 costs 7.150 CFP for 2 hours, 9.200 CFP for 4 hours, 11.000 CFP for 8 hours and 12.600 CFP for 24 hours. These rates cover unlimited mileage and third-party insurance. Gas and flat tires are not included.

Fare Piti Rent A Car is at the boat dock in Faanui, *Tel. 67.65.28/67.71.58*, where the inter-island ships arrive from Tahiti, in Vaitape, *Tel. 67.77.17*, and at Le Maitai Polynesia, *Tel. 67.69.69*. The lowest car rental price for a Peugeot 106 is 6.000 CFP for 2 hours and 8.000 CFP for 8 hours. Scooter rentals are 4.000 for 2 hours and 6.000 CFP for 8 hours. These rates include unlimited mileage and insurance. Gas is extra.

Bicycles

Fredo & Fils Rent A Car, Tel. *67.70.31*, rents bicycles at several hotels for 1.730 CFP for 4 hours and 2.310 CFP for 8 hours.

Europcar, *Tel. 67.70.15/67.70.03*, rents mountain bikes for 1.300 CFP for 2 hours, 1.500 CFP for 4 hours and 1.850 CFP for 8 hours.

Fare Piti Rent A Car, *Tel. 67.65.28*, rents mountain bikes for 1.000 CFP for 2 hours, 1.350 CFP for 8 hours and 2.000 CFP for 24 hours.

Mautara Location, in Tiipoto, *Tel. 67.73.16*, also has bikes for rent.

Taxis

Taxi service is provided by **Dino's Island Tours & Cab**, *Tel. 79.29.65;* **Simplet Taxi**, *Tel. 79.19.31/73.85.72;* **Bora Bora Tours**, *Tel. 67.70.31, 20.35.88 or 78.31.74;* **Jacques Isnard**, *Tel. 67.72.25*, **Gilles Taxi**, *Tel. 72.01.01*, **Otemanu Tours**, *Tel. 67.70.49*, **Charley Taxi**, *Tel. 67.64.37 or 78.27.71*, and **Jeannine Buchin**, *Tel. 67.74.14*. See more information under *Circle Island Tours* in this chapter.

Le Truck

Each hotel and pension has its own *le truck* or mini-van service between the hotel and the boat dock in Vaitape or Faanui, coordinating their runs with the arrivals and departures of Air Tahiti and the inter-island ferries. Some of them may stop for you if you flag them down, but there is no official public transportation service on Bora Bora.

Where to Stay
ON THE MAIN ISLAND
Deluxe

HOTEL BORA BORA, *B.P. 1, Bora Bora 98730. Tel. 689/60.44.60; Fax 689/60.44.66; E-mail: Central Reservations Office: Tel.; 689/60.44.11; Fax 689/60.44.22. E-mail: reservations@hotelborabora.pf. North America Reservations: Tel. 800/421-1490, Los Angeles Tel. 818/587-9650; Fax 818/710-0050; E-mail: hotelborabora@aol.com; www.amanresorts.com. Beside the lagoon at Raititi Point, 14 kilometers (8.7 miles) from the airport and 5.8 kilometers (3.6 miles) from the village of Vaitape. Round-trip transfers provided from airport to hotel by private launch. 54 bungalows. EP Rates single/double through March 31, 2005 and from (April 1, 2005-March 31, 2006): superior bungalow $700 ($700); pool fare $875 ($900); overwater bungalow $925 ($950); premium beach fare $975 ($1,000). Add $75 per day for additional person. Add 5% hotel tax to room rates and 6% value added tax to room rates, plus 150 CFP municipal tax per person per day. A 10% value added tax is applicable to other services. All major credit cards. Note: US $ rates are converted to local currency at time of billing.*

The Hotel Bora Bora was the first international class hotel built on Bora Bora, and naturally, the owners chose the best spot on the island. It is located on Point Raititi, a private peninsula that faces the southwest, with sunset views of the neighboring island of Maupiti. The famous Matira Beach is just an extension of one of the hotel's three private white-sand beaches.

This exclusive resort offers 50 individual Polynesian style guest bungalows and *fares* (villas) that are situated in tropical gardens with ocean views on one of the three beaches or resting on columns over the water. All accommodations are spaciously designed and elegantly but simply appointed to maximize guest comfort. Each bungalow has air-conditioning, ceiling fans, bathtub and separate shower, hairdryer, private bar, coffee and tea facilities, telephone with Internet connection, radio/cassette/CD player and personal safe. The management of the Hotel Bora Bora takes pride in not putting television sets in the guest rooms as they find this is a good selling point; however, there is a satellite television in the Fare Raititi lounge.

The Hotel Bora Bora was the first hotel to introduce overwater accommodations to the island more than three decades ago, and more recently, they were the first hotel in French Polynesia to introduce the *fare* concept of a Tahitian home with a private swimming pool.

The hotel's facilities include the Matira Terrace restaurant overlooking Bora Bora's spectacular lagoon; the adjacent Matira Bar bar offers tropical beverages from 5pm; the Pofai Beach Bar is open from 10:30am for lunches, cocktails and sunsets, and there is also room service available from 7am to 9:30pm. Afternoon tea is served on the beach. A Manager's Cocktail Party is held at 6pm each Tuesday on the Pofai Beach. The Hotel Bora Bora presents special evenings on the beach several nights a week. See information under *Where to Eat* in this chapter.

Activities and excursions available include: Aquascope, Boat Rental, BBQ Picnic, Beauty & Body Treatments (Massage), Bicycle Rental, Car Hire, Canoeing, Deep Sea Fishing, Fly Fishing, Glass Bottom Boat, Helicopter Tours, Helmet Dive, Hiking, Horse Riding, Helicopter Trips, Island Tours, Jet Skiing, Jeep Safari, Jungle Bike, Lagoon Fishing, Lagoon Cruise, Parasailing, Photo Services, Private Outrigger Tours, Sailing, Scuba Diving, Shark Feeding, Snorkeling, Submarine, Sunset Cruise, Scooter Rental, Tennis and Water Skiing. There is also a library, pool table, games, television and video player. Other services include a boutique and black pearl shop, laundry, baby-sitting and foreign exchange. Honeymoon packages and Polynesian «wedding» ceremonies are also available. See more information in the *Best Places to Stay* chapter.

INTERCONTINENTAL MOANA BEACH RESORT BORA BORA, *B.P. 156, Bora Bora 98730. Tel. 689/60.49.00; Fax 689/60.49.99; in US 800/327-0200. E-mail: reservations_borabora@interconti.com; www.borabora.interconti.com. Beside the lagoon on Point Matira. 64 bungalows. 2005 Low Season (High Season) EP Rates for bungalows single/double: beach junior suite bungalow 65.450 CFP (71.150 CFP); overwater lagoon junior suite bungalow 83.350 CFP (91.600 CFP); overwater horizon suite bungalow 94.350 CFP (102.600 CFP); additional person 15 years and over 8.000 CFP; no charge for child under 15 sharing parents' bungalow suite. Beach junior suite with living room 91.500 CFP (99.500 CFP); overwater junior suite with living room 123.350 CFP (134.100 CFP); "Heremoana" beach junior suite 157.000 CFP (170.700 CFP); "Poe Va'i" overwater junior suite 214.900 CFP (233.600 CFP). Note: Low Season is January 1-May 31, 2005 and December 1-31, 2005. High Season is June 1-November 30, 2005. Continental breakfast 2.290 CFP; American breakfast 2.810; 3-course set luncheon menu 4.295 CFP; 3-course set dinner menu 6.315; meal plan with breakfast and dinner 8.860 CFP per person; meal plan with breakfast, lunch and dinner 11.890 CFP per person. Child under 12 years 50% discount on meal plans. Round-trip airport transfers by boat 5.000 CFP per person. Rates quoted include 5% hotel tax on room rates and 6% value added tax on room rates, meal plans and transfers. Add 150 CFP municipal tax per person per day. A 10% value added tax is applicable to other services. All major credit cards.*

The Bora Bora Beachcomber InterContinental Resort was designated a "Connoisseur's Choice" for 2004 by the world renowned publication *Resorts & Great Hotels, The Connoisseur's Guide to the World's Best*. This 64-unit hotel shared the honor with the 143-room Moorea Beachcomber InterContinental Resort. The Bora Bora Beachcomber Intercontinental Resort also topped the list of 10 "Five-star fantasy hotels" on the Internet website Expedia.com.

By the end of 2004 the name of this hotel will be changed from Bora Bora Beachcomber Intercontinental Resort back to its original name of Moana Beach, preceded by Intercontinental. When the new 112-unit Hotel Intercontinental Bora Bora opens in March 2006 on Motu Tiarepuomu, it will be referred to as the Intercontinental, while the former Beachcomber will be called Moana Beach, as it is now referred to by most residents of Bora Bora.

During an extensive building and renovation project that was completed in 2003, the Moana Beach added 14 more bungalows, as well as a swimming pool and 4 day rooms. This hotel now has a total of 64 individual units that are junior suite size with air conditioning: 12 beach bungalows and 1 beach suite called "Heremoana"; 48 overwater bungalows and 1 overwater suite called "Poe Va'i". These suites can be rented as two single bungalows or as a family bungalow with a kitchen, dining table and lounge in the middle. All the bungalows feature a large sun terrace, living room, bedroom and attractive bathroom/dressing area that is decorated with live vanilla vines growing on a trellis above the bathtub and separate open shower. In addition to the dressing table and stool, there is also a makeup mirror, electric razor outlet, hairdryer and a complimentary selection of Kinu toiletries in this area, which is brightened daily with red hibiscus flowers. The toilet is separate and there is a door between the bedroom and bathroom.

The bungalows are built in a modern Polynesian style of pointed pandanus thatch roofs and are beautifully furnished with contemporary wood and wicker furniture, live plants, natural fabrics, appliqué *tifaifai* bedspreads, and paintings by resident artists. There are ambient lights beside the bed and adjustable reading lights on the headboard of woven wood. Teak panels slide to cover the picture window in the bedroom when you wish to block out the bright sunshine and give the room a cozier atmosphere. A king-size bed can be converted into twin beds, and in the living room is a sofa that can sleep a third person. This room also contains a writing desk, fully stocked mini-bar and coffee and tea facilities. Each unit is furnished with two satellite televisions with video channel, CD and DVD players, two telephones with voice mail and dataports for Internet. They also have an iron, ironing board and personal safe. One beach bungalow and one overwater bungalow can accommodate handicapped guests.

The overwater bungalows are the perfect haven for lovers. Room service is available 24/24 and you can even treat yourself to a Royal Canoe Breakfast for Two, with an American breakfast delivered by outrigger canoe to your private terrace. This treat costs 6.390 CFP per person. Two lounge chairs on the spacious terrace are ideal for hand-in-hand star-gazing. Step down from your sun deck into the warm embrace of the clear lagoon for the feel of paradise. Or look through your glass table in the living room and watch the fish swimming around in the crystalline lagoon. An experiment of implanting coral in the sandy bottom is being carried out under each overwater unit.

Should you lovers decide to visit the rest of the hotel, you will discover that it has a lovely white sand beach, an inviting swimming pool, and a cool oasis of greenery to welcome you when you arrive by car. You need only walk across the road from the entrance to watch a spectacular sunset from the western side of Matira Beach.

Big changes have also taken place in the hotel's public facilities. A circular driveway brings you to the entrance, which is now covered, and a newly designed reception area allows for a faster and more pleasant check-in. Reception is open 24/24. The Noa Noa Restaurant and Terrace opens onto the patio that overlooks the white sand beach and lagoon, providing an enlarged dining space. The Vini Vini Bar now leads to the new 2-level swimming pool, which has one overflowing pool with a concrete bottom and a sandy bottom pool. This area is enhanced with a waterfall and tropical vegetation. Four fully equipped transit bungalow units are available for day visitors or guests arriving before the 2pm check-in or departing after the 11am check-out. The Te Anuanua boutique has been moved outside the hotel entrance and is now easily accessible to the public without them having to come into the hotel grounds. Tahiti Pearls has a boutique adjacent to the hotel's reception area. There is also a separate room for the guest relations/ activities center, which includes a car rental desk, business center and computer for guest use with Internet connection that costs 700 CFP for 10 minutes. A Concierge service is now available, providing professional assistance to guests. This is one of the very few hotels in French Polynesia offering such a personalized service.

The Fare Plage (Beach Desk) is open from 8am to 5pm for beach towels and snorkeling equipment. The Beach Boys will give you pointers on how to use the complimentary outrigger paddle canoes for two, windsurf boards and kayaks. The Activities and Excursion Lounge is open from 8am to 7pm. The Activities Director will explain the full range of land and water sports available, which include shark- and ray-feeding safaris, and a visit to the Lagoonarium. You can take a catamaran cruise, sailing cruise, sunset cruise, glass-bottom boat ride, guided island tour by sea scooter, go water-skiing, scuba diving, snuba diving, deep-sea or lagoon fishing, parasail above the lagoon, picnic on a *motu* islet, ride horses, explore the mountains by jeep safari or Quad excursion, and ride around the island on a guided bus tour. You can also rent a car or bike around the island and discover Bora Bora's charms on your own. Or you can just remain in your private overwater bungalow, order from room service and be romantic.

The Vini Vini Bar has special cocktails and a musical duo, who play their guitars and ukuleles in the bar and during dinner in the Noa Noa Restaurant, while you dine on a gourmet meal of French specialties and *la nouvelle cuisine Tahitienne*, an imaginative alliance of local seafood and fruit prepared with a French flair. Entertainment includes a *pareo* show, demonstrations of Tahitian cooking, or a slide show presenting the hotel's activities and excursions. A snooker lounge and board games are also available for your enjoyment.

Special theme evenings include a Tuesday night Barbecue Buffet and the spectacular Maohi Nui group with fire dancing. Thursday night is Polynesian night with traditional foods and local entertainment. "La Soirée Merveilleuse" takes place on Saturday nights, which is a seafood buffet followed by a Polynesian dance show on the beach. For more information see *Where to Eat* in this chapter.

Honeymooners are especially welcome in this romantic setting. On making a reservation at the Intercontinental Moana Beach Resort, when you mention "Honeymoon" on the reservation document as well as on the voucher, you will receive special complimentary gifts on the day of your arrival: tropical flowers arranged in the bedroom and bathroom of your bungalow and a half bottle of French champagne on ice. Honeymooners staying four to ten nights receive even more gifts.

Anne De Saint Pierre, the hotel's very efficient French manager, will happily orchestrate a Polynesian wedding ceremony for you on the beach at sunset, should you so desire. This traditional Polynesian wedding ceremony is called "Te Arii" and is complete with a Tahitian priest, singers, dancers and musicians, traditional costumes and *pareos*, flower leis and bouquet. Once the couple has exchanged their wedding vows, the priest baptizes them with their Tahitian names and hands them a marriage certificate on an authentic sheet of *tapa* bark cloth. The bride and groom are then covered with a Tahitian *tifaifai* wedding quilt (rented). Following the ceremony, a bottle of champagne and a wedding cake are served in their bungalow, where they will find a beautiful arrangement of tropical flowers covering the bed. Starting at 7pm a gastronomic dinner will be served at a specially prepared table on the hotel's private beach. This full ceremony will cost 180.000 CFP. "Te Tama" is a mini version of the Polynesian Wedding Ceremony and costs 125.000 CFP. A 20-minute "No Te Hau" ceremony and renewal of vows is 80.000 CFP. A photographer can prepare a souvenir album of photos, digital pictures or make a video film of any of these ceremonies. A "Royal" ceremony on a private motu with a traditional oven is the unique experience of a lifetime, and costs 297.500 CFP. A most unusual choice for getting married underwater is provided during a "Neptune" ceremony. First you'll have to take snuba training the day before the big event, and your wedding certificate is even waterproof. This celebration of romance is priced at 200.000 CFP and involves three divers, including the cameraman, who will make a DVD or videotape of the ceremony.

Romantic canoe breakfasts, tours, picnics and special dinners for two can be arranged at your request. A "Romance in Bora Bora" dinner served in the Noa Noa Restaurant, with candles and flowers and a special romantic menu, includes a bottle of champagne, for 23.000 CFP per couple. A "Moonlight Gastronomic Dinner", served by torchlight on the hotel beach, also includes a bottle of champagne, for 28.000 CFP per couple. A "Gastronomic Dinner" served on the terrace of your bungalow is 40.000 CFP for two, and includes the dinner, exotic cocktails and a bottle of champagne. Other "Romantic Ideas" can be ordered, such as a bed of flowers or a Tahitian musical duo for one hour. The hotel will happily send you a list of suggestions.

Superior
    HOTEL SOFITEL MARARA, *B.P. 6, Bora Bora 98730. Tel. 689/60.55.00;
Fax 689/67.74.03; E-mail: ho564-gm@accor-hotels.com. Reservations: 689/
41.04.04; Fax 689/41.05.05; in US Tel. 800/SOFITEL (763-4835); E-mail:
reservation_tahiti@accor-hotels.com; www.sofitel.com. Beside the lagoon at
the end of Taahana Bay, north of Point Matira on the east side. 2005 Low
Season (High Season) EP Rates single/double: garden bungalow 30.000 CFP
(34.600 CFP); beach bungalow 40.000 CFP (46.000 CFP); overwater bungalow (shallow water) 43.000 CFP (49.000 CFP); overwater bungalow (deep
water) 46.000 (53.000 CFP. Third adult add 5.000 CFP. Note: Low Season is
from January 1-June 30, 2005 and from November 1-December 31, 2005.
High Season is from July 1-October 31, 2005. American breakfast 2.400 CFP;
lunch 2.950 CFP; dinner 5.050 CFP. No room charge for children under 12
sharing room with parent; children's meals are half-price. Round-trip transfers
4.000 CFP per person. Add 5% hotel tax to room rates and 6% value added
tax to room rates, plus 150 CFP municipal tax per person per day. A 10% value
added tax is applicable to other services. All major credit cards.*

This is the last hotel in the area generally known as Matira, at the end of
a long white sand beach. At publication time there were 64 units, consisting
of 32 garden bungalows, 11 beach bungalows and 21 overwater bungalows,
all with thatched roofs. If all goes as planned, there will soon be 77 bungalows.
A long-awaited and much needed renovation project was scheduled to begin
in November 2004 and be finished by October 2005. This improvement
program will involve destroying all the overwater bungalows and rebuilding
them further out into the lagoon. The restaurant will be redone, a new bar will
be built beside the beach and a Japanese restaurant will be added where the
bar is presently located. The swimming pool will also be enlarged and
transformed into an infinity pool. This work will be done in two stages and part
of the hotel will be closed during the construction work. When the changes
are all completed the hotel will also have a spa and an overwater conference
area.

Each bungalow has air-conditioning, a ceiling fan, direct dial telephone,
individual safe, tea and coffee facilities, mini-bar, bathroom with shower and
separate toilet, hair dryer, beach towels and Sofitel brand coconut soaps,
monoi oils and other amenities. The large overwater bungalows are attractively decorated with bamboo furniture and contain king-size beds, with a
sliding window between the bathroom and bedroom so that you can see the
lagoon from the dressing area. There is piped in music in the overwater
bungalows if you want it, and room service is also available. Snorkeling gear
is also provided in these units. From the big semi-circular sun decks of the
overwater bungalows you can see Tahaa and Raiatea on the horizon, as well

as the Sofitel Motu, which is off limits to the public, including guests at the Sofitel Marara.

Until the renovation project is finished and the new overwater bungalows are built further away from the road and kitchen area, I prefer the beach bungalows at this hotel because they are just as attractively decorated as the overwater units and have most of the same facilities and amenities. You will hear the lap-lap of the gentle waves on the white sand beach rather than the cars, motorcycles and scooters on the road. There are no screens on the windows but electric mosquito repellent machines are provided. Some of the beach units also have lighted extension makeup mirrors. There are two chairs and a table on the terrace and an outside faucet to wash off the sand when you come back from the beach.

The ambiance at the Marara is lively, with a list of daily activities that are posted in the reception area. From the fresh water swimming pool you have views of the lagoon and *motu* islets. Guests also have free use of snorkeling equipment, kayaks, outrigger paddle canoes, windsurf boards, tennis, ping-pong, beach volley ball, frisbie, badminton, board games and an exchange library. The activities desk can book any land tour or lagoon excursion you want, plus rent you a car or bicycle. A shuttle bus to Vaitape village is 600 CFP per person and leaves the hotel at 9am, 11am and 2pm. The Maradive center is located on the premises, providing three outings a day to scuba dive in the lagoon, pass and open ocean, for 6.500 CFP per dive. There is something going on every evening, with nightly entertainment at the bar, and a Happy Hour is held every evening from 5 to 6pm and from 9 to 10pm. Buy one drink at Le Corail bar and get the second one free. At 6:30pm you can learn all about the Tahitian black pearls, how to tie a pareo, make *poisson cru*, open and grate a coconut and dance Tahitian style.

La Perouse Restaurant restaurant serves French and international cuisine. An "Around the World" buffet is served every Tuesday evening, followed by the "Mamas" Polynesian show at 8:30pm; an Ocean buffet is served on Thursday evening, followed by a fashion show or Heiva Marara; and a Saturday evening Polynesian buffet features *maa Tahiti* cooked in an underground oven, followed by traditional songs and dances.

You can honeymoon at the Marara with a VIP welcome and non-binding Polynesian wedding ceremonies are performed in the traditional wedding *fare* beside the beach. This ceremony costs 75.000 CFP, and includes flower leis and crowns, two white *pareos*, Polynesian musicians and two dancers, wedding ceremony, tapa wedding certificate, two fruit juice cocktails, a special dinner for two including a wedding cake. Another wedding choice takes place on the decorated beach or by the swimming pool and costs 110.000 CFP. This includes all the above plus the arrival of the groom by outrigger canoe, local musicians and dancers performing the fire dance, two dinners with wedding cake and champagne, a video tape of the ceremony, and a floral decoration in the bungalow. Contact the hotel directly for details and rates.

Moderate to Superior
   LE MAITAI POLYNESIA, *B.P. 505, Bora Bora 98730. Tel. 689/60.30.00; Fax 689/67.66.03; E-mail: booking@bora.hotelmaitai.com; www.hotelmaitai.com. At Taahana Beach in the Matira area, 15 kilometers (9 miles) from the ferry dock and 12 kilometers (6 miles) from Vaitape. Round-trip transfers to/from Vaitape and hotel 1.500 CFP per person. 74 units. EP Rates: single/double: air-conditioned room 25.500 CFP; air-conditioned room with ocean view 34.000 CFP; beach bungalow 41.000 CFP; overwater bungalow 51.000 CFP; Third person 6.438 CFP. Continental breakfast 1.750 CFP; American breakfast 2.150 CFP; meal plan with breakfast and dinner 6.800 CFP; meal plan with breakfast, lunch and dinner 9.100 CFP. Add 5% hotel tax to room rates and 6% value added tax to room rates and prepaid meal plans, plus 150 CFP municipal tax per person per day. A 10% value added tax is applicable to other services. All major credit cards.*

   This hotel opened in June 1998 and added more rooms in 2000, offering four types of lodging. There are 28 air-conditioned garden view rooms and 20 air-conditioned ocean view rooms on the mountainside, 7 beach bungalows and 19 overwater bungalows. The air-conditioned rooms with a garden view are located in 2-level concrete buildings behind the reception, Haere Mai Restaurant and Manuia Bar. The air-conditioned rooms with an ocean view are located in adjacent buildings, which are across the road from the lagoon, offering a lovely view of the Bora Bora lagoon. The mountainside rooms are not recommended for anyone who has difficulty walking, as there are stone steps leading up to these units. The mountainside rooms have 312 square feet (29 square meters) of living space and provide either twin or king size beds. The ocean view rooms also have a day bed that can sleep a third person.

   The beach bungalows and overwater bungalows are all 323 square feet (30 square meters) in size and are built in the traditional Polynesian style, with thatched roofs and woven pandanus walls. These units all have ceiling fans but no air-conditioning and they also have king-size beds plus a daybed that can accommodate a third person. All the hotel's rooms and bungalows are furnished with a writing desk, blackout curtains, television and in-house video, mini-bar fridge, direct dial telephone with data jack, personal safe, shower with massage nozzle, hair dryer, bath and beauty amenities, extension mirror and full length mirror in bathroom and sliding glass door onto a private terrace or balcony. The overwater bungalows have a glass viewing table that enables you to see the fish swimming in the clear water below, steps providing direct access into the lagoon and a shower on the landing below the terrace.

   Maitai means 'all is well,' and you'll certainly have a good feeling about this place from the moment you enter the reception area and are welcomed by a smiling Tahitian hostess, who offers you a refreshing fruit punch cocktail. The reception desk, Haere Mai Restaurant and Manuia Bar are all under one huge woven pandanus roof. Vivid shades of bougainvillea, hibiscus, colored leaves, tree ferns and hanging baskets of exotic ferns fill the gardens of the hotel and the South Seas setting is completed with a decor of tapa, bamboo and huge chandeliers of seashells. Breakfast and dinner are served in the Haere Mai Restaurant, and a Wednesday night Seafood Buffet is a popular event, accompanied by a Polynesian dance show and a fire dance. The Manuia Bar is a gathering place during Happy Hour, when the musicians play island tunes and demonstrations are given on how to make *poisson cru* or tie the *pareo*. The Tama'a Maitai Restaurant is located on the beach side of the property, providing non-stop service from 11:30am to 8:30pm. Room service is available from 7am to 9:30pm. The hotel also provides next day laundry service, luggage room, fax and photocopy facilities.

Keana boutique and jewelry shop are also located on the premises. You can rent a car or bicycle from the Fare Piti Agency in front of the main building, and there is an activity desk in the lobby, where you can book your tours and excursions. Guests have free use of the hotel's snorkeling equipment, kayaks and outrigger paddle canoes.

TOP DIVE RESORT, *B.P. 515, Bora Bora 98730. Tel. 689/60.50.50, cell 78.98.55; Fax 689/60.50.51; E-mail: info@topdive.com; www.topdive.com. Located beside the bay on the north end of Vaitape village, 5 minutes from the boat dock. 9 bungalows. EP Rates: garden bungalow 29.000 CFP single/ double; 34.800 CFP triple; overwater bungalow 39.000 CFP single/double; 44.700 CFP triple. Children under 12 years free of charge. Meal plan with breakfast and dinner 5.500 CFP per person; meal plan with breakfast, lunch and dinner 8.000 CFP per person. Round-trip transfers to/from quay provided. Rates include all taxes except 150 CFP municipal tax per person per day. A 10% value added tax is applicable to other services. All major credit cards.*

This hotel opened in August 1999, providing lodging for guests who want a scuba diving vacation with accommodations. This is also a convenient location if you want to be close to Vaitape village. The six garden bungalows and the three overwater bungalows are all built very close together, adjacent to an overflowing swimming pool and one of the best restaurants on the island. All the bungalows are sturdily built of wood and have a pandanus roof. The furniture is made of dark kohu wood, and each bungalow is air-conditioned, with a tile floor, and is furnished with a king-size bed and a single bed covered with a Tahitian *tifaifai* patchwork quilt, which adds some needed color to the room. The bathrooms are equipped with a bathtub/shower, double sinks, private toilet and hair dryer. The rooms also have a mini-bar fridge, a personal safe, coffee and tea facilities, writing desk, reading lights, telephone, and television. The garden bungalows have a bidet and a small garden. All the rooms have terraces.

There is also a black pearl boutique, a bar and dive shop in the main building. The TOPdive center offers introductory dives and lessons either inside the lagoon or in the swimming pool, using Scubapro equipment. Nitrox diving is also available. Guests staying at the TOPdive Resort receive a 15% rebate on all dive prices and 20% reduced rates for car rental. For more information see *Scuba Diving* in this chapter.

Moderate
NOVOTEL BORA BORA BEACH RESORT, *B.P. 174, Bora Bora, 98730. Tel. 689/60.59.55; Fax 689/60.59.51. Reservations TAHITIRES Tel 689/ 86.66.66; Fax 689/41.05.05; E-mail: reservation_tahiti@accor-hotels.com; www.sofitel.com. Located between the Bora Bora Beach Lodge and Sofitel Marara in the Matira area. 2005 Low Season (High Season) EP Rates single/ double: 21.600 CFP (28.800 CFP) for an air-conditioned room. Note: Low Season is from January 1-June 30, 2005 and from November 1-December 31, 2005. High Season is from July 1-October 31, 2005. American breakfast 1.700 CFP per person; lunch 2.600 CFP; dinner 3.900 CFP. Half-price on meals for child 3-12 years. Round-trip bus transfers 1.550 CFP per person. Add 5% hotel tax to room rates and 6% value added tax to room rates, plus 150 CFP municipal tax per person per day. A 10% value added tax is applicable to other services. All major credit cards.*

This hotel opened in May 2003 as the Bora Bora Beach Resort, replacing the former Bora Bora Beach Club that was supposed to have been taken over by the French company, Les Nouvelles Frontières, to be rebuilt as a Paladian hotel. In August 2004 it was taken over by the Accor group as a 3-star Novotel outlet and put under the management of Sofitel, which also has the 4-star Sofitel Marara just next door to this hotel, and the 5-star Sofitel Motu, a 5-minute boatride from the Novotel.

There are 80 rooms in two story concrete motel-like buildings on the mountain side of the road, and the reception, restaurant, bar and activities center are on the lagoon side. The rooms are equipped with individual air-conditioning, a double bed or 2 twin beds and a sofa bed, a big writing desk with lamp, a satellite television, direct dial telephone with Internet plug, in-room safe, coffee/tea facilities, and a tiled bathroom with a lavabo, shower, separate toilet and hair dryer. The furniture is teak and kohu wood and the curtains and bed covers are beige or natural. Each unit has a small balcony or terrace overlooking the gardens. There are 4 rooms for handicapped guests and 3 communicating rooms for a family or for use as a suite.

The reception area is large and there is an activity center, a beachfront and outdoor restaurant for 180 diners, a beachfront bar and a swimming pool. Nautical activities depart from the overwater pier and the Nemo World Diving center is located on the white sand beachfront. Free activities include snorkeling equipment, outrigger paddle canoes, transfers to the motu, and entertainment several nights a week, especially on weekends, where there is music for dancing. Guests can also go next door to watch the Polynesian dance shows at the Sofitel Marara.

HOTEL MATIRA, *B. P. 31, Bora Bora 98730. Tel. 689/67.70.51/67.78.58, cell 79.15.95; Fax 689/67.77.02; E-mail: hotel.matira@mail.pf; www.hotelmatira.com. On Matira Beach at the turnoff to Point Matira. Round-trip transfers on arrival and departure; child 5-11 years 1.113 CFP; child or adult over 12 years 2.226 CFP. 14 bungalows. EP Rates single/double: standard bungalow 21.090 CFP; garden view bungalow 26.640 CFP; lagoon view bungalow 31.080 CFP; beach bungalow 35.520 CFP; third person, child 5-11 years 4.440 CFP; child or adult over 12 years 8.325 CFP. Add 5% hotel tax to room rates and 6% value added tax to room rates, plus 150 CFP municipal tax per person per day. A 10% value added tax is applicable to other services. American Express, Mastercard, Visa.*

Look for the Hotel Matira sign on the beach side of the road just before you turn right to go to Point Matira. The hotel reception was formerly located in the same building as the Restaurant Matira, but since March 2004 it has moved to Point Matira where 14 brand new bungalows are built in the garden and facing the white sands of Matira Beach. There are 2 beach bungalows, 4 with a lagoon view, 5 with a garden view and 3 standard units near the parking lot. Each of the bungalows has two double beds in the bedroom, a sofa bed in the living room, ceiling fan, small refrigerator, coffee and tea facilities, bathroom with hot water shower, and a terrace. There is no air-conditioning and no television or telephone. An iron and hair dryer are available at reception.

The hotel no longer has a restaurant, but there are several good restaurants and snacks very close by and some of them provide pick-up service for dinner. There is also a food store within easy walking distance and an excellent roulotte sets up shop practically across the street every evening. All activities and excursions, such as lagoon trips and mountain safaris are available.

CLUB MED BORA BORA, *B.P. 34, Bora Bora 98730. Tel. 689/60.46.04; Fax 60.46.11; E-mail: clubmed@mail.pf; www.clubmed.com. Reservations: 689/41.32.34; Fax 689/42.16.83; in US 800/528-3100. Beside the lagoon on Faaopore Bay, between the villages of Anau and Faanui, on the east coast. 150 twin-share units. AP Rates: garden room and all meals 21.400-26.200 CFP single occupancy, 17.900-21.900 CFP per person double occupancy; beach bungalows and all meals 25.600-31.400 CFP single occupancy, 21.400-26.200 CFP per person double occupancy. Reduced rates for children. Rates vary according to seasons. Add 150 CFP municipal tax per person per day. All major credit cards.*

The Club Med Bora Bora has always attracted a different kind of tourist from the GM (*gentil membre*) who used to choose Club Med Moorea for their all-inclusive holiday. The rah-rah, let's make noise and have fun every second atmosphere that used to prevail at Club Med villages has also disappeared. People of all ages and from many countries choose the Club Med Bora Bora because it offers a great vacation package in an attractive, amiable environment. Only in the bar and disco will you find any noise, and you can join in or do your own thing without any pressure.

The Club Med Bora Bora has 92 garden rooms and 58 beach rooms in one or two story motel-style concrete buildings and stand-alone bungalows, all painted in pastel shades of yellow, chartreuse and mauve, intended to resemble a coral garden. The units are well spaced throughout the village, each with a view of the lagoon. Honeymooners enjoy the privacy of the beachfront bungalows, which are more elaborate and will soon be transformed into deluxe rooms. Each room has air-conditioning, a ceiling fan, twin beds that can be transformed into a king size bed, Polynesian *tifaifai* bed covers, reading lights overhead and on the bedside tables, a writing desk, small refrigerator, telephone with computer modem hookup to Internet, and a cable television with an inhouse video channel that introduces each G.O (*gentil organisateur*) by name and job. Ample closet space and shelves are provided in the dressing area and there also is a safety box in the closet. The bathroom contains shelves for cosmetics, a hair dryer and personal amenities. The shower has an overhead nozzle plus a hand held nozzle, and a full length mirror covers the door to the separate toilet. A blackout shade provides privacy when it is pulled down to cover the sliding glass door that leads to the balcony or terrace. Laundry service is available and drinks can be ordered from room service for a minimum of 2.000 CFP. The village is fumigated every evening at dusk, and there is also an anti-mosquito electric plug in each room.

An enormous thatched-roof beachside pavilion is the central gathering place, with the reception, boutiques, dining room, bar and nightclub located here. A full range of Club Med activities is presented, free of charge, including snorkeling equipment, boat shuttles to the motu, Hobie Cat sailing, windsurfing, kayaking, paddling an outrigger canoe and fitness classes. There are optional sailboat excursions with a picnic on the motu, shark feeding, water skiing, jet skiing, scuba diving, fishing in the lagoon, Aquascope lagoon excursion, horseback riding, safari tours, helicopter flights and shuttle service twice a day to Vaitape village. You can even get a massage, hydrotherapy treatment, anti-cellulite wrap, sea mud application, facial, pedicure and other beauty treatments at Club Med Bora Bora. And if you still have the energy in the evening, you can party in the disco bar following the Club Med show presented by the G.O.'s nightly except Thursday and Sunday, when you can watch a Polynesian dance group perform on stage.

For more information see *Where to Eat* in this chapter.

Small Family Hotels, Family Pensions, Guest Houses, Guest Rooms, Dormitories, Camping on the Main Island
BORA BORA BEACH LODGE, *B.P. 180, Bora Bora 98730. Tel. 689/ 67.78.21; Fax 689/67.77.57; E-mail:courrier@boraborabeachlodge.pf; www.boraborabeachlodge.com. Beside the Taahana lagoon and white sand beach in Matira area, 15 kilometers (9 miles) from the ferry dock and 7 kilometers (miles) from Vaitape. 8 units. Round-trip transfers between Vaitape and pension 1.000 CFP per person. EP Rates: studio 14.040 CFP single/double; apartment 18.375 CFP single/double; beach bungalow 20.440 CFP single/double. Third person 3.820 CFP. Child from 5 to 12 years 1.650. Add 6% value added tax to room rates and 50 CFP per person per day for municipal tax. American Express, JCB, Mastercard, Visa.*

Peter Eberhardt bought this small family hotel in September 2001 and immediately began a renovation project and facelift. He plans to install air-conditioners in each apartment, but when I talked to Peter in February 2004, he said that he had not yet done that. The thatched roof Polynesian style units include four studios, each with a queen-size bed with sitting area, bathroom with hot water shower and fully equipped kitchens with a large refrigerator; three apartments can sleep four adults, featuring a separate bedroom with a queen-size bed, a living/dining area with a single sofa bed, kitchen and private bathroom with hot water, and private balcony. A separate bungalow on the beach can sleep up to three adults, and has a kitchen and the same amenities as the units. Daily maid service and house linens are furnished. All units are equipped with ceiling fans and have private terraces.

Bora Bora Beach Lodge does not have a restaurant, but a food market is across the road and there are several restaurants and snack bars very close by, as well as big hotels with a wide range of activities. You can rent a bicycle from the Bora Bora Beach Lodge and there are several activity catalogs at the front desk. The receptionist will help organize your land or lagoon excursions and tours. Upon your arrival at the Vaitape boat dock you will find several mini-vans waiting for passengers, and you can easily negotiate transfers to the Matira area for a very reasonable fee.

VILLAGE TEMANUATA, *B.P. 544, Bora Bora 98730. Tel. 689/67.75.61; Fax 689/67.62.48; cell 70.93.33; E-mail: village.temanuata@mail.pf; www.letahititraveler.com.*

Beach: *On the beach side at Point Matira, just past the turnoff to Intercontinental Moana Beach Resort. Round-trip transfers 1.100 CFP per person. EP Rates: garden bungalow, 12.720 CFP single/double; beach bunga-low 15.900 CFP single/double; family bungalow with kitchen 15.900 CFP single/ double; 18.550 CFP triple; extra bed 2.120 CFP per day. All taxes included except municipal tax of 50 CFP per person per day. Mastercard and Visa.*

This is a good location on Matira Beach. The 11 Polynesian style thatched roof bungalows sit in a spacious grassy area between the white sand beach and the road, adjacent to Restaurant Fare Manuia. Seven are garden bungalows, two are on the beach, and there are two family units in the garden, which are small suites with a kitchen and accommodations for five people. All of the bungalows have a terrace, private bathroom with hot water, double or single beds, a closet, refrigerator, coffee and tea making facilities and a fan. They are attractively decorated with pareo curtains and bedspreads and cleaned daily. This pension is very close to all the Matira Beach restaurants and activities and there is a supermarket across the road. You can rent a bicycle at reception and Martine, the manager, will happily help you arrange your tours and excursions.

Lagoon: On the mountain side between Hotel Bora Bora and Point Matira. Round-trip transfers 1.100 CFP per person. EP Rates: 19.610 CFP single/double; extra bed 2.120 CFP per day. All taxes included except municipal tax of 50 CFP per person per day. Mastercard and Visa.

Four large thatched roof bungalows are located in a private garden setting across the road from Matira Beach and the lagoon. These well furnished units for one or two people are equipped with a king size bed, ceiling fan, coffee and tea making facilities, television, house linens, private bathroom with hot water, kitchen and a terrace. Bungalows are cleaned daily. Two complimentary bicycles are provided for each bungalow.

MOON BED & BREAKFAST, *B.P. 307, Bora Bora 98730. Tel. 689/ 67.74.36; E-mail: moonbungalow@netcourrier.com; munanui- teriitehau@hotmail.com. Beside lagoon in Pofai Bay, between Vaitape village and Hotel Bora Bora. Free round-trip transfers. EP Rates: room and breakfast 8.500 CFP single/double. Camping 2.000 CFP per person per night. Minimum stay 2 nights. Add 6% value added tax to room rates and 50 CFP per person per day for municipal tax. No credit cards.*

Muna Teriitehau's bed and breakfast and campground is beside the lagoon adjacent to Galerie Alain and Linda. You will receive a warm Polynesian welcome here. There are three modern and clean bungalows built with private bathroom facilities and kitchens. Campers can pitch a tent in the yard at the water's edge and share the kitchen and bathroom facilities.

VILLAGE PAULINE, *B.P. 215, Bora Bora 98730. Tel. 689/67.72.16; Fax 689/67.78.14; E-mail: vpauline@mail.pf. Located on the mountainside at Pk. 8.3 in Pofai Bay, behind Bora Kaina Hut restaurant. Round-trip transfers to/ from Vaitape and pension 1.000 CFP per person; 10 units plus dormitory and campground. EP rates: Small garden cabin with communal bathroom (cold water) and kitchen 7.000 CFP single/double; private room 7.000 CFP single/ double; garden family bungalow with private bathroom (hot water) and kitchen 12.000 CFP single/double/triple; Turama deluxe bungalow with private bathroom (hot water), kitchen and television 15.000 CFP double; dormitory 3.000 CFP per person per day; camping 2.300 per person per day.*

Child up to 10 years free. Check-out time 10am. Add 6% value added tax to room rates and 50 CFP per person per day for municipal tax. Mastercard, Visa.

Village Pauline offers the facilities of a small family hotel, guest room, backpacker's dormitory and campground, just 1 1/2 kilometers (.9 mile) from Matira Beach, a five-minute bike ride or a 20-minute walk. The Polynesian style thatched roof and wooden structures provide 4 small cabins, each with a double bed. There are also 3 rooms containing a double bed and a single bed, a dormitory with 8 beds, and a campground. All these guests share the kitchen, dining areas and bathrooms with cold water showers. There are also two family bungalows with private bathrooms and hot water. These units have a double bed and fan, plus a kitchen corner with a 3-burner hot plate and a refrigerator, and a terrace on the front where the guests can enjoy their meals. For people who like the comfort of hotel rooms at pension rates, Pauline has added the Turama bungalow, which is attractively built with wood and bamboo. It contains a queen size bed covered by a mosquito net, a ceiling fan, bedside lamp, tiled bathroom with a hot-water shower and a separate toilet, plus a well-equipped kitchen with a refrigerator and stove. You can sit on the front terrace and admire the lovely flower garden of tropical blossoms that Pauline planted.

Covered tables are scattered around the spacious village and another table sits beside the bay, for sunset watching. You can also eat your meals here if you wish. A grocery truck stops at Village Pauline every day at 7:30 and 11am and again at 5:30pm. The Bora Kaina Hut is located on the premises beside the road, serving lunch and dinner. See *Where to Eat* in this chapter.

You can rent bicycles at the reception. A really big plus for this very clean pension is Nir Shalev, the manager, who is extremely friendly, knowledgeable, helpful and cheerful. He rents sea kayaks and he can also book guided hiking tours, land tours, outrigger canoe circle island tours, scuba diving, snorkeling excursions or any other activity or tour that is available on Bora Bora. The drivers will stop at Village Pauline to pick you up.

CHEZ TEIPO, *B.P. 270, Bora Bora 98730. Tel. 689/67.78.17; Fax 689/ 67.73.24; E-mail: teipobora@mail.pf. At Pk 12 beside the lagoon in Anau, 200 meters (656 feet) from Club Med. Free round-trip transfers. 6 units. EP Rates: bungalow with cold water shower 7.000 CFP single; 8.500 CFP double; bungalow with hot water shower 11.000 CFP up to four people. Additional person 1.000 CFP. Rates include all taxes except municipal tax of 50 CFP per person per day. Mastercard, Visa.*

Six small thatched roof bungalows, each containing a double bed and private bathroom. Two units have hot water and the other four have cold water showers. Each unit also has a kitchen and coffee facilities are provided. House linens are also furnished. Bicycles, line fishing and reef fishing are available. This guest house is clean and has a good reputation, even though it is far from the activity center of Matira and there is no beach here. Bicycles and kayaks are available for guest use.

PENSION ROBERT ET TINA, *Vaitape, Bora Bora 98730. Tel. 689/ 67.63.55; Fax 689/67.72.92; cell 79.22.73/73.53.89. Beside the lagoon at Point Matira. Round-trip transfers 1.000 CFP per person. EP Rates: room 5.200 CFP single; 8.300 CFP double; 9.300 CFP triple; child 3 to 5 years 1.600 CFP; child 6 to 11 years 2.100 CFP. Add 6% value added tax to room rates and 50 CFP per person per day for municipal tax. Mastercard, Visa.*

This Polynesian family has 3 individual houses with a total of 12 rooms for rent right at the tip end of Point Matira. One house has 6 rooms with a double bed and a single bed, 3 private bathrooms with cold water and 2 equipped kitchens. Each of the other two houses has 3 bedrooms with double or single beds, one or two bathrooms with cold water and equipped kitchens. All three houses are furnished with house linens and electric fans. You can rent a room and share the bathroom and kitchen or rent the entire house. A circle island tour by outrigger canoe or boat includes shark feeding, visit to sting rays and manta rays, snorkeling in coral garden and picnic on a motu. This costs 6.750 CFP per adult and 3.375 CFP for child 3 to 11 years. A half day excursion is 5.500 CFP for adults and 2.750 CFP for children.

PENSION BORA LAGOONARIUM, *B.P. 56, Bora Bora 98730. Tel. 689/ 67.71.34, Fax 689/67.60.29, cell 79.73.67/79.22.90/79.15.82; E-mail: lagonarium@mail.pf; www.boraboraisland.com. Beside lagoon in Anau village 900 meters (2,952 feet) after Club Med. Transfers by Le Truck 500 CFP one-way. EP rates: room 6.000 CFP single/double; bungalow 8.000 CFP single/double, extra bed 2.000 CFP; dormitory 2.500 CFP per person per day; camping 2.000 CFP per tent per day. Add 6% value added tax to room rates and 50 CFP per person per day for municipal tax. No credit cards.*

Three garden bungalows are furnished with a double bed, a mini-fridge and private bathroom with cold water shower. There are four rooms with a double bed and single bed in each room, and you will share the bathroom facilities with campers and those guests staying in the 20-bed dormitory. All guests share the kitchen and dining areas.

The pension, dorm and campground are owned by the same people who operate a water park called the Lagoonarium, which is located on a motu near Le Méridien hotel. Claudine Teheiura, one of the owners, said that they are not too fond of computers and do not readily answer e-mail inquiries. They said it's not usually necessary to make reservations to stay in the pension. Just show up.

CHEZ NONO, *B.P. 282, Bora Bora, 98730. Tel. 689/67.71.38; Fax 689/ 67.74.27; E-mail: nono.leverd@mail.pf. On the white sand beach of Point Matira, facing the Hotel Bora Bora and the distant island of Maupiti, 13 kilometers (8 miles) from the ferry dock and 6.8 kilometers (4.2 miles) from Vaitape village. Round-trip transfers Vaitape/Chez Nono 1.000 CFP per* *person. 6 rooms and 4 bungalows. EP Rates: room in big house 5.500 CFP single; 6.500 CFP double; 8.500 CFP triple; twin bungalow with private bathroom 8.500 single/double; round bungalow with private bathroom 12.000 CFP single/double. Third person 2.000 CFP Breakfast 800 CFP. Add 6% value added tax to room rates and 50 CFP per person per day for municipal tax. Mastercard, Visa.*

This guest house is probably the best choice for a budget accommodation on Bora Bora, because of its excellent location right on the white sand beach of Matira, facing Maupiti and the sunset sea. A grocery store and several restaurants and snack bars are within a 10-minute walk. Most of the guests stay in the big house, which has bedrooms on two levels. The communal kitchen and bathroom have solar hot water. There are also two twin bungalows, each with a queen-size bed and private bathroom with solar hot water; and two round bungalows, each with a king-size and single bed and private bathroom with solar hot water. Every room and bungalow has a fan and all guests can use the kitchen. House linens are provided. The family bungalows are especially recommended because they are each a Polynesian style *fare*, with a big thatched roof and half-walls of woven bamboo, overlooking the incredibly beautiful lagoon. The biggest drawback here is lack of privacy, as Matira Beach is Bora Bora's only public beach. Nono operates Teremoana Tours and has a motorized outrigger canoe that he uses to take his guests around the island with a picnic on a motu. His very popular excursions depart from the beach in front of his pension at 9:30am and return at 4:30pm. A lunch of *poisson cru*, grilled fish, coconut bread, cake, fresh fruit and po'e is served on the *motu*. The cost is 8.000 CFP per person. Nono also operates a 4-wheel drive safari tour.

CHEZ MAEVA MASSON, *B.P. 33, Bora Bora 98730. Tel./Fax 689/ 67.72.04. Beside the beach at Point Matira, 13 kilometers (8 miles) from the ferry dock and 6.8 kilometers (4.2 miles) from Vaitape village. 5 rooms plus dormitory. EP Rates: room on ground level 6.500 CFP single/double; upstairs room 6.500 CFP single/double; bed in dormitory 3.250 CFP. Child under 4 years free; 5 to 10 years 1.600 CFP, 11 years up 3.250 CFP per day. Add 1.000 CFP per person for one night stay in all categories. Add 6% value added tax to room rates and 50 CFP per person per day for municipal tax. Mastercard, Visa.*

This is a very good location on Matira Beach, close to the Intercontinental Moana Beach Resort. It was the former home of artist Rosine Temauri-Masson and her late husband, the painter Jean Masson, and it still has the decor and warmth of a home. The two-story wooden house has two bedrooms on the ground floor, each containing a double bed and the four rooms upstairs each have a double bed; plus there is a 3-bed dormitory; and a sofa bed in the living room. The bathroom with hot shower and the kitchen are communal. House linens are provided. Use of the washing machine costs 1.000 CFP and the iron is also 1.000 CFP. There is a grocery store across the road and several restaurants and snacks are within easy walking distance. Transfers are available from the airport boat dock in Vaitape village for 500 CFP per person with luggage and 300 CFP without luggage.

CHEZ ROSINA, *B.P. 51, Bora Bora 98730. Tel./Fax 689/67.70.91; E-mail: adesaintpierre@mail.pf. At Pk 4.5, on mountain side in Paparoa section of Pofai Bay, 8 kilometers (5 miles) from the ferry dock and 4.5 kilometers (2.8 miles) from Vaitape village. Free round-trip transfers. 7 rooms. EP Rates: room with communal bathroom 5.000 CFP single, 6.000 CFP double; room with private bathroom 5.500 CFP single, 7.000 CFP double; child under 12 years half-rate; breakfast and dinner 3.500 CFP per person. Add 6% value added tax to room rates and 50 CFP per person per day for municipal tax. No credit cards.*

This clean family pension is located on the mountainside in Povai Bay, just before Village Pauline when coming from Vaitape. There are 4 bedrooms with private bath, hot water and a fan, and 3 rooms sharing a bathroom with hot water. You also have use of the living room, dining room and kitchen. House linens are provided.

CHEZ HENRIETTE, *B.P. 267, Bora Bora 98730. Tel./Fax 689/67.71.32; Fax 689/67.60.29, cell 21.34.57. Beside the lagoon in Anau over the hill from Club Med. Arrival transfers free. Departure transfer 500 CFP per person. EP Rates: room 10.000 CFP up to 4 people; bed in dormitory 2.500 CFP; camping 1.800 CFP per camper per day. Add 6% value added tax to room rates and 50 CFP per person per day for municipal tax. No credit cards.*

Very basic accommodations for backpackers and campers include 5 rooms, a 12-bed dormitory and a campground, a communal bathroom with cold water and shared kitchen and dining facilities. There is no beach here, but Stellio Vaiho, the owner, has a *le truck* and provides free transfers to the beach every morning, returning to the pension at 5pm. He also provides circle island tours by air-conditionedcar, by 4x4 vehicle or le truck, as well as lagoon tours, all at extra cost.

Condos on the Main Island

BORA BORA CONDOMINIUMS, *Tel./Fax 689/67.61.21, cell 70.75.60; E-mail: marcolunci@mail.pf. Facing the airport on the north side of Bora Bora's main island, between Faanui village and Point Taihi.*

This is a complex of 16 condos built over the lagoon and up the mountain side. Most of these units are rented by the year, but there are 3 condos available for weekly or monthly rental. One of these is the Black Pearl Condo, described below.

BLACK PEARL CONDO, *in US Tel. 408/209-3900 and ask for Frank; www.a1vacations.com. You can also contact Isabelle at Bora Bora Condo-*

miniums (see information above). Weekly rates for 2005 are $2,100 for two people, and $300 for each additional day. A cleaning fee of $50 is extra.

This is a fully equipped condo with 1,400 square feet of living space, built over the lagoon in Bora Bora. It is part of a small luxury complex and features a large bedroom with a queen size bed, a bathroom, living room and kitchen, all overlooking the turquoise waters through panoramic bay windows and sliding doors. Custom imported tiles cover the floor and bathroom walls. Large bamboo furniture completes the South Seas island feel. A covered terrace overlooks the lagoon and is furnished with quality outdoor furniture and a gas barbecue. You can dive into the water from your own private dock, just four steps down from your terrace. The condo has central air-conditioning, ceiling fans, satellite television, VCR, CD player, radio, ice-maker, washing machine, ironing board, optional maid service, and many more extras.

Hotels on the Motu
Prestige
BORA BORA NUI RESORT & SPA, *B.P. 502, Bora Bora 98730. Tel. 689/ 60.33.00; Fax 689/60.33.01. Reservations: in Tahiti, Tel. 689/86.48.49; E-mail: info@boraboranui.com; www.boraboranui.com; in US and Canada Tel. 800/782-9488; www.starwoodtahiti.com; www.luxurycollection.com. On Motu Toopua, southeast of the main island of Bora Bora, six miles from Motu Mute domestic airport. Round-trip airport transfers by private launch 6.500 CFP per person. 2005 Low Season (High Season) EP Rates single/double with breakfast included: Lagoon View Suite 62.000 CFP (68.500 CFP); Beach Villa 73.800 CFP (82.000 CFP); Villa-Spa Horizon View 100.800 CFP (112.000 CFP); Overwater Villa-Spa Horizon View 122.400 CFP (136.000 CFP); Royal Villa Lagoon View 202.500 CFP (225.000 CFP); Overwater Royal Villa Horizon View 247.500 CFP (275.000 CFP); third person add 13.000 CFP per day. Note: 2005 Low Season is January 1-March 31 and November 1-December 22; High Season is April 1-October 31 and December 23, 2005-January 1, 2006. American breakfast for third person 3.302 CFP. Meal plan with breakfast and dinner add 6.132 CFP; meal plan with breakfast, lunch and dinner add 9.906 CFP per person per day. Child under 18 years of age pays half price for meals taken with parents. Add 5% hotel tax to room rates, 6% value added tax on rooms and prepaid meal plans and 150 CFP municipal tax per person, per day. A 10% value added tax is applicable to other services. All major credit cards.*

This 5-star hotel with 120 ultra-luxurious suites is owned by Louis Wane of Tahiti, who also owns the Sheraton hotels on Tahiti and Moorea. It is part of the Starwood Hotels Luxury Collection. The Bora Bora Nui Resort & Spa was named one of the "100 Best New Hotels in the World" in the May 2004 *Conde Nast Traveler* magazine. It was also chosen as one of the Top Resort Spas in the World by *Modern Bride* magazine's Seventh Annual Honeymoon Survey of U.S. Travel Agents. Starwood Hotels & Resorts Worldwide, Inc. was named the World's Leading Hotel Group at the 10th Annual World Travel Awards in 2003.

The Bora Bora Nui Resort & Spa is located on 16 acres of lush, terraced hillside and on the water of a private, protected cove. The white sand beach is 600 meters (1,968 feet) long, one of the longest hotel beaches on the island of Bora Bora. The 82 Overwater Villa-Spa Horizon View units have 94 square meters (1,012 square feet) of living space, and two Overwater Royal Villas with a Horizon View are 135 square meters (1,453 square feet) large, offering the finest overwater suites in French Polynesia. Twelve Beach Villas of 85 square meters (915 square feet) are just steps from the lagoon and 16 Lagoon View Suites of 95 square meters (1,023 square feet) offer breathtaking views of the lagoon. Seven Villa-Spa Horizon View units of 85 square meters are nestled on the slopes of Toopua Island, offering panoramic views of the lagoon and the islands of Taha'a and Raiatea. Private entrances and lush gardens provide guests with a secluded retreat. A Royal Villa of 135 square meters (1,453 square feet) is built on the hillside and has the best lagoon view of all. Among the 120 units there are 80 non-smoking rooms, 4 rooms for handicapped guests and 16 twin-rooms.

The meticulously planned decor in the bungalow suites features stylish Polynesian decor with rich, exotic woods (Indonesian yellow balau walls, mahogany furniture, merbau decks, and teak outdoor furniture), plus Polynesian and Asian shell chandeliers. I stayed in one of the 82 Overwater Villa-Spa units with a Horizon View, which had a living room with a daybed-sofa, two end tables with a glass viewing panel to see into the lagoon below, a big wide coffee table, satellite color television concealed in a carved cabinet, with a radio/tape/CF player on top. The mini-bar is set up to bill your room the instant you remove an item from its place. There is a ceiling fan here and you can also benefit from the air-conditioner, which is located in the bedroom. There is an entrance foyer with a narrow table and a carved mirror on the wall. Paintings by resident painters adorn the walls in the living room and bedroom, and wood craft objects were created by local artists. Tapa covered sconces are fixed in the corners of the living room, tapa covered sliding doors lead to the bathroom and there is a tapa covered lamp on the desk in the bedroom.

The bedroom is furnished with a kingside bed with a dark wooden frame. There are two mattresses together that seem to be thicker than normal and are so dreamy comfortable to sleep on. There is another television in the bedroom, a wall of closets and shelves, and inside the closet are two sets of snorkeling gear, a basket table for breakfast in bed, two plastic raincoats, shoe polish, personal safe, iron and board. There are three telephones — in the living room, bedroom and toilet, all with DDD, voice mail and computer data ports. The pink marble bathroom is huge and very well lit. The floor and walls are tiled and there is a see-through window into the lagoon behind the bathtub. There are dressing counters and lavabos on two opposite walls. On one side there is a magnified lighted makeup mirror, hair-dryer and a generous supply of Aveda personal amenities, including a vanity kit, mending kit and shower cap. On the other counter are two pots for making coffee and tea, along with the supplies. Underneath the counter is a bathroom scale. The bath fixtures are French and the Jacuzzi spa bathtub is wide enough for two skinny people or one really big person. The toilet and bidet are in a large separate room. There is also a separate shower with an overhead shower head with a soft spray and a hand held shower nozzle with a jet spray. Electric outlets are provided for both 110 and 220 volt AC.

The terrace is partically covered with a thatched roof and there is also space for a sundeck. All the outdoor furniture is teak and includes two padded lounge chairs, a teacart and table and two dining chairs. A fish and coral viewing panel is built into the deck and a ladder leads to a lower platform, where there is a shower. From there you can dive into the deep water or descend slowly on another ladder to snorkel among the coral gardens in the lagoon. Should you decide to spend your entire day in your villa, be assured there is 24-hour room service. You can even order the romantic Canoe Breakfast to be delivered by outrigger canoe.

The resort's public facilities are just as impressive as the bungalows, however, and as well decorated. Louis Wane's wife Lulu oversaw the landscape design of this resort, as well as its interior design. Among 600 coconut trees and hundreds of other palms, pandanus trees and tropical plants are two restaurants and two of the three bars, a meeting room, library and computer room with free Internet access, a fitness center with juice bar facilities, a 10,000 square foot infinity-edge swimming pool, a gift boutique, art gallery, Tahiti Perles shop, beauty salon with manicure and pedicure, a wedding chapel, and a Mandara Spa built on the hillside. An overwater check-in area is set in a natural aquarium, and the Upa Upa Bar is also built over the water. Secretarial and other business services are available, as well a tour and travel desk, same day laundry service, two-day dry-cleaning, daily maid service and nightly turn-down service, baby-sitting, private boat transfers between the airport and resort, private shuttle boat service for Vaitape village, electric shuttle carts and a heliport. Special Honeymoon/Romance, Scuba diving and Spa packages are available on request. See information on *Where to Eat* in this chapter.

Deluxe

BORA BORA LAGOON RESORT & SPA, *B.P. 175, Bora Bora 98730. Tel. 689/60.40.00; Fax 689/60.40.01; E-mail: info@bblr.pf. US and Canada Reservations: Orient Express 800/860-4095 or 843/965.8600. www.boraboralagoon.com; www.orient-express.com. 79 units. 2005 EP Rates single/double: garden bungalow 47.135 CFP; beach bungalow 59.068 CFP; one bedroom suite 93.077 CFP; overwater bungalow 80.546 CFP; end* *pontoon overwater bungalow 93.077 CFP; villa 184.961 CFP; extra bed 6.000 CFP. Buffet breakfast 2.983 CFP per person per day; MAP with breakfast and dinner 10.143 CFP; AP with breakfast, lunch and dinner 13.723 CFP. Roundtrip boat transfers from Bora Bora Airport to hotel are not included. Add 5% hotel tax to room rates and 6% value added tax to room rates, plus 150 CFP municipal tax per person per day. A 10% value added tax is applicable to other services. All major credit cards.*

This hotel originally opened in June 1993 as a Nara Resort, and in April 1997 Orient-Express Hotels took over operation under management contract, adding the Bora Bora Orient-Express as one of the Leading Hotels of the World. Orient-Express acquired the Bora Bora Lagoon Resort in 2001, and has since closed the hotel twice for extensive additions, renovations and enhancment programs.

This very exclusive hideaway hotel is located on the sunset point of Motu Toopua, a small, roadless coral island a mile across the bay from Bora Bora's main island. A quarter-mile stretch of white sand beach fronts the resort, which is set amid 12 acres of lush tropical gardens. Since a 2004 improvement program took place these gardens contain an even greater number of carefully chosen indigenous flora, as well as meandering streams, fountains and waterfalls. The most outstanding new addition to the waterworld scene on the hotel grounds is a Tahitian style special events facility that is reached by a wooden footbridge that takes you across a lily pond in a very zen-like setting. This conference center can accommodate 100 people. A Chapiteau (marquee) on the beach can accommodate up to 120 guests, and there are three other possible meeting areas on the premises.

Following the extensive work carried out in the first quarter of 2004 there are now 79 guest bungalows, including a new Presidential villa with 2-bedrooms and 2-bathrooms. It faces the beach and has its own swimming pool in front and a rock wall and garden in the back. Three bungalow suites have also been added, each with one bedroom and a swimming pool. The older units consist of 5 garden bungalows, 20 beach bungalows, 44 overwater bungalows and 6 overwater bungalows on the end of the pontoon. The bungalows are built in the traditional Tahitian *fare* style, with thatched roofs and are arranged in three groupings, each with easy access to the village center. Some of the bungalows face Motu Tapu and the Teavanui Pass, while others face the main island and Bora Bora's famous Otemanu Mountain. All the units are air-conditioned and have ceiling fans. Features include yucca wood floors, floor-to-ceiling louvers and timber blinds. The furniture is made of wood and wicker, and the upholstery and draperies are neutral with lots of accent cushions, as well as tikis, wooden carvings and other South Seas artifacts decorating the walls. Each room contains a wonderfully comfortable king-size bed and a day bed, writing desk, bathroom with bathtub, separate shower, double basins, mini-bar, private safe, hair dryer, lighted makeup mirror, tea and coffee facilities, international direct dial telephones including one beside the toilet. The satellite television offers more choices than most of the other hotels in Bora Bora and there is also an in-house video channel and a video player that will also play DVD music. The overwater bungalows have glass-bottom coffee tables, private sun decks and steps leading into the lagoon, with fresh water showers on the landing. These older bungalows will eventually be remodeled one by one, as they lack sufficient storage space in the closets, drawers and bathroom counter for two people. There is a lot of floor space between the bed and the television, but you can sit in a chair if you want to get closer to the screen.

Guest services include ice delivery, laundry, nightly turndown, baby-sitting, boat transfers between the Bora Bora airport and the hotel and a motor launch transfer between the hotel and Vaitape village. Room service is available 24-hours a day with a casual menu of sandwiches, salads, seafood, pastries and drinks. A special treat for lovers staying in the overwater bungalows is to have a Continental breakfast of tropical fruits, pastries and juices delivered to their sundeck by outrigger canoe.

Otemanu Restaurant, Bora Bora Lagoon Resort's 92-seat restaurant, is poised over the lagoon with breathtaking views on every side. It has now been improved with new windows that maximize views of Mt. Otemanu, and its terrace has new stonework and new outdoor seating, purposely designed with lovers in mind who wish to take in the *motu*'s superlative sunsets. It is open daily for dinner, offering fine dining on Continental cuisine with a distinctive Polynesian influence. A Tahitian Dinner Show is presented each Thursday evening and a Seafood Buffet with local entertainment takes place each Saturday night when the hotel has a lot of in-house guests.

Café Fare offers informal indoor/outdoor dining for breakfast and lunch beside the swimming pool. You can order your favorite libation from the Rotopa Bar, which is conveniently located between the pool and both beaches. The Hiro Lounge seats 50 and is open from 6 to 11pm, with live music featured nightly. You can sit in a very high chair of wood and leather at the hand-crafted wooden bar, relax in a big comfortable masculine chair, or enjoy the fresh breezes on the terrace while sipping your favorite libation. The Pavilion library/lounge can also be used for private dining and meetings for small groups. This newly refurbished room contains a pool table, dart board, card table, computer with Internet connections and a large screen television and video. A DVD player will be added, as well as the entire National Geographic collection of films. The Putari Boutique carries gift items, film and clothing and there is a Sibani Perles shop in the main building.

An all-new Fitness Center was added in 2004, complete with air-conditioning, television and 14 technogym machines. The activities manager will help you with your exercise programs. The 160-foot long swimming pool is now even bigger and is supposedly the largest fresh water pool in Bora Bora.

All the tiling around the pool was also enlarged. Guests also have free use of two floodlit tennis courts, beach volleyball, snorkeling equipment, Tahitian outrigger paddle canoes, kayaks, windsurf boards and Hobie cats.

Another addition that was completed in 2004 was the creation of Marú, the Polynesian inspired treehouse spa. Four treatment rooms are on the waterfront and two massage rooms are built into the branches of two almost mythic Banyan trees. Spa services include Tahitian based treatments using herbs and remedies that have been practiced in the South Pacific for hundreds of years. An 80-minute Shiatsu massage is 15.400 CFP and you can combine your massage with a bath of aromatic oils, sand, milk or flowers. A special treat for lovers is the flower-perfumed bath and a sunset massage for two. You can even enjoy Bora Bora's spectacular sunset in the comfort of a private boat while sipping champagne and enjoying a relaxing 50-minute massage for two. This unforgettable experience costs 74.930 CFP.

The hotel's reception area has a newly designed sophisticated lighting system and throughout the public rooms and hallways of this building are sculptures and paintings by Bora Bora's celebrated artist, Garrick Yrondi. There are also chairs made from polished tree trunks, carved wooden tikis and primitive art from various parts of the South Pacific. A separate discussion area has been created at the Activities Desk, where you can book any of the island's regular tours and excursions. You can book a shark feeding tour, boat rental, catamaran cruise, coral garden snorkeling excursion, jet ski tour, fishing expedition, glass bottom boat tour, helicopter tour, circle island tour, mountain safari tour, mountain bike tour, whale watching tour (in season), go parasailing, water-sailing, scuba diving, snuba diving, drift snorkeling, hiking, horseback riding, visit the Lagoonarium, or go shopping for black pearls. The hotel provides free shuttle boat service to Vaitape village.

In addition, the hotel offers some exclusive activities. The *Hippocampe II* is a catamaran based at the Bora Bora Lagoon Resort & Spa that is available for a Sunset Cruise from 4:45 to 6:45pm for 10.000 CFP per person. You can also have a half-day cruise for 15.000 CFP per person, or a full-day cruise for 24.000 CFP per person. Moonlight Cruises can also be arranged. A most unusual romantic activity for lovers is an exclusive Motu Barbecue Picnic. Your guide will take you in his boat to a lovely spot on a motu islet, where you can snorkel and swim in the turquoise waters while the host sets up a gourmet lunch, complete with tables, chairs, parasol, fine linens, china and silverware, all in two feet of water. The barbecue also stands in the water, and the ice bucket stands nearby. You can watch the brightly colored fish swimming around you while you dine on lobster and beef and share a bottle of champagne. You leave the hotel at 10am and return at 3pm and you'll pay 70.000 CFP a couple for this memorable experience.

Tahitian Weddings may be performed on the hotel's main beach at 4:30pm, followed by a Sunset Cruise in an outrigger canoe and a special

Romantic Dinner served in the Otemanu Restaurant. The full-on ritual with Tahitian singers and dancers costs 156.250 CFP per couple and includes photos of the non-binding ceremony. You can also have a Tahitian Wedding performed on a private *motu* islet for 218.750 CFP, which includes a Sunset Cruise and Champagne Dinner served on the *motu*. The hotel offers 5-night packages called the "Tahitian l'Esprit d'Amour" that include such romantic touches as a flower decorated bed on arrival, a bottle of French champagne, a sunset cruise for two, and a one-hour massage for two. For details and rates contact the hotel directly.

The Bora Bora Lagoon Resort made the *Condé Nast Traveler's* "The World's Best Place to Stay" Gold List for 2003 and 2004, with a score of 100 for "The Best by Location" and a high score for "The Best Activities". In June 2003 this hotel was voted by readers of *Travel & Leisure* as one of the "Top Hotels for Service, in Australia, New Zealand and the South Pacific." In October 2004 Travel & Leisure's World's Best Spas report named the hotel's Marú Spa as "one to Watch". The hotel was named one of the "Top 5 Australia, New Zealand and South Pacific Hotels" on the 2003 Platinum List in *Celebrated Living*. Other awards were given in 2003 and 2004 by *Departures Magazine*, *Modern Bride*, World Travel Awards, Travel Channel, and Zagat's Top International Hotel, Resorts & Spa Surveys. These are just the most recent of a long list of praises sung in the honor of a hotel that has even been voted the #1 "Top Exotic Spot" Luxury Destination in the 1999 Robb Report.

HOTEL SOFITEL MOTU, *B.P. 516, Bora Bora 98730. Tel. 689/60.56.00; Fax (689) 60.56.66; E-mail: h8989@accor-hotels.com; Reservations: 689/ 41.04.04; Fax 689/41.05.05; in US Tel. 800/SOFITEL (763-4835); E-mail: reservation_tahiti@accor-hotels.com; www.sofitel.com. On Motu Piti Uu'uta, across lagoon from Sofitel Marara. 30 bungalows. 2005 Low Season (High Season) EP Rates single/double: deluxe bungalow 66.000 CFP (75.600 CFP); overwater bungalow 84.300 CFP (96.500 CFP); Suite 101.200 CFP (115.800 CFP) Third person add 5.000 CFP. Note: Low Season is from January 1-June 30, 2005 and from November 1-December 31, 2005. High Season is from July 1-October 31, 2005. American breakfast 2.950 CFP; lunch 3.250 CFP; dinner 6.450 CFP. Children under 12 half-price. Round-trip transfers 4.000 CFP per person. Add 5% hotel tax to room rates and 6% value added tax to room rates, plus 150 CFP municipal tax per person per day. A 10% value added tax is applicable to other services. All major credit cards.*

This luxury resort opened in August 1999 on the private islet of Motu Piti Uu'uta, set in the middle of the Bora Bora lagoon, facing the Sofitel Marara and the mesmerizing mountains of Otemanu and Pahia. This secluded *motu* features three beaches, one of which has sun all day long for sunbathing and snorkeling in the coral gardens surrounding the *motu*. People who have stayed here claim that the best snorkeling in Bora Bora is in the aquarium right beside this islet. Honeymooners quickly discovered the charms of this very private place and now it is fully booked practically year-round, even though the room rack rates escalated 23% for the overwater bungalows and 26% for the deluxe units between 2002 and 2004. Guests who read the Tahiti forums on the Internet websites soon learn that the choice bungalows are number 128 and 129. From these end units you have a fabulous view of the mountains of Bora Bora as well as the rising sun and all the vivid colors of the romantic tropical sunsets.

There are 20 overwater bungalows and 10 deluxe bungalows built on high stilts over the beach or hillside, which offer you choices of the sunset, sandy beach or sunset views. The hotel is built of Indonesian kohu wood, which is similar to teak, and all the roofs are made of woven pandanus leaves. The sturdy furniture was made in Bora Bora and there is no bamboo used in the construction, although woven pandanus peue mats cover the walls. You have a choice of two twin beds or a king-size bed when they are pushed together. A big wooden headboard has tattoo designs painted across the top and individual reading lights are also placed on the headboard. There is also a day bed, which is covered in a homey salmon colored upholstery to match the bedspread, cushion covers and draperies. Each bungalow has the luxury of air conditioning and a ceiling fan, a private safety box, mini-bar, satellite television and video channel, plus coffee and tea facilities and two-line phones with a modem plug. At publication time there were no CD or DVD players provided. The bathroom floor is covered with polished black volcanic stones and an enormous showerhead provides a relaxing massage in the very spacious shower. A long bathroom counter of kohu wood contains two lavabos and a selection of Sofitel amenities. There is also a lighted magnified makeup mirror, a hairdryer and a full length wall mirror. A telephone is installed in the private toilet area. The overwater bungalows each contain a round glass window on the floor for prime viewing of the natural marine life in the lagoon below. The rich coral gardens here attract parrotfish, mullets, jackfish, picassofish, butterflyfish and needlefish. Stairs from the covered terrace lead you directly into the inviting water and snorkeling gear and beach towels are provided in each room. There is an outdoor shower on the lower sundeck.

Because this particular *motu* is a natural reserve of the reef heron, *egretta sacra*, this graceful bird is used as the hotel's logo. It is called Manu Tuki in the Paumotu language of the Tuamotu atolls, which is also the name of the hotel's hilltop restaurant and bar. You will enjoy spectacular views of the multihued lagoon as well as the highly praised cuisine served here. This restaurant is open to outside guests for dinner only on reservation. For more information see *Where to Eat* in this chapter. Room service is also available. A new bar has been added on the terrace that connects with the restaurant. The stone steps leading to the reception, restaurant and bar have also been improved.

Exclusivity is the by-word of the Sofitel Motu because the management wants their guests to find the privacy they seek as they realize their dreams of being in an authentic natural environment, where you can swim, and walk around the *motu* and climb the hill to gaze beyond the reef at the neighboring islands of Tahaa and Raiatea to the east and Maupiti to the west.

Kayaks are complimentary for the guests staying at the Sofitel Motu, and they can also enjoy all the amenities, activities, and excursions that are available at the Sofitel Marara. A complimentary on demand shuttle service takes you from the *motu* to the main island in less than five minutes.

This hotel provides the perfect honeymoon hide-away, which you can celebrate with a VIP welcome. Upon arrival you will receive a cold drinking coconut, a basket of tropical fruits and two Sofitel *pareos*, and Tahitian musicians will come to your bungalow and serenade you. A romantic dinner for two will be served in your bungalow or in the restaurant, complete with a bottle of French champagne. You can also get married Polynesian style on the Sofitel Motu beach or in the gardens of the Sofitel Marara. Contact the hotel for details and rates.

HOTEL LE MERIDIEN BORA BORA, *B.P. 190, Bora Bora 98730. Tel. 689/ 60.51.51; Fax 689/60.51.52. Reservations 689/47.07.27; Fax 689/47.07.28; E-mail: reservations@lemeridien-tahiti.com; www.lemeridien-bora.com; in US and Canada 800/543-4300; E-mail: sales@lemeridien-tahiti.com. 100 units. 2005 EP Rates single/double: beach bungalow 65.000 CFP; overwater bungalow 75.000 CFP; premium overwater bungalow 85.000 CFP. Meal plan with breakfast and dinner 8.290 CFP; meal plan with breakfast, lunch and dinner 12.340 CFP. American buffet breakfast 2.900 CFP; set luncheon menu 4.050 CFP; set dinner menu 5.970 CFP. Round-trip airport transfers 4.000 CFP per person. Add 5% hotel tax to room rates and 6% value added tax to room rates and prepaid meal plans, plus 150 CFP municipal tax per person per day. A 10% value added tax is applicable to other services. All major credit cards.*

This 5-star hotel opened in June 1998, and for several years it was one of the most reclusive international class hotels on Bora Bora. If you hurry up and visit, you can still find some of this tranquillity, without being disturbed by the activity of cruise ship tenders, airport boats, excursion canoes and jet skis zooming past at frequent intervals. New hotels are now under construction on either side of Le Méridien, with a June 2005 opening planned for the 100-unit Ritz-Carlton and a March 2006 completion date scheduled for the 112-suite Intercontinental Bora Bora. Hopefully, by the time the stiff competition moves in next door, Le Méridien will have found the funds to do some much needed updating in their bungalows, as the wood needs a touch up and the original furnishings are looking rather worn. There's not much that can be done, however, to stop the overwater bungalows from shaking each time the maids or room service personnel drive their electric carts onto the pier that leads to these units.

With more than 1 kilometer (.6 miles) of white sand beach, accessible only by a 20-minute boat ride from the airport or 5 minutes by boat from the main island of Bora Bora, Le Méridien covers more than 9.5 hectares (23.5 acres) on the southern end of Motu Piti Aau, an islet across the lagoon from the village of Anau. It is located between the sea and lagoon, with 82 overwater bungalows and 18 beachside bungalows surrounding a shallow interior lagoon. Everywhere you look is absolutely beautiful, from the miki miki bushes, pandanus, sea grape and flowering trees to the blinding white beaches and the blues and greens of the sparkling lagoon.

Each bungalow contains 60 square meters (646 square feet) of living space, which includes a large bedroom with a sitting area, a walk-in closet and a spacious bathroom. There is also a partially covered outside deck, and for the bungalows over water, there are steps leading into the lagoon. Instead of the standard glass table that allows you to watch the fish in the lagoon underneath the overwater bungalows, Le Méridien has gone a step further and built a large glassed surface into the polished wood floor. Once you get used to it, then you may enjoy the feeling of walking on water or in space, and a rug is provided to cover the glass floor if you don't like looking at all that water under your feet. Some of the guests who have stayed here rave about the thrill they had lying on the windowed floor and watching all the fish that swim around underneath the bungalow at 2am.

The 100 deluxe bungalows are built with natural materials of pandanus-thatched roofs and precious kohu wood, which is dark and heavy, similar to teak. Unlike many other hotels in these islands, the bungalows contain no bamboo, and their decor is more Indonesian than Polynesian. Each bungalow is air-conditioned and has a ceiling fan, and they are furnished with two twin beds that pushed together to make a king-size bed. There is also a sofa bed, a big desk with a recessed make-up mirror, blackout curtains, satellite television and video, a mini-bar fridge, separate liquor or snack cabinet, international direct dial telephone, personal safe, coffee and tea facilities, a bathtub and separate shower, private toilet, a full length mirror, magnified makeup mirror, hair dryer and a selection of Le Méridien toilet amenities. Wooden louvers in the windows enable you to control the flow of light and air into the room. Next day laundry service is also provided. The 16 premium overwater bungalows are the same size as the other overwater units, but they are located at the end of the deck with a direct view of Bora Bora's famous mountains. An experience in establishing coral under the bungalows on stilts is being carried out at Le Méridien Bora Bora, and guests are asked not to touch them in order to optimize their growth rate.

An unusual addition to this hotel is the construction of a levy on the ocean side, which is 3.5 meters (11.5 feet) high and 20 meters (66 feet) wide. This serves as a protective barrier in the event of big ocean swells, and it is camouflaged with sand and planted with trees to enhance the visual aspect of the wall. The boat-shaped central building is therefore high and can be reached by a flight of stairs or a concrete driveway leading to the reception area, activities desk, an air-conditioned lounge and television room, the Miki Miki Bar, boutique and Sibani black pearl shop, and a lending library and game room with billiards table. In the center of this complex is a lily pond where small colorful fish dart to and fro in the green-shaded water.

Breakfast and dinner are served in the restaurant Le Tipanier, which can seat 180 people and looks out onto the inner lagoon, complete with hungry *nape* fish looking for a handout. The chef caters to the taste preferences of the hotel guests, who are primarily French, Italian, American and Japanese, providing international and local cuisine. A theme buffet is served in the Honu (turtle) section of Le Tipanier restaurant each evening, and is priced at 6.000 CFP. An à la carte gourmet dinner is served each evening in the Tiare section of the restaurant, and reservations must be made in advance to be seated in this section. Entertainment includes a Polynesian dance show each Tuesday and Friday night, and a local band plays music during dinner on Wednesday nights. Le Te Ava, the 120-seat beachside restaurant adjacent to the fresh water swimming pool, serves a Parisian breakfast from 10 to 11:30am, and lunch is available from 11:30am to 3pm. The atmosphere here is informal and friendly, and you sit in rocking chairs at the tables with your feet in the sand. Snacks are available in the Miki Miki bar from 3 to 9pm. and at the Beach Tupa snack bar between 10am and 5pm. Room service is available 24 hours a day, with a limited menu between 10pm and 6am, and you can even order picnic baskets to take with you while exploring the delights of the beautiful white sand beach and aquamarine waters of Bora Bora's incredible lagoon.

The choices of activities and excursions available at Le Méridien include the fresh water swimming pool, free snorkeling equipment, pedal boats, windsurf boards, kayaks, Polynesian outrigger canoes and a special Hawaiian sailing canoe. You can rent a 14-foot Hobie Cat for 2.000 CFP per hour. The activities desk can arrange your land and lagoon activities. You can also go sailing or parasailing, water skiing or jet skiing, go deep-sea fishing, scuba diving, shark feeding or horseback riding on the *motu*. A specialty at Le Méridien is the 65-foot sailing catamaran *O'Hana* that is used for day sailing and snorkeling excursions and for romantic sunset sailing cruises. You can visit the turtle nursery on the hotel property and watch dozens of large and small sea turtles being fed each morning. You can even swim with the turtles inside the clear waters of a *hoa* channel that flows from the ocean into the lagoon. The Lagoonarium is just a five-minute walk from the hotel property along the white sand beach, where, for an entrance fee, you can swim with the wild creatures that live inside this enclosure. One of the hotel's beach bungalows has been transformed into a massage and body care salon called Espace Bien-Etre, a place of well-being. It is open daily except Sunday, and you can indulge your hedonistic nature with a rubdown with coconut fiber, crushed coffee beans or sand perfumed with oils, followed by an aromatic bath or floral bath, a seaweed wrap, facial and a choice of massages. A 50-minute relaxing massage is 11.000 CFP and an outdoor massage at twilight is 13.000 CFP for 50 minutes.

Honeymoon couples from Japan and other countries, who have already been legally married in their country, have their formal wedding ceremony in Bora Bora filmed in a romantic little chapel on the hotel grounds. Polynesian Wedding Ceremonies are performed on the beach at Le Méridien on request. The "Otemanu" wedding sells for 178.000 CFP and includes the ceremony, 12 pictures taken by a professional photographer, a champagne sunset sail aboard a catamaran, with a romantic dinner served that evening on the balcony of your bungalow or in the restaurant. The bride and groom are dressed in traditional *pareos* and fragrant flowers, with entertainment provided by Polynesian singing and dancing. For further details you should contact the hotel directly.

BORA BORA PEARL BEACH RESORT, *B.P. 169, Bora Bora 98730. Tel. 689/60.52.00; Fax 689/60.52.22; Reservations: Tel. 689/50.84.53; Fax 689/ 43.17.86; E-mail: sales@spmhotels.pf; www.pearlresorts.com. 80 bunga- lows. 2005 *Low Season (High Season) EP Rates single/double: garden pool suite 51.000 CFP (51.000 CFP); premium pool suite 58.000 CFP (58.000 CFP; beach suite 67.000 CFP (72.000 CFP); overwater bungalow 68.000 CFP (75.000 CFP); premium overwater bungalow 78.000 CFP (85.000 CFP); third person 10.000 CFP. Meal plan with breakfast and dinner 8.700 CFP per person; meal plan with breakfast, lunch and dinner 11.700 CFP. Children under 12 sharing the bungalow with their parents are free and pay half-price for meals. Full American breakfast 2.500 CFP; Continental breakfast 2.200 CFP; lunch (set menu) 3.000 CFP; dinner (set menu) 6.200 CFP; fruit basket 4.025 CFP. One-way transfers between the airport and hotel 2.500 CFP per person. Private boat transfer 12.500 CFP. Add 5% hotel tax to room rates and 6% value added tax to room rates and prepaid meal plans, plus 150 CFP municipal tax per person per day. A 10% value added tax is applicable to other services. All major credit cards. *Low Seasons are from January 1-May 31, 2005 and November 1-December 31, 2005. High Season is June 1-October 1, 2005.*

This beautiful five-star hotel opened in June 1998, on 19 hectares (47 acres) of land between the ocean and lagoon on Motu Tevairoa, facing Faanui Bay. The hotel has recently been renovated and is well maintained. There are 20 overwater bungalows, 30 premium overwater bungalows, 10 beach suites with Jacuzzi, and 6 garden suites with pools and 14 premium pool suites. The entire hotel is built in the traditional Polynesian style, with pandanus thatched roofs, local woods, woven pandanus wall coverings and a decor that includes tapa wall hangings and paintings and sculptures by Polynesian artists.

All the bungalows have air-conditioning as well as ceiling fans, a well-stocked refrigerated mini-bar, coffee and tea making facilities, bathroom amenities, hair dryer, safety box, stereo with CD player, satellite television with a hotel movie channel, DVD player, and international direct dial telephone. There are twin beds or a king size bed and a day bed in each unit, as well as writing desks and reading lights.

Honeymooners will prefer the 30 overwater bungalows that are classified as Premium, because they offer the best views of the mountain and lagoon. These attractively decorated bungalows have 658 square feet (61 square meters) of living space, with not only a glass bottom table to observe the eco-system of the lagoon below, but you can also watch the fish feeding on the coral from a window through the vanity area in the bathroom. This will keep you mesmerized while you're soaking in your bathtub. All the overwater units have a bathtub and a separate shower, and the telephones are equipped for Internet connections. Guests staying in the overwater bungalows may also have the pleasure of their breakfast being delivered by outrigger canoe. Four overwater bungalows are equipped for handicapped guests in wheelchairs, and there is an elevator in the main building, from the reception area to the restaurant and bar upstairs.

The very popular beach suites provide 786 square feet (73 square meters) of living space and they are equipped with a shower, private sundeck and a Jacuzzi. A much appreciated touch in the beach units is the wall that encloses the sundeck and Jacuzzi. It is high enough to truly offer the privacy you seek, so that you can sunbathe or walk around in the nude if you so desire. The bedroom, where the air-conditioning is located, can be completely closed off from the living room and bath area. Anyone sitting or sleeping in the living room, which has a day bed, will have the benefit of a ceiling fan but no air-conditioning. This room is cleverly designed to provide a quiet, sheltered space in the afternoon and a romantic setting in the evening, when you can watch the dazzling view of the water and mountain through your picture window that you can open or close with bamboo shutters. This room has direct access to the white sand beach if you feel like walking hand in hand under the shade of the sacred old *tamanu* trees that line the beach.

The premium and garden pool suites are all the same size, providing 872 square feet (81 square meters) of living space. This includes a gazebo type shelter with a table and benches, a sundeck with two lounge chairs, a private plunge pool and a small tropical garden. A privacy fence surrounds this area and another wall protects the outdoor shower in the garden adjoining the bathroom. The bedroom can be closed off from the bathroom to take full advantage of the air-conditioning. These large garden suites may be preferable for families, but you should know that there are some hungry mosquitoes living back here in this area. Although the maintenance staff sprays the grounds every afternoon, the mosquitoes don't seem to pay much attention, and in the early evening it is difficult to sit on the sundeck without being chewed up. You also have to keep the doors and windows shut, as the only screening is on the window in the toilet.

The Restaurant Tevairoa is the main restaurant, which sits 20 feet (6 meters) above sea level and overlooks the myriad hues of the blues and greens of the Bora Bora lagoon. It is open for breakfast and dinner, serving a refined international menu. Special evenings are presented on Monday and Friday, when a group of musicians and dancers comes over from the main island to dance for you. A luncheon menu of salads, sandwiches, seafood and meat dishes is served beside the pool at the Miki Miki Restaurant and Bar, and the Taurearea Bar upstairs provides the perfect setting to admire the sunset as you gaze at the peaks of Otemanu and Pahia mountains. You can reach this bar and the main restaurant by taking the elevator or stairs. Room service is also available. See more information on *Where to Eat* in this chapter.

The hotel also has a gift shop, Sibani Jewelry pearl boutique, game room with billiards table and library. There is a conference center and a movie theater for 40 people, but this room is mostly being used as a computer room with Internet service. The Bora Bora Pearl Beach Resort features one of the largest fresh water swimming pools on Bora Bora (5,220 square feet), situated at the base of a water cascade. There is also a Jacuzzi pool in this area. The hotel guests have free use of the snorkeling equipment, outrigger paddle canoes, kayaks, Ping Pong, bacci ball, badminton and society games. They can use the tennis court, which is floodlit for night games, or play mini-golf. The Bora Bora Blue Nui Dive Center is located on the hotel premises and optional excursions and tours can be arranged at the hotel's activity desk. And if you feel like just lying back and being pampered, you can have a relaxing Swedish massage in your bungalow.

The Bora Bora Pearl Beach Resort is a favorite destination for honeymooners and other lovers who appreciate the romantic setting of this hotel. To make those moments together even more magical, you can begin your visit with a Romantic Welcome, choosing a Tipanier Welcome for 18.133 CFP, a Hibiscus Welcome for 43.067 CFP, or a Tiare Welcome for 64.600 CFP. Suggestions for a Romantic Interlude include breakfast served to your overwater bungalow by outrigger canoe, for 8.613 CFP for two. A Romantic dinner served in the restaurant is 18.700 CFP per couple, or you may prefer to have dinner under the stars on the overwater terrace of your bungalow for 34.567 CFP for two. A romantic dinner served aboard a catamaran is 63.467 CFP for two. Romantic Escapades will take you lovers on a private champagne sunset cruise aboard a catamaran for 53.833 CFP. A full day catamaran cruise with lunch for two is 124.667 CFP, and a private boat tour to Taha'a is 226.667 CFP. These are just a sample of private possibilities.

A new addition to this resort is a little wedding chapel. Should you prefer a more unusual setting for your vows, Polynesian wedding ceremonies can be performed on the beach or on a private *motu*, which are priced at 116.733 CFP for "Te Ruau," 187.000 CFP for "Te Mana" and 198.333 CFP for a Sunset Motu ceremony. You can even have a Robinson Crusoe day for honeymooners, complete with a wedding on the motu, for 243.667 CFP. Scuba divers sometimes choose to say "I do" during an Underwater Itiraa Mahana Ceremony, for 143.933 CFP. Check with the hotel directly for details on these non-binding blessings, which are also appropriate for renewal of vows.

Moderate
   BORA BORA EDEN BEACH HOTEL, *B. P. 191, Bora Bora 98730, Tel. 689/60.57.60; Fax 689/67.69.76; E-mail: borabora@mail.pf; www.boraborahotel.com. 15 bungalows. EP Rates single/double: garden or ocean view bungalow 25.000 CFP; beach bungalow 35.000 CFP. Boat transfers from Anau land base to hotel 500 CFP per person; meal plan with breakfast and dinner 6.100 CFP; meal plan with breakfast, lunch and dinner 8.000 CFP per person per day; lunch 1.900 CFP; dinner 4.100 CFP. Add 5% hotel tax to room rates and 6% value added tax to room rates and prepaid meal plans, plus 150 CFP municipal tax per person per day. A 6% value added tax is applicable to transfers and 10% VAT is added to other services. All major credit cards.*

   This property opened in October 2001 on Motu Piti Aau, a 15-minute boat ride across the lagoon from Anau village. It was formerly promoted by South Pacific Management (who also manage the Pearl Resorts), as an environmental friendly eco-tourist hotel, completely autonomous with solar power, desalinization plant, a water-catchment system and recycling facilities. Owner Vlada Zidek then took over the management of his hotel and when I was in Bora Bora in March 2004 I learned that all the employees had left because they were not getting paid. Soon after that Zidek was advertising for a new manager. The Tahiti forums on the Internet printed complaints from unhappy people who had stayed there, and at publication time the hotel was reportedly up for sale. Hervé and Morgan Guillard became the hotel's new managers in September 2004, so let's hope that everything will improve under their care.

   There are seven bungalows on the white sand beach, four garden bungalows in the coconut grove and four bungalows face the ocean side of the *motu* islet. All construction is of local woods and bamboo, with thatched pandanus roofs in the traditional Polynesian style. Each bungalow is equipped with a bathroom with hot water shower, a covered terrace and ceiling fan. There is a communal television in the main building, but the rooms have no television and no hair dryers. Remember that this hotel was built as a 2- to 3-star resort. Small refrigerators and coffee and tea making facilities were added long after the hotel opened, although the original brochures claimed to already have these amenities.

The restaurant, bar, kitchen, game room, boutique and office are located in the main building on the beach, and a small fresh water swimming pool is built on the sun deck. The hotel provides snorkeling gear, windsurf boards and sails, outrigger canoes and kayaks for the guests, and there are facilities for playing volley ball and bacci ball. Boat transfers between the hotel and the main island cost 500 CFP each way, and one of the main complaints made by former guests is that the shuttle boat does not leave the hotel at lunchtime until 2:30pm, after all the restaurants are closed on the main island, therefore forcing the guests to eat mediocre food at the hotel. Check it out well before making your reservations to stay here.

Other Lodgings on the Motu

PRIVATE ISLAND, *B.P. 511, Bora Bora 98730. Tel./Fax 67.74.50, cell 79.26.39; E-mail: tevanessa@private-island.net; www.private-island.net. On Motu Haapiti Rahi, a private islet five minutes by boat from the airport and five minutes from the ferry dock. Free round-trip transfers to/from the airport. EP Rate: 50.000 CFP per day. Breakfast and dinner 5.000 CFP; breakfast, lunch and dinner 7.000 CFP per person per day. Breakfast 1.000 CFP, lunch 2.000 CFP, dinner 4.000 CFP. Add 6% value added tax to room rates and meal plan and 50 CFP per person per day for municipal tax.*

Teva Victor owns this small *motu* and lives on the islet with his lovely companion, Vanessa. Teva grew up on Motu Tane, the adjacent islet, which was owned at the time by his parents, the famous French explorer Paul-Emile Victor and his wife, Colette. Following in his parents' footsteps, Teva and Vanessa have added a second villa to their property, which can sleep five people. The main area of this very private and luxuriously decorated *fare* consists of a living area with a dining table, a library, a Hi-Fi Stereo system, a fully equipped open kitchen and a bar leading to the overwater terrace. On the mezzanine is a lounge area with television and DVD player, a desk and a double bed. The two bedrooms (with a double bed and a single bed) both lead to the rear of the villa, where you'll find an outdoor shower room with a little garden. Kayaks and snorkeling equipment are also provided. If you don't want to cook for yourself, Vanessa will prepare your meals.

MAI MOANA ISLAND, *B.P. 164, Bora Bora 98730. Tel. 689/67.62.45, Fax 689/67.62.39, cell 73.75.73; E-mail: stan@mail.pf; www.mai-moana-island.com. On Motu Mute Iti, a private islet five minutes by boat from airport and 10 minutes from ferry dock. Boat transfers from airport 1.500 CFP per couple. One-way boat transfer to main island 2.500 CFP. 3 bungalows. EP Rates: Beach bungalow 24.000 CFP single/double. Third person 8.000 CFP per day. MAP: Beach bungalow with breakfast and dinner 34.000 CFP double; AP: Beach bungalow with breakfast, lunch and dinner 38.800 CFP double. Breakfast 1.200 CFP per person; lunch 2.400 CFP per person; dinner 3.800 CFP per person. Bungalow for a couple who wants to be alone, with no other* guests on the island, 45.000 CFP including breakfast. Bungalow with breakfast and dinner 52.400 CFP. Add 6% value added tax to room rates and meal plan, plus 50 CFP per person per day for municipal tax. Mastercard, Visa. No children allowed.

This lodging is classified as a small family hotel. Owner Stan Wisnieswski speaks English, French, German, Russian and Polish, and he's a ham radio operator. His private paradise gets a lot of good comments from people who have stayed at Mai Moana Island, which is dotted with coconut palms and ironwood trees and surrounded by a white sand beach, with no dock. There are three Polynesian style deluxe thatched roof *fares*, each with a double bedroom with mosquito nets over the beds, ceiling fan, mini-bar, telephone, television, dressing room, hair dryer and private bathroom with solar hot water, and a covered terrace. House linens are furnished. A fresh water swimming pool is adjacent to the sunset bar and library. There is a small panoramic restaurant and bar on the premises. Stan and his young Polish wife, Malgorzata, are proud of their cuisine, which is French with a Polynesian touch. Snorkeling equipment and two kayaks are available for guest use.

Special lovers who want to honeymoon on a desert island are welcomed with flowers, a bottle of French champagne, and Tahitian musicians who arrive by outrigger canoe, all for 12.000 CFP for two people. A candlelight dinner for two is served on a beautifully set table with crystal glasses and costs 12.000 CFP. If notified in advance, Stan will serve your favorite French wine. Tahitian wedding ceremonies can also be performed.

BLUE HEAVEN ISLAND, *Bora Bora 98730. Tel. 689/72.72.61; E-mail: john@blueheavenisland.com; www.blueheavenisland.com. On a motu near the airport in Bora Bora. Contact owners for rates.*

This private island is owned by John Gunsen and Monique Lavoie, who have five small Polynesian style bungalows that will accommodate 10-15 people, providing an ideal setting for group events, from private scuba diving trips and yoga retreats to honeymoon parties and family reunions. Each unit is equipped with all the amenities for a comfortable stay, including king size beds or twin beds, television and DVD, private bathrooms, large closets and ceiling fans. Cell phone service is available for an additional cost. There is an outdoor common living room area and a full kitchen where you can cook your own meals or groups can have meals prepared for an additional cost. There is also a washing machine for guest use. Each bungalow has a view of the lagoon and there are kayaks for cruising the lagoon.

RELAIS MATIE, *B.P. 521, Bora Bora 98730. Tel. 689/77.50.26. On ocean side of Motu Piti Aau, a 15-minute boat ride from the airport. Free airport transfers. EP Rates: Matie room, 16.000 CFP; Moana room, 15.000 CFP; Fenua room, 14.000 CFP. Extra mattress 2.000 CFP. Breakfast and dinner add 4.500 CFP per person per day; breakfast, lunch and dinner add 6.000 CFP per person per day. Special rates for child up to 12 years. Add 6% value added* *tax to room rates and meal plan and 50 CFP per person per day for municipal tax. No credit cards.*

There are three guest rooms in a white colonial style house with a red roof, built on the ocean side of Motu Piti Aau, between Hotel Eden Beach and the Intercontinental Hotel Bora Bora, which is under construction. You can see the Eden Beach pier from Relais Matie, but not the hotel itself. From the ocean side of the motu you can see the islands of Taha'a and Raiatea, as well as humpback whales during the months of July to late October. Each guest room is 15 square meters (161 square feet) and can sleep 3 people and one room can accommodate 4 people. There are three private bathrooms with hot water provided by solar panels, and the electricity is also solar. Meals are served family style. Guests can enjoy the swimming pool and kayaks are provided, and Rodolphe Tranchard said that all the comforts are available. He charges 2.500 CFP for a boat transfer if you want to go somewhere specific on the main island, such as to Vaitape village, or you can ride for free when he makes his twice-daily runs to the closest shore.

LE PARADIS, *B.P. 243, Bora Bora 98730. Tel./Fax 689/67.75.53, cell 78.27.87; E-mail: haere-mai@mail.pf; www.haere-mai.com. On Motu Paahi, a private islet five minutes by boat from the Motu Mute airport and 10 minutes from the ferry dock. Free round-trip boat transfers between airport and motu. Paid boat transfers to Vaitape. 7 bungalows. EP Rates: fare 10.000 CFP single; 15.000 CFP double; family fare 17.000 CFP double/triple. Meal plan with breakfast and dinner is 3.500 CFP per person. Add 6% value added tax to room rates and meal plan and 50 CFP per person per day for municipal tax. No credit cards.*

Tehapai and Tipea Pahuiri, the Tahitian family who own this little pension, have a very good reputation for their local style cuisine, especially the *maa Tahiti* they prepare in the underground oven. The 7 thatched roof bungalows have bamboo walls and are located on a pretty white sand beach. Five small bungalows have beds for 2 people and two larger bungalows can sleep 3 people. They are all clean and have a mosquito net over each bed and house linens are supplied. Each unit has its own private bathroom with hot water, and all guests share the kitchen and dining room.

Where to Eat

A value added tax of 10% will be added to all restaurant prices quoted below unless otherwise indicated.

Hotel Restaurants on the Main Island

HOTEL BORA BORA, *Tel. 60.44.60. All major credit cards.*

Matira Terrace Restaurant. This is the main restaurant of the Hotel Bora Bora, located on the top level of the building that houses the reception, business office, and sundries boutique. While you dine you can enjoy a panoramic view of the multi-hued lagoon and talk to the hotel's pet cat, who makes the rounds of the tables each mealtime, looking for free handouts. Open daily serving breakfast from 7 to 10:30am, lunch from 12 to 2pm, and dinner from 6:30 to 9:30pm. Breakfast is also served for early morning departures. You can order room service from the same menu as the restuarant serves for breakfast, lunch and dinner, for an additional 20 percent cost.

Your breakfast is brought from the buffet to your table or you can order à la carte. The Continental breakfast is 3.000 CFP, an American breakfast is 4.000 CFP, and the menu lists a plate of seasonal fresh fruits or a glass of fresh fruit juice for 825 CFP, French toast, waffles or pancakes with maple syrup for 950 CFP, and omelette or Eggs Benedict with smoked salmon or ham for 1.675 CFP, and a cup of coffee or tea for 425 CFP.

Luncheon may be light or substantial fare, with such choices as chilled tomato gaspacho with fresh mint for 1.400 CFP, poisson cru with coconut milk for 1.900 CFP, fresh tuna sashimi for 2.000 CFP, a choice of pasta and sauces for 1.700 CFP, grilled fish of the day or grilled beef steak for 2.800 CFP, or you can order a wok dish of sweet and sour pork, marinated chicken breast with ginger, lime and herbs, or sauteed lamb with Thai basil and fresh tomato, priced from 2.400-2.500 CFP. Luncheon desserts include coconut pie with chocolate coulis, lemon tartlet with raspberry coulis and fresh fruits with mint, from 950-1.100 CFP.

Dinner at the Matira Terrace is not just a meal—it's a privilege. Soups are priced from 1.800 to 1.900 CFP, cold starter courses and salads are 1.900 to 2.400 CFP, and warm appetizers from 2.000 to 2.400 CFP, including Tahitian style octopus and prawn ragout, and brochettes of scallop and smoked duck. Fish and shellfish dishes range from 3.400 to 3.600 CFP. Roasted lobster tails and pineapple chutney flavored with Bora Bora chili and balsamic syrup is 6.500 CFP. Meats and poultry, priced from 3.400 to 6.800 CFP, include roasted lamb fillet, noisette of veal sauteed with chanterelle, light tarragon sauce and Neapolitan Tagliatelle, grilled beef served with Béarnaise sauce and Gratin Dauphinois, and rib roast grilled with teriyaki sauce for two. The dessert menu may tempt you to try a warm preserved pineapple crumble served with its raspberry coulis, a black chocolate mousse stuffed with Morello cherry marinated in brandy, or a warm chocolate cake served with coconut ice cream. These treats are priced from 900 to 1.300 CFP.

Friday night is Spice Night at Restaurant Matira, when the chef invites you to sample the flavors all of the main course proposals in different bowls, or for your main course you can pick the one dish that tempts you the most. A Sampling of Spices Around the World is followed by a Trilogy of Sweet Temptations, and the price is 7.500 CFP per person, which includes coffee or tea.

The wine cellar has the right wine for every dish, with selections from California, Chile, Australia, New Zealand, South Africa, Spain, Italy and France.

Prices range from 2.400 CFP for a Beaujolais-Village to 70.000 CFP for a bottle of the special Reserve of the opening of the Hotel Bora Bora in 1961. This is a Châteaux Beycheville, St. Julien A. Fould, France 1961. They also carry a menu of Cuban cigars for another special treat.

Pofai Beach Bar. *Open daily for lunch and snacks. Special theme evenings.*

This restaurant-bar is located on the white sand beach below the Hotel Bora Bora's main restaurant. You can order sandwiches, salads, *poisson cru*, fruit salads, milkshakes, a fresh drinking coconut, cold beer or exotic cocktails, and enjoy your lunch while you take a break from sunbathing. Throughout the years, every time I go to Bora Bora, I make it a point to stop here to eat a mahi mahi burger with fries and drink a draft beer while enjoying the scenery of the hotel grounds, beach and lagoon. A kitchen has been added, which provides much faster service than before when everything had to be carried from the kitchen upstairs, and the menu is now more varied. Salads are priced from 1.450-2.100 CFP, a choice of 3 pizzas is 1.650-1.800 CFP, a traditional Amanresorts beef or cheese burger is 1.850 CFP, a fish burger with tomato and lettuce heart is 1.850 CFP, and an order of french fries is 1.000 CFP.

A Manager's Cocktail Party is held at 6pm each Tuesday on the Pofai Beach. A special theme menu is served here for dinner, which includes a main dish, dessert and a glass of wine for 6.500 CFP per person. Polynesian Night takes place each Wednesday evening on Pofai Beach. A Beach Barbecue and buffet dinner starts at 7pm and is followed by a traditional Polynesian show and fire dancing, priced at 8.000 CFP. On Thursdays you can try the Surf and Turf menu, which includes a starter course, a main dish, dessert and glass of wine under the stars, for 7.500 CFP per person. Starting at 5:30pm on Friday evenings at the Beach Bar there is the very special Mamas of Bora Bora Song and Dance Show, along with the spectacular Bora Bora sunset. Following this entertainment a dinner of typical Polynesian food is served on the beach, with a starter course, main course, dessert and glass of wine priced at 7.500 CFP per person.

INTERCONTINENTAL MOANA BEACH RESORT BORA BORA, *Tel. 60.49.00. All major credit cards.*

Noa Noa Restaurant and Terrace. *Open daily for breakfast, lunch and dinner.*

An Express breakfast is 1.240 CFP, a Continental breakfast is 2.290 CFP and a full American breakfast is 2.810 CFP. A Canoe breakfast delivered to your overwater bungalow is 6.390 CFP per person. A 3-course set luncheon menu is 4.295 CFP and a 3-course set dinner menu is 6.315 CFP. The MAP meal plan rate for breakfast and lunch is 8.860 CFP and the AP meal plan rate for three meals a day is 11.540 CFP. Light snacks are served on the Vini Vini Bar Terrace for lunch and the *a la carte* dinner menu in the Noa Noa Restaurant lists hot and cold appetizers from 2.280 to 2.720 CFP, fish and seafood dishes from 3.360 to 3.930 CFP, meat and poultry selections from 3.320 to 3.990 CFP, lobster for 4.990 CFP, desserts for 1.100 to 1.200 CFP, and mini-sweets for 500-600 CFP. A lavish seafood buffet under the stars is served each Saturday evening, during the *Soirée Merveilleuse* (marvelous evening), followed by a Polynesian dance show on the beach. The cost is 7.800 CFP. A barbecue and buffet dinner highlights each Tuesday evening, with a Tahitian dance show and fire dancing, for 6.225 CFP. Each Thursday evening is Polynesian Night, with a Tahitian dinner and local entertainment for 6.315 CFP.

LE MAITAI POLYNESIA, *Tel. 60.30.00. All major credit cards.*

Haere Mai Restaurant, *in main building of Le Maitai Polynesia. Open daily 6:30 to 10am and 6:30 to 9pm.*

This is an open-air thatched roof restaurant, very attractively decorated with bamboo, tapa, big shell chandeliers and ceiling fans. Lush gardens of tropical flowers, colored leaves and hanging baskets of ferns complete the pleasant Polynesian scene. A generous American breakfast buffet is served each morning for 2.150 CFP, a Continental breakfast is 1.750 CFP, or you can order à la carte. A Seafood & Polynesian Specialties Buffet is presented each Wednesday night, followed by the Maohi Nui Tahitian dancers and fire dance show, for 5.900 CFP. A Barbecue Buffet is served on Saturday evenings when the hotel's occupation rate is high. The dinner menu on other nights features international cuisine with a French touch.

Tama'a Maitai Restaurant, *on beach at Hotel Le Maitai Polynesia. Open daily with non-stop service from 11:30am to 9pm.*

This is a big open sided restaurant with a thatch roof, situated between the road and beach in the Matira area. The burger bar atmosphere is very casual, with indoor/outdoor seating at Formica tables. You can order a selection of soups, salads and burgers for lunch or dinner. The burgers are served on sesame buns and are good, priced from 1.300 to 1.350 CFP, including fries. *Poisson cru* is 1.390 CFP, pasta dishes are 1.390 to 1.850 CFP, sashimi is 1.550, a sirloin steak with green pepper sauce is 1.850 CFP, and a grilled shrimp kebab is 1.950 CFP. The menu also lists a Maitai Polynesia salad with raw vegetables, fish and grilled chicken for 1.500 CFP, spring rolls and samoussa for 1.550 CFP, wahoo fish with local fruit for 2.650 CFP, plus veal scallops and grilled lamb chops. The most expensive dish is pan fried lobster and mahi mahi filet for 2.800 CFP. Desserts are 450 to 920 CFP, including coconut pie, a chocolate eclair, and strawberries and whipped cream. You can also order fresh fruit juices, a glass of beer or house wine, or a bottle of wine.

NOVOTEL BORA BORA BEACH RESORT, *Tel. 60.59.55. All major credit cards. Open daily for breakfast, lunch and dinner.*

You can sit inside the hotel's 180-seat restaurant or on the terrace by the beach. A Continental breakfast is 1.500 CFP and an American breakfast is 1.700 CFP. Lunch is served between 12 and 2pm, with choices of poisson cru for 1.200 CFP, a fish burger, Club sandwich, roasted pepper sandwich or steak teriyaki sandwich for 1.300 CFP, a Reuben sandwich, bistro burger, smoked turkey sandwich or pizza for 1.400 CFP, Texas style chicken wings for 1.000 CFP, rib-eye steak for 1.500 CFP or Alaska king crab legs for 2.200 CFP. A set luncheon menu is 2.600 CFP. The dinner menu lists starter courses from 950 to 1.900 CFP, fish from 1.800 to 2.400 CFP, meats from 1.800 to 2.900 CFP and desserts from 800 to 1.000 CFP. The chef's specials when I stayed at the hotel and ate in the restaurant included shrimp glazed with ginger liqueur for 2.200 CFP, seafood stew for 2.400 CFP, a butcher's plate of rib eye steak, filet mignon, lamb chops or roasted breast of duck in Huahine honey, for 2.900 CFP. A set dinner menu is 3.900 CFP per person. Let's hope that the new Sofitel management doesn't change the menu too much because it is a good one.

HOTEL SOFITEL MARARA, *Tel. 60.55.00. All major credit cards.*
La Perouse Restaurant. *Open daily from 5:30 to 10:30am for breakfast, 12 to 3:30pm for lunch, and 7 to 9:30pm for dinner.*
The restaurant and bar are built on stilts over the lagoon, next to the swimming pool, facing Tahaa and Raiatea. An American breakfast is 2.400 CFP, the set luncheon menu is 2.950 CFP and the set dinner menu is 5.050 CFP. An Around-the-World buffet is served each Tuesday evening, followed by a «Mamas» show; for 5.200 CFP; an Ocean Buffet is held each Thursday, priced at 6.500 CFP, and is followed by the Heiva Marara band or a fashion show; and a Polynesian Buffet for 4.876 CFP and a traditional dance show take place each Saturday evening, starting at 6pm with the opening of the underground oven. The dance shows begin at 8:30pm.
Café Nui serves a light lunch and snacks from 11am to 9:30pm. A Club sandwich is 990 CFP, a panini sandwich is 1.100-1.290 CFP and burgers are 1.290-1.490 CFP. You can also order a fruit salad with kiwi sorbet for 990 CFP.
CLUB MEDITERANNEE, *Tel. 60.46.04. Open daily for breakfast, lunch and dinner. Tel. 67.49.00. All major credit cards.*
Even if you are not staying at Club Med you can go for breakfast, lunch or dinner. The breakfast buffet costs 2.180 CFP; lunch or dinner is 6.100 CFP for each meal and 3.910 CFP for children under 12. Beer and wine are included. The breakfast buffet is truly a groaning board of fresh, dried and stewed fruits, dry cereals, hot porridge, juices, yogurt, eggs, bacon, sausages, pancakes, crêpes, all kinds of bread and rolls, raw or steamed vegetables, cheeses, cold cuts and Japanese breakfast items: Japanese omelets, noodles, fish fried in soy sauce, pickled vegetables, Cantonese rice and miso soup.
Should you wish to have lunch and spend the afternoon at Club Med it is open to the public between 10:15am and 7pm. Dinner is served between 7:30-9pm. Theme buffets are served nightly with choices of Asian, French or Italian specialties. You may start with fresh New Zealand oysters on the half shell, smoked salmon or foie gras and toast, and proceed to the tables laden

with delicious choices of cold and hot food. Each Thursday and Sunday night is Polynesian night, featuring traditional Tahitian foods cooked in an underground oven and a Tahitian dance show. A nightly show is presented by the Club Med staff except when there is a Tahitian dance show. Starting at 9:30pm you can attend the shows and spend an evening dancing without eating when you buy a *carnet* of bar tickets for 1.980 CFP. All rates include taxes.

TOP DIVE RESORT RESTAURANT, *Tel. 60.50.50. Located beside the bay on the north end of Vaitape village, 5 minutes from the boat dock. Open for breakfast, lunch and dinner. American Express, Mastercard, Visa. Free pick-ups nightly from hotels and boat docks.*

This 47-seat restaurant bills itself as the "best table" in Bora Bora and most of the people who have dined here will agree whole-heartedly. They get a magical feeling when they walk into the restaurant at night and see the 18-meter (59-foot) high ceiling and the soft glow of lights. Through the floor to ceiling windows you can watch the boats in the harbor or the swimmers in the hotel's fresh water pool while you dine on roasted red tuna with pineapple chutney for 1.800 CFP; spicy shrimp soup with croutons for 1.950 CFP, scallops and shrimp layered in pastry with curry and coconut milk sauce for 3.150 CFP, veal filet Rossini, home made mashed potatoes with Basque country ham for 3.500 CFP; or roasted lobster with butter, chives and seasonal vegetables for 6.250 CFP. The hot or cold appetizers are priced from 1.800-2.800 CFP; the fish and seafood dishes are 2.900-3.250 CFP; the meats and poultry are 2.950-3.600 CFP; and desserts are 1.150-1.450 CFP, including a selection called Flower of Strawberries with crunchy pastry and pistachio cream. Can you resist? They also have an exotic menu for 6.000 CFP, and a taster's menu for 9.800 CFP. The menu changes every three months. The cave includes unique selections of exceptional wines from Bordeaux and other vineyards of France, and they also serve wines from the USA, Australia, and Chile. The food served here is *la nouvelle cuisine française*, which means small portions of excellent food beautifully served on a decorated plate. So if you are hungry, you'll be more satisfied with a 3- or 4-course meal. Bring the plastic!

Hotel Restaurants on the Motu
BORA BORA LAGOON RESORT & SPA, *Tel. 60.40.00. All major credit cards.*

Otemanu Restaurant. *Open daily for dinner only. Proper attire is necessary.*

This hotel restaurant is on Motu Toopua, facing the main island of Bora Bora and its famous mountain peaks. Fresh seafood is imported from around the world and is prominent on the menu of gastronomic Continental cuisine with a distinctive Polynesian influence. Starter courses are priced from 1.500 to 2.900 CFP, with new menu items chosen by the executive chef that include mildly spicy ceviche with mahi mahi, corn and steamed *fei* banana, shrimp fritters filled with preserved tomato and basil, seasonal salad, and black olives vinaigrette, and duck breast carpaccio, beetroot salad with anise star and walnut vinaigrette. Ravioli and pasta dishes, from 1.800 to 2.100 CFP, give you choices such as gratin of cannelloni filled with young vegetables and mushrooms in an herb sauce, or penne rigate, slices of chicken breast with paprika, and caramelized julienne of bell peppers, or ravioli filled with Bora Bora shrimp, sautéed fennel with pastis, and a crustacean cappuccino sauce. Fish and seafood dishes are 2.000 to 3.000 CFP, including grilled filet of mahi mahi, roasted wahoo (ono), lagoon fish and seafood cassolette in a coconut milk broth with Indian curry and steamed Basmati rice. Meats may be roasted rack of lamb with potatoes and gravy for 2.900 CFP, or grilled beef tenderloin, leek and bacon samosas, asparagus au gratin and red wine sauce for 3.200 CFP. You can order a glass of wine for 500 to 900 CFP, a glass of champagne for 1.800 CFP, or select a bottle of wine from France, Italy, the USA, Chile, New Zealand or Australia. Prices range from 2.600 to 28.545 CFP, and French champagnes are 10.450 to 41.580 CFP. The bar carries Davidoff Ambassadrice cigars for 1.920 CFP each, a Partagas cigar is 5.000 CFP and a Bolivar Churchill cigar is 5.400 CFP.

When the hotel has a good occupancy rate a Seafood Buffet under the stars is held each Saturday evening on the Otemanu terrace, and also includes sushi and sashimi prepared by the Japanese Chef. This is priced at 8.500 CFP. The popular Tahitian feast, which is held on Thursday evenings, is known for its authentic and elegantly presented Polynesian delicacies such as suckling pig, fresh lobster, locally caught fish and sauces made from a variety of exotic fruits. The menu has been further expanded by the chef to incorporate elements that reflect more of the island's complex history, and the Maohi Nui dancers present traditional dancing, including an exciting fire dance. This costs 8.000 CFP per person.

Café Fare. *Open daily for breakfast and lunch.*

This restaurant offers informal indoor/outdoor dining, serving from an open air kitchen with service pool side. The American breakfast buffet is 2.983 CFP. The luncheon menu suggests appetizers for 1.300 to 2.100 CFP, including red tuna tartar, poisson cru and shrimp cocktail served in an avocado. Salads are 1.200 to 2.600 CFP; pizzas and pasta dishes are 1.400 to 2.100 CFP; and the main courses are priced from 1.700 to 2.500 CFP. These include a Club sandwich with turkey ham for 1.900 CFP, a cheeseburger, fries and salad for 1.900 CFP, a grilled New York steak for 1.800 CFP, and broiled filet of mahi mahi for 2.200 CFP. For dessert you will pay 1.000 CFP for either home made ice cream and sorbet, a crunchy Polynesian banana, a Pineapple piña colada style, or crème brulée and a sauce made with vanilla from Tahaa.

BORA BORA NUI RESORT & SPA, *Tel. 60.33.00. All major credit cards.*
Tamure Grill is a big open sided restaurant with a thatched roof and a

floor of white sand, located next to the swimming pool and white sand beach. Breakfast is served from 6 to 11:30am, offering a choice of a Continental breakfast for 3.000 CFP, an American buffet for 4.000 CFP, a Fitness breakfast for 4.000 CFP, or a Japanese breakfast for 4.000 CFP. You can also eat lunch at one of the tables inside the Tamure Grill or outside on the terrace. Sandwiches are priced from 1.700 to 2.200 CFP, burgers are 2.000 CFP, pasta is 1.800 to 3.200 CFP, pizza is 1.900 CFP, and grilled fish, chicken, steak and lobster are 2.500 to 3.600 CFP. A salad bar is 2.500 CFP, and desserts are 1.200 CFP.

Tamure Snacks are also available at the **Ta'ie'ie Beach Bar**, which is at one end of the Tamure Grill, where you can sit at a table or on polished coconut stumps at the monkeypod bar. The bar employees are friendly and efficient. The Tamure grill is also open nightly for dinner. A 3-course set dinner is 5.800 CFP and a 3-course vegetarian dinner is 5.600 CFP. The Manager's Cocktail Party is held each Tuesday evening, followed by a Tahitian traditional feast in the Tamure Grill, with entertainment provided by Kevin's Polynesian dance show, for 8.500 CFP per person. A Seafood and Japanese Buffet is presented on Friday evening for 8.500 CFP a person. Sometime during the week, depending on what else is happening, the Tamure Grill presents a Surf 'N Turf à la carte dinner. This special evening starts with appetizers for 1.500 CFP, which include a choice of barbecued chicken wings, Vietnamese spring rolls, Asian prawn salad with pickled ginger and Thai dressing, and beef carpaccio with chicken or shrimp. Grilled mahi mahi, shrimp, calamari steak, chicken, pork chops and beef sirloin are priced from 2.500 to 2.800 CFP, and desserts are 900 CFP. Vegetarian dishes can be ordered à la carte. To accompany your meal, the bar and wine cellar are stocked with a good choice of mineral waters, soft drinks and juice, beers, wine by the glass, half bottle and bottle, as well as champagnes.

Iriatai is a panoramic restaurant on the upper level of the central building. Dinner is served here nightly except Tuesday and Friday, when there are special theme evenings being held in the Tamure Grill. The Iriatai features contemporary Italian cuisine, with antipasti or starter courses priced from 1.700 to 2.500 CFP, pasta and risotto dishes from 1.700 to 2.800 CFP, fish and seafood from 3.000 to 5.300 CFP, and meats from 2.600 to 3.600 CFP. Daily specials, such as swordfish (meka) with mushroom croute and blue cheese potatoes, are about 3.000 CFP. Desserts are 1.000 CFP each, and you can order wines from Napa Valley, California, New Zealand, Australia, South Africa, Chile, Italy, and all the wine producing regions of France. In addition to an impressive list of Grands Crus from Bordeaux, there are also 13 choices of French champagnes available.

While you are enjoying your quiet romantic dinner by candlelight, you are being serenaded by Wesley Smith, a very gifted pianist from Ohio who has lived in Tahiti for many years. The owners of Bora Bora Nui Resort & Spa enticed

Wesley to come to Bora Bora for the special enjoyment of their guests. Let him know if you have a musical request, for he knows all your favorite songs. He's the best.

Following your dinner, why not adjourn to the bar for a digestif of 1923 Laberdolive Armagnac at 18.500 CFP a serving, or a sip of Nº 11 champagne from the AE dor collection, for 26.000 CFP. This would go well with a Cohiba Robusto cigar, that sells for 5.200 CFP.

HOTEL SOFITEL MOTU, *Tel. 60.56.00. All major credit cards.*

Manu Tiki Restaurant. *Open daily for breakfast, lunch and dinner for guests staying at Hotel Sofitel Motu, and open for dinner only to outside guests who must reserve in advance.*

This restaurant is built on stilts on the hilltop of a *motu*, granting spectacular views of Bora Bora and its famous lagoon and mountains. An American breakfast is 2.950 CFP, the set luncheon menu is 3.250 CFP and the set dinner menu is 6.450 CFP per person. The cuisine is French with a Polynesian accent and has earned a good reputation for quality. Starter courses for the dinner menu include creamy pumpkin soup and crispy bacon and scallops for 1.700 CFP and lobster salad with artichokes and sweet potato chips and creamy ginger sauce for 2.700 CFP. Fish dishes are priced from 2.600-2.800 CFP, and meat choices range from 2.600-3.400 CFP, including crispy pan fried lamb filet with curry, bananas and coconut milk and pan fried breast of duck with apple chips and mashed sweet potatoes. Lobster canneloni with parmesan cheese for 4.900 CFP consists of two taco-like rolls with the mixture inside and melted cheese on the outside. Very rich. Desserts are 1.300-1.650 CFP and include banana pie and homemade chocolate truffles with Tiare flower perfume.

HOTEL LE MERIDIEN BORA BORA, *Tel. 60.51.51. All major credit cards.*

Le Tipanie Restaurant. *Open daily from 6:45 to 10am for breakfast and from 6:30 to 9:30pm for dinner.*

An American Breakfast Buffet is 2.900 CFP. You can feed the fish in the interior lagoon while dining in this 180-seat restaurant, where you can choose your favorite dishes from the buffet tables. A Fish and Seafood Buffet is served on Monday, a Pacific Buffet is presented each Tuesday, followed by a Polynesian dance show, a Mediterranean Buffet is featured on Wednesday, accompanied by live music, a Parisian Buffet is the theme for Thursdays, a Barbecue Buffet on Friday night is followed by a Polynesian dance show, a Market of the Day Buffet is featured on Saturday evenings, and an Asian Buffet is served on Sundays. All the buffets are priced at 6.000 CFP per person.

An à la carte menu is also available each evening in the Honu (turtle) section of Le Tipanie Restaurant, where you can watch the sea turtles and lagoon fish swimming in the lagoon just below your table. You must reserve in advance to dine here and a set dinner menu is 5.970 CFP. Starter courses are priced from 2.000 to 2.940 CFP, and may include cold avocado cream served with shredded crab meat, crayfish salad with diced exotic fruits and a cold creamy seafood sauce, or hot pan-fried foie gras with a passion fruit sauce. Fish and seafood dishes are 2.700 to 3.250 CFP, offering grilled red tuna tournedos with shallots and risotto for 2.950 CFP, and pan-fried prawns marinated in pesto served on a bed of Provencal vegetables with a balsamic caramel, for 3.250 CFP. The meat choices range from 3.100 to 3.900 CFP, including chicken, filet of deer, grilled rack of lamb and roast beef filet. The gourmet menu changes frequently and always includes some interesting vegetarian dishes, such as vegetable lasagna, grilled vegetable skewers flavored with pesto, and wild mushroom risotto, priced from 2.400 to 3.150 CFP. Desserts for 1.500 CFP include the traditional crème brûlée served with coffee ice cream, chocolate mousse, moist chocolate fondant, steamed banana, strawberries and vanilla wrapped in a banana leaf and served with rum sherbet, as well as a roasted Granny Smith apple stuffed with pan-fried dices of caramelized apples and vanilla ice cream. A cheese selection is 1.700 CFP. To accompany these delicacies you can order from an interesting list of wines from France, Chile, Australia and California.

Te Ava Restaurant is Le Méridien's 120-seat beachside restaurant adjacent to the fresh water swimming pool. This outdoor restaurant with a big thatch roof and open sides offers a very relaxing atmosphere, where you sit in a rocking chair and dig your toes into the white sand. A Parisian breakfast of coffee and croissants is served daily between 10 and 11:30am. A salad bar and special luncheon theme is featured daily from 11:30am to 3pm, with such choices as gazpacho, miso soup with scallops, Chinese style *poisson cru*, Greek salad with feta cheese, hamburgers, grilled fish and meats, a barbecue plate or roasted prawns with spicy butter. A set luncheon menu is 4.050 CFP. The **Miki Miki Bar** at Le Méridien is open from 3 to 11pm, and you can order snacks and pizzas here between 3-9pm. You can also order sandwiches and drinks from the **Fare Tupa** snack bar between 10am and 5pm.

BORA BORA PEARL BEACH RESORT, *Tel. 60.52.00. All major credit cards.*

Tevairoa Restaurant is the hotel's main dining room, which has an elevated view of the overflowing swimming pool, beach and overwater bungalows, plus the electric blues of the Bora Bora lagoon and the stately Otemanu mountain across the bay. You can admire the morning-softened scenery or the velvet night sky and reflected lights in the lagoon while dining on international cuisine.

Breakfast is served from 6:30 to 10am with a choice of Continental breakfast for 2.200 CFP or full American breakfast for 2.500 CFP, and an omelet station is the center of attention each morning. A 3-course set dinner menu is 6.200 CFP. An *a la carte* menu suggests gaspacho or pumpkin-vanilla soup for 1.200 CFP, *poisson cru* for 1.800 CFP or prawn fritters with sweet chili sauce for 1.900 CFP. The fish and seafood courses are 2.900-3.300 CFP, with pan seared mahi mahi served on vegetables from Provence and laced with a pesto sauce for 3.100 CFP, filet of red snapper scented with thyme, accompanied by asparagus spears and gnochi potatoes for 3.200 CFP. Meat dishes are 2.800-3.900 CFP and include Tandoori chicken with lemon flavored rice and chutney for 2.800 CFP, grilled beef tenderloin with polenta and glazed pearl onions for 3.200 CFP.

You must remember to save room for one of the excellent desserts prepared by the hotel's pastry chef, who is already famous for his Pearl Beach chocolate cake with a warm soft center, served with ice cream flavored with vanilla from Tahaa. All desserts are 1.500 CFP, and you can order a glass of dessert wine or champagne to accompany your sweets. The wine list contains some of the *grands crus* from the Bordeaux vineyards of France, as well as selections from Italy, Australia, California, Chile and New Zealand. There is also a selection of Cuban cigars on the menu, as well as imported coffees. A Polynesian dance/cultural show is presented in the Tevairoa Restaurant every Monday and Friday at 8pm. A Polynesian Buffet is served each Monday at 7pm for 6.600 CFP, and a Seafood Buffet is presented each Friday at 7pm, for 7.100 CFP.

Teavanui Restaurant and Bar are located beside the swimming pool. This is a great place to hang out during a hot tropical day, sipping cold Hinano pression beer and munching on cheeseburgers, club sandwiches, poisson cru, fish and chips, or grilled sirloin steak. Most of the guests sitting at the friendly bar or at the tables on the terrace are American honeymooners or young French families with children. The atmosphere here is very casual.

Private Restaurants on the Main Island
Deluxe
LA VILLA MAHANA, *Tel. 67.50.63; E-mail: damien_rinaldi@villamahana.com; www.villamahana.com. At the art gallery of Garrick Yrondi, behind the Gauguin boutique on the mountainside between Vaitape village and the Hotel Bora Bora. Open for lunch and dinner. Closed all day Tuesday and at noon on Wednesday. Reserve well in advance. American Express, Mastercard, Visa.*

A 28-year old Corsican chef de cuisine named Damien Rinaldi Dovio opened this 5-table gastronomic restaurant in April 2004 and it became an immediate success. Residents and tourists alike are reserving up to 4 days in advance and when they leave the restaurant in a dreamy state of contentment, their comments in his guest book and by word of mouth are full of praise. This is indeed a unique experience that you don't want to miss when you visit Bora Bora because people are saying that Damien, who studied at the prestigious Institut Paul Bocuse in Lyon, France, served them the best meal they have ever eaten.

Damien has placed 5 small tables on the courtyard terrace of Garrick Yrondi's art gallery, which resembles a scene from the Mediterranean, with

Yrondi's paintings and sculptures decorating the walls and garden. The gourmet menu features light cuisine influenced by Damien's origins, combined with Polynesian products and associated with the use of spices to magnify the flavors. He suggests several tempting menus, but his piece de resistance is the Menu Royal, which is very popular with tourists, even though it costs 8.500 CFP per person. You start with a light salad of shellfish and caviar on toast, followed by fried foie gras with sherry and fleur de sel, served with green asparagus. The next course is Langouste Royale grillée aux Saveurs exotiques, followed by filet of roast beef, gnocchi with the essence of truffle, and red wine sauce infused with Grande Caravane sweet spices. Dessert for this feast is pure Caribbean dark chocolate fondant served with homemade ice cream with Tahitian vanilla. Damien also has an impressive wine list to accompany your meal.

Superior

FARE MANUIA, *Tel. 67.68.08. On the lagoon side at Point Matira, just past the turnoff at Point Matira. Open daily 11:30am-2pm and 6-10pm. Mastercard and Visa. Free pick-up for dinner.*

This attractive little restaurant is built of coconut trunk walls, with a huge chandelier of bamboo and mother-of-pearl shells hanging from the crossbeams under a thatched roof. Half of the customers are local residents who appreciate the fine French cuisine served here, and many visitors agree that this is one of the best restaurants on the island.

The luncheon choices include burgers and fries for 1.100-1.600 CFP, *poisson cru* for 1.500 CFP and grilled tuna Niçoise salad for 1.900 CFP. The starter courses on the dinner menu are 1.500-2.400 CFP, the fish dishes are 2.500-3.500 CFP and the meats are priced from 1.900-3.900 CFP. Among these choices you will find pan fried shrimp with pastis butter, a fisherman platter for 3.500 CFP. Provençale rack of lamb with ratatouille for 2.900 CFP, and roast rib of beef for 3.900 CFP. The desserts are reportedly delicious and one that may be hard to pass up is the strawberry rhubarb crumble for 1.000 CFP. Special theme evenings feature specialties from Alsace, Toulouse and Breton.

BLOODY MARY'S, *Tel. 67.72.86. On the mountainside in Pofai Bay, 5 kilometers (3 miles) from Vaitape and 1 kilometer (.62 miles) from the Hotel Bora Bora. Open for lunch and dinner. Closed Sunday. American Express, Mastercard and Visa. Free dinner transportation is provided from select locations.*

Bloody Mary's is the kind of funky and fun place where people get to know one another very easily. You can't be too reserved while you are sitting on a tree stump at the bar under a huge thatched roof or wiggling your toes in the white sand floor while eating your dinner or watching to see which movie star or television personality will walk through the door. A long list of celebrities who have dined at Bloody Mary's is posted beside the road. And they keep on coming, because Bloody Mary's truly is world famous.

The dinner service starts at 6pm, when the daily catch of the local fishermen of Bora Bora is displayed on ice. After an explanation of exactly what's available on your particular evening, your host, Craig Goold, an American expatriate, takes your order directly with the chef. Appetizers start at 1.250 CFP, and include grilled shrimp, garlic crab, charred peppered sashimi, teriyaki fish kabob, and the house specialty, a very tender calamari steak, that is breaded and sautéed in capers and white wine for 1.400 CFP. Fish choices are priced from 2.650-3.200 CFP and usually include mahi mahi, salmon of the gods (moonfish), albacore tuna, wahoo (ono), meka (broadbill swordfish), striped marlin and mako shark. Should you prefer lagoon fish the choices are parrotfish, grouper, jackfish or red snapper, for 3.000 CFP. Fresh New Zealand beef may be ribeye steak, New York steak or short ribs, for 3.000 CFP. You can also order grilled chicken for 2.650 CFP or a vegetarian plate for 2.000 CFP. Fresh local lobster is 6.000 CFP or you can combine lobster and your choice of fish for 5.500 CFP. The main courses are accompanied by green salad, white rice, hot vegetables and fresh fruit. The dessert menu will tempt you with warm coconut pie and ice cream, chocolate mousse and chocolate cake. You won't leave this restaurant hungry!

The bar is open from 9:30am to 11pm and you'll certainly want to try the house specialty, a famous Bloody Mary for 600 CFP, or an excellent frozen Margarita for 900 CFP, or perhaps a Bloody Mary's maitai for 1.200 CFP. A cold draft beer (Hinano *pression*) is 350 CFP. Lunch is served between 11am and 3pm, which consists of salads, great burgers. and homemade tortilla pie. Their wine list is very impressive and they also carry three kinds of Cuban cigars.

Moderate to Superior

LE PANDA D'OR, *Tel. 67.62.70. On mountainside in Vaitape village. Open 11am-1pm and 6-9pm. Closed Sunday. Mastercard, Visa.*

This Chinese restaurant, which means the Golden Panda, opened in June 2001, serving refined Cantonese cuisine and seafood prepared by chefs from Hong Kong and China. The air-conditioned restaurant is attractively decorated and can seat almost 200 people. The extensive menu is impressive, with such tempting seasonal delicacies as shrimp and lobster sautéed with broccoli for 3.800 CFP, sweet and sour crab for 3.800 CFP, and lobster for 3.800 CFP. The crustacean dishes start at 1.800 CFP for cuttlefish and go up to 2.990 CFP for Coquille St. Jacques (scallops). Chinese soups are 1.090; Vietnamese *nems* are 1.250 CFP and breaded fried shrimp is 2.550 CFP. Meat dishes are 1.650 to 2.300 CFP and you can also order a vegetarian plate. The wine list includes some of the *grand crus* of Bordeaux for 8.200 to 19.500 CFP. Carry-out orders are possible.

BORA KAINA HUT, *Tel. 67.54.06, cell 77.19.38; E-mail: vpauline@mail.pf. is on the mountainside in Pofai Bay. Open daily for lunch and dinner. Visa.* A big thatch roof covers this open-sided Polynesian style restaurant beside the road. It has a sandy floor, coconut wood furniture, pretty shell chandeliers and lots of plants and flowers, and is owned by Pauline Youssef, who also owns Village Pauline just behind the restaurant. Sacha, the manager/chef, is a well-known *artiste* in the kitchen, complete with mood swings, but he serves excellent food that you won't find anywhere else in Bora Bora. Starter courses include 6 sushis for 980 CFP, tuna carpaccio for 1.500 CFP, the chef's raw vegetables for 1.600 CFP, tuna tartar and sushi for 1.700 CFP, *poisson cru* for 1.800 CFP, Kaina special salad for 1.800 CFP, and a Japanese mix with red and white cabbage, sashimi, spicy sushi, tuna tartar and Japanese rice for 1.800 CFP. The house specialty is a Millennium roll for 2.300 CFP, which consists of hot smoked salmon and sushi. Main courses are 1.800-3.900 CFP, including grilled wahoo with tomatoes *rougaille* for 1.800 CFP, pork caramel spare ribs for 1.900 CFP, mahi mahi with lemon grass sauce for 2.100 CFP, and grilled lobster for 3.900 CFP. Mouth-watering desserts include coconut pie for 900 CFP and a banana split for 1.100 CFP. A snack menu lists hamburger or cheeseburger and fries for 1.600 CFP and a fishburger and fries for 1.800 CFP. Every Saturday night a Pacific Buffet of grilled meat and fish is served, accompanied by local vegetables and live Polynesian music.

BAMBOO HOUSE, *Tel./Fax 67.76.24. On the mountainside in Pofai Bay, 3.5 kilometers (2 miles) from Vaitape toward Matira. Open daily except Sunday lunch from 11:30am to 2pm and for dinner from 6:30 to 9pm. American Express, Mastercard and Visa. Free dinner transportation provided from your hotel or boat.*

The decor here is what the name implies, a little house made of bamboo walls and a thatched roof. Dining is inside, on the covered terrace or outdoors in the courtyard. This restaurant gets high ratings from tourists as well as the residents of Bora Bora and manager Yann Pendezec and his team give a warm welcome to visitors. Luncheon choices suggest burgers and chips, salads and *poisson cru*. I ate an excellent *salade Niçoise* with a slice of grilled tuna. The dinner menu features French cuisine and fresh fish, crab and lobster specialties from the Bora Bora lagoon. Appetizers are 1.500-1.900 CFP and pasta dishes are priced from 2.350-3.000 CFP, which include a delicious shrimp fettucine. Fish dishes are 2.700-2.950 CFP, with choices of Atlantic salmon in a white wine butter sauce or a grilled shark steak with a vanilla-lemon-herb sauce. Seafood is 3.100 CFP and grilled lobster is 6.000 CFP. Meat courses are 2.900-3.500 CFP. Cheese fondue for a minimum of 2 people is 2.800 CFP per person, and beef fondue is 3.300 to 3.500 CFP. You can even grill your own barbecue for 3.300 CFP and a new menu features cooking your fish, shrimp and meats on a hot "pierrade" stone. The two chocolates-cake is one of the dessert favorites.

Moderate

RESTAURANT PATOTI, *Tel. 67.61.99, cell 79.30.10, on mountainside in Matira, just past Hotel Sofitel Marara. Open daily for lunch and dinner. Mastercard, Visa. Pick-up service provided for dinner.*

This started out as a local style snack, and now that Agnès and Guy have taken it over it has become one of the most popular restaurants on the island. This couple formerly owned Chez Agnès & Guy restaurant in Raiatea and French chef Guy also cooked at Le Pêcheur in Raiatea and at the Marina Iti in Tahaa. The dinner menu includes fresh fish soup for 1.300 CFP, fish and seafood dishes for 1.700-2.400 CFP, and meat selections for 1.900-2.300 CFP. Specialities may feature lamb chops or veal scallop flambée. Hamburgers and fries are 1.100 CFP, *poisson cru* is 1.350 CFP and chao mein is 1.500 CFP.

LA BOUNTY, *Tel. 67.70.43; E-mail: labounty@mail.pf. On mountainside in Matira, close to Hotel Le Maitai Polynesia and Bora Bora Beach Lodge. Open for lunch and dinner. Closed Monday. Mastercard and Visa.*

This is a popular restaurant with a good location, close to several hotels and pensions. Crêpes have been added to the menu and are priced from 700-1.050 CFP. Starter courses are 950 to 1.300 CFP, pizza costs 1.150 to 1.650 CFP, fish selections are 1.550 to 2.100 CFP, and meat dishes range from 1.400 to 1.800 CFP.

RESTAURANT MATIRA, *Tel. 67.53.79. On the beach between the Hotel Bora Bora and Point Matira. Open daily for breakfast, lunch and dinner. American Express, Mastercard and Visa. Free pick-up for dinner.*

This is a great place to watch the action on the beach while eating your meal on the covered dining terrace. The sunsets from this viewpoint are often spectacular. This restaurant is no longer managed by the owners of Hotel Matira and the meal rates have now been reduced. A French breakfast is 800 CFP, a tropical breakfast is 1.300 CFP and an American breakfast costs 1.900 CFP. You can also order a shrimp omelette for 1.200 CFP. Hamburgers are 500 CFP and a Club Sandwich with fries is 950 CFP. The dinner courses vary from 1.200 to 1.800 CFP, and Cantonese style Chinese food is 1.000-1.800 CFP. Lobster is 3.800 CFP.

AU COCOTIER, *Tel. 67.74.18. On mountainside in Vaitape, between Chin Lee's market and the pharmacy. Open Monday through Saturday 7:30am to 8:30pm. Closed Sunday. Mastercard and Visa.*

Visitors usually have no trouble finding their way to this small restaurant, as it is conveniently located in the center of Vaitape village. They serve burgers and fries for 950 to 1.150 CFP, a choice of six *casse-croûte* sandwiches for 1.100 CFP, and steak and fries for 1.400 CFP. They have *poisson cru*, sashimi, tuna tartare, tuna carpaccio, tuna teriyaki, and six choices of *meka* (the non-fighting swordfish, which is melt-in-your-mouth delicious), Meat dishes are 1.100 to 2.000 CFP. Their main menu, however, features local Chinese and Tahitian dishes, as well as exotic dishes for 1.900 to 2.000 CFP. These specialties include shrimp and broccoli, shrimp curry, stuffed eggplant, tamarind duck, pork with oyster sauce and lemon chicken. Wines are available for 2.000 to 3.000 CFP a bottle.

L'APPETISSERIE, *Tel. 67.78.88; E-mail: lappetisserie@mail.pf. In Pahia Center in Vaitape village. Open 6am to 6pm Monday through Saturday. Closed Sunday. No credit cards.*

You'll find just the treat for your sweet tooth on the terrace of this popular pastry shop. In addition to cakes, ice cream and sorbets, you will also find homemade croissants, quiches, pizza and daily specials. Owner Marc-André Zani also operates a Cybercafé here. (For E-mail access see information under Cybercafé-Internet Service).

PIRATE'S BAR, *Tel. 60.52.52, beside the water at Royal Helen's Bay Center in Vaitape village. Open Monday through Friday from 8am to 3pm and from 5pm to midnight, and non-stop on Saturday from 8am to 1am. Closed Sunday. No credit cards.*

This is a comfortable hang-out any time of the day as you can benefit from the refreshing ocean breezes while sitting at the bar, on the terrace or outside in the small garden area next to the bay. This is a good place to watch the boats going by or to gaze at the sunset. You can order eggs for breakfast for 450 CFP, omelettes are 500-700 CFP, ham or bacon is 550 CFP, coffee is 300 CFP and fresh fruit juice is 650 CFP. A Continental breakfast is 800 CFP. Burgers are 800-900 CFP, six choices of salads are priced from 400-1.600 CFP, pasta is 1.500-1.700 CFP, sashimi or tuna tartare is 1.500 CFP, grilled fish is 1.600 CFP, a seafood plate is 2.200 CFP, and desserts include homemade apple pie with vanilla ice cream and chocolate sauce for 900 CFP. A Hinano draft beer is 400 CFP and a bottle of beer is 500 CFP, scotch, gin, vodka or tequila is 700 CFP, a cocktail is 1.000 CFP and a liter of wine is 1.600 CFP. Bottled wines are also available for 1.950-6.700 CFP.

Economy

BEN'S PIZZA HUT, *Tel. 67.74.54. On mountainside in Matira, between Hotel Bora Bora and Point Matira. Open at 11am and close at 5pm on Tuesday, Thursday and Saturday. Open until 8pm on Monday, Wednesday, Friday and Sunday nights. No credit cards.*

Ben Teraitepo, from Bora Bora, and his American wife, Robin, gave up their busy life in Southern California to settle in Bora Bora in 1987. They are now busier than ever, cooking for the diners on their front terrace, across the road from the white sandy beach. Their menu includes pizzas from 850 to 1.500 CFP, spaghetti with different types of sauces for 900 to 1.300 CFP, and lasagna for 1.000 CFP, as well as Mexican fajitas, quesadillas, tacos, hot dogs, cheeseburgers, submarine sandwiches, chowder and *poisson cru*.

CHEZ MICHEL, *Tel. 67.71.43. On the northern end of Vaitape about 90 meters (100 yards) from Le Pahia Commercial Center. Open Monday to Friday from 6-11am. Closed Saturday and Sunday. No credit cards.*

This little snack serves some of the best local style dishes you'll find on Bora Bora and the price is right. Daily specials include chow mein, steak and fries, and *maa tinito*, (Chinese food), which is a delicious combination of red beans, pork, vegetables and macaroni. It's very filling. The specials cost 750 to 950 CFP and you can get a chow mein *casse-croûte* for 120 CFP or a ham-and-cheese sandwich for 100 CFP. Bora Bora residents say that Michel serves the best *poisson cru* on the island (750 CFP) and it is often sold out before noon. So get there early!

BORA BORA BURGERS, *No phone. Next door to the post office in Vaitape. Open Monday through Friday 7:30am to 5pm and on Saturday morning. Closed Saturday afternoon and Sunday. No credit cards.*

You can sit on a coconut barstool or at one of the tables on the sidewalk in front of this small fast food stand and eat your burgers and fries. The prices are reasonable for Bora Bora.

SNACK MATIRA, *Tel. 67.77.32, which is also known as Chez Julia, is on Matira Beach, across the road from Ben's Pizza Hut. Open 10am to 4pm. Closed Monday. No credit cards.*

This beach snack became so popular that the owner expanded to 80 tables. Casse-croûte sandwiches on baguette bread cost 200-700 CFP, burgers are 450-600 CFP, *poisson cru* is 600-1.100 CFP and pizza is 1.200-1.500 CFP. Beer is served with food only.

ROULOTTES. There are at least four *roulottes* (mobile diners) in Vaitape village at night, where you can enjoy a full meal for 1.200 CFP or less. They all serve steak and fries, *brochettes* (kebabs), barbecued chicken legs, *poisson cru* and grilled fish. Roulotte Matira, across the road from the Moana Beach Intercontinental, charges 1.400 CFP up for a meal.

Seeing the Sights

To explore the island by car, scooter or bicycle, start at the Vaitape boat dock, if you head south around the island. All along the water's edge of Pofai (or Povai) Bay you will see spectacular views of the **Otemanu Mountain**. Beside the lagoon at the edge of the town center of Vaitape you will see a two-story white building that houses the Tahiti Perles boutique. Robert Wan, the owner, plans to open a Black Pearl Museum here eventually. Along the edge of Pofai Bay you will see Moon B&B just before coming to Alain and Linda's Art Gallery on the right. There are usually gaily-painted *pareos* hanging on a line in front of the boutique. Across the road from the nearby soccer field and gymnasium is a path that leads over the island to the village of Anau. The interior roads can only be traversed by mountain bike or on foot. The Ellacott

Marina is also located in this bay and is a terminal for some of the hotel shuttle boats.

If you stay on the **circle island road** you'll see Village Pauline, Bora Kaina Hut, Bamboo House Restaurant, Gauguin Boutique and Garden, Chez Rosina, Bloody Mary's Restaurant and Moana Art. Look to the right across the bay toward the point of Motu Toopua Iti and you will see some of the overwater bungalows at the Bora Bora Nui Resort & Spa. Continuing south on the main road, at Raititi Point, you will pass the entrance to the luxurious Hotel Bora Bora.

Go past Bora Diving Center, Bora Bora Gallery and Alain Despert's gallery and you'll see the Restaurant Matira beside the lagoon. When the American Armed Forces were stationed on Bora Bora during World War II they installed a battery of coastal defense guns on the hillside. You can reach them in just a 10-minute hike up a walking trail east of the hotel property. Ben's Place serves American food on the mountainside and Snack Matira serves local style dishes beside the lagoon. A sign indicates the turnoff at Point Matira, where you can visit the Intercontinental Moana Beach Resort and the Hotel Matira and have a swim at Matira Beach. Chez Nono has a pension right on the white sand beach and Chez Robert & Tina have 3 rental houses right at the tip of Point Matira. Back on the main road, you'll see Chez Maeva Masson and the excellent Fare Manuia Restaurant on the right, next to Village Temanuata, and Matira Pearls is on the left (the selection and prices are good).

Heading along the east coast of Matira, Le Maitai Polynesia hotel is on both sides of the road, with beach, mountain and overwater bungalows. La Bounty Restaurant, Tiare Market, Bora Bora Beach Lodge, Nemo World dive shop, Novotel, Sofitel Marara, Maradive and Snack Patoti are all located on either side of this short stretch of road. Out on the motu in front of the Sofitel Marara is the deluxe Sofitel Motu, a haven for honeymooners.

A steep hill leads you behind the Club Med Coral Garden Village at **Faaopore Bay**, just before Paoaoa Point. You can visit a lookout point on a ridge above the bay by taking Club Med's private tunnel under the road or by walking up the steps just beyond the Boutique Hibiscus (now closed) on the left side of the road. A trail to the right of the hill will take you down to Marae Aehautai, where you will have a good view of Otemanu Mountain and the islands of Tahaa and Raiatea beyond the reef. Other *marae* are also located in this vicinity, as well as coastal guns from World War II. Shortly after Club Med you will come to Chez Teipo and Pension Bora Lagoonarium, both on the lagoon side.

The road continues on to **Anau village**, which has a general store, service station, a couple of roadside stands where you can buy shells and *pareos*, a church, school and some very modest homes, which are often unpainted. Beside the lagoon is the land base for Hotel Eden Beach and nearby is the land base for Le Méridien Bora Bora, whose luxurious overwater bungalows you can see on the *motu* opposite the village. On this same long *motu* are the Eden Beach, Relais Matie and the Hotel InterContinental Bora Bora, now under construction and due to open in March 2006. The Lagoonarium is built beside a motu just past Le Méridien, and further along you will soon see the Four Seasons hotel project on Motu Tofari and the Ritz Carlton hotel that is under construction on Motu Ome. After passing a few houses on the road beyond Fitiiu Point, you'll come to l'Espadon Restaurant (now closed) on Taimoo Bay and the Revatua Club across the street, which is no longer operated as a hotel.

For the next few miles the only thing you will see are scattered houses, coconut plantations and *tupa* crabs, until you come to the *Musée de la Mer*, the Marine Museum, which has replicas of famous ships that have visited Tahiti and Bora Bora.

Just before Point Taihi you'll see a steep track that leads up to a World War II radar station on top of Popoti Ridge. Across the lagoon you can see the Bora Bora airport on Motu Mute. Continuing on the circle island road you'll pass the Bora Bora Condos, which consist of 4 overwater bungalows and 11 mountainside apartments on stilts. Marlon Brando's estate owns 2 overwater bungalows and 1 on the mountainside. These condos are available for visitors who wished to spend a week or more on the island.

At Tereia Point in **Faanui Bay** you'll see an old shipping wharf and a seaplane ramp that were built by the American Seabees during the war. Another US coastal gun is located on the hill above the concrete water tank, and right after the former submarine base is the Marae Fare-Opu, between the road and the bay. The stones of the temple are engraved with turtle petroglyphs. A road beside the Protestant church at the head of the bay runs inland, narrowing into an unmarked track that you can follow with a guide over the saddle of the ridgetop to Bora Bora's east coast of Vairau Bay, south of Fitiiu Point.

On the western end of Faanui Bay is the main shipping wharf, where inter-island ferries and cargo vessels from Tahiti dock. This wharf was also built during the war. Just 100 meters west of the quay is the Marae Marotetini, a coastal *marae* that was restored by Dr. Yosihiko Sinoto in 1968. This was a royal temple and members of Bora Bora's chiefly families are buried nearby.

Around the bend from the Faanui boat dock is the Bora Bora Yacht Club, whose restaurant, bar and bungalows are closed until it is sold. Yachts can still anchor here and use the showers and washing machine. On the hillside facing the island's only pass are two defense guns left over from the war. The Safari Tour excursions will take you to visit these guns. On two *motu* islets across the lagoon you will see the Bora Bora Pearl Beach Resort and the Bora Bora Lagoon Resort, as well as Motu Tapu, which is now the private domain of the Bora Bora Nui Resort & Spa. This little *motu* is famous for its white sand beach and is located just beside the Teavanui Pass, the only navigable entrance through the protective necklace of coral reef surrounding the island.

Just before you reach Vaitape village you will see the Topdive Resort, with its excellent restaurant, on the seaside. You will also find a good little *patisserie* in the modern Centre Commercial Le Pahia, or you can shop at Magasin Chin Lee, which is truly an establishment of village life in Bora Bora. In addition to cold juices and drinks you can choose a *casse-croûte,* sandwich, Tahitian and Chinese pastries or a take-away container of good hot food, usually rice and fish, chicken or meat. Royal Helen's Bay is another small shopping center beside the lagoon in Vaitape, where you will find the Pirate's Bar and artisan shops.

To end your do-it-yourself tour around the island, spend a little time in Vaitape village and you will be able to observe the daily drama of life on a small island. You'll discover that Bora Bora is not just a tourist island, but the residents have their own private interests, as well as looking after visitors from all over the world. You may see the children bursting from the confines of their schoolrooms into the Bora Bora sunshine. Their parents or big brother or sister, auntie or grandmother may be waiting for the little ones in the car or on a scooter parked in the shade of a flamboyant tree.

Have a look at the fruits and vegetables the vendors have carefully placed on small tables beside the road. Take a picture of the brightly colored lagoon fish strung on a line that the fisherman and his family are selling. Watch the adolescent boys playing basketball on the court beside the road and enjoy the flirting that goes on between them and the young *vahines*. Walk down to the *mairie* (town hall) and you'll see the stately Polynesians coming and going, taking care of business that involves division of their land, or the marriages, births and deaths of family members. At the post office you'll see local residents standing in line to pay their telephone bills or mail a letter. Even if they're in a hurry to check their mailboxes, they always have time to greet a friend with kisses on both cheeks, and to share a bit of gossip and a joke. Then go to the arts and crafts center beside the wharf, which is adjacent to the Bora Bora Tourist Bureau. While you're looking at the hand painted *pareos* and dresses, the shell necklaces and woven hats, be sure to exchange smiles with the "mama" who spends all day here, waiting to make a sale. Just lifting your eyebrows is a form of greeting and you'll be happy with the response when you see her eyes light up with friendly warmth. This is Bora Bora at its best.

Circle Island Tours

To fully appreciate the history and beauty of Bora Bora, climb aboard an excursion bus or *le truck* and settle back to listen, learn and enjoy as the English-speaking guide tells all about this little island and its colorful past, exciting present and plans for tomorrow. While passing through the little villages on the 29-kilometer (18-mile) circuit, you will see modest homes surrounded by pretty flower gardens, small snack stands and little boutiques selling *pareos* and shells.

The *marae* temples, where Polynesians used to worship in pre-Christian days, are pointed out, along with the Quonset huts, naval base and heavy artillery guns, left behind by the 5,000 American soldiers, sailors and Seabees who made a "friendly invasion" of Bora Bora during World War II, who also left many blue-eyed children. If you book through your hotel activity desk you will pay 2.500-3.000 CFP for a circle island tour by Le Truck, 3.000-3.500 CFP by air-conditioned van or bus, 5.720 CFP for a private tour by Le Truck and up to 12.700 CFP for a private tour in an air-conditioned Mercedes. Circle island tours can be booked with the following companies:

Bora Bora Tours, *Tel. 67.70.31; E-mail boraboratours@mail.pf*, has a 2-hour excursion that departs in the morning and afternoon from the Hotel Bora Bora and several other hotels. Transfers are also available.

Otemanu Tours, *Tel. 67.70.49; E-mail: otemanu.tours@mail.pf;* provides a 2 1/2-hour circle island tour daily, using air-conditioned vans or *le truck* to show you the island. If you are on a ship or yacht they will pick you up on the dock in front of your tender at 10am and 2pm.

Dino's Island Tours & Cab, *Tel. 79.29.65; Fax 689/67.74.70; E-mail: dexterdino@yahoo.fr,* is operated by Dino Dexter, a handsome young man from Bora Bora who was the first Mister Tahiti in 2001. He also won second runner-up in the Mister France 2002 competitions. Dino speaks excellent English and charges 2.500 CFP for a 2 hour and 15-minute tour around the island in his air-conditioned van. He was named after Dean Martin and is also a crooner.

Simplet Taxi, *Tel. 79.19.31/73.85.72; E-mail: kayhaut@yahoo.fr,* is operated by Matahi "Simplet" Tefana, who worked as guest relations manager for Sofitel Marara for years until he retired. He also speaks good English and will drive you around the island in his air-conditioned 4x4 vehicle.

You can also take a circle island tour with **Charley Transports**, *Tel. 67.64.37;* **Isnard Transports**, *Tel. 67.72.25 or 79.29.78;* **Maire Tours**, *Tel. 67.71.32 or 21.34.57;* and **Matira Tours**, *Tel. 67.74.14.*

Mountain Safari 4x4 Excursions

Viewing Bora Bora's majestic beauty takes on new dimensions when you bounce up and down the rutted mountain trails in a Land Rover or Jeep on a photographic safari excursion. Your guide will tell you the story of the American military base that was established in Bora Bora during World War II and you'll visit the gun emplacements and radar station on Popoti Ridge. At the end of the trail you walk uphill through the bush, where you are rewarded with a 360 degree panoramic vista of an ancient volcano crater, the lagoon and coral reefs around Bora Bora and the neighboring islands of Tahaa, Raiatea, Huahine, Maupiti and the atoll of Tupai, which are all clearly visible from this height. These tours also circle the island, where your guide points out the *marae* stone temples used by the ancient Polynesians, and the war relics used by the Americans. These are very interesting and scenic tours, but are not for the faint-hearted, pregnant or lazily inclined tourist.

Tupuna Mountain Expeditions, *Tel. 67.75.06; E-mail: tupuna.bora@mail.pf; www.safaribora.com*. Owner Dany Leverd has several 4-wheel drive (4x4) vehicles and good guides. This half-day morning or afternoon tour is a highlight of a visit to Bora Bora and costs 6.500 CFP per adult and half-price for children under 12 years.

Patrick's Activities, *Tel. 67.69.94/79.19.11, E-mail: patrick.bora@mail.pf*. Patrick Tairua was a guide for Tupuna Mountain Expeditions for several years, and his warm and friendly personality so impressed visitors that they wrote "Mauruuru Award" letters to the *Tahiti Beach Press*, singing his praises. Patrick now has his own Jeep that he uses for private half-day Nature Tours or à la carte tours. Rather than following the beaten path around the island and up into the valleys, Patrick has discovered new sights and sites for his passengers to enjoy. For people who are really interested in the history and legends of Bora Bora, Patrick will lead you on a walking tour to an archaeological site that is located on private property in Povai Bay. First you walk to a botanical garden of tropical fruits and plants, and then on to the jungle. Patrick has cleared the area around an ancient marae, whose name is unknown, and he will show you the petroglyphs of turtles carved into the basaltic rocks in this sacred place. He will take you to the Queen's Bath, which is a fresh water spring. It is said that Princess Teura, who was the wife of the Polynesian god Oro, used to bathe here. A private Safari Tour is sold for 48.800 CFP to 52.000 CFP at the hotel activity desks. On request Patrick can also combine a Jeep Safari with a Lagoon Excursion. See information under *Private Lagoon Excursions* and *Wedding Ceremonies*.

Bora Bora 4WD Safari, *Tel./Fax 67.71.32; cell 73.26.81/27.10.08*. Leone and Stellio Vaiho have four 8-seater Jeeps to show you the highlights and high spots of Bora Bora.

Jungle Bike, ATV, Quad Mountain Tours

Most of the hotel activity desks can arrange guided excursions in the mountains with a Jungle Bike or quad all-terrain vehicle. A half-day tour will take you inland on a hidden trail where few people venture and you will experience the tropical wilderness of Bora Bora. No experience is required. A 1 1/2 hour excursion for a minimum of two people is 12.100 CFP per quad. A private tour for two people is 48.400 CFP for two quads for the 1 1/2 hour excursion. You can also rent a quad at Matira Jet Tours on Matira Beach, *Tel. 77.63.63*.

Helicopter Tours

Polynesia Hélicoptères, *Tel. 67.62.59, E-mail: helico-bora@mail.pf* is next door to the Air Tahiti office on the Vaitape quay. A 6-seat AS 350 BA

Squirrel "Ecureuil" helicopter provides 15-minute flights over Bora Bora for 15.180 CFP per person. A 30-minute flight-seeing tour of Bora Bora and the nearby atoll of Tupai costs 25.500 CFP per person for a minimum of 4 people. These tours are available daily except Sunday. A private 15-minute ride for up to 5 passengers is 60.720 CFP for the helicopter and a 30-minute ride is 102.000 CFP. You can also visit the neighboring islands by helicopter, which is rented by the hour for 152.340 CFP. Helicopter transfers are available from the Bora Bora airport to the Hotel Bora Bora, the Bora Bora Nui Resort and Spa or Le Méridien Bora Bora for 35.420 CFP for 1-4 passengers. Helicopter transfers will also take you from Bora Bora to Le Taha'a Private Island et Spa (Relais et Chateaux).

Special Activities & Sightseeing Stops

Alain Gerbault's grave opposite the *gendarmerie* on Vaitape quay will be pointed out to you during all guided land tours. This is a Frenchman who had sailed the seven seas aboard his yacht *Firecrest* before dropping anchor in Bora Bora. He was most attracted to the young boys of Bora Bora, to whom he introduced the game of soccer. Due to the politics of war Gerbault left Bora Bora in 1941, and died on the island of Timor. His remains were brought back to his beloved Bora Bora in 1947, and a small tomb in the form of a *marae* was built in his honor.

Ancient temples of coral stone called *marae* are scattered around the island and on a few of the surrounding *motu* islets. The most easily accessible of these pre-historic sites of worship and human sacrifice are: **Marae Marotetini**, on a point by the lagoon between the Bora Bora Yacht Club and the Faanui boat dock; **Marae Taianapa**, on private property well off the mountain side of the road in Faanui, close to the Electra power plant; and **Marae Aehautai**, located on the beach at Fitiiu Point overlooking Anau Bay. **Fare Opu**, "House of the Stomach" is located between the lagoon and the road, close to the old navy docks in Faanui, immediately before the Faanui village. Petroglyphs of turtles are incised into two of the coral slabs. Turtles were sacred to the Maohi ancestors of today's Polynesians.

Matira Beach begins at the Hotel Bora Bora and continues past the Hotel Matira and Chez Nono at Point Matira, and on around the point past the Intercontinental Moana Beach Resort. It joins Taahana Beach at Le Maitai Polynesia and the Sofitel Marara, but most people still refer to the entire area as Matira Beach. This is where you will find a concentration of hotels, pensions, boutiques, black pearl shops and all kinds of nautical activities.

The west side of Matira Beach, facing the Hotel Bora Bora, is Bora Bora's most popular beach. The soft, white powdery sand slopes gently into the aquamarine lagoon, where the water is very shallow until you see the deepening shades of blue. Point Matira was named in memory of a British ship named *Mathilda* that was wrecked on Moruroa Atoll in the Tuamotus in 1792.

Three of the survivors remained in Tahiti, forming the first European colony. One of the crew, James O'Connor, married King Pomare's cousin, and their granddaughter was named Mathilda. She married a chief of the Leeward Islands and they settled in Bora Bora, where part of their property included the beautiful point and sand beach now called Matira, the Tahitian pronunciation of Mathilda.

Tupapau

"Many vestiges of ancient times still linger on Bora Bora. The belief in **tupapau** (TWO-pow-pow), ghosts of the dead, is prevalent among the islanders. Walk alone on a dark Bora Bora night and you'll see why. It is still a common practice to keep a lamp lit at night to ward off these evil spirits.

In 1973 my son Tom and I discovered a human arm and a portion of jawbone in front of the altar of Marae Marotetini. They had been pushed to the surface by land crabs digging their burrows. Despite warnings from the locals, we took the bones as souvenirs. Shortly after the discovery, my right arm became swollen to twice its normal size, followed by a swelling of the right side of my jaw. Upon taking the bones back to Los Angeles, Tom's leg was broken in several places during a freak motorcycle accident. This was followed by a period of family sickness and bad luck that didn't cease until we returned the bones to Marae Marotetini in 1976.

In 1981, several giant human footprints were discovered at the water's edge near Marae Taianapa. The discovery was important enough to bring government officials and newsmen from Papeete to examine the huge prints and wonder at their origin. The elders of Bora Bora didn't wonder. They knew. The prints were an omen from the distant past." – From cinematographer Milas Hinshaw's booklet **"Bora Bora E."**

Musée de la Marine is on the back side of the island, between the villages of Faanui and Anau, *Tel. 67.75.24*. French architect Bertrand Darasse displays his collection of ship models, which includes the *Mayflower*, dated 1615, the *H.M.S.Endeavour* that brought James Cook to Tahiti in 1769, the *Boudeuse* and *Etoile*, commanded by **Louis Antoine de Bougainville**, **Captain Bligh's** famous *Bounty*, and **Alain Gerbault's** *Firecrest*, which he sailed to Bora Bora. There are also models of outrigger sailing canoes, *bonitiers* and *poti marara* boats that are still used in these islands. Admission to the maritime museum is free.

Nightlife & Entertainment

All the big hotels have entertainment several nights a week. Details are given under *Where to Eat* in this chapter. The bar at Bloody Mary's is a very friendly place, where you can be assured of meeting other English-speaking people. A nightly show is presented by the Club Med staff except on Thursdays and Sundays, when there is a Tahitian dance show. You can attend the shows and spend an evening dancing without eating when you buy a *carnet* of bar tickets for 1.980 CFP. All rates include taxes.

In addition to his *à la carte* excursions and wedding ceremonies, Patrick Tairua and his Maohi Nui dance group perform at several of the hotels. You can watch their thrilling fire dance each Sunday night at Club Med, on Tuesday at the Intercontinental Moana Beach, on Wednesday at Le Maitai Polynesia and also at the Hotel Bora Bora, each Friday night at the Bora Bora Nui Resort, and on Saturdays at the Bora Bora Lagoon Resort & Spa. These programs are subject to change, so be sure to check with your hotel or pension when you get to Bora Bora.

LE RÉCIF, *Tel. 67.73.87, north of Vaitape towards Faanui.*

This is Bora Bora's only disco and it is open on Friday and Saturday nights. The ambiance in this dark and crowded room is very Tahitian. If you are curious as to how the locals whoop it up, there's an entry fee of 1.000 CFP, which includes a drink. The drinking and dancing goes on until the wee hours of the morning. You'll probably enjoy it more if you go with some local residents. Some of the young people who work at the hotels may be happy to go with you.

Heiva in Bora Bora – Where the Fête Goes On and On

During the month of July, the island of Bora Bora pulsates to the rhythm of the **Heiva**, which means festival in Tahitian. Some people still call this event the Fête or Tiurai, the Tahitian word for July. Whatever name you choose to call it, this is the most colorful time to visit Bora Bora.

Most of the islands have their own Heiva celebrations, but the Fête in Bora Bora is the best, because the villagers put so much enthusiasm and effort into building their *baraques* (barracks). These are carnival type stalls or booths that are made of thatched roofs and walls woven of palm fronds. They are decorated with multicolored *tifaifai* wall hangings, ferns, bright blossoms and *ti* leaves. These *baraques* are transformed into restaurants, pool halls, shooting galleries and carnival booths with a roulette-type wheel called *taviri*. If you place a bet you may win a bar of soap, sack of rice or sugar, bolt of *pareo* cloth, or even a live suckling pig.

Each village presents a singing group and a troupe of dancers in the Heiva competitions. Some of these performers are just as talented as the professional entertainers in Tahiti, as Bora Bora has long been recognized for producing excellent dancers, choreography and costumes. The competitions are a big social event, when old friends get together to catch up on the latest happenings and to swap a choice bit of gossip. Seats are provided for the officials and those who wish to pay to sit down. Everyone else sits on the grass or white sand at Place Vaitape. The bicycle races around the island are fun to watch on July 14, as the supporters stand beside the road and spray the riders with water. The fruit-carriers' race, javelin-throwing contest, soccer matches and outrigger sailing canoe races are just warm-up events for the outrigger paddle canoe races.

July 14 is a good combination of old style Polynesian celebrations and the French version of honoring Bastille Day in the tropics. This is the time to drink champagne at the mayors office, aboard a visiting French ship and at the glamorous resort hotels. A huge fireworks display ends the day's festivities, and an all-night ball gets underway a little later. Although there are only two or three weeks of planned events during the Heiva in Bora Bora, the Fête still goes on and on, well into the month of August. After all, building the *baraques* did require a lot of work. What's more, they provide a great meeting place.

Sports & Recreation
Hiking & Trekking
Mont Pahia Excursions is operated by Otemanu Tours, *Tel. 67.70.49; E-mail: otemanu.tours@mail.pf*. Your guide will meet you in Vaitape village or pick you up at your hotel. The Tahitian guide may not speak very good English but he is experienced in mountain climbing, and will lead you up the Pahia Mountain, where you will sometimes have to crawl on hands and knees and use a cord to climb and repel. You should be in very good physical shape to attempt this challenge, which can last from 3 to 6 hours, depending on the hikers. The cost begins at 15.000 CFP (plus 10% VAT) per person for 1 to 10 people.

Amae Hiking Excursion (A.H.E.), *Tel. 24.03.96*, is operated by Erico and Alan, who will guide 2-10 people up Mata Pua mountain (235 meters or 770 feet) on Monday and Saturday and up Mount Pahia (661 meters 2,168 feet) on Tuesday and Thursday. Departure is at 9am and you'll return at 4:30pm. The Mata Pua hike starts from Tiipoto and the Mount Pahia climb departs from Vaitape. You must be fit, in good health, and not prone to vertigo. Children younger than 12 years are not allowed. Bring a sandwich and a bottle of water and wear mountain shoes or boots.

Horseback Riding
Reva Reva Ranch is located on Motu Piti A'au across the lagoon from the village of Anau, *Tel. 67.63.63* or *78.26.36; E-mail: dom@mail.pf*. Olivier Ringeard will take you riding along secluded white sand beaches on New Zealand horses, with a choice of English and Western saddles. A 1-hour ride is 6.600 CFP and a 1 1/2 hour ride is 8.000 CFP, including transfers. There are

four rides daily and you can also take a romantic ride along the beach during the full moon, from 8 to 10pm, for 11.000 CFP. A 1 1/2 hour private ride is 48.000 CFP and a private moonlight ride is 66.000 CFP.

Taxi Boat and Boat Rental
   Taxi Motu, *Tel. 67.60.61, cell 77.33.23, Fax 67.61.01; E-mail: taximotu@hotmail.com.* Patrick Labataille operates a boat shuttle transfer service from the beach to the coral gardens or a *motu* for 2.000 CFP per person. He also provides Taxi Boat service on request for 15.000 CFP per hour for 1-4 passengers. A private Taxi Boat transfer from the airport to your hotel is 9.010 CFP for two passengers.
   If you want to pilot your own boat, Patrick rents aluminum boats for four people, with a 6 HP engine, which cost 6.500 CFP for 2 hours, 7.500 CFP for 3 hours, 8.500 CFP for a half-day and 12.000 CFP for a full day. No permit is required to operate this boat. A 15 HP boat does require a license, and rents for 8.500 CFP for 2 hours and up to 14.000 CFP for a full day. Add 10% Value Added Tax to all rates.
   Moana Adventure Tours, adjacent to the Hotel Bora Bora, *Tel. 67.61.41*, provides boat transfers upon request from the airport and resort hotels or private lodgings. The cost of transporting up to 3 passengers from the Bora Bora Airport to your hotel is 15.400 CFP in a 17-foot Boston Whaler and 19.800 CFP for up to 6 people in a 21-foot Bayliner. A 17-foot Boston Whaler with sun top can be rented with a pilot, who will take you to places in the lagoon that visitors normally never get to see. Rates are 22.000 CFP for 2 hours, 28.050 CFP for 3 hours, and up to 50.600 CFP for 8 hours for a maximum of 6 passengers. Rental of a 6-passenger 21-foot Bayline "Orama" with sun top starts at 33.000 CFP for 2 hours and goes up to 81.400 CFP for 8 hours, pilot included. They also rent 4-person dinghys without a pilot for day cruises. A 4-passenger boat with 6HP engine starts at 6.500 CFP for two hours, with no license required. A 6-passenger boat with a 15 HP engine is 8.500 CFP for 2 hours and 14.000 CFP for 8 hours, and a license is required.

Lagoon and Coastal Fishing
   Moana Adventure Tours, *Tel. 67.61.41/67.75.97* or *78.27.37*, uses a 17-foot Boston Whaler for fishing close to the outside reef, where currents and high seas attract bonito, tuna, mahi mahi, jacks, barracudas and wahoo. Private half-day excursions are 35.200 CFP for lagoon fishing and 38.500 CFP for a maximum of 2 people when fishing offshore.

Deep Sea Fishing
   Sports fishing around Bora Bora is a very popular activity and the local fishing clubs hold tournaments throughout the year. There is even a Vahine Sport Fishing Club for the ladies, and any visiting female angler is welcome to

join the competitions and fun. The fishing grounds are only 20 minutes away outside the barrier reef, and the waters around Bora Bora are filled with marlin, yellowfin tuna, sailfish, wahoo, mahi mahi and bonito. The marlin are tagged and released at the anglers' request. Inter-island cruises are provided on request. The sea captains listed below all speak very good English.

Taravana is a 50-foot prototype sportfishing/sailing catamaran owned by American expatriate, Richard Postma, which is based at the Hotel Bora Bora, *Tel. 67.77.79 (evening) or cell 689/72.30.99 (day); Fax 689/60.59.31; E-mail: taravana@mail.pf; www.taravana.com.* Richard said that *Taravana* (which means 'crazy' in Tahitian) is the world's first sportfishing sailboat and has proven to be successful with an impressive record of tournament wins. The boat is equipped with the best gear, 20 custom rods from 8 lbs. to 130 lbs. test line, Penn international reels, custom gaffs, and 2 custom fighting chairs. She's tournament ready. A half-day's deep-sea fishing excursion costs 95.400 CFP and a full-day's outing is 127.200 CFP for a maximum of 8 people. See more information under *Day Sailing Excursions and Sunset Cruises* in this chapter and in the chapter on *Planning Your Trip.*

Luna Sea is a Black Watch 34 that is also owned by Richard Postma of Island Sport Charters Bora Bora. *Tel. 67.77.79 (evening) or cell 689/72.30.99 (day); Fax 689/60.59.31; E-mail: taravana@mail.pf; www.taravana.com.* In spite of its name, this is a No Nonsense Big Game Fishing Boat built specifically for serious charter fishing in French Polynesian waters off the Leeward Society Islands. "Luna Sea" is based in Bora Bora but can easily fish the neighboring islands of Tahaa, Raiatea, Huahine, Tupai and Maupiti. The boat is dry, smooth, stable and very quick, and is equipped with Melton International Tackle custom built rods from 8 lb. to 130 lb. test with Shimano Tiagra 2-speed reels and Shimano spinning reels. She has Top Shot gaffs and a Relax Marine fighting chair and outriggers. Captain Tepoe Pere has more than 25 years of local and international experience and his goal is to give you the very best service possible. A half-day sportfishing excursion for up to 6 passengers is 84.800 CFP for the boat, and 116.600 CFP for a full-day charter. A full-day tour to Tahaa and Raiatea for up to 5 passengers is 127.200 CFP for the boat.

Jessie L is a Luhrs 35 based at the Ellacott Marina close to Vaitape, *Tel. 67.75.22/67.74.04; E-mail: alainloussan@mail.pf; www.moanatours.com.* Owner Alain Loussan can take four passengers on board for half-day fishing expeditions at 77.000 CFP and full-day charters for 132.000 CFP for the boat. No food or drinks included.

Tai San is a 54-foot Bertram Sport Fisherman that is based at the Bora Bora Nui Resort & Spa, *Tel. 60.32.41; Fax 67.51.12; E-mail: jeanne.pahuiri@boraboranui.com.* There are 3 cabins, 2 ensuites with head and showers, a salon, dining area, galley, phone, fax, television, video and game fishing gear. The boat is ideal for tough fishing expeditions or leisure cruises of several days for 4-6 passengers. It can accommodate 10 passengers for day excursions. A half-day fishing charter for 2-8 passengers is 120.000 CFP for the boat, and an all-day fishing charter is 195.000 CFP for the boat. A private sunset cruise is 79.000 CFP for the boat.

Lagoon Excursions by Outrigger Canoe or Speedboat

Bora Bora's lovely lagoon offers many surprises, pleasures and photographic treasures. **A Boat Trip Around the Island** normally includes time for snorkeling, exploring a small Motu islet, walking on the living Coral Reef, searching for the graceful Manta Rays, sharing a kiss with the Sting Rays, diving for the Giant Mussels buried in the white sand lagoon bottom (the mussels are not removed from their habitat) and donning mask and snorkel to view the fish and coral in the Natural Aquarium. **Feeding the Sharks and Stingrays** is included in most **Circle Island Tours**, and is Bora Bora's most popular and thrilling excursion. A **Picnic on a Motu** combined with your boat tour can mean you eat freshly grilled fish and fruit and drink coconut water, or you may be served a gourmet lunch, complete with cold drinks and wine. All lagoon activities depend on the whim of the weather and sea. Each of the following tour operators offers something different:

Bora Bora Lagoonarium, *Tel. 67.71.34; E-mail: lagoonarium@mail.pf; www.boraboralagoonarium.com.* A half-day excursion operated by Teura and Claudine Teheiura departs at 9:15am and returns you to your hotel at 12:45pm. Your destination is to their Lagoonarium on the northern point of Motu Piti A'au. Fenced-in sections of the lagoon contain fish, sea turtles, rays, and a huge moray eel that likes to play kissy face when you feed it some fish. The cost of the morning tour is 7.800 CFP and the afternoon tour is 6.600-7.000 CFP, depending on where you book. Or you can stay all day and enjoy a picnic on the white sand beach, returning to your hotel at 5pm. The full-day package is 11.000 CFP, including a picnic and *pareo* show.

Marona Tours, *Tel. 67.72.26/60.40.16*, is owned by Marona Atiu, who has two locally built motorized outrigger canoes for 4-22 passengers and a 22-foot Starline motor boat. He speaks very good English and is a good guide. Marona works with the Bora Bora Lagoon Resort & Spa and they charge 9.000 CFP for a half-day lagoon excursion and 13.000 CFP for a full-day picnic excursion. Both tours include shark feeding and sting ray feeding.

Moana Reva Tours, *Tel. 67.60.27*, is operated by Eric Moasen, who will take you around the island by outrigger speed canoe, motu hopping with a picnic on a white sand beach, and feed the sharks while you photograph this exciting event. He leaves Le Maitai Polynesia at 9:30am and returns at 3:30pm, and the cost is 8.000 CFP for adults and half-price for children under 12 years old.

Raanui Tours, *Tel. 67.61.79* or *79.43.14*, is operated by Arieta Onee *in Anau village.* He has two motorized outrigger canoes for half-day excursions that include shark and ray feeding and snorkeling. A 3-hour tour is 4.000 CFP per person.

Shark Boy of Bora Bora, *Tel. 67.60.93* or *78.27.42; E-mail: sharkboy@mail.pf*, is owned by Evan Temarii, whose has 4 outrigger canoes for 12 passengers, a locally built canoe for 30 people and a catamaran for 60 passengers. He works with the Bora Bora Intercontinental Moana Beach Resort, Bora Bora Pearl Beach Resort and cruise ships, making half-day excursions around the island, for 7.200 CFP per person. Full-day excursions leave the hotels at 9:30am and return at 4:30pm, with a picnic lunch served on a *motu*, and costs 8.800 CFP. On all the excursions you will be able to swim with the rays and watch the sharks being fed. Evan has starred in two movies filmed in Bora Bora: starting when he was 11 years old with *Heart*, made for the Wonderful World of Disney, followed by *Call It Courage* when he was 18. He traps the sharks with his bare hands and holds them over his head out of

Bora Bora's Shark Feeding Show

Feeding the sharks is one of the most popular excursions on Bora Bora. Each morning the tourists board outrigger canoes to speed across the lagoon toward the barrier reef. When you make your own shark feeding tour, you will put on a mask and snorkel, and step into the clear waters of the warm lagoon, just inside the fringing reef. With just a few steps in water about 1.2 meters (4 feet) deep you will reach a rope that has been tied around two huge coral heads. You hold onto the rope for stability and watch through your mask as your guide performs the daily shark feeding show.

Thousands of tropical fish of all colors rush over to have a nibble at the huge head of tuna or mahi mahi that the guide holds out to them. You will see rainbow colored butterfly fish, black and white striped manini, the blue and yellow empress angel fish, the variegated and very territorial Picasso fish, plus many other families of more than 300 species of fish that inhabit the Bora Bora submarine gardens.

Gasps and squeals from the audience announce the arrival of the sharks as they appear for their breakfast. Sometimes you can see as many as a dozen sharks, about 1.5 meters (5 feet) long. These are the Carcharhinus Melanopterus, commonly known as the **blackfin** or **blacktip reef shark**.

The shark feeding show is so fascinating that you may forget your fear. As you are upcurrent of the sharks and the Tahitian guides keep their attention diverted with the proffered fish breakfast, the sharks normally pay little attention to their observers. If you are bold enough, you can even help to feed these hungry beasts. And if your nerve fails you, then the outrigger canoe is just a few steps away.

&

the water for the photographers. He was the first one to tame the stingrays, and even taught them how to kiss.

Teremoana Tours, *Tel. 67.71.38*, is operated by Noel "Nono" Leverd, who also owns Chez Nono pension on Matira Beach. His very popular excursions aboard a 36-foot outrigger speed canoe depart from the beach in front of his pension at 9:30am and return at 3:30pm. A lunch of *poisson cru*, grilled fish, coconut bread, cake, fresh fruit and *po'e* is served on the *motu*. The cost is 8.000 CFP per person.

Private Lagoon Excursions and Picnics on the Motu

Etienne, *Tel./Fax 67.63.14; cell 79.22.62*, was the first tour operator to provide a picnic in the water, and his private lagoon excursions and barbecues on the motu are highly praised by guests staying at the Bora Bora Lagoon Resort & Spa, his exclusive client. Etienne's tour begins with a trip around the lagoon, where you can feed the rays and sharks and admire the manta rays. Then he takes you to a truly private motu, where you will be the only people swimming and snorkeling in the water and sunbathing on the white sand beach. While you are enjoying this lovely site, Etienne is preparing your lunch. He places a small table and two chairs in the shallow lagoon water, shades them with a big umbrella, dresses the table with a linen cloth and place settings, sets up his barbecue grill in the water and ices down the champagne in a bucket standing in the lagoon next to the table. The stylish lunch starts with mixed salad and poisson cru with coconut milk, and is followed by grilled lobster, mahi mahi and steak, accompanied by potatoes, and followed by a dessert of fresh fruit. There is beer, pineapple juice, Sprite and Coke in the cooler, and you can have wine if you prefer that to champagne. Etienne's brother Motai and their sister Merita have now joined the family business, to the delight of the tourists. This activity is available daily except Saturday, departing Bora Bora Lagoon Resort & Spa at 10am and returning at 3pm. The cost is 70.000 CFP for two. Etienne said that you can contact him directly for a better rate. He also told me that most of the so-called private picnic tours, except for Patrick's Activities, take place on a motu near the Lagoonarium, and you can see other couples or small groups while swimming and dining.

Keishi Tours, *Tel. 67.67.31, cell 79.26.56,* is owned by Pierrot Taati, who has two motorized outrigger canoes, 32 feet and 35 feet long. He works with some of the hotels, taking their guests on boat excursions around the island with a private picnic on a *motu*, and the tourists are very happy with Pierrot's excursions. The Pearl Beach charges 55.000 CFP for this outing. The Sofitel Marara charges 30.000 CFP for a Keishi Tour and 60.000 CFP with a picnic in the water. Contact Pierrot directly for better rates.

Moana Adventure Tours, *Tel. 67.61.41*. Owner Franck Sachsse has a 2 hour and 15 minute snorkeling safari, which includes feeding the rays and sharks, for 6.600 CFP per person. He also provides 3-hour private snorkeling, ray and shark excursions for 44.000 CFP to 52.800 CFP for the boat. The Blue Lagoon Cruise is a private speed boat tour around the island to watch the ray ballet, visit the reef sharks, discover manta rays and much more. Soft drinks and a bottle of champagne are included for two people. A 4-hour excursion for two is 55.000 CFP in a 17-foot Boston Whaler and 77.000 CFP in his 21-foot Bayliner "Orama" boat. The Hotel Bora Bora has also asked Franck to take care of their guests who wish to enjoy a barbecue picnic on a private beach. Each Tuesday and Friday Franck takes a minimum of 4 passengers to visit the barrier reef and go snorkeling while he prepares lunch on the motu. This 6-hour excursion costs 13.310 CFP per person. The Hotel Bora Bora charges 55.220 CFP for two people who sign up for a private barbecue picnic on a private beach, and Franck takes them to the motu for a full day's outing.

Ben Heriteau of **Diveasy**, *Tel. 79.22.55; Fax 67.69.36; E-mail: diveasy@mail.pf*, handles the Private Picnic tours for the Intercontinental Moana Beach Resort, who sells this "Table set in the Water" excursion for 61.600 CFP a couple. The boat leaves the hotel at 11am and returns at 3pm. This Romantic Idea activity includes snorkeling beside a private motu, the table and chairs in the water, the shady umbrella, chilled champagne and grilled fish on the barbecue.

Teiva Tours, *Tel. 67.64.26, cell 73.75.74; E-mail: teivatours@ifrance.com*. Teiva Mullatier has an open outrigger speed canoe that takes tourists around the island, stopping for snorkeling and shark feeding for 7.700 CFP for a half-day excursion. The full-day tour is 16.000 CFP per person and includes a picnic on the motu. He also does private tours for two, which are priced at 46.000 CFP with a cold buffet lunch served on a motu, or 56.000 CFP for two if you want a barbecue lunch on the motu.

Patrick's Activities / Maohi Nui Private Excursions, *Tel. 67.69.94, cell 79.19.11; E-mail: patrick.bora@mail.pf*. Patrick Tairua is well known and appreciated in Bora Bora for his Famous Nature Tours by 4x4 Jeep and outrigger canoe, his ma'a Tahiti feasts on a private motu, his Polynesian Wedding Ceremonies, and his spectacular fire-dancing when he performs with his Maohi Nui dancers at the hotels several nights a week. Patrick is indeed a busy man because he is really good at what he does and he's dependable; therefore, he is in demand by the hotels and individual clients.

The Hotel Bora Bora and Bora Bora Lagoon Resort & Spa propose a 3 1/2 hour Private Outrigger Tour for up to 8 people, which sells for 44.000 CFP for the boat. Patrick speaks good English and he will tell you about the Polynesian culture and legends of Bora Bora as he takes you around the lagoon in his famous yellow outrigger speed canoe with a roof of coconut palm fronds. You can snorkel in the coral gardens, watch the ballet of the graceful manta rays inside the lagoon in Anau, feed the sting rays and eagle rays and go ashore on the white sandy beach of a motu islet, where Patrick will refresh you with some tropical fruit. Bring a beach towel, shoes or sandals, sunscreen and your cameras.

A Polynesian Tour is also one of the excursions that Patrick leads for the guests of the Hotel Bora Bora and Bora Bora Lagoon Resort & Spa, which begins with a cruise by outrigger canoe all around the island for snorkeling and sightseeing. Then you land on the white sand beach of a motu islet where your ma'a Tahiti feast of traditional foods will be served. These include pork, chicken, tropical vegetables and local fruits and the food is cooked in banana leaves, buried under the ground in a natural ahima'a oven. You can also request a barbecue if you prefer that to a Tahitian feast. The all-inclusive cost of a 4-hour outing is 75.000 CFP for 2-4 people and 90.000 CFP for up to 8 people. A 5 1/2 hour excursion is 84.000 CFP for 2-4 people and 101.500 CFP for up to 8 people, which includes a complimentary bottle of champagne. A 7-8 hour excursion is 107.500 CFP for 1-4 people and 125.000 CFP for up to 8 people, which also includes a bottle of champagne. The Intercontinental Moana Beach sells Patrick's tour as a Private Picnic Tamaara'a for 92.400 CFP. See information under *Mountain Safaris and 4x4 Excursions* and *Wedding Ceremonies*.

Sailing Charter Yachts

There is no big yacht charter company based in Bora Bora. You can rent a sailboat from one of the charter companies based in Tahiti, Moorea or Raiatea and sail to Bora Bora, or you can arrange for a yacht to be delivered to Bora Bora in time for your arrival. See Chapter 6, *Planning Your Trip*, section on Cruises.

Day Sailing Excursions & Sunset Cruises

Atara Royal, *Tel. 66.17.74/78.23.74; Fax 66.17.67; E-mail: myc@mail.pf; www.tahiti-motoryacht.com*. Day charters aboard this 46-foot Grand Banks Europa motor yacht will take you to visit the lagoon of Bora Bora, the coral garden and stopping for snorkeling and swimming. Lunch is served on board. An 8 and 1/2 hour cruise for two people is 220.000 CFP for the boat, and each additional person is 6.600 CFP.

If you would like to spend a day visiting the "Vanilla Island" of Taha'a, you can take a 15-minute helicopter ride from Bora Bora to Motu Tau Tau in Taha'a, where the prestigious Le Taha'a Private Island & Spa is located. There you will board the *Atara Royal* and navigate to moor in front of a private motu, where you will swim in the lagoon and have lunch on the motu. Then you will visit a pearl farm and a vanilla plantation and cruise around Taha'a until you return to Motu Tau Tau. You can fly back to Bora Bora by helicopter or sail back on board the *Atara Royal*. The cost of the 9-hour outing with a round-trip helicopter ride is 256.000 CFP for two people and 26.100 CFP for each additional person. If you fly one way by helicopter and sail one way by motor yacht the 10 1/2 hour trip for two is 292.999 CFP, and 41.100 CFP for an extra person.

The *Atara Royal* will also make transfer cruises between Bora Bora and Taha'a or Taha'a-Bora Bora. This 8 1/2 hour excursion includes a welcome cocktail and canapé on board, mineral water, soft drinks and lunch on the yacht, plus time for swimming and snorkeling. Departure time is at 9am from either island and the cost for two people is 200.000 CFP, and 6.600 CFP for each additional person.

The *Atara Royal* can be chartered for short or long cruises in the Leeward Islands or to other archipelagoes of French Polynesia. It was built in 1999 and has two Caterpillar 375 horsepower engines. Accommodations include double cabins plus crew quarters, air-conditioning, water maker, washing machine, microwave oven, television, video and DVD players, satellite telephone/fax, two stereos, dinghy with 30 horse-power engine, plus equipment for fishing and water skiing. A Honeymoon cruise for a minimum of 4 days and 3 nights is 90.000 CFP per night for the Groom and 65.000 CFP per night for the Bride. An "a la carte cruise" through the Leeward Islands is 180.000 CFP per night for 2 passengers and 195.000 CFP per night for 4 passengers, all meals included. A minimum of 4 days/3 nights is required.

Hippocampe II, *Tel./Fax 67.73.48; cell 77.24.82; E-mail: bluelagoonchart@mail.pf; www.bluelagooncharter.pf.* Michel Bordier operates Blue Lagoon Charter and his Privilege 45 cruising catamaran is based at the Bora Bora Lagoon Resort & Spa. *Hippocampe II* is available daily except Saturday for morning or afternoon half-day cruises, which cost 15.000 CFP per person, or for full-day cruises with a picnic included for 24.000 CFP per person. She is also used for sunset cruises between 4:45 and 6:45pm, for 10.000 CFP per passenger. This luxurious sailing boat is also equipped for cruising charters for a week or more, with accommodations in 5 double cabins for 8 passengers. Dive cruises in the Tuamotu atolls can also be organized.

O'Hana, *Tel. 67.52.26, cell 79.19.42; E-mail: info@ohanatahiti.com; www.ohanatahiti.com.* This 65-foot Ocean Voyager sailing catamaran is based at Le Méridien Bora Bora. Half-day sailing excursions are scheduled five mornings a week for 8.250 CFP per passenger. A sunset cruise is 9.900 CFP. Private charters are available. **O'Hana Excursions** is owned by Bernard Marmillon, who also has two locally built motorized outrigger canoes for 6 to 50 passengers.

Taaroa III, *Tel./Fax 67.64.30; E-mail: boravoil@netcourrier.com.* Sylvie and Pascal at Bora Bora Fun own this Formula 40 Fleury Michon racing catamaran that can accommodate 2-10 people for the morning excursions around the island and 16 passengers for a sunset sailing cruise. A sail around the island, from 8:45am to 12:30pm, costs 6.500 CFP, and includes a swim in the lagoon. Sunset cruises for 2-16 passengers are from 4:30 to 5:15pm or

6:30 to 7pm daily except Sunday, for a cost of 3.800 CFP per person. The boat can be chartered for 50.000 CFP for private excursions.

Taravana, *Tel. 67.77.79 (evening) or cell 689/72.30.99 (day); Fax 689/ 60.59.31; E-mail: taravana@mail.pf; www.taravana.com* is a 50-foot prototype sportfishing/sailing catamaran based at the Hotel Bora Bora. Captain Richard Postma is an American who has lived in Bora Bora for about 25 years, and he works with several of the big hotels and passenger ships, offering half-day and full-day cruises. The sunset cruises for up to 20 people aboard the *Taravana* are ideal for lovers, departing each Tuesday, Thursday and Saturday from the Hotel Bora Bora boat dock at 5pm for a 2-hour sail on the flat, calm lagoon waters inside the protected reef. This excursion costs 6.890 CFP and a complimentary beverage. The boat can be chartered for private sunset cruises for 68.900 CFP for a maximum of 8 passengers. Half-day sailing and fishing charters are 95.400 CFP for the boat and 127.200 CFP for full-day cruises.

Famous Hollywood stars who want to get away from it all find the privacy and tranquillity they seek when they charter the *Taravana* for an overnight sail. The cost of this romantic cruise is 233.200 CFP for two people or 275.600 CFP for four passengers for one day and one night. A cruise of 2 days and one night for 2 passengers is 381.600 CFP for the trip. The rates include meals and drinks, which are served by a staff of two professionals. Some movie stars have even gotten married aboard Richard's famous catamaran "far from the madding crowd."

You can also enjoy a full-day sail and dive expedition to the atoll of Tupai, the island closest to Bora Bora. It takes 1 1/2 hours to cross the 10-mile channel and you can sportfish on the way to the reef, enjoy superb snorkeling and have lunch on board when you reach the calm side of the atoll. Once the boat reaches Tupai you can go for two scuba dives with your private instructor. The cost of the boat, instructor and equipment for two dives is 186.160 CFP for the day for up to 4 people. The rates quoted here are those charged if you book through the Hotel Bora Bora. Contact Captain Richard Postma for further rates and details. See more information under *Deep-Sea Fishing* in this chapter.

Malibu is an open speedboat with an inboard engine that is used for private Romantic Sunset cruises, leaving the Intercontinental Moana Beach pier at 4pm and returning at 7pm. Champagne and music add to the feeling of romance, and the cost is 31.900 CFP for the boat.

Scuba Diving

Bora Bora's six scuba diving clubs have qualified diving instructors who will introduce you to a large variety of diving spots inside the lagoon and beyond the barrier reef. Visibility is usually 20 to 30 meters, with an abundance of marine life, including manta rays, sharks, barracuda, dolphins and turtles. The lagoon of Bora Bora is the only one in the world where a family of manta rays lives year-round. Initiation dives, fun dives and night dives are available, with up to four outings a day.

Bora Bora Blue Nui is based at the Bora Bora Pearl Beach Resort, *Tel. 67.79.07 or 79.22.72; Fax 67.79.07; E-mail: boraborablue nui@mail.pf; www.bluenui.com.* Gilles Petre, who manages the Blue Nui Dive Centers in Bora Bora, Taha'a, Manihi and Tikehau, has almost 20 years' experience diving in French Polynesia and he speaks very good English. His American wife, Wendy, works with him at the dive shop. Gilles is an international CMAS ** monitor, State instructor BEES 1, PADI instructor and OWSI. He can give exams for CMAS, PADI and FFESM certificates. The center has two fast 115 HP covered aluminum boats for 16 divers, and the rates are 6.700 CFP for one dive, 7.500 CFP for an initiation dive, and 8.000 CFP for a night dive, including all the equipment. Blue Nui offers packages that can be used in any or all of the four Blue Nui Dive Centers. These packages sell for 31.000 CFP for 5 dives and 59.000 CFP for 10 dives.

Bora Diving Center, *Tel. 67.71.84/67.74.83; Fax 67.74.83; E-mail: boradiving@mail.pf; www.boradive.com* is managed by Michel and Anne Condesse, adjacent to the Hotel Bora Bora on Matira Beach. International CMAS *** monitor, State instructor BEES1, PADI instructor. You can get certified for CMAS and PADI in three days. They have free pickup daily at 8:30am and 1:30pm and offer 10 dive sites with depths from 9 to 200 feet. There are 7 multi-lingual instructors and 5 comfortable dive boats with all the necessary safety equipment. A video cameraman accompanies the divers, and the center has an individual viewing service. They also make day trips to dive around Tupai atoll. A regular dive is 6.500 CFP, a 2-tank dive is 12.000 CFP, a 5-dive package is 30.000 CFP and a private boat is 36.000 CFP.

Diveasy is located at the end of Point Matira, *Tel. 79.22.55; Fax 67.69.36; E-mail: diveasy@mail.pf.* Owner Ben Heriteau offers private dives for 1-4 people, and this is reportedly a good dive center for beginners. He is a State Instructor BEES 1, Class II B. Examinations are given for ANMP and CMAS certification. He is equipped with an underwater communications system to allow comments during the dive. He charges 10.000 CFP per dive. He leads initiation dives with the manta rays, ocean dives with sharks and reef exploration dives. Underwater camera rental is available. Bora Bora Nui Resort & Spa and Bora Bora Lagoon Resort & Spa book Diveasy private dives with personalized guidance for 25.000 CFP for one person and 30.000 CFP for two divers. Intercontinental Moana Beach also uses Diveasy for private dives and charges 12.000 CFP for an initiation or exploration dive and 10.000 CFP for a snorkeling excursion.

Maradive, *Tel./Fax 67.74.83; E-mail: boradiving@mail.pf; www.boradive.com.* This friendly dive center is located at the Sofitel Marara and is operated by Anne and Michel Condesse of Bora Diving Center, along with Eric Poupion. The staff speaks English, French, Japanese and Spanish and are qualified PADI, CMAS, FFESSM and ANMP dive instructors. There is one dive boat with a 225 HP engine that can accommodate up to 12 divers for the 2-4 dives per day. An exploratory dive is 6.500 CFP, a night dive is 7.500 CFP, a 2-tank dive is 12.000 CFP, and a 5-dive package is 30.000 CFP.

Nemo World Bora Bora, *Tel. 67.77.85; E-mail: mail@nemoworld.pf; www.nemodivebora.com.* This dive center is managed by Katia Labat, whose staff includes a qualified international CMAS *** monitor, State instructor BEES 1, PADI instructor, OWSI and ANMP. Examinations are given for certification in ANMP, CMAS and PADI. Their clients usually come from Le Méridien and they provide free land transfers from your hotel, pension or boat. There are two morning dives for certified divers, for 12.000-13.000 CFP, and one dive in the afternoon for initiation and lessons, which costs 6.500-7.000 CFP. Video films can also be made of your dive.

TOPdive Bora Bora, *Tel. 60.50.50; Fax 60.50.51; E-mail: info@topdive.com; www.topdive.com.* This is the biggest dive center in Bora Bora and they also work with Club Med Bora Bora. The TOPdive center offers introductory dives and lessons either inside the lagoon or in the swimming pool. Lessons in theory are given in the classroom next to the patio beside the pool. The equipment used is Scubapro, with 121 steel tanks and 8 tanks for children eight years or older. There are four completely equipped dive boats to take you to special dive sites inside the lagoon or outside the coral reef. You can dive up to four times a day, and night dives in the lagoon are also organized. Certification courses in CMAS and PADI are given, but it is best to check with the resort to find out when each course will begin. Public rates for scuba diving start at 6.500 CFP for an introductory dive, fun dive or night dive; a CMAS* (one star) course is 49.900 CFP; and a package of 10 dives is charged at the rate of nine dives, which comes to 58.500 CFP. The diving rates include taxes and all equipment. This package can be used at TOPdive centers in Bora Bora, Moorea, Rangiroa, Fakarava and Tahiti. Nitrox scuba diving is also available and costs 7.900 CFP for an exploratory dive, 15.500 CFP for 2 tank dives, 29.000 CFP for Nitrox certification and 71.100 CFP for a Nitrox Interisland 10-dive package.

Snuba, *Tel.60.59.16, Fax 60.59.15, E-mail: snubaborabora@mail.pf; www.marcus-diving.com.* Marc Biehler is a professional underwater instructor BEES 2 who will teach you all about Snuba, which is a cross between snorkeling and scuba diving. It is fun for the whole family and doesn't require any special training or diploma. You can dive down to six meters (18 feet) inside the lagoon of Bora Bora, and instead of wearing the air tank on your back, it remains on a float above the water while you breathe through an attached tube. Marc leads private half-day Snuba trips for a maximum of 6 people. He will pick you up at your hotel in a 24-foot long covered boat with a 150 HP engine, and the tour includes a stop for snorkeling and another stop at a private motu islet where you can practice the Snuba technique. The cost of this excursion is 30.000 CFP for two people and 5.000 CFP for each additional person.

Marc Biehler also leads private **Scuba** diving trips for a maximum of 4 people. The 2005 price for one dive is 15.000 CFP a person and a two-tank dive is 30.000 CFP for one person, 45.000 CFP for two people, and 12.000 CFP for an additional person. He can arrange a picnic on a private motu or special trips on request.

You can even get married underwater with the Snuba concept. A "Neptune" wedding at the Intercontinental Moana Beach Resort is 220.000 CFP.

Other Ways to Discover Bora Bora's Marine World

Aqua Safari, *Tel. 67.71.84/67.74.83; E-mail: aquasafari@mail.pf.* Anne and Michel Condesse at Bora Diving Center offer you an unusual way in which to discover what's under Bora Bora's world-famous lagoon. You put a funny looking square yellow helmet over your head and you can walk on the lagoon bottom at a 3-meter (10-foot) depth, without getting your head wet. And you don't even have to know how to swim or dive to discover this new sensation. The helmet is attached to air bottles just like the divers wear, only the bottles remain on the boat while you wander around under the water, breathing as you normally do. A bilingual guide accompanies 4 to 5 people while a dive master stays aboard the boat to check on the air supply. This 1 hour and 15-minute Undersea Walk takes you to a part of the lagoon called the Aquarium, or close to Toopua Island, where you can see families of rays swimming in the blue depths. The hotels charge 6.500-7.000 CFP for this Helmet Dive. A private helmet dive can be combined with snorkeling during a 3-hour tour for two, which costs 66.000 CFP for the boat.

Aquascope Bora Bora, *Tel. 67.61.92/78.27.92,* operates the *Moana View*, a 10-passenger air-conditioned glass-bottom semi-submerged boat that offers a 180-degree view of Bora Bora's underwater gardens during a 50-minute excursion. There are five departures daily, for 5.000-5.400 CFP per adult and about 3.500 CFP for a child from 4 to 12 years. A Blue Safari 3-hour excursion inside the lagoon and outside the pass is also available for a minimum of 6 passengers, which includes a snorkeling excursion in the lagoon and refreshments served on board the power boat. This is priced at 11.000 CFP for adults and 7.000 CFP for 4-12 year olds.

Bora Bora Submarine, *Tel. 67.55.55, cell 74.99.99; Fax 67.65.67; E-mail: spiritofpacific@mail.pf; www.spiritofpacific.com.* Spirit of Pacific is a yellow submarine that will take 4 to 6 passengers down to 25 meters (82 feet) below the water's surface to observe the world of corals and their animal life. You may see sting rays, eagle rays, blue jackfish, bat fish, surgeon fish, unicorn fish, convict tangs, Moorish idols, butterfly fish, blue damselfish, and schools of snappers. The cabin is air-conditioned with a 360 degree viewing port. You are transferred by boat to the submarine, which remains inside the protected lagoon between Bora Bora's main island and Motu Toopua. There are five outings per day and the hotels charge 13.000-15.000 CFP for 30 minutes, and 18.500-20.000 CFP for 45 minutes, including transfers. Children under 12 years old pay half price. A private tour is 100.000 CFP.

Glass Bottom Boat Excursions
Moana Adventure Tours, *Tel. 67.61.41* or *78.27.37*, has a covered glass bottom boat that operates tours from all the hotels on Monday, Wednesday and Saturday, between 9:45am and 12pm., for 3.850CFP, and half-price for children under 12 years.

Jet-Ski or Wave-Runner Excursions
You can rent a jet ski for 1 or 2 hours, with guides to take you around the island inside the lagoon. You'll stop on the *motu* islets, snorkel in beautiful coral gardens, feed the fish, visit the aquarium and even dive with the sharks and stingrays. The rental costs are 16.500 CFP for one hour and 17.900-20.500 CFP per jet for two hours when you book through the hotels, and less if you contact the operators directly. The hotels charge 82.000 CFP for a private 2-hour tour for up to 4 people on two jets.

Matira Jet Tours, *Tel. 67.62.73* or *77.63.63*, is operated by Rainui Besineau on Point Matira. **Miki-Miki Jet Tours**, *Tel. 67.76.4* or *79.11.78* is owned by Karl Chang, also on the beach at Point Matira.

Sea Kayaks
Bora Bora Kayak, *Tel. 67.72.16; Fax 67.78.14; E-mail: info@boraborakayak.com; www.boraborakayak.com* is managed by Nir Shalev, who also manages Village Pauline in Pofai Bay. He rents single Dolphin kayaks and double Aqua Terra kayaks for a half or full day, and he is the only one on the island with sea kayaks for rent. Included with the kayak: storage space, paddles, snorkeling gear, lifevests. Backrests, dry bags, fishing poles, cooler and guided tour are optional. Group rates or long term rentals possible. **Note**: Due to restructuring, Nir cannot rent any kayaks until he gets an all-new setup into operation in July 2005.

Water-Skiing & Wakeboard
Bora Bora Laguna Ski, *Tel. 73.53.77, E-mail: bobwaterski@mail.pf*, is operated by Karen Bonnevie, who works several hotels, providing all levels of waterskiing: bi-ski, mono-ski, wakeboard, barefoot and buoy skiing. A 15-minute tour is 6.000 CFP, a 30-minute session is 11.000 CFP, and a 20-minute lesson for beginners is 9.000 CFP. A private 2-hour boat ride around the island is 33.000 CFP for up to 4 people, which includes water-skiing and a snorkeling stop. A 3-hour water-skiing island tour is 46.000 CFP for up to 4 people and a 6-hour tour with boat and instructor is 78.000 CFP.

Parasailing
   Bora Bora Parasail, *Tel. 67.70.34, cell 78.27.10; E-mail: parasail@mail.pf,* is located adjacent to the Sofitel Marara. You can soar solo or duo from 330 to 990 feet high above the Bora Bora lagoon for a fabulous view. The take-off and landing is gentle and you won't even get wet. No experience required. A 15-minute flight up to 100 meters (330 feet) costs 12.500 CFP for one person and 20.500 CFP for two. A 30-minute flight up to 300 meters (990 feet) is 19.500 CFP solo and 28.500 CFP duo. There is no age limit to this thrilling flight, which was tested and approved by Walt Disney World.

Shopping
Art Galleries
   Galerie D'Art Alain and Linda, *Tel./Fax 67.70.32, cell 79.15.89; E-mail: alain-linda@mail.pf.* This interesting art gallery is on the beach side of Pofai Bay, between Vaitape village and the Hotel Bora Bora. Linda, who is German, attended the Beaux Arts and the Sorbonne in Paris and her paintings were exhibited during the opening of the Ministry of Culture in Tahiti in 2003. She also had a showing in Italy that year. Alain, her French husband, worked for world renowned artists in leading galleries throughout Paris before moving to Bora Bora with his bride Linda more than 35 years ago. Now he paints the *pareos* and tee shirts that they sell. Their gallery has a collection of paintings, sculptures, pottery, etchings and lithographs by the finest artists from the Polynesian islands. They also carry art books and tapa bark paintings. Both of these friendly folks enjoy meeting people and Linda has a lot of stories to tell you about the legends and life of the island. She's one of those magical people you'll love to meet.

   Garrick Yrondi has a gallery in the center that also contains the Bamboo House Restaurant and Art du Pacifique, between Vaitape and the Hotel Bora Bora, *Tel. 60.57.15.* His paintings, sculptures and bronzes are on display. Yrondi created the pink marble statue of *vahine ei'a*, the fish woman, which you should look for at the edge of the Motu Mute lagoon by the airport. This is the protector of Bora Bora.

   Moana Art and Pearls Gallery, *Tel. 67.66.00,* is adjacent to the Hotel Bora Bora beside Pofai Bay. This is the realm of photographer Erwin Christian, now retired, who has produced several beautiful and informative coffee table books on Bora Bora and all the islands in French Polynesia. In his boutique you will find Erwin's signed photographs and books, as well as his post cards and posters and greeting cards. They also feature hand-picked Polynesian carvings and artifacts from the Marquesas as well as a lovely selection of black pearls.

   Art du Pacifique, *Tel. 67.76.23,* is in the same complex with the Yrondi gallery, the Bamboo House and the gastronomic restaurant Villa Mahana. This collection of South Seas primitive art includes ceremonial masks, drums and war clubs from the tribes of Papua New Guinea and other Melanesian and Polynesian islands.

Emmanuel Masson, *Tel. 67.65.31*, learned to paint from his father, Jean Masson, who was a very well known French artist who first discovered Tahiti in 1938. Years later he met Rosine Tamauri from Bora Bora, who became his favorite model and student, and together they had four children. Emmanuel exhibits his paintings of Polynesian people and Bora Bora scenery in his art gallery called **Paarara Mountain**, which is located above Faanui Bay, overlooking the lagoon and the Bora Bora Pearl Beach Resort. All the Safari tours stop at his gallery and if you want to rent a car and drive there, you should turn off the main road beside the church in Faanui and follow the winding road up the mountain until you see his sign. You can even picnic in his garden and gaze at the lovely view.

Other galleries include: **Tamanu Galerie d'Art**, *Tel. 67.66.89*, next to the post office in Vaitape; **Alain Despert**, *Tel. 60.48.15*, on mountainside between Hotel Bora Bora and Point Matira, **Bora Bora Gallery**, *Tel. 67.66.75*, on mountainside between Hotel Bora Bora and Point Matira; and **Bora Bora Art Naea Studio**, on mountainside in Faanui, *Tel. 67.71.17*.

Black Pearls, Clothing & Souvenirs

Matira Pearls & Fashions,*Tel. 67.79.14; Fax 67.70.45; E-mail: mpfpearl@mail.pf; www.matirapearls.com*. Look for this pearl shop and clothing boutique on the mountainside at Point Matira, just past the turnoff sign for the Intercontinental Moana Beach Resort, if you are coming from Vaitape, The two American owners are both named Steve. Steve Fearon's family used to own the Hotel Bora Bora and the Hotel Tahara'a in Tahiti, and Steve Donnatin also worked in the hotel and restaurant business in Bora Bora before getting into the black pearl business. Stop by and meet them and have a look at their big collection of high quality black pearls, which they sell at the best possible prices. Their pearls for all budgets are mounted in 18 karat gold or white gold, and they also have a large selection of loose (unset) pearls.

Bora Pearl Company, *Tel./Fax 67.75.01; E-mail: map@mail.pf; www.borapearls.com* has four black pearl shops. These include **Bora Pearl**, *Tel. 67.76.35*, in Vaitape village; **Moana Art & Pearls**, *Tel. 67.66.00*, next to the Hotel Bora Bora; **Keana**, *Tel. 67.54.03*, at Le Maitai Polynesia hotel; and **Bora Original**, *Tel. 67.54.02*, also at Le Maitai Polynesia. A complimentary shuttle service is available to take you to any of these locations. The sales manager is Miri Kelley from Moorea, whose father, the late Hugh Kelley, was one of the founders/builders/owners of the Bali Hai hotels.

Some of the big name black pearl companies from Tahiti, such as **Sibani, Tahiti Perles** and **Perlissima** also have outlets in Bora Bora, and you will find black pearls in almost every shop you wander into.

Royal Helen's Bay Center and Pahia Center are two small shopping centers beside the lagoon in Vaitape village, with more pearl shops, a few clothing boutiques and miscellaneous gift shops. All around the island you will find little boutiques and thatched roof stands that sell hand-printed *pareos*, tee-shirts, swimwear and all kinds of creative souvenir items that were actually made on Bora Bora. Don't be fooled into buying an authentic made-in-Bali carving that has the name Bora Bora stamped on it. **Boutique Paiki** sells Marquesan Art on the mountainside in Matira between Fare Manuia and Le Maitai Polynesia. Look for **Boutique Gauguin** and **Pakalola Boutique** in Vaitape, and **Keana Boutique** has several locations.

The **Arts and Crafts Center** at the Vaitape quay has grass skirts and coconut bras, shell jewelry and woven hats and bags that are handmade by the people who sell them, even though most of the seashells were imported.

Camera Rental

Jean-Luc Camera Shop, *Tel. 67.64.82/67.76.63, cell 72.01.23,* is located on the Vaitape pier adjacent to the Air Tahiti office. He rents cameras for all occasions. A snorkeling camera with automatic flash and 36 exposure film included is 5.500 CFP per day. A scuba diving professional Nikonos V camera with 36 exposure film included rents for 8.800 CFP for a half-day and 11.000 CFP for a full day. A Sony video 8mm land camera rents for 8.800 CFP for a half-day and 11.000 CFP for a full day. Jean-Luc also sells film and provides express photo development. He can handle digital transfers and can help you with your video and DVD requirements. Jean-Luc works with several of the top hotels, to photograph or film any occasion such as weddings, anniversaries, gatherings, reunions or whatever you want for your souvenir album. The photos can be delivered on paper, put on a CD-ROM or DVD-edited with sound effects.

Special Services – Massage, Natural Therapy, Relaxation & Spa Treatments

Bora Bora Just Relax, *Tel. 67.65.90, cell 78.66.31; E-mail: borajustrelax@hotmail.com.* Lucette Couderc has a massage room and offers spa services at the Novotel hotel and she will also come to your hotel room to give you a relaxing massage and aromatic bath.

Ethy Kalombe, *Tel. 67.62.61,* is a physical therapist and chiropractor who gives relaxing Swedish massages, Chinese accupressure, reflexology of the feet, back and head, clears the lymphatic system, stretching massages, and a traditional massage with aromatic oils. You can also be a true hedonist and treat yourself to one of her special baths.

Mandara Spa, *Tel. 60.33.00,* is built on the hillside at the Bora Bora Nui Resort & Spa. There are 3 private and luxurious treatment bungalows hidden within the lush vegetation. You have an unsurpassed view of the azure waters of Bora Bora's world famous lagoon and Otemanu mountain from one terrace and a panoramic sweeping view of the lagoon and Pacific Ocean from the other side of the spa. Each bungalow is equipped with its own Jacuzzi and all of the world-famous Mandara Spa treatments are available, such as Aromatherapy full body massage, Vea Vea Stone Massage, Facials, Body Scrubs and much more.

Marú Spa, *Tel. 60.40.00, ext. 4094*, is a unique treehouse spa that opened in August 2004 at the Bora Bora Lagoon Resort & Spa. It features six treatment rooms: four waterfront and two massage rooms built into two Banyan trees. Services include massages, body scrubs, facials, hair and scalp massages, manicures, pedicures, and waxing treatments. You can also have a Reva Jet Lag treatment for 17.000 CFP, or a romantic bath for two where you are immersed in coconut milk and flower blossems. This indulgent experience is followed by a relaxing 50-minute couples massage for 18.000 CFP a person.

Espace Bien-Etre, *Tel. 60.51.51, ext. 1103,* is a massage and body care center located at Lé Meridien, and is open Monday through Saturday. A 30-minute aromatic bath costs 6.000 CFP, a 50-minute massage is 11.000 CFP, an 80-minute body scrub and massage is 18.000 CFP, and a 3-hour Polynesian Treasure body scrub, shower massage, facial and aromatic bath treatment is 30.000 CFP. Hand and foot care is also available.

Hotel Bora Bora, *Tel. 60.44.04*, offers massages and body treatments in your bungalow, on the terrace or in their Taurumi Fare #39. Classical massages start at 12.000 CFP for an hour's deep massage, or you can try a traditional Polynesian "taurumi" massage that includes a rubdown with monoi (coconut oil and flowers). A full body taurumi massage is 12.000 CFP for one hour and a customized taurumi is 22.000 CFP for a 2-hour massage. Beauty treatments include facials for 10.600 CFP, a manicure for 8.500 CFP and a pedicure for 9.000 CFP.

Club Med, *Tel. 60.46.04*. Massages, hydrotherapy treatments and beauty treatments are available on the premises. You can get an anti-cellulite wrap, a sea mud application on your neck, shoulders and spine, various facials, foot and hand care, depilation treatments, waxing, or revitalizing massages.

Tattoo Artists

Marama Traditional Tattoo, *Tel. 67.66.73* or *72.03.75*, is located on the lagoon side in Matira between Point Matira and Le Maitai Polynesia. Teriimarama Olson is a half-American half-Polynesian native of Bora Bora who designs the tattoo to suit the individual.

Tattoo Fati, *Tel. 71.54.84; E-mail: fatitattoo@hotmail.com.* Look for Boutique Paiki in Matira, where Fati's Marquesan sculptures are on display. He does guaranteed hygienic tattoos by appointment.

Practical Information

Banks
Bora Bora has three banks, which are all located in Vaitape village. **Banque de Tahiti**, *Tel. 60.59.99*, **Banque Socredo**, *Tel. 60.50.10*, and **Banque de Polynésie**, *Tel. 60.57.57*. All the banks have ATM windows.

Books, Magazines, Newspapers, Cigars
Maison de la Presse, *Tel. 60.57.75*, is located on the mountainside in Vaitape village, adjacent to the Gendarmerie. In addition to coffee table books, travel guides, local and international newspapers and magazines, you will find cigars from Cuba, the Dominican Republic and Honduras, as well as Dunhill cigarettes.

Cybercafé/Internet Service
You can check your E-mail while enjoying your morning coffee and croissant at L'Appetisserie in the Centre Commercial Le Pahia in Vaitape village, which is operated by Marc-André Zani, *Tel/Fax 67.78.88; E-mail lappetisserie@mail.pf*. He speaks American English.

Most hotels also have computers and internet service available for their clients, and you can also plug in your laptop to the telephone in your room.

Doctors
There are five private doctors and a dentist at the Medical Cabinet in Nunue and a new government operated dispensary is located in Vaitape, *Tel. 67.70.77*. Two dentists are located in the Pahia Center, *Tel. 67.70.55*.

Drugstore
Pharmacie Bora Bora, *Tel. 67.70.30*, is located on the mountainside of the road in Vaitape village. It is open Monday to Friday from 8am to 12pm and 3:30 to 6pm; on Saturday from 8am to 12pm and 5 to 6pm; and on Sunday from 9 to 9:30am.

Police
The French *gendarmerie* is on the mountainside opposite the quay in Vaitape, *Tel. 60.59.05*.

Post Office & Telecommunications Office
The Post Office is in Vaitape village on the circle island road near the quay, *Tel. 67.70.74*. Hours are 8am to 3pm on Monday, 7:30am to 3pm Tuesday through Friday, and 8 to 10am on Saturday. All telecommunications and postal services are available here.

Tourist Bureau

The **Bora Bora Visitors' Bureau** is on the quay in Vaitape, *Tel. 67.76.36; E-mail: info-bora-bora@mail.pf.* Hours are 8am to 4pm Monday through Friday. They are closed on weekends but will open for a half day if there is a ship in port on Saturday.

Wedding Ceremonies

Patrick's Activities, *B.P. 261, Vaitape, Bora Bora, 98730. Tel. 689/ 67.69.94, cell phone 79.19.11; patrick.bora@mail.pf; www.boraboraisland.com.* I watched Patrick Tairua perform a Polynesian wedding ceremony on the beach at one of the resort hotels in Bora Bora, and I thought it was the most touching, romantic sensation a couple in love could experience. The bride and groom were dressed in white pareos and wore a crown of flowers on their heads. Patrick, the *tahua* priest, was dressed in a yellow costume with a necklace of mother-of-pearl and feathers. He conducted the ceremony in Tahitian and translated the words into English, with a gentle look at the couple he was marrying (unofficially). It was a magical moment for everyone who watched this performance. The Polynesians use the word *mana* to describe a sacred power, and Patrick is definitely filled with this presence, this *mana*.

Patrick has created his own programs of ceremonies that are very popular with young couples who want to be married in the traditional Polynesian style or anniversary twosomes who wish to renew their vows. He meets the couple at their hotel and transports them in a flower-decorated canoe to a private motu islet. Two Tahitian warriors come to carry the couple ashore and they are then dressed in pareos and flowers for the ceremony. After repeating their vows, Patrick gives the newly united couple a Tahitian name, as well as a "wedding' certificate printed on tapa bark cloth. The Maohi Nui dancers then perform for the newlyweds, and they sip their French champagne while Patrick takes them on a cruise to another motu, where lunch is served at a shaded table in the lagoon. A full-day outing, with the wedding, dancing, champagne cruise and lunch, varies from 218.750 CFP to 327.250 CFP, depending on which hotel you go through and how many extras you want included. A 30-minute ceremony performed by Patrick on a hotel beach is priced from 113.500 CFP to 198.000 CFP and photographers are available on request to capture this big event on film.

Bora Bora Pearl Beach Resort, Bora Bora Nui Resort & Spa and Le Méridien have wedding chapels for more classic type ceremonies. You can also get married on a catamaran or underwater in Bora Bora. But no matter how romantic or bizarre your ceremony is, it is still not legal unless you go meet all the requirements outlined under **Getting Married** in the *Basic Information* chapter of this guide.

Chapter 19

MAUPITI

If you appreciate the beauty of Bora Bora but not the mass tourism, **Maupiti** offers similar scenery, peace and tranquility, as well as an authentic Polynesian experience, with genuinely friendly people who are not burned out by seeing too many tourists. If you want to find out what Bora Bora was like 30 years ago, then go to Maupiti. It offers so much more than sunshine, white sand beaches and a turquoise lagoon. The rhythm of life is slow and easy. There's gentleness to the place and the people that will answer a longing inside you to know the "real Polynesia." The villagers still smile and say "Ia Ora Na" when you meet. The longer you stay in Maupiti, the longer you will want to stay.

Lying just 40 kilometers (25 miles) west of bustling Bora Bora, Maupiti is considered the hidden jewel in the necklace of emerald islands and atolls that make up the Society Islands. Some people say it's one of the prettiest islands in the South Seas.

Like Bora Bora, Maupiti has a central island with a high mountain range of volcanic origins, and is surrounded by a shallow, sparkling lagoon with five long offshore *motu* islets bordered by beautiful white sand beaches. **Onoiau** is the name of a narrow pass leading into the lagoon. This formerly dangerous pass is more easily navigable since channel markers were added, but it can still be hazardous during high seas. The clear turquoise lagoon has pretty coral gardens, a plentiful supply of edible fish, lobsters, tridacna clams, *vana*, an edible sea urchin, and even *varo*, a sea centipede that is sought by gourmets. The *motus* provide coral gardens for watermelon and cantaloupe plantations, as well as secluded white sand beaches for sunbathing and excellent snorkeling grounds a few feet into the lagoon.

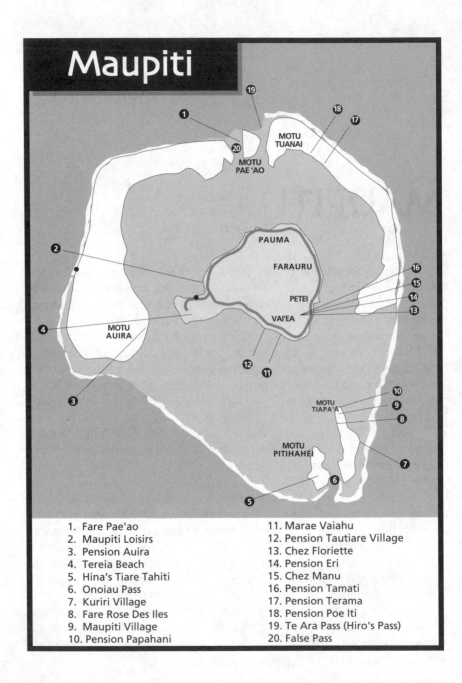

Maupiti

MOTU TUANAI

MOTU PAE 'AO

PAUMA

FARAURU

PETEI

VAI'EA

MOTU AUIRA

MOTU TIAPA'A

MOTU PITIHAHE

1. Fare Pae'ao
2. Maupiti Loisirs
3. Pension Auira
4. Tereia Beach
5. Hina's Tiare Tahiti
6. Onoiau Pass
7. Kuriri Village
8. Fare Rose Des Iles
9. Maupiti Village
10. Pension Papahani

11. Marae Vaiahu
12. Pension Tautiare Village
13. Chez Floriette
14. Pension Eri
15. Chez Manu
16. Pension Tamati
17. Pension Terama
18. Pension Poe Iti
19. Te Ara Pass (Hiro's Pass)
20. False Pass

Mount Teurafaatiu rises 380 meters (1,246 feet) above the central island, and is relatively easy to scale for panoramic views. **Point Tereia** on the main island is a lovely white sand beach in a natural environment, a favorite swimming site for the young people from the villages. Some of the older folks compare this beach to what Point Matira in Bora Bora was like 50 years ago. From here you can walk across the lagoon to the *motu*, in waste-deep water. Although you may encounter a few curious sharks, just hit the water hard with the palm of your hand and yell at them, and they will swim away. It works for the locals, and no tourists have been injured to date by the "friendly" sharks that grew up inside the lagoon.

Geologists say that Maupiti is the oldest of the high islands in the Society archipelago, and was formed some four million years ago.

Dr. Yosihiko H. Sinoto and Dr. Kenneth P. Emory of the Bernice P. Bishop Museum in Honolulu excavated a burial site in Maupiti in 1962 and 1963, unearthing 13 skeletons from the ninth century. Inside the tombs on Motu Paeao were adzes, fishhooks, lures and sperm whale tooth pendants that date back to circa 850 AD. This is one of the oldest archaeological sites in the Society Islands, and one of the most important. Doctor Sinoto said that the whale tooth pendants were the first material cultural link between the Society Islands and the New Zealand Maoris.

Other archaeological sites include two more *marae* on the *motus* and two *marae* on the high island. In the valley of Heranae are petroglyphs representing turtles, a sacred animal for the ancient Maohi people.

At one time there were nine districts and nine royal Maohi chiefs on Maurua Ite Ra, as Maupiti was then called. Chiefs came from other islands to meet at the royal Marae Vaiahu for gatherings that included investiture ceremonies. A huge boulder at the stone temple has been engraved with the names of these nine chiefs, who came from Rimatara, Raivavae, Rapa, Atiu in the Cook Islands, and Hawaii. One of these kings was said to have come from Malaysia.

The Dutch explorer Roggeveen discovered Maupiti in 1722; 45 years before Samuel Wallis discovered Tahiti. It was united with Bora Bora during the reign of the last royal family. The nine villages of ancient times have dwindled to the three contiguous villages of Vai'ea, Farauru and Pauma, where most of the 1,191 inhabitants live.

Arrivals & Departures
Arriving By Air
Air Tahiti, *Tel. 86.42.42/86.41.84* in Tahiti; *Tel. 60.15.05/67.81.30* in Maupiti, has a flight from Tahiti to Maupiti each Tuesday, two flights on Friday and one Sunday flight, all with stops in Raiatea. During the high seasons there are non-stop flights from Tahiti to Maupiti on Monday and Wednesday, and an additional flight on Friday with a stop in Raiatea. The Maupiti airstrip is

located on a *motu* islet across the lagoon from the main village. If you have reservations for a place to stay then you will be met at the airport and taken by boat to the pension. Otherwise, you can catch a ride with one of the taxi boats that goes to the airport for each flight arrival. The one-way airfare between Tahiti and Maupiti is 14.200 CFP and the round-trip fare is 26.000 CFP. The one-way between Raiatea and Maupiti is 6.500 CFP. There is no longer any scheduled flight service between Bora Bora and Maupiti.

You can also get to Maupiti by chartering an airplane in Tahiti from **Wan Air**, *Tel. 50.44.17, cell 77.03.79*; **Air Archipels**, *Tel. 81.30.30*; or **Air Tahiti**, *Tel. 86.42.42*.

Polynesia Hélicoptères, *Tel. 689/67.62.59; E-mail: helico-bora@mail.pf*, provides helicopter transfers from Bora Bora to Maupiti on request.

Arriving By Boat
Maupiti Express II, *Tel. 689/67.66.69 (Bora Bora); cell phone 689/78.27.22*. This new 140-passenger ship began service at the end of September 2004, transporting passengers between Raiatea, Tahaa, Bora Bora and Maupiti. The *Maupiti Express II* leaves Bora Bora on Tuesday, Thursday and Saturday at 8:30am, arriving in Maupiti at 10:15am. The one-way fare from Bora Bora is 2.500 CFP. Passengers under 12 years pay half-fare. If you want to take a day-trip from Bora Bora to Maupiti, you should contact Gérald Sachet at the above cell phone number. He is the owner/captain of *Maupiti Express II* and his wife runs the Pension Poe Iti, which serves as a land base for day-trippers. They have a small boat that is used for exploring the lagoon and motu islets. See information under *Where to Stay* and *Lagoon Tours* in this chapter.

Departing By Air
Air Tahiti, *Tel. 60.15.05/67.81.30*; Tahiti Reservations *Tel. 86.42.42/86.41.84*. Air Tahiti has four flights from Maupiti to Papeete each week, stopping at Raiatea on Tuesday, twice on Friday and once on Sunday. During the high seasons there are direct flights to Tahiti each Monday and Wednesday.

Departing By Boat
Maupiti Express II, *Tel. 67.66.69, cell phone 78.27.22*, leaves Maupiti at 4pm for Bora Bora each Tuesday, Thursday and Saturday. The trip takes 1 hour and 45 minutes and the one-way fare is 2.500 CFP. Passengers under 12 years pay half price.

Orientation
The main village is **Vai'ea**, where the town hall, schools, Air Tahiti office, post office, church, school, airport boat dock, family pensions and a few small stores are located, as well as the only snack shop, Snack Tarona. This village

suffered severe destruction in November 1997 when Cyclone Osea destroyed 95 percent of the houses and buildings on the island. Most of the houses are now of the MTR variety, which is a box-like 'anti-cyclone' design, built on stilts. Each family adds their own touch of flowers and colored leaves planted around the houses to make them more attractive.

Getting Around Maupiti
Bicycles
Arieta Firuu, *Tel. 67.80.63*, is a very friendly Polynesian vahine who rents bicycles at the public boat dock in Vai'ea village. When the *Maupiti Express* arrives from Bora Bora with day visitors who want to explore the island by bicycle, Arieta welcomes them with a lei of Tiare Tahiti flowers. She also gives them fruit, continuing the traditional Polynesian custom of sharing the abundance of Nature. People from the yachts or family pensions get the same treat, and the price is also right. She charges 1.000 CFP per day for a bike. The bicycles may have been moved away from the boat dock by the time you arrive as the *mairie* (town hall) has not given their permission to rent bicycles in that public place.

Loana Manuarii, *Tel. 67.81.46*, also rents bicycles on the boat dock for 1.000 CFP a day.

Maupiti Loisirs, *Tel. 67.80.95*. Ui and Simone rent bicycles at their family pension for 1.000 CFP per day and guests staying with them get free use of bicycles starting on the second day of their sojourn.

Puanere Locations, *Tel. 67.81.68*. Suzanne Tetuahiti has rental bicycles for 1.000 CFP per day. Look for the sign in front of her house in the village.

Transport Service
Arieta Firuu, *Tel. 67.80.63*, has a 10-passenger Toyota in which she transports visitors around the island, stopping at the *marae* and petroglyphs along the way. If you want a bite to eat she will stop at Snack Tarona, the only place in the village where you can get food if you're not staying in a family pension. Then she will drop you at Tereia beach and come back to get you later. She charges only 1.000 CFP per person for all this service. I was told by another Maupiti resident involved in tourism that Arieta does not have the proper permits to transport tourists. Hopefully, this will soon be sorted out.

Where to Stay & Eat
ON THE MOTUS
Moderate
FARE PA'EAO, *B.P. 33, Vai'ea, Maupiti 98732. Tel./Fax 689/67.81.01; E-mail: fare.pae.ao@mail.pf. On Motu Pa'eao, 10 minutes by boat from the airport. Round-trip boat transfers between airport and pension 1.100 CFP per person; round-trip boat transfers to boat dock 1.500 CFP per person. Rates:*

bungalow with breakfast and dinner 13.770 CFP single; 17.340 CFP double; 22.440 CFP triple; family rates available. Rates include taxes. No credit cards.

This pension was totally destroyed during Cyclone Osea in 1997 and reopened in August 2001 with six bungalows of the FEI type that have become the standard Polynesian bungalow promoted by and partially financed by the local government. These attractive new units, which are wooden with a wood shake roof, consist of a double bed and a single bed, a ceiling fan, an electric anti-mosquito device, a mosquito net over the beds, a terrace and a private bathroom with cold water shower. Breakfast and dinner are served in the communal dining room and Janine Tavaearii, the owner, will make you a casse-croute sandwich for lunch on request. Free kayaks are provided for guests. The snorkeling is very good here.

KURIRI VILLAGE, *B.P. 23, Vai'ea, Maupiti 98732. Tel. 689/74.54.54; Fax 689/67.82.23; E-mail: kuriri@mail.pf; www.maupiti-kuriri.com. Beside the ocean on Motu Tiapa'a, an islet 15 minutes by boat from the airport. Free round-trip boat transfers between airport and pension. Rates: bungalow with half-pension, including breakfast and dinner 11.400 CFP person; bungalow with full-pension, including breakfast, lunch and dinner 13.800 CFP person. Half-price for child under 11 years. Add 6% value added tax to room rates and meals. A 10% value added tax is applicable to other services. No credit cards.*

This lodging changed hands in 2000 and again in 2002 and is now owned by yet another French couple who sailed their boat around the world before settling down in Maupiti. Their plans are to renovate the 5 aging bungalows that face the beach or the garden. Three of the *fares* contain a double bed or two twin beds and a private bathroom with cold water. The two family *fares* have a double bed, mattresses on the mezzanine, a living room and a private bathroom with cold water. All the beds are covered by a mosquito net.

Rather than facing the inner lagoon, the view you'll have here is of the open ocean and Bora Bora in the distance, and if you get up early in the morning you can watch the sunrise behind Bora Bora. There is even a panoramic lookout deck built above the seaside dining area, for gazing at the sea and sky. The beach on the ocean side is always cooled by the trade winds and you can take a nice siesta under the thatched roof of the cushioned contemplation deck overlooking the sea. However, if you are visiting between July and October you may want to remain vigilant and be on the lookout for humpback whales. Snorkeling equipment, a kayak and an outrigger paddle canoe are available for guest use. Paid activities include drag fishing in the lagoon, speedboat tours of the lagoon, mountain hikes, and snorkeling excursions.

PENSION PAPAHANI, *B.P. 1, Vai'ea, Maupiti 98732. Tel. 689/60.15.35; Fax 689/60.15.36. On Motu Tiapa'a, 15 minutes by boat from the airport. Round-trip boat transfers included. Rates: small garden bungalow with breakfast and dinner 8.000 CFP, with all meals 9.000 CFP per person per day;*

big garden bungalow with breakfast and dinner 11.000 CFP, with all meals 12.000 CFP per person per day; big beach bungalow with breakfast and dinner 12.000 CFP, with all meals 13.000 per person per day. Meal plans are half-price for child 6-12 years and 2.500 CFP per day for child 3-6 years. Add 6% value added tax to room rates and meals. A 10% value added tax is applicable to other services. No credit cards.

This pension is located on the lagoon side of the *motu* facing the pass and the village, and it has a beautiful beach of fine white sand on a point of land. Some of the old *fares* were destroyed by a cyclone in 1997 and two are still standing. Three new bungalows have also been built. The bungalows are very close together and are simply furnished with a double bed in the smaller units and a double bed in the family bungalows. Another bed can be added to the larger units on request. All the bungalows have a bathroom with a cold water shower, and house linens are supplied. Family style meals are served at a thatched roof dining shelter beside the beach and boat excursions are available.

Vilna and Denis Tuheiava own this pension and everything runs smoothly when they are on the *motu*. The parents built the bungalows for their sons to manage, however, and half the time it's only the young people who are in charge. Their son Rudy acts as guide on boat tours and mountain hikes.

PENSION AUIRA, *B.P. 2, Vai'ea, Maupiti 98732. Tel./Fax 689/67.80.26. On Motu Auira, 20 minutes by boat from the airport. Round-trip boat transfers 2.000 CFP per person. Rates: garden fare with breakfast and dinner 8.500 CFP per person; beach fare with breakfast and dinner 9.500 CFP per person. Child 3-11 years 4.750 CFP. Camping 2.000 CFP. Breakfast 1.500 CFP; dinner 3.500 CFP. Add 6% value added tax to room rates, meals and transfers. A 10% value added tax is applicable to other services. No credit cards.*

The beach here is very beautiful when it is clean, with soft white powdery sand and clear shallow water in the lagoon that is deep enough for swimming if you walk out into the blue water several feet distant. All of the former *fares* were destroyed by the cyclone in 1997, and Edna Terai and her husband Gilbert have rebuilt 5 bungalows: three on the beach and two in the garden. All the fares are furnished with a double bed, a private bathroom with cold water and mosquito screens. House linens are provided and there is a restaurant-bar on the premises. Campers can pitch their tent in the shaded garden or on the beach and they also have bathroom facilities with a cold water shower and can cook their meals in the kitchen, which has a refrigerator.

Edna can arrange for your boat excursions with a picnic or to watch the manta rays and feed the sharks and stingrays inside the lagoon. Her husband will take you by boat to the village on request, where you can bike around the island or hike in the mountains.

PENSION ROSE DES ILES, *B.P. 55, Vai'ea, Maupiti 98732. Cell 689/ 70.50.70; Fax 689/67.82.00. Beside the lagoon on Motu Tiapa'a, 15 minutes* *by boat from the airport. Round-trip boat transfers 1.500 CFP to airport and 1.000 CFP to village. Rates: Room and breakfast 5.000 CFP per person; room, breakfast and dinner 8.000 CFP per person. Bungalow and breakfast 7.000 CFP per person; bungalow, breakfast and dinner 10.000 CFP, and with all meals 13.000 CFP per person per day. Half-price for child 2-12 years old. Camping 1.000 CFP per day. Breakfast 1.500 CFP, lunch or dinner 3.000 CFP. Taxes included. No credit cards.*

This property is located near the pass on the pretty white sand beach of Motu Tiapa'a. There is a big beach bungalow built of bamboo and a thatched roof that can sleep five people, and it has two bathrooms with cold water showers, as well as four showers outdoors. A "Romantic Room" for two is located in a tropical garden of flowers. Mosquito nets are provided on request. A maximum of two tents can be set up close to the lagoon, and there is also a shower on the beach.

Guests have complimentary use of snorkeling equipment, kayaks, rainy day games and a small library of books. Paid activities include bicycle or automobile tours around the main island, mountain walks, boat excursions and fishing.

PENSION POE ITI, *B.P. 39, Vai'ea, Maupiti 98732. Tel. 689/67.83.14. On Motu Tuanai, 5 minutes by boat or car from the airport and 5 minutes by boat from the village. Rates: Bungalow 5.000 CFP single/double/triple. Breakfast 700 CFP, lunch 2.000 CFP and dinner 2.500 CFP per person. Add 6% value added tax to room rates and meals. A 10% value added tax is applicable to other services. No credit cards.*

This pension opened in October 2004, with 4 bungalows built in a garden setting on the same motu where the airport is located. The wooden bungalows with wood shake roofs are the government approved and subsidized FEI type units that are modern and attractive. Electricity is provided by wind generators. Each bungalow has a king size bed and a single bed, air-conditioning, television and DVD player, a private bathroom with hot water shower and a private covered terrace facing the white sand beach and lagoon. The kitchen and restaurant/bar are located in separate buildings, and the spacious dining area can accommodate day visitors who come over from Bora Bora on board the *Maupiti Express II*, whose captain, Gérald Sachet, is also owner of Pension Poe Iti and Maupiti Poe Iti Tours. His wife, Joséphine Ah-Yun manages the pension and takes care of guests. The snorkeling equipment is complimentary, as well as the outrigger paddle canoes, kayaks, windsurf boards and society games. She provides free boat transfers to the village twice a day. Maupiti Poe Iti Tours will drop you at Motu Tiapa'a and return later to pick you up for 1.000 CFP per person, or you can join a boat tour around the island for 2.000 CFP, and even have a picnic on an uninhabited motu if you wish.

MAUPITI VILLAGE, *Vai'ea, Maupiti 98732. Tel./Fax 689/67.80.08; Cell 689/70.13.69/76.03.69. On Motu Tiapa'a, 5 minutes by boat from the airport and 3 minutes by boat from the village. Round-trip transfers 1.750 CFP per person. Rates: Bungalow with all meals 9.000 CFP; room with all meals 6.500 CFP; dormitory with all meals 5.500 CFP per person. Add 6% value added tax to room rates and meals. A 10% value added tax is applicable to other services. No credit cards.*

There are two simple plywood bungalows beside a pretty beach and the rooms are often rented by French people from Raiatea or Bora Bora. There is plenty of fresh water and solar electricity day and night. Audine Colomes, the owner/manager, speaks a little English and serves fresh seafood, and every Sunday there is a feast of "maa Tahiti" served. Boat transfers to the main village are 1.250 CFP per person. Activities can be arranged.

PENSION TERAMA, *Vai'ea, Maupiti 98732. Tel. 689/67.81.96. On Motu Puaterama, 5 minutes by boat from the airport and the village. Free round-trip transfers. Rates: Room with breakfast and dinner 6.500 CFP per person; half price for child up to 11 years. Casse-croute sandwich for lunch 350 CFP. Add 6% value added tax to room rates and meals. A 10% value added tax is applicable to other services. No credit cards.*

Melissa Firuu and her French husband, Marc Pinson, have built a 3-bedroom concrete house in the middle of a Tiare Tahiti plantation on the airport motu, but there are no neighbors and no noise in this remote area. There is a double bed in two of the guest rooms and three single beds in the other room. Both the interior and exterior bathrooms with cold water showers are shared. The kitchen is separate and a *fare pote'e* shelter is being built for the dining room. Guests have use of the kayaks and can hop a ride to the village when Marc goes there to shop. He will also take you to collect *pahua* (tridacna clams) on the reef and will take you on a tour of the lagoon for 1.000 CFP. On request he can arrange for you to accompany some local fishermen in their *poti marara* boat when they fish for mahi-mahi and tuna in the open ocean. A half-day outing is 2.500 CFP and an all-day fishing trip is 5.000 CFP per person. Both Melissa and Marc speak some English and are very open and friendly.

On the Main Island

PENSION TAUTIARE VILLAGE, *B.P. 16, Vai'ea, Maupiti 98732. Tel./Fax 689/67.83.58, Cell 689/72.24.29; E-mail: pension-tautiare@mail.pf. On seaside in Hurumanu, 2 kilometers (1.2 miles) from the village. Round-trip boat transfers 1.500 CFP per person. Rates: Room and breakfast 5.000 CFP per person; room with breakfast and dinner 6.500 CFP; room with all meals 8.000 CFP per person per day; half-price for child 3-12 years. Add 6% value added tax to room rates and meals. A 10% value added tax is applicable to other services. No credit cards.*

David and Dawn Domingo have built two new houses on the main island, located between the white sand beach of Tereia and the Vaiahu Marae. There are 4 guest bedrooms with a private bathroom and hot water shower in one of the houses, and 1 guest bedroom in the other house, which is shared with the owners, including the bathroom. Each house has a big covered terrace and the living room and dining room are also communal.

Snorkeling equipment and kayaks are available for guest use. Bicycles are 1.000 CFP per day. Paid activities include boat excursions to the motu, with a picnic included for 2.500 CFP per person, and boat tours around the island for 2.000 CFP.

CHEZ FLORIETTE, *B. P. 43, Vai'ea, Maupiti 98732. Tel./Fax 689/ 67.80.85. Beside lagoon in Vai'ea village, one kilometer (.62 miles) from the ferry dock and three kilometers (1.9 miles) from the airport. Round-trip boat transfers included. Rates: bungalow with breakfast and dinner 6.500 CFP per person; bungalow with all meals 7.500 CFP per person. Add 6% value added tax to room rates and meals. A 10% value added tax is applicable to other services. No credit cards.*

This lodging is in the middle of the village and is quite noisy during the daytime because it is adjacent to the school and basketball court, but it is convenient to small food stores and the boat landing. Floriette has been running a pension for many years, speaks a little English and is a good hostess. She has two bungalows for guests, with a double and single bed in one unit and a double bed and two single beds in the other unit. Guests share the living room with a television, dining room and communal bathroom with cold water. House linens are furnished.

PENSION ERI, *Vai'ea, Maupiti 98732. Tel. 689/67.81.29. Beside the lagoon in Vai'ea village, 700 meters (763 yards) from the ferry dock and three kilometers from the airport. Round-trip boat transfers from airport 1.000 CFP per person; from boat dock 500 CFP. Rates: Room with breakfast 3.000 CFP person; room with breakfast and dinner 5.000 CFP per person; room with all meals 6.500 CFP per person. Half-price for child under 12 years. Add 6% value added tax to room rates and meals. A 10% value added tax is applicable to other services. No credit cards.*

This is a popular pension with young French people and other travelers who want to stay on the main island, but it is noisy here in the heart of the village. The four-bedroom house is very clean, with a double bed in each room. Guests share the kitchen, living room and bathroom with cold water. House linens are furnished. Eri Mohi's family has a farm where they grow their own fruit and vegetables. She and her two daughters take care of the pension. Snack Tarona is also close by. You can rent a bicycle or kayak, go by boat to the *motu*, fishing in the lagoon or on picnics to a white sand beach.

MAUPITI LOISIRS, *B.P. 66, Vai'ea, Maupiti 98732. Tel./Fax 689/67.80.95. The house is 4 kilometers (2.5 miles) from the village on the main island and* *the camping area is on Motu Auira, 20 minutes by boat from the airport. Round-trip boat transfers provided. Rates: room with breakfast and dinner 5.000 CFP per person; camping on the motu 2.000 CFP per person per day. No credit cards.*

Ui Teriihaunui and Simone Chan welcome guests in their *fare* MTR, which is a 2-bedroom house like you will find everywhere on Maupiti. These "anti-cyclone" houses were constructed after Cyclone Osea wiped out 95 percent of the homes in November 1997. There are ceiling fans in each bedroom and each bed is covered by a mosquito net, plus you have a choice of electric anti-mosquito devices or the traditional burning coils. Everyone shares the bathroom with cold water shower and another shower is outside. Ui and Simone have made a sleeping area for themselves in a hangar behind the house, rather than sleeping on mattresses in the living room as they previously did when they had clients. Meals are served family style and dinner consists of three courses. The white-sand beach of Tereia is easily reached by foot or bicycle, which you can rent from Ui and Simone for 1.000 CFP the first day and use free of charge after that. Ui has also applied for a permit to operate mini-bus tours around the island.

Ui has an 18-foot locally made fiberglass boat with a flat bottom that he uses to take people all the way around the island, a feat that cannot be accomplished by big boats unless it's at high tide. Ui's all-day excursion includes swimming in the sparkling lagoon, a visit to the petroglyphs carved in basaltic stone and a lunch stop at Snack Tarona, the island's only snack stand. In the afternoon he will take you to snorkel in the "false pass" and to visit the Vaiahu Marae ("sacred stone") if it is still low tide, as the marae is covered by water during high tide. Ui is a well-informed historian who loves to share his knowledge of Maupiti with others. I met him in 1977 when I first visited the island and he taught me a lot about the legends and culture of Maupiti.

This lodging is not on the Tahiti Tourism list of approved pensions, but visitors (including Americans) who have stayed here are still writing to Ui and Simone and sending them gifts because they enjoyed themselves so much. Simone, who is mostly Chinese, is from Tahiti and was a schoolteacher until she met Ui and moved to Maupiti. She speaks English, but you'll appreciate Ui's many stories much more if you speak French. Ui always greets their guests at the Maupiti airport with leis of Tiare Tahiti from their garden, and when they leave the island, he sends them off with another fragrant Tiare Tahiti lei around their necks. They also give their guests lots of fresh fruit from the garden.

Campers who are seeking a "sauvage" site to pitch their tent will enjoy the seclusion they'll find at Ui's property on Motu Auira. You can camp on the beach, under the trees or under a shelter. There is a protected area where you can cook your meals, and a stove and petrol refrigerator have been provided, as well as a toilet, shower and water tank. There are also four double mattresses available and you have free use of the kayaks. If you want to get "lost" for a while and just enjoy the beauty of nature on a small *motu* islet, this is a good place to do it. A huge bonus for this spot is that you can watch the sun drop behind the horizon every evening, and there's not anything to impede that view. It's all wide-open space—just the sky and the sea and the wonderful magic of an incredible tropical sunset.

Other Bed and Breakfast Lodgings on the Main Island
   CHEZ MANU (formerly Chez Mareta), *Tel. 689/67.82.32*, who has 2 bedrooms for 4.000 CFP MAP; **PENSION TAMATI**, *Tel. 689/67.80.10*, an old 2-story house with 9 rooms and private bathrooms for 4.500 CFP MAP.

Seeing the Sights
   You can walk around the main island of Maupiti in about two or three hours, depending on your pace, and how many times you stop to take pictures, shake down a ripe mango from a roadside tree or stop for a swim in the inviting lagoon. A road circles the island for 9.6 kilometers (5.9 miles). You can also bike around the island and visit the petroglyphs of turtles, the family and royal *marae* stone temples and other archaeological sites. The *maraes* are located on some of the *motu* islets, as well as the central island.
   The hosts at each pension normally organize the activities for their guests, which include snorkeling and shelling, outrigger paddle canoes, fishing in the lagoon and pass for lobster and fish, and picnics on the *motu*.

Lagoon Tours
   Maupiti Loisirs, *Tel. 67.80.95*, is operated by Ui and Simone Teriihaunui, who have an 18-foot fiberglass flat-bottom boat for excursions. An all-day outing by land and lagoon is 3.500 CFP per person. See information under *Where to Stay* in this chapter.
   Maupiti Poe Iti Tours, *Tel. 67.83.14*, is owned by Gérald Sachet, who owns *Maupiti Express* and Pension Poe Iti. He has a 20-foot long aluminum boat that is used for lagoon tours and transfers to Motu Tiapa'a. A circle island tour by boat includes fruit tasting and coconut water for 2.000 CFP, and you can also have a picnic on request. The boat will drop you off on Motu Tiapa'a and pick you up later for 1.000 CFP per person. See information on *Where to Stay* in this chapter.
   Richard Excursions is owned by Richard Tefaatau, *Tel. 67.80.62*, who takes groups on lagoon excursions, with a picnic on the *motu* if requested. He charges 2.500 CFP plus the cost of the food. Richard also makes trips on request to visit Mopelia, an atoll just west of Maupiti.
   Manuela Mohi at Pension Manu (Chez Mareta), *Tel. 67.82.32*, also takes visitors on lagoon tours, or provides boat transfer service if they want to spend some time alone on the motu.

Sports & Recreation
Mountain Climbing
   Tefarerii Excursions, *Tel./Fax 67.81.83; E-mail: nicolerichardo@mail.pf*, is operated by Auguste Taurua. He can take from 1 to 10 people on hikes to the cliff of Hotu Parata, which is 165 meters (541 feet) above the village of Vai'ea. Mango, wild hibiscus and Tahitian chestnut trees shade the fairly steep trail, but you have glimpses of the panorama of motu islets and the varying shades of the lagoon and coral gardens as you ascend. The path becomes harder and more dangerous to climb as you go higher and the crumbling rock sometimes causes landslides before you reach the end of the cliff. But once you get there and look out to the neighboring islands and infinity, you'll feel it was definitely worth the effort.

Chapter 20

TUAMOTU ISLANDS

The 77 atolls and one upraised island that form the **Tuamotu Archipelago** are mere specks of land out in the heart of the trade wind, lost in the vastness of the blue Pacific. Sprinkled across ten latitudes and covering a length of 1,500 kilometers (930 miles) and a width of 500 kilometers (310 miles), these are some of the most remote islands in the world.

This vast collection of coral islets conjures up castaway dreams on a tropical isle, the ultimate get-away for rejuvenation of the body and soul. Tiny green oases floating in the desert of the sea, with names as exotic as the trade winds and coconut trees. Wild windswept beaches, the sea and sunshine. And only the sound of the surf and the cries of the sea birds for company. Fragrant *miki miki* blends their perfume with aromas of salt spray and blossoms from the *tiare kahaia*, *geo geo* and *gapata* trees. The lagoons shimmer with a brilliance of light and color unsurpassed, and a submerged landscape of untouched magic and awesome beauty awaits beneath the sun-gilded waters tinged in turquoise.

Polynesian explorers, sailing from their homeland in the West, settled on the lonely shores of these atolls centuries ago. Pakamotu, they called their new home—a cloud of islands. Outcast chiefs from Tahiti and the Marquesas Islands named them Paumotu, the Submissive or Conquered Islands, the isles of Exiles. European ships from many nations rode the treacherous reef in this maritime maze, thus adding the names Low or Dangerous Archipelago and the Labyrinth. The **Paumotu people** now call their home the Tuamotu—many islands.

More than 400 varieties of fantastic, rainbow-hued fish glint like ornaments of gold in the iridescent waters of the sheltered lagoons, providing hours of enchantment for snorkelers and scuba divers. On many of the atolls you can visit black pearl farms and fish parks inside the lagoons, take boat tours to visit the various *motu* islets and picnic under the black-eyed gaze of the white fairy tern.

You may also be invited to join in the volleyball and soccer games played by the villagers. You can go along on fishing expeditions, hunt for tiny shells to string into pretty necklaces, learn to weave hats, mats and baskets from palm fronds, and eat delicious seafood direct from its shell while you stand at the edge of a Technicolor reef. In the evening you can sit beside the Paumotu musicians under a starlit sky, watching the Southern Cross as you listen to melodic island tunes being played on guitars and ukuleles. Their songs tell of old gods and heroes, the spirits of sharks and fish, destructive hurricanes, people lost at sea, shipwrecks on the treacherous reef, *vahines* and *l'amour*.

More than two dozen of these atolls have airstrips and regular air service from Tahiti, and several inter-island trading schooners transport supplies and passengers. The lack of potable water remains a problem on many of these remote islands, while solar energy provides electricity and hot water for villages and remote pearl farms. This archipelago is rapidly being developed, with modern telecommunications services now reaching even the most distant of the settled islands.

"Many Lagoons" by Ralph Varady

You have to see an atoll to get its feeling. It leaves a vastly different impression than a high island does. There is something about the atolls that is magnetic. They are lost and, for the greater part, deserted, full of flies and copra bugs. They are remote, a death trap in a hurricane, a danger to navigation and often inaccessible except by small boat. They offer the minimum of human comfort, their maximum asset being their copra; and yet there is something wonderful about them, and truly they belong to the list of nature's wonders.

Many of the islands are uninhabited and seldom visited. Nevertheless, the traveler who wanders into this maritime maze will be rewarded by what he sees. These Dangerous Islands are not sizable or comfortable, but they are rich in the realm of color. The debauch of color found in the Tuamotu lagoons is incomparable to that of any other island group.

Personally, I hope that these islands never have "facilities" so that they will be kept as they are now: unspoiled, beautiful and natural. It is good to know that some of these islands will remain out of reach of a fast-moving civilization."

౨

The atolls of Rangiroa, Manihi, Tikehau and Fakarava, which are described in this chapter, offer international class hotels, small hotels, pensions, houses or a room in a family home, where guests can find simple accommodations. These are the destinations most frequently visited by travelers, but the number of visitors in the Tuamotus is so minute that these islands still offer a natural environment and miles of empty beaches.

You will also find accommodations in family homes and pensions on the atolls of Ahe, Anaa, Apataki, Arutua, Hao, Kaukura, Mataiva, Takaroa and Takapoto. Unfortunately, we are not able to give the details of each atoll in this book, but you can obtain a list of lodging facilities from Tahiti Manava Visitors Bureau in Papeete, with rates for each small hotel, pension, hostel, guest house and campground that exists in French Polynesia. The contact numbers are listed in the *Basic Information* chapter under *Where to Find More Information About Tahiti & French Polynesia*.

RANGIROA

Rangiroa, also called **Rairoa**, means 'long sky' in the Paumotu dialect, the language of the Polynesian inhabitants. The coral ring encircling the pear-shaped atoll of Rangiroa contains more than 240 *motu* islets, separated by at least 100 very shallow *hoa* channels and three passes. The Tiputa Pass and Avatoru Pass on the north of the atoll are deep and wide enough for ships to enter the lagoon, and the Tivaru Pass on the west is narrow and shallow. A vast inland sea measures approximately 75 kilometers (47 miles) long by 25 kilometers (16 miles) wide, covering a distance of 1,020 square kilometers (393 square miles). This is the largest atoll in the Southern Hemisphere and the second largest in the world, after Kwajalein atoll in the Marshall Islands of Micronesia.

Cultivation pits and *marae* temples of coral stone are remains of settlements that existed on Rangiroa during the 14th and 15th centuries. To protect themselves from the aggressive 'Parata' warriors from the atoll of Anaa, the Rangiroa inhabitants took refuge on the southwest side of the atoll, close to Motu Taeo'o, known today as the Blue Lagoon. This village was destroyed by a natural disaster, probably a *tsunami*, in 1560, and the entire population disappeared.

Rangiroa and its surrounding atolls made up small independent kingdoms in the 17th and 18th centuries, and were known as the Mihiroa. Political relations were established with Tahiti, but the bloody battles with Anaa exterminated most of Rangiroa's population by 1800. The ancestors of Tahiti's King Pomare I were Anaa chiefs, and through his intervention the marauders ended their aggressions and cannibalism with their rival clans. The surviving Rangiroans went to the nearby atoll of Tikehau and to Tautira in Tahiti Iti, and returned to their atoll between 1823 and 1826.

The Dutch explorer Le Maire discovered Rangiroa in 1616, but the first European settlers did not arrive until 1851. The missionaries insisted that the population be grouped in Avatoru and Tiputa rather than dispersing in small villages around the atoll, where they could more likely continue their heathenistic

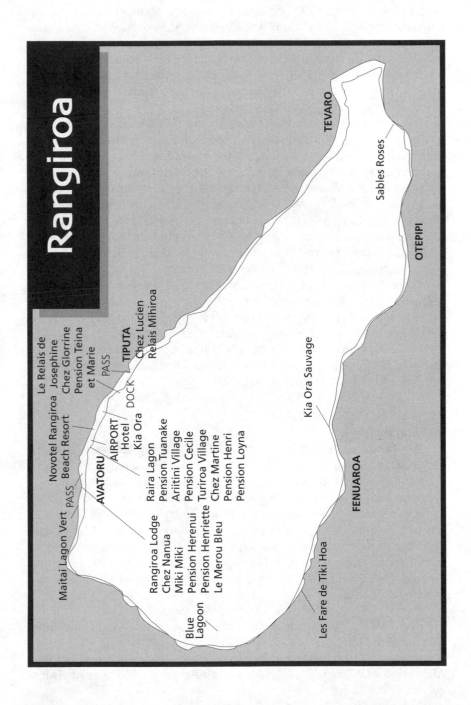

Rangiroa

Maitai Lagon Vert
Le Relais de Josephine
Novotel Rangiroa Beach Resort
Chez Glorrine
Pension Teina et Marie
PASS
AVATORU
PASS
TIPUTA
Chez Lucien
Relais Mihiroa
AIRPORT
DOCK
Hotel Kia Ora
Raira Lagon
Pension Tuanake
Ariitini Village
Pension Cecile
Turiroa Village
Chez Martine
Pension Henri
Pension Loyna
Rangiroa Lodge
Chez Nanua
Miki Miki
Pension Herenui
Pension Henriette
Le Merou Bleu
Blue Lagoon
Kia Ora Sauvage
TEVARO
Sables Roses
OTEPIPI
FENUAROA
Les Fare de Tiki Hoa

practices. A cyclone in 1906 destroyed the village of Tivaru, and today the population of 2,530 inhabitants reside in the villages of Avatoru and Tiputa.

Rangiroa is the administrative center of the northern Tuamotu atolls. Children from the small atolls are sent to junior high school and technical schools in Rangiroa, where they are lodged throughout the school year, some of the students returning to their homes only during the two-month vacation in July and August.

Rangiroa's lagoon is world famous for unsurpassed scuba diving in the warmest and clearest water you can dream of. Favorite excursions include "shooting the pass," where hundreds of fish, moray eels and sharks swim beside and below you, swept along by the strong currents. You can view this exciting spectacle aboard a glass-bottom boat, or jump into the water with mask, snorkel, fins or even scuba diving bottles. Vacation memories are also made while paddling a kayak or outrigger canoe, sailing inside the lagoon, line or drag fishing, on boat excursions to the pink sand beach of Vahituri, while admiring the fossilized coral formations on Reef Island, and during a full day picnic trip to the Blue Lagoon or Green Lagoon.

Among this wealth of scenery is an attractive selection of international resort hotels, small hotels with thatched roof bungalows and simple family owned pensions with fresh lagoon fish on the menu. Across the lagoon from the villages are very basic sleeping facilities in camp like settings that can be reached only by boat, where you can walk on beaches as remote as Robinson Crusoe's. On these beautiful little islets you can live a *sauvage* simplified life with lots of fresh food from the reef and lagoon.

Arrivals & Departures
Arriving By Air
Air Tahiti has one to four direct ATR flights daily between Tahiti and Rangiroa. The 55-minute non-stop flight is 15.300 CFP one-way for adults, and 28.000 CFP round-trip, tax included. You can also fly from Bora Bora to Rangiroa with 70-minute direct flights on Monday, Tuesday, Wednesday, Friday and Sunday, and with one stop in Tikehau on Thursday, for 23.000 CFP one-way. Flight service is also provided to Rangiroa from Manihi each Wednesday, Saturday and Sunday, for 10.000 CFP. There are direct flights from Tikehau to Rangiroa each Tuesday, Wednesday, Thursday, Friday and Saturday for 5.200 CFP, and you can fly direct from Fakarava to Rangiroa each Monday for 5.200 CFP.

If you have reservations with a hotel, pension or yacht charter company, then you will be met at the airport and driven to your hotel. **Air Tahiti reservations**: Tahiti, *Tel. 86.42.42.*

You can also get to Rangiroa by chartering an airplane in Tahiti from **Wan Air**, *Tel. 50.44.17, cell 77.03.79;* **Air Archipels**, *Tel. 81.30.30;* or **Air Tahiti**, *Tel. 86.42.42.*

Arriving By Boat

Mareva Nui, *Tel. 42.25.53, Fax 42.25.57*, is a 181-foot steel ship that transports cargo between Tahiti and the Tuamotu atolls. It leaves Tahiti every 15 days, arriving in Rangiroa three days later. There are 12 berths for the maximum number of passengers allowed, but no cabins on board. The one-way fare to Rangiroa is 5.700 CFP. Add 2.200 CFP per person per day for three meals.

St. Xavier Maris Stella III, *Tel. 42.23.58*, can transport 12 passengers who have to sleep on the deck until the berths are repaired. The fare from Tahiti to Rangiroa is 7.710 CFP per person, including 3 meals a day. Sometimes Rangiroa is the first stop after a 20 hour crossing from Tahiti, and on other voyages it may be the third island visited. The ship leaves Papeete every 15 days.

Vai Aito, *Tel. 43.99.96*, Fax 43.53.04, makes two to three voyages to the Tuamotus a month, with Rangiroa the second port-of-call after Tikehau. They are also limited to 12 passengers. There are no cabins on board and the cost of sleeping on the deck starts at 5.353 CFP per day, including three daily meals. See more information in Chapter 6, *Planning Your Trip*.

Departing By Air

Air Tahiti has one to five flights daily from Rangiroa to Tahiti, including at least one direct flight per day, which are either direct flights or with only one stop. You can fly direct from Rangiroa to Manihi on Monday, Wednesday, Friday and Sunday, direct from Rangiroa to Tikehau on Monday, Wednesday, Friday, Saturday and Sunday, and direct from Rangiroa to Fakarava on Monday and Friday. There is a flight from Rangiroa to Bora Bora each Monday and Friday, and a direct flight from Rangiroa to Nuku Hiva each Saturday, continuing on to Hiva Oa. *Tel. 93.11.00* in Rangiroa. Tickets can be purchased at the airport. If you already have reservations and a ticket, reconfirmations should be made one day in advance, and most hotels will take care of this for you. Check-in time at the airport is one hour before scheduled departure.

Departing By Boat

The *Mareva Nui, Tel. 42.25.53, Fax 42.25.57*, calls at 11-12 other atolls after leaving Rangiroa each 15 days. A berth costs from 3.850 to 8.200 CFP, depending on how long the journey takes, and three daily meals are 2.200 CFP extra. *St. Xavier Maris Stella III, Tel. 42.23.58*, leaves Rangiroa every 15 days for Ahe, Manihi, and all the western Tuamotu atolls, before returning to Papeete. You can sleep on the deck with three daily meals included. Fares are determined by length of voyage to Tahiti. *Vai Aito, Tel. 43.99.96*, leaves Rangiroa twice a month for Ahe, Manihi, Aratika, Kauehi, Fakarava and Papeete. You'll pay from 5.353 to 18.735 CFP to sleep on the deck, which includes all meals. The total round-trip fare is 27.560 CFP, including taxes.

Orientation

The villages of **Avatoru** and **Tiputa** are located on the northern coast of Rangiroa atoll, where most of the population lives beside the two deep passes, a 45-minute boat ride apart. A flat paved road 10 kilometers (6.2 miles) long extends from the Avatoru Pass to the Tiputa Pass, with the ocean on one side and the lagoon on the other side. Most of the hotels and pensions are on the lagoon side of this road and the airport is about halfway between the two passes. You will find churches, schools, post offices and small food stores in both villages and it is easy to walk around once you are there, but you will probably find that the people in Tiputa village are friendlier to visitors.

You can explore Avatoru village to the Tiputa Pass by car, scooter or bicycle. You have to take a boat across the Tiputa Pass to get to Tiputa village, which can be easily discovered in a short walk. Overlooking the Tiputa Pass is **Ohotu Point**, which is also called Ohutu Point, complete with benches and shade trees. This is a favorite destination in late afternoon, when dolphins can often be seen playing in the swift current that flows through the pass, between the open ocean and the interior lagoon.

Getting Around Rangiroa

The hosts at the hotels and pensions meet their guests at the airport and provide transportation to the lodging. A *le truck* service is operated by Manatea, *Tel. 79.81.26*, providing public transportation from Ohutu Point to Avatoru village and return. This service operates 7/7 from 6am to 6pm. A one-way trip can take up to 1 1/2 hours when there are lots of passengers, as stops are made at the airport, the hospital and at the old and new *mairies* (town halls). Although this service is primarily for the local inhabitants, visitors can also make use of it for a 300 CFP fare. Although Manatea has a program for this service, he frequently modifies the schedule according to the destination of his passengers. Therefore, it is best to get a French speaking person to call in advance if you want to go by *le truck*.

To get to Tiputa from Ohutu Point on the Avatoru side you can take a taxi boat, which costs tourists 1.000 CFP per person for a one-way trip. Contact Maurice Snow direct at *Tel./Fax 96.76.09* or *cell 78.13.25*. From the Hotel Kia Ora to Tiputa dock the fare is 1.500 CFP. You can also try to catch a ride aboard one of the speedboats that travels between the Ohutu Point boat dock, adjacent to Pension Glorinne, and Tiputa village.

Car, Scooter & Bicycle Rentals

Europcar Rangiroa (also called **Rangi Rent-A-Car**) has an office near Avatoru village, *Tel./Fax 96.03.28, cell 20.17.89*, and a desk at the Hotel Kia Ora, *Tel.93.11.11*. A 2-passenger 3-wheel Fun Car rents for 4.500 CFP for 2 hours, 5.500 CFP for 4 hours and 6.500 CFP for 8 hours. A 2-passenger Mini Car rents for 6.000 CFP for 2 hours, 7.000 CFP for 4 hours and 8.500 CFP for

8 hours. A 5-passenger air-conditioned Saxo costs 8.000 CFP for 4 hours and 9.500 CFP for 8 hours. Scooters rent for 4.000 CFP for 2 hours, 5.000 CFP for 4 hours and 6.000 CFP for 8 hours. Rates for cars and scooters include unlimited mileage, insurance and gas. Bicycles cost 900 CFP for 4 hours and 1.500 CFP for 8 hours. Bicycles with a baby chair are 1.200 CFP for 4 hours and 1.800 CFP for 8 hours.

Arenahio Locations is operated by Pomare Temaehu, at Carole Pareo in Avatoru, *Tel./Fax 96.82.45*; *E-mail: carpom@mail.pf*. A 4-passenger air-conditioned Peugeot 106 or a 4-passenger air-conditioned Citroën rents for 6.200 CFP for 4 hours and 8.400 CFP for 24 hours. Gas is not included. Scooters rent for 4.200 CFP for 4 hours and 5.200 CFP for 24 hours. Bicycles with baskets cost 700 CFP for a half-day and 1.300 CFP for a full day.

Bicycles can also be rented from several of the hotels and pensions.

Where to Stay
Deluxe
HOTEL KIA ORA RANGIROA, *B.P. 198, Avatoru, Rangiroa 98775. Tel. 689/93.11.11; Fax 689/96.04.93; Reservations: Tel. 689/93.11.17; Fax 689/ 96.02.20; E-mail: resa@hotelkiaora.pf; www.hotelkiaora.com. 63 units beside the lagoon at Ohotu Bay, 2 kilometers (1.2 miles) east of the airport. EP Rates single/double: garden bungalow 30.000 CFP; family size garden suite bungalow 36.000 CFP; beach bungalow 44.000 CFP; beach suite bungalow 52.000 CFP; overwater bungalow 65.000 CFP. Additional person 5.000 CFP. Meal plan: breakfast 2.400 CFP; lunch 3.000 CFP, dinner 5.000 CFP per person. A supplementary cost is added to meal plan for Christmas and New Year's Eve. Add 5% hotel tax to room rates and 6% value added tax to room rates and prepaid meal plans, plus 150 CFP municipal tax per person per day. A 10% value added tax is applicable to other services. Round-trip transfers from/to airport are provided. All major credit cards.*

Like a lovely jewel sparkling in the sunshine, the Hotel Kia Ora beams an invitation to you if you are sitting on the left side of the Air Tahiti flight when the plane approaches the airport in Rangiroa. Viewed from the air or from the roadside, the 40 acres of gardens and coconut trees and the white sand beach almost a mile long make a perfect setting for a Polynesian style hotel. And the coral studded lagoon that is the center of this precious gem glitters in agreement.

The Hotel Kia Ora was the first international class hotel on Rangiroa. Three former Club Med employees with foresight opened the Kia Ora Village in 1973. Laris Kindynis, Robin Angely and Serge Arnoux ran a successful operation for almost two decades, before selling the 30-bungalow hotel to the Tokyo Coca-Cola Bottling Company in 1990. The new management has continued to improve and expand the property, and has dropped "Village" and added "Hotel" to the name.

The hotel's present capacity of 63 units includes 23 garden bungalows and 5 garden suites spread throughout a coconut grove and Tiare Tahiti bushes. The garden bungalows can sleep two in a king-size bed and the garden suites have accommodations for four adults, with a king-size bed in the bedroom and a sofa bed in the lounge.

The 22 beach bungalows have a bedroom with a king size bed and a living room with a single bed or day bed, with sliding doors to separate the two rooms. The 3 prestige beach units have a bedroom downstairs and another bedroom with two twin beds in the loft, plus a separate lounge, providing accommodations for four people. All beach units have a Jacuzzi on the sundeck, facing a very white sand beach. You can relax here and sip your favorite cocktail while watching the sunset over the lagoon, as there is no fence around the terrace.

The 10 overwater bungalows are so beautiful, comfortable and romantic you'll never want to leave. They stand on a wooden pontoon over the jade and blue water and are made of thatched roofs, local woods and woven bamboo walls. They are spacious junior suites with a separate lounge and a glass bottom coffee table for fish watching. That can be a full-time occupation in Rangiroa's lagoon, with its wealth of marine flora and fauna. The decor is a subtle Polynesian design in cool colors to complement the blues and greens of the lagoon. Each overwater unit has a shiny, modern bathroom, telephone and safe, plus a big terrace and a private solarium, with steps leading into the inviting lagoon, a huge liquid playground of a thousand delights.

All the bungalows are built in a traditional Polynesian style that blends noble and precious materials with international class comfort. All units now include air conditioning and ceiling fans and they are equipped with telephones, safety boxes, refrigerator/mini bar, and tea and coffee making facilities. In the beach and overwater bungalows a door separates the bedroom from the large bathroom. All the bathrooms have a big tiled hot water shower and walls that are decorated with coral and mother-of-pearl shell. There is a hairdryer and the range of toiletries is replenished daily. Room service is provided on request.

Even if you're not staying in an overwater bungalow you can still fish watch through the floor of the spacious bar and lounge, or walk along the pier to see a variety of brightly colored tropical fish as they swim through the coral gardens in the translucent water. Or you can don mask and snorkel and jump in with them. You can also float lazily in the fresh water swimming pool, daydream in the adjacent Jacuzzi, or snooze on a lounge chair under the shade of an umbrella on the pool deck. The hotel provides free snorkeling equipment for its guests, outrigger paddle canoes, tennis, volleyball, petanque (French bowls), arts and crafts exhibits and frequent shows of Tahitian songs and dances. The Kahaia Lounge is equipped with a pool table, wide screen television with DVD and VCR players and films, library, and board games such as chess, backgammon, scrabble and dice. Another free service provided is round-trip transportation to attend services held each Sunday at the Catholic Church in Avatoru. Optional activities include bicycle, scooter and car rentals, glass bottom boat rides to snorkel and feed the sharks, fish watching in an air-conditioned Aquascope, lagoon tours to visit the dolphins and drift through the passes, picnic excursions to *motu* islets on the other side of the lagoon, deep-sea fishing, scuba diving, visits to a black pearl farm, boat rentals and excursions to visit the Kia Ora Sauvage. After a full day's activities, you can relax while enjoying a Thai body massage in a new beauty center on the beach.

You can sign up for your tours and excursions at the activities counter across the lobby from the reception desk. These two facilities are located in a big open-air building that also houses the Kahaia lounge and game room, the Missir black pearl shop and La Boutique, as well as the hotel management offices. Jean Pierre Naegelen, a decorator of renown from Tahiti, created a magnificent work of art in the lobby, using all local materials such as kauri, maru maru and other semi-precious woods, bamboo carved with Polynesian designs, and trimmed with coconut fiber, mother-of-pearl shells and white coral from the Rangiroa beach. His *piéce de resistance* is a huge round sphere that is covered with the dried branches of the miki miki bushes that grow on the seashore. Naegelen said that this sphere represents the world, as the Hotel Kia Ora is open to all the people of the world. It also represents a pearl, and all the elements that signify a coral atoll are present, with a coral pedestal over a fountain of water. You will also see Naegalen's distinctive work in the overwater bar, where he created a chandelier of 70,000 seashells, and in the magnificent decor of the bungalows.

The 120-seat open-air dining room faces the swimming pool and shining lagoon, and the menu selections have been chosen to please the discerning clientele, who do come from all parts of the world. Local fish and lobster are favorite choices, along with the fine French cuisine and the sumptuous buffets that are served each Wednesday and Sunday. The wine cellar contains just the right vintage to enhance your meal, and the service provided by the friendly staff is also commendable. See more information under *Where to Eat* in this chapter.

The Kia Ora team is headed by Gerard Garcia, of Spanish and French origin, who was born in Australia and grew up in Vancouver, Canada. He worked for seven years at the Hotel Bora Bora as food and beverage manager, and helped open the Bora Bora Lagoon Resort, before coming to the Hotel Kia Ora in October 1998.

HOTEL KIA ORA SAUVAGE RANGIROA, *Hotel Kia Ora, B.P. 198, Avatoru, Rangiroa 98775. Tel. 689/93.11.11; Fax 689/96.04.93; Reservations: Tel. 689/93.11.17; Fax 689/96.02.20; E-mail: resa@hotelkiaora.pf; www.hotelkiaora.com. 5 bungalows on a private motu islet, two kilometers (1.2 miles) east of the airport to Hotel Kia Ora, then one hour by boat across* the lagoon to Motu Avea Rahi, 40 kilometers (25 miles) from main village. Round-trip car transfers included between airport and Hotel Kia Ora. Round-trip boat transfers to Kia Ora Sauvage are 10.000 CFP per person. Rates: beach bungalow single/double 40.000; third person add 5.000 CFP. AP Meal plan with breakfast, lunch and dinner included is compulsory for 7.600 CFP per person. Half-price for children under 12 years. A supplementary cost is added to meal plan for Christmas and New Year's Eve. Add 5% hotel tax to room rates and 6% value added tax to room rates and meal plan, plus 150 CFP municipal tax per person per day. A 10% value added tax is applicable to other services. All major credit cards.

Here is your ultimate Robinson Crusoe Island. There are only five bungalows for a maximum of 12 guests. What you don't have here is of primary importance for your tranquility and totally relaxed getaway. No electricity, no telephones, no jet-skis, no excursion boats or helicopters buzzing around and overhead the lagoon, no cars, motorcycles and other traffic noises, and no roosters to crow all night. Your host and hostess and a staff of two assistants will take care of your meals, which are served family style in the restaurant-bar or on the beach. Your bungalow is an attractive thatched roof fare built of local woods, and contains a king-size bed and a single bed, a private bathroom with hot water shower and a terrace overlooking the white sand beach. Two kerosene lamps are placed on your front steps each evening.

Activities include boat trips to nearby motu islets, fishing for dinner in the lagoon and trips to the reef for appetizers. You can also paddle an outrigger canoe, windsurf or feed the sharks. This little hotel is a favorite retreat for honeymooners and other travelers in the know. See more information in Best Places to Stay chapter.

Superior

NOVOTEL RANGIROA BEACH RESORT, B.P. 17, Avatoru, Rangiroa 98775. Hotel Tel. 689/93.13.50, Fax 689/93.13.51; Reservations: TAHITIRES Tel. 689/86.66.66, Fax 689/41.05.05; E-mail: reservation_Tahiti@accor-hotels.com. Beside the lagoon, 150 meters (492 feet) from the airport. Round-trip transfers 1.650 CFP per adult, 750 CFP for child under 12 years. Rates: garden room 24.500 CFP single/double/triple; garden bungalow 28.800 CFP single/double/triple; beach front room 34.200 CFP single/double/triple. American breakfast 2.300 CFP. Set lunch menu 2.600; set dinner menu 3.900 CFP; Meal plans available; half-fare meals for child 3-12 years. Supplement for New Year's Eve dinner 13.200 CFP. Prices include all taxes except a city tax of 150 CFP per person per day. All major credit cards.

This hotel offers an alternative choice between a deluxe hotel and the bed and breakfast type accommodations found on Rangiroa. It opened to the public in April 2004 as a Polynesian Resort Hotel, and because it was originally supposed to have been a Paladien hotel, the residents of Rangiroa still call it by that name. The French group Accor took over management in August 2004 and it is now operated as a Novotel. The clientele includes a number of scuba divers, as the room and bungalow rates are the same for single, double or triple occupancy.

The accommodations consist of 22 garden rooms with terrace, 10 garden bungalows and 6 beach bungalows with terrace. These units include 4 adjoining rooms for a family or can be used as a suite, and there are also 2 rooms for physically challenged guests. The twin beds can also be transformed into one king size bed, and the sofa beds in the beach and garden bungalows can sleep a third person. The furniture is teak. All units include individual air conditioning, cable television, direct dial phone, safety boxes, refrigerator/ mini-bar and coffee and tea making facilities. The bathrooms are tiled, have a separate toilet, hot water shower and lavabo, a hair dryer and a range of toiletries.

The compact bungalows and rooms are built of wood that is almost the color of the coconut palm trunks. The public facilities include a reception area, where you will also find the activities desk and car rental center, as well as a small boutique and board games area. The beachfront and outdoor restaurant offers European and Polynesian food made with local products. The menu also includes Chinese dishes, as well as fresh fish specialties. A tropical buffet is served at breakfast, a snack menu or a full meal are available at lunchtime, so that you can order sandwiches, salads, pizzas, or grilled meats and fish. Barbecue buffets and Polynesian buffets will be featured on some evenings, alternating with "a la carte" service. The beachfront bar is open daily from 10am to 11pm, serving Polynesian cocktails as well as standard drinks and fresh fruit juice.

Recreational activities and sports include complimentary use of snorkeling equipment, sea kayaks and outrigger canoes. The hotel also offers petanque (French bowls), and beach volleyball. Optional activities include bicycle, scooter and car rentals, boats and jet skis, line fishing, angling, deep-sea fishing, day cruising on the lagoon with a skipper, picnics to the distant motu islets and scuba diving. Local musicians and Tahitian dance shows are also featured on special evenings.

Moderate
LES RELAIS DE JOSEPHINE, *B.P. 140, Avatoru, Rangiroa 98775. Tel./Fax 689/96.02.00; E-mail: relaisjosephine@mail.pf; http://relaisjosephine.free.fr. Beside the Tiputa pass close to Pension Glorinne and the Ohutu boat dock, 5 kilometers (3.1 miles) from the airport. Rates: bungalow with breakfast and dinner 13.860 CFP per person; add 10.400 CFP for third adult in bungalow and 6.930 CFP for child 2-12 years sharing bungalow with parents. Lunch is available at extra cost. Free round-trip transfers. Add 6% value added tax to*

room rates and meal plan and 50 CFP per person per day for municipal tax. A 10% value added tax is applicable to other services. All major credit cards.

Six attractive bungalows with thatched roofs are built in the garden and beside the beach in a sheltered cove along the lagoon opening of Tiputa pass. Each cozy unit is furnished in a colonial style with a canopied double bed and single bed, a private bathroom with hot water and separate toilet, a dressing room with individual safe, a ceiling fan, coffee and tea facilities and private terrace. The bar terrace overlooks the pass, where dolphins can often be seen dancing in the waves. The French owners, Madame Denise Thirouard and her husband, a doctor with a practice in Rangiroa, like to entertain in the evening with piano recitals. You might think you are in Paris or New York with their wine tastings and introduction to Oenologie (study of wine) Their clients are mostly French and Japanese, who appreciate the refined atmosphere, gourmet cuisine and wines served in their restaurant, Le Dauphin Gourmand. Activities can be arranged with the hosts and there is a scuba diving center nearby.

LE MEROU BLEU, *B.P. 163, Avatoru, Rangiroa 98775. Tel./Fax 689/ 96.84.62, cell 79.16.82; E-mail: lemeroubleu@mail.pf; http://le-merou-bleu.ifrance.com. Beside the Avatoru pass, five minutes from the village. Free round-trip transfers from airport and Ohutu boat dock. Rates: bungalow with cold water shower, breakfast and dinner, 10.000 CFP per person; bungalow with hot water shower, breakfast and dinner, 12.000 CFP per person. Children 3-12 years half-price if sharing bungalow with parents. Add 6% value added tax to room rates and meal plan and 50 CFP per person per day for municipal tax. A 10% value added tax is applicable to other services. No credit cards.*

The name of this pension means "Blue Spotted-Grouper" in English or "Roi" in Tahitian. The owners are Pierre and Sonya Friedrich from Alsace, who have built three traditional style thatched roof bungalows right beside Avatoru pass. You can lie in the hammock on your terrace and listen to the steady roar of the ocean while watching the surfers riding the waves, or you can join them in their sport, as this is "the" surfing spot on Rangiroa. This is also an excellent place to snorkel and look for that special seashell in the white sand below the clear water.

Two of the bungalows can sleep a maximum of three people and the honeymoon bungalow is ideal for two. All beds are protected by mosquito nets and electricity is provided by solar lighting and electric generator. Each room contains an ice chest. Pierre is a decorator and has added his special touch to each bungalow with the use of local woods, bamboo, sea urchin shells, and mother-of-pearl and dolphin mobiles. Sonya had a restaurant in France and serves guests her specialties of couscous, West Indian dishes and local foods. Bicycles are free for guests and lagoon outings are arranged with Tane Excursion at Chez Henriette in Avatoru village. You can easily walk to the village and check out the small boutiques. A gift is offered to young honeymooners who stay at least three days. The owners speak French and German, but very little English; however, their daughter Emmanuelle, *Tel. 96.82.36*, speaks English and will be happy to translate.

RAIRA LAGON, *B.P. 87, Avatoru, Rangiroa 98775. Tel. 689/93.12.30; Fax 689/93.12.31; E-mail: rairalag@mail.pf; www.raira-lagon.pf. At PK 1.5, beside the lagoon in Avatoru commune, 6.5 kilometers (4 miles) from the Ohutu boat dock and 800 meters (2,624 feet)) west of the airport. Rates: a fare with breakfast and dinner (obligatory) costs 10.800 CFP per person, half-price for children 3-12 years and no charge for younger children. Free round-trip transfers. Rates include taxes. American Express, Mastercard, Visa.*

There are 10 small *fares* for couples or families, with single or double beds and electric fans and anti-mosquito gadgets, which are also electric. Each bungalow has a private bathroom with hot water shower, and there is a sliding glass door leading onto a small terrace. Rooms are cleaned daily. Le Margouillat restaurant is on the beach, serving a Continental breakfast, salads and sandwiches for lunch and gastronomic French cuisine for dinner. There is also a small bar in the restaurant. Beach chairs for guests are placed under the shade trees or on the coral beach and snorkeling equipment is provided. Scooters and bicycles can be rented on the premises. Scooters are 1.700 CFP per hour, 4.400 CFP for a half day and 7.800 CFP for a full day. Bicycles rent for 700 CFP for a half day and 1.300 CFP for a full day. See more information on *Where to Eat* in this chapter.

PENSION TUANAKE, *B. P. 21, Avatoru, Rangiroa 98775. Tel. 689/ 93.11.80; Fax 689/93.11.81; E-mail: tuanake@mail.pf; www.tuanake.fr.st. Beside the lagoon in Avatoru, 2.5 kilometers (1.6 miles) from the airport and 7.5 kilometers (4.7 miles) from the boat dock at Ohutu. Free round-trip transfers. EP Rates: fare 6.300 CFP single; 9.500 CFP double; 11.600 CFP triple. Fare with breakfast and dinner: 10.300 CFP single; 15.500 CFP double; 20.600 CFP triple. Family bungalows with 5-6 beds also available. EP rates for children 4-11 years 2.500 CFP per day; MAP for children 4-11 years 5.150 CFP per day. Add 6% value added tax to room rates and meal plan and 50 CFP per person per day for municipal tax. A 10% value added tax is applicable to other services Mastercard, Visa.*

There are six *fares* or bungalows on the white sand beach, two with two single beds, and four family *fares* with accommodations for five or six people. Each *fare* is very clean and has a fan and private bathroom with cold water or a separate hot water shower outside. House linens are furnished. All guests share the big open-air living room with television and the dining room. There is also a pay phone for guests.

Roger Terorotua has served two terms as president of the Haere Mai Association, which represents the small hotels and pensions in French Polynesia. Therefore, he is very interested in tourism and presenting a good tourist product. His son Vetea now helps takes care of the pension. A friendly, comfortable atmosphere reigns here, with beach chairs to read in the shade or sunbathe on the white coral beach. The cuisine is also recommended, which is served in an attractive dining room overlooking the beach and lagoon. A *hoa* channel runs from the ocean to the lagoon on one side of the property and Gauguin's Pearl farm is on the other side.

LES FARE DE TIKI HOA, *B.P. 235, Avatoru, Rangiroa 98775. Tel. 689/ 73.80.13/73.63.10; E-mail: tikihoa@mail.pf; www.fare-tikihoa.pf. on Motu Tairua Manahune, 19 kilometers (11.8 miles) across the lagoon from the airport and 15 kilometers (9.3 miles) from the boat dock. Round-trip boat transfers 2.000 CFP per person. Rates: bungalow only 6.000 CFP per person; bungalow with breakfast, lunch and dinner 12.500 CFP per person per day. Taxes included. Mastercard, Visa.*

This small family hotel was scheduled for completion in July 2004 on the northwest side of the lagoon, a 30-minute boat ride from Avatoru village. It is located on Motu Tairua Manahune, the same motu islet where the former Sans Souci hotel was built, but more to the north, according to Michel Tavernier, who is in charge of this project. He said that the 10 bungalows are of high standard and are 29 square meters (312 sq. ft.) with a terrace, and are constructed of wood on concrete pilings, with a niau roof of thatched coconut fronds. The sliding glass door also has a mosquito screen and the bungalows are supposedly very airy as they are built beside the lagoon, facing the wind. Each unit contains a double bed and private bathroom with cold water shower (actually tepid in this climate), and electricity is provided by solar panels and an electric generator. There is also a reception area, kitchen, dining terrace and bar, as well as a small boutique. There is a small lake on the property and the hotel grounds are sprayed on a regular basis against mosquitoes. The emphasis here on this remote motu is being close to nature. Guests will enjoy walks along the white sand beach beside the lagoon and various methods of fishing will be included in the choices of things to do. Boat excursions will take you to other uninhabited motu, including the popular Blue Lagoon, which is much closer to this hotel than to the villages. Scuba divers can be transported by boat to the dive centers on the Avatoru side of the lagoon.

PENSION CECILE, *B. P. 98, Avatoru, Rangiroa 98775. Tel. 689/93.12.65, Fax 689/93.12.66. In Avatoru, 7.5 kilometers (4.7 miles) from the Ohutu boat dock and 2.5 kilometers (1.6 miles) from the airport. Free round-trip transfers. Rates: bungalow 4.500 CFP per person; bungalow with breakfast and dinner 8.000 CFP person; half-price for child under 12 years. Add 6% value added tax to room rates and meal plan and 50 CFP per person per day for municipal tax. A 10% value added tax is applicable to other services. Mastercard, Visa.*

There are nine bungalows beside the beach and lagoon and in the garden, including four new units of the standard government approved FEI model. Eight bungalows contain a double and single bed, a private bathroom and cold water. There is also a family bungalow with one double and one single bed, plus mattresses on the mezzanine, and a private bathroom with cold water. House linens and snorkeling equipment are supplied. Guests share the living room with television and meals are served in an open-air dining room. Throughout the years Cecile has been very much appreciated by visitors because of her warm welcome and excellent meals. Her husband has now taken over as host and cook because Cecile has gone to France for three years for medical treatment.

Activities can include a visit to a pearl farm, fishing in the lagoon and lagoon excursions aboard the pension's own boat. They charge 7.500 CFP for a picnic trip to the Blue Lagoon or to Reef Island, 8.000 CFP to visit the old village and 10.000 CFP to the Pink Sand Beach.

PENSION MARTINE, *B.P. 68, Avatoru, Rangiroa 98775. Tel. 689/ 93.12.25; Fax 689/93.12.26; cell 79.71.52; E-mail: pensionmartine@mail.pf. On the lagoon side near the airport and 5 kilometers (3.1 miles) from the village of Avatoru. Free round-trip transfers. Rates: bungalow with breakfast 6.000 CFP single; 5.000 CFP per person double or triple; bungalow with breakfast and dinner 7.000 CFP single; 8.000 CFP per person double or triple. Half-price for children under 12 years. No charge for children under four years. Add 6% value added tax to room rates and meal plan and 50 CFP per person per day for municipal tax. A 10% value added tax is applicable to other services. Mastercard and Visa.*

This pension has a good reputation in Rangiroa and with former guests, including a young couple from Tahiti who spent their honeymoon there and wrote a "Mauruuru Award" letter to the *Tahiti Beach Press* to thank Martine for her warm hospitality. There are three attractive and clean little bungalows, including a unit for singles, built beside the beach and lagoon. Each bungalow has a private bathroom with a ceiling fan, hot water shower and terrace, and all house linens are furnished. Two of the units have a double bed and a single bed. All guests share the living room and eat their meals in the dining room. Your hosts will take you to visit their family pearl farm if you wish.

TURIROA VILLAGE, *B.P. 26, Avatoru, Rangiroa 98775. Tel. 689/96.02.46, Fax 689/96.04.27, cell 78.90.19; E-mail: pension.turiroa@mail.pf. Beside the lagoon in Avatoru, six kilometers (3.7 miles) from the airport and 5 kilometers (3.1 miles) from Avatoru village. Free round-trip transfers. EP Rates: fare without kitchenette 6.000 CFP for one to two people; bungalow with kitchenette 8.000 CFP for one to four people; add 2.750 CFP per person for breakfast and dinner. Half-price for children under 12 years. Add 6% value added tax to room rates and meal plan and 50 CFP per person per day for municipal tax. A 10% value added tax is applicable to other services. No credit cards.*

There are two garden and two beach bungalows, each containing a double bed and a mezzanine with single beds. These units also have a kitchenette, private bathroom with cold water, and a terrace. There is also a small *fare* with two single beds and a terrace, with a private bathroom and hot water outside. House linens are furnished. Everyone shares the living room with television and the laundry room. If you don't want to cook your meals will be served in the communal dining room, which is built over the lagoon. Your hostess, Mrs. Olga Niva, will take you to visit her family pearl farm and she also offers free transfers daily to the village.

ARIITINI VILLAGE, *B.P. 18, Avatoru, Rangiroa 98775. Tel. 689/96.04.41, Fax 689/96.04.40. Located beside the lagoon at PK 4 in Avatoru, 5.6 kilometers (3.5 miles) from the Ohutu boat dock and 500 meters (1,640 feet) from the airport. Free round-trip transfers. Rates: bungalow with breakfast and dinner 8.000 CFP per person per day; half-fare for children under 12 years. Taxes included. No credit cards.*

Felix and Judith Tetua have 6 bungalows in a garden setting beside the beach and lagoon. Each unit has a double bed and a single bed, a private bathroom with cold water shower and a small terrace. They also have two boats that are used for excursions to the Blue Lagoon, Reef Islet and the Sables Roses.

RELAIS MIHIROA, *B.P. 51, Tiputa, Rangiroa 98775. Tel. 689/96.72.14, Fax 689/93.12.70, E-mail: relaismihiroa@mail.pf. Beside lagoon on Tiputa side of pass, 4 kilometers (2.5 miles) from Tiputa village and 15 minutes by boat from airport. Round-trip boat transfers 1.000 CFP per person. Rates: bungalow with breakfast and dinner 7.600 CFP per person per day; half-price for children 3-12 years and no charge for children under 3 years. Camping space 1.500 CFP per person per day, tent and camping space 3.000 CFP per person per day. Add 6% value added tax to room rates and meal plan and 50 CFP per person per day for municipal tax. A 10% value added tax is applicable to other services. Mastercard, Visa.*

If you want to get away from the village, this family pension and campground offers a good choice. There are four bungalows with a double bed and single bed in each unit, as well as a fan, mosquito machine and private bathroom with cold water shower. House linens are supplied and there is a large fare with a dining room and equipped kitchen that can be shared by campers or other guests who want to cook their own meals. Monique Guitteny, your hostess, will also serve lunch on request. She can also arrange for you to visit the distant motu islets by boat with a picnic on the motu.

PENSION GLORINNE, *Avatoru, Rangiroa 98775. Tel. 689/96.04.05; Fax 689/96.03.58; E-mail: pensionglorine@mail.pf; http://glorine.site.voila.fr. Beside the lagoon just 50 meters from the Ohotu quay near Tiputa Pass and five kilometers (3.1 miles) east of the airport. Rates: bungalow with breakfast 4.500 CFP per person, bungalow with breakfast and dinner 7.500 CFP per person; half-price for child under 12 years. Round-trip transfers 800 CFP per vehicle. Add 6% value added tax to room rates and meal plan and 50 CFP per* *person per day for municipal tax. A 10% value added tax is applicable to other services. No credit cards.*

For many years this was the most popular pension on Rangiroa and Glorinne has long been noted for her delicious food. Her daughter has now taken over some of the workload, but Glorinne is still there as well and many tourists are still choosing this pension for their vacation. The biggest drawback here is the noise generated by the inter-island boats that bring fuel and other supplies to Rangiroa. They unload at the dock beside the pension, which may be disturbing to some guests, but they are not there every night. There is no beach here but the fascinating Tiputa pass is right beside the pension. Rangiroa Paradive is located adjacent to the pension.

There are six small thatched roof Polynesian style bungalows: four for two people, one for four people and one for six people. Each smaller fare has a private bathroom and cold water shower, and a veranda, and the family bungalow has a hot water shower. Mosquito nets, fans and house linens are furnished in all the rooms. A communal sitting room with television and a covered terrace have brochures and information on activities and excursions available and paperback books to exchange. Beach chairs are scattered throughout the shaded and sunny lawn. Meals are served in a covered dining area right beside the lagoon. You can rent a bicycle for 1.500 CFP for 4 hours.

Economy
MAITAI LAGON VERT, *B.P. 54, Avatoru, Rangiroa 98775. Tel./Fax 689/ 96.84.73; Cell 689/79.24.66/77.28.85. On a motu at Lagon Vert (Green Lagoon), a 10-minute boat ride from Avatoru village. Free ground transfers from airport to boat dock and 1.000 CFP per person for round-trip boat transfers to the motu. Rates: fare with breakfast and dinner 5.500 CFP per person; fare with breakfast, lunch and dinner 6.500 CFP per person. Campers pay 1.050 CFP per person if they cook their own meals, or 4.500 CFP per person per day for breakfast and dinner. Rates include taxes. No credit cards.*

Punua and Moana Tamaehu have built three simple Paumotu style *fares* of coconut fronds and kahaia wood on a motu islet called Lagon Vert (Green Lagoon). There is also camping space here. Each fare has a private bathroom with cold water shower. Gas lamps are used for lighting, as there is no electricity.

Punua provides boat excursions to visit the Blue Lagoon or Reef Islet for 7.500 CFP or to Sables Roses (Pink Sand) motu for 9.500 CFP. A picnic is included in each of these outings. He will also take you to visit the Lagoonarium and Sharky Park for 3.500 CFP without picnic and you pay 4.500 CFP for this same excursion with a picnic lunch. A special fishing expedition takes place every October, when Punua and his friends beat the surface of the lagoon with sticks to round up the fish.

CHEZ LUCIEN, *B.P. 69, Tiputa, Rangiroa 98776. Tel./Fax 689/96.73.55; E-mail: pensionlucien@mail.pf; http://pensionlucien.free.fr. Near the pass in Tiputa village, 10 minutes by boat from the airport. Round-trip boat transfers 1.000 CFP per person. Rates: bungalow with breakfast 4.500 CFP per person; bungalow with breakfast and dinner 6.500 CFP per person; half-price for child under 12 years. Add 6% value added tax to room rates and meal plan and 50 CFP per person per day for municipal tax. A 10% value added tax is applicable to other services. No credit cards.*

This well maintained pension is facing the lagoon at the edge of the Tiputa Pass. Lucien Pea has built two small bungalows and a 2-bedroom family bungalow, all with covered porches that overlook the pass. Each of the smaller bungalows has two double beds, a mezzanine with a double bed, a refrigerator and a bathroom with hot water. The family bungalow has a double bed in each bedroom, 3 double beds on the mezzanine, a living room, refrigerator and a communal bathroom with cold water. House linens are furnished. The meals are generous and pleasant, served in a covered dining room beside the lagoon.

RANGIROA LODGE, *Avatoru, Rangiroa 98775. Tel. 689/96.82.13. Beside the lagoon in Avatoru village, 8 kilometers (5 miles) from the Ohutu boat dock and 6 kilometers (3.7 miles) from the airport. Free round-trip transfers. EP Rates: double room with communal bathroom 2.000 CFP single; 4.000 CFP double; double room with private bath 5.000 CFP one or two people per day; dormitory 1.700 CFP per person per day. Add 6% value added tax to room rates and meal plan and 50 CFP per person per day for municipal tax. A 10% value added tax is applicable to other services. No credit cards.*

Because of its location and facilities, this is probably the best inexpensive pension for low-budget travelers who want to stay in Avatoru and be able to cook their own meals. There are four simple rooms and two 3-bed dormitories built between the lagoon and the road—very close to the road. There is also an equipped kitchen and a dining room on the coral beach. Reaching the owner by telephone is very difficult, so it is best to go to the site and make arrangements with the guardian.

Other Pensions

The pensions I have listed above are the most popular of the family lodgings that were available in Rangiroa at publication time. The other pensions near Avatoru village are: **PENSION HENRI**, *Tel./Fax 96.82.67;* E-mail: pensionhenri@mail.pf; **PENSION HENRIETTE**, *Tel. 689/72.31.51;* **PENSION HERENUI**, *Tel./Fax 96.84.71;* **PENSION LOYNA**, *Tel./Fax 96.82.09;* E-mail: pensionloyna@mail.pf; **CHEZ MIKI MIKI**, *Tel. 96.83.83; Fax 96.82.90;* **CHEZ NANUA**, *Tel./Fax 96.83.88;* **CHEZ TEINA & MARIE**, *Tel. 96.03.94, Fax 96.84.44.*

Where to Eat

Deluxe

HOTEL KIA ORA, *Tel. 93.11.11. Open daily for breakfast, lunch and dinner. All credit cards.*

This 120-seat restaurant caters to international palates, served in an open air setting beside the lagoon. A breakfast buffet includes fresh fruits, yogurt, croissants and a choice of juices, for 2.000 CFP, and an American breakfast with eggs and bacon is 2.400 CFP.

The luncheon menu features burgers with fries from 1.250 to 1.400 CFP, or pizza, pasta, chow mein, lagoon fish and a fresh fruit plate. You can also order a sirloin steak for 2.550 CFP or shrimp curry with sweet potatoes for 2.450 CFP. The dinner menu offers several different choices each evening, which usually include fresh fish from the lagoon or deep ocean, with a good selection of fine wines. The *soupe du jour* is 850 CFP, appetizers are 1.200 to 1.750 CFP, fish and seafood dishes are 2.450 to 3.250 CFP, meat and poultry selections range from 2.150 to 3.500 CFP and roast lobster is 3.950 CFP. The pastry chef creates an appealing dessert buffet for 950 CFP and ice creams and sorbets are 750 CFP per order. A barbecue buffet of grilled meat, chicken and fish is served on Wednesday and Sunday night, and a Polynesian dance show is performed during the buffet. The cost for each event is 5.500 CFP per person. The overwater bar is open daily from 9am to 11pm, serving almost any drink you want to order, plus their own exotic creations, such as Blue Lagoon, Pink Sands, Lagoon Secret and Rangiroa Blue Sky.

Moderate

LE KAI KAI, *on lagoon side next door to Pension Martine and across road from L'Atelier Corinne, Tel. 96.03.39. Open for lunch and dinner daily except Wednesday. Mastercard, Visa.*

This restaurant is managed by Gaëlle Coconnier, who serves her guests French home cooking on an outdoor terrace with a thatch roof and coral floor. The starter courses are priced from 1.000 to 1.500 CFP and include sashimi and *poisson cru*. Fish dishes are 1.200 to 2.000 CFP, with choices of grilled mahi mahi, shrimp curry or shrimp with ginger sauce. A dish of Paumotu style roast pork is excellent and is served with roast *fei*, green beans and french fries for 1.500 CFP. Beef filet with Roquefort sauce is 2.000 CFP. Wines are priced from 2.000 to 6.800 CFP a bottle, and an extensive dessert menu has tempting choices from 450 to 600 CFP. Round-trip transfers are provided.

LE MARGOUILLAT, *at Pension Raira Lagoon, Tel. 93.12.30. Open daily. Reservations. American Express, Mastercard, Visa.*

This beachfront restaurant is popular with local residents because they can choose from an *a la carte* menu and the French gourmet cuisine is well prepared. The average price for dinner is around 3.000 CFP per person. They specialize in fresh fish from the lagoon and ocean, as well as lobster and seafood, and they also serve New Zealand beef. Sandwiches and salads are available at lunchtime.

VAIMARIO, *Tel. 96.05.96, is located on the ocean side of the road between the Hotel Kia Ora and the airport. Open for lunch and dinner except on Tuesday when they are closed all day and at noon on Saturday. Mastercard, Visa.*

Dominique Soupot, who formerly worked at the Hotel Kia Ora, took over this restaurant and bar in 2003 and prepares French cuisine and pizzas for his clientele, who always include a number of local residents. His wife Marcella manages the restaurant and takes orders for the *confits*, *magret de canard*, escargots and fresh fish dishes, as well as *poisson cru* and the daily specials. Burgers are 900 CFP, pizzas are 950-1.100 CFP, pasta is 1.200 CFP, appetizers are priced from 850-1.350 CFP, fish and shrimp dishes are 1.600-2.250 CFP, meats are 1.600-2.400 CFP, desserts are 500-700 CFP, and wine is priced from 1.400-12.350 CFP a bottle. A Tahitian brunch is served on Sundays. Free pick-up service is provided from the hotels and pensions.

Economy

CHEZ AUGUSTE & ANTOINETTE, *Tel. 96.85.01, is on your right, next to the Shell Station, when coming from the airport toward Avatoru village. Open Monday through Friday from 6am to 10pm. No credit cards.*

Chinese food is the specialty here, with chow mein, lemon chicken, tamarind duck and other mouth-watering dishes prepared to eat in the restaurant or take with you. Prices range from 950 to 1.200 CFP a plate.

CHEZ BEATRICE, *Tel. 96.04.12, is in Avatoru village. Open daily for breakfast, lunch and dinner except on Wednesday. No credit cards.*

You have a choice of Chinese and local dishes or French cuisine and you can eat in the small restaurant or take it with you. Breakfast is served from 6 to 9am and is priced from 1.000 to 1.500 CFP, according to your selection, which can include fried fish, *taioro*, *pahua* and *maoa*, or a more conventional breakfast if you wish. Lunch is served from 11am to 2pm and dinner is from 6 to 9pm. Chinese dishes are priced from 950 to 1.680 CFP per plate and French foods, mostly steak, are 1.000 to 1.150 CFP. Tahitian food is served on Sundays for 1.200 CFP a plate. Alcoholic beverages are also available.

SNACK TAUIRARII, *Tel. 96.83.33, is at the Avatoru marina. Open daily except Tuesday and Sunday for lunch and dinner. No credit cards.*

You can buy steak-frites, chow mein, *poisson cru* with coconut milk, or grilled fish and meats for 1.000 - 1.200 CFP a plate. You can get food to go, or you can stay and play *petanque* with the locals.

SNACK RELAIS OHOTU *is a snack on the Ohotu quay, across the road from Pension Glorinne, overlooking the Tiputa Pass. Open Monday through Saturday 8am to 5pm, and on Sunday from 5:30 to 7:30am. No credit cards.*

Fruit juices, beer, *casse-croûtes*, omelets, grilled chicken, steak, shish kebabs, fish and hamburgers are served on the overwater terrace.

SNACK AGNES is located at the Rangiroa airport.
You can buy Hinano beer, soft drinks and a ham and cheese casse-croûte sandwich.

Roulottes open up for business when the sun goes down. You can usually find one of these mobile diners parked beside Snack Relais Ohutu and another one near Pension Chez Martine and Le Kai Kai Restaurant. They serve steak-frites, poisson cru, grilled fish and chicken and chow mein.

Sports & Recreation
Motor Boat Rental
   Oviri Excursions, Tel./Fax 96.05.87, is owned by Ugo Angely and three of his friends, who have two boats that are 28-feet and 32-feet long that they use for various excursions. These boats with skipper can be chartered for private tours.
   Maurice Taxi Boat, Tel./Fax 96.76.09 or cell 78.13.25. Maurice Snow operates a non-stop taxi boat service between Ohutu boat dock, Tiputa village and the airport daily from 6am to 5pm. If you deal directly with Maurice, the round-trip fare from Ohutu to Tiputa is 1.000 CFP per person. He has another boat that is used for excursions. He charges 1.500 CFP to visit the dolphins, 2.500 CFP for drift snorkeling in the pass, 8.000 CFP for a round-trip excursion to Reef Islet, 8.500 CFP to go to the Blue Lagoon, 10.000 CFP to Sables Rose and 10.000 CFP for an excursion to Otepipi, the site of an ancient village, where the inhabitants once lived. The old Catholic church of Sainte-Anne is still standing, the white sand beach has fine sand and small paths lead into the jungle on the motu. All the full day excursions include a picnic lunch of fresh lagoon fish and grilled meats, rice salad, dessert and drink.

Deep Sea Fishing
   Ava, Tel. 96.04.49/79.24.82; E-mail: elihiria@mail.pf. Hiria Arnoux has a 36-foot polyester bonito type boat that he uses for a maximum of 7 passengers. He offers half-day deep sea fishing charters in the afternoons only for 50.000 CFP for the boat. He also has 3-hour fishing expeditions in the late afternoon for 30.000 CFP, which can begin between 2:30 and 3pm or you can wait until 4:30pm for a sunset outing.
   Toohi II, Tel. 70.45.14, is a 30-foot Arcoa boat owned by Willie and Pascale, who work out of the Hotel Kia Ora. A maximum of 4 passengers can rent the boat for a minimum of 2 hours for deep sea fishing excursions, which costs 30.000 CFP for the boat. A half-day excursion is 50.000 CFP and a full-day is 80.000 CFP. Bring your own lunch and drinks. You can also fish inside the lagoon for 7.500 CFP per hour for a minimum of 2 hours.

Glass Bottom Boat Excursions
Matahi Excursions, *Tel. 96.84.48*, based at Ohotu Point on the Avatoru side of the Tiputa pass, is operated by Matahi Tepa and his daughter. They have two glass bottom boats that provide 2-hour excursions, with departures made according to the incoming current in the pass. You'll view the amazing wealth of sea life from the dry comfort of the boat as you drift through the pass and stop at the fishermen's *motu* islet inside the pass, where you can watch the shark feeding. The cost is 2.500 CFP per person. Line fishing is available on request. Round-trip transfers are provided from your lodging to the boat.

Toohi III, *Tel. 70.45.14*, is a 24-foot glass bottom boat owned by Willie and Pascale, who provide 1 1/2 hour excursions for a maximum of 12 people, departing at 2 pm from the Hotel Kia Ora dock. The cost is 2.500 CFP per person. Or you can take a half-day excursion from 9am to 1pm, which includes a picnic lunch served on board the covered boat, for 5.900 CFP per person.

Fafarua Rangiroa, *Tel. 20.62.43*, is an air-conditioned Aquascope for six passengers, which is based near the Hotel Kia Ora. Free transfers are provided from the hotels and pensions for the four daily outings inside the lagoon. A 1/2-hour excursion costs 3.300 CFP per person.

Lagoon Excursions
The most popular destination of the lagoon excursions is the **Blue Lagoon**, which is an hour's boat ride from the hotels and pensions in Rangiroa, on the western edge of the atoll. This lagoon within a lagoon is formed by a natural pool of aquamarine water on the edge of the reef, known locally as Taeo'o. Several *motu* islets are separated by very shallow *hoa* channels, and you can walk from one white sand beach to another. Each hotel or pension has its own private *motu* used for barbecue picnics. The cost of an all-day picnic excursion to the Blue Lagoon ranges from 7.500 to 9.900 CFP per person, depending on your hotel or pension. Be sure to take along your T-shirt, hat, sunscreen, mosquito repellent, protective shoes and snorkeling gear. And don't forget your camera.

Reef Islet, also called **île aux Récifs** and **Motu Ai Ai**, are on the south end of Rangiroa, an hour's boat ride across the lagoon. Here you can walk through razor sharp raised coral outcrops called *feo* that resemble miniature fairy castles formed during four million years of erosion. This excursion is also sold for 7.500 to 9.900 CFP, including a picnic on the beach.

The pink sand beaches of **Vahituri**, or **Les Sables Roses**, are 1 1/2 or 2 hours by boat from Avatoru to the southeastern edge of the lagoon. The pink reflections in the sand are caused by Foraminifera deposits and coral residues. You'll enjoy swimming and snorkeling in the lagoon in this lovely area. The cost of this excursion ranges from 9.500 CFP to 11.900 CFP, including a picnic.

The following excursions will take you to discover the wonders of the Rangiroa lagoon.

Oviri Excursions, *Tel./Fax 96.05.87*, is owned by Ugo Angely and three of his friends, who have two boats that are 28-feet and 32-feet long that they use for various excursions. They work out of the Hotel Kia Ora as well as providing private tours that start from the Ohutu quay. They will take you on a 3-hour snorkeling excursion aboard one of their powerful motorboats to drift dive through the Tiputa Pass and the Avatoru Pass. This is 5.000 CFP a person with a minimum of four people. A full-day picnic excursion to Taeo'o (Blue Lagoon) is 8.000 CFP (9.900 CFP when booking through the hotel) and includes a visit to Shark City, where you can see up to 100 sharks. Ugo considers two lemon sharks the stars of the show whenever they appear. His rate for the excursion to Motu Ai Ai (Reef Islet) is also 8.000 CFP (9.900 CFP at Hotel Kia Ora), and he charges 10.000 CFP per person for the excursion to the pink sand beach of Vahituri, while the hotel charges 11.900 CFP per person. A minimum of four people is required when booking through Ugo and the hotel asks for a minimum of six passengers. Ugo's father, Robin Angeley, was one of the original owners of the Kia Ora, and Ugo grew up at the hotel. His English is very good.

Pa'ati Excursions, *Tel. 96.02.57*, is operated by Leon Revault. His picnic excursion for 4-10 people starts from Ohutu quay or the Hotel Kia Ora. His direct charges are 7.500 CFP to take you to Reef Islet and 10.000 CFP for the longer trip to the pink sands of Vahituri (Sables Roses).

Rangiroa Activities, *Tel. 96.03.31/71.02.98; E-mail: p.rohde@mail.pf; www.dolphin-watch.pf; www.snorkeling.pf*. Pascal and Cosetta Rohde, a young French and Italian couple, will take you on 2-hour boat excursion to the pass and for dolphin watching. When the current is incoming from the ocean to the lagoon Pascal will take you through the Tiputa Pass, where you can drift snorkel through the pass into the lagoon. When the current is outgoing you can watch the dolphins riding the current to the open ocean. You may see the big dolphins (Tursiops truncatus), a family of spinner dolphins (Stenella longirostris), or more rarely, the black and white dolphins (Peponocephala electra) that live around the coast of Rangiroa.

A drift-snorkeling excursion is 4.500 CFP and the dolphin watch excursion is also 4.500 CFP, or you can combine the two activities. Between the months of July and November they will take you to look for the humpback whales that come up from Antarctica to breed or give birth in tropical waters.

Raumati Excursions (Hei Hei Te Vahine Te Pua Excursions), *Tel. 96.83.23*, is operated by Raumati Sanford, who has two 12-passenger boats used for excursions. He works with the Hotel Kia Ora as well as the family pensions. He will take a minimum of six people to the Blue Lagoon or Reef Island for 7.500 CFP per person, or to the pink sand beach of Vahituri (Sables Roses) for 10.000 CFP per person. Each excursion includes a barbecue picnic on his private motu. Rates for these excursions are higher if you book through the hotel.

Maurice Taxi Boat, *Tel./Fax 96.76.09* or *cell 78.13.25*. See information under *Motor Boat Rental*.

Ariitini Excursions, *Tel. 96.04.41*, is owned by Judith and Felix Tetua and is located at the Ariitini Village pension. They have two excursion boats for a minimum of six passengers. You can join one of these outings even if you are staying in another pension.

Tane Excursions, *Tel. 72.31.51*, is operated by Marcel Tane Tamaehu, whose wife owns Pension Henriette, close to the Avatoru Marina. He has two locally built boats that he uses for lagoon fishing, deep-sea fishing, shooting the pass or for picnic excursions to Blue Lagoon or Reef Islet for 7.500 CFP per person or to Sables Rose (pink sand beach) for 9.500 CFP per person. I was told by other boat operators in Rangiroa that Tane puts too many people in his boats during these excursions, at the risk of the passengers' safety.

Pearl Farms
  Gauguin's Pearl, *Tel. 93.11.30/78.79.78, Fax 93.11.36; E-mail: phcab@mail.pf*, is operated by Philippe Cabrall. Free guided visits to this black pearl farm, which is built over the lagoon close to the airport, are given Monday through Friday at 8:30am and 2pm. The pearl boutique is open Monday through Saturday from 9am to 5:30pm, and on Sunday from 10am to 12pm and from 2:30 to 5pm. They also work in conjunction with Missir Pearls at Hotel Kia Ora.

Sailing Charter Yachts
  Archipels Cruises (Archipels Croisières), *Tel. 689/56.36.39, Fax 689/ 56.35.87; E-mail: archimoo@mail.pf; www.archipels.com* has a yacht based permanently in Rangiroa. A Tuesday to Friday 4-day/3-night Tuamotu cruise inside the atoll of Rangiroa is 124,000 CFP in the low season and 133.500 CFP per person during the high season. A Saturday to Monday 3-day/2-night cruise inside the lagoon 93.000 CFP to 102.000 CFP per person according to season. These cruises operate all year except in January and the first half of February. One-week cruises on board a Marquises 57 catamaran are also available from Fakarava to Toau and Rangiroa, boarding in Fakarava on Saturday morning and disembarking in Rangiroa at noon on Friday. The cruise dates are scheduled in conjunction with the full moon and guaranteed departure for a minimum of two passengers. The per person cost of this cruise is 220.500 CFP, including taxes, meals and hotel services on board in double cabin occupancy, airport/yacht transfers at boarding and landing sites, as well as all excursions and events specified in program.

Scuba Diving

The lagoon of Rangiroa offers world-class diving. It is essentially a huge inland sea, with a maximum depth of about 27 meters (90 feet), which offers the finest and most abundant of nature's aquaculture. The two passes of **Tiputa** and **Avatoru** are submarine freeways for the passage of fish between the open ocean and the lagoon. The ocean normally has a moderate swell running and near the passes a five-knot current enters or exits rhythmically with the rise and fall of the tide. Static dives in or near the passes can only be done twice a day when the water is still and clear, which is normally at 12-hour intervals. Drift dives are possible on nearly any day, and these "shooting the pass" dives are exhilarating, as you are surrounded by hordes of fish, jacks, tuna, barracuda, manta rays, eagle rays, turtles, dolphins and sharks.

Between December and March huge hammerhead sharks gather to mate outside Tiputa Pass, and the graceful manta rays are most plentiful during their mating season between July and October. There are 15 popular dive sites inside the lagoon, in the passes and on the outer coral reef of Rangiroa. The following diving clubs have qualified instructors who speak English and schedule their dives between 8am and 2pm, depending on the tides, currents, swell and wind conditions. They all accept credit cards and dive packages are available. Equipment is included, but you may feel more secure if you bring your own buoyancy compensator, regulator and depth gauge. You'll also need to bring you certification papers and bring a medical certificate if you are not certified. Transportation is usually provided from your hotel or pension to the dive center.

Blue Dolphins Diving Center, *Tel./Fax 96.03.01, E-mail: bluedolphins@mail.pf; www.bluedolphinsdiving.com.* This busy dive shop, located at the Hotel Kia Ora, offers initiation, exploration and night dives with instructors who speak French, English, German, Spanish, Italian, Japanese or Tahitian. The dive masters are qualified PADI instructors as well as CMAS, BEES1, FFESSM, IANTD and TDI qualified. International certifications are given, including Nitrox Diver, Buddy Diver and Recycler Drager Diver certificates. A fun dive is 7.150 CFP, an introductory dive is 7.700 CFP, and a night dive is 8.800 CFP, plus tax. The dive equipment is 100 percent Scubapro that is renewed every two years.

Raie Manta Club, *Tel. 96.84.80; Cell 72.31.45; Fax 96.85.60; E-mail: raiemantaclub@mail.pf; http://raiemantaclub.free.fr.* The main office is beside the lagoon near Avatoru village, between Pension Herenui and Rangiroa Lodge and there is an annex next to Chez Teina and Marie beside Tiputa Pass. Yves Lefevre is a PADI instructor and international CMAS two-star monitor, French State BEES, 1st level monitor and sea guide. He was the first dive master to open a scuba diving center on Rangiroa in 1985, and his dive centers on Rangiroa, Tikehau and Rurutu are popular throughout the world. Yves and his team of State licensed guides are qualified to give all international examinations at any level and they use complete Scubapro equipment. Video films of your dive are also available. An introductory dive or a fun dive costs 6.000 CFP and a night dive is 7.800 CFP. A 10-dive package is 56.000 CFP.

Rangiroa Paradive, *Tel. 96.05.55; Fax 96.05.50; E-mail: paradive@mail.pf; www.chez.com/paradive.* This dive center is next door to Pension Glorinne near the Tiputa Pass. Bernard Blanc is a PADI Open Water Instructor, international CMAS two-star monitor, French State BEES second level monitor, sea guide and FFESSM instructor. He and his assistant instructors also offer PADI and CMAS training and picnic dives. He charges 6.300 CFP for a normal dive.

The Six Passengers, *Tel. 96.03.05; Tel/Fax 96.02.60; E-mail: the6passengers@mail.pf; www.the6passengers.com.* This dive center is located between the Hotel Kia Ora and Ohotu Point by the Tiputa Pass and is owned by Ugo Mazzavillani. Nanou Chapuisat, the international CMAS two star monitor, is also a BEES 1 and PADI instructor. As the name implies, their boats accommodate only six passengers for dives and diving picnics. They charge 6.400 CFP for one dive, 6.800 CFP for an introductory dive, 7.800 CFP for a night dive, 30.500 CFP for 5 dives and 58.000 CFP for 10 dives. All dives are videotaped and shown at the center when you return. They also feature special honeymoon dives with a video film to take home.

TOPdive, *Tel. 96.05.60/72.39.55; E-mail: info@topdive.com; www.topdive.com* is located beside the lagoon, just a one minute walk to the right of Hotel Kia Ora. Frenchman Eric Bressan, the dive master, is a CMAS two star monitor and PADI Open Water instructor, and is assisted by another qualified French instructor. They have modern equipment including two Zodiacs for eight to nine divers per boat and they provide free pick-up service from the hotels and pensions. They charge 5.900 CFP for any type of dive and a 10-dive package is 53.000 CFP, which can be used in any of the three Topdive centers on Moorea, Bora Bora or Rangiroa. They do not offer night dives.

Cruise & Dive Charters

Tahiti Aggressor, *US contact: Tel. 800/348-2628; Fax 985/384-0817; E-mail: tahiti@aggressor.com; www.aggressor.com.* The *Tahiti Aggressor* is a 106-foot, 18 passenger catamaran that is based year-round in Rangiroa, offering a live-aboard dive program that takes guests to explore the passes and channel entrances of the Tuamotu Atolls. Depending on the weather the itinerary includes departures from Rangiroa or Fakarava, with diving in the passes of Apataki, Toau, Fakarava and Rangiroa. The boat offers state-of-the-art diving facilities and luxurious personal accommodations such as 9 double cabins with private bathroom, a spacious salon with entertainment center, and a partially covered sun deck. For details and rates see chapter on *Planning Your Trip*.

Cruise and Surf/Fish Charters
Cascade, *Tel./Fax 689/43.70.70; cell 689/73.78.10; 881631468727 sat/phone on boat; E-mail: chris@tahitianbluewaterdream.com; www.tahitianbluewaterdream.com / www.wavehunters.com/tuamotus.*

Cascade is a 64-foot steel motor vessel with 4-star live-aboard accommodations for 10 surfers or fishermen in 6 cabins. 60 professional surfboards, top of the line fishing tackle, Jet Ski, kite surfer, kayaks, snorkel and spearfishing gear are also provided. Scuba divers can link up with licensed dive operators in the Tuamotu atolls. Live aboard charters for 10 surfers or deep-sea fishing begin in Rangiroa or Fakarava according to the seasons. Singles can also book. Specialized trips can be made to suit those who charter the whole boat for surfing, diving, adventure and fishing excursions. For details and rates see chapter on *Planning Your Trip.*

Shopping

Atelier Corinne is in Avatoru, across road from Restaurant Le Kai Kai and Pension Martine, *Tel. 96.03.13.* Open daily. She sells black pearl jewelry.

Au Petit Coin de Paradis is a boutique in Avatoru village, selling clothes and gift items.

Black Pearl Island is close to the airport, *Tel. 96.02.99,* with displays of black pearl jewelry.

Carole Pareo is close to Avatoru village, *Tel. 96.82.45,* and shares the same premises as the Arenahio Locations for rental cars, bicycles and motorbikes. Most of the clothing is imported, but you will also find a few local items.

Ciao Rangiroa Video in Avatoru, *Tel./Fax 96.02.60,* rents waterproof video cameras to record your scuba diving memories.

La Boutique located at Hotel Kia Ora, *Tel. 96.03.84,* sells local style clothing, curios, video film, post cards and jewelry.

Lagoon Pearl Boutique, *Tel. 96.04.26,* is between the airport and Novotel Rangiroa Beach Resort, selling black pearl jewelry and clothes.

Ocean Passion, between the airport and Novotel Rangiroa Beach Resort, *Tel./Fax 96.02.72,* sells beautiful original T-shirts, *pareos* and wall hangings of dolphins, rays, fish and the coral gardens of Rangiroa's lagoon. Caroline, the very talented owner of this small shop, will also paint portable size tableaux for you, as well as a specially designed *pareo* or tee shirt, if you will place your order at the beginning of your stay in Rangiroa. Mastercard and Visa accepted.

Raie Manta Club Boutique is adjacent to the scuba diving center in Avatoru, between Pension Herenui and Rangiroa Lodge, *Tel. 96.84.80.* Here you will find a good selection of wildlife postcards, underwater video films, tee shirts and posters.

Taaroa Bijoux, *Tel. 96.03.04,* is beside the lagoon between Hotel Kia Ora and Point Ohutu, offering an interesting selection of black pearl jewelry.

Une Fille A La Vanille Boutique is adjacent to the Six Passengers Dive Center between Hotel Kia Ora and Ohutu Point. It is operated by Madame Denise Thirouard, who also owns Les Relais de Josephine.

Vai Boutique is in Avatoru village, *Tel. 96.85.61*. You will find a few homemade dresses and shirts, tee shirts and hand painted *pareos*.

Practical Information
Banks
Banque de Tahiti has an office in Avatoru village close to the Catholic Church and the *mairie* (town hall), *Tel. 96.85.52*. It is open Monday, Wednesday and Friday, from 8 to 11am and 2 to 4pm, and on Tuesday and Thursday from 8 to 11:30am. Closed on Tuesday and Thursday afternoon. In Tiputa village the Banque de Tahiti operates from the *mairie* on Tuesday from 1:30 to 4pm, and on Thursday from 8 to 11:30am.

Banque Socredo is located beside the *mairie* of Avatoru, *Tel. 96.85.63*, and is open on Monday, Wednesday and Friday from 8am to 12pm, and on Monday through Thursday from 1:30 to 4:30pm. Banque Socredo, *Tel. 96.75.57*, also has an office at the *mairie* in Tiputa, which is open Monday and Thursday, 8am to 12pm.

Doctors
Dr. Guy Thirouard has an office in Avatoru, *Tel. 96.85.85*, residence *Tel. 96.04.43*, or cell phone *71.70.74*.

Dentist
Dr. Philippe Pujol, *Tel. 96.05.00*, has an office next to Lagoon Pearl Boutique, between the airport and Novotel Rangiroa Beach Resort.

Hospitals
A government operated medical center is located in Avatoru village, *Tel. 96.03.75* between 7:30am and 3:30pm and on Friday from 7:30am to 2:30pm. Outside these hours you can reach emergency service at *78.60.18*. The hospital has an ambulance. There is an infirmary in Tiputa village, *Tel. 96.03.96*.

Internet
Taaroa Web, *Tel. 96.03.04*, is operated by Florent Legeron, who speaks English and provides the only Internet service in the Tuamotu Archipelago. His office is located in the same building with Taaroa Bijoux, between Hotel Kia Ora and Point Ohutu. Open daily 9am to 7pm. He charges 350 CFP for each 15 minutes spent on-line. You can bring your own laptop and hook it up to his facilities and he also has a web camera and printer.

Magasins (Food Stores)
Magasin Daniel is the best-stocked store in Avatoru village and sells wine, beer and a few fresh vegetables.
Magasin Heiura, *Tel. 96.04.75*, is a new food store located in the airport area close to the Novotel Rangiroa Beach Resort.
Magasin Kahaia is a small store located on the lagoon side of the road between Hotel Kia Ora and Point Ohutu.

Pharmacy
The **Pharmacie de Rangiroa**, *Tel. 93.12.35*, is a new building in Avatoru village, across the road from the Catholic Church. It is open Monday-Friday from 7am to 12:30pm and from 2:30 to 6:30pm; on Saturday from 7am to 12:30pm and 4:30 to 6:30 pm; and on Sunday from 10 to 11:30am.

Police
The French *gendarmerie* is beside the lagoon between Hotel Kia Ora and the airport, *Tel. 96.03.61 or cell phone 78.82.45*.

Post Office & Telecommunications Office
A Post Office is located in Avatoru village, *Tel. 96.83.81* and another is in Tiputa village, *Tel. 96.73.80*.

MANIHI
This is one of the friendliest villages in the Tuamotu Islands. The children love to smile at visitors, greeting them with "Bonjour, Madam," "Bonjour, Monsieur." The first black pearl farm was started in **Manihi** in 1968, and with the development of the black pearl industry in the Tuamotu Archipelago, the pretty little atoll of Manihi has become synonymous with the *po'e rava*. This is the Tahitian name for the rare and beautiful Tahitian black pearl. Manihi's famous lagoon, which is 5.6 kilometers (3 1/2 miles) wide by 30 kilometers (19 miles) long, is as lovely as the high quality rainbow-hued pearls that are produced in the black pearl farms that are built on stilts around the periphery of the transparent lagoon. There were 66 of these farms in 2004, but only a few of them were still operating, due to the high taxes demanded by the government and the low investment return for the small pearl farmer.

Seen from the air, the lagoon of Manihi presents a picturesque palette of glimmering greens and blues, with white and pink beaches in a framing of feathery green coconut palms. A close range view of this crystal clear lagoon is even better, as you can see the vividly painted tropical fish feeding in the coral gardens on the white sand bottom, several feet below the water's surface.

You can fly to Manihi from Tahiti in just one hour and fifteen minutes or hop aboard a cargo boat for a cruise of 520 kilometers (322 miles). Should you

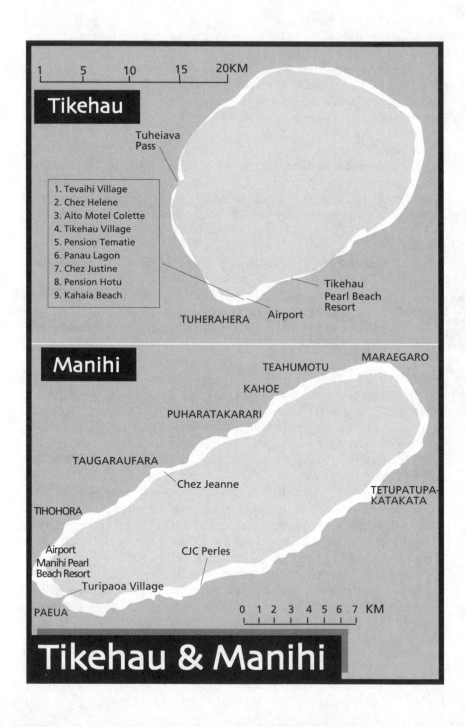

20KM

Tikehau

Tuheiava
Pass

1. Tevaihi Village
2. Chez Helene
3. Aito Motel Colette
4. Tikehau Village
5. Pension Tematie
6. Panau Lagon
7. Chez Justine
8. Pension Hotu
9. Kahaia Beach

TUHERAHERA

Airport

Tikehau
Pearl Beach
Resort

Manihi

MARAEGARO

TEAHUMOTU

KAHOE

PUHARATAKARARI

TAUGARAUFARA

Chez Jeanne

TETUPATUPA-
KATAKATA

TIHOHORA

Airport
Manihi Pearl
Beach Resort

CJC Perles

Turipaoa Village

PAEUA

0 1 2 3 4 5 6 7 KM

Tikehau & Manihi

choose to fly, you will be transferred by mini-bus or electric car from the airport to the Manihi Pearl Beach Resort, or by boat to the village of Turipaoa or some distant *motu*, depending on where you are staying.

Turipaoa is a sun-baked little village with colorful houses of limestone and clapboard lining the two streets that run straight through the village for about two blocks along the ocean on one side and the lagoon on the other side. The houses are shaded by breadfruit trees and bordered with frangipani, hibiscus and bougainvillea. This village is home to some of Manihi's 789 inhabitants, while others remain on the pearl farms an hour's boat ride from the village. The favorite hangout in Turipaoa village is under the shade of a giant *tou* tree with orange flowers beside the Turipaoa pass. The old folks sit on benches under the tree and watch the comings and goings of the supply ships from Tahiti and the boats from the pearl farms. This is more interesting to them than sitting at home watching television.

Just a few years ago almost everyone who lived in Manihi was involved in the pearl business, even though they may have had other jobs as well. Some of the pearl farms are now abandoned since the market for pearls took a dive, and all around the lagoon you can see the buoys that once floated on the surface, marking the presence of pearl oysters suspended below the water in wire baskets. These buoys have drifted onto the shores of the motu islets, creating a new form of pollution. Many of the Paumotu people, including grown men and women and even babies, wear necklaces, bracelets, earrings and rings of 18 karat gold and exquisite pearls of peacock blue, fly-wing green, aubergine or shiny black.

The warm waters of Manihi are ideal for swimming, snorkeling, or diving at any time of the year. You can spear fish on the reef or line fish in the lagoon. You can even watch the brilliantly colored parrotfish as they nibble their lunch in the live coral gardens. Manihi Blue Nui is a scuba diving center based at Manihi Pearl Beach Resort with a CMAS and PADI instructor, which offers diving in the lagoon, at the pass or outside the coral reef, plus night dives and underwater filming excursions.

Arrivals & Departures
Arriving by Air
Air Tahiti flies from Tahiti to Manihi seven days a week, with a 75-minute direct flight on Tuesday and during the high season on Friday and Sunday. The other flights stop in Rangiroa or Ahe. You can fly from Bora Bora to Manihi every Monday, Wednesday, Friday and Sunday, with an aircraft change in Rangiroa on Wednesday and Sunday. From Tikehau to Manihi the Wednesday flight stops first in Rangiroa and there is a direct flight on Saturdays. The one-way fare from Tahiti to Manihi is 18.500 CFP and 26.000 CFP from Bora Bora to Manihi. The one-way fare from Rangiroa or Tikehau to Manihi is 10.000 CFP.

Air Tahiti reservations: Tahiti, *Tel. 86.42.42*; in Manihi *Tel. 96.43.34/ 96.42.71*.

The airport is on a *motu islet* and part of the airstrip is still covered over by big blocks of coral that occurred during a tropical depression a few years ago. The ATR-42 airplanes have to stop before the good part of the runway ends and when you descend from the airplane you will board an electric car or mini-bus to be driven to the Manihi Pearl Beach Resort, if that is your destination. All other passengers will be driven to the old airport terminal, where you have to wait for your baggage to arrive. If you have reservations with a pension or yacht charter company, then you will be met at the airport and driven to your lodging or transferred by boat. Otherwise, you can catch a boat ride to the village with some of the residents who have come to meet arriving family members. Air Tahiti does not provide any boat transportation from the airport to the village, and they are not responsible for your baggage once it is delivered to the airport terminal.

You can also get to Manihi by chartering an airplane in Tahiti from **Wan Air**, *Tel. 50.44.17, cell 77.03.79*; **Air Archipels**, *Tel. 81.30.30*; or **Air Tahiti**, *Tel. 86.42.42*.

Arriving By Boat

Mareva Nui, *Tel. 42.25.53, Fax 42.25.57*, is a 181-foot steel ship that transports cargo between Tahiti and the Tuamotu atolls. It leaves Tahiti every 15 days for the 8-day round-trip voyage, and calls at Manihi after stopping at several atolls, which may include Makatea, Mataiva, Tikehau, Rangiroa and Ahe. There are 12 berths but no cabins and the one-way fare from Tahiti to Manihi is 8.200 CFP, plus 2.200 CFP per day for three meals.

St. Xavier Maris Stella III, *Tel. 42.23.58, Fax 43.03.73*, can transport 12 passengers who sleep on the bridge for 8.484 CFP between Tahiti and Manihi, including three meals a day. The ship leaves Papeete every 15 days and the itinerary varies, taking from 7 to 10 days for the round-trip voyage.

Vai Aito, *Tel. 43.99.96, Fax 43.53.04*, visits Tikehau, Rangiroa and Ahe before calling at Manihi during the 7-8-day round-trip voyages from Tahiti to the Tuamotu Islands. The cost from Tahiti to Manihi is 10.706 CFP per person including three meals daily and taxes.

See more information in Chapter 6, *Planning Your Trip*. All the ships stop at the Turipaoa quay beside the pass in Manihi.

Departing By Air

Air Tahiti flies from Manihi to Rangiroa and Papeete on Monday, Wednesday, Saturday and Sunday, and from Manihi to Ahe and Papeete on Tuesday and Thursday. There is a direct Manihi-Papeete flight on Friday and Sunday during the holiday seasons. There is a Manihi-Tikehau-Bora Bora flight each Monday and a Manihi-Tikehau-Raiatea-Bora Bora flight each Friday. **Air**

Tahiti reservations in Manihi: *Tel. 96.43.34* and the airport number is *Tel. 96.42.71*. The Air Tahiti office is located in Jean Marie's supermarket in the village. If you are staying in the village or on a motu islet you should be at the airport one hour and 30 minutes prior to departure, and your luggage will have to be transferred from the old airport terminal to the landing strip in time for the arrival of the airplane. If you are staying at Manihi Pearl Beach Resort they will take care of getting your luggage to the airport, then drive you direct to the waiting shelter 30 minutes before departure.

Departing By Boat
     St. Xavier Maris Stella III, *Tel. 42.23.58*, leaves Manihi every 15 days, stopping at several of the western Tuamotu atolls before returning to Papeete. Meals are served on board. *Mareva Nui*, *Tel. 42.25.53*, *Fax 42.25.57*, calls at 9-10 other atolls after leaving Manihi each 15 days. A berth costs up to 8.200 CFP, depending on how long the journey takes, and three daily meals are 2.200 CFP extra. *Vai Aito*, *Tel. 43.99.96*, may visit Ahe, Aratika or Kauehi and Fakarava before returning to Papeete. You'll sleep on deck and pay according to the number of days it takes. Meals are served on board.
     See more information under *Inter-Island Cruise Ships, Passenger Boats and Freighters* in Chapter 6, *Planning Your Trip*.

Orientation
     The airport is at the southwest end of Manihi, on the same *motu* where the Manihi Pearl Beach Resort is located. Transfers from the airport to the Manihi Pearl Beach Resort are made by electric car, just a two-minute ride. Manihi's only village, **Turipaoa**, is across the lagoon from the airport, a 15-minute boat ride from the airport. The village is built next to the Tairapa Pass, which provides the only navigable entry into the lagoon. A sheltered basin provides moorings for several boats and has lights at night. In the village you will find a *magasin* store, a bakery and a restaurant-snack.

Where to Stay
Deluxe
     MANIHI PEARL BEACH RESORT, *B.P. 1, Manihi Tuamotu. Tel. 689/ 96.42.73; Fax 689/96.42.72; E-mail: welcome@manihipearlbeach.pf. Reservations: Tel. 689/50.84.52; Fax 689/43.17.86; E-mail: carine.keck@smphotels.pf; www.pearlresorts.com. 41 units. EP Rates single/double: standard beach bungalow 28.000 CFP, superior beach bungalow 38.000 CFP; overwater bungalow 52.000 CFP; premium overwater bungalow 60.000 CFP; third person 5.000 CFP; meal plan with breakfast and dinner 7.500 CFP per person; meal plan with breakfast, lunch and dinner 10.000 CFP per person per day; Continental breakfast, 1.800 CFP; American breakfast 2.400 CFP; lunch (set menu) 2.500 CFP per person; dinner (set menu) 5.100 CFP per person; bottle of wine 3.500*

CFP; bottle of champagne 11.000 CFP. One-way transfer to/from airport 1.000 CFP. One or two children between 3 and 12 years old sharing parent's room are free of charge on accommodation basis and have 50% discount on AP/MAP plans (excluding beverages) and Airport/Hotel/Airport transfers when provided by the hotel. Babies and children under 3 years old are free of charge on accommodation, meal plans and transfers. Cribs are free. Add 5% hotel tax to room rates and 6% value added tax to room rates and prepaid meal plans, plus 150 CFP municipal tax per person per day. A 10% value added tax is applicable to other services unless otherwise specified. All major credit cards.

The five-star hotel is located on the same *motu* as the airport, and is 4 kilometers (2.5 miles) across the lagoon from the main village. There are 5 standard beach bungalows, 17 superior beach bungalows, 14 deluxe overwater bungalows and 5 premium overwater bungalows, all built in the traditional Polynesian style of pointed pandanus thatched roof and local woods. Each of the very attractively decorated bungalows has a ceiling fan, a mini-bar refrigerator, coffee/tea facilities, hot water shower, hair-dryer, international direct dial telephone, television with two channels and DVD player, individual safe and sundeck. All bungalows have electric mosquito repellent plugs. Laundry service is also available.

All the overwater bungalows have a glass bottom table so that you can watch the colorful parrotfish, Picassofish and ever-hungry *nape* (diamond-scaled mullet) feeding in the clear lagoon below. The five premium overwater bungalows are the same size as the deluxe overwater bungalows (51m² or 549 square feet) but they are further apart, providing just a little more privacy. In addition to having the same amenities as the other units, these premium bungalows also have a CD player. They are decorated with plants and bathrobes are provided for guests' use while in residence. There are two overwater bungalows designed for physically challenged guests in wheel-chairs, and the hotel's public areas and pool are also wheelchair accessible. The hotel staff will assist handicapped guests when being transferred by boat between the hotel and village or other boat excursions.

The first-class Poe Rava restaurant serves French cuisine, seafood and local specialties. The bar, boutique, black pearl shop and billiards room are all located in separate buildings. Beside the white sand beach and the lagoon is a large fresh water swimming pool, and the Manihi Blue Nui scuba diving center is adjacent to the pier. A snorkeling pier has been added, with steps leading into the lagoon and a shower on the pier. This is where guests feed the fish, so you'll be sure to find a welcome party of brightly painted lagoon fish waiting to accompany you while you snorkel.

Free activities for hotel guests only include use of bicycles, outrigger paddle canoes and kayaks, snorkeling gear, swimming pool, bacci ball court, volleyball, badminton, billiards and mini-golf. Paid excursions and activities include a visit to a black pearl farm for 2.500 CFP, a picnic on an uninhabited motu islet for 8.500 CFP, hand line fishing for 1.900 CFP, a tour of the atoll by boat for 5.500 CFP, drift snorkeling in the pass for 1.900 CFP, boat rental with captain for 9.500 CFP per hour, a sunset cruise for 2.000 CFP and deep sea fishing for 15.000 CFP per hour with a 2-hour minimum requirement. Boat rentals are for hotel guests only. Following your scuba dive outings with Manihi Blue Nui you can watch a video film of Manihi's underwater world at 7pm each evening in the dive center.

Feeding the fish is a daily pleasure each morning at 9:30am at the swimming pontoon. A coconut show, pareo tying demonstration, traditional weaving lessons and tamure dance lessons are scheduled regularly at the Miki Miki bar. Tahitian dance shows are presented twice a week during dinner. See more information in *Where to Eat* in this chapter and *Best Places to Stay* chapter.

Manihi Pearl Beach Resort is one of French Polynesia's most popular destinations for honeymooners and other loving couples. The hotel offers a number of suggestions for Romantic Interludes. A Romantic Breakfast for two can be served on your terrace for 8.500 CFP per couple, and if you are staying in an overwater bungalow, you will certainly want to order a Canoe Breakfast, which is delivered by outrigger paddle canoe and served on your terrace. This costs 8.500 CFP per couple. A Private Cocktail party for two is 7.820 CFP and a Champagne Heaven party is 15.300 CFP for two. A Candlelight Dinner in the restaurant is 23.800 CFP for two and a private Starlight Dinner with champagne is served on your terrace for 28.333 CFP. Romantic Escapades programs include a Sunset Cruise for two for 26.633 CFP, a private boat tour of the lagoon for 53.833 CFP and a Barbecue Picnic on the Motu that includes champagne served at an elegantly dressed table, for 77.633 CFP per couple.

A Polynesian Wedding Ceremony is the ultimate touch of romance for honeymooners or couples who wish to renew their vows. The hotel offers a Maohi wedding package for 77.633 CFP per couple, a Miki Miki wedding for 107.100 CFP or a Poe Rava wedding for 130.900. These rates all include 10% VAT. Contact the hotel for details on Romantic Gateway and be sure to have a look at their website as they have installed a webcam to entice you.

Moderate

CHEZ JEANNE, *Turipaoa, Manihi 98771. Tel. 689/96.42.90, Fax 689/ 96.42.91, E-mail: motel.chez.jeanne@caramail.com. On Motu Tangaraufara, a private islet, 10 kilometers (6.2 miles) from the airport and 14 kilometers (8.7 miles) from the village. Free round-trip boat transfers. EP Rates: beach bungalow 10.000 CFP single/double/triple; overwater bungalow 14.000 CFP single/double. Breakfast and dinner 2.100 CFP; breakfast, lunch and dinner 3.900 CFP per person per day. Add 6% percent value added tax to room rates. A 10% value added tax is applicable to other services. Mastercard, Visa.*

Jeanne and Guy Huerta have two clean beach bungalows, each with a double and single bed, and private bathroom with cold water. A sliding glass door leads onto a small terrace and there are no screens on windows and doors. They also have a "Honeymoon Suite", which is an overwater bungalow with a double bed, kitchenette and private bathroom with cold water and a sun deck over the lagoon. House linens are furnished. Electricity is provided by solar panels and electric generator and each bungalow has an electric fan.

Meals are provided on request and will be delivered to your bungalow. Do not expect fresh lagoon fish as Guy, a Frenchman, said that he doesn't have time to go fishing or to arrange for someone to deliver fish to the pension. He is usually busy taking care of his pearl farm and his other equipment. Although the water is supposedly potable, you should include a sufficient supply of bottled water for your needs. Beach chairs are provided to sit under the shade of the palm trees or on the white sand beach, and kayaks are available for exploring the lagoon. Scuba divers are charged 3.000 CFP per person for boat transfers to the Manihi Pearl Beach Resort to dive with Manihi Blue Nui. A visit to the family's pearl farm is included in your room charge. A small boutique on the premises includes paintings by the Huerta daughter as well as a few pieces of black pearl jewelry.

Economy

PENSION VAINUI PERLES, *Turipaoa, Manihi 98771. Tel. 689/96.42.89; Fax 689/96.43.30; E-mail: pension-vainui@mail.pf. On Motu Marakorako, 12 kilometers (7.5 miles) from the airport and main village. Round-trip boat transfers 1.000 CFP per person. AP Rates: fare or room with all meals included 10.000 CFP per person. Half-fare for child 3-12 years. Add 6% percent value added tax to room rates and meals. A 10% value added tax is applicable to other services. Mastercard, Visa.*

This is a private motu in a remote location 30 minutes by boat from the airport. Very basic accommodations are available in 8 rooms facing the lagoon, including 2 single rooms and 3 bungalows with two bedrooms in each unit. All guests share the bathroom with cold water shower. House linens are furnished. Meals are served on a shaded terrace next to the beach of white and pink sand. This pension is managed by an older Polynesian man, who is assisted by his daughter and a worker. Although the food served is very good, complaints in April 2004 reported that the rooms are old and decrepit, smell of mildew and are filled with cockroaches. Although their brochure advertises several activities there are none available, and there is no longer a family pearl farm to visit.

Where to Eat

POE RAVA RESTAURANT *at Manihi Pearl Beach Resort, Tel. 96.42.73. Open daily, serving breakfast from 6:30 to 9:30am, lunch from 12 to 3pm, and dinner from 7 to 9pm. All credit cards.*

A Continental breakfast is 1.800 CFP and the breakfast buffet with a full

American breakfast is 2.400 CFP. The luncheon menu offers *poisson cru*, sashimi, Caesar salad with chicken, burgers and fries, grilled lagoon fish and grilled sirloin steak. The set lunch menu is 2.500 CFP and the set dinner menu is 5.100 CFP. A local band plays island style music in the restaurant during dinner on Tuesday and Friday, and a Tahitian dance show is presented at 8pm each Wednesday and Saturday.

Sports & Recreation

See information for Manihi Pearl Beach Resort under *Where to Stay* in this chapter.

Scuba Diving

Manihi Blue Nui Dive Center is located at the Manihi Pearl Beach Resort, *Tel./Fax 96.42.17; E-mail: Manihi.blue.nui@mail.pf*. This well equipped dive shop has showers, lockers, hangers for wet suits and a covered aluminum boat for 16 divers. The diving gear is Sherwood brand, with 30 tanks and a complete range of equipment. Waterproof lights are available for rent for 500 CFP per dive. Gilles Petre, who is based primarily in Bora Bora, manages all the Blue Nui Dive Centers. His staff in Manihi includes dive master Thierry Cadeau, who is a PADI, BEES and CMAS qualified diving instructor. The rates are 6.700 CFP for one dive, initiation dives are 7.500 CFP, and night dives are 8.000 CFP, including all the equipment. The Blue Nui Dive Centers in Manihi, Tikihau, Iahaa and Bora Bora all offer dive packages that can be used in any or all of the centers. These packages sell for 31.000 CFP for 5 dives and 59.000 CFP for 10 dives.

A Paumotu Picnic

As beautiful as they are to look at, the parrot fish and some of the other fish species in Manihi are reportedly dangerous to eat because of **ciguatera**, which I was told is caused by the iron fencing used for all the black pearl farms that now blanket the lagoon. Some of the pearl farmers who live on motu islets on the opposite side of the lagoon from the village say that they have no trouble eating any of the fish. When you take a lagoon excursion to the motu for a barbecue picnic, your guide will spear some fish for the grill. He knows which ones to choose, which will usually be grouper, a sweet tasting fish. If you don't like the idea of peeling away the charred skin with your fingers, and looking at the fish head and eyes, or fighting the flies for your meal, then choose a piece of chicken or steak instead. But if you want to have a Paumotu-style picnic on the motu, then you'll squeeze some lime juice on the fish and fan the flies away with a leaf and dig in for a delightful meal.

Manihi offers excellent diving conditions in shallow, warm, clear water, with mild currents in the pass. The dive sites are only five minutes away from the dive center, reached by a comfortable speedboat that is custom designed for diving. The pass is south to north with the main wind from the east, and for beginners, a site outside the reef is used that is protected from the main wind by the village of Turipaoa.

Tairapa Pass is one of the most popular dive sites, offering drift dives with the incoming or outgoing currents. You'll feel as though you are soaring through space with the tuna, sharks, schools of barracuda, jack fish, rays and turtles. **The Drop Off** is a wall dive on the ocean side of Manihi, which descends from 3 to 1,350 meters (10 to 4,500 feet) deep. This site abounds with gray sharks, Napoleon fish, giant jack fish, schools of snapper and sea pike barracuda, plus the deep-sea fish like tuna and marlin. Each July thousands of groupers gather here to breed, offering one of the most fascinating underwater events in the world.

The Circus is the name given to a location between the pass and the lagoon, which is a favorite hangout for eagle and manta rays. Underwater photographers can get close to the graceful manta rays as they glide up and down in an average underwater depth of 9 meters (30 feet). These curious and friendly creatures sometimes have a wingspan up to four meters (13 feet) wide, and remain here all year long.

A scenic dive on the **West Point** of the ocean side reveals fire coral, antler coral and flower petal coral, among others, which are visible for up to 60 meters (200 feet) in the incredibly clear water. Shark feeding is best at **The Break**, a large cut in the outer reef, where a coral amphitheater provides the scenery for a multitude of reef sharks, including black tip, white tip, gray sharks and an occasional hammer head, who show up for the free handouts of tuna heads.

Shopping

The Manihi Pearl Beach Resort has the Vahine Purotu Boutique and Pearls by Corrion sells pearls and pearl jewelry on the premises. Just a five-minute walk or an even quicker bike ride from the hotel is La Boutique Mareva, *Tel./Fax 689/96.43.28; E-mail: marevacoquille@hotmail.com.* This is the home of Mareva and Guy Coquille, who formerly owned and managed the Kaina Village. Mareva has a nice selection of black pearl jewelry.

You can also buy pearls in Turipaoa village, where you may encounter some of the pearl farmers who have set jewelry as well as loose pearls. It is best to learn something about pearls first, so that you will be able to determine if the pearl is not a reject or a pearl that has been harvested early for control purposes. The best quality pearls stay inside the oyster for 18 months, and have a lovely orient or luster. See more information under Shopping in the *Basic Information* chapter.

Visits to a Pearl Farm

Although there are dozens of black pearl farms inside the lagoon of Manihi, these operations are not generally open to the public. You cannot just rent a boat and visit a pearl farm with the expectation of buying a pearl at a discount rate direct from the owner. He sells his pearls in bulk to the wholesale buyers in Tahiti, or to buyers who come from Japan, Switzerland, the United States and other countries to buy in quantity for big jewelry companies. Some of the pearl farms in Manihi, such as **Pai Moana Pearls**, have their own retail outlets in Papeete and other islands.

Pearls by Corrion, also known as **CJC Perles,** is the only pearl farm in Manihi that allows regular visits, which are conducted each Monday, Wednesday and Friday morning. The boat leaves the Manihi Pearl Beach Resort at 8am, with a minimum of two people, and the excursion lasts 2 1/2 hours. During this time you will learn practically all there is to know about the *Pinctada Margaritifera* black lipped oyster that gives us this precious gift from the rainbow-hued lagoon of Manihi. The guide is well informed, as she also works in the Pearls by Corrion boutique located at the hotel, where you can buy black pearls from the farm. Please do not expect to fly into Manihi at noon and be taken to a pearl farm that afternoon. It just doesn't work that way because the farm is on the other side of the lagoon and the boat and pilot may be otherwise occupied. The guided boat tour to the pearl farm costs 2.500 CFP per person.

Practical Information

Banks

There are no banks in Manihi.

Hospital

A government-operated infirmary is located in Turipaoa village, *Tel. 96.43.67.* The nurse is on duty from 7-11am and from 4-6pm.

Post Office

A new **Post Office and Telecommunications Office** is located in Turipaoa village facing the marina, *Tel. 96.42.22.* You'll find telephone booths in this building, as well as a couple more in the village and at the airport, and a public phone is located at the Manihi Pearl Beach Resort. They all accept phone cards.

TIKEHAU

Tikehau is a South Sea island dream come true, an escapist's haven of seclusion that is less than an hour's flight from Tahiti and just 20 minutes by plane from Rangiroa. Tikehau is one of the most popular atolls in the Tuamotu Archipelago, because of its natural beauty and the friendliness of the 400 inhabitants.

In the Paumotu language Tikehau means "peaceful landing" and when the Russian navigator Kotzbue discovered the atoll in 1815, he named it Krusenstern Island. The old village was destroyed by a cyclone in 1906 and the residents moved to higher ground and built their homes in Tuherahera on the southwest side of the atoll. This is a clean, quiet and pretty little village, with lots of flowers and fruit trees surrounding the large concrete houses that are situated on big lots, with lots of lawn space between neighbors. Here you'll find the *mairie* (town hall), post office and telecommunications center, school, infirmary, three *magasin* stores, bakery, Protestant temple, Catholic church, Seventh-Day Adventist church, Sanito temple and most of the pensions and guest houses. There is no bank in Tikehau. Three coral sand roads connect Tuherahera with the airport and the road follows the coast line around the *motu*, where you will see new settlements of the anti-cyclone MTR houses, as well as new concrete houses, which are built by the new generation who have moved back to the old village.

Most of the guesthouses or pensions are located between the airport and a pretty white sand beach. Tall, stately ironwood trees, *Casuarina equisetifolia*, also known as Australian pine or *aito*, border the beaches, and you can hear the wind whistling through the branches while you watch the white fairy terns soaring overhead.

The barrier reef surrounding Tikehau is almost continuous and 150-meter (492-feet) wide Tuhieava Pass, on the west coast, is the only entrance into the lagoon. Immediately to the left of the pass is Motu Teonai, which contains a small village of about 10 houses belonging to fishing families. Copra is produced in the old village of Maiai, on the northeast side of the atoll, and this is where you will find a religious community called Eden, where cruise boats are usually welcomed. Many members of this sect are Chinese from Tahiti who gather here during holidays and long weekends.

Tikehau's lagoon is rich with sea life, whose forms and hues defy even the most active imagination. There are brain coral and stag horn corals, in a myriad of shapes and colors. Soft corals and sponges, tubeworms with lively colored feathered tips. Reef clams with blue, brown, purple and green mantles, orange crown-of-thorn starfish, pink sea anemones, and a whole parade of brightly painted fish.

When **Jacques Cousteau's** research group made a study of the Polynesian atolls in 1987, they declared the lagoon of Tikehau to contain the most fish of any of the lagoons in French Polynesia. Two scientific studies of the fishing industry were made in 2003, reporting that of Tikehau's 510 inhabitants each adult consumes an average of 140 kilos (308 lbs.) of fish per year and that 95% of the fish eaten come from wire enclosures in the lagoon called fish parks. Some 12.5 tons of fish are caught in the Tikehau lagoon each year and 8.5 tons of this number are sent to Tahiti. There has been no evidence of ciguatera fish poisoning in Tikehau, and all the lagoon fish are considered edible. The choice fish include parrotfish, grouper, long-nose emperor fish, soldier fish and jack fish. Most of the family-owned pensions serve a variety of fresh fish to their guests, with little or no meat or chicken on the menu. A few attempts were made to harvest the *Pinctada Margaritifera* oyster that produces black pearls, but due to a lack of plankton in the lagoon, most of these pearl farms are now closed. Surfers seek the swells of the sea as it crashes on the reef beside Tuheiava Pass.

Arrivals & Departures

Arriving by Air

Air Tahiti flies direct from Tahiti to Tikehau each Tuesday, Wednesday, Thursday (during holiday seasons), Friday and twice on Saturday, with 55-minute flights. Each Monday, Friday, Saturday and Sunday one of the ATR-42 flights from Tahiti to Tikehau stops in Rangiroa. There is a direct flight from Manihi to Tikehau each Monday and Friday. You can fly direct from Bora Bora to Tikehau each Thursday, and with a stop in Rangiroa on Monday, Wednesday, Friday, Saturday and Sunday. You'll have to change aircraft in Rangiroa on Monday and Friday. **Air Tahiti reservations**: Tahiti, *Tel. 86.42.42*, in Tikehau *Tel. 96.22.66*.

The one-way airfare from Tahiti to Tikehau is 15.300 CFP, the one-way fare from Rangiroa to Tikehau is 5.200 CFP, the one-way fare from Manihi to Tikehau is 10.000 CFP, and the one-way fare from Bora Bora to Tikehau is 23.000 CFP.

You can also get to Tikehau by chartering an airplane in Tahiti from **Wan Air**, *Tel. 50.44.17, cell 77.03.79*; **Air Archipels**, *Tel. 81.30.30*; or **Air Tahiti**, *Tel. 86.42.42*.

Arriving by Boat

Mareva Nui, *Tel. 42.25.53, Fax 42.25.57*, is a 181-foot steel ship that transports cargo between Tahiti and the Tuamotu atolls. It leaves Tahiti every 15 days, stopping in Makatea and Mataiva before arriving in Tikehau. There are 12 berths on board but no cabin. The one-way fare from Tahiti to Tikehau is 3.850 CFP and three meals a day cost 2.200 CFP per person.

St. Xavier Maris Stella III, *Tel. 42.23.58*, can transport 12 passengers who have to sleep on the deck until the berths are repaired. The fare from Tahiti to Tikehau is 7.710 CFP per person, including 3 meals a day. The ship leaves Papeete every 15 days for 7-10 day voyages.

Vai Aito, *Tel. 43.99.96, Fax 43.53.04*, calls at Tikehau 2-3 times a month, providing overnight service from Papeete. It costs 5.353 CFP for deck space for 12 passengers, which includes three meals a day.

See more information in Chapter 6, *Planning Your Trip*.

Departing by Air
Air Tahiti flies direct from Tikehau to Tahiti each Monday, Wednesday, Thursday (during holiday seasons), Friday, Saturday and twice on Sunday. The flight from Tikehau stops in Rangiroa enroute to Tahiti on Tuesday, Wednesday, Friday and Saturday. You can fly from Tikehau to Manihi on Wednesday, changing planes in Rangiroa, and direct on Saturday. There is a non-stop flight from Tikehau to Bora Bora on Monday and Friday for 23.000 CFP and a direct flight from Tikehau to Raiatea on Friday, for 23.000 CFP. **Air Tahiti reservations** in Tikehau, *Tel. 96.22.66.*

Departing by Boat
Mareva Nui, Tel. 42.25.53, calls at 12 other atolls after leaving Tikehau each 15 days, and the trip back to Tahiti takes 7 days. *St. Xavier Maris Stella III, Tel. 42.23.58,* leaves Tikehau every 15 days for Fakarava and several other western Tuamotu atolls before returning to Papeete. You can sleep on the deck with three daily meals included. Fares are determined by length of voyage to Tahiti. *Vai Aito, Tel. 43.99.96,* leaves Tikehau twice a month for Ahe, Manihi, Aratika, Kauehi or Fakarava, and arrives in Papeete after about six days. Meals are served on board.
See more information under *Inter-Island Cruise Ships, Passenger Boats and Freighters* in Chapter 6, *Planning Your Trip.*

Orientation
Most of the residents of Tikehau live in **Tuherahera village** on the southern end of the atoll, where small boats can enter the lagoon through a pass in the coral reef. The almost circular interior lagoon is 26 kilometers (16 miles) wide, bordered by white sand beaches. A 10-kilometer (6.2-mile) dirt road circles the *motu* of Tuherahera, which you can explore on bicycle.

Where to Stay & Eat
Deluxe
TIKEHAU PEARL BEACH RESORT, *B.P. 20, Tuherahera, Tikehau 98778. Tel. 689/96.23.00; Fax 689/96.23.01; E-mail: welcome@tikehaupearlbeach.pf; www.pearlresorts.com. Reservations: Tel. 689/50.84.54; Fax 689/43.17.86; E-mail: raina.plantier@spmhotels.pf. 38 units. EP Rates single/double: beach bungalow 38.000 CFP, deluxe beach bungalow 45.000 CFP; overwater bungalow 48.000 CFP; premium overwater bungalow 60.000 CFP; overwater suite 70.000 CFP; third person 5.000 CFP; Continental breakfast 1.800 CFP; American breakfast 2.400 CFP; lunch (set menu) 2.500 CFP; dinner (set menu) 5.100 CFP; MAP meal plan with breakfast and dinner 7.500 CFP per person; AP meal plan with breakfast, lunch and dinner 10.000 CFP per person; one-way boat transfer to or from airport 2.000 CFP per person. One or two children between 3 and 12 years old sharing parent's room are free of charge*

on accommodation basis and have 50% discount on AP/MAP plans (excluding beverages) and Airport/Hotel/Airport transfers when provided by the hotel. Babies and children under 3 years old are free of charge on accommodation, meal plans and transfers. Cribs are free. Add 5% hotel tax to room rates and 6% value added tax to room rates and prepaid meal plans, plus 150 CFP municipal tax per person per day. A 10% value added tax is applicable to other services unless otherwise specified. All major credit cards.

This 4-star hotel is located on Motu Tianoa, 3 kilometers (1.9 miles) east of Tuherahera village in a group of islets called Ohotu. The hotel opened in 2001 with 8 beach bungalows, 6 deluxe beach bungalows with air-conditioning, 8 overwater bungalows and 8 premium overwater bungalows. A 2004 project added 8 premium overwater suites with air-conditioning. All the bungalows have thatched roofs, walls of woven palm fronds, woven pandanus matting on the ceiling and split bamboo on the walls inside the bungalows. The furniture is made of rich-toned local woods and consists of a king-size bed or two twin beds, a single daybed, writing desk, small table and chairs. There is a ceiling fan, telephone satellite television, mini-bar, coffee-tea making facilities, safe, umbrella and snorkeling gear in each room. The bathrooms in the beach bungalows open onto a garden and a high coral wall, and there are doors between the bedroom and bathroom. Each bathroom has a hair-dryer and Pearl Resorts amenities that are replenished daily when the rooms are cleaned. One of the nicest features of the beach bungalows is the partially covered terrace overlooking a beautiful white sand beach. You can recline in the lounge chairs on the sundeck and watch the sunrise or sunset, depending on which unit you have, and rarely do you see another person on the beach, nor even a passing boat. The very inviting lagoon is just a few steps away. This is the gentle side of the motu, so typical of the South Seas scenery that makes you dream of trade winds singing through the coconut palms, white sandy beaches that turn pink with the setting sun and a crystalline lagoon the color of green silk, turquoise and jade

The spacious overwater bungalows are 55m² (595 square feet), and are built over a *hoa* channel where the current flows from the ocean into the lagoon. Because the water can be as deep as 2 meters (6.6 feet) underneath some of the bungalows, the hotel management advises guests against swimming here when the current is very strong. Some of these units have a sunbathing platform and steps leading into the lagoon. The sea breezes are very energizing and guarantee a cool night's rest even without air-conditioning. You can stand on your balcony and see the waves crashing onto the coral reef and watch a family of reef herons fishing on a small motu finger of land. The overwater bungalows have a glass window in the floor for fish watching. These units have all the same amenities as the beach units, with the addition of CD players in the premium overwater bungalows. Two of the overwater units are equipped for guests in wheelchairs. The new overwater suites are

93m² (1001 square feet) and are built over the lagoon adjacent to the beach bungalows. These units have bathtubs as well as direct access into the lagoon.

In addition to the Poreho Restaurant and Bar Tianoa, the hotel also has an activities desk at the reception area, plus an all-purpose room that can be used for meetings or a game room with a wide screen television and VCR. There is also a sundries gift shop and a jewelry shop. Room service is offered for breakfast, and there is a 48-hour laundry service and a secretarial service.

In addition to a swimming pool, the hotel's other complimentary activities include kayaks, snorkeling gear, volleyball, badminton and petanque (bacci ball). For optional excursions and activities you can take a boat trip to visit a lagoonarium for 3.500 CFP, visit Bird Island on Motu Puarua and snorkel in the lagoon for 6.000 CFP, join a barbecue picnic on a pink-sand motu for 8.500 CFP, or join a boat excursion to visit the lagoon and motu islets for 11.000 CFP. A local fisherman will also take one to four people for line fishing (15.000 CFP) or trawling (27.500 CFP). Prices are for the boat. You can join a sunset cruise, and you can also order a picnic lunch and drinks for a Robinson Crusoe picnic on an uninhabited motu. You will be supplied with a walkie-talkie before being dropped off for the day. The boat ride without picnic is 3.000 CFP.

Scuba divers can sign up for a nice choice of dives with Tikehau Blue Nui Dive Center, which is based at the hotel. They can also take you snorkeling for 3.500 CFP. The hotel operates a daily boat service between the village and the hotel, providing 5 round-trip shuttles. The first boat leaves the hotel at 6:30am and the last boat returns from the village at 5:30pm. You can take this shuttle to the village and pick up a bicycle at the boat dock. You pay 2.000 CFP for each bike at the hotel and get a ticket to give to the person who manages the bicycle rentals in the village. A bike ride around the village motu takes about 45 minutes and it is a lovely trip. The people of Tikehau are very friendly to one another and to visitors.

The Tikehau Pearl Beach Resort is a favorite destination for honeymooners and other loving couples. The hotel offers a number of suggestions on ways to celebrate your romance. Why not a Romantic Welcome, with a private boat transfer from the airport to the hotel, during which you toast one another with a half bottle of French champagne. This costs 23.800 CFP per couple. You can also have a Romantic Breakfast for two served on your terrace for 8.500 CFP per couple. Or you may prefer a Blue Lagoon Breakfast served in the water for 8.840 CFP per couple. A Romantic Lunch for Lovers served on the private terrace of your bungalow is 10.540 CFP per couple, and a Barefoot Beach Lunch is served at a private table set on the white sand beach, for 11.107 CFP per couple. Sunset Cocktails and an array of hors d'œuvres can be served on your private terrace for 7.140 CFP for two. A Romantic Dinner with champagne and wedding cake can be served in the hotel dining room for 16.433 CFP per couple, and a private Starlight Dinner with champagne is 28.900 CFP for two. A Picnic on the Motu lets you play "castaway" in a secluded natural paradise while you enjoy a lunch artfully prepared by the hotel chef, for 30.600 CFP per couple. A Gourmet Picnic on the Motu includes champagne served at an elegantly dressed table, for 41.933 CFP per couple.

A Polynesian Wedding Ceremony is the ultimate touch of romance for honeymooners or couples who wish to renew their vows. The hotel offers a Te Pa'ari Wedding package for 96.333 CFP per couple, or Te Pa'ari II Wedding package for 109.933 CFP per couple. Add 10% VAT to these prices. Contact the hotel for details on Romantic Gateway.

Economy

These pensions are listed in the order in which they are located, starting in the village and extending past the airport and to the adjacent motu.

TEVAIHI VILLAGE, *B.P. 42, Tuherahera, Tikehau 98778. Tel./Fax 689/ 96.23.04, cell 74.85.29; E-mail: tevaihivillage@mail.pf; www.yozz-online.com/ tevaihivillage. Beside lagoon in Tuherahera village, five minutes from the airport and 400 meters (1,312 feet) from the quay. Free round-trip transfers. Rates: bungalow only 5.000 CFP; bungalow with breakfast and dinner 8.500 CFP; bungalow with breakfast, lunch and dinner 10.500 CFP per person per day. Half-fare for children under 12 years. Add 6% percent value added tax to room rates and meal plans. A 10% value added tax is applicable to other services. No credit cards.*

Noella Poetai operates the newest of Tikehau's family pensions, which consists of four bungalows of the FEI type government approved models, which are built on stilts facing a pretty beach of white sand. This is the only pension to the left of the boat dock. Each unit has a double bed and a single bed and a bathroom with cold water shower. You can sit on the covered terrace and watch flocks of sea birds as they fish in the lagoon and you can also watch the sunrise from here.

Meals are served in an open-air restaurant on the beach and you can order a bottle of wine for 2.500 CFP to accompany your dinner. You can rent a bicycle from Noella for 1.000 CFP a day and ride around the village or the island. She will also arrange your boat excursions on request.

CHEZ HELENE, *Tuherahera, Tikehau 98778. Tel. 689/96.22.52, Fax 689/ 96.22.78. 4-room house in the village of Tuherahera, 2 kilometers (1.2 miles) from the airport. Free round-trip transfers between airport and pension. Rates: room with shared bath plus breakfast and dinner 5.500 CFP per person; room with shared bath and all meals 6.500 CFP; room with private bath, breakfast and dinner 6.500 CFP; room with private bath and all meals 7.500 CFP; half-fare for children 3 to 11 years. Add 6% percent value added tax to room rates and meal plans. A 10% value added tax is applicable to other services. No credit cards.*

Hélène Teakura has a big 4-bedroom concrete house in the center of the main village, one block from the lagoon and one block from a *magasin* food

store. She renovated her family pension in 2004 to provide better accommodations and service to her guests. There is a double bed and single bed in three
of the four bedrooms, with a communal bathroom and cold water. The fourth
bedroom has a double bed and a private bathroom with cold water shower.
Guests share the living room with television and a covered terrace. Meals are
served family style on a covered terrace or in the dining room. House linens
are furnished. Bicycles and outrigger paddle canoes are available at no cost.

Hélène also has land on the motu beside the Tuheiava Pass, where surfers
can pitch a tent and ride the waves. The cost for one camper is 800 CFP per
day and for two people it's 1.000 CFP per day. Teakura Excursions, which is
operated by this family, provides round-trip boat transfers from the village to
the campsite for 4.000 CFP per person. For further information see *Nautical
Activities* in this chapter.

AITO MOTEL COLETTE, *Tuherahera, Tikehau 98778. Tel. 689/96.23.07;
Tel./Fax 689/96.22.47. Beside lagoon between Tuherahera village and the
airport. Free round-trip transfers. Rates: bungalow only 6.000 CFP single,
8.000 CFP double/triple; bungalow with breakfast and dinner 7.800 CFP per
person; bungalow with all meals 9.600 CFP per person per day; half-fare
meals for child under 12 years. Breakfast is 1.000 CFP, lunch is 2.000 CFP and
dinner is 2.500 CFP. Add 6% percent value added tax to room rates and meal
plans. A 10% value added tax is applicable to other services. No credit cards.*

Colette has five thatched-roof A-frame bungalows built on stilts on the
beach within easy walking distance from the village. Tall Australian pine trees
(called Aito in Tahitian) line the beach, providing shade and the melody of their
whispering sounds as their feathery fronds sway in the ocean breeze. Two
bungalows contain two double beds, two bungalows have one double bed,
and one bungalow has a double bed and a sofa. Each unit has a private
bathroom with a cold water shower. There is a restaurant and bar on the
beach where you can enjoy Colette's delicious cooking, which includes lagoon
fish and rock lobsters—no meat or chicken. Colette doesn't speak English,
although she works at the airport for each Air Tahiti flight arrival and
departure, so she can manage to communicate with non-French speaking
guests. She can arrange for boat excursions on request.

TIKEHAU VILLAGE, *Tuherahera, Tikehau 98778. Tel./Fax 689/96.22.86.
Beside the beach in Tematie village, 600 meters (654 yards) from the main
village of Tuherahera and 400 meters (436 yards) from the airport. Rates:
single beach bungalow with breakfast and dinner 8.000 CFP; single beach
bungalow with all meals 9.500 CFP; double beach bungalow with breakfast
and dinner 6.500 CFP per person; double beach bungalow with all meals
8.000 CFP per person; family-size beach bungalow with breakfast and dinner
9.000 CFP per person; bungalow with all meals 10.500 CFP per person. Half-
price for child under 12 years and free for child less than 4 years. Free round-*

trip transfers. Add 6% percent value added tax to room rates and meal plans. A 10% value added tax is applicable to other services. Mastercard, Visa.

This small family hotel is also called Chez Paea and Caroline, and is located between Aito Motel Colette and Chez Tematie on a pretty white sand beach next to the airport. There are 9 thatched roof *fares* built facing the beach. All rooms have tiled floors, ceiling fans and private bathrooms with cold water showers, and terraces. You have a choice of double or twin beds and mosquito nets are available on request, as the louvered or Plexiglas windows are not screened. House linens are furnished.

This pension has the only public restaurant and bar on the main island, and you can eat in the open-air dining room even if you are not staying here. This is a popular place with residents of Tahiti, who stay here because the food is good. When business is good they have buffet dinners twice a week and a Tahitian feast is also prepared weekly, complete with Paumotu music.

Guests enjoy feeding the sharks and rays that come to the edge of the lagoon beside the white sand beach in search of handouts. Boat trips can be arranged with Teakura Excursion to take you to visit other motu islets inside the lagoon, complete with a picnic. The Raie Manta Club diving center is located on the hotel premises.

PENSION TEMATIE, *Tuherahera, Tikehau 98778. Tel./Fax 689/96.22.65. Beside the beach in Tematie village, 400 meters (436 yards) from the airport and 2 kilometers (1.2 miles) from the main village of Tuherahera. Rates: bungalow only 5.000 CFP single; 7.000 CFP double; bungalow with breakfast and dinner 8.000 CFP per person; bungalow with all meals 10.000 CFP per person; half price for child under 12 years. Free round-trip transfers. Add 6% percent value added tax to room rates and meal plans. A 10% value added tax is applicable to other services. No credit cards.*

This original style pension opened in March, 1999, between Tikehau Village and Panau Lagoon, right on the pretty white sand beach that is shaded by *aito* trees (Australian pines) that whisper in the refreshing sea breezes. Owner Nora Hoiore is originally from Tikehau and her French husband, Yves-Marie Dubois, is an engineering consultant for airport landing strips. After living in Africa, St. Kitts, Indonesia and other countries for several years, they returned to Tikehau and built 3 bungalows for guests. Two of these units are octagon shaped and the walls are made of broken coral they collected from the reef. The smaller bungalows have a double bed and a single bed, and the family bungalow also has a mezzanine that will sleep two people. All the bathrooms are tiled and private, with cold water showers. The windows are screened and there is a portable fan. The bungalows are attractively decorated with Polynesian bed covers and woodcarvings.

Meals are served in the communal dining room, and these consist of local fish and seafood dishes as well as quiche, fresh pasta, crêpes and an occasional dinner of fish or leg of lamb. Activities include bicycle and kayak rentals and boat trips can be arranged to visit the lagoon. They both speak some English.

PANAU LAGON, *Tuherahera, Tikehau 98778. Tel./Fax 689/96.22.99. Beside the white sand beach in Hotu Panau village, adjacent to the airport. Rates: beach bungalow 4.000 CFP per person; bungalow with breakfast and dinner 6.000 CFP per person; bungalow with breakfast, lunch and dinner 7.000 CFP per person; half-price for child under 12 years. Free round-trip transfers. Add 6% percent value added tax to room rates and meal plans. A 10% value added tax is applicable to other services. No credit cards.*

There are six small *fares*, four with a double bed and single bed and private bathroom with cold water; one *fare* with two rooms and communal bathroom with cold water; and one *fare* with two double beds and communal bathroom. All have ceiling fans and a small terrace facing the pretty white sand beach. House linens and mosquito nets are furnished and meals are served in a communal dining room. Owner Arai Natua is the local policeman and he has a big boat for excursions to the *motu* islets, fish parks, pink sand beach and diving in the pass,

CHEZ JUSTINE, *Tuherahera, Tikehau 98778. Tel./Fax 689/96.22.87; cell 72.02.44. Beside the white sand beach in Hotu Panau village, 200 meters (656 feet) from the airport. Free round-trip transfers. Rates: room only 4.000 CFP single/double; room with breakfast and dinner 6.890 CFP per person; room with breakfast, lunch and dinner 8.480 CFP per person; half fare for child 3-12 years; camping and breakfast 3.000 CFP per person per day. Taxes included except for a municipal tax of 50 CFP per person per day. Master card, Visa.*

This pension is located between Panau Lagon and Pension Hotu, across the road from the airport, along a pretty white sand beach. Justine speaks a little English. Two concrete and plywood duplex accommodations face one another several feet from the beach, providing four rooms that are clean and attractively decorated with Polynesian fabrics. Each of the rooms has tiled floors, screened louvered windows, a double bed, private bathroom with cold water, and terrace. There are also three separate bungalows right on the beach, which are well located for enjoying the ocean breezes. All house linens are provided. You can pitch a tent on the beach. The dining room is right at the water's edge and the meals feature fish and other local style foods. You can rent a bicycle here for 500 CFP for a half-day and 1.000 CFP for all day.

PENSION HOTU, *Tuherahera, Tikehau 98778. Tel. 689/96.22.89. Beside the white sand beach in Hotu Panau village, 200 meters (656 feet) from the airport and two kilometers (1.2 miles) from Tuherahera village. Free round-trip transfers. Rates: fare only 4.000 CFP per person; fare with breakfast and dinner 6.000 CFP per person; fare with all meals 8.000 CFP per person; half-price for child 6-12 years. Add 6% percent value added tax to room rates and meal plans. A 10% value added tax is applicable to other services. No credit cards.*

This pension is also known as Chez Isidore and Nini. It is adjacent to Panau Lagon and is the last pension in the airport area before the end of the road. This is one of the most attractive, as well as one of the cleanest of the lodgings on the beach, and the lagoon swimming here is also good. The three thatched roof *fares* are built of concrete and plywood and are basically furnished. Two units contain a double bed and sofa and a private bathroom with cold water. The third bungalow has two double beds, a private bathroom with cold water and a terrace. The louvered windows in the bungalows are unscreened, but you can have a mosquito net, and there are mats on the floors and locks on the doors. The hand-painted Polynesian style bed covers lend an attractive air and the terraces have small gardens. House linens are provided. The kitchen is equipped and shared by all guests, and meals are served in the bright and clean dining *fare*, which consist primarily of fish dishes.

Nini and her husband operated another pension in the main village for several years, and she can manage in English. She is also outgoing and friendly and greets her guests at the airport with Tiare Tahiti floral leis. When they leave she gives them a shell lei that she has made herself. You can rent a bicycle for 700 CFP a day. There are two boats available to take you on lagoon excursions and to visit the fish parks and *motu* islets around the lagoon.

KAHAIA BEACH, *Tuherahera 98778. Tel. 689/96.22.77; Fax 689/ 96.23.75. Beside the beach on the private Motu Kahaia, across channel from the end of the airport runway and five minutes by boat from Tuherahera quay. Free round-trip car and boat transfers. Rates: bungalow with breakfast and dinner 6.500 CFP per person; bungalow with breakfast, lunch and dinner 8.000 CFP per person; half-price meals for child under 10 years. Add 6% percent value added tax to room rates and meal plans. A 10% value added tax is applicable to other services. No credit cards.*

Motu Kahaia is located across a narrow *hoa* channel of water just five minutes by boat from the main village, at the end of the road that leads to the airport and village. Six thatched or sheet metal roof bungalows situated along a white sand beach have single or double beds and a mattress on the mezzanine. House linens are furnished. There are mosquito nets over some of the beds and each unit has a private bathroom with cold water shower, but the water is turned off at night. There is electricity in the bungalows but it isn't very reliable; therefore, you will be given a hurricane lamp for your room. Be sure to bring a good flashlight, a powerful mosquito repellent and sunscreen. I cannot recommend this place for anyone who requires a hygienic atmosphere and lots of looking after. This is a lot like summer camp, complete with sandy floors and do-it-yourself housekeeping. Cleanliness is not a major concern in this family pension, but it certainly offers an "authentic" Polynesian experience in other ways.

Owners Merline and Pita Natua do not speak any English. Pita's usual attire is a swimsuit and a T-shirt and he loves to joke and pretend to flirt with the pretty ladies. In his younger days he played guitar and sang with the band at Quinn's Tahitian Hut in Papeete, which closed in 1973. He still likes to join his guests after dinner and serenade them with Polynesian melodies while he strums his guitar.

Local dishes are served family style in the communal dining room, often to the sound of an electric generator during dinner. Breakfast consists of Nescafé instant coffee and *firifiri* (Tahitian doughnuts) or baguettes. If you've caught your own breakfast fish Merline will cook it for you. Fresh lagoon fish is served each evening as *poisson cru*, *beignets*, fried or grilled, and it is all delicious. You can take your drinks to put in the refrigerator box outside the kitchen. Pita will take you to the village to buy food and wine and beer. I spent Easter weekend here with two friends and Pita was absent when we arrived by boat from another hotel. One of my friends had to paddle a kayak with the remains of a shark-eaten paddle to the other side of the channel and tow the outrigger canoe back to our beach. Then we poled the canoe across the channel and drove Pita's rickety pick-up truck into the village to buy supplies for our lunch and drinks.

Pita will take you spear fishing or line fishing inside the lagoon. You can also feed the sharks at the pension beach as they are ever present wherever fish has been cleaned and scraps thrown into the water or left on the dock. There is also camping space on the motu.

Seeing the Sights

You can view the beauty of the fish and submarine gardens through a snorkeling mask or while scuba diving with qualified instructors. Take a boat to **Motu Ohihi**, which is surrounded by shallow *hoa* channels and has a pink sand beach. Go to **Motu Puarua** and **Oe Oe**, the Bird Island where snowy white fairy terns and noddy birds nest. Snorkeling is especially good in Tikehau's crystal clear lagoon.

Boat excursions will take you to visit the fish parks and past one or more of the pearl farms, and you have a choice of *motu* islets for a memorable picnic. You can fish by line or spear, and Tuheiava Pass is a good surfing spot in December and January. On the main island bike through the coconut groves to the rose-colored reef, and take a guided land tour to the old village and surrounding area. Hina's Bell is a big rock beside the beach that resounds like a chime when struck. This is a lovely place to watch the sunset. And under the light of the tropical stars it becomes a romantic spot for lovers to meet.

Sports & Recreation
Scuba Diving

Raie Manta Club Tikehau is located in an overwater bungalow at Tikehau Village, *Tel./Fax 96.22.53; E-mail: raiemantaclub@mail.pf; http://raiemantaclub.free.fr*. Eric Roubeaud is a qualified English-speaking diving instructor, who charges 6.500 CFP for an introductory dive with lessons, and 6.000 CFP or an exploration dive, using complete Scubapro equipment. He takes a maximum of five divers for each outing, just a 20-minute boat ride from the village. You can dive twice in one day for 11.000 CFP, which also includes the boat, crew, diving instructor, and a stop at noon for a picnic on a *motu*. Bring your own lunch and drinks. A 10-dive package is 56.000 CFP. Open water dives are possible, and Bertrand can give you exams for CMAS certification. Diving in the Tuheiava Pass is an exciting experience, where you will be surrounded by white tip reef sharks, leopard rays, eagle rays, tunas, barracudas, jackfish, black surgeon fish, big groupers, napoleons and other brilliantly colored schools of tropical fish. You may even see the graceful manta rays gliding by.

Tikehau Blue Nui, *Tel. 96.22.40; Fax 96.23.01; E-mail: tikehaubluenui@mail.pf; www.bluenui.com* has their dive center at the Tikehau Pearl Beach Resort, *Tel. 96.23.00.* Gilles Petre is in charge of all the Blue Nui Dive Centers at the Pearl Resorts and Franck Poilper is the resident dive instructor. He is a CMAS** international monitor, a French State Instructor BEES1, and a PADI OWSI. Examinations are given for CMAS, CEDIP and PADI certificates. The rates are 6.700 CFP for a certified dive, 7.500 CFP for an introductory dive and 8.000 CFP for a night dive. Dive packages can be used at any of the Blue Nui centers in Tikehau, Manihi, Bora Bora and Tahaa. A 5-dive package is 31.000 CFP and a 10-dive package is 59.000 CFP. You can also contact Franck for a snorkeling excursion, which is 3.500 CFP per person.

Nautical Activities

Teakura Excursion, *Tel. 689/96.22.52, cell 71.25.53; E-mail: tahitidream_16@hotmail.com.* Tuheiava is your guide aboard his boat *Aotearoa*, which has a sun roof, to take you across the lagoon for a half-hour ride to visit Bird Island, where hundreds of sea birds come to lay their eggs in the sand or on the bare limb of a tree. He will prepare a Paumotu style picnic on another motu and then take you to visit the pink sand beach of Motu Ohihi. This outing leaves the village boat dock at 9am and returns around 3:30pm and costs 6.000 CFP per adult and 3.000 CFP for children less than 12 years. You can also substitute a visit to the fish parks instead of going to Bird Island, and you will pay only 5.500 CFP per person, which also includes a picnic.

Surfers can be transported from the village to Tuheiava Pass. The round-trip fare is 4.000 CFP per person and you can pitch a tent here for 800 CFP per day for one person and 1.000 CFP per day for two people.

Practical Information

There are no banks and no *gendarmes* in Tikehau. The *mairie* (town hall) is located in Tuherahera village, adjacent to the post office and school.

Food Stores
There are two stores in Tuherahera village that provide frozen products, canned foods, a few fresh vegetables, wine and beer. You can buy fresh baguettes of French bread each morning. Yachts can find a limited quantity of fuel in the stores. A municipal cistern at the foot of the wharf can supply yachts with water.

Medical Services
There is no doctor and no infirmary in Tikehau.

Post Office
The **Post Office and Telecommunications Office** is in Tuherahera village, *Tel. 96.22.22.* There is an automatic telephone cabin here.

FAKARAVA
Fakarava is the second largest atoll in the Tuamotu Archipelago, after Rangiroa, and its rectangular-shaped lagoon is 60 kilometers (37 miles) long by 25 kilometers (15 miles) wide. The atoll is 488 kilometers (303 miles) east-north-east of Tahiti and southeast of Rangiroa in the central Tuamotus.

A direct flight from Tahiti to Fakarava is just one hour and ten minutes, which is helping to turn this atoll into a dream location for those who seek vacation experiences off-the-beaten path, especially scuba divers and other "water babies" who love tropical islands. The airport runway has been lengthened to allow easy access for Air Tahiti's ATR 72 planes and landing lights were installed for night flights. The lagoon of Fakarava is a magnificent marine realm of sharks, graceful manta rays, giant sized fish and a whole parade of beautiful tropical fish. This atoll is protected as a biosphere reserve classified by UNESCO. Its special features are columns of water in the lagoon and ocean and the importance and diversity of its fauna and flora, including the kingfisher, the Tuamotu palm tree and the lagoon crustaceans, such as *varo* (squill or sea centipede) and *tiane'e* (slipper lobster).

The **Garuae Pass** on the northwest coast is one kilometer (.62 miles) wide. It is the largest pass in French Polynesia and gives access to anchorages for yachts and even big passenger liners, such as the 35,000 ton *Europa* or the *Queen Elizabeth 2*, which have both dropped anchor in front of the village of **Rotoava** on the northeast coast facing the pass. The *Aranui III* calls here every few weeks, the last stop of 16-day round-trip voyages between Tahiti and the Marquesas Islands. The public quay was enlarged in 2003, paved and embellished with street lamps and a marina for fishing boats. The lights and pavement were destroyed in November 2003 by the high seas and strong winds of a 6-hour storm that sank or battered three boats, including the boat belonging to the pension Motu Aito Paradise. Rotoava village is home to most of the atoll's 689 population. This is where you will find an international class hotel, several family pensions, a couple of *magasin* stores as well as a new super market, the post office, grade school, churches and town hall. A scuba dive center is also located in Rotoava village, offering experienced divers a selection of dives among some of the most abundant fish life in all of French Polynesia. In anticipation of a visit from President Jacques Chirac in July 2003, some 22 kilometers (13.6 miles) of road was paved between the airport and property owned by the local government, where a villa was also built for the French President. Chirac's busy schedule prevented him from going to Fakarava, but the new road makes driving more comfortable—and faster. Tahiti's local French language publications have also announced that Tahiti's President Gaston Flosse plans to build an 18-hole golf course on a 30-hectare (7,413 acres) piece of land belonging to the government and rumors report plans to build a 5-star hotel on this atoll.

On the southeast side of the atoll is **Tumakohua Pass**, which is 200 meters (656 feet) wide and 12 to 15 meters (39 to 49 feet) deep. The distance from pass to pass is 58 kilometers or 35 nautical miles and takes 1 1/2 to 2 hours by speedboat. Several decades ago Fakarava was the social, religious and cultural capital of the Tuamotu Archipelago, and was known to the *Paumotu* people in ancient times as Havaiki Nui. **Tetamanu** village was formerly the principal settlement on Fakarava. It is located on a very small *motu* beside the Tumakohua Pass, and only a couple of families live here today. There are two pensions plus some simple accommodations for local folks who also seek the solitude of this remote paradise. There are no shops, no boutiques, nowhere to go on land except to visit the vestiges of the old village. There is the coral shell of an old Catholic Church that was built in 1862, the remains of a building that was a prison and the walls of the former Residence of the French Administrator of the Tuamotu Archipelago. Another church is dated 1876 and is more intact, but no mass is celebrated here anymore. A cemetery behind the church contains a few tombstones.

Inside the reef surrounding the atoll are 94 motu islets, mostly uninhabited except for sea birds. At the southern extremity is a very special motu called Hirifa, where the lagoon provides a magical luminescence, a mirror reflection of hundreds of coconut palms that grow beside the beach that stretches on and on for several miles. Koka Koka motu is a favorite picnic destination for those in the know. Like many of the motu islets in Fakarava it is surrounded by pink sands, and in the crystalline lagoon you'll find a wealth of succulent fish that can be grilled for lunch. The forests are filled with trees that provide precious wood for building and carving: *kahaia*, *puatea*, *miro*, *tou*, *gnao gnao* and *autera'a*. Chances are you will also see a white fairy tern with black button eyes perched on the branch of a *tou* tree, along with her newly hatched chick. She provides no nest, but lays a solitary egg in the crook of a tree limb. Drinking coconuts are within easy reach without shinnying up the trunk. This is the domain of the *kaveu*, the giant coconut crab, which makes a very tasty dinner.

So, you see, there are interesting things to do even if you are not a diver. You can join boat trips to visit a fish park, which is a wire enclosure designed to allow fish to swim in with the currents, then they are trapped inside and live there until chosen for dinner. You can also visit a black pearl farm if you are staying in a pension that owns a farm. You can lie on the pristine beach and contemplate the clouds; watch flocks of seabirds fishing in the lagoon or resting on the pink sandbars. Watch the rainsqualls in the distance and hear it approach, then take a delightful warm shower in the rain. It's good to cool off this way!

Whatever you do and wherever you stay in Fakarava, do not miss seeing the Southern end of the atoll. It is totally overwhelming. Bring your camera and lots of film. You probably won't even need mosquito repellent here, but you should bring your own booze and munchie snacks.

Arrivals & Departures
Arriving by Air
Air Tahiti flies direct from Tahiti to Fakarava each Monday, Wednesday, Thursday, Saturday and Sunday, with 70-minute flights. There are also direct flights on Tuesday and Friday during holiday seasons. Each Tuesday and Friday the ATR flight from Tahiti to Fakarava stops in Rangiroa, with a change of aircraft on Tuesday. You can fly from Bora Bora to Fakarava on Tuesday and Friday with a stop in Rangiroa each day and a change of aircraft on Friday. **Air Tahiti reservations**: Tahiti, *Tel. 86.42.42* in Fakarava, *Tel. 98.42.30/98.42.64*.

The one-way airfare from Tahiti to Fakarava is 16.500 CFP, the one-way fare from Rangiroa to Fakarava is 5.200 CFP, and the one-way fare from Bora Bora is 26.000 CFP. The airport is four kilometers (2.5 miles) from Rotoava village, connected by a paved road.

You can also get to Fakarava by chartering an airplane in Tahiti from **Wan Air**, *Tel. 50.44.17, cell 77.03.79*; **Air Archipels**, *Tel. 81.30.30*; or **Air Tahiti**, *Tel. 86.42.42*.

Arriving by Boat
Mareva Nui, *Tel. 42.25.53, Fax 42.25.57*, is a 181-foot steel ship that transports cargo between Tahiti and the Tuamotu atolls. It leaves Tahiti every 15 days, arriving in Fakarava after stopping at 8 atolls in the Western Tuamotu Archipelago. There are 12 berths on board but no cabin. The one-way fare from Tahiti to Fakarava is 5.700 CFP and three meals a day cost 2.200 CFP per person.

St. Xavier Maris Stella III, *Tel. 42.23.58*, can transport 12 passengers who have to sleep on the deck until the berths are repaired. The fare from Tahiti to Fakarava is 11.830 CFP per person, including 3 meals a day. The ship leaves Papeete every 15 days for 7-10 day voyages.

Vai Ato, *Tel. 43.99.96, Fax 43.53.04*. From Tahiti this ship stops in Tikehau, Rangiroa, Ahe, Manihi, Aratika and Kauehi before arriving in Fakarava. The one way cost for sleeping on the deck and three meals daily is 18.735 CFP per person, including 3 meals a day.

See more information in Chapter 6, *Planning Your Trip*.

Departing by Air

Air Tahiti flies direct from Fakarava to Tahiti each Tuesday, Wednesday, Thursday, Friday, Saturday and Sunday. The Monday flight from Fakarava stops in Rangiroa enroute to Tahiti. **Air Tahiti reservations** in Fakarava, *Tel. 98.42.30*.

Departing by Boat

Mareva Nui, *Tel. 42.25.53*, calls at five or more atolls after leaving Fakarava each 15 days, and the trip back to Tahiti takes 4 days or more. The cost is determined by the number of days required and 3 meals a day are 2.200 CFP per person. *St. Xavier Maris Stella III, Tel. 42.23.58*, leaves Fakarava every 15 days for Papeete following an itinerary determined by freight to deliver or pick up. You can sleep on the deck with three daily meals included. *Vai Aito, Tel. 43.99.96*, will usually bring you straight from Fakarava to Tahiti, unless there is freight to deliver or pick up on another atoll.

See more information under *Inter-Island Cruise Ships, Passenger Boats and Freighters* in Chapter 6, *Planning Your Trip*.

Where to Stay

Superior

HOTEL MAITAI DREAM FAKARAVA, *B.P. 19, Rotoava, Fakarava 98763. Tel. 689/98.43.00; Fax 689/98.43.01; E-mail: info@fakarava.hotelmaitaifa.com; www.hotelmaitai.com. Beside lagoon 10.5 kilometers (6.5 miles) from airport. 30 bungalows. EP Rates single/double: Garden bungalow 26.000 CFP; Beach bungalow 31.000 CFP; Premium beach bungalow 37.000 CFP; third person 6.500 CFP per day. Add 6.500 CFP per person per day for breakfast and dinner, and 9.000 CFP for breakfast, lunch and dinner. Round-trip airport transfers 2.500 CFP per person. Add 5% hotel tax to room rates and 6% value added tax to room rates and prepaid meal plans, plus 150 CFP municipal tax per person per day. A 10% value added tax is applicable to other services unless otherwise specified. All major credit cards.*

Fakarava's first hotel opened in September 2002, offering international class lodging and services just a 15-minute ride on the paved road from the airport and a 15-minute boat ride from the Garuae Pass, which offers nirvana for scuba divers in the kilometer-wide opening through the coral reef.

The bungalows are built on raised islands above the wide white sand beach in groups of three. There are 9 premium beach bungalows and 6 beach bungalows facing the magnificent lagoon, and behind them are 15 Tiare bungalows, set in a garden of Tiare Tahiti bushes. All the bungalows have 45 square meters (484 square feet) of living space, plus a covered terrace. The only difference in price is where they are placed. The walls and roofs are constructed with rich teakwood from Bali. Each unit is furnished with a king size bed or twin beds and a sofa bed, an office desk and chair, a ceiling fan, international direct dial telephone, satellite television, refrigerator with mini-bar on request, coffee and tea making facilities, and individual safe. The furniture is made of coconut wood from Bali. The bathroom is decorated with coral and has a hot water shower and hair dryer. There are also facilities for physically challenged guests.

The Kura Ora restaurant and Kiri Kiri bar overlook the lagoon. Buffet or à la carte meals are served in the 48-seat dining room or on the open terrace, and these include a large selection of fresh fish from the lagoon and deep sea. The bar is open from 10 am to 10:30pm, serving your favorite cocktails. Musical entertainment adds a Polynesian touch during special evenings. A long pier is built over the lagoon in front of the hotel, which is the departure point for boat trips to visit black pearl farms, fish parks, remote motu islets, picnics on deserted beaches, deep-sea fishing and other lagoon excursions. Guests have free use of snorkel gear, kayaks and outrigger paddle canoes. You can rent a bike or arrange for a village tour or lagoon excursion at the front desk. Fakarava Diving Center is based at the hotel, offering a range of exciting dives to explore the wealth of big sea life in the passes and lagoon.

Moderate/Economy

I have listed the Pensions on the North side of Fakarava atoll in order of their proximity to the airport.

RELAIS MARAMA, *B.P. 16, Rotoava, Fakarava 98763. Tel./Fax 689/ 98.42.51, cell 72.09.42/70.81.98; E-mail: teavanui@divingfakarava.com. On seaside in Rotoava village, 3.5 kilometers (2.2 miles) from airport. EP Rates: room 3.600 CFP single, 5.400 CFP double, 7.800 CFP triple; ocean side bungalow 4.200 CFP single, 6.600 CFP double, 9.000 CFP triple; camping 1.600 CFP per person per day; half-rate for child under 12 years. Rates include free round-trip transfers, breakfast, bicycles and taxes. No credit cards.*

This is a popular bed and breakfast lodging with backpackers, campers and other budget travelers who prefer to spend a minimum amount on their sleeping facilities and save their money for scuba diving in one of the world's most spectacular lagoons. Owners Jacques Sauvage, a Frenchman, and Marama Teanuanua, a Paumotu man from Fakarava, speak English, French and Tahitian. They have built 6 bungalows and a 3-bedroom house, with two twin beds in each room. Camping space for 12 tents is available in a clearing overlooking the ocean. There are 4 communal bathrooms and 2 showers with cold water and guests can also use the washing machine. A *fare potee* shelter contains a kitchen/dining area that is well equipped with two gas burners and two refrigerators, plus a sink and tables. There is also a barbecue grill. Guests can cook their own food here as the bungalows are rented without meals included, but you can order dinner or barbecue for 2.000 CFP per person. Be sure to reserve before 2pm. Rainwater is used for drinking. There is a public telephone on the premises, and there are 3 snacks, a new supermarket and two small stores in the village. Lagoon excursions are handled by Ato of Pension Paparara and the owners of Relais Marama recommend Te Ava Nui Plongée for anyone who wants to go scuba diving.

VAHITU DREAM, *B.P. 9, Rotoava, Fakarava 98763, Tel. 689/98.42.63, Fax 689/98.42.50. On seaside at edge of Rotoava village, 4 kilometers (2.5 miles) from airport. Rates: room and breakfast 3.500 CFP per person; room and all meals 7.500 CFP single, 14.000 CFP double; half-rate for child under 12 years. Free round-trip transfers. Rates include taxes. No credit cards.*

This is a big old house with 6 rooms for guests, 3 showers with cold water and 2 toilets. There are mosquito nets over the beds and fans in each room. House linens are furnished. Owner/hostess Jacqueline Moeroa serves local style meals at a big table in the communal dining room, which also serves as the television room. She has a boutique in the sitting room at the front of her house, where she sells the clothes and *tifaifai* bed covers she makes when she's not making shell necklaces or taking care of several other chores. Her clients are often Polynesians who come to Fakarava on business. She rents bicycles for 600 CFP for 4 hours and 1.200 CFP for a full day. You can swim in the lagoon and walk to the stores in the village. She also has a house for rent with 2 bedrooms, kitchen and private bedroom.

PENSION HAVAIKI, *Rotoava, Fakarava 98763. Tel/Fax 689/98.42.16, cell 74.16.16; E-mail: havaiki@mail.pf; http://chez.mana.pf~havaiki. Beside lagoon 5 kilometers (3.1 miles) from airport and 600 meters (1,968 feet) past Rotoava village. AP Rates: bungalow with breakfast, lunch and dinner 13.000 CFP single, 19.000 CFP double, 27.000 CFP triple; half-price for child 3 to 12 years. Free round-trip transfers. Rates include taxes. American Express, Visa.*

This is the most popular family pension in Fakarava and definitely my favorite place to stay on the north side of the atoll. Owners Clotilde (Havaiki) and Joachim Dariel truly deserve the praise they receive from satisfied guests. Their 5 well-built plywood bungalows are lined up at the edge of a pretty white sand beach, overlooking one of the most beautiful views of the lagoon and sky that Nature has created in these islands. Each bungalow contains a double bed and a single bed. Woven bamboo mats cover the walls and woven palm leaf mats cover the ceiling. A lavabo and pretty shell-framed mirror are in a corner of the room and the toilet and cold water shower are separate, hidden behind a curtain of *pareo* cloth. Lights are provided by solar panels. The windows can be propped open by sticks at the top and bottom and there is no need for a fan here, because the ocean breezes are delightful, wafting through the room even during the day. Strands of orange, yellow, gold and white seashells hang over the bed and here and there, decorating the room and terrace. These lovely creations are made by Clotilde's mother, who lives in Rotoava village and they are for sale. There are also fresh flowers in the rooms. Clotilde has the prettiest garden of all the pensions and baskets of bright blossoms hang under the eaves of each bungalow.

The grafting *fare* for their black pearl farm sits overwater at the end of a very long and narrow pier. There are very few coral heads in this area of soft white sand and the shallow water sparkles like diamonds in the sunshine and reflects the pink of the trade wind clouds at sunset. You can sit on the covered terrace of your bungalow or at the edge of the lagoon and watch the sun setting right in front of you, as the pension faces the Garuae pass.

A road is just outside the bungalows, but it is seldom used by through traffic, as there is another road beside the ocean a block away. However, you can occasionally hear a scooter go by, not even 10 feet from your bed. Clotilde has placed big planters of hot pink bougainvillea, yellow and purple alamanda and other colorful flowers on both sides of the road to mark the limits of her land. She and Joachim live on the ocean side of the road and the delicious meals are served family style at a table in their dining room or at a picnic table beside the road. Fresh fish is the highlight of each meal, even for breakfast if you wish. Clotilde's brother grows vegetables and Joachim also has a small vegetable garden, so the plentiful meals are well balanced.

Joachim is half-English, half-French and speaks English. He lived in Bora Bora and Raiatea when he was a child, and his father, Nicolas Dariel, who was a goldsmith, sculptor and painter, had a pearl shop in Bora Bora. You can visit Joachim's black pearl farm and have a look at his harvest if you are looking to buy pearls. He's been in the business for more than 13 years. Bicycles and kayaks are provided for guest use, and they can organize excursions on request.

VEKEVEKE VILLAGE, *Rotoava, Fakarava 98763. Tel./Fax 689/98.42.80 (Fakarava), Tel. 689/82.03.36 (Tahiti), Fax 689/82.44.14 (Tahiti); cell 79.13.77; E-mail: vekevekevillage@mail.pf. Beside lagoon 9 kilometers (6 miles) from airport. Rates: bungalow with breakfast and dinner 10.000 CFP single, 18.000 CFP double, 27.000 CFP triple; add 2.000 CFP per person for dinner. Half-price for child under 12 years. Round-trip airport transfers 1.000 CFP per bungalow. Rates include taxes. No credit cards.*

Owners Lenick Tau and Thierry Amo have built 4 plywood bungalows beside a pretty cove with a narrow beach. Two beach bungalows have a double bed, one bunk bed and private bathroom with cold water shower. Two semi over-water bungalows each have a double bed, 2 single mattresses in upper level mezzanine and private bathroom with cold water shower.

Meals are served in a dining *fare* at the water's edge and electricity is provided by solar panels, with an electric generator for backup power. Bicycles and kayaks are provided free of charge to guests staying in the pension. All optional excursions and picnics can be arranged. Lenick Tau is president of the Noho Ariki association that represents all the family pensions in Fakarava.

PENSION PAPARARA, *B.P. 88, Rotoava, Fakarava 98763. Tel./Fax 689/ 98.42.66 or cell phone 74.69.10; E-mail: fakaravaexplorer@hotmail.com; www.haere-mail.pf. Beside lagoon past Rotoava village, 10 kilometers (6.2 miles) from the airport. Rates: room only 2.200 CFP, room with breakfast and dinner 6.000 CFP, room with all meals 8.000 CFP per person per day; bungalow only 3.200 CFP; bungalow with breakfast and dinner 7.000 CFP; bungalow with all meals 9.000 CFP per person per day; half-price for child under 12 years. Breakfast 530 CFP, lunch 2.120 CFP, dinner 3.200 CFP. Round-trip transfers 1.500 CFP per person. All taxes included. Credit cards accepted.*

This Polynesian owned pension is located beside the lagoon just before the Hotel Matai Dream Fakarava and has been in operation for 15 years. There are three bungalows including an A-shaped *fare* in the garden that is on stilts and is very airy. The double mattress is on a low bed and there is a table outside on a floor of coral. Another garden *fare* also has a double bed. The bungalow next to the lagoon has a big bed on the ground level and a double mattress on the mezzanine. The ground level floor is made of coral. From the terrace you can watch the parrotfish nibbling at the coral heads in the shallow water. All three of these units have mosquito nets over the beds.

Corina Lenoir cooks local style meals for her guests, which they can eat at a picnic table beside the lagoon or in the kitchen with a coral floor. The communal bathroom is tiled and has a shower with cold water. Lights are provided by solar panels and the electric generator is used for washing clothes and other household needs when the guests are absent. Corina's husband Ato takes them in his boat for lagoon excursions, picnics and deep-sea fishing. They also have a pearl farm in the lagoon in front of the pension. Corina makes and sells shell jewelry and mirrors bordered with seashells.

TOKERAU VILLAGE, *B.P. 53, Rotoava, Fakarava 98763. Tel./Fax 689/ 98.41.09/88.06.82, cell 70.82.19/71.17.04. Beside lagoon 11 kilometers (6.8 miles) from airport. AP Rates: bungalow with all meals 15.000 CFP single, 26.000 CFP double per day. A minimum of 2 nights required. Rates include airport transfers and taxes. American Express, Mastercard, Visa.*

This attractive pension opened in February 2003 and is located beside the lagoon just after the Hotel Maitai Dream Fakarava. It is owned by Flora and Patrick Bordes, who are assisted by their daughter, Gahina, who speaks English. The 4 new bungalows built on stilts are the government approved and financed models (*fond d'entraide aux îles*-FEI) that consist of shingle shake roofs and wooden walls, a modern Polynesian style with *pueu* mats from Indonesia covering the walls, and room for a double bed and a single bed, desk and clothes closet in the bedroom/sitting room. The rooms are colorfully decorated with *tifaifai* bed covers and photographs of old Tahiti hang on the walls. Each bungalow is decorated in a different color scheme and named after the three daughters of the Bordes family: Mere, Maea, Gahina, and their niece, Hina. The private bathrooms have a cold water shower and lights are provided by solar panels. A covered terrace overlooks the French style garden with sculpted bushes and there are flowers everywhere.

Meals are served in a shared dining room near the beach, and you can come here to eat even if you are not staying in the pension. Bicycles and kayaks are provided free of charge for guests and car and boat excursions can be arranged on request. The scuba dive centers will come here to pick up clients who wish to dive.

VAIAMA VILLAGE, *B.P. 25, Rotoava, Fakarava 98763. Tel./Fax 689/ 98.41.13, cell 70.56.41. Beside lagoon 15 kilometers (9.3 miles) from the airport and 6 kilometers (3.7 miles) past Rotoava village. AP Rates: bungalow with all meals 8.000 CFP per person per day; half-price for child under 12 years. Round-trip transfers from airport 2.000 CFP per couple or family. Rates include taxes. No credit cards.*

Tuaana Amaru manages this pension, which is the last one on the north side of Fakarava atoll. There are 4 very simple *fares* whose roofs and walls are made of palm fronds. Two of these *fares* are on stilts and one is 2-story, providing basic Tuamotu style accommodations for two to four people, and the beds are covered by mosquito nets. All the *fares* have private bathrooms with cold water showers and some of the bathrooms are outside and have coral floors.

Breakfast is served at a picnic table on the beach and the dining room and kitchen are located inside a big *fare pote'e* shelter. Bicycles, kayaks and outrigger paddle canoes are provided free of charge for guests, and you can also visit the family's black pearl farm and see the oysters being grafted for production. Ato of Pension Paparara is part of the family and he takes care of the lagoon excursions, including a picnic on a *motu*, which is additional to the full-board meal plan.

Pensions on the South side of Fakarava atoll, close to Tumakohua Pass
TETAMANU VILLAGE, *B.P. 6534, Faaa, Tahiti 98702. Tel. 689/43.92.40/ Fax 689/42.77.70, cell 77.10.06; E-mail: tetamanuvillage@mail.pf; www.tetamanuvillage.pf. Beside the pass in Tetamanu village, 55 kilometers (34 miles) by boat from the airport and main village. AP Rates per person: bungalow with all meals for 2 nights 35.000 CFP, 3 nights 48.500 CFP, 4 nights 62.000 CFP, 5 nights 69.000 CFP, 6 nights 77.000 CFP, and 7 nights 86.000 CFP; half-fare for child under 12 years. Round-trip boat transfers between airport and pension, all excursions and taxes are included. Minimum stay 3 nights for one or two people; minimum of 2 nights for four people. Packages for lodging, meals, transfers, taxes and scuba diving range from*

48.000 CFP for 3 nights and 3 dives up to 122.000 CFP per person for 7 nights and 12 dives. No credit cards.

Sané and Annabelle Richmond make the 90-minute boat trip from their pension on the south side of Fakarava atoll each Monday, Tuesday, Friday and Saturday to transfer their guests to and from the airport on the north shore. Then they head back across the lagoon with new faces and more food supplies. Annabelle is a very exuberant young Paumotu woman who lived in the States and speaks good English. She is in charge of promotion, guest relations, ordering supplies and overseeing the kitchen and housekeeping. She does a wonderful job of feeding her guests and staff, who all eat together at the same table. Sané, who is a Paumotu man of the sea, built this pension about 15 years ago. He certainly chose the right spot for observing the very lively tropical aquarium.

Tetamanu Village consists of six simple bungalows with thatched coconut palm roofs built on stilts at the edge of the Tumakohua pass. Each unit has solar lighting and contains a double bed and single bed, a lavabo and mirror in the bedroom, and a separate bathroom with the toilet and cold water shower. The brackish water is okay for washing your body, hair and clothes, but not for drinking. Bring soap for salt water if you want it to lather. The windows prop open with a stick and there's a mosquito net over the bed, as well as mosquito coils. Mosquitoes and nonos are rare in Fakarava when the trade winds blow. A terrace overlooks the strong current that flows in and out of the pass. This is like a giant aquarium filled with schools of fish of every shape, size and color. Without even getting into the water you can see parrotfish, yellow butterfly fish, electric blue damselfish and blue moray eels swimming in their magical world of purple and pink coral. It's amazing to watch the current change direction as the incoming flow slows to a standstill and then reverses; then the current inside the lagoon begins rushing outward through the pass into the open ocean.

The dining terrace, bar and kitchen are in a separate overwater *fare*. Sané Richmond has tamed two huge and beautiful blue-green Napoleon fish (wrasse) that he and Annabelle hand feed from the dining terrace every morning during breakfast. They pet each 200-pound fish on top of the head while it eats fresh fish. The water around the restaurant is also a rendezvous point for small sharks that come in search of food in the morning and late afternoon. They eat leftover scraps from the table, in addition to the fresh fish they get when the workers filet the day's fresh catch for lunch or dinner. A private pontoon is built over the water for line fishing and swimming. The activities are centered on Tumakohua pass, offering the ultimate scuba diving experience just a 5-minute boat ride from this pension. Tetamanu Diving Center is on the hotel premises and Sané is training to become a diving instructor. You can also accompany the Paumotu workers when they go spear fishing, or you can request a fishing expedition to fish inside the pass. Sané may even take you along with him to visit his black pearl farm. Sunday is picnic day, when Sané and Annabelle take their guests on a boat ride to the south end of the atoll for an unforgettable picnic on a desert isle surrounded by a pristine beach and a sparkling clear lagoon. As the sun lowers in the sky the sands turn vivid pink to match the overhead clouds. No one can remain untouched by this magnificent show of nature.

The remains of the old Tetamanu village are right beside the bungalows of the pension. You can visit this site and walk on around the motu to look at the pass from the shore, which is shaded by centuries old sacred *tamanu* trees.

TETAMANU SAUVAGE has the same contact information, rates and activities as Tetamanu Village. This extension is located on a neighboring motu islet that can be reached from Tetamanu Village in five minutes by wading across a *hoa*, a shallow and narrow channel of water that flows from the ocean to the lagoon. There are six bungalows whose roofs and walls are made of coconut palm fronds. Each unit has a double bed and a single bed, a bathroom with a cold water shower, solar lighting and a terrace overlooking the water. There is a dining fare and also a covered pier where guests can eat their meals as they watch the fish swimming by.

Note: I have written about the Tetamanu pension in a positive way, but it seems that the volatile on-again-off-again situation between Sane and Annabelle cannot be ignored when it affects the clients. I have had negative reports from a Canadian couple and a couple from Alaska, who are all very well seasoned travelers to the outer reaches of French Polynesia, including previous visits to Tetamanu Village. One couple was there when both owners were absent, and the other couple stayed there when Annabelle had run off with another man and Sane was alone and despondent. Although they agreed that the location is probably the best anywhere for snorkeling, the accommodations and food were far from satisfactory. They were given bungalows that had not been cleaned after the previous guests had left, including slept-on sheets. The food was very basic, without even coconut cream for the *poisson cru*, and they had only rainwater to drink. One American couple got lost in the lagoon in the pouring rain for eight hours before they could get back to the pension, and all of the boats were out of commission during the visit of the couple from Alaska, when Sane was there. It is rumored that Sane wants to sell the pension, so it would be best to verify the conditions before you make a reservation to stay here.

MOTU AITO PARADISE, *B.P. 12, Rotoava, Fakarava 98763. Tel./Fax 689/41.29.00; E-mail: motu-aito@mail.pf; www.fakarava.org. On Motu Aito near the Tumakohua Pass and Tetamanu village, 55 kilometers (34 miles) by boat from the airport and Rotoava village. AP Rates: bungalow with breakfast, lunch and dinner 13.000 CFP single, 26.000 CFP double, 39.000 CFP triple and 40.000 CFP for four people per day; half-price for child under 12* *years. Minimum stay 3 nights. Round-trip boat transfers between airport and pension, 3 meals a day, excursions and taxes are included. No credit cards.* Manihi and Tila Salmon have five good reasons for adding "Paradise" to the name of their pension. There are no mosquitoes or nonos. Calmness is assured because you are in the heart of Nature, with no telephone and no neighbors. You will be warmly welcomed with a very cordial greeting. The environment is user-friendly, with a convivial family atmosphere. The setting is very exotic—even paradisiacal!

I call it the Garden of Tranquility. I haven't stayed here yet, but I have several friends who have, and they just loved it. I look forward to doing so myself, because I appreciated the peaceful calm that I felt when I visited their motu and spent some time with this very together couple. They are both Polynesians who lived in New Zealand for 10 years and they speak very good English. Their three children are now grown and the two boys are professional tattoo artists in Tahiti. See information on Aroma Tattoo Art and Manu Tattoo Art under *Tattoos* in the *Tahiti* chapter.

When the Salmon family settled on Motu Aito almost 20 years ago, the islet was only sand and coral. Today it is an oasis bordered by *aito* trees (also known as Casaurina, ironwood or Australian pine) that have been trimmed. There are also *tamanu* and *tou* trees, as well as papaya trees, flowering Tiare Tahiti bushes, frangipani and lovely green bird's nest ferns. The main abode is a big concrete house with an enormous family lounge filled with sofas or beds to accommodate the Salmon children and grandchildren when they come to visit, or to provide extra sleeping space for friends and an overflow of guests.

Manihi has built six Polynesian style bungalows for clients, which are very well constructed and thoughtfully decorated with driftwood, coral and seashells. Each *fare* contains a double bed and a single bed and a mattress can be added if needed. Each unit is different and very originally designed, with walls and ceiling of woven palm frond and terraces trimmed with the very useful *kahaia* wood found in the atolls. Manihi also built the furniture, using local woods. There is an individual bathroom for each bungalow, with a private outdoor shower in a little garden of ferns and other green plants. Two enormous concrete tanks catch the rain and provide a plentiful supply of water for showers.

Both Manihi and Tila practice yoga on a daily basis and welcome others who want to join them. Throughout the day they take care of their guests. He will take you in his boat to visit Pension Tetamanu, the old village of Tetamanu and the adjacent Tumakohua Pass, where he will join you if you want to snorkel or dive. You can accompany him on a tuna fishing expedition in the open ocean, or you can help him choose dinner from the abundant selection of fish in his fish trap. Manihi grills fresh fish on a barbecue every evening and everyone eats together at a big table on the dining terrace.

It is also easy to get away on your own. You can walk across a shallow channel to visit adjacent motu islets. Yours will be the only footsteps in the sand, as these are truly desert isles. Tila will pack you a picnic lunch and Manihi will drop you off on the pink sand beach of still another uninhabited paradise and pick you up whenever you wish. You'll have all the privacy you desire.

Be sure to bring your own booze, and they will cool your beer and supply you with ice, but they do not sell alcoholic beverages. While you're packing for the trip across the lagoon to Motu Aito Paradise, you'd better throw in a few extra cans of Hinano for Manihi. He also likes to party.

RAIMITI, *B.P. 1, Haapiti, Moorea 98729. Tel. 689/55.05.65; Fax 689/ 55.05.67; E-mail: linareva@mail.pf; www.linareva.com. On a big motu in the Tetamanu district, 60 kilometers (37.2 miles) from the main village of Rotoava and 15 kilometers (9.3 miles) from the nearest neighbor.*

This was still a project at publication time, but construction was due to begin before the end of 2004, with hopes of opening this family pension in June 2005. The owners of Pension Linareva and Le Bateau Restaurant in Moorea have bought 6 hectares (14.8 acres) of land on a very large motu that is bordered on the east by the Pacific Ocean, on the west by the lagoon, on the north by an immense coconut forest and untouched natural environment and on the south by Irifa, one of the most beautiful beaches in Fakarava. Raimiti means between the sky and sea. The only way to get to this isolated area is by boat, which takes about an hour. Plans include building 6 bungalows on the lagoon side and 3 on the reef side. These carefully decorated units will provide such comforts as hot water showers, natural ventilation and electric fans. There will also be a partially covered restaurant beside the lagoon, leaving some open space to barbecue under the tropical night sky. A boutique featuring local arts and crafts will be included and the white sand beach below the restaurant will serve as an outdoor cocktail lounge. Activities will include kayaks, snorkeling, small boat rentals, picnics on a neighboring motu, visits to the old village of Tetamanu, scuba diving in the pass, and visits to fish parks inside the lagoon. Once this place opens it should be an instant success, as the Linareva fellows, Eric Lussiez and Florian Pilloud, have had 20 years' experience in pleasing their guests.

Sports & Recreation
Cruise and Surf/Fish Charters

Cascade, *Tel./Fax 689/43.70.70; cell 689/73.78.10; 881631468727 sat/ phone on boat; E-mail: chris@tahitianbluewaterdream.com; www.tahitianbluewaterdream.com / www.wavehunters.com/tuamotus. Cascade* is a 64-foot steel motor vessel with 4-star live-aboard accommodations for 10 surfers or fishermen in 6 cabins. Charters begin in Rangiroa or Fakarava according to the seasons. For details and rates see information under *Rangiroa* in this chapter as well as chapter on *Planning Your Trip*.

Cruise & Dive Charters
  Aqua Tiki. Contact Patrice Poiry at Aqua Polynésie, *Tel. 689/73.47.31;* *Sat/phone on boat 06 60525060; E-mail: aquapol@club-internet.fr;* *www.aquatiki.com.* Aqua Tiki is a 46-foot Bahia deep-sea catamaran that provides 8-day/7-night dive cruises in the Tuamotu atolls. You embark in Fakarava and visit the north and south ends of the atoll, then sail to Kauehi, Toau and back to Fakarava, where you disembark. The 10-day/9-night cruises take you from Fakarava to Tahanea, Kauehi, Toau and back to Fakarava, and the 14-day/13-night cruises start in Fakarava and visit Toau, Aratika, Kauehi, Tahanea and back to Fakarava. Six passengers/divers can sleep in the 3 double cabins, each with its own bathroom. There is a television and VCR player on board, as well as full scuba diving equipment. Low season rates are about 34.000 CFP per day for each diver and 29.833 CFP for each non-diver or each diver in a group of six. Other cruises are available.
  Archipels Cruises (Archipels Croisières), *Tel. 689/56.36.39, Fax 689/ 56.35.87; E-mail: archimoo@mail.pf; www.archipels.com.* One-week cruises on board a Marquises 57 catamaran are available from Fakarava to Toau and Rangiroa, boarding in Fakarava on Saturday morning and disembarking in Rangiroa at noon on Friday. The cruise dates are scheduled in conjunction with the full moon and guaranteed departure for a minimum of two passengers. The per person cost of this cruise is 220.500 CFP, including taxes, meals and hotel services on board in double cabin occupancy, airport/yacht transfers at boarding and landing sites, as well as all excursions and events specified in program.
  Tahiti Aggressor, *US contact: Tel. 800/348-2628; Fax 985/384-0817; E-mail: tahiti@aggressor.com; www.aggressor.com.* The *Tahiti Aggressor* is a 106-foot, 18 passenger catamaran that offers live-aboard dive programs departing from Fakarava or Rangiroa. For details and rates see information under *Rangiroa* in this chapter as well as chapter on *Planning Your Trip.*

Scuba Diving
  Fakarava Diving Center, *Tel. 98.43.23, cell 73.38.22; E-mail showald@mail.pf; www.fakarava-diving-center.pf* is located on the premises of the Hotel Maitai Dream Fakarava. Serge and Carine Howald are the two qualified instructors who welcome first time divers who wish to get their first, second or third level permit from the National Association of Diving Instructors. Private lessons on request. Dives are made inside the lagoon, in the two passes of Fakarava, on the outer reef, deep sea and on the neighboring atoll of Toau, a 45-minute boat ride across the open ocean. The 26-foot long semi-rigid boat is comfortable and spacious. The club provides all necessary diving gear and charges 6.000 CFP per dive. A 2-dive outing for 4-5 people includes a picnic on a motu and costs 15.000 CFP per person.

Te Ava Nui Plongée, *Tel./Fax 689/98.42.50, cell 79.69.50; E-mail:teavanui@divingfakarava.com; www.divingfakarava.com.* This dive center opened in 1999 in Rotoava village and is operated by Frenchman Jean-Christophe Lapeyre, who is an international CMAS three-star monitor and BEES 1 professional dive master. He is assisted by two qualified instructors and a local boat pilot and has two fast unsinkable boats available to take small groups of divers to explore some of the best dive sites in the wide and deep passes, inside the lagoon and outside the Garuae pass. You can also visit several of the motu islets, which are bordered by white sand beaches. The diving center provides modern and state of the art Aqualung equipment and this is a Nitrox station. They charge 6.000 CFP per dive.

Tetamanu Diving, *Tel. 689/43.92.40/Fax 689/42.77.70, cell 77.10.06; E-mail: tetamanuvillage@mail.pf; www.tetamanuvillage.pf.* This dive center is located at Tetamanu Village pension and has a 22-foot boat with a 50 h.p. outboard engine and a 12-foot Boston Whaler for dive excursions in the Tumakohua pass and inside the lagoon on the south end of Fakarava. A fun dive costs 6.000 CFP, 6 dives are 5.750 CFP per dive, 10 dives are 5.000 CFP per dive and more than 10 dives are 4.500 CFP per dive. All equipment is supplied. It is recommended to verify in advance whether a qualified diving instructor will be available during your visit as they tend to come and go. Sané Richmond, owner of Tetamanu Village and Tetamanu Sauvage, is training to become a dive instructor so that his clients will be able to dive at any time of the year. For rates on dive and accommodation packages see information on Tetamanu Village. **Note**: Please read comments about this pension under *Where to Stay* in this chapter.

Shopping

Each month when the *Aranui III* arrives in Fakarava and the passengers come ashore for a picnic on the beach, some of the pearl vendors set up tables of black pearl jewelry and loose pearls at the picnic site. This scene is repeated for any ships that call. Otherwise you need only mention the word "pearls" and you will be escorted to someone's house to look at the pearls that came from their family's pearl farm. Some of these may be good quality pearls, but very often they are pearls of very poor quality. You can learn the difference by reading about Tahitian Black Pearls in the *Basic Information* chapter in this book. You should also be aware that jeweler's glue is not always used to set the pearls in these remote atolls, and you risk losing your pearl just hours after you buy it. If you cannot resist a piece of jewelry, then have a jeweler reglue it once you get home. Some of the unset pearls are magnificent and sell at bargain prices.

Jacqueline Moeroa at Pension Vahitu Dream makes clothes and *tifaifai* bed covers, which she sells in her little boutique at the front of her pension.

Corina Lenoir at Pension Paparara makes shell jewelry and mirrors bordered with seashells.

Go to see Clotilde Dariel at Pension Havaiki if you want to buy some pretty shell necklaces. She sells them for her mother who lives in Rotoava village. These are made from the deep yellow, gold and orange shells that are found only on certain atolls in the Tuamotu Archipelago.

Practical Information

There are no banks and no *gendarmes* in Fakarava. The *mairie* (town hall) is located in the center of Rotoava village, *Tel. 98.42.81.*

Food Stores

In addition to a new supermarket there are two well stocked stores in Rotoava village that provide frozen products, canned foods, a few fresh vegetables, wine and beer. You can buy fresh baguettes of French bread each morning. One of the magasins sells fuel (diesel by the 200-liter drum only). They will deliver it to the quay for visiting yachts. Snack Teanuanua serves good food beside the lagoon in Rotoava village.

Hospital

An infirmary is located in Rotoava village, *Tel. 98.42.24.*

Post Office

The **Post Office and Telecommunications Office** is in Rotoava village, *Tel. 98.42.22.* There are automatic telephone cabins here.

Chapter 21

MARQUESAS ISLANDS

The South Seas Island images of tranquil lagoons protected by coral reefs are not part of the scenery in the **Marquesas Islands**. Rising like a mirage from the swells of the cobalt blue Pacific, the rugged volcanic cliffs soar like rock fortresses thousands of feet above the thundering sea. The wild ocean beats endlessly against the craggy, sculpted coasts, unbroken by any barriers for almost 6,400 km. (4,000 miles).

Beyond the tumbling breakers lie the fjord-like bays, the narrow shores and curving beaches of golden black sand. Sheltered coves reveal a turquoise tide with pink and white sand beaches. Behind the seaside cliffs the electric green grasslands wander gently upward. Brooding and black with frequent rains, the jagged peaks and spires become a fairy castle in the clouds of the setting sun.

Lying north-northwest by south-southeast along a 350-kilometer (217-mile) submarine chain, the Marquesas Islands are all of volcanic origin. Scientists believe that these islands rose from the oceanic depths and their foundations are submerged 4,000 meters (13,120 feet) below sea level. The island of Fatu Hiva is the youngest of the chain, with an age of only 1.35 million years, while the most ancient island in the Marquesas group is the uninhabited island of Ei'ao, which was formed 5.2 to 7.5 million years ago. This is the youngest group of islands in French Polynesia and the farthest removed from any continent.

The Marquesas Islands are 7.50 to 10.35 degrees south of the Equator, and 138.25 to 140.50 degrees west longitude. They form two geographical groups about 111 kilometers (69 miles) apart, with a combined land area of 1,279 square kilometers (492 square miles) for the 20 or so islands.

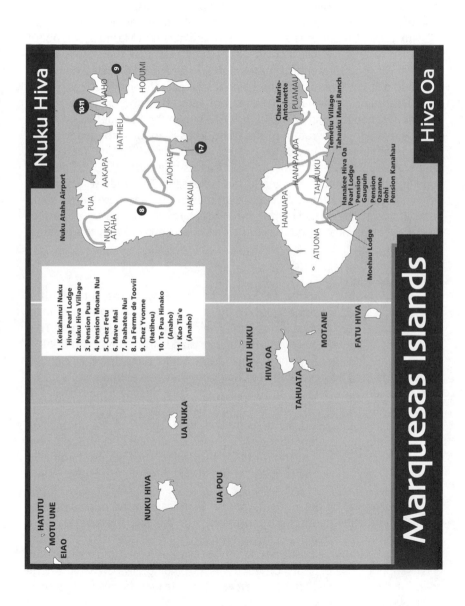

Nuku Hiva

Nuku Ataha Airport

ANAHO

HOOUMI

HATIHEU

AAKAPA

PUA

TAIOHAE

HAKAUI

NUKU ATAHA

Hiva Oa

Chez Marie-Antoinette

PUAMAU

Temetiu Village
Tahauku Maui Ranch

Hanakee Hiva Oa
Pearl Lodge
Pension Gauguin
Pension Ozanne
Rohi
Pension Kanahau

HANAPAAOA

TAHAUKU

HANAIAPA

ATUONA

Moehau Lodge

1. Keikahanui Nuku
   Hiva Pearl Lodge
2. Nuku Hiva Village
3. Pension Pua
4. Pension Moana Nui
5. Chez Fetu
6. Mave Mai
7. Paahatea Nui
8. La Ferme de Toovii
9. Chez Yvonne
   (Hatiheu)
10. Te Pua Hinako
    (Anaho)
11. Kao Tia'e
    (Anaho)

Marquesas Islands

HATUTU
MOTU UNE
EIAO

NUKU HIVA

UA POU

UA HUKA

FATU HUKU

HIVA OA

TAHUATA

MOTANE

FATU HIVA

The southern group consists of the three inhabited islands of **Hiva Oa**, **Tahuata** and **Fatu Hiva**, plus a few smaller islets. The northern group comprises the three principal islands of **Ua Pou**, **Nuku Hiva** and **Ua Huka**, and several uninhabited islands, including **Eiao** and **Hatutu**, which lie about 80 kilometers (50 miles) northwest of the other islands in the northern group.

Nuku Hiva, the administrative center of the northern Marquesas, is about 1,500 kilometers (932 miles) northeast of Tahiti. Hiva Oa, the main island in the southern group, lies approximately 1,400 kilometers (868 miles) northeast of Tahiti, a 3 1/2-hour flight by Air Tahiti's 48-passenger ATR 42 airplanes. Marquesan time is one-half hour ahead of the rest of the islands in French Polynesia. When it is 6am in Tahiti, it is 6:30am in the Marquesas.

The average temperature of the Marquesas is about 27 degrees Celsius (80 degrees Fahrenheit), with the hottest weather in March and the coolest temperatures in August. Although there is usually more than 80 percent humidity, the climate is healthy and fairly pleasant. The trade winds prevail between April and October, but at other times of the year there can be some hot, calm days. The annual rainfall varies greatly and is unevenly distributed. Fatu Hiva is the most verdant island of all because it receives the greatest amount of rain.

Land of the Men

Maohi people, whom the Europeans called Polynesians, settled in the valleys of these islands some 2,000 to 2,500 years ago, sailing their double-hulled canoes from Samoa or Tonga. Their legends tell of the god **Tiki**, ancestor of man, who conjured up a dozen islands from the ocean depths. These proud and fierce warriors were divided into clans, living in isolated valleys, separated by steep, knife-edge ridges. They had abundance, but also seasons of draught, famine and tribal wars. They tattooed their bodies in intricate patterns learned from their god Tiki. As they evolved they made exquisite carvings in wood, stone, ivory and bone. They built their homes on *paepae* platforms, worshipped their gods in *me'ae* temples of stone, and were feared cannibals. In the northern islands they called their adopted home *Te Henua Te Enata*, and in the southern group it was *Te Henua Te Enana*, "Land of the Men."

In later years the descendants of The Men learned the origins of their islands from their legends, and had a story for the way their islands were named. Folklore tells that the islands were born of a marriage between the sea and sky. Their god Atua built a house: Nuku Hiva was its pointed roof; Ua Pou was its support posts or pillars; Ua Huka was the binding; Hiva Oa was the ridge pole; Fatu Hiva was the thatched roof; and Tahuata was the celebration of its completion.

European Conquerors

The history of the Marquesas with the arrival of the Europeans was varied and often tragic. In 1595 Spanish explorer Alvaro de Mendaña discovered the southern group, which he named Las Marquesas de Mendoza—in honor of the wife of his patron, Don Garcia Hurtado de Mendoza, Marquis de Canete, Viceroy of Peru. When Mendaña sailed away 200 islanders lay dead on the beach of Tahuata.

Captain James Cook claimed the southern group for England in 1774, estimating the population at 100,000. Joseph Ingraham of Boston discovered the northern group in 1791, and explorers from France, Germany and Russia also planted their flags on these distant shores.

These islands became a regular port-of-call for the men sailing the Pacific—crews hungry for a touch of land, women and recreation. Australians seeking the valuable sandalwood that grew in abundance in the valleys of the Marquesas brought their sailors to these shores. Later the American whaling ships arrived, often leaving behind those deserters who had jumped ship. Over the years there were all kinds of blackbirders, profiteers, beachcombers and adventurers who sought refuge in the Marquesas. They brought guns, alcohol, opium, smallpox, syphilis and other deadly diseases, which almost decimated the entire population.

In 1842 the whole archipelago was annexed to France under the name *Iles Marquises*. Catholic missionaries were installed and a new rule began. Yet the decline of the population continued. When the French took control in 1842 there were 20,000 people living in the Marquesas Islands. Thirty years later that number dropped to 6,200. The all-time low of 2,225 people was recorded in 1926, and 131 of this number were non-natives. The population of the 1996 census was 8,064; still only a fraction of what it was a century and a half before that, but on the rise again. The latest census of November 2002 was 8,712, showing a migratory deficit of 173 inhabitants and a natural growth rate of 8%. Most of the inhabitants are Catholics. The 2002 studies also revealed that the Marquesas Islands received only 2.8% of the total number of tourists to visit French Polynesia that year. Most of these tourists were passengers on the *Aranui*, which calls at all six of the inhabited islands in the Marquesas archipelago.

Modern Marquesas

The Marquesas Islands today are quite modern, with electricity, international communications services, a radio and television station and efficient boat docks in the larger villages for the supply ships that provide regular service from Tahiti. The islands of Nuku Hiva, Hiva Oa, Ua Pou and Ua Huka have airports, and projects to build airports on Tahuata and Fatu Hiva are still in the planning stage.

Farming and fishing are carried out on a family scale. The villagers live mostly from the land and sea, earning money for purchased supplies by copra production. A recent addition to the cash economy is generated by the wild pickings of the *noni*, the *Morinda Citrifolia*, a potato-like fruit that grows on a tall bush. The juice from this fruit is sold as a tonic to cure anything from sore throats to syphilis, or as a panacea to heal a wide range of ailments from colds to cancers. While encouraging the exploitation of this business, the local government tries to discourage the islanders from abandoning their subsidized copra plantations in favor of planting *noni* to be shipped primarily to the US market.

The *Aranui* cruises to the Marquesas Islands 16 times a year during its 16-day round-trip voyages from Tahiti. The ship calls at every principal valley and many smaller ones on each inhabited island. This is the most practical and enjoyable way to make a brief visit to the Marquesas, as the costs of land and sea transportation are very expensive for individual travelers. See information on the *Aranui* under *Inter-Island Cruises, Passenger Boats and Freighters* in the chapter on *Planning Your Trip*.

Accommodations are available in small hotels, pensions and family homes on each island, and two international class hotels opened in 1999 on Nuku Hiva and Hiva Oa. The 6-bungalow Keikahanui Inn that was owned by Rose Corser in Taiohae was closed in April 1998, rebuilt, and opened in September 1999, as the four-star **Keikahanui Nuku Hiva Pearl Lodge**, with 20 bungalows. The 6-bungalow Hotel Hanakee in Atuona, owned by Serge Lecordier, was also transformed into a 20-bungalow four-star hotel that opened in September 1999, as the **Hanakee Hiva Oa Pearl Lodge**. Lecordier has since taken back management of 6 bungalows, leaving 14 bungalows operating as a Pearl Resort. Both of these hotels are associated with the Financière Hôtelière Polynésienne (FHP) of Tahiti, and are managed by South Pacific Management of Tahiti.

Activities in the Marquesas Islands include 4-wheel drive excursions, helicopter flights, horseback riding, hiking over mountain trails and to inland cascades, picnics on the beach or in the mountains. You can go deep-sea fishing, on motorboat rides, scuba diving, visit the restored archaeological sites and stone tikis, and go to the workshops of crafts people to buy woodcarvings and tapa hangings.

A fragrant bouquet of flowers and herbs is worn in the hair or around the necks of the Marquesan women. This is called *kumu hei* in the northern group and *umu hei* in the southern islands. Their *monoi* is a delightful blend of coconut oil, sandalwood, spearmint, jasmine, gingerroot, pineapple, sweet basil, gardenia, pandanus fruit, ylang-ylang and other mysterious herbs. This is used as perfume, for massages, to seduce a boyfriend or to ward off mosquitoes.

For further information on the hotels, pensions, restaurants, rental cars, boats, horses, and boat or land excursions, the E-mail address is: *tourisme@marquises.pf* and their website is *www.marquises.pf.* You can also find information on the family pensions and guesthouses at: *haere-mai@mail.pf* and *www.haere-mai.pf.*

NUKU HIVA

In Marquesan mythology, **Nuku Hiva** was the first island to be raised from the ocean depths by the god Tiki, who created a wife from a pile of sand. Even today this beautiful emerald isle, located about 1,500 kilometers (932 miles) northeast of Tahiti, is the leader of the Marquesas archipelago.

Captain Joseph Ingraham from Boston discovered Nuku Hiva in 1791, followed the same year by French Etienne Marchand. When Russian Admiral Krusenstern landed in Taiohae Bay in 1804 they found an Englishman and a Frenchman who had deserted their ships to settle in Nuku Hiva. Cabry, the Frenchman, was tattooed from head to foot, just like his hosts in Taiohae.

With a surface area of 330 square kilometers (127 square miles), Nuku Hiva is the largest island of the Marquesas group. The beauty of Nuku Hiva is truly breathtaking, whether viewed from the sea or the mountain heights. On the crenellated north coast is Taiohae Bay, a spectacular giant amphitheater dominated by emerald peaks and waterfalls. This is a welcome haven for cruising yachts from all over the world that drop anchor here after a month or more at sea. Taiohae is a pleasant village bordering the sea and serves as the administrative, economic, educational and health center of the Marquesas Islands. Here are the French and Territorial administrators, government buildings, *gendarmerie*, post office, general hospital, town hall, Air Tahiti office, banks and schools.

The 2,652 inhabitants live in the villages of Taiohae, Taipivai, Hatiheu, Aakapa, Pua, Ho'oumi, Anaho and Hakaui, which are separated by serrated mountain ranges, and connected by rutted roads best suited for four-wheel drive vehicles and horses. These residents work for the government, the community, Catholic church or school system, or for themselves—chopping copra high in the mountains, fishing, raising cattle and other livestock, or sculpting bowls, platters, Marquesan ceremonial clubs, tikis and ukuleles.

The Notre-Dame Cathedral of the Marquesas Islands contains magnificently carved sculptures by craftsmen from each of the Marquesas Islands. You can visit the sculptors' workshops and arts and crafts centers in the villages of Taiohae, Hatiheu and Taipivai. You can rent a horse, a 4WD or pickup truck with chauffeur or a speedboat with pilot. A scuba diving center is located in Taiohae and the waters surrounding the island are rich with big fish, manta rays and an exciting variety of sharks. You can hang glide from the peaks of Nuku Hiva or take a helicopter flight to Hakaui Valley, with its steep gorges and Ahuii waterfall, one of the world's highest cascades, at an altitude of 350 meters (1,148 feet). Near Hatiheu and Taipivai are ceremonial platforms, stone tikis and petroglyphs hidden deep in the valleys.

In addition to the 20 bungalows at the Keikahanui Nuku Hiva Pearl Lodge, accommodations are available in small hotels and pensions. Taiohae has a few restaurants and snack bars, and stores well stocked with fresh produce, canned and frozen food, clothing and household items. In Hatiheu you will find one of the best restaurants in the Marquesas Islands, as well as one of the most important ceremonial sites.

Arrivals & Departures
Arriving By Air
Air Tahiti, *Tel. 86.42.42*, in Nuku Hiva *Tel. 91.02.25/92.01.45*, flies ATR 42 turbo jet planes from Tahiti to Nuku Hiva once a day in 3 1/2 hours. All the flights are direct except for the Friday flight, which stops in Hiva Oa, and the Saturday flight, which stops in Rangiroa enroute to Nuku Hiva. Do not forget that the Marquesas Islands time is 30 minutes ahead of Tahiti. The one-way airfare from Tahiti to Nuku Hiva is 27.200 CFP, and the round-trip fare is 49.600 CFP. From Rangiroa to Nuku Hiva the one-way fare is 27.200 CFP.

You can fly from Atuona to Nuku Hiva by ATR or Dornier planes daily except Saturday for a one-way fare of 10.000 CFP. You can also fly to Nuku Hiva from Ua Pou on Monday, Wednesday, Thursday, Friday and Sunday aboard a Dornier, and from Ua Huka each Wednesday, Thursday and Sunday, also by Dornier. The one-way fare for the 25- to 30-minute flights from Ua Pou or Ua Huka to Nuku Hiva is 6.000 CFP. In 2004 a 19-passenger Twin Otter Dornier was based permanently in the Marquesas and the inter-Marquesas flights correspond to the schedule of the ATR 42 flights to Tahiti. See further information under *Hiva Oa*, *Ua Pou* and *Ua Huka* in this chapter.

The 48-kilometer (30-mile) road between the Nuku Ataha airport and Taiohae village takes about two hours in a four-wheel drive vehicle. The unpaved road winds across the Toovii Plateau and is rutted, often very muddy and always uncomfortable. Most people prefer to take the helicopter shuttle service.

You can also get to Nuku Hiva by chartering an airplane in Tahiti from **Wan Air**, *Tel. 50.44.17, cell 77.03.79*; **Air Archipels**, *Tel. 81.30.30*; or **Air Tahiti**, *Tel. 86.42.42*.

Arriving By Boat
The *Aranui* includes stops at Taiohae, Hatiheu and Taipivai, and sometimes at Anaho and Aakapa, during its 16-day round-trip cruise program from Tahiti to the Marquesas. The *Taporo VI* includes Taiohae in its 10-day round-trip voyages from Tahiti. See details in section on *Inter-Island Cruise Ships and Cargo/Passenger Boats* in Chapter 6, *Planning Your Trip*.

Departing By Air
There is a direct ATR 42 flight between Nuku Hiva and Tahiti daily except Saturday, when the plane stops in Atuona. There are also direct flights by 19-passenger Dornier from Nuku Hiva to Atuona on Monday, Tuesday, Thursday and Saturday. The Dornier flight on Wednesday from Nuku Hiva to Atuona stops in Ua Pou and the flights on Friday and Sunday stop in Ua Huka. **Air Tahiti reservations** in Taiohae, *Tel.* 91.02.25; Nuku Ataha airport, *Tel. 92.01.45.*

Departing By Boat
The *Aranui* arrives in Taiohae Bay on the sixth day of its 16-day voyage from Tahiti to the Marquesas Islands. An alternative to taking the entire trip is to fly to Nuku Hiva and join the ship there, which will give you the opportunity of visiting all the inhabited islands in the Marquesas, with a stop in Rangiroa on the return trip to Tahiti. Or you can make the round of the Marquesas on board the ship and fly back to Tahiti. If you're just looking for a one-way passage from the Marquesas to Tahiti, the *Aranui* calls at Nuku Hiva on the 11th and 12th day of its schedule, and from there goes to Ua Pou, Fakarava and Tahiti, which will give you only three nights aboard the ship. See details in section on *Inter-Island Cruise Ships and Cargo/Passenger Boats* in Chapter 6, *Planning Your Trip.*

Orientation
Nuku Ataha airport is a 3 1/2-hour direct flight from Tahiti, and can also be reached from Hiva Oa, Ua Pou and Ua Huka, as well as Rangiroa. The principal town of **Taiohae** is 48 kilometers (30 miles) from the airport at La Terre Deserte. A twisting dirt road from the airport winds through the mountains and the Toovii plateau, 800 meters (2,624 feet) above the valleys of ferns, giant mango trees and coconut palms.

The village of Taiohae follows the semicircular curve of **Taiohae Bay** for about 3.5 kilometers (2 miles), from the ship dock on the east to the **Keikahanui Nuku Hiva Pearl Lodge** on the west. During the summer months flowering flamboyant trees shade the road that passes through the village between the bay and the administrative buildings, hospital, church, school, post office, bank, shops, boutiques and small hotels.

Sundays and holidays are just as busy as any work day, when the villagers drive back and forth along the seafront road in their four-wheel drive vehicles, calling out to their friends and stopping to join the game of petanque being played beside the black sand beach. Nearby the women sit under a shelter and play bingo, while the children splash in the rollers that crash onto the beach.

Getting Around Nuku Hiva

Helicopter Flights

Polynesia Hélicoptères, *Tel. 92.02.17, Fax 92.08.40 Taiohae office; Tel. 92.04.40 Nuku Ataha airport; E-mail: helico-nuku@mail.pf*. An AS 355 helicopter can transport five passengers for sightseeing tours over Nuku Hiva or for air transport between the Nuku Ataha Airport and Taiohae Village, or between the airport and the Nuku Hiva villages of Taipivai, Hatiheu and Aakapa. The one-way transfer is 7.500 CFP per passenger. Reservations are required and the baggage limit is 15 kilograms (33 pounds) per person and 20 kilograms (44 pounds) if you are in possession of an international airline ticket. Inter-island flights between Taiohae and Ua Pou are made each Monday, Wednesday, Thursday and Sunday for 12.500 CFP per person. A 20-minute helicopter ride will take you on a flight-seeing tour of the island of Nuku Hiva, for 16.700 CFP per person if there are four passengers minimum.

Taxi & Transport Service

Heiatea Tours, *Tel. 98.08.22, Cell 74.42.23*. Jean Claude Dupont can transfer you from the airport to Taiohae village aboard his Discovery Land Rover. The cost from the airport to Taiohae by way of Toovii Plateau is 4.000 CFP a person, and if you wish to go by way of Aakapa, Hatiheu and Taipivai to Taiohae, the cost is 5.000 CFP per passenger.

Huki Location, *Tel. 92.04.89 / 72.86.70 / 72.02.65*. The one-way taxi fare between the Terre Deserte airport to Taiohae village is 4.000 CFP per person. Owner Justin Otto charges 10.000 CFP for a half-day excursion with driver or 20.000 CFP for a full day tour.

Nuku Hiva Transports, *Tel. 92.06.80/77.32.81*, is owned by Marcel Huveke, who operates a taxi and excursion service. He charges 4.000 CFP per person for a 4WD-vehicle transfer from the airport to Taiohae village.

Teiki Transports, *Tel. 92.03.47*, in Taiohae village is operated by Joseph Teiki Puhetini. He will drive you from Taiohae to Taipivai, Hatiheu or to Aakapa and back to Taiohae, or to the Nuku Ataha airport. Be prepared to pay a minimum of 10.000 CFP and often much more when you hire a car with chauffeur.

Other chauffeur-driven vehicles you can hire include: **Kimitete Transports**, *Tel. 92.05.22*, and **Rose-Marie Transports**, *Tel. 92.05.96/74.36.76*. See more information under *Land Tours* in this chapter.

Rental Cars

You can rent a self-drive 4WD vehicle from **Huki Location**, *Tel. 92.04.89/ 72.86.70/ 72.02.65*. He charges 13.000 CFP for 24 hours. **Moana Nui Location**, *Tel. 92.03.30/72.86.65*, and **Tapuama Location**, *Tel. 92.03.24* also have 4WD vehicles for rent without driver. Guests staying at **Pension Mave Mai**, *Tel. 92.08.10/73.76.01*, can rent a 4WD for 10.000 CFP per day.

Where to Stay

Superior

KEIKAHANUI NUKU HIVA PEARL LODGE, *B.P. 53, Taiohae, Nuku Hiva 98742, Marquesas Islands. Tel. 689/92.07.10; Fax 689/92.07.11; E-mail: keikahanui@mail.pf; www.pearlresorts.com. Reservations: South Pacific Management, B.P. 2460, Papeete, Tahiti 98713; Tel. 689/50.84.53; Fax 689/ 43.17.86; E-mail: carine.keck@spmhotels.pf. 20 bungalows overlooking Taiohae Bay, 2 kilometers (1.2 miles) from the Taiohae pier and 48 kilometers (30 miles) from the airport. EP Rates single/double: standard garden bungalow 18.000 CFP; bayview bungalow 22.000 CFP; premium bayview bungalow 35.000 CFP; add 5.000 CFP for third person. Meal plan with breakfast and dinner add 7.200 CFP per person; meal plan with breakfast, lunch and dinner add 9.900 CFP per person; American breakfast 2.200 CFP; lunch (set menu) 2.700 CFP; dinner (set menu) 5.000 CFP; fruit basket 2.900 CFP; bottle of champagne 9.200 CFP; one-way transfer from airport to Taiohae village by helicopter 7.500 CFP; one-way transfer from helipad in Taiohae village to hotel by 4WD 1.000 CFP; one-way transfer from airport to hotel by 4WD 4.500 CFP per person. A private transfer is 15.000 CFP. One or two children between 3 and 12 years old sharing parents' room are free of charge on accommodation basis and have 50% discount on AP/MAP plans (excluded beverages) and Airport/Hotel/Airport transfers when provided by the hotel. Babies and children under 3 years old are free of charge on accommodation, meal plans and Airport/Hotel/Airport transfers when provided by the hotel. Add 5% hotel tax to room rates and 6% value added tax to room rates, prepaid meal plans and transfers. A 10% value added tax is applicable to other services. All major credit cards.*

This four-star hotel opened in September 1999, with 20 local style bungalows built on stilts on the hillside overlooking Taiohae Bay. The grounds cover six hectares (15 acres) of tropical gardens of fruit trees and flowers. There are 6 Garden bungalows, 6 Bay View bungalows and 8 Premium Bay View Bungalows. Each bungalow has a bedroom with a king size bed or two twin beds and an extra bed, plus a separate bathroom with hot water shower, and a terrace facing the bay. The bamboo walls and shingle roof of the bungalows are complemented by an interior of pandanus and tapa, which are beautifully blended to create a very pleasant decor. Each bungalow has air-conditioning, a mini-bar refrigerator, satellite television, in-house movie channel, tea and coffee making facilities, international direct dial telephone, safe and hair dryer. Two Bay View rooms are well equipped for disabled guests using a wheelchair. Room service, laundry service and baby-sitting services are available.

The public facilities include Le Pua Enana gourmet restaurant and Le Tiki bar, the reception, boutique and tour desk, plus the fresh water swimming pool, from where you can gaze out at the lovely scenery of Taiohae Bay. The

Keikahanui Museum / Boutique is located on the road leading to the beach. Stop in and meet Rose Corser, an American woman who, with her husband, built the original Keikahanui Inn, which had six bungalows. The boutique features a large variety of art objects as well as tapa and original paintings by local artists. Rose also has a small library and museum of Marquesan artifacts and handcrafts, and she loves to share her wealth of information about life in the Marquesas Islands.

The hotel's tour desk can help you arrange excursions and outings to visit the island by land or sea or air. You can walk around Taiohae village and visit Colette Bay, Goat Park, Tahuna Nui and Koueva, and you can walk up the hill for a panoramic view from the archaeological site of Koueva. A 2-hour guided horseback ride is 5.800 CFP and a full day's ride is 9.800 CFP. Half-day excursions by 4WD vehicle to visit Taiohae village are 3.600 CFP, and a half-day excursion to Taipivai is 7.500 CFP. Full-day excursions by 4WD include a visit to Toovii Plateau for 9.500 CFP without lunch or 11.500 CFP with lunch; and you can visit Hatiheu for the day for 10.000 CFP without lunch and 12.800 CFP with lunch. A half-day boat excursion to Hakapaa bay is 9.500 CFP, and a full-day boat trip to Hakaui valley is 10.000 CFP. A full-day boat tour around the island of Nuku Hiva is 25.000 CFP and you can go by boat to the island of Ua Pou for the day for 25.000 CFP. Scuba diving with a qualified instructor costs 5.500 CFP for one dive and packages are available for 5 and 10 dives. See more information in the sections on *Land Tours*, *Horseback Riding*, *Motor Boat Rental*, and *Scuba Diving* in this chapter.

As in all the Pearl Resorts, the Nuku Hiva Keikahanui Pearl Lodge has a special program for honeymooners and other romantic couples. A Starlight dinner served on the terrace of your bungalow is 23.800 CFP for two. A Romantic Escapade will take you to Colette Bay where you will be served lunch for 17.907 CFP per couple, and a Sunset cruise for two is 47.600 CFP. Traditional Polynesian wedding ceremonies can also be performed for 102.000 CFP. Extras include a Marquesan tattoo for 12.013 CFP, digital camera photos for 3.627 CFP and a cassette of your wedding song for 3.627 CFP. For details please contact the hotel directly.

Moderate
NUKU HIVA VILLAGE, *B.P. 82, Taiohae, Nuku Hiva 98742, Marquesas Islands. Tel. 689/92.01.94; Fax 689/92.05.97; E-mail: nukuvillage@mail.pf. On mountain side, 2 kilometers (1.2 miles) from the Taiohae pier and 48 kilometers (30 miles) from the airport. Round-trip transfers: 8.000 CFP per person by 4WD; 15.000 CFP per person by helicopter. 6 bungalows. EP Rates: bungalow 6.500 CFP single; 7.500 CFP double, 8.500 CFP triple. Meal plan with breakfast and dinner add 3.800 CFP per person; meal plan with breakfast, lunch and dinner add 5.100 CFP per person. Rates include taxes for*

room, meal plan and transfers. A 10% value added tax is applicable to other services. No credit cards.

There are 15 thatched roof bungalows spread out on a big grassy lawn facing Taiohae Bay, but only 6 units are available for short-term rentals. These are typically Polynesian style *fares*, with woven bamboo walls and a private terrace. Each room contains a double bed and a single bed, a private bathroom with hot water and a ceiling fan. The restaurant and bar are very popular with local residents, especially on weekends, when there may be music and singing and dancing. This hotel is owned by the Gendron family, who also own Moorea Village and it is managed by Marcel Gendron.

MAVE MAI, *B.P. 378, Taiohae, Nuku Hiva 98742, Marquesas Islands. Tel./Fax 689/92.08.10; Cell 689/73.76.01; E-mail: pension-mavemai@mail.pf. On mountainside overlooking Taiohae Bay, 100 meters (328 feet) from the boat dock and 48 kilometers (30 miles) from the airport. Airport transfer by 4WD 5.500 CFP per adult one-way and 2.500 CFP for child 2-12 years. Free transfers from heliport in Taiohae to pension. EP Rates: room 6.200 CFP single, 7.200 CFP double; 8.400 CFP twin; 2.800 third adult; 1.000 CFP for child up to 5 years and 1.400 CFP for child 5-12 years. Add 800 CFP per person for breakfast; 2.600 CFP for breakfast and dinner, and 5.200 CFP for all meals. No food charge for child under 5 years and half-fare for child 6-11 years. Rates include taxes for room, meal plan and transfers. A 10% value added tax is applicable to other services. Mastercard, Visa.*

This is a big concrete white house with 8 rooms that is conveniently located close to the shops and restaurants in Taiohae village. There are 5 clean and cheerfully decorated bedrooms on the ground floor, with a small terrace, and 3 nice rooms on the upper level with a balcony. Every room overlooks the bay. All the rooms are equipped with air-conditioning, a ceiling fan, a private bathroom with hot water shower, one double and one single bed, and house linens. A big covered terrace can seat 30 people for meals and the former dining room has been transformed into a lounge for guests, where you can read and watch television or video films on the Marquesas Festival and the Survivor TV series that was filmed in Nuku Hiva.

Your hosts, Jean-Claude and Régina Tata, will drive you to the Keikahanui Nuku Hiva Pearl Lodge to visit Rose Corser's museum, and they will also provide free transportation for you to dine out in the restaurants in Taiohae. They will arrange day excursions for you on request or you can rent a 4WD vehicle from them for 10.000 CFP per day and drive yourself around. Please see details under *Land Tours* in this chapter.

PENSION MOANA NUI, *B.P. 33, Taiohae, Nuku Hiva 98742, Marquesas Islands. Tel. 689/92.03.30; Fax 689/92.00.02; Cell 689/72.86.65. E-mail: pensionmoananui@mail.pf; www.ifrance.com/pensionmoananui. On mountain side 600 meters (654 yards) from the boat dock and 48 kilometers (30 miles) from the airport. Round-trip transfers: 8.000 CFP per person by 4WD;*

15.000 CFP per person by helicopter. EP Rates: room with breakfast 6.360 CFP single; 6.890 CFP double; room with breakfast and dinner 9.010 CFP single, 12.190 CFP double; room with breakfast, lunch and dinner 11.660 CFP single, 15.370 CFP double. Rates include taxes for room, meal plan and transfers. A 10% value added tax is applicable to other services. All major credit cards.

This two-story renovated building has seven rooms upstairs, with single or double beds and private bathrooms with hot water showers. Four rooms have air conditioning. Each room has a television and terrace and house linens are furnished. The restaurant and bar downstairs serves three daily meals, which may be steak and fries, Marquesan seafood specialties or pizza. The manager, Charles Mombaerts, also has a one bedroom air-conditioned bungalow for rent, with a double bed and a single bed, private bathroom with hot water shower, a living room and dining room. There's nothing fancy about this hotel, but it's conveniently located if you want to be in Taiohae village. The owner also rents self-drive 4WD vehicles.

PENSION PUA, *B.P. 99, Taiohae, Nuku Hiva 98742, Marquesas Islands. Tel. 689/92.06.12; Fax 689/92.01.35; Cell 689/21.47.53; E-mail: claudepua@mail.pf. On the grounds of Nuku Hiva Village 2 kilometers (1.2 miles) from the Taiohae pier and 48 kilometers (30 miles) from the airport. Round-trip transfers: 8.000 CFP per person by 4WD. EP Rates: small bungalow 4.000 CFP single, 7.500 CFP double; large bungalow with kitchen 5.500 CFP single, 7.500 CFP double; add 1.000 CFP for third person. Rates include taxes for room and transfers. A 10% value added tax is applicable to other services. No credit cards.*

Georges Pua Taupotini, who operates Pua Excursions, also has 5 bungalows for rent in the hotel complex known as Nuku Hiva Village. Two of the bungalows have kitchens and the other three are simple rooms. All units have private bathrooms with hot water showers and a terrace. Meals are served in the restaurant of the Nuku Hiva Village. See Pua for transfers and sightseeing.

Economy
PAAHATEA NUI (CHEZ JUSTIN & JULIENNE), *B.P. 201, Taiohae, Nuku Hiva 98742, Marquesas Islands. Tel. /Fax 689/92.00.97; E-mail: paahateanui@mail.pf. Overlooking the bay at the west end of Taiohae village, 3 kilometers (1.9 miles) from the quay and 45 kilometers (28 miles) from the airport. Round-trip transfers: 8.000 CFP per person by 4WD; 15.000 CFP per person by helicopter. EP Rates: room and breakfast 3.500 CFP per person; bungalow and breakfast 4.400 CFP per person. No lunch or dinner served. Room, meal and transfers include taxes. A 10% value added tax is applicable to other services. No credit cards.*

This bed and breakfast pension has three rooms and six bungalows in a garden setting with access to the sea. One of the bedrooms and all six bungalows are equipped with a private shower and toilet, and the other two rooms share the bathroom facilities. Hot water is available and house linens are provided on request. One of the family bungalows has a kitchen. Everyone shares the communal dining room and terrace.

CHEZ FETU, *B.P. 322, Taiohae, Nuku Hiva 98742, Marquesas Islands. Tel. 689/92.03.66. On mountain side in Taiohae village, 1.5 kilometers (.9 miles) from the boat dock and 48 kilometers (30 miles) from the airport. Round-trip transfers: 8.000 CFP per person by 4WD; 15.000 CFP per person by helicopter. EP Rates: Bungalow 2.000 CFP single, 4.000 CFP double, 6.000 CFP triple. Taxes included in transfer and room rates. A 10% value added tax is applicable to other services. No credit cards.*

This is a bungalow with a one double bed and two single beds, a kitchen, terrace and private bathroom with cold water shower. House linens are furnished on request. It is in the center of Taiohae village and you can easily walk to the stores, banks, cathedral and beach.

Lodging Outside Main Village

LA FERME DE TOOVII, *B.P. 5, Taiohae, Nuku Hiva 98742, Marquesas Islands. Tel. 689/92.07.50; Fax 689/92.00.04; E-mail: ferme-auberge@mail.pf. EP Rates: room with breakfast 3.000 CFP single, 5.000 CFP double; bungalow with breakfast 6.000 CFP single, 8.000 CFP double; bungalow with breakfast and dinner 8.000 CFP single, 12.000 CFP double; bungalow with all meals 10.000 CFP single, 16.000 CFP double. Add 6% value added tax to room rates and meal plans. A 10% value added tax is applicable to other services. American Express, Master Card, Visa.*

Toovii Farm is in the center of the island, in the cool heights of Toovii Plateau, 800 meters (2,624 feet) above sea level, yet it is only 22 kilometers (13.6 miles), from Taiohae village, less than an hour's drive by 4WD. You can get a taxi from the airport or Taiohae village to reach the auberge, which consists of 5 bungalows in the midst of 300 hectares (741 acres) of pastureland and pine forests. Each bungalow is furnished with a double bed and a single bed, closets, television and a private bathroom with hot water shower.

The restaurant serves food grown on the farm or gathered locally, such as goat cooked in coconut milk, grilled pig, river shrimp, lobster and beef steaks, plus the tasty vegetables from their fertile gardens and the strawberries from their own fields. They make their own ice creams; yogurts, butter and jams, and they gather honey from beehives on their land. You can follow one of the many trails and walk around the private domain as you breathe in the fresh air and scent of pine. You can rent a bicycle for 1.000 CFP for a half-day, or a horse for 2.500 CFP for a half-day's ride, with a guide if you prefer. Ismael, the friendly Marquesan manager, also speaks English.

CHEZ YVONNE (HINAKO NUI,) *B.P. 199, Taiohae, Nuku Hiva 98742, Marquesas Islands. Tel. 689/92.02.97; Fax 689/92.01.28; E-mail:*

hinakonui@mail.pf. On mountain side in Hatiheu village, 500 meters (545 yards) from the Hatiheu boat landing, 75 kilometers (47 miles) from the airport and 28 kilometers (17 miles) from Taiohae Bay. Round-trip transfers: 8.000 CFP per person by 4WD; 15.000 CFP per person by helicopter. EP Rates: Bungalow plus breakfast 5.000 CFP single, 7.000 CFP double; bungalow with breakfast and dinner 11.000 CFP single, 15.000 CFP double; bungalow with all meals included 18.000 CFP single, 24.000 CFP double. Taxes included in room rates, meal plans and transfers. A 10% value added tax is applicable to other services. No credit cards.

These five bungalows facing the sea and the restaurant next door are usually called "Chez Yvonne" and are owned by Yvonne Katupa, who is also the mayor of Hatiheu. Yvonne is reputed for serving the best food in all the Marquesas Islands. Four of the five little bungalows have a double bed and a private bathroom with a cold water shower, and there is one family bungalow with a double bed and a single bed, a private bathroom and cold water shower. House linens are included. This pension is in the center of Hatiheu village and you can walk to the church, archaeological sites, to a small museum and to the artisan center. A black sand beach is across the dirt road in front of the bungalows. Be sure to protect yourself against the vicious nonos. Guided 4WD excursions start at 3.000 CFP per person and a boat excursion to Anaho village is 7.000 CFP per person for a maximum of 5 passengers.

TE PUA HINAKO (CHEZ JULIETTE), *B.P. 202, Taiohae, Nuku Hiva 98742, Marquesas Islands. Tel. 689/92.04.14. Beside the beach in Anaho Bay, 2 kilometers (1.2 miles) from Hatiheu village, 30 kilometers (19 miles) from Taiohae Bay and 77 kilometers (48 miles) from the airport. Round-trip transfers by boat between Hatiheu Bay and Anaho Bay 12.000 CFP for 1-6 passengers; round-trip helicopter transfers between airport and Anaho 15.000 CFP per person. EP Rates: Room 2.500 CFP per person; room with breakfast and dinner 4.000 CFP per person; room with all meals 5.500 CFP per person per day. Taxes included in room rates, meal plans and transfers. A 10% value added tax is applicable to other services. No credit cards.*

It's worth staying here just to swim in the beautiful Anaho Bay, bordered by a beach of soft pink sand. Juliette Vaianui has a 2-bedroom house with both single and double beds, and a communal bathroom with cold water shower. House linens are furnished. Free activities include line fishing, swimming and shelling. You can hike the trail along the beach to Atuatua Bay and to the peaks overlooking the bay. You can also find a horse to ride along the beach if you just ask Juliette. Her son Raymond owns the Kao Tia'e pension next door, and his brother Leopold takes care of feeding the guests in both pensions.

KAO TIA'E, *B.P. 290, Taiohae, Nuku Hiva 98742, Marquesas Islands. Tel. 689/92.00.08. Beside the beach in Anaho Bay, 2 kilometers (1.2 miles) from Hatiheu village, 30 kilometers (19 miles) from Taiohae Bay and 77 kilometers (48 miles) from the airport. Round-trip boat transfers between Hatiheu Bay* *and Anaho Bay 12.000 CFP for 1-6 passengers; round-trip helicopter transfers between airport and Anaho 15.000 CFP per person. EP Rates: bungalow 2.500 CFP per person; breakfast 500 CFP, lunch 1.500 CFP and dinner is 1.800 CFP. Taxes included in room rates, meal plans and transfers. A 10% value added tax is applicable to other services. No credit cards.*

Kao tia'e is Marquesan for the Tiare Tahiti bud. This five-bungalow pension opened in June 1998, at Anaho Bay. Each bungalow is furnished with a double bed and a private bathroom with hot water, a terrace and house linens. See information on Te Pua Hinako, as Juliette is the mother of Raymond Vaianui, the man who owns this pension. They combine meals and activities for their respective guests.

Where to Eat

KEIKAHANUI NUKU HIVA PEARL LODGE, *Tel. 92.03.82. On hillside in Taiohae. All major credit cards.*

Le Pua Enana restaurant is open daily for breakfast, lunch and dinner. The Marquesan chef studied in France and presents high gourmet cuisine, combining the best of France and the Marquesas. This restaurant is getting very good recommendations from guests who have stayed at the hotel or just stopped in for an excellent meal. An American breakfast costs 2.200 CFP; the set luncheon menu is 2.700 CFP and the set dinner menu is 5.000 CFP. Le Tiki Bar has a bartender who is trained to make your favorite cocktail.

NUKU HIVA VILLAGE, *Tel. 92.01.94. Across road from waterfront in Taiohae. No credit cards.*

Open daily for breakfast, lunch and dinner. French and local cuisine is served, which an emphasis on Marquesan specialties.

MOANA NUI, *Tel. 92.03.30. On the waterfront street of Taiohae village. All major credit cards.*

Open daily except Sunday for breakfast, lunch and dinner. In addition to pizzas, local and French cuisine and buffet dinners are served. This is the most popular gathering place in the village.

LE KOVIVI, *Tel. 92.01.14. On the waterfront street of Taiohae village. Reserve. No credit cards.*

Open daily except Sunday for breakfast, lunch and dinner. The menu includes French and local cuisine, and you can get take-away meals.

CHEZ YVONNE (HINAKO NUI), *Tel. 92.02.97 in Hatiheu village. Reservations are a must at this popular restaurant. No credit cards.*

Open for breakfast, lunch and dinner. Although this popular restaurant is now called Hinako Nui, most people still refer to it as Chez Yvonne Katupa, because that's the name that earned it the reputation of serving the best food in the Marquesas Islands. The specialty here is the fresh water shrimp that are caught in the river nearby, which are battered and fried. The restaurant also serves very tasty barbecued chicken legs, tuna fritters and grilled lobster. This is where the *Aranui* passengers eat when they come to Hatiheu.

AUBERGE DE TOOVII, *Tel. 92.07.50, is on Toovii Plateau in center of island, less than an hour's drive above Taiohae Bay. Open daily for breakfast, lunch and dinner. American Express, Mastercard, Visa.*

The food served is grown on the Toovii Farm. Choices may offer goat cooked in coconut milk, grilled pig, river shrimp or lobster. They also grill steaks from their own cattle. These main courses are accompanied by fresh vegetables from their gardens and fruits in season, which may include strawberries. They make their own ice cream, yogurts, butter and jams, and they gather honey from beehives on their land. Lunch and dinner prices range from 2.000 to 4.000 CFP. This is a lunch good stop while exploring the heights of Nuku Hiva by 4WD, on horseback or when hiking.

Seeing the Sights

The **Notre-Dame Cathedral of the Marquesas Islands** is located in the Catholic mission on the west side of Taiohae village. The cathedral was built in 1977, using stones from all the inhabited islands in the archipelago. The magnificent carvings were made by several of the local sculptors.

The **Herman Melville memorial** is a wooden sculpture made by Kahee Taupotini in 1992, which is on the bayside between the cemetery and the nautical club at the west end of the village. Melville wrote two books, *Typee* and *Omoo*, based on his short visit to Nuku Hiva in 1842, when he jumped ship from an American whaler and lived among the Taipi cannibals in Taipivai Valley for three weeks.

The **Koueva** and **Temehea** sites in Taiohae were used for ceremonies during the 5th Marquesas Festival of Arts in December 1999. The *tohua* Koueva was the ancient site for public festivities in ancient times, and during the 1800s the Temehea was the residence of one of the great chiefs of Taiohae Bay. You can see the carved stones at each site, as well as the millennium tree that was planted at Temehea.

Behind Taiohae village you can have a panoramic view of Taiohae Bay and the island of Ua Pou from the summit of **Muake Mountain,** which rises 864 meters (2,834 feet). You can get there on foot, by horse or by 4WD.

Hakaui Valley is on the southern coast, about a 20-minute boat ride from Taiohae. You'll have to hike inland over stones for about two hours to reach the **Ahuii waterfall**. This is one of the world's highest cascades, with a single jet of water tumbling from the basaltic rock at an altitude of 350 meters (1,148 feet). You can also reach Hakaui from Taiohae on horseback, riding 12 kilometers (8 miles) along a bridleway that ranges from 400 to 500 meters (1,312 to 1,640 feet) in altitude. You'll appreciate the refreshing pool of water when you get to the waterfall. It's best to go with a guide, and take mosquito repellent, plastic shoes and your swimsuit with you. This valley was featured in the "Survivor" television series that was filmed in Nuku Hiva in 2001 and telecast in 2002.

Hatiheu, on the northern coast, is 28 kilometers (17 miles) from Taiohae and 12 kilometers (7.5 miles) from Taipivai. The road between the two villages has been improved and now offers a smoother and easier trip by 4x4. Hatiheu was the favorite village of the Scottish writer, **Robert Louis Stevenson**, when he visited the Marquesas Islands in 1888 aboard his yacht *Casco*. This is also my first choice on Nuku Hiva, for the beauty and layout of the village, for the food at Chez Yvonne Katupa's restaurant (also called Restaurant Hinako Nui) and for the **Hikokua** *tohua* in the valley, beside the road to Taipivai. This archaeological site is about one kilometer (.62 miles) from Chez Yvonne, and it was restored for the Marquesas Festival of Arts that was held in Nuku Hiva in 1999. It is a large flat surface 120 meters (394 feet) long, used for dances and other public ceremonies. The *me'ae* are decorated with ancient stone tikis and modern sculptures also decorate the *paepaes*.

At the entrance to the site is a phallic-shaped fertility tiki. It is said that infertile women who touch the tiki will soon become pregnant. A 20-minute walk further up the road from Hikokua brings you to **Kamuihei**, a sacred place shaded by numerous trees, including an impressive old banyan tree that is 14 meters (46 feet) wide and said to be more than 600 years old. **Dr. Robert Suggs** found skulls in the branches of this tree when he was doing archaeological research in Nuku Hiva in the 1950s. The **Te i'ipoka** *me'ae* of boulders and stone platforms is located near the banyan tree in a mysterious dark jungle setting of *purau*, mango, breadfruit and *mape* chestnut trees, with giant ferns and *ape* leaves. There are also big pits that were used for storing "ma", a paste made from fermented breadfruit. In a riverbed behind the banyan tree are boulders carved with petroglyphs of fish, turtles and humans. After crossing a log bridge on the main path below the banyan tree you will come to Kamueihei *me'ae*, where you can hear the *upe'e* pigeons hooting in the banyan forest and smell the fragrance of the slim yellow flowers of the ylang ylang trees bordering two *tohua* complexes.

In Hatiheu village a small **museum** inside the *mairie* (town hall) has a collection of traditional artifacts found in the valley. A French priest brought a white statue of the Virgin Mary to Hatiheu in three pieces in 1872, and it was placed on one of the cathedral-shaped peaks overlooking the village, some 300 meters (984 feet) above the sea. Once a year people from Hatiheu climb the peaks to clean the Virgin Mary statue. The Catholic Church in this village was rebuilt in 2003 and is ideally situated, facing the sea with a backdrop of rolling hills carpeted in shades of green.

Anaho is just a 10-minute easy boat ride from Hatiheu, and you can also get there by 4WD, horse or hiking the difficult 2-kilometer (1.2-mile) trail, which takes about 90 minutes round trip. Anaho Bay is one of the loveliest spots in the Marquesas Islands, with good swimming in tranquil turquoise water and a crescent-shaped beach with golden-pink sand. Only a few families live in this valley, and the simple little chapel here is perhaps the smallest church in French Polynesia. The manta rays and leopard rays live in the depths of this bay, and the dreaded *nono* hangs out in the beach area. Bring your repellent.

Ha'atuatua Valley can be reached by hiking from Anaho beach, and the best way to visit it is with Dr. Robert Suggs, who is a guest lecturer aboard the *Aranui* two or three times a year. Dr. Suggs will lead you to the archaeological site he excavated on the Ha'atuatua beach in 1956 and 1957-58. In addition to the human bones, basalt adzes, fishhooks, mother of pearl ornaments and basalt flake tools he uncovered, he also found potsherds of a type of pottery that is known as "Polynesian Plain Ware." This undecorated household ware belongs to the Lapita pottery category of ceramics that was used by the Lapita peoples in Eastern Indonesia and Western Melanesia as far back as 2000-1900 BC. The pieces of potsherds that Dr. Suggs found at the Ha'atuatua site were believed to be brought by the first Polynesian settlers, which radiocarbon dating of the pottery indicates was around 125 BC. For more information on this subject you should read Dr. Suggs' books, which are listed in the chapters on *Basic Information* and *Ecotourism*.

A dirt road was built in 2000 that connects the Nuku Ataha airport in the **Terre Déserte** with **Aakapa** village, opening a 20-kilometer stretch of virgin land. The wind-battered bushes, dried grasses and red earth in this desert land make you think you've been transported to an African savanna, and the only living beings you normally see are herds of wild goats. The panoramic scenery is incredible, with vistas of Motu Ehe and its bay edged with a beach of fine white sand. You pass through the sacred valley of Pua, where the last queen is buried, and the road leads up to a hill where you can look out over the bays of Akahea and Hapapani with a pink sand beach and turquoise waters. Then you see the sentinel peaks of Aakapa and follow the road into the little village.

The **Paeke archaeological site** in Taipivai has two *me'ae* temples and 11 tikis of reddish colored stone. The trailhead, about four kilometers (2.5 miles) from where the valley begins, is not marked, so it is best to go with a guide. In 1957 American archaeologist Dr. Robert Suggs excavated **Te Ivi o Hou**, a *tohua* ceremonial site that is 274 meters (300 yards long). You'll need a guide to reach this hidden site, way back in the valley. **Pukiki**, a guide who lives in Taipivai, is familiar with both sites. Protect yourself against *nonos* in the valleys as well as on the beaches.

Taipivai Valley is 16 kilometers (10 miles) northeast of Taiohae, which you can reach in 30 minutes by boat from Taiohae, or by 4WD over a now improved road that crosses the **Toovii Plateau**, which has an average altitude of 800 meters (2,624 feet). A navigable river connects Contrôleur Bay with the village boat dock and follows the single dirt road through the village into the valley. American writer Herman Melville made this village famous with his published account of the Taipi tribe who welcomed him into their village in

1842. A **'Cite Melville'** sign marks the place where Melville was supposed to have stayed during his three-week visit. It's on the left side of the Hatiheu road about 4.5 kilometers (2.8 miles) from the bridge in Taipivai village.

Land Tours

Jocelyne Henua Enana Tours, *Tel. 92.08.32, Cell 74.42.23; Fax 92.00.52; E-mail: jocelyne@mail.pf; www.marquises.com.pf.* Jocelyne Mamatui provides full-day safari excursions by 4WD vehicle to Taipivai, Ho'oumi, Hatiheu and the Aakapa lookout, for 16.000 CFP for one person, 9.000 CFP each for two, 6.500 CFP each for three and 4.750 CFP each for up to six passengers. An optional lunch at Chez Yvonne is 2.500 CFP or 3.000 CFP per person. Half-day tours will take you from Taipivai to Ho'oumi for 13.000 CFP for one passenger, 6.500 CFP per person for two, 4.750 CFP for three, and 4.000 CFP per person for four to six passengers. You can go to Muake Mountain and the Toovii Plateau during a half-day excursion for 4.750 CFP per person for six passengers, or to visit Taiohae village, the artisans and the Koueva site, for 3.250 CFP per person for one to three passengers and 2.750 CFP per person for four to six passengers. Jocelyne also has all-inclusive package programs available to visit the other islands in the Marquesas group.

Nuku Hiva Excursions, *Tel. 92.06.80, Fax 92.06.44, Cell 77.32.81,* is owned by Marcel Huveke in Taiohae. He will drive you from Taiohae to Taipivai to visit the Paeke archaeological site, the three cascades and a panoramic view of Taipivai valley, for 16.000 CFP per vehicle. His tour from Taiohae to Hatiheu is 20.000 CFP, and includes stops at the Kamuihei and Hikokua sites and a view of Anaho Bay. You'll stop for a Marquesan type lunch at Chez Yvonne's restaurant. The cost of a tour to Aakapa is 25.000 CFP and takes you to look over Taanui and a visit to the archaeological sites. He will drive you from Taiohae to Anaho for 30.000 CFP and for 20.000 CFP you can visit the Toovii Plateau, where you can walk in the forest, visit the farm and have lunch in the restaurant at the Toovii auberge. An island tour starting from Taiohae is 30.000 CFP for the vehicle.

Pua Excursions Nuku Hiva is operated by Georges Pua Taupotini, *Tel. 92.06.12/92.06.87; Fax 92.01.35; Cell 21.47.53/21.74.50; E-mail: info@puaexcursions.pf; www.puaexcursions.pf.* A day's outing with Pua will take you by 4WD to Hatiheu, where you will then continue on to Anaho Bay by speedboat, a ride of 20 minutes. Lunch will be served on the beach in Anaho, featuring lobster if the season is right. Then you have time for swimming in the coral gardens. Be sure to bring a snorkel. The cost of 12.000 CFP per person does not include drinks. Another excursion choice takes you by speedboat from Taiohae Bay to Hakaui Valley, where you will hike to the Ahuii waterfall. Here you will have a picnic lunch before hiking back to the boat for the return trip to Taiohae. The price of 12.000 CFP per person includes the boat and guide, but not the picnic. Pua also leads 3-day and 8-day guided excursions by 4WD, horseback or hiking for a minimum of 2 people.

Mave Mai Tours, *Tel./Fax 92.08.10, Tel. 92.00.01; Cell 73.76.01; E-mail: pension-mavemai@mail.pf. Mastercard and Visa accepted.* Jean-Claude and Régina Tata, who own the Pension Mave Mai, also provide excursions by 4WD, which are sometimes combined with boat trips and hiking. You can take an archaeological tour by 4WD to visit the sites of Taipivai and Hatiheu and stop at the Aakapa Col for a panoramic view. At noon you will be taken by boat from Hatiheu to Anaho Bay where you will have a picnic of casse-croûte sandwiches and drinks, as well as time for swimming and enjoying the lovely white sand beach. This tour is 9.500 CFP for one person for a minimum of three people. For 6.500 CFP per person you can visit the valleys without including the boat trip to Anaho.

Sports & Recreation
Horseback Riding
The Ranch is operated by Patrice Tamarii, *Tel. 92.06.35, E-mail: danigo@mail.pf,* who has horses for rent. He charges 2.000 CFP per hour and 8.000 CFP for a full-day ride with a picnic. Children pay half-price. He can arrange 2-day excursions to Hakahui Cascade and to Hakatea, where you spend the night on the white sand beach. His 3-day outings will take you to the Terre Déserte.

Sabine and **Louis Teikiteetini** in Taiohae village, *Tel. 92.05.68/21.24.15,* have Marquesan horses for rent for one hour, half-day or full-day rides. They will organize excursions for you to explore the valleys by horseback.

Alphonse Teikiteetini, *Tel. 92.02.37,* also has horses for rent by the hour, half- or full day.

Motor Boat Rental, Fishing and Excursions
Marquises Plaisance, *Tel./Fax 92.07.97, Cell 73.23.48, E-mail: e.bastard@mail.pf; www.marquises.pf,* is owned by Eric Bastard, who has a 23-foot long boat named *Hitiaa* that is used for excursions. He charges 25.000 CFP for 1-2 passengers and 30.000 CFP for up to 5 people to visit Anaho Bay for a swim and picnic on the beach (picnic not included). He also combines a boat tour with hiking when he takes you to the Ahuii waterfall in Hakaui Valley. On the return boat trip you'll stop for a swim in Hakatea Bay. The cost begins at 13.000 CFP for 1-2 people and is 22.500 CFP for 5 people. A half-day outing to the Southwest coast of Nuku Hiva also includes a swim at Hakatea Bay, and a half-day excursion to the Southeast coast of the island will take you from Taiohae to the site of the dolphins.

Jocelyne Henua Enana Tours, *Tel. 92.08.32, Cell 74.42.23; Fax 92.00.52; E-mail: jocelyne@mail.pf.* Jocelyne Mamatui's boat, **Nils 1**, is a 26-foot polyester hull motorboat that will take you to the Hakatea Valley and the

Cascade of Hakaui, a 7-hour excursion that costs 13.000 CFP for one or two people, 5.250 CFP per person if there are three or four passengers, and 4.750 CFP per person for five to seven passengers. Bring your own sandwich and drinks. A 2 1/2-hour outing will take you to Hakatea for a swim and to see the waterfall for the same rates as listed above. You can also take a boat tour around the island with a picnic at Anaho beach. This all-day excursion is 32.000 CFP for one to two people, 13.000 CFP per person for three to four passengers, and 9.000 CFP per person for five to six passengers. A new excursion, that is available from May to November or according to the sea during the other months, takes you on a swim and picnic to Heinanii beach. This all-day tour is 28.000 CFP for one or two people, 10.000 CFP per person for three to four passengers, and 7.500 CFP per person for five to six passengers. You can drag a fishing line or go deep sea fishing aboard the *Nils I* for 16.000 CFP for one or two people, 7.000 CFP per person for three to four passengers, and 9.000 CFP for five to six passengers.

Mave Mai Tours, *Tel./Fax 689/92.08.10; E-mail: pension-mavemai@mail.pf*, also offers boat excursions to Hakatea Bay, Tikapo, Hakapaa, in combination with land tours by 4x4 vehicle. A boat trip to Ua Pou is 40.000 CFP and lasts all day. They accept Mastercard and Visa.

Heetai is a locally built 40-foot tuna fishing boat based at the Taiohae Marina, owned by Laurent Teiki Falchetto, *Tel. 92.05.78*. He will take a maximum of eight passengers to Ua Pou or Ua Huka or to the airport on request.

Makuita is a 33-foot Fiberglas boat owned by Xavier Curvat, *Tel. 92.00.88*, who also operates the scuba diving center. He can take a maximum of 15 passengers on round-trip inter-island excursions to Ua Pou and Ua Huka, or to the Nuku Ataha airport.

Ati Toka is a 25-foot polyester hull boat for six passengers owned by Francis Falchetto, *Tel. 92.01.51*, which is based at the Taiohae wharf.

Prisca is a 30-foot Bertram owned by Joseph Kavee, *Tel. 92.03.55*, that will take up to 12 people on excursions.

Scuba Diving

Centre de Plongee Marquises (CPM) is based at the Taiohae Quay, *Tel./Fax 92.00.88, E-mail: marquisesdives@mail.pf; www.marquises.pf*. Xavier Curvat is a French Federal Instructor who has lived in the Marquesas Islands for 18 years. He is a PADI OWSI, BEES 1 and CMAS two-star instructor, and he can give exams for diving certificates. His dive boat is the 33-foot *Makuita*, with complete equipment for 15 divers, plus a compressor and additional bottles. He can take you to more than 20 dive sites in the immediate proximity of Taiohae, or on day trips to Ua Pou, Ua Huka and the other islands in the northern Marquesas group. The water temperature in the Marquesas Islands is 28º C (82º F) all year.

You can see an abundance of marine life near the rocky points, where the water is oxygenated continuously by the surf. Among the profusion of color, species and movement, you may see red snappers, groupers, perch and other rock fish seeking shelter in the hollows of rock slides and caves sculpted in volcanic stones, hiding from their predators—tuna, surgeon fish, lionfish and four kinds of jacks or trevally. Curious manta rays, with their graceful ballet movements, will approach you for a closer look. And everywhere you will see sting, eagle and marble rays, lobsters, sponges and rare seashells. A little deeper you can observe barracudas and sharks. These may include reef sharks, silvertip sharks, Galapagos and silky sharks, hammerhead sharks and melon-head whales. You may even see one or more orcas, as they have been regular visitors in this area for the past five years.

The rates for scuba diving are 5.500 CFP for an exploration dive, 6.000 CFP for an introductory dive, 10.000 CFP for a double-tank dive, 25.000 CFP for five dives and 50.000 CFP for 10 dives. All equipment is included.

Shopping

Boutique Keikahanui Pearl Lodge is operated by Rose Corser, *Tel. 92.03.82*, in an annex building on the hotel grounds. Rose, who is American, has lived in Nuku Hiva since the 1970s and she buys carvings from the best sculptors in the Marquesas, which are on display in her museum or for sale in her boutique. She also sells tapa bark paintings and other original works of art.

La Galerie d'Art des Marquises, *Tel. 92.08.62*, in Taiohae, is operated by Renaud Coquille and his wife, who present the works of the best contemporary artists in the Marquesas Islands.

You can visit the sculptors' workshops to buy carved bowls, platters, saddles, tikis, ceremonial clubs and intricately carved tables. You can also visit the arts and crafts centers to buy woodcarvings. **Damien Haturau**, *Tel. 92.05.56*, is the best known of the Marquesan sculptors. His works include the statues in the cathedral in Taiohae and the Virgin with Child at the Vaitahu church in Tahuata.

Other noted wood carvers and stone sculptors include: **Brice Haiti**, *Tel. 92.05.19*; **Edgard Tamarii**, *Tel. 92.01.67*; **Tahiahui Haiti, Charles Deane**, *Tel. 92.04.13*; **Damien Huukena, Bernard Taupotini**, *Tel. 92.01.07*; **Pierrot Keuvahana**, *Tel. 92.05.58*; and **Philippe Utia**, *Tel. 92.00.51*. **Raphael Ah-Scha**, *Tel. 92.03.33*, is a wood carver and tattoo artist. If you're a serious collector, you can get a list of sculptors and arts and crafts centers from the Nuku Hiva Visitors' Bureau.

Practical Information

Banks

Banque Socredo, *Tel. 92.03.63*, has a branch office in Taiohae. You can exchange currency and make credit card withdrawals here. The ATM machine is inside the bank.

Hospitals
There is a government-operated hospital in Taiohae, *Tel. 92.03.75*, and a dental center. The villages of Hatiheu and Taipivai each have an infirmary.

Police
The French gendarmerie has an office in Taiohae, *Tel. 92.03.61 or 17*.

Post Office & Telecommunications Office
All telecommunications and postal services are available at the post office, which is close to the boat dock in Taiohae, *Tel. 92.03.50*. It is open Monday to Thursday from 8am to 3pm and on Friday from 7:30am to 4:30pm.

Tourist Bureau
Nuku Hiva Visitors Bureau is located on the mountainside between the marina and *mairie* (town hall) in Taiohae village and is open in the mornings only, Monday through Friday. Deborah Kimitete is the president, *Tel. 92.02.20/ 92.01.95; Fax 92.08.25; E-mail: tourisme@marquises.pf; www.marquises.pf*. She speaks English.

Yacht Services & Internet Connections
Rose Corser, *B.P. 21 Taiohae, Nuku Hiva, (ZIP 98742), Marquesas Islands; Tel. 689/92.03.82, Fax 689/92.0074, E-mail: rose.corser@mail.pf*.
Rose Corser is an American woman who sailed to Tahiti in the mid-1970s with her husband Frank aboard their yacht *Corser*. They settled in Nuku Hiva, where they bought land and built a 6-bungalow hotel called the Keikahanui Inn. Rose continued to run the hotel after her husband's death, until she formed a partnership to build the 20-bungalow hotel that opened in Taiohae in September 1999. You can find Rose these days in her small museum, boutique and library of Marquesan artifacts, handcrafts and history, which is located near the beach on the road going up to the Hotel Keikahanui Pearl Lodge. In addition to providing a service for mail and packages, she also has facilities and equipment for Faxes, E-mail and Internet connections for cruising yachts, Rose will be happy to answer your questions about the islands. She is very knowledgeable and helpful.
Nuku Hiva Yacht Services, *B.P. 461 Taiohae, Nuku Hiva 98742, Marquesas Islands. Tel./Fax 689/91.01.50; E-mail: anneragu@hotmail.com*.
This service is operated by Ronald Lasson and Anne Ragu at the quay in Taiohae, who welcome the people who arrive aboard cruising yachts. In addition to Fax, E-mail and Internet connections, they can help visiting yachts with entry formalities, visa extensions, provide general information on the weather, the Marquesas Islands and French Polynesia. They do mechanical repairs for boats, repair sails, and advise on where to buy duty free fuel, do the boat laundry, shop for provisions, rent a car, boat, horse or helicopter. They can

organize hikes, guided excursions, visits to the wood sculptors' workshops and other arts and crafts vendors and can even send you to a good tattoo artist.

UA POU

When the Polynesians first settled on the island of **Ua Pou** they named it for the pillars of rock that resemble great cathedral spires. The mountain called Oave Needle, the tallest of the fantastic monoliths, thrusts 1,232 meters (4,040 feet) into the clouds, and Ua Pou's dramatic silhouette is visible from Nuku Hiva, 35 kilometers (22 miles) across the sea, and even from Ua Huka, some 56 kilometers (35 miles) distant.

From the time of the old Polynesian chiefs Ua Pou has always been different from the rest of the Marquesas Islands. Although they formed tribes in the isolated valleys they recognized the authority of a single chief. The people seemed to be more peaceful, more unified and friendly, and the girls of Ua Pou are still considered the prettiest in all of Polynesia.

Ua Pou is the third largest island in the Marquesas archipelago, with 114 square kilometers (44 square miles) of surface area. The 2,200 inhabitants live in the villages of Hakahau, Hakahetau, Haakuti, Hakamaii, Hakamoui, Hakatao, Hohoi and Anahoa. Air Tahiti has 20-minute flight connections to Nuku Hiva and 35 minute flights to Hiva Oa.

The first stone church built in the Marquesas was constructed in Hakahau in 1859, and in Haakuti and Hakahetau villages there are small Catholic churches built on top of old *paepae* platforms. The main village of **Hakahau** has a dispensary, *gendarmerie*, bank, post office, food stores, boutiques, Air Tahiti office, port facilities, schools, small family pensions, plus a few simple restaurants and bars.

Ua Pou has experienced a cultural revival within the past several years. **Paepae Teavatuu** is a restored meeting platform in Hakahau, where traditional reenactments are held. **Rataro** is a talented young singer from Ua Pou, who has become very popular throughout the Polynesian triangle and beyond. Videotapes and musical cassettes featuring his all-male performers are fast selling items throughout the islands.

The **Kanahau Trio** is another popular singing group from Ua Pou. The sculptors sell their wood or stone carvings from their homes and in the handcraft centers in the villages. Horseback or 4x4 vehicle excursions can be arranged to visit the **Valley of the Kings** at Hakamoui, archaeological sites in the interior valleys, to picnic on the white sand beach of Anahoa or to discover the flower stones (*phonolitis*) of Hoho'i, with their multi-colored drawings. Boats with pilot can be chartered for offshore fishing or to visit **Motu Ua**, a bird sanctuary on the south coast.

The 7th **Marquesas Festival of Arts** will be held in Ua Pou in 2007.

Arrivals & Departures

Arriving By Air

Air Tahiti, *Tel. 86.42.42* in Tahiti and *Tel. 91.52.25/92.51.08* in Ua Pou, has daily ATR 42 flights from Tahiti to the Marquesas Islands of Nuku Hiva and Hiva Oa. A Twin Otter 19-passenger Dornier is based in the Marquesas Islands, providing air connections from Nuku Hiva to Ua Pou on Monday, Wednesday, Thursday and Sunday, and from Hiva Oa to Ua Pou on Monday, Wednesday, Thursday, Friday and Sunday. From Ua Huka to Ua Pou there is a direct flight on Friday and one-stop service on Wednesday and Sunday. One-way airfare from Tahiti to Ua Pou is 30.400 CFP; the one-way fare from Hiva Oa to Ua Pou is 7.500 CFP; the one-way fare from Nuku Hiva to Ua Pou is 6.000 CFP; and from Ua Huka to Ua Pou the cost is also 6.000 CFP.

If you have reservations with a pension then you will be met at the Ua Pou's Aneou airport and driven to your lodging. Otherwise, you can get a taxi or hitch a ride. It's a 45-minute trip between the airport and Hakahau.

Polynesia Hélicoptères, *Tel. 92.02.17, Fax 92.08.40 Taiohae office; Tel. 92.04.40 Nuku Ataha airport; E-mail: helico-nuku@mail.pf*. An AS 355 helicopter can transfer a minimum of 4 passengers between the Nuku Ataha Airport and Ua Pou for 12.500 CFP per person. These flights are made in connection with the ATR flights from Tahiti each Monday, Wednesday, Thursday and Sunday.

Arriving By Boat

The *Aranui* includes stops at Hakahetau and Hakahau during its 16-day round-trip cruise program from Tahiti to the Marquesas. The *Taporo VI* includes Ua Pou in its 10-day round-trip voyages from Tahiti. See details in section on *Inter-Island Cruise Ships and Cargo/Passenger Boats* in Chapter 6, *Planning Your Trip*.

Motorboats can be rented in Nuku Hiva for trips to Ua Pou. See details in *Nuku Hiva* section.

Departing By Air

The **Air Tahiti** office in Ua Pou is in Hakahau at the Kanahau Boutique, *Tel. 91.52.25/92.51.08*. The Dornier departure flight leaves from the Aneou airfield each Monday, Wednesday, Thursday, Friday and Sunday, and flies direct to Nuku Hiva to connect with the departure schedule of the ATR 42 flights to Tahiti. On Wednesday, you can fly the Dornier from Ua Pou to Atuona, Hiva Oa, or you can take the flight on Monday, Thursday, Friday or Sunday, which has one or two stops before reaching Atuona. There are no direct flights from Ua Pou to Ua Huka, but you can fly to Ua Huka on Wednesday and Friday via Atuona, and the Sunday flight stops in Nuku Hiva on the way to Ua Huka.

Heli-Inter Marquises, *Tel. 92.02.17*, flies from Ua Pou to Nuku Hiva to connect with the ATR 42 flight schedule. The cost is 12.500 CFP per person for a minimum of 4 passengers.

Departing By Boat
See information on the *Aranui* and *Taporo VI* in Chapter 6, *Planning Your Trip* (section on Inter-Island Cruise Ships and Passenger Boats). It is also possible to make arrangements with the numerous speedboats and *bonitiers* that frequently make the crossing from Ua Pou to Nuku Hiva.

Orientation

The **Aneou airport** is located between Hakahetau and Hakahau, half an hour's distance to the main village. **Hakahau** is spread along the Bay of Hakahau and continues inland for several blocks. Sailboats drop anchor in the bay, adjacent to a concrete dock for inter-island ships. The "pillars" rise above the seaside cliffs, and are often covered by clouds. A paved road leads from the boat dock throughout the village, and it is also an easy walk from the dock to the village center, where you'll find *magasins*, a few snack bars and the Catholic Church in the south end of the village.

A 22-kilometer (14-mile) dirt road from Hakahau to the airport and **Hakahetau** continues on to the tiny valley of **Haakuti** on the southwest side of the island, with a track from there to the village of **Hakamaii**, which is more accessible by boat. The dirt road from Hakahau to the south leads to the villages of **Hakamoui, Haakau** and **Hoho'i**. A track leads from this road to **Pa'aumea**, but all the villages along this southeast coast are better reached by boat. The white sand beach of **Anahoa** is a 25-minute walk east of Hakahau. This is also a nice ride on horseback, where you have panoramic views of the volcanic mountains and Hakahau Bay. Look for the Restaurant Pukue'e sign, which also gives directions to Anahoa Beach.

Getting Around Ua Pou

Taxi & Transport Service

Gilbert Kautai, *Tel. 92.51.80*, and **Jules Hituputoka**, *Tel. 92.53.33*, provide taxi service in Hakahau village, and **Bertrand Ah-Lo**, *Tel. 92.51.97*, has a taxi in Hakahetau.

Car Rentals

Pukue'e Locations, *Tel. 92.50.83* and **Jules Hituputoka**, *Tel. 92.53.33*, both in Hakahau village, provide rental 4WD vehicles.

Where to Stay
HAKAHAU
Moderate
PENSION PUKUE'E, *B.P. 31, Hakahau, Ua Pou 98745, Marquesas Islands. Tel./Fax. 689/92.50.83; E-mail: pukuee@mail.pf;* http://chez.mana.pf/ *~pukuee. Overlooking Hakahau Bay, 12 kilometers (7.5 miles) from the airport and 300 meters (984 feet) from the boat dock. Round-trip transfers between airport and pension 4.000 CFP per car. Rates: room 3.000 CFP single, 5.500 CFP double; Continental breakfast 500 CFP per person; American breakfast 1.000 CFP per person; lunch or dinner 2.500 CFP each meal. Half-price for child 5-12 years. Add 6% value added tax to room rates and meal plans. A 10% value added tax is applicable to other services. No credit cards.*

This is also known as Chez Hélène et Doudou. A big 5-room house sits on a hill overlooking the boat harbor, with a good view of the sugar-loaf mountains of Ua Pou. The motif is more Japanese than Marquesan, with shoji screens and unadorned wood. Three rooms have a double bed, one room has two single beds and there is one single bed in the other room. Guests share the two bathrooms with hot water. A very spacious terrace is also used as a dining area for the restaurant. Hélène Kautai is from Ua Pou and spent several years in France with her French husband, before coming home to open her own pension. She serves French cuisine and local products with a French flavor and takes very good care of her guests, who are often government officials from Tahiti who are visiting the Marquesas as part of their duties as *fonctionnaires*. You can rent a 4WD vehicle here or sign up for a guided excursion for 15.000 CFP per car. Meals are not included in these outings, but if you pay 500 CFP more, you can have a casse croûte sandwich. Hikes can also be organized, as well as a weekend camping trip in a deserted valley, for 30.000 CFP per person.

CHEZ DORA, *Hakahau, Ua Pou 98745, Marquesas Islands. Tel. 689/ 92.53.69; Fax 689/92.53.99. 500 meters (1,640 feet) from the quay of Hakahau and 10 kilometers (6.2 miles) from the airport. Round-trip transfers 4.000 CFP per vehicle. Rates: room 3.500 CFP single with (free) breakfast; room with (free) breakfast and dinner 5.500 CFP single; room with all meals 7.500 CFP single. Bungalow with (free) breakfast 4.000 CFP per person; room with (free) breakfast and dinner 6.000 CFP; room with all meals 8.000 CFP. Add 6% value added tax to room rates, meal plans and transfers. A 10% value added tax is applicable to other services. No credit cards.*

This is the home of Dora Teikiehupoko, who has a 2-story white house in the heights of Hakahau at the end of the village. One of the three rooms she rents to guests is large and comfortable and has a private bathroom with a hot water shower. The other two rooms are also large and the bath facilities are shared. A big covered terrace overlooks the bay. There are also two bungalows on the premises, each with a private bathroom and cold water shower. Dora has a reputation of preparing some of the best local style meals in town, which are served in the communal dining room.

PENSION VEHINE, *B.P. 54, Hakahau, Ua Pou 98745, Marquesas Islands. Tel. 689/92.50.63; Fax 689/92.53.21. Overlooking Hakahau Bay, 800 meters (2,624 feet) from the quay of Hakahau and 13 kilometers (8 miles) from the airport. Round-trip transfers 4.000 CFP per person. EP Rates: room 3.000 CFP single, 5.500 CFP double; room with breakfast and dinner 5.500 CFP single; room with all meals 7.500 CFP. Bungalow 4.000 CFP single, 7.500 CFP double; bungalow with breakfast and dinner 6.500 CFP single; bungalow with all meals 8.500 CFP. Add 6% value added tax to room rates, meal plans and transfers. A 10% value added tax is applicable to other services. No credit cards.*

This pension in the center of Hakahau village is also called Chez Claire, and is owned by Marie-Claire and Georges "Toti" Teikiehuupoko, who are both involved in the cultural activities in Ua Pou. Claire rents out 2 rooms in a big two-story house and in 2 new separate bungalows. The rooms contain a double bed and a single bed and guests share the living room, dining room, terrace and bathroom with hot water. The bungalows are equipped with twin beds and a private bathroom with hot water. House linens are provided. Meals are served on the big covered terrace upstairs or you can eat in Snack Vehine on the ground floor, which Claire also manages.

PENSION LEYDJ KENATA, *B.P. 105, Hakahau, Ua Pou 98745, Marquesas Islands. Tel. 689/92.52.66; Fax 689/92.53.19. On the hillside in Hakahetau village, overlooking the Bay of Hakahetau, 17 kilometers (10.6 miles) from the airport. Round-trip transfers 4.000 CFP per person. EP Rates: room with breakfast 3.500 CFP single, 5.000 CFP double; room with breakfast and dinner 5.500 CFP per person; room with all meals 7.000 CFP per person. Add 6% value added tax to room rates, meal plans and transfers. A 10% value added tax is applicable to other services. No credit cards.*

You have a choice of 2 average size bedrooms or 2 big rooms, all with a double bed. Guests share a bathroom with hot water, plus the kitchen, dining room, living room and terrace. Tony Tereino, the owner, has a restaurant-bar on the premises, and meals are served family style on the covered terrace of his big white house. He also operates Ua Pou Evasion, organizing hikes, 4x4 excursions and horseback riding.

Where to Eat

CHEZ HAEAPA, *Tel. 92.51.77, in the center of Hakahau village. Open daily for lunch and dinner. No credit cards.*

This was formerly known as Chez Rosalie, and since Rosalie has pretty much retired from the scene, her granddaughter Jeannine has taken charge of this popular restaurant. This is where the passengers from the *Aranui* have a Marquesan feast when the ship arrives in port. This delicious buffet features

shrimp, *poisson cru,* roast pork, beef or goat with coconut milk and vegetables, octopus, *uru, fei,* banana *po'e,* mangoes and papaya. A fantastic *kai
kai* for only 2.500 CFP per person. You can order from the a la carte menu,
which includes fish dishes for 900 CFP, shrimp for 1.100 CFP or steak and
vegetables for 1.100 CFP. Reserve in the morning for local style food at lunch.
    SNACK VAITIARE, *Tel. 92.50.95. No credit cards.*
    This snack serves good food.
    SNACK VEHINE HOU, *Tel. 92.53.21, on the ground level of Pension
Vehine in the center of Hakahau village. No credit cards.*
    Breakfast is 500 CFP, lunch is 1.500 CFP and dinner is 1.500-2.000 CFP,
which consists of Marquesan, Chinese and French cuisine.

Seeing the Sights
    Saint Etienne Catholic Church in Hakahau village is on the site where
the first church in the Marquesas Islands was built in 1859. The carvings inside
this stone and wood church include a pulpit of *tou* wood that represents the
prow of a boat with a fishnet filled with fish. Adam and Eve and the serpent
in the Garden of Eden and other Biblical designs are also presented. The statue
of Christ rests his feet on the head of a tiki and the Virgin Mary and Christ child
have Polynesian faces. Alfred Hatuuku, who lives in Hakahau, created these
exquisite carvings.
    Excursions by horseback or four-wheel drive vehicle will take you to visit
the white sand beach of **Anahoa** and the flower stones of **Hohoi**. These
amber colored stones are pieces of volcanic *phonolite* that make a pinging
noise when struck. They were formerly used to make carving tools and as
weapons. Recent studies show that these *phonolites* are 2.9 million years old
and the light colored basalt, which is very rich in black minerals, is different
from that found in other places. In the vicinity of Hakahetau and Hakamaii a
very unusual basaltic stone was dated as 4 million years old. Archaeological
sites in the **Valley of the Kings** in Hakamoui and Hakaohoka valley include
paepae platforms, *tohua* ceremonial plazas, *me'ae* temples and tikis.
    Above the village of **Haakuti** a small Catholic Church is built on a high
paepae stone terrace. **Hakahetau** also has an interesting Catholic Church
with a red tower. Hakanai Bay, 11 kilometers (7 miles) from Hakahau, below
the track leading to Hakahetau, is a good picnic spot. This cove is also called
Shark Beach.
    Te Menaha Taka'oa is the site of what was once a holy temple, dedicated
to Te Atua Heato, one of the Polynesian gods worshipped by the ancient
Marquesans. The German ethnologist Karl von den Steinen visited this sacred
site in the 1800s, when it was still *tapu* (forbidden). Georges Toti Teikiehuupoko,
Tel. 92.53.21, can guide you there.

Sports & Recreation

Horseback Riding

Tony Tereino in Hakahetau, *Tel. 92.51.68; Fax 92.52.66*, can arrange horseback rides on request. A 1-2 hour ride costs 1.000-1.500 CFP, depending on your knowledge of riding horses. An all-day ride is 6.000 CFP, with a picnic on request.

Cultural, Hiking and Eco Tours

Georges "Toti" Teikiehuupoko, *Tel. 92.50.63/92.53.21*, speaks good English and enjoys sharing his knowledge of Marquesan culture and history. He is a schoolteacher and president of Motu Haka, the Society for the Preservation of Marquesan Culture, and he is also director of l'Académie Marquisienne. Toti is an excellent contact for information on local sites, history and archaeology. His wife, Claire, who runs Pension Vehine and Snack Vehine, is also leader of a Marquesan dance group in Hakahau.

Oatea was created by Pascal Erhel Hatuuku, *Tel./Fax 92.51.28; E-mail: oatea@mail.pf or pascal@mail.pf.* Pascal was born in Ua Pou and educated in France, then returned to Ua Pou in 1997 to discover his own island and culture and learn the Marquesan language. Oatea is an Eco-Tourism agency he started in 2001 that specializes in cultural hikes and "green" excursions with a team of Marquesan guides whom Pascal has helped train, complete with English lessons. His guides will lead you on walking tours from Hakahau to the Vaiea waterfall, or from Hakahetau to Hakahau, over the mountains and through the woods, along the seashore and beach of Hakanai, following a cleared path that takes you to the Pokoio pass and through the Keaoa valley, where you will be tempted to climb the Poumaka peak for a breathtaking panoramic view of the island and sea. This 4-hour walk is relatively easy for most people, but you can also go by 4WD if you prefer. Pascal organized the cultural center in Ua Pou, bringing in exhibits from the Museum of Tahiti and Her Islands and getting the school students interested in participating. He also works as a guide for the *Aranui 3* as well as German tour operators and yachting groups. He can arrange lodging, transfers and excursions for private or professional groups or solo-travelers, reporters, scientists, tour operators and travel agents.

Ua Pou Evasion, *Tel. 92.53.19/92.51.68; Fax 92.52.66*, is operated by Tony Tereino, who will guide you on half- or full-day walks to discover the flora and fauna, archaeology and history of the island. You can also join him for a 2-3 day trek, visiting the wood carvers and fishing in the traditional manner. Six-day treks will take you to the mountains, where you will stay with a local family. A half-day walk is 2.000 CFP per person and a full-day's outing is 3.000 CFP. Tony doesn't speak much English.

Motor Boat Rental & Fishing Excursions
The following locally built speedboats are available for inter-island transfers between Ua Pou and Taiohae or the Nuku Ataha airport on Nuku Hiva, for excursions around the island, and for fishing trips.
Oceane is a 24-foot Fiberglas boat owned by Antoine Tata, *Tel. 92.54.87* that he uses for fishing expeditions and other charters.
Kukupa is a 24-foot 8-passenger Fiberglas boat owned by Rudla Klima, *Tel. 92.53.86; Fax 92.53.37*, that is available for deep-sea fishing and boating excursions or transfers.
Tahia O Te Tai is a 24-foot 8-passenger Fiberglas boat owned by François Keuvahana, *Tel./Fax 92.53.31* that can be chartered for fishing and guided excursions.

Shopping
Tehina Boutique in Hakahau, *Tel. 92.55.25,* sells curios, local clothing and perfumes. There is an arts and crafts center near the boat dock in Hakahau. Some two dozen wood or stone sculptors live on the island of Ua Pou, and you can visit their workshops beside their homes. One of the finest sculptors is Alfred Hatuuku, *Tel. 92.52.39,* who carved the pulpit in the Catholic Church. He lives between the seafront and Snack Vehine Hou.
In Hakahau village **William Aka**, *Tel. 92.53.90,* makes and sells jewelry, small tikis, lizards and miniature saddles of semi-precious woods. Artisans in Hakahetau village include **Marcel Kautai**, *Tel. 92.52.37*, **Beo Makario**, *Tel. 92.52.54*; **Tony Tereino**, *Tel. 92.53.19*; **Jacques Kaiha**, *Tel. 92.50.31*; in Hakamaii village **Eloi Hikutini**, *Tel. 92.52.53*, carves wood sculptures and **Kina Vaiauri**, *Tel. 92.50.32*, does tattoos. **Jean-Marc N'guyen** of Hakahetau and **Lino Taerea** of Hakahau, *Tel. 92.50.86*, were chosen to represent the Marquesas Islands during an art show of jewelry that was held in Tahiti in 2004. Tahia and Eugene Hapipi are in charge of the **Ua Pou Artisans Committee**, *Tel. 92.52.71.*

Practical Information
Bank
Banque Socredo, *Tel. 92.53.63,* is located in the same building as the Hakahau Mairie. The bank is open Monday to Thursday from 7:30 to 11:30am and 1:30 to 4:30pm, and on Friday from 7:30am to 2:30pm.

Hospital
A government operated dispensary with a medical team and dentist is located in Hakahau, *Tel. 92.53.75,* and every village has an infirmary.

Information Centers

The **Ua Pou Tourism Committee** is presided by Madame Tina Klima, *Tel. 92.53.86; Fax 92.53.41.* The Syndicat d'Initiative of Ua Pou is headed by Madame Tapita Gueret, *Tel./Fax 92.54.81.*

Police

There is a French *gendarmerie* in Hakahau, *Tel. 92.53.61.*

Post Office & Telecommunications Office

The post office is in Hakahau and all telecommunications and postal services are available here. Phonecard telephone booths are located beside the post office, on the quay and opposite the Air Tahiti office.

UA HUKA

Welcome to **Ua Huka**, Marquesan cowboy country by the sea. On the southern coast untamed horses gallop freely in the wind on the tablelands. Herds of cows and goats graze in the ferns, wild cotton and scrub brush that grows in the desert-like topography on a vast plateau. Above this incredible and beautiful scene rises Mount Hitikau, the highest mountain at 855 meters (2,804 feet). Breathtaking panoramas of the rugged coast and the sparkling sea greet the eye at every turn on the narrow winding mountain road that connects Vaipae'e, Hane and Hokatu, the three valleys where the 584 inhabitants live.

Ua Huka lies 35 kilometers (22 miles) east of Nuku Hiva, and 56 kilometers (35 miles) northeast of Ua Pou. It is the smallest of the inhabited islands in the northern Marquesas group, with just 81 square kilometers (31 square miles) of land. This crescent-shaped island is 8 kilometers (5 miles) long and 14 kilometers (8.7 miles) wide.

Ua Huka is one of the most interesting of all the Polynesian islands. The fern-covered valleys conceal *tohua* ceremonial plazas, *me'ae* stone temples and *tokai* burial platforms for women who died while pregnant or giving birth. Among the ruins from the seven tribes who formerly inhabited the island are petroglyphs that can be seen at the archeological site of Vaikiki valley. From Auberge Hitikau (Chez Fournier) in Hane you can hike uphill for half an hour or so to **Me'ae Meiaiaute**, a restored temple terrace where you will see three *tiki* that are sculpted from slabs of red tuff. A fourth *tiki* is a smaller version of the Maki'i Tau'a Pepe statue found in Puamau Valley on Hiva Oa, only this one in Ua Huka has been beheaded. (Read *Manuiota'a*, a book that was written by **Dr. Robert C. Suggs** and **Burgle Lichtenstein**, for more information on this subject).

In 1964 and 1965, **Dr. Yosihiko H. Sinoto**, Senior Anthropologist at the Bishop Museum in Honolulu, excavated a coastal village in Hane that was buried under sand dunes two meters (6.6 feet) high. Among his findings were two fragments of pottery, dating from around 380 AD, which Dr. Sinoto said is the oldest site yet discovered by anyone in Eastern Polynesia, and an important link between Western and Eastern Polynesia. Other renowned archaeologists believe that the Marquesas were settled between 500-200 BC. When Dr. Suggs excavated the Ha'atuatua site in Nuku Hiva between 1956-58, he discovered the first pieces of pottery ever found in Eastern Polynesia. The radiocarbon technique dated these shards at 125 BC.

An archaeological site named Manihina is located on a sandy beach not far from the arboretum in Ua Huka. Dr. Sinoto first noticed this site in 1964 when he was excavating the sand dune in Hane. In 1991 the mayor of Ua Huka wanted to take sand from the beach to use in construction. Before doing so he notified the department of archaeology at the Centre Polynésien des Sciences Humaines (CPSH) in Tahiti. Their research in three stages uncovered a burial site at Manihina that contained 39 human skeletons of both sexes, along with skeletons of two dogs and 11 pigs. Studies date this site between 1000 and 1400 AD. Although these were robust people in general, some of the human skeletons revealed that the old folks suffered from rheumatism and one of them had leprosy.

Captain Joseph Ingraham, of the American trading ship *Hope*, sailed by Ua Huka in 1791. The northern Marquesas islands were then visited in quick succession by Captain Marchand of the French ship *La Solide*; Lieutenant Hergest aboard the *Doedalus*, who surveyed the islands, and by Captain Josiah Roberts of the American ship *Jefferson* in 1793. Ua Huka was spared most of the carnage wreaked on the other Marquesas Islands by European discoverers, whalers and sandalwood seekers. During this period of discovery Ua Huka was named Ile Solide, Washington Island, Massachusetts, Ouahouka, Riou, Roahouga and Rooahooga.

Accommodations for tourists are available in the villages of Vaipae'e, Hane and Hokatu. These lodgings are located in separate houses and small bungalows, or in family homes or pensions. There was formerly talk about building a small five-star hotel for 40 guests before the year 2000, but that still hasn't materialized. The site chosen is just two minutes from the airport at a place by the sea called Tetumu, the former habitat of wild goats.

Arrivals & Departures
Arriving By Air
Air Tahiti, *Tel. 86.42.42*, has daily ATR 42 flights from Tahiti to the Marquesas Islands of Nuku Hiva and Atuona. From Nuku Hiva you can connect directly to Ua Huka by 19-passenger Dornier each Wednesday, Thursday and Sunday. From Atuona there are direct flights to Ua Huka each Friday and Sunday, and the Wednesday flight makes a stop in Nuku Hiva and Ua Pou before the Dornier reaches Nukumoo airport in Ua Huka. There are no direct flights between Ua Pou and Ua Huka, but you can make the connection by

flying from Ua Pou to Atuona and then to Ua Huka. One-way airfare from Tahiti to Ua Huka is 30.400 CFP; the one-way fare from Nuku Hiva to Ua Huka is 6.000 CFP; the one-way fare from Atuona to Ua Huka is 7.500 CFP, and from Ua Pou to Ua Huka the cost is 6.000 CFP. If you have reservations with a pension then you will be met at the Ua Huka airport and driven to your lodging.

Helicopter Service is provided by **Polynesia Hélicoptères** in Taiohae, Nuku Hiva, *Tel. 92.02.17*, on request.

Arriving By Boat

The *Aranui* includes stops at Vaipae'e and Hane in its 16-day round-trip cruise program from Tahiti to the Marquesas. The *Taporo IV* includes Ua Huka in its 10-day round-trip voyages from Tahiti. See details in the section on Inter-Island Cruise Ships and Cargo/Passenger Boats in Chapter 6, *Planning Your Trip*. Motorboats can be rented in Nuku Hiva for trips to Ua Huka. See details in Nuku Hiva section.

Departing By Air

Air Tahiti reservations in Ua Huka is *Tel. 92.60.44/92.60.85*. The 30-minute flight aboard a 19-passenger Dornier leaves Ua Huka each Wednesday, Thursday and Sunday, connecting in Nuku Hiva for a direct flight to Tahiti on board the ATR plane. There are direct flights from Ua Huka to Atuona each Friday and Sunday, and a direct flight to Ua Pou on Friday.

Departing By Boat

See information on the *Aranui* and *Taporo VI* in Chapter 6, *Planning Your Trip*, section on Inter-Island Cruise Ships and Passenger Boats.

Motorboats can be rented in Ua Huka to visit Nuku Hiva. Please see information in this chapter under Motor Boat Rentals.

Orientation

Ua Huka's three villages of **Vaipae'e**, **Hane** and **Hokatu** are connected by an unpaved road that winds along the edge of the cliffs for 14 kilometers (8.7 miles). Four-wheel drive vehicles (4x4) and horses are the means of transportation. The surf crashes against the steeply rising rocks of the coastline, creating a continuous spray that splashes high into the sky, reflecting the sun in multiple shades of blue. After a rain the hills and plains glimmer in varying shades of green, but the plateaus become brown and desolate during the arid seasons.

If you arrive by ship you will probably disembark in **Vaipae'e Bay**, also called Invisible Bay, because a wall of basaltic rock protects the bay from the open sea. Landings are made by small boat onto a concrete pier. Vaipae'e is the largest village on Ua Huka, with the *Mairie*, post office and the Vaipae'e Archaeological Museum of Marquesan artifacts all in the same complex. The

Catholic Church in Vaipae'e is worth a stop to see the artwork in the windows. An addition was made in time for Easter of 2002. The new window consists of six panels that were designed by Deanna de Marigny, an American woman who lives in Tahiti. The illustrations of the Immaculate Conception feature a Marquesan Mary against a background of the Invisible Bay, and she is complete with tattoos and a ukulele, while the panels are bordered by figures from the petroglyphs found in the valleys. The Catholic Church in Hane village was given a new sculpture in 2002 by Jean Yves Teikihuavanaka and Joseph Vaatete, when a big tamanu tree was blown down by strong winds in the valley. They carved a 3-toed sculpture for the Stations of the Cross.

The Nukumoo airport is located between Vaipae'e and Hane villages and the arboretum is close to the small airstrip. **Hane Bay** is distinguished by Motu Hane that sits just offshore facing the pretty little village. This is a dark violet and red rock 152 meters (508 feet) high, shaped like a sugar loaf. A structure of stones on top of this huge rock looks like a giant tiki has been carved there. In Hane there is a post office, an infirmary, schools and churches. Small *magasins* offer limited food supplies in Vaipae'e, Hane and Hokatu. Handcrafts centers and wood carvers' shops are found in each village.

The coast off Haavei is rich in sea life, filled with sharks, dolphins, manta ray, big turtles, lobster and a variety of fish. Boats with captains can be rented for deep-sea fishing and excursions to Anaa Atua grotto and the islets of Teuaua and Tiotio. On these bird islands thousands of white and sooty terns (*kaveka*), red-footed booby birds, blue noddy birds, frigates, tropic birds, petrels and shearwaters lay their eggs. They screech and squawk as they feed on the abundance of fish in this area, while their fluffy white fledglings sit on the hard ground of the upraised *motu* islets, waiting for dinner to be served.

Getting Around Ua Huka

Here is a partial list of the people who have 4-wheel drive vehicles. Some of them can be rented without a driver, but most of the cars come with a chauffeur. The rates are 6.000 to 10.000 CFP per day, depending on where you are staying when you rent the 4x4.

Alexis Scallamera, *Tel. 92.60.19*, **Paul Teatiu**, *Tel. 92.60.88*, **Maurice Rootuehine,** *Tel. 92.60.55*, **Jonas Teikihuavanaka**, *Tel. 92.60.57*, **Denis Fournier,** *Tel. 92.60.62*, **Marie-Louise Fournier**, *Tel. 92.61.08*, and **Firmin Teikiteepupuni**, *Tel. 92.61.07*.

Where to Stay

Moderate

MANA TUPUNA VILLAGE, *Vaipae'e, Ua Huka 98744, Marquesas Islands. Tel. 689/92.60.08, Tel./Fax 689/92.61.01; E-mail: manatupuna@mail.pf. In Vaipae'e valley, 5.5 kilometers (3.4 miles) from the airport and 2 kilometers (1.2 miles) from the Vaipae'e boat landing. Round-trip transfers 2.000 CFP.*

Rates: bungalow only 5.000 CFP single; 9.000 CFP double; bungalow with breakfast and dinner 7.000 CFP single, 11.000 CFP double; bungalow with all meals 9.500 CFP single, 16.000 CFP double per day. Half-price for child under 12 years and free for child less than 5 years. Add 6% value added tax to room rates, meal plans and transfers. A 10% value added tax is applicable to other services. No credit cards.

Three small wooden A-frame bungalows on stilts overlook Vaipae'e valley, where you can see goats and horses roaming freely and feeding on wild grass. Each of these *ha'e* contains a double bed and a single bed, a private bathroom with hot water, and a covered terrace. The furniture is made of bamboo and the posts on the terrace are sculpted coconut trunks from Ua Huka. House linens are provided and there is a restaurant and bar on the premises serving local style food. Karen Taiaapu-Fournier is your hostess at Mana Tupuna Village, and she is also head of the Visitors Bureau in Ua Huka. She speaks good English and Spanish.

LE REVE MARQUISIEN, *Vaipae'e, Hane 98744, Marquesas Islands. Tel./ Fax 689/92.61.84; Cell 689/79.10.58/71.52.95. In Pahataua valley, 800 meters (2,624 feet) from Vaipae'e village, 5 kilometers (3.1 miles) from the airport, 1 kilometer (0.62 miles) from the museum, 2 kilometers (1.2 miles) from the arboretum and 1.5 kilometers (0.93 miles) from the boat dock. One-way transfers between airport and pension 2.000 CFP per person. Rates: bungalow 3.500 CFP per person; bungalow with breakfast and dinner 6.000 CFP per person; bungalow with all meals 8.000 CFP per day. Add 6% value added tax to room rates, meal plans and transfers. A 10% value added tax is applicable to other services. No credit cards.*

Marie-France and Charles Aunoa opened this new pension and restaurant in 2003, which consists of 4 bungalows in the middle of a bird sanctuary. Each unit has a double bed, electric fan, mosquito net, private bathroom with hot water and a terrace. A sofa bed can be added for a third person and house linens are furnished. Guests can watch television or DVD films in a communal room and enjoy their meals in the restaurant. The hosts will organize sports activities, deep-sea fishing and walking excursions.

AUBERGE HITIKAU, *Hane, Ua Huka 98744, Marquesas Islands. Tel./Fax 689/92.61.74. In Hane village, 7 kilometers (4.3 miles) from the airport and 11 kilometers (7 miles) from the Vaipae'e boat landing. Round trip transfers between boat landing and pension 2.000 CFP. EP Rates: room 2.000 CFP single, 3.000 CFP double; add 3.200 CFP per person per day for breakfast and dinner; add 5.200 CFP per person per day for breakfast, lunch and dinner. Add 6% value added tax to room rates and meal plans. A 10% value added tax is applicable to other services. No credit cards.*

This is a concrete building, constructed especially for use as a pension and restaurant. The 3 bedrooms are clean and spacious, each containing a double bed, closet and desk, with curtains over the entry to each room. Shared bath facilities have cold water showers. House linens are furnished. A big terrace in front is also shared by guests who come to eat local style cuisine in the Hitikau restaurant and bar, also operated by the Fournier family.

Economy

CHEZ ALEXIS, *Vaipae'e, Ua Huka 98744, Marquesas Islands. Tel./Fax 689/92.60.19. In Vaipae'e valley, 5.5 kilometers (3.4 miles) from the airport and 2 kilometers (1.2 miles) from the Vaipae'e boat landing. Round-trip transfers 2.000 CFP per person. EP Rates: room 2.000 CFP per person; air-conditioned room 4.000 CFP; add 2.700 CFP per person for breakfast and dinner; add 4.700 CFP for all meals. Half-price for child under 12 years. Add 6% value added tax to room rates and meal plans. A 10% value added tax is applicable to other services. No credit cards.*

This is a concrete house with four rooms for rent beside the main road in Vaipae'e village. Look for the sign on the right. Each room contains a double bed. The living room with television, the large kitchen, terrace and two bathrooms with hot water are shared. House linens are furnished. You can rent a 4x4 vehicle with a driver for 6.000 CFP per day. Alexis will organize hikes for you on request.

CHEZ MAURICE & DELPHINE, *Hokatu, Ua Huka 98744, Marquesas Islands. Tel./Fax. 689/92.60.55. In Hokatu valley, 7 kilometers (4.4 miles) from the airport, 13 kilometers (8 miles) from the boat landing of Vaipae'e and 2 kilometers (1.2 miles) from Hane village. At the entry to Hokatu it's the first house on the left. Round-trip transfers between airport and pension 2.000 CFP per person. Rates: room 2.000 CFP single, 4.000 CFP double; bungalow 3.000 CFP single, 6.000 CFP double; room with breakfast and dinner 4.700 CFP single, 9.500 CFP double; bungalow with breakfast and dinner 5.700 CFP single, 11.500 CFP double. Add 6% value added tax to room rates, meal plans and transfers. A 10% value added tax is applicable to other services. No credit cards.*

Three bungalows overlooking the sea and Mount Hane contain a double bed, private bathroom with cold water, and a terrace. There is also a bedroom in a concrete house, with a double bed. Guests share the living room, equipped kitchen, terrace and two bathrooms with cold water. House linens are furnished. A 4x4 (4WD vehicle) is available for rent with driver for 6.000 CFP a day, or 10.000 CFP a day if you are not staying in this pension.

CHEZ CHRISTELLE, *Vaipae'e, Ua Huka 98744, Marquesas Islands. Tel. 689/92.60.04, Fax 689/92.60.85. In Vaipae'e valley, 7 kilometers (4.4 miles) from the airport and 2 kilometers (1.2 miles) from the boat landing. It's the seventh house on the left from the bridge, 5 meters (16 feet) after Chez Alexis. Round-trip transfers 2.000 CFP per person. Rates: room 2.000 CFP single, 4.000 CFP double; room with breakfast and dinner 4.700 CFP single, 9.400 CFP double; room with all meals 6.700 CFP single, 13.400 CFP double.*

Breakfast is 700 CFP, lunch or dinner is 2.000 CFP each. Half-rate for child 5-12 years. House can also be rented by the month for 90.000 CFP. Add 6% value added tax to room rates, meal plans and transfers. A 10% value added tax is applicable to other services. No credit cards.

This is a 4-bedroom concrete house, with a double bed in each room. Guests share the living room, equipped kitchen where you can cook your own food, dining room, two bathrooms with cold water shower, and terrace. House linens are furnished. There is also a large garden here. You can rent a 4WD vehicle with or without driver for 6.000 CFP per day.

Where to Eat

In Vaipae'e village each morning around 9am, Christelle sells *casse-croûtes* from her white pickup truck. She also has fried chicken legs, meats, fish, banana fritters and a selection of sandwiches.

When the *Aranui* arrives in Vaipae'e, the mamas of the village sell soft drinks and *casse-croûtes* at the boat landing around 10am.

For more extensive meals, try:

MANA TUPUNA VILLAGE, *Vaipae'e, Tel. 92.61.01/92.60.08. No credit cards.*

Breakfast is 800 CFP, lunch is 2.000 CFP and dinner is 1.500 CFP. Reserve if you are not staying in the pension.

CHEZ ALEXIS, *Vaipae'e village, Tel. 92.61.16.* If you reserve in advance, Alexis can prepare you some of his specialties, which include grilled lobster with *uru* fries, grilled fish, goat in coconut milk, sashimi, *poisson cru*, banana fritters or fruit salad. Breakfast is 700 CFP; lunch and dinner are 2.000 CFP each.

LE REVE MARQUISIEN, Pahataua valley, *Tel. 92.61.84/79.10.58/71.52.95.* Marie-France and Charles Aunoa serve refined cuisine in their restaurant, specializing in Marquesan, Tahitian, Chinese and French specialties. Breakfast is 800 CFP, lunch is 2.500 CFP and dinner is 2.500 CFP.

AUBERGE HITIKAU, Hane village, *Tel. 92.61.74. Advance reservations are needed for all meals. No credit cards.*

Breakfast is 700 CFP, and lunch and dinner are each 2.500 CFP. Feasts are prepared for groups, such as the *Aranui* passengers. These buffets may include kaveka (sooty tern) omelets, hard boiled kaveka eggs, goat cooked in coconut milk, *poisson cru*, roast pig, goat and fish cooked in an underground oven, plus rice, *fei, uru*, banana po'e, *sashimi*, cake and wine and coffee.

CHEZ MAURICE & DELPHINE, Hokatu village, *Tel. 92.60.55.*

You can eat three meals a day or arrange for an individual meal by calling in advance. Breakfast is 700 CFP and lunch and dinner each costs 2.000 CFP.

Seeing the Sights

Papuakeikaha Arboretum, between Vaipae'e and Hane, *Tel./Fax 92.61.51*, is a botanical and plant nursery with more than 400 species of flora, including 144 varieties of citrus plants. Leon Lichtle, who is now the mayor of Ua Huka, started this nursery in the early 1970s. The gardens comprise 23 hectares (57 acres) and contain every kind of plant and flower you can think of that grows in this climate. There are huge trees of *miro* (rosewood), *tou*, bamboo, banyan, *uru*, teak, *puatea*, *pakai*, *cerrettes*, *tutui*, allspice, acacia, mangoes, mountain apples, custard apples, star apples, carambola and guava. You'll find several species of bananas and plantains, pomegranates, coffee, cacao, vanilla, hot peppers, hibiscus, auti and jasmine. Plus there are many bushes of Tiare Tahiti and Tiare Moorea. This is a refreshing stop in the shade of the lovely trees, as well as a very interesting and informative botanical lesson. The arboretum is open to the public from 8am to 3pm Monday through Friday. There is no admission charge.

Vaipae'e Archaeological Museum is adjacent to the Mairie or town hall of Vaipae'e on the left of the main road from the boat landing, *Tel. 92.60.74, Fax 92.60.39*. At the entryway is a small sandalwood tree, one of only a few that you will see in the Marquesas Islands. The small museum is filled with old photographs and ancient Marquesan artifacts, including replicas of a chief's burial grotto and a Marquesan stove. A collection of reproductions of ancient sailing canoes and outrigger canoes represents all the Polynesian archipelagoes. A contest is held each year at the end of June, when the sculptors carve reproductions of old Marquesan artifacts. The winner of this competition has the pleasure of seeing his creation sent off to Tahiti to be displayed in the Museum of Tahiti and Her Islands. Master sculptor Joseph Vaatete takes care of the museum in Vaipae'e, which is open Monday to Friday from 8am to 3pm.

Hane Maritime Museum, *Tel. 92.60.74; Fax 92.60.39*, is managed by Joseph Vaatete, and is located beside the sea in Hane village. This small museum contains an old anchor, fishnets, ancient fishhooks, reproductions of outrigger canoes, and drawings of the Polynesian triangle, retracing the route of the first Polynesian sailors who settled the South Pacific islands. An arts and crafts center shares the building with the Musée de la Mer.

Hokatu Geological Museum, *Tel./Fax 92.60.55*, is managed by Maurice Rootuehine, and is open Monday through Friday, 8am to 3pm.

Museum of Wood "Jardin", *Tel. 92.60.13*, is another project realized by Léon Lichtle, the mayor of Ua Huka, who planted the first seeds in the botanical nursery in the 1970s. This museum is in the magnificent setting of the Arboretum and pays homage to trees. Contact Joseph Vaatete if you want to visit, as it is open on request.

Hokatu Stone Museum, *Tel. 92.60.13*, is also managed by Joseph Vaatete and open on request. Here you will see a display of petroglyphs carved into basaltic stone.

Land Excursions
Land tours will take you to visit the three villages, the archaeological sites, arboretum, museums and the arts and crafts shops. To arrange for an excursion by four-wheel drive vehicle (4x4) you can ask at the pension where you're staying, or you can hire the following people: in Vaipae'e valley contact Jean Tamarii, *Tel. 92.60.67*, or Benoît Teatiu, *Tel. 92. 61.22*; in Hane village contact Léon Fournier, *Tel. 92.60.61*, or Richard Teikihuavanaka, *Tel. 92.60.78*. Also see the names under the *Ua Huka* section in *Getting Around*. These drivers are also available for land tours.

In Hokatu valley arrangements can be made at *magasin* Maurice, *Tel. 92.60.55*, for land tours, horseback riding and boat rentals.

Sports & Recreation
Horseback Riding
Seeing Ua Huka on horseback is the way to go. The small Marquesan horses you see wandering around the desert-like plains are descendants from Chilean stock imported in 1856. You can ride bareback or astride wooden saddles softened by piling on copra sacks. The cost of horseback riding in Ua Huka is 5.000 CFP per day, plus 2.000-3.000 CFP for a guide. The following men rent horses and will accompany you on your outing.

Alexis Fournier in Vaipae'e, *Tel. 92.60.05*, rents riding horses for half- and full-day excursions. Horses can also be rented from **Edmond Lichtle** in Vaipae'e, *Tel. 92.60.87*, **Pierre Brown** and **François Brown**, *Tel. 92.61.31*.

Motor Boat Rental
Offshore excursions can be made by speedboat to visit Ua Huka's unusual sites. Half-day excursions and all-day outings with picnics are also possible. Boats with captains can be rented for deep-sea fishing and excursions to **Anaa Atua** grotto and the bird islands of **Teuaua** and **Tiotio**.

Bird Island or **Teuaua Motu** is a steep rock 6 meters (20 feet) high, 150 meters (492 feet) long and 100 meters (328 feet) wide, lying offshore Haavei valley. Attracted by the numerous fish in this area, millions of sooty terns lay their eggs on the open ground on top of this small island. You have to climb to the top by rope, which is very tricky and dangerous. The small eggs are white with black spots and the yolk is very orange. People gather these eggs by the bucket to boil or use in omelets.

The imprint of human footsteps can be seen in the sand at low tide in the **Anaa Atua** grotto and they disappear during high tide. Petroglyphs can be visited at the pretty beach of **Hatuana**. The **Pahonu beach** near the airport is a good place to swim and can be reached by boat.

Alexis Fournier, in Vaipae'e, *Tel. 92.60.05/92.60.72*, has a locally built 20-foot fishing boat for six passengers. Excursions around Ua Huka include half-day outings to Bird Island and Anaa Atua grotto. Full-day excursions around the island of Ua Huka also include a picnic.

Other boat owners in Vaipae'e are **Venance Ah-Sha**, *Tel. 92.61.54;* and **Nestor Ohu**, *Tel. 92.60.18.*

Maurice Rootuehine, in Hokatu, *Tel. 92.60.55,* has a locally built 25-foot fishing boat for 7 passengers, which is available for inter-island round-trips between Ua Huka and Nuku Hiva, and excursions around Ua Huka. Also in Hokatu you can rent a boat from **Paul Teatiu**, *Tel. 92.60.88.*

Shopping

Arts and crafts centers are located in the villages of **Vaipae'e, Hane** and **Hokatu**. The prices here are less expensive than in the other islands. You can also visit the sculptors' workshops at their homes. There are a dozen wood sculptors living in Hane Village, 14 wood sculptors living in Hokatu, and up to a dozen wood sculptors living in Vaipae'e village.

You will also find artisans who carve stone and bones. **Joseph Vaatete**, *Tel. 92.60.74,* is one of the most noted sculptors in wood and stone, who makes pieces for the museums in Ua Huka. He lives in Hane village, a couple of blocks from the sea, on the left side of the road that goes up the valley. You can recognize his house by the tree trunks and pieces of wood and stone in his yard. Two of Joseph's statues are located at the International Airport of Tahiti-Faaa, and another carving is located at the *Mairie* of Papeete. Joseph also takes care of the Vaipae'e Archaeological Museum adjacent to the *Mairie* of Vaipae'e, the Hane Maritime Museum, the Museum of Wood and the Hokatu Stone Museum. **Daniel Naudin**, *Tel. 92.61.03/92.61.35,* the best-known sculptor in Ua Huka who carves bones, lives in Vaipae'e. He creates designs combining wood and bone.

Magasin stores are located in each village and are also open on Sundays.

Practical Information

Infirmary

A government-operated infirmary is located in the village of Hane, *Tel. 92.60.58.*

Post Office & Telecommunications Office

A Post Office is located in the main village of Vaipae'e, *Tel. 92.60.26,* and in Hane village, *Tel. 92.60.46.* All telecommunications and postal services are available here.

Visitors Bureau

You can get tourist information from the association A Hee I Ua Huka, *Tel./Fax 689/92.61.01.* Karen Taiaapu-Fournier is the president and she speaks good English and Spanish. She also owns the pension Mana Tupuna Village.

HIVA OA

According to some Marquesan legends, **Hiva Oa** was the first island in this archipelago settled by the Polynesians before they reached Nuku Hiva. Archaeological findings support this theory, based on a charcoal sample taken from a fireplace in a rock shelter at Anapua. This site was excavated in 1981 by Pierre Ottino of the ORSTOM research center in Tahiti, and the charcoal dates 150+-95 years BC. This is one of the oldest dates thus uncovered reflecting the presence of human occupancy in Eastern Polynesia.

Hiva Oa is located 1,400 kilometers (868 miles) northeast of Tahiti. It is one of the youngest islands in the Marquesas chain, and has been described as a seahorse whose head faces the setting sun. The island measures 40 kilometers (25 miles) long east to west and averages 10 kilometers (6.2 miles) north to south. Atuona sits in the center of three adjoining craters, and Temetiu, whose peak reaches into the clouds 1,190 meters (3,900 feet), crowns the ridge of mountains above the picturesque bays. The steep slopes of high altitude interior plateaus dominate this large fertile island of 330 square kilometers (127 square miles). The 2,015 inhabitants live in the villages of Atuona, Puamau, Hanaiapa, Hanapaaoa, Nahoe, Tahauku and Taaoa, which are separated into isolated valleys by the dorsal spine and ridges.

The French painter **Paul Gauguin** came to Hiva Oa in 1901 in search of a primitive culture and savage wildness, and here he died in 1903. He is buried in Calvary Cemetery on a hill behind Atuona village. Fragrant petals from a gnarled old frangipani tree shower down on the simple grave, and a statue of Oviri, "the savage" stands at the head of the tombstone.

In the village of Atuona you can visit the **Paul Gauguin Center,** a complex of three large buildings on the original site where Gauguin lived. This new center was inaugurated on May 8, 2003, during the commemorative services to honor the 100th anniversary of Gauguin's death in Atuona. The Gauguin Museum has some 100 reproductions of the French artist's paintings made in Tahiti and Hiva Oa, as well as sculptures, drawings, photographs, letters and other souvenirs of Gauguin. The entry charge is 600 CFP for adults and 300 CFP for 12-18 year olds. A replica of Gauguin's house, which he named **La Maison du Jouir** (House of Pleasure), is built beside the well into which Gauguin used to keep his liquor bottles, and there is a bamboo pole hanging out the window upstairs, which represents the pole Gauguin used to fetch a bottle from the well. This dried pit was uncovered during construction of this complex, and was filled with broken bottles, old paintbrushes and other cast off items. An open-sided shelter was erected near the sea for visiting artists, a replica of Gauguin's *Atelier des Tropiques,* where the ocean breezes fanned him as he painted. These Gauguin copyists are lodged in four bungalows on the premises. Across the street from the Gauguin Center is the Magasin Gauguin, where he used to buy his supplies.

A few graves distant from Gauguin's tombstone in Calvary Cemetery is the final resting place of the famous Belgian singer **Jacques Brel**, who lived in Atuona from 1975 until his death in 1978. Many of Brel's European fans make a pilgrimage to his grave, which is always decorated with flowers. When Brel was buried his mistress, Maddly Bamy, placed a plaque on his tombstone that contained an engraving of the two devoted lovers. This was the image visitors to his grave photographed for 20 years, until Brel's family changed the plaque in 1999, replacing it with the names of his wife, their three daughters and their children. Maddly then returned to Hiva Oa and put the original plaque back up, which was then removed again and replaced by the family plaque. Maddly changed plaques again before the 25th anniversary of Jacques Brel's death was commemorated in August 2003. The **Jacques Brel Memorial** is a black marble stele set in a stone overlooking the Hanakee Pearl Lodge and Atuona Bay east of Atuona. Brel wanted to build his house on this hillside, but was unable to do so because of his illness. There are two tracks leading to the site, and it is best to get clear directions before setting off on foot.

Jacques Brel's Beechcraft airplane, Jo Jo, has been restored and is on display in the **Jacques Brel Space** adjacent to the Gauguin Center. The **Traditional Arts Museum** (entrance is 400 CFP for adults and 200 CFP for 12-18 year olds) and an arts and crafts center are found in the area facing the **Pepeu** *tohua* meeting ground, where the ceremonies and dances were held during the Marquesas Festival of Arts in December 2003.

Atuona is the administrative center for the southern Marquesas. Framed in a theater of mountains with the Tahauku Bay providing safe anchorage, Atuona is a favorite port of call for yachts and copra/cargo ships. Atuona village has a *gendarmerie*, infirmary, new post office, bank, weather station, Air Tahiti office, restaurants and snack bars, stores and shops. There is a Catholic mission with a boarding school and a Protestant church.

You can rent a car with or without a driver or you can join an excursion by 4-wheel drive vehicle and visit the bays of Nahoe and Hanamenu, the black sand beach of Taaoa and the lovely white sand beach of Hanatekua. Near the little village of Hanaiapa is a cascade that splashes down a 249-meter (800-foot) cliff into the surging sea, wetting the black rocks so they sparkle like vaults of mica. Petroglyphs carved on stone have been found in the valleys of Eiaone and Punaei, and many other archaeological sites exist all over the island of Hiva Oa.

Gauguin's descendants still live in the Puamau valley, 48 kilometers (30 miles) from Atuona. The restored archaeological site of I'ipona is also located in this valley. In this religious sanctuary is a *me'ae* on two large terraces, with five huge stone tikis. The most famous stone tiki represents the god Takai'i.

Carved from porous red rock, this statue is 2.35 meters (7.7 feet) tall, and is the largest stone tiki in French Polynesia.

You can also go deep-sea fishing, explore woodcarvers' shops, ride along a black sand beach on a Marquesan horse or charter a boat for a trip to visit nearby islands, including **Motane**, the sheep island. Accommodations on Hiva Oa are found in a 4-star hotel overlooking the cobalt blue Pacific and in small family pensions near the villages.

Arrivals & Departures
Arriving By Air
Air Tahiti, *Tel. 86.42.42* in Tahiti, *Tel. 91.70.90/92.72.31* in Atuona, flies ATR 42 turbo jet planes from Tahiti direct to Hiva Oa each Friday and Sunday. The flights from Tahiti on Monday, Wednesday, Thursday and Saturday have one or two stops before reaching Atuona, and some of them involve a change of aircraft. The one-way fare from Tahiti to Atuona is 30.400 CFP and the round-trip fare is 55.500 CFP. You can fly from Rangiroa to Atuona each Saturday, with a stop in Nuku Hiva, for a one-way fare of 27.200 CFP. The fare from Ua Pou to Atuona is 7.500 CFP, flying by Twin Otter 19-passenger Dornier direct on Wednesday, via Nuku Hiva on Monday and Thursday, and stopping in both Nuku Hiva and Ua Huka on Friday and Sunday. You can also fly direct from Ua Huka to Atuona on Friday and Sunday, and you'll stop in Nuku Hiva and Ua Pou on Wednesday. The one-way fare is 7.500 CFP.

You can also get to Nuku Hiva by chartering an airplane in Tahiti from **Wan Air**, *Tel. 50.44.17*, cell *77.03.79*; **Air Archipels**, *Tel. 81.30.30*; or **Air Tahiti**, *Tel. 86.42.42*.

Arriving By Boat
The *Aranui* includes stops at Atuona, Puamau, and Hanaiapa in Hiva Oa during its 16-day round-trip cruise program from Tahiti to the Marquesas. The *Taporo VI* includes Hiva Oa in its 10-day round-trip voyages from Tahiti. See details in section on *Inter-Island Cruise Ships and Cargo/Passenger Boats* in Chapter 6, *Planning Your Trip*.

The communal boats from Tahuata and Fatu Hiva connect their islands with Atuona once or twice a week. See further information for these two islands in this chapter.

Departing By Air
Air Tahiti reservations in Atuona, *Tel. 91.70.90/92.72.31*. You can take an ATR plane from Atuona direct to Tahiti each Saturday and Sunday. On Friday the ATR makes a stop in Nuku Hiva before heading to Tahiti. On Monday, Wednesday and Thursday you board a Dornier-19 passenger plane in Atuona and fly to Nuku Hiva to connect with the ATR-42 flight to Tahiti. You can fly the 19-passenger Dornier direct from Atuona to Ua Pou each

Wednesday, and the Dornier flights on Monday, Thursday, Friday and Sunday stop in Nuku Hiva. The Twin Otter also takes you from Atuona to Ua Huka with direct flights on Friday and Sunday and with two stops on Wednesday.

Departing By Boat

Tahuata Nui is a 48.6-foot long aluminum hull boat that can transport 60 passengers between Atuona and Tahuata. The boat leaves the quay of Atuona at 12pm each Tuesday for Vaitahu, and each Thursday the boat leaves Atuona at 12pm for Vaitahu and Hapatoni. The one-way fare is 2.000 CFP. Reserve at the Mairie of Tahuata, *Tel. 689/92.92.19; Fax 689/92.92.10.*

Auona II, *Tel. 92.80.23; Fax 92.80.39*, is the 51-foot communal catamaran of Fatu Hiva. It can transport 30 passengers and when it is not broken down the boat leaves Atuona each Wednesday around 12pm for Fatu Hiva. The one-way fare is 4.000 CFP.

See information under *Boat Excursions & Deep Sea Fishing* in this chapter.

Orientation

A road 17 kilometers long (10.5 feet) is built on the **Tepuna Plateau**, 440 meters (1,443 feet) above the sea, connecting the airport with **Atuona village**. The town is at the north end of Taaoa Bay, 3 kilometers (1.9 miles) from **Tahauku Bay**, also known as Traitors' Bay, which provides a safe harbor for yachts and the inter-island cargo vessels that dock at the concrete pier.

Three paved roads pass through Atuona and it is easy to walk around the town center, where most of the businesses and administrative offices are concentrated, as well as the medical facilities, churches and Catholic schools.

Getting Around Hiva Oa

When you make reservations with a hotel or pension your hosts will meet you at the airport or boat dock on your arrival. You can also organize your excursions at the place where you're staying. The cost of transfers and land tours varies according to the lodgings, which are listed under *Where to Stay*.

Taxi Service

Ida Clark, *Tel. 92.71.33, Cell 72.34.73*. She charges 1.700 CFP per person for transfers between the airport and Atuona village and she can also drive you to visit the valleys and sites around the island.

Land Tours & 4x4 Safari Excursions

Gabriel Heitaa of Pension Temetiu Village, *Tel. 91.70.60,* has guided 4x4 excursions to Puamau for a maximum of 4 passengers for 20.000 CFP per vehicle. The 2 1/2-hour ride to Puamau is a one-way distance of 48 kilometers (30 miles). You will be taken to visit the famous tikis, the queen's grave, and return by way of Jacques Brel's stele. This is an all-day trip and you can include lunch for 2.000 CFP per person. You'll pay an entry fee of 200 CFP at the archaeological site of Oipona. Another excursion takes you to the restored archaeological site of Taaoa, for 8.000 CFP per vehicle. This is a distance of 7 kilometers (4.4 miles) and a 15-20 minute ride from Atuona. It costs 12.000 CFP per 4WD to visit the village of Hanaiapa, where you can buy tapa bark paintings and woodcarvings.

André Teissier at Pension Gauguin, *Tel. 92.73.51*, leads excursions to the historical sites in Hiva Oa.

Etienne Heitaa, *Tel. 92.75.28*, in Puamau.

Car Rentals

With advance reservations a car can be delivered to the airport for your arrival. The gas station is located at the cargo ship dock at Tahauku Bay. Make sure there is a stockage of fuel on hand before signing your contract.

Atuona Rent-A-Car, *Tel. 92.76.07, Cell 72.17.17*, operated by Rosine Numa, has self-drive 4WD vehicles.

David Locations, *Tel. 92.72.87; E-mail: davidkmk@mail.pf*, is owned by David Kaimuko, next to Magasin Chanson in Atuona. He has a 4WD self-drive vehicle for 15.000 CFP per day.

Gabriel Heitaa of Temetiu Village, *Tel. 91.70.60; E-mail: heitaagabyfeli@mail.pf* rents a 4x4 vehicle for 13.000 CFP per day. American Express, Mastercard, Visa.

Where to Stay

Superior

HANAKEE HIVA OA PEARL LODGE, *B.P. 80, Atuona, Hiva Oa 98742, Marquesas Islands. Tel. 689/92.75.87, Fax 689/92.75.95; E-mail: hiva.oa.pearl@mail.pf; www.pearlresorts.com. Reservations: South Pacific Management, B.P. 2460-98713 Papeete, Tahiti; Tel. 689/50.84.54; Fax 689/43.17.86; E-mail: carine.keck@spmhotels.pf. On hillside overlooking Tahauku Bay, 7 kilometers (4.4 miles) from airport and 2 kilometers (1.2 miles) from boat dock. 14 bungalows. EP Rates: mountain view bungalow 22.000 CFP single/double; premium ocean view bungalow 35.000 CFP; add 5.000 CFP for third person; add 7.200 CFP per person for breakfast and dinner; add 9.900 CFP per person per day for all meals; full American breakfast 2.200 CFP; one-way transfer from airport by 4WD 2.400 CFP per person. One or two children between 3 and 12 years old sharing parents' room are free of charge on accommodation basis and have 50% discount on AP/MAP plans (excluded beverages) and Airport/Hotel/Airport transfers when provided by the hotel. Babies and children under 3 years old are free of charge on accommodation, meal plans and Airport/Hotel/Airport transfers when provided by the hotel. Add 5% hotel tax to room rates and 6% value added tax to room rates,* *prepaid meal plans and transfers. A 10% value added tax is applicable to other services. All major credit cards.*

This 4-star hotel is built on the hillside overlooking Tahauku Bay, above the port for the inter-island ships. It has 6 mountain view bungalows and 8 premium ocean view bungalows, all with air-conditioning, ceiling fan, satellite television, in-house video system, a mini-bar refrigerator, tea and coffee making facilities, international direct dial telephone, in-room safe, shower with hot water, hair dryer and a sundeck. Laundry service is available and you can get a babysitter on request. Two of the ocean view bungalows are equipped for handicapped guests in wheelchairs.

The main building houses the reception, boutique and a desk for excursions and car rentals. There is a gourmet restaurant and bar, and a swimming pool overlooks Traitors Bay, the Bordelais canal and the small island of Hanakee.

If you want to really appreciate the nature and special beauty of Hiva Oa, then you will want to take a tour by mountain bike. The activity desk at the hotel can suggest a dozen trails that offer various levels of physical exertion and you'll even have a guide to show you the way. The rental rates on the all-terrain bikes are 800 CFP for a half-day and 1.500 CFP for a full day. Guided excursions cost 2.300 CFP to visit the Tehueto Petroglyphs, 2.300 CFP to go to Jacques Brel's stele, 3.500 CFP for a half-day ride to the Taaoa Valley and 6.500 CFP for a full-day's bike ride to Hanaiapa village and Hanatekua Beach.

Should you prefer a 4-wheel drive excursion, you can visit the Tehueto Petroglyphs or Jacques Brel's stele for 2.300 CFP each, the smiling tiki and paepae for 2.300 CFP, or the Makamea sites for 2.900 CFP, and you can take a half-day tour to the Taaoa valley for 3.500 CFP. Other half-day excursions by 4x4 take you to Hanaiapa valley for 4.500 CFP, or to visit Atuona village for 2.900 CFP. A full-day trip to Puamau valley and the Oipona sites is 10.500 CFP, and an all-day excursion will take you to Vaipikopiko waterfall for 6.500 CFP.

You can visit the island of Tahuata by boat for 15.000 CFP, and if there are more than four passengers, the cost is 12.000 CFP each. Horseback rides are 7.000 CFP for a half-day outing, and your choices include Punaei Creek, Tehueto petroglyphs and the Belvedere lookout of Jacques Brel's stele.

You can also rent a 4WD car to drive yourself to see the historical and archaeological sites, the famous stone tiki in Puamau, and the picturesque scenes of Marquesan horses swimming in the lovely bays or galloping down a black sand beach.

Romantic Rendez-vous at the Hiva Oa Hanakee Pearl Lodge include a Romantic Sunset for 9.500 CFP, Romantic Dinner for 15.300 CFP, and Starlight Dinner for 23.800 CFP. A Romantic Escapade will take you on a private tour by boat to the island of Tahuata for 49.867 CFP. Prices quoted are per couple. The hotel can also arrange Polynesian Weddings. The Matiri Wedding is 113.333 CFP and the Matiri Wedding and Dinner is 138.267 CFP. Other romantic touches available include a fruit basket for 2.900 CFP, a bottle of wine for 3.500 CFP, and a bottle of champagne for 9.200 CFP. Contact the hotel directly for details on the Romantic programs.

Moderate
PENSION KANAHAU, *B.P 101, Atuona, Hiva Oa 98741, Marquesas Islands. Tel. 689/91.71.31; Cell 689/70.16.26; Fax 689/91.71.32; E-mail: pensionkanahau@mail.pf; www.ifrance.com/pensionkanahau. Bungalow 9.646 CFP single; 11.448 CFP double; 14.310 CFP triple. Breakfast 848 CFP, lunch or dinner 2.968 CFP each meal; half-price for child under 12 years. Round-trip transfers between airport and pension 3.000 CFP per person. Rates include taxes. No credit cards.*

This 4-bungalow family pension managed by Stèphania Dubreuil opened in 2003 on the hillside of Atuona, overlooking Tahuku Bay, 9 kilometers (5.6 miles) from the airport and 1 kilometer (0.62 miles) from the boat dock. Two of the wooden bungalows on stilts have a double bed and the other two units have two twin beds. Each unit also has a ceiling fan, a convertible sofa, a private bathroom with hot water, a television, electric anti-mosquito machine and a terrace. Meals are served on a big terrace with a marvelous view of the bay. Free activities include accompanied excursions to visit the points of interest in Atuona village, include the artisan workshops. They will also introduce you to the local cuisine, weaving, tapa making and Marquesas dancing.

TEMETIU VILLAGE, *B.P. 52, Atuona, Hiva Oa 98741, Marquesas Islands. Tel. 689/91.70.60; Fax 689/91.70.61; E-mail: heitaagabyfeli@mail.pf. EP Rates: room 6.180 CFP single, 8.240 CFP double; add 2.060 CFP for third person or child more than 12 years old; add 1.030 CFP for child under 12 years and 515 CFP for a baby. Breakfast is 1.000 CFP and lunch or dinner costs 2.800 CFP per person for each meal; half-price for child under 12 years. Round-trip airport transfers 3.000 CFP per person. Add 6% value added tax to room rates, meal plans and transfers. A 10% value added tax is applicable to other services. American Express, Mastercard, Visa.*

Seven neat and clean bungalows sit on the hillside in Atuona village, with a beautiful view of Tahauku Bay. Three bungalows have two bedrooms with 3 single beds in each room and a bathroom with hot water. Four bungalows have a double bed, a wardrobe and table, plus a private bathroom with hot water. All bungalows have a television. There is also a communal living room with a television, video and books. Meals are served on the covered dining terrace overlooking the bay. You can rent a self-drive 4x4 vehicle for 13.000 CFP a day.

This is a favorite lodging because of its location, but mainly because of the owners, who are warm and welcoming. "Gaby" owns the *Pua Ote Tai* boat that provides transportation service to other villages and islands. He is the former president of the Tourism Committee in Hiva Oa. His wife speaks English and will guide you on a complimentary tour of Atuona village and the other main points of interest. Gaby also has an Excursion business. See information under *Boat Excursions & Deep Sea Fishing*, and *Land Tours & Safari 4x4 Excursions* in this chapter.

RELAIS MOEHAU, *B.P. 50, Atuona, Hiva Oa 98741, Marquesas Islands. Tel. 689/92.72.69; Cell 689/70.16.34; Fax 689/92.77.62; E-mail: moehaurelais@mail.pf; www.relaismoehau.pf. On mountainside in Atuona, 15 kilometers (9.3 miles) from the airport and 3 kilometers (1.9 miles) from Atuona quay. Round-trip transfers between airport and pension 3.000 CFP per person. Rates: room with breakfast and dinner 9.760 CFP single, 17.890 CFP double; 23.960 CFP for three adults. Child up to 2 years old pays 890 CFP per night and 2-11 years 4.880 CFP. Rates include all taxes. Mastercard, Visa.*

Gisèle and Georges Gramont, who are from the Tuamotu Islands, inaugurated their big 2-story white house in November 2000. Their guests have a choice of a double bed or two single beds in the 8 spacious rooms upstairs. Each room has a ceiling fan, television with an in-house video channel, plus a private bathroom with hot water shower. The rooms are cleaned daily. A big terrace spans the length of the house, offering a lovely view of Traitors Bay and Hanakee Rock.

Meals are served in the restaurant on the premises, which is equipped with a wood-burning pizza oven. Breakfast is 955 CFP and lunch or dinner costs 3.710 CFP for each meal, including taxes. An *a la carte* menu features Marquesan, Polynesian and French cuisine. Excursions and guided tours can be organized on request to visit Hiva Oa and the sister island of Tahuata.

PENSION TAHAUKU MAUI RANCH, *B.P. 40, Atuona, Hiva Oa 98741, Marquesas Islands. Tel./Fax 689/92.71.04; Cell 689/73.47.45; E-mail: tahuku@mail.pf; www.chez.mana.pf:odscd. Bungalow 5.500 CFP single; 7.600 CFP double; add 1.900 CFP for third person or child over 12 years; add 1.000 CFP for child under 12 years and 500 CFP for baby. Breakfast 800 CFP; lunch or dinner 2.500 CFP each meal. Round-trip transfers between airport and pension 3.000 CFP per person. Add 6% value added tax to room rates, meal plans and transfers. A 10% value added tax is applicable to other services. American Express, Mastercard, Visa.*

Four new FEI type government approved bungalows are located in Tahauku Valley, on the corner that goes to the airport. The pension sits in a grove of orange trees and herds of goats graze nearby. They belong to Priscille Rauzy and her companion, Coleano Teriinohorai, who also run the pension and act as guides for their guests. Each wooden bungalow is built on stilts and contains a double bed and a single bed, a ceiling fan, private bathroom with hot water and a covered terrace. House linens are furnished and guests can watch television in a communal living room and eat their meals in a shared dining room. Free transfers are provided to Atuona village. Maui Ranch is located nearby and your hosts will accompany you for horseback rides to see the petroglyphs in Tehueto for 4.000 CFP per person, the Punaei for 4.500 CFP, and to the stele of Jacques Brel for 5.000 CFP. Guided 4WD excursions are also available to the archaeological site of Taaoa for 8.000 CFP or to see the tikis in the Oipona site of Paumau for 20.000 CFP.

PENSION GAUGUIN, *B.P. 34, Atuona, Hiva Oa 98741, Marquesas Islands. Tel./Fax 689/92.73.51; E-mail: pens.gauguin@mail.pf. Rates: room 3.700 CFP per person; breakfast 750 CFP; room with breakfast and dinner 6.900 CFP per person; room with all meals 9.400 CFP per person per day. Round-trip airport transfers 3.600 CFP per person. Add 6% value added tax to room rates, meal plans and transfers. A 10% value added tax is applicable to other services. No credit cards.*

This popular small hotel overlooks the road that leads to Tahauku port at the eastern end of Atuona Bay, 7 kilometers (4.4 miles) from the airport and 2.5 kilometers (1.6 miles) from the boat dock. The 2-story building has 6 rooms, each with a double bed and a single bed, sharing 4 bathrooms, the living room and dining room. The house linens are furnished. A big terrace has a panoramic view of the bay. The atmosphere is very homey and clean and the meals are good. The Make Make Snack is also close by, should you want a change. André Teissier, your host, will organize interesting excursions for you to visit the sites in Hiva Oa and to spend the day on Tahuata.

Economy

PENSION OZANNE, *B.P. 43, Atuona, Hiva Oa 98741, Marquesas Islands. Tel/Fax 689/92.73.43. Rates: room 4.000 CFP; bungalow 5.000 CFP. Meal plans available. Round-trip airport transfers 3.000 CFP per person. Add 6% value added tax to room rates, meal plans and transfers. A 10% value added tax is applicable to other services. No credit cards.*

This pension is on the hillside on the eastern edge of Atuona, providing accommodations in a 2-bedroom house and 2 bungalows. In the house there is a double bed in each room, and guests share the living room, terrace and a communal bathroom with cold water. The bungalows each have two rooms, with sleeping accommodations for four people, including a mezzanine. They also have a TV, private kitchen, bathroom with cold water shower and two balconies. House linens are furnished. The Marquesan style meals are eaten with the family under a *fare pote'e* shelter overlooking the black sand beach and ocean. John Ozanne Rohi will rent you a 4WD vehicle and you may want to join him aboard his *Denise III* boat for deep-sea fishing, picnics and visits to Tahuata and Fatu Hiva. He's very nice and friendly.

PENSION CHEZ MARIE-ANTOINETTE, *Puamau, Hiva Oa 98741, Marquesas Islands. Tel. 689/92.72.27. Rates: room with breakfast and dinner 5.500 CFP per person; room with all meals 6.500 CFP per person per day; half price for child under 12 years. Round-trip transfers between airport and* *pension 34.000 CFP per car. Add 6% value added tax to room rates, meal plans and transfers. A 10% value added tax is applicable to other services. No credit cards.*

This pension is in the valley of Puamau, on the northeast coast of Hiva Oa, 40 kilometers (25 miles) from the airport and 3.5 kilometers (2.2 miles) from the quay in Puamau. It is on the right hand side of the road that leads to the I'ipona or Oipona archaeological site with the five big tikis. There are two simply furnished rooms in the home of the former mayor, Bernard "Vohi" Heitaa, with a double and a single bed in each room. The bathroom with hot water is shared, as well as the living room and dining room. Marie-Antoinette cooks the meals and spends most of her time planting and picking noni fruit to earn a little money. She also has a big yard with lots of other kinds of fruit trees and flowers. Marie-Antoinette serves lunch for 2.000 CFP per person to those who stop here during day excursions to Puamau valley.

According to Marie-Antoinette, the tomb of Vehine Tetoiani, the last queen of Puamau valley, is also located on her property in the **Tohua Pehe Kua.** Although the queen was given a Christian burial when she died in 1926, two *ti'i* statues are placed beside her tomb and a *paepae* is also close by. Other guidebooks say that the last ruler of the valley was named Te Hu Moena and when she died in 1916 she was buried along with her two bicycles. Vohi Heitaa claims that the grave decorated with the small tikis is that of Te Hau Moena, the father of the last queen. Marie-Antoinette admitted that she and her husband just go along with whatever version of the story anyone has heard and doesn't try to change it for them.

Where to Eat

HANAKEE HIVA OA PEARL LODGE, *Tel. 92.75.87. Open daily for breakfast, lunch and dinner. All major credit cards.*

An American breakfast is 2.200 CFP; the set luncheon menu is 2.700 CFP and the set dinner menu is 5.000 CFP. The chef's specialties include fresh fish and locally caught seafood. You can sit on the terrace overlooking the bay and listen to Jacques Brel music during Happy Hour, which is held at the bar every Friday evening. There is a Marquesan dance show on special evenings.

HOA NUI, *in Atuona village, Tel. 92.73.63. No credit cards. Reserve.*

This is where the *Aranui* passengers eat when they visit Atuona. They get to enjoy Marquesan feasts of lobster, curried goat, fresh river shrimp, smoked red chicken, *fafa poulet*, macaroni fritters, fried breadfruit, banana *po'e* and other delicious treats. Dinner costs around 2.000 CFP.

TEMETIU VILLAGE, *Tel. 92.73.02. Reservations are necessary. American Express, Mastercard, Visa.*

Breakfast, lunch and dinner are served on their terrace overlooking Tahauku and Taaoa bays. Breakfast is 800 CFP and lunch or dinner costs 2.500

CFP. Lobster and shrimp specialties are featured, along with goat in coconut milk and other Marquesan foods.

SNACK KAUPE, *Tel. 92.70.62, adjacent to Magasin Gauguin in the center of Atuona village. Open during the day Tuesday-Sunday and for dinner on Friday-Saturday. No credit cards.*

Besides pizzas, Chinese dishes and fish, you can order spicy specialties from Réunion Island to eat there or to take away. Prices vary from 1.100-1.650 CFP per dish. Interested yachties should ask the manager, who speaks some English, about the laundry service they provide for cruising yachts.

SNACK MAKE MAKE (**SNACK ATUONA**), *Tel. 92.74.26, on the mountainside in the center of Atuona village. Open Monday through Friday. Closed at night and on weekends. No credit cards.*

They serve fresh fish, Chinese dishes, *poisson cru*, burgers and sandwiches, all very reasonably priced. The quality is good and there's plenty of food on your plate.

Seeing the Sights

In the center of Atuona you can visit the Paul Gauguin Museum and Maison du Jouir in the Gauguin Center, Jacques Brel Cultural Center, Traditional Arts House, arts and crafts center and the sacred site of Tohua Pepeu, which was restored for the 1991 Marquesas Festival of Arts and used again as a stage during the 2003 Marquesas Festival of Arts. In Calvary Cemetery behind Atuona village you can visit the graves of French artist Paul Gauguin and Belgian singer Jacques Brel. The tourist office erected a stele or memorial to Brel in 1993 on a piece of open ground a few kilometers east of Atuona, overlooking the Hanakee Hiva Oa Pearl Lodge. This can be visited by 4WD, horseback on foot.

Sightseeing highlights away from Atuona include a visit to **Puamau Valley** to see the giant tikis at the **I'ipona** (or Oipona) archaeological site; the tiki and *paepae* platforms of **Taaoa Valley**; the petroglyphs on the **Tehueto** site in the **Faakua Valley**; the **Moe One tiki** in **Hanapaaoa Valley**; and the *paepae* and pretty little village of **Hanaiapa Valley,** where you can visit wood carvers' workshops and watch the surfers riding the waves in this recently discovered surf spot.

Sports & Recreation
Horseback Riding

Maui Ranch Tahauku, *Tel. 92.74.92*, has guides who will accompany you on horseback rides to see the petroglyphs in Tehueto for 4.000 CFP per person, the Punaei Creek for 4.500 CFP, and to the stele of Jacques Brel for 5.000 CFP.

Lucien "Pako" Pautehea, *Tel. 92.70.57*, leads "green tourism" expeditions by horseback to explore any of the dozen trails he knows, starting from

Atuona. He is a nature lover and enjoys sharing his knowledge of the Marquesan fauna and flora with small groups of three or four riders.

Etienne Heitaa, *Tel. 92.75.28*, has Marquesan horses for rent in Puamau, with a guide if requested. Check with your hotel or pension for other possibilities of renting a horse.

Boat Excursions & Deep Sea Fishing

Pua O Te Tai, *Tel. 91.70.60; Fax 91.70.61; E-mail: heitaagabyfeli@mail.pf*, is a locally built 30-foot bonito fishing boat owned by Gabriel Heitaa of Atuona, which can transport 10 passengers. He will take you on a day tour of Tahuata to visit the wood and bone carvers in Hapatoni village and the main village of Vaitahu, with its church and little archaeological museum. The cost of 8.635 CFP per person also includes a picnic on a white sand beach and time for swimming. You can also charter the boat to visit Fatu Hiva.

Denise III, *Tel./Fax 92.73.43*, is a locally built 39-foot bonito fishing boat owned by John Ozanne Rohi of Atuona. He charges 20.000-25.000 CFP for a round-trip to Tahuata and 55.000 CFP to visit Fatu Hiva. Deep-sea fishing and picnics on request for a maximum of 13 passengers.

Tehinaonaiki is a 36-foot bonito boat owned by Médéric Kaimuko, *Tel. 92.74.48 that* will hold 8 passengers.

Shopping

One of several arts and crafts centers in Atuona is adjacent to the Gauguin Museum and a very good handcraft shop and boutique is across the road. You can buy tee shirts with Marquesan designs, hand-painted pareos, *monoi* oil made with sandalwood and a thousand flowers, and *mille fleurs* honey. Artisan shops are also located in Puamau and Taaoa.

If you want to buy woodcarvings you can visit the sculptors at their home workshops. The Atuona artisans include: **Jean-Marie Otomimi,** *Tel. 92.74.35*; **Gilbert "Tuarai" Peterano**, *Tel. 92.70.64*; **Antoine Tohetiaatua**, *Tel. 92.73.74*; **John** and **Axel Kimitete**, *Tel. 92.72.48*; and **Norbert Huhina**, *Tel. 92.77.50*. **Jean-Noël Scallamera**, *Tel. 92.71.19*, is in Tahauku, and **Gabriel Bonno**, *Tel. 92.72.55*, and **Paul O'Connor**, *Tel. 92.74.51*, live in Taaoa. This is only a partial list. For further information contact **Véronique Kohumoetini** of "Te Tuhuka O Te Henua Enana Artisanal Federation", *Tel. 41.39.89* in Tahiti, or the "Service de l'Artisanat," *Tel. 42.32.25*, also in Tahiti.

Practical Information

Banks

Banque Socredo, *Tel. 92.73.54*, has a branch on the main street in Atuona, next to the Air Tahiti office. Business hours are Monday, Tuesday, Thursday and Friday 7:30 to 11:30am, and 1:30 to 4pm, Wednesday 7:30 to 11:30am.

Hospitals
There's a government-operated infirmary in Atuona, *Tel. 92.73.75*, a dental center, *Tel. 92.78.17*, an infirmary in Puamau, *Tel. 92.74.96*, and first aid stations in Nahoe and Hanaiapa.

Information
Hiva Oa Tourism Committee, *Tel. 92.78.93; E-mail: comtourismhiva@yahoo.fr* is located in a small building in front of the Paul Gauguin Center in the village of Atuona. Georges Gramot of Relais Moehau is the president.
Ernest Teapuaoteani works for the Mairie (town hall) of Atuona, *Tel. 92.73.32*, and he is a good source of information on Marquesan culture, dance and history. He speaks English.

Police
The French *gendarmerie* has a brigade in the center of Atuona, *Tel. 92.73.61*.

Post Office & Telecommunications Office
The post office is located adjacent to the town hall (*mairie*) in the center of Atuona village, *Tel. 92.73.50*. It is open Monday-Thursday from 7:30 to 11:30am and from 1:30 to 4:30pm, and on Friday until 3:30pm; on Saturday it is open from 7:30-8:30am.

TAHUATA
Tahuata has the only coral gardens in the Marquesas and the prettiest white sand beaches. There is no airport, although plans are underway to construct a runway on this island. Nor is there any helicopter service, but you can easily reach Tahuata by boat from Hiva Oa, which is just an hour's ride across the Bordelais Channel. This is a popular port-of-call for cruising yachts that drop anchor in coves with beautiful secluded beaches accessible only by boat. The *Aranui* passengers enjoy visiting the friendly little village of Hapatoni and playing on the beach at Hanemoenoe.

Tahuata is the smallest populated island in the Marquesas archipelago, with only 50 square kilometers (19 square miles) of land. A central mountain range crowns the crescent shaped island, reaching 1,040 meters (3,465 feet) into the ocean sky.

It was in Tahuata's Vaitahu Bay that Alvaro de Mendaña's expedition of four caravels anchored in 1595. He named the island group *Las Marquesas de Garcia de Mendoza de Canete*, in honor of the wife of Peru's viceroy. The Spanish explorer came ashore at Vaitahu Bay, which he named *Madre de Dios*, Mother of God. It was here that the first crosses were raised and mass was held. When the Spanish-Peruvian ships set sail, 200 inhabitants lay massacred on the beach.

Following Captain James Cook's visit in 1774, Vaitahu's harbor was named Resolution Bay. When the first Protestant missionaries came in 1797, the generous local chief left his wife with missionary John Harris, with instructions that he should treat her as his own wife. Harris fled when the wife and five of her women friends visited his room.

The French took possession of the Marquesas in Vaitahu, establishing a garrison at Fort Halley in 1842. Monuments, ruins and graves of the French soldiers killed during the skirmishes can be seen in Vaitahu, but no indication is given to the Marquesans who lost their lives. The Catholic missionaries chose Tahuata as the site of their first Marquesan church. The Catholic Church that stands today in Vaitahu was built in 1988 with funds from the Vatican. It has a stained-glass window depicting a Marquesan Madonna, plus carvings from the wood sculptors.

Although Tahuata's past has been violent and grim, the 677 inhabitants live a quiet life today, working peacefully in their verdant valleys, raising livestock and making copra. The rich waters surrounding the island attract an amazing variety of fish, sharks and even whales.

Boat day in Tahuata's small villages is a main event, when the copra ship arrives with food and supplies. Getting ashore in Hapatoni has always been dangerous, and this process is now easier with the addition of a jetty that was built to protect the enlarged concrete quay so that the new communal boat can dock here. The 60 residents of Hapatoni are especially welcoming, and the seafront road is shaded by the sacred *tamanu* trees, which are made almost entirely of ancient paved stones.

Arrivals & Departures
Arriving By Boat
The **Aranui 3** includes stops at Vaitahu and sometimes at Hapatoni and Hanemoenoe during its 16-day round-trip cruise program from Tahiti to the Marquesas. The *Taporo VI* includes Tahuata in its 10-day round-trip voyages from Tahiti. See details in section on *Inter-Island Cruise Ships and Cargo/ Passenger Boats* in Chapter 6, *Planning Your Trip*.

The 48.6-foot long **Tahuata Nui** is a new aluminum hull boat operated by the Commune of Tahuata that transports 60 passengers between Atuona and Tahuata. The boat leaves the quay of Atuona at 12pm each Tuesday for Vaitahu, and each Thursday the boat leaves Atuona at 12pm for Vaitahu and Hapatoni. The one-way fare is 2.000 CFP. Reserve at the Mairie of Tahuata, *Tel. 689/92.92.19; Fax 689/92.92.10.*

Departing By Boat
Tahuata Nui departs Vaitahu each Tuesday and Thursday at 6:30am for

Atuona. The boat stops at Hapatoni village each Thursday enroute to Hiva Oa. The one-way fare is 2.000 CFP and reservations are a must. See information above under *Arriving by Boat*.

Orientation

You can walk from the boat landing to the small village of **Vaitahu**. **Hapatoni** is just a 10-minute boat ride from Vaitahu, or you can take the new road between the two villages. The **Valley of Hanatehau** is a 30-minute horse ride from Hapatoni. A track joins Vaitahu and **Motopu** in the northeast, a distance of about 17 kilometers, which is ideal for riders. **Hanatetena** was formerly approachable only by boat and getting ashore through the turbulent surf is a dangerous maneuver. A road is under construction to connect this small valley with Hapatoni, Motopu and Vaitahu.

Where to Stay

PENSION AMATEA, *Vaitahu, Tahuata 98743, Marquesas Islands. Tel. 689/92.93.68; Tel./Fax 689/92.92.84. Located in the center of Vaitahu village, with access to the sea. Free transfers from quay. EP Rates: room with breakfast 3.500 CFP per person; breakfast 500 CFP; lunch or and dinner 2.000 CFP. Add 6% value added tax to room rates and meal plans. A 10% value added tax is applicable to other services. No credit cards.*

This pension opened in April 2001, offering five bedrooms in a big white concrete house owned by Marguerite Kokauani and her husband. Each room contains a double bed and guests share the bathroom with cold water shower, the living room, dining room and terrace. The beach is close by and you can easily walk around the village from here. Land and sea activities are also available on request.

Seeing the Sights

Vaitahu is the main village, and the small museum **Haina Kakiu** is located in the *mairie* (town hall), which contains exhibits, photos and illustrations of an archaeological site excavated in Hanamiai. **Monuments** in Vaitahu commemorate the 400th anniversary of the Spanish discovery of the Marquesas Islands; the 150th anniversary of **Iotete**, the first Marquesan chief; French Admiral Dupetit-Thouars; and the French-Marquesan battle of 1842. There are also the remains of a French fort and the graves of French sailors.

The big **Meipe Eia** in Hapatoni was renovated by the youths from the village. **Petroglyphs** can be found in the Hanatu'una valley, which can be reached by boat or horseback from Hapatoni. There are also stone **petroglyphs** in Hanatehau and **archaeological sites** in Vaitahu valley.

In front of the **Notre Dame de l'Enfant Jesus Catholic Church** in Vaitahu is a wooden statue of the *Virgin with Child* that is nearly four meters

(13 feet) tall. This beautiful work of art was carved by **Damien Haturau** of Nuku Hiva, whose Christ child is holding an *uru* (breadfruit) as an offering.

Shopping

A specialty of Tahuata is the fragrant *monoi* oil made from coconuts, herbs and flowers, sandalwood, pineapple and other aromatic plants. You will also enjoy the smoke flavored dried bananas wrapped in leaves. Wood carvers have their workshops in the valleys of Vaitahu, Hapatoni, Hanatetena and Motopu.

One of the best bone carvers in the Marquesas is Teiki Barsinas, *Tel. 92.93,24*, who lives in Vaitahu. Other noted sculptors in Vaitahu are: Edwin Fii, *Tel. 92.93.04*; Felix Fii, *Tel. 92.92.14*, In Hapatoni contact Frédéric Timau, *Tel. 92.92.55*, Ernest Teikipupuni, *Tel. 92.92.51*, Paul Vaimaa, *Tel. 92.93.20*, Jules Timau, and Sébastien "Kehu" Barsinas, *Tel. 92.92.38*. Be sure to visit the handcrafts center in Hapatoni for woodcarvings.

Felix Barsinas in Vaitahu, *Tel. 92.93.23*, is one of the best tattoo artists in the Marquesas and passengers aboard the *Aranui 3* can arrange to get a tattoo during their time ashore, providing it doesn't take too long. Edwin and Felix Fii are also tattoo masters whose designs are very original.

FATU HIVA

The beautiful island of **Fatu Hiva** will show you the mysterious Marquesas you have dreamed of discovering. Deep within **Hanavave Bay** you may feel that you are inside a gigantic cathedral, a green mansion of moss and fern covered mountains, often encased in misty rain. White patches of goats and sheep look down from their green mansions above the quiet harbor. Nature's chiseled image of the Polynesian god Tiki is visible in the mountain formations, which may give inspiration to the talented sculptors of wood and stone. This is the famous Bay of Virgins, so named by Catholic missionaries, who said that the phallic shaped stone outcrops were formed as veiled virgins.

When the Spanish explorer Alvaro de Mendaña sighted the island of Fatu Hiva in 1595, he believed he had discovered Solomon's kingdom, complete with gold mines. He named the island La Magdalena and killed his first Polynesian on the shore of Omoa village.

The wild, spectacularly beautiful island of Fatu Hiva is the most remote, the furthest south and the wettest and greenest of the Marquesas Islands. Stretching 15 kilometers (9.3 miles) long, a rugged mountain range is topped by Mt. Tauaouoho, at 960 meters (3,149 feet), overlooking 80 square kilometers (31 square miles) of land.

Fatu Hiva is about 70 kilometers (43 miles) south of Hiva Oa, and can be reached by communal catamaran, private bonito boats or inter-island ships. Although government plans include building an airport here sometime in the future, the only approach is still by sea, and this view alone is worth a trip to the Marquesas Islands.

The jungle greenery begins at the edge of the sea, which is like blue glass after a rain. Narrow ravines, deep gorges and luxuriant valleys briefly open to view as your boat glides past, close to the sheer cliffs that plunge straight into the splashing surf.

Due to the abundant rain and rich, fertile soil, sweet and juicy citrus fruits fill the gardens. Large, tasty shrimp live in the rivers that rush through each valley and rock lobsters are plentiful in the submerged reefs offshore Omoa.

Fatu Hiva is a center of Marquesan crafts. In the villages you will see the women producing tapa cloth from the inner bark of mulberry, banyan or breadfruit trees. They hammer the bark on a log until the fibers adhere, and when it is dry they paint it with the old Marquesan designs like their ancestors wore as tattoos. Sculptors carve the semi-precious woods of rosewood, *tou* and sandalwood, as well as coconuts, basaltic stones and bones. They produce bowls, platters, small canoes, turtles, tiki statues and war clubs. You are welcome to visit their workshops at their homes.

A rare collection of ancient Marquesan woodcarvings can be viewed at a private museum in Omoa for a small entrance fee. You can rent a horse for a bareback ride into the valley, charter a motorized outrigger canoe to explore the coastline and line fish, swim in the rivers or open ocean, go shrimping or lobstering with the locals, and if you're really adventurous, you can join a Marquesan wild pig hunt.

Smoke flavored dried bananas are a specialty of the industrious people of **Omoa village**. Fatu Hiva's special bouquet is the *umu hei*—a delightful blend of sandalwood powder, spearmint, jasmine, ginger root, pineapple, vanilla, sweet basil, gardenia, pandanus fruit, ylang-ylang and other mysterious herbs. This seductive concoction is all tied together and worn around your neck or in your hair.

Arrivals & Departures
Arriving By Boat

The *Aranui* includes stops at Hanavave Bay and Omoa during its 16-day round-trip cruise program from Tahiti to the Marquesas. See details in Chapter 6, *Planning Your Trip*, section on Inter-Island Cruise Ships and Cargo/Passenger Boats.

Auona II is a locally built 51-foot catamaran owned by the Commune of Omoa, *Tel. 92.80.23* that can transport 30 passengers. The boat leaves Atuona, Hiva Oa, each Wednesday around 12pm for Fatu Hiva. The round-trip cost is 4.000 CFP. You can also charter a boat in Atuona that will cost you 50.000 CFP each way to visit Fatu Hiva.

Departing By Boat
The best advice is to leave on the boat that brought you here, unless you're staying a long time and have made other arrangements that you can count on. You can take the *Auona II* catamaran to Atuona from Omoa or Hanavave each Wednesday around 5:30-6am, for 4.000 CFP per person for the round-trip voyage. Reserve at the *mairie* in Omoa, *Tel. 92.80.23.*

Orientation
The 584 inhabitants of Fatu Hiva live in the villages of **Omoa** and **Hanavave**, which are separated by five kilometers (3 miles) of sea. Omoa, in the south of the island, is a wide-open valley with a black sand beach lined with several outrigger canoes painted blue. Just behind the beach are a soccer field and a paved road that leads through the village past the little Catholic Church, which has a red roof and a lovely background of mountainous peaks and spires. Beautiful flower gardens, pamplemousse (grapefruit) trees, citrons and oranges, bananas and other tropical fruit trees surround almost every house. This village is clean and the people are open and friendly. A spring-fed river runs through the village, bordered by ferns and flowers, and villagers say it is safe to swim in this water, as there are no pigpens beside the river.

Getting ashore in Omoa can be an adventure in itself, as the small boat landing is slippery. When the ocean is wild, as it often is, the whaleboat bobs up and down beside the pier and you have to time your jump with the crest of the waves.

A protective seawall has been built on the left bank of Hanavave Bay, which greatly facilitates the problem of getting ashore. The whaleboat discharges passengers at a new concrete quay, where they are welcomed by the artisan group. The tourists are led to the arts and crafts center, where tables are covered with tapa cloth paintings, sculptures, monoi oil, dried bananas, seashells and other wares for sale. The people of Hanavave village, who were formerly closed and wouldn't talk with tourists, are now open and friendly to strangers. This change came about because the women in the artisan groups traveled to Papeete for arts and crafts exhibits and they observed how the "mamas" in other groups enjoyed singing and dancing and being friendly to everyone. Then they returned home to their villages and initiated the same practices among their neighbors.

Hanavave village is narrow and closed in between the fantastic rock formations that resemble the sculpted faces of tikis. Most of the houses are old and shabby. Hanavave has more children than any other village in the Marquesas. A Marquesan guide told me that this is because they had the same nurse for 20 years and she was a devout Catholic who refused to give the women birth control pills. Now that she has retired the pills have become available for those who want to take them. There are still some cases of leprosy found in this valley and it also has had more than the average amount of incest, child molestation, wife beating and other similar activities. One explanation for the behavioral problems is said to be due to the charismatic practices that the Catholic Monseigneur introduced several years ago. The people went too far with it and got into some dark energy and the movement turned negative. The Monseigneur has since put a stop to the charismatic movement and the people seem to be better off now. You should still be cautious when shopping in the village here because the price of a seashell can be quoted at 1.000 CFP if you speak English and sold for 200 CFP if you speak French. This is the only place in the Marquesas where the children beg for money and you should also watch your backpack or back pockets in this village.

A serpentine path winds over the mountains between Omoa and Hanavave, offering a 17-kilometer (10.5-mile) challenging hike and panoramic views through the curtains of rock. Majestic waterfalls are visible from the path deep inside **Vaie'enui Valley**. In Hanavave valley you should avoid swimming in the basin at the bottom of the waterfall, as it is polluted and you risk catching leptospirosis. Facilities include food stores, a post office, a town hall and primary schools in each village.

Getting Around Fatu Hiva
Car Rentals
Henri Tuieinui, *Tel. 92.80.23*, **Didier Gilmore**, *Tel. 92.80.86*, **Xavier Gilmore**, *Tel. 92.82.08*, **Roberto Maraetaata**, *Tel. 92.81.02*, and **Joseph Tetuanui**, *Tel. 92.80.09*, all have a 4WD vehicle they will use to drive you to Hanavave. Cars have to be rented with a chauffeur, as the roads are very rugged.

Where to Stay
Economy
CHEZ NORMA ROPATI, *Omoa, Fatu Hiva 98740, Marquesas Islands. Tel./Fax 689/92.80.13. Rates: room 1.500 CFP per person; room with demi-pension (breakfast and dinner) 3.500 CFP; room with pension complète (all meals) 5.000 CFP per person. Free round-trip transfers from boat landing to pension. Add 6% value added tax to room rates and meal plans. A 10% value added tax is applicable to other services. No credit cards.*

Norma's guesthouse is in the middle of the village, across the road from Chez Cecile. It is totally surrounded by beautiful flowers and colorful bushes and shrubs. The 6-bedroom house has a double bed in four rooms, and two single beds in two rooms. The living room, dining room, terrace and communal bathroom with hot water are all shared. The house linens are furnished. Norma's Marquesan style meals are generous and very tasty. She will also wash your clothes on request.

PENSION CHEZ LIONEL, *Omoa, Fatu Hiva 98740, Marquesas Islands. Tel./Fax 689/92.81.84. EP Rates: room and breakfast 4.500 CFP single, 5.500*

CFP double, third person 1.500 CFP; bungalow and breakfast 6.000 CFP single, 7.500 CFP double, third person 2.000 CFP. Restaurant on premises. Free round-trip transfers from boat landing to pension. Add 6% value added tax to room rates and meal plans. A 10% value added tax is applicable to other services. No credit cards.

This pension and restaurant is the last residence in the village, located beside a river 1.5 kilometers (.9 mile) from the quay. Lionel and Bernadette Cantois rent one room in the main house, which has a double bed and a single bed. As in many Polynesian homes, the walls do not go all the way to the ceiling. You share the bathroom with hot water and the living room with the family. A small bungalow next to the house has a double bed and a single bed, a fan, kitchenette and tiled bathroom with hot water. Two rooms can also be rented in their son's house on the premises, sharing the bathroom and kitchen. Meals are served on a big covered dining terrace in the main house. Lionel has a 4WD that he uses to take guests over the mountain road to Hanavave for 10.000 CFP. You can also include a picnic lunch on this excursion. He will also take you to visit Omoa valley where there are waterfalls, ancient paepae and petroglyphs. He also has a small boat and can take guests fishing. He can take you hunting by horseback if you stay 8 days. You can also take a refreshing bath in the spring-fed river that gurgles behind his house.

PENSION HEIMATA, *Omoa, Fatu Hiva 98740, Marquesas Islands. Tel./ Fax 689/92.80.58. Rates: room with breakfast 2.500 CFP per person; room with breakfast and dinner 4.000 CFP per person; room with all meals 5.500 CFP per person. Free round-trip transfers from boat landing to pension. Add 6% value added tax to room rates and meal plans. A 10% value added tax is applicable to other services. No credit cards.*

This two-bedroom house is beside the road in the village, and is very clean, homey and brightly decorated. There's a double bed in each room, a living room, dining room, terrace and bathroom with hot water. House linens are furnished and Albertine's husband, Teva Tetuanui, will arrange excursions for you on request. Albertine serves good Marquesan food, which includes lots of fresh fish, fruits and vegetables.

Other pensions in Omoa village include: **CHEZ MARIE-CLAIRE**, *Tel. 689/ 92.80.75,* who has a 2-bedroom house with kitchen for rent; **PENSION MANAUEA**, *Tel./Fax 689/92.80.02,* who has 2 rooms for rent; and **CHEZ CECILE GILMORE**, *Tel. 689/92.80.54,* who has a 2-bedroom house with a kitchen in the center of the village. All the lodgings in Fatu Hiva are fairly basic.

PENSION VAIHAU, *Tel. 689/92.81.84,* is planned to open in 2005 in Hanavave valley, providing a 2-bedroom house with kitchen and bathroom for guests. Désirée and Jacques, who will be the hosts, will offer outrigger canoe trips from the Bay of Virgins to Omoa, and hikes or horseback rides to visit the waterfall in the valley. Désirée presently works in conjunction with Pension Lionel to provide excursions for his guests.

Where to Eat

You'll eat very well for budget costs at the family pensions Chez Lionel, Chez Norma Ropati and Pension Heimata. There are two *magasin* stores in Omoa village that sell food supplies and cold beer, and there is also a *boulangerie* that bakes long *baguette* loaves of French bread. There are no snacks or restaurants.

Seeing the Sights

The most beautiful sight in Fatu Hiva is the **Bay of Virgins** in Hanavave, which is best seen from the sea. In Omoa a giant **petroglyph** featuring a huge fish and stick figures is engraved in a boulder at the edge of the village, and there are stone *paepae* house terraces in the valleys. A private collection of ancient Marquesan woodcarvings that belonged to former chief **Willie Grelet** are on display in a house owned by his grandchildren in Omoa. The **Catholic Church** in Omoa, with its red roof, white walls and rock fence, is one of the most picturesque scenes in any Marquesan village.

A 17-kilometer (10.5-mile) **hiking trail** will lead you across the rugged mountains between Omoa and Hanavave village. Walking alone in the mountains of Fatu Hiva is not recommended, even if you are an experienced hiker.

Sports & Recreation
Horseback Riding

In Omoa village you can rent a Marquesan horse with a wooden saddle for daily excursions to Hanavave Bay or to ride around Omoa Valley. Contact Roberto Maraetaata, *Tel. 92.81.02*, or Isidore Mose, *Tel. 92.80.89.*

Boat Rental

You can rent an outrigger canoe with an engine and guide to get from Omoa to Hanavave Bay or vice-versa. Skimming across the incredibly blue water close to the untamed shore and gazing up at the rock formations and the wild cattle and goats staring down at you are moments to remember forever.

Auona II, *Tel. 92.80.23; Fax 92.80.39*, is a 51-foot aluminum catamaran that is operated by the commune of Fatu Hiva. It makes a round-trip voyage from Fatu Hiva to Atuona, Hiva Oa, each Wednesday, and the round-trip cost is 4.000 CFP. This boat can also be chartered for special trips. The big joke in Fatu Hiva is that their communal boat spends more time on land than it does in the sea, due to so many repairs it has had to undergo.

Lionel Cantois at Pension Lionel, *Tel. 92.81.84*, has a small boat he uses to take his guests fishing. Other rental boats: in Omoa contact Xavier Gilmore, *Tel. 92.81.38*, or his brother Napoléon. They have an aluminum speedboat.

Joel Coulon, *Tel. 92.81.17*, has a locally made *poti marara* fishing boat, and Roberto Maraetaata, *Tel. 92.81.02*, has a boat for hire. Jacques Tevenino, *Tel. 92.80.71*, Mathias Pavaouau, *Tel. 92.80.45*, also have boats. In Hanavave call Daniel Pavaouau, *Tel. 92.80.60*.

Deep Sea Fishing
The Marquesan men are experienced fishermen and you can arrange with your pension to accompany one of them. Most of the boats used for fishing are the outrigger speed canoes or *poti marara* wooden boats.

Shopping
Most of the women in Fatu Hiva make tapa bark paintings, which they sell in their arts and crafts center adjacent to the *mairie* (town hall). They also take or send their tapa creations to Papeete for arts and crafts exhibits. Appoline Tiaiho, *Tel. 92.80.66*, in Omoa village is one of the most noted tapa makers. When passengers from the *Aranui 3* or other ships visit the village, she demonstrates how the bark cloth is made. Marie-Noëlle Ehueinana, who also lives in Omoa, has won prizes for her tapa paintings.

Their *monoi* is a delightful blend of coconut oil, sandalwood, spearmint, jasmine, gingerroot, pineapple, sweet basil, gardenia, pandanus fruit, ylang-ylang and other mysterious herbs. This is used as perfume, for massages, to seduce a boyfriend or to ward off mosquitoes. Some of the men even consider drinking it. The women wear an *umu hei* bouquet of flowers and herbs in their hair or around their necks, which has an enticing aroma. Dried bananas are also a specialty here.

In the village of Hanavave the artisans have started displaying their tapa, carvings and other handcrafts on tables near the dock whenever a ship comes to call.

Fatu Hiva has several sculptors in both villages. They carve wood, stone, shell and even coconuts, creating lovely designs taken from the ancient Marquesan tattoos. There are at least a dozen sculptors in Omoa village and two or three in Hanavave. Some of the noted sculptors are: Stéphane Tuohe, *Tel. 92.80.11*, David Pavaouau, *Tel. 92.80.45*, and Marc Barsinas, *Tel. 92.80.44*.

Practical Information
Doctors
There is a new government-operated **infirmary** in Omoa village, *Tel. 92.80.36*, and a **First Aid Station** (*Poste de Secours*) in Hanavave village, *Tel. 92.80.61*.

Post Office and Telecommunications Office
There is a **post office** in Omoa Village, *Tel. 92.83.74*.

Chapter 22

THE AUSTRAL ISLANDS

In the Polynesian language the **Austral Islands** of French Polynesia are collectively known as *Tuhaa Pae*, referring to the five parts or islands that make up the archipelago. Folklore tells of Maui, the South Seas Superman, who fished up this chain of islands from the sea, using a magical fishhook that now forms the tail of Scorpio in the sky. This same hero is said to have cut away the great octopus that held the earth and the sky together, and he pushed up the sky so that people could walk upright. The arms of this octopus fell to the earth to form the Austral Islands, with Tubuai as its head.

Tane was a powerful god who used his many colored seashells to help separate the earth and sky, decorated the Austral heavens with twinkling stars, a golden sun and silvery moon, cool winds and billowing clouds. R'o, God of Agriculture and the Harvest, can be seen as a gilded rainbow and heard as the voice of thunder. Ruahatu-Tinirau, a Polynesian Neptune known as God of the Ocean and Lord of the Abyss, is said to have a man's body joined to a swordfish tail. Everyone knows that this powerful god lives in the reefs of Raivavae. And Tuivao, a fishing hero from Rurutu, sailed on the back of a whale to an enchanted island ruled by the goddess Tareparepa. Fleeing her spell Tuivao rode his whale to the island of Raivavae, where the mammal landed so hard on the beach that its imprint is still seen there today.

Past and present blend in harmony in the Austral Islands today. Islands of quiet beauty, peace and pride; these are Polynesia's Temperate Isles.

The Austral Islands include the high islands of **Rurutu, Tubuai, Rimatara, Raivavae** and **Rapa**, plus the low, uninhabited islands of **Maria** (or Hull) and the **Marotiri** (or Bass) **Rocks**. These islands lie on both sides of the Tropic of Capricorn, extending in a northwest-southeasterly direction across 1,280 kilometers (794 miles) of ocean. They are part of a vast mountain range, an

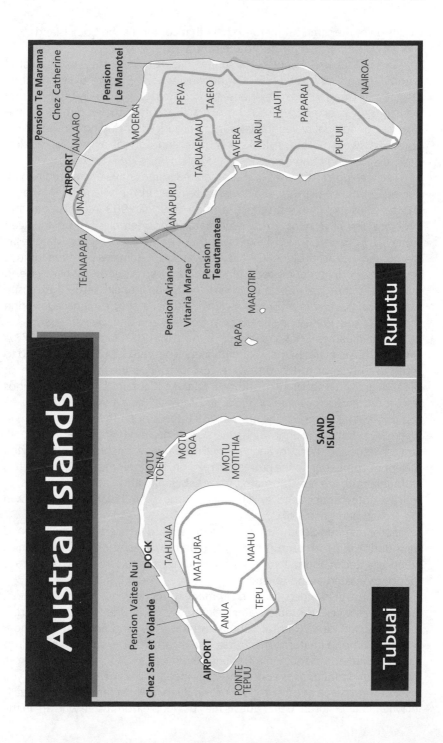

Austral Islands

Rurutu

Pension Te Marama
Chez Catherine
Pension Le Manotel
AIRPORT
ANAARO
MOERAI
PEVA
TAERO
TAPUAEMAU
AVERA
NARUI
HAUTI
PAPARAI
NAIROA
PUPUII
UNAA
TEANAPAPA
ANAPURU
Pension Ariana
Vitaria Marae
Pension Teautamatea
RAPA
MAROTIRI

Tubuai

Pension Vaitea Nui
Chez Sam et Yolande
DOCK
TAHUAIA
MOTU TOENA
MOTU ROA
MOTU MOTITHIA
SAND ISLAND
MATAURA
ANUA
MAHU
TEPU
AIRPORT
POINTE TEPUU

extension of the same submerged chain that comprises the Cook Islands 960 kilometers (595 miles) further to the northwest.

The 141 square kilometers (54 square miles) of land surface in the Austral Islands is home to some 6,386 Polynesians, who live peaceful lives in their attractive villages, where their houses and churches are usually built of coral limestone or concrete. Due to the rich soil and the cooler climate of the Australs, good quality vegetables can be produced, including taro, manioc, potatoes, sweet potatoes, leeks, cabbage and coffee, as well as apples, peaches, figs and strawberries.

Archaeological diggings in these isolated islands have uncovered habitation sites, council platforms and *marae* temples in the village of Vitaria on Rurutu, showing man's presence around the year 900 A.D. Tubuai and Rimatara also have ruins of open-air *marae* stone temples, and giant sized stone *tikis* have been found on Raivavae that resemble those in the Marquesas Islands and on Easter Island. On Rapa there are the remains of seven famous *pa* fortresses on superimposed terraces that were found nowhere else in Polynesia except New Zealand where the Maori people settled. Exquisite woodcarvings, now in museums, tell of an artistic people highly evolved in their craft, who were also superb boat builders and daring seafarers.

Captain James Cook discovered Rurutu in 1769 and Tubuai in 1777. Fletcher Christian and his band of mutineers from the H. M. S. *Bounty* tried to settle in Tubuai in 1789, but were forced to flee the island because of skirmishes with the men of Tubuai. Spanish Captain Thomas Gayangos discovered lovely Raivavae in 1775 and remote Rapa was first sighted by English Captain George Vancouver in 1791. Rimatara, the lowest of the high islands, was not found until 1821, when Captain Samuel Pinder Henry of Tahiti arrived, returning the following year with two native teachers who converted the entire population to the Protestant religion. Evangelism still predominates, although there are now Mormon, Adventist, Sanito and Catholic churches, as well as Pentecost and Jehovah's Witnesses. The Austral Islands have all flown the French flag since 1901.

European and South American crews aboard whalers and sandalwood ships during the 19th century brought epidemic diseases to the islands, which practically decimated the strong, proud and highly cultured Polynesian race that once existed in the Australs.

The Austral Islanders today have many of the advantages of civilization, including electricity, potable water, telephone service and television. There is regular air service to Rurutu, Tubuai and Raivavae, and an airstrip is under construction on Rimatara. The Tuhaa Pae II cargo ship from Papeete brings supplies to all the islands on a frequent basis.

Accommodations for visitors are provided in small pensions, where you will often eat, sleep and live in close proximity to the host family, which usually includes small children. Other guests may be people from Tahiti who are in the islands on business for the local government, school system or a church group. They may be technicians who have come to repair some broken machinery or bakery oven, or traveling salesmen called demarcheurs who take orders for school books and other supplies. Or it's just as likely you'll meet a couple of travelers from Norway who have come here to write a book.

RURUTU

Rurutu is the most northerly of the Austral Islands, lying at 22º27' Latitude South and 151º21' Longitude West, 572 kilometers (355 miles) southwest of Tahiti. A very pretty island with a circumference of 30 kilometers (19 miles), Rurutu is an upthrust limestone island with steep cliffs rising dramatically from the sea. The crannies in these bluffs were formerly used as shelters and burial chambers. There are also caves and grottoes decorated with stalactites and stalagmites. Rurutu's highest mountain, **Manureva**, reaches an elevation of 385 meters (1,263 feet), and the coral reefs that surrounded the island eons ago are now raised *makatea* bluffs some 90 meters (300 feet) high above the sea. Rurutu does not have the wide lagoons found in the Society Islands or in Tubuai and Raivavae. Swimming and snorkeling are still possible in certain areas, however, and there are a few white sand beaches.

The original name of this island was *Eteroa*, which means a long measuring string. The current name of *Rurutu tu noa* is an old Polynesian saying that means a mast standing straight. *Manureva* (soaring bird) was formerly the name of one of Rurutu's famous sailing boats that carried produce between the islands. The men are still noted sailors, and several of them work aboard the inter-island cargo ships that serve as a lifeline between Tahiti and the remote islands of French Polynesia.

The people of Rurutu were also highly skilled wood carvers, but no longer practice this craft. Most of the ancient tiki statues were destroyed by the missionaries, and one of them, the statue of the Rurutu ancestor god A'a, was taken to London by John Williams, one of the pioneering missionaries. This original tiki, which is 45 inches tall and weighs 282 pounds, is in the Museum of Mankind in London, but five plaster of Paris molds of the A'a statue were made by the British Museum. One of them was willed to the people of Rurutu by an American man who died a few years ago. This statue is now on display in the Mairie in Moerai village. Christi's has evaluated each of the A'a tiki statues to be worth $50,000. A Rurutu dance group made a wooden replica of the A'a tiki for a Heiva performance in Tahiti and this big statue now stands as guardian in front of Pension Le Manotel in Moerai.

In the old village of **Vitaria** is the **Marae Taaroa** or Arii, which dates from the year 900. This is the oldest known site of man's habitation in the Austral Islands. Nearby is a council platform and 70 house sites of a former village and warriors' house. In ancient times the warriors of Rurutu were feared for their strength. Today they are admired for their industriousness, seamanship, dancing skills and physical beauty.

The 2,104 handsome, intelligent and industrious Polynesians who live in the three villages of Moerai, Avera and Hauti, have houses of white concrete or coral limestone, bordered by flower gardens and low fences of white limestone.

In the main village of **Moerai** there is a *gendarmerie*, a post office and infirmary with a doctor and dentist, a bank, primary and junior high schools, a few small *magasin* stores, bakeries, snack bars and roulottes (mobile diners). Each village is dominated by a Protestant temple, with smaller churches for the Catholic, Mormon, Adventist, Pentecostal and Jehovah's Witness faiths.

The men harvest their taro, potatoes, tapioca, sweet potatoes, cabbages, leeks and carrots. The women form artisan groups to weave specially grown fibers of *paeore* pandanus into attractive hats, bags and mats, which are sold both locally and in Tahiti. The people of Rurutu enjoy a pleasant communal spirit, working together, singing *himenes* in their Evangelical churches, and pitching in to prepare a big feast.

A New Year's custom on Rurutu is to visit each house in the village, where you are sprinkled with talcum powder before entering to partake of the refreshments and to admire the women's nicest woven products and *tifaifai* bed covers and wall hangings. Also during the month of January the youth groups of the Protestant churches participate in a ritual called the *Tere*. A long caravan of flower-decorated pickup trucks, 4-wheel drive vehicles and motorcycles makes a tour of the island, stopping at each historical site, where one of the orators recites the legends of each significant stone or cave. One of the stops is on top of a mountain, where you have a lovely view of the village of Avera. Here is the Ofai Maramaiterai (intelligence that lightens the sky), which folklore claims is the center and origin of the island.

During the *Tere* circle island tour and also during the 2-week Heiva Festival in July the young men and women of each village prove themselves in a show of strength. Following a custom called *amoraa ofai*, unique to Rurutu, they attempt to lift huge volcanic stones to their shoulders. The village champions hoist one sacred stone that weighs 150 kilograms (330 pounds). This accomplishment is followed by exuberant feasting and dancing.

Another big event in Rurutu, as well as in all the Austral Islands, takes place during the month of May, when the Protestant parishioners gather in their temples for a religious fête called Me. The "mamas" dress for this occasion in their white gowns and elaborate hats and blend their voices with those of the men to sing their *himenes* and to donate money to support the church's projects for the coming year.

Activities on Rurutu include horseback riding and hiking to waterfalls, where refreshing showers cascade into fern bordered pools. The limestone grottoes form a natural stage for cultural reenactment ceremonies and cinematographers from all parts of the world come here to film these natural formations. Circle island tours by four-wheel drive vehicle wind over concrete or dirt roads into cool valleys where fields of wild miri (sweet basil) scent the breeze. Picnic lunches can be packed for these trips or to play in the sun on deserted white sand beaches. Humpback whales can be seen offshore Rurutu during the austral winter months of July-October, and observation platforms have been built across the bluffs overlooking the ocean at each end of Moerai village.

The aroma of pineapple mingles pleasantly with *ylang ylang*, Tiare Tahiti, wild *miri* basil and *avaro*, some of the fragrant flowers, fruits and spices that are used to make the welcoming leis you will smell as soon as you arrive on this island of fragrant perfumes.

Arrivals & Departures
Arriving By Air
Air Tahiti has a 1 1/2 hour direct flight from Tahiti to Rurutu each Wednesday and Friday, and a flight each Sunday via Tubuai. During the high seasons there is a flight daily except Monday. The one-way airfare from Tahiti to Rurutu is 18.500 CFP and the fare from Tubuai to Rurutu is 9.500 CFP. **Air Tahiti reservations**: *Tahiti Tel. 86.42.42/86.41.84; Rurutu Tel. 93.02.50.*

You can also get to Rurutu by chartering an airplane in Tahiti from **Wan Air**, *Tel. 50.44.17, cell 77.03.79*; **Air Archipels**, *Tel. 81.30.30*; or **Air Tahiti**, *Tel. 86.42.42.*

Arriving By Boat
Tuhaa Pae II, *Tel. 50.96.09, Fax 42.06.09; E-mail: snathp@mail.pf* makes 3 voyages a month from Tahiti to the Austral Islands, calling at Tubuai, Rimatara, Raivavae and Rurutu, then returning to Papeete. This itinerary may change according to the freight requirements of each voyage. The one-way fare to Rurutu is 4.046 CFP on the deck, 5.664 CFP in a berth on deck, and 7.789 CFP for a berth in a cabin. Meals are 3.080 CFP per day in the cafeteria and 5.060 CFP per day in the officers' dining room. Rates include taxes. See further information in Chapter 6, *Planning Your Trip.*

Departing By Air
You can fly from Rurutu direct to Tahiti on Wednesday and Sunday, and there is a flight to Tubuai and Tahiti each Friday. During the high seasons there are daily flights except on Monday. **Air Tahiti reservations** in Rurutu, *Tel. 93.02.50.*

Departing By Boat
The **Tuhaa Pae II** calls at Moerai village in Rurutu on its way back to Papeete or enroute to the other Austral Islands, according to the needs of the islanders. You can purchase your ticket on board the ship.

Orientation

The oblong-shaped island of Rurutu is 10 kilometers (6.2 miles) long and 5.5 kilometers (3.4 miles) wide, or 36 square kilometers (14 square miles) in circumference. The main village of **Moerai** on the east coast is about four kilometers (2.5 miles) from the airport, connected by a paved road, which also extends to the village of **Hauti,** also on the east coast. Another concrete road links Moerai with **Avera**, a village 6 kilometers (3.7 miles) distant, located on the western coast. Avera has a small harbor for fishing boats, within the island's only real bay. The road around the island does not circle the coastline, but climbs up and down, from sea-level to almost 200 meters (656 feet), with panoramic views of white sand beaches and lagoons alternating with craggy cliffs and limestone caves and grottoes. The interior roads are bordered by fields of potatoes and taro and plantations of pandanus, bananas, coffee and noni. There are also several off-track dirt roads that can be explored by 4WD, horseback or on foot.

Getting Around Rurutu
Car, Scooter & Bicycle Rentals

If you reserve a room at a family pension they will provide free round-trip transportation between the airport and the lodging. They charge for other transfers requested. **Rurutu Rent A Car**, *Tel. 93.02.80, Fax 93.02.81, E-mail: pensiontemarama@mail.pf*, is located at Pension Temarama in Unaa, between the airport and Moerai, where you can rent a 2- or 4-seat Suzuki 4WD for 7.100 CFP for 4 hours, 8.700 CFP for 8 hours, or 10.900 CFP for 24 hours. Weekly and monthly rates are also available. Bicycles rent for 1.100 CFP for 4 hours, 1.500 CFP for 8 hours, 1.800 CFP for 24 hours, and 9.800 CFP for 7 days. Monthly rates also possible.

Rauaru, *Tel./Fax 94.03.02*, in Avera village, also has rental cars.

Where to Stay

PENSION TE MARAMA, *B.P. 68, Moerai, Rurutu 98753. Tel. 689/93.02.80, Fax 689/93.02.81; cell 689/72.30.20; E-mail: pensiontemarama@mail.pf. On mountainside in Unaa with access to the sea, 2 kilometers (1.2 miles) from the airport and 500 meters (1,640 feet) from the village of Moerai. EP Rates: room 4.000/5.000 CFP single, 5.000/5.700 CFP double, 6.700 CFP triple and 7.700 CFP for 4 people; room with breakfast and dinner from 7.800 CFP single; 12.600 CFP double; room with breakfast, lunch and dinner from 9.800 CFP single, 16.600 CFP double per day. Child 4 to 10 years pays 2.100 CFP on MAP and 3.100 CFP on AP. Free round-trip transfers between airport and pension. Add 6% value added tax to room rates and meal plans. A 10% value added tax is applicable to other services. Mastercard, Visa.*

Landry and Tania Chong transformed their family home into a bed and breakfast lodging in 1998 and they have already earned a good reputation for taking very good care of their guests. Landry, who is half-Chinese and half-Rurutu, speaks some English.

This is a big two-story white house with six bedrooms located just outside the main village of Moerai. Three very attractively decorated and furnished bedrooms are on the ground floor and three are upstairs, and each room has a private bathroom and hot water shower. The rooms have one or two double beds and some rooms also have a single bed, as well as a writing desk, a ceiling fan and a pandanus mat on the floor. The rooms are cleaned daily and freshly laundered towels are placed on the bed every day. Each floor also has a living room with sofas, a television and bookshelves. A long, wide covered balcony outside the rooms overlooks the ocean, which is only about a block from the pension. A bar and restaurant are on the ground floor, where Tania's delicious and well-prepared meals are served family style. Dinner is accompanied by a pitcher of red wine. They also operate Rurutu Rent A Car on the premises, and either Landry or Tania will drive you around the island or to a special picnic site, and they can also help you arrange your other activities, such as hiking, horseback riding, fishing and diving.

PENSION LE MANOTEL, *B.P. 11, Moerai, Rurutu 98753. Tel. 689/ 93.02.25, Fax 689/93.02.26; E-mail: manotel@mail.pf. On the mountainside of road, 6 kilometers (3.7 miles) from the airport and 2 kilometers (1.2 miles) from the boat dock in Moerai village. EP Rates: bungalow 5.775 CFP single, 6.300 CFP double, 6.825 CFP triple; bungalow with breakfast and dinner 8.925 CFP single, 12.600 CFP double, 16.275 CFP triple; bungalow with all meals 11.025 CFP single, 16.800 CFP double, 22.575 CFP triple. Free round-trip transfers between airport and pension. Rates include all taxes on room rates and meal plans. A 10% value added tax is applicable to other services. Mastercard, Visa.*

Hélène and Yves Gentilhomme inaugurated their new pension in May 2003, which is located in an area called Peva, across the road from a long white sand beach that is shaded by tamanu trees. The four FEI type government model wooden bungalows are built on stilts in a lovely garden of flowers and ferns. Each colorfully decorated unit has a double bed, a single bed, a fan and television, a private bathroom with hot water shower and a covered terrace with two lounge chairs. Yves plans to add 4 more bungalows in 2005. A restaurant and bar is also open to the public, serving à la carte meals and daily specials, which can be accompanied by your favorite beverage, including a choice of wines.

Yves is retired from the French military and is also president of the Rurutu Visitors Bureau. He and Hélène ran Pension Catherine for a few years and they both speak a little English. Yves provides half- and full-day land tours by 4WD and will take you to visit the grottoes, caves, beaches and blowhole, with or without lunch included. He can also put you in touch with a qualified hiking guide. Just across the road from Le Manotel you can easily see the humpback whales swimming close to shore during their visit each July through October.

PENSION TEAUTAMATEA, *B.P. 35, Moerai, Rurutu 98753. Tel./Fax 689/93.02.93; E-mail: pensionteautamatea@mail.pf; www.haere-mai.com. Across the road from the sea in Vitaria, 3 kilometers (1.9 miles) from the airport and 6 kilometers (3.7 miles) from Moerai quay. EP Rates: room 4.500 CFP single, 6.000 CFP double, 7.500 CFP triple; room with breakfast and dinner 7.500 CFP single, 12.000 CFP double, 16.500 CFP triple; room with breakfast, lunch and dinner 9.500 CFP single, 16.000 CFP double, 22.500 CFP triple. Free round-trip transfers between airport and pension. Add 6% value added tax to room rates and meal plans. A 10% value added tax is applicable to other services. No credit cards.*

This is a modern house situated in a magnificent coconut grove in an ancient royal archaeological site in Vitaria. There are five guest bedrooms, either on the ground level or upstairs, with one or two double beds. There are four private bathrooms and one communal bathroom, all with hot water showers. All guests share the living room, dining room and terrace. Snorkeling equipment and an outrigger paddle canoe are free for guests and bicycles can be rented for 1.000 CFP a day. You can also go horseback riding in the mountains for 5.000 CFP for a half-day, or take an hour's ride along the beach for 2.500 CFP. A half-day excursion by 4WD vehicle is 4.000 CFP. There is a pretty white sand beach here that faces the setting sun. The owner, Viriamu Teuruarii, is a nice looking young Polynesian man who will show you the royal *marae* temple on his property, which he maintains himself. Be sure to pay attention to the well-made wooden furniture that Viriamu built from pandanus, coconut wood, wild hibiscus trees and bamboo. The beds upstairs are antique iron bedsteads and the house is filled with Viriamu's creative decorations and the woven hats made by his pretty sister, Darianne, who also takes care of the pension and cooks the meals. They both speak a little English.

PENSION ARIANA, *B.P. 23, Moerai, Rurutu 98753. Tel. 689/94.06.69; Fax 689/94.07.14; www.haere-mai.com. Beside the lagoon in Vitaria, 1 kilometer (.6 mile) from airport and 3 kilometers (1.9 miles) from Moerai village and quay. EP Rates: room 5.000 CFP single, 6.500 CFP double; room with breakfast and dinner 9.000 CFP single, 14.500 CFP double; room with all meals 11.500 CFP single, 19.500 CFP double. Bungalow 6.000 CFP single, 7.500 CFP double; bungalow with breakfast and dinner 10.000 CFP single, 15.500 CFP double; bungalow with all meals 12.500 CFP single, 20.500 CFP double. Free round-trip airport transfers. Add 6% value added tax to room rates and meal plans. A 10% value added tax is applicable to other services. No credit cards.*

Ariana Vidal has 7 simple bungalows and a 4-bedroom house to rent in a jungle setting that slopes down the hill from the road to the white sand beach and lagoon in the small village of Vitaria. Each of the bungalows contains a double bed and one or two single beds, plus a private bathroom with hot water. A 2-story house with four bedrooms is also available for guests who don't want to walk down the uneven rocky steps that lead to the beach. Beside the road is the restaurant, bar, boutique and reception. Although she is in her late 60s Madame Vidal still runs her pension all by herself, as her strong character chases employees away after only a few days. She cooks local style foods, which means plenty of fresh fish, breadfruit, fei, taro and tropical fruits. If you speak French and are limber enough to negotiate the hillside slopes, she will happily show you around her botanical garden, which she takes care of by herself. She will also give you cultural demonstrations in her artisan's shop and will arrange for your visits to the highlights of Rurutu's attractions. She rents bicycles for 800 CFP for 4 hours and 1.600 CFP for 8 hours, and a circle island tour by 4WD is 4.000 CFP per person.

CHEZ CATHERINE, *Moerai, Rurutu, 98753. Tel. 689/94.02.43. In Moerai village facing the port. MAP Rates: room with breakfast and dinner 7.500 CFP single, 11.550 CFP double; AP Rates: room with all three meals 9.700 CFP single, 15.550 CFP double. Add 6% value added tax to room rates and meal plans. A 10% value added tax is applicable to other services. No credit cards.*

Catherine ran this pension for several years before leasing it to other managers. It was closed in 2002 for repairs and renovation, and now Catherine has taken it back over and put her young grandson, Raymond, in charge, although the renovation still remains to be done. There was a time when you could sit on the front terrace and watch the ocean while listening to the *himene* singing coming from the Protestant church in the center of Moerai village, just a few steps away. A concrete wall now hides the view from the terrace, but the singing continues still.

Seven very basic rooms contain a double bed or two single beds, a closet and a private bathroom with a hot water shower. House linens are furnished. The windows are unscreened except at the top, where a little air can enter even though you may wisely close the windows at night. The main building contains a living/dining room and Raymond hopes to get a cook soon. There's nothing at all fancy about this place, but it is convenient for non-picky guests who want to be in Moerai village. You can walk around the village or along the road beside the sea, up to the limestone caves overlooking the ocean. Raymond can arrange a circle island tour by 4WD for 4.000 CFP a person.

Where to Eat

RESTAURANT LE MANOTEL, *Tel. 93.02.25*, is a public restaurant and bar located at Pension Le Manotel. Open daily serving breakfast for 735 CFP, lunch for 2.310 CFP, and dinner for 2.836 CFP, taxes included. Mastercard, Visa.

PENSION TEMARAMA, *Tel. 93.02.80*. Breakfast 800 CFP, lunch 2.000 CFP, dinner 3.000 CFP, plus 6% tax. Reserve. Mastercard, Visa.

PENSION TEAUTAMATEA, Tel. 93.02.93. Breakfast 800 CFP, lunch 2.800 CFP, dinner 3.000 CFP, plus 6% tax. Reserve. No credit cards. PENSION ARIANA, Tel. 94.06.69. Breakfast 1.000 CFP, lunch 2.500 CFP, dinner 3.000 CFP, plus 6% tax. Reserve. No credit cards.

Snack Paulette, Tel. 94.05.82 / 72.30.06, is a roulotte at the port in Moerai. She serves breakfast, lunch and dinner, featuring fresh local fruits and vegetables and fish. A traditional meal is served once a week. No credit cards. Snack Tetua Line, Tel. 94.07.82, is in Moerai on the road leading to the college (junior high school), and Vanina's roulotte, Tel. 94.06.90, is close to the primary school in Moerai village. The Omiri Ferme (Farm), Tel. 94.02.39, in Moerai, makes various kinds of goat cheese, yogurt and confitures, and on Friday nights you can get pizzas and fresh homemade pasta to go. Snack Te Auti is on the mountainside in Vitaria, across the road from Chez Ariana.

There are 9 Chinese stores or magasins on Rurutu and most of them sell prepared dishes to go. It's best to shop before noon. There are also 3 bakeries turning out fresh baguettes daily.

Seeing the Sights

Some of the interesting sites you will want to visit in Rurutu are the grottoes and marae temples of Vitaria, the Tetuanui Plateau and dam, the beautiful view of Matotea between Vitaria and Avera, the Lookout Point at Taura'ma, where you can see the villages of Avera and Hauti, the Trou de Souffleur (spouting hole) and the beautiful white sand beaches of Naairoa, Narui and Peva, the Vairuauri Grotto al Paparai, and the Underwater Grotto of Te Ana Maro at Teava Nui.

You may also be interested in visiting the final resting-place of Eric de Bisschop, a French explorer who was noted for his ocean voyages in unseaworthy rafts. He died at Rakahanga in the Cook Islands in 1972, and is buried in the second cemetery of Moerai, off the main road, south of the village. All the pensions can provide a 4WD excursion to visit the highlights of Rurutu. The cost is 4.000 CFP per person.

Hiking

At this writing Rurutu has two trained guides to take you on hiking excursions, which may include a visit to the Metuari'i domain on the north coast of the island. You can visit the Matonaa promontory overlooking Moerai village, and climb to the summits of Teape, Taatioe and Manureva mountains, which shouldn't present any major difficulty unless you are subject to vertigo. The Ana Aeo grotto in Vitaria resembles a baroque cathedral with its stalactites and stalagmites. President François Mitterand came here in 1990 when he was still president of France, and this grotto became a stage where the traditional songs and dances of Rurutu were performed. Following this visit the residents now calls this Mitterand Grotto. The Pito circuit covers the beautiful south end of the island, with its numerous beaches of white sand. You will climb plateaus and explore numerous grottoes, cross the cliffs and follow a road that takes you from Avera to Auti villages. The Peva circuit between the villages of Moerai and Auti is the shortest hike in distance, but the richest in various kinds of sites. This is where you will find the most beautiful grottoes on the island, complete with stalactites and stalagmites. The Varirepo grotto is comprised of two immense chambers with a ceiling that is 20 meters high. One of the calcite formations is in the amazing shape of a giant sized *cocoro* (penis) that stands 2 meters high.

Horseback Riding
Viriamu Teuruarii at Pension Teautamatea in Vitaria, *Tel. 93.02.93*. You can ride a horse along the white sand beach for an hour for 2.500 CFP, and a half-day ride in the mountains is 5.000 CFP per person.

Sports & Recreation
Boat Rentals & Excursions
Rurutu Excursions, *Tel. 94.07.91*, is a new activity that began in September 2004, with the arrival of the new Bertram fishing boat, *Princesse Inanui*. This 16-passenger boat will be used for whale watching excursions between the months of July and October, for deep-sea fishing and trips around the island. The Polynesian owners are also planning to offer weekend camping and fishing trips to the uninhabited atoll of Maria Island, a 7 1/2 hour boat ride from Rurutu. This will interest adventurers who want to play Robinson Crusoe, providing only minimal comforts while you fish, search for lobsters and other crustaceans on the reef, and cook your meals over a campfire under the stars. The captain and crew are all certified in first aid and life saving at sea.

Adrien Manuel in Moerai, *Tel. 94.05.52*, and **Pierre Harua** in Avera, *Tel. 94.06.36*, also have boats to rent with a skipper.

Diving
Raie Manta Club Rurutu operates only during the whale-watching season from July through October, when the humpback whales (*Megaptera novaeangliae*) come up from the cold Antarctic waters to breed or give birth in the warmer waters of the tropics. Yves Lefevre, who owns the Raie Manta Clubs in Rangiroa and Tikehau, sends a qualified PADI scuba diving instructor and Sea Guide to Rurutu and they rent a house for the season. Contact Raie Manta Club Rangiroa at *Tel. 689/96.84.80; Cell 689/72.31.45; Fax 689/96.85.60; E-mail: raiemantaclub@mail.pf; http://raiemantaclub.free.fr.*

Two observation platforms have been built on either side of Moerai village to watch the humpback whales, which are easily sighted as the reef is close to the shore. The islanders say that when the orange flowers of the African tulip tree start to blossom this is a sure sign that the whales will arrive at any moment. Although the air temperature in Rurutu may drop to 15 degrees Celsius (59º F.) in July and August, the ocean temperature doesn't get any cooler than 21 to 22 degrees Celsius (70 to 72º F). Visitors from several countries make their reservations months in advance so that they can dive with the humpback whales in Rurutu.

Shopping

The "mamas" of Rurutu are noted for their finely made hats, baskets, tote bags, mats and other woven products. You can visit the arts and crafts shops and you will also see the women sitting together on the grass or on their front terraces, creating an outlandish hat for them to wear to church or a beautiful traditional hat for you to buy. The Association of Artisans of Rurutu is located at the airport, the Vaipurua Association is in Moerai village, and the Tiare Porea association is in Auti village. Pension Ariana and Pension Teautamatea in Vitaria also have arts and crafts exhibits.

Taofe Tapiti, *Tel. 94.07.03*, is on the mountainside in Unaa, past the airport heading toward Vitaria. This is a small shop where you can learn how coffee is grown and ground and you can even taste the different coffees that are produced in the Austral Islands. Here you can buy coffee and confitures made in Rurutu. In some of the *magasins* you can also buy 500-gram (1 lb.) bags of Cafe Teautoa, which is 100% Arabica Cafe de Rurutu.

Practical Information

Banks

Banque Socredo, *Tel. 94.04.75*, has an agency in Moerai village, with an ATM inside the bank.

Doctors

There is a small medical center in Moerai, *Tel. 94.03.12*, and an infirmary in Avera village, *Tel. 94.03.21*.

Police

The French *gendarmerie* of Rurutu, *Tel. 94.03.61*, is located in Moerai.

Post Office

There is a Post Office and Telecommunications Center in Moerai, *Tel. 94.03.50*.

Tourist Bureau

Rurutu Visitors Bureau is at Le Manotel Pension in Moerai, *Tel. 93.02.25, Fax 93.02.26, E-mail: manotel@mail.pf*, is in Moerai. Yves Gentilhomme is president.

TUBUAI

Tubuai is 568 kilometers (352 miles) due south of Tahiti, located just above the Tropic of Capricorn in the center of the Austral Island group, offering a pleasant combination of the tropics and Temperate Zone.

This is the largest of the Austral Islands, with a land area of 45 square kilometers (17 square miles) and a population of 1,979 inhabitants. An immense turquoise lagoon is bordered by brilliant white sand beaches and dotted by seven palm shaded *motu* islets, surrounded by superb snorkeling grounds. From the village of Mahu the reef is 5 kilometers (3 miles) from the shore. These shallow lagoon waters provide an ideal nursery for colorful and delicious tropical fish, clams, sea urchins and lobsters. There are three main passes and several smaller passes through the coral reef into the lagoon, and cargo ships can offload supplies at a concrete pier near Mataura village. This sheltered harbor is located close to the former site where Fort George was established by Fletcher Christian and his mutineers from the *H.M.S. Bounty* when they tried to settle on Tubuai in 1789. This was one of the most important events in the history of Tubuai, when the mutineers tried twice to settle on the island, but were fought off by the unfriendly warriors of the island. This event is re-enacted every two years and will take place again in May 2006.

Captain James Cook discovered Tubuai in 1777 during his third voyage to Tahiti, but he did not go ashore. The London Missionary Society sent native teachers to the island to convert souls to Christianity in 1822 and the Protestant faith is still predominant in Tubuai. The first Mormon missionary to settle in these islands arrived in Tubuai in 1844, and this religion is today an important part of the lifestyle.

Tubuai is the administrative center for the archipelago, and the main village of **Mataura** has the administrative offices, town hall, gendarmerie, small hospital, post office, schools and some of the churches. Chinese families operate the island's 5 grocery stores and 2 bakeries. Electricity and hot water are provided in the small bed and breakfast pensions, where you can also share lunch and dinner with the host family in their big dining room. Activities can be arranged at your pension to visit the island by car or bicycle or to explore the motu islets and lagoon by boat. Hiking is popular here and can easily be accomplished without a guide.

Tubuai is a pretty island with gentle slopes and contours. It does not have the dramatic coastlines of Rurutu, Raivavae and Rapa, and the people here seem to lack the zestful spirit, the *joie de vivre* that you'll find on Rurutu. This is one of the few remaining islands in French Polynesia where the untreated tap water is still totally safe for consumption, even for babies.

Arrivals & Departures

Arriving By Air

Air Tahiti has a 1 hour and 40 minute direct flight from Tahiti to Tubuai each Sunday and Monday, a flight each Wednesday via Raivavae and each Friday via Rurutu. More flights are added during the high seasons and school vacation periods. The one-way airfare from Tahiti to Tubuai is 20.700 CFP, the fare from Rurutu to Tubuai is 9.500 CFP, and from Raivavae to Tubuai the one-way fare is 9.300 CFP. **Air Tahiti reservations**: *Tel. 86.42.42 (Tahiti), Tel. 93.22.75 (Tubuai).*

You can also get to Tubuai by chartering an airplane in Tahiti from **Wan Air**, *Tel. 50.44.17, cell 77.03.79*; **Air Archipels**, *Tel. 81.30.30*; or **Air Tahiti**, *Tel. 86.42.42.*

Arriving By Boat

Tuhaa Pae II, *Tel. 50.96.09, Fax 42.06.09; E-mail: snathp@mail.pf* makes 3 voyages a month from Tahiti to the Austral Islands, calling at Tubuai, Rimatara, Raivavae and Rurutu, then returning to Papeete. This itinerary may change according to the freight requirements of each voyage. The one-way fare to Tubuai is 4.046 CFP on the deck, 5.664 CFP in a berth on deck, and 7.789 CFP for a berth in a cabin. Meals are 3.080 CFP per day in the cafeteria and 5.060 CFP per day in the officers' dining room. Rates include taxes. See further information in Chapter 6, *Planning Your Trip.*

Departing By Air

You can fly direct from Tubuai to Tahiti each Wednesday and Friday. The Monday departure from Tubuai makes a brief stop in Raivavae before returning to Tahiti and the Sunday flight stops in Rurutu on its way to Tahiti. More flights are added in July and August. **Air Tahiti reservations** in Tubuai, *Tel. 93.22.75.*

Departing By Boat

The **Tuhaa Pae II** calls at Tubuai enroute to the other Austral Islands or on its way back to Papeete. You can purchase your ticket on board the ship.

Orientation

Tubuai is an oval shaped island with no indented bays. Two mountain ranges rise from the heart of the island, with **Mount Taitaa** the highest peak at 422 meters (1,393 feet) in altitude. A 24-kilometer (15 mile) paved road circles the island, connecting the quiet villages of **Mataura, Taahuaia** and **Mahu**. The airport is about four kilometers (2.5 miles) west of Mataura village and the ship wharf is on the east side of Mataura. Beside the pretty mint green Protestant church in the center of Mataura village a transversal road heads inland and crosses the island from Mataura to Mahu, passing through fertile plains and marshlands, where taro, potatoes, sweet potatoes and peaches grow alongside coffee, corn and oranges. The island is bordered by soft sandy beaches that range in color from white to rose and yellow to ochre, an artist's palette of at least 8 varying shades. Most of the houses are built on the mountain side of the road because of the high seas and strong winds during the winter months of July and August. Australian pine trees and hedges of white lilies are planted on the beach side of the road to serve as wind breaks.

Getting Around Tubuai

You will be met at the airport or boat dock by someone from the pension where you've reserved accommodations. There is no public transportation system on Tubuai and no taxi service outside the pensions. Check with your host for car and bicycle rentals.

Where to Stay

CHEZ SAM ET YOLANDE, *B.P. 23, Mataura, Tubuai, 98754. Tel./Fax 689/95.05.52. On the mountainside in Mataura, 2 kilometers (1.2 miles) from the airport and 3 kilometers (1.9 miles) from the boat dock. EP Rates: room with breakfast and dinner 7.500 CFP per person; room with all meals 8.000 CFP per person. Round-trip transfers 1.000 CFP. Add 6% value added tax to room rates and meal plans. A 10% value added tax is applicable to other services. No credit cards.*

This modern, clean and attractive 2-story concrete house is the pension of choice in Tubuai, with 2 rooms to rent on the ground floor and 3 rooms upstairs. Each room has nice furniture, with a double bed and a single bed, a private bathroom and hot water shower. House linens are furnished but there is no place to hang your clothes. Two of the rooms have air-conditioners and the others have ceiling fans. The communal dining room and living room with television are on the ground floor and there is also a tiled lounge upstairs, well furnished with big wicker sofas and chairs. This big room also has a microwave oven, double sink and a glass top table for 8 people, where you can have tea, coffee or a snack in between meals. A big open terrace overlooks the lagoon across the road.

A little knowledge of French would be helpful here as very little English is spoken. Sam Tahuhuterani died in December 2003 and his widow, Yolande, lives alone in a big house behind the pension, which is normally very quiet. She takes care of the students' meals in the school in Mataura village and she is also active in the Mormon Church. During her absence her pension guests are looked after by her employees. The maid will wash your clothes for 500 CFP per machine load. You can rent a bicycle for 1.500 CFP per day; a circle island tour by car is 1.500 CFP per person. and Yolande can arrange boat excursions on request. This pension has an excellent reputation for its cuisine, which is sumptuous. Yolande joins the table for meals and to talk with her guests. There's no smoking at the table in this pension.

PENSION VAITEA NUI, *B.P. 141, Mataura, Tubuai, 98754. Tel. 689/ 93.22.40; Fax 689/93.22.42; E-mail: bodin.m@mail.pf; www.vaiteanui.com.*

Beside the cross-island transversal road in Mataura, 5 kilometers (3 miles) from the airport and a 10-minute walk inland from the circle island road in the heart of Mataura village. EP Rates: room 3.150 CFP single, 5.250 CFP double; 6.850 CFP triple; special rates for children. MAP breakfast and dinner 3.200 CFP per person; AP breakfast, lunch and dinner 5.000 CFP per person. Half-price meals for child under 12 years. Round-trip transfers included. Add 6% value added tax to room rates and meal plans. A 10% value added tax is applicable to other services. No credit cards.

This is a 5-room one-story motel-like concrete structure in a big yard behind the family house. The rooms are clean and simply furnished with a double bed with a foam rubber mattress, a bedside table and lamp, a wardrobe and private bathroom with hot water, plus a couple of wooden folding chairs on the long front terrace. The louvered windows are screened and house linens are furnished. A drawback for the location of the rooms is that they are built too close to the family house and restaurant, and you can hear all the sounds from the kitchen, as well as the conversations of friends and family who sit outside the kitchen. That's not a problem if you are out of your room during the day. But the walls between the bedrooms are very thin and you can hear the noises from the adjacent rooms, including all-night snoring. Meals are served in the big family style dining room, shared with the lively and active Bodin family of six adults, two children (at this writing) and various and sundry relatives and friends, most of whom speak English, and who smoke lots of cigarettes at the table.

Melinda Bodin, the mother, takes charge of promotion for the family pension. Vaiana and her sister Heinui run the pension, and Vaiana's husband, Alphonse Tiaipoi, handles the excursions. Vaiana, Alphonse and Heinui have all worked in tourism in Tahiti for several years. This pension is conveniently located near the post office, food stores, banks, hospital, pharmacy, churches and town hall. Guests have free use of the bicycles and can rent a car for 5.000 CFP a day. For activities see *Sports & Recreation* in this chapter. Melinda is president of the Tubuai Visitors Bureau and will happily tell you all about the 1789 visit of the *Bounty* and its crew of mutineers. She organizes a re-enactment program of this event every two years during the month of May. The next celebration will be in May 2006.

Where to Eat

TE MOTU, *Tel. 95.05.27*, in Taahuaia village. Must reserve. No credit cards. Serves lunch and dinner, featuring French and local cuisine. Take away pizzas 700 to 1.000 CFP. Closed on Sunday.

CHEZ SAM & YOLANDE, *Tel. 95.05.52*, in Mataura village. Please reserve. No credit cards. French, Chinese and local cuisine. Beer and wine available. This pension has a very good reputation for the quality of its cuisine, which is served family style.

VAITEA NUI, *Tel. 93.22.40*, in Mataura village. Please reserve. No credit cards. Serves family style meals, which may be raw or cooked fish, chicken or sausages served with rice, baked breadfruit and spaghetti with ketchup. A breakfast of instant coffee, baguette, butter and jam is 800 CFP, lunch is 1.900 CFP, dinner is 2.000 CFP per person, which is cheaper than the MAP and AP rates charged for meals. Beer and wine available.

Snack Vahine Arii is across the road from the boat dock at Mataura port. There are a few other snack stands in Mataura and Taahuaia that open and close according to what's happening on the island. **Libre Service Tien Hing** is the biggest magasin on the island, and each morning they sell casse-croûte baguettes and prepared dishes such as chow mein and *ma'a tinito* (Chinese food).

Seeing the Sights

A car tour around the island costs 1.500 CFP at Chez Sam & Yolande and 1.800 CFP at Pension Vaitea Nui, the latter including an English-speaking guide. A tour by 4WD is also available at Pension Vaitea Nui for 4.500 CFP, which takes you off the road and up the mountain tracks. **Mount Taitaa** is an attraction for hikers, who will enjoy the view from the summit, which is 422 meters (1,384 feet) high. Your pension host will drop you off beside the track and it's an easy round-trip hike of 3 hours to get to the top. Other hiking trails are also interesting and easily reached.

Sports & Recreation

Boat Rentals, Lagoon Excursions, Fishing and Picnics on the Motu

Alphonse Tiaipoi at Pension Vaitea Nui in Mataura, *Tel. 93.22.40*, will take you by boat to visit the motu islets for 6.000 CFP or drop you off at a motu and come back for you later, for 3.500 CFP. A picnic on the motu is 6.000 CFP and a picnic on one of the main island's beaches is 2.500 CFP. A boat tour around the island is 8.000 CFP per person, and a boat ride to watch the humpback whales (between August and October) is 7.000 CFP per person. You can rent a boat for 12.000 CFP for a half-day or 20.000 CFP for a full day of fishing inside the lagoon or outside the reef. Alphonse will also take you camping on a motu for 7.000 CFP per person.

Scuba Diving

La Bonne Bouteille, *Tel/Fax 95.08.41, cell 74.90.97; E-mail: labonnebouteille@mail.pf; www.polynesia-diving.com.* "The Good Bottle" is operated by Laurent Juan de Mendoza, originally from Nice, who is a BEES 1 sports educator instructor and has been a Sea Guide since 1994. His boat is specially equipped for scuba divers and he has all the necessary diving equipment available in his center located near the marina. He teaches scuba diving and also has free-dive outings, as well as diving with the humpback whales between July and late October.

Te Moana Sub, *Tel. 77.15.94 or 93.22.40*, is also operated by Alphonse Tiaipoi, who is a qualified English-speaking scuba diving instructor. He will take you on a discovery dive inside the lagoon of Tubuai for 5.000 CFP. You can also have a baptism dive for 3.500 CFP if you are inexperienced or haven't been diving in a while.

Shopping

Tubuai no longer has any organized arts and crafts groups or centers, although some of the women still make woven hats, mats, bags, clothing, *pareos* and *tifaifai* bed covers. Ask your hostess at the pension where you are staying and she will direct you to the best place to buy locally made products.

Practical Information

Banks

Banque Socredo, *Tel. 95.04.86/95.06.88*, has an agency in Mataura village behind the Protestant church. **Banque de Tahiti**, *Tel. 95.03.63*, in Mataura village, serves all the Austral Islands.

Doctors

There is a hospital in Mataura, which serves all the Austral Islanders, *Tel. 93.22.50*.

Police

French *gendarmerie*, *Tel. 93.22.05*.

Post Office

There is a Post Office and Telecommunications Center in Mataura, *Tel. 95.03.50*.

Tourist Bureau

The **Tubuai Visitors Bureau**, *Tel. 93.22.40*, is in Mataura, presided by Melinda Bodin, who speaks English.

RIMATARA

When the *Tuhaa Pae II* anchors offshore **Rimatara** every few weeks to bring supplies, the passengers come ashore by whaleboat, surfing over the reef in turbulent waves that beat against the island's limestone cliffs. Upon landing on the beautiful white sand beach of Amaru the visitors are required to follow an old custom of the island and walk through a cloud of smoke to purify them before being welcomed ashore.

The *Vaeanu II* was wrecked on the reef in Rimatara in April 2002 and the ship is still sitting there.

Far removed from the beaten path of tourists and even cruising yachts, Rimatara has no sheltered boat harbor or dock, and no hotel. For some of the island's 811 inhabitants (2002 census), who live in blissful isolation from the world's problems and turmoil, Rimatara is a joyful and tranquil refuge. Several of the young people, however, are slowly leaving their island for Tahiti, where they can find jobs and a livelier lifestyle. An airport is currently under construction, which will bring a new rhythm to the island's easy-going pace when Air Tahiti starts a regular service between Tahiti and Rimatara. This work advances slowly, however, because there is no ship available that is capable of transporting the necessary equipment for the work. In 2003 the administrative ship *Tahiti Nui IV* (ex-*Meherio II*) sank on its way to Rimatara while carrying equipment to build the new airstrip. Seven people died during this accident, including the captain.

Located 538 kilometers (334 miles) southwest of Tahiti and 150 kilometers (93 miles) west-south-west of Rurutu, the circular island of Rimatara is the smallest and lowest of the inhabited Austral Islands. The land surface is only 8 square kilometers (3 square miles) and Mount Vahu is the highest peak at 83 meters (274 feet). A narrow fringing reef hugs the uneven shore of the island and there is no lagoon.

Amaru is the principal village, with the town hall, *gendarmerie*, post office and infirmary, plus a school and a couple of stores. **Anapoto** and **Mutuaura** villages are reached by dirt roads. There is a severe water shortage during dry seasons. At publication time there were no pensions, guesthouses, bed and breakfasts, restaurants and bars or rental bicycles and cars on Rimatara. However, if you really want to stay here and can communicate in French or Tahitian, the Polynesian people will always find a place for you to sleep. Just bring your own supplies.

Arrivals & Departures

Tuhaa Pae II, *Tel. 50.96.09, Fax 42.06.09; E-mail: snathp@mail.pf* makes 3 voyages a month from Tahiti to the Austral Islands, calling at Tubuai, Rimatara, Raivavae and Rurutu, then returning to Papeete. This itinerary may change according to the freight requirements of each voyage. The one-way fare to Rimatara is 4.046 CFP on the deck, 5.664 CFP in a berth on deck, and 7.789 CFP for a berth in a cabin. Meals are 3.080 CFP per day in the cafeteria and 5.060 CFP per day in the officers' dining room. Rates include taxes. See further information in Chapter 6, *Planning Your Trip*.

RAIVAVAE

Raivavae is one of the most exquisite islands in the South Pacific, rivaling even Bora Bora with its natural beauty. Fern covered Mount Hiro reaches 437 meters (1,442 feet) into the mist of clouds. Sea birds soar around some two dozen picturesque islets that seem to float on the emerald lagoon protected by a distant coral reef. Beaches of soft white powdery sand surround these motus, forming graceful swirling patterns of lagoons within lagoons. Raivavae remained aloof from the world of tourism until November 2002, when the small airport opened, providing Air Tahiti connections to Papeete two to three times a week, depending on the season. Although the new airport represents a giant step forward into modern times, tranquility still reigns on Raivavae, even in the four pretty villages of **Rairua**, **Mahanatoa**, **Anatonu** and **Vaiuru**. These neat and clean villages, with their pastel colored limestone houses, are home to the island's 995 inhabitants. The women of Raivavae compete with one another to see who can make the most original hat to wear to the Evangelical church services. Some of the decorations consist of plastic fruit, golf balls and even blinking lights.

Located 632 kilometers (392 miles) southeast of Tahiti, this island of 16 square kilometers (6 square miles) can also be reached by cargo/passenger boat service from Tahiti.

Raivavae has long held the attention of anthropologists, archaeologists and biologists, who come here to study the people and their customs, the remains of stone temples and tiki statures or to make an inventory of the birds, snails and aquatic insects. These included J. Frank Stimson in 1917, Thor Heyerdahl in 1956 and Donald Marshall in 1957. John Stokes of the Bishop Museum in Hawaii led an archaeological mission to Raivavae in 1921 to record the oral traditions and inventory the archaeological sites. The people agreed to loan five of their tikis to the Bishop Museum, which have never been returned. Thor Heyerdahl's expedition resulted in the loss of seven more tikis that were carried away without permission of the local authorities and are now in the Museum of Oslo. Two of the tikis from Raivavae were brought to Tahiti in 1933 and are now standing on the grounds of the Paul Gauguin Museum in Tahiti. Edmundo Edwards made an inventory of the sites in 1986 and 1991 on behalf of the Culture and Patrimony Service at the Museum of Tahiti and Her Islands and his findings are reported in his book published in September 2003: *Ra'ivavae: Archaeological Survey of Ra'ivavae, French Polynesia*. More than 600 archaeological structures have been found on Raivavae, including 80 marae still remaining. A short walk inland from the coastal road, just to the west of Mahanatoa village you can see Raivavae's only remaining tiki, which is 2 meters high. There are 20 tikis on Pomoavao marae, which is on the Matahariua land facing the airport, but these are incomplete fragments like the only tiki that was not voluntarily destroyed, stolen or sold.

Raivavae's climate and fertile soil are ideal for growing crops of taro, potatoes, carrots, cabbages, coffee and citrus fruits. Sandalwood trees are also numerous on this island. There is a plentiful variety of seafood in the lagoon, including lobster, sea snails and tridacna clams. Due to a high level of ciguatera that affects fish caught from certain parts of the lagoon, most of the pensions serve only deep-sea fish at their tables.

Arrivals & Departures

Arriving By Air

Air Tahiti flies has a 1 hour 45 minute direct flight from Tahiti to Raivavae each Wednesday and on Saturday during the high seasons. There is also a flight each Monday that stops in Tubuai. The one-way airfare from Tahiti to Raivavae is 23.300 CFP and the fare from Tubuai to Raivavae is 9.300 CFP. There is no flight between Raivavae and Rurutu. **Air Tahiti reservations**: *Tahiti Tel. 86.42.42/86.41.84; Raivavae Tel. 95.44.33.*

You can also get to Rurutu by chartering an airplane in Tahiti from **Wan Air**, *Tel. 50.44.17, cell 77.03.79*; **Air Archipels**, *Tel. 81.30.30*; or **Air Tahiti**, *Tel. 86.42.42*.

Arriving By Boat

Tuhaa Pae II, *Tel. 50.96.09, Fax 42.06.09; E-mail: snathp@mail.pf* makes 3 voyages a month from Tahiti to the Austral Islands, calling at Tubuai, Rimatara, Raivavae and Rurutu, then returning to Papeete. This itinerary may change according to the freight requirements of each voyage. The one-way fare to Raivavae is 5.832 CFP on the deck, 8.164 CFP in a berth on deck, and 11.226 CFP for a berth in a cabin. Meals are 3.080 CFP per day in the cafeteria and 5.060 CFP per day in the officers' dining room. Rates include taxes. See further information in Chapter 6, *Planning Your Trip*.

Departing By Air

You can fly from Raivavae direct to Tahiti on Monday, and the Wednesday flight stops in Tubuai enroute to Tahiti. There is also a Saturday flight via Tubuai during high seasons. **Air Tahiti reservations** in Raivavae, *Tel. 95.44.33.*

Departing By Boat

The **Tuhaa Pae II** calls at Raivavae on its way back to Papeete or enroute to the other Austral Islands, according to the needs of the islanders. You can purchase your ticket on board the ship.

Orientation

The island of Raivavae is 9 kilometers (5.6 miles) long and 2 kilometers (1.2 miles) wide. On the western shore of the island is Rairua village, where there is a new port for cargo vessels, a new *mairie* (town hall), small infirmary, post office, *gendarmerie*, primary school and a couple of old Chinese stores with a poor selection of supplies. A partially constructed Protestant church was built too close to the edge of the lagoon, and work has stopped until a landfill is approved by the government. The houses in this village have no running water because the communal pipes have rusted out. They catch rainwater into cisterns or drill wells for their water supply. A road, either concrete or dirt, connects the villages and a cross-island road provides a shortcut route over a mountain saddle from Rairua on the western side to Vaiuru on the southern coast. The airport is 6 kilometers (3.7 miles) from the ship dock, built on a landfill between Rairua and Vaiuru.

Most of the houses are built on the mountain side of the coastal road and hedges of white spider lilies border the beach side to serve as a windbreak. Tall Australian pine trees also help to protect homes from the strong austral winds and big ocean swells that arrive during the winter months of July and August. Picturesque Protestant churches adorn each village, where the faithful parishioners gather several times a week to sing and pray.

Getting Around Raivavae

You will be met at the airport or boat dock by someone from the pension where you've reserved accommodations. There is no public transportation system on Raivavae and no taxi service outside the pensions. Check with your host for car and bicycle rentals or read information on *Where to Stay* in this chapter.

Seeing the Sights

No matter where you stay in Raivavae your hosts can arrange for a circle island tour by 4WD and they can usually find someone with a boat who will take you to visit the fabulous motu islets on the southern and eastern parts of the reef. Do not miss going to Motu Vaiamanu, which the islanders call motu piscine. This is the most beautiful motu I have ever seen in all my island hopping days in the South Seas. You arrive by boat from the main island and step onto a perfect white sand beach of white powdery sand. Then you walk a few feet through the shady grove of ironwood trees (Australian pines) to the other side of the motu, and a breathtaking vision opens up before you that will make you very happy you brought your camera equipment along. This lagoon within a lagoon is better than Blue Lagoon in Rangiroa. Miles of soft white sand beach mingle with the shallow water of the tides, which reflect the patterns of white clouds. You can walk across this swimming pool to another motu that is closer to the reef or you can follow the curve of the beach to the spot where the tridacna clams are still found in abundant plenty in knee-deep water. You can picnic here or continue on to explore some of the other motus, and you can also camp out on many of these uninhabited islets.

Archaeological sites on the main island include the one remaining big stone tiki, in a clearing just west of Mahanatoa village, Marae Maunauto on the south coast, where there is the grave of a princess, and Marae Pomoavao, facing the airport. You'll need a guide to take you to Marae Poupou at Vai Otorani stream in the valley, a short walk inland from the transversal road.

Many of the big slabs of volcanic stone are still standing around this immense structure. A private museum is operated by the Vavitu Association in the courtyard of the Vivi family home. This little bamboo structure has an exhibit of artifacts found around the island, including a rock that was supposedly used by a warrior from Mahanatoa to kill his enemy from Anatonu during a battle. There are also stones carved with petroglyphs and a stone tiki of a pregnant woman, as well as woven hats, purses, floor mats, hand embroidered fabrics, various seashell jewelry and a few sculptures. Entry is 500 CFP.

Where to Stay & Eat

RAIVAVAE TAMA RESORT, *B.P. 17, Vaiuru, Raivavae 98750. Tel./Fax 689/95.42.52. Beside the sea in Anatonu village, 6 kilometers (3.7 miles) from the airport and 8 kilometers (5 miles) from the boat dock. AP Rates: bungalow or room with all meals 10.000 CFP per person, including taxes, transfers and activities. No credit cards.*

Emmy Teupoo White and her American husband, Dennis, have built 1 wooden bungalow overlooking the beach in Anatonu village, across the road from their house, where they also have two bedrooms and a bathroom with hot water shower that can be used by guests. The bungalow is furnished with a comfortable double bed, closet, bamboo chair and coffee table, ceiling fan and a bathroom that will soon have hot water for the shower. There is also a sundeck where you can sit and watch the lagoon, or you can walk a few steps past a row of *aito* trees (Australian pines) and you are on a white sand beach. This is the only place on the island where you can stay beside the beach, and you are lulled to sleep at night by the gentle murmur of the waves.

Emmy's delicious and generous meals are served family style in their dining room in the main house. She worked in the San Bernardino, California school system for 15 years, in nutrition, cafeteria and catering, before returning home to Raivavae in 2001. She was also president of the Friends of Tahiti association in California.

Fare Toa Angelique, a magasin store that is run by their daughter and son-in-law, is across the road from the bungalow, and besides being well stocked with supplies, provides fax service. A phone booth is on the corner and the Protestant church is just next door.

When I visited Raivavae in July 2004, the Whites were ready to build 4 FEI government model bungalows on their property 200 meters high (656 feet) on the hillside in Vaiuru, 2.3 kilometers (1.4 miles) from the airport, which should all be finished in early 2005. These bungalows will have a double bed and a single bed, private bathroom with hot water shower, ceiling fan and a covered terrace where you can sit and look at the beautiful lagoon and motu islets. There will also be a communal dining room. Emmy and Dennis will take you in one of their big 4WD's to visit the island and Emmy's brother has a boat, so you'll be able to visit the exquisitely lovely Motu Vaiamanu and help collect fresh *pahua* (tridacna clams) from the knee deep water just inside the reef. The residents of Raivavae call this shallow lagoon a piscine, as it resembles a vast swimming pool. They will also take you camping on Motu Ruahoa, where they will make a fire on the beach at night and you can sing under the stars. On request, Emmy will also drop you off at a motu all by yourself and bring you food every couple of days. Otherwise, you will have all the privacy you wish.

PENSION LINDA ET NELSON, *Rairua, Raivavae 98750. Tel. 689/88.30.81; Tel./Fax 689/95.44.25; E-mail: pensionlindanelson@yahoo.fr. Across the road from the lagoon in Rairua village, close to the airport. MAP Rates: room with breakfast and dinner 6.700 CFP single, 12.200 CFP double; AP room with breakfast, lunch and dinner 9.100 CFP single, 17.000 CFP double. Round-trip transfers and taxes included. No credit cards.*

Four rooms are rented to guests in a big white concrete house in Rairua village, with a choice of 2 twin beds, a double bed or a double and single bed. There is a bathroom for guests inside the house and you can also share the outside bathroom with Linda and Nelson, a young couple with a baby. There is also a living room with television, video and DVD machine. Meals are served family style in the open sided dining room, which is covered by an immense roof and overlooks the beach across the road. Unfortunately, the lagoon is not nice in this area and the water is muddy because of the disturbances caused while the airstrip was under construction.

Nelson and Linda have 2 kayaks that can be used by guests at no charge, and they also have a windsurf you can use if you are experienced in this sport. Nelson will drop you off on the motu without a picnic lunch for 1.000 CFP per person, and he charges 2.400 CFP per person for a boat excursion to the motu, including a picnic of fish, taro, breadfruit, banana and *pahua* (reef clams). He will take you on a boat tour around the island for 1.500 CFP and around the island by 4WD for no charge. You can also rent a bicycle here for 500 CFP a day, rent a scooter for 2.500 CFP per day or rent a car for 6.000 CFP per day. A guided hiking excursion is 1.500 CFP per person.

They plan to build two bungalows on their property by the end of 2004 and will keep 2 of the rooms in the house for their family. The bungalows will have a double bed and single bed, a ceiling fan and a private bathroom with hot water shower. Nelson's mother, Jeanine Tavaearii, owns Fare Pa'eao in Maupiti, and he grew up in the family pension business and speaks a little English.

PENSION ATAHA, *B.P. 37, Rairua, Raivavae 98750. Tel./Fax 689/ 95.43.69. Across road from lagoon in Rairua village, 2.5 kilometers (1.6 miles) from the airport. MAP Rates: room with breakfast and dinner 6.500 CFP per person; AP room with breakfast, lunch and dinner 8.500 CFP per person. Cabin on Motu Rani 1.500 CFP per person. Round-trip airport or boat dock transfers included. Add 6% value added tax to room rates and meal plans. A 10% value added tax is applicable to other services. No credit cards.*

Terani Tamaititahio runs the pension and keeps the baby while his wife, Odile, teaches school. Terani says that he doesn't speak any English at all, but he is an enthusiastic and friendly young man who is also constructing what he calls Ataha 2, a new house containing 3 rooms, living room, dining room, shared bathroom and terrace. Ataha 1, which he now rents to guests, is a one-story concrete house beside the road, with 2 bedrooms containing a double bed and fan, a shared bathroom with a very small bathtub and hot water, small living/dining area and an open terrace facing the lagoon.

Terani prepares the meals for the guests, serving local style food and deep-sea fish such as tuna and mahi mahi. Guests can do their laundry in his washing machine for 1.000 CFP per load. He has 5 bicycles that he rents for 500 CFP for a half-day, and he charges 1.000 CFP per person for a cross-island tour by car. He has kayaks for guests located at Ataha 1 and also on Motu Rani, where Ataha 3 is located. This is a small cabin with no kitchen and no electricity. There is no charge to take you there by boat and you can buy a *casse croûte* sandwich for 250 CFP and a bottle of water for 150 CFP and spend the day by yourself on the motu. Or you can have a prepared picnic for 2.000 CFP.

PENSION RAU'URU, *Rairua, Raivavae 98750. Tel./Fax 689/95.42.88. Across road from the lagoon in Rairua village, 1.5 kilometers (.9 miles) from the airport. Tel./Fax 689/95.42.88. Rates: studio with breakfast and dinner 6.000 CFP per person; studio with all meals 8.000 CFP per person per day; room in the house with breakfast and dinner 5.500 CFP per person; room with all meals 7.500 CFP per person per day. Round-trip transfers included. Add 6% value added tax to room rates and meal plans. A 10% value added tax is applicable to other services. No credit cards.*

Edmond and Maitu Flores have a big white house on the mountainside of the road in Rairua village, in view of the airport runway. Each of the two guest rooms in the house has a double bed, single bed, cupboard closet, and a private bathroom with hot water shower. There is also a studio with a bedroom, living room, kitchen, private bathroom with hot water and a balcony. Maitu is a schoolteacher and doesn't have much time for her guests and there is a lot of coral in the lagoon across the road.

PENSION MOANA, *Mahanatoa, Raivavae 98750. Tel. 689/95.42.66. Across private road from white sand beach, 8 kilometers (5 miles) from airport and 3 kilometers (1.9 miles) from Rairua dock. EP Rates: room 2.500 CFP single, 4.000 CFP double, 1.000 CFP for extra bed; room with breakfast and dinner 5.000 CFP single; 6.500 CFP double; room with all meals 7.000 CFP single, 8.500 CFP double. Round-trip airport or boat dock transfers included. Add 6% value added tax to room rates and meal plans. A 10% value added tax is applicable to other services. No credit cards.*

This is a light green concrete house with red and white trim that is located on a point of land bordered by Australia pine trees and small strips of white sand beach. Madame Haamoeura Teehu is a very pretty 60-something woman who rents out her house with 3 bedrooms, a living room, dining room, kitchen, covered terrace and communal bathroom with hot water. House linens are furnished as well as a washing machine, and there is a television, video, stove, microwave oven, refrigerator and other kitchen equipment and dishes, so that you can prepare your own meals if you prefer. Madame Teehu will cook for you on request, as she stays in another nearby house whenever guests occupy her rental house. You can easily walk to the magasin stores in Mahanatoa village for your supplies or to the Protestant church to listen to the *himene* singing. Although she doesn't speak any English, your hostess can arrange for your excursions to discover Raivavae. This pension is not recommended for young single women traveling alone, as there is a problem with one or more young men in the neighborhood who try to crawl through the window at night.

Other Guest Lodgings
Chez Vaiete, *Tel. 689/95.42.85*, who has 4 rooms with meals in Mahanatoa; and **Pension Taina**, who has a 2-story house with 5 rooms to rent without meals, plus a magasin where you can buy food products.

Shopping
There are at least eight arts and crafts associations in the villages around the island of Raivavae. Their handcrafts centers are located in Mahanatoa, Vaiuru, Rairua and Anatonu, but they are not open except for special occasions. Contact Madame Heiarii Mahaa in Mahanatoa, *Tel. 95.42.42*, who represents the Federation of Artisans in Raivavae.

RAPA
Remote **Rapa** stands proudly alone 1,074 kilometers (666 miles) southeast of Tahiti, below the tropical zone, where the temperature can drop to 5 degrees Celsius (41 degrees Fahrenheit) during the austral winter in July and August. Rapa-Iti, as the island is also called, has a strong cultural connection to Rapa-Nui, the Polynesian name for Easter Island. Archaeological ruins include strong *pa* fortresses built among volcanic pinnacles. **Mount Perehau**, the tallest of six peaks, reaches 650 meters (2,145 feet) above the island, whose fjord-like coastline has 12 deeply indented bays. Several sugar loaf-shaped islets lie just offshore and there is no fringing reef in these cold waters. White puffs of sheep and wild goats perch on precipitous cliffs over the sea and bay, and herds of cattle roam the velvety green mountain ranges.

Rapa's 497 inhabitants live in **Haurei Village** and in the smaller village of Area, which is reached only by boat one kilometer distant across Haurei Bay. There is a town hall, post office, infirmary, weather station and school. A cooperative store provides the villagers with basic supplies and many of the homes have television and telephone service. There is no airport in Rapa, and the *Tuhaa Pae II* supply ship docks in Haurei Bay every 6-8 weeks, the island's only regular connection to the outside world. This ship usually stays only a few hours at the dock before returning to Tahiti.

Arrivals & Departures

Tuhaa Pae II, *Tel. 50.96.09, Fax 42.06.09; E-mail: snathp@mail.pf* calls at Rapa once every two months during its visits to the Austral Islands. This itinerary may change according to the freight requirements of each voyage. The one-way fare from Tahiti to Rapa starts at 7.974 CFP on the deck, and escalates up to 15.330 CFP for a berth in a cabin. A round-trip voyage from Tahiti to Rapa and return is 23.361 CFP for one person, plus meals. Meals are 3.080 CFP per day in the cafeteria and 5.060 CFP per day in the officers' dining room. Rates include taxes. See further information in Chapter 6, *Planning Your Trip*.

Where to Stay & Eat

CHEZ TITAUA, *Ahurei, Rapa 98751. Tel. 689/95.72.59; Fax 689/95.72.60. Beside lagoon in Ahurei village. EP Rates: 4.000 CFP single/double per day; 60.000 CFP per month. Add 6% value added tax to room rates. A 10% value added tax is applicable to other services. No credit cards.*

This is a one-bedroom house with a living room, dining room, kitchen, terrace and private bathroom with hot water. House linens are furnished.

Chapter 23

THE GAMBIER ISLANDS

MANGAREVA

If you have a quest for remote islands in temperate climes, **Mangareva** may qualify as your Garden of Eden. This island, which is 1,650 kilometers (1,023 miles) southeast of Tahiti, is the largest of the **Gambier Archipelago**, just above the Tropic of Capricorn. The climate in these southern latitudes is very pleasant, with cooler temperatures than in Tahiti.

Mangareva and the other high islands of Aukena, Akamaru and Taravai are partially enclosed by a barrier reef that stretches for 80 kilometers (50 miles). Also sharing this protected lagoon are six smaller islands and 25 *motu* islets surrounded by white coral sand beaches. Three passes lead into the sun-gilded waters of the turquoise lagoon, which are a haven for the *Pinctada Margaritifera*, the black-lipped oyster that produces some of the world's finest black pearls in the farms of Mangareva and its neighboring islands.

In addition to raising cows and pigs, coffee, oranges and watermelons, many of the 1,097 inhabitants of the Gambier Islands are employed in the black pearl business.

History

Polynesian oral tradition claims that expeditions of Polynesians from the eastern and western Pacific used to stop at Mangareva, and that it was settled by people from the Marquesas Islands during three migratory waves. Archaeologists have found similarities between the Marquesas Islands stone temples and the *marae* found on the islet of Temoe, 50 kilometers (31 miles) southeast of Mangareva, outside the protective coral reef. Carbon-14 dating confirms human occupations on Mangareva around the year 1200.

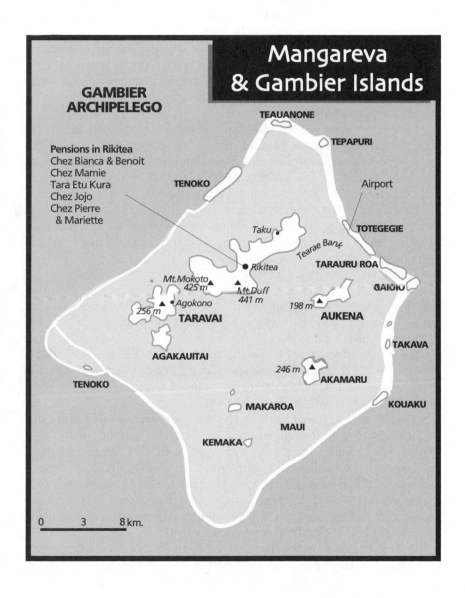

Mangareva & Gambier Islands

GAMBIER ARCHIPELEGO

TEAUANONE

TEPAPURI

Pensions in Rikitea
Chez Bianca & Benoit
Chez Mamie
Tara Etu Kura
Chez Jojo
Chez Pierre
 & Mariette

TENOKO

Airport

Taku

Tearae Bank

TOTEGEGIE

Rikitea

TARAURU ROA

Mt.Mokoto
425 m

Mt.Duff
441 m

GAIOIO

256 m

Agokono

198 m

TARAVAI

AUKENA

TAKAVA

AGAKAUITAI

246 m

AKAMARU

TENOKO

MAKAROA

KOUAKU

MAUI

KEMAKA

0   3   8 km.

English Captain Wilson of the London Missionary Society's (LMS) chartered ship, *H.M.S. Duff*, sailed past Mangareva in May, 1797, and named it after **Captain Gambier**, a descendant of the French Huguenots who had supported the LMS expedition. F. W. Beechey, another Englishman, landed on the island in 1826, and the island became a popular port-of-call for ships who traded for the mother-of-pearl shell from the lagoon.

Mangareva's history is strongly connected with Catholic missionaries from the Sacred Heart of Picpus, who arrived in the Gambler Islands in 1834. Under the staff of Father Honoré Laval, these docile, gentle people were converted to Catholicism and taught to spin, weave, print, construct boats, and above all, to build churches.

Laval organized a native police force, commanded the girls to become nuns and the men to become monks, and forced the islanders to work night and day to construct a neo-gothic city of coral and stone. Great blocks of coral were used to build a cathedral large enough for 2,000 people and a church replaced every *marae* altar that existed on the island.

Also constructed were chapels, a convent, a monastery, a school, triumphal arches of great size, and a large number of palatial and unhealthy stone houses for King Maputeoa and the aristocrats of the island. Laval also had a number of houses built for his own use.

The people began to die under the enforced labor, and in 1864, the new Governor of Tahiti, Comte Emile de la Roncière, visited Mangareva to investigate the stories he had heard of Laval's behavior, which included trafficking in pearls and shell. When the governor ordered the prisons opened, he found two boys in a dungeon. Their offense had been to laugh during Mass.

Laval's rule ended in 1871 when he departed for Tahiti, where he died in 1880. Some 116 coral and stone buildings of the neo-gothic design still stand today. These include the 2,000-seat St. Michel Cathedral, another silent witness to Father Laval's driving need to build.

It was thanks to Father Laval and his assistant François Caret that Tahiti was brought to the attention of the French government. Soon after they arrived in the Gambier Islands the two priests went to Tahiti to establish a Catholic mission in the staunch English Protestant territory. They were literally removed from the island, which began a mighty dispute between the English Protestants and French Catholics, and resulted in France establishing a protectorate over the islands in 1842. The Gambier Islands remained relatively independent until their official annexation in 1881.

In 1982 the Frères of the Sacred Heart of Québec opened a **Center for Education and Development** in Mangareva, to train the youths in mechanics and carpentry. A visit to the sculptors' workshop in the village is one of the activities provided for visitors.

The inhabitants of the Gambier Islands have their own language, which is called *reo mangareva*. They also have food specialties, such as *popoi* (taro poi), *kokori ota* (raw nacre), *ika ogi* (smoked fish) and *puaka tao* (pig cooked in the underground oven). Their *pei* style of repetitive dancing is very different from what you'll see in Tahiti and the other Society Islands. The artisans of Mangareva are very creative in making their handcrafts, and their mother-of-pearl necklaces and other shell jewelry sell quickly when they have exhibits in Tahiti.

Lodging is available in the main village of **Rikitea**, where comfortable and clean cottages or modern style houses welcome the traveler, with a choice of European or local-style cuisine.

Arrivals & Departures
Arriving By Air
Air Tahiti flies from Tahiti to the Gambier Islands each Tuesday, using ATR turbo jets for the 3 hour and 40 minute flights. The flight leaves Tahiti at 5:50am and arrives in Mangareva at 10:30am local time, which is an hour ahead of Tahiti time. An additional flight is added each Friday during the high seasons. The cost of a one-way fare from Tahiti is 30.400 CFP, and round-trip is 55.500 CFP. **Air Tahiti reservations**: in Tahiti, *Tel. 86.42.42/86.41.84*. The airport of Totegegie is built on one of the flat *motu* islets across the lagoon from Rikitea, the principal village of Mangareva. A communal boat transfers passengers between the airport and Rikitea village, a 15-minute ride across the lagoon that costs 500 CFP per person each way, or someone from your pension will come to meet you at the airport.

You can also get to Mangareva by chartering an airplane in Tahiti from **Wan Air**, *Tel. 50.44.17, cell 77.03.79*. Robert Wan owns several pearl islands and pearl farms in the Gambier-Tuamotu archipelago and his planes make frequent trips to Mangareva. **Air Archipels**, *Tel. 81.30.30*; or **Air Tahiti**, *Tel. 86.42.42* also has charter flights available.

Arriving By Boat
Nuku Hau, *Tel. 54.99.54; Fax 45.24.44*. This is a 210-foot cargo ship that can take 12 passengers from Tahiti to the eastern Tuamotu and Gambier Islands during the 20-day round-trip voyages it makes once every 25 days. There is no cabin space but you will be served three meals a day on board. The one-way fare is 7.950 CFP for deck space, plus 1.950 CFP per day for breakfast, lunch and dinner. The ship docks at the wharf near Rikitea village after 10 days at sea and visiting various atolls in the Tuamotu Archipelago. If you have reservations in a pension your hosts will meet you at the pier.

Taporo VIII, *Tel. 42.63.93; Fax 42.06.17*. This 213-foot steel ship carries freight and passengers to the eastern atolls of the Tuamotu Archipelago and to Rikitea village on the island of Mangareva. The ship leaves Papeete once a month for the 23-day round trip voyage, and can carry 12 passengers on deck. There are no cabins. The one-way fare to Rikitea in the Gambier Islands is

33.534 CFP, including meals served on board. For further information see the chapter on *Planning Your Trip*.

Departing By Air

Air Tahiti's weekly departure from Mangareva is at 11am each Tuesday morning. The plane stops at Hao in the Tuamotus and arrives in Papeete at 2:50pm Tahiti time. The high season Friday flight leaves Mangareva at 10:50am and flies direct to Tahiti, arriving at 1:50pm. Be sure to set your watch back an hour. **Air Tahiti reservations** in Rikitea, *Tel. 97.82.65.*

Departing By Boat

Nuku Hau calls at Tematangi, Anuanuraro, Nukutepipi and Hereheretue on the return trip to Tahiti, and may stop on request at other atolls.

Taporo VIII stops at Marutea Sud, Tureia, Reao, Tatakoto, Vahitahi, Nukutavake, Pinaki, Vairaatea, Hao and Hereheretue on the way back to Papeete. The itinerary is subject to change according to the cargo destinations.

Orientation

Mangareva is 8 kilometers (5 miles) long and 1.5 kilometers (.9 miles) wide. A road encircles the island for 28 kilometers (17.3 miles), offering picturesque views of the luminescent bays and inlets and other islands. **Mount Duff**, at 441 meters (1,455 ft.) high, is the highest point on Mangareva. The hillsides of the island turn yellowish-brown during the dry seasons. **Rikitea**, the main village, is a quiet little oasis of verdure and a new road is being built to create a pedestrian zone on the waterfront.

Where to Stay & Eat

CHEZ BIANCA & BENOIT, *B.P. 19, Rikitea, Mangareva, 98755. Tel. 689/ 97.83.76/88.08.81; Fax 689/97.83.76; E-mail: biancabenoit@mail.pf; www.tahitilive.com. Rates: Room with breakfast and dinner 6.560 CFP single; 12.320 CFP double; 18.080 CFP triple; room with all meals 9.200 CFP single, 17.600 CFP double, 26.000 CFP triple. Round-trip transfers airport to village 1.000 CFP person. Same MAP or AP rates apply for bungalow and meals on Temoe Island. Add 6% value added tax to room rates and meals. A 10% value added tax is applicable to other services. No credit cards.*

This large, modern, white concrete house is on an elevated position in Rikitea village, at the foot of Mount Duff, with a magnificent panoramic view of Rikitea Bay, Aukena and a few pearl farms. The top floor is reserved for visitors and contains three bedrooms, each with a double bed and a single bed. Guests share the living room, kitchen, terrace and bathroom with hot water. House linens are furnished. The dining terrace overlooks the bay, providing a lovely view. The food is European and local cuisine.

Your hostess, Bianca Urarii, will arrange for your guided tours to visit the St. Michel Cathedral, the old churches and other historic ruins and natural sites on Mangareva Island. You can be dropped off by boat at a motu where you can spend the day in blissful isolation with a casse-croute and water, for 3.000 CFP or 4.000 CFP per person, depending on your meal plan. You can also discover the islands of Aukena, Akamaru, Taravai and Tauna on a day's boat excursion and picnic on one of the motu islets. This costs 5.500 CFP or 7.500 CFP depending on your meal plan. A 2-day excursion takes you to Aukena, Pohue and Tauna (bird island) on the first day and to Akamaru, Mekiro and Taravai on the second day, for 3.000 CFP or 5.000 CFP, according to your MAP or AP choice.

Bianca and Benoit have also built 4 Polynesian style wooden bungalows on Temoe Island. This is a low coral atoll 3.5 miles long and 2 miles wide, located 50 kilometers (31 miles) East-South-East of Mangareva, and is noted for the *marae* temples that have remained intact. Each of the bungalows has a king size bed and a single bed, a private bathroom with hot water shower and a covered terrace. The rooms are nicely decorated and even have mosquito nets over the beds. Half-pension (MAP) or full-pension (AP) meals are served, according to your choice. Activities include fishing in lagoon and visiting other uninhabited motus.

CHEZ JOJO, *B.P. 1, Rikitea, Mangareva, 98755. Tel./Fax 689/97.84.69/ 97.82.61. On mountainside 5 kilometers (3 miles) from Rikitea village. Rates: room with breakfast and dinner 10.345 CFP per person; room with breakfast, lunch and dinner 13.271 CFP per person. Bungalow with breakfast only 10.600 CFP per person. Round-trip transfers 1.000 CFP per person, tax included. No credit cards.*

There is one bedroom with a double bed and single bed for rent in a two-story house, and guests share the living room, dining room and terrace, as well as the bathroom with hot water shower. There are also two twin bungalows at the edge of the lagoon, each unit with a double bed and single bed, a television and private bathroom with hot water shower. Bicycles are free for guests and your hostess, Madame Jocelyne Mamatui, will show you the village and take you on an island tour free of charge. You can also rent a kayak from her. Fishing, free diving and boat excursions to the motu with a picnic can be arranged on request.

CHEZ MAMIE "TARA ETU KURA", *Rikitea, Mangareva 98755. Tel./Fax 689/97.83.25. Beside the lagoon at Point Teonekura. Rates: bungalow with breakfast and dinner 7.500 CFP per person; bungalow with breakfast, lunch and dinner 9.500 CFP per person. single. Round-trip transfers 1.000 CFP per person. Add 6% value added tax to room rates and meals. A 10% value added tax is applicable to other services. No credit cards.*

Madame Erena Marae-Schmidt has a rental bungalow for 3 guests in a big garden beside the lagoon in Rikitea village. It has a double bed and a single bed, plus a convertible sofa in the living area. There is a kitchenette and the private bathroom has a hot water shower. Meals available on request.

CHEZ PIERRE AND MARIETTE PAEAMARA, *Rikitea, Mangareva 98755. Tel. 689/97.82.87. At the foot of Mount Duff, 100 meters (328 feet) from the boat landing in Rikitea. Rates: room 3.200 CFP; room with breakfast and dinner (demi-pension) 5.500 CFP; room with all meals (full-pension) 7.500 CFP. Round-trip boat transfers 1.000 CFP per person. Add 6% value added tax to room rates and meals. A 10% value added tax is applicable to other services. No credit cards.*

This hospitable couple has a concrete house with three bedrooms that can accommodate up to 3 people in each room, a lounge with color television, a fully equipped kitchen and two communal showers with hot water and toilets. The hosts will take you around the island by private car, or by boat to visit a motu, go fishing and tour the family-owned pearl farm. This pension is not included on the Tahiti Tourism list of recommended places to stay because their papers to operate a family pension are not in order, but former guests have highly recommended this lodging.

Seeing the Sights

Activities include lagoon excursions by outrigger speed canoe, boat trips to visit the various *motu* islets around the island, fishing, and visits to the family-owned pearl farms, land tours of the island, with stops at the religious and historic sites. You can also hike up the mountains and visit the sculptors' workshop for mother-of-pearl carvings. Local surfers have tried to keep it a well-guarded secret, but the word is now out that there are some good surfing waves in the passes.

Practical Information

Doctor
There is a government-operated infirmary in Rikitea, *Tel. 97.82.16.*

Police
The French *gendarmerie* is located in Rikitea, *Tel. 97.82.68.*

Post Office & Telecommunications Office
The post office is located in Rikitea, *Tel. 97.82.22.*

Tourist Bureau
Bianca Urarii is president of the Comite du Tourisme in the Gambier Islands, *Tel./Fax 689/97.83.76 / 88.08.81; E-mail: biancabenoit@mail.pf.*

Chapter 24

GLOSSARY

The Tahitian alphabet contains 13 letters. A is pronounced ah, as in father, E is pronounced e, as in fate, F is pronounced fa as in farm, H is pronounced he as in heaven, I is pronounced i as me, M is pronounced mo as in mote, N is pronounced nu as in noon, O is pronounced o as in go, P is pronounced p as in pat, R is pronounced ro as in rode, T is pronounced t as in time, U is pronounced u as in rule, V is pronounced v as in veer.

The Tahitian dialect abounds in vowels, such as Faaa, the name of Tahiti's largest commune, where the international airport is located. This is pronounced Fah-ah-ah, but most people lazily forget the last syllable. Tahitian words have no "s" for the plural. There are no hard consonants in the Tahitian alphabet, such as the letter "B;" however, the name Bora Bora is accepted as the legal name for the island that was formerly called Pora Pora.

a'ahi - tuna, *thon* on French menus
ahima'a - underground oven used for cooking traditional Polynesian food; also *hima'a*
ahu - the most sacred place on a marae, an altar that took many forms, including pyramid shaped
aita - Tahitian for "no"
aita e peapea - no problem; also used as "you're welcome"
aita maitai - no good
aito - ironwood tree, also a strong warrior
aparima - a Polynesian story-telling group dance
api - new, young
arii - Polynesian high chief, a sacred being or princely caste
arioi - a religious sect or fraternity in the Society Islands in pre-Christian days

atoll - a low coral island, usually no more than six feet above sea level
atua - Polynesian gods
baguette - long loaf of crusty French bread
barrier reef - coral reef between the shoreline and the ocean, separated from the land by a lagoon
belvédère - panoramic lookout
bonitier - bonito boat
BP - *bôite postale*, post office box
breadfruit - a football-size starchy green fruit that grows on a breadfruit tree, eaten as a staple with fish, pork or canned corned beef and coconut milk
bringue - a party or fête, usually with lots of music, singing, dancing and Hinano beer
cascade - French for waterfall
casse-croûte - sandwich made with *baguette* bread
CEP - *Centre d'expérimentation du Pacifique*; the French nuclear-testing program that was carried out in French Polynesia from 1966-1996
CFP - *cours de franc Pacifique*; the French Pacific franc is the local currency
chevrette - French for sea shrimp, as opposed to fresh water *crevettes*
CMAS - *Confédération Mondiale des Activités Subaquatiques*; the World Underwater Federation, France's scuba diving equivalent to PADI
copra - dried coconut meat used to make oil and monoi
coral - a white calcareous skeletal structure inhabited by Madreporaria, organisms that comprise the living polyps inside the skeletal pores, giving color to the coral
croque madame - also called *croque vahine*, is a toasted ham and cheese sandwich with a fried egg on top
croque monsieur - toasted ham and cheese sandwich
cyclone - tropical storm rotating around a low-pressure 'eye'; the equivalent to a typhoon in the western Pacific and a hurricane in the Caribbean
demi-pension - half board (bed, breakfast and dinner), see also *pension complète*
demis - half caste Tahitian-European
e - Tahitian for "yes"
espadon - French for sword fish
faa'amu -to feed; an informal child adoption system in Polynesia
faa'apu - farm
fafa - the green tops of the taro plant, similar to spinach
fafaru - stinky fish dish
fare - traditional Polynesian house, home, hut
fare iti - little house, outdoor toilet
fare manihini - visitor's bureau
fare moni - bank
fare ohipa - office

fare pape - bathroom
fare pote'e - chief's house or community meeting place, oval shaped
fare pure - church
fare purera'a rahi - cathedral
fare rata - post office
fare taoto -sleeping house
fare toa - store
fare tutu - kitchen
fei - plantain, Tahitian cooking banana
fête - festival, party, celebration
fiu - bored, fed up
fringing reef - a coral reef along the shoreline
FFESSM - *Fèderation Française des Activités Subaquatiques*, or French Underwater Federation of Scuba Divers
gendarmerie - French national police station
goëlette - French for schooner; inter-island cargo or freighter ships
haere mai - come here
haere maru - take it easy
haura - swordfish or marlin
heiva - festival, an assembly for dancing
heiva vaevae - big festival parade
here here - romance
high island - an island created by volcanic action or geological upheaval
himenes - Tahitian for songs or hymns
hinano - flower of the pandanus tree, girl's name, Tahiti's favorite beer
Hiro - Polynesian god of thieves; Raiatea's first king was named Hiro
hoa - shallow channel across the outer reef of an atoll that carries water into or out of the central lagoon at high tide or with big ocean swells
hoe - ceremonial canoe paddle
honu - turtle
ia ora na - hello, good morning, good afternoon, good evening, pronounced similar to "your honor" (yore-ronah)
ia'ota - marinated fish salad, *poisson cru*
ipo - a dumpling made with breadfruit and coconut water
iti - small, little
kaina - a slang term similar to hick or hillbilly, usually applied to out-islanders; country music
kava - mildly intoxicating drink made from the root of piper methysticum, the pepper plant; a fruit tree
kaveu - coconut crab
keshi - a pearl without a nucleus
lagoon - a body of normally calm water inside a coral reef
leeward - on the downwind side, sheltered from the prevailing winds

le truck - Tahiti's public transportation system

LMS - London Missionary Society, the first Protestants to bring the Gospel to Tahiti in 1797

ohipa - work

opani - out of order, broken, closed

maa - food, also spelled **ma'a**

maa tahiti - traditional Tahitian food

maa tinito - Chinese food

maa tinito haricots rouge - a popular dish with red beans, macaroni, pork or chicken

mabe - blister pearl that is grown inside the mother-of-pearl shell

maeva; manava - greetings, welcome

magasin - small food store

mahi mahi - dolphinfish, *dorade Coryphène*

mahu - Tahitian for transvestite or female impersonator

maitai - good; also a potent rum drink

maiore - another name for uru or breadfruit

mana - spiritual power

manahune - the common people or peasant class in pre-European Polynesia; servants, tillers of the soil, fishermen, prisoners of war and slaves

manuia - cheers, a toast to your health

mako, mao - shark

maniota - manioc root

manu - bird

maoa - sea snails

Maohi - Tahitian Polynesians; the ancestors of today's Tahitians, some of whom sailed to New Zealand and are called Maori

mape - Tahitian chestnut

maraamu - southeast trade winds that can often blow for days, bringing rain, rough seas and cooler weather

marae - traditional Polynesian temple of coral or basaltic stone, usually built with an ahu altar at one end

marara - flying fish

mauruuru - thank you

mauruuru roa - thank you very much

me'ae - Marquesan word for marae

mei'a - banana

meka - a melt-in-your-mouth swordfish from the ocean depths. French menus sometimes list it as *espadon de nuit*

miti ha'ari - fresh coconut milk poured over traditional Tahitian foods

miti hue - a fermented coconut milk used as a dipping sauce for breadfruit, taro, fei, bananas, fish, pork and canned corned beef

mona mona - sweet, candy

monoi - oil made from coconut oil, flavored with Tiare Tahiti, ylang ylang, pitate and other flowers, also with sandalwood powder or vanilla. It is used as an emollient, perfume, hair dressing, suntan oil and mosquito repellent

mo'o - lizard

mo'o rea - yellow lizard, name of the island of Moorea

more - Tahitian grass skirts made from the purau tree

mou'a - mountain

motu - a coral islet inside the lagoon, between the outer reef and a high island

mutoi - Tahitian municipal police

nacre - mother-of-pearl shell

naissain - larva of an oyster

nao nao -mosquito

navette - shuttle boat

nehenehe - pretty; handsome

neo neo - stinky smell

noa noa - fragrant, sweet smelling

nohu - stone fish

noni - Marquesan for *Morinda citrifolia*, a plant whose juice is used as a tonic

nono - sand flea; also Tahitian word for *Morinda citrifolia*

nucleus - a small sphere of calcium carbonate that is grafted into the gonads of the pearl oyster to produce a pearl. The fresh water mussel from the Mississippi River provides the best nucleus and helps to produce the finest black pearls

nui - big, new

oa oa - happy, joyful, merry

ono ono - barracuda

Oro - Polynesian god of war who demanded human sacrifices at the *marae* in pre-Christian days

otea - legendary group dance performed in grass skirts

PADI - Professional Association of Diving Instructors, the American system of scuba diving

pae pae - stone paved floor of pre-European houses or meeting platforms

pahua - clam; *bénitier* on French menus

painapo - pineapple, *anana*

pandanus - palm tree with aerial roots whose leaves are used for weaving roofs, hats, mats and bags

pape - water

pareo, pareu - a sarong-like garment that is hand-painted or tie-dyed

pass - channel through the outer reef of an atoll or the barrier reef around a high island that allows water to flow into and out of the lagoon

Paumotu - inhabitants of the Tuamotu atolls

peapea - problems, worries

pension - boarding house, hostel
pension complète - full-board (bed and all meals)
penu - pestle
pétanque - also known as *boules* or bocci-ball; a French game of bowls, where metal balls are thrown to land as near as possible to a target ball. A very competitive sport in Tahiti
peue - mats woven of coconut or pandanus fronds
pia - beer
pirogue - French word for outrigger canoe
PK - *poste kilometre*, the number of kilometers from the *mairie* or post office
plat du jour - daily special, plate of the day
po'e - a sticky pudding made with papaya, bananas or pumpkin, corn starch and coconut milk
poe rava - black pearl that comes from the *Pinctada Margaritifera*, the black-lip oyster
poisson cru - fish marinated in lime juice and served cold with tomatoes, onions, carrots, cucumbers and coconut milk. In Tahitian it's *i'a ota*
popaa - foreigner, Europeans, westerners, white people
popoi - fermented breadfruit eaten as a bread substitute or sweetened with sugar and coconut cream as a dessert
poulet - French for chicken
poulet fafa - chicken cooked with taro leaves and coconut milk
pu - conch shell blown to announce the arrival of a delegation, dancers, or the fish truck
puaa - pig, the basic food for all Tahitian *tamaara'a* feasts
pua'a'toro - beef; canned corned beef, the staple of the South Seas
purau - wild hibiscus tree, whose inner bark is used to make grass skirts
rae rae - a slang term for *mahu*, usually implying homosexuality
raatira - the intermediary caste of the ancient Polynesian society, between the *arii* and the *manahune*
rori - sea slug, sea cucumber
roulotte - mobile dining van
sennit - woven fiber from coconut husks
siki - dark skinned people
Taaroa - Polynesian creator god
tahua - priests of ancient Polynesian religion
taioro - fermented grated coconut sauce that may contain *pahua* clams or *maoa* sea snails
tamaara'a - Tahitian feast
tama'a maitai - enjoy your meal, *bon appetit*
tamure - Tahiti's national hip swiveling, rubber-legging dance
tane - man, husband, boyfriend, Mr.

tapa - bark-cloth, traditional clothing of the pre-European Polynesians; wall hangings

tapu - tabu, taboo, sacred, forbidden

taramea - crown-of-thorns starfish that eats the coral animals and destroys the reefs

taro - root vegetable that is one of the staple foods in Polynesia

tarua - a tuber usually cooked in the *ahima'a* oven

tatau - Tahitian word for tattoo

tiane'e - slipper lobster; *cigalle de mer* on French menus

tiare - flower

Tiare Tahiti - fragrant white petalled *gardenia taitensis*, Tahiti's national flower

tifaifai - colorful bed and cushion covers or wall hangings sewn in patchwork or appliquéd designs

tii - Tahitian name for human-like wooden or stone statues that had a religious significance in pre-European Polynesia

tiki - a Marquesan word for the Tahitian *tii*; some of these statues are still found on the *me'ae* in the Marquesas Islands

Tinito - Tahitian name for Chinese

tiurai - Tahitian for July, the major festival of July

TPE - *traitement paiement electronique*, an automatic teller machine equivalent to the ATM. Nobody calls this a TPE, however, but a *distributeur*

toe toe - cold

toere - wooden slit drum played for Tahitian dance shows

tohua - a place for meetings or festivals in pre-European Polynesia

tupa - land crab

tupapau - spirit ghosts of the Polynesian religion, still feared by some people

ufi - a huge root vegetable similar to yams, cooked in underground *ahima'a* oven

umara - sweet potato

umete - wooden dish or bowl used for serving foods or holding fruits and flowers

upa upa - music

uru - breadfruit

vaa - Tahitian word for outrigger canoe

vahine - Tahitian word for woman, wife, Ms.

vehine- Marquesan word for woman, wife, Ms.

vana- black sea urchin whose meat is good to eat

vanira - vanilla

varo - sea centipede, a gourmet's delicacy

V.A.T. - value added tax; called T.V.A. in French Polynesia

vea vea - hot

vivo - nose flute

VTT or vélo or tout terrain - mountain bike
windward - facing the wind; the opposite of leeward
4x4 or 4WD - a 4-wheel drive vehicle, such as a Landrover, Jeep or pick-up
truck

GENERAL INDEX

LODGING INDEX

Travel Notes

Things Change!

Phone numbers, prices, addresses, quality of food, etc, all change. If you come across any new information, we'd appreciate hearing from you. No item is too small! Drop us an email note at: jopenroad@aol.com, or write us at:

Tahiti & French Polynesia Guide
Open Road Publishing, P.O. Box 284
Cold Spring Harbor, NY 11724